KV-013-730

LIVERPOOL JMU LIBRARY

3 1111 01528 1759

THE OXFORD HANDBOOK OF

OFFENDER DECISION MAKING

THE OXFORD HANDBOOKS IN CRIMINOLOGY AND CRIMINAL JUSTICE

GENERAL EDITOR: MICHAEL TONRY

THE OXFORD HANDBOOKS IN CRIMINOLOGY AND CRIMINAL JUSTICE offer authoritative, comprehensive, and critical overviews of the state of the art of criminology and criminal justice. Each volume focuses on a major area of each discipline, is edited by a distinguished group of specialists, and contains specially commissioned, original essays from leading international scholars in their respective fields. Guided by the general editorship of Michael Tonry, the series will provide an invaluable reference for scholars, students, and policy makers seeking to understand a wide range of research and policies in criminology and criminal justice.

Other titles in this series:

THE OXFORD HANDBOOK OF

OFFENDER DECISION MAKING

Edited by

WIM BERNASCO,
JEAN-LOUIS VAN GELDER,
and
HENK ELFFERS

OXFORD
UNIVERSITY PRESS

OXFORD
UNIVERSITY PRESS

Oxford University Press is a department of the University of Oxford. It furthers
the University's objective of excellence in research, scholarship, and education
by publishing worldwide. Oxford is a registered trade mark of Oxford University
Press in the UK and certain other countries.

Published in the United States of America by Oxford University Press
198 Madison Avenue, New York, NY 10016, United States of America.

© Oxford University Press 2017

All rights reserved. No part of this publication may be reproduced, stored in
a retrieval system, or transmitted, in any form or by any means, without the
prior permission in writing of Oxford University Press, or as expressly permitted
by law, by license, or under terms agreed with the appropriate reproduction
rights organization. Inquiries concerning reproduction outside the scope of the
above should be sent to the Rights Department, Oxford University Press, at the
address above.

You must not circulate this work in any other form
and you must impose this same condition on any acquirer.

Library of Congress Cataloging-in-Publication Data
Names: Bernasco, Wim, 1961- author. | Van Gelder, Jean-Louis, author. | Elffers, H., author.
Title: The Oxford handbook of offender decision making / Wim Bernasco,
Jean-Louis Van Gelder, and Henk Elffers.
Description: New York : Oxford University Press, [2017] | Series: The Oxford
handbooks in criminology and criminal justice ; 6 | Includes bibliographical references and index.
Identifiers: LCCN 2016036115 (print) | LCCN 2016051574 (ebook) |
ISBN 9780199338801 (hardback) | ISBN 9780199338818 (ebook)
Subjects: LCSH: Criminal psychology. | Decision making. | Choice (Psychology) | Criminology.
Classification: LCC HV6080 .B447 2017 (print) | LCC HV6080 (ebook) | DDC 364.3—dc23
LC record available at https://lccn.loc.gov/2016036115

3 5 7 9 8 6 4 2
Printed by Sheridan Books, Inc., United States of America

Contents

PREFACE

WITH great pleasure, we present this new addition to the *Oxford Handbooks in Criminology and Criminal Justice* series. Offender decision making and the assumption of human agency embedded within it go straight to the heart of our discipline. When we were invited in 2012 by *Oxford Handbooks* series general editor Michael Tonry to edit an entire volume devoted to this topic, we accepted the opportunity without precisely knowing what was ahead of us. Although each of us had studied offender decision making extensively, our methods and theoretical perspectives had been very different. As we started to develop a draft outline and to consider potential authors, it dawned on us that the breadth and depth of the subject went far beyond our own experiences. Yet, to our knowledge, very few resources existed that integrated this body of knowledge. Of course, this was why Michael asked us to take up the project in the first place. As a result of this relative ignorance on our part, editing this handbook has been not only a pleasant and exciting but certainly also a rewarding and instructive journey for us.

In addition to an editors' introduction, the *Handbook* comprises 32 contributions, each devoted to one or more aspects of offender decision making. The topics range from "traditional" rational choice-based perspectives to the latest insights from neuroscience, from the influence of stable offender dispositions on criminal choice to fleeting emotional experiences impacting on decision processes, and from victim selection to weapon use. Furthermore, a series of chapters address the different methods that have been and can be used to investigate offender decision making. Several chapters are included that address decision making in specific types of crime. All in all, we think our efforts have resulted in an encompassing, yet by no means exhaustive, resource for those researchers, professionals, and students who share an interest in this topic.

There are many people to whom we are indebted for making *The Oxford Handbook of Offender Decision Making* possible. First, we thank Michael Tonry for providing us with the opportunity to edit this handbook. Second, we owe much debt to all the reviewers who so kindly devoted their time and effort to provide input to help improve the various contributions. They are, in alphabetical order, Martin Andresen, Ronet Bachman, Eric Beauregard, Michael Benson, Giulia Berlusconi, Arjan Blokland, Remi Boivin, Jeffrey Bouffard, John Braithwaite, Jeff Brantingham, Fiona Brookman, Gerben Bruinsma, Vincent Buskens, Peter Carrington, Heith Copes, Mary-Louise Corr, Veroni Eichelsheim, Paul Ekblom, Els Enhus, Lyn Exum, Richard Felson, Frank van Gemert, Charlotte Gerritsen, Paul Gill, Stephanie van Goozen, Liz Groff, Cory Haberman, Jan Hendriks, Scott Jacques, Erich Kirchler, Eward Kleemans, Katy de Kogel, Marieke Liem, Marie Rosenkrantz Lindegaard, Tamara Madensen, Jean McGloin, Geert Mesters,

Frank Morgan, Daniel Nagin, Claire Nee, Lieven Pauwels, Jill Portnoy, Travis Pratt, Danielle Reynald, Jason Roach, Job van der Schalk, Shaul Shalvi, Aiden Sidebottom, Sally Simpson, Wouter Steenbeek, Jeffrey Stuewig, Milind Tambe, Marie Tillyer, George Tita, Kyle Treiber, Frank Weerman, Brandon Welsh, Johan van Wilsem, and Richard Wortley. Their careful reading and helpful suggestions have been pivotal in the end result.

We also thank our editor at Oxford University Press, James Cook, for his efforts and patience in getting this handbook together. Finally, and most important, we express our sincere gratitude to all the contributors of this handbook.

Wim Bernasco
Jean Louis van Gelder
Henk Elffers

Contributors

Robert Apel is Associate Professor of Criminal Justice at Rutgers University. His research interests include the economy, crime control policy, and the life course.

Lauren A. Austin is a doctoral student in the Public Policy program at the University of North Carolina at Charlotte. Her research interests include at-risk youth, resiliency, and the history of North Carolina's public health policies. She is currently completing her dissertation on the risk and protective factors of resilient at-risk youth.

Margit Averdijk is a senior research associate at the Jacobs Center for Productive Youth Development of the University of Zurich. Her research interests include the study of victimization, social contexts of crime, and individuals' development of violent behavior.

Ronet Bachman is a professor in the Department of Sociology and Criminal Justice at the University of Delaware. She has published several books on research methods, statistics, and violence and victimization. Her most recent federally funded research examined the long-term desistance patterns of a drug-involved cohort of offenders.

Eric Beauregard is a professor in the School of Criminology at Simon Fraser University and Director of the Centre for Research on Sexual Violence. His research interests include the crime-commission process, decision making, criminal investigation, as well as the factors influencing criminal outcomes for different types of sex offenders.

Wim Bernasco is a senior researcher at the Netherlands Institute for the Study of Crime and Law Enforcement (NSCR) and Professor of "spatial analysis of crime" in the Department of Spatial Economics of the Vrije Universiteit Amsterdam. He studies spatial aspects of crime, including offenders' travel behavior and target selection. His work also comprises research on situational causes of crime, including the analysis of crime captured on camera.

Daniel Birks is a lecturer in the School of Criminology and Criminal Justice, Griffith University, and a research fellow at the Griffith Criminology Institute. His research interests are broadly based in the fields of environmental criminology, crime analysis, and computational social science.

Wouter van den Bos is a research scientist at the Max Planck Institute for Human Development. His research focuses on the neural underpinnings of reward-based learning and social decision making across adolescent development.

Jeffrey A. Bouffard is a professor in the College of Criminal Justice at Sam Houston State University and Research Director for the Correctional Management Institute of Texas. His research interests include offender decision making, criminological theories, and offender rehabilitation.

Iain R. Brennan is a senior lecturer in criminology and psychology at the University of Hull. His research interests include weapon use, alcohol-related violence, and victim responses to crime.

Fiona Brookman is Professor of Criminology at the University of South Wales and Director of the Criminal Investigation Research Network (CIRN). Her major research interests are homicide, violence, and the police investigation of homicide. She is currently undertaking ethnographic research on the role of forensic science and technology in homicide investigations in the United Kingdom.

Paolo Campana is University Lecturer in Criminology and Complex Networks at the Institute of Criminology, University of Cambridge. His research interests include the study of organized crime and forms of extralegal governance as well as the application of network analysis techniques to the research of organized forms of criminality.

Gabriel T Cesar is a doctoral candidate in the School of Criminology and Criminal Justice at Arizona State University. His research explores child welfare, youth development, violence, and policing as sources of formal and informal social control.

Megan Eileen Collins is a doctoral student in the Department of Criminology and Criminal Justice at the University of Maryland. Her research interests include gun violence and markets, procedural justice, policing, and public policy.

Heith Copes is a professor in the Department of Justice Sciences at the University of Alabama at Birmingham. His research addresses the criminal decision-making strategies of offenders and understanding the ways that offenders make sense of their lives and crimes.

Timothy Coupe works at the Institute of Criminology, Cambridge University. His research interests are policing, crime detection and investigation, and burglary.

Scott H. Decker is Foundation Professor in the School of Criminology and Criminal Justice at Arizona State University. His main research interests are in the areas of gangs, violence, criminal justice policy, and the offender's perspective.

John E. Eck is Professor of Criminal Justice at the University of Cincinnati. His work encompasses investigations management, problem-oriented policing, and preventing crime at high crime places, focusing on practical solutions to crime problems based on sound research and rigorous theory.

Paul Ekblom is Professor Emeritus of Design Against Crime at Central Saint Martins University of the Arts. His research interests include criminal adaptability and coevolution with crime prevention, developing conceptual frameworks for crime prevention theory and practice, designing products and places to resist crime, and horizon scanning.

Henk Elffers is a senior researcher at the Netherlands Institute for the Study of Crime and Law Enforcement (NSCR); Emeritus Professor in the Department of Criminal Law and Criminology, Vrije Universiteit Amsterdam; and Adjoint-Lecturer at Griffith University, Mount Gravatt. He works on rational choice, guardianship, spatial criminology, and the interaction between judges and the general public.

Justin D. Franklin is a graduate of the Master of Science program in Criminal Justice at the University of North Carolina at Charlotte. His interests include rehabilitation strategies that target juvenile offenders.

Jean-Louis van Gelder is a senior researcher at the Netherlands Institute for the Study of Crime and Law Enforcement (NSCR). His research interests include the interplay of affect and cognition in criminal decision making, multiple self models, the application of novel methods and technologies in criminological research, and informality.

Berna Güroğlu is Associate Professor in Developmental Psychology and a principal investigator in the Brain and Development Laboratory at Leiden University. Her research focuses on the neurocognitive development of social decision making across childhood, adolescence, and young adulthood. She is particularly interested in the role of peer relationships and their links with socioemotional functioning.

Wim Huisman is Professor of Criminology at the Vrije Universiteit Amsterdam. His research interests are organizational and white-collar crime, among which the involvement of business in serious human rights violations, fraud, and corruption.

Shayne Jones is Associate Professor in the School of Criminal Justice at Texas State University. His research interests include the relationship between personality and offending, the extent to which criminological constructs mediate and moderate this relationship, and factors that influence various actors (juries, judges, and criminal defendants) in making legal decisions.

Eduard T. Klapwijk is a PhD candidate in the Department of Child and Adolescent Psychiatry at the Leiden University Medical Center. His research focuses on the neurocognitive mechanisms of empathy and social decision making in adolescents with conduct disorder and adolescents with autism spectrum disorders.

Marie Rosenkrantz Lindegaard is a senior researcher at the Netherlands Institute for the Study of Crime and Law Enforcement (NSCR) and an Associate Professor at the Department of Sociology of the University of Copenhagen. Her research interests are situational aspects of crime, agency, street culture, qualitative methods, use of camera footage for crime research, and urban ethnography in South Africa.

Thomas A. Loughran is Associate Professor in the Department of Criminology and Criminal Justice at the University of Maryland. His research interests include offender decision making and deterrence, illegal market participation, public policy, and methods for inferring treatment effects from nonexperimental data.

M. Lyn Exum is Associate Professor in the Department of Criminal Justice and Criminology at the University of North Carolina at Charlotte. His research interests include criminal decision making and the forces that impact those cognitive processes.

Tamara D. Madensen is Associate Professor in the Department of Criminal Justice at the University of Nevada, Las Vegas. Her research interests are problem-oriented policing, crime opportunity structures, place management, and crowd violence.

Chae Mamayek is a doctoral student in the Department of Criminology and Criminal Justice at the University of Maryland. Her research interests include offender decision making, statistical methodology, deterrence, and public policy.

Daniel S. Nagin is Teresa and H. John Heinz III University Professor of Public Policy and Statistics at the Heinz College, Carnegie Mellon University. His research focuses on the evolution of criminal and antisocial behaviors over the life course, the deterrent effect of criminal and noncriminal penalties on illegal behaviors, and the development of statistical methods for analyzing longitudinal data.

Nicole Niebuhr is a doctoral student in the College of Criminal Justice at Sam Houston State University. Her research interests include offender rehabilitation, re-entry, life course theory, and program evaluation.

Ray Paternoster is a professor in the Department of Criminology and Criminal Justice at the University of Maryland. He is interested in rational choice models of offender decision making, the transition from adolescence to adulthood, desistance theory and research, and issues related to capital punishment.

Lieven J. R. Pauwels is Professor of Criminology in the Department of Criminology, Criminal Law and Social Law at Ghent University. He is interested in crime causation theories, unifying frameworks and empirical tests, philosophy of causation, and innovative methods in quantitative criminology.

Heiko Rauhut is Associate Professor of Social Theory and Quantitative Methods at the Institute of Sociology, the University of Zurich. His substantial research interests include social norms, the evolution of cooperation, crime, punishment, and control. His methodological research interests are experimental game theory, quantitative social research methods, and analytical sociology.

Carter Rees is Assistant Professor of Sociology at Brigham Young University. His research focuses on social networks, juvenile delinquency, and the structure of adolescent friendships.

Danielle M. Reynald is a senior lecturer in the School of Criminology and Criminal Justice at Griffith University and a criminologist at the Griffith Criminology Institute in Brisbane, Australia. Her research focuses on how guardianship functions as a crime control mechanism in a variety of domains including in residential, workplace, public, and cyber contexts; crime prevention through environmental design; and offender decision making.

Stijn Ruiter is Senior Researcher at the Netherlands Institute for the Study of Crime and Law Enforcement (NSCR) and Professor of Social and Spatial Aspects of Deviant Behavior at Utrecht University. His research focuses on spatiotemporal aspects of crime and the role of activity patterns in crime target selection.

Aiden Sidebottom is a lecturer in the Department of Security and Crime Science at University College London. His research interests are evidence-based policing, situational crime prevention, and crime prevention evaluation.

Robert Svensson is Professor in the Department of Criminology at Malmö University. His research interests include crime and deviance, particularly crime and deviance among adolescents.

L. Thomas WinfreeJr is Professor Emeritus of Criminal Justice at New Mexico State University, having retired in 2012. He has contributed extensively to the criminological literature, particularly in juvenile delinquency. His research interests include youth gangs, both domestically and internationally.

Nick Tilley is Professor in the Department of Security and Crime Science at University College London and Adjunct Professor at Griffith University, Mount Gravatt. His research concerns problem-oriented policing, prevention, community policing, and evaluation research.

Kyle Treiber is University Lecturer in Neurocriminology at the Institute of Criminology, University of Cambridge, and Deputy Director of the Peterborough Adolescent and Young Adult Development Study (PADS+). Her research interests include the (bio)mechanics of decision making and the interaction between neurocriminological and social environmental factors and their influence on cognition and behavior, both at the point of action and throughout development and the life course.

Sarah B. van Mastrigt is Associate Professor in the Department of Psychology and Behavioral Sciences, Aarhus University. Her research interests include co-offending, developmental and life-course criminology, and the social psychology of crime and punishment.

Frank M. Weerman is a senior researcher at the Netherlands Institute for the Study of Crime and Law Enforcement (NSCR) and Endowed Professor at the Department of Criminology of the Erasmus University Rotterdam. His research focuses on the explanation of juvenile delinquency, co-offending and youth gangs, and the role of delinquent peers.

Michelle Wright is a Chartered Psychologist and Senior Lecturer in Forensic Psychology at Manchester Metropolitan University. Her research focuses on furthering understanding of homicide and criminal investigation processes to inform policing, policy. and practice.

THE OXFORD HANDBOOK OF

OFFENDER DECISION MAKING

CHAPTER 1

EDITORS' INTRODUCTION

WIM BERNASCO, JEAN-LOUIS VAN GELDER, AND HENK ELFFERS

For several decades, criminologists have been studying offender decision making. This research has yielded new and profound insights, at times produced counterintuitive findings, and also generated practical prescriptions regarding the way people can be discouraged or prevented from committing crime. The study of offender decision making has proven to be inherently interdisciplinary, with insights from disciplines such as psychology, economics, and, recently, the cognitive sciences enhancing our understanding of how and why offenders make their decisions.

Several features of criminological studies on decision making set it apart from other fields of criminological thought. Perhaps the most prominent of these features is the ubiquity of decision making. Virtually every discussion about crime or law enforcement is guided by beliefs about how people make decisions in one way or another. Can potential offenders be deterred by the prospect of sanctions? How do they deal with uncertainty about the consequences of a planned crime? Will lethal violence decline if guns are banned? How do emotions facilitate crime? What emotional experiences can prevent crime? Do offenders learn to commit crime from their own previous experiences or from those of others? Is juvenile crime the result of impulsive decisions?

Given this ubiquity and despite the importance of offenders' decision making for our understanding of crime and the effects of law enforcement, there are few resources that integrate information about the role of human decision making in crime. To address this void in the literature, the *Oxford Handbook of Offender Decision Making* aims to be a comprehensive resource of theoretical, methodological, and substantive empirical knowledge about decision making as it relates to criminal behavior. It offers state-of-the-art reviews of the main paradigms in offender decision making, such as rational choice theory, but also includes more recent approaches, such as game theory and dual-process models of decision making. In addition, the handbook contains up-to-date reviews of empirical research on decision making with respect to a wide range of decision types—addressing not only criminal initiation and desistance but also choice of location and time, co-offenders, victims, and modus operandi—and specific types of crime, including homicide, carjacking, burglary, sexual offending, and white-collar crime. Importantly, the handbook includes in-depth treatments of the principal research methods that have been used, and can be used, to study offender decision making: experimental designs, observation studies, surveys, offender interviews, and simulations.

Another prominent feature of the decision-making literature as it relates to crime regards the central role that rational choice perspectives and their situational derivatives have traditionally played in theorizing on this particular topic, paying tribute to arch-fathers Adam Smith (1759/1982) and Jeremy Bentham (1789/1889). The dominance of these perspectives is in fact so great that criminologists at times tend to equate rational choice with offender decision making. In this handbook, the importance of rational choice theory in its different manifestations for study of offender decision making is reflected in the various chapters that devote attention to it. Chapters 2–5, for example, all deal with rational choice. However, as the editors, we also thought it befitting to make an effort to extend the scope of this book beyond rational choice-based perspectives. A variety of chapters discuss alternative approaches that in some cases can be considered as extensions of rational choice theories but in other cases are better conceived of as deviations from the models of human behavior proposed in the classic works of Becker (1968) and Cornish and Clarke (1986) that provided the foundations for rational choice in criminology. In this context, we think criminology is following a trend that could be observed earlier elsewhere. Economist Gary Becker was awarded the 1992 Nobel Prize for his work on rational choice in the prediction of crime, and the same prize was awarded in 2011 to decision theorist and psychologist Daniel Kahneman, who is famous for his work showing how human behavior often *deviates from* the rationality assumptions posited by classical economists. Of course, this succession of Nobel laureates not only reflects the progress of the field of human decision making as a whole but also attests to the importance of understanding decision processes in all domains of human behavior. We hope this handbook can form a modest contribution in this respect.

I. Framing Decision Making: Individual, Situation, Choice, and Outcome

Offender decision making is a process that links an individual to a situation in which a choice must be made among two or more alternatives, which results in one of the multiple potential outcomes (figure 1.1). This requires that the individual perceives at least two alternatives from which to choose, at least one of them involving a criminal act. The choice depends on stable and temporary characteristics of the decision maker, characteristics of the situation, and the perception and evaluation of the alternatives.

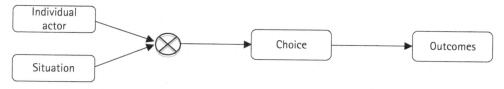

FIGURE 1.1 Elements of a decision-making situation.

Characteristics of the *individual* are important because not all individuals evaluate the same situation equally. Some individuals give more weight to certain aspects (e.g., morals and social norms), some are better at assessing the consequences of their choices (e.g., through knowledge and experience), and some people have a longer time horizon than others (e.g., impulsivity and present-orientation). Characteristics of the *situation* are also important because they may have an impact on the outcomes of decisions. A resilient victim, a capable guardian, or the presence of barriers between the offender and the prospective target may all impact the decision. Finally, the *perception and evaluation of alternatives* by the individual is relevant. Even if the objective situation is given, the individual is not necessarily aware of the utility of the consequences, the probability and severity of sanctions, or the reputation enhancement or damage that they generate. This characterization of offender decision making is in part reflected in the structure of this handbook.

II. ORGANIZATION OF THIS HANDBOOK

This handbook is divided into five parts, each consisting of a series of chapters. Part I discusses various theoretical perspectives of decision making. The chapters that comprise this part deal with perspectives that have been developed as criminological perspectives, such as situational crime prevention, but also with perspectives that have their origins in other disciplines, such as psychology (e.g., dual-process models) or behavioral economics (e.g., game theory). Part II of the handbook revolves around how characteristics of the offender influence decisions to commit crime, from stable individual dispositions that characterize offenders' personalities to the neural mechanisms triggering adolescents' delinquent decisions. Part III focuses on the criminal choice situation. The chapters in this part not only deal with aspects such as the role of victims, guardians, and co-offenders but also address the influence of alcohol, weapons, and law enforcement on the choice process. Part IV discusses the research methods that have been employed to examine decision making in the context of crime, such as observational methods and experimental designs but also secondary data and simulation studies. Part V addresses criminal decision making with respect to specific types of crime, from burglary to sex offending. As the editors, we have made every effort to be encompassing, although we acknowledge that the vastness of the field implicates that certain specific topics may have been overlooked or not received the amount of attention they were due.

A. Part I: Theories of Criminal Decision Making

The first part of the handbook comprises eight contributions that address various theories of human decision making as they relate to crime and rule-breaking in general. Given that the decision process forms the core of rational choice theory, it should not be surprising that it plays a central role in this part of the handbook as the main focus, as the starting point for an extension, or as the counterpoint to a competing perspective.

In chapter 2, Megan Collins and Thomas Loughran review the knowledge that has been gained during the past decades from research on human decision making under uncertainty. The authors consider the various heuristics and biases that can lead offenders to depart from rationality in their criminal decision making.

Paul Ekblom takes an evolutionary approach to the role of rationality in offender decision making in chapter 3. His work is influenced by the natural sciences, in which optimal decision making is typically viewed as an element of the evolutionary explanation of observed behavior patterns.

In chapter 4, Henk Elffers reviews a number of common misinterpretations of rational choice theory in the social sciences in general and criminology in particular. He demonstrates that the classic rational choice theorists described human behavior as "purposive action" without any strict claims about its rationality and with place for emotions as drivers of the decision process, a position that is also attributed to Elster.

In chapter 5, Aiden Sidebottom and Nick Tilley investigate to what degree rational choice theory is a necessary and sufficient underpinning of one of the dominant methods for reducing opportunities for crime by manipulating the immediate environment—the situational crime prevention approach.

In chapter 6, Kyle Treiber discusses the biosocial underpinnings of criminal decision making. In addition to providing an overview of relevant biosocial findings, this chapter argues that such findings are best viewed and understood in the context of a theoretical model of the decision process. It focuses on three key components of this process—motivation, perception and choice—and compares how they are portrayed in models of criminal decision making with what is currently known about their biomechanics.

Robert Apel and Daniel Nagin provide an overview of the broad scope of perceptual deterrence scholarship in chapter 7. After reviewing the basic perceptual elements of criminal choice models, the determinants of sanction perceptions are discussed. Specific attention is devoted to the overall accuracy of sanction perceptions, the degree to which an individual's sanction perceptions are updated in response to his or her experiences as a successful or unsuccessful offender, and research traditions speaking to situational influences on sanction perceptions.

In chapter 8, Heiko Rauhut addresses game theory, a perspective that has strongly influenced theory development in economics, political science, and sociology. Game theory is a generalization of rational choice theory that is useful in situations in which the optimal decision of an individual depends on what others do. Rauhut explains its basic elements and mechanisms and reviews applications of game theory to offender decision making.

Dual-process models of criminal decision making are discussed by Jean-Louis van Gelder in chapter 9. He argues that this type of model, which is common in social psychology and the cognitive sciences, offers a more accurate account of the decision process than the traditional choice models in criminology, such as rational choice and deterrence frameworks, and can overcome some of their limitations.

B. Part II: Attributes of the Criminal Decision Maker

Although theories of human decision making are generic, different people often make different decisions in the same situation. Thus, many criminological theories that address inter-individual differences in criminal behavior suggest that there is variability in cognitive and moral capabilities and characteristics that should be taken into account when discussing individual decision making.

In chapter 10, Shayne Jones, in addition to reviewing the literature on personality and offender decision making to introduce this body of thought to a criminological readership, makes an effort to demonstrate the importance of personality characteristics as embodied by the main theoretical models, such as the Big Five and HEXACO models of personality, to criminological inquiry more generally. The chapter also contains suggestions regarding how personality can be better integrated into criminology.

In chapter 11, Chae Mamayek, Ray Paternoster, and Thomas Loughran provide an overview of temporal orientation as it relates to the discounted utility model and describe how these concepts may have implications for the celerity principle of deterrence. Temporal discounting is proposed as one way to explain how an individual may consider immediate rewards and underweight future sanction costs, allowing criminal behavior in the present to become a rational choice under expected utility theory.

In chapter 12, Robert Svensson, Lieven Pauwels, and Frank Weerman address the relevance of moral beliefs and moral emotions to criminal decisions. Shame and guilt are two painful emotions that have been historically linked to individual differences in criminal propensity. Reviewing both theoretical frameworks and empirical findings, the authors focus on the effect of anticipated shame and guilt on the decision to offend.

In chapter 13, Eduard Klapwijk, Wouter van den Bos, and Berna Güroğlu summarize what is known about neurocognitive mechanisms that affect criminal decision making in adolescents. After reviewing the neural basis of decision making in adolescence, they compare the cognitive and affective capacities of delinquent and nondelinquent adolescents, concluding that delinquent adolescents mainly display affective deficits. The authors suggest that future research should focus on specific subgroups of offenders and include environmental factors.

In chapter 14, Carter Rees and Thomas Winfree provide an overview of the role of choice and human agency in social learning theory, and they explain how these concepts can help us understand delinquency and crime. Particular attention is devoted to the matching law, which relates the rate of behavioral response to the rate of reward.

C. Part III: Elements of the Choice Situation

The third part of the handbook shifts the focus from the offenders to the situations in which they make their decisions. It also discusses how characteristics of victims, co-offenders, guardians, and places, as well as the availability of weapons and the arousal of offenders, may influence the decisions made.

In chapter 15, Margit Averdijk reviews offenders' decisions on victim selection. She investigates the theoretical contributions of the structural-choice model of victim selection, social interactionism, and target congruence, and she discusses data sources on victim selection. After an overview of empirical findings on victim selection evidence, she provides an inventory of contemporary gaps in our knowledge and how to address them in the future.

In chapter 16, Sarah van Mastrigt reviews theory and research on co-offending as it relates to offender decision making, including the decision to (co)-offend, the selection of accomplices, and the choices that shape the criminal event (planning, target selection, and seriousness). She concludes by identifying gaps in our current knowledge and directions for future research.

The focus of chapter 17, by Danielle Reynald, is on the role of informal guardians in influencing the decision space of offenders. She highlights what we can learn from empirical research about the way offenders perceive informal guardianship and about how it affects their criminal choices. She also reviews a number of specific crimes by way of example.

In chapter 18, it is the turn of the formal guardians, in this case the police, to be investigated with regard to what role they play in offender decision making. John Eck and Tamara Madensen, starting from the scheme shown in figure 1.1, propose a new framework for thinking about and researching the manifold roles police guardianship may have in delimiting or changing offenders' choices. They emphasize the primary importance of the way the police behave vis-à-vis offenders.

In chapter 19, the perspective changes to the location where offenders choose to execute their crimes. Stijn Ruiter reviews spatial criminal choice research, with an emphasis on the discrete spatial choice framework, making a plea for incorporating the time dimension in future work.

In chapter 20, Iain Brennan describes the contradictory roles that weapons play in offender decision making by their capacity to serve both offensive and defensive purposes. Brennan provides an analysis of weapon carrying and use based on rational choice, contrasting it with research evidence suggesting that culture and availability are important influences on behavior related to weapons. The chapter concludes with a review of the effectiveness of weapons in reducing victim resistance and retaliation, showing that weapon use is a high-reward, high-cost activity.

In chapter 21, Lyn Exum, Lauren Austin, and Justin Franklin describe how alcohol and sexual and emotional arousal impact on offender decision making from a neuro-economic perspective. This chapter reviews the literature and discusses how alcohol and arousal impact neurological functioning and the effects they may have on the identification and evaluation of criminal consequences.

In chapter 22, Jean-Louis van Gelder reviews the empirical and theoretical criminological literature on the role of emotions in crime causation. He also draws from other disciplines in the behavioral and cognitive sciences that have examined the influence of emotions on human decision making, devoting special attention to appraisal theories of emotion.

D. Part IV: Methodology of Criminal Decision-Making Research

This part of the handbook is dedicated to the various ways by which knowledge can be obtained about offender decision making. Each of the five chapters describes a particular method (or methods) and discusses how the method is used to gain insight into offender decision making, addressing its advantages and disadvantages.

In chapter 23, Jeffrey Bouffard and Nicole Niebuhr discuss research that has used experimental designs to examine offender decision making. Most of these studies have used hypothetical vignettes. The authors discuss how this research has shown various situational and individual-level factors to influence both the content and the process of offender decision making in important ways.

Chapter 24 is devoted to the use of observational methods in offender decision-making research. Marie Rosenkrantz Lindegaard and Heith Copes argue that the use of camera footage of criminal events is a promising method augmenting the more conventional but rather seldomly used ethnographic methods (participant observation and researcher as observer). They discuss merits and shortcomings of each approach within the context of the positivistic turn in criminology.

In chapter 25, Ronet Bachman and Ray Paternoster discuss the use of survey, interview, and life calendar methodologies in offender decision-making research. This chapter provides a review of such research using samples from the general population of adolescents and young adults as well as samples of adolescents at a higher risk of offending and adult offenders in correctional settings.

In chapter 26, Daniel Birks discusses the use of agent-based modeling (ABM) and agent-based social simulation (ABSS) in studying how offenders decide in criminal events. The chapter outlines how ABM can be used to construct formal models of offenders and the decisions they make. Subsequently, it proposes that ABSS provides unique means to formally assess the explanatory capacity of proposed crime event decisions.

Chapter 27 addresses the use of secondary data in offender decision modeling. Wim Bernasco reviews the use of police and other law enforcement records as well as that of population registries that contain data on birth, death, family composition, schooling, employment, finances, and health. The chapter reviews the use of secondary data in research on the decision of whether to offend and on the decision of where to offend.

E. Part V: Studies on Decision Making About Various Types of Crimes

Whereas the preceding parts of this handbook focus on the common characteristics of crime in general, and thus describe criminal decision making in generic terms, the final part of the handbook discusses criminal decision making with respect to a variety of specific types of crime: homicide, carjacking, sexual crimes, burglary, white-collar crime, and organized crime. Each chapter in this part addresses aspects of decision making that are pertinent to the particular type of crime.

In chapter 28, Fiona Brookman and Michelle Wright take up the challenge of characterizing the decision making of homicide offenders. Given the paucity of literature on this topic, they also include sublethal violent offenses and present case studies to illustrate the cognitive, affective, and situational factors that influence decision making in lethal and near-lethal events.

In chapter 29, Gabriel Cesar and Scott Decker analyze the decision-making behaviors of carjackers, arguing that a theoretical framework to explain this type of choice behavior is currently lacking. They provide their own theoretical account based on a hot/cool approach of offender decision making and discuss its implications for both policy and prevention.

In chapter 30, Eric Beauregard provides a review of the literature on decision making involved in sexual crimes, focusing specifically on the decision making involved before, during, and following the crime. He argues that sex offenders are "reasoning" offenders and that the long-standing assumptions that sex offenders suffer from mental disorders and are mainly driven by an uncontrollable impulse to sexually offend contradict accumulating evidence showing the versatility among this group of offenders.

In chapter 31, Timothy Coupe discusses the literature on burglar decision making, distinguishing between burglary event decisions, decisions leading up to the burglary, and burglary characteristics that provide insights into them. The chapter reviews empirical evidence, highlights gaps in the current knowledge base, discusses methodologies and aspects of theory, and identifies avenues for future research.

As Wim Huisman states in chapter 32, corporate crimes are offenses that employees commit in the interest of their company, whereas white-collar crimes are those they commit for personal benefit. What these crimes have in common is that they are typically perpetrated in an occupational or business-related setting. His review of the literature closely follows the framework sketched in this introduction, as he consecutively addresses the characteristics of the decision makers, the characteristics of situations, and the perception of action alternatives in the context of corporate and white-collar crimes.

In chapter 33, Paolo Campana applies a rational choice perspective to explore the key mechanisms of organized crime, with a special focus on protection rackets. He defines organized crime in terms of market monopolies and discusses the factors that facilitate criminal monopolies. After discussing the distinctive features of protection rackets, he addresses the challenges faced by illegal protectors.

III. Where Do We Stand Now?

Where do we stand now, after having digested all the contributions in this book? Offender decision making as a field of research is in full swing. It may be expected that criminology will see further work on theory, methodology, and applications in this field. We hope that the current handbook will be useful for scientists wishing to contribute—possibly by expanding on some of the work in the chapters or by firmly challenging what is proposed in this handbook. We as editors are looking forward to it.

References

Becker, G. S. 1968. "Crime and Punishment: An Economic Approach." *Journal of Political Economy* 76:169–217.

Bentham, J. 1889. *An Introduction to the Principles of Morals and Legislation*. Oxford: Clarendon Press. (Originally published 1789.)

Cornish, D. B., and R. V. Clarke. 1986. *The Reasoning Criminal: Rational Choice Perspectives on Offending*. New York: Springer-Verlag.

Kahneman, D. 2011. *Thinking, Fast and Slow*. New York: Farrar, Straus and Giroux.

Smith, A. 1982. *The Theory of Moral Sentiments*. Indianapolis, IN: Liberty. (Originally published 1759.)

CHAPTER 2

....

RATIONAL CHOICE THEORY, HEURISTICS, AND BIASES

....

MEGAN EILEEN COLLINS
AND THOMAS A. LOUGHRAN

WHEN confronted with equitable conditions, why is it that two similarly motivated offenders may reach disparate conclusions with regard to what is "rational"? For example, how can it be that when two burglars encounter the same set of circumstances, such as an alarmed but empty house on a well-trafficked street, one views it as a suitable target, whereas the other perceives it as being too risky? Could an offender's prior experience with the criminal justice system or knowledge of the likely punishment for getting caught in the act of burgling the house influence his or her perceptions of risk? An expanding body of criminological literature seeks to answer such questions and enhance our understanding of the elements that contribute to offender decision-making processes.

For instance, in a review article, Piquero et al. (2011) crafted an argument for a refinement of traditional deterrence theory, specifically focused on the deterrent effect of sanctions on offender decision making. The authors' key point is that the question is not whether or not sanctions deter but, instead, under what conditions, for which kind of persons, and when and for whom do (or do not) sanctions deter? The main conclusion offered by Piquero et al. is that the deterrent effect of sanctions can be thought of as *heterogeneous*. One such set of instances in which this heterogeneity is present is across a "kinds-of-people dimension," or individual differences such as level of social bonding, morality, impulsivity and time preference, social network position, and decision-making ability. Similarly, Mamayek, Paternoster, and Loughran (chapter 11, this volume) expand on this issue of individual heterogeneity with respect to the role of certain conceptualizations of time orientation in the offender decision-making process.

However, a second set of instances in which deterrent effects of sanctions may operate in a heterogeneous manner is situational. Beyond individual differences, a growing body of research on deterrence is aimed at studying the use of *heuristic biases*, or cognitive shortcuts taken in certain situations, when offenders make decisions in the face of uncertainty. Kahneman (2011) defined a heuristic as "a simple procedure that helps find adequate, though often imperfect, answers to difficult questions" (p. 98) and framed the "heuristic question" as a simpler question, the answer to which is substituted in place of the answer to a more difficult and thought-intensive target question.[1] The idea is that when offenders (or any individuals) are contemplating uncertain decisions with limited time, information, or resources to make a rational choice calculus, heuristics enable a suitable decision to be reached quickly. However, often heuristics can lead to biases, errors, preference reversals, or suboptimal decisions.

This chapter explores the concepts of departures from rational behavior, and heuristics and biases, and how such instances have been integrated into the study of offenders' choice calculus. It begins with an overview of rational choice and then reviews how biases and deviations have been routinely observed when studying offender decisions.

I. Overview of Economic Rational Choice Theory

Rational choice theory asserts that criminals engage in a form of cost–benefit analysis to determine whether to commit a crime. It is based on the expected utility principle in economic theory, which states that people will make rational decisions based on the extent to which they expect the choice to maximize benefits and minimize costs. Perhaps the earliest example of theorizing about this type of rational offender can be identified in Bentham's (1789/1843) philosophy of utilitarianism. This thinking suggested that individuals apply a felicific calculus—to determine the amount of pleasure something is likely to produce—when estimating the moral standing of any particular action.[2] Describing this notion, Bentham wrote, "The profit of the crime is the force which urges man to delinquency: The pain of the punishment is the force employed to restrain him from it. If the first of these forces be the greater, the crime will be committed; if the second, the crime will not be committed." (p. 399). Bentham's work was expanded upon by twentieth-century social scientists who have further developed the discussion of individual-level risk calculus. Notably, economist Gary Becker introduced a neoclassical economic approach to crime, assuming that people are self-interestedly rational, opting to commit crime when it provides the greatest benefit to them. Becker argued that the frequency of crime is determined by three factors: (a) the costs of crime associated with arrest, probability of conviction, state punishment, and loss of income that could be gained from legal employment; (b) the benefit of financial, personal, or social gain from offending; and (c) the many variables that influence one's motivation or willingness to offend. These factors vary according to individuals' values and preferences, as individuals seek to maximize their personal welfare as they perceive it. Actions are limited by factors such as income, time, imperfect memory and calculating abilities, and opportunities (Becker 1968, 1993).

Thus, when heterogeneity and influence of values, beliefs, preferences, situations, and the like are considered, rational choice becomes a much richer, more complex process than a crude cost–benefit calculus. Economic notions of rational choice assume that crime can be understood as if people use the same principles of a cost–benefit calculus to decide if they are going to commit crime as they use when selecting legal behaviors (Becker 1968; Ehrlich 1974; McCarthy 2002).[3]

A utility function can be applied to standardize various costs and benefits of crime into comparable units (von Neumann and Morgenstern 1944; Becker 1968). A utility of a particular action or behavior is determined by evaluating the costs and benefits, weighted by the probability of receiving consequences and the probability of receiving benefits. A generic utility model would take a form such as the following:

$$\left[U\left(c_1, c_2\right) = \pi_1 * u\left(c_1\right) + \pi_2 * u\left(c_2\right)\right]$$

This utility model depicts the weighting of a course of action, dependent on two conditions (c_1 and c_2). When extended to estimating the costs and benefits of committing crime, the expected utility model may be rewritten as follows:

$$\left[U\left(\text{crime}\right) = \pi_1 * u\left(\text{benefits of crime}\right) + \pi_2 * u\left(\text{costs of crime}\right)\right]$$

Under these conditions, deterrence from crime is most likely to occur when the expected disutility of costs, which is weighted by the likelihood of receiving sanctions, exceeds the benefits of the offense.

An individual's perceptions of costs and benefits are limited by his or her "bounded" rationality, which is constrained by limited time, ability, and availability of relevant information. Bounded rationality refers to the cognitive, information, and computational limitations that may influence the process of making a "rational" decision (Simon 1982). The factors considered by offenders are not uniform and are instead informed and influenced by their individual socialization and experiences. One's costs can include both formal and informal sanctions in addition to moral costs, whereas benefits may be interpreted differently based on different individual and situational perceptions. In addition, benefits are not necessarily instrumental in nature. Offenders may obtain emotional or mental benefits (e.g., status) that are intangible and seemingly beyond the scope of deterrence (Katz 1988). People have preferences for particular outcomes (e.g., goods, services, and states of being), which may be influenced by their orientation to present versus future outcomes (McCarthy 2002). However, as indicated by the expected utility model, these outcomes are probabilistic and generally lack a guarantee that they will be realized.[4]

McCarthy (2002) asserted that people base assessments of costs and decisions on information they collect, noting that gathering information is a cost in itself. For actions to be considered rational, they must be consistent with their assessments of costs, benefits, and preferences (because this can be situational and individual, behaviors cannot be described a priori as rational). Thus, "rational choice" does not mean that people cannot or do not act irrationally (i.e., acting in a way that is inconsistent with expected utilities). It does mean that there is a relationship between preferences and choices; these choices are not deterministic and may vary depending on individual preferences, information, and approaches and responses to risk.

This utilitarian literature provides a foundation for the criminological rational choice theory as well as for the cognitive processes, such as heuristics and biases, that inform offender decision making. Criminological rational choice theory is only briefly introduced in the following section; it is presented in greater detail in chapter 4.

II. Emergence of Criminological Rational Choice Theory

The assumptions of rational choice theory, as described in the economic literature, are consistent with those of classical criminology and deterrence. The rational choice theory of offending in the criminological literature is thus a product of both Enlightenment era (e.g., Bentham and Beccaria) and microeconomic (e.g., Becker) influences.[5] However, the criminological model expands on a fundamental explanation of deterrence and instead seeks to provide a general, inclusive explanation of engaging in and refraining from crime (Cornish and Clarke 1986).[6] According to rational choice theory as described by Cornish and Clarke, the decision to engage in criminal acts is a two-stage process. First, individuals decide whether they are willing to engage in crime in order to satisfy their needs. This "initial involvement model" indicates that individuals may consider an array of ways to satisfy their needs (both criminal and noncriminal), which may be influenced by their personal beliefs, experiences, and knowledge. Second, once individuals decide to engage in crime, they must target a particular offense that meets their specific need ("the criminal event model") (Cornish and Clarke 1986). Subsequently, motivated offenders engage in "situational selection," in which they select certain situations for engaging in crime, largely based on the perceived costs and benefits (Birkbeck and LaFree 1993).

This consideration of costs and benefits is derived from the aforementioned economic literature. As the probability of being sanctioned increases, the net benefits from offending decrease. Typically, this calculus assumes that the benefits from offending are not contingent on avoiding detection—just sanction—and that all costs from offending rely on apprehension by official entities. For example, in a qualitative assessment of repeat property offenders, Tunnell (1990, 1992) found that these offenders believed they would gain income (benefits) from engaging in property crime and that they either would not get caught or would not serve much prison time if they were caught and sanctioned. However, these reports did not entirely align with earlier notions of rational choice theory because it was clear that many of the offenders did not engage in rational calculations of costs and benefits, with little forethought about planning or consideration of potential risks.

Importantly, perceptions of costs and benefits, and estimates of the ratio of one to the other, are not universal. Previous research has established that people generally respond to situational factors and risks of offending quite differently. As such, an average effect of outcomes such as sanction severity may not provide much information regarding processes, given the individual nature of decision making (Piquero et al. 2011). There exists great heterogeneity in offender perspectives, experiences, and competencies that influence their individual decision-making processes. For example, this was demonstrated when Nagin and Paternoster (1993) surveyed approximately 700 undergraduate students, presenting them with three hypothetical scenarios involving drunk driving, larceny, and sexual assaults. They found that persons low in self-control (as indicated by the 24-item scale developed by Grasmick et al. [1993]) perceived higher utility for offending because the rewards were immediate, discounted the costs because they were delayed, and appeared insensitive to social censure. These findings indicate that poor self-control plays an important role in explaining variation in intentions to offend.

Thus, contemporary criminological research has taken early notions of rational choice and deterrence theories (Bentham 1789/1843; Cornish and Clarke 1986) and begun to account for individual heterogeneity and differing perceptions of costs and benefits. This individual variation has been the focus of recent inquiries (for a review, see Paternoster 2010) and has introduced questions regarding which individual differences and cognitive processes matter most (Piquero et al. 2011).

III. MODELING COGNITIVE PROCESSES INFLUENCING RATIONAL CHOICE

In an effort to better understand the individual and situational contexts that impact one's decision-making processes, and the potential for deterrence, criminologists have expanded the initial focus on utility and reason to a wide-ranging exploration of cognitive processes. These contemporary areas of inquiry include integrating concepts of microeconomics and heuristics into explanations of crime. Noting this shift, Oldfather (2007) posited, "Behavioral law and economics replaces one model incorporating an assumption about human behavior—that people act rationally—with another that likewise incorporates an assumption about human behavior—that people act irrationally in predictable ways" (p. 253).

Generalizations concerning thought processes and behaviors that influence this "predictably irrational" conduct are classified as heuristic biases. Specifically, these cognitive tools require one's subjective assessment of the probability of a particular outcome or event occurring (Tversky and Kahneman 1974). Individual differences in cognitive processes and susceptibility to irrational behavior are not uniformly distributed but are instead understood to be the product of individual or situational contexts (Mitchell 2002; Oldfather 2007).

Assessments of probability are typically based on imperfect data, which are then interpreted according to heuristic rules (Tversky and Kahneman 1974). For example, when attempting to apply reason to everyday problems, people typically use statistical heuristics, or judgmental tools that are intuitively comparable to statistical principles. The likelihood of using statistical heuristics and reasoning may be affected by the clarity of the sample space and processes, recognition of the operation of chance factors, cultural prescriptions, and the role of generalizing from instances (Nisbett et al. 1983).[7] Tversky and Kahneman (1974) outlined three heuristics that are often utilized when making judgments under uncertainty: representativeness (to determine the probability that an object or event belongs to a particular class or process), availability of instances or scenarios (to assess frequency or probability of a class or event), and adjustment from an anchor (for numerical predictions).

Use of heuristics such as these can correct for individuals' overconfidence and self-serving interpretations of information when confronted with uncertain outcomes (Weinstein 2003; Covey 2007). However, they can also lead to systematic and predictable errors (i.e., biases), which include insensitivities to prior outcome probabilities, sample size, chance, and predictability (Tversky and Kahneman 1974).

As heuristics and cognitive bias take on stochastic processes rather than determinism, they provide an explanation of how people make many of their decisions, without the assumption that all choices can be anticipated or explained. Individuals' choices can thus vary, even when confronted with the same preferences, information, and approaches to risk (McCarthy 2002). Thus, biases vary across people and situations, and although experienced statisticians are unlikely to make the same errors as laymen, such as the "gambler's fallacy," they are still susceptible to biases that stem from more complex problems (Tversky and Kahneman 1974). The remainder of this chapter introduces several examples of heuristics that may be utilized when offenders make decisions, and it provides illustrations of how biases can contribute to heterogeneous actions in the face of equitable circumstances.

IV. Examples of Modeling Decision-Making Processes

One way in which rational choice and decision making have been modeled as a cognitive process is through prospect theory. Devised by Kahneman and Tversky (1979), this microeconomic model is considered to be a more psychologically accurate representation of decision-making processes that attempts to addresses some of the limitations and violations of the expected utility model. These violations include overweighting certain outcomes compared to probabilistic outcomes (violating expected utility); over-weighting extremely low probabilities (and failing to differentiate between them); pre-ferring certain gains over probabilistic gains, while choosing probabilistic losses over certain losses; and failing to consider the marginal utility of a gain as less than the mar-ginal utility of an equivalent loss.[8] In other words, Kahneman and Tversky contend that individuals consider gains and losses differently and that when two equal choices are presented—one phrased in terms of gains and one in terms of losses—people are more likely to choose the former.

Kahneman and Tversky's (1979) prospect theory attempts to overcome these vio-lations through a two-stage choice process. In the first phase (the "editing phase"), competitive outcomes are re-evaluated and ordered according to a certain heuristic.[9] Through the editing process, people determine which outcomes are equivalent, and they set a threshold or "reference point" separating losses from gains. In doing so, fram-ing effects and other phenomena that might contribute to inaccurate utility assessments are addressed. In the "evaluation phase," people estimate a utility based on potential outcomes and respective probabilities, and they choose the outcome with the higher respective probability.

Loughran and colleagues (2012) assessed the relationship between perceptions of risk and self-reported offending, and they identified a threshold as described by Kahneman and Tversky (1979). Initial analyses revealed a negative relationship between risk per-ceptions and self-reported offending. Deterrence only occurs when one's estimated risk of sanction reaches a certain threshold or "reference point" (i.e., between 0.3 and 0.4), with an accelerated deterrence effect appearing at the high end of the perceived risk continuum. The nonlinearity of this relationship conforms to the assumptions of pros-pect theory. This concept of a tipping point—that is, a point at which one's perception of the risk certainty must exceed or else there will be no deterrent effect of risk—has been alluded to in prior work by Tittle and Rowe (1974) at a macro level. This also implies that very small levels of risk may not be enough to deflect offender behavior if such levels are simply ignored. Thus, according to prospect theory, when selecting a target, burglars would first assess potential gains relative to costs (e.g., the value of the heist relative to the chance of being caught) and then evaluate the values and perceived probabilities of the gains and losses. This individual assessment and evaluation process, as well as the preference for gains over losses, can explain why offenders may violate the expected util-ity model or make other "irrational" decisions.

A number of methods that are less explicitly economic have also been applied in an effort to describe or explain the individual process of decision making. For exam-ple, McCarthy (2002) cited game theory as a way to model the interacting dynamics that contribute to decision-making processes, suggesting that it can be used to provide and assess explanations of crime. This approach to decision making is unique in that it assumes people are strategic in their interactions, aware that their actions affect one another. Furthermore, game theory approaches assume that the people making deci-sions are rational, have preferences, and understand the characteristics of the process in which they are involved (McCarthy 2002).

In some instances, game theory may treat crime as a heuristic device, providing the foundation of a game to more broadly explore individuals' assumptions about social organization, social change, peoples' behavior, or game theoretic concepts (Brams 1994; Hoffman 2001).These game theoretic situations treat human behavior as a rational reaction to a constantly changing environment. Because different environments may be associated with different risks or rewards, individuals must adapt accordingly (Tsebelis 1990). Unlike economic models, however, game theory approaches to decision making include an additional actor—the police. Rather than limiting decisions to an individual's weighting of costs and benefits, the crime scenario is conceived of as a game in which criminals and police modify their behaviors (and assessments of risk) in response to one another. In its simplest form, each party has two possible actions: The criminal can violate or not violate the law, and the police can enforce or not enforce the law (Tsebelis 1990). Decisions in this context vary with the completeness of information available, environment, and strategy employed by either party.

Another game theoretical approach is Brams' theory of moves (TOM), which is used to predict decision making regarding mugging incidents in which victims would or would not resist and muggers would or would not use force. Data reveal that nonresistance of victims is more likely than resistance regardless of whether the mugger is armed, and likelihood of the use of force by the mugger is inversely related to being armed. Victims' responses are largely unaffected by the type of weapon, whereas the muggers' behavior appears to become less violent the better armed they are. When modeling the risk–payoff matrix, Brams used the TOM model to weigh probabilities of using force and resistance and found that when resistance becomes relatively less costly, muggers are more likely to use force (Brams 1994; Hoffman 2001). As such, game theory may be considered a heuristic in the sense that it can aid with one's cognitive processing of potential costs and outcomes when making a rational decision regarding offending.

V. Individual Decision Making and Biases

In addition to the process itself, differences in decision-making *competence* have often been described in the context of an individual-level trait or characteristic. "Thoughtfully reflective decision making" (TRDM; Paternoster and Pogarsky 2009) describes the process of rational decision making in four phases: thinking about the most important alternatives to one's goals, collecting information about possible alternatives, thinking intelligently about how likely it is each alternative will allow for goal achievement, and revisiting the decision and learning from it (Paternoster and Pogarsky 2009; Paternoster, Pogarsky, and Zimmerman 2011). Paternoster and Pogarsky hypothesize that TRDM is positively related to prosocial outcomes, such as pursuit of higher education, and negatively related to maladaptive outcomes, such as crime. Paternoster and colleagues (2011) furthered this hypothesis to suggest that the relationship between TRDM and crime is mediated by capital accumulation; those who engage in thoughtfully reflective decision making are more likely to gain social, cultural, and human capital (i.e., access to support through relationships, positive communication, education, and other skills). Paternoster et al. demonstrated that TRDM was inversely related to short-term (one year) and long-term (three year) participation in crime. Specifically, TRDM was positively related to the formation of personal, cultural, and social capital; those who engaged in TRDM were more likely to make investments in different forms of capital, inversely associated with offending.

Another common cause of individual bias has to do with the tendency to overvalue one's own level of skill or expertise; this is commonly referred to as self-serving bias. Dunning, Heath, and Suls (2004) reviewed multiple areas in which self-assessment has been demonstrated to be flawed, noting that an individual's ability to introspectively self-assess is not very accurate. For instance, humans routinely overrate their own performance across a wide range of abilities, from intelligence and academic skill (Chemers, Hu, and Garcia 2001) to driving proficiency (Rutter, Quine, and Albery 1998). This type of overconfidence has been repeatedly shown to affect individual behavior to the point at which unwise or irrational behavior is undertaken (Thaler 1988). It is no surprise, then, that offenders often overvalue their own abilities and that this level of overconfidence can lead to increases in offending behavior outside of traditional rational behavior in which costs and risk are carefully weighed. For example, studies by Wright and Decker (1997) and Tunnell (1992) indicated that feelings of overconfidence tended to drive the decisions of residential burglars.[10]

Early work on perceptual deterrence by Waldo and Chiricos (1972) noted an important distinction between one's subjective beliefs about the risk certainty for an average person and one's subjective beliefs about the risk certainty for oneself. Loughran et al. (2013) exploited this distinction in a sample of active offenders who reported both sets of perceptions for getting caught (i.e., risk to others and risk to self) for a range of crimes. Loughran et al. calculated the difference between these two sets of perceptions and argued that those who perceived the risk to one's self was lower than the risk to others displayed a self-serving bias. Specifically, these individuals tended to think of their own skill at avoiding detection to be somehow better than average. Loughran et al. found that self-serving bias was highly related to the future offending behavior, even after controlling for mean levels of subjective risks.

Notably, there is now growing evidence that individual perceptions about offending (e.g., sanction risks) are dynamic and malleable and, more important, responsive to one's personal or even vicarious experiences. For example, Piquero and colleagues (2011) noted that although the process of Bayesian updating has been demonstrated in a number of studies that show that people update risk perceptions, the mean effect of this updating is generally small in magnitude (Pogarsky and Piquero 2003; Pogarsky, Piquero, and Paternoster 2004; Matsueda, Kreager, and Huizinga 2006; Lochner 2007; Anwar and Loughran 2011). Anwar and Loughran found that individuals update their perceptions of the risk of receiving sanctions based on current information, or what they refer to as an offending "signal"—that is, the ratio of arrests to crimes committed. They found that an individual who commits one crime and is arrested will increase his or her perceived probability of being caught by 6.3 percent compared with if he or she had not been arrested. Thus, one's prior experiences with being arrested impact the degree to which one updates how he or she processes new information. Others have found similar evidence of rational updating of offending perceptions (Matsueda et al. 2006; Lochner 2007). These findings contribute to the perceptual deterrence framework in that the perception of certainty of apprehension or sanction is related to an individual's offending; people update their perceived risk based on previous experiences.

Although Bayesian updating is a hyperrational behavior in that it implies individuals are fully integrating all learned information via personal experience into their subjective beliefs, it appears that not all offenders seem to update in such a manner. Anwar and Loughran's (2011) research was expanded upon to assess whether the deterrent effect of arrest has a differential impact across individuals based on some observable factors. Yet more recent work by Thomas, Loughran, and Piquero (2013) suggests that the degree to which individuals are influenced by new information in the form of their offending signal is perhaps not entirely rational in that it may be moderated by individual-level differences such as criminal propensity. Specifically, the authors found that high-propensity individuals are more responsive to official sanctions in terms of updating their posterior risk perceptions. These findings suggest that certain individual factors can perhaps be determinant in the process of updating, specifically in terms of how individuals may predictably deviate from rational updating, a necessary condition for deterrence.

With regard to issues of time, Loughran, Paternoster, and Weiss (2012) examined the phenomena of intertemporal decision making (i.e., decisions involving costs and benefits that occur at different points in time). Using data from a scenario-based survey instrument completed by 478 university students, Loughran and colleagues found evidence for hyperbolic time preferences. Specifically, when respondents indicated preferences related to a drunk driving scenario, Loughran et al. found hyperbolic time preferences for both costs and rewards; the discount function appeared to operate independently of changes in the risk certainty for detection. When the benefit was delayed by 1 week, the self-reported intention to offend increased by nearly 10 percent; however, when delayed by 1 month, the intent to offend increased by only 4 percent. A weaker effect was identified for delayed costs. Thus, time and other contextual variations have important effects on individuals' perceptions of risk.

VI. Conclusions and Future Directions

Clearly, the decision to offend is a complex process, which may be influenced by situational context; timing; individual differences in intelligence, education, financial stability, and experience; and one's perceptions of the associated risks, costs, and benefits. Contrasting the crude risk calculus posited in early rational choice models, the study of cognitive biases is viewed by some as better explaining the often irrational behavior of criminals compared to the miscalculation of costs and benefits that emerge from one's "bounded rationality" (Simon 1982). Examples presented in this chapter, such as prospect theory and game theory, provide more comprehensive illustrations of cognitive mechanisms that may influence decision making and account for seemingly irrational behavior. Similarly, sources of individual heterogeneity and bias, such as self-serving bias and updating based on past experiences, can help explain why individual offenders confronted with equitable circumstances can arrive at two different but "rational" decisions. For example, again consider the discussion of the two burglars presented at the beginning of the chapter. There are many reasons why one may find a given target to be suitable, whereas another does not—for instance, subjective perceptions of risk of getting caught, which vary between the two individuals based on their own actual experiences with apprehension, or factors such as their inability to rationally update these subjective beliefs based on their different degree of self-serving bias.

Our understanding of the heuristics that drive these diverse perceptions and subsequent behaviors relies on research across social and behavioral science disciplines. Specifically, the study of offender decision making has revealed an important set of predictable biases that appear to be instrumental in offending behavior. However, this body of work is relatively new and still quite narrow. We advocate for a continued agenda to study these issues. In order to understand the unobservable or latent processes behind individual decision-making processes, continued innovation and theorizing across economics, cognitive science, psychology, and criminology are necessary.

NOTES

1. For instance, Kahneman (2011) gives an example of a target question, "How happy are you with your life these days?" and an analog heuristic question, "What is my mood right now?"
2. The felicific calculus algorithm was generated by Bentham (1789) and includes seven variables or "circumstances" in the calculation: intensity, duration, certainty or uncertainty, propinquity or remoteness, fecundity (probability it will be followed by sensations of the same kind), purity (probability it will not be followed by opposite sensations), and extent (number of people affected).
3. Therefore, the decision to offend is influenced by individuals' preferences; attitudes toward risk and time discounting; and estimates regarding the availability, costs, and benefits of an illegal opportunity and how these returns compare to a legal alternative (McCarthy 2002).
4. As such, the expected utility function reflects three important features of preferences for outcomes: People's preferences are influenced by the potential (as opposed to the assured) benefits of an outcome relative to its costs; economists recognize several types of potential costs and benefits, many of which are nonmonetary—however, decision-making models typically assign them monetary values; and calculating an expected utility for an action involves multiplying a person's utility of each possible outcome by the possibility it will occur (if an action is chosen) and then summing across all possible outcomes.
5. There are some exceptions to the argument that criminological rational choice is derived from the economic model. For example, Akers and Sellers (2013) note that there have been

some cases of rational choice concepts emerging from criminological research; for example, "aleatory risk" was born from sociologists' study of delinquency (Strodtbeck and Short 1964; Short and Strodtbeck 1965).

6. Some criminologists have questioned the contribution of an economic approach to explaining crime. For example, Gottfredson and Hirschi (1990) stated that "the theoretical contribution of the new economic positivism is not as impressive as it is to its authors" (p. 72), arguing that economic analyses related to crime are of little value to the field.

7. Nisbett and colleagues (1983) note that statistical heuristics generally rely on training in statistics so that it may be a part of one's cognitive process. Training increases the likelihood people will take a statistical approach to a given problem and the quality of the statistical solutions. Adults who lack a formal understanding of statistical principles still seem to reason in statistical ways about events, other than those produced by a randomizing machine.

8. Kahneman and Tversky (1979) attempted to explain why people commonly violate basic statistical principles during basic inductive reasoning tasks. Reasons for these violations included that people consistently overlook statistical variables such as sample size, correlation, and base rate when solving inductive reasoning problems (Nisbett et al. 1983).

9. Editing processes include coding, combination, segregation, cancellation, simplification, and dominance (Kahneman and Tversky 1979).

10. A corollary to the concept of self-serving bias is a tendency to take credit for successes but blame failures on external events, a theme echoed by the subject of Tunnell's (1992) interview. When the burglar was asked if he worried about getting caught, he answered, "No. . . . No-o-o. I didn't give a damn. And the police couldn't catch a damn cold if it wasn't for the snitches" (p. 89).

REFERENCES

Akers, R. L., and C. S. Sellers. 2013. *Criminological Theories: Introduction, Evaluation, and Application*. Oxford: Oxford University Press.

Anwar, S., and T. A. Loughran. 2011. "Testing a Bayesian learning theory of deterrence among serious juvenile offenders." *Criminology* 49:667–98.

Becker, G. S. 1968. "Crime and Punishment: An Economic Approach." *Journal of Political Economy* 76J:169–217.

Becker, G. S. 1993. "Nobel Lecture: The Economic Way of Looking at Behavior." *Journal of Political Economy* 101:385–409.

Bentham, J. 1843. *An Introduction to the Principles of Morals and Legislation*. Oxford: Clarendon Press. (Originally published 1789.)

Birkbeck, C., and G. LaFree. 1993. "The Situational Analysis of Crime and Deviance." *American Review of Sociology* 19:113–37.

Brams, S. J. 1994. *Theory of Moves*. Cambridge: Cambridge University Press.

Chemers, M. M., L. Hu, and B. F. Garcia. 2001. "Academic Self-Efficiency and First-Year College Student Performance and Adjustment." *Journal of Educational Psychology* 93:55–64.

Cornish, D. B., and R. V. Clarke. 1986. *The Reasoning Criminal: Rational Choice Perspectives on Offending*. New York: Springer-Verlag.

Covey, R. 2007. "Reconsidering the Relationship Between Cognitive Psychology and Plea Bargaining." *Marquette Law Review* 91:213–47.

Dunning, D., C. Heath, and J. Suls. 2004. "Flawed Self-Assessment: Implications for Health, Education, and the Workplace." *Psychological Science in the Public Interest* 5:69–106.

Ehrlich I. 1974. "Participation in Illegitimate Activities: An Economic Analysis." In *Essays in the Economics of Crime and Punishment*, edited by G. S. Becker and W. M. Landes, pp. 68–134. New York: Columbia University Press.

Gottfredson, M. R., and T. Hirschi. 1990. *A General Theory of Crime.* Stanford, CA: Stanford University Press.

Grasmick, H. G., C. R. Tittle, R. J. Bursik, and B. J. Arneklev. 1993. "Testing the Core Empirical Implications of Gottfredson and Hirschi's General Theory of Crime." *Journal of Research in Crime and Delinquency* 30:5–29.

Hoffman, R. 2001. "Mixed Strategies in the Mugging Game." *Rationality and Society* 13:205–12.

Kahneman, D. 2011. *Thinking Fast and Slow.* New York: Farrar, Straus, and Giroux.

Kahneman, D., and A. Tversky. 1979. "Prospect Theory: An Analysis of Decision Under Risk." *Econometrica* 47:263–91.

Katz, J. 1988. *Seductions of Crime: Moral and Sensual Attractions in Doing Evil.* New York: Basic Books.

Lochner, L. 2007. "Individual Perceptions of the Criminal Justice System." *American Economic Review* 97:444–60.

Loughran, T. A., R. Paternoster, and D. Weiss. 2012. "Hyperbolic Time Discounting, Offender Time Preferences, and Deterrence." *Journal of Quantitative Criminology* 28:607–28.

Loughran, T. A., G. Pogarsky, A. R. Piquero, and R. Paternoster. 2012. "Re-examining the Functional Form of the Certainty Effect in Deterrence Theory." *Justice Quarterly* 29:712–41.

Loughran, T. A., R. Paternoster, A. R. Piquero, and J. Fagan. 2013. "'A Good Man Always Knows His Limitations': The Role of Overconfidence in Criminal Offending." *Journal of Research in Crime and Delinquency* 50:327–58.

Matsueda, R. L., D. A. Kreager, and D. Huzinga. 2006. "Deterring Delinquents: A Rational Choice Model of Theft and Violence." *American Sociological Review* 71:95–122.

McCarthy, B. 2002. "New Economics of Sociological Criminology." *Annual Review of Sociology* 28:417–42.

Mitchell, G. 2002. "Why Law and Economics' Perfect Rationality Should Not Be Traded for Behavioral Law and Economics' Equal Incompetence." *Georgetown Law Journal* 67:83–7.

Nagin, D. S., and R. Paternoster. 1993. "Time and Punishment: Delayed Consequences and Criminal Behavior." *Journal of Quantitative Criminology* 20:295–317.

Nisbett, R. E., D. H. Krantz, C. Jepsen, and Z. Kunda. 1983. "The Use of Statistical Heuristics in Everyday Inductive Reasoning." *Psychological Review* 90:339–63.

Oldfather, C. M. 2007. "Heuristics, Biases, and Criminal Defendants." *Marquette Law Review* 91:249–62.

Paternoster, R. 2010. "How Much Do We Really Know About Criminal Deterrence?" *Journal of Criminal Law and Criminology* 100:765–824.

Paternoster, R., and G. Pogarsky. 2009. "Rational Choice, Agency and Thoughtfully Reflective Decision Making: The Short- and Long-Term Consequences of Making Good Choices." *Journal of Quantitative Criminology* 25:103–27.

Paternoster, R., G. Pogarsky, and G. Zimmerman. 2011. "Thoughtfully Reflective Decision Making and the Accumulation of Capital: Bringing Choice Back In." *Journal of Quantitative Criminology* 27:1–26.

Piquero, A. R., R. Paternoster, G. Pogarsky, and T. A. Loughran. 2011. "Elaborating the Individual Difference Component in Deterrence Theory." *Annual Review of Law and Social Science* 7:335–60.

Pogarsky, G., and A. R. Piquero. 2003. "Can Punishment Encourage Offending? Investigating the 'Resetting' Effect." *Journal of Research in Crime and Delinquency* 40:95–120.

Pogarsky, G., A. R. Piquero, and R. Paternoster. 2004. "Modeling Change in Perceptions About Sanction Threats: The Neglected Linkage in Deterrence Theory." *Journal of Quantitative Criminology* 20:343–69.

Rutter, D. R., L. Quine, and I. P. Albery. 1998. "Perceptions of Risk in Motorcyclists: Unrealistic Optimism, Relative Realism and Predictions of Behavior." *British Journal of Psychology* 89:681–96.

Short, J. F., and F. L. Strodtbeck. 1965. *Group Process and Gang Delinquency*. Chicago: University of Chicago Press.

Simon, H. A. 1982. *Models of Bounded Rationality*. Cambridge, MA: MIT Press.

Strodtbeck, F. L., and J. F. Short. 1964. "Aleatory Risks Versus Short-Run Hedonism in Explanation of Gang Action." *Social Problems* 12:127–40.

Thaler, R. H. 1988. "Anomalies: The Winner's Curse." *Journal of Economic Perspectives* 2: 191–202.

Thomas, K. J., T. A. Loughran, and A. R. Piquero. 2013. "Do Individual Characteristics Explain Variation in Sanction Risk Updating Among Serious Juvenile Offenders? Advancing the Logic of Differential Deterrence." *Law and Human Behavior* 37:10–21.

Tittle, C. R., and A. R. Rowe. 1974. "Certainty of Arrest and Crime Rates: A Further Test of the Deterrence Hypothesis." *Social Forces* 52:455–62.

Tsebelis, G. 1990. "Penalty Has No Impact on Crime: A Game-Theoretic Analysis." *Rationality and Society* 2(3): 255–86.

Tunnell, K. D. 1990. "Choosing Crime: Close Your Eyes and Take Your Chances." *Justice Quarterly* 7:673–90.

Tunnell, K. D. 1992. *Choosing Crime: The Criminal Calculus of Property Offenders*. Chicago: Nelson-Hall.

Tversky, A., and D. Kahneman. 1974. "Judgment Under Uncertainty: Heuristics and Biases." *Science* 185:1124–31.

von Neumann, J., and O. Morgenstern. 1944. *Theory of Games and Economic Behavior*. Princeton, NJ: Princeton University Press.

Waldo, G., and T. Chiricos. 1972. "Perceived Penal Sanction and Self-Reported Criminality." *Social Problems* 19:522–40.

Weinstein, I. 2003. "Don't Believe Everything You Think: Cognitive Bias in Legal Decision Making." *Clinical Law Review* 9:783–834.

Wright, R. T., and S. H. Decker. 1997. *Armed Robbers in Action: Stickups and Street Culture*. Boston: Northeastern University Press.

CHAPTER 3

....

EVOLUTIONARY APPROACHES TO RATIONAL CHOICE

....

PAUL EKBLOM

DOBZHANSKY (1973) stated that "nothing in biology makes sense except in the light of evolution." It arranges apparently disjointed facts in natural history as a coherent body of knowledge explaining and predicting many facts about life. We should therefore consider how far the evolutionary perspective illuminates human rationality, including that of offenders.

As other chapters in this handbook elaborate, the rational choice perspective (RCP) is a lynchpin of crime science and especially of situational crime prevention (SCP). It focuses on the here and now of criminal decision making with its agenda of maximizing reward and minimizing risk and effort (Clarke 2014). Offender motivation is taken as given, and detailed mental mechanisms of perception, motivation, and choice are underemphasized in pursuit of "good enough theory" (Clarke 2014) centered on crime as opportunity. Intended for practitioners, this heuristic has been considered insufficient for leading-edge science (Bouhana 2013; Ekblom and Hirschfield 2014). Moreover, richer understanding of *offenders* may be necessary to help refine *situational* interventions (Ekblom 2007)—for example, how and why adolescents handle risk differently compared to adults should inform interventions targeted on this age group. One radical path to enrichment is to research the *evolutionary* connections of RCP. This not only facilitates importing theories, findings, and research methods from diverse disciplines into crime science but also helps view the familiar from fresh angles.

Forays into evolution and biological ecology in crime science are rare. They include Cohen, Vila, and Machalek (1995) on evolutionary expropriative strategies; Ekblom (1997, 1999, 2015) on arms races; Felson (2006) on crime and nature; optimal foraging theory (e.g., Bernasco, 2009); and a guide by Roach and Pease (2013); see also Sagarin and Taylor (2008) for an exploration of "natural security" by biologists. As will be discussed in this chapter, evolution can unfold in domains beyond the biological. Hence, *cultural* evolution, with cumulation and transmission through ideas or memes rather than genes (Aunger 2000; Caldwell and Millen 2008), also pertains to the evolution of rationality. These processes interact through gene–cultural coevolution or dual inheritance (Henrich and McElreath 2003). It is worth noting that this line of thought is still evolving: Jablonka and Lamb (2014) distinguish *four* dimensions of evolution, namely genetic, epigenetic, behavioral, and symbolic.

This chapter proceeds as follows. Basic concepts of evolution are introduced, covering brain and behavior, levels and types of explanation, the strained relationship with social science, and the evidencing of evolutionary processes. Next, the focus shifts to rationality, covering decision making; the wider suite of capacities and processes needed to understand rationality in action; and specific discussions on cooperation, humans' wider "sociocognitive niche," and development. Although evolutionary issues are addressed throughout, the penultimate section covers how rationality in the broadest sense has unfolded over evolutionary history and the significant connection between maximization of utility in contemporary rational choice and maximization/optimization of fitness in evolution. The conclusion raises practical, empirical, and theoretical questions for crime science.

Several points should be kept in mind when reading this chapter. First, although crime-related illustrations are emphasized, processes and capacities peculiar to crime are rare. This is unsurprising because evolution explains what is common to humans as one species compared to others rather than focusing on individual differences. RCP and SCP particularly chime with this because they view offenders as essentially normal people with broadly normal motives/preferences and psychological makeup acting in situations occasioning criminal opportunities. However, broader approaches, such as situational action theory (Wikström 2014), also cover differences in criminal propensity, and it is the *capacity* to develop criminal propensity under certain conditions that may be universal. Second, in this chapter, the biological evolution of behavioral tendencies is treated as equivalent to that of anatomy and physiology—obvious given that individual thought and action occur through neurological mechanisms. However, learning and cultural evolution are also highly significant and are often brought in. Last, crossing disciplinary boundaries challenges terminology: References here to agents, organisms, and creatures are equivalent.

I. What Is Evolution?

Biological evolution is a threefold process undergone by all organisms. Generation of *variation* in anatomy, physiology, or behavioral tendency among individual members of a species is followed by natural or sexual *selection* in terms of differential probability of survival and reproduction in the species' habitat, which may challenge individuals with competition for resources or mates, conflict, and predation. Variants better adapted to their environment—or alternatively stated, meeting appropriate fitness criteria—tend to survive and reproduce more than their conspecifics. Mechanisms of *inheritance*—predominantly through encoding of DNA in genes—transmit the properties of the variants to subsequent generations. All this produces a gradual increase in the proportion of variants in a given breeding population that possess features fitter for survival and reproduction. This mechanism operates over many generations, where the species as a whole, and particularly its genes, "learns" what it takes to flourish in its normal habitat. Variety may be generated by recombination of gene variants via sexual reproduction or through point mutations and other copying errors in DNA.

Of course, an organism's *genotype* is not the only influence on its *phenotype* (adult form). Individual genes interact with one another and with the environment in successively more complex ways as the organism develops from fertilized egg to maturity. Nature and nurture are inseparable (just as disposition and situation combine in generating contemporary behavior). In humans particularly, much of the environment to which individuals must adapt is social—that is, comprising other people.

Fergusson et al. (2011) illustrate how genetic inheritance and early life experience interact. They show that the probability of maltreated children developing violent and antisocial tendencies is mediated by the genetically varying activity of monoamine oxidase A (MAOA)—an enzyme that breaks down dopamine. However, the apparent violence-promoting effect of low-activity MAOA appears only if individuals experience maltreatment during childhood; hence, this is a genetic effect contingent on proximal causes.

A. Evolution, the Brain, and Behavior

Because the human brain has evolved like the hand or eye, and because its neurological structure and operation underlie psychological processes, it is reasonable to suppose that psychological mechanisms and the behavior they generate may partly derive from evolutionary experience, as transmitted by genes. As Cosmides and Tooby (1994) neatly state,

> The applicability of evolutionary biology is based on a simple but powerful idea. Form follows function: The properties of an evolved mechanism reflect the structure of the task it evolved to solve. This approach has teeth because there is only one class of problems that evolution produces mechanisms for solving: *adaptive* problems. These are problems that recurred across many generations during a species' evolutionary history, and whose solution statistically promoted reproduction in ancestral environments. By identifying and modelling the adaptive problems humans faced during their evolution, researchers can make educated guesses about the designs of the complex computational devices the human brain embodies, and about many of the specific design features they required to be able to solve these problems. (p. 329, emphasis in original)

The approach known as *evolutionary psychology* (Tooby and Cosmides 2005) holds that natural selection has equipped humans with some specific evolved psychological mechanisms—a "Swiss army knife" of modules—that conferred adaptive advantage in the past. Each supports specialized thinking about a particular kind of technical or social problem repeatedly confronting our Paleolithic ancestors (what crime scientist would not warm to the problem-specific orientation?). Each applies a distinctive set of rules and representations, and each is a kind of "reasoning instinct." To quote Cosmides and Tooby (1994) again,

> Although instincts are often thought of as the polar opposite of reasoning, a growing body of evidence indicates that humans have many reasoning, learning, and preference circuits that (i) are complexly specialized for solving the specific adaptive problems our hominid ancestors regularly encountered; (ii) reliably develop in all normal human beings; (iii) develop without any conscious effort; (iv) develop without any formal instruction; (v) are applied without any awareness of their underlying logic; and (vi) are distinct from more general abilities to process information or behave intelligently. . . . They make certain kinds of inferences just as easy, effortless and "natural" to make as spinning a web is to a spider or building a dam is to a beaver. (p. 330)

The hypothesized conditions under which our distinctively human mental adaptations arose are termed the "environment of evolutionary adaptedness" (EEA [Bowlby 1969]; equivalent to the historically "expected" habitat). They occurred mostly in the Pleistocene epoch (1.8 million to 11,000 years before present). Then, modern humans and their predecessors lived in small hunter–gatherer tribes, all of whose members knew each other intimately; there was no permanent settlement, agriculture, private property, large interacting populations, or mass communication. The proposed problems that modules evolved to solve include habitat selection, foraging, competition from small armed groups, parental care, language acquisition, contagion avoidance, sexual rivalry, and social exchange (Cosmides and Tooby 1994). Several of these are of obvious significance to crime scientists.

In combination with contemporary developmental and environmental factors, these modules influence how we interpret and behave in different situations. Cosmides and Tooby (1994; see also Pinker 1994) claim that massive modularity and its repertoire of specialist problem-solving methods are more powerfully adaptive for organisms than the rational decision-making methods of logic, mathematics, and probability theory. They further argue that the massive modularity approach eclipses the perspectives of *bounded rationality*—that is, rationality modified by a series of limitations and biases (Simon 1955; Kahneman 2003)—and *heuristics*, an alternative and long-standing approach to understanding adaptive behavior based on satisficing (Simon 1976; Kahneman, Slovic, and Tversky 1982). Chapter 2 in this handbook covers both.

From an evolutionary perspective, neither boundedness of rationality nor heuristics are shortcomings from some absolute standard of perfect rationality. They are an optimization solution, juggling brainpower (and the energy and material requirements to build and run powerful brains), time to decide, and availability of information against the overall contribution to survival and reproduction. For example, heuristics are simple, shallow but effective rules of thumb, which are effective most of the time in the EEA and occupy relatively little of the brain's limited processing capacity. Gigerenzer and Gaissmaier (2011) even demonstrate that in some circumstances, ignoring part of the information relevant to decisions can lead to more accurate judgments. According to Schulz (2011), few economists consider decision-making speed and frugality alongside accuracy; however, the whole package is important for survival.

Proponents of these diverse perspectives battle on. Gintis (2009) holds that cognitive biases and irrationalities undermine the rational actor perspective underlying economic theory. Brighton and Gigerenzer (2012), advocates of heuristics, maintain that rational choice models work only in "small worlds," in which the dimensions of the problem to be decided are pre-given, but fail in "large worlds," in which the dimensions themselves have to be defined and clarified.

Mention must also be made of Ormerod's (2012) agent-based modeling approach to games. He views *imitation* as an efficient alternative adaptive process to rationality in complex environments in which the payoff to various strategies is constantly changing. This relates to the "costly information hypothesis" (Henrich and McElreath 2003), which sees trade-offs in effort and advantage between acquiring behaviorally useful information about the environment via individual learning and the social equivalent.

However, the massive modularity approach to evolutionary psychology (EP) has itself been challenged from the opposite direction by Heyes (2012*b*) and colleagues, under a "new thinking" label. Rather than merely addressing relatively recently arisen differences between humans and hominid apes, this takes a longer historical perspective, reaching way before the Pleistocene, offering wider cross-species comparison. In strong contrast to what it calls "high church evolutionary psychology" (Heyes 2012*b*, p. 2092), it suggests that rather than recently emerged cognitive *modules*, humans are endowed with uniquely powerful, *domain-general* cognitive–developmental mechanisms. She offers the metaphor of the human hand in contrast to the Swiss army knife of modularity—the hand being of far longer and more gradual evolution and being both highly functionally and structurally integrated and extremely adaptable. The "new thinking" also highlights the importance of coevolution and cultural evolution in generating gradual, incremental change. A related critique is in Jablonka and Lamb (2014) who argue that apparently-inherited modules can be accounted for by processes of social/cultural construction.

This divergence of models has implications for crime science—for example, whether the "risk, effort, and reward" dimensions of criminal choice are universal or differ between module domains; whether and when the decisions of criminal involvement, commission, or desistance can be viewed as small-world or large-world related (perhaps the latter applies to innovative crime); and whether we should attend more to *imitation* as an alternative to rational choice.

B. Levels and Types of Explanation

Different levels of explanation were used previously; to avoid confusion, we must distinguish between them. Suppose, for example, that people are predisposed to prefer sweet foods. Tinbergen (1963) describes four ways of understanding this pattern of behavioral preference. *Functional* explanations consider here-and-now benefits to individuals of acquiring sweet foods for survival and reproduction. In nonhumans, these are unconscious. In humans, often these may be processed as cognitively mediated goals involving reflectivity and symbolic thought. (Nevertheless, until the scientific era, it was known only that humans liked sweet foods, not why.) *Mechanistic* explanations refer to contemporary underlying causes, whether proximal (active in situations immediately preceding or hosting the behavior—for example, a state of hunger or the sight of chocolate) or more distal (e.g., the market price of sugar). (Note that goal-directed behavior is ultimately reducible to causal mechanisms, but these involve feedback loops homing in on the desired end-state. Note also that psychological mechanisms may in turn be redescribed in neurological/biochemical terms—for example, glucose sensors in the hypothalamus.) *Developmental* explanations describe how individuals acquire the behavioral tendency while progressing from egg to adolescent to adult and, more generally, through learning (as such, they are an instance of distal). *Ultimate* causes cover evolutionary history, relating to the period when the behavior first evolved and the preference for sweet things emerged and conferred adaptive advantage on those individuals who possessed the genetic variants that underlay it. This historical account resembles the functional, but it becomes significant when environmental conditions change, generating dysfunctional lags. Thus, uninhibited pursuit of sweetness was an excellent adaptation in the EEA when such treats were rare and to be rapidly consumed at every opportunity. However, in the abundant present, our scarcity-derived preferences jeopardize survival (e.g., via obesity).

Because genetically transmitted influences must act via the development of the phenotype in each successive generation, evolutionary approaches to cognition often adopt developmental perspectives. It is during development, and the extended juvenile learning period in higher animals, that environmental influences also exert themselves (whether as prolonged processes such as deprivation or critical incidents such as traumatic events): Information about the here-and-now environment is incorporated in the organism's competences and acquired goals. In this respect, higher cognitive development is less "canalized" than, for example, the basic development of vision, making room for cultural inputs (discussed later).

C. Evolution and Social Science

Whichever of the rival EP perspectives prevails, we should refute the argument that EP views significant human psychological/behavioral tendencies as mere "wired-in" fixed action patterns. This has underlain much of the criticism from conventional social science, long resistant to evolutionary explanations (for a refutation, see Roach and Pease 2013). The dominant assumption has been that the young mind is free of any content that does not originate in the senses and the social world, and it is equipped only with a few content-independent rules of inference (Cosmides and Tooby 1994). But from the

EP perspective, these assumptions are false. Also, each mechanism envisaged by EP is primed to detect and react to specific, distinct, environmental stimuli. As James and Goetze (2001) stated, "Different environmental stimuli trigger different mechanisms, and we may have a large number of such mechanisms. If indeed this is the correct way to understand human psychology and associated behaviors, then any complete explanation will necessarily involve a discussion of environmental stimuli and activated mental mechanisms" (pp. 9–10).

Thus, EP approaches are entirely compatible with *situational* approaches to crime. The *developmental* emphasis in the "new thinking" approach additionally views the emergence of the general-purpose cognitive capacity of humans as a product of protracted childhood interactions between genetic potential and environmental experience. Because most of humans' environment is social, this allows much scope for transmission, through social learning, of *cultural* influences, and indeed the evolution of culturally/linguistically mediated layers of cognitive ability, including logic or moral reasoning. These "add-ons" may underlie "everyday" rational choice processes for most of us, although their culturally advanced equivalents in economics or moral philosophy are rarely used by criminals.

This prompts consideration of wider Darwinian evolutionary processes than the biological/genetic model: Although all follow the same "evolutionary algorithm" (Dennett 1995), they are mediated by different mechanisms. Cultural evolution can be viewed as the variation, selection, and replication of "memes" (Dawkins 1976; Aunger 2000). Analogous to genes, these are ideas, designs for tools and weapons, tunes, and complexes such as religious or moral causes. Cultural replication itself works through several mechanisms operating on different scales. Godfrey-Smith (2012) distinguishes imitative selection from the population of intracultural variants of behavior (i.e., individuals choosing what/who to copy); cumulative cultural adaptation (e.g., adjustments to climate change); and the most macro-level, "cultural phylogenetic change" (e.g., the Neolithic revolution shifting from hunting–gathering to farming).

"Gene–culture coevolution" or "dual-inheritance" theories (Cavalli-Sforza and Feldman 1981; Boyd and Richerson 1985) envisage interactions between biological and cultural processes, the classic example being the evolution of dairying culture in Neolithic northern Europe alongside genetic tolerance for lactose (milk sugar) previously indigestible by adults. Of more particular interest, Sterelny (2012) states the importance of *techno-social* coevolution in bestowing language on hominins (those species, ourselves and extinct relatives, that split from apes on the distinctively human line of descent) and turning them into cooperative foragers. He argues that improvements in technical (foraging) and social skills (gestural communication) were mediated by common cognitive processes controlling complex sequences of action. Pressure for improvement in technical competence enhanced social as well as technical skills, and vice versa, in a positive feedback loop.

Complex action sequences include scripts, a significant field in crime science (Cornish 1994), but script performance generally requires a string of decisions, some of which will have salient "rational choice" aspects. Proficiency with weapons and tools, communication, collaboration, and foraging have clear implications for emergence of competence at both committing and defending against crime-like behavior. The last phrase is used because obviously the cultural, societal, and institutional definition of *crime* as we know it did not exist in the hunter–gatherer bands in which humans emerged.

In summary, both cultural and developmental processes and the significance of situational triggers firmly link EP to contemporary social phenomena—if not always recognized by the academics who study them. As will be shown, biological and cultural evolutionary processes have supported the evolution of rationality, in the course of which they have imposed their imprints on it.

D. Establishing Evidence for Evolutionary Psychology Influences

Gould and Lewontin (1979) and others have attacked facile "evolutionary just-so stories"' (as in Kipling's "how the elephant got its trunk") in which evolutionary enthusiasts have uncritically posited adaptive functions and evolutionary histories behind a range of behavioral and anatomical features of particular organisms, including humans. In the present context, we risk overattributing aspects of rationality and other crime-related features to specific evolutionary circumstances and processes.

Gould's point is now broadly accepted. Evidence for EP influences must be triangulated from diverse sources—experimental, comparative, developmental, archaeological, genetic, physiological, and so forth. Specifically, Heyes (2003), drawing on Pinker (1997) and others, describes how a candidate for cognitive evolution is assumed to be phylogenetic (i.e., evolved and inherited) if (a) there is evidence of "poverty of the stimulus"—that is, the adaptive properties of the cognitive process could not have arisen through experience alone because that experience supplied too little information to account for the complexity of the process—or (b) the adaptive properties are genetically heritable. Conversely, it is classed as ontogenetic (arising developmentally) if the evidence suggests "wealth of the stimulus"—that is, the adaptive properties could be products of experience—and if there is no evidence of genetic heritability. Heyes states, "Research relevant to the poverty or wealth of the stimulus compares the development of cognitive processes across species, cultures, and subgroups within a population. Wealth is indicated by correlated variation in experience and development, whereas poverty is implied by invariant development in the face of experiential diversity" (p. 715).

Nonetheless, the evidentiary issue remains unsettled. Shulz (2011) warns that evidentially, simple heuristic models (à la Gigerenzer) suffer from an ongoing lack of crucial information about our past, a shortcoming he generalizes to all evolutionary approaches to rationality.

Subtler approaches to evidence and analysis are required. For example, Heyes (2003), discussing adaptive specialization of cognitive processes, distinguishes between *constructive* and *inflectional* processes. The first refers to qualitatively different cognitive mechanisms, whereas the second refers to same mechanisms but processing different input (e.g., from the perceptual system and ultimately from the outside environment). The evidence trail for these distinctions is complex and painstaking—no just-so stories here.

II. RATIONALITY

Rationality relates to organisms, their mental processes and behavior (and perhaps their tools; Ekblom 2016). It is variously a process of generating rational behavior, a capacity and/or a state of mind for so doing ("He is not entirely rational"), or a description of a particular item of thought or behavior ("That act was irrational"). Rationality is addressed elsewhere in this handbook; here, the interest lies in the process and capacity, its function, and its evolutionary history.

Rationality is addressed through diverse disciplines: Kacelnik (2006; see also Houston, McNamara, and Steer 2007) distinguishes *PP-rationality* (psychology and philosophy, centering on mental mechanisms/processes rather than outcomes), *E-rationality* (economics, centering on behavioral outcomes/choices leading to utility maximization), and *B-rationality* (biology, centering on evolutionary/ecological aspects of organisms' adaptation to their habitat). Attempts have been made to explore the relationship between these in considering whether biological insights can support or illuminate economic thinking on rationality (Cosmides and Tooby 1994; Schulz 2011) or vice versa (Okasha and Binmore 2014). RCP in crime science has elements of both E-rationality (risk, effort, and reward) and PP-rationality (boundedness and hot and cool decisions) (van Gelder et al. 2014) but has barely touched on B-rationality.

Psychological (PP-) studies of the mediation of rationality have come to distinguish between diverse mechanisms—experiential versus analytic (Slovic et al. 2004)—and the related "system 1 versus system 2 thinking" (Kahneman 2011). (These are further discussed in chapter 9.) System 1 is fast, automatic, frequent, emotional, stereotypic, and subconscious; system 2 is slow, effortful, infrequent, logical, calculating, and conscious. Extremes of system 1 may connect, for example, to Katz's (1988) account of the emotional and phenomenological processes of, for example, righteous, enraged murder.

In contrast to PP-rationality, E-rationality, used in economics, is predominantly instrumental, with the goal being the maximization of expected utility. This can be used to predict patterns of behavior without paying much attention to underlying mechanisms. However, to class someone as rational, we must assume, or seek evidence for, the goals the person is pursuing and how they relate to one another in terms of priority, transitivity, and so on. The divergence of focus between psychological process (PP) and economic outcomes/goals (E) relates to the dual "caused agent" perspective (Ekblom 2010): The offender as *caused* by environmental and/or internal mechanisms (perceptions of risk, states of intoxication or arousal, etc.) but simultaneously *causing*—that is, actively constructing and executing plans and goals.

The third discourse, B-rationality, is mainly a subsidiary of E-rationality in which outcomes relate to costs and benefits in an ecological context. We revisit this later.

A. Decision Making

The discussion of rationality usually centers on the process of decision making, often involving issues of risk/uncertainty. We find choices straightforward to talk about both scientifically and in the vernacular. However, we must first ask what exactly decisions are and how they fit within an evolutionary framework; we must also consider the wider "rationality suite" of processes and systems within which they act, develop, and have evolved with.

Decisions are taken at various stages of cognition. We are continually making *perceptual* decisions—for example, "Is it a police car or an ambulance siren?" The outcome of perceptual decisions may inform more general *action* decisions. Prey species have evolved to cope with knife-edge balancing of feeding versus fleeing in deciding whether lions, for example, are hunting or just ambling past. Here, the action choices are predetermined and merely await input from the perceptual decision regarding which is activated. Less critical situations allow time for weighing action choices in terms of risk, effort, and reward.

With action decisions, the mechanisms are diverse. We have already noted the system 1/system 2 duality. A partially related phenomenon addressed by van Gelder et al. (2014) is the distinction between decision making undertaken in "hot" versus "cool" states of mood or emotion. However, even the most calculating and cool of decisions appears to rely on *affect* or "gut feeling" to swing the choice one way or another, with affect described by Slovic et al. (2004) as a "faint whisper of emotion" (p. 312). Strong evidence for this derives from people with particular brain damage who, whilst perfectly articulating the advantages and disadvantages, cannot make decisions. This led Damasio (Bechara, Damasio, and Damasio, 2000) to contend that rationality is a product of both the analytical and the experiential mind and, particularly, to develop the "somatic marker" theory in which all thoughts (perceptual and symbolic images) become marked with positive or negative affect, whether through experience, evolutionary pre-programming (think snakes), or some combination. One evolved function of emotions—affect especially—thus seems to be integral to decision making rather than an alternative, even with "instrumental" behavior, in which visceral emotional processes are absent (cf. van Gelder et al. 2014).

At the functional level, why take decisions at all? The answer must relate an organism's evolved needs for survival and reproduction to its contemporary mechanisms for delivering those outcomes in relation to ecological factors in its habitat. Decision making is pervasive: Bacteria decide whether to secrete an enzyme to exploit a particular foodstuff when that becomes available; plants decide when to drop leaves in relation to drought. With humans—foraging for food, tackling an opponent, or burgling a house—the decisions are more numerous, interlinked, and subtle.

Fundamentally, decisions are needed because organisms have multiple goals to juggle. Their priority and urgency may shift dynamically over various timescales (e.g., the state of their energy reserves; Houston 2014) and as a function of immediate or anticipated environmental conditions that may make demands, supply resources, or place constraints on the organism. These goals, and the behaviors that serve them, may well be in conflict or competition. This threatens paralysis or vacillation if some capacity is not available to routinely detect or anticipate such circumstances and force a choice to resolve the affair.

The decision-making capacity of contemporary organisms has diverse origins. A core capacity has evolved *genetically*: Any organism incapable of making ecologically relevant decisions is unlikely to survive and replicate. However, additional decision-making capacity built on genetic inheritance is acquired *developmentally*. This may partly be sourced from individual learning undertaken during a single lifetime, partly (in humans) from social learning/instruction. The last may draw on cultural knowledge that has itself evolved over multiple generations, including the invention of formal logic and economic theory.

Cultural inputs also supply *motivational, emotional,* and *reputational influences* in valuing decisiveness and strong planning and execution; however, occasionally the opposite occurs in subcultures of "anti-rationality" as documented by Wright and Decker (1994). Generally, the psychological "handles" on which emotions tug have evolutionary origins. Fearless animals or those that do not like their food are likely to die sooner, and individual members of group-living species that are unconcerned with status are less likely to breed.

The *time* dimension of rationality is important. Decision making generally addresses the future, anticipating that particular harmful or beneficial events may happen, necessitating prior action. The capacity to anticipate, and the content of assumptions and predictions made, will usually derive from the past. Biological evolution as a whole resembles a learning process (Hammerstein and Stevens 2012) in which the genes defining a particular species have learned about stable features of their habitat (e.g., climate or terrain), and over generations the resulting phenotype is appropriately adapted.

Only ecological variations that are stable over many generations can be addressed by genetic learning, leading in higher organisms to the evolution of "instincts." However, variations too rapid for genes to track can be picked up by cultural evolution and the fastest by individual within-lifetime processes of learning. Plotkin (1997) makes an interesting point that rationality of any kind can only evolve if there is "predictable unpredictability"—that is, variation of the food supply, for example, or the population of predators, within a normal range. Total chaos makes anticipatory decisions impossible; total certainty makes rationality superfluous to survival. Plotkin states, "Learning and memory mechanisms, or some further capacity for rationality, are the way in which the problem of the uncertain physical future is solved" (p. 149). The intimate connection between risk and decision making is noteworthy.

B. The Wider Rationality Suite

The decision-making capacity has not evolved in isolation. It is embedded in a wider suite of tendencies, capacities, and processes that together enable agents to cope and flourish in their habitat. A fuller understanding of the current function and working of decisions and rationality, their development from birth, and their evolutionary history must embrace these internal and external contexts in which decisions are made and acted on. Crime science focuses on problem-solving approaches to prevention, but problem-solving by offenders is equally relevant (Ekblom 2016).

Rational choice can function only if the chooser has an array of *preferences* or goals. Criticisms of RCP in criminology have sometimes mistakenly equated these preferences exclusively with material ones (money, goods, etc.), whereas immaterial rewards such as status are also relevant. In fact, rationality is about *relations* between goals/preferences and the behavior for realizing them; it makes no presumptions about which preferences the chooser has. Economists term such factors *exogenous*. Many of these preferences are claimed to derive from our evolutionary history, as with the sweetness example discussed previously.

The options brought to the offender's attention for decision may be shaped by *perceptual* factors involving the assessment of uncertain possibilities, costs, threats, and risks (Slovic et al. 2004). According to Wikström's (2014) situational action theory, certain criminal options simply do not occur to many people. However, morality is not always automated. *Moral reasoning* may impose constraints and skew choices. Johnson (2014) argues that we have evolved to be moral creatures in order to survive and flourish in groups: Ethical reasoning is a form of problem solving primarily concerned with situations in which our values and interests conflict with those of others. Any social species encounters such situations, so morality is not uniquely human, although our own morality is more complicated, subtle, and reflective compared with that of other animals. In particular, we have evolved, culturally and genetically, what Johnson calls a capacity for *imaginative moral deliberation*—a simulation of alternative courses of action and their ethical consequences.

Broader reasoning/inference processes underlie both system 1 and system 2 decisions, although the latter takes more explicit and complex routes (Heyes 2003). Indeed, van Gelder et al. (2014) prefer the phrase "reasoned choice" over "rational choice." The evolution of human linguistic/symbolic capacity is another component in supporting sophisticated and communicable reasoning.

The rationality process must operate on *knowledge*. The basis of choice must be knowledge of both generic and specific operating environments/habitats, knowledge in the form of a behavioral repertoire and the advantages and disadvantages of alternatives, and self-knowledge of one's own capacity for tackling an adversary of particular strength.

Heylighen (1991) combines evolution and cybernetics to enrich understanding of the ecological function of decisions. As adaptive systems, organisms often face a situation in which maintenance or achievement of a particular goal state is jeopardized or "perturbed" by some circumstance. They must therefore choose items from their action repertoire that are most likely to compensate that particular perturbation. Knowledge of both actions and environment enables them to choose the former from the variety of alternatives at their disposal that are most likely to fit the latter, in taking (or returning) them to their desired goal state. According to Heylighen, knowledge substitutes for real encounters with the environment; thus, following a perspective presented by Campbell (1974), knowledge serves as a "vicarious selector." It represents, and allows anticipation of, the selective action of the environment, whether a lion lurking on the path home or police monitoring a drug den. *Natural* selection is in effect internalized; Popper (1972) has a related view of anticipated action, namely "ideas dying in our stead," that will be revisited. The more varied and complex the environment that agents must control, the greater the variety of responses they need at their disposal—an expression of Ashby's (1957) law of requisite variety—and thus the more sophisticated the decision-making capacity must become, along with the planning and design capacities to generate the variety of responses and fit them to purpose.

Due to the salience of opportunity in RCP and SCP, it is important to connect it to the rationality concept. The default understanding of opportunity is as a property of the environment. However, deeper reflection suggests that, like the larger scale ecological concept of the niche (Brantingham and Brantingham 1991), it is a conjoint property of the following: the particular goals of the offender (that is, opportunity to achieve what?), the properties of the environment, the knowledge and wider psychological capacity of the offender to perceive the opportunity (affordance) in that environment, and the material resources and psychological capacity of the offender (Ekblom and Tilley 2000) to cope with the hazards and exploit the vulnerabilities the environment contains. Implicit or explicit reasoning processes may connect possible coping and exploitative actions to the offender's goals. What becomes an opportunity thus depends on the evolving resources of the agent to perceive and exploit it and changes in the environmental components over time, including, other people and organizations. With criminal arms races (Ekblom 1997, 1999, 2015; Sagarin and Taylor 2008), these coevolve.

Typically, many individual crimes are viewed as impulsive, gain-now/pay-later affairs. Making decisions through system 2 often involves exercise of some kind of self-control or *executive function* to actively impose longer time frames and consideration of broader issues, including moral ones, on the estimation of costs and benefits. What happens after decisions is also important: It is pointless to carefully make a rational, utility-maximizing choice with delayed gratification if one cannot then stick to that choice over the appropriate time period. Ambitious, organized crimes in particular may require considerable self-control and patience in execution and also complex crime scripts involving a cascade of linked decisions as the scripts are adapted on-the-fly to current environmental contingencies. Whether such capacities are used for good or bad purposes, Jablonka, Ginsburg, and Dor (2012) view their origins in the requirement to develop strong inhibitory control to serve both the finicky, patience-demanding requirements of tool-making and those of "alloparenting," in which individuals besides the actual parents look after children (think of the patience of kindergarten teachers).

Pre-decisional neutralization in anticipation of guilt feelings and post-decisional rationalization are also relevant here, presumably psychologically/culturally uniquely human. Whether these offer any adaptive advantage is debatable: They may serve respectively to make decisions easier and to maintain them once made. Generally, neutralization and rationalization are examples of "metacognition," the processes by which we monitor and influence our own thinking and that of others (for review, see Frith 2012), with clear adaptive value, especially in group living.

More strategic decisions on criminal involvement, continuance, and desistance may last decades (although some of the lock-in may derive from the sustained response of the environment to the choice made—for example, persistent relationships with criminal associates or wider criminal reputation). Their mediating mechanisms may differ from those underwriting criminal tactical choices.

C. Rationality and Cooperation

Research (Nowak 2011) has emphasized the cooperative, altruistic nature of humans, which is unusual in the animal world. Schneier (2012) takes this up in the security field, noting that we should study cooperation in both the wider society and within groups of criminals.

Specifically, Gold (2014) reviews theories of "team reasoning," a perspective developed to account for apparently nonrational choices of players in game theory experiments. Gold proposes that players come to identify with their team and make choices that maximize team rather than individual benefit. Gold connects the switching between individual- and team-mindedness with the controversial issue within evolutionary science of multilevel selection (especially selection not just between individuals but also between groups). However, for crime science, immediate implications surely center on whether studying rational choice among cooperating co-offenders or offending organizations might benefit from a distinct team reasoning perspective.

D. Rationality and the Wider Human Sociocognitive Niche

Cooperation is part of a wider picture that informs what our rationality deals with today and how it evolved. Whiten and Erdal (2012) ask how a moderately sized ape, lacking the formidable anatomical adaptations of professional hunters such as lions, could compete over the same prey. The conventional answer (Tooby and DeVore 1987) revolves around the elaboration of a new cognitive niche based on intelligence and technology (e.g., the advanced inferential reasoning in tracking prey—how many, whether wounded, how long ago they passed, and the refinement of weapons for the kill). This enables humans to mount what Tooby and DeVore refer to as "evolutionary surprise attacks" that escalate the arms race such that prey cannot keep up through their own biologically evolving counteradaptations, which are slower to emerge and more limited in scope.

Whiten and Erdal (2012) argue, however, that cognition alone is insufficient. They present evidence that a fuller answer

> lies in the evolution of a new socio-cognitive niche, the principal components of which include forms of cooperation, egalitarianism, mindreading (also known as "theory of mind"), language and cultural transmission, that go far beyond the most comparable phenomena in other primates. This cognitive and behavioral complex allows a human hunter–gatherer band to function as a unique and highly competitive predatory organism. (p. 2119)

Whiten (2006) termed the complex "deep social mind" to emphasize the core features of mental interpenetration and adjustment of individual to group-level goals (as with "team reasoning" discussed previously). The consequent fitness benefits and positive feedback between the individual elements may explain the tripling of human brain size in the past 2.5 million years.

Note that the reason for much of this boost in brain size was less for dealing with other prey or predator species than for dealing with fellow humans. Indeed, such foraging and predatory capacity used by individuals or groups against other humans and their assets is what makes human criminals potentially so resourceful and adaptive (Cohen et al. 1995; Ekblom and Tilley 2000; Ekblom 2007) and capable of running those arms races against one another. Another relevant EP factor is human concern with reputation (Wilson and Daly 1985; Schneier 2012), which may have either criminocclusive or criminogenic consequences depending on whether the reputation is judged by wider society or fellow gang members.

E. Rationality and Development

Breland and Breland's (1961) famously titled article, "The Misbehavior of Organisms," describes numerous examples of different species' readiness to learn particular associations or actions but resistance to others. Humans are more versatile, but conventional EP suggests we will most easily learn what our inherited mental modules have prepared us for. For example, we should be better at learning how to spot cheats than to do some more abstract logical equivalent (Tooby and Cosmides 2005).

As previously noted, the process of development from birth to adulthood offers a distinct level of explanation for the decision-making and rational capacities of individuals traversing each stage. Personal and social learning of individually and culturally acquired knowledge play significant roles in such development—but what of biological evolution? The discipline known as "evo-devo" (Carroll 2005) studies how evolutionary changes are realized through their effects on developmental pathways. It has long been obvious that individuals' rational capacity increases from childhood through maturity.

Findings on adolescence, and its associated changes in neuroanatomy and perception of and appetite for risk, have reached an interesting stage (regarding evolution and the age–crime curve, see Steinberg 2005; Slovic et al. 2004; Roach and Pease 2013; regarding criminal decision making of juveniles, see chapter 13, this volume). Current research (Steinberg 2005) strongly suggests that adolescents undergo a phase in which

> changes in arousal and motivation brought on by pubertal maturation precede the development of regulatory competence in a manner that creates a disjunction between the adolescent's affective experience and his or her ability to regulate arousal and motivation. To the extent that the changes in arousal and motivation precede the development of regulatory competence—a reasonable speculation, but one that has yet to be confirmed—the developments of early adolescence may well create a situation in which one is starting an engine without yet having a skilled driver behind the wheel. (p. 70)

The major question with regard to "ultimate" explanations from evolutionary history is whether this disjunction is currently or previously *adaptive* or just an accidental outcome of other pressures with no, or negative, benefit for survival or reproduction. Risk-taking has been postulated to serve various adaptive functions despite its potentially high cost, with risky behaviors (including crime-related ones) largely driving elevated adolescent mortality rates across diverse species (Spear 2010). Set against these costs, these adaptive functions have been claimed to include increasing the probability of reproductive success among human and other species' males (Steinberg and Belsky 1996). In humans, this is hypothesized to stem from social status mechanisms originating in sexual selection (the "young male syndrome"; Wilson and Daly 1985). Steinberg (2005) notes that evidence in animal and human studies supports a link between increasing levels of reproductive hormones and sensitivity to social status, a fact consistent with the link between puberty and risk-taking. These fit an evolutionary pattern.

Whether adaptive or otherwise, this shifting relationship between emotion, risk perception/appetite, and behavioral control means that what may be effective situational influences on offenders during adolescence may differ from those that work during adulthood. Similar risk-related considerations could apply with gender differences, but this dimension has so far awakened little interest in SCP.

III. The Relationship Between Evolution and Rationality

This section discusses two issues central to the relationship between evolution and rationality: the elaboration of rationality throughout evolutionary history and the ahistorical relationship between maximizing utility and maximizing evolutionary fitness.

A. Evolutionary History

Biological evolution builds on prior art, extending here, simplifying there, finding a new adaptive function for anatomical or behavioral features originating in some other context (e.g., our upright walking stance may derive from tree-climbing). The result is a succession of modifications that weave a very crooked ascent to some peak in the "fitness landscape." Biological evolution is blind, and every new step must convey immediate adaptive advantage to the generation inaugurating it. Therefore, that peak may not be the theoretically highest one in the totality of fitness space. Biological evolution may be trapped at a local peak because once there, all alterations take the species downhill in fitness terms before it can ascend a higher peak. Evolutionary processes as much involve conserving what works as finding something better (some vital enzymes have remained essentially unchanged over millions of years and those transplanted from humans into yeasts may still function). This contributes to "evolutionary lag."

Slovic et al. (2004) give an example of how the "affect heuristic" (i.e., managing risks through gut feelings alone) hits the fitness limits: "It works beautifully when our experience enables us to anticipate accurately how we will like the consequences of our decisions. It fails miserably when the consequences turn out to be much different in character than we anticipated" (p. 321). They identify two ways in which experiential/system 1 thinking misguides us. One results from the deliberate manipulation of our affective reactions by those who wish to control our behaviors (as in advertising and con-tricks); the other results from the existence of stimuli in our environment that are simply not amenable to valid affective representation. Slovic et al. state, "If it was always optimal to follow our affective and experiential instincts, there would have been no need for the rational/analytic system of thinking to have evolved and become so prominent in human affairs" (p. 319).

Only human learning and cultural evolution are capable of looking, and leaping, across the deep valley that may separate a local fitness maximum from a far higher distant peak. Dennett's (1995) "tower of generate and test" conveys a key evolutionary sequence spanning the range from biological to individual and cultural learning. This is an imaginary tower in which each floor has creatures able to find better and smarter moves and find them more quickly and efficiently:

1. Darwinian creatures, on the ground floor, rely only on *genetically inherited* knowledge, and they die when this fails to predict or avoid trouble in their environment. The faulty knowledge is thus filtered out.
2. Skinnerians on the next floor are less likely to die but with simple trial-and-error learning "kill off" *behavior* that does not work and preserve that which does.
3. Popperian creatures on the next floor can *imagine* outcomes in their heads and solve problems by thought. In Popper's (1972) words, this ability "permits our hypotheses to die in our stead" (p. 244). Evolutionary pressure is not halted but, rather, taken offline from the real world into protective environments and recast in acts ranging from intuitive imagination to research and development. This is how we can leap across to higher peaks.

4. Gregorian creatures are named after psychologist Richard Gregory, who noted that *cultural artifacts* not only require intelligence to produce them but also enhance their owner's intelligence (Gregory 1981). Such artifacts can include tangible objects such as scissors or calculators, but as Dennett (1995) noted, they also include "mind tools" such as verbal/symbolically mediated logic and rationality. With these, Gregorian creatures can find good moves and evolve new behaviors much faster.

5. Scientific creatures rigorously, collectively, and publically *test hypotheses and undertake "rational" design* based on understanding of causal mechanisms.

The creatures in this sequence are successively more intelligent and efficiently innovative, and the process and scope of decision making expand at each floor. In fact, this is a case of the "evolution of evolvability" (Dawkins 2003), in which certain adaptations boost adaptive potential. Ekblom and Pease (2014) and Ekblom (2016) discuss this concept further with regard to adaptive criminals, citing Gregorian socio-technological examples such as 3D printers and "script kiddies" (software kits that enable amateurs to generate effective computer viruses). Related "bootstrapping" concepts feature in Henrich and McElreath's (2003) notion of the "evolution of cultural evolution."

"Better" decisions, covering more issues in more detail and perhaps over longer timescales, may only confer adaptive advantage if a species is committed to an intelligence-based strategy. (Some are not: Sea squirts begin as mobile larvae but on maturity settle on rocks and promptly digest their now-redundant brain. Also recall the previous discussion of the advantages of frugality and speed.)

Pressure to ascend the tower may come from competition, conflict, or the struggle for survival in a rapidly changing environment, as arguably happened due to cycles of drought and damp in East Africa's Rift Valley during the past few million years of human evolution (Shultz and Maslin 2013). Such changes effectively reshape the fitness landscape, removing the peaks that organisms had climbed and substituting others elsewhere. Continual change (evolutionary "disturbed ground") makes for *adaptable* generalists like ourselves rather than highly *adapted* specialized species that die out when their EEA disappears. Humans are creating the same perpetually disturbed circumstances for favoring opportunist species such as rats—and maybe opportunist fellow humans including criminals—through disruptive technologies, business models, and social media.

The cybernetician Heylighen (1991) considers the evolving requirements of mental control systems, where what these seek to control is some combination of the agent's environment, and their own behavior in that environment. As the level of complexity of a mental control system, and the variety of responses it can generate, exceeds a threshold, the agent encounters problems, as with the previously discussed example by Slovic et al. (2004). Heylighen therefore posits the need for higher levels of control to arise, via a "metasystem transition," with the emergence of a new system controlling the controls of the level below. He argues that the emergence of higher control leads to an increase in response variety, whereas the increase in variety, if it is large enough, stimulates the emergence of yet a higher control, in a positive feedback cycle.

Our own, uniquely human, rational level of control relies on symbolic concepts abstracted from their perceptual origins (e.g., "essence of cat" as opposed to the whole vision of claws, dead birds, litter trays, etc.). This provides generative creativity, producing a huge variety of action possibilities from which to choose—a fact exploited by offenders (Cropley et al. 2010)—and also, for practical purposes, free will. Heylighen (1991) also muses about the current emergence of a new level: our ability to design and use collective rational models. (These range from the deliberate design of new antibiotics to climate change models and certain frameworks in crime prevention; e.g., Ekblom 2011). Whether and how offenders might come to use such models in their decision making is debatable, but sophisticated cybercrime and fraud are likely possibilities.

As Heylighen (1991) describes it, the emergence and imposition of new, higher control systems seems rather neat and bloodless; however, the process, and the resultant composite systems, can be messy. The systems 1 and 2 model and the tower of generate and test discussed previously illustrate the "layering" often encountered particularly in biological evolution, in which old and new layers function alongside one another. In humans, the layers may conflict, as with impulsive versus reflective decisions and/or emotionally hot versus cool ones (van Gelder et al. 2014). Cultural layers and influences add to the fray.

Slovic et al. (2004) hold that effective rational decision making requires good integration of these modes of thought. Perhaps human mental conflicts over decisions are inevitably messy or are currently acute simply because the evolutionarily new cognitive layers have had insufficient time to "shake down" into full coordination with the earlier layers. Apart from guiding our understanding of situational precipitators (Wortley 2017) and decision-swayers, such conflicts between layers originating at different periods in evolutionary history constitute a rich source of literature ranging from fiction to moral philosophy and the Freudian entities of Id, Ego, and Superego. The diverse array of interactions between immediate situations, wider circumstances (e.g., prolonged stress), and humans' capacity to switch psychological states in terms of affect, moods, emotions, and visceral feelings (e.g., sexual arousal or rage) has powerful effects on our rationality that are well documented in van Gelder et al. (2014).

Biological evolution of complex organisms is slow, and changes from the EEA can leave them lagging behind, as discussed previously. With humans, the lag is continually stretched by environmental changes from our own accelerating techno-social evolution. This now places us in situations lacking natural environmental inhibitors for behaviors such as road rage and Internet trolling (empathic stimuli from face-to-face interaction are missing). The ongoing cultural evolution of our own rationality dooms humans to experience perpetual perturbation in our conflicting control systems at both individual and collective levels, unless and until Heylighen's metasystem transitions provide temporary relief.

However, the evolutionary literature is not yet settled. According to Dayan (2012), the clash of different decision-making mechanisms may not be just an evolutionary lag but also a beneficial adaptation. He views this struggle as providing valuable redundancy against errors in computing and maladaptive properties of the individual models on which the computations are based. Such internal competition thus may help to maintain robust decision making. Of course, such robustness may be especially helpful in our self-complicated circumstances.

The scope for both cultural perturbations and adaptations to them may be wider than some evolutionary biologists imagine. The controversy between massive-modularity protagonists (e.g., Tooby and Cosmides) and those supporting general cognitive capacity was noted previously. Heyes (2012a) especially questions the widespread assumption that it is biological evolution that produced and maintains the core cognitive processes enabling cultural inheritance. Using evidence from comparative psychology, developmental psychology, and cognitive neuroscience, she argues that the development of imitation and other processes of social learning is remarkably similar to the development of literacy, and that the cognitive processes enabling cultural inheritance are themselves significantly culturally inherited rather than exclusively and directly genetic. This instance of "evolutionary bootstrapping" can perhaps be likened to a switch from hardware evolution to software evolution.

Whatever the case, crime scientists should be cautious in assuming the universality and fixity of rational thinking across cultures and across situations. Brighton and Gigerenzer (2012) suggest that there is no such thing as "one true rationality" because rationality principles are invented, not discovered. The implications of this idea for RCP are that we must reconsider whether the simple table of "risk, effort, and reward" and so on at the heart of, for example, the 25 techniques of SCP remains entirely good enough (as argued by Tilley 2014) or should be decomposed into columns for specific kinds of risks, effort, and rewards.

B. Maximizing Utility, Maximizing Fitness?

Many writers (Becker 1976; Okasha 2011; Sterelny 2014) highlight the apparent similarity between maximization of utility, central to RCP especially within economics, and maximization/optimization of evolutionary fitness in biology. Cosmides and Tooby (1994) talk of evolution creating the mental equipment whereby individuals' economic choices create the market: One invisible hand creating the other. Gintis (2014) argues that the "rational actor" model integrates seamlessly with evolutionary biology, discounting on evolutionary grounds the received psychological view that human cognitive biases *undermine* the applicability of RCP. Indeed, Nettle (2012) argues that an evolutionary approach via error management theory predicts the sorts of contexts in which biased decision making might be anticipated: those with important implications for evolutionary fitness. The link, if valid, promises dividends in transfer of ideas, research methods, and practice between these disciplines. However, there are complications.

Both utility and fitness maximization concern an organism's success in dealing with its environment, and both are claimed to play similar theoretical roles in their respective disciplines (Schulz 2014). In RCP, agents are assumed to make choices that maximize their utility, whereas in evolutionary theory, natural selection "chooses" between alternative phenotypes, or genes, in line with fitness maximization. Consequently, evolved organisms often exhibit behavioral choices apparently designed to maximize their fitness, which suggests that rational choice principles might be applied to study nonhumans (Okasha and Binmore 2014).

Crime science may gain from traffic in the opposite direction—for example, in importation of thinking from the ecologically based optimal foraging theory (OFT). This was initially used in behavioral ecology to explain how animals search, choose, and process food; it was extended to deal with how they handle predators, competitors, and so on. The conceptual heart of OFT, as with RCP, concerns goal-oriented behavior, with contemporary goals derived ultimately through natural selection acting over evolutionary history. Optimizing foraging strategies involves making (rational) choices in terms of the budgeting of resources, including time and energy, which maximize reproductive success and hence evolutionary fitness. In other words, the *capacity* to forage optimally can be viewed as a fitness-enhancing outcome of evolution; exercising that capacity in the everyday *conduct* of optimal foraging should enhance survival and reproductive success. Unfortunately, few OFT studies show that decision making leads to different fitness outcomes; one exception is that by Altman (1998).

The OFT–RCP link is explored in detail by Bernasco (2009), who utilized OFT to derive hypotheses on offense specialization, the use of time and space by property offenders, and the influence of police presence on offender behavior. The fruitfulness of this approach led him to conclude that although OFT in itself adds relatively little that is not already in RCP, the importation of perspectives and methods from behavioral ecology that the link enables, enriches the approach to research and helps complete the wider picture of causal factors that the abstract RCP does not specify. Gintis (2014) holds that a complete theory of behavioral choice must go beyond the rational actor model to incorporate ideas from both evolutionary biology and social psychology.

However, the specific OFT–RCP linkage and the more general utility/fitness equivalence are not straightforward. Bernasco (2009) identifies differences between OFT as applied to humans versus animals. *Legal* behaviors almost always remain an alternative human choice, and criminal involvement is usually embedded in a lifestyle mostly comprising legal behavior—a distinction irrelevant to other animals. Animal choices are generally closer to life-or-death issues such as obtaining the next meal while avoiding becoming one, whereas with humans, committing a (foraging-relevant) crime is a matter of less intense and immediately consequential choice—except, for example, with drug dependency. However, Bernasco's latter distinction may diminish in significance if foraging is held to include choice switching between immediate survival necessities and the pursuit of reproductive opportunities. (Here are echoes of Maslow's hierarchy of needs; e.g., see Tay and Diener 2011.) The animal will not die if it misses out on the latter (although it may feel frustrated), but seeking and courting a mate may jeopardize its personal survival (the extreme case being certain species of spiders in which copulating males become "wedding breakfast" for their partners).

However, more general questions remain. Houston et al. (2007) state that we cannot expect natural selection, lacking foresight, to shape organisms to act rationally in all circumstances but only in those circumstances they encounter in their natural setting. Therefore, fitness-maximizing behavior might not appear when animals are placed in novel contexts. For animals, this may be in laboratory experiments; for humans, our own techno-social change is continually subjecting us to novelty.

Okasha and Binmore (2014) ask *when* it is possible to identify economists' notion of utility with biologists' notion of fitness—a question that needs addressing, for example, in relation to the import of OFT to crime science. Sterelny (2012) maintains that their coincidence depends on whether information is transmitted vertically (between generations) or horizontally (between peers) and on whether or not group selection is a prevalent factor. From another angle, Schulz (2014) identifies two processes affecting the equivalence of fitness and utility. In "niche construction," organisms modify their environment to fit their needs; in the process of "adaptive preferences," animals change their desires to make them fit what is available. The former is the subject of active debate in fundamental evolutionary thought (Laland et al. 2009). It relates to criminal activity, for example, in corruption, in which offenders subvert crime preventers; the latter is less clear but, speculating, may have some link to sex offending, criminal involvement, or displacement choices.

IV. Conclusions: Implications for Crime Science

This chapter has only touched the surface of the evolution/rationality field, which remains in considerable ferment. It is hoped that this chapter will encourage and assist crime scientists to undertake their own explorations. The field is uniquely challenging because of its recursive nature—thus, for example, we have the evolution of rationality as a fitness-optimizing *process*, ultimately generating *products* in the form of brains, which themselves support rational, utility-maximizing decision *processes* that in turn feedback to biological evolution via improved prospects of survival and reproduction. The brains themselves adapt to more rapid changes in the social and physical environment through individual lifetime development and learning and cumulative cultural change and transmission. The mechanisms and preparedness for learning have significant components from biological evolution but in turn support a "bootstrapping" process in which tools for learning, instruction, and decision making evolve culturally. At both biological and cultural levels, there is evidence for evolution of evolvability; and biological and cultural coevolution has been shown to occur where each drives the other. All this makes human evolution exciting to study.

The evolutionary perspective on rationality raises numerous issues for crime science. The research evidence is currently too limited to supply firm answers, and we cannot know to what extent those eventual answers will be tweaks on contemporary research and practice or something more disruptive. However, we can at least suggest questions to answer by our own research and by "watching this space" in evolutionary studies:

- What are the particular *triggers* in the social and/or physical environment that might precipitate criminal behavior, and once the criminal is ready to offend, how might they affect criminal decision making? How might this differ for hot versus cool decision processes?
- How are risk, effort, and reward preferences *primed*—what is risky, what is effortful, and what is rewarding as a function of evolutionary history as opposed to other more recent influences? How flexible is that priming during development and maturity?
- How has the very *capacity* for assessing risk, effort, and reward, and for integrating these through decisions, evolved in, for example, foraging behavior? Has evolutionary history left its imprint on these? Does it make a difference whether inherited massive modularity, heuristics, or general-purpose rationality underlie decision making?
- How long can we continue to treat the risk, effort, and reward columns of the 25 techniques of SCP as *universals* rigidly applicable across all crime situations or differing contextually by their triggering stimuli and/or their perception/estimation processes as these have evolved biologically, culturally, or through learning?
- Should we be investigating *team reasoning* in co-offending and organized crime?
- Should we consider *imitation* as an alternative/complementary source for criminal behavior to rational choice?
- What factors influence the *development* and the *shape* of rationality in individuals, especially but not exclusively during adolescence? Are any of these sensitivity factors evolutionarily informed? Do they relate differently to strategic versus tactical criminal decisions?
- Does (criminal) rationality differ between *small-* and *large-world decisions*, and do the latter inform studies of criminal innovation?
- Are there wider evolutionary influences on the performance of the *executive control system* that we should consider? What implications do these have for crimes usually committed under low self-control versus high self-control?
- Should we further examine whether the concepts of *niche construction* and its mirror-image *adaptive preference* can be applied to crime science—for example, on corruption, our understanding of opportunity, and (non)displacement?

Once we start answering these questions, we can apply them to crime prevention—testing them through practice. This contributes to Campbell's (1974) evolutionary epistemology.

However, we should heed the evidentiary warnings on over-attribution to EP and to outdated retention of adaptations to the EEA. We should keep abreast of rapid changes in evolutionary science, paying special attention to thinking on the fitness/utility relationship. We should not expect answers to be simple and unconditional. We should not consider rationality in isolation but, rather, in its wider social/ecological/technical context—the context to which our brains and our cultures have adapted. We should consider in parallel biological and cultural evolution and individual learning and development.

It is hoped that this chapter has demonstrated two distinct benefits for crime science from linking rationality with evolution: (a) extending and refining the specific content of our theoretical, empirical, and practical address to crime and its prevention and (b) viewing the entire field from an entirely fresh perspective. Let's keep our ideas evolving—generating variety but also being selective.

REFERENCES

Altman, S. 1998. *Foraging for Survival: Yearling Baboons in Africa.* Chicago: University of Chicago Press.

Ashby, W. R. 1957. *An Introduction to Cybernetics.* London: Chapman and Hall.

Aunger, R., ed. 2000. *Darwinizing Culture: The Status of Memetics as a Science.* Oxford: Oxford University Press.

Bechara, A., H. Damasio, and A. Damasio. 2000. "Emotion, Decision Making and the Orbitofrontal Cortex." *Cerebral Cortex* 10:295–307.

Becker, G. 1976. *The Economic Approach to Human Behavior.* Chicago: University of Chicago Press.

Bernasco, W. 2009. "Foraging Strategies of Homo Criminalis: Lessons from Behavioral Ecology." *Crime Patterns and Analysis* 2:5–16.

Bouhana, N. 2013. "The Reasoning Criminal vs. Homer Simpson: Conceptual Challenges for Crime Science." *Frontiers in Human Neuroscience* 7:682.

Bowlby, J. 1969. *Attachment and Loss.* New York: Basic Books.

Boyd, R., and P. Richerson. 1985. *Culture and the Evolutionary Process.* Chicago: University of Chicago Press.

Brantingham, P., and J. Brantingham. 1991. "Niches and Predators: Theoretical Departures in the Ecology of Crime." Paper presented at Western Society of Criminology, Berkeley, CA.

Breland, K., and M. Breland. 1961. "The Misbehavior of Organisms." *American Psychologist* 16:681–84.

Brighton, H., and G. Gigerenzer. 2012. "Are Rational Actor Models 'Rational' Outside Small Worlds?" In *Evolution and Rationality: Decisions, Co-operation, and Strategic Behaviour,* edited by S. Okasha and K. Binmore, pp. 84–109. Cambridge: Cambridge University Press.

Caldwell, C., and A. Millen. 2008. "Studying Cumulative Cultural Evolution in the Laboratory." *Philosophical Transactions of the Royal Society B: Biological Sciences* 363(1509): 3529–39.

Campbell, D. 1974. "Evolutionary Epistemology." In *The Philosophy of Karl Popper,* edited by P. Schlipp, pp. 413–63. LaSalle, IL: Open Court.

Carroll, S. 2005. *"Endless Forms Most Beautiful: The New Science of Evo Devo and the Making of the Animal Kingdom."* New York: Norton.

Cavalli-Sforza, L., and M. Feldman. 1981. *Cultural Transmission and Evolution: A Quantitative Approach.* Princeton, NJ: Princeton University Press.

Clarke, R. 2014. "Affect and the Reasoning Criminal: Past and Future." In *Affect and Cognition in Criminal Decision Making; Between Rational Choices and Lapses of Self-Control,* edited by J.-L. van Gelder, H. Elffers, D. Reynald, and D. Nagin, pp. 20–41. New York: Routledge.

Cohen, L., B. Vila, and R. Machalek. 1995. "Expropriative Crime and Crime Policy: An Evolutionary Ecological Analysis." *Studies on Crime and Crime Prevention* 4:197–219.

Cornish, D. 1994. "The Procedural Analysis of Offending and Its Relevance for Situational Prevention." *Crime Prevention Studies* 3:151–96.

Cosmides, L., and J. Tooby. 1994. "Better Than Rational: Evolutionary Psychology and the Invisible Hand." *American Economic Review* 84(2): 327–32.

Cropley, D., A. Cropley, J. Kaufman, and M. Runco. 2010. *The Dark Side of Creativity.* Cambridge: Cambridge University Press.

Dawkins, R. 1976. *The Selfish Gene.* Oxford: Oxford University Press.

Dawkins, R. 2003. "The Evolution of Evolvability." In *On Growth, Form and Computers*, edited by S. Kumar and P. Bentley, pp. 239–55. London: Academic Press.

Dayan, P. 2012. "Robust Neural Decision Making." In *Evolution and the Mechanisms of Decision Making*, edited by P. Hammerstein and J. Stevens, pp. 151–68. Cambridge, MA: MIT Press.

Dennett, D. 1995. *Darwin's Dangerous Idea.* London: Penguin.

Dobzhansky, T. 1973. "Nothing in Biology Makes Sense Except in the Light of Evolution." *American Biology Teacher* 35(3): 125–29.

Ekblom, P. 1997. "Gearing Up Against Crime: A Dynamic Framework to Help Designers Keep Up with the Adaptive Criminal in a Changing World." *International Journal of Risk, Security and Crime Prevention* 2:249–65.

Ekblom, P. 1999. "Can We Make Crime Prevention Adaptive by Learning from Other Evolutionary Struggles?" *Studies on Crime and Crime Prevention* 8:27–51.

Ekblom, P. 2007. "Making Offenders Richer." In *Imagination for Crime Prevention: Essays in Honour of Ken Pease. Crime Prevention Studies 21*, edited by G. Farrell, K. Bowers, S. Johnson, and M. Townsley, pp. 41–58. Monsey, NY: Criminal Justice Press.

Ekblom, P. 2010. "The Conjunction of Criminal Opportunity Theory." In *Sage Encyclopedia of Victimology and Crime Prevention*, vol. 1, pp. 139–46. Thousand Oaks, CA: Sage.

Ekblom, P. 2011. *Crime Prevention, Security and Community Safety Using the 5Is Framework.* Basingstoke: Palgrave Macmillan.

Ekblom, P. 2015. "Terrorism—Lessons from Natural and Human Co-evolutionary Arms Races." In *Evolutionary Psychology and Terrorism*, edited by M. Taylor, J. Roach, and K. Pease, pp. 70–101. London: Routledge.

Ekblom, P. 2016. "Technology, Opportunity, Crime and Crime Prevention—Current and Evolutionary Perspectives." In *Crime Prevention in the 21st Century*, edited by B. Leclerc and E. Savona, pp. 319–43. New York: Springer.

Ekblom, P., and A. Hirschfield. 2014. "Developing an Alternative Formulation of SCP Principles—The Ds (11 and Counting)." *Crime Science* 3:2.

Ekblom, P., and K. Pease. 2014. "Innovation and Crime Prevention." In *Encyclopedia of Criminology and Criminal Justice*, edited by G. Bruinsma and D. Weisburd, pp. 2523–31. New York: Springer.

Ekblom, P., and N. Tilley. 2000. "Going Equipped: Criminology, Situational Crime Prevention and the Resourceful Offender." *British Journal of Criminology* 40:376–98.

Felson, M. 2006. *Crime and Nature.* Cullompton, UK: Willan.

Fergusson, D., J. Boden, L. Horwood, A. Miller, and M. Kennedy. 2011. "MAOA, Abuse Exposure and Antisocial Behaviour: 30-Year Longitudinal Study." *British Journal of Psychiatry* 198:457–63.

Frith, C. 2012. "The Role of Metacognition in Human Social Interactions." *Philosophical Transactions of the Royal Society B* 367:2213–23.

Gigerenzer, G., and W. Gaissmaier. 2011. "Heuristic Decision Making." *Annual Review of Psychology* 62:451–82.

Gintis, H. 2009. *The Bounds of Reason: Game Theory and the Unification of the Behavioral Sciences.* Princeton, NJ: Princeton University Press.

Gintis, H. 2014. "An Evolutionary Perspective on the Unification of the Behavioral Sciences." In *Evolution and Rationality: Decisions, Co-operation, and Strategic Behaviour*, edited by S. Okasha and K. Binmore, pp. 213–45. Cambridge: Cambridge University Press.

Godfrey-Smith, P. 2012. "Darwinism and Cultural Change." *Philosophical Transactions of the Royal Society B* 367:2160–70.

Gold, N. 2014. "Team Reasoning, Framing and Cooperation." In *Evolution and Rationality: Decisions, Co-operation and Strategic Behaviour*, edited by S. Okasha and K. Binmore, pp. 185–212. Cambridge: Cambridge University Press.

Gould, S. J., and R. Lewontin. 1979. "The Spandrels of San Marco and the Panglossian Paradigm: A Critique of the Adaptationist Programme." *Proceedings of the Royal Society of London* Series B: Biological Sciences 205(1161): 581–98.

Gregory, R. 1981. *Mind in Science: A History of Explanations in Psychology and Physics.* London: Weidenfeld and Nicholson.

Hammerstein, P., and J. Stevens. 2012. "Six Reasons for Invoking Evolution in Decision Theory." In *Evolution and the Mechanisms of Decision Making*, edited by P. Hammerstein and J. Stevens, pp. 1–20. Cambridge, MA: MIT Press.

Henrich, J., and R. McElreath. 2003. "The Evolution of Cultural Evolution." *Evolutionary Anthropology* 12:123–35.

Heyes, C. 2003. "Four Routes of Cognitive Evolution." *Psychological Review* 110:713–27.

Heyes, C. 2012a. "Grist and Mills: On the Cultural Origins of Cultural Learning." *Philosophical Transactions of the Royal Society B* 367:2181–91.

Heyes, C. 2012b. "New Thinking: The Evolution of Human Cognition." *Philosophical Transactions of the Royal Society B* 367:2091–96.

Heylighen, F. 1991. "Cognitive Levels of Evolution: From Pre-rational to Meta-rational." In *The Cybernetics of Complex Systems—Self-Organization, Evolution and Social Change*, edited by F. Geyer, pp. 75–91. Salinas, CA: Intersystems.

Houston, A. 2014. "Natural Selection and Rational Decisions." In *Evolution and Rationality: Decisions, Co-operation and Strategic Behaviour*, edited by S. Okasha and K. Binmore, pp. 50–66. Cambridge: Cambridge University Press.

Houston, A., J. McNamara, and M. Steer. 2007. "Do We Expect Natural Selection to Produce Rational Behaviour?" *Philosophical Transactions of the Royal Society B* 362(1485): 1531–43.

Jablonka, E., and M. Lamb. 2014. *Evolution in Four Dimensions. Genetic, Epigenetic, Behavioral, and Symbolic Variation in the History of Life* (revised edition). Cambridge, MA: MIT Press.

Jablonka, E., S. Ginsburg, and D. Dor. 2012. "The Co-evolution of Language and Emotions." *Philosophical Transactions of the Royal Society B* 367:2152–59.

James, P., and D. Goetze. 2001. *Evolutionary Theory and Ethnic Conflict.* Westport, CT: Praeger.

Johnson, M. 2014. *Morality for Humans: Ethical Understanding from the Perspective of Cognitive Science.* Chicago: University of Chicago Press.

Kacelnik, A. 2006. "Meanings of Rationality." In *Rational Animals?* edited by S. Hurley and M. Nudds, pp. 87–106. Oxford: Oxford University Press.

Kahneman, D. 2003. "A Perspective on Judgment and Choice: Mapping Bounded Rationality." *American Psychologist* 58(9): 697–720.

Kahneman, D. 2011. *Thinking, Fast and Slow.* New York: Farrar, Straus and Giroux.

Kahneman, D., P. Slovic, and A. Tversky. 1982. *Judgment Under Uncertainty: Heuristics and Biases*. Cambridge: Cambridge University Press.

Katz, J. 1988. *The Seductions of Crime*. New York: Basic Books.

Laland, K., J. Odling-Smee, M. Feldman, and J. Kendal. 2009. "Conceptual Barriers to Progress Within Evolutionary Biology." *Foundations of Science* 14(3): 195–216.

Nettle, D. 2012. "Error Management." In *Evolution and the Mechanisms of Decision Making*, edited by P. Hammerstein and J. Stevens. Cambridge, MA: MIT Press.

Nowak, M. 2011. *Supercooperators: Altruism, Evolution, and Why We Need Each Other to Succeed*. New York: Free Press.

Okasha, S. 2011. "Optimal Choice in the Face of Risk: Decision Theory Meets Evolution." *Philosophy of Science* 78:83–104.

Okasha, S., and K. Binmore. 2014. *Evolution and Rationality: Decision, Cooperation, and Strategic Behaviour*. Cambridge: Cambridge University Press.

Ormerod, P. 2012. "Terrorist Networks and the Lethality of Attacks: An Illustrative Agent Based Model on Evolutionary Principles. *Security Informatics* 1:16.

Pinker, S. 1994. *The Language Instinct*. New York: Morrow,

Pinker, S. 1997. *How the Mind Works*. New York: Norton.

Plotkin, H. 1997. *Darwin Machines and the Nature of Knowledge*. Cambridge, MA: Harvard University Press.

Popper, K. 1972. *Objective Knowledge: An Evolutionary Approach*. Oxford: Clarendon.

Roach, J., and K. Pease. 2013. *Evolution and Crime*. Crime Science Series. London: Routledge.

Sagarin, R., and T. Taylor. 2008. *Natural Security. A Darwinian Approach to a Dangerous World*. Berkeley: University of California Press.

Schneier, B. 2012. *Liars and Outliers: Enabling the Trust That Society Needs to Thrive*. New York: Wiley.

Schulz, A. 2011. "Gigerenzer's Evolutionary Arguments Against Rational Choice Theory: An Assessment." *Philosophy of Science* 78:1272–82.

Schulz, A. 2014. "Niche Construction, Adaptive Preferences, and the Differences Between Fitness and Utility." *Biology and Philosophy* 29(3): 315–35.

Shultz, S., and M. Maslin. 2013. "Early Human Speciation, Brain Expansion and Dispersal Influenced by African Climate Pulses." *PLoS One* 8(10): e76750.

Simon, H. 1955. "A Behavioral Model of Rational Choice." *Quarterly Journal of Economics* 69:99–118.

Simon, H. 1976. "Rationality as Process and Product of Thought." *American Economic Review* 8(21): 1–11.

Slovic, P., M. Finucane, E. Peters, and D. MacGregor. 2004. "Risk as Analysis and Risk as Feelings: Some Thoughts About Affect, Reason, Risk, and Rationality." *Risk Analysis* 24(2): 1–12.

Spear, L. 2010. *The Behavioral Neuroscience of Adolescence*. New York: Norton.

Steinberg, L. 2005. "Cognitive and Affective Development in Adolescence." *Trends in Cognitive Sciences* 9(2): 69–74.

Steinberg, L., and J. Belsky. 1996. "An Evolutionary Perspective on Psychopathology in Adolescence." In *Rochester Symposium on Developmental Psychopathology 7; Adolescence: Opportunities and Challenges*, edited by D. Cicchetti and S. Toth, pp. 93–124. Rochester, NY: University of Rochester Press.

Sterelny, K. 2012. "Language, Gesture, Skill: The Coevolutionary Foundations of Language." *Philosophical Transactions of the Royal Society B* 367:2141–51.

Sterelny, K. 2014. "From Fitness to Utility." In *Evolution and Rationality: Decisions, Co-operation and Strategic Behaviour*, edited by S. Okasha and K. Binmore, pp. 246–73. Cambridge: Cambridge University Press.

Tay, L., and E. Diener. 2011. "Needs and Subjective Well-Being Around the World." *Journal of Personality and Social Psychology* 101(2): 354–65.

Tilley, N. 2014. "Review of 'The Reasoning Criminal: Rational Choice Perspectives on Offending,' by D. Cornish and R. Clarke (2014 reprint of 1986), New York: Springer-Verlag." http://clcjbooks.rutgers.edu

Tinbergen, N. 1963. "On Aims and Methods of Ethology." *Zeitschrift für Tierpsychologie* 20:410–33.

Tooby, J., and L. Cosmides. 2005. "Conceptual Foundations of Evolutionary Psychology." In *Handbook of Evolutionary Psychology*, edited by D. Buss, pp. 5–67. Hoboken, NJ: Wiley.

Tooby, J., and I. DeVore. 1987. "The Reconstruction of Hominid Behavioral Evolution Through Strategic Modelling." In *The Evolution of Human Behavior: Primate Models*, edited by W. Kinzey, pp. 183–227. New York: State University of New York Press.

van Gelder, J.-L., H. Elffers, D. Reynald, and D. Nagin. 2014. *Affect and Cognition in Criminal Decision Making; Between Rational Choices and Lapses of Self-Control.* New York: Routledge.

Whiten, A. 2006. "The Place of 'Deep Social Mind' in the Evolution of Human Nature." In *Human Nature*, edited by M. Jeeves, pp. 207–22. Edinburgh: Royal Society of Edinburgh.

Whiten, A., and D. Erdal. 2012. "The Human Socio-Cognitive Niche and Its Evolutionary Origins." *Philosophical Transactions of the Royal Society B* 367:2119–29.

Wikström, P.-O. 2014. "Situational Action Theory." In *Encyclopedia of Criminology and Criminal Justice*, edited by G. Bruinsma and D. Weisburd, pp. 4845–52. New York: Springer.

Wilson, M., and M. Daly. 1985. "Competitiveness, Risk Taking, and Violence: The Young Male Syndrome." *Ethology and Sociobiology* 6(1): 59–73.

Wortley, R. 2017. "Situational Precipitators of Crime." In *Environmental Criminology and Crime Analysis*, edited by R. Wortley and M. Townsley, 2nd ed, pp. 62–86. London: Routledge.

Wright, R., and S. Decker. 1994. *Burglars on the Job: Street Life and Residential Break-Ins.* Boston: Northeastern University Press.

CHAPTER 4

....

MULTIPLE INTERPRETATIONS OF RATIONALITY IN OFFENDER DECISION MAKING

....

HENK ELFFERS

I. Emotions and the Rational Choice Perspective

....

THE rational choice perspective on criminal offending views the occurrence of crimes as a choice process. The choice is between engaging in a criminal event or staying on the right side of the law. According to the theory, such a choice is made on the basis of a cost–benefit analysis by the potential offender.[1] The approach has divided the community of criminologists. On the one hand, we find the proponents of rational choice theory, who are satisfied that the approach has empirically proven its usefulness—it is a "good enough" theory (Cornish and Clarke 1986, 2008). On the other hand, we find opponents who believe they cannot engage with the approach because, in their opinion, it offers no place for "emotions" in describing or explaining criminal involvement, which in their view is a natural and absolute necessity for a fruitful theory. The following are two exemplary quotes from the opposing side: "By disregarding the role of norms, values, and moral emotions like guilt and shame and leaving aside these normative and emotional elements of decision making, the rational choice perspective seems to misrepresent the nature of the action it explains in terms of rational choice" (De Haan and Vos 2003, p. 33) and "Neither the theory nor the method [of the rational choice perspective] allows for the inclusion of emotions as elements in human behavior" (Scheff 1992, p. 104).

I challenge these characterizations of the rational choice perspective. Rational choice theory is not at all neglecting emotions, let alone the notion that there is not a place for them in the theory. First, the founding fathers of rational choice decision making in social sciences—Dirck Coornhert,[2] Adam Smith, and Jeremy Bentham—introduced in their original writings their perspectives in terms of norms, guilt, conscience, pity, and other affects. Coornhert (1587/1985, p. 75) argues that offenders prefer the short, quick, sudden death of capital punishment over the long-lasting misery of a slow death that is a life lived in grim poverty. When considering Smith's work, even the title of his treatise, *The Theory of Moral Sentiments* (Smith 1759/1982), is an illustration of the point. Bentham discusses benevolence, malevolence, sympathy, and social affection (Bentham, 1789/1879, pp. 40–41), and indeed, his well-known maxim, "Nature has placed mankind under the governance of two sovereign masters, pain and pleasure. It is for them alone to point out what we ought to do, as well as to determine what we shall do" (p. 1), demonstrates how much he was thinking in terms of emotions.

In present times, there are scores of criminological publications that incisively analyze the role of emotions in the context of rational choice criminal decision making. An edited volume taking stock of arguments and evidence in this respect is that by van Gelder et al. (2014).

These classical as well as modern authors make a strong case for the statement that the rational choice paradigm in criminology is, and always has been, strongly pervaded with emotions.

It appears that much disagreement is a consequence of a hidden difference of opinion regarding what the concept of "rational choice" contains or should contain and how it may or may not be used in explaining the occurrence of crime. This chapter intends to provide some clarity about this issue by discussing various elements that may have generated disagreement about content and scope of the rational choice approach. The chapter does not cover in detail the many interesting contributions that various authors have made[3] but focuses instead on what is, could, or should be the contribution of rational choice theory to criminal choice theory.

II. What Is Rational Choice Theory?

In the book *Nuts and Bolts for the Social Sciences*, Jon Elster (1989) summarizes the theory of rational choice deceptively simply in the sentence, "When faced with several courses of action, people usually do what they believe is likely to have the best overall outcome" (p. 22). Much misunderstanding on what exactly rational choice theory would mean, or should mean, is packed in the term "rational." Let us first then ponder on the less controversial part, "choice theory." I wonder whether many people would object against the structure of the previous statement—that is, that people tend to choose what they think will turn out as most advantageous. However, people tend to disagree about what "the best overall outcome" would mean. Elster's formulation is rather to the point: What counts is what the person making the choice believes is best—meaning best for him- or herself. Some people may consider in their own "overall outcome" the benefits and costs of others (Hessing and Elffers 2000), whereas others may consider only themselves. Elster sees no reason to deny that some people view their "self-interest" increased by other people's well-being: "In fact, his preferred option might be one that gives pleasure to others and none to himself" (pp. 23–4). His formulation is a bit off course; I prefer to state that the pleasure given to himself is indeed identical to the pleasure he thinks the choice will give to relevant others.

Let us now concentrate on another term in Elster's (1989) description: "belief on what is the best outcome." Elster is not addressing here a difference in perception of what might be the state of the world but, rather, a difference in evaluating how much pleasure and pain is the result of that state of the world—that is, whether an outcome is to the taste of a decision maker. We are well aware that tastes are personal: What seems to me to be the best overall outcome for me is not necessary equal to what you perceive to be the best overall outcome for you. People may have different tastes, so they have different appreciations of the same outcome. For example, Jeremy happens to prefer an orange over an apple, whereas Adam may well choose the apple. Nobody would be surprised if that happened to be the case; indeed, everybody would infer that Jeremy likes oranges best, whereas Adam has a taste for apples. Both choices fall readily within Elster's definition: Adam and Jeremy choose what they, individually, appreciate to be the best outcome for themselves. Everybody is well accustomed to the idea that there is no accounting for tastes, and nobody would classify Adam or Jeremy as behaving strange. Because both of them choose what they think would be subjectively best for them, we certainly will not classify their behavior as not rational.

III. PAINS AND PLEASURES

Within economic discourses, there is a tendency to represent the possible outcomes of choices in monetary terms. For example, in his article, often considered as having put rational choice back into criminology, Becker (1968) tries to monetize all costs and benefits. Notice, however, that nothing in Elster's formulation points to a necessity to restrict rational choice to a balancing of monetary costs and benefits only. On the contrary, the previous treatment did not even mention money. Jeremy is not considering the pleasure of eating an orange as equivalent to more monetary wealth for him than he would get out of eating an apple; he simply anticipates more pleasure. Outcomes to be considered may be of all sorts, as long as they fall in Bentham's classical categories of pain and pleasure. Adam expects more joy, more pleasure (or less pain), from eating an apple than from eating an orange, whereas for Jeremy it is the other way around. They simply have different preferences. The fact that people may have different preferences is, of course, one of the basic observations we all have made during our life. Indeed, Aristotle (1894) observes in his *Nicomachean Ethics* that people may make different choices in identical situations (which he then analyses not in the context of different preferences but, rather, as showing that their degrees of virtuousness differ).

IV. Perceptions and Preferences

We should recognize that people do not only differ in preferences but also may differ in what they expect when facing the same choices—their perceptions of what will be the outcomes of their choices. Becker (1968) states that people make different choices "because their benefits and costs differ" (p. 176). From his treatment, it is not quite clear whether he aims at different perception by various persons of identical costs and benefits or at an objective difference in costs and benefits holding for different people. That is irrelevant for the present argument, however. In both cases, people may have different preferences because they experience different costs and benefits. For example, although we know that, in general, Jeremy would prefer oranges over apples, he may in a given case distrust the quality of the orange offered to him. Although he indeed prefers good oranges over good apples, he also prefers good apples over bad oranges, and if he perceives this particular orange to be of inferior quality, whereas the apple is above suspicion, he will choose the apple. Likewise, Adam may change his choice if he distrusts the apple. Notice that Adam and Jeremy may have different opinions of the qualities of the fruit offered to them and hence perceive different benefits. In general, when the outcome of a choice is not known beforehand—that is, when uncertainty plays a role—people may form different opinions about the outcomes of identical states of the world.

V. Taste Dimensions and Objective Dimensions of Choice

Is rational choice theory thus only a subjective theory? To a considerable degree it is, but it is not only subjective. In this section, it is argued that there are some elements in what everybody personally views as the best overall outcome for themselves that should observe certain restrictions within persons. Let us consider an example. If Cesare, facing the choice between buying a book for $25 and buying the same title for $30, would buy the more expensive version, we would be surprised. We all maintain that there is a clear subordination of the choice for the more expensive copy to the choice for the cheaper one, *ceteris paribus*, for all people. In fact, if we observed Cesare paying the higher price, we would immediately wonder what were his motives to do so and probably hypothesize "other (dis)advantages of the choices" not previously known to us but evidently perceived by Cesare. Examples of such hidden advantages may be that Cesare has discovered a quality in the more expensive copy that has escaped our attention or that he likes to see the second seller benefit from his clientele (e.g., because that seller is a good friend of his or a person to whom he owes a favor). The mere fact that we believe that such hidden reasons must exist immediately demonstrates that we classify the $25 choice without further ado as objectively being the better overall outcome. It also shows that we are ready to take into account the word "overall" in Elster's formulation. We admit that it may well be the case that having to spend $25 without further ado may be a less good overall outcome than spending $30 while simultaneously letting a friend benefit. What we would not accept as being reasonable behavior, however, is a case in which all other things equal except for the money to be spent on a choice, Cesare would choose the most expensive option.

It is here that the term "rational" comes into play. The rank ordering of choices on certain dimensions, all other things being equal, is not experienced as up to the taste of the decision maker. Unlike the rank ordering of choices on dimensions of taste, which is considered to be a personal affair, we tend to reject what is viewed as an illogical treatment of choices on various other dimensions. The following are dimensions on which we implicitly seem to hold that a logical ordering of different positions exist: More monetary costs are less preferable than less costs, more monetary benefits are preferable over less benefits, more labor to be done is less attractive than less labor, more status to be gained is better than less status, and more punishment received is worse than less punishment. Such dimensions are usually perceived by all as "objective dimensions" of choice.[4] We can very well accept that Jeremy prefers oranges over apples, while the reverse holds for Adam, because we classify taste in fruits as a taste dimension. We reject a state of affairs in which Jeremy prefers to pay more for an orange over paying less: It is an objective dimension. For objective dimensions, it holds that we know beforehand which of a pair of outcomes on such a dimension is preferable for all people. The rationality of the rational choice theory boils down to this observation: On objective dimensions, we commonly think we know what everybody in his or her right mind would prefer. Notice, however, that this rationality prescription is still applicable only under the stringent condition of the *ceteris paribus* clause. If the clause does not hold, things may turn out differently. For example, we can accept that less punishment is not preferable over more punishment if, and only if, the latter goes hand in hand with other expected benefits, which may be ratable on either an objective ("rational") dimension or a subjective ("taste") dimension. An example of the first is if Gary prefers 6 months in prison plus an undiscovered loot of $10,000 (waiting to be collected by him when released) over not going to jail but losing the loot (i.e., a case of conflicting rationalities on separate dimensions). We accept that it is up to Gary, not us, to balance these two (dis)advantages on different dimensions and to choose his course of action accordingly. Indeed, we would not be surprised to hear that Dirck, in the same situation, would prefer the other choice, inferring then that Dirck evidently values his freedom more than his monetary wealth. Again, other dimensions of evaluating outcomes, other than monetary, may come into play as well. An example of the latter is if Gary prefers 6 months in prison plus the pride of not having betrayed his companion in crime, Dirck, over one month in prison plus giving evidence against Dirck (i.e., a case of a negative balance on an objective dimension together with a positive balance on a taste dimension).

VI. Subjectively Combining Dimensions

Next to when evaluating uncertain outcomes, subjectivity comes into play in two other respects as well. First, regarding taste dimensions, we are accustomed to the fact that different people may have different subjective positions. Second, subjectivity comes into play because the way people weigh several dimensions may be different as well. In fact, how people subjectively combine (dis)advantages on various scales is a major problem; hence, it is difficult to foresee a person's final choice. That problem arises even when we consider combining objective dimensions. If Sally can chose between buying a two-year-old used bike of a certain brand for $200 and a brand-new one of the same brand for $800, what will she do? Objectively, $200 is less than $800, but also objectively, used bikes are worse than new ones. How, then, does she combine the outcomes on these two dimensions and weigh the counteracting advantages and disadvantages? That may very well differ between persons, and again we do not classify somebody as behaving irrational, whatever she happens to do. Sally may buy the new bike because she is afraid that a secondhand bicycle will soon incur expenses of more than the saved $600. Just as well, Patricia may choose the cheaper used one because she simply does not think that two years of wear and tear on a bike outweighs the price difference. Again, weighing the various dimensions involved in determining the overall value of various choices is a personal, subjective matter. The same holds, *a fortiori*, when we consider situations in which taste dimensions come into the equation. If Sally wants to impress her friends by owning a bike that is currently very fashionable, she has to take into account that very personal dimension as well, whereas Patricia may be indifferent about what her friends think of her means of transportation. However, even if both of them like to impress their friends, which counts as an argument for choosing the new bike, it is by no means given that both of them would evaluate equally that advantage in comparison to the financial disadvantage of the new bike choice. There is not an objective common yardstick with which the perceived advantages and disadvantages of choices on various dimensions may be measured.

VII. Outcomes of Offending

The reader may have observed that in the previous treatment I hardly addressed offending. Rational choice theory is indeed a general theory of choice, not a theory of criminal choice as such. Being a general theory, it may be applied to matters of criminal choice as well. Decisions about committing a crime have a general characteristic in common that distinguishes them from many, if not most, noncriminal choices: The choice for offending is not morally neutral, and committing a crime will in general come with social disapproval and possibly with reactions by the legal authorities. Thus, offending comes with a cost. Again, such cost will be evaluated subjectively. In this situation, the difficulty of combining various dimensions becomes even more salient: The potential offender has to also weigh various possible reactions from the side of law enforcement and from his social environment and integrate them with the expected advantage of offending. With respect to law enforcement, breaking a law implies a certain likelihood that negative consequences will occur in terms of arrest, prosecution, conviction, and serving punishment. Again, people may well differ considerably with regard to how they perceive and weigh these latter dimensions, and we may even wonder which of these consequences should be viewed as objective or as taste dimensions. Trevor may believe those consequences to be very unlikely to happen, assuming that he will not be caught; Richard may laugh about a fine; Marie may fear prison more than anything else; and Jody is well aware that she is only facing community service if convicted. Analogously, this holds for the reaction of one's social environment, which may again differ across persons and be weighted different by individuals. Danielle may well be ashamed if her parents see her misbehaving; George would loath to set a bad example for his children; Scott may indeed relish being seen misbehaving because it demonstrates to the gang to which he wishes to join that he is indeed one of them; and Marcus assumes that his neighbors do not monitor his behavior at all. Last, people may face moral costs in the form of guilty feelings and losing self-respect—again, totally person dependent. Repeat offenders may well be bothered less by guilt compared to those considering offending for the first time. Notice that again there are many examples of nonmonetary aspects that we propose have a natural place within the rational choice perspective.

VIII. The Time Perspective

In his description of rational choice, Elster speaks of "the best overall outcome." What about the time frame over which a decision maker is summing up his or her expectations as the "overall outcome"? It is here that we may anticipate a distinction between cases of deliberate planning of an offense and acting on the spur of the moment. It is sometimes argued that cases of sudden violence, such as a violent bar brawl when somebody thinks another patron is not displaying due respect, do not fit in the rational choice perspective. The argument then is that from an objective point of view, it is unwise to engage in drunken violence because its expected costs (removal from the bar, prosecution, and bodily harm) outweigh the gains. The observation that indeed bar brawls do occur then leads to the conclusion that they are incompatible with rational choice. However, maybe the tipsy bar client is actually summing up his options—fighting or not—over a small time period, possibly not more than a minute, and disregards what may occur later. This is indeed rather likely when people are under the influence of alcohol or other drugs. Within that short interval, the option of fighting may well seem to be the rationally preferable choice because it will provide returns such as restoring hurt pride and self-esteem, even if the price of a black eye and a severe rebuke by the bouncer are taken into consideration. However, other consequences, such as arrest and prosecution, fall outside the time horizon during which the prospective offender is considering advantages and disadvantages. Notice that consequences on an objective dimension, such as expected punishment, become manifest usually outside such a short time perspective. The morning after, it might be different, but in the moment that the troublemaker decides, he may well choose fighting because it appears to be the better alternative. Again, this is a case in which the length of the time interval considered by a would-be offender may differ considerably among individuals, which makes it difficult for an outsider to predict whether a certain person will or will not make a drunken row. The applicability of rational choice over a short time horizon is not at stake, however.

IX. Rational Choice Theory "Strict"

Different from the previous treatment, it has been argued that there should not be a place for taste or subjective elements in a decent rational choice theory (Stigler and Becker 1977). This is associated with a difference in language usage of such authors compared to that of the treatment discussed previously (Anand, Pattanaik, and Puppe 2009). In the latter, we distinguished expected outcomes on objective and subjective (taste) scales, observing that most decisions are made using a combination of both types of dimensions, and argued that both can play a role in the Elsterian concept of rationality as governing decisions in terms of subjective expected outcomes. Those who prefer the use of the term "rational" for objective dimensions of choice situations only should recognize that they are using the term not only in a different meaning than proposed here but also different from the usage of the founding fathers of rational choice in criminology, such as Coornhert and Bentham, as previously illustrated. Note that the previous analysis indeed already classified social disapproval, the influence of law enforcement, and formal punishment as "taste dimensions," and those concepts are central to criminal decision making. Many economists try to solve the problem of combining taste and objective dimensions by generalizing their outcomes to an abstract "utility" scale in an attempt to address the "lack of common yardstick problem." As long as no operational definition is available on how to translate different dimensions of preference into utility, the concept is too abstract to be of use in combining heterogeneous dimensions.

Within economics, a more strict usage of the term rationality is common in what broadly is called the economic theory of expected utility maximization—a line of thought that argues that when facing a choice, people are guided by an objective computation of the expected value of both outcomes, based on an infinite time horizon and complete information on all consequences, given their preferences (Becker 1968; Mongin 1997). This paradigm is sometimes called (neo)classical economy, and it is perhaps the dominant school in economics. Although this strict rationality approach has demonstrated its merits within economics, this is not much of an argument to prefer a "strict" rationality approach over a "lighter," Elsterian rational choice approach of criminal decision making. The criticism that rational choice theory of criminal decision making has no place for emotion is perhaps aimed at the strict version, but there seems to be no compelling reason to identify "light" and "strict" rational choice, so arguments for or against one of these are not necessarily valid against or in favor of the other. Note that the strict utility maximization paradigm also has not gone undisputed in economics. Behavioral economics and economic psychology have eloquently argued that real people do not behave according to that model (Kahneman and Tversky 1979; Weigel, Hessing, and Elffers 1987; Gigerenzer, Todd, and the ABC Group 1999; Gigerenzer 2000; Kirchler 2007; Altman 2015).

Optimizing over an infinite time horizon and having complete information is, of course, rather at odds with people's everyday experience with choices. Simon (1955) proposed to consider rational choice within a framework of incomplete information and optimizing over a finite time interval, which has become known as "bounded rationality" or the "satisficing" approach. In a way, Simon's proposal brings into the equation all the previously discussed topics about differences between the way people may weigh different qualities of the various choice options. I suggest that the debate between "full" and "bounded" rationalists has little relevance for criminology. In fact, the rational choice approach within criminology as outlined previously seems only compatible with the concept of bounded rationality. More important, it deviates even further from "full" rationality than Simon's proposals in allowing subjective elements as well as deeming them essential for a defendable theory. It is up to the individual person how he or she weights costs and benefits on various dimensions, which is in line with the use of finite periods: Most people do not attach weight to consequences that seem too distant, and they may well differ with respect to the degree that they are sensitive to deferred gratification, for example, or are impulsive.

X. Emotions

Having argued that emotions are at the center of the classical rational choice approach, we now carefully consider in more detail the role of emotions in rational choice theory of criminal decision making. In fact, there is ample empirical evidence of the role of emotions in criminal decision making (van Gelder et al. 2014; see also chapters 9 and 20 in this volume). Note that in previous examples, just as in the original treatment of Bentham or Smith, emotions such as fear, shame, and pity did enter the discussion. In fact, taste dimensions are usually closely connected to emotions.

A. Anticipated and Immediate Emotions

Loewenstein et al. (2001) stressed the difference between anticipated and immediate emotions. Anticipated emotions are those expected to occur due to the consequences of the choice made. In the case of criminal choices, guilt feelings and shame are examples of anticipated emotions. Immediate emotions are of a different type: They occur at the very moment of (pondering about) the decision and are connected to the actual decision making as well as to the situation in which the decision maker finds him- or herself. An example is anger about the situation in which a decision has to be made (Elster 1998; Lowenstein et al. 2001; van Gelder, Reynald, and Elffers 2014).

Conceptually, anticipated emotions fit seamlessly in the rational choice framework as consequences of choices being evaluated by the decision maker in a personal, subjective way. In fact, Jeremy seems to prefer an orange over an apple because he is anticipating the pleasure it will give him to taste an orange—a pleasure that he anticipates to be larger than the pleasure he believes he will derive from eating an apple. We can even suggest that evaluating options is inherently connected to emotions. It seems not to be for the saved $5 itself that Cesare prefers paying $25 for a book over paying $30 but, rather, for the anticipated emotion of pleasure he can gain (or anticipated pain he can evade) by using the $5 spared for another purpose and still have the pleasures expected as a result of buying that book. These examples, like the ones concerning feeling guilty or having pride in not snitching on friends, seem to fit well in terms of anticipated emotions to be gotten from various choices. Of course, it is an empirical question to what degree anticipated versus immediate emotions explain decision making.

In the context of criminal acts, a decision maker considering the choice of law transgressing has to face the possibility of being sent to prison along with anticipated emotions associated with a lack of freedom, tediousness, being confined, lacking contact with loved ones, and so on, in addition to the anticipation of possibly being ashamed or feeling guilt. Coornhert (1587/1985) analyzed why the threat of capital punishment did not stop prospective offenders. He observed that their lives were so miserable that a quick death by the hand of the executioner was preferred by them over continuing life in dreadful circumstances. (Incidentally, Coornhert therefore argued for punishment more grievous than a quick death—in this case, lifetime forced labor as a rower on galleys).

Immediate emotions fit less well in the framework of evaluating possible outcomes of choices because they are a direct consequence of the situation of having to make a decision and have already occurred, whatever choice is finally made. In fact, it has been demonstrated that both types of emotions, anticipated and immediate, may independently influence decision making (this is captured by so-called dual-process models; Treiber 2014; van Gelder and de Vries 2014; see also chapter 9 in this volume). We could interpret this as showing that an exclusionary claim of the rational choice approach should be rejected: It is not only expected consequences but also the state of mind in which consequences are evaluated that count. Note, however, that the dual paradigm fits closely to the traditional rational choice framework: It does not deny the claim that decisions are made on the basis of weighing consequences, but it recognizes that this weighing may turn out differently in different emotional states, in terms of immediate emotions. For example, when angry, a decision maker may value the choice of applying violence much higher than when he is in an emotionally neutral state. Note that the notion is linked to what happened before the moment of decision making. It is concerned with the route by which the decision maker reached that decision moment—that is, what led him into his current emotional state. It then considers how this state affects the weighing of future consequences. As such, it comes close to the type of considerations we discussed with regard to the planning horizon: Angry, slighted, indignant people have no concern for future consequences.

Sorting out the interplay between immediate and anticipatory emotions seems a fruitful area for further research (van Gelder, Reynald, and Elffers 2014).

XI. Rational Choice Theory as a Conceptual Framework and its Application

When we accept that people may choose on the basis of a combination of various objective dimensions and taste dimensions, and that how to weigh the various dimensions and over what time frame are personal preferences, we realize that rational choice theory is not able to predict in "real-life" situations which decision individual people will choose. According to the theory, whether Ron will evade his taxes or not, in a given situation, is governed by his evaluation of expected outcomes in terms of his perceived effort, returns, social (dis)approval, law enforcement, and feelings of guilt—each being weighted with Ron's subjective weights. It is unlikely that we can adequately measure all elements that play a role in his decision; hence, we cannot predict his choice.[5]

In fact, rational choice theory is not so much a theory. It is first and foremost a conceptual framework within which we can discuss various dimensions and their relations. It is a powerful mechanism for structuring our thoughts in certain *ceteris paribus* conditions. For example, irrespective of how Derrick values the monetary outcome of burglary, or his feelings about being a criminal, in comparison to his perceived likelihood of being caught and prosecuted, we may infer that when facing targets with equal expected proceeds, he will prefer the one for which he believes he has a better chance of executing his burglary without being apprehended. In such a case, it may be worthwhile to ponder which of the targets considered indeed provides, in objective terms, that better chance of not being apprehended. Will Derrick subjectively classify those targets as providing less chance of apprehension that are, in an objective sense, better hardened against burglary? Indeed, the most incisive (although not the only) use of the framework is in comparing situations *within persons*. Such applications can be found, for example, within environmental criminology, in which it is attempted to investigate the influence of the physical or social environment on the occurrence of crime by comparing either empirically or in the form of a thought experiment how various environments may influence a decision maker.

By way of example (Elffers 2004), consider when closed-circuit television (CCTV) will be helpful in preventing vandalism. It is not helpful in the case of people whose evaluation of the outcome of vandalism is negative at the outset: They will not do it whether or not a camera is present. Neither will the presence of CCTV be helpful in the case of those whose evaluation in terms of rewards is extremely positive. They may well perceive a diminished expected return in the condition that a camera is present (due to an increased chance of apprehension), but they will still remain on the positive side and hence go for it. It is the group of people in between, for whom vandalism is just slightly more advantageous than remaining law-abiding, who may decide that the advantage of committing vandalism has vanished due to the greater chance of apprehension with the presence of CCTV and therefore refrain from vandalism, at least in this particular situation. The example shows that by thinking in rational choice terms, we may realize that we do not know enough about certain aspects in the valuation of expected consequences. How much target hardening will delay prospective burglars enough so that they prefer not too burgle? Can we answer this question by speaking to burglars or observe the victimization of various targets with different degrees of hardening?

In general, the rational choice perspective can be helpful in considering how to alter situations. For example, if we examine bike theft and distinguish direct costs/benefits, social costs, law enforcement costs, and moral costs, we may question which costs can be increased and which benefits can be decreased, and we may question whether that would be enough to inhibit different types of offenders. Paradoxically, whereas I have previously argued that emotions form an indispensable part of the rational choice paradigm, I here conclude that the practical use of the paradigm is in comparing situations within persons, thus canceling out the unknown, but equal within a person, values of emotional aspects.

For those who try to sell oranges to apple-loving Adam, it seems a more fruitful approach to provide juicier oranges than to try to alter Adam's preference. We can apply the same type of reasoning to criminal choices. Trevor may remain on the right side of the law if we can convince him that the probability of being caught is higher than he thinks, or we may decide that we should increase that probability (if Trevor was correct after all). That will not work for Scott, who secretly hopes to be caught. A rational choice analysis can help in understanding under what circumstances people are likely to misbehave, and it provides us with a framework to consider what costs can be raised and whether that will help in preventing crime. As such, it can be of great practical value because there is nothing so practical as a good theory.

Notes

1. A concise introduction to the rational choice approach in the field of criminal decision making is given by Collins and Loughran in chapter 2 of this handbook.
2. Dirck Volckertszoon Coornhert (1522–1590) was a sixteenth-century Dutch philosopher, theologian, and politician. In 1567, he became a political prisoner as a result of the

political unrest and riots preceding the Dutch Revolt (1568–1648). During his imprisonment, he proposed a reform of criminal punishment in his manuscript "*Boeventucht*" or "*On Disciplining Villains,*" which was published in 1587 (Coornhert 1587/1985; Coornhert et al. 2009). He grounds his proposals on his conviction that offending is a rational choice in the circumstances in which most offenders live. By introducing a rational choice argument in criminal law, he precedes Smith and Bentham by a good two hundred years (Elffers 2005).

3. There are many excellent publications available about the rational choice approach in criminology. In addition to Coornhert's work, cited previously, I mention the following: Cornish and Clarke (1986, 2008), Nagin and Paternoster (1993), Hessing and Elffers (2000), Piquero and Tibbets (2002), Dahlbäck (2003), Elffers (2005), van Gelder et al. (2014), Clarke (2014), and Leclerc and Wortley (2014). The current handbook contains a number of chapters that discuss rational choice: chapter 2 (Collins and Loughran), chapter 3 (Ekblom), chapter 5 (Sidebottom and Tilley), and chapter 7 (Apel and Nagin). The role of emotions within the paradigm is discussed by van Gelder in chapters 9 and 22. When looking outside criminology, there is an avalanche of publications available. In addition to the previously mentioned works by Smith (1759/1982) and Bentham (1789/1879) are those by Simon (1955), Elster (1989, 1998), and Coleman and Fararo (1992). The law and economics approach to criminal decision making is presented in Schmidt and Witte (1984) and Becker (1968). Outright rejection of the approach may be found in circles of cultural criminologists, including De Haan and Vos (2003) and Ferrell, Hayward, and Young (2008); not all authors in this line use a civil tone.

4. Notice, however, that it is not too difficult to imagine people or cases for whom those "objective" dimensions after all have a different, subjective meaning: People with a strong desire to be punished for their evil deeds may prefer more punishment over less, Calvinists may perhaps prefer more labor over less, and so on. In that respect, the objectivity of objective dimensions is not set in stone.

5. It may be argued that the strength of rational choice "strict" in comparison to "light" lies in contexts in which it is indeed possible to measure or deduct the utility of choices—that is, where personal subjective preferences are of minor or no importance—in which case the full analytical mechanism of maximization can be successfully applied.

REFERENCES

Altman, M. 2015. *Handbook of Contemporary Behavioral Economics: Foundations and Developments*. New York: Routledge.

Anand, P., P. Pattanaik, and C. Puppe, eds. 2009. *The Handbook of Rational and Social Choice*. Oxford: Oxford University Press.

Aristotle. 1894. *Ethica Nicomachea*. Oxford: Clarendon Press.

Becker, G. S. 1968. "Crime and Punishment: An Economic Approach." *Journal of Political Economy* 76:169–217.

Bentham, J. 1879. *An Introduction to the Principles of Morals and Legislation*. Oxford: Clarendon Press. (Originally published 1789.)

Clarke, R. V. 2014. "Affect and the Reasoning Criminal." In *Affect and Cognition in Criminal Decision Making*, edited by J.-L. van Gelder, H. Elffers, D. Reynald, and D. Nagin. Crime Science Series 14, pp. 20–41. New York: Routledge.

Coleman, J. S., and Th. J. Fararo, eds. 1992. *Rational Choice Theory: Advocacy and Critique.* Newbury Park, CA: Sage.

Coornhert, D. V. 1985. *Boeventucht* [*The Discipline of Misbehavior*]. Muiderberg, Netherlands: Coutinho. (Originally published 1587.)

Coornhert, D. V., W. Freund, R. Deacon, and E. Verbaan. 2009. "Boeven-Tucht: The Discipline of Misbehaviour: Or the Means to Reduce the Number of Harmful Idlers." *Theoria: A Journal of Social and Political Theory* 56(118): 89–104.

Cornish, D. B., and R. V. Clarke, eds. 1986. *The Reasoning Criminal: Rational Choice Perspectives on Offending.* New York: Springer.

Cornish, D. B., and R. V. Clarke. 2008. "The Rational Choice Perspective." In *Environmental Criminology and Crime Analysis*, edited by R. Wortley and L. Mazerolle, pp. 21–47. Cullompton, UK: Willan.

Dahlbäck, O. 2003. *Analyzing Rational Crime—Models and Methods*, vol. 36. New York: Springer.

De Haan, W., and J. Vos. 2003. "A Crying Shame: The Over-rationalized Conception of Man in the Rational Choice Perspective." *Theoretical Criminology* 7:29–54.

Elffers, H. 2004. "The Rational Offender Under a CCTV-Camera: Conceptual Clarification.: In *Forensic Psychology and Law: Facing the Challenges of a Changing World*, edited by A. Czerederecka, T. Jaśkiewicz-Obydzińska, R. Roesch, and J. Wójcikiewicz, pp. 92–99. Kraków, Poland: Institute of Forensic Research Publishers.

Elffers, H. 2005. *De rationele regelovertreder* [*The Rational Rule Transgressor*]. Inaugural lecture Antwerp University. The Hague, Netherlands: Boom Juridische uitgevers.

Elster, J. 1989. *Nuts and Bolts for the Social Sciences.* Cambridge, UK: Cambridge University Press.

Elster, J. 1998. "Emotions and Economic Theory." *Journal of Economic Literature* 36(1): 47–74.

Ferrell, J., K. Hayward, and J. Young. 2008. *Cultural Criminology: An Invitation.* Thousand Oaks, CA: Sage.

Gigerenzer, G. 2000. *Adaptive Thinking: Rationality in the Real World.* New York: Oxford University Press.

Gigerenzer, G., P. M. Todd, and the ABC Research Group, eds. 1999. *Simple Heuristics That Make Us Smart.* New York: Oxford University Press.

Hessing, D. J., and H. Elffers. 2000. "Mens Rea or Mens Insana: Theoretical Explorations Into the Good, the Bad, the Ugly and the Fool." In *Rationality, Information and Progress in Law and Psychology: Liber Amicorum Hans F. M. Crombag*, edited by P. J. van Koppen and N. H. M. Roos, pp. 91–114. Maastricht, Netherlands: Metajuridica.

Kahneman, D., and A. Tversky. 1979. "Prospect Theory: An Analysis of Decision Under Risk." *Econometrica: Journal of the Econometric Society* 47:263–91.

Kirchler, E. 2007. *The Economic Psychology of Tax Behaviour.* Cambridge, UK: Cambridge University Press.

Leclerc, B., and R. Wortley. 2014. *Cognition and Crime: Offender Decision Making and Script Analyses.* New York: Routledge.

Loewenstein, G. F., E. U. Weber, C. Hsee, and N. Welch. 2001. "Risks as Feelings." *Psychological Bulletin* 127(2): 267–86.

Mongin, P. 1997. "Expected Utility Theory." In *Handbook of Economic Methodology*, edited by J. Davis, W. Hands, and U. Maki, pp. 42–350. London: Elgar.

Nagin, D. S., and R. Paternoster. 1993. "Enduring Individual Differences and Rational Choice Theories of Crime." *Law and Society Review* 27(3): 467–96.

Piquero, A. R., and S. G. Tibbets, eds. 2002. *Rational Choice and Criminal Behavior: Recent Research and Future Challenges*. New York: Routledge.

Scheff, T. J. 1992. "Rationality and Emotion, Hommage to Norbert Elias." In *Rational Choice Theory: Advocacy and Critique*, edited by J. S. Coleman and T. J. Fararo, pp. 101–17. Newbury Park, CA: Sage.

Schmidt, P., and A. D. Witte. 1984. *An Economic Analysis of Crime and Justice: Theory, Methods and Applications*. Orlando, FL: Academic Press.

Simon, H. A. 1955. "A Behavioral Model of Rational Choice." *Quarterly Journal of Economics* 69(1): 99–118.

Smith, A. 1982. *The Theory of Moral Sentiments*. Indianapolis, IN: Liberty. (Originally published 1759.)

Stigler, G. J., and G. S. Becker. 1977. De Gustibus Non Est Disputandum. *American Economic Review* 67(2): 76–90.

Treiber, K. 2014. "A Neuropsychological Test of Criminal Decision Making: Regional Prefrontal Influences in a Dual Process Model." In *Affect and Cognition in Criminal Decision Making*, edited by J.-L. van Gelder, H. Elffers, D. Reynald, and D. Nagin, pp. 193–220. Crime Science Series 14. New York: Routledge.

van Gelder, J.-L., and R. E. de Vries. 2014. "Rational Misbehavior? Evaluating an Integrated Dual-Process Model of Criminal Decision Making." *Journal of Quantitative Criminology* 30:1–27.

van Gelder, J.-L., H. Elffers, D. Reynald, and D. Nagin, eds. 2014. *Affect and Cognition in Criminal Decision Making*. Crime Science Series 14. New York: Routledge.

van Gelder, J.-L., D. Reynald, and H. Elffers. 2014. "Anticipated Emotions and Immediate Affect in Criminal Decision Making: From Shame to Anger." In *Affect and Cognition in Criminal Decision Making*, edited by J.-L. van Gelder, H. Elffers, D. Reynald, and D. Nagin, pp. 161–78. Crime Science Series 14. New York: Routledge.

Weigel, R. H., D. J. Hessing, and H. Elffers. 1987. "Tax Evasion Research: A Critical Appraisal and Theoretical Model." *Journal of Economic Psychology* 8:215–35.

CHAPTER 5

SITUATIONAL CRIME PREVENTION AND OFFENDER DECISION MAKING

AIDEN SIDEBOTTOM AND NICK TILLEY

I. BACKGROUND

HUMAN choice is a central topic in the social sciences. Different disciplines tend to view the choices we make in different ways. Psychologists are inclined to try to understand how people choose between the options available to them (with relatively little interest in the range of choices and their sources). Sociologists are more inclined to try to understand which choices are and are not available to particular groups of people and where those that are available come from (with relatively little interest in how selections from them are made). For many in both disciplines, however, the term "decisions" may overstate the degree to which those acting knowingly elect to do one thing or another. For such skeptics, people *behave* and mostly do so in response to inner urges, habits, or external stimuli. The notions of choice making and decision taking imply a degree of voluntarism that is deemed largely illusory. For others, choices are not so much "there" or "not there" as "seen" or "not seen": In this view, they are individual or social constructions rather than brute givens. Thus, in principle, many more may be available than the perceived set from which individuals make a selection, albeit the range of choices is not unlimited.

Criminologists are similarly interested in human choice, most notably the decision to commit crime (or not). What factors influence this decision is a fundamental criminological question, and as with psychology and sociology, different branches of criminology have attempted to answer this question from contrasting perspectives. The dominant approach has been to explain criminal behavior in terms of dispositional factors: Most crimes are universally condemned, and so those that engage in crime must harbor criminal dispositions, the source of which likely resides in an individual's genes, upbringing, and wider social conditions. Efforts to reduce crime therefore hinge on altering criminal motivation by effecting changes in the social conditions assumed to dispose some to become criminal through early intervention for individuals judged to exhibit greater risks of participating in crime or, retrospectively, in attempts to rehabilitate known offenders.

An alternative and complementary perspective, albeit one that is less fashionable among traditional criminologists, assumes that crime need not follow inexorably from a disposition to commit crime, whether that disposition derived from individual attributes, social forces, or some combination of both, but instead can be traced to the immediate environment in which crime takes place. The dominant view from this perspective is that crime is a choice, and individuals make decisions about whether to commit crime in much the same way as any other behavior, responsive to and influenced by opportunities and temptations in the immediate situation. This account of offender decision making is known as the *rational choice perspective*. Simply stated, this perspective argues that an individual is more likely to commit crime if the expected rewards are greater than the perceived losses. It follows that crime can be prevented by altering the immediate environment in ways that influence the choices of prospective offenders, without having to address the "root causes" of criminal disposition, in whatever ways those root causes are construed. This approach is known as *situational crime prevention*.

Few would deny that situational crime prevention and the rational choice perspective have made significant contributions to both criminological thinking and the practical task of reducing crime. In 2015, Ron Clarke, a central figure in the development of both concepts, was awarded the prestigious Stockholm Prize in Criminology (along with Patricia Mayhew). As the awarding committee reports, "Rarely has so much direct application of criminological research occurred so quickly, and with so much apparent benefit in crime reduction."[1] However, situational crime prevention and the rational choice perspective have also received much criticism, both independently and in combination. In this chapter, we explore the development of and relationship between situational crime prevention and the rational choice perspective, drawing on cognate fields with an interest in decision making, such as economics, sociology, and psychology. We begin by recounting the origins of situational crime prevention and its expansion to include the rational choice perspective (for more detailed overviews, see Clarke 2008; Leclerc and Wortley 2014; Tilley and Sidebottom 2014).[2] We then consider three related questions. First, is rational choice the only possible theoretical underpinning for situational crime prevention? Second, is it sufficient as a model of offender decision making for the purposes of crime prevention research and practice? Third, should the rational choice account of offender decision making be supplemented, and if so, with what?

II. On the Marriage of Situational Crime Prevention and the Rational Choice Perspective

Situational crime prevention (SCP) was first articulated in the 1970s. As mentioned previously, it is most associated with the work of Ron Clarke, although efforts to ward off undesirable behaviors through situational techniques have a much longer history—consider the fortress design of castles or the thorns and prickles of certain plants. Clarke (1997) defines SCP as

> opportunity-reducing measures that (1) are directed at highly specific forms of crime, (2) involve the management, design and manipulation of the immediate environment in as systematic and permanent a way as possible, (3) make crime more difficult and risky, or less rewarding and excusable as judged by a wide range of offenders. (p. 4)

A key study in the initial formulations of SCP concerns gas supply and suicide. Until the early 1960s, the gas supplied to most households in England and Wales for cooking and heating was toxic. It provided a convenient opportunity for suicide through self-gassing. Advancements in the gas industry (e.g., improved production processes and a shift from manufactured to natural gas) initiated a gradual change in domestic gas supply to less toxic forms. This produced some unexpected effects, particularly a commensurate reduction in the rate of suicide. There was no reason to assume that there had been an equivalent reduction in the motivation to commit suicide precisely during the period in which detoxification of the gas supply occurred. The change in gas supply did not, of course, remove all opportunities for suicide: Many other methods remained available. Gas, however, had certain commonsense advantages. It was on tap, painless, and non-disfiguring. Once the choice of self-gassing as a method for committing suicide was removed, the overall suicide rate declined simply because a readily available and widely known choice was removed, with little displacement to alternative suicide methods. Removing one popularly used opportunity for suicide was thus sufficient to lead to a reduction in the number of suicides overall (for an overview, see Clarke and Lester 1988). In addition to the drop in suicides following the removal of the toxic gas supply, reductions have also occurred with the decline in availability of other suicide commission methods, including the use of catalytic converters in cars (which made exhaust fumes less toxic), the introduction of blister packs for paracetamol (which made taking handfuls of tablets less convenient), and blocking off access to high bridges and buildings (which made lethal locations from which to jump more scarce). Even desperate behavior, presumably consequent on deep feelings leading to a disposition to kill oneself, was found to be strongly affected by the choices of methods available. This was a profoundly counterintuitive finding.

Complementary evidence for arguably more mundane behaviors supported the notion that situational contingencies are important in understanding behavioral choices. In one of the first publications on SCP, *Crime as Opportunity*, Mayhew et al. (1976) provide several examples of unwanted behaviors (e.g., cheating and absconding) that appear to be responses to "provocations, attractions, and opportunities of the immediate situation" (p. 1). At the same time, doubt had been cast on the effectiveness of efforts to reduce crime by altering the disposition of offenders, famously encapsulated by Robert Martinson's (1974) "nothing works" slogan. Beyond criminal behavior, accumulating evidence from psychology and sociology demonstrated the significance of the immediate situation for behavior. At a macro level, patterns of social mobility appear to be largely conditioned by changing occupational structures. An expanding white-collar sector and a shrinking blue-collar sector change the opportunity structure and thereby facilitate upward social mobility (Goldthorpe, Llewellyn, and Payne 1987; Goldthorpe 2000). At a micro level, the famous experiment by Asch (1955) on conformity and the notorious experiments by Milgram (1974) and Zimbardo (2007) on obedience and anonymity, respectively, showed how individuals' behavior is shaped by their immediate situations. Most of us recognize this in our daily lives. If something we like, such as chocolate, is easily accessible, then even if we know it is bad for us, we are easily tempted to eat it even as we recognize what is happening. We may try to forestall the availability of that option by choosing not to buy it or even not to walk down the aisle in which it is displayed in order to avoid situations in which the choice is readily at hand.

No grand psychological or sociological theory of the individual or of society is needed to grasp the salience of situations and of the choices they present in shaping behavior. In many respects, what is odd (and in need of explanation) is why so many people have had such difficulty accepting that this is the case. The "fundamental attribution error" has been invoked for this purpose (Ross 1977). It refers to the general tendency to overestimate disposition in others' undesirable behaviors rather than the situational contingencies at work—a tendency that is less frequent in accounts of one's own behavior. The fundamental attribution error has itself been subject to some critical discussion. It comprises a label for a general tendency rather than an explanation of underlying cognitive processes. The following may be the case: When unwanted or undesirable behavior is undertaken by those we dislike (or know little of), we tend to invoke internal causes deriving from some personal pathology (thereby blaming them); when we engage in unwanted or undesirable behavior or those we like or admire do so, we tend to invoke external situational contingencies (thereby exculpating ourselves or those close to us); when those we dislike (or know little of) engage in desirable behaviors, we are apt to invoke external situational contingencies (to avoid commending them); and when we or those we like or admire engage in desirable behaviors, we tend to invoke internal causes (and thereby celebrate the virtues of ourselves or others with whom we identify) (Pettigrew 1979). In some cases, those we admire or like behave in ways that we find appalling; in which case they move from liked to disliked and explanations move to internal rather than external causes (as with those found to have acted improperly toward children, who are bestowed the status of pedophile). All this could be easily explained as a result of efforts to reduce cognitive dissonance.

The fundamental attribution error may explain why SCP only emerged in the 1970s and, more generally, why dispositional theories of crime outnumber their situational counterparts. However, buoyed by developments in related fields and following the initial recognition and demonstration that (a) opportunity plays a part in explaining patterns of unwanted behavior (including crime) and (b) reducing opportunity can prevent that behavior rather than simply divert it elsewhere, a more general account of how situations foster or foreclose crime was developed by Ron Clarke and Derek Cornish. They drew on rational choice theory. Rational choice has a strong pedigree in the social sciences. It had been assumed in classical economics. It had been a cornerstone of exchange theory. It had formed the starting point for Weberian sociology. It is founded on the notion of *utility*, taken to mean decision outcomes that are favorable to the decision maker. Rational choice theory proposes that humans make decisions based on an appraisal of the utility of available options, choosing that which affords maximum utility.

Since its inception, rational choice has been widely considered to be at best a workable approximation that could usefully be drawn upon to better understand and model behavioral choices. Moreover, rational choice theory could easily be rendered unfalsifiable by the simple expedient of defining observed behavior as necessarily that which is, in the eye of the agent, expected to yield the greatest utility. This is a simple trick if utility is defined broadly enough to include the nonmaterial as well as the material, the afterlife as well as this life, a sense of self-satisfaction at helping others as well as satisfaction from receiving help from them, and so on. If someone did X, even if it seems to an observer to be against their better interests, that can be explained as a function of the utilities that the person values more highly than those we otherwise impute to him or her and his or her ideas about how best to achieve those utilities. Suicide bombing is a case in point.

Rational choice is thus generally considered to be a *normative* model rather than a *descriptive* one. In other words, it outlines the decisions that we *should* make under perfect conditions as opposed to providing an accurate account of what people ordinarily do in reality. It has emerged that we are far from perfect in our calculations of what will achieve greatest utility. A raft of experimental work has shown that miscalculation is rife, often in predictable ways (Kahneman 2011). Moreover, situational contingencies play a part in limiting our capacity for utility estimation—life is too short and calculations are too complex for us to work through what will serve us best at each decision point.[3] Standing decisions, rules of thumb, and faulty reasoning against a backdrop of time pressures and incomplete information are all part of the stock-in-trade of human agents. All this is captured in the innocent-sounding notion of "bounded rationality" (Simon 1955). The rational choice, utility-maximizing assumption remains, but departures from it in the ebb and flow of everyday life are acknowledged and have been the focus of analysis.

Clarke and Cornish's (1985) version of rational choice and crime was initially that risk, effort, and reward fed into the calculation of whether or not a given crime would be committed in the circumstances facing someone who might contemplate crime commission. Expected effort and risk are balanced against anticipated reward (broadly defined) to work through whether or not to commit a crime in the presenting circumstances. Marginal changes in the risk/reward/effort equation are expected to effect marginal changes in the calculations made by prospective offenders, leading to alterations in decisions about whether or not to commit a particular crime in a given context. Conclusions will vary across offenders according to their appetite for risk taking, values for rewards, and the perceived level of effort required for them to commit the crime.

From the outset, Cornish and Clark treated rational choice as a heuristic as opposed to a descriptive *theory* of offender decision making—hence the term *perspective*. They privileged pragmatism and viewed rational choice as a "good enough" account of how the decision to commit crime is influenced by situational factors, with the central purpose of informing crime prevention. It is a point they repeatedly reiterated, lest there be any confusion (for numerous illustrative quotations, see Wortley 2013, pp. 237–39).

Cornish and Clarke (2008, p. 24) set out the following six assumptions that characterize the rational choice perspective of offender decision making:

1. *Criminal behavior is purposive*: Individuals make a deliberate decision to commit crime and do so with the expectation of reaping some form of benefit, be that monetary, social, or psychological.
2. *Criminal behavior is rational*: When faced with alternatives, individuals will opt for that which they consider offers the best means of achieving their goals at that time, accepting that mistakes will happen.
3. *Criminal decision making is crime specific*: Different crimes are often carried out for different reasons, requiring different resources and in the expectation of receiving different benefits. Treating crime as a single homogeneous phenomenon runs roughshod over the nuances associated with particular crime types, and it stymies thinking about how best to prevent them. Being crime specific affords a greater understanding of the criminal decision-making process.
4. *Criminal choices are classified into two broad groups—"involvement" and "event" decisions*: The decisions to embark, continue, and desist from crime (involvement decisions) are qualitatively different from the decisions associated with performing a particular type of crime (event decisions) in a particular set of circumstances. The two should be distinguished and studied separately.
5. *There are separate stages of involvement*: It is advantageous to think of criminal involvement as comprising three stages—initiation, habituation, and desistance—with different factors being brought to bear on decisions made at each stage.
6. *Criminal events unfold in a sequence of stages and decisions*: It is tempting (and common) to reduce "event decisions" to only the most salient features of a particular crime—for example, the theft of the car, the sale of the drug, and the abduction of the child. However, the process of committing crime invariably involves numerous decision points occurring before, during, and after these central stages. Deconstructing crime types into their necessary stages provides a fuller range of

the criminal choices associated with particular crimes and how they might be influenced by situational intervention.[4]

Rational choice is a well-established criminological theory in its own right. It lies at the heart of deterrence theory, which in turn underpins many efforts to reduce crime. In their ambitious attempt to determine the extent to which statistical models derived from different criminological theories explain crime—measured using the R-squared statistic from papers published in *Criminology*, the premier journal in the field— Weisburd and Piquero (2008) find rational choice theory to exhibit the largest average R-squared statistic (0.782).[5] Our interest in this chapter, however, is limited to rational choice as the dominant model of offender decision making underpinning SCP, about which questions remain regarding the necessity of and profit from this relationship. Here, we consider three key questions. First, is rational choice the only possible theoretical underpinning for SCP? Second, is it true enough as a general working assumption for further (and fruitful) research and practice? Third, does it need to be supplemented?

A. Is Rational Choice the Only Possible Theoretical Underpinning for Situational Crime Prevention?

The propositions built into SCP were certainly not derived specifically or formally from rational choice. The initial formulations of SCP (Mayhew et al. 1976; Clarke 1980) predate references to and the application of rational choice (Clarke and Cornish 1985). Instead, responsiveness to situations was observed (as with the suicide example), and it was noted that this opened the way to prevent crime without having to focus on dispositions presumed to foster criminality. The key theoretical point was that the assumptions of the then dominant dispositional theories (that crime will inevitably be committed by those liable to offend because of deep-seated social and psychological causes) are mistaken.

Nevertheless, it might be argued that rational choice is implicit in SCP or that rational choice is the only assumption that could make sense of the effects of situations on criminal behavior. Neither position can be sustained. Evolutionary theory, for example, would have it that those behaviors that probabilistically favor survival persist *because* they favor survival; those that did not were weeded out by the sieve of natural selection.[6] Behavioral ecology has shown how animal behaviors are shaped by the benefits they bring for survival of the organism and their genes. Responsiveness to frequently encountered situations clearly confers advantages. Although ecologists speak of choices in these circumstances, the use of the term is metaphorical. Optimal foraging theory, for example, does not propose that flies, frogs, and foxes carefully assess predation threats, energy expenditure, and so on. The cause lies in the hardwired mechanisms of the brain that underpin behavioral responses that have persisted (or been selected) because of their survival-enhancing advantages. Skinnerian behaviorists likewise show how animals respond to the contingencies surrounding them.

The notion that pigeons and rats *decide* to move in the patterns to which they have been conditioned by the artfully designed rewards given in response to their more or less random movements makes little sense.

Furthermore, at least some behavioral possibilities emerge and then cease to be available, thereby altering the set from which any choice can be made. In this case, situational contingencies do not so much affect choices as the range from which choices can be made. As Felson (1986, p. 119) stated, "People make choices, but they cannot choose the choices available to them." Indeed, much SCP may not so much influence *choice making* as *choice availability*. For example, the invention of automobiles, the Internet, mobile phones, credit cards, bank notes, customs duties, airplanes, postal services, and self-service shops furnished new crime opportunities that were not available prior to their invention. Likewise, there can sometimes be a reduced supply of crime possibilities (Walsh 1994). Coin clipping was a widespread crime in the seventeenth century, punishable by hanging. Milled edges made it difficult. The use of base metals later made it pointless. The crime became obsolete. Regicide is no longer possible in countries that have become republics. The removal of customs borders between two countries means that smuggling to avoid duty payable ceases to be available as a crime. Failure to vote is a crime only in jurisdictions in which voting is compulsory. This broadly sociological position holds that elections to take advantage of available choices may be of many different kinds, most of which are easy to grasp—for example, stealing objects because one needs or covets them, hitting or killing people because one dislikes them or is thwarted by them, or damaging objects because they are frustrating us. In these ways, doing things one wants to do but that may be unlawful is more or less self-explanatory. What matters is the supply of options rather than the reason for exercising choices that happen to comprise infractions of rules. Moreover, there is no need to invoke or assume or propose any single theory of the person to explain the range of reasons why a decision is made to act in ways that a jurisdiction has deemed criminal.

What might be more accurate is that efforts to prevent specific crimes turn on changing situations to introduce considerations that may not previously have figured. These would make the exploitation of a given opportunity less attractive. These considerations introduced in the changed situation very often broadly relate to potential offenders' calculations about whether or not the costs or effort involved have become so large or any prospective benefits have become so small that at least a proportion of offenders act differently and forgo the crime they would otherwise have committed. In this way, marginal changes in the costs and benefits may alter the rates of those behaviors for individuals for whom costs and benefits are a major factor in informing actions and for whom the change is sufficient to tip the balance in favor of refraining from a crime that would otherwise have been committed. Of course, a small marginal change for those for whom the costs are low in relation to the prospective benefits (hence, expected returns are high) would be unlikely to be effective. Other changes in prospective offenders' circumstances might also alter the cost–benefit equation through the life course: More is to be lost, for example, when a significant other (e.g., a wife or girlfriend) expresses disapprobation at criminal involvement or when work yielding regular utility is put in jeopardy by involvement in crime and the risk that this may lead to apprehension, prosecution, and conviction.

B. Is Rational Choice True Enough as a General Working Assumption for Further (and Fruitful) Crime Prevention Research and Practice?

Oddly for a man emphasizing that scientific progress is achieved with the production of falsifiable propositions that are then subject to rigorous empirical tests to provoke the production of better ones, Karl Popper championed the pragmatic value of what he referred to as the "rationality principle." Although it is clearly false, he argued that we should retain it because of its explanatory fecundity. The rationality principle, of course, equates to rational choice. Let us examine whether Popper's case holds specifically for research and practice in relation to crime and SCP.

The pragmatic value of rational choice is clear. It provided SCP with a well-established theoretical base. Through emphasizing that human decision making is influenced by situational contingencies, it shone a light on the pervasive neglect of opportunities as a causal factor in crime. It provided a convenient framework for organizing and describing general techniques that could be considered by those trying to deal with specific crime problems. It accorded with much common sense and experience: We all know from our everyday lives what is involved in working through options with different balances of cost, risk, and expected benefits. It has been easily taught and now is widely presented as the theoretical base for SCP when this is introduced to students, policymakers, and practitioners. It may also have helped recognize that the ways in which offenders think and make decisions are not alien to the ways in which ordinary law-abiding people think and make decisions. Idle assumptions that those who offend are pathological monsters are difficult to sustain. In this way, rational choice assumptions are humanizing in their conception of criminals.

Just as in classical economics, even if not absolutely true as an account of how individual behaviors are produced, rational choice may possess enough truth (i.e., it may be roughly correct as a working principle) both to explain and predict many patterns of crime and to inform crime prevention. For example, the increases in shop theft, car theft, and phone theft, respectively, when self-service rather than counter-run displays were being established, when cars were becoming commonplace, and when mobile telephony was becoming widespread are all easily explained by rational choice in the face of new opportunities. Likewise, the precipitous international drop in car theft during the past two decades is easily explained by the increasing difficulty and risk of stealing cars consequent on improvements in vehicle security and in the locations where they tend to be parked (Farrell et al. 2011). The recent scandal in Britain concerning excessive expenses claims made by many politicians—most (in)famously for moat maintenance—are equally readily explained by the ease with which they could be made and the low risk that they would be queried.

From a prevention perspective, the accumulated evidence in support of reducing crime through situational means is considerable. Across a variety of contexts and crime types, advocates can point to numerous anthologies (Clarke 1992, 1997) and reviews (Smith, Clarke, and Pease 2002; Guerette 2009; Guerette and Bowers 2009) that generally converge on the finding that thoughtfully conceived and correctly implemented situational interventions are an effective crime reduction method. Often, the impact is immediate and confidently attributable to the situational measures put in place, such as the near disappearance of bus robberies following the installation of drop safes introduced as part of a wider shift toward an exact fare system (Chaiken et al. 1974, as cited in Clarke 2008). This is not always the case for many other crime control efforts in which greater uncertainty exists regarding the causal mechanisms that link intervention to any crime reductions observed (e.g., see Weisburd et al.'s [2015] discussion of broken windows policing). Although comparisons between different crime reduction methods are limited, in a randomized controlled trial on the effectiveness of various police strategies at crime hot spots in Lowell, Massachusetts, Braga and Bond (2008) found that situational interventions outperformed misdemeanor arrests and social service-oriented interventions in terms of reductions in calls for service.

The scope of SCP is widening. This can be seen in the application of SCP to terrorism (Clarke and Newman 2006), cybercrimes (Newman and Clarke 2003), wildlife poaching (Lemieux 2014), maritime piracy (Shane, Piza, and Mandala 2015), and sex offenses against children (Wortley and Smallbone 2006). It is difficult to isolate the influence of rational choice on the formulation of situational interventions for these problems; many may well have been designed in ignorance of the rational choice perspective.[7] However, we believe that it is reasonable to assume that at least some of the many forms of SCP were formulated with some awareness of the effort, risk, and reward calculus supplied by the rational choice model.

Attaching primacy to rational choice, even where its lack of verisimilitude is known in advance, has a strong pedigree. Max Weber argued for it in sociology while recognizing that actions always also include elements of habit, affect, and value. In modern bureaucratic and market societies, in particular, Weber argued that means–ends rationality (at the heart of rational choice) tended to prevail over other aspects of action that might prevail in other times, places, and conditions. As we have seen, Popper endorsed the rationality principle, whilst at the same time knowing its assumptions to have been falsified. Rational choice remains the default position in economics, whilst much research explores its limits and exceptions. Imre Lakatos (1978) would understand rational choice to have been (and maybe still is) a "scientific research program" that is "progressive" in the sense that it is still yielding new findings (and for an account of rational choice as part of the scientific research program in economics, see Latsis 1976).

Thus, for much research and practice, rational choice remains good enough, even if known not strictly to be true. Changing situations so that specific crime options are either removed or become marginally less attractive to potential offenders in terms of risk, effort, and reward has proved to be an effective way to prevent much crime. This brings us to our third question.

C. Does Rational Choice Need to Be Supplemented as a Means of Understanding Crime Patterns and Finding Ways of Preventing Crimes by Altering the Situations in Which They Are Committed?

Even if the explanatory, policy, and practice default is rational choice for the reasons already given, there may be good reasons (as with Weberian sociology, analytical sociology, and behavioral economics) to focus attention on nonrational action consequent on situational cues. Indeed, there has already been some tacit recognition of this in extensions made to the early typology of situational measures.

Consistent with the tenets of "substantive rationality" emphasized in classical economics (Simon 1996), the first formulations of SCP stressed only risk, effort, and reward—those considerations germane to determining what course of action will maximize utility. Later formulations referred to "rule reminders" (Clarke and Homel 1997). Rule reminders acknowledge that social life occurs in and through adherence to rules of behavior that we learn. We internalize these rules as they are taught to us and mostly take them for granted. Mores, those rules deemed most important, are enshrined in law; if we breach them, we are both shamed and formally penalized. However, where conformity involves costs by forgoing utilities we might otherwise expect, we can be tempted to break rules. In situations in which the operation of rules appears to have been suspended (e.g., during a riot in which looting is occurring or on a freeway where the prevailing rate of travel exceeds the speed limit), their salience is liable to diminish. Moreover, we are adept at rationalizing breaches of rules with a repertoire of excuses—so-called "techniques of neutralization" (Sykes and Matza 1957).

Rule reminders in situations in which there might be temptations to breach rules remind potential offenders of the rule they might otherwise break. These techniques are widely used in British trains and railway stations, where weaknesses in the transport network are liable to produce extreme frustration and violence. Posters remind travelers that assaulting staff members is an offense. The presence of rule reminders comprises an acknowledgment that most of the time, most of us adhere to most rules. We learn them and accept that there is a general obligation to behave in ways that accord with widely accepted moral principles, especially where these are enshrined in law. Rule reminders act as situational prompts where there may momentarily be high levels of temptation or provocation to behave criminally.

The reference to "provocation" brings us to a second supplement to the initial classification of SCP techniques. Wortley (2001, 2008) suggests four ways in which situations may *precipitate* criminal action. First, situations may contain cues that *prompt* individuals to act unlawfully, such as when exposure to violence-related imagery stimulates aggression-related feelings, thereby priming an individual for violence (the so-called weapons effect; see Berkowitz 1983). Second, situations may convey social *pressures* that are criminogenic, such as when an individual commits crime in accordance with the (perceived) wishes of an authority figure. Third are *permissions*, which refer to situations rich in material that can be invoked or exploited to justify committing criminal behavior, such as alcohol, drugs, and unclear rules. Most relevant to this chapter is the fourth type of situational precipitator, *provocations*. Here, crime may be engendered not because of the expected utility but because a nerve has in some way been touched. The frustrated, angry, and potentially violent British rail traveler is a case in point. His or her aggression is "expressive" rather than "instrumental." It will not reduce the (all too frequent) delay to the rail service. Modifying situations liable to provoke in ways that make them less provocative comprises a SCP technique that speaks to emotion rather than reason. Signage of the sort previously mentioned is a response to a situation that arouses crime-engendering feelings but does nothing to lessen those feelings. Other situational interventions are similarly put in place to avoid generating those feelings or to assuage them should they arise. For example, managing queues for taxis, buses, and in bars reduces frustration and therefore provocation. Likewise, provision for seating in bars creates conditions in which customers are less likely to collide with one another or upset one another. Soothing music at the end of a disco aims to leave patrons in a calm frame of mind, where they might otherwise be liable to act aggressively. Removing sweets from counters easily accessible to impecunious young children avoids stimulating their appetite and hence temptation to steal them. Provocation speaks to pushes toward criminal behavior rather than the pull of expected utility based on calculated risk, effort, and reward.

Max Weber referred to habit as a source of action. Habits or routines describe behaviors undertaken unreflectively, although they are not undertaken automatically in that those behaving habitually could have acted otherwise. Consider the case of the accomplished concert pianist. She does not reflect on the placement of each finger in the course of playing a piece. However, she could certainly act otherwise. The action is intentional and in that sense willed, even though it is undertaken unreflectively. Much crime prevention and crime commission seem to fall into this category. For example, locking of our car doors and windows at night or when going out and activating the central locking system have become routines that reduce risk of victimization. Of course, the householder or driver is not acting compulsively. They could do otherwise, but they are acting unreflectively as a matter of habit. As law-abiding citizens, for the most part we do not work out whether there is an opportunity to commit crime that would maximize our expected utility. Instead, we have a standing decision to obey the law. We pay for goods in shops, buy tickets on buses and trains, pay for meals in restaurants, and ignore provocations at railway stations without a moment's thought, even though we could do otherwise. Likewise, the "habitual criminal" is apt to take advantage of criminal opportunities as and when they arise as a matter of routine, again unreflectively, albeit that they could act otherwise. It is easy to miss the importance of routine because, like routine itself, it is taken for granted.

Routines are important for a number of reasons. The economist Geoffrey Hodgson (1997, p. 665) lists the following seven:

1. *Optimization*—where the choice set is known and it is possible to employ procedures and decision rules to find an optimum
2. *Extensiveness*—where the information may be readily accessible and comprehensible but the search for it requires the application of substantial time and other resources
3. *Complexity*—where there is a gap between the complexity of the decision environment and the analytical and computational capacity of the agent
4. *Uncertainty*—where crucial information and probabilities in regard to future events are essentially unobtainable
5. *Cognition*—the general problem of dealing with and interpreting sense data
6. *Learning*—the general process of acquiring crucial knowledge about the world
7. *Communication*—the general need to communicate regularly with others

The first five are self-explanatory. The sixth, learning, refers to the preexisting analytic frameworks that shape the ways in which we apprehend new information: We are not Bayesian learning machines adapting to new information to modify our estimates of risk, effort, and reward; instead, we are apt to interpret new information in terms of our existing cognitive frameworks. These frameworks (and the neural circuitry that underpin them), however, are themselves subject to change on the basis of experience that challenges prior assumptions. Once new frameworks are formed, albeit that initially they require conscious thought, they eventually become automatic frameworks for interpreting new events. The seventh reason, communication, refers to the kind of routine signalling that occurs in humans and animals to convey behavioral intentions. It is sometimes conscious and sometimes hardwired. Hodgson gives examples that are directly relevant to SCP: the messages "Never negotiate with terrorists" and "Never give in to terrorists." In both cases, the behavior could otherwise be different (and in specific instances may be suboptimal), but the communicative routine is oriented toward achieving a wider preventive outcome.

In a later paper, Hodgson (2010, p. 2) relates the development of routines to evolutionary principles, quoting no less than Charles Darwin as saying, "Men are called 'creatures of reason,' more appropriately they would be 'creatures of habit'" (Darwin 1974, pp. 85, 115). Habitual behaviors make evolutionary sense: Making decisions exacts costs (time, cognitive effort, etc.); repeating responses that proved advantageous when previously encountering similar stimuli (e.g., avoiding snakes and cliff faces) frees our brains to consider other issues while simultaneously executing said behavior (see chapter 3 in this volume). In this view, habit comes first and (rational) choice then emerges, at least at the margins.

Habits can prove hard to break, however. Entire industries have been established on devising effective methods to extricate difficult-to-dislodge habitual behaviors such as smoking and gambling. Most relevant here is whether habitual aspects of human behavior are open to situational intervention. The fact that routines are unthinking but enduring makes them less promising than rational choice calculations or rule reminders or provocation reduction, all of which speak to the immediate situation and the prompts within it to act in one way or another. For the potential victim, it is easier to understand how establishing and acting on routines can be important. Well-designed situational measures, such as central locking for cars, can facilitate the establishment of precautionary routines. For the habitual offender, the question is whether situational measures can be put in place that will undermine taken-for-granted offending routines. There may be a few possibilities:

1. Disruption of habituated offending: It is a sobering fact that most criminal behavior goes unpunished. In England and Wales, it is estimated that only a tiny proportion of crime (approximately 3 percent) results in a criminal conviction or caution (Barclay and Tavares 1999; see also Burrows et al. 2005). From the perspective of the offender, Cook (1980) argues that "if active criminals find that they are rarely arrested, unlikely to be convicted if arrested, and unlikely to be sentenced to prison terms if convicted, then they may acquire a justified sense of invulnerability" (p. 224). Pioneering work by Ken Pease and colleagues on offender self-selection (Chenery, Henshaw, and Pease 1999), David Kennedy's (2008) work on targeted deterrence, and strategies implemented by Durham (UK) police to disrupt organized crime families (Tilley 2014) all undermine routine offending patterns by altering the taken-for-granted context sustaining the routines (patchy enforcement, gang culture legitimating violence, and community intimidation and collusion).

2. Randomized crackdowns/checks: High-rate randomized breath tests undermine the notion that driving while intoxicated can be routinely undertaken with little risk that the driver will be caught (Homel 1994, 1995). This may also apply for random passenger searches at airports and for random speed traps leading to automatic prosecution and the risk that one's driver's license will be revoked.

3. The signalling that neither blackmail nor terrorist demands will receive case-by-case attention but, rather, will be routinely ignored (as noted by Hodgson). This amounts to mobilization of routines as against rational acts.

4. The randomization/variation of routes and times for wages collections or payment into banks to undermine victim-availability routines (Smith and Louis 2010). This amounts to artful creation of nonroutines as against routines that reflect rational decisions.

5. Restriction of staff tenure—for example, of police and accounting roles—to disrupt the creation of mutually rewarding fraud and corruption routines (Mundy 1999).

6. Broken windows policing: The signs permitting routine incivilities are removed, thereby impeding decisions underpinning routinized, unthinking antisocial behavior (Wilson and Kelling 1982).

7. Puncture pluralistic ignorance: When we routinely behave in ways that accord with what we deem others routinely to approve, our behaviors can be altered if misconceptions of what others believe are persuasively punctured (Prentice and Miller 1993).

This section suggested that although rational choice remains an invaluable default position for understanding crime patterns and for thinking about preventive interventions, it can usefully be supplemented with rule reminders and excuse removers, provocation removal and reduction, and routine mobilization and disruption.

III. CONCLUSION

Much can be learned about crime patterns and crime prevention by examining only opportunity distribution, without attending to the ways in which opportunities are apprehended. The early work on SCP (notably *Crime as Opportunity* by Mayhew et al. 1976) was indifferent to the internal processes behind decisions to take advantage of opportunities to offend. It was enough to note that opportunity made a difference to rates of criminal (and other unwanted) behaviors. The retrofitting of rational choice to try to open the black box of opportunity use has served SCP well. It was good enough to create a preliminary heuristically useful classification of preventive techniques that could be drawn on by those trying to think through preventive strategies. It was also good enough to drive explanatory efforts in relation to many patterns of offending.

This chapter, however, suggested that recent developments in SCP have, in some cases tacitly, acknowledged that rational choice is insufficient to explain crime patterns and particularly the ways in which situational contingencies can influence criminal behavior without being mediated through *rational* choice. The term "choice" may still be relevant in that the person could have acted differently, but the choices need not be altogether conscious and also may be informed by considerations other than utility maximization.

The next chapter of SCP will need to build on what has been achieved so far. It needs to include a wider range of cues to behavior than those associated with traditional rational choice, some of which relate to reasoning that is not focused on utility maximization and others that work "behind the backs" of potential offenders to shape behavior in ways they will not ordinarily recognize consciously (but of which they could become aware). This suggests a research agenda that does not assume offenders know fully how they are deciding what to do and that teases out grounds for decision making that are not oriented to extrinsic utility maximization. It also broadens the range of techniques that policymakers and practitioners might draw on in trying to prevent specific crimes. The acknowledgment of rule reminders and provocation reduction are moves already made in this direction, but there is scope to broaden this further to include methods of disrupting (or mobilizing) habitual behavior and also measures that trigger responses that are subconscious (e.g., see Thaler and Sunstein [2008] and the literature on "nudges"). In making these moves, SCP would be following the direction already taken in economics, which has come to embrace the findings and methods of the broader behavioral sciences as well as other relevant disciplines.

What we are suggesting is certainly no repudiation of SCP. What we hope it might stimulate, however, is greater and more explicit research attention to techniques whose underlying mechanisms operate at a subconscious level or that involve the removal of options. In both cases, reasoning and choice making are taken out of the equation. Even where rational choice is at work in offending behaviors, in practice it might sometimes be more practical to focus situational measures on the non-decision-making cues that lie behind the criminal acts or on the removal of any option to choose to commit the crimes.

Acknowledgments

We thank Lieven Pauwels, Richard Wortley, and two anonymous reviewers for their helpful comments on earlier drafts of this chapter.

Notes

1. This quotation is taken from http://www.su.se/english/about/news-and-events/press/press-releases/criminology-prize-winners-pioneers-of-situational-crime-prevention-1.208593. A video of Professor Clarke's prize winners' lecture is available at https://www.youtube.com/watch?v=edjQXdoFmfE.
2. We recognize that other theories have also made important contributions to the development of situational crime prevention—most notably the routine activity approach (Cohen and Felson 1979) and crime pattern theory (Brantingham and Brantingham 2008)—but given the focus of this handbook, we limit our discussion to the rational choice perspective.
3. To elaborate, with the exception of the most rudimentary of tasks, the number of possible consequences resulting from real-world decisions is too many to confidently assume perfect rationality. Psychologists refer to this as a *combinatorial explosion*. Chess is a helpful game to illustrate this principle. Colman (1995) describes how in a standard game of chess there are usually approximately 30 options per move, with each player usually performing approximately 40 moves in the course of a game (80 in total). That equates to a total number of chess moves of approximately 30^{80}. To put this in perspective, there are an estimated 10^{80} particles in the universe.
4. Crime scripts have emerged as a popular tool for parsing specific crime types into their necessary stages (Cornish 1994).
5. Weisburd and Piquero (2008) are quick to point out that this statistic was generated from only two articles that met their definition of testing rational choice theory.
6. This also seems to have been Milton Friedman's (1953) view of economics. He said, "Let the apparent immediate determinant of business behavior be anything at all—habitual reaction, random chance, or whatnot. Whenever this determinant happens to lead to behavior consistent with rational and informed maximization of returns, the business will prosper and acquire resources with which to expand; whenever it does not, the business will tend to lose resources and can be kept in existence only by the addition of resources from outside" (p. 22).
7. A study by Wartell and Gallagher (2012) on crime analysts' familiarity with concepts from environmental criminology is relevant here, albeit with the usual caveat of concerns

regarding generalizability. In their survey of more than 100 analysts affiliated with the Association of Crime Analysts, 19 percent of respondents had never heard of the rational choice perspective. For repeat victimization and crime pattern theory, the same response was given by 4 and 7 percent of the sample, respectively.

REFERENCES

Asch, S. E. 1955. "Opinions and Social Pressure." *Scientific American* 193(5):31–5.

Barclay, G. C., and C. Tavares. 1999. *Digest 4: Information on the Criminal Justice System in England and Wales.* London: Home Office.

Berkowitz, L. 1983. "The Experience of Anger as a Parallel Process in the Display of Impulsive, 'Angry' Aggression." In *Aggression: Theoretical and Empirical Reviews*, edited by R. Geen and E. I. Donnerstein, pp. 103–33. New York: Academic Press.

Braga, A. A., and B. J. Bond. 2008. "Policing Crime and Disorder Hot Spots: A Randomized Controlled Trial." *Criminology* 46:577–607.

Brantingham, P. J., and P. L. Brantingham. 2008. "Crime Pattern Theory." In *Environmental Criminology and Crime Analysis*, edited by R. Wortley and L. Mazerolle, pp. 78–93. Cullompton, UK: Willan.

Burrows, J., M. Hopkins, R. Hubbard, A. Robinson, M. Speed, and N. Tilley. 2005. *Understanding the Attrition Process in Volume Crime Investigations.* Home Office Research Study 295. London: Home Office.

Chenery, S., C. Henshaw, and K. Pease. 1999. *Illegal Parking in Disabled Bays: A Means of Offender Targeting.* Home Office Policing and Reducing Crime Unit, Briefing Note 1/99. London: Home Office.

Clarke, R. V. 1980. "Situational Crime Prevention: Theory and Practice." *British Journal of Criminology* 20:136–47.

Clarke, R. V., ed. 1992. *Situational Crime Prevention: Successful Case Studies.* Albany, NY: Harrow and Heston.

Clarke R. V., ed. 1997. *Situational Crime Prevention: Successful Case Studies*, 2nd ed. Guilderland, NY: Harrow and Heston.

Clarke, R. V. 2008. "Situational Crime Prevention." In *Environmental Criminology and Crime Analysis*, edited by R. Wortley and L. Mazzerole, pp. 178–94. Cullompton, UK: Willan.

Clarke, R. V., and D. B. Cornish. 1985. "Modeling Offenders' Decisions: A Framework for Research and Policy." In *Crime and Justice: An Annual Review of Research*, vol. 6, edited by M. Tonry and N. Morris, pp. 147–85. Chicago: University of Chicago Press.

Clarke, R. V., and R. Homel. 1997. "A Revised Classification of Situational Crime Prevention Techniques." In *Crime Prevention at a Crossroads*, edited by S. P. Lab, pp. 17–27. Highland Heights/Cincinnati, OH: Academy of Criminal Justice Sciences/Anderson.

Clarke, R. V., and D. Lester. 1988. *Suicide: Closing the Exits.* New York: Springer-Verlag.

Clarke, R. V., and G. R. Newman. 2006. *Outsmarting the Terrorists.* New York: Praeger.

Cohen, L. E., and M. Felson. 1979. "Social Change and Crime Rate Trends: A Routine Activities Approach." *American Sociological Review* 44:588–608.

Colman, A. 1995. *Game Theory and Its Applications.* Oxford: Butterworth-Heinemann.

Cook, P. J. 1980. "Research in Criminal Deterrence: Laying the Groundwork for the Second Decade." In *Crime and Justice*, vol. 2, edited by N. Morris and M. Tonry, pp. 211–68. Chicago: University of Chicago Press.

Cornish, D. B. 1994. "The Procedural Analysis of Offending and Its Relevance for Situational Prevention." In *Crime Prevention Studies*, vol. 3, edited by R. V. Clarke, pp. 151–96. Monsey, NY: Criminal Justice Press.

Cornish, D. B., and R. V. Clarke. 2008. "The Rational Choice Perspective." In *Environmental Criminology and Crime Analysis*, edited by R. Wortley and L. Mazzerolle, pp. 21–47. Cullompton, UK: Willan.

Darwin, C. 1974. *Metaphysics, Materialism, and the Evolution of Mind: Early Writings of Charles Darwin*, transcribed and annotated by Paul H. Barrett with a commentary by Howard E. Gruber. Chicago: University of Chicago Press.

Farrell, G., A. Tseloni, J. Mailley, and N. Tilley. 2011. "The Crime Drop and the Security Hypothesis." *Journal of Research in Crime and Delinquency* 48:147–75.

Felson, M. 1986. "Linking Criminal Choices, Routine Activities, Informal Control, and Criminal Outcomes." In *The Reasoning Criminal*, edited by D. Cornish and R. V. Clarke, pp. 119–28. New York: Springer-Verlag.

Friedman, M. 1953. "The Methodology of Positive Economics." In *Essays in Positive Economics*, edited by M. Friedman, pp. 3–43. Chicago: University of Chicago Press.

Goldthorpe, J. 2000. *On Sociology*. Oxford: Oxford University Press.

Goldthorpe, J., C. Llewellyn, and C. Payne. 1987. *Social Mobility and Class Structure*. Oxford: Clarendon.

Guerette, R. T. 2009. "The Pull, Push and Expansion of Situational Crime Prevention Evaluation: An Appraisal of Situational Crime Prevention of Thirty-Seven Years of Research. In *Evaluating Crime Reduction Initiatives*, vol. 24, *Crime Prevention Studies*, edited by N. Tilley and J. Knutsson, pp. 29–58. Monsey, NY: Criminal Justice Press.

Guerette, R. T., and K. Bowers. 2009. "Assessing the Extent of Crime Displacement and Diffusion of Benefit: A Systematic Review of Situational Crime Prevention Evaluations." *Criminology* 47(4): 1331–68.

Hodgson, G. 1997. "The Ubiquity of Habits and Rules." *Cambridge Journal of Economics* 21:663–84.

Hodgson, G. 2010. "Choice, Habit and Evolution." *Journal of Evolutionary Economics* 20:1–18.

Homel, R. 1994. "Drink-Driving Law Enforcement and the Legal Blood Alcohol Limit in New South Wales." *Accident Analysis and Prevention* 26(2): 147–55.

Homel, R. 1995. "Can Police Prevent Crime?" In *Contemporary Policing: Unpeeling Tradition*, edited by K. Bryett and C. Lewis, pp. 7–34. Sydney: Macmillan.

Kahneman, D. 2011. *Thinking Fast and Slow*. New York: Farrar, Straus and Giroux.

Kennedy, D. M. 2008. *Deterrence and Crime Prevention: Reconsidering the Prospect of Sanction*. New York: Routledge.

Lakatos, I. 1978. *The Methodology of Scientific Research Programmes*. Cambridge: Cambridge University Press.

Latsis, S. 1976. *Method and Appraisal in Economics*. Cambridge: Cambridge University Press.

Leclerc, B., and R. Wortley. 2014. "The Reasoning Criminal: Twenty-Five Years On." In *Cognition and Crime: Offender Decision Making and Script Analysis*, edited by B. Leclerc and R. Wortley, pp. 1–11. London: Routledge.

Lemieux, A. M., ed. 2014. *Situational Crime Prevention of Poaching*. Abingdon, UK: Routledge.

Martinson, R. 1974. "What Works? Questions and Answers About Prison Reform." *The Public Interest* 35:22–54.

Mayhew, P. M., R. V. Clarke, A. Sturman, and J. M. Hough. 1976. *Crime as Opportunity*, Home Office Research Study no. 34. London: Her Majesty's Stationary Office.

Milgram, S. 1974. *Obedience to Authority: An Experimental View*. New York: Harper and Row.

Mundy, G. 1999. *Tenure Policy and Practice*, Police Research Series Paper 106. London: Home Office.

Newman, G., and R. V. Clarke. 2003. *Superhighway Robbery: Preventing Ecommerce Crime*. London: Willan.

Pettigrew, T. 1979. "The Ultimate Attribution Error: Extending Allport's Cognitive Analysis of Prejudice." *Personality and Social Psychology Bulletin* 5(4): 461–76.

Prentice, D., and D. Miller. 1993. "Pluralistic Ignorance and Alcohol Use on Campus: Social Consequences of Misperceiving the Social Norm." *Journal of Personality and Social Psychology* 64(2): 243–56.

Ross, L. 1977. "The Intuitive Psychologist and His Shortcomings: Distortions in the Attribution Process." *Advances in Experimental Social Psychology* 10:173–220.

Shane, J. M., E. L. Piza, and M. Mandala. 2015. "Situational Crime Prevention and Worldwide Piracy: A Cross-Continent Analysis." *Crime Science* 4:21.

Simon, H. 1955. "A Behavioural Model of Rational Choice." *Quarterly Journal of Economics* 69:99–118.

Simon, H. 1996. "From Substantive to Procedural Rationality." In *Method and Appraisal in Economics*, edited by S. Latsis, pp. 129–48. Cambridge: Cambridge University Press.

Smith, L., and E. Louis. 2010. *Cash in Transit Armed Robberies*. Trends and Issues in Crime and Criminal Justice no. 397. Canberra: Australian Institute of Criminology.

Smith, M. J., R. V. Clarke, and K. Pease. 2002. "Anticipatory Benefit in Crime Prevention." In *Analysis for Crime Prevention*, vol. 13, *Crime Prevention Studies*, edited by N. Tilley, pp. 71–88. Monsey, NY: Criminal Justice Press.

Sykes, G. M., and D. Matza. 1957. "Techniques of Neutralization: A Theory of Delinquency." *American Sociological Review* 22(6): 664–70.

Thaler, R. H., and C. R. Sunstein. 2008. *Nudge: Improving Decisions About Health, Wealth, and Happiness*. New Haven, CT: Yale University Press.

Tilley, N. 2014. "There Is Nothing So Practical as a Good Theory: Teacher–Learner Relationships in Applied Research for Policing. In *Applied Police Research: Challenges and Opportunities*, edited by E. Cockbain and J. Knutsson, pp. 141–52. London: Routledge.

Tilley, N., and A. Sidebottom. 2014. "Situational Crime Prevention." In *Encyclopedia of Criminology and Criminal Justice*, edited by G. Bruinsma and D. Weisburd, pp. 4864–74. New York: Springer-Verlag.

Walsh, D. 1994. "The Obsolescence of Crime Forms." In *Crime Prevention Studies*, vol. 2., edited by R. V. Clarke. Monsey, pp. 149–64. NY: Willow Tree Press.

Wartell, J., and K. Gallagher. 2012. "Translating Environmental Criminology Theory Into Crime Analysis Practice." *Policing* 6(4): 377–87.

Weisburd, D., J. Hinkle, A. Braga, and A. Wooditch. 2015. "Understanding the Mechanisms Underlying Broken Windows Policing: The Need for Evaluation Evidence." *Journal of Research in Crime and Delinquency* 52(4): 589–608.

Weisburd, D., and A. Piquero. 2008. "How Well Do Criminologists Explain Crime? Statistical Modeling in Published Studies." *Crime and Justice* 17:453–502.

Wilson, J., and G. Kelling. 1982. "Broken Windows." *The Atlantic Monthly* March:29–38.

Wortley, R. 2001. "A Classification of Techniques for Controlling Situational Precipitators of Crime." *Security Journal* 14(4): 63–82.

Wortley, R. 2008. "Situational Precipitators of Crime." In *Environmental Criminology and Crime Analysis*, edited by R. Wortley and L. Mazerolle, pp. 48–69. Cullompton, UK: Willan.

Wortley, R. 2013. "Rational Choice and Offender Decision Making: Lessons from the Cognitive Sciences." In *Cognition and Crime: Offender Decision Making and Script Analyses*, edited by B. Leclerc and R. Wortley, pp. 237–51. New York: Routledge.

Wortley, R., and S. Smallbone, eds. 2006. *Situational Prevention of Child Sexual Abuse*, vol. 19, *Crime Prevention Studies*. Monsey, NY: Criminal Justice Press.

Zimbardo, P. 2007. *The Lucifer Effect*. New York: Random House.

CHAPTER 6

BIOSOCIAL CRIMINOLOGY AND MODELS OF CRIMINAL DECISION MAKING

KYLE TREIBER

I. INTRODUCTION: CONTEMPORARY APPROACHES IN BIOSOCIAL CRIMINOLOGY

BIOSOCIAL criminology is an emerging field of criminological enquiry that aims to integrate knowledge and methods from neuroscience, genetics, and evolutionary science into the study of crime (for overviews, see Walsh and Beaver 2009; Beaver and Walsh 2011; Raine 2013; Beaver, Barnes, and Boutwell 2015). It has opened up new directions for criminological research and paradigmatically shifted criminological thinking about the etiology of crime involvement. It has the potential to contribute significantly to our understanding of criminal decision making, but so far its application in this arena has been surprisingly limited.

One reason is that biosocial criminology tends to take a *correlational approach*, focusing on statistical relationships in order to predict crime (e.g., who will commit crime) but paying less attention to the processes such as action decision making that link those correlates to criminal actions. This is in contrast to an *analytical approach*, which focuses on those processes (causal mechanisms) in order to explain why acts of crime happen (Wikström and Treiber 2013).

A second reason is that when biosocial criminology has made steps to model these processes, which it has done increasingly in recent years, it has tended to do so by incorporating biological factors into existing criminological theories without giving due consideration to the serious problems that plague those theories, including endemic fragmentation, gross and unfounded assumptions, and a lack of adequate action mechanisms that explain how biological or social factors actually produce (i.e., move people to commit) acts of crime (Walsh 2009a, 2009b; Beaver and Walsh 2011; Beaver et al. 2015; Rocque, Posick, and Felix 2015).

Clarke and Cornish (1985) were among the first to recognize that the missing link was a model of criminal decision making. Their solution was a rational choice model that they have argued is "good enough" to explain why people decide to commit acts of crime (Clarke and Cornish 1985; Cornish and Clarke 2008). This model has been widely adopted, both explicitly and implicitly, by criminological theories (e.g., routine activity theory, see Clarke and Felson 1993; self-control theory, see Gottfredson and Hirschi 1990; deterrence theory, see Nagin and Pogarsky 2001 and Paternoster 2010; and even as its own theory, see Loughran et al. 2016) and many biosocial criminologists (e.g., Armstrong and Boutwell 2012). But is it good enough? Advances in knowledge about cognition and behavior and their biological underpinnings may help answer this question.

II. THE RELATIONSHIP BETWEEN BIOLOGICAL FACTORS AND CRIME

A growing body of interdisciplinary research demonstrates reliable statistical relationships between a wide range of biological factors and criminal behavior. This smorgasbord of "biomarkers" includes genetic polymorphisms; neurotransmitters and hormones; structural and functional brain characteristics; autonomic indicators such as heart rate and skin conductance; and factors relating to birth, development, and general health (for a monumental overview, see Ellis, Beaver, and Wright 2009; see also Raine 2002; Patrick 2008). These relationships are intriguing and warrant closer consideration. However, although there is a growing interest in relevant causal mechanisms, efforts to theoretically address and empirically test those mechanisms remain limited, underdeveloped, and generally lackluster (see Barnes, Boutwell, and Beaver 2015; Chen et al. 2015). Many biomarkers cannot be causes of crime (e.g., attributes such as sex and race and symptoms such as minor physical anomalies, a low resting heart rate, or a low 2D:4D ratio) and therefore, regardless of how well they may predict crime, give us little direct insight into why crime happens and what we can do to prevent it (Wikström and Treiber 2013). A strong theoretical framework that delineates key causal processes may help us separate causal from correlational relationships between biological factors and crime and better understand their usefulness for explaining and preventing crime or as proxies and predictors.

So what is currently known about biological factors and their role in criminal decision making? Neurological factors have the most direct association with criminal decision making. Studies exploring brain structures and functioning have demonstrated a consistent link between certain brain regions and crime involvement (Wahlund and Kristiansson 2009; Wright et al. 2009; Chen et al. 2015), especially the prefrontal cortex

(Ishikawa and Raine 2003; Yang and Raine 2009), limbic system (DeLisi 2009), and, the basal ganglia (Buckholtz et al. 2010; Glenn et al. 2010)—regions that are all strongly implicated in action cognition. Recent advances in neuroimaging have also drawn attention to the interplay between these regions and the brain structures and neural pathways through which they communicate (Craig et al. 2009; Motzkin et al. 2011; Pujol et al. 2012; Yang et al. 2012).

The prefrontal cortex (PFC) is the most anterior region of the neocortex and the latest brain region to evolve. It is responsible for the organization and active maintenance of action-relevant information during decision making, and it can exert control over the action process through "executive" functions (Alexander, DeLong, and Strick 1986; Cardinal et al. 2002; Koechlin, Ody, and Kouneiher 2003; Daw, Niv, and Dayan 2005; Frank et al. 2009; Balleine and O'Doherty 2010; de Wit et al. 2012; Hofmann, Schmeichel, and Baddeley 2012; Smith and Graybiel 2013). These higher level cognitive capacities include the ability to inhibit various cognitive and behavioral processes, selectively shift the distribution of cognitive resources (e.g., attention), represent information internally (think abstractly), and organize and integrate information relevant to action (e.g., relating to action goals, situational factors, and previous experiences) (Tranel, Anderson, and Benton, 1994; Fuster 1997; Goldberg 2009). It is therefore not surprising that executive functioning is one of the strongest and most consistent neuropsychological correlates of crime, with delinquent populations performing on average half a standard deviation below the norm on executive function measures (Moffitt and Henry 1989; Moffitt 1990; Henry and Moffitt 1997; Morgan and Lilienfeld 2000; Toupin et al. 2000; Nigg and Huang-Pollock 2003; Ogilvie et al. 2011).

Some of criminology and criminal law's most colorful case studies (e.g., Phineas Gage, see Harlow 1868; Donta Page, see Raine 2013) involve individuals with prefrontal deficits, and neuroimaging studies report disproportionate rates of prefrontal deficits among offenders, one of the most striking being Raine et al.'s (1997, 1998) positron emission tomography study of convicted murderers. There is also an interesting association between the age–crime curve, which peaks between the teenage and adult years, and the developmental timing of the prefrontal cortex, which undergoes the last stages of its development from adolescence into young adulthood (Spear 2000; Steinberg 2008; Walsh 2009b; Shulman et al. 2016).

A substantial body of literature also links the limbic system to crime (DeLisi 2009; Yang et al. 2009; Pardini et al. 2014). This group of subcortical structures, which includes the amygdala and hippocampus, is situated at the center of the brain and supports key emotive and mnemonic processes. The amygdala, which plays a central role in emotional experiences and perception, has received particular attention due to its association with key psychopathic traits (DeLisi 2009; Yang et al. 2009; Pardini et al. 2014) and reactive aggression (Davidson, Putnam, and Larson 2000). It has also been implicated in important social learning processes as it plays a key role in emotional memory and autonomic arousal, which will be discussed shortly (Furmark et al. 1997; Critchley, Mathias, and Dolan 2002).

Recent criminological attention has also been drawn to the basal ganglia, another set of subcortical structures implicated in reward response and expectation. Key structures include the striatum, which plays a fundamental role in habit formation and exclusion of the PFC from action guidance, and the nucleus accumbens, a major component of the brain's reward circuit (Koob et al. 2004; Everitt and Robbins 2005). Although the link between these structures and crime involvement has not been as widely studied as that between crime and the PFC and limbic system, growing interest in criminal action as well as criminal propensities, along with increasing knowledge about the important role of the basal ganglia in key action processes (Balleine and O'Doherty 2010; Haber 2011; Smith and Graybiel 2013), means they are gaining increasing criminological attention.

Recent evidence suggests it is not only the functioning of these key brain regions in isolation but also as an action network that predicts crime involvement. Studies have associated activity in intermediary structures (e.g., the cingulate and insular cortices) and the white matter tracts through which the PFC, limbic system, and basal ganglia communicate with criminal propensities and crime involvement (Craig et al. 2009; Motzkin et al. 2011; Yang et al. 2012).

The link between structural and functional brain abnormalities and crime is generally explained by the logic that these abnormalities "give rise to risk factors that in turn predispose to antisocial and criminal behavior" (Chen et al. 2015, p. 356). These risk factors typically take the form of specific cognitive deficits, such as impulsivity, volatility, and callousness, which are overrepresented among offenders. There is a natural connection between such deficits and criminal decision making, but how this is framed and ultimately interpreted depends on the decision-making model applied. To date, biosocial criminologists have tended to rely on a traditional rational choice model. Thus, when they consider the link between neurocognitive deficits and criminal decision making, this tends to be in the context of a cost–benefits analysis of potential rewards and consequences—for example, how such deficits influence whether people consider, and how they perceive and value, rewards and consequences.

Another category of neurological deficits consistently associated with crime are autonomic deficits. The autonomic nervous system is responsible for involuntary physiological processes both at rest (e.g., resting heart rate and respiration) and when aroused (e.g., heart rate reactivity and skin conductance response). Evidence suggests that some offenders may experience a diminished autonomic response referred to as *underarousal* (Zuckerman 2006; Patrick 2008; Raine 2013). Markers of underarousal include a low resting heart rate, renowned as "the best-replicated biological correlate to date of antisocial behavior in children and adolescents" (Ortiz and Raine 2004, p. 154); low heart rate reactivity (Armstrong et al. 2009; Wilson and Scarpa 2011; Armstrong and Boutwell 2012); a reduced skin conductance response (Herpertz et al. 2005; Fairchild et al. 2008; Gao et al. 2010); and abnormal brain wave patterns (e.g., reduced alpha and beta and increased theta waves and reduced or delayed event-related potentials; Houston and Stanford 2005; Gao and Raine 2009).

As with other neurocognitive deficits, explanations of the link between underarousal and crime tend to be framed in relation to rational decision making (Armstrong and

Boutwell 2012). Poor fear conditioning leading to undervalued costs is one widely considered mechanism (Mednick and Christiansen 1977; Raine and Venables 1981; Veit et al. 2013). Alternatively, sensation seeking leading to overvalued rewards has also been proposed, and there is evidence that it may be a stronger mediator than fear conditioning (Portnoy et al. 2014), although the basic relationship between sensation seeking and crime appears to be quite weak (Sijtsema et al. 2010; Wilson and Scarpa 2011). It is difficult to reconcile these two mechanisms because the former implies an abnormal lack of motivation in situations that would normally generate a response, and the latter implies an abnormal level of motivation in situations that would not. Both propositions also rely on a number of assumptions regarding socialization and motivation that warrant further exploration (e.g., the situational relevance of deterrence, the motivational properties of underarousal, and the arousing capacities of antisocial behavior).

A final category of neurocognitive deficits that have been linked to crime involvement are those associated with the hypothalamic–pituitary–adrenal (HPA) axis, which governs the stress response (Susman 2006). When a person experiences stress, the HPA axis triggers the release of cortisol, a hormone that has wide-ranging physiological effects that support the "flight or fight" response but can be detrimental over time (Miller, Chen, and Zhou 2007). Consequently, a protective feedback loop lowers the responsivity of the HPA axis under conditions of chronic stress (Susman 2006; Miller et al. 2007), which can result in underresponsiveness to chronic stress-inducing stimuli, with parallels to underarousal. At the same time, HPA allostasis has also been linked to enhanced sensitivity to acute stressors (van Goozen et al. 2000; Marin et al. 2007) and therefore sensitivity to friction and reactive aggression (van Goozen and Fairchild 2006).

Many other biomarkers are linked to crime through their association with the HPA axis, autonomic nervous system, prefrontal cortex, limbic system, or basal ganglia. This includes the activity of many hormones, such as testosterone; neurotransmitters (neuroactive chemicals that excite or inhibit neural activity; see Collins 2011), such as serotonin and dopamine; and enzymes involved in their regulation, such as monoamine oxidase A (MAO-A) and catechol-O-methyltransferase (COMT).

The relationship between testosterone and crime involvement remains unclear (Mehta and Beer 2010; Carré, McCormick, and Hariri, 2011). Prenatal testosterone has been linked to later aggression (Cohen-Bendahan, van de Beek, and Berenbaum, 2005; Cohen-Bendahan et al. 2005). The 2D:4D digit ratio is not infrequently used as a marker for exposure to testosterone in utero, although it has been strongly criticized (e.g., it cannot definitively distinguish between males and females; Berenbaum et al. 2009; Breedlove 2010). Situationally, some studies suggest testosterone is linked to aggression only under certain circumstances (e.g., in response to certain kinds of provocation; Mehta and Beer 2010; Carré et al. 2010, 2011; Eisenegger, Haushofer, and Fehr 2011; Montoya et al. 2012). Others suggest this depends on an interaction between testosterone and cortisol, which increases the reactivity of the amygdala (Montoya et al. 2012; Denson, Mehta, and Ho Tan 2013). Explanations again tend to draw on rational conceptualizations of behavior; for example, Carré et al. (2010) suggest a link between testosterone and heightened expectations of reward from aggression.

Serotonin (5-HT) and dopamine (DA) are the most studied neurotransmitters in criminology. Serotonin is associated with inhibition, whereas dopamine is associated with arousal, and the balance of the two, particularly in prefrontal and limbic regions, has been associated with the balance of executive and emotive controls (Steinberg 2008; Wahlstrom et al. 2010; Dalley and Roiser 2012). Enzymes that break down 5-HT and DA, such as MAO-A and COMT, have also been extensively studied in relation to crime involvement (Caspi et al. 2002; Kim-Cohen et al. 2006).

The vast majority of genes associated with crime involvement are linked to the functioning of these neurochemicals—their production, reception, transport, and decomposition (Jackson and Beaver 2012). For example, findings suggest that variants of serotonergic genes (e.g., 5-HTTLPR and TPH; Manuck et al. 1999; Beitchman et al. 2006; Haberstick, Smolen, and Hewitt 2006; Vaughn et al. 2009; Duke et al. 2013; Ficks and Waldman 2014), dopaminergic genes (e.g., DRD2, DRD4, and DAT1; Guo, Roettger, and Shih 2007; Vaughn et al. 2009; Beaver et al. 2012), and MAO-A and COMT genes (Brunner et al. 1993; Caspi et al. 2002; Kim-Cohen et al. 2006; Guo et al. 2008; Eme 2013; Ficks and Waldman 2014; Stetler et al. 2014) carry a heightened risk for crime involvement. However, many studies question the nature and strength of the relationship between any one gene and antisocial behavior as evidence suggests most genetic effects involve the expression and interaction of many genes and, crucially, the interaction between those genes and environmental factors (Duncan and Keller 2011; Tielbeek et al. 2012; Vassos, Collier, and Fazel 2014). Environmental factors provide molecular building blocks and energy, trigger gene expression, and can even change a gene's molecular structure (e.g., through epigenetic processes such as methylation) with lasting and even heritable but potentially reversible effects on gene expression (Walsh 2009a). Although much of this science is still in its infancy, seminal studies such as that by Caspi et al. (2002) have greatly changed our thinking about the interdependent roles of biological and environmental factors in people's personal propensities and subsequent behavior. One overarching conclusion is that the genes most relevant to behavior are those that affect susceptibility to environmental influences (Belsky and Pluess 2009; Ellis and Boyce 2011; Ellis et al. 2011; Simons et al. 2011; Simons, Beach, and Barr 2012).

It is difficult to square these findings with the core aims and findings of behavioral genetics, one of the most active branches of biosocial criminology. Behavioral genetics seeks to portion out the roots of variation in a particular behavior in a given population to genetic and environmental effects, and a consistent and key finding is that at least half of that variation is attributable to genetic effects (Rhee and Waldman 2002; Polderman et al. 2015). Separating genetic and environmental effects seems a Sisyphean task if those effects are highly interactive, and the assertion that genes are independently responsible for half the variation in criminal behaviors conflicts with findings from molecular genetics that show very small, if any, effects when actual genes are assessed (Maher 2008; Tielbeek et al. 2012; Zuk et al. 2012; Burt and Simons 2014, 2015). More careful consideration of the biosocial mechanisms involved is needed to resolve these incongruities.

The relationship between brain functioning and underlying hormones, neurotransmitters, and ultimately genes and their expression and behavior at the point of action is one important level of association that biosocial criminology explores; another is how people come to differ in these biological factors. Especially because of the implications for crime prevention, development has emerged as a key area of exploration in biosocial criminology. This includes research on prenatal influences (e.g., maternal stress, substance use, and birth complications), general health (e.g., malnutrition, maltreatment, exposure to pathogens, and head injuries), and puberty (e.g., timing, hormonal changes, and neurodevelopment) (Ellis et al. 2009; Raine 2002; Tibbetts 2011; Chen et al. 2015). These factors can be seen as causes of the causes because they are only indirectly related to cognitive and behavioral outcomes.

Another set of indirect factors that has captured the attention of biosocial criminology are evolutionary factors (Vila 1994; Kanazawa 2009; Ferguson 2010;Ellis et al. 2011). Evolutionary science draws attention to the process by which our cognitive and behavioral capacities have been selected based on the kinds of environmental pressures our ancestors encountered. Although far removed from our immediate actions, these processes have shaped how our brains engage with our environments—for example, the stimuli that draw and hold our attention, and that we intrinsically value or are averse to, and the ways in which we learn from our experiences. These processes have shaped the general blueprint of our cognitive and behavioral machinery, but perhaps most intriguingly, they have left that machinery responsive to the content it receives, developmentally as well as situationally, so that our biology and behavior are products of our environments and our experiences as well as our genes, which is why a truly biosocial approach to explaining human behavior and action decision making is crucial (Belsky and Pluess 2009; Simons et al., 2011, 2012).

For some time, an economical or rational explanation of action decision making has seemed to fit naturally with evolutionary science and assumptions of self-interest that tend to go hand-in-hand with the concept of "survival of the fittest." However, advances in evolutionary science show that the reality of social behavior, and hence the evolution of social organisms (and their cognitive and behavioral capacities), is much more complex and nuanced (Hamilton 1963, 1964a, 1964b; Axelrod 1984; Wright 2001; Rilling 2013).

In summary, biosocial criminology has advanced in leaps and bounds in the past few decades. Our knowledge about biosocial correlates of crime is well-developed. Our knowledge about the mechanisms linking those correlates to crime is far more limited and arguably constrained by a lack of attention to action decision making as the key intermediary process. It is important that we actively engage with a robust model of criminal decision making if we are to better understand the role of biosocial factors in crime causation.

III. The Action Process

At the core of biosocial criminology is the assertion that people's actions depend on their biological characteristics as well as characteristics of the social environments (settings) in which they act and, importantly, develop. However, people still remain the sources of their actions; people *decide* to act in certain ways.[1] Action decision making—the cognitive process by which people form intentions to act—is arguably the central process (mechanism) that links (the characteristics of) people and settings to actions, including their biological traits and acts of crime (Wikström 2006). Hence, a robust explanation of action (e.g., acts of crime) requires a robust model of how people make action decisions (e.g., to commit or not commit an act of crime) that specifies the real driving forces, subprocesses, and major constraints.

Action decision making can be subdivided into three key subprocesses: motivation, perception, and choice (figure 6.1). *Motivation* directs attention toward an action goal, initiating the action process. *Perception* is the process through which a person identifies possible action alternatives for obtaining a particular action goal in response to a

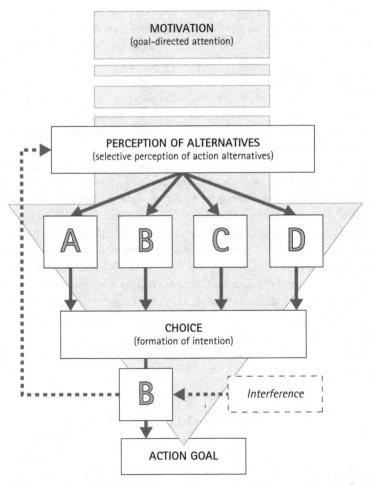

FIGURE 6.1 Subprocesses of action decision making: motivation, perception and choice.

motivation. *Choice* is the process through which a person selects which alternative to pursue, forming an action intention, which he or she will carry out if there is no interference[2] (Wikström 2006).

Most criminological theories have not forwarded an explicit model of action because they have tended to focus on either crime-relevant characteristics of people (criminality) or environments (criminogeneity) and their roots, and they have paid less attention to actions and the mechanism that generates them. Cornish and Clarke's rational choice perspective (RCP; Clarke and Cornish 1985; Cornish and Clarke 1986) has served as a stand in for this mechanism, despite the fact that it was not intended to represent or explain how people actually make action decisions but, rather, to serve as a tool for predicting the places and circumstances in which crimes are and are not likely to occur (Cornish and Clarke 2008). Nevertheless, it is considered by many criminologists to provide a "good enough" model of the action process,[3] and it serves as a mechanism in several leading theories (e.g., self-control theory, routine activity theory, and deterrence theory; see Akers 1990; Gottfredson and Hirschi 1990; Clarke and Felson 1993; Nagin and Pogarsky 2001). The core assertions of RCP are that people's actions are (1) fundamentally self-interested (directed toward obtaining personal benefits and avoiding personal costs), (2) chosen based on their personal utility, and (3) chosen through a rational costs–benefits assessment of action alternatives (Cornish and Clarke 1986, 2008; Clarke 2014).

RCP continues to dominate criminological thinking despite the fact that a number of alternative models have been proposed and received empirical support, including the social information processing (SIP) model (Crick and Dodge 1994, 1996; Fontaine and Dodge 2006; Fontaine 2007, 2008), situational action theory (SAT; Wikström 2006, 2010; Wikström et al. 2012), the model of frame selection (MFS; Kroneberg 2006), and dual systems models (Kahneman 2003, 2012; Steinberg 2010; van Gelder and de Vries 2014; Shulman et al. 2016; see also chapter 9, this volume). These alternative models bring into question core assumptions of RCP and make different assertions about motivation, perception, and choice. These include the proposition that people's actions are (1) fundamentally rule-guided (directed toward satisfying wants and needs in personally and socially acceptable ways) (Wikström 2006); (2) chosen preferentially within the constraints of personal and social rules (Fontaine and Dodge 2006; Kroneberg 2006; Wikström 2010); (3) from action alternatives that are selectively perceived as a result of the interplay between personal and social rule guidance (Fontaine and Dodge 2006; Kroneberg 2006; Wikström 2010); (4) through either deliberate (considered) or habitual (automatic) choice processes (Kroneberg 2006; Kahneman 2012; Wikström et al. 2012; Shulman et al. 2016).

The following section explores these propositions and considers their viability in light of current knowledge about the biological mechanisms that underlie motivation, perception, and choice. Any valid framework for action decision making must be consistent with available knowledge about the underlying biological mechanisms ("biomechanics"); this seems particularly obvious for a model that aims to explain the action relevance of biological factors. An inaccurate model would, at best, be inefficient or ineffective, wasting limited resources; at worst, it could mislead crime policy and practice, with potentially significant implications for those involved in and affected by crime.[4]

IV. ACTION SUBPROCESSES

A. Motivation: What Induces Action Decision Making?

Motivation is the impetus for action and occurs when a person's attention is directed toward an action goal (Crick and Dodge 1994; Wikström 2006). In criminological theory, the concept and role of motivation in action often lack clarity. One reason is that many prominent criminological theories do not engage with the reality of differential motivation. Many assume that people share similar action goals, wants, and needs and therefore under similar conditions are similarly motivated. This motivation is typically presumed to revolve around self-interests; acquiring personal benefits and avoiding personal costs are presumed to be universal action goals, and personal capital such as money, status, material goods, and sex are presumed to be universally valued (this is most explicitly stated in Gottfredson and Hirschi 1990, but is implicit in many other models, including Hirschi 1969; Sampson and Laub 1993; Nagin and Pogarsky 2001; Felson 2006). Such assumptions have led to the importance of motivation being overlooked in many models of criminal decision making while the importance of other variables, such as opportunities and deterrents, has been overstated (Hirschi 1969, p. 32; Gottfredson and Hirschi 1990, p. 95; Clarke 2005, p. 41; Felson 2006, p. 54; Felson and Boba 2010, p. 50).

Models of criminal decision making that do recognize differences in motivation tend to confound motivation with characteristics of people (e.g., "motivated" offenders; Cohen and Felson 1979, Clarke and Felson 1993; Cornish and Clarke 2003, 2008) or places (e.g., "opportunities" that include motivation as a prerequisite; see Cohen and Felson 1979; Felson and Clarke 1998; Felson and Boba 2010; Clarke 2012).[5] Alternatively, Wikström (2006, 2010) has argued that motivation is a *situational concept*—something that characterizes person–environment interactions—and therefore cannot be fully explained solely by personal characteristics or the features of the settings people encounter; people differ in their desires and commitments (wants and needs) and sensitivities, and these shape their action goals only when activated by relevant opportunities or frictions. This is similar to Crick and Dodge's (1994) assertion that people bring goal-related tendencies with them into a setting "but also revise those goals and construct new goals in response to immediate social stimuli" (p. 87). This is not dissimilar to the notion of "prompts" and "precipitators" discussed in later versions of RCP, although according to Cornish and Clarke (2003, p. 60), these are only relevant "in limited circumstances."

The notion of motivation as a situationally variable concept is consistent with what we know about the biomechanics of motivation, which suggests that people are not solely or even predominantly driven by self-interest but, rather, differ in their motivations, many of which are socially oriented. A growing body of research suggests that contrary to general assumptions of self-interest, people's goal-directed attention is regularly directed toward the interests of others and, furthermore, that the balance of social interests and self-interests may be calibrated by social experiences (Vila 1994; Van Voorhees and Scarpa 2004; Susman 2006; Ellis et al. 2011; Rilling 2013; Tottenham 2015).

Evidence points to a number of biomechanisms that support social interests in social organisms, co-opting mechanisms that originally supported self-interests, most likely through the evolution of parenting behaviors (Churchland 2011; Rilling 2013). Examples include alarm mechanisms associated with self-preservation that also respond to threats to others; mechanisms associated with place preferences that respond to the presence (or absence) of others; a reward circuit that responds to positive social stimuli and a stress response system that responds to negative social stimuli; and the dedication of valuable cognitive resources to functions that gauge others' perspectives, feelings, and behavioral intentions (Eisenberger and Lieberman 2004; Lamm, Decety, and Singer 2010; Panskepp 2010; Churchland 2011; Rilling 2013; Smith et al. 2014). The fact that social interests and self-interests are underpinned by the same physiological processes means they are perceived/experienced in similar ways, making them comparable behavioral drivers (Eisenberger and Lieberman 2004).

Additional regulatory mechanisms manage conflict between self-interests and social interests, some more deliberate (e.g., moral judgments) and some more intuitive (e.g., moral emotions) (Moll and de Oliveira-Souza 2003; Greene et al. 2004; Woodward and Allman 2007; Moll, de Oliveira-Souza, and Zahn 2008). Many of these functions bias people's attention, values, and perception toward *social* interests, even when this incurs a personal cost. However, there is also evidence that people adopt more self-interested strategies when social behaviors are consistently ineffectual or detrimental—for example, when a person's efforts at social behavior are not appropriate or his or her social environment is not receptive (van Voorhees and Scarpa 2004; Susman 2006; Rutter et al. 2007).

These assertions require further exploration (e.g., through more targeted experimental and developmental research), but it seems clear that self-interest is not the only, and may not even be the most important, driving force behind human behavior, and assuming it is simply is not "good enough."

Whether our action goals are selfish or social, our motivation to pursue them manifests through the same neurocognitive processes, which depend primarily on activity in the limbic system and the basal ganglia, with some prefrontal oversight. The limbic system plays a crucial role in priming people for action in response to external cues, orienting people toward important action goals (whether selfish or social) and galvanizing them to recognize and respond to important stimuli (e.g., which signal opportunities or create friction) (Robbins and Everitt 1996; Adolphs Baron-Cohen, and Tranel 2002; Cardinal et al. 2002). The amygdala plays a key role in emotive processes that direct attention and energy toward action goals, while another limbic structure, the hippocampus, plays a key role in memory processes that encode action experiences and inform expectations (e.g., recognition of opportunities that are likely to satisfy particular desires). The close association between emotive and mnemonic brain structures and functions is integral to learning from personally significant experiences, which may be important for future action decisions (Phelps 2004).

The basal ganglia contain the nucleus accumbens, the hub of the brain's reward circuit, and therefore also play a crucial role in reward processing and action–outcome associations, signalling expectations. Importantly, reactivity of the reward circuit to a given motivator is experience dependent. The basal ganglia and certain sections of the PFC (e.g., the orbitofrontal cortex, or OFC) work together to form and inform expectations about situational stimuli and the outcomes with which they have previously co-occurred (Balleine and O'Doherty 2010; Haber 2011). This suggests people will vary in their response to particular motivators depending on their experiences.

The limbic system and basal ganglia often provide preliminary action guidance, initiating the action process and activating primed response options, but the PFC may inhibit selection of these responses and exert executive control. The PFC has important connections to the limbic system through which it receives information about motivation in order to shape response guidance but also through which it can suppress motivation; consequently, the PFC plays a key role in the management of motivation in relation to other action-relevant information. Indeed, one of its fundamental functions is to establish an optimal balance (in terms of efficacy and efficiency) between action-inducing motivational functions and action-controlling executive functions—for example, by assessing the need for control and harnessing the appropriate level (Ochsner & Gross 2005; Heatherton and Wagner 2011; Munakata et al. 2011; Hofmann et al. 2012; Ochsner, Silvers, and Buhle 2012). Both motivation and control can be important sources of action guidance; hence, their effective coordination is crucial, and there is evidence that a lack of coordination may lead to antisocial behaviors (Shulman et al. 2016).

This evidence derives from the vast amount of literature relating to neurocognitive and behavioral changes during adolescence (Spear 2000; Steinberg 2008; Wahlstrom et al. 2010; Blakemore and Robbins 2012; Crone and Dahl 2012; Shulman et al. 2016). Between late childhood and early adulthood, prefrontal and limbic connections are rewired, refining executive control. While this takes place, prefrontal and limbic functions become uncoordinated. Increases in active dopamine levels lead to hyperactivity in the limbic system and reward circuit and hypoactivity in the PFC; consequently, young people experience heightened reward sensitivity and greater risk-taking (particularly in social domains) alongside reduced executive control. Although this may serve an adaptive purpose in galvanizing social independence, it can also lead to maladaptive behavior and may contribute significantly to the shape of the well-established age–crime curve (Hirschi and Gottfredson 1983; Walsh 2009b; Sweeten, Piquero, and Steinberg 2013).

The coordination of prefrontal and limbic/basal ganglia activity is reflected in the coordination of dopaminergic (DA) and serotonergic (5-HT) functioning. DA plays a key role both in activating the reward circuit and in modulating the reactivity of the amygdala (Takahashi et al. 2010; Wahlstrom et al. 2010). These excitatory effects are counteracted and hence regulated by inhibitory neurotransmitters, including 5-HT, which are utilized by the PFC to suppress subcortical activity (Hariri et al. 2002; Hariri and Holmes 2006; van Goozen et al. 2007; Caspi et al. 2010; Schardt et al. 2010).

Biosocial criminology has highlighted the importance of DA and 5-HT activity for behavioral control (e.g., reactivity, affectivity, impulsivity, and the ability to exercise self-control) (Burt and Mikolajewski 2008; Raine 2008; Beaver, Ratchford, and Ferguson 2009; Craig and Halton 2009; Collins 2011; Wright, Moore, and Newsome 2011; Jackson and Beaver 2012). Although these findings are often interpreted in terms of differences in people's ability to exercise self-control, they may also tap into differences in people's motivation—that is, their need to exercise self-control. Given the large number of studies that link serotonin- and dopamine-related variables to crime involvement, a better understanding of their role in motivation, and of motivation in action, seems a promising direction for research.

The following conclusions can be drawn from the biomechanics of motivation: (1) People are not purely self-interested, and (2) people may differ in their motivations as a consequence of both biological and experiential differences. This may help us better explain the association between key biological factors (e.g., those relating to dopaminergic, serotonergic, limbic, and basal ganglia functioning) and people's crime involvement by separating our thinking about the action goals that people are moved to satisfy and how they set the stage for the perception of action alternatives from our thinking about how action alternatives and their potential to achieve action goals are evaluated, which occurs later in the action process (Fontaine and Dodge 2006; Wikström 2006).

B. Perception: The Role of Rules in Criminal Decision Making

Motivation to obtain an action goal activates the perception process that populates the field of alternatives from which a person will choose his or her action. Perception is often overlooked in models of criminal decision making, which tend to either (1) presume all people perceive crime as an option (at least in certain circumstances, i.e., those that are criminogenic) or (2) only explain action decisions in which people do perceive crime as an option. Assuming that everyone views crime as an option that some (indeed most) people actively choose not to act upon is clearly unsupportable. For example, the last time you needed money, did you consider robbing a bank or selling drugs? The last time you were sexually aroused, did you consider committing date rate or watching child pornography? The last time you were strongly opposed to an ideology, did you consider committing an act of terrorism? These action alternatives probably do not occur to most people even in these circumstances, or if they do, they are not seriously considered. Hence, the reason most people do not pursue such actions is not because they choose not to do so (e.g., after calculating the costs and benefits) but, rather, because they do not perceive such actions as viable action alternatives, despite their motivations.

How the field of perceived alternatives is populated remains largely undiscussed in criminology. Some models (e.g., SAT, SIP, and MFS; Fontaine and Dodge 2006;

Kroneberg 2006; Wikström 2010) suggest it occurs via a selection process through which a person becomes aware of and retains certain alternatives to be considered for action. Attention undoubtedly plays a role; some alternatives may simply not occur to the actor regardless of whether or not he or she might consider and even choose them if they did occur to him or her. Other factors, such as plausibility, may serve as filters that quickly direct attention, and therefore cognitive resources, away from certain alternatives (Fontaine and Dodge 2006). Wikström (2010) suggests that a *moral filter* may be particularly important in the perception of crime as an alternative. According to SAT, this filter is determined by the interplay between the moral rules that apply to the setting and the moral rules to which the actor ascribes, and it rules out certain alternatives as morally unacceptable ways of satisfying the given motivation under the given circumstances (Wikström 2010). This selective process is mostly unconscious and/or automatic and should not be confused with more elaborate moral reasoning.[6]

Wikström (2010) argues that the moral filter represents an important facet of *rule guidance*. Models of criminal decision making typically relegate rule guidance to the costs–benefits analysis, suggesting it is only relevant in relation to the consequences of rule-breaking and, therefore, to the process of choice.[7] However, it has been suggested that rule use is more fundamental to human behavior than rational choice and, therefore, understanding how rules influence action decision making is crucial for understanding crime involvement, the defining characteristic of which is that it breaks the rules of the law (Wikström 2010).

The SIP model also describes a process by which people access and filter out response options (Crick and Dodge 1994; Fontaine and Dodge 2006, 2009). Steps 4 and 5 of this model detail "response access and construction" and "response decision," respectively, with the former being more focused on quantity and the latter on the quality of response options (Crick and Dodge 1994). According to Fontaine and Dodge (2006, p. 609), an action alternative must satisfy three criteria to be considered for enactment: it must be situationally relevant, situationally applicable, and sufficiently congruent with a person's "internal standards." Fontaine and Dodge (2006) argue that "normative beliefs are of important utility in filtering out behaviors that are deemed unacceptable or incongruent with internal standards" (p. 608), which is similar to Wikström's (2010) assertion that personal morality may lead to the filtering out of action alternatives that a person thinks would be wrong. However, Fontaine and Dodge (2006) do not recognize the interplay between these beliefs and the moral context of the setting, suggesting "they are independent of situational specificity" (p. 608), which contrasts with Wikström's argument that this interplay is fundamental to the operation of the moral filter.

The MFS describes a process of *script selection* for identifying response options, with scripts being "mental models of sequences of action" (Kroneberg 2006, p. 10). Script selection occurs through two "modes"—a reflecting–calculating mode through which scripts are perceived based on their situationally relevant *subjective expected utility* and an automatic–spontaneous mode through which they are identified based on their *activation weight* or salience. Under conditions of strong rule guidance, scripts will be selected through the automatic–spontaneous mode, but weaker beliefs may lead to, although still influence, reflecting–calculating script selection (Kroneberg 2006). This is similar to Wikström's (2010) argument that when moral beliefs are strong, only morally acceptable alternatives will be perceived.

Evidence abounds that rule guidance is fundamental to social behaviors and rule-relevant functions are pervasive in human action cognition (Bunge 2004; Bunge and Wallis 2008; Wendelken et al. 2012). Rule guidance is primarily governed by the PFC, although the basal ganglia and limbic system support relevant functions such as associative learning (Wallis and Miller 2003; Bunge et al. 2005; Yin and Knowlton 2006; Bhanji, Beer, and Bunge 2010). More complex situation-contingent rules require advanced capacities for abstract thinking, a core executive function. This apples to the rules governing social behavior, including the law.

All regions of the PFC support rule use. Lateral regions are specifically implicated in practical aspects of rule guidance. The ventrolateral PFC communicates with other brain regions (e.g., parietal and temporal lobe storage areas) to encode rules during rule learning (e.g., moral education) and to retrieve and maintain rule-relevant information in preparation for action (e.g., for use in moral filtration or moral reasoning) (Bunge et al. 2003; Donohue et al. 2005). The dorsolateral PFC is then implicated in using those rules to designate response options (actual moral filtration) and switching attention between different rule sets and contingencies (e.g., to manage conflicting rule guidance) (Wallis and Miller 2003; Bunge 2004). Medial prefrontal regions, such as the ventro-medial PFC (vmPFC) and particularly its orbitofrontal subdivision (OFC), assist in learning new rules, drawing on connections to the limbic system to provide information on emotional salience (e.g., the importance of rules, reflected in shame and guilt) and connections to the basal ganglia to monitor and update information on expected and unexpected outcomes (e.g., prediction errors) (Bhanji et al. 2010; Kayser and D'Esposito 2013; Amarante and Laubach 2014; Strait, Blanchard, and Hayden 2014).

One of the most important functions of the PFC is to populate and update working memory, which serves as a cognitive scratchpad for active action information, including rules and action alternatives (Baddeley 2001, 2010). A key individual difference in prefrontal functioning is processing efficiency—how quickly the PFC can integrate or eliminate information from working memory (Kail and Salthouse 1994; Demetriou et al. 2002). This capacity may be particularly relevant in regard to the filtering of action alternatives in preparation for the process of choice. Less efficient processing may mean criminal alternatives are not adequately filtered, or noncriminal alternatives are filtered inappropriately.

Rational choice models focus predominantly on the consequences of rule-breaking,[8] but the biomechanics of rule use suggest this may not be the most important way that rules influence action decision making (Bunge 2004). The suggestion that rule guidance plays a particularly important role in the perception of alternatives is consistent with prefrontal functions that manage and triage information during action decision making. Importantly, these functions appear to be sensitive to action contexts; evidence suggests the PFC supports the specification of abstract rule representations across compound situational contingencies (Bunge and Zelazo 2006; Badre 2008; Badre et al.

2012). This brings into question assumptions that the perception of crime as an action alternative will not vary across settings or people and that situations in which crime is not perceived are not of criminological relevance.

The following conclusions can be drawn: (1) people differ in the alternatives they perceive for action, including acts of crime; and (2) rule-related cognitive functions may play an important role. Although the link between executive functioning and crime is typically interpreted in relation to the ability to exercise self-control, tests of executive functioning often tap into prefrontal functions involved in rule guidance. It may therefore be interesting and important, given that rule-breaking is the common characteristic of acts of crime, to pay closer attention to the mechanics of rule guidance and their implications for how people perceive as well as choose their alternatives for action.

C. Choice: A Twofold Process

People form action intentions via the process of choice, which of all action processes has received the lion's share of criminological attention. However, to adequately frame the process of choice requires taking upstream processes of motivation and perception into account because the former determines the goal that an action choice aims to achieve and the latter provides the set of possible action alternatives from which a choice is made. Relying on major assumptions about these preceding processes may distort perspectives on action choices.

Most criminological models assume choices are made through a rational process in which an actor evaluates the costs and benefits of means and ends and ranks alternatives based on their utility (typically, but not necessarily, in relation to self-interests; Cornish and Clarke 1986). However, a plethora of literature has argued and evidenced that choice processes are not singularly rational but, rather, dualistic, composed of one more considered (e.g., rational/deliberate) process and one automatic (e.g., habitual/intuitive) process (see chapter 9, this volume; see also Epstein et al. 1996; Kroneberg 2006; Sloman 1996; Kahneman 2003, 2012; Strack and Deutsch 2004; Daw et al. 2005; Woodward and Allman 2007; Graybiel 2008; Evans and Frankish 2009; Balleine and O'Doherty 2010; Treiber 2011). Different frameworks name and model these processes (systems/strategies) in different ways (e.g., deliberate vs. habitual, considered vs. automatic, rational vs. intuitive, model-based vs. model-free, or representation outcome vs. stimulus response) and vary in the extent to which they present both processes working in parallel or one dominating the other. Taken as a whole, this literature generally suggests that (1) one process is definitely not rational, (2) a not insignificant proportion of action decisions utilize this process, (3) this is beneficial in most day-to-day activities, and (4) both processes can be clearly delineated in the brain. These dual-process and dual-systems models are gaining theoretical and empirical momentum and clearly need to be incorporated in any comprehensive model of action decision making.

Such a model must specify the conditions under which each system operates. Evidence suggests that more cognitively demanding evaluative processes are likely the exception rather than the rule and that they are initiated only when more assiduous consideration is warranted—for example, in unfamiliar action contexts or when the actor needs to manage competing or conflicting action information (Daw et al. 2005; Kahneman 2012). This suggests the perception of alternatives may play an important role in which system becomes activated because it determines whether competing alternatives are perceived or alternatives that conflict with personal or social rules are perceived (Wikström and Treiber 2009a).

When people do deliberate, it is important to understand what action information is most relevant and influential. Traditional rational choice models emphasize personal costs and benefits. Other models incorporate elements of rule guidance, suggesting that people's perception of right and wrong ways to respond to a motivation plays an important role in their ranking of alternatives (Fontaine and Dodge 2006; Kroneberg 2006; Wikström 2010). Which is correct has implications for understanding the role and relevance of controls because it establishes what needs to be controlled and therefore what kind of control is needed.

Control, or a lack thereof, is often presented as one of the most important factors in criminal choices, if not the most important (Hirschi 1969; Clarke and Cornish 1985; Gottfredson and Hirschi 1990; Sampson and Laub 1993; Nagin and Pogarsky 2001; Felson and Boba 2010;). Although rarely explicitly defined, control refers to the ability to manage conflict regarding an action alternative under consideration. In rational choice models, this generally refers to conflict between immediate and future outcomes; self-control and deterrence make actors aware of long-term costs and benefits that may offset short-term costs and benefits. Other models argue that the most important source of conflict in deliberate criminal choices is between incitements to offend and moral rules of conduct (Wikström and Treiber 2013; Wikström 2014); self-control manages conflict between personal moral rules and external incitements, whereas deterrence manages conflict between the rules of a setting and personal incitements.

An important implication is that RCP models suggest self-control and deterrence are relevant to all criminal decisions, whereas other models suggest they are conditionally relevant and thus irrelevant to some criminal decisions (Wikström and Treiber 2007; Wikström 2008; Wikström and Svensson 2010; Wikström, Tseloni, and Karlis 2011). Situational action theory (Wikström 2010) refers to this as the principle of the conditional relevance of controls, which states that when the morals of the actor and (perceived) setting correspond (i.e., both promote or oppose rule-breaking), no conflict is registered, and thus controls are irrelevant: People are either unlikely to view crime as an alternative (when both discourage acts of crime) or choose to commit an act of crime without bothering/needing to consider other alternatives (when both encourage acts of crime). There is growing support for these assertions (Antonaccio and Tittle 2008; Kroneberg, Heintze, and Mehlkop 2010; Svensson et al. 2010; Wikström and Svensson 2010; Wikström et al. 2011; Svensson 2015), which brings into question models of action decision making that emphasize consequences and their controlling effects. Some people may not need to be controlled, whereas others may be oblivious.

Better understanding the biomechanics of choice may provide further clarity regarding these propositions. Deliberate choices are effortful and to a large extent conscious. They require goal maintenance, evaluation, and integration of personal and contextual information; representation and comparison of action alternatives; and prognostication of outcomes. At a neurological level, this means they engage the PFC and executive control.

During deliberate decision making, the PFC draws on its ventral, medial, and lateral aspects—as well as its connections to all sensory cortices and key subcortical structures, including the limbic system and basal ganglia—to activate, integrate, and organize action-relevant information into an *internal representation* of the action context. This representation, which it has been suggested may be the unifying executive function (Goldman-Rakic 1987; Treiber 2011), qualifies and supplements perceived external information with the actor's knowledge and experiences, creating an enhanced guide for the action choice (Case 1992; Tranel et al. 1994; Fuster 1997; Koechlin et al. 2003; Koechlin and Summerfield 2007; Goldberg 2009; Haber 2011; Hofmann et al. 2012). Using an internal representation to guide action choices is deliberate but not necessarily fully rational. Although an important function of internal representation may be to identify and assess expected costs and benefits, any rational calculus is neither comprehensive, being limited by cognitive capacity, nor objective, being qualified by intuitive affective valences. It is also likely that this bounded rationality is impinged upon (often heavily) by rule guidance and habitual/intuitive processes (Epstein et al. 1996; Wikström and Treiber 2007; Treiber 2011; Kahneman 2012). The former means that deliberate choices are constrained not only by expected outcomes but also by rules, which exert their own efficacy on preferred choices for action; the latter means that choices are typically neither fully considered nor fully automated.

Action responses must be temporarily withheld for action choices to be deliberate, which means motivational impulses must be regulated long enough to accommodate more time-intensive cognitive processes. The PFC is hierarchically placed to inhibit motivational centers and take control of action decision making and can even be "recruited" by the limbic system and basal ganglia (e.g., via the anterior cingulate cortex) to guide decision making when action information is conflicting or unclear (Ochsner and Gross 2005; Carter and van Veen 2007; Heatherton and Wagner 2011; Munakata et al. 2011; Hofmann et al. 2012; Ochsner et al. 2012). Whether it is recruited may depend on whether conflict is detected between perceived action alternatives and relevant action goals—for example, if those alternatives include actions that break personal or social rules (Cardinal et al. 2002; Greene et al. 2004; Carter and van Veen 2007).

Intuitive choice processes have been less explored in criminology, and their role in criminal decision making is consequently less well understood (Betsch 2008; Wikström and Treiber 2009b; Kahneman 2012). Over time, repeated actions become associated with an action context and experienced outcomes. These actions can become primed in those contexts and may "skip" deliberate processing (Epstein et al. 1996; Kahneman

2003; Betsch 2008; Glockner 2008; Plessner and Czenna 2008; Fineberg et al. 2014). This is known as habituation.

The striatum, a key structure in the basal ganglia, plays a critical role in habituation (Cardinal et al. 2002; O'Doherty et al. 2004; Faure et al. 2005; Yin et al. 2005; Yin and Knowlton 2006; Tricomi, Balleine, and O'Doherty 2009; Balleine and O'Doherty 2010; Haber 2011; Dolan and Dayan 2013; Smith and Graybiel 2013). As a behavior is successfully repeated, the striatum oversees transition of the dopamine reward from receipt of the outcome to perception of a key stimulus (Daw et al. 2005; Yin and Knowlton 2006; Graybiel 2008; Graybiel and Smith 2014; Voon et al. 2015). In essence, the brain intuitively jumps to the conclusion that the primed alternative will obtain that outcome.

As a behavior habituates, it solicits less guidance from the PFC regarding future outcomes and relies increasingly on the striatum and its information regarding past experiences (Graybiel 2008; Smith and Graybiel 2013). However, habits do not completely lack prefrontal involvement; the vmPFC plays an important role in consolidating goal values based on experienced outcomes and contextual contingencies (e.g., motivations and situational constraints) (Balleine and O'Doherty 2010; Haber 2011). The striatum then keeps track of when expectations are and are not met, and it uses this information to determine whether habitual or deliberate processes are activated (the former when they are, and the latter when they are not). However, just as it can suppress motivation, the PFC can exert top-down control to suppress habitual responses—for example, when conflict is perceived (Greene et al. 2004; Carter and van Veen 2007; Balleine and O'Doherty 2010; de Wit et al. 2012).

It can be concluded that the human brain is clearly designed to support decision making through both habitual/intuitive and, when necessary, reasoned/deliberate processes. Limitations on information processing (e.g., time and cognitive resources) make habitual/intuitive shortcuts not only practical but often preferable. Thus, a purely rational choice model likely does not capture key elements of action choice that may be crucial for understanding, and influencing, criminal decision making. This includes the nuances of controls. Top-down prefrontal involvement is highly implicated in the more rational forms of control typically described in criminological theories, but it does not appear to be activated in all action decisions. This has implications for the relevance of self-control and deterrence and therefore their relevance for explaining and preventing crime. An important future step for criminology is to better specify what is meant by "control" so the concept can be better aligned with what is known about neurocognitive control processes.

Another important element of criminal decision making is risk-taking. In a traditional RCP model, risk-taking is interpreted in relation to the certainty, celerity, and severity of rewards and consequences. A dual-systems model, however, suggests it may have more to do with the interplay of motivation and control and the balance of intuitive and deliberate processes. Another important future step for criminology, then, may be to better understand the extent to which choices draw on limbic or striatal functions in addition to, or rather than, prefrontal functions and therefore depend on motivation in addition to, or rather than, control.

V. Conclusions: What Does a Biologically Informed Model of Action Decision Making Look Like?

Action decision making is what links people and environments to actions; therefore, all factors of relevance to crime exert their influence through the action process—that is, through motivation, perception, and choice (or interference) (see figure 6.1). Thus, when we think about how a biological factor such as a low resting heart rate, executive dysfunction, or a specific gene might influence crime involvement, we should consider how it might influence criminal decision making.

There is still much theoretical and empirical work to do to establish a fully detailed model of criminal decision making, and far more knowledge to draw on from relevant biological as well as social sciences. However, this chapter highlights a few fundamental points that any knowledge-based model must account for: (1) people are not universally motivated by self-interest, and they differ in their response as well as their exposure to potential sources of motivation; (2) people differ in the alternatives they perceive for action in response to their motivations and what alternatives they perceive constrain their action choices and hence their actions; and (3) people make their action choices using both intuitive and reasoned processes, and therefore controls are not always needed or influential. Unless we take these assertions seriously in criminological theories and theory testing, we are unlikely to derive a good enough explanation of why people decide to commit acts of crime and how we can influence them to decide not to do so. As a consequence, we will also not be able to derive a good enough model of the role that biological factors play in crime causation and could play in crime prevention.

Notes

1. This does not mean they have complete autonomy; people experience many personal and environmental constraints on their actions that influence the decision process.
2. An action is not inevitable once a choice is made; circumstances may still interfere with its execution and/or reactivate decision making to take new information into account, which may lead to the formation of a new intention.
3. "Good-enough theories" emphasize "clarity and parsimony over comprehensiveness" (Cornish and Clarke 2008, p. 38). Although Clarke and Cornish (1985) admit that such theories "may not necessarily be the most appropriate or satisfactory for more comprehensive explanations of criminal behavior" (p. 178), they contend that these theories may "still be 'good enough' to achieve . . . important policy and research purposes" (p. 147).
4. A presumption of rationality, for example, affects how we perceive criminal responsibility, with implications for penal policy, the judicial process, and the treatment of offenders.
5. See Wikström and Treiber (2015) for a more detailed discussion.

6. This is not to say that people are never aware of alternatives that they find morally unacceptable, but these are not seriously considered for action. If they are, they are clearly not totally unacceptable. This is why notions of cognitive dissonance and neutralization are misspecified (Maruna and Copes 2005).

7. Later versions of Cornish and Clarke's RCP accept that "moral scruples" may influence people's "readiness to offend" (i.e., criminal dispositions) through anticipated moral emotions (consequences) and that "rule settings" potentially moderate opportunities for some types of offenders ("mundane offenders"), but RCP does not view moral rules as particularly important for the explanation of crime because it does not view rule guidance as part of the process of criminal decision making ("involvement decisions") but, rather, simply part of the content (Cornish and Clarke 2003, 2008).

8. But see footnote 7.

References

Adolphs, R., S. Baron-Cohen, and D. Tranel. 2002. "Impaired Recognition of Social Emotions Following Amygdala Damage." *Journal of Cognitive Neuroscience* 14(8): 1264–74.

Akers, R. L. 1990. "Rational Choice, Deterrence, and Social Learning Theory in Criminology: The Path Not Taken." *Journal of Criminal Law and Criminology* 81(3): 653.

Alexander, G. E., M. R. DeLong, and P. L. Strick. 1986. "Parallel Organization of Functionally Segregated Circuits Linking Basal Ganglia and Cortex." *Annual Review of Neuroscience* 9:357–81.

Amarante, L. M., and M. Laubach. 2014. "For Better or Worse: Reward Comparison by the Ventromedial Prefrontal Cortex." *Neuron* 82(6): 1191–93.

Antonaccio, O., and C. R. Tittle. 2008. "Morality, Self-Control, and Crime." *Criminology* 46(2): 479–510.

Armstrong, T. A., and B. B. Boutwell. 2012. "Low Resting Heart Rate and Rational Choice: Integrating Biological Correlates of Crime in Criminological Theories. *Journal of Criminal Justice* 40(1): 31–39.

Armstrong, T. A., S. Keller, T. W. Franklin, and S. N. Macmillan. 2009. "Low Resting Heart Rate and Antisocial Behavior: A Brief Review of Evidence and Preliminary Results from a New Test." *Criminal Justice and Behavior* 36(11): 1125–40.

Axelrod, R. 1984. *The Evolution of Cooperation*. New York: Basic Books.

Baddeley, A. 2001. "Is Working Memory Still Working?" *American Psychologist* 56:851–64.

Baddeley, A. 2010. "Working Memory." *Current Biology* 20:R136–40.

Badre, D. 2008. "Cognitive Control, Hierarchy, and the Rostro-Caudal Organization of the Frontal Lobes." *Trends in Cognitive Sciences* 12(5): 193–200.

Badre, D., B. B. Doll, N. M. Long, and M. J. Frank. 2012. "Rostrolateral Prefrontal Cortex and Individual Differences in Uncertainty-Driven Exploration." *Neuron* 73(3): 595–607.

Balleine, B. W., and J. P. O'Doherty. 2010. "Human and Rodent Homologies in Action Control: Corticostriatal Determinants of Goal-Directed and Habitual Action." *Neuropsychopharmacology* 35(1): 48–69.

Barnes, J. C., Boutwell, B. B., and K. M. Beaver. 2015. "Contemporary Biosocial Criminology: A Systematic Review of the Literature, 2000–2012." In *The Handbook of Criminological Theory*, edited by A. R. Piquero, pp. 75–99. Chichester, UK: Wiley-Blackwell.

Beaver, K. M., J. C. Barnes, and B. B. Boutwell. 2015. *The Nurture Versus Biosocial Debate in Criminology: On the Origins of Criminal Behaviour and Criminality*. London: Sage.

Beaver, K. M., M. Ratchford, and C. J. Ferguson. 2009. "Evidence of Genetic and Environmental Effects on the Development of Low Self-Control." *Criminal Justice and Behavior* 36(11): 1158–72.

Beaver, K. M., J. E. Shutt, M. G. Vaughn, M. DeLisi, and J. P. Wright. 2012. "Genetic Influences on Measures of Parental Negativity and Childhood Maltreatment: An Exploratory Study Testing for Gene × Environment Correlations." *Journal of Contemporary Criminal Justice* 28(3): 273–92.

Beaver, K. M., and A. Walsh. 2011. *The Ashgate Research Companion to Biosocial Theories of Crimes*. Surrey, UK: Ashgate.

Beitchman, J. H., L. Baldassarra, H. Mik, V. De Luca, N. King, D. Bender, S. Ehtesham, and J. L. Kennedy. 2006. "Serotonin Transporter Polymorphisms and Persistent, Pervasive Childhood Aggression." *American Journal of Psychiatry* 163:1103–05.

Belsky, J., and M. Pluess. 2009. "Beyond Diathesis Stress: Differential Susceptibility to Environmental Influences." *Psychological Bulletin* 135:885–908.

Berenbaum, S. A., K. K. Bryk, N. Nowak, C. A. Quigley, and S. Moffat. 2009. "Fingers as a Marker of Prenatal Androgen Exposure." *Endocrinology* 150:5119–24.

Betsch, T. 2008. "The Nature of Intuition and Its Neglect in Research on Judgment and Decision Making." In *Intuition in Judgment and Decision Making*, edited by H. Plessner, C. Betsch, and T. Betsch, pp. 3–22. London: Taylor and Francis.

Bhanji, J. P., J. S. Beer, and S. A. Bunge. 2010. "Taking a Gamble or Playing by the Rules: Dissociable Prefrontal Systems Implicated in Probabilistic Versus Deterministic Rule-Based Decisions." *Neuroimage* 49(2): 1810–19.

Blakemore, S. J., and T. W. Robbins. 2012. "Decision-Making in the Adolescent Brain." *Nature Neuroscience* 15(9):1184–91.

Breedlove, S. M. 2010. "Minireview: Organizational Hypothesis: Instances of the Fingerpost." *Endocrinology* 151:4116–22.

Brunner, H. G., M. Nelen, X. O. Breakefield, H. H. Ropers, and B. A. Van Oost. 1993. "Abnormal Behavior Associated with a Point Mutation in the Structural Gene for Monoamine Oxidase A." *Science* 262(5133): 578–80.

Buckholtz, J. W., M. T. Treadway, R. L. Cowan, N. D. Woodward, S. D. Benning, R. Li, M. S. Ansari, R. M. Baldwin, A. N. Schwartzman, E. S. Shelby, C. E. Smith, D. Cole, R. M. Kessler, and D. H. Zald. 2010. "Mesolimbic Dopamine Reward System Hypersensitivity in Individuals with Psychopathic Traits." *Nature Neuroscience* 13:419–21.

Bunge, S. A. 2004. "How We Use Rules to Select Actions: A Review of Evidence from Cognitive Neuroscience." *Cognitive, Affective and Behavioral Neuroscience* 4(4): 564–79.

Bunge, S. A., I. Kahn, J. D. Wallis, E. K. Miller, and A. D. Wagner. 2003. "Neural Circuits Subserving the Retrieval and Maintenance of Abstract Rules." *Journal of Neurophysiology* 90(5): 3419–28.

Bunge, S. A., and J. D. Wallis. 2008. *Neuroscience of Rule-Guided Behavior*. Oxford: Oxford University Press.

Bunge, S. A., J. D. Wallis, A. Parker, M. Brass, E. A. Crone, E. Hoshi, and K. Sakai. 2005. "Neural Circuitry Underlying Rule Use in Humans and Nonhuman Primates." *Journal of Neuroscience* 25(45): 10347–50.

Bunge, S. A., and P. D. Zelazo. 2006. "A Brain-Based Account of the Development of Rule Use in Childhood." *Current Directions in Psychological Science* 15(3): 118–21.

Burt, C. H., and R. L. Simons. 2014. 'Pulling Back the Curtain on Heritability Studies: Biosocial Criminology in the Postgenomic Era." *Criminology* 52(2): 223–62.

Burt, C. H., and R. L. Simons. 2015. "Heritability Studies in the Postgenomic Era: The Fatal Flaw Is Conceptual." *Criminology* 53(1): 103–12.

Burt, S. A., and A. J. Mikolajewski. 2008. "Preliminary Evidence That Specific Candidate Genes Are Associated with Adolescent-Onset Antisocial Behavior." *Aggressive Behavior* 34(4): 437–45.

Cardinal, R. N., J. A. Parkinson, J. Hall, and B. J. Everitt. 2002. "Emotion and Motivation: The Role of the Amygdala, Ventral Striatum, and Prefrontal Cortex." *Neuroscience and Biobehavioral Reviews* 26(3): 321–52.

Carré, J. M., J. D. Gilchrist, M. D. Morrissey, and C. M. McCormick. 2010. "Motivational and Situational Factors and the Relationship Between Testosterone Dynamics and Human Aggression During Competition." *Biological Psychology* 84:346–53.

Carré, J. M., C. M. McCormick, and A. R. Hariri. 2011. "The Social Neuroendocrinology of Human Aggression." *Psychoneuroendocrinology* 36:935–44.

Carter, C. S., and V. van Veen. 2007. "Anterior Cingulate Cortex and Conflict Detection: An Update of Theory and Data." *Cognitive, Affective and Behavioral Neuroscience* 7(4): 367–79.

Case, R. 1992. "The Role of Frontal Lobe Maturation in Cognitive and Social Development. *Brain and Cognition* 20(1): 51–73.

Caspi, A., A. R. Hariri, A. Holmes, R. Uher, and T. E. Moffitt. 2010. "Genetic Sensitivity to the Environment: The Case of the Serotonin Transporter Gene and Its Implications for Studying Complex Diseases and Traits." *American Journal of Psychiatry* 167(5): 509–27.

Caspi, A., J. McClay, T. E. Moffitt, J. Mill, J. Martin, I. W. Craig, A. Taylor, and R. Poulton. 2002. "Role of Genotype in the Cycle of Violence in Maltreated Children." *Science* 297(5582): 851–54.

Chen, F. R., Y. Gao, A. Glenn, S. Niv, J. Portnoy, R. Schug, Y. Yang, and A. Raine. 2015. "Biosocial Bases of Criminal and Antisocial Behavior." In *The Handbook of Criminological Theory*, edited by A. R. Piquero, pp. 355–79. Chichester, UK: Wiley-Blackwell.

Churchland, P. 2011. *Braintrust: What Neuroscience Tells Us About Morality*. Princeton, NJ: Princeton University Press.

Clarke, R. 2005. "Seven Misconceptions of Situational Crime Prevention." In *Handbook of Crime Prevention and Community Safety*, edited by N. Tilley, pp. 39–70. Collumpton, UK: Willan.

Clarke, R. 2012. "Opportunity Makes the Thief. Really? And So What?" *Crime Science* 1(3): 1–9.

Clarke, R. 2014. "Introduction." In *The Reasoning Criminal: Rational Choice Perspectives on Offending*, edited by D. Cornish and R. Clarke, pp. ix–xvi. Piscataway, NJ: Transaction Publishers.

Clarke, R., and D. Cornish. 1985. "Modelling Offenders' Decisions: A Framework for Research and Policy." *Crime and Justice* 6:147–85.

Clarke, R., and M. Felson. 1993. *Routine Activity and Rational Choice. Advances in Criminological Theory Volume 5*. Piscataway, NJ: Transaction Publishers.

Cohen, L., and M. Felson. 1979. "Social Change and Crime Rate Trends: A Routine Activity Approach." *American Sociological Review* 44(4): 588–608.

Cohen-Bendahan, C. C. C., J. K. Buitelaar, S. H. M. van Goozen, J. F. Orlebeke, and P. T. Cohen-Kettenis. 2005. "Is There an Effect of Prenatal Testosterone on Aggression and Other Behavioral Traits? A Study Comparing Same-Sex and Opposite-Sex Twin Girls." *Hormones and Behavior* 47:230–37.

Cohen-Bendahan, C. C. C., C. van de Beek, and S. A. Berenbaum. 2005. "Prenatal Sex Hormone Effects on Child and Adult Sex-Typed Behavior: Methods and Findings." *Neuroscience and Biobehavioral Reviews* 29:353–84.

Collins, R. E. 2011. "Neurotransmitters: Indirect Molecular Invitations to Aggression." In *The Ashgate Research Companion to Biosocial Theories of Crimes*, edited by K. Beaver and A. Walsh, pp. 135–65. Surrey, UK: Ashgate.

Cornish, D., and R. Clarke. 1986. *The Reasoning Criminal: Rational Choice Perspectives on Offending*. New York: Springer-Verlag.

Cornish, D., and R. Clarke. 2003. "Opportunities, Precipitators and Criminal Decisions: A Reply to Wortley's Critique of Situational Crime Prevention." *Crime Prevention Studies* 16:41–96.

Cornish, D., and R. Clarke. 2008. "The Rational Choice Perspective." In *Environmental Criminology and Crime Analysis*, edited by R. Wortley and L. Mazerolle, pp. 21–47. Abingdon, UK: Routledge.

Craig, I. W., and K. E. Halton. 2009. "Genetics of Human Aggressive Behaviour." *Human Genetics* 126(1): 101–13.

Craig, M. C., M. Catani, Q. Deeley, R. Latham, E. Daly, R. Kanaan, M. Picchioni, P. K. McGuire, T. Fahy, and D. G. M. Murphy. 2009. "Altered Connections on the Road to Psychopathy." *Molecular Psychiatry* 14:946–53.

Crick, N. R., and K. A. Dodge. 1994. "A Review and Reformulation of Social Information-Processing Mechanisms in Children's Social Adjustment." *Psychological Bulletin* 115(1): 74–101.

Crick, N. R., and K. A. Dodge. 1996. "Social Information-Processing Mechanisms in Reactive and Proactive Aggression." *Child Development* 67: 993–1002.

Critchley, H. D., C. J. Mathias, and R. J. Dolan. 2002. "Fear Conditioning in Humans: The Influence of Awareness and Autonomic Arousal on Functional Neuroanatomy." *Neuron* 33:653–63.

Crone, E. A., and R. E. Dahl. 2012. "Understanding Adolescence as a Period of Social-Affective Engagement and Goal Flexibility." *Nature Reviews Neuroscience* 13(9): 636–50.

Dalley, J. W., and J. P. Roiser. 2012. "Dopamine, Serotonin and Impulsivity." *Neuroscience* 215:42–58.

Davidson, R. J., Putnam, K. M., and C. L. Larson. 2000. "Dysfunction in the Neural Circuitry of Emotion Regulation—A Possible Prelude to Violence." *Science* 289:591–94.

Daw, N. D., Y. Niv, and P. Dayan. 2005. "Uncertainty-Based Competition Between Prefrontal and Dorsolateral Striatal Systems for Behavioral Control." *Nature Neuroscience* 8(12): 1704–11.

de Wit, S., P. Watson, H. A. Harsay, M. X. Cohen, I. van de Vijver, and K. R. Ridderinkhof. 2012. "Corticostriatal Connectivity Underlies Individual Differences in the Balance Between Habitual and Goal-Directed Action Control." *Journal of Neuroscience* 32(35): 12066–75.

DeLisi, M. 2009. "The Criminology of the Amygdala." *Criminal Justice and Behavior* 36(11): 1241–52.

Demetriou, A., C. Christou, G. Spanoudis, and M. Platsidou. 2002. "The Development of Mental Processing: Efficiency, Working Memory, and Thinking." *Monograms of the Society for Research in Child Development* 67(1): 1–155.

Denson, T. F., P. H. Mehta, and D. Ho Tan. 2013. "Endogenous Testosterone and Cortisol Jointly Influence Reactive Aggression in Women." *Psychoneuroendocrinology* 38:416–24.

Dolan, R. J., and P. Dayan. 2013. "Goals and Habits in the Brain." *Neuron* 80(2): 312–25.

Donohue, S. E., C. Wendelken, E. A. Crone, and S. A. Bunge. 2005. "Retrieving Rules for Behavior from Long-Term Memory." *Neuroimage* 26(4): 1140–49.

Duke, A. A., Bègue, L., Bell, R., and T. Eisenlohr-Moul. 2013. "Revisiting the Serotonin–Aggression Relation in Humans: A Meta-Analysis." *Psychological Bulletin* 139: 1148–72.

Duncan, L. E., and M. C. Keller. 2011. "A Critical Review of the First 10 Years of Candidate Gene-by-Environment Interaction Research in Psychiatry." *American Journal of Psychiatry* 168(10): 1041–49.

Eisenberger, N. I., and M. D. Lieberman. 2004. "Why Rejection Hurts: A Common Neural Alarm System for Physical and Social Pain." *Trends in Cognitive Sciences* 8(7): 294–300.

Eisenegger, C., J. Haushofer, and E. Fehr. 2011. "The Role of Testosterone in Social Interaction." *Trends in Cognitive Science* 15:263–71.

Ellis, B. J., and W. T. Boyce. 2011. "Differential Susceptibility to the Environment: Toward an Understanding of Sensitivity to Developmental Experiences and Context." *Developmental Psychopathology* 23:1–5.

Ellis, B. J., W. T. Boyce, J. Belsky, M. J. Bakermans-Kranenburg, and M. H. Van Ijzendoorn. 2011. "Differential Susceptibility to the Environment: An Evolutionary-Neurodevelopmental Theory." *Development and Psychopathology* 23(1): 7–28.

Ellis, L., K. Beaver, and J. Wright. 2009. *Handbook of Crime Correlates.* San Diego: Academic Press.

Eme, R. 2013. "MAOA and Male Antisocial Behavior: A Review." *Aggressive and Violent Behavior* 18:395–98.

Epstein, S., R. Pacini, V. Denes-Raj, and H. Heier. 1996. "Individual Differences in Intuitive-Experiential and Analytical-Rational Thinking Styles." *Journal of Personality and Social Psychology* 71(2): 390–405.

Evans, J., and K. Frankish. 2009. *In Two Minds: Dual Processes and Beyond.* Oxford: Oxford University Press.

Everitt, B. J., and T. W. Robbins. 2005. "Neural Systems of Reinforcement for Drug Addiction: From Actions to Habits to Compulsion." *Nature Neuroscience* 8:1481–89.

Fairchild, G., S. H. van Goozen, S. J. Stollery, and I. M. Goodyer. 2008. "Fear Conditioning and Affective Modulation of the Startle Reflex in Male Adolescents with Early-Onset or Adolescence-Onset Conduct Disorder and Healthy Control Subjects." *Biological Psychiatry* 63: 279–85.

Faure, A., U. Haberland, F. Conde, and N. El Massioui. 2005. "Lesion to the Nigrostriatal Dopamine System Disrupts Stimulus-Response Habit Formation." *Journal of Neuroscience* 25(11): 2771–80.

Felson, M. 2006. *Crime and Nature.* Thousand Oaks, CA: Sage.

Felson, M., and R. Boba. 2010. *Crime and Everyday Life.* London: Sage.

Felson, M., and R. Clarke. 1998. *Opportunity Makes the Thief: Practical Theory for Crime Prevention.* London: Home Office, Policing and Reducing Crime Unit, Research, Development and Statistics Directorate.

Ferguson, C. J. 2010. "Genetic Contributions to Antisocial Personality and Behavior: A Meta-Analytic Review from an Evolutionary Perspective." *Journal of Social Psychology* 150: 160–80.

Ficks, C. A., and I. D. Waldman. 2014. "Candidate Genes for Aggression and Antisocial Behavior: A Meta-Analysis of Association Studies of the 5HTTLPR and MAOA-uVNTR." *Behavioral Genetics* 44:427–44.

Fineberg, N. A., S. R. Chamberlain, A. E. Goudriaan, D. J. Stein, L. J. Vanderschuren, C. M. Gillan, S. Shekar, P. A. Gorwood, V. Voon, S. Morein-Zamir, D. Denys, B. J. Sahakian, F. G. Moeller, T. W. Robbins, and M. N. Potenza. 2014. "New Developments in Human Neurocognition: Clinical, Genetic, and Brain Imaging Correlates of Impulsivity and Compulsivity." *CNS Spectrums* 19(1): 69–89.

Fontaine, R. G. 2007. "Toward a Conceptual Framework of Instrumental Antisocial Decision-Making and Behavior in Youth." *Clinical Psychology Review* 27(5): 655–75.

Fontaine, R. G. 2008. "On-line Social Decision Making and Antisocial Behavior: Some Essential But Neglected Issues." *Clinical Psychology Review* 28(1): 17–35.

Fontaine, R. G., and K. A. Dodge. 2006. "Real-Time Decision Making and Aggressive Behavior in Youth: A Heuristic Model of Response Evaluation and Decision (RED)." *Aggressive Behavior* 32(6): 604–24.

Fontaine, R. G., and K. A. Dodge. 2009. "Social Information Processing and Aggressive Behavior: A Transactional Perspective." In *The Transactional Model of Development: How Children and Contexts Shape Each Other*, edited by A. J. Sameroff, pp. 117–35. Washington, DC: American Psychological Association.

Frank, M. J., B. B. Doll, J. Oas-Terpstra, and F. Moreno. 2009. "Prefrontal and Striatal Dopaminergic Genes Predict Individual Differences in Exploration and Exploitation." *Nature Neuroscience* 12(8): 1062–68.

Furmark, T., H. Fischer, G. Wik, M. Larsson, and M. Fredrikson. 1997. "The Amygdala and Individual Differences in Human Fear Conditioning." *NeuroReport* 8:3957–60.

Fuster, J. 1997. *The Prefrontal Cortex: Anatomy, Physiology and Neuropsychology of the Frontal Lobe*. Philadelphia: Lippincott-Raven.

Gao, Y., and A. Raine. 2009. "P3 Event-Related Potential Impairments in Antisocial and Psychopathic Individuals: A Meta-Analysis." *Biological Psychology* 82:199–210.

Gao, Y., A. Raine, P. H. Venables, M. E. Dawson, and S. A. Mednich. 2010. "Reduced Electrodermal Fear Conditioning from Ages 3 to 8 Years Is Associated with Aggressive Behavior at Age 8 Years." *Journal of Child Psychology and Psychiatry* 51:550–58.

Glenn, A., A. Raine, P. S. Yaralian, and Y. Yang. 2010. "Increased Volume of the Striatum in Psychopathic Individuals." *Biological Psychiatry* 67:52–58.

Glockner, A. 2008. "Does Intuition Beat Fast and Frugal Heuristics? A Systematic Empirical Analysis." In *Intuition in Judgment and Decision Making*, edited by H. Plessner, C. Betsch, and T. Betsch, pp. 309–25. London: Taylor and Francis.

Goldberg, E. 2009. *The New Executive Brain: Frontal Lobes in a Complex World*. Oxford: Oxford University Press.

Goldman-Rakic, P. S. 1987. "Circuitry of Primate Prefrontal Cortex and Regulation of Behaviour by Representational Memory." In *Handbook of Physiology: The Nervous System, Volume 5, Part 1: Higher Functions of the Brain*, edited by V. Mountcastle, F. Plum, and S. Geiger, pp. 373–417. Bethesda, MD: American Psychological Society.

Gottfredson, M., and T. Hirschi. 1990. *A General Theory of Crime*. Stanford, CA: Stanford University Press.

Graybiel, A. M. 2008. "Habits, Rituals, and the Evaluative Brain." *Annual Review of Neuroscience* 31:359–87.

Graybiel, A. M., and K. S. Smith. 2014. "Good Habits, Bad Habits." *Scientific American* 310: 38–43.

Greene, J. D., L. E. Nystrom, A. D. Engell, J. M. Darley, and J. D. Cohen. 2004. "The Neural Bases of Cognitive Conflict and Control in Moral Judgment." *Neuron* 44(2): 389–400.

Guo, G., X. M. Ou, M. Roettger, and J. C. Shih. 2008. "The VNTR 2 Repeat in MAOA and Delinquent Behavior in Adolescence and Young Adulthood: Associations and MAOA Promoter Activity." *European Journal of Human Genetics* 16(5): 626–34.

Guo, G., M. E. Roettger, and J. C. Shih. 2007. "Contributions of the DAT1 and DRD2 Genes to Serious and Violent Delinquency Among Adolescents and Young Adults." *Human Genetics* 121:125–36.

Haber, S. N. 2011. "Neuroanatomy of Reward: A View from the Ventral Striatum. In *Neurobiology of Sensation and Reward*, edited by J. A. Gottfried. Boca Raton, pp. 235–61. FL: CRC Press.

Haberstick, B. C., A, Smolen, and J. K. Hewitt. 2006. "Family-Based Association Test of the 5HTTLPR and Aggressive Behavior in a General Population Sample of Children." *Biological Psychiatry* 59:836–43.

Hamilton, W. D. 1963. "The Evolution of Altruistic Behavior." *American Naturalist* 97:354–56.

Hamilton, W. D. 1964a. "The Genetical Evolution of Social Behaviour I." *Journal of Theoretical Biology* 7:1–16.

Hamilton, W. D. 1964b. "The Genetical Evolution of Social Behaviour II." *Journal of Theoretical Biology* 7:17–52.

Hariri, A. R., and A. Holmes. 2006. "Genetics of Emotional Regulation: The Role of the Serotonin Transporter in Neural Function." *Trends in Cognitive Sciences* 10(4): 182–91.

Hariri, A. R., V. S. Mattay, A. Tessitore, B. Kolachana, F. Fera, D. Goldman, M. F. Egan, and D. R. Weinberger. 2002. "Serotonin Transporter Genetic Variation and the Response of the Human Amygdala." *Science* 297(5580): 400–03.

Harlow, J. 1868. "Recovery from the Passage of an Iron Bar Through the Head." In *Publications of the Massachusetts Medical Society*, vol. 2. Boston: David Clapp and Sons. Reprinted in MacMillan, M. 2000. *An Odd Kind of Fame: Stories of Phineas Gage*, pp. 329–346. London: MIT Press.

Heatherton, T. F., and D. D. Wagner. 2011. "Cognitive Neuroscience of Self-Regulation Failure." *Trends in Cognitive Sciences* 15(3): 132–39.

Henry, B., and T. E. Moffitt. 1997. "Neuropsychological and Neuroimaging Studies of Juvenile Delinquency and Adult Criminal Behavior." In *Handbook of Antisocial Behavior*, edited by D. Stoff, J. Breliing, and J. Maser, pp. 280–88. New York: Wiley.

Herpertz, S. C., B. Mueller, M. Qunaibi, C. Lichterfeld, K. Konrad, and B. Herpertz-Dahlmann. 2005. "Response to Emotional Stimuli in Boys with Conduct Disorder." *American Journal of Psychiatry* 162:1100–07.

Hirschi, T. 1969. *Causes of Delinquency*. Berkeley, CA: University of California Press.

Hirschi, T., and M. Gottfredson. 1983. "Age and the Explanation of Crime." *American Journal of Sociology* 89(3): 552–84.

Hofmann, W., B. J. Schmeichel, and A. D. Baddeley. 2012. "Executive Functions and Self-Regulation." *Trends in Cognitive Sciences* 16(3): 174–80.

Houston, R. J., and M. S. Stanford. 2005. "Electrophysiological Substrates of Impulsiveness: Potential Effects on Aggressive Behavior." *Progress in Neuro-Psychopharmacology and Biological Psychiatry* 29: 305–13.

Ishikawa, S. S., and A. Raine. 2003. "Prefrontal Deficits and Antisocial Behavior: A Causal Model." In *Causes of Conduct Disorder and Juvenile Delinquency*, edited by B. Lahey, T. Moffitt, and A. Caspi, pp. 277–304. New York: Guilford.

Jackson, D., and K. Beaver. 2012. "Candidate Genes for Criminal and Delinquent Behaviour." In *Psychology of Adolescence: New Research*, edited by L. Baris and O. Uzun, pp. 49–74. New York: Nova Science.

Kahneman, D. 2003. Maps of Bounded Rationality: A Perspective on Intuitive Judgment and Choice. *Les Prix Nobel. The Noble Prizes 2002*, T. Frangsmyr. Stockholm, Nobel Foundation.

Kahneman, D. 2012. *Thinking, Fast and Slow*. London: Penguin.

Kail, R., and T. A. Salthouse. 1994. "Processing Speed as a Mental Capacity." *Acta Psychologica* 86(2): 199–225.

Kanazawa, S. 2009. "Evolutionary Psychology and Crime. In *Biosocial Criminology: New Directions in Theory and Research*, edited by A. Walsh and K. M. Beaver, pp. 90–110. London: Routledge.

Kayser, A. S., and M. D'Esposito. 2013. "Abstract Rule Learning: The Differential Effects of Lesions in Frontal Cortex." *Cerebral Cortex* 23(1): 230–40.

Kim-Cohen, J., A. Caspi, A. Taylor, B. Williams, R. Newcombe, I. W. Craig, and T. E. Moffitt. 2006. "MAOA, Maltreatment, and Gene–Environment Interaction Predicting Children's Mental Health: New Evidence and a Meta-Analysis." *Molecular Psychiatry* 11(10): 903–13.

Koechlin, E., C. Ody, and F. Kouneiher. 2003. "The Architecture of Cognitive Control in the Human Prefrontal Cortex." *Science* 302(5648): 1181–85.

Koechlin, E., and C. Summerfield. 2007. "An Information Theoretical Approach to Prefrontal Executive Function." *Trends in Cognitive Sciences* 11(6): 229–35.

Koob, G. F., S. H. Ahmed, B. Boutrel, S. A. Chen, P. J. Kenny, A. Markou, L. E. O'Dell, L. H. Parsons, and P. P. Sanna. 2004. "Neurobiological Mechanisms in the Transition from Drug Use to Drug Dependence." *Neuroscience and Biobehavioral Review* 27:739–49.

Kroneberg, C. 2006. "The Definition of the Situation and Variable Rationality: The Model of Frame Selection as a General Theory of Action." *SonderForschungsBereich* 504, Discussion Paper No. 06–05:1–44.

Kroneberg, C., I. Heintze, and G. Mehlkop. 2010. "The Interplay of Moral Norms and Instrumental Incentives in Crime Causation." *Criminology* 48(1): 259–94.

Lamm, C., J. Decety, and T. Singer. 2011. "Meta-Analytic Evidence for Common and Distinct Neural Networks Associated with Directly Experienced Pain and Empathy for Pain." *Neuroimage* 54(3): 2492–2502.

Loughran, T. A., R. Paternoster, A. Chalfin, and T. Wilson. 2016. "Can Rational Choice Be Considered a General Theory of Crime? Evidence from Individual-Level Panel Data." *Criminology* 54:86–112.

Maher, B. 2008. "Personal Genomes: The Case of the Missing Heritability." *Nature* 456:18–21.

Manuck, S. B., J. D. Flory, R. E. Ferrell, K. M. Dent, J. J. Mann, and M. F. Muldoon. 1999. "Aggression and Anger-Related Traits Associated with a Polymorphism of the Tryptophan Hydroxylase Gene." *Biological Psychiatry* 45:603–14.

Marin, T. J., T. M. Martin, E. Blackwell, C. Stetler, and G. E. Miller. 2007. "Differentiating the Impact of Episodic and Chronic Stressors on Hypothalamic–Pituitary–Adrenocortical Axis Regulation in Young Women." *Health Psychology* 26:447–55.

Maruna, S., and H. Copes. 2005. "What Have We Learned from Five Decades of Neutralization Research?" *Crime and Justice* 32:221–320.

Mednick, S. A., and K. O. Christiansen. 1977. *Biosocial Bases of Criminal Behavior*. Oxford: Gardner Press.

Mehta, P. H., and J. Beer. 2010. "Neural Mechanisms of the Testosterone–Aggression Relation: The Role of Orbitofrontal Cortex." *Journal of Cognitive Neuroscience* 22:2357–68.

Miller, G. E., E. Chen, and E. S. Zhou. 2007. "If It Goes Up, Must It Come Down? Chronic Stress and the Hypothalamic–Pituitary–Adrenocortical Axis in Humans." *Psychological Bulletin* 133:25–45.

Moffitt, T. E. 1990. "The Neuropsychology of Juvenile Delinquency: A Critical Review." *Crime and Justice* 12:99–169.

Moffitt, T. E., and B. Henry. 1989. "Neuropsychological Assessment of Executive Functions in Self-Reported Delinquents." *Developmental Psychopathology* 1:105–18.

Moll, J., and R. de Oliveira-Souza. 2003. "Morals and the Human Brain: A Working Model." *NeuroReport* 14(3): 299–305.

Moll, J., R. de Oliveira-Souza, and R. Zahn. 2008. "The Neural Basis of Moral Cognition: Sentiments, Concepts, and Values." *Annals of the New York Academy of Sciences* 1124:161–80.

Montoya, E. R., D. Terburg, P. A. Bos, and J. van Honk. 2012. "Testosterone, Cortisol, and Serotonin as Key Regulators of Social Aggression: A Review and Theoretical Perspective." *Motivation and Emotion* 36:65–73.

Morgan, A., and S. Lilienfeld. 2000. "A Meta-Analytic Review of the Relation Between Antisocial Behavior and Neuropsychological Measures of Executive Function." *Clinical Psychology Review* 20:113–36.

Motzkin, J. C., J. P. Newman, K. A. Kiehl, and M. Koenigs. 2011. "Reduced Prefrontal Connectivity in Psychopathy." *Journal of Neuroscience* 31:17348–57.

Munakata, Y., S. A. Herd, C. H. Chatham, B. E. Depue, M. T. Banich, and R. C. O'Reilly. 2011. "A Unified Framework for Inhibitory Control." *Trends in Cognitive Sciences* 15(10): 453–59.

Nagin, D. S., and G. Pogarsky. 2001. "Integrating Celerity, Impulsivity, and Extralegal Sanction Threats Into a Model of General Deterrence: Theory and Evidence." *Criminology* 39(4): 865–92.

Nigg, J. T., and C. L. Huang-Pollock. 2003. "An Early-Onset Model of the Role of Executive Functions and Intelligence in Conduct Disorder/Delinquency." In *Causes of Conduct Disorder and Juvenile Delinquency*, edited by B. Lahey, T. Moffitt, and A. Caspi, pp. 227–53. London: Guildford.

Ochsner, K. N., and J. J. Gross. 2005. "The Cognitive Control of Emotion." *Trends in Cognitive Sciences* 9(5): 242–49.

Ochsner, K. N., J. A. Silvers, and J. T. Buhle. 2012. "Functional Imaging Studies of Emotion Regulation: A Synthetic Review and Evolving Model of the Cognitive Control of Emotion." *Annals of the New York Academy of Sciences* 1251:E1–24.

O'Doherty, J., P. Dayan, J. Schultz, R. Deichmann, K. Friston, and R. J. Dolan. 2004. "Dissociable Roles of Ventral and Dorsal Striatum in Instrumental Conditioning." *Science* 304(5669): 452–54.

Ogilvie, J. M., A. L. Stewart, R. C. K. Chan, and D. H. K. Shum. 2011. "Neuropsychological Measures of Executive Function and Antisocial Behaviour: A Meta-Analysis." *Criminology* 49:1063–1107.

Ortiz, J., and A. Raine. 2004. "Heart Rate Level and Antisocial Behavior in Children and Adolescents: A Meta-Analysis." *Journal of the American Academy of Child and Adolescent Psychiatry* 43(2): 154–62.

Pardini, D. A., A. Raine, K. Erickson, and R. Loeber. 2014. "Lower Amygdala Volume in Men Is Associated with Childhood Aggression, Early Psychopathic Traits, and Future Violence." *Biological Psychiatry* 75(1): 73–80.

Paternoster, R. 2010. "How Much Do We Really Know About Criminal Deterrence?" *Journal of Criminal Law and Criminology* 100:765–824.

Patrick, C. J. 2008. "Psychophysiological Correlates of Aggression and Violence: An Integrative Review." *Philosophical Transactions of the Royal Society of London B Biological Science* 363:2543–55.

Phelps, E. A. 2004. "Human Emotion and Memory: Interactions of the Amygdala and Hippocampal Complex." *Current Opinion in Neurobiology* 14(2): 198–202.

Plessner, H., and S. Czenna. 2008. "The Benefits of Intuition." In *Intuition in Judgment and Decision Making*, edited by H. Plessner, C. Betsch, and T. Betsch, pp. 251–65. London: Taylor and Francis.

Polderman, T. J. C., B. Benyamin, C. A. de Leeuw, P. F. Sullivan, A. van Bochoven, P. M. Visscher, and D. Posthuma. 2015. "Meta-Analysis of the Heritability of Human Traits Based on Fifty Years of Twin Studies." *Nature Genetics* 47:702–09.

Portnoy, J., A. Raine, F. R. Chen, D. Pardini, R. Loeber, and J. R. Richard. 2014. "Heart Rate and Antisocial Behavior: The Mediating Role of Impulsive Sensation Seeking." *Criminology* 52:292–311.

Pujol, J., I. Batalla, O. Contreras-Rodríguez, B. J. Harrison, V. Pera, R. Hernández-Ribas, E. Real, L. Bosa, C. Soriano-Mas, J. Deus, M. López-Solà, J. Pifarré, J. M. Menchón, and N. Cardoner. 2012. "Breakdown in the Brain Network Subserving Moral Judgment in Criminal Psychopathy." *Social Cognitive and Affective Neuroscience* 7(8): 917–23.

Raine, A. 2002. "Annotation: The Role of Prefrontal Deficits, Low Autonomic Arousal, and Early Health Factors in the Development of Antisocial and Aggressive Behavior in Children." *Journal of Child Psychology and Psychiatry* 43:417–34.

Raine, A. 2008. "From Genes to Brains to Antisocial Behavior." *Current Directions in Psychological Science* 17(5): 323–28.

Raine, A. 2013. *The Anatomy of Violence: The Biological Roots of Crime*. London: Penguin.

Raine, A., M. Buchsbaum, and L. LaCasse. 1997. "Brain Abnormalities in Murderers Indicated by Positron Emission Tomography." *Biological Psychiatry* 42:495–508.

Raine, A., J. R. Meloy, S. Bihrle, J. Stoddard, L. LaCasse, and M. S. Buchsbaum. 1998. "Reduced Prefrontal and Increased Subcortical Brain Functioning Assessed Using Positron Emission Tomography in Predatory and Affective Murderers." *Behavioral Science and Law* 16:319–32.

Raine, A., and P. H. Venables. 1981. "Classical Conditioning and Socialization—A Biosocial Interaction." *Personal and Individual Differences* 2:273–83.

Rhee, S. H., and I. D. Waldman. 2002. "Genetic and Environmental Influences on Antisocial Behavior: A Meta-Analysis of Twin and Adoption Studies." *Psychological Bulletin* 128: 490–529.

Rilling, J. K. 2013. "The Neural and Hormonal Bases of Human Parental Care." *Neuropsychologia* 51(4):731–47.

Robbins, T. W., and B. J. Everitt. 1996. "Neurobehavioural Mechanisms of Reward and Motivation." *Current Opinion in Neurobiology* 6(2): 228–36.

Rocque, M., C. Posick, and S. Felix. 2015. "The Role of the Brain in Urban Violent Offending: Integrating Biology with Structural Theories of 'the Streets.'" *Criminal Justice Studies* 28:84–103.

Rutter, M., C. Beckett, J. Castle, E. Colvert, J. Kreppner, M. Mehta, S. Stevens, and E. Sonuga-Barke. 2007. "Effects of Profound Early Institutional Deprivation: An Overview of Findings from a UK Longitudinal Study of Romanian Adoptees." *European Journal of Developmental Psychology* 4(3): 332–50.

Sampson, R. J., and J. Laub. 1993. *Crime in the Making: Pathways and Turning Points Through Life*. London: Harvard University Press.

Schardt, D. M., S. Erk, C. Nusser, M. M. Nothen, S. Cichon, M. Rietschel, J. Treutlein, T. Goschke, and H. Walter. 2010. "Volition Diminishes Genetically Mediated Amygdala Hyperreactivity." *Neuroimage* 53(3): 943–51.

Shulman, E. P., A. R. Smith, K. Silva, G. Icenogle, N. Duell, J. Chein, and L. Steinberg. 2016. "The Dual Systems Model: Review, Reappraisal, and Reaffirmation." *Developmental Cognitive Neuroscience* 17:103–17.

Sijtsema, J. J., R. Veenstra, S. Lindenberg, A. M. van Roon, F. C. Verhulst, J. Ormel, and H. Riese. 2010. "Mediation of Sensation Seeking and Behavioral Inhibition on the Relationship Between Heart Rate and Antisocial Behavior: The TRAILS Study." *Journal of the American Academy of Child and Adolescent Psychiatry* 49(5): 493–502.

Simons, R. L., R. H. Beach, and A. B. Barr. 2012. "Differential Susceptibility to Context: A Promising Model of the Interplay of Genes and the Social Environment." *Advances in Group Processes* 29:139–63.

Simons, R. L., M. K. Lei, S. R. Beach, G. H. Brody, R. A. Philibert, and F. X. Gibbons. 2011. "Social Environmental Variation, Plasticity Genes, and Aggression: Evidence for the Differential Susceptibility Hypothesis." *American Sociological Review* 76:833–912.

Sloman, S. 1996. "The Empirical Case of Two Systems of Reasoning." *Psychological Bulletin* 119(1): 3–22.

Smith, K. E., E. C. Porges, G. J. Norman, J. J. Connelly, and J. Decety. 2014. "Oxytocin Receptor Gene Variation Predicts Empathic Concern and Autonomic Arousal While Perceiving Harm to Others." *Social Neuroscience* 9(1): 1–9.

Smith, K. S., and A. M. Graybiel. 2013. "A Dual Operator View of Habitual Behavior Reflecting Cortical and Striatal Dynamics." *Neuron* 79(2): 361–74.

Spear, L. P. 2000. "The Adolescent Brain and Age-Related Behavioral Manifestations." *Neuroscience and Biobehavioral Reviews* 24(4): 417–63.

Strack, F., and R. Deutsch. 2004. "Reflective and Impulsive Determinants of Social Behavior." *Personality and Social Psychology Review* 8(3): 220–47.

Strait, C. E., T. C. Blanchard, and B. Y. Hayden. 2014. "Reward Value Comparison via Mutual Inhibition in Ventromedial Prefrontal Cortex." *Neuron* 82(6): 1357–66.

Steinberg, L. (2008). "A social neuroscience perspective on adolescent risk-taking." *Developmental review* 28(1): 78–106.

Steinberg, L. A. 2010. "A dual Systems Model of Adolescent Risk-Taking." *Developmental Psychobiology* 52:216–24.

Stetler, D. A., C. Davis, K. Leavitt, I. Schriger, K. Benson, S. Bhakta, L. C. Wang, C. Oben, M. Watters, T. Haghnegahdar, and M. Bortolato. 2014. "Association of Low-Activity MAOA Allelic Variants with Violent Crime in Incarcerated Offenders." *Journal of Psychiatric Research* 58:69–75.

Susman, E. J. 2006. "Psychobiology of Persistent Antisocial Behavior: Stress, Early Vulnerabilities and the Attenuation Hypothesis." *Neuroscience and Biobehavioral Reviews* 30(3): 376–89.

Svensson, R. 2015. "An Examination of the Interaction Between Morality and Deterrence in Offending: A Research Note." *Crime and Delinquency* 61(1): 3–18.

Svensson, R., L. Pauwels, and F. Weerman. 2010. "Does the Effect of Self-Control on Adolescent Offending Vary by Level of Morality? A Test in Three Countries." *Criminal Justice and Behavior* 37(6): 732–43.

Sweeten, G., A. R. Piquero, and L. Steinberg. 2013. "Age and the Explanation of Crime, Revisited." *Journal of Youth and Adolescence* 42: 921–38.

Takahashi, H., H. Takano, F. Kodaka, R. Arakawa, M. Yamada, T. Otsuka, Y. Hirano, H. Kikyo, Y. Okubo, M. Kato, T. Obata, H. Ito, and T. Suhara. 2010. "Contribution of Dopamine D1 and D2 Receptors to Amygdala Activity in Humans." *Journal of Neuroscience* 30(8): 3043–47.

Tibbetts, S. G. 2011. "Birth Complications and the Development of Criminality: A Biosocial Perspective." In *The Ashgate Research Companion to Biosocial Theories of Crime*, edited by K. M. Beaver and A. Walsh, pp. 273–90. Abingdon, UK: Ashgate.

Tielbeek, J. J., S. E. Medland, B. Benyamin, E. M. Byrne, A. C. Heath, P. A. Madden, N. G. Martin, N. R. Wray, and K. J. Verweij. 2012. "Unraveling the Genetic Etiology of Adult Antisocial Behavior: A Genome-wide Association Study." *PLoS One* 7:e45086.

Tottenham, N. 2015. "Social Scaffolding of Human Amygdala-mPFC Circuit Development." *Social Neuroscience* 10(5): 489–99.

Toupin, J., M. Déry, R. Pauzé, H. Mercier, and L. Fortin. 2000. "Cognitive and Familial Contributions to Conduct Disorder in Children." *Journal of Child Psychology and Psychiatry* 41:333–44.

Tranel, D., S. Anderson, and A. Benton. 1994. "Development of the Concept of 'Executive Function' and Its Relationship to the Frontal Lobes." In *Handbook of Neuropsychology, Volume 9, Section 12: The Frontal Lobes*, edited by F. Boller and H. Spinnler, pp. 125–48. Oxford, UK: Elsevier.

Treiber, K. 2011. "The Neuroscientific Basis of Situational Action Theory." In *The Ashgate Research Companion to Biosocial Theories of Crime*, edited by A. Walsh and K. Beaver, pp. 213–45. Abingdon, UK: Ashgate.

Tricomi, E., B. W. Balleine, and J. P. O'Doherty. 2009. "A Specific Role for Posterior Dorsolateral Striatum in Human Habit Learning." *European Journal of Neuroscience* 29(11): 2225–32.

van Gelder, J.-L., and R. E. de Vries. 2014. "Rational Misbehavior? Evaluating an Integrated Dual-Process Model of Criminal Decision Making." *Journal of Quantitative Criminology* 30:1–27.

van Goozen, S. H. M., and G. Fairchild. 2006. "Neuroendocrine and Neurotransmitter Correlates in Children with Antisocial Behavior." *Hormones and Behavior* 50:647–54.

van Goozen, S. H. M., G. Fairchild, H. Snoek, and G. T. Harold. 2007. "The Evidence for a Neuro-biological Model of Childhood Antisocial Behavior." *Psychological Bulletin* 133(1): 149–82.

van Goozen, S. H. M., W. Matths, P. T. Cohen-Kettenis, J. K. Buitelaar, and H. van England. 2000. "Hypothalamic–Pituitary–Adrenal Axis and Autonomic Nervous System Activity in Disruptive Children and Matched Controls." *Journal of the American Academy of Child and Adolescent Psychiatry* 39:1438–45.

van Voorhees, E., and A. Scarpa. 2004. "The Effects of Child Maltreatment on the Hypothalamic–Pituitary–Adrenal Axis." *Trauma, Violence, and Abuse* 5(4): 333–52.

Vassos, E., D. A. Collier, and S. Fazel. 2014. "Systematic Meta-Analyses and Field Synopsis of Genetic Association Studies of Violence and Aggression." *Molecular Psychiatry* 19(4): 471–77.

Vaughn, M. G., M. DeLisi, K. M. Beaver, and J. P. Wright. 2009. "DAT1 and 5HTT Are Associated with Pathological Criminal Behavior in a Nationally Representative Sample of Youth." *Criminal Justice and Behavior* 36:1113–24.

Veit, R., L. Konicar, J. G. Klinzing, B. Barth, O. Yilmaz, and N. Birbaumer. 2013. "Deficient Fear Conditioning in Psychopathy as a Function of Interpersonal and Affective Disturbances." *Frontiers of Human Neuroscience* 7:706.

Vila, B. 1994. "A General Paradigm for Understanding Criminal Behavior: Extending Evolutionary Ecological Theory." *Criminology* 32(3): 311–59.

Voon, V., K. Derbyshire, C. Ruck, M. A. Irvine, Y. Worbe, J. Enander, L. R. Schreiber, C. Gillan, N. A. Fineberg, B. J. Sahakian, T. W. Robbins, N. A. Harrison, J. Wood, N. D. Daw, P. Dayan, J. E. Grant, and E. T. Bullmore. 2015. "Disorders of Compulsivity: A Common Bias Towards Learning Habits." *Molecular Psychiatry* 20(3): 35–52.

Wahlstrom, D., P. Collins, T. White, and M. Luciana. 2010. "Developmental Changes in Dopamine Neurotransmission in Adolescence: Behavioral Implications and Issues in Assessment." *Brain and Cognition* 72(1): 146–59.

Wahlund, K., and M. Kristiansson. 2009. "Aggression, Psychopathy and Brain Imaging—Review and Future Recommendations." *International Journal of Law and Psychiatry* 32:266–71.

Wallis, J. D., and E. K. Miller. 2003. "From Rule to Response: Neuronal Processes in the Premotor and Prefrontal Cortex." *Journal of Neurophysiology* 90(3): 1790–1806.

Walsh, A. 2009a. "Criminal Behaviour from Heritability to Epigenetics: How Genetics Clarifies the Role of the Environment." In *Biosocial Criminology: New Directions in Theory and Research*, edited by A. Walsh and K. Beaver, pp. 29–49. London: Routledge.

Walsh, A. 2009b. "Crazy by Design: A Biosocial Approach to the Age–Crime Curve." In *Biosocial Criminology: New Directions in Theory and Research*, edited by A. Walsh and K. M. Beaver, pp. 154–75. London: Routledge.

Walsh, A., and K. Beaver. 2009. "Introduction to Biosocial Criminology." In *Biosocial Criminology: New Directions in Theory and Research*, edited by A. Walsh and K. Beaver, pp. 7–28. London: Routledge.

Wendelken, C., Y. Munakata, C. Baym, M. Souza, and S. A. Bunge. 2012. "Flexible Rule Use: Common Neural Substrates in Children and Adults." *Developmental Cognitive Neuroscience* 2(3): 329–39.

Wikström, P.-O. H. 2006. "Individuals, Settings, and Acts of Crime: Situational Mechanisms and the Explanation of Crime." In *The Explanation of Crime: Context, Mechanisms and Development*, edited by P.-O. H. Wikström and R. J. Sampson, pp. 61–107. Cambridge, UK: Cambridge University Press.

Wikström, P.-O. H. 2008. "Deterrence and Deterrence Experiences: Preventing Crime Through the Threat of Punishment." In *International Handbook of Penalty and Criminal Justice*, edited by S. G. Shoham, pp. 345–78. Boca Raton, FL: Taylor and Francis.

Wikström, P.-O. H. 2010. "Explaining Crime as Moral Action." In *Handbook of the Sociology of Morality*, edited by S. Hitlin and S. Vaysey, pp. 211–39. New York: Springer-Verlag.

Wikström, P.-O. H. 2014. "Why Crime Happens: A Situational Action Theory." In *Analytical Sociology: Actions and Networks*, edited by G. Manzo, pp. 74–94. West Sussex, UK: Wiley.

Wikström, P.-O. H., D. Oberwittler, K. Treiber, and B. Hardie. 2012. *Breaking Rules: The Social and Situational Dynamics of Young People's Urban Crime*. Oxford: Oxford University Press.

Wikström, P.-O. H., and R. Svensson. 2010. "When Does Self-Control Matter? The Interaction Between Morality and Self-Control in Crime Causation." *European Journal of Criminology* 7(5): 395–410.

Wikström, P.-O. H., and K. Treiber. 2007. "The Role of Self-Control in Crime Causation: Beyond Gottfredson and Hirschi's General Theory of Crime." *European Journal of Criminology* 4(2): 237–64.

Wikström, P.-O. H., and K. Treiber. 2009a. "Violence as Situational Action." *International Journal of Conflict and Violence* 3(1): 75–96.

Wikström, P.-O. H., and K. Treiber, 2009b. "What Drives Persistent Offending? The Neglected and Unexplored Role of the Social Environment." In *The Development of Persistent Criminality*, edited by J. Savage, pp. 389–420. Oxford: Oxford University Press.

Wikström, P.-O. H., and K. Treiber. 2013. "Towards an Analytical Criminology: A Situational Action Theory." In *Kriminologie—Kriminalpolitik—Strafrect: Festschrift für Hans-Jürgen Kerner zum 70. Geburtstag*, edited by K. Boers, T. Feltes, J. Kinzig, et al., pp. 319–30. Tübingen, the Netherlands: Mohr Siebeck.

Wikström, P.-O. H., and K. Treiber. 2015. "Situational Theories: The Importance of Interactions and Action Mechanisms in the Explanation of Crime." In *Handbook of Criminological Theory*, edited by A. R. Piquero, pp. 415–44. Hoboken, NJ: Wiley-Blackwell.

Wikström, P.-O. H., A. Tseloni, and D. Karlis. 2011. "Do People Comply with the Law Because They Fear Getting Caught?" *European Journal of Criminology* 8(5): 401–20.

Wilson, L. C., and A. Scarpa. 2011. "The Link Between Sensation Seeking and Aggression: A Meta-Analytic Review." *Aggressive Behavior* 37(1): 81–90.

Woodward, J., and J. Allman. 2007. "Moral Intuition: Its Neural Substrates and Normative Significance." *Journal of Physiology, Paris* 101(4–6): 179–202.

Wright, J. P., D. Boisvert, K. Dietrich, and M. D. Ris. 2009. "The Ghost in the Machine and Criminal Behavior: Criminology for the 21st century." In *Biosocial Criminology: New Directions in Theory and Research*, edited by A. Walsh and K. M. Beaver, pp. 73–89. London: Routledge.

Wright, J. P., K. Moore, and J. Newsome. 2011. "Molecular Genetics and Crime." In *The Ashgate Research Companion to Biosocial Theories of Crimes*, edited by K. Beaver and A. Walsh, pp. 93–114. Surrey, UK: Ashgate.

Wright, R. 2001. *Nonzero: The Logic of Human Destiny*. New York: Random House.

Yang, Y., and A. Raine. 2009. "Prefrontal Structural and Functional Brain Imaging Findings in Antisocial, Violent, and Psychopathic Individuals: A Meta-Analysis." *Psychiatry Research— Neuroimaging* 174:81–88.

Yang, Y., A. Raine, A. A. Joshi, S. Joshi, Y. T. Chang, R. A. Schug, D. Wheland, R. Leahy, and K. L. Narr. 2012. "Frontal Information Flow and Connectivity in Psychopathy." *British Journal of Psychiatry* 201:408–09.

Yang, Y., A. Raine, K. L. Narr, P. Colletti, and A. W. Toga. 2009. "Localization of Deformations Within the Amygdala in Individuals with Psychopathy." *Archives of General Psychiatry* 66(9): 986–94.

Yin, H. H., and B. J. Knowlton. 2006. "The Role of the Basal Ganglia in Habit Formation." *Nature Reviews Neuroscience* 7:464–76.

Yin, H. H., S. B. Ostlund, B. J. Knowlton, and B. W. Balleine. 2005. "The Role of the Dorsomedial Striatum in Instrumental Conditioning." *European Journal of Neuroscience* 22(2): 513–23.

Zuckerman, M. 2006. "Biosocial Bases of Sensation Seeking." In *Biology of Personality and Individual Differences*, edited by T. Canli, pp. 37–59. New York: Guilford.

Zuk, O., E. Hechter, S. R. Sunyaev, and E. S. Lander. 2012. "The Mystery of Missing Heritability: Genetic Interactions Create Phantom Heritability." *Proceedings of the National Academy of Sciences of the USA* 109:1193–98.

CHAPTER 7

....

PERCEPTUAL DETERRENCE

....

ROBERT APEL AND DANIEL S. NAGIN

In theory, punishments that are more severe, applied with greater certainty, and more swiftly carried out will not only better deter future offending of the punished individual ("specific deterrence") but also deter offending by the public writ large ("general deterrence"). These are the three (among several more) principles of punishment rooted in the Classical School of criminology that form the basis of the modern theory of deterrence (Beccaria 1764/1963; Bentham 1789/1988). Underlying the utilitarian principles of the Classical School is a theory of choice in which would-be offenders weigh the potential rewards of criminal conduct against the potential losses (Becker 1968). Crime is said to be deterred when the probability of punishment, the intensity of sanction, or the promptness of administration lowers the expected utility of crime just enough to make noncriminal behavior the preferred course of action.

It is important to bear in mind that certainty and severity are subjective rather than strictly objective properties of punishment. Modern criminological interest in sanction perceptions arose in the 1970s and 1980s as researchers sought to more clearly delineate the link between criminal punishments and individual criminal behavior. Scholars observed that deterrence is, fundamentally, a process of information transmission intended to discourage law violation (Geerken and Gove 1975; Gibbs 1975). From this long-standing interest has arisen a rich tradition of research in perceptual deterrence, acknowledging the importance of perceptions as an intermediate link between sanctions and behavior (Waldo and Chiricos 1972). Indeed, Nagin (1998, p. 18) observed that "behavior is immune to policy manipulation" to the degree that there is no link between policy and perceptions, and he viewed the formation and malleability of sanction perceptions as among the least understood features of the deterrence doctrine.

In this chapter, we consider theory and evidence on the perceptual principles of deterrence theory, drawing liberally from our own prior work (Nagin 1998, 2013; Apel and Nagin 2011; Apel 2013). This review is also intended to accompany other chapters in this volume, namely chapters 2 and 4. We begin with a basic description of how sanction perceptions are incorporated into decision-making models, and we provide a brief review of early research with respect to the deterrent effect of those perceptions on criminal offending. We then step back and consider the determinants of sanction perceptions in their own right, doing so in three parts. We first survey the research with respect to the accuracy of sanction perceptions. We next survey the research on perceptual updating in response to crime and arrest. We finally survey the research on the situational malleability of sanction perceptions. We close the chapter with consideration of emerging perspectives on the perceptions–behavior relationship, as well as concluding thoughts and suggestions for further developments in the study of perceptual deterrence.

I. The Deterrent Effect of Sanction Perceptions

It is helpful to begin with a brief formulaic description of the rational choice model. Crime decision making involves forming expectations about the future concerning potential rewards (i.e., benefits and incentives) as well as potential punishments (i.e., costs and disincentives). Because these outcomes are uncertain—potential punishments in particular, because they require discovery and often follow quite some time after the act itself—crime decisions also entail corresponding probabilities of the rewards and punishments. These considerations give rise to the expected utility model of criminal behavior:

$$E(U) = (1 - \pi_p) \times U(\text{reward}) - \pi_p \times U(\text{punishment})$$

According to this model, a person chooses to commit crime when the expected returns from illegal behavior, discounted by punishment risk, exceed the expected returns from law-abiding behavior such as legitimate employment (Becker 1968). In the model, $U(\cdot)$ represents an individual's utility function, which refers to the (un)happiness or overall (dis)satisfaction that he or she achieves from a particular outcome. The rewards comprise the pecuniary benefits from the successful commission of a crime (namely the "loot") as well as the possible value of the thrill of committing the crime or the satisfaction of humiliating, injuring, or even killing the victim. The costs refer to the pecuniary costs of punishment, for example, fines, asset forfeiture, or the costs of legal representation as well as social costs such as enduring stigma. The probability parameter, π_p, denotes the likelihood that the individual will be caught and punished for the crime, which would trigger the punishment portion of the expected utility model. The net or expected utility of crime therefore indexes all of the potential rewards, less the potential losses, with each scaled by its corresponding probability.

It is important to bear in mind that the rewards, costs, and probabilities comprising the rational choice model are subjective rather than objective properties of the punishments (Piliavin et al. 1986). For example, whereas the expected utility model assumes that π_p (the punishment probability) is objectively known, the "subjective expected utility model" allows individuals to have a subjective probability distribution, $f(\pi_p)$, substituting an estimate in place of π_p, usually the mean or expected value of this distribution, $E(\pi_p)$.

In a recent elaboration of the rational choice model, Nagin (2013) provides a fuller accounting of opportunities, rewards, and punishments, as well as their perceptual properties. The decision-making process that he outlines has three intersecting possibilities: successful completion versus noncompletion of the criminal act, apprehension versus non-apprehension given that the offender completes the act, and conviction versus nonconviction given that the offender is apprehended. This elaboration clarifies the unique trade-off of the perceived rewards and costs associated with sequential outcomes, as well as their corresponding probabilities. It also further clarifies the nature of the manifold perceived costs associated with the loss portion of the crime decision—the perceived costs of crime commission (e.g., planning, effort, and victim resistance), the perceived economic and social costs of apprehension (e.g., pretrial detention, legal fees, and disapproval of loved ones), and the perceived formal and informal costs of conviction (e.g., incarceration and job loss).

A. Empirical Status of the Perceptions–Crime Link

The most relevant research on the deterrent effects of perceptions on behavior derives from two forms of inquiry: panel surveys and vignettes (Nagin 1998). Panel surveys are designed to untangle temporal priority for the perceptions–behavior link by relating perceptions in one time period to actual behavior in a subsequent time period. Findings from panel surveys tend to show that the perceptions–behavior correlation is fairly small and often diminishes to nonsignificance with the inclusion of control variables (Paternoster 1987). However, there are notable exceptions. An example of this approach is provided by Wright and colleagues (2004), who found long-term perceptual deterrent effects on behavior in a cohort of New Zealand youth. They found that the perceived risk of getting caught for criminal behavior in late adolescence was inversely and significantly correlated with criminal behavior at age twenty-six years.

Vignette research provides respondents with a detailed, hypothetical crime scenario and then asks them about their perceptions of the certainty and severity of punishment for the crime, as well as their own behavior if they found themselves in the same situation. A unique feature of this design is that situational characteristics can be experimentally manipulated in order to study how subjects respond to a variety of incentives, disincentives, and opportunity structures. To consider one example in detail, Nagin and Pogarsky (2001) administered a scenario describing an incident of drunk driving to university students, in which they experimentally manipulated the severity and celerity of punishment. Respondents given a scenario with a longer length of license suspension upon conviction for drunk driving (higher severity) reported a significantly lower likelihood of driving drunk, although this effect appeared to be diminished among individuals who were more present-oriented or impulsive (i.e., those with a higher "discount rate"). On the other hand, a shorter delay between conviction and the suspension period (higher celerity) was unrelated to drunk-driving intentions. When the authors inquired about subjects' own estimated likelihood of being apprehended and convicted for drunk driving (a measure of certainty) under the conditions described in the scenario, they found that it was a robust predictor of intentions to drive drunk.

Research on the perceptual deterrent effects of punishment has produced two other sets of findings that are important to understanding the sources of deterrence. The first concerns the comparative deterrent effects of the certainty and severity of punishment. The perceptual deterrence literature finds more consistent evidence of the certainty of punishment as a crime deterrent relative to the severity of punishment. The second concerns the role of informal sanctions in the deterrence process. Zimring and Hawkins (1973) observe that formal punishment may best deter when it sets off informal sanctions: "Official actions can set off societal reactions that may provide potential offenders with more reason to avoid conviction than the officially imposed unpleasantness of punishment" (p. 174). Much perceptual deterrence research confirms this linkage. This research has consistently found that individuals who report higher stakes in conventionality are more strongly deterred by their perceived risk of punishment for law violation.

A salient example of research supporting the priority of sanction certainty, as well as untangling the link between formal and informal sanctions, concerns tax evasion. In the United States, civil enforcement actions by tax authorities are a private matter unless the taxpayer appeals the action. Because tax authorities are scrupulous about maintaining the confidentiality of tax return information, for civil enforcement actions noncompliers are gambling only with their money and not their personal reputations. In a study by Klepper and Nagin (1989a), a sample of generally middle-class adults were posed a series of tax noncompliance scenarios. The scenarios laid out the essential features of a tax report—income from different sources, number of exemptions, and various deductions. They then experimentally varied the amount and type of noncompliance (e.g., overstating charitable deductions or understating business income) across tax return line items and found that a majority of respondents reported a non-zero probability of taking advantage of the noncompliance opportunity described in the scenario. The latter finding indicated that this sample of respondents was generally willing to consider tax noncompliance when only their money was at risk. They also seemed to be calculating: The attractiveness of the tax noncompliance gamble was inversely related to the perceived risk of civil enforcement.

The one exception to the rule of confidentiality of enforcement is criminal prosecution. As with all criminal cases, criminal prosecutions for tax evasion are a matter of public record. Here, Klepper and Nagin (1989a) found evidence of a different decision calculus: Seemingly all that was necessary to deter evasion was the perception of a non-zero chance of criminal prosecution. Stated differently, if the evasion gamble also involved putting reputation and community standing at risk, the middle-class respondents were seemingly unwilling to consider taking the noncompliance gamble. This might help explain the common finding that the certainty of punishment may be a stronger deterrent than its severity. If the social and economic costs of punishment were strictly proportional to the punishment received—for example, if the cost to the individual of a two-year prison term was twice that of a one-year sentence—certainty and severity would equally affect expected cost. However, the Klepper and Nagin study suggested that people do not perceive costs to be proportional to potential punishment. Instead, they apparently perceive there to be a fixed cost associated with merely being convicted or even apprehended if it was public record.

Each of the previously discussed examples concerns the deterrent effect of the threat of detection and/or apprehension. Based on this observation, Nagin (2013) argues an important refinement of the certainty principle. The certainty of punishment is the product of a series of conditional probabilities that correspond closely to the stages of the criminal justice system—the certainty of apprehension given crime commission, the certainty of conviction given apprehension, and the certainty of various types of punishment given conviction. Virtually all the evidence on the deterrent effect of certainty pertains to the certainty of apprehension (or detection). Thus, Nagin restates the certainty principle as "it is the certainty of apprehension not the severity of the ensuing consequences that is the more effective deterrent" (p. 199).

In summary, research on perceptual deterrence does suggest that sanction perceptions are an important source of law-abiding behavior. In the remaining sections of this chapter, we turn our attention away from studies in which sanction perceptions are an independent variable and instead consider studies in which sanction perceptions can be conceived as the dependent variable. We are particularly interested in the degree to which sanction perceptions are sensitive to objective sanction risk, personal and vicarious experiences with crime and punishment, and incidental features of crime situations. We consider each in turn.

II. Correspondence Between Objective and Subjective Sanctions

In order for a sanction policy to influence behavior in a predictable manner, individual perceptions of the certainty and severity of sanctions must have some grounding in reality (Nagin 1998). Implicit in the rational choice model is an assumption known as "rational expectations." The highly stylized version of this assumption is that individuals contemplating a crime possess complete information about sanction risk, comprising punishment probabilities (certainty) and penalty magnitude (severity). In practice, the assumption instead requires that the aggregate of perceived certainty or severity estimates in a sample of respondents (e.g., the mean) conforms to its objective counterpart. In other words, an individual's perceptions are accurate or rational, in the sense that an average person knows the true sanction certainty or severity.

An important research tradition therefore entails estimation of the correspondence between area-level measures (city, county, or state) of criminal punishment and individual perceptions of the certainty and severity of sanction risk. Manski (2004) refers to these as "calibration studies" because they are concerned with the degree to which the perceptions of sanction risk are accurately calibrated to objective sanction risk or otherwise responsive to short- or long-term changes in objective sanction risk. Based on this research, it would seem that most people are not particularly well informed about criminal penalties. Some notable studies in this tradition are summarized here, but for a more extensive review, readers are referred to Apel (2013).

In 1967, in the first study of its kind as far as we are aware, the California Assembly examined the deterrence effectiveness of its criminal penalties (Assembly Committee on Criminal Procedure 1968). One component of the study was a survey of how knowledgeable different groups of respondents were of the prevailing statutory penalties for criminal behavior. The sample included more than 1,500 subjects and comprised noninstitutionalized civilians, college students, high school students (stratified by low- and high-delinquency schools), institutionalized youth, and institutionalized adults. Of the six offenses studied—assault with a deadly weapon, second-degree burglary, first-degree robbery, forcible rape, joyriding, and fraudulent check writing—the mean percentage of respondents who identified the correct maximum penalty was just 27 percent. Among the six subgroups in the study, the worst calibration was attained by the noninstitutionalized civilians and low-delinquency high school youth (mean of 22 and 23 percent, respectively, across the six offenses), whereas the best calibration was attained by the institutionalized adults (mean of 62 percent). In addition, between 21 and 28 percent of the noninstitutionalized civilians were unable to provide a maximum sentence, and among those who did so incorrectly, the predominant tendency was to underestimate the statutory penalty.

The committee also inquired about public knowledge concerning legislative activity for three offenses for which the penalties had recently increased (rape, robbery, and burglary), along with two offenses for which the penalties had not changed (marijuana possession and driving under the influence). The mean percentage of respondents who answered correctly about whether or not the penalties had recently changed was 28 percent. Again, the most knowledgeable subjects were the institutionalized adults, among whom 52 percent responded correctly. In addition, between 35 and 49 percent of the noninstitutionalized civilians reported that they did not know whether the legislature had acted on these offenses. Among those who responded but did so incorrectly, the universal pattern was to report that the severity of the penalty had decreased. Among those who correctly responded that the penalty had increased, the overwhelming tendency was to understate the magnitude of the statutory change. The committee's conclusion concerning recent legislative changes was blunt: "While the Legislature had supposedly responded to public appeal and increased the penalties for crime of violence to victims, this was not known by the public" (Assembly Committee on Criminal Procedure, 1968, p. 14).

Ross (1973) reported on the findings of a public opinion survey conducted before and after passage of the British Road Safety Act (BRSA) of 1967. The BRSA included a number of provisions: A fixed blood alcohol level was adopted as the legal definition of impairment, a field breath test followed by laboratory analysis of the motorist's blood or urine was to provide the evidence of impairment, and motorists were required to submit to a breath test when an officer had reasonable cause to suspect drunkenness or else face the same penalties as if they had failed the test (e.g., loss of driver's license and arrest). In addition to the widespread publicity generated by legislative deliberation, the British government embarked on a large-scale campaign to inform the public about the provisions of the BRSA, utilizing newspaper and television announcements as well as dissemination of brochures. Surveys of randomly chosen adults, administered both before and after the law's passage, indicated that the percentage of respondents who were aware of the blood alcohol limit increased from 22 to 39 percent. In the post-BRSA survey, 99 percent of respondents knew that a breath test was the basis for prosecution, and 95 percent knew that refusal of a breath test could lead to arrest.

MacCoun et al. (2009) pooled data from the National Survey on Drug Use and Health, in which respondents were asked to report the maximum penalty in their state for first-time possession of one ounce or less of marijuana (fine, probation, community service, possible prison sentence, or mandatory prison sentence). The authors compiled information on each state's laws, classifying them by the exact statutory penalties assessed (e.g., fine amount, jail time, and diversionary and expungement provisions). Residents of states that decriminalized marijuana possession, compared to states in which marijuana possession was still criminalized, did indeed report significantly more lenient sanctions for violation, but the actual differences were very modest. For example, excluding the "don't know" responses (approximately one-third of the sample), among residents of states with a decriminalization policy, 44 percent still reported that the maximum penalty included the possibility of a jail or prison sentence, compared to 49 percent among residents of states without a decriminalization policy. Interestingly, the state's arrest rate for marijuana possession was uncorrelated with perceived sanctions, indicating that "prescribed punishments" (statutes) were more strongly correlated with perceptions than were "actual punishments" (enforcement) (for the distinction, see Gibbs 1975).

To briefly summarize the research on perceptual calibration, when survey respondents are asked about the statutory applicability of specific criminal penalties (e.g., fine and prison), there is only modest correspondence between perceptions and reality. Although the evidence was not reviewed here, there is also a consistent tendency for survey respondents to overestimate arrest or clearance rates (an oft-used measure of sanction certainty) and to underestimate the maximum penalties (the standard measure of sanction severity) (Apel, 2013). (However, for a critique of clearance rates as a measure of apprehension risk, see Nagin, Solow, and Lum, 2015.) Therefore, whereas the public does, at best, only a fair job of knowing what criminal penalties are statutorily allowed, it does a very poor job of estimating the probability and magnitude of the penalties. Thus, the observation made long ago by Zimring and Hawkins (1973) is apparently still relevant: "The moment of truth in the life of a potential delinquent will seldom take place in a law library" (p. 149).

The lack of strong correspondence between punishment perceptions and punishment actualities is discouraging for perceptual deterrence. If people are only vaguely aware of the criminal punishments in their city or state, then the perceptual deterrence rationale of punishment is seriously undermined. However, there are many weaknesses in calibration studies, suggesting there is still much to be learned about how or if individuals calibrate their sanction perceptions with respect to objective punishment likelihoods (Apel 2013). Foremost among them is the fact that most of the public is not "in the market" for the kinds of criminal offenses that have been the subject of many calibration studies. In rational choice parlance, most survey respondents are not "on the margin" for crime—they are committed law abiders. Consequently, there is no a priori reason to expect that their perceptions will be the least bit accurate (i.e., "rational"), simply because criminal offending is not even a remotely realistic possibility for them.

Anticipating these conclusions, Cook (1980) observed that although the public might have some vague sense of the overall effectiveness of the criminal justice system, it is highly unlikely that "each arrest and criminal disposition has some marginal (infinitesimal) effect on the perceptions of all potential criminals" (p. 225). Instead, it is more plausible that criminal justice actions have "local" rather than "general" effects on sanction perceptions. In other words, it is more plausible that "each arrest and disposition has a relatively large effect on the perceptions of a small number of potential criminals (including the arrestee himself), and goes essentially unnoticed by all others" (p. 225). Lochner (2007) similarly observes that "while beliefs are largely unresponsive to most outside influences, they do respond to an individual's own experiences with crime and police" (p. 459). This suggests that one promising place to search for evidence with respect to perceptual deterrence is among individuals who are involved in criminal offending.

III. The Influence of Crime and Arrest on Sanction Perceptions

A finding that emerged quite early from survey research was that perceived sanctions were significantly lower among youth who were involved in delinquent behavior compared to their nondelinquent counterparts (Claster 1967). At first glance, this is evidence for perceptual deterrence—the lower perceived risk of delinquents might very well have precipitated their law violation, consistent with the doctrine. However, critics noted that failure to ensure proper temporal ordering left doubt about whether perceptions were the cause or the consequence of behavior. The latter was dubbed an "experiential effect" of unlawful behavior on sanction perceptions, in contrast with the deterrent effect of sanction perceptions on unlawful behavior (Saltzman et al. 1982). Panel surveys indicate that there is indeed a pronounced experiential effect, and in fact it is often substantially stronger than the deterrent effect (Paternoster 1987).

Stafford and Warr (1993) postulated that sanction perceptions are formed, in part, on the basis of personal experiences with punishment as well as punishment avoidance.

Ample evidence confirms that, other things being equal, sanctioned offending is correlated with higher risk perceptions, whereas unsanctioned offending is correlated with lower risk perceptions. For example, in a study by Horney and Marshall (1992), offenders with higher "arrest ratios" (i.e., more reported arrests among reported offenses) reported higher subjective probabilities of detection. In other words, offenders with more successful criminal careers—with success defined as avoidance of arrest—had substantially lower risk perceptions. Stafford and Warr also observed that individuals' risk perceptions are partially formed on the basis of the crime and punishment experiences of their acquaintances. They referred to these as indirect or vicarious experiences of punishment and punishment avoidance.

The ongoing interest in perceptual deterrence has spawned a new generation of research concerned with the development and testing of formal models of perceptual change as a consequence of personal and vicarious experiences with, and avoidances of, arrest and punishment. These studies employ panel designs and appeal to a Bayesian or experiential model of learning. A Bayesian updating model of sanction perceptions and criminal behavior begins with individuals' initial assessments of the likelihood of apprehension for unlawful behavior. This is known as the prior probability of the risk of arrest (among other sanctions). The perceptual deterrence literature strongly suggests that the prior risk probability of individuals without offending experience substantially overstates the true risk of apprehension. Over time, however, as some of these individuals initiate their criminal careers, they will accumulate personal or vicarious experiences (or both) with punishment and punishment avoidance (Stafford and Warr 1993). The expectation is then that these individuals will update their assessment of the risk of apprehension based on their experiences. The resulting posterior risk probability is a weighted function of the individual's prior risk probability (based on past experiences) and his or her current experiences as a successful or unsuccessful offender.

Matsueda et al. (2006) studied belief updating among youth in the Denver Youth Survey. In models of the "perceived probability of being picked up by the police" for theft and violence, they compared different groups of offenders to naive individuals who had neither offended nor been arrested. First, among arrested individuals, they found that those who had lower "experienced arrest certainty" (the ratio of the number of times arrested or questioned to the number of crimes committed) reported lower subjective arrest probabilities. For example, those individuals with the fewest arrests per crime reported a mean subjective probability that was more than 15 points lower than that of naive individuals, whereas individuals with the most arrests per crime were indistinguishable from non-offenders. Second, among non-arrested individuals, more frequent offending was inversely correlated with subjective arrest probabilities. For instance, individuals who reported the most unsanctioned offenses had a mean subjective probability that was more than 10 points lower than that of naive individuals, whereas the least prolific unsanctioned offenders were no different than non-offenders. Furthermore, youth who had friends who were more extensively involved in criminal behavior reported significantly lower subjective arrest probabilities.

Lochner (2007) used the National Longitudinal Survey of Youth 1997 (NLSY97) and the National Youth Survey (NYS) to estimate belief updating models of the probability of arrest among male respondents. In the NLSY97 analysis, he reported that individuals adjusted their subjective probabilities (of the risk of arrest for auto theft) upward in response to arrest in the previous year and downward in response to criminal behavior in the previous year, which, by controlling for arrest, signified successful or unsanctioned offending. Subjective probabilities were less responsive to the crime and arrest experiences of male siblings, although there was weak evidence that subjective probabilities were adjusted downward in response to sibling crime in the previous year (as reported by siblings themselves). In the NYS analysis, Lochner reported that the perceived probability of arrest (in 1986) for four different crimes (theft less than $50, theft greater than $50, breaking into a building or car, and aggravated assault) was significantly lower among males who had committed each of the offenses in the past two years. Although the impact of prior arrests on subjective probabilities was consistently large and positive, as expected, it failed to attain statistical significance.

Anwar and Loughran (2011) also tested a Bayesian updating model. Their sample comprised approximately 1,300 adjudicated youth from Arizona and Pennsylvania. These youth were interviewed a total of eight times in five years, and they provided information about their perceived likelihood of being caught and arrested for seven different crimes (each on a 0–10 scale), as well as their self-report frequency of involvement in seventeen different crimes. They then calculated arrest ratios as the ratio of officially recorded arrests to the number of self-report crimes. The findings were threefold. First, Anwar and Loughran found that during periods in which youth were criminally active, being arrested significantly increased subjective probabilities, although the effect diminished as more crimes were committed during the reference period. For example, youth who committed a single crime and were arrested increased their subjective probability by four points, and this magnitude was inversely proportional to the number of crimes. Second, they showed that experienced offenders placed relatively more weight on their prior subjective probabilities and therefore "updated less" in response to new arrests. Inexperienced offenders, by contrast, "updated more" by placing more weight on their arrest ratios and less weight on their prior subjective probabilities. The impact of arrest was therefore more salient (i.e., a stronger deterrent) early in one's criminal career. Third, Anwar and Loughran concluded that the impact of arrest on subjective probabilities was crime specific, or at least specific within a class of criminal behaviors. Specifically, youth arrested for "aggressive crimes" did not update their subjective probabilities concerning "income-generating crimes." Thus, there was no evidence of spillover effects of arrests for one class of crime to subjective probabilities about other classes of crime.

By way of summary, whereas research on the strength of the correlation between objective sanctions and risk perceptions (reviewed in the previous section) has revealed that individuals are typically poor judges of the certainty and severity of punishment (or at least imperfect estimates thereof), panel research on the experiential component of the perceptual deterrence model has revealed that personal experiences and, to a lesser degree, vicarious experiences with crime and punishment are salient determinants of changes in risk perceptions.

The consensus from risk updating research is that criminally naive individuals possess unusually high estimates of the subjective probability of arrest compared to experienced offenders. Naive individuals who then go on to initiate a "criminal career" tend to learn that the actual risk of apprehension is lower than they initially expected (their prior probability), and they therefore update (downward) their subjective certainty in later periods to bring it closer in line with their experiences (their posterior probability). On the other hand, the experience of arrest tends to lead to upward adjustments in subjective certainty. Stated simply, offenders update their subjective probabilities of arrest risk upward as a result of sanctioned offending, but they update them downward as a result of unsanctioned offending.

The nature of this perceptual updating process depends on at least two factors (Anwar and Loughran 2011). First, the impact of an arrest on perceived risk depends on the number of crimes committed within a reference window. For example, being arrested once leads to more updating for an offender who committed only one crime as opposed to an offender who committed ten crimes. In the case of the former, the "experienced arrest certainty" (Matsueda et al. 2006) is 100 percent, whereas in the case of the latter it is only 10 percent. Second, the impact of an arrest on perceived risk depends on how much criminal experience one has accumulated to a given point. Any given arrest is accorded less weight in the updating process as individuals accumulate a more extensive criminal history. In other words, the risk perceptions of experienced offenders are highly stable over time relative to those of novice offenders. These individuals have learned that they can offend with impunity, even if they do get caught on occasion.

IV. Situational Influences on Sanction Perceptions

The review of research to this point has concerned the impact that the objective and experiential features of punishment have on subjective probabilities of apprehension. We next consider the impact that situational characteristics have on subjective probabilities of punishment in specific circumstances. Studies of the situational context of criminal choice focus on the responsiveness of would-be offenders to immediate environmental cues. Of particular interest is the malleability of risk perceptions to proximal influences that include, but are not limited to, objective sanction risk. Three research traditions are considered: offender interviews, vignette research, and laboratory experiments.

A. Offender Interviews

Interviews with offenders have yielded many insights into situational decision making. This research tradition includes in-depth interviews with felony offenders who had recently been incarcerated (Shover and Thompson 1992), as well as active street criminals recruited by informants (Wright and Decker 1994, 1997; Jacobs and Wright 1999). A recurring theme in many such interviews is that offenders commonly experience an intense, pressing need for cash that borders on desperation (Shover and Thompson 1992; Wright and Decker 1994; Jacobs and Wright 1999). This suggests that much crime has an economic motivation but not in the sense that offenders face financial hardship and are pushed by circumstances beyond their control. On the contrary, Jacobs and Wright observed that many offenders are immersed in a street culture that rewards "fast living," which encompasses "fetishized consumption" of status-enhancing luxury goods and cash-intensive "every night is a Saturday night" illicit activities (e.g., gambling, heavy drinking, and hard drug use). Financial desperation arises when offenders need a quick infusion of cash in order to keep the party going, as it were. Crime is often the most efficient means available to resolve an offender's present financial crisis.

These observations are relevant from a perceptual deterrence perspective because such a lifestyle might constrain available options as perceived by offenders, as well as neutralize sanction threats in the offender's mind. For example, some offenders suppress their fear of getting caught by deliberately committing their offenses under the influence of alcohol or drugs. This has the consequence of robbing the threatened sanctions of their deterrent value (Wright and Decker 1994, 1997).

B. Vignette Research

As defined previously, vignette research provides respondents with hypothetical crime scenarios and asks them to imagine that they are the protagonist portrayed in the scenario. A unique feature of vignette research for the study of sanction perceptions is that investigators can vary the objective properties of punishment in order to determine the degree to which sanction perceptions are sensitive to situational information.

Klepper and Nagin (1989b) disseminated tax noncompliance scenarios to approximately 160 graduate students enrolled in a master's program in public management. Two basic noncompliance scenarios were studied: understating self-employment income by 25, 50, and 90 percent and overstating charitable deductions by 25, 50, and 90 percent. The investigators randomized actual self-employment income ($5,000 or $15,000) and actual charitable contributions ($1,000 or $5,000) across subjects and then inquired about subjects' perceived chance that the Internal Revenue Service would detect at least half of the noncompliance gamble, as well as the chance that the protagonist in the scenario would be criminally prosecuted if at least half of the gamble were detected. They found that the perceived risks of detection and prosecution were an increasing function of the percentage of the noncompliance gamble, whereas the perceived risk of detection was also influenced by the amount (in absolute dollars) of the noncompliance gamble. In the charitable deduction scenario, perceptions of detection risk were additionally shaped by the size of the noncompliance gamble for self-employment income. Klepper and Nagin also found that respondents who had been audited in the recent past reported a significantly higher probability of detection, but only in the self-employment income model.

Bachman, Paternoster, and Ward (1992) provided sexual assault scenarios to approximately 100 male undergraduates. After reading a set of scenarios in which six situational circumstances were varied, subjects reported the likelihood that the offender would be arrested as well as the likelihood that the offender would be dismissed from school, which were then combined into a summary scale of perceived risk of formal sanction. Bachman and colleagues found that subjects reported a significantly higher likelihood of formal sanction when the offender threatened or used physical force, when the offender injured the victim, when the victim did not permit the offender to kiss or fondle her, and when the offender and victim were not in a dating relationship. In other words, more serious offense circumstances were correlated with higher perceived sanction risk. Close inspection of the responses led the investigators to surmise that under the four aforementioned circumstances, subjects reported higher sanction risk because they believed the victim was more likely to report the offense.

C. Laboratory Experiments

Vignette research has demonstrated that it is feasible to randomize the situational features of hypothetical scenarios in order to study risk perceptions and crime decision making. Laboratory experiments provide an alternative approach by randomizing features of the situations that participants actually experience.

Loewenstein, Nagin, and Paternoster (1997) examined the degree to which male college students' state of physical arousal modified their risk perceptions in a scenario involving date rape. Before reading the sexual assault scenario, participants were randomly assigned to one of three arousal conditions: An "immediate arousal" group was exposed to sexually arousing material before reading the scenario, a "no arousal" group was exposed to sexually neutral material, and a "prior arousal" group was exposed to sexually arousing material a day prior to reading and reacting to the scenario. The scenario described a situation in which a male and a female had been drinking, returned to the female's apartment, and engaged in sexual foreplay, at which time the female expressed that she did not wish to have intercourse but did not physically resist. The participants were the male referent in the scenario, and they were asked how likely it is they would try to verbally coax the female to remove her clothes and how likely it is they would have sex with her even if she protested. Participants were then asked about their perceptions of the benefits (level of fun and vividness) as well as the negative consequences (discovery, arrest, dismissal from the university, and loss of respect from friends and family) of having sex with the scenario female. Unexpectedly, the investigators found that there were no significant differences in the perceived benefits or perceived risks by arousal condition. However, there was some indication that arousal level affected the weighing of the benefits and risks in the scenario. In particular, males in the arousal condition were more strongly deterred by the perceived risks in their intentions to be sexually aggressive in the scenario.

Gardner and Steinberg (2005) studied the impact of peer presence on the situational decision making of adolescents (ages 13–16 years), young adults (ages 18–22 years), and adults (ages 24+ years). Participants were randomly assigned to a group condition (with two same-aged peers) or to a sole participant condition, and then they completed a number of tasks, one of which involved completing a questionnaire measuring the relative benefits and risks of a variety of scenario behaviors. Participants in the group condition completed individual questionnaires, but they were allowed to discuss the scenarios with each other and were able to see the responses chosen by their counterparts. Individuals participating in groups assigned significantly greater weight to the perceived benefits as opposed to the costs of five risky activities (e.g., having sex without a condom, riding in a car driven by someone who has been drinking, and trying a new drug that one does not know anything about). Moreover, these differences were not age graded, confirming all decision makers were sensitive to a "risky shift" in their perceptions of risk in the presence of their peers.

The findings from the foregoing research traditions speak to the malleability of risk perceptions to the proximal features of crime contexts. There are three situational contingencies that are worthy of elaboration. One such contingency that emerges quite readily from in-depth interviews with offenders is the importance of substance use and abuse. Heavy use of alcohol and drugs negatively impacts a would-be offender's decision-making process by foreshortening consideration of the potential risks. Yet many would-be offenders resort to alcohol and drugs precisely because they are fully aware of the risks, and they require an ample amount of "liquid courage" before they are prepared to proceed with the criminal act. Abuse of alcohol and drugs desensitizes would-be offenders to considerations of failure or the risk of apprehension.

A second situational contingency concerns the susceptibility of individual perceptions to group processes. This has clear relevance for criminological research in light of the importance of co-offenders in criminal behavior, especially among youthful law violators. The "risky shift" phenomenon suggests that the presence of peers leads to changes not only in risky behavior but also in risk perceptions and the relative weighing of rewards and punishments (Gardner and Steinberg 2005).

A third contingency with respect to situational decision making is a person's level of affective and emotional arousal. Scholars have observed that individuals under "visceral control" can act without regard for their long-term self-interest, "often with full awareness that they are doing so" (Loewenstein 1996, p. 273). This has stark implications for the study of risk perceptions because most designs allow participants the opportunity to deliberate on the rewards and punishments of different courses of action, in the absence of environmental distractions, emotional arousal, and altered states of consciousness. Ariely and Loewenstein (2006) suggest that individual perceptions of benefits and risks under such conditions can produce misleading and error-prone results in decision-making research (for further discussion, see Nagin 2007).

V. A Dual-Process Perspective from Judgment and Decision-Making Research

Modern decision research appeals to choice models that push the boundaries beyond expected utility. This is because in some contexts, outcomes are evaluated in ways that are not strictly consistent with utility maximization, because decision makers possess "bounded rationality," and "satisfice" rather than optimize (Simon 1955). For example, some individuals do not sum the products of utilities and subjective probabilities in the manner anticipated by the expected utility model (Carroll 1978). Instead, the dimensions of crime opportunities (reward, punishment, reward probability, and punishment probability) tend to be evaluated additively. In addition, individuals exhibit "dimensional preferences" that are strongly tilted toward potential rewards as opposed to potential punishments and probabilities (Carroll 1978). Other crime-related limitations of the expected utility model concern the capacity that individuals have to form realistic subjective probabilities that obey the rules of probability theory, the cross-situational stability (transitivity) of preferences, and the global concavity of risk preferences (Johnson and Payne 1986; Lattimore and Witte 1986).

Alternatives to the expected utility model allow for decision making that is intuitive as opposed to strictly normative. For example, an early contribution by Tversky and Kahneman (1974) identified heuristics that individuals utilize in their formation of judgments about uncertain outcomes. Although these heuristics render decision making more efficient, under certain circumstances, they have the potential to introduce bias in subjective probabilities. The prospect theory of Kahneman and Tversky (1979) represented one formal effort to account for perceptual and behavioral anomalies that are not well predicted by the expected utility model. Although a thorough survey is beyond the scope of the present review, a number of empirical investigations of the use of heuristics in crime decision making have devoted attention to such judgment biases as the base rate fallacy (Scheider 2001), the gambler's fallacy (Pogarsky and Piquero 2003), and self-serving bias (Nagin and Pogarsky 2003).

Inspired by the departures from the more stylized version of rational choice, a tradition of research lying at the intersection of psychology and economics probes the cognitive underpinnings of risky decision making (Kahneman 2003). Of most relevance for criminologists is the development of dual-process models of decision making that integrate two cognitive systems—reasoned decision making (analytical, deliberative, "cold" state) and reactive decision making (intuitive, affective, "hot" state). Reasoned decision making, consistent with the prototypical rational choice model, is "based on conscious, deliberate evaluation of the costs and benefits of choice alternatives" (Albert and Steinberg 2011, p. 215). Yet as observed in the foregoing section, certain situational contingencies—pharmacological, interpersonal, and emotional ones—have a demonstrated tendency to override this cognitive system, leading to an imbalance in which decision making is less reasoned and more reactive.

Reactive decision making characterizes behavior "in the heat of the moment" and tends to be more heavily influenced by habit, heuristics, and social desirability. This type of decision making has the capacity to narrow one's perceived behavioral options, restrict the nature or source of acquired information, alter perceptions of rewards and punishments, or tip the reward–punishment balance in favor of the former (Loewenstein 1996). Interest in the reactive component of the dual-process model has been especially pronounced in developmental psychology, in which concerns are routinely voiced about psychosocial maturity and criminal responsibility with respect to adolescent decision making (Steinberg and Scott 2003). This research tradition has contributed to the integration of neuropsychological concepts into developmental models of risky decision making (Steinberg 2008). Yet the model has applicability well beyond adolescence, and it can be fruitfully invoked by researchers who are generally interested in situational influences on risk perceptions and crime decision making.

The dual-process model has important implications for understanding the degree to which risk perceptions are incorporated into decision making. For example, van Gelder and de Vries (2014) explain that reasoned decision making is responsive to risks, rewards, and probabilities, whereas reactive decision making is "largely unresponsive to outcomes and probabilities" (p. 4), and that the two cognitive modes can yield very different outcomes (see also van Gelder 2013).

VI. Discussion and Conclusion

Deterrence is the behavioral response to the perception of sanction threats. In virtually every major review of deterrence theory, emphasis is placed on the importance of research on the perceptual underpinnings of compliance with the law (Cook 1980; Nagin 1998, 2013; Paternoster 2010). Indeed, devising sensible deterrence-based crime policies requires knowledge of the determinants of sanction perceptions, as well as how those perceptions are incorporated into crime decision making. Our review in this chapter has been an attempt to consider several facets of sanction perceptions, including their accuracy, updating, and situational malleability.

In our view, a great deal of promise is held in the consideration of situational influences on perceptions and behavior, coupled with the development of dual-process models of decision making. The findings from this research tradition speak to the malleability of risk perceptions to the proximal features of crime contexts. There are three situational contingencies on which we elaborate here: substance use and abuse, group dynamics, and emotional arousal. These research developments promise to enrich the study of situational decision making with respect to criminal behavior.

One situational contingency that emerges quite readily from in-depth interviews with offenders is the importance of substance use and abuse. The most obvious implication is that heavy use of alcohol and drugs negatively impacts a would-be offender's decision-making process by foreshortening consideration of the potential risks. However, there is a less obvious take-away point from this research. Many would-be offenders resort to alcohol and drugs because they are fully aware of the risks and require an ample amount of "liquid courage" before they are prepared to proceed with the criminal act. Interviews with active offenders reveal that the devotion of conscious thought to the possibility of failure or the risk of apprehension is a serious liability during the criminal act. Abuse of alcohol and drugs desensitizes would-be offenders to such considerations.

A second situational contingency is the susceptibility of individual perceptions to group dynamics. This has clear relevance for criminological research in light of the importance of co-offenders in criminal behavior, especially among youthful law violators. The "risky shift" phenomenon suggests that the presence of peers leads to changes not only in risky behavior but also in risk perceptions and the relative weighing of rewards and punishments (Gardner and Steinberg 2005).

A third contingency with respect to situational decision making is a person's level of affective and emotional arousal (Loewenstein 1996; Ariely and Loewenstein 2006). Scholars have observed that individuals under "visceral control" can act without regard for their long-term self-interest, "often with full awareness that they are doing so" (Loewenstein 1996, p. 273). This has stark implications for the study of risk perceptions because most designs allow participants the opportunity to deliberate on the rewards and punishments of different courses of action, in the absence of environmental distractions, emotional arousal, and altered states of consciousness. Ariely and Loewenstein suggest that individual perceptions of benefits and risks under such conditions can produce misleading and error-prone results in decision-making research (for further discussion, see Nagin 2007).

The perceptual deterrence tradition in criminology has been reinvigorated by recent efforts, across several disciplines, to better understand the perceptual underpinnings of risky behavior. There remains much to be learned, and the jury is still out on whether perceptual deterrence research will yield findings that are truly actionable with respect to crime control policy (for discussion, see Paternoster 2010). However, there can be little doubt that this research will enrich criminology.

REFERENCES

Albert, D., and L. Steinberg. 2011. "Judgment and Decision Making in Adolescence." *Journal of Research on Adolescence* 21:211–24.

Anwar, S., and T. A. Loughran. 2011. "Testing a Bayesian Learning Theory of Deterrence Among Serious Juvenile Offenders." *Criminology* 49:667–98.

Apel, R. 2013. "Sanctions, Perceptions, and Crime: Implications for Criminal Deterrence." *Journal of Quantitative Criminology* 29:67–101.

Apel, R., and D. S. Nagin. 2011. "General Deterrence: A Review of Recent Evidence." In *Crime and Public Policy*, edited by J. Q. Wilson and J. Petersilia, 4th ed, pp. 411–36. New York: Oxford University Press.

Ariely, D., and G. Loewenstein. 2006. "The Heat of the Moment: The Effect of Sexual Arousal on Sexual Decision Making." *Journal of Behavioral Decision Making* 19:87–98.

Assembly Committee on Criminal Procedure. 1968. *Deterrent Effects of Criminal Sanctions.* Sacramento, CA: Assembly of the State of California.

Bachman, R., R. Paternoster, and S. Ward. 1992. "The Rationality of Sexual Offending: Testing a Deterrence/Rational Choice Conception of Sexual Assault." *Law and Society Review* 26:343–72.

Beccaria, C. 1963. *On Crimes and Punishments,* translated by Henry Paolucci. New York: Macmillan. (Originally published 1764.)

Becker, G. S. 1968. "Crime and Punishment: An Economic Approach." *Journal of Political Economy* 76:169–217.

Bentham, J. 1988. *The Principles of Morals and Legislation.* Amherst, NY: Prometheus. (Originally published 1789.)

Carroll, J. S. 1978. "A Psychological Approach to Deterrence: The Evaluation of Crime Opportunities." *Journal of Personality and Social Psychology* 36:1512–20.

Claster, D. S. 1967. "Comparison of Risk Perception Between Delinquents and Non-delinquents." *Journal of Criminal Law and Criminology* 58:80–86.

Cook, P. J. 1980. "Research in Criminal Deterrence: Laying the Groundwork for the Second Decade." *Crime and Justice: An Annual Review of Research* 2:211–68.

Gardner, M., and L. Steinberg. 2005. "Peer Influence on Risk Taking, Risk Preference, and Risky Decision Making in Adolescence and Adulthood: An Experimental Study." *Developmental Psychology* 41:625–35.

Geerken, M. R., and W. R. Gove. 1975. "Deterrence: Some Theoretical Considerations." *Law and Society Review* 9:497–513.

Gibbs, J. P. 1975. *Crime, Punishment, and Deterrence.* New York: Elsevier.

Horney, J., and I. H. Marshall. 1992. "Risk Perceptions Among Serious Offenders: The Role of Crime and Punishment." *Criminology* 30:575–93.

Jacobs, B. A., and R. Wright. 1999. "Stick-up, Street Culture, and Offender Motivation." *Criminology* 37:149–73.

Johnson, E., and J. Payne. 1986. "The Decision to Commit a Crime: An Information-Processing Analysis." In *The Reasoning Criminal: Rational Choice Perspectives on Offending,* edited by D. B. Cornish and R. V. Clarke, pp. 170–85. New York: Springer.

Kahneman, D. 2003. "Maps of Bounded Rationality: Psychology for Behavioral Economics." *American Economic Review* 93:1449–75.

Kahneman, D., and A. Tversky. 1979. "Prospect Theory: An Analysis of Decision Under Risk." *Econometrica* 47:263–91.

Klepper, S., and Nagin, D. 1989a. "The Deterrent Effect of Perceived Certainty and Severity Revisited." *Criminology* 27:721–46.

Klepper, S., and Nagin, D. 1989b. "Tax Compliance and Perceptions of the Risks of Detection and Criminal Prosecution." *Law and Society Review* 23:209–40.

Lattimore, P., and A. Witte. 1986. "Models of Decision Making Under Uncertainty: The Criminal Choice." In *The Reasoning Criminal: Rational Choice Perspectives on Offending,* edited by D. B. Cornish and R. V. Clarke, pp. 129–55. New York: Springer.

Lochner, L. 2007. "Individual Perceptions of the Criminal Justice System." *American Economic Review* 97:444–60.

Loewenstein, G. 1996. "Out of Control: Visceral Influences on Behavior." *Organizational Behavior and Human Decision Processes* 65:272–92.

Loewenstein, G., D. Nagin, and R. Paternoster. 1997. "The Effect of Sexual Arousal on Expectations of Sexual Forcefulness." *Journal of Research in Crime and Delinquency* 34: 443–73.

MacCoun, R., R. L. Pacula, J. Chriqui, K. Harris, and P. Reuter. 2009. "Do Citizens Know Whether Their State Has Decriminalized Marijuana? Assessing the Perceptual Component of Deterrence Theory." *Review of Law and Economics* 5:347–71.

Manski, C. F. 2004. "Measuring Expectations." *Econometrica* 72:1329–76.

Matsueda, R. L., D. A. Kreager, and D. Huizinga. 2006. "Deterring Delinquents: A Rational Choice Model of Theft and Violence." *American Sociological Review* 71:95–122.

Nagin, D. S. 1998. "Criminal Deterrence Research at the Outset of the Twenty-First Century." *Crime and Justice: A Review of Research* 23:1–42

Nagin, D. S. 2007. "Moving Choice to Center Stage in Criminological Research and Theory: The American Society of Criminology 2006 Sutherland Address." *Criminology* 45:259–72.

Nagin, D. S. 2013. "Deterrence in the Twenty-First Century." *Crime and Justice: A Review of Research* 42:199–263.

Nagin, D. S., and G. Pogarsky. 2001. "Integrating Celerity, Impulsivity, and Extralegal Sanction Threats Into a Model of General Deterrence: Theory and Evidence." *Criminology* 39:865–91.

Nagin, D. S., and G. Pogarsky. 2003. "An Experimental Investigation of Deterrence: Cheating, Self-Serving Bias, and Impulsivity." *Criminology* 41:167–93.

Nagin, D. S., R. M. Solow, and C. Lum. 2015. "Deterrence, Criminal Opportunities, and Police." *Criminology* 53:74–100.

Paternoster, R. 1987. "The Deterrent Effect of the Perceived Certainty and Severity of Punishment: A Review of the Evidence and Issues." *Justice Quarterly* 4:173–217.

Paternoster, R. 2010. "How Much Do We Really Know About Criminal Deterrence?" *Journal of Criminal Law and Criminology* 100:765–823.

Piliavin, I., C. Thornton, R. Gartner, and R. L. Matsueda. 1986. "Crime, Deterrence, and Rational Choice." *American Sociological Review* 51:101–19.

Pogarsky, G., and A. R. Piquero. 2003. "Can Punishment Encourage Offending? Investigating the 'Resetting' Effect. *Journal of Research in Crime and Delinquency* 40:95–120.

Ross, H. L. 1973. "Law, Science, and Accidents: The British Road Safety Act of 1967." *Journal of Legal Studies* 2:1–78.

Saltzman, L. E., R. Paternoster, G. P. Waldo, and T. G. Chiricos. 1982. "Deterrent and Experiential Effects: The Problem of Causal Order in Perceptual Deterrence Research." *Journal of Research in Crime and Delinquency* 19:172–89.

Scheider, M. C. 2001. "Deterrence and the Base Rate Fallacy: An Examination of Perceived Certainty." *Justice Quarterly* 18:63–86.

Shover, N., and C. Y. Thompson. 1992. "Age, Differential Expectations, and Crime Desistance." *Criminology* 30:89–104.

Simon, H. A. 1955. "A Behavioral Model of Rational Choice." *Quarterly Journal of Economics* 69:99–118.

Stafford, M. C., and M. Warr. 1993. "A Reconceptualization of General and Specific Deterrence." *Journal of Research in Crime and Delinquency* 30:123–35.

Steinberg, L. 2008. "A Social Neuroscience Perspective on Adolescent Risk-Taking." *Developmental Review* 28:78–106.

Steinberg, L., and E. S. Scott. 2003. "Less Guilty by Reason of Adolescence: Developmental Immaturity, Diminished Responsibility, and the Juvenile Death Penalty." *American Psychologist* 58:1009–18.

Tversky, A., and D. Kahneman. 1974. "Judgment Under Uncertainty: Heuristics and Biases." *Science* 185:1124–31.

van Gelder, J. L. 2013. "Beyond Rational Choice: The Hot/Cool Perspective of Criminal Decision Making." *Psychology, Crime and Law* 19:745–63.

van Gelder, J. L., and R. E. de Vries. 2014. "Rational Misbehavior? Evaluating an Integrated Dual-Process Model of Criminal Decision Making." *Journal of Quantitative Criminology* 30:1–27.

Waldo, G. P., and T. G. Chiricos. 1972. "Perceived Penal Sanction and Self-Reported Criminality: A Neglected Approach to Deterrence Research." *Social Problems* 19:522–40.

Wright, B. R. E., A. Caspi, T. E. Moffitt, and R. Paternoster. 2004. "Does the Perceived Risk of Punishment Deter Criminally Prone Individuals? Rational Choice, Self-Control, and Crime." *Journal of Research in Crime and Delinquency* 41:180–213.

Wright, R. T., and S. H. Decker. 1994. *Burglars on the Job: Streetlife and Residential Break-Ins.* Boston: Northeastern University Press.

Wright, R. T., and S. H. Decker. 1997. *Armed Robbers in Action: Stickups and Street Culture.* Boston: Northeastern University Press.

Zimring, F. E., and G. J. Hawkins. 1973. *Deterrence: The Legal Threat in Crime Control.* Chicago: University of Chicago Press.

CHAPTER 8

....

GAME THEORY

....

HEIKO RAUHUT

I. FOUNDATIONS OF GAME THEORY

....

MOST research on crime acknowledges that offender decision making does not take place in a vacuum. Nevertheless, most analytically oriented research applies decision theory to understand offenders. Tsebelis (1989) illustrates why this is a problem by using two examples: the decision to stay at home when rain is probable and the decision to speed when one is in a hurry. The first seems an appropriate problem for decision theory. An actor evaluates the probability of rain and the missed utility when staying at home and then selects the alternative with the highest expected utility. The point here is that the probability of rain is independent of the strategy of the actor.

In contrast, the decision to speed is not such a game against "nature." Speeding can result in two different outcomes: getting to work faster or getting caught, fined, and delayed. The probability of getting caught is not a "random," independent event; it depends on the activities of policemen, particularly their resources and their strategy when and where to control speeding. For example, policemen will try to anticipate when and where speeders are frequent and may control more at trafficked streets during rush hours than at remote places early in the morning. This may be anticipated by speeders, however, who may rather take side streets and drive faster at less obvious times. This, in turn, may also be anticipated by speed controllers and so on. In addition, there may even be further actors involved, such as victims, bystanders, judges, politicians, and even journalists, whose actions may influence the actions of lawbreakers and guardians likewise.

Speeding, similar to many other offenses, should therefore be analyzed by a theory of interdependent decision making. Game theory provides a useful methodology for analyzing the interactional dynamics of interdependent decision makers. It enables deriving predictions of the decisions of offenders and law enforcers and fosters the understanding of the emerging macrostructural patterns of crime and control. Game theory has become influential in economics, political science, and sociology. It is valuable for criminology because it forces theorists to make explicit assumptions about preferences and constraints of offenders, co-offenders, victims, guardians, and law enforcement agents. This allows theorists to model explicitly the strategic interaction structure between the involved players. This provides novel, interesting, and testable hypotheses, which are derived from deep assumptions about interdependent decision making.

Game theory provides tools for analyzing how actors decide as if they tried to realize their preferences as good as possible under given restrictions. In particular, actors are assumed to take the preferences and restrictions of all other involved players into account. Hence, it is assumed that everybody forms beliefs about the others' preferences and payoffs and maximizes own payoffs under these restrictions.

Game theory can be described as a universal language for the unification of the social and behavioral sciences (Gintis 2000, 2007). It may be described as a branch of rational choice theory, although the term "rational" is not necessary and may be confusing. It is also possible to describe game theory as a branch of "analytical sociology" (Hedström and Bearman 2009) or as a branch of law and economics (Baird, Gertner, and Randal Picker 1994). In general, it is a rigorous, mathematical approach for analyzing social interactions.

Game theory can be described by five elements (see also Diekmann and Voss 2004; Raub and Buskens 2004; Voss 2006). The most basic prerequisite of game theory is that actors hold resources that they can use for their goals. This requires at least two choice alternatives from which actors can select. Resources can refer to opportunities and restrictions, such as time, money, market prices, institutions, social norms, legal rules, general policies, contracts, and social control. They can also refer to probabilities of certain events, such as detection of norm violations and expected severity of punishments.

Goals are typically referred to as "preferences." The most basic ones may be physical well-being and social approval. However, other-regarding preferences can be included, such as inequity aversion (Fehr and Schmidt 1999), altruism (Andreoni 1989), and social value orientation (Van Lange 1999; Murphy and Ackermann 2014). Risk preferences can be specified in terms of risk neutrality, risk aversion, and risk seekingness.

An important scope condition of game theory is its focus on situations of strategic interdependence. The probability that actor A reaches a certain goal depends on the strategies of all other involved actors B, C, . . ., Z. Different from the case of assessing the probability of rain, the probability of reaching a goal in interdependent social situations depends on the behavior and beliefs of other actors. A has to anticipate the decisions of B, C, . . ., Z, and they have to anticipate the decision of A, given their own beliefs about the beliefs of A (and so on).

The theory also specifies a decision rule. In general, actors are assumed to use their resources such that they reach their goals "as good as possible." As good as possible could mean to maximize own utility, to maximize subjective expected utility, or to merely satisfice a certain threshold under "bounded rationality." The most well-known decision rule is the Nash equilibrium (Nash 1951). The Nash equilibrium is a combination of strategies in which all players maximize their expected utility, given all others' strategies. In equilibrium, no player has an incentive to unilaterally change his or her strategy. In other words, the combination of all strategies in equilibrium are best replies to each other. Note that the equilibrium is simultaneously a decision rule for individual actors and an aggregation rule, specifying how all decisions interact and generate a social structure.

In summary, game theory can be described by the following five elements:

1. The basic units of investigation are actors.
2. Actors hold resources, have preferences, and can select among at least two alternatives.
3. The scope refers to situations of strategic interdependence, in which the probability of reaching a goal depends on the decisions of all other involved actors.
4. Actors hold beliefs about the preferences, resources, choice alternatives, and beliefs of the other actors.
5. The theory specifies a decision rule—how all actors decide. The decision rule is simultaneously the aggregation rule, specifying how all decisions aggregate to emergent social structures.

Note that these prerequisites do not imply specific assumptions about selfishness, far-sightedness, or rationality. Game theory is quite flexible and offers a general framework for analyzing social interactions. There is a whole branch of game theory that analyzes how altruistic or prosocial actors decide in interdependent social situations (Camerer 2003). It is also not required that actors are assumed to be rational. Actors can be myopic (Jackson and Wolinsky 1996; Eaton and Wen 2008), bounded rational (Simon 1955), or even backward-looking learners (Macy and Flache 2002).

The specification of strategic interaction situations requires a minimal set of definitions (see also Braun and Gautschi 2011, p. 147f):

Players refer to actors who engage in the same interaction situation. They can represent individuals but also corporate actors such as organizations including the mafia, the police, or political parties. Sometimes, "nature" is a fictitious additional player, referring to a random event.

Choice alternatives refer to the moves each player can make at a certain stage of the game. There are games in which players move simultaneously and others in which they move sequentially one after each other.

Information refers to the knowledge of each player at a certain stage of the game. "Common knowledge" refers to situations in which decision rules of all players, the structure of the game, and the moves by nature are all known by all players and all players know that everybody knows (and so on). Incomplete information refers to the case in which at least some parts of the structure of the game or the types of players are unknown to at least some players.

Strategies are complete rules that specify for each stage of the game which action is to be taken by the players. A pure strategy is a deterministic rule of action. A mixed strategy is a random distribution over pure strategies.

Payoffs refer to the utility players receive after everybody has decided about all alternatives at each stage of the game.

The following sections present intuitive applications of game theory in the fields of offender decision making, criminology, and sociology of social norms, deviance, and crime. For in-depth introductions to game theory, see Dixit and Skeath (2004) and Gintis (2000); for game theory textbooks with a focus on law and crime, see Baird et al. (1994); and for a textbook about its empirical validity and development toward "behavioral game theory," see Camerer (2003).

II. APPLICATIONS OF GAME THEORY TO OFFENDER DECISION MAKING

The examples presented in this section illustrate how game theory can be used for analyzing offender decision making. The examples are structured by three fundamental categories of games. The first category refers to *simultaneous games*. Here, each actor chooses his or her alternative without knowledge of the actions of all other players. The problem here is to build the best possible expectations about the others' behaviors to get the best out of the situation.

Simultaneous strategic interaction situations are fundamentally different from *sequential games*. If games are sequential, at least one player has multiple moves, whose sequence is determined by at least one move of the opponent. The later players have at least some information of the moves of the earlier players so that they can make their strategy contingent on what the others have done.

The third class of examples refers to games with *incomplete information*. Here, at least some parts of the structure of the game are unknown to at least some players. I discuss cases in which *alter* can have different types and this is only known to alter and not to *ego*. Ego has to move first but can observe either a credible or an unreliable signal of alter.

A. Simultaneous Games

Security games are an important application of simultaneous games to offender decision making. A key characteristic of crime is that it cannot be controlled omnipotently. There are not enough resources to protect ports, airports, buses, trains, warehouses, schools, and other infrastructure facilities around the clock. This means that security resources have to be deployed selectively. Speed controls on streets, drug controls in trains, and targeted weapons controls at airports operate at specific times and locations. However, any systematic pattern is likely to be exploited by adversaries. If speed patrols are always on the same street on Wednesdays at 5 p.m., rushed commuters will soon realize it, drive slowly only on Wednesdays at the exact control spot, and speed home at all other times and on all other streets. Similarly, terrorist attackers will observe control patterns at airports and try to exploit systematic patterns.

Security games can be defined by two players, the defendant and the attacker, who have reversed payoffs. If the attacker attacks a target while the defendant protects it, the attacker has worse payoffs than when it was not covered. The defender has the opposite payoff structure and is better off if he or she protects the target during an attempted attack. The defender's best strategy is to randomize such that control cannot be anticipated by the attacker. Randomization, however, is difficult for humans to do and may require computational support in complex situations. Security games are extensively studied by Tambe (2011), whose research group has also developed a number of computational programs to assist airports, ports, and other infrastructure to randomize their control and optimize their fielding of resources. Note that security games are also quite similar to inspection games (Tsebelis 1989; Rauhut 2009), which are extensively discussed later. It is obvious from the description of security games that the players do not know the choices of their opponents when they have to select their own choices. Hence, the strategic interaction situation can be described by a simultaneous game.

B. Sequential Games

In contrast to simultaneous games, sequential games refer to situations in which actors decide one after each other and have at least some information about the previous moves of their opponents. A widespread application of a sequential game is the problem to place and honor trust.

Trust can be modeled by the so-called trust game (Camerer and Weigelt 1988; Dasgupta 1988; Coleman 1990; Buskens and Raub 2002). There are two players. The trustor moves first and has to decide whether to place trust in the trustee or not. If trust is denied, the interaction terminates and the status quo remains. If trust is placed, the trustee can decide whether to honor or abuse trust. If trust is placed and honored, both players earn a higher payoff than the status quo. However, the trustee has a temptation to abuse trust because he or she receives an even higher payoff than when honoring trust. In this case, the trustor receives the worst payoff. If this is anticipated by the trustor, trust is not placed and both cannot enjoy welfare gains. This payoff structure defines the trust problem and reveals two dilemmas (Raub 2009). By placing trust, the trustor risks being abused; however, if trust is not placed, both are worse off than if trust had been placed and honored.

Examples of trust games are sending deficient products or delaying payments on eBay (Diekmann et al. 2014), economic fraud committed in second-hand markets for used cars (Buskens and Weesie 2000), and taxi drivers who risk being deceived or assaulted by customers (Gambetta and Hamill 2005). An interesting and classical instructive example of a serious offense is the strategic interaction between kidnapper and victim. Schelling (1960) depicts a kidnapper who has to decide to kill or return her hostage after having received the ransom money. The kidnapper prefers not to kill her hostage due to empathy and lower punishment in case of conviction. However, the hostage has seen the kidnapper's face and could reveal distinguishing marks to the police. The hostage promises to keep silent; however, once she has been released, her promise is not credible anymore. A solution to this problem is that the kidnapper chooses a remarkable hostage, such as a person who has committed a crime with the kidnapper as the only witness: "If the victim has committed an act whose disclosure could lead to blackmail, he may confess it; if not, he might commit one in the presence of his captor, to create the bond that will ensure his silence" (Schelling 1960, pp. 42–43).

Another important application of sequential games to offender decision making is the "norm game" (Heckathorn 1989; Coleman 1990; Voss 2001; Fehr and Gächter 2002). In situations in which non-cooperative behavior and norm violations are observable by bystanders but social control and punishment have to be enforced by informal observers, enforcement is often costly. The decision to admonish a polluter, to report a cheating student to the professor, to report a shoplifter to the store, or to stop an aggressor harming his victim in a public street are all actions that entail costs to the informal enforcer. Third-party enforcers may prefer that offenders are stopped and sanctioned. However, enforcement is often costly or risky. It often does not pay off to enforce a norm, especially if strangers interact who will never see each other again so that future cooperative behavior of the norm violator cannot be enjoyed by the enforcer. This makes enforcement not credible, which is anticipated by offenders, making norm violations more likely. Game theory can help predict under which conditions control and punishment are more likely to be performed and more likely to induce cooperative behavior (Camerer 2003; Fehr and Gintis 2007; Diekmann, Przepiorka, and Rauhut 2015).

C. Games with Incomplete Information

In games with complete information, all players know all choice alternatives, payoffs, and other characteristics of the game of all players at any point in time. Games with *incomplete information* can be characterized by a preceding move by *nature*, which is unobserved by at least one player. A move by nature means that there is a random event by which the game structure or by which the types of players are determined.

An important class of games with incomplete information is *signalling games*. Signalling theory analyzes an elementary problem of communication: "How can an agent, the receiver, establish whether another agent, the signaler, is telling or otherwise conveying the truth about a state of affairs or event which the signaler might have an interest to misrepresent?" (Gambetta 2009b, p. 168). A typical problem is to find out the type of the opponent: Is he or she trustworthy or undeserving, cooperative or selfish, honest or dishonest, strong or weak, risk-seeking or risk-averse, hardworking or lazy, well connected or solitary, patient or impulsive, smart or naive? This class of games is particularly important for the analysis of offender decision making because there are many traits and actions that criminals, victims, and police agents have an interest to hide.

Applications of signalling theory have to satisfy four conditions (Gambetta 2009b, pp. 172, 175):

1. There is some action the receiver can do that benefits the signaler, whether or not he or she has a certain quality or type.
2. This action benefits the receiver if and only if the signaler truly has the property and otherwise hurts him or her.
3. There is information asymmetry between the signaler, who knows his or her type, and the receiver, who does not.
4. The signaler can commit an action with a cost that is sufficiently high so that it discriminates between truthful signalers and pretending mimicries. The action must have a sufficient cost differential between what a truthful signaler can and what a mimicry cannot afford to pay to receive the benefit of the receiver.

Instructive applications of signalling theory to offender decision making are given by Gambetta (2009a). Reviews and summaries of Gambetta's work are given by Przepiorka (2010) and Dixit (2011). An interesting example is the "job market" for criminals. It is risky to find trustworthy, serious co-offenders. Offenders want to avoid "wannabes" and undercover agents. An extreme, but in the mafia, ubiquitous signal of seriousness is to commit a murder in the presence of others. Although a serious offender aiming at a long-standing criminal career may afford such a signal, an undercover agent would never commit a murder just to establish trust.

This example fulfills all four conditions of signalling theory mentioned previously: First, the criminal employer (the receiver) can give a job in the criminal organization to the applicant (the sender), which benefits the applicant whether or not he is serious. Second, this action only benefits the employer if the applicant is a serious offender and negatively affects him if the applicant is an undercover agent or a wannabe. Third, the applicant knows his type, but the employer does not. Fourth, the applicant can commit a murder to establish trust. The risk of conviction and the moral cost of committing a murder are outweighed by a long criminal career for a serious offender. An undercover agent cannot afford the risk and the costs of committing a murder because this would not be covered by his agency. A wannabe cannot afford the risk and the costs of committing a murder because he is not serious and ruthless enough.

Another interesting example by Gambetta (2009a) is communication and fighting among prison inmates. One important goal of inmates is to establish good standing in the prison hierarchy. One way of doing so is to engage in fights. However, fights are costly, so prison inmates do not want to waste energy fighting opponents who are too weak and do not want to risk losing against opponents who are too strong. Fighting ability can be communicated truthfully by scars from knife stabs or bullet wounds, indicating that the signaler has been in and survived many fights. It is also possible to derive structural hypotheses from signalling theory about the level of aggression in different prison regimes. Interestingly, fights are more likely to occur in prisons with strict regimes, in which encounters between prisoners are rare. Here, information about fighting ability is more difficult to communicate by signals, so it has to be experienced directly by participating in many fights.

III. Crime and Punishment from a Game Theoretical Perspective

This section presents an in-depth example of a game theoretical model on crime and punishment, provides results from several experiments of the model, and discusses a number of theoretical and practical implications of the results. This shall illustrate the benefits (and problems) of game theoretical models in the area of offender decision making. This section also presents the formal model and shows how point predictions can be derived. By using monetary payoffs in experimental games, these predictions can be translated into real, detailed interaction situations in which behaviors of people can be compared with predictions. This allows empirical corroborations with high internal validity.

The impact of punishment severity on crime is a key topic for criminology and for understanding offender decision making. Game theory can offer novel insights on how punishment severity affects both the level of crime and the level of control. This yields a novel understanding of the strategic interaction structure between criminals and guardians.

The model is motivated by the fact that a certain proportion of offenses and crimes go undetected. Examples include tax evasion, doping in sports, fare dodging, and many other forms of criminal behaviors. These socially undesirable behaviors are often monitored by inspectors such as policemen, conductors, guards, night watchmen, private detectives, or doping testers. In these situations, offenders and inspectors typically have opposite incentive structures. Whereas inspectors are rewarded for successful detections of crimes, offenders try to pass undetected.

A crucial problem is to find the right incentives to increase law abidance. Standard approaches are to increase punishment severity (Becker 1968; Clarke 1995; Friedman 1995; Levitt 2002) or to increase rewards for successful inspectors (Allingham and Sandmo 1972; Andreoni, Erard, and Feinstein 1998). However, empirical deterrence research has shown that crime and control incentives do not affect respective behavior in such a simple and direct way (Cook 1980; Williams and Hawkins 1986; Nagin 1998; Doob and Webster 2003). It seems that punishment severity has relatively little impact on crime, whereas subjective beliefs about the detection likelihood are much more important (Kahan 1997; Lochner 2007). A game theoretical perspective can contribute a micromechanism showing how beliefs about detection probabilities of offenders and control agents interact dynamically so that they can explain some of the findings in empirical deterrence research.

A. Models Without Interdependent Decision Making

In classical rational choice theory, punishment severity and detection probability are the key variables for explaining crime. However, in the traditional approach, there is no interactive element—what matters is the utility maximization of offenders. The probability of punishment is typically fixed and not determined by beliefs and decisions of control agents.

The seminal article by Gary Becker (1968) builds the basis of such a "non-interdependent" decision-making model on crime and punishment. Becker regards crime as rational behavior, accessible to standard market equilibrium analysis. Criminals are regarded as utility maximizers who optimize their payoffs under restrictions and risk. Criminals have clear incentives for criminal conduct; they gain material utility for theft or burglaries and also immaterial gains, such as for assaults.

The basic model of Becker (1968) can be specified as follows. Let offender i receive the combined monetary and psychic payoff y from a certain crime. Let her face conviction probability c to receive punishment p. Therefore, the expected utility π from crime for offender i is denoted by $\pi_i = c(y - p) + (1 - c)(y)$ (Becker 1968, p. 177). This means that with probability c, crime is detected and punishment costs have to be paid, which is more loss than what is to be gained by crime. With the reversed probability $1 - c$, payoffs from crime can be enjoyed without punishment costs.[1]

Now let s_i denote the likelihood that offender i commits the crime. Utility maximization of risk-neutral offenders implies that offenders commit crimes for sure (i.e., $s_i = 1$) when the expected utility from crime is positive (i.e., $y - cp > 0$). If expected payoffs from crime are negative (i.e., $y - cp < 0$), offenders refrain from crime (i.e., $s_i = 0$). By rearranging terms, the payoff of offender i can be written as follows:

$$\pi_i = (s_i) = s_i (y - cp) \tag{8.1}$$

From this perspective, higher punishment and higher conviction probabilities decrease crimes. Becker (1968) used this model to derive "optimal" levels of crime for a society for given punishment costs and harm done to victims.

Although Becker's (1968) analysis focuses on offenders' decisions, it completely neglects decisions of control agents. However, the detection probability is largely driven by beliefs and decision making of control agents. This implies that crime is a strategic interaction problem between offenders and control agents. Crime cannot be analyzed by only focusing on offenders' decisions. More generally, if decision theoretical problems are confounded with problems of strategic interaction, conclusions are often misguided. Tsebelis (1989) termed this confusion between decision and game theoretical reasoning the Robinson Crusoe fallacy. For the case of crime and punishment, there may be a lack of incentives for individual police officers to make major inspection efforts.

B. Game Theoretical Model of Interdependent Decision Making

The model of Becker (1968) ignores interdependent decision making: The detection probability is modeled as an exogenous factor. This ignores that detection probability is generated by the beliefs and the decision making of inspectors.

A specific model of strategic interdependent decision making between offenders and control agents is the so-called "inspection game." The inspection game has been theoretically developed by Tsebelis (1989, 1990). Earlier, Graetz, Reinganum, and Wilde (1986) proposed a similar game with respect to tax compliance. Notable is also early work by Wittman (1985), who exemplifies counterintuitive results in games with mixed strategies (although he does not explicitly apply these games to inspection situations). Holler (1993) discusses an inspection game structure with respect to pollution, in which polluters play against enforcers. The first experimental test of inspection games was contributed by Rauhut (2009). Agent-based simulations of learning models in inspection games and their experimental test are given by Rauhut and Junker (2009). A review of the mathematical properties of inspection games is given by Andreozzi (2010).

The inspection game is based on the assumption that the payoffs of offenders and control agents are in complete conflict, where success of one party implies failure for the other. Rational and selfish offenders will commit crimes when they believe they will not be caught, and rational and selfish control personnel will make inspection efforts when they believe offenders will commit crimes. The underlying payoff structure is formally called a "zero-sum game."

The inspection game can be formalized as follows. The offender part is similar to the rational choice model of Becker (1968). Offender i can decide to commit a crime with payoff y and punishment costs p if caught. If she does not commit a crime, her payoffs remain unchanged.

The novel part in the game theoretical model is the specification of the decision-making structure of control agents. Inspectors can decide to inspect offenders. Inspector j has to invest inspection costs k to detect the action of offender i. If an inspector catches the offender for having committed a crime, the inspector receives the reward r. If not successful, inspection costs are lost. If she does not inspect, she remains at her payoff level. It is further assumed that undetected crime is attractive and punishment is a real threat—that is, $p > y > 0$.[2] Likewise, inspectors are assumed to gain from successful inspections—that is, $r > k > 0$. The strategic interaction between offenders and control agents is illustrated by the two-by-two game matrix in the so-called "normal form" (Table 8.1). Normal form

Table 8.1 The inspection game

		inspector j	
		inspect	not inspect
offender i	crime	$y-p$, $r-k$ ⇐	y , 0
		⇓	⇑
	no crime	0 , $-k$ ⇒	0 , 0

with $p > y > 0$, $r > k > 0$.

means a matrix in which the choice alternatives of row and column players are written in respective rows and columns. The payoffs of the strategy combinations of row players are written on the left and payoffs of column players on the right side of the comma.

The payoff structure has the implication that rational, selfish, and payoff-maximizing offenders commit a crime if not inspected, and they abide the law if inspected. In contrast, rational, selfish, and payoff-maximizing inspectors perform inspections if offenders commit a crime and do not inspect if offenders do not commit a crime. This has the consequence that there is no "dominant strategy." This means that there is no best decision regardless of the decision of the opponent. The absence of a dominant strategy is illustrated by the arrows in Table 8.1. They indicate that ego always has a reason to change her strategy, once the strategy of alter has changed. However, once ego updates her strategy and changes her behavior, alter becomes a reason to change her strategy as well, giving another reason for ego to change again, and so on.

These circling, indefinite changes of best responses can be demonstrated as follows. Let us start in the upper left corner of Table 8.1. If the inspector inspects and the offender commits a crime, the offender receives a punishment that exceeds the reward from crime. This strategy combination is not in equilibrium. Therefore, the offender decides to change her strategy and commits no crime. In this case, the inspector pays inspection costs k without receiving the reward r. Hence, the inspector changes to the better response not to inspect the offender. In this case, however, the offender receives an incentive to commit a crime because she would receive payoffs from crime y without punishment p. This strategy combination, however, gives the inspector an incentive to change her strategy to inspection, yielding for her the better payoff $r - k$, which is more than nothing. Yet, this strategy combination has been the starting point of our analysis and is no equilibrium in pure strategies either—that is, the offender changes to no crime and so on.[3]

This demonstrates that there is no combination of strategies in which both actors have no incentive to unilaterally change their strategy. In this case, actors can "mix" their strategies. This means that players choose a certain probability to perform one of their alternatives. The best way to do this is to respond with the best possible strategy mix given the mix of the opponent. If both parties optimize their respective probability to commit a crime and to perform inspections, the equilibrium in probabilities is such that offenders choose the probability for crime at the indifference point of inspectors and inspectors choose the probability of inspection at the indifference point of offenders.

The intuition for the equilibrium of optimal crime and inspection probabilities may be illustrated by the following consideration: An offender who commits crimes no matter what will sooner or later receive many punishments in a row. On the other hand, a "big brother" control regime, in which the inspector invests in omnipresent inspection, will be highly inefficient because crimes will decrease up to a minimum and control activities will no longer amortize. As a consequence, both parties will choose a mixed rather than a "pure" (fixed and deterministic) strategy.[4]

The equilibrium in mixed strategies has the interesting, counterintuitive implication that more severe punishments do not decrease the crime rate. The point is that a mix of strategies is only in equilibrium if both actors make their opponent indifferent between their two alternatives. If one actor is not indifferent, he will take advantage and exploit the other, which gives an incentive for the other to change her strategy and so on. The only stable probability combination is such that the opponent is indifferent between both alternatives. This is why the payoffs of alter determine the probability choice of ego.

The equilibria in mixed strategies can be formalized as follows. Let s_i denote the probability that offender i commits the crime and c_j the probability that inspector j inspects offender i. A value of zero means no action (no crime and no inspection), a value of one means a fixed action (crime or inspection), and values between zero and one mean that the actor chooses a probabilistic (mixed) strategy.

This allows for the payoff functions for offenders and inspectors to be defined in the following way. The payoff function π for offender i who plays against inspector j is given by

$$\pi_i\left(s_i, c_j\right) = s_i\left(y - c_j p\right).$$

The payoff function ϕ for inspector j who plays against offender i is

$$\phi_j\left(s_i, c_j\right) = c_j\left(s_i r - k\right).$$

The payoff functions consist of the payoffs from Table 8.1 and the strategies specified previously. For example, if offender i chooses to commit a crime ($s_i = 1$) and the inspector chooses to inspect offender i ($c_j = 1$), then the payoff for offender i is $y - p$ and the payoff for inspector j is $r - k$. Another example is that the offender chooses a probabilistic strategy of 50 percent to commit a crime ($s_i = 0.5$) and the inspector does not inspect ($c_j = 0$). Then, the offender's payoff is $0.5 \times y$ and the inspector's payoff is zero.

The best response is the best strategy for a given choice of the opponent. Best responses of offenders are calculated by the first partial derivative of the payoff function—that is, $\partial \pi_i / \partial s_i$:

$$s^*_i\left(c_j\right) = \begin{cases} 1 & \text{if } y - c_j p > 0 \\ [0,1] & \text{if } y - c_j p = 0 \\ 0 & \text{if } y - c_j p < 0 \end{cases} \tag{8.2}$$

EQUATION 8.2 Offender's best crime responses for given inspection decisions

From the first line, it can be seen that the offender's best response is to commit a crime for sure if the expected payoff is positive, thus if the payoff from crime y is higher than the expected loss from punishment ($c_j \times p$). The expected loss from punishment is simply given by the probability that the inspector chooses to inspect (c_j), which is multiplied with the punishment cost p. From the third line, it can be seen that the offender's best response is to commit no crime for sure if the expected payoff is negative, thus if the payoff from crime y is lower than the expected loss from punishment ($c_j \times p$). The second line shows that the offender is indifferent for the case that the payoff from crime y is equal to the expected losses from punishment ($c_j \times p$). Indifference means that any probability to commit a crime yields the same payoffs for the offender. Thus, the offender's best response is anything between no crime ($s_i = 0$), crime with some probability ($0 < s_i < 1$), and crime for sure ($s_i = 1$).

Inspector's best responses j are calculated in a similar way, using the first partial derivate of the inspector's payoff function $\partial \pi_j / \partial c_j$. This yields

$$c^*_j\left(s_i\right) = \begin{cases} 1 & \text{if } s_i r - k > 0 \\ [0,1] & \text{if } s_i r - k = 0 \\ 0 & \text{if } s_i r - k < 0 \end{cases} \qquad (8.3)$$

EQUATION 8.3 Inspector's best inspection responses for given crime decisions

From the first line, it can be seen that the inspector chooses to inspect for sure ($c_j = 1$) if the expected payoff from inspection ($s_i \times r$) is larger than the inspection costs k. The expected payoffs from inspection are simply given by the probability that the offender chooses to commit a crime (s_i), which is multiplied by the reward for successful inspection r. From the third line, it can be seen that the inspector's best response is not to inspect for sure if the expected payoffs from inspection ($s_i \times r$) are lower than the inspection costs k. The second line shows that the inspector is indifferent for the case that the payoff from inspection ($s_i \times r$) is equal to the inspection cost k. Thus, any probability to choose inspection yields the same payoffs for the inspector. Therefore, the inspector's best response is anything between no inspection ($c_j = 0$), inspection with some probability ($0 < c_j < 1$), and inspection for sure ($c_j = 1$).

The best response analysis reveals that there are no pure strategies in equilibrium. If the offender chooses to commit a crime for sure ($s_i = 1$), the inspector's best response is to inspect for sure ($c_j = 1$), for which the best response for the offender is to commit no crime for sure ($s_i = 0$), for which the best response for the inspector is to perform no inspection for sure ($c_j = 0$). Therefore, both have to choose a probabilistic strategy. The only stable strategy combination is that both are indifferent between their choices. The second line of the best response functions in equations (8.2) and (8.3) indicates the indifference conditions. The combination of indifference points yields the equilibrium in mixed strategies. This equilibrium implies for offenders to choose a crime with probability

$$s^*_i = \frac{k}{r} \qquad (8.4)$$

EQUATION 8.4 Predicted probability of offenders to commit crimes

This shows that the crime rate depends on only the inspector's payoffs—that is, the inspection cost k and the inspection reward r.

This effect is called the "strategic incentive effect." This term denotes the prediction that ego's incentives only affect alter's behavior and vice versa. The strategic incentive effect has the counterintuitive implication for inspection games that punishment does not affect crime rates. Crime rates are affected only by inspection incentives and inspection costs.

Game theoretical prediction 1: Punishment severity has no impact on crime.
Game theoretical prediction 2: The stronger the inspection incentives, the lower the crime rate.

The equilibrium in mixed strategies for inspection is calculated by the indifference condition of the offender. Thus, the inspector chooses to perform an inspection with probability

$$c_j^* = \frac{y}{p}. \tag{8.5}$$

EQUATION 8.5 Predicted probability of enforcers to perform inspections

Therefore, the rate of controls only depends on offenders' payoffs, thus on gains from crime y and punishment costs p. Hence, the "strategic incentive effect" also holds for inspections.

Game theoretical prediction 3: The level of inspection incentives has no effect on inspection behavior.
Game theoretical prediction 4: More severe punishments cause less inspections.

The counterintuitive implication is that inspection incentives do not affect inspection rates. Inspection rates are affected only by criminal gains and punishments.

C. Backward-Looking Rationality

The strategic incentive effect that more severe punishment reduces control and stronger inspection incentives reduce crime occurs for perfectly farsighted actors right from the start. Farsighted means that actors form a belief about the future behavior of their opponent and perform a payoff-maximizing strategy throughout all future interactions given their current belief. This actor type is also called "forward-looking" (Macy and Flache 2009).[5]

The strategic incentive effect also occurs for actors who are not farsighted but who learn the behavior of their opponent step by step by experience. These "rational learners" form a belief based on their previous experience and perform a payoff-maximizing choice given their experience. They also update their beliefs throughout the course of all upcoming interactions. This actor type is also called "backward-looking" (Macy and Flache 2009). This requires fewer assumptions. The forward-looking game theoretical reasoning assumes that (1) actors anticipate the behavior of their opponent correctly and (2) all actors know the payoffs of their opponents. In the learning model, actors are not perfectly farsighted but, rather, learn the detection probability by experience. Furthermore, learning actors do not have to know the payoffs of their opponent but, rather, react on the previous choices of their opponent by a payoff-maximizing response.[6]

It can be shown that forward-looking and backward-looking rationality predict equivalent dynamics:[7] (1) More severe punishment does not affect crime but reduces control, and (2) stronger inspection incentives do not affect inspections but reduce crimes. The dynamics—in which individual offenders and enforcers make reasonable decisions given the information they have—leads to the strategic incentive effect for farsighted agents in the first time step and for rational learners after some time. Perfectly farsighted agents anticipate the complete course of the dynamics at once, and rational learners go through some learning periods after which they show the same aggregate behaviors.

IV. Empirical Evidence
on Inspection Games

The game theoretical model is difficult to test in the field. In field settings, it is easier for researchers to obtain information about policy than about actual enforcement efforts by control personnel. Relatedly, it is difficult to obtain data on offenders' reactions to actual enforcement levels. Furthermore, it is difficult to observe the dynamic interplay of behaviors in the field. These likely data limitations in conjunction with other factors that may covary mean that it is difficult to track the feedback loops between criminal activity and control efforts. In addition, it is difficult to solve the endogeneity problem in the field: Do high crime rates affect the level of punishment severity or does punishment severity drive the level of crime?

In the laboratory, these methodological concerns can be addressed.[8] Rauhut (2009) conducted experiments that manipulated the severity of punishment and another series that manipulated the incentives for law enforcement to pursue criminals (Rauhut 2015). Because the laboratory setting allows the manipulation of punishment severity, the endogeneity problem that the crime rate may cause changes in punishment severity is eliminated. In addition, the experiments enabled measuring the decisions of both offenders and control agents—which is often difficult to do in natural settings—so that feedback loops between crime and control could be tracked. Both experimental series had a similar structure. Two offenders and two law enforcers were randomly matched in each period (so-called "stranger matching"). Participants were randomly assigned to be in either the offender or the law enforcer position throughout the entire experiment. The participants interacted with each other for 30 rounds. In each round, offenders had the opportunity to steal money from each other. Also in each round, law enforcers were able to investigate crime—that is, to determine whether theft occurred. Law enforcers earned money by catching criminal offenders, and criminal offenders were subject to monetary fines.

The experimental treatments varied the level of punishment severity and law enforcement incentives and their order. In the first series of experiments (Rauhut 2009), punishment severity was varied between mild and severe. In one condition, the first 15 periods were mild punishment and the next 15 periods were severe punishment. In the second condition, the order was reversed, starting with 15 periods of severe punishment followed by 15 periods of mild punishment. In the second series of experiments (Rauhut 2015), inspection incentives were varied with the same structure: In one condition, 15 periods of little inspection incentives were followed by 15 periods of strong inspection incentives, and in the other condition the order was reversed.

What happened? In the first experiment, more severe punishment led to lower rates of enforcement. When collapsed over both orders of treatments, the average enforcement rate for mild punishment was 56 percent; when punishment was severe, the average enforcement rate decreased to 42 percent. This 14 percent decrease in inspections for more severe punishments was statistically significant at the 0.1 percent level.[9]

Increasing the severity of punishment also discouraged theft, however. Taking the average over both orders of treatments, severe punishment yielded a theft rate of 43 percent and mild punishment a theft rate of 65 percent. This 22 percent decrease in thefts for more severe punishments was also statistically significant at the 0.1 percent level.[10] Note that the severity of punishment affected crime more than expected, suggesting that subjects were not good at anticipating that law enforcers were going to reduce their efforts.

The second experiment produced complementary results and provided additional support for the proposed mechanism (Rauhut 2015). It showed that as rewards for enforcement were increased, crime rates decreased from 52 to 40 percent. Enforcement efforts also increased from 38 to 66 percent in regimes with strong enforcement incentives. These percentages denote the averages over all periods and both orders of treatments. The decline in crimes by 12 percent and the increase in inspections by 28 percent for increased inspection incentives were statistically significant at the 0.1 percent level, computed by logistic random intercepts models.

The different strategic interaction patterns between offenders and enforcers for control regimes with different levels of punishments and enforcement incentives can also be analyzed dynamically. Figures 8.1 and 8.2 show the dynamics of crime and inspection decisions over time. Figure 8.1 shows crime and inspection dynamics for the treatments with 15 consecutive periods of mild and 15 consecutive periods of severe punishment from the data of Rauhut (2009). Figure 8.2 shows crime and inspection dynamics for little and strong inspection incentives from the data of Rauhut (2015). For both figures, the data are pooled with respect to treatment order. Thick lines show the predicted mixed Nash equilibria, and error bars denote 95% confidence intervals of each rate during each period.

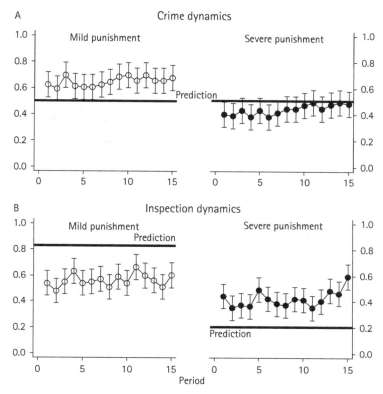

FIGURE 8.1 Crime and inspection rates over time for mild versus severe punishment conditions. (A) Theft rates over 15 periods with mild punishment (left) and 15 periods with severe punishment (right). (B) Respective inspection rates (left, mild punishment; right, severe punishment). Rates are collapsed over the order of punishment severity treatments (experiment 1 with mild punishment as first condition and experiment 2 with severe punishment as first condition). Thick black lines show respective predictions from mixed Nash equilibria. Error bars denote 95% confidence intervals for each rate at each period (consisting of 98 observations each).

Source: Data from Rauhut (2009).

The dynamics show that there is a sharp change in behaviors when punishment and inspection incentives are changed. After the strong behavioral change, however, crime and inspection rates do not converge toward predictions over time but, rather, remain relatively stable.

Taken together, these experiments provide evidence that incentives (punishments for criminals and rewards for enforcers) not only have direct effects on behavior but also have indirect effects. Because offenders and control agents have opposing interests, each is sensitive to the incentives of the other. They change their behaviors in response to the behaviors of others. However, the results also suggest that people are not as sensitive to the payoffs of their opponent as the theory would predict—people seem to be slow in updating their beliefs about the detection probability.

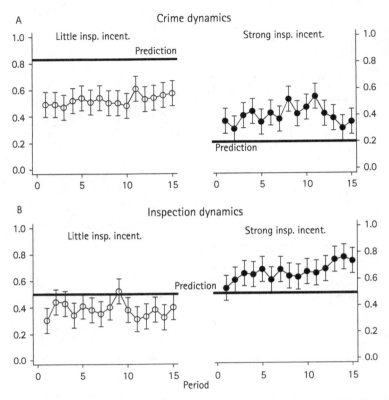

FIGURE 8.2 Crime and inspection rates over time for little versus strong inspection incentive conditions. (A) Theft rates over 15 periods with little inspection incentives (left) and 15 periods with strong inspection incentives (right). (B) Respective inspection rates (left, little inspection incentives; right, strong inspection incentives). Rates are collapsed over the order of inspection incentive treatments (experiment 1 with little inspection incentives as first condition and experiment 2 with strong inspection incentives as first condition). Thick black lines show respective predictions from mixed Nash equilibria. Error bars denote 95% confidence intervals for each rate at each period (consisting of 100 observations each).

Source: Data from Rauhut (2015).

V. Discussion

Most rational choice theories on offender decision making imply that more severe punishments cause lower crime rates. However, many field studies could not confirm strong effects of punishment severity on crime. A game theoretical perspective offers an explanation by a mechanism linking offender decision making with decision making of control agents. The game theoretical argument focuses on the opposite incentive structure between criminals and control agents. Due to this zero-sum game between criminals and control agents, incentives of both parties have counterintuitive effects. From a theoretical standpoint, offenders' incentives only affect control agents' decisions and control agents' incentives only affect offenders' decisions. This reversed effect of ego's payoffs on alter's behavior is also called strategic incentive effect. This has two major implications: More severe punishments reduce control behaviors, and stronger control incentives reduce criminal behaviors.

The game theoretical mechanism is difficult to test in the field. Much crime is undetected, and offenders do not freely report their decision making and beliefs in offender surveys. Relatedly, it is difficult to elicit precise information about enforcement efforts by control personnel and their beliefs about offender decision making. Field data also have an endogeneity problem in the sense that it is not known whether crime rates affect the level of punishment severity or whether punishment severity drives the level of crime. Furthermore, field data often cannot disentangle unrelated covariates from causal factors, leading to spurious correlations that may be falsely interpreted as confirming or disconfirming evidence for theories of offender decision making. However, much of the empirical research in criminology and law relies on official crime statistics, surveys, and observational data, which are often limited to descriptive evidence of the correlates of crime (Sampson 2000). Laboratory experiments are able to test causal relations and mechanisms and help illuminate mechanisms at the micro level and their aggregation to macro-level patterns of behavior.

The results from the laboratory experiments by Rauhut (2009) show that more severe punishment causes lower inspection rates, supporting the main game theoretical implication. However, not only inspection but also crime is affected by punishment. If punishment is more severe, there is less control and less crime. Hence, there is both a strategic incentive effect (higher punishment causes less control) and an own incentive effect (higher punishment causes less crime). These findings are qualitatively supported in the second series of laboratory experiments (Rauhut 2015). Here, stronger inspection incentives cause less crime. However, stronger inspection incentives also increase control. This series complements the findings from the punishment experiments, confirming strategic and own incentive effects.

The own incentive effect could partly be explained by less sophisticated calculations and less anticipatory reasoning by offenders. Instead, offenders may primarily use rules of thumb and "heuristics" in decision making (Gigerenzer and Goldstein 1996; Todd and Gigerenzer 2000). Such offender heuristics specify easier decision rules. A simple example of an offender heuristic is a reversed tit-for-tat strategy: Commit a crime if no inspection occurred previously, and do not commit a crime if there has been an inspection recently. Respective follow-up experiments (Rauhut and Jud 2014) show that this can partly explain the findings. However, there are also offender types who care about payoffs of other offenders. This other-regarding type cares about becoming a victim of crime and retaliates by committing more crimes to any others than what would be individually payoff maximizing.

Another approach to explain the own incentive effect is to assume that people expect others to make errors and do not behave in a perfectly farsighted and calculating way. Therefore, they may form beliefs about the probability of each of their opponents' choice alternatives. This can be modeled by the so-called "quantal response equilibrium" (McKelvey and Palfrey 1995). The intuition behind this model is that errors of the opponent can become very costly if ego does not anticipate these errors and take them into account in calculating expected payoffs from choice alternatives. For example, if the punishment is very high, citizens may doubt that inspectors indeed perform only very few controls. If citizens err on this side, they face a very high punishment, which they may try to avoid. Conversely, if the control incentive is very low, inspectors may doubt that criminals perform many crimes. If inspectors err on this side, their control efforts may not amortize so that they may decide to control less if there are only little incentives for control. Nosenzo et al. (2012) support predictions from this so-called quantal response equilibrium with data from simpler versions of the inspection game than presented here.

In addition to contributing to actor models in the social sciences, the game theoretical framework also has implications for political decision makers. Deterrence policies are often based on too simple theoretical mechanisms. The rhetoric of politicians frequently focuses on arguments based on the own incentive effect: Punishment severity is thought of only as a crime deterrence and not as an inspection deterrence. Likewise, inspection rewards are typically created in order to motivate inspections, neglecting their effect on crime. Especially if crime is on the rise or if single criminal events are widely discussed in the press, politicians often make the narrow argument that more severe punishment would help to reduce crime.

Given the results of the human subject experiments, policy recommendations should take two considerations into account: (1) Crime is an interdependent strategic interaction situation between offenders and enforcers, and (2) both actor types should be assumed to behave according to behavioral rather than classical game theory. This means that the creation of incentives should always take all involved players into account. In addition, these players should be modeled to be less calculating, less adaptive, and less farsighted but more prosocial, more other-regarding, and more sensitive to others' mistakes than what is assumed by classical rational choice models.

The presented game theoretical framework may also have implications for a welfare analysis of optimal control. For example, it may be cheaper to increase rewards for police and other control agents with the main aim to deter crime. Utilizing the strategic incentive effect for the design of crime deterrence policies could give rise to more effective and cheaper deterrence. Deterrence policies should carefully take these considerations into account to be efficient and successful.

NOTES

1. Note that criminal gains are still received when punished. This is the case in the original model by Becker (1968) and is also kept in the later game theoretical model. This may reflect crimes whose benefits remain to some extent—for example, assaults or murder. It can also be argued that some benefit always remains—for example, keeping a loot or gaining criminal experience. See the original article by Becker for further arguments.

2. If the cost of punishment p would be smaller than the payoff from crime, then a payoff-maximizing actor would always commit a crime, whatever the likelihood of punishment. For example, if the punishment of fare dodging would be less than the ticket price and no extra ticket price would be taken if fare dodgers were detected, then a payoff-maximizing passenger would never buy a ticket. If this situation were modeled in a game with payoff-maximizing agents, the offender would always offend. This means that punishment severity (between nothing and the ticket price in this example) would not affect the rate of offending, which would always be 100%.

3. Note that strategic settings without dominant strategies and ones without Nash equilibria in pure strategies are formally not the same. Dominance means that a strategy is better regardless of what the opponent chooses. Combinations of dominant strategies are always Nash equilibria. Nash equilibria in pure strategies are more general and can also specify strategy combinations, in which mutual best replies are contingent on the other player's move. For example, driving on the right side if the other is also driving on the right side, and driving on the left side if the other is driving on the left side.

4. There is discussion regarding whether mixed strategies are a plausible prediction in zero-sum games. Holler (1990, 1993) argued that maximin strategies were more plausible. See the discussion therein and the summary by Andreozzi (2010).

5. Note that the inspection game has also been extended to a sequential version, in which the inspector can commit him- or herself to a probability of inspection. This is beyond the scope of this chapter; see Andreozzi (2004) for details.

6. The learning model can be described as backward-looking rationality because actors adapt their behavior with a best response to the past behavior of their opponent. This model is also known as fictitious play (Fudenberg and Levine 1998) or Bayesian updating. Note that there are also alternative backward-looking learning models, some of which are described in Macy (1991, 1993) and Macy and Flache (2002).

7. For the precise learning dynamics, see Rauhut (2015), Rauhut and Jud (2014), and Rauhut and Junker (2009).

8. For a more in-depth discussion of how laboratory experiments can be used for studying crime and law, see Horne and Rauhut (2013); for an extensive discussion of their validity, see Rauhut and Winter (2012).

9. Statistical significance here is estimated by a logistic random intercepts model.

10. Statistical significance is again estimated by a logistic random intercepts model.

References

Allingham, Michael G., and Agnar Sandmo. 1972. "Income Tax Evasion: A Theoretical Analysis." *Journal of Public Economics* 1:323–38.

Andreoni, James. 1989. "Giving with Impure Altruism: Applications to Charity and Ricardian Equivalence." *Journal of Political Economy* 97(6): 1447–58.

Andreoni, James, Brian Erard, and Jonathan Feinstein. 1998. "Tax Compliance." *Journal of Economic Literature* 36:818–60.

Andreozzi, Luciano. 2004. "Rewarding Policemen Increases Crime: Another Surprising Result from the Inspection Game." *Public Choice* 121:69–82.

Andreozzi, Luciano. 2010. "Inspection Games with Long-Run Inspectors." *European Journal of Applied Mathematics* 21:441–58.

Baird, Douglas G., Robert H. Gertner, and Randal C. Picker. 1994. *Game Theory and the Law*. Cambridge, MA: Harvard University Press.

Becker, Gary S. 1968. "Crime and Punishment: An Economic Approach." *Journal of Political Economy* 76:169–217.

Braun, Norman, and Thomas Gautschi. 2011. *Rational Choice Theorie*. Weinheim, Germany: Juventa.

Buskens, Vincent, and Werner Raub. 2002. "Embedded Trust: Control and Learning." *Advances in Group Processes* 19:167–202.

Buskens, V., and J. Weesie. 2000. "An Experiment on the Effects of Embeddedness in Trust Situations—Buying a Used Car." *Rationality and Society* 12:227–53.

Camerer, Colin. 2003. *Behavioral Game Theory: Experiments in Strategic Interaction*. Princeton, NJ: Princeton University Press.

Camerer, Colin, and Keith Weigelt. 1988. "Experimental Tests of a Sequential Equilibrium Reputation Model." *Econometrica* 56:1–36.

Clarke, R. V. 1995. "Situational Crime Prevention." *Crime and Justice* 19:91–150.

Coleman, James S. 1990. *Foundations of Social Theory*. London: Belknap

Cook, Philip J. 1980. "Research in Criminal Deterrence: Laying the Groundwork for the Second Decade." *Crime and Justice* 2:211–68.

Dasgupta, Partha. 1988. "Trust as a Commodity." In *Trust: Making and Breaking Cooperative Relations*, edited by Diego Gambetta. Vol. 4, pp. 49–72. Oxford: Blackwell.

Diekmann, Andreas, Ben Jann, Wojtek Przepiorka, and Stefan Wehrli. 2014. "Reputation Formation and the Evolution of Cooperation in Anonymous Online Markets." *American Sociological Review* 79:65–85.

Diekmann, Andreas, Wojtek Przepiorka, and Heiko Rauhut. 2015. "Lifting the Veil of Ignorance: An Experiment on the Contagiousness of Norm Violations." *Rationality and Society* 27(3): 309–33.

Diekmann, Andreas, and Thomas Voss. 2004. "Die Theorie rationalen Handelns. Stand und Perspektiven." In *Rational-Choice-Theorie in den Sozialwissenschaften: Anwendungen und Probleme*, edited by Andreas Diekmann and Thomas Voss. Munich: Scientia Nova.

Dixit, Avinash. 2011. "A Game-Theoretic Perspective on Diego Gambetta's Codes of the Underworld." *Global Crime* 12:134–45.

Dixit, Avinash K., and Susan Skeath. 2004. *Games of Strategy*. 2nd ed. New York: Norton.

Doob, Anthony N., and Cheryl M. Webster. 2003. "Sentence Severity and Crime: Accepting the Null Hypothesis." *Crime and Justice* 28:143–95.

Eaton, B. Curtis, and Jean-Francois Wen. 2008. "Myopic Deterrence Policies and the Instability of Equilibria." *Journal of Economic Behavior and Organization* 65:609–24.

Fehr, Ernst, and Simon Gächter. 2002. "Altruistic Punishment in Humans." *Nature* 415:137–40.

Fehr, Ernst, and Herbert Gintis. 2007. "Human Motivation and Social Cooperation: Experimental and Analytical Foundations." *Annual Review of Sociology* 33:43–64.

Fehr, Ernst, and Klaus M. Schmidt. 1999. "A Theory of Fairness, Competition, and Cooperation." *Quarterly Journal of Economics* 114:817–68.

Friedman, David. 1995. "Rational Criminals and Profit-Maximizing Police: The Economic Analysis of Law and Law Enforcement." In *The New Economics of Behavior*, edited by Mariano Tommasi and Kathryn Ierulli, pp. 43–58. Cambridge: Cambridge University Press.

Fudenberg, Drew, and David K. Levine. 1998. *The Theory of Learning in Games*. Cambridge, MA: MIT Press.

Gambetta, Diego. 2009a. *Codes of the Underworld: How Criminals Communicate*. Princeton, NJ: Princeton University Press.

Gambetta, Diego. 2009b. "Signaling." In *The Oxford Handbook of Analytical Sociology*, edited by Peter Hedström and Peter Bearman, pp. 168–94. New York: Oxford University Press.

Gambetta, Diego, and Heather Hamill. 2005. *Streetwise: How Taxi Drivers Establish Customer's Trustworthiness*. New York: Russell Sage Foundation.

Gigerenzer, Gerd, and Daniel G. Goldstein. 1996. "Reasoning the Fast and Frugal Way: Models of Bounded Rationality." *Psychological Review* 103:650–69.

Gintis, Herbert. 2000. *Game Theory Evolving: A Problem-Centered Introduction to Modeling Strategic Behavior*. Princeton, NJ: Princeton University Press.

Gintis, Herbert. 2007. "A Framework for the Unification of the Behavioral Sciences." *Behavioral and Brain Sciences* 30:1–61.

Graetz, Michael J., Jennifer F. Reinganum, and Louis L. Wilde. 1986. "The Tax Compliance Game: Toward an Interactive Theory of Law Enforcement." *Journal of Law, Economics, and Organization* 2:1–32.

Heckathorn, Douglas D. 1989. "Collective Action and the Second-Order Free-Rider Problem." *Rationality and Society* 1:78–100.

Hedström, Peter, and Peter Bearman. 2009. *The Oxford Handbook of Analytical Sociology*. New York: Oxford University Press.

Holler, Manfred J. 1990. "The Unprofitability of Mixed-Strategy Equilibria in Two-Person Games: A Second Folk-Theorem." *Economics Letters* 32:319–23.

Holler, Manfred J. 1993. "Fighting Pollution When Decisions Are Strategic." *Public Choice* 76:347–56.

Horne, Christine, and Heiko Rauhut. 2013. "Using Laboratory Experiments to Study Law and Crime." *Quality and Quantity* 47:1639–55.

Jackson, Matthew O., and Asher Wolinsky. 1996. "A Strategic Model of Social and Economic Networks." *Journal of Economic Theory* 71:44–74.

Kahan, D. M. 1997. "Social Influence, Social Meaning, and Deterrence." *Virginia Law Review* 83:349–95.

Levitt, Steven D. 2002. "Deterrence." In *Crime: Public Policies for Crime Control*, edited by James Q. Wilson and Joan Petersilia, pp. 435–50. San Francisco: Institute for Contemporary Studies Press.

Lochner, Lance. 2007. "Individual Perceptions of the Criminal Justice System." *American Economic Review* 97:444–60.

Macy, Michael W. 1991. "Learning to Cooperate: Stochastic and Tacit Collusion in Social Exchange." *American Journal of Sociology* 97:808–43.

Macy, Michael. W. 1993. "Backward-Looking Social-Control." *American Sociological Review* 58:819–36.

Macy, Michael W., and Andreas Flache. 2002. "Learning Dynamics in Social Dilemmas." *Proceedings of the National Academy of Sciences of the USA* 99:7229–36.

Macy, Michael W., and Andreas Flache. 2009. "Social Dynamics from the Bottom Up: Agent-Based Models of Social Interaction." In *The Oxford Handbook of Analytical Sociology*, edited by Peter Hedström and Peter Bearman. New York: Oxford University Press.

McKelvey, Richard D., and Thomas R. Palfrey. 1995. "Quantal Response Equilibria for Normal Form Games." *Games and Economic Behavior* 10:6–38.

Murphy, Ryan O., and Kurt A. Ackermann. 2014. "Social Value Orientation: Theoretical and Measurement Issues in the Study of Social Preferences." *Personality and Social Psychology Review* 18(1): 13–41.

Nagin, Daniel S. 1998. "Criminal Deterrence Research at the Outset of the Twenty-First Century." *Crime and Justice* 23:1–42.

Nash, John. 1951. "Non-cooperative Games." *Annals of Mathematics* 2:286–95.

Nosenzo, Daniele, Theo Offerman, Martin Sefton, and Ailko van der Veen. 2012. "Encouraging Compliance: Bonuses Versus Fines in Inspection Games." CeDEx Discussion Paper Series, pp. 1–30.

Przepiorka, Wojtek. 2010. "Diego Gambetta: Codes of the Underworld: How Criminals Communicate." *Rationality, Markets and Morals* 1:9–11.

Raub, Werner. 2009. "Commitments by Hostage Posting." In *Perspectives in Moral Science*, edited by M. Baurmann and B. Lahno, pp. 207–25. Frankfurt, Germany: Frankfurt School Verlag.

Raub, Werner, and Vincent Buskens. 2004. "Spieltheoretische Modellierungen und empirische Anwendungen in der Soziologie." Kölner Zeitschrift für *Soziologie und Sozialpsychologie* 44:560–98.

Rauhut, Heiko. 2009. "Higher Punishment, Less Control? Experimental Evidence on the Inspection Game." *Rationality and Society* 21:359–92.

Rauhut, Heiko. 2015. "Stronger Inspection Incentives, Less Crime? Further Experimental Evidence on Inspection Games." *Rationality and Society* 27:1–41.

Rauhut, Heiko, and Silvana Jud. 2014. "Avoiding Detection or Reciprocating Norm Violations? An Experimental Comparison of Self- and Other-Regarding Mechanisms for Norm Adherence." *Soziale Welt* 65:153–83.

Rauhut, Heiko, and Marcel Junker. 2009. "Punishment Deters Crime Because Humans Are Bounded in Their Strategic Decision-Making." *Journal of Artificial Social Systems and Societies* 12(3): 1.

Rauhut, Heiko, and Fabian Winter. 2012. "On the Validity of Laboratory Research in the Political and Social Sciences: The Example of Crime and Punishment." In *Experimental Political Science: Principles and Practices*, edited by Bernhard Kittel, Wolfgang Luhan, and Rebecca Morton, pp. 209–32. Palgrave Research Methods Series. London: Palgrave Macmillan.

Sampson, Robert J. 2000. "Whither the Sociological Study of Crime." *Annual Review of Sociology* 26:711–14.

Schelling, Thomas C. 1960. *The Strategy of Conflict*. Cambridge, MA: Harvard University Press.

Simon, Herbert A. 1955. "A Behavioral Model of Rational Choice." *Quarterly Journal of Economics* 69:99–118.

Tambe, Milind. 2011. *Security and Game Theory: Algorithms, Deployed Systems, Lessons Learned*. Cambridge: Cambridge University Press.

Todd, Peter M., and Gerd Gigerenzer. 2000. "Precis of Simple Heuristics That Make Us Smart." *Behavioral and Brain Sciences* 23:727–80.

Tsebelis, George. 1989. "The Abuse of Probability in Political Analysis: The Robinson Crusoe Fallacy." *American Political Science Review* 1:77–91.

Tsebelis, George. 1990. "Penalty Has No Impact on Crime: A Game Theoretic Analysis." *Rationality and Society* 2:255–86.

Van Lange, P. A. M. 1999. "The Pursuit of Joint Outcomes and Equality in Outcomes: An Integrative Model of Social Value Orientation." *Journal of Personality and Social Psychology* 77:337.

Voss, Thomas. 2001. "Game-Theoretical Perspectives on the Emergence of Social Norms." In *Social Norms*, edited by Michael Hechter and Karl-Dieter Opp. New York: Russell Sage Foundation.

Voss, Thomas. 2006. "Game Theory." In *International Encyclopedia of Economic Sociology*, edited by Jens Beckert and Milan Zafirovski, pp. 296–99. Abingdon, UK: Routledge.

Williams, K. R., and R. Hawkins. 1986. "Perceptual Research on General Deterrence—A Critical Review." *Law and Society Review* 20:545–72.

Wittman, Donald. 1985. "Counter-intuitive Results in Game Theory." *European Journal of Political Economy* 1:77–89.

CHAPTER 9

DUAL-PROCESS MODELS OF CRIMINAL DECISION MAKING

JEAN-LOUIS VAN GELDER

IMAGINE the following situation: At work, John has an argument with his boss, who accuses John of not doing his job. When John explains that this was not the case and that it was actually a colleague who forsook his duties, his boss accuses him of lying and a lack of loyalty toward his fellow workers. Driving home later that day, a car cuts him off and forces him to slam on the brakes to avoid an accident. When he pulls up next to the car at a red light down the road, the driver of the other car starts swearing at him. John pulls the other driver out of his car and punches him square in the face.

Now consider another situation: Jane is at the airport returning from a trip overseas. One of the reasons she went on the trip was because she was interested in buying some local artifacts. However, before leaving, she did not check whether it was legal to import them. As she proceeds to take her luggage off the belt, she notices a billboard indicating that it is forbidden to bring cultural goods into the country without an export license from the country of departure. Jane did not get such a license, which means she is now faced with the choice of declaring the artifacts she bought and have them confiscated or taking her chances and not declaring them. By not declaring them, she risks not only the confiscation of the items but also a hefty fine. Jane sits down for a moment to consider the situation and then decides to take her chances and to "forget" to declare her newly bought artifacts.

Is the choice for crime or noncrime in these cases guided more by how John and Jane think about the situation and how they rationally evaluate the costs and benefits involved or by their intuitions and emotions at the time of decision? This question stands as the basis of an incipient debate in criminology. According to the traditional decision-making perspectives, the decision is guided by a thoughtful or rational evaluation in both situations. These perspectives posit a reasoning decision maker who evaluates different alternatives to arrive at a decision (Becker, 1968; Cornish and Clarke, 1986). According to these perspectives, feelings play little, if any, role beyond perhaps how they influence the evaluation of cost and reward parameters. For example, if John and Jane would anticipate regretting their choice, this would count as a cost factored into their calculation. Conversely, should they think they would enjoy punching someone in the face or the thrill of trying to get away with not declaring the items, this would count as a benefit. The net balance of the anticipated thrills, joys, and regrets in conjunction with any other potential perceived costs and benefits are determinative of the choice to commit crime or to abstain from it. In short, ultimately the choice to engage in crime according to most criminal decision-making perspectives is a rational one based on a cost–benefit trade-off.

However, there is increasing empirical evidence that this portrayal of the decision process is inaccurate or at least incomplete. According to an emerging view of criminal decision making, emotions play an important role in crime causation and do so in ways that are difficult to reconcile with rational choice-based models (for an overview of rational choice theory, see chapters 2 and 4, this volume). The answer to the question as to what guides the choice for crime or noncrime in the previous examples according to this emerging view is *both* rational "cool" thinking and "hot" affect. That is, similar to decisions that involve risk in other behavioral domains, both feelings about a situation and cool rational thought provide input guiding the choice at hand. According to this alternative view, even in the case of the ostensibly calculated choice by Jane not to declare her artifacts, her feelings are likely to play a role. Later in this chapter, a model of criminal decision making is drawn out that accommodates both the influence of "cool" rational thought and "hot" affect on decisions to offend. Next, however, is a discussion of the theoretical and empirical underpinnings of the dual-process hypothesis.

I. THE DUAL-PROCESS HYPOTHESIS

Emerging insights from research on information processing and decision making demonstrate the fundamental role of affect (i.e., feelings) as a driver of virtually all human decisions, also absent a state of intense emotional arousal, and that cognition and affect appear to pertain to two relatively independent modes of mental information processing.[1] So-called dual-process or dual-system theories, which are common in cognitive and social psychology (Epstein 1994; Chaiken and Trope 1999; Metcalfe and Mischel 1999; Kahneman 2003, 2011; Strack and Deutsch 2004; van Gelder, de Vries, and van der Pligt, 2009; Evans and Stanovich 2013) and which are also encountered in the behavioral economics literature (Thaler and Shefrin, 1981; Loewenstein and O'Donoghue, 2004; Fudenberg and Levine, 2006), revolve around the idea that activities as diverse as making attributions, solving problems, evaluating risks, or deciding on a course of action involve two qualitatively different modes of mental processing, each of which has unique properties.[2] Whereas dual-process models tend to describe two modes of information processing in a specific behavioral domain, dual-system models posit two mental systems that guide behavior in general.

In this chapter, it is argued that these models can also significantly contribute to our understanding of offender decision making and overcome some of the limitations of rational choice-based models. Next, the general properties of the dual-process paradigm are outlined before discussing its application to criminal behavior focusing on one recently proposed model in particular.

II. General Properties of Dual-Process and Dual-System Models

Due to sometimes significant differences between the various dual-process and dual-system models that have been proposed throughout the years, it is more accurate to view them as a class of models that share several basic principles that set them apart from single-system models rather than as a specific theory. Perhaps the most important common principle underlying dual-process and dual-system models is the idea that human behavior is not the result of reasoning, habit, drive, or motivation but, instead, is guided by more than one underlying process (Strack and Deutsch 2004). The different models are also generally in agreement that one of the processing modes or systems is based on automatic, fast, and heuristic reasoning, whereas the other is based on deliberative, slow, and systematic thinking (Gerrard et al. 2008; but see Evans and Stanovich 2013).[3] In the words of Smith and Neumann (2005), most models "share the general theme that one of the processing modes operates automatically and preconsciously to structure people's conscious experiences with little dependence on attention or cognitive resources," whereas the other mode "operates optionally, uses more powerful inferential means, and requires attention and subjective effort" (p. 292).

Another important assumption of duality models is that both modes may trigger compatible responses but may also generate opposite responses. An example of the former is when the sight of food activates the affective state of hunger and the cognition, "What shall I cook for dinner tonight?" (Loewenstein and O'Donoghue 2004). An example of an opposite response occurs when the sight of food activates the affective state of hunger and the cognitive state of "I'm on a diet" (Loewenstein and O'Donoghue 2004).

A. Application of Dual-Process and Dual-System Models in Criminology

Recently, several researchers have started to apply dual-process and dual-system models in crime research (Thomas and McGloin 2013; Treiber 2013; van Gelder and de Vries 2014). Thomas and McGloin applied a dual-systems approach to examine differential susceptibility to peer influences, arguing that adolescents at both extremes of the impulsivity spectrum are differentially susceptible to peer influences due to their differential reliance on one of the systems. Adhering to the system 1 (fast and automatic) versus system 2 (slow and effortful) distinction (Stanovich and West 2002; Kahneman 2003, 2011), the authors found that individuals high in impulsivity are more susceptible to situational influences and immediate considerations, whereas those low in impulsivity are more influenced by deviant normative influence in their decision to engage in delinquency, which ties in with the consideration of longer term consequences as "peers have the capacity to define an adolescent's values regarding delinquency and structure a social reinforcement contingency that ties delinquent acts to the acquisition of goals that extend past the immediate situation, such as social acceptance, status, and respect" (Thomas and McGloin 2013, pp. 440–441). The authors conclude that high-impulsivity individuals are more led by stimuli in their immediate environment and are therefore more inclined to rely on system 1, whereas for those low in impulsivity, decisions to engage in crime are more deliberate. These individuals consequently tend to rely more on system 2.

Treiber (2013) employed a neurocognitive perspective to tap into the intuitive/emotive functions versus the reasoned/rational functions of the prefrontal cortex, a brain area strongly implicated in decision making, and linked them to self-reported and police-recorded criminal involvement of adolescents. That is, Treiber argues that the functions of intuitive/emotive and reasoned/rational decision making can be localized in two separate anatomical regions of the prefrontal cortex—the ventromedial and dorsolateral cortices, respectively. The results show weak to modest relations between the neurocognitive measures that reflect localized activity in the prefrontal cortex and criminal involvement, but the author notes, "Considering the number of factors and processes which intercede between specific neurocognitive functions ... and rare behaviors such as acts of crime, the fact that any statistically significant relationship is apparent speaks to the importance of these functions for action" (p. 210).

Van Gelder and de Vries (2014) tested the dual-process-based framework of criminal decision making suggested by van Gelder (2013), which is discussed in detail in the next section. Using a priming manipulation, the authors induced either a cool cognitive or a hot affective processing mode in participants. Processing mode was manipulated by having participants rely on either their thinking or their feelings when deciding on whether or not to make a criminal choice. Following the manipulation, participants were presented a series of criminal choice scenarios. In line with their hypotheses, the authors found that priming an affective processing mode led to feelings of insecurity, worry, and fear, which proved to be a significantly stronger predictor of criminal choice than the cognitive measure of perceived risk of sanction—that is, punishment probability and severity. Conversely, priming a cognitive processing mode led perceived risk of sanction to more strongly predict criminal choice. In other words, the priming of processing mode was found to moderate the relations between negative affect and perceived risk and criminal choice.

Given the topic of this chapter, in the present context we are particularly interested in those duality models that emphasize the distinction between the cognitive nature of one of the modes or systems and the affective nature of the other (Epstein 1994; Metcalfe and

Mischel 1999; Loewenstein and O'Donoghue 2004; Slovic et al. 2005; van Gelder et al. 2009; van Gelder 2013). The next section discusses a recently proposed model of criminal decision making (van Gelder 2013) that draws from and builds on these particular models (and which should therefore not be taken to be representative of dual-process or dual-system models in general).

III. The Hot/Cool Perspective of Criminal Decision Making

Situations that require self-control are particularly suitable to demonstrate the usefulness of the dual-process paradigm because they are typically experienced as a conflict between two antagonistic forces that exert incompatible influences: one force pulling toward what is thought or believed to be reasonable and the other pushing toward what pleasure dictates (Hofmann, Friese, and Strack 2009, p. 162; see also Thaler and Shefrin 1981; Metcalfe and Mischel 1999; Fudenberg and Levine 2006). Consequently, given the ubiquity of impulsivity and self-control in criminal conduct, dual-process notions of criminal choice are well positioned to understand offender decision making. Precisely this is also the point of departure of the hot/cool framework of criminal decision making, which distinguishes between a "cool," cognitive (i.e., thinking-based) mode of information processing and a "hot," affective (i.e., feeling-based) mode.

A central assumption of the hot/cool framework, which was recently proposed by van Gelder (2013) and which borrows its terminology from Metcalfe and Mischel (1999), regards the difference, and potential discrepancy, between people's cognitive evaluations of a criminogenic situation and their affective reactions to it. In line with the dual-process hypothesis, these are assumed to be the result of two qualitatively distinct modes of processing. Higher order executive functions such as planning and analytic thinking belong to the domain of the cool, cognitive mode, which resembles (but is not identical to) system 2, type 2 processing, or the reflective system in other models (Hofmann et al. 2009; Kahneman 2011; Evans and Stanovich 2013). The effortful and controlled processes of the cool mode include deliberate judgments and evaluations and potentially inhibiting or overriding of impulses generated by the hot mode, which resembles what is referred to as system 1, type 1 processing, or the impulsive system in other models. The cool mode is therefore sensitive to considerations such as risk probabilities and social costs such as anticipated guilt and disapproval. It is therefore likely to respond to variations in sanction severity and certainty. The cool mode is also capable of weighing costs against benefits and making projections about the long-term consequences of decisions. The cool mode therefore reflects the contents of rational choice and deterrence models (van Gelder, 2013, p. 8).

The hot, affective mode, on the other hand, evaluates prospects in a more intuitive and automatic way and remains largely unresponsive to probabilities and the content of outcomes. The hot mode recognizes only whether an outcome is possible, and it is relatively insensitive to variations in the range of probabilities that lie in between certainty and impossibility. As emotion theorist Nico Frijda (1988) phrases it, "Emotions know no probabilities. They do not weigh likelihoods. What they know, they know for sure" (p. 355). Emotions, and by implication the hot mode, are influenced by variables that play only a minor role in cognitive evaluations, such as the time interval between a decision and the realization of outcomes, physical proximity, and the degree to which a risk is known or controllable (Loewenstein et al. 2001; Loewenstein and O'Donoghue 2004). Fear and anger belong to the domain of the hot mode. The hot mode has no counterpart in the existing choice models of crime.

The hot mode, similar to system 1 (Kahneman 2011), type 1 (Evans and Stanovich 2013), associative (Sloman 1996), or impulsive processing (Strack and Deutsch 2004) in other duality models, operates automatically and is fast and only partially conscious. Whereas the cool mode operates optionally, the hot mode's operations are nonvolitional in nature (Smith and Neumann 2005). An intuitive response generated by the hot mode may or may not be followed by a response of cool mode because the latter operates optionally and requires attention and effort (Epstein 1994; Evans and Stanovich 2013). As Zajonc (1980) argues, although feeling is generally not entirely free of thought, and thought is not entirely free of feelings, affect is always present as a companion to thought, whereas the converse is not true for cognition. The hardwiring of the brain allows for an emotional reaction without the participation of a cognitive appraisal (LeDoux 1996; Zajonc 1998, p. 597). As Treiber (2013, p. 195) also notes, affective content can guide behavior spontaneously, drawing attention to preferred courses of action and sweeping aside undesirable alternatives even before cognitive energy is spent on deliberation.

The fact that the hot mode is relatively insensitive to the input variables of rational choice models explains why an individual's criminal or normative behavior can deviate from or, as shown later, even directly contradict what would be a beneficial course of action in terms of perceived utility and long-term considerations. The operations of the hot mode, in short, lie outside the explanatory realm of rational choice and deterrence models, and the influence of emotions and other affective states on behavior stretches far beyond simply influencing the perception of cost and reward parameters of the decision-making situation.

Again, in line with other dual-process and dual-system models, both modes are interrelated and work together. For example, an opportunity for embezzlement of company assets that presents itself may be processed by the cool mode as a low-risk and high-yield option while simultaneously triggering feelings of entitlement or excitement in the hot mode. In such a case, both modes favor choosing the criminal option. In a similar vein, the consideration of possible negative consequences following criminal conduct may go hand in hand with feelings of worry and fear that are evoked by this prospect, and both may therefore work against making a criminal choice (van Gelder and de Vries, 2012, 2014). However, the two modes may also cue diverging responses and compete for control over behavior. The cool mode may try to prevent the execution of the behavior that was impulsively activated by the hot mode. For example, feelings of desire aroused by the offer of a tempting bribe may be accompanied or followed by the cognition that it is better not accepted out of risk of detection, resulting in a choice dilemma that may go either way depending on which of the two modes succeeds in overriding the other (van Gelder and de Vries 2015).

A. An Alternative to Rational Choice-Based Models

How do dual-process models, and the hot/cool model in particular, offer a more realistic account of criminal decision-making processes than the common single-system models of criminal decision making, and how can they explain criminal behaviors that are difficult to account for in terms of rational choice?

One case in point regards the distinction between anticipated and immediate emotions (Loewenstein et al. 2001; Loewenstein and Lerner, 2003; for a more elaborate discussion, see chapter 22, this volume). Anticipated emotions, such as regret, guilt, or shame, are a component of the expected consequences of a decision. Such emotions are expected by the decision maker to be felt when outcomes are experienced rather than feelings experienced at the time of decision. Immediate emotions, in contrast, are experienced at the time of decision and can arise from contemplating decision consequences, such as feelings of fear and dread when visualizing potential negative outcomes, or they can be the result of incidental influences unrelated to the decision itself, such as the mood of an individual at the moment of decision making (think of the example of John at the beginning of this chapter). This distinction elucidates why anticipated emotions such as shame and guilt can be incorporated into rational choice models but immediate emotions, such as anger and fear, cannot. As predictions about future emotional states, regret and shame are essentially costs that can be entered in a cognitive calculus, and the decision process remains modeled as the implicitly cognitive task of predicting future emotions and weighing them in terms of the expected utility of the different possible courses of action (Loewenstein et al. 2001). In terms of the hot/cool model, the consideration of potential future emotions, like estimates of probability and severity, regards thoughts *about* feelings rather than feelings experienced at the moment. As such, they belong to the domain of the cool mode (van Gelder 2013).

Anger and fear, in contrast, are felt at the time of decision and therefore implicate the hot mode. Such emotional experiences and their influence on the decision process are difficult, if not impossible, to plausibly model as costs or benefits. We may not even be consciously aware of the (more subtle) emotional states we are in.

Another way in which the hot/cool model can make sense of behavior that is more difficult to explain in strictly rational terms is the experience of inner conflict between what is thought to be the best course of action and the choice that is felt as most desirable. Such competition is likely to emerge when the short- and long-term hedonic properties of the choice at hand are negatively correlated, which is often the case with crime. That is, most crime tends to carry immediate benefits, whereas its costs tend to be more remote (Gottfredson and Hirschi 1990; Hirschi 2004; van Gelder et al., 2015). Recall that the hot mode is geared toward the here and now and lacks the ability to consider the hypothetical consequences of a choice. Hence, the cool mode needs to be able to override the prepotent response of the hot mode to prevent a crime from occurring.

Consider by way of example again the situation of road rage described at the outset of this chapter: John may have been perfectly aware that he should not punch the other driver in the face and that it would be likely to cause him trouble, but he may have been unable to convert this cognitive awareness into action. Alternatively, John's anger may have gradually crept up on him without him being even aware of it, and hence cognitive processing occurred at a minimum level, if at all. Framed in terms of the hot/cool perspective, the hot mode prompted the "decision" to lash out at the other driver, and his cool mode was unable to override this behavioral response. Note that in rational choice parlance, John's expected subjective costs clearly outweighed anticipated gains that militate against the use of force. Hence, the "irrational" behavior of John is difficult to explain in terms of rational choice.

These examples illustrate the partial independence of both modes of processing and also the possibility of competition between the modes for control over overt behavior, and they elucidate why we can think about something one way but feel about it differently. Furthermore, because many affective processes occur below the level of our awareness, they are not consciously experienced, which makes it difficult for people to gage them and control for their influence (LeDoux 1996). This also casts some doubt on the premise of informed cost–benefit analyses that precede choice as assumed by rational choice models.[4]

Another striking illustration of the power of unconscious processes in the context of offending is provided by Ward and Hudson (2000) in their work on serial sex offenders, in which they argue that some offenders' planning is explicit, systematic, and analytical, whereas for others it appears to be implicit, covert, and intuitive. These latter offenders engage in decision making that "has the appearance of automaticity, that is, decision making that is implicit, fast, relatively autonomous, frequently associated with a lack of control, effortless, and occurring without conscious awareness" (p. 189). Their implicit decision making leads them to highly risky situations in which they are exposed to temptation and that trigger further automatic mental scripts resulting in offending behavior. In terms of dual-processing, it could be argued that an affectively laden past experience gets reactivated by a stimulus that initially receives little conscious attention (perhaps because it is but one element in a crowded mental scene), leading to an affective state for which the perceiver is unable to assign a cause (Smith and Neumann 2005). For example, a sex offender who chooses to exercise at 3 p.m. and passes a children's playground may be unaware of the destination and the unconscious goal to enable the offending process, even though he is conscious of going for a walk (Ward and Hudson 2000). The offender subsequently finds himself in a high-risk situation that triggers an affective state, sexual arousal, which requires conscious effort (i.e., intervention by the cool mode) and self-restraint to abandon (Nee and Meenaghan 2006). In terms of the hot/cool framework, this is again a situation in which the cool and hot modes trigger opposite responses. Furthermore, as discussed previously, even if an actor is ultimately aware of the influence of affect on his or her behavior, it may be only partially subject to cognitive control.

These processes are unlikely to be restricted to sex offenders and may be paralleled in many different types of offending behavior. For example, a convicted street robber who is motivated to abstain from future offending may unwittingly return to situations conducive to his earlier offending. These situations may evoke different kinds of associations that trigger the hot mode, such as feelings of desire or enticement felt by the prospect of the quick money that can be made when an easy target is spotted, which can lead to the breakdown of restraint (Lofland 1969; Wright an Decker 1994, 1997; Topalli and Wright 2013). Nor are these processes restricted to states of strong arousal.

In closing, we can consider again the situation, discussed at the beginning of this chapter, of Jane, who had unknowingly bought artifacts abroad that upon arrival at the airport turned out to be illegal without an export license from the country of departure. The question that was posed was whether Jane's choice to take her chances and not declare the items was largely the result of a rational evaluation of the costs and benefits involved or guided more by her intuitions and emotions at the time of decision. The previous discussion has made clear that even though very different from the highly emotionally charged situation of John, the same competition for control of the hot and cool mode may be operative. Jane may experience a conflict between her awareness that she is best off declaring her items and be unwilling to violate the law, on the one hand, and her feelings of attachment toward her newly purchased goods or even the excitement of trying to get away with smuggling her items into the country, on the other hand. Alternatively, she may not even be aware of the fact that her hot mode leads her to consider only those options that she considers desirable while ignoring undesirable alternatives.

B. Practical Implications

There are several practical implications that follow from the previous discussion. For example, a failure to acknowledge the influence of affect on behavior and unrealistic optimism regarding one's ability to control impulses in future situations may imply that convicted offenders fail to optimally utilize their possibilities to protect themselves against the temptations of crime and may return to situations that contributed to their initial offenses, even when they are committed to abstain from offending (Dhami et al. 2006; van Gelder 2013).

The hot/cool perspective can elucidate research findings that are difficult to accommodate in terms of rational choice and deterrence frameworks. The premise underlying deterrence is that people will abstain from offending when costs of offending in terms of sanction probability, severity, and celerity outweigh the gains. As explained previously in this chapter, appeals to consider external and particularly longer term costs are directed at the cool, cognitive mode. When decisions to offend are cued by the hot mode and the cool mode is unable to override the response of the hot mode, deterrence will fail to generate the desired effect. This also speaks to the situational nature of the hot/cool framework with regard to explaining crime. In other words, an offender may not be deterred by considerations of punishment severity and probability "in the heat of the moment," even though he or she may be perfectly able to abstain from such acts in an emotionally neutral or "cold" state. Foreshadowing the advent of dual-process models, Zimring and Hawkins (1973) perfectly described this point in their classic work on deterrence: "Decisions about criminal conduct that are made when a person is in circumstances which provoke great emotional arousal may be less amenable to threats than decisions that occur when the potential criminal is less aroused, because very high degrees of emotional arousal may eclipse thoughts of future consequences by riveting all of the potential criminal's attention on his present situation" (p. 136).

IV. Conclusion

This chapter discussed some of the limitations of the dominant choice models in criminology, which by and large tend to be rational choice based, in accommodating for the pervasive influence of our feelings on human behavior, specifically rule-violating behavior. The chapter drew from dual-process and dual-system models to be able to theoretically account for this influence and explain findings in the criminological literature on criminal decision making that are difficult to explain in terms of rational choice. The chapter provided an alternative perspective based on dual-process models of information processing, paying particular attention to a recently proposed framework of criminal decision making that explains how hot affect influences decisions alongside cool cognitive factors. It was argued that an encompassing understanding of offender decision making requires the consideration of both.

Interestingly, the dualism between feeling and thinking is an ancient one, dating back more than two millennia to the ancient Greeks, who chronicled how people's short-sighted passions got them into trouble when obscuring reason and led them to engage in behavior that ran counter to their best interests. For Descartes (1649/1989), too, passions could contradict deliberation and, if intense enough, be self-defeating by overpowering the mind's countervailing efforts. In a similar vein, Adam Smith (1759/1976) described human behavior as the outcome of a struggle between the "passions" (i.e., emotions and drives such as hunger and desire) and the "impartial spectator," which he envisioned as an internal voice of reason able to moderate the passions. Hume (1739/1896, p. 217) also referred to the dualism, arguing that "reason is, and ought only to be the slave of the passions, and can never pretend to any other office than to serve and obey them." Freud (1923/1962) expressed the inner tension as a conflict between an ego, which represents the rational and conscious self and obeys a reality principle, and a pleasure-seeking id. All these perspectives have embedded in them the notion of a divided mind guided by both ratio and affect, or reason and passion, and to a greater or lesser extent map onto several of the key principles underlying the dual-process hypothesis.

However, during the course of the twentieth century, the notion that feelings can be important drivers of behavior got somewhat lost to psychologists, sociologists, and economists, and in their wake criminologists, who increasingly came to rely on strictly cognitive choice models, thereby excluding from consideration the potential influence of affect on our decisions and actions. Tracing the origins of the insistence on models limited to rational thought and cognition, Karstedt (2011) notes that "criminology as a science is a descendant of the Enlightenment, and is as such committed to the ideals of reason and reasonable discourse" (p. 1). The upshot of this commitment has been a view of the offender as a largely rational decision maker—a view that sits uneasy with the accumulating empirical evidence showing that emotions are fundamental inputs in the decision process.

In their classic work, *The Reasoning Criminal*, the architects of the rational choice perspective in criminology argued that it is rooted in the psychological tradition of information processing and decision making (Cornish and Clarke 1986). However, since the introduction of this seminal work by Cornish and Clarke in the 1980s, it has received only sparse updating. Consequently, insights from approximately three decades of research in the very same tradition that forms its basis have gone relatively unnoticed in criminal decision-making research (van Gelder et al. 2013). Ironically, much of this research has shown that affect—that is, emotions, moods, and related visceral drive factors such as sexual arousal and drug craving—plays a fundamental role in human decision processes, which seems to imply that the rational choice model is in need of updating (van Gelder et al. 2013).

Following the logic underlying the dual-process hypothesis, and the hot/cool perspective in particular, it is clear why choice models of offending behavior restricted to that part of our mental operations that pertains to thinking or cool rational processing amount to a rather limited and one-sided view of decision processes under risk and uncertainty, with a crippled understanding of criminal choice processes as a result. As shown in this chapter, treating emotions as just another form of cost or benefit that people weigh in their calculation when deciding to offend or not does not accurately reflect what is now known about how emotions influence thinking and behavior (Benson and Sams 2012).

It is hoped that this chapter has not only shown that there is more to the criminal decision process than rational choice but also that the extension of the standard choice perspectives in criminology with affective, automatic, and intuitive processes does not imply an incomprehensible amalgam of irrational forces (van Winden and Ash, 2012). Although we should acknowledge the multitude of environmental factors that can influence criminal choice and render the relation between affect and behavior to not be clear-cut, it is also important to recognize that the influence of affect on behavior is systematic rather than random in nature and therefore, to a certain extent, predictable. The current challenge is to develop research designs that aim to better understand the interaction between cognition and affect and to consider how this knowledge can serve as imput for crime prevention and deterrence policies and offender treatment. As we become more adept at developing instruments for measuring cognitive and affective variables, at both the explicit level and the implicit level, we can now work toward a more precise decision-making framework that moves from theory toward the development of policy.

NOTES

1. Note that "affect" is a broad term that includes not only emotions but also feeling states such as moods (e.g., feeling good, bad, or anxious) and visceral drives states (e.g., hunger, thirst, pain, drug craving, and sexual arousal). For a more elaborate discussion, see chapter 22 of this volume.
2. For a critique on dual-process and dual-system models, see Kruglanski and Gigerenzer (2011).
3. Evans and Stanovich (2013) argue that the commonly used terms "system 1" and "system 2" are actually misnomers because they imply that what is being referred to is a singular system, whereas each actually refers to a set of systems in the brain. Deutsch and Strack (2006) add that the assumption that there are exactly two processes is not implied by duality theories. Systems are regularly interacting groups of processes that share the same computations or functions. Accordingly, the two systems entail multiple processes.
4. Note that although rational choice-based theories remain faithful to the utilitarian notion that individuals tend to behave in ways that maximize benefits and minimize cost, it is often acknowledged that they do not engage in elaborate assessments of all the advantages and disadvantages of various alternative courses of action. Instead, they exhibit "bounded rationality" (Simon 1957) and may resort to the use of cognitive heuristics that may result in error (Kahneman and Tversky 1982). Nonetheless, feelings are largely viewed as unrelated to the decision-making process by rational choice-based explanations.

REFERENCES

Becker, G. S. 1968. "Crime and Punishment: An Economic Approach." *Journal of Political Economy* 76:169–217.

Benson, M. L., and T. L. Sams. 2012. "Emotions, Choice and Crime." In *The Oxford Handbook of Criminological Theory*, edited by Francis T. Cullen and Pamela Wilcox, p. 494. Oxford: Oxford University Press.

Chaiken, S., and Y. Trope. 1999. *Dual-Process Theories in Social Psychology*. New York: Guilford Press.

Cornish, D. B., and R. V. Clarke. 1986. *The Reasoning Criminal: Rational Choice Perspectives on Offending*. New York: Springer-Verlag.

Descartes, R. 1989. *The Passions of the Soul*. Indianapolis, IN: Hackett Publishing. (Originally published in French: *Les passions de l'âme*, 1649).

Deutsch, R., and F. Strack. 2006. "Duality-Models in Social Psychology: From Opposing Processes to Interacting Systems." *Psychological Inquiry* 17:166–72.

Dhami, M. K., D. R. Mandel, G. Loewenstein, and P. Ayton. 2006. "Prisoners' Positive Illusions of Their Post-Release Success." *Law and Human Behavior* 30:631–47.

Epstein, S. 1994. "Integration of the Cognitive and Psychodynamic Unconscious." *American Psychologist* 49:709–24.

Evans, J. S. B., and K. E. Stanovich. 2013. "Dual-Process Theories of Higher Cognition Advancing the Debate." *Perspectives on Psychological Science* 8:223–41.

Freud, S. 1962. *The Ego and the Id.* New York: Norton. (Originally published in German: *Das Ich und das Es*, 1923).

Frijda, N. H. 1988. "The Laws of Emotion." *American Psychologist* 43:349–58.

Fudenberg, D., and D. K. Levine. 2006. "A Dual-Self Model of Impulse Control." *American Economic Review* 96:1449–76.

Gerrard, M., F. X. Gibbons, A. E. Houlihan, M. L. Stock, and E. A. Pomery. 2008. "A Dual Process Approach to Health Risk Decision Making: The Prototype Willingness Model." *Developmental Review* 28:29–61.

Gottfredson, M., and T. Hirschi. 1990. *A General Theory of Crime.* Palo Alto, CA: Stanford University Press.

Hirschi, T. 2004. "Self-Control and Crime." In *Handbook of Self-Regulation: Research, Theory, and Applications*, edited by R. F. Baumeister and K. Vohs, pp. 537–552. New York: Guilford.

Hofmann, W., M. Friese, and F. Strack. 2009. "Impulse and Self-Control from a Dual-Systems Perspective." *Perspectives on Psychological Science* 4:162–76.

Hume, D. 1896. *A Treatise of Human Nature.* Oxford: Clarendon Press. (Originally published 1739).

Kahneman, D. 2003. "Perspectives on Judgment and Choice: Mapping Bounded Rationality." *American Psychologist* 58:697–720.

Kahneman, D. 2011. *Thinking Fast and Slow, 2011.* New York: Farrar, Strauss and Giroux.

Kahneman, D., and A. Tversky. 1982. "Judgment Under Uncertainty: Heuristics and Biases." In *Judgment Under Uncertainty: Heuristics and Biases*, edited by Daniel Kahneman, Paul Slovic, and Amos Tversky, pp. 3–20. Cambridge: Cambridge University Press.

Karstedt, S. (2011). "Handle with Care: Emotions, Crime and Justice." In *Emotions, Crime and Justice*, edited by S. Karstedt, I. Loader, and H. Strang. Onati International Series in Law and Society, pp. 1–19. Oxford: Hart Publishing.

Kruglanski, A. W., and G. Gigerenzer. 2011. "Intuitive and Deliberate Judgments Are Based on Common Principles." *Psychological Review* 118:97–109.

LeDoux, J. E. 1996. *The Emotional Brain.* New York: Simon and Schuster.

Loewenstein, G., and J. Lerner. 2003. "The Role of Affect in Decision Making. In *Handbook of Affective Sciences*, edited by R. J. Davidson, K. R. Scherer, and H. H. Goldsmith, pp. 619–642. New York: Oxford University Press.

Loewenstein, G., and T. O'Donoghue. 2004. "Animal Spirits: Affective and Deliberative Influences on Economic Behavior." Working paper. Pittsburgh, PA: Department of Social and Decision Sciences, Carnegie Mellon University. https://ssrn.com/abstract=539843

Loewenstein, G., E. Weber, C. Hsee, and N. Welch. 2001. "Risk as Feelings." *Psychological Bulletin* 127:267–86.

Lofland, J. 1969. *Deviance and Identity.* Englewood Cliffs, NJ: Prentice-Hall.

Metcalfe, J., and W. Mischel. 1999. "A Hot/Cool System Analysis of Delay of Gratification: Dynamics of Willpower." *Psychological Review* 106:3–19.

Nagin, D. S. 2007. "Moving Choice to Center Stage in Criminological Research and Theory: The American Society of Criminology 2006 Sutherland Address. *Criminology* 45:259–72.

Nee, C., and A. Meenaghan. 2006. "Expert Decision Making in Burglars." *British Journal of Criminology* 46:935–49.

Simon, H. A. 1957. *Administrative Behaviour.* New York: Macmillan.

Sloman, S. A. 1996. "The Empirical Case for Two Systems of Reasoning." *Psychological Bulletin* 119:3–22.

Slovic, P., E. Peters, M. L. Finucane, and D. G. MacGregor. 2005. "Affect, Risk, and Decision Making." *Health Psychology* 24:35–40.

Smith, A. 1976. "The Theory of Moral Sentiments." Indianapolis, IN: Liberty Classics. (Originally published 1759).

Smith, E. R., and R. Neumann. 2005. "Emotion Processes Considered from the Perspective of Dual-Process Models." In *Emotion and Consciousness*, edited by Lisa Barrett Feldman, Paula M. Niedenthal, and Piotr Winkielman, pp. 287–311. New York: Guilford.

Stanovich, K. E., and R. F. West. 2000. "Individual Differences in Reasoning: Implications for the Rationality Debate." *Behavioral and Brain Sciences* 23:645–65.

Strack, F., and R. Deutsch. 2004. "Reflective and Impulsive Determinants of Social Behavior." *Personality and Social Psychology Review* 8:220–47.

Thaler, R. H., and H. M. Shefrin. 1981. "An Economic Theory of Self-Control." *Journal of Political Economy* 89:392–406.

Thomas, K. J., and J. McGloin. 2013. "A Dual-System Approach for Understanding Differential Susceptibility to Processes of Peer Influence." *Criminology* 51(2): 435–74.

Topalli, V., and R. Wright. 2013. "Affect and the Dynamic Foreground of Predatory Street Crime: Desperation, Anger and Fear." In *Affect and Cognition in Criminal Decision Making*, edited by J. L. van Gelder, H. Elffers, D. Reynald, and D. S. Nagin, pp. 42–57. Abingdon, UK: Routledge.

Treiber, K. 2013. "A Neuropsychological Test of Criminal Decision Making: Regional Prefrontal Influences in a Dual Process Model." In *Affect and Cognition in Criminal Decision Making*, edited by J. L. van Gelder, H. Elffers, D. Reynald, and D. S. Nagin, pp. 193–221. Abingdon, UK: Routledge.

van Gelder, J. L. 2013. "Beyond Rational Choice: The Hot/Cool Perspective of Criminal Decision Making." *Psychology, Crime and Law* 19:745–63.

van Gelder, J. L., and R. E. de Vries. 2012. "Traits and States: Integrating Personality and Affect into a Model of Criminal Decision Making." *Criminology* 50:637–71.

van Gelder, J. L., and R. E. de Vries. 2014. "Rational Misbehavior? Evaluating an Integrated Dual-Process Model of Criminal Decision Making." *Journal of Quantitative Criminology* 30:1–27.

van Gelder, J. L., and R. E. de Vries. 2015. "Traits and States at Work: Lure, Risk and Personality as Predictors of Occupational Crime." Unpublished manuscript.

van Gelder, J. L., R. E. de Vries, and J. van der Pligt. 2009. "Evaluating a Dual-Process Model of Risk: Affect and Cognition as Determinants of Risky Choice." *Journal of Behavioral Decision Making* 22:45–61.

van Gelder, J. L., H. Elffers, D. Reynald, and D. S. Nagin. 2013. "Affect and Cognition in Criminal Decision Making: Between Rational Choices and Lapses of Self-Control." In *Affect and Cognition in Criminal Decision Making*, edited by J. L. van Gelder, H. Elffers, D. Reynald, and D. S. Nagin, pp. 1–19. Abingdon, UK: Routledge.

van Gelder, J. L., E. C. Luciano, M. Weulen Kranenbarg, and H. E. Hershfield. 2015. "Friends with My Future Self: A Longitudinal Vividness Intervention Reduces Delinquency." *Criminology* 53(2): 158–79.

van Winden, F., and E. Ash. 2012. "On the Behavioral Economics of Crime." *Review of Law and Economics* 8:181–213.

Ward, T., and S. M. Hudson. (2000). "Sexual Offenders Implicit Planning: A Conceptual Model." *Sexual Abuse: A Journal of Research and Treatment* 12:189–202.

Wright, Richard, and Scott H. Decker. 1994. *Burglars on the Job: Streetlife and Residential Break-ins.* Boston: Northeastern University Press.

Wright, Richard, and Scott H. Decker. 1997. *Armed Robbers in Action: Stickups and Street Culture.* Boston: Northeastern University Press.

Zajonc, R. B. 1980. "Feeling and Thinking: Preferences Need No Inferences." *American Psychologist* 35:151–75.

Zajonc, R. B. 1998. "Emotions." In *Handbook of Social Psychology*, edited by D. Gilbert, S. T. Fiske, and G. Lindzey, pp. 591–634. New York: Oxford University Press.

Zimring, F. E., and G. E. Hawkins. 1973. *Deterrence: The Legal Threat in Crime Control.* Chicago: University of Chicago Press.

CHAPTER 10

PERSONALITY AND OFFENDER DECISION MAKING

The Theoretical, Empirical, and Practical Implications for Criminology

SHAYNE JONES

As evidenced throughout this handbook, there are a variety of explanations and pathways that link decision making to offending. This chapter focuses on the role of personality and how it can influence the choice to engage in offending. The chapter begins by defining personality and providing some basic background information. This is followed by a discussion of structural models of personality, with particular emphasis given to the five-factor model (FFM) and the HEXACO model of personality. As will be demonstrated, both are reliably associated with antisocial behavior. The next section describes theoretical pathways that underscore the role of decision making in explaining the relationship between personality traits and offending. This is followed by a review of the empirical evidence that offers either direct or indirect support for the mediating role of decision making. The final section focuses on the role of personality within mainstream criminology, with specific recommendations on how and why criminologists should more widely use this construct in their theories, research, and application. Although there remains much work to be done, this chapter demonstrates that personality is an important construct that can provide insights into the decision making of offenders as well as advance criminology inquiry.

I. DEFINING PERSONALITY

Within criminology, and compared to numerous other constructs, personality has not been a focal concern. Perhaps part of the reason for this is that the concept of personality is not well understood. Some individuals view the glass as half full and are optimistic, whereas others view it as half empty and are more pessimistic. Some individuals interpret an ambiguous stimulus (e.g., being bumped into by another person) as an accident, whereas other individuals perceive this as a slight. Some individuals are easily emotionally aroused, whereas others are better able to maintain a cool and calm demeanor. Some individuals walk by a bakery and immediately rush in to purchase a sweet treat, whereas other individuals never go inside because they are trying to avoid unnecessary calories. Why are individuals so different in their behavior and interpretations? To be sure, one's life experiences play some role. However, another very compelling and empirically validated reason is that individuals vary in personality. Each of the previously mentioned differences can be reliably explained by personality.

A more formal definition of personality is the relatively enduring patterns of thinking, feeling, and behaving exhibited within individuals. Such patterns demonstrate remarkable stability over time (Roberts and DelVecchio 2000), although changes can and do occur with sufficient regularity that it is unreasonable to conceive of personality as crystalized at any point in the life course (Roberts, Caspi, and Moffitt 2001). Thus, the term *relative* is used here to denote such possibilities. It is also important to distinguish between absolute and relative stability. Absolute stability suggests that the level of a trait is precisely the same at different time points within the same individual. In contrast, relative stability refers to the notion that between-individual differences will be maintained over time. For instance, the rank order between two individuals, one exceptionally high on a given trait and another who is extraordinarily low on the same trait, will likely be preserved over time. Although absolute levels of the trait for both individuals can change over time, the one scoring higher will typically show greater levels of the trait than the one with less of the trait years afterwards (Caspi, Roberts, and Shiner 2005).

As an enduring pattern, it is crucial to distinguish personality traits from states. States can be influenced by something situational or outside the individual. Public speaking, being unfairly accused of wrongdoing, or the loss of a loved one will elicit common reactions from many people. The thoughts, feelings, and actions resulting from these experiences are transient, however, because they are tied to specific situations. Yet some individuals experience anxiety, resentment, or depression on a regular basis, and these do not wax and wane as a function of situational factors. Instead, they are relatively enduring patterns that characterize the person. In short, these differences are due to personality.

It is also important to note that the situations and environments to which individuals are exposed are not random. In fact, personality influences situations and environments in important ways. Caspi and Roberts (2001) described three processes that help to understand the relationship between personality and environments. First, there are reactive person–environment transactions. This suggests that two individuals can experience the same situation differently depending on their traits. As mentioned previously, public speaking can elicit anxiety from many, if not most, people. Someone low in trait anxiety, however, might only be modestly affected by public speaking (or not at all). Conversely, someone high in trait anxiety will find the experience debilitating. Second are evocative person–environment transactions. This process suggests that others respond in similar ways to an individual's disposition. For example, aggressive children are often avoided/rejected by prosocial children (Dodge et al. 2003). That is, the aggressive behavior of the child leads prosocial others to react in a predictable and consistent way—avoidance and rejection. Third, there are proactive person–environment transactions. These occur when individuals seek out environments consistent with their personalities. For example, sensation seekers (generally) would prefer to spend an evening at an amusement park riding roller coasters rather than taking part in a book club (Zuckerman 1994). These different processes underscore that environments are influenced by personality. Later in the chapter, these processes are used to demonstrate relationships between personality and mainstream criminological constructs.

Having established what personality is and is not, the following section shifts to describing how personality is operationalized and measured in the contemporary personality literature. There is also a focus on the empirical relationships between personality traits and offending.

II. STRUCTURAL MODELS OF PERSONALITY

There are a variety of ways personality has been conceptualized (for review, see Pervin and John 1999), but arguably the most influential in the contemporary personality psychology literature are structural models of personality. These models purport to capture all personality traits and, by way of different techniques (discussed later), place them into distinct components. That is, not all personality traits can be captured under one unifying structure. Instead, there are some traits that are similar to one another but different from others. By identifying these different components (or factors), personality can be organized along meaningful axes. At the broadest levels are domains, each of which is composed of several more precise facets. (The precise number of facets within a domain varies depending on the specific model.)

Numerous structural models have been developed throughout the years, with many early models consisting of three main dimensions. During the 1980s and 1990s, there was an emerging consensus that there are five domains. From the five-factor model (FFM), the domains are Neuroticism, Extraversion, Openness to Experience, Agreeableness, and Conscientiousness (John and Srivastava 1999). Neuroticism refers to the tendency to experience negative affect, such as depression and anxiety. Extraversion describes the degree to which an individual seeks the company of others and engages with the world. Openness to Experience taps into one's willingness to consider different values and ideas. Agreeableness describes the tendency to relate to and interact with others in a prosocial manner. Conscientiousness refers to being dependable and possessing self-control.

John and Srivastava (1999) provide a thorough overview of the origins, development, and measurement associated with the five domains. The following is a brief overview of their work. The origins of models based on these five domains are found in the lexical approach, which suggests that any trait that is important to understanding personality can be found in the natural language. Personality psychologists explored the English language for any words that could describe a trait (e.g., friendly and diligent) that could distinguish one individual from another. Throughout the years, researchers paired down the number of traits. One means of doing so was to eliminate items that appeared to be synonyms and to group similar items together. Another approach, facilitated by the advancement of computers and software, was to employ factor analytic techniques. What resulted were the five broad factors noted previously—labeled the Big Five[1]. One of the most widely used and researched varieties of this framework is the FFM (Costa and McCrae 1992). Originally, the FFM consisted of three domains, based on factor analyses (Neuroticism, Extraversion, and Openness). With the evidence of five domains, the FFM added Agreeableness and Consciousness. (The Big Five and the FFM are not identical. The Big Five represents a conceptual taxonomy of personality, whereas the FFM refers to a specific theoretical and measurement approach. Although often used interchangeably, there are some differences between the original Big Five and the FFM. For instance, Openness from the FFM is broader than the Intellect or Imagination factor in the Big Five; see John and Srivastava [1999] for a discussion of similarities and differences.) Underlying the five broad domains are six lower order facets (table 10.1).

Two meta-analyses have been conducted that addressed the extent to which personality traits are related to antisocial behavior. Miller and Lynam (2001) examined several different structural models of personality, including the Eyesenck's PEN model, Tellegen's Multidimensional Personality Questionnaire, Cloninger's Seven-Factor Temperament Model, and Costa and McCrae's FFM. Components from each model demonstrated significant relationships with antisocial behavior, but the authors noted that each of the significant findings could be explained in terms of the FFM traits. For instance, Constraint (from the Multidimensional Personality Questionnaire) was significantly negatively related to antisocial behavior. However, Constraint substantially overlaps with Conscientiousness from the FFM. Thus, their conclusions were framed in the language and measurement of the FFM. To that end, Agreeableness and Conscientiousness were moderately and negatively related to antisocial behavior, whereas Neuroticism demonstrated a positive, weak relationship. Extraversion and Openness to Experience were unrelated to antisocial behavior.

A subsequent follow-up of FFM studies published since the 2001 meta-analysis was performed by Jones, Miller, and Lynam (2011), in which they focused on antisocial behavior and aggression separately. Their results confirmed and extended the results of the previous meta-analysis. As before, Agreeableness, Conscientiousness, and Neuroticism demonstrated the largest and most consistent effects across both outcomes. Interestingly, Extraversion and Openness to Experience were weakly and negatively related to aggression. Jones et al. also examined the relationship between all 30 FFM facets and these outcomes. All six facets from Agreeableness and Conscientiousness were significantly negatively related to both outcomes. Three facets from Neuroticism—Angry Hostility, Depression, and Impulsiveness—were positively related to both outcomes. Another facet from Neuroticism—Anxiety—was negatively related to antisocial behavior only, whereas another Neuroticism facet—Vulnerability—was positively related to aggression only. As they noted, some facets from Neuroticism were positively related to the outcomes,

Table 10.1 FFM Domains and Facets

Neuroticism

Anxiety
Angry hostility
Depression
Self-consciousness
Impulsiveness
Vulnerability

Extraversion

Warmth
Gregariousness
Assertiveness
Activity
Excitement seeking
Positive emotions

Openness to Experience

Fantasy
Aesthetics
Feelings
Actions
Ideas
Values

Agreeableness

Trust
Straightforwardness
Altruism
Compliance
Modesty

Tender-Mindedness

Conscientiousness
Competence
Order
Dutifulness
Achievement striving
Self-discipline
Deliberation

whereas others were negatively related. Moreover, some Neuroticism facets were more strongly related to one outcome than the other. This explains why Neuroticism demonstrated relatively weaker effects in the first meta-analysis (Miller and Lynam 2001). A similar argument was advanced by Jones et al. to explain differences between the domain and facet level analyses for Extraversion and Openness. Overall, there is compelling evidence that FFM traits are related to antisocial outcomes.

A relatively newer structural model of personality, the HEXACO, includes six domains: Honesty–Humility, Emotionality, Extraversion, Agreeableness, Conscientiousness, and Openness (table 10.2). As noted by the developers of this model (Ashton et al., 2004),

Table 10.2 HEXACO Model of Personality Domains and Facets
Honest–Humility
Sincerity
Fairness
Greed avoidance
Modesty
Emotionality
Fearfulness
Anxiety
Dependence
Sentimentality
Extraversion
Social self-esteem
Social boldness
Sociability
Liveliness
Agreeableness
Forgiveness
Gentleness
Flexibility
Patience
Conscientiousness
Organization
Diligence
Perfectionism
Prudence
Openness to Experience
Aesthetic appreciation
Inquisitiveness
Creativity
Unconventionality

there was evidence consistently emerging from psycholexical studies that a six-factor model might be more appropriate than the dominant five-factor solutions. Specifically, using the lexical approach in languages other than English, a sixth factor consistently emerged.[2]

Although there is overlap between the FFM and HEXACO, there are some important differences as well. Two studies help to further understand the similarities and differences between the FFM and HEXACO model of personality. An abbreviated version of the FFM (i.e., the NEO Five-Factor Inventory; Costa and McCrae 1992) was compared to the 60-item version of the HEXACO Personality Inventory (HEXACO-PI; Lee and Ashton 2004). Lee, Ashton, and de Vries (2013) found that Extraversion ($r = .72$), Conscientiousness ($r = .76$), and Openness ($r = .79$) across the two measures were strongly related to one another. Agreeableness domains across the two models were moderately related to one another ($r = .62$). However, FFM Agreeableness also demonstrated a moderate relationship with Honesty–Humility ($r = .42$). FFM Neuroticism was moderately related to both HEXACO Emotionality ($r = .51$) and Extraversion ($r = -.54$). In a separate study (Gaughan, Miller, and Lynam 2012), the full measures of FFM (i.e., the NEO Personality Inventory–Revised; Costa and McCrae 1992) and HEXACO (HEXACO Personality Inventory–Revised; Lee and Ashton 2004) were examined for their overlap. Four domains demonstrated strong convergent correlations: Extraversion ($r = .86$), Openness to Experience ($r = .76$), Conscientiousness ($r = .87$), and Agreeableness ($r = .68$). Emotionality and Neuroticism were moderately related ($r = .52$). Honesty–Humility, the unique domain within the HEXACO model, was related most strongly to Agreeableness ($r = .67$; the only other significant correlation with this domain was Neuroticism, $r = -.23$). These findings suggest that, on the one hand, there is a notable overlap between the different models/measures, but on the other hand, there are important differences.

In addition to the empirical relationships between these models, there are some important conceptual distinctions between them. Ashton et al. (2014) provide an excellent review in this regard. They note that Openness, Extraversion, and Conscientiousness across both models are quite similar. However, the remaining domains share only modest resemblance. For instance, HEXACO Agreeableness shares overlap with FFM Agreeableness, but it does not include the sentimentality of FFM Agreeableness. Also, the anger-related traits from FFM Neuroticism are found in HEXACO Agreeableness. HEXACO Emotionality includes the sentimentality traits (from FFM Agreeableness) and removes the anger-related traits (from the FFM). This distinction between the two conceptualizations might also explain why some FFM Neuroticism traits (e.g., Angry–Hostility) are positively related to antisocial behavior, whereas others (e.g., Anxiety) are negatively related. Finally, Ashton and colleagues argue that HEXACO Honesty–Humility is not captured well by the FFM, despite some modest correlation with FFM Agreeableness. They demonstrate the distinction between HEXACO Honesty–Humility and FFM Agreeableness by discussing cooperative efforts under different circumstances. Someone who is low in Honesty–Humility will tend to exploit another when the opportunity exists.

Conversely, someone low in Agreeableness will be more exploitative when she believes the other is trying to take advantage of her. Thus, the difference is proactively taking advantage of another (low in Honesty–Humility) versus taking advantage of someone else only when the individual perceives she might be the victim of such behavior (low in Agreeableness).

All of the empirical studies discussed in this chapter relied on either the FFM or HEXACO. However, because these models overlap substantially in some respects, in many instances findings provide insight across models. For example, evidence regarding the relationship between FFM Conscientiousness and antisocial behavior can also be applied to HEXACO Conscientiousness. Greater caution should be exercised regarding findings focused on Neuroticism/Emotionality, Agreeableness, and Honesty–Humility. Despite being correlated at some level, they appear to be tapping into somewhat different aspects of personality (Lee and Ashton 2004; Gaughan et al. 2012). The similarities and differences across these models are summarized in table 10.3.

Although still relatively new, the HEXACO model has also been found to be related to antisocial behavior. Ashton and Lee (2008) found that Honesty–Humility, Emotionality, and Conscientiousness were negatively related to delinquency. Van Gelder and de Vries (2012, 2014) found that Honesty–Humility was related to the likelihood of making criminal choices, as were Emotionality and Conscientiousness (van Gelder and de Vries, 2012). The relationship between the HEXACO domains and workplace antisocial behavior has also been explored in several studies. Honesty–Humility, Emotionality, Conscientiousness, Openness to Experience, and Agreeableness (at least in one of two samples) were negatively related to unethical business decisions (Lee and Ashton 2008). Honesty–Humility, Emotionality, and Agreeableness were related to antisocial behavior directed at individuals (e.g., being rude toward a coworker), and Honesty–Humility,

Table 10.3 Similarities and Differences Between the FFM and HEXACO Structural Models of Personality

FFM	HEXACO
Neuroticism	Emotionality, Agreeableness, Extraversion
Openness	Openness
Extraversion	Extraversion
Agreeableness	Agreeableness, Neuroticism, Honesty–Humility
Conscientiousness	Conscientiousness
Agreeableness	Honesty–Humility[a]

[a]Ashton et al. (2014) argue that this domain is only peripherally related to FFM Agreeableness and that it is largely unaccounted for by FFM.

Emotionality, and Conscientiousness were related to antisocial behavior directed at the organization (e.g., not fulfilling work obligations dutifully; Lee, Ashton, and Shin 2005). Lee, Ashton, and de Vries (2005) found that Honesty–Humility was consistently negatively related to workplace delinquency across three samples. In addition, Emotionality was negatively related to workplace delinquency in two (of three) samples, and Openness to Experience was positively related in one (of three) samples.

Beyond the direct relationships between the HEXACO and antisocial behaviors, there is also evidence linking this model of personality to measures of criminal propensity. One analysis revealed that the Honesty–Humility dimension was negatively related to psychopathy (Lee and Ashton 2005). However, results from two other studies indicated that not only Honesty–Humility but also Emotionality, Agreeableness, and Conscientiousness were negatively related to psychopathy (de Vries and van Kampen 2010; Gaughan et al. 2012). In addition, de Vries and van Kampen found that Openness was positively related to psychopathy. Because psychopathy is a robust correlate of offending, it seems reasonable to assume that the traits related to psychopathy might also be related to offending.

The FFM has been used in numerous studies since the 1980s, whereas the HEXACO was initially described in 2004. Therefore, there is much more research regarding the FFM than the HEXACO. It is only a matter of time before there is more research linking the HEXACO to antisocial behavior. In fact, there are several reasons to suspect this will be the case.

Although the two structural models share overlap on some domains, there are some advantages for criminologists (and other researchers) in choosing the HEXACO model over the FFM. The most important reason is that the HEXACO appears to account for more variation in antisocial behavior and propensity compared to the FFM (Lee et al. 2005; de Vries and van Kampen 2010; Gaughan et al. 2012). Second, the HEXACO is freely available for research purposes (http://hexaco.org). However, the most widely used measure, the NEO Personality Inventory–Revised (NEO-PI-R), is proprietary and has professional qualification requirements for purchase and use. These factors might result in less access to that specific measure, especially compared to the HEXACO. Third, the HEXACO has three different versions based on length: There are 60-, 100-, and 200-item versions. The 60-item version takes 12 minutes to complete, whereas the 100-item version requires 20 minutes. The 200-item version is best if researchers want to capture the facets well. Like the NEO-PI-R, the HEXACO has several more specific traits within each domain. Specifically, each of the six domains is composed of four traits at the facet level (table 10.2). Fourth, the HEXACO is currently available in several different languages. Finally, the HEXACO can explain more variation in the NEO-PI-R than vice versa (Gaughan et al. 2012), so researchers who use the HEXACO are able to capture much of what they would get from using the NEO-PI-R. Given these factors, the HEXACO might be the better choice. (See Ashton and Lee [2007] for additional advantages of the HEXACO model of personality.)

The purpose of this section was to introduce readers to the notion of structural models of personality, with a focus on the FFM and HEXACO models in particular.

Both models demonstrate utility in understanding antisocial behavior. From the FFM, Agreeableness and Conscientiousness are the most consistently related to antisocial behavior. For the HEXACO, Honesty–Humility demonstrates the most robust association with antisocial behavior. In the following sections, the focus shifts to explain how the traits and models noted previously can influence decision making and lead to offending. As will be demonstrated, some empirical evidence exists that has addressed this issue, although much work remains to be done.

III. Exploring the Link Between Traits and Antisocial Behavior

According to McCrae and Costa (1999), traits are biologically based, and there is sufficient evidence that traits are heritable (i.e., they have a genetic basis; Jang et al. 1998). But traits, in and of themselves, do not directly produce behavior. Instead, they lead to characteristic adaptations. These adaptations are culturally prescribed and include factors such as attitudes and beliefs (McCrae and Costa 1999). Thus, traits themselves do not cause behavior directly, but they influence perceptions, attitudes, and relationship choices (see also the previous discussion of the person–environment transaction). Some examples help to illustrate this. Jones and Quisenberry (2004) examined whether self-control (measured with the Grasmick scale), an interstitial trait that has been extensively linked to antisocial behavior (Pratt and Cullen 2000), might also be related to risky but prosocial behaviors. They found that self-control was negatively related to engaging (or intending to engage) in Thrill and Adventure Seeking behavior (e.g., bungee jumping and skydiving; for this scale, see Zuckerman 1994). Importantly, however, they found evidence that although low self-control might manifest itself in prosocial, risky behaviors, it could also be expressed in antisocial behavior. Moreover, it did not appear that those lower in self-control who engaged in antisocial behaviors were the same ones who engaged in risky, prosocial behaviors. Similar arguments have been advanced with regard to being pathologically low in fear arousal. Lykken (1995) suggests that the psychopath and the hero share something in common—exceptionally low fear arousal. Although these two have similar dispositions (on fear arousal), one might become a violent criminal, whereas the other one might become a daring fighter jet pilot serving in the Armed Forces. Psychopathic traits, especially in terms of Fearless Dominance, have even been ascribed to US presidents (Lilienfeld et al. 2012). Thus, traits certainly influence behavior, but the precise behavioral expression of the traits will be affected by factors other than the traits.

Not only can similar dispositional attributes lead to different outcomes but also similar outcomes can be explained by different traits. This is perhaps best typified by the notion of impulsivity. Various behaviors can be described as impulsive, including overindulging in food or drink, watching television instead of studying for an exam, deciding to take a weekend trip at the last moment, and, of course, choosing to commit a crime. While sharing some degree of phenotypic similarity (i.e., they are impulsive behaviors), these behaviors stem from different personality traits. Whiteside and Lynam (2001), in an effort to bring some clarity to the elusive notion of impulsivity, found that there are four distinct traits that can lead to impulsive behavior. Moreover, these four traits are captured in the FFM of personality. The traits are Urgency, Premeditation, Perseverance, and Sensation Seeking. Urgency (from Neuroticism) describes impulsive behavior that stems from negative affect. Premeditation (from Conscientiousness) refers to impulsive behavior that results from failing to consider the negative consequences of a behavior. Perseverance (from Conscientiousness) denotes impulsive behavior that results from failing to maintain focus on a difficult or boring task when more appealing alternatives exist. Sensation seeking (from Extraversion) relates to impulsive behavior that is based on a desire to seek out novel and exciting experiences. Some of these traits are more strongly related to antisocial behaviors than others. Lynam and Miller (2004) found that Premeditation and Sensation Seeking were the two impulsive traits most consistently related to antisocial behaviors.

It is also worth noting that the relationship between traits and behavior is not likely to be direct in most instances. Instead, traits are mediated by other factors. For instance, those lower in Premeditation are less likely to consider the negative consequences of antisocial behavior. To determine this, however, one must introduce some measure of perceptions of negative consequences that mediates the relationship between this trait and antisocial outcomes. This is true for other traits as well. In the next section, a series of theoretical mechanisms are discussed that focus on decision making in particular, and this discussion is followed by the presentation of empirical evidence speaking to the veracity of some of these claims.

IV. THEORETICAL SPECIFICATIONS

With the caveat that the manifestation of a trait is contingent on several factors, there are ways of linking traits, decision making, and antisocial behavior. One way to understand how the five factors, in particular, might influence offender decision making is to explore the facets noted in the FFM. Based on the work of Jones et al. (2011) noted previously, the focus here is on some of the facets that demonstrated the most consistent significant relationships with antisocial and aggressive outcomes. From the Neuroticism domain, Angry–Hostility and Impulsiveness were positively related to these outcomes. Such individuals are more likely to experience negative, angry affect and respond rashly to that affect. For such individuals, their antisocial behavior can be viewed as a means of coping with and reducing this emotion. For instance, their decision to lash out at others might be an attempt to alleviate the negative affect they are experiencing.

From the Extraversion domain, low Warmth was related to antisocial and aggressive outcomes (Jones et al. 2011). Individuals low in Warmth are disinterested and unwelcoming toward others. Such individuals have little to lose in antisocial/aggressive exchanges because they are relationally distant from others and are unconcerned if others feel positive affect in their presence. Excitement Seeking was positively related to antisocial behavior, and such individuals crave novel, thrilling, and exciting activities. The decision to offend could be viewed by such individuals as a rewarding means of satisfying those desires (Katz 1988).

Each of the facets from Conscientiousness demonstrated significant relationships with both outcomes (Jones et al. 2011), and it is not difficult to understand how they could influence the decision to engage in offending. Two of the strongest facets from this domain that were related to antisocial behaviors were Deliberation and Dutifulness. Individuals low in these traits are characterized by failing to consider the consequences of their actions before acting and failing to meet one's obligations, respectively. Individuals low in Deliberation might fail to consider the costs or place too much weight on the potential rewards, both of which could lead to antisocial behavior. Possessing low Dutifulness could lead to antisocial outcomes because such individuals place too little emphasis on meeting moral obligations that constrain such behavior among those higher in this trait. From the perspective of people low on this trait, the obligation they have toward others simply might not enter into their decision making. Stated alternatively, those higher on this trait might not offend because they perceive such behavior as a failure to meet one's moral obligation.

Like Conscientiousness, each of the six domains from Agreeableness was related to antisocial and aggressive behavior (Jones et al. 2011). The six facets included in this domain are Trust, Straightforwardness, Altruism, Compliance, Modesty, and Tender-Mindedness. Linking these traits to antisocial decision making is not difficult to do. For individuals lower in these traits, their interpersonal interactions and relationships are characterized by greater conflict, less emotional attachment, and more self-centeredness. When making the decision to aggress against another, there is a substantial risk in compromising or dissolving the relationship with that person. For individuals lower in Agreeableness, either these risks are not considered or they are weighted so little that such thoughts are not sufficient to inhibit the aggression.

As noted previously, the HEXACO model includes the trait of Honesty–Humility. Again, by examining this trait at the facet level, it is not difficult to ascertain why such individuals engage in antisocial behavior. Sincerity refers to being genuine and straightforward in interpersonal interactions. Fairness describes the tendency to avoid cheating and corruption as a means of acquiring something. Greed Avoidance conveys the penchant to not be interested in accumulating wealth and showing it off. Modesty denotes the predisposition to be unassuming. Those scoring lower on these four traits are manipulative and dishonest, want to be perceived as social/economic elites, and feel entitled. An individual with such a disposition views others as objects to be used and therefore is not deterred from offending against them. These people are also self-centered, and it might be the case that their decision to aggress against someone is based on their own needs with little consideration of others' needs. In addition, because such individuals value wealth and status, they might perceive offending (e.g., theft) as a viable strategy for reaching their goals. It is very likely that other facets from the HEXACO model of personality are related to antisocial behavior. Gaughan et al. (2012) found modest negative correlations between antisocial behavior (as measured in the Antisocial facet of the Self-Report Psychopathy Scale) and Fearfulness, Sentimentality, and Prudence. As described in detail later, van Gelder and de Vries (2012, 2014) found relationships between specific HEXACO facets and criminal choice. It is only a matter of time before more research is directed at the relationship between HEXACO facets and antisocial behavior, and this will lead to new insights.

This section provided a conceptual basis for understanding how the influence of personality traits on antisocial behavior can be explained through decision-making processes. Although much of this remains theoretical, empirical accounts offer support for these propositions. That is the focus of the following section.

V. Empirical Links Between Traits, Decision Making, and Behavior

Whereas there is a great deal of empirical data linking personality traits to antisocial behavior, the research on the mechanisms linking the two has not received as much attention (Miller and Lynam 2001). This is especially true when considering how decision-making processes might mediate the relationship. Nonetheless, there are several empirical accounts that offer insights and guidance. The following sections provide a summary of studies that have linked traits to decision making in various contexts, including interpersonal interactions, affective states, perceived risks and rewards, and cognitive distortions.

A. Interpersonal Interactions: A Focus on Agreeableness and Affect

Several studies have explored how Agreeableness affects interpersonal interactions. The work of Jensen-Campbell and colleagues is informative in this regard. Adolescents in middle school who were higher in Agreeableness used more constructive conflict resolution tactics (e.g., compromise) and fewer destructive tactics (e.g., threats). Such individuals also appeared more motivated to maintain positive relations with others (Jensen-Campbell and Graziano 2001). In terms of decision making, these findings suggest that those higher in Agreeableness are able to access and utilize more prosocial conflict resolution tactics as well as place greater value on such interactions. Conversely, those lower in Agreeableness might make decisions based on limited information (e.g., not knowing how to minimize conflict) or failing to consider the importance of getting along with others. Jensen-Campbell and Graziano also noted that those higher in Emotional Stability (i.e., lower in Neuroticism) were less likely to endorse the use of physical force and undermining the esteem/position of their rival as a means of retaliation. This suggests that those with greater Emotional Stability can cognitively and behaviorally suppress aggressive responses better than those who are emotionally unstable.

Similar results were obtained among younger children (fifth and sixth graders; Jensen-Campbell et al. 2002). Agreeableness was related to being more accepted by peers as well as having more peers. Jensen-Campbell et al. suggested that agreeable children might hold more positive attitudes toward others. Thus, the decision to not aggress against their peers seems to be based, at least in part, on the value agreeable individuals place on maintaining prosocial relationships.

A related, but distinct, set of findings offers support for this interpretation. Individuals low in Agreeableness express less sympathy and empathy toward others (Graziano et al. 2007), and they are less likely to forgive others and experience guilt (Strelan 2007). Such individuals are less likely to offer assistance to someone in need, and this finding was amplified when the costs to the person offering assistance created negative affect (Graziano et al. 2007).

Graziano and colleagues (2007) suggested that individuals low in Agreeableness appeared to be more interested in alleviating their own negative affect than helping others resolve their distress. In other words, such individuals place their own needs above those of others. This is also consistent with a model of aggression advanced by Blair, Mitchell, and Blair (2005) that explains the violence exhibited by psychopathic individuals. They suggest that the violence perpetrated by such individuals could be the result of failing to perceive and accurately interpret the distress of others. In terms of basic personality traits, psychopathy can be conceived of as a combination of low Agreeableness and Conscientiousness from the FFM (Widiger and Lynam, 1998; Gaughan et al. 2012) and low Honesty–Humility, Emotionality, Agreeableness, and Conscientiousness from the HEXACO (Gaughan et al. 2012).

The role of affect in explaining the links between Agreeableness and interpersonal interactions has been underscored by others as well. Ode and Robinson (2009) noted that disagreeable persons appear to have difficulty regulating negative affect. Based on their findings, as well as those of other studies, they suggest that the reason highly agreeable individuals have more prosocial relationships is because they can effectively reduce negative affect that occurs in the face of conflict. For those lower in Agreeableness, their difficulty in suppressing negative affect during conflict can lead to aggression, which may compromise the relationship.

Côté and Moskowitz (1998) provide additional evidence and understanding of the complexity affect plays. They found that high Agreeableness was associated with less negative affect, more agreeable behavioral interactions, and less quarrelsome behavior. However, they suggest another layer of nuance in their behavioral concordance model. This model suggests that consistent trait–behavior relationships lead to more positive affect, but inconsistent trait–behavior relationships result in more negative effect. In support of this model, those higher in Agreeableness experienced more positive affect when engaging in agreeable interactions with others, and they experienced more negative affect when engaging in quarrelsome behaviors. Thus, one of the reasons agreeable individuals engage in more prosocial behavior is because it provides positive affective experiences, and they avoid conflict because of the negative affect that stems from it. Those lower on Agreeableness failed to exhibit much positive affect when engaging in agreeable behavior, and their level of negative affect was not increased by engaging in quarrelsome behavior.

The role of negative affect has been extended in laboratory studies by Meier, Robinson, and Wilkowski (2006). Individuals lower in Agreeableness demonstrated the typical pattern of being more likely to aggress against another, in this case by employing a louder sound blast directed at another person in an experiment. However, this effect was exacerbated when those low in Agreeableness were also primed before the task with aggression-related words (e.g., "torture"). In the context of interpersonal conflict, when aggression-related cues are likely present, individuals lower in Agreeableness appear to be especially prone to respond with aggression.

The role of affect and priming has been discussed by others as well. Van Gelder and de Vries suggest there are two types of modes for processing information—hot and cool. (The "cool" mode of information processing is described in the following section in detail.) The "hot" mode of information processing focuses on how affect that is associated with emotional arousal can influence behavior. Specifically, they assessed the extent to which negative state affect might mediate the relationship between various traits and criminal choice. Negative state affect was assessed by asking respondents to imagine what kind of negative feelings they would expect to experience if they committed a crime. They found that Honesty–Humility and self-control (van Gelder and de Vries 2012, 2014), as well as Emotionality (Van Gelder and de Vries, 2012), were positively related to negative state affect, which was negatively related to criminal choice. Furthermore, negative state affect significantly mediated the effect of these traits on criminal choice. In addition, the mediating potential of negative state affect was more pronounced (compared to perceived risks) when participants were primed with affectively laden terms.

Many of the previously discussed findings are consistent with the social information processing model developed by Dodge and Schwartz (1997). They found that aggressive individuals display consistent social–cognitive patterns that can explain why they aggress. First, aggressive individuals are more likely to attend to aggressive cues in the environment. Second, they interpret ambiguous stimuli as aggressive, which Dodge and Schwartz refer to as a hostile attribution bias. Third, aggressive individuals have a tendency to select goals that are more aggressive in nature (e.g., dominance). After selecting a goal, the next stage involves response access and construction. Not only do aggressive individuals generate fewer possible responses in the face of conflict but also the responses they do create are more aggressive. In the last stage, response evaluation and decision, aggressive individuals evaluate aggressive behavior more positively.

Consistent with the social information processing model, Wikowski et al. (2006) noted that individuals low in Agreeableness tend to be drawn toward antisocial cues and have greater difficulty suppressing the antisocial thoughts generated by such cues. It might very well be the case that antagonistic individuals are more likely to perceive and process threatening and antisocial stimuli, allow these negative perceptions to dominate their thoughts, and use them as a basis for aggressing. There is some empirical evidence to support this view. Miller, Lynam, and Jones (2008) explored the relationships between personality traits (i.e., Agreeableness and Conscientiousness), laboratory tasks, and externalizing behaviors (e.g., antisocial behavior and aggression). One of the laboratory tasks involved reading a series of vignettes in which something unpleasant happened to the protagonist. Participants were then asked to answer questions about how they perceived the event and how they might respond. Miller et al. found that Agreeableness was negatively related to more hostile attributions, generating more aggressive responses, and choosing to enact an aggressive response. In turn, these laboratory tasks were related to various antisocial behaviors (e.g., substance use and aggression). These findings were consistent with the social information processing paradigm, and they suggest that one pathway linking personality traits and aggression is through social–cognitive models of decision making.

In the same study, Miller and colleagues (2008) examined whether a different laboratory task might explain the link between personality and antisocial behavior. They used the Hypothetical Money Choice Task, which was designed for the purpose of identifying differences among individuals in choosing an immediate, lower value reward or a larger reward after a longer delay. They hypothesized that Conscientiousness would be related to this measure of behavioral discounting. Instead, they found that Agreeableness was consistently and positively related to this task, indicating those higher on Agreeableness were more likely to choose a delayed, larger reward. Only one facet from Conscientiousness—Deliberation—was negatively related, but this effect was weaker than the relationships observed for every facet from the domain of Agreeableness. They speculated that this pattern of findings might be explained by the fact that individuals low in Agreeableness are suspicious and distrustful, and perhaps in this study, such individuals did not believe a better reward would come if they waited. With respect to decision making and offending, this finding might be extended in future research. Specifically, because individuals lower in Agreeableness are wary of others in their interpersonal interactions, they might be less prone to develop strong prosocial ties and empathy toward others. This line of thinking is consistent with the findings from several studies noted previously.

In addition to how traits influence the manner in which individuals interact with others, there is evidence that traits can affect with whom individuals associate and the kinds of access they have to criminogenic opportunities. Wilcox et al. (2014) examined how personality traits influence offending and victimization, with a focus on antisocial peers and access to illegal goods as potential mediators. They found that the relationship between Agreeableness and offending and victimization partially operated through both mediators. That is, those higher in Agreeableness reported fewer antisocial peers and less access to illegal goods, both of which, in turn, predicted less offending and victimization. The findings regarding Conscientiousness were more mixed. The effect of Conscientiousness on offending and victimization operated through antisocial peers, similar to the manner in which Agreeableness did so. Access to illegal goods did not mediate the relationship between Conscientiousness and offending and victimization. Individuals lower in Agreeableness (in particular) and Conscientiousness (to a lesser extent) might decide to offend because they find themselves surrounded with greater opportunity to do so.

The focus in this section was on how traits influence interpersonal interactions. The roles of Agreeableness and affect appear to be particularly important in this regard. Perhaps the most straightforward way to understand this is by noting why individuals higher in Agreeableness do not decide to aggress against others. Such individuals value prosocial relationships with others, actively avoid conflict, can better de-escalate conflict when it does occur, perceive others as less threatening, evaluate conflict less positively, avoid antisocial peers, and can effectively regulate their affect. For antagonistic individuals, none of these barriers exist and therefore do not enter into their decision making. As detailed in the following section, however, the decision to offend is not based only on the value one places on prosocial interactions.

B. Perceived Risks and Rewards and Cognitive Distortions

An area that has received attention with regard to the link between traits, decision making, and antisocial behavior is the role of perceptions of risk and reward. Maslowsky et al. (2011) examined the relationship between sensation seeking and risky behavior (some of which were acts of delinquency) among adolescents. They also focused on whether the perception of benefits and costs mediated this effect. They found that individuals higher in sensation seeking viewed risky behavior as leading to more benefits than risks. This cost–benefit measure also significantly mediated the relationship between sensation seeking and engagement in risky behaviors. Because they relied on a combined measure of benefits and risks, it was not clear whether sensation seekers were attracted to risky activities because of the perceived rewards or because of a failure to consider the costs or both.

Other research has been able to separate costs and benefits and examine their unique influences. Jones, Lynam, and Piquero (2015) examined the effects of two traits linked to impulsive behavior—Premeditation and Thrill and Adventure Seeking (from Eysenck's short form and Zuckerman Sensation Seeking Scale-V). These constructs are captured within the FFM domains of Conscientiousness and Extraversion, respectively. They also included perceptions of both rewards and costs for substance use. They found that the effect of Premeditation on substance use was primary driven by the perception of rewards. The role of perceived costs in explaining the Premeditation–substance use relationship was often not significant. Even in instances in which it demonstrated some effect, it was weaker than perceived rewards. Thus, individuals lower on Premeditation were more likely to use substances because they perceived such behavior as very rewarding, with perceived costs playing little, if any, role. In contrast, the relationship between Thrill and Adventure Seeking and substance use was consistently mediated by perceptions of both costs and rewards, with some analyses indicating that perceived costs exerted a stronger mediating effect. Thus, those higher in Thrill and Adventure Seeking use substances because they perceive such activity as rewarding but, even more important, because they fail to view such behavior as producing many costs.

Weller and Tikir (2011) examined several traits from the HEXACO model of personality, the effect these traits exerted on ethical risk-taking, and the roles of risk perceptions and perceived benefits. They found that Honesty–Humility affected ethical risk-taking, in part, because individuals lower in this domain had lower perceptions of the risk inherent in this action, as well as higher perceptions of the benefits for engaging in such behavior. Although they did not test whether the mediating effects of perceived risks or benefits were significantly different from one another, the coefficients presented suggested that perceived benefits were stronger. After accounting for the pathways linking Honesty–Humility to ethical risk-taking, the effect of Conscientiousness exerted only a direct effect on ethical risk-taking. Finally, they found the relationship between Emotionality and ethical risk-taking was mediated through perceptions of risk.

Similar results were obtained by Weller and Thulin (2012). They examined both risk-taking gain and risk-taking loss. Risk-taking gains involved a hypothetical situation in which participants chose between a sure gain (e.g., win $50 for certain) and taking a risk to acquire even more, but with the potential of getting nothing. The risk-taking loss conditions involved choosing between losing a certain amount (e.g., $50) and taking a risk to lose nothing, but with the potential to lose even more than the guaranteed amount they would lose. They found that Honesty–Humility was negatively related to risk-taking losses but only marginally related ($p < .10$) to risk-taking gains.

Additional evidence of the role of risk-taking preferences in mediating the relationship between traits and behavior has been generated by van Gelder and de Vries. In the previous section, their affectively driven "hot" mode of information processing was discussed. Here, the focus is on the "cool" mode, which describes a more rational and cerebral decision-making process. Using the HEXACO model, van Gelder and de Vries (2012) found that the relationships between Emotionality, Honesty–Humility, and Conscientiousness and criminal choice were significantly mediated by perceived risk (operationalized as punishment probability multiplied by punishment severity). That is, those higher in each of these traits perceived more risk associated with offending, which in turn decreased the likelihood of choosing a criminal action. In a separate study (van Gelder and de Vries 2014), they replicated the finding whereby the relationship between Honesty–Humility and criminal choice was significantly mediated by perceived risk. In addition, in this study, they were able to manipulate whether participants relied more heavily on perceived risk than on an emotional component (negative state affect; discussed previously). When participants were primed with cognitive-related words, the relationship between traits and criminal choice was mediated more strongly by perceived risk (compared to affective state).

In both studies, van Gelder and de Vries (2012, 2014) explored whether the relationship between self-control and criminal choice was mediated by perceived risk as well. They derived a measure of self-control using the following domains (and facets) from HEXACO: Honesty–Humility (Fairness and Modesty), Conscientiousness (Prudence and Diligence), Agreeableness (Flexibility and Patience), Emotionality (Fearfulness), Extraversion (Social Self-Esteem), Openness to Experience (Inquisitiveness), and the interstitial scale Altruism. This measure of self-control was significantly positively related to perceived risk, which was significantly negatively related to criminal choice. In addition, perceived risk significantly mediated the effect of self-control on criminal choice. Although not a focus in either study, an interesting possibility was raised by their findings. It could be that perceived risk is a significant mediator of other traits from the HEXACO when examined at the facet level. That is, more specific causal pathways might be uncovered in future research linking facets, perceived risk, and offending.

Beyond the perceptions of risks and rewards, the role of cognition has been theorized as a key component in understanding how traits exert their influence. Cognitive factors (e.g., attitudes and schemas) appear to mediate the relationship between traits and various life outcomes (other than crime; Ozer and Benet-Martinez 2006), leading some to suggest that personality and cognitive models should be integrated (Nigg 2000). Such suggestions have empirical support. Giancola, Mezzich, and Tarter (1998) found that executive functioning (which focuses on higher order mental processes, such as planning and concentration) mediates the relationship between difficult temperament (temperament is the precursor to personality) and physical aggression among females with conduct disorder.

More direct evidence of the relationship between traits and cognitive distortions has been noted by others. Koolen, Poorthuis, and van Aken (2012) examined proactive and reactive aggression among sixth graders and the roles that cognitive distortions and personality played in explaining these forms of aggression. Agreeableness was related to both forms of aggression, whereas Conscientiousness was related to neither. This latter finding stands in contrast to those of most other studies (Jones et al. 2011). They also found that Agreeableness was related to various cognitive distortions, including self-centeredness, minimizing, blaming others, and assuming the worst. Conscientiousness was not related to any of these distortions. Although the results they provided did not address the mediating potential of cognitive distortions on the relationship between Agreeableness and aggression, the results are suggestive that such a relationship exists. That is, it is possible that individuals lower in Agreeableness possess more cognitive distortions, which in turn increase the likelihood of aggression.

The work of Otter and Egan (2007) suggests similar relationships. To assess cognitive distortions associated with offending, they relied on the Psychological Inventory of Criminal Thinking Styles (PICTS) scale (Walters 2002). They suggested (based on factor analyses) that the PICTS scale was composed of two broad dimensions of antisocial cognition—impulsive thoughtlessness and callousness. Agreeableness and Conscientiousness were negatively related to both types of antisocial cognitions, whereas Neuroticism was positively related to impulsive thoughtlessness and callousness. This offers preliminary support for the notion that one mechanism linking traits and behavior is through antisocial cognitions. Specifically, those lower in Agreeableness and Conscientiousness, and higher in Neuroticism, are more likely to possess cognitions that are higher in impulsive thoughtlessness and callousness, which may in turn lead to antisocial behavior.

Additional evidence of cognitive problems linking personality and behavior can be gleaned from the psychopathy literature. From an FFM personality perspective, psychopathy can be thought of as a combination of low Agreeableness and Conscientiousness (Widiger and Lynam 1998), and from the HEXACO model, it can be described as low Honesty–Humility, Emotionality, Agreeableness, and Conscientiousness (de Vries and van Kampen 2010; Gaughan et al. 2012). One consistent finding is that psychopathic individuals experience response modulation deficits (Lorenz and Newman 2002). These deficits describe a process whereby once a dominant response for reward has been established, psychopathic individuals have difficulty inhibiting their behavior. This is true even when environmental cues suggest the behavior be stopped. In the context of decision making and offending, it would appear that after psychopathic individuals are pulled in by the rewards of offending, they have difficulty interrupting their approach behavior, even when contingencies change and the rewards are not apparent or punishment is impending. Lynam and Derefinko (2006) speculated that the response modulation deficit is likely the result of low Conscientiousness characteristic of psychopathy. Heritage and Benning (2013) found evidence of this in that the impulsivity component of psychopathy led to response modulation deficits because individuals high in impulsivity failed to cognitively process cues that promoted stopping behavior.

This section described the cognitive factors linking specific traits to antisocial behavior. There appears to be some consensus that impulsivity-related traits (e.g., Premeditation, Sensation Seeking, and Conscientiousness) from the FFM, and Honesty–Humility from the HEXACO, influence the perception of risks and rewards. These same traits are also related to cognitive distortions, although other traits (Agreeableness and Neuroticism) are involved as well. As suggested previously, future research might benefit from examining traits at the facet levels instead of the domain level. Such explorations might yield more precise pathways. In addition, future research should include the role of affective modes of processing.

VI. Discussion

This chapter has focused predominantly on how personality is related to offending and the role of decision making in mediating this relationship. However, this is only one way to understand the importance of personality and how it can be integrated with other criminological theories and constructs. This section highlights the different ways personality can be used in criminological research.

As mentioned previously, personality has not played a prominent role in criminology. One piece of evidence that supports this view is that relatively few articles that underscore the role of personality have appeared in the top criminological journals. Although there are some historical reasons for this, the criticisms of yesteryear have been addressed (Caspi et al. 1994). Still, few criminologists have become reacquainted with personality or used it in their research. Some might argue that personality, as conceptualized through self-control, has played a major role in criminological research. In fact, self-control (as typically operationalized) can be conceived of as a trait. More accurately, it is a multidimensional or interstitial trait composed of related, but distinct, personality traits (van Gelder and de Vries, 2012, 2014; de Vries and van Gelder 2013). Although the influence of self-control in the literature suggests an interest in personality among criminologists, there are several problems with assuming that the multidimensional construct of self-control is all that is needed in criminology. First, Hirschi (2004) suggested moving away from conceptualizations of self-control that rely on traits. To the extent that criminologists agree, there will be less attention devoted to personality-based self-control. Second, self-control includes different dimensions from distinct domains of personality (van

Gelder and de Vries, 2012, 2014; de Vries and van Gelder 2013). Although there is nothing inherently wrong with creating such an interstitial trait, collapsing different traits into one superordinate trait can lead to ambiguities. For instance, Jones, Cauffman, and Piquero (2007) found divergent interaction patterns when different elements of self-control were examined separately. Specifically, parental support was a stronger deterrent to offending among those lower in impulse control. However, parental support was a weaker deterrent among those lower in consideration of others. Impulse control and consideration of others are conceptually similar to the impulsivity and self-centeredness components of self-control (as initially described in the general theory of crime), respectively. Although Jones and colleagues did not test this, if these two elements of self-control were examined together, the opposing signs of the interaction effect might have washed each other out. Therefore, it is recommended that individual traits be used to better understand how, and under what circumstances, personality is related to offending. Third, personality is a construct that is much broader than what is represented in self-control. In terms of construct validity, relying only on self-control is very limiting. For all these reasons, it is argued here that using broader measures of personality will advance the discipline.

Of course, self-control was placed within a theoretical framework by its co-creators (Gottfredson and Hirschi 1990). Perhaps the neglect of other traits, or anything much beyond self-control, is because criminologists are unaware of the theoretical linkages between personality and offending. Some of the preceding sections were designed to demonstrate that. Beyond those specific accounts, personality is clearly linked to numerous other criminological constructs. For instance, Caspi and Roberts (2001) described person–environment transactions (discussed previously). To reiterate, there are reactive, proactive, and evocative person–environment transactions, and there are some instances in the empirical literature that include mainstream criminological constructs. The most often tested empirical accounts support the notion of reactive person–environment transactions. For instance, the effects of neighborhoods on individual-level offending vary by impulsivity (Lynam et al. 2000; Meier et al. 2008; Jones and Lynam 2009). Parenting also varies in its effects as a function of impulsivity (Jones et al. 2007) and self-control (Wright et al. 2001). In addition, Wright and colleagues noted that the deterrent effects of education, employment, and romantic partnerships are stronger among those with lower self-control, whereas the criminogenic effect of antisocial peers is stronger among those lower in self-control. Although the evidence is mixed, some researchers have found that the effects of morality are weaker at higher levels of self-control (Wikström and Svensson 2010; Pauwels 2012). Several empirical accounts have found that deterrence exerts stronger effects among those lower in self-control (Piquero and Pogarsky 2002; Wright et al. 2004). Thus, the constructs from several criminological theories (including social bonding, social learning, deterrence, and social disorganization) are moderated by personality traits.

Other research has noted that the effects of low empathy interact with parenting. Wooten and colleagues (1997) found that good parenting was an effective means of reducing conduct problems, but only among those children with lower levels of callous–unemotional traits. Similarly, Jones et al. (2007) noted that parental efficacy was related to lower antisocial behavior among incarcerated adolescents, but only for those scoring higher in consideration of others. Parenting, in some capacity, plays a role in several criminological theories (e.g., social bonding, social learning, and strain). Based on the evidence noted previously, its influence on offending might very well be limited among callous, self-centered individuals.

Theoretical arguments consistent with reactive person–environment transactions were advanced by Wright et al. (2001). They suggested that the interactions between several criminological constructs and self-control can be explained by two processes highlighted in their life course interdependence model. The first is the social amplification effect, whereby criminogenic risk factors are more strongly related to offending for the most at-risk individuals (e.g., those low in self-control). The second process is the social protection effect, which suggests that protective factors play a more influential role in reducing offending among those most at risk. Although there are some methodological issues that require greater attention in order to assess the veracity of the reactive person–environment transactions (Ousey and Wilcox 2007; Yarbrough et al. 2012), there is initial evidence supportive of them.

More limited evidence exists for the proactive person–environment transaction in the criminological literature. The aforementioned study by Wright et al. (2001) found that those lower in self-control were more likely to have compromised relationships (including with peers, employers, parents and family, and romantic partners). That is, low self-control led to more antisocial ties and fewer prosocial ties, both of which were related to subsequent delinquency. A burgeoning literature has emerged that has tested whether low self-control is related to antisocial peer formation. However, as Young (2011) noted, much of that literature does not directly test the hypothesis that "birds of a feather flock together." His research calls into question whether self-control has any effect on peer formation and instead suggests that triad closure offers a superior account of why peer groups form. Triad closure refers to a process whereby friendships emerge due to a common acquaintance. Thus, according to Young, two individuals are drawn together not because they share a common trait (i.e., self-control) but, instead, because they share a common friend. Despite the mixed findings from the criminological literature, several studies from the psychological literature (that do not focus on offending) support the notion of proactive person–environment transactions (Caspi and Roberts 2001). More methodologically rigorous research is needed in criminology to determine how personality and offending can be understood by proactive person–environment transactions.

The least studied person–environment transaction in the criminological literature is the evocative type. In fact, the author is not aware of any such research. However, there are psychological studies that are very suggestive. For instance, children with conduct disorder are more likely to elicit negative parenting practices (Lytton 1990). Jaffe et al. (2004) further decomposed this process whereby child misbehavior affects parenting. Specially, they found that corporal punishment, but not maltreatment (a more severe variant that results in physical injury), can be influenced by the child's disruptive behavior. There is also evidence that aggressive children are more likely to be avoided and ostracized by prosocial peers (Dodge et al. 2003). This might help explain the formation of deviant peer groups. Much more work remains to be done in criminology to test evocative person–environment transactions.

Beyond the theoretical and empirical connections between personality and main-stream criminological theories and constructs, there are important reasons to consider personality in applied research and settings. One of the Big Four (Andrews and Bonta 2010) correlates of offending is antisocial personality. The other three—antisocial peers, cognitions, and history—have received substantial attention within the criminological literature. However, personality is not often examined, and there is little or no explanation of why this is the case. Not only is personality one of the most robust correlates of offending but also it plays an important role in recidivism. Psychopathy is a personality disorder characterized by interpersonal and emotional deficits, as well as impulsive, irresponsible lifestyles and history of antisocial behavior (Hare 2003). It is also one of the best predictors of recidivism (Olver and Wong 2015), and it is included in the most widely validated violence risk measures (e.g., HCR-20 and VRAG). In terms of treatment effects, psychopathy is perceived as a barrier to successful treatment (Polaschek and Daly 2013). It might very well be that some treatments are very effective at reducing recidivism among those lower in psychopathic traits but substantially less effective (or even ineffective) among those higher in these traits. Thus, some of the inconsistencies in treatment effects could be due to the personality traits of specific offenders. Note that theoretical and empirical accounts of psychopathy are virtually nonexistent in the criminological literature. (For notable exceptions, see DeLisi [2009] and volume 43, issue 4 of the *Journal of Criminal Justice*.) To this author's knowledge, studies focusing on psychopathy have never appeared in the discipline's flagship journal, *Criminology*.

This section highlighted the many ways in which the construct of personality can be used in criminological theory, research, and practice. Not only does personality exert reliable, moderate direct effects on offending but also it interacts with other criminological constructs (e.g., neighborhoods), explains why some individuals are attached/attracted to prosocial or antisocial others and institutions, and influences the way others perceive and react to individuals. These are in addition to the fact that personality is related to offender decision making.

VII. Conclusion

The primary goal of this chapter was to explain how personality influences offender decision making. A related, secondary goal was to stress the importance and value of including personality in mainstream criminology theory and inquiry, beyond its relationship with offender decision making. As Osgood (1998) suggested nearly two decades ago, we should draw upon important and valuable ideas, concepts, theories, and perspectives from our colleagues in other fields. I recommends borrowing personality from our fellow psychologists. There is absolutely nothing to lose, and much to gain, by doing so. Perhaps if criminology follows this advice, theoretical accounts will become more nuanced, empirical findings can be extended, criminal justice practice will be more effective, and criminology can better reach its goal of being a truly interdisciplinary field.

NOTES

1. Some versions of the Big Five (a similar but different conceptualization of personality compared to the FFM) are also available free of charge, such as the Big Five Inventory (John and Srivastava 1999) and various versions that can be generated through the International Personality Item Pool (http://ipip.ori.org).
2. The HEXACO model of personality has been validated in English as well as in 11 other languages since the original development of this measure (Lee and Ashton 2008).

REFERENCES

Andrews, D. A., and J. Bonta. 2010. *The Psychology of Criminal Conduct.* 5th ed. New Providence, NJ: LexisNexis.

Ashton, M. C., and K. Lee. 2007. "Empirical, Theoretical, and Practical Advantages of the HEXACO Model of Personality Structure." *Personality and Social Psychology Review* 11:150–66.

Ashton, M. C., & K. Lee. 2008. "The Prediction of Honesty–Humility-Related Criteria by the HEXACO and Five-Factor Models of Personality. *Journal of Research in Personality* 42:1216–28.

Ashton. M. C., K. Lee, and R. E. de Vries. 2014. "The HEXACO Honesty-Humility, Agreeableness, and Emotionality Factors: A Review of Research and Theory." *Personality and Social Psychology Review* 18:139–52.

Ashton, M. C., K. Lee, M. Perugini, P. Szarota, R. E. de Vries, L. Di Blas, et al. 2004. "A Six-Factor Structure of Personality-Descriptive Adjectives: Solutions from Psycholexical Studies in Seven Languages." *Journal of Personality and Social Psychology* 86:356–66.

Blair, J., D. Mitchell, and K. Blair. 2005. *The Psychopath: Emotion and the Brain.* Malden, MA: Blackwell.

Caspi, A., T. E. Moffitt, P. A. Silva, M. Stouthamer-Loeber, R. F. Krueger, and P. S. Schmutte. 1994. "Are Some People Crime-Prone? Replications of the Personality–Crime Relationship Across Countries, Genders, Races, and Methods. *Criminology* 32:163–95.

Caspi, A., and B. W. Roberts. 2001. "Personality Development Across the Life Course: The Argument for Change and Continuity." *Psychological Inquiry* 12:49–66.

Caspi, A., B. W. Roberts, and R. L. Shiner. 2005. "Personality Development: Stability and Change." *Annual Review of Psychology* 56:453–84.

Costa, P. T., and R. R. McCrae. 1992. *Revised NEO Personality Inventory (NEO-PI-R) and NEO Five-Factor Inventory (NEO-FFI) Professional Manual.* Lutz, FL: Psychological Assessment Resources.

Côté, S., and D. Moskowitz. 1998. "On the Dynamic Covariation Between Interpersonal Behavior and Affect: Prediction from Neuroticism, Extraversion, and Agreeableness." *Journal of Personality and Social Psychology* 75:1032–46.

de Vries, R. E., and J. L. van Gelder. 2013. "Tales of Two Self-Control Scales: Relations with Five-Factor and HEXACO Traits. *Personality and Individual Differences* 54:756–60.

de Vries, R. E., and D. van Kampen. 2010. "The HEXACO and 5DPT Model of Personality: A Comparison and Their Relationships with Psychopathy, Egoism, Pretentiousness, Immorality, and Machiavellianism." *Journal of Personality Disorders* 24:244–57.

DeLisi, M. 2009. "Psychopathy Is the Unified Theory of Crime. *Youth Violence and Juvenile Justice* 7:256–73.

Dodge, K. A., J. E. Lansford, V. S. Burks, J. E. Bates, G. S. Pettit, R. Fontaine, and J. M. Price. 2003. "Peer Rejection and Social-Information Processing Factors in the Development of Aggressive Behaviors in Children. *Child Development* 74:374–93.

Dodge, K. A., and D. Schwartz. 1997. "Social Information Processing Mechanisms in Aggressive Behavior." In *Handbook of Antisocial Behavior*, edited by D. Stoff, J. Breiling, and J. Maser, pp. 171–80. New York: Wiley.

Gaughan, E. T., J. D. Miller, and D. R. Lynam. 2012. "Examining the Utility of General Models of Personality in the Study of Psychopathy: A Comparison of the HEXACO-PI-R and NEO PI-R." *Journal of Personality Disorders* 26:513–23.

Giancola, P. R., A. C. Mezzich, and R. E. Tarter. 1998. "Executive Cognitive Functioning, Temperament, and Antisocial Behavior in Conduct-Disordered Adolescent Females." *Journal of Abnormal Psychology* 107:629–41.

Gottfredson, M. R., and T. Hirschi. 1990. *A General Theory of Crime*. Stanford, CA: Stanford University Press.

Graziano, W., M. Habashi, B. Sheese, and R. Tobin. 2007. "Agreeableness, Empathy, and Helping: A Person × Situation Perspective." *Journal of Personality and Social Psychology* 93:583–99.

Hare, R. D. 2003. *Manual for the Revised Psychopathy Checklist.* 2nd ed. Toronto: Multi-Health Systems.

Heritage, A. J., and S. D. Benning. 2013. "Impulsivity and Response Modulation Deficits in Psychopathy: Evidence from the ERN and N1." *Journal of Abnormal Psychology* 122:215–22.

Hirschi, T. 2004. "Self-Control and Crime." In *Handbook of Self-Regulation: Research, Theory, and Application*, edited by R. F. Baumeister and K. D. Vohs. New York: Guilford.

Jaffe, S. R., A. Caspi, T. E. Moffitt, M. Polo-Tomas, T. S. Price, and A. Taylor. 2004. "The Limits of Child Effects: Evidence for Genetically Mediated Child Effects on Corporal Punishment But Not on Physical Maltreatment." *Developmental Psychology* 40:1047–58.

Jang, K. L., R. R. McCrae, A. Angleitner, R. Riemann, and W. J. Livesley. 1998. "Heritability of Facet-Level Traits in a Cross-Cultural Twin Sample: Support for a Hierarchical Model of Personality." *Journal of Personality and Social Psychology* 74:1556–65.

Jensen-Campbell, L. A., R. Adams, D. G. Perry, K. A. Workman, J. Q. Furdella, and S. K. Egan. 2002. "Agreeableness, Extraversion, and Peer Relations in Early Adolescence: Winning Friends and Deflecting Aggression." *Journal of Research in Personality* 36:224–51.

Jensen-Campbell, L. A., and W. Graziano. 2001. "Agreeableness as a Moderator of Interpersonal Conflict." *Journal of Personality* 69:323–62.

John, O. P., and S. Srivastava. 1999. "The Big Five Trait Taxonomy: History, Measurement, and Theoretical Perspectives." In *Handbook of Personality: Theory and Research*, edited by L. A. Pervin and O. P. John, 2nd ed., pp. 102–38. New York: Guilford.

Jones, S., E. Cauffman, and A. Piquero. 2007. "The Influence of Parental Support Among Incarcerated Adolescent Offenders: The Conditioning Effects of Impulse Control and Empathy." *Criminal Justice and Behavior* 34:229–45.

Jones, S., and D. R. Lynam. 2009. "In the Eye of the Impulsive Beholder: The Influences of Neighborhood Perceptions and Impulsivity on Offending Behavior." *Criminal Justice and Behavior* 36:307–21.

Jones, S., D. R. Lynam, and A. R. Piquero. 2015. "Substance Use, Personality, and Inhibitors: Testing Hirschi's Predictions About the Reconceptualization of Self-Control. *Crime and Delinquency* 61(4): 538–58.

Jones, S., J. D. Miller, and D. R. Lynam. 2011. "Personality, Antisocial Behavior, and Aggression: A Meta-Analytic Review." *Journal of Criminal Justice* 39:329–37.

Jones, S., and N. Quisenberry. 2004. "The General Theory of Crime: How General Is It?" *Deviant Behavior* 25:401–26.

Katz, J. 1988. *Seductions of Crime: Moral and Sensual Attractions in Doing Evil*. New York: Basic Books.

Koolen, S., A. Poorthius, and M. A. G. van Aken. 2012. "Cognitive Distortions and Self-Regulatory Personality Traits Associated with Proactive and Reactive Aggression in Early Adolescence." *Cognitive Theory and Research* 36:776–87.

Lee, K., and M. C. Ashton. 2004. "Psychometric Properties of the HEXACO Personality Inventory." *Multivariate Behavioral Research* 39:329–58.

Lee, K., and M. C. Ashton. 2005. "Psychopathy, Machiavellianism, and Narcissism in the Five-Factor Model and the HEXACO Model of Personality Structure." *Personality and Individual Differences* 38:1571–82.

Lee, K., and M. C. Ashton. 2008. "The HEXACO Personality Factors in the Indigenous Personality Lexicons of English and 11 Other Languages." *Journal of Personality* 76:1001–53.

Lee, K., M. C. Ashton, and R. E. de Vries. 2005. "Predicting Workplace Delinquency and Integrity with the HEXACO and Five-Factor Models of Personality Structure." *Human Performance* 18:179–97.

Lee, K., M. C. Ashton, and R. E. de Vries. 2013. "Prediction of Self- and Observer Report Scores on HEXACO-60 and NEO-FFI Scales." *Journal of Personality Research* 47:668–75.

Lee, K., M. C. Ashton, and K. Shin. 2005. "Personality Correlates of Workplace Anti-social Behavior." *Applied Psychology: An International Review* 54(1): 81–98.

Lilienfeld, S. O., I. D. Waldman, K. Landfield, A. L. Watts, S. Rubenzer, and T. R. Faschingbauer. 2012. "Fearless-Dominance and the U.S. Presidency: Implications of Psychopathic Personality Traits for Successful and Unsuccessful Political Leadership." *Journal of Personality and Social Psychology* 103:489–505.

Lorenz, A. R., and J. P. Newman. 2002. "Deficient Response Modulation and Emotional Processing in Low-Anxious Caucasian Psychopathic Offenders: Results from a Lexical Decision Task." *Emotion* 2:91–104.

Lykken, David T. 1995. *The Antisocial Personalities*. Hillsdale, NJ: Erlbaum.

Lynam, D. R., A. Caspi, T. E. Moffitt, P. H. Wikstrom, R. Loeber, and S. Novak. 2000. "The Interaction Between Impulsivity and Neighborhood Context on Offending: The Effects of Impulsivity Are Stronger in Poorer Neighborhoods." *Journal of Abnormal Psychology* 109:563–74.

Lynam, D. R., and K. J. Derefinko. 2006. "Psychopathy and Personality." In *Handbook of Psychopathy*, edited by C. J. Patrick, pp. 133–55. New York: Guilford.

Lynam, D. R., and J. D. Miller. 2004. "Personality Pathways to Impulsive Behavior and Their Relations to Deviance: Results from Three Samples." *Journal of Quantitative Criminology* 20:319–41.

Lytton, H. 1990. "Child and Parents Effects in Boys' Conduct Disorder: A Reinterpretation." *Developmental Psychology* 26:683–97.

Maslowsky, J., E. Buvinger, D. P. Keating, L. Steinberg, and E. Cauffman. 2011. "Cost–Benefit Analysis Mediation of the Relationship Between Sensation Seeking and Risk Behavior Among Adolescents." *Personality and Individual Differences* 51:802–6.

McCrae, R. R., and P. T. Costa Jr. 1999. "A Five-Factor Theory of Personality." In *Handbook of Personality: Theory and Research*, edited by L. A Pervin and O. P. John, 2nd ed., pp. 139–53. New York: Guilford.

Meier, B., M. Robinson, and B. Wilkowski. 2006. "Turning the Other Cheek: Agreeableness and the Regulation of Aggression-Related Primes." *Psychological Science* 17:136–42.

Meier, M. H., W. S. Slutske, S. Arndt, and R. J. Cadoret. 2008. "Impulsive and Callous Traits Are More Strongly Associated with Delinquent Behavior in Higher Risk Neighborhoods Among Boys and Girls." *Journal of Abnormal Psychology* 117:377–85.

Miller, J. D., and D. R. Lynam. 2001. "Structural Models of Personality and Their Relation to Antisocial Behavior: A Meta-Analysis." *Criminology* 39:765–98.

Miller, J. D., D. R. Lynam, and S. Jones. 2008. "Externalizing Behavior Through the Lens of the Five Factor Model: A Focus on Agreeableness and Conscientiousness." *Journal of Personality Assessment* 90:158–64.

Nigg, J. T. 2000. "On Inhibition/Disinhibition in Developmental Psychopathology: Views from Cognitive and Personality Psychology and a Working Inhibitory Taxonomy." *Psychological Bulletin* 126:220–46.

Ode, S., and M. Robinson. 2009. "Can Agreeableness Turn Gray Skies Blue? A Role for Agreeableness in Moderating Neuroticism-Linked Dysphoria." *Journal of Social and Clinical Psychology* 28:436–62.

Olver, M. E., and S. C. P. Wong. 2015. "Short- and Long-Term Recidivism Prediction of the PCL-R and the Effects of Age: A 24-Year Follow-Up." *Personality Disorders: Theory, Research, and Treatment* 6:97–105.

Osgood, D. W. 1998. "Interdisciplinary Integration: Building Criminology by Stealing from Our Friends." *The Criminologist* 23:1, 3, 4, 41.

Otter, Z., and V. Egan. 2007. "The Evolutionary Role of Self-Deceptive Enhancement as a Protective Factor Against Antisocial Cognitions." *Personality and Individual Differences* 43:2258–69.

Ousey, G., and P. Wilcox. 2007. "The Interaction of Antisocial Propensity and Life-Course Varying Predictors of Delinquent Behavior: Differences by Method of Estimation and Implications for Theory." *Criminology* 45:313–54.

Ozer, D. J., and V. Benet-Martinez. 2006. "Personality and the Prediction of Consequential Outcomes." *Annual Review of Psychology* 57:401–21.

Pauwels, L. 2012. "How Similar Is the Interaction Between Low Self-Control and Deviant Moral Beliefs in the Explanation of Adolescent Offending? An Inquiry in Subgroups by Gender and Immigrant Background." In *Psychology of Morality*, edited by A. S. Fruili and L. D. Veneto, pp. 141–54. Hauppauge, NY: Nova.

Pervin, L. A., and O. P. John. 1999. *Handbook of Personality: Theory and Research*, 2nd ed. New York: Guilford.

Piquero, A., and G. Pogarsky. 2002. "Beyond Stafford and Warr's Reconceptualization of Deterrence: Personal and Vicarious Experiences, Impulsivity, and Offending Behavior." *Journal of Research in Crime and Delinquency* 39:153–86.

Polaschek, D. L. L., and T. E. Daly. 2013. "Treatment and Psychopathy in Forensic Settings." *Aggression and Violent Behavior* 18:592–603.

Pratt, T. C., and F. T. Cullen. 2000. "The Empirical Status of Gottfredson and Hirschi's General Theory of Crime: A Meta-Analysis." *Criminology* 38(3):931–64.

Roberts, B. W., A. Caspi, and T. E. Moffitt. 2001. "The Kids Are Alright: Growth and Stability in Personality Development from Adolescence to Adulthood." *Journal of Personality and Social Psychology* 81:670–83.

Roberts, B. W., and W. F. DelVecchio. 2000. "The Rank-Order Consistency of Personality Traits from Childhood to Old Age: A Quantitative Review of Longitudinal Studies." *Psychological Bulletin* 126:3–25.

Strelan, P. 2007. "Who Forgives Others, Themselves, and Situations? The Roles of Narcissism, Guilt, Self-Esteem, and Agreeableness." *Personality and Individual Differences* 42:259–69.

van Gelder, J. L., and R. E. de Vries. 2012. "Traits and States: Integrating Personality and Affect into a Model of Criminal Decision-Making." *Criminology* 50:637–71.

van Gelder, J. L., and R. E. de Vries. 2014. "Rational Misbehavior? Evaluating an Integrated Dual-Process Model of Criminal Decision-Making." *Journal of Quantitative Criminology* 30:1–27.

Walters, G. D. 2002. "The Psychological Inventory of Criminal Thinking Styles (PICTS): A Review and Meta-Analysis." *Assessment* 9:278–91.

Weller, J. A., and Tikir, A. 2011. "Predicting Domain-Specific Risk Taking with the HEXACO Personality Structure." *Journal of Behavioral Decision Making* 24:180–201.

Weller, J. A., and E. W. Thulin. 2012. "Do Honest People Take Fewer Risks? Personality Correlates of Risk-Taking to Achieve Gains and Avoid Losses in HEXACO Space." *Personality and Individual Differences* 53:923–26.

Whiteside, S. P., and D. R. Lynam. 2001. "The Five-Factor Model and Impulsivity: Using a Structural Model of Personality to Understand Impulsivity." *Personality and Individual Differences* 30:669–89.

Widiger, T. A., and D. R. Lynam. 1998. "Psychopathy and the Five-Factor Model of Personality." In *Psychopathy: Antisocial, Criminal, and Violent Behaviors*, edited by T. Millon, E. Simonsen, M. Birket-Smith, and R. D. Davis, pp. 171–87. New York: Guilford.

Wikström, P.-O. H., and R. Svensson. 2010. "When Does Self-Control Matter? The Interaction Between Morality and Self-Control in Crime Causation." *European Journal of Criminology* 7:395–410.

Wilcox, P., C. J. Sullivan, S. Jones, and J. van Gelder. 2014. "Personality and Situational Opportunity: An Integrated Approach to Offending and Victimization." *Criminal Justice and Behavior* 41:880–901.

Wilkowski, B. M., M. D. Robinson, and B. P. Meier. 2006. "Agreeableness and the Prolonged Spatial Processing of Antisocial and Prosocial Information." *Journal of Research in Personality* 40:1152–68.

Wootton, J., P. Frick, K. Shelton, and P. Silverthorn. 1997. "Ineffective Parenting and Childhood Conduct Problems: The Moderating Role of Callous-Unemotional Traits." *Journal of Consulting and Clinical Psychology* 65:301–8.

Wright, B., A. Caspi, T. Moffitt, and R. Paternoster. 2004. "Does the Perceived Risk of Punishment Deter Criminally Prone Individuals? Rational Choice, Self-Control, and Crime." *Journal of Research in Crime and Delinquency* 41:180–213.

Wright, B., A. Caspi, T. Moffitt, and P. Silva. 2001. "The Effects of Social Ties on Crime Vary by Criminal Propensity: A Life-Course Model of Interdependence." *Criminology* 39:321–51.

Yarbrough, A., S. Jones, C. J. Sullivan, C. S. Sellers, and J. K. Cochran. 2012. "Social Learning and Self-Control: Assessing the Moderating Potential of Criminal Propensity." *International Journal of Offender Therapy and Comparative Criminology* 56:191–202.

Young, J. T. N. 2011. "How Do They 'End Up Together'? A Social Network Analysis of Self-Control, Homophily, and Adolescent Relationships." *Journal of Quantitative Criminology* 27:251–73.

Zuckerman, M. 1994. *Behavioral Expressions and Biosocial Bases of Sensation Seeking*. Cambridge: Cambridge University Press.

....

CHAPTER 11

TEMPORAL DISCOUNTING, PRESENT ORIENTATION, AND CRIMINAL DETERRENCE

....

CHAE MAMAYEK, RAY PATERNOSTER, AND THOMAS A. LOUGHRAN

I. INTRODUCTION

....

THROUGHOUT the history of criminological theory, from the earliest classical school ideas to the theories of today, there has been a belief that those who commit criminal offenses differ from law-abiding citizens in their decision-making process. Some theorists have assumed that offenders are too present oriented, others that they lack patience or willpower, some believe that offenders are too impulsive, and still others think there are more general cognitive limitations among offenders. Although there are important differences among concepts such as willpower, self-control, impulsivity, and time orientation, there are important areas of common ground. With few exceptions, individuals with these characteristics are thought by criminological theorists to be more difficult to deter because when choosing a course of action, they value the here and now rather than the potential future consequences of their actions. That is, they place greater weight on immediate consequences and underweight consequences that are delayed in time. This distinction is particularly problematic for deterrence theory because it has long been realized that the benefits of criminal offending arrive in the short term, whereas the potential costs do not occur until some later time in the future. It is this deficit in the capacity to adequately weight longer term consequences of behavior that has been seen by many a criminologist to be a major contributor to criminal offending (Wilson and Herrnstein 1985).

Long ago, Beccaria (1764/1985) announced that the most important dimension of punishment was its certainty.[1] However, what many criminology scholars may not realize is that Beccaria was well aware of the fact that even a certain punishment had to be contemplated in the mind of an offender at the same time as the imagined benefits in order to counteract its effect on the mind. In other words, the offender had to have the ability to both imagine the punishment that would arrive in the future and bring it fully into the mind during the present and imagine that this connection was key to the effectiveness of punishment as a deterrent. This recognition that the contemplation of punishment had to be brought into the present so that it could be considered as a consequence of the crime was anchored in associationist psychology common in the eighteenth century and developed by Hume (*An Enquiry Concerning Human Understanding*) and Locke (*An Essay Concerning Human Understanding*), whereby the mind is able to recall events that are sequential and contiguous (Warren 1916). With respect to punishment for crimes, Beccaria argued that in order to deter crime, the would-be offender must have the facility to contemplate in his or her mind that the act brought on the punishment—that there is a causal connection between the two:

> The more promptly and the more closely punishment follows upon the commission of a crime, the more . . . useful will it be. I have said that the promptness of punishments is more useful because when the length of time that passes between the punishment and the misdeed is less, so much the strong and more lasting in the human mind is the association of these two ideas, crime and punishment; they then come insensibly to be considered, one as the cause, the other as the necessary inevitable effect. (pp. 55–56)

Of course, if punishment was made swift–that is, an offender was rapidly arrested, tried, convicted, and punished—then, at least theoretically, the causal connection between crime and punishment would more likely be made in the mind of the would-be offender and deterrence enhanced. However, Beccaria was mindful of the fact that although the objective swiftness of punishment was important, the perception of swift punishment in the mind of the offender was what really mattered.

However, Beccaria's (1764/1985) associationism also allowed for the fact that there are individual-level differences in persons' capacity to make this association between crime and punishment. Some persons have a deficit in their ability to contemplate future consequences during the present. They may be easily able to consider the immediate benefits of their actions but lack the capacity to pull future events into the present, and those who are lured by the immediate and less mindful of the future—the "vulgar"—are more at risk for crime:

> The more men depart from general ideas and universal principles, that is, the more vulgar they are, the more apt are they to act merely on immediate and familiar associations, ignoring the more remote and complex ones that serve only men strongly impassioned for the object of their desires; the light of attention illuminates only a single object, leaving the others dark. . . . Of utmost importance is it, therefore, that the crime and punishment be intimately linked together, if it be desirable that, in crude, vulgar minds the seductive picture of a particularly advantageous crime should immediately call up the associated idea of punishment. Long delay always

produces the effect of further separating these ideas; thus, though punishment of a crime may make an impression, it be less as a punishment than as a spectacle, and will be felt only after the horror of the particular crime. (pp. 56–57)

Punishment must be perceived to be swift, therefore, to enable even those who are tempted by the "seductive picture of a particularly advantageous crime" to contemplate the possibility of punishment as well as gain. Although we think of Beccaria as a moral or even political philosopher, he had for his time a fairly articulate notion of the more positivist idea that some people find it more difficult than others to think of long-term consequences and so are seduced by the immediate anticipated gains of crime. In the words of today, they are impulsive, shortsighted, present oriented, low in self-control, or have a high discount rate, and they may be particularly difficult to deter from crime. In summary, Beccaria recognized the importance of, to give it a general term while ignoring quibbles about differences, one's temporal orientation as it pertains to deterrence.

In the decades since Beccaria, with some important exceptions (Nagin and Paternoster 1991; Piquero and Tibbetts 1996; Piquero et al. 2011), deterrence theorists and scholars have tended to ignore this psychological dimension of his thought and have focused on his more obvious deterrence hypotheses: The greater the certainty, severity, and celerity of punishment, the greater the deterrence. Of course, there is an implied *ceteris paribus* here, but, as suggested previously, Beccaria recognized that other things are not the same. People differ in their orientation to time, and this difference has major implications for how decisions are made, including decisions to commit crime. It may have been the disciplinary myopia of scholars trained as sociologists that led to this dimension being ignored, but these ideas have been picked up more recently by scholars interested in deterrence but who also are psychologists or economists. Specifically, by including time orientation or discounting, researchers have started to examine the vast implications that celerity may have as an instrument of deterrence and, even more broadly, how discounting may influence individual choice in many types of behaviors.

This chapter provides a general overview of how temporal orientation can influence decision making through linking the deterrence concept of celerity with the notion of individual difference in what has been referred to as time orientation. In sequential order, this chapter provides an overview of deterrence, discusses the empirical validity of deterrence theory, and provides an overview of discounting. The chapter then provides a summary of some types of discounting that have been presented thus far in the literature and discusses the various policy implications. Finally, the chapter provides commentary on the many avenues for future research.

II. OVERVIEW OF DETERRENCE THEORY

Interest in deterrence as a justification for punishment is most often traced to the work of Cesare Beccaria (1738–1794). Particularly concerned with eighteenth-century injustices of the law, courts, and arbitrary sanctions and punishments, Beccaria sought to reform a volatile, harsh, and inefficient legal system. In an essay on penology titled *On Crimes and Punishments*, Beccaria (1764/1985) outlined government inefficiencies in the procedural law and punishment for crimes and proposed ideas for reform. His thoughts were premised on what would become basic classical criminology principles: Individuals exercise free will, are able to think rationally, and are guided by self-interest. It was also believed that the purpose of the justice system was to deter crime. It then followed that penalties delivered by the criminal justice system would most effectively deter if the sanctions were *severe, certain,* and *swift* enough to outweigh any rewards obtained from criminal activity, where severity refers to the magnitude of the punishment, certainty refers to the likelihood of detection, and swiftness (also referred to as celerity) describes how quickly a sanction is applied following an offense. By increasing the cost of crime, potential offenders would be deterred.

III. THE EMPIRICAL VALIDITY OF DETERRENCE THEORY

Modern criminology continues to examine the principles of severity, certainty, and celerity in relation to specific and general deterrence. Historically, deterrence theory has evolved from an almost exclusive focus on death penalty research (Sellin 1959) to a more expansive examination of the principles of deterrence using objective properties of punishment (Gibbs 1968; Tittle 1969; Chiricos and Waldo 1970; Waldo and Chiricos 1972) and, ultimately, to a theory that was restated as a perceptual theory (Geerken and Gove 1975). Although there were some exceptions, the perceptual studies that followed found that offending is lower for people who perceive higher sanctioning risks and costs, again finding certainty to be a much more robust property of punishment than severity (Grasmick and Bursik 1990; Bachman, Paternoster, and Ward 1992). Research on criminal justice policy has reached similar conclusions based on findings that increasing certainty of punishment through police enforcement in localized high-crime areas, known as "hot spot" policing (Sherman and Weisburd 1995), and police crime-specific crackdowns (Sherman 1990) have had a crime-reducing effect. Not surprisingly, the evidence for increasing severity, such as increasing prison incarceration, has been more mixed (Zimring and Hawkins 1995; Levitt 1996). Pratt and colleagues' (2006) meta-analysis demonstrated that measures of perceived certainty have a stronger deterrence effect than measures of perceived severity and overall that the main effect sizes for deterrent variables tend to be weaker than variables typically associated with other criminological theories. In summary, although deterrence research does not always support a deterrent effect, it appears that overall the research suggests that the cumulative criminal justice system seems to have some effect on individuals' offending decisions (Nagin 1998, 2013; Paternoster 2010). What stands out in this body of research for our purposes is a lack of discussion regarding the celerity principle. For a more detailed overview of deterrence, see chapter 7, this volume.

IV. ELABORATION OF DETERRENCE THEORY

The historical origin of the rational choice model can be traced to the British philosopher, Jeremy Bentham (1748–1832). In *An Introduction to the Principles of Morals and Legislation*, Bentham's (1789/1988) outlook on human nature suggested that there are many pleasures and pains that individuals consider when making decisions. Using rational calculation, potential offenders weigh the potential pains and likelihood of being caught against the possible pleasure of committing a crime, and they make a reasoned decision to do the act that returns the greatest utility.

In 1968, Gary Becker incorporated this concept into criminology using an economic perspective. Specifically, in his paper titled "Crime and Punishment: An Economic Approach," Becker (1968) illustrated that the same methods economists had been using to study purchasing decisions could be applied to the decision to commit a crime. The economics-based method of choice analysis Becker outlined would later be referred to as the *expected utility model* (Schoemaker 1982). Within this model, rational individuals make decisions based on expectations that they will maximize benefits and minimize costs. Therefore, it follows that an offender will offend as long as the benefits of committing a crime are greater than the potential costs:

$$U\left(\text{benefits}\right) > pU\left(\text{costs}\right)$$

where p is the perceived risk of being sanctioned.[2] Importantly, this model recognizes that individuals are faced with limitations on their ability to make decisions because they are faced with realistic constraints and uncertainty. For instance, it is unlikely that when making a decision, a person has all the information or unlimited time in which to make a decision. It is for this reason that Simon (1957) introduced the concept of *bounded rationality*, in which individuals are bounded or face restrictions in their decision making that may result in collecting or interpreting information imperfectly. Due to their imperfect decision making, in an attempt to minimize costs and maximize benefits, individuals will "satisfice" rather than optimize. What an individual considers to be beneficial and costly is also subjective; thus, this model has also been referred to as the *subjective expected utility model* (Ramsey 1931; Savage 1954).

The expected utility model was largely developed in the sphere of criminology through the work of Cornish and Clarke (1986). In an effort to establish a perspective with many practical implications, these theorists developed a situation-based theory of crime that focuses on costs and benefits associated with specific offenses and locations. The authors believed that criminals are at least somewhat rational; crime requires some level of planning; and when deciding to commit a crime, offenders weigh costs and benefits of committing a crime against alternative outcomes. Through paying close attention to which factors make a criminal opportunity more costly (therefore increasing risk and certainty), criminal offenses theoretically can be prevented. For a more thorough discussion, see chapter 4, this volume.

V. Time Discounting

It is not difficult to imagine how an individual's impulsivity, self-control, or time orientation could influence decision making and the overall effectiveness of deterrence. Central to this discussion is the idea that crime almost always provides immediate gratification, whereas any legal or social cost associated with the crime often will occur at a later point in time. Wilson and Herrnstein (1985) may have been the first to bring to light the importance of time discounting, or devaluating the future, in order to best explain criminal behavior. They claimed that individuals differ in the extent to which they discount the future, suggesting that "the more impulsive a person is, the more likely he or she is to find occasions when crime will seem to be more rewarding than non-crime, other things equal" (p. 51). Similarly, Gottfredson and Hirschi (1990) state, "What classical theory lacks is an explicit idea of self-control, the idea that people also differ in the extent to which they are vulnerable to temptations of the moment" (p. 87). Gottfredson and Hirschi further detail that criminal acts provide immediate and simple gratification that requires relatively little skill or planning. Among other things, individuals low in self-control will be impulsive and shortsighted. The "here and now" or present orientation of those with low self-control makes them likely to be less affected by the threats and punishments of sanctions (Gottfredson and Hirschi 1990; Grasmick et al. 1993; Piquero and Tibbetts 1996).

Quite often in the criminological literature, the concepts discounting, impulsivity, and self-control are used interchangeably to describe a present-orientated person. Nagin and Pogarsky (2004), however, argued that there is a need for a clear distinction between discounting and impulsivity. Discounting is the tendency to deliberately devalue the future,[3] whereas impulsivity is the failure to consider the future.[4] Using data from the National Longitudinal Survey of Adolescent Health, those authors found that although both forms of present orientation were independently significant in predicting outcomes, high discounting was a better predictor of deliberate or future-orientated outcomes, whereas poor impulse control better predicted urge drive behaviors that required little forethought (Nagin and Pogarsky 2004). In addition, only poor impulse control predicted violent offending (threatening with a weapon, creating a public disturbance, and participating in a group fight), whereas both impulsivity and high discounting were related to property offending (shoplifting, car theft, and burglary); however, high discounting was a stronger predictor (Nagin and Pogarsky 2004). This research indicates there may be a need to differentiate more carefully between these two constructs because they were found to predict different criminal behaviors and could have separate and specific policy implications. If it is assumed that there is a time lapse in which the benefits of crime occur in the present and the costs of crime (legal or informal sanctions) occur in the future, individuals who devalue the future in turn devalue sanctions. This has direct implications for the effectiveness of deterrence because it would follow that those who may highly devalue sanctions are less receptive to deterrence.

VI. The Discounted Utility Model and Intertemporal Choice

Wilson and Herrnstein (1985) provide an excellent example of how future costs can have little influence on an individual's behavior: "Millions of cigarette smokers ignore the (possibly) fatal consequences of smoking because they are distant and uncertain. If smoking one cigarette caused certain death tomorrow, we would anticipate a rather sharp reduction in tobacco consumption" (p. 49).

In behavioral economics and psychology, a trade-off between costs and benefits that occur at different points in time is referred to as an *intertemporal choice*. When making an intertemporal choice, individuals are thought to have a time preference with a present or future orientation. Traditionally, criminological evaluation of deterrence from a rational choice perspective had largely ignored the concept of intertemporal choice and that individuals may have varying levels of impulsivity, self-control, or time discounting that may influence decision making. Nagin and Pogarsky (2001) made a leap to remedy this exclusion through incorporating a discount rate into the traditional expected utility (EU) model, which is known as the *discounted utility* (DU) model. Within the DU model, it is often assumed that individuals are present oriented or prefer rewards quickly, even immediately, and prefer costs to be delayed into the future.

The deterrence concept of celerity is closely tied to time orientation or time preference. If a swift punishment effectively deters, it then follows that offenders must prefer slow or deferred sanctions. Nagin and Pogarsky (2001) define the celerity effect as "the sooner the sanction is expected to commence, the greater its current costliness and resulting deterrent potential" (p. 868). Nagin and Pogarsky incorporated the celerity of punishment by inserting a discount factor, δ, into the EU model:

$$U(\text{benefits}) > \delta_t \, pU(\text{legal costs} + \text{extralegal costs})$$

$$\delta_t = \left(\frac{1}{(1+r)}\right)^t$$

where the discount factor (δ_t) allows a weight to be added to the future costs. The amount of weight applied to costs is dependent on t, the number of time periods a sanction is delayed (the celerity), and r, which is an individual's discount rate. The discount rate is the extent to which a person decreases future values—in the case of deterrence, future sanctions. Those with a high discount rate, such as the smokers from the previous quotation, are very present orientated and therefore less patient. An individual's discount rate, r, can be determined by finding the future value that would make an individual indifferent to waiting a period t. This model makes the assumption that the discount rate is positive ($r > 0$). The discount factor δ_t is a function of r, and both values therefore can vary from individual to individual.

Nagin and Pogarsky (2001, p. 872) provide an example illustrating how the discount rate affects the cost of crime: Imagine an individual is issued a fine of $1,000 (table 11.1). If the individual's discount rate is .10 ($r_i = .10$), and his or her fine is delayed thirty days or one period ($t = 1$),[5] the individual's discount factor becomes .91, as demonstrated here:

$$\frac{1}{(1+.10)} = .9091 \approx .91$$

When the discount factor (.91) is multiplied by the original fine of $1,000, the present value of the fine decreases to $910. If the discount rate were to increase (a more "present-orientated" or impatient person) and become $r_i = .20$, the discount factor becomes .83 (where $.8333 = 1 / 1.20$), and the present value of the future fine decreases to a lower value of $830.

The previous model, which allows for the discounting of future costs and benefits, is an exponential model of time preference. In summary, holding the period constant (t), an increase in discount rate causes the present-day equivalent of a fine to decrease in value. In addition, holding the discount rate constant as the delay of punishment (t) increases the value of the fine also decreases. This means that the further into the future a fine is delayed, the less valuable the cost is toward producing disutility. Also, consistent with the rational choice model, the utility of crime decreases as the legal and extralegal costs increase or the perceived certainty of punishment (p) increases.

Table 11.1 Applied Example of Discounted Utility

Expected Payment Period	Discount Factor (δ_i)		Present Value of $1,000	
	$r_i = .10$	$r_i = .20$	$r_i = .10$	$r_i = .20$
$t = 1$	.91	.83	$910	$830
$t = 2$	.83	.69	$830	$690
$t = 3$	.75	.58	$750	$580

Source: Nagin and Pogarsky (2001, p. 872).

VII. NEGATIVE DISCOUNT RATE

Frederick, Loewenstein, and O'Donoghue (2002) discussed inconsistencies within the discounted utility model ("DU anomalies") that have given rise to alternative models of discounting, one of which is centered around the potential for a negative discount rate. Generally, the DU model such as the one put forth by Nagin and Pogarsky (2001, 2004) draws from the classical theory of deterrence and is consistent with the traditional celerity effect. Recall that this theory makes the assumption that individuals have a positive discount rate ($r > 0$), which means they prefer immediate or short-term benefits and to defer costs into the future. However, the DU positive discount rate assumption has been challenged conceptually, with claims there may be disutility in postponing cost. Similarly, Gibbs (1975) expressed that any delay in punishment would be more painful for offenders because of the psychological stress they would undergo while waiting and thinking about their future punishment. Furthermore, drawing from Bentham (1789/1988), Loewenstein (1987) underscored anticipation as a key source of pleasure and pain. Contradictory to DU, the negative discount model emphasizes the idea that there is utility involved in anticipating a future reward, such as a vacation, and thus an individual would prefer to wait for and *savor* this future beneficial outcome. Correspondingly, negative discounting makes the assumption that there is disutility in postponing a negative event such as punishment, exercise, or possibly giving a public speech. Because there may be *dread* associated with waiting for a negative outcome, an individual may tend to prefer to "just get it over with" quickly. Loewenstein found empirical support for negative discounting preferences when examining nonmonetary outcomes. In his experiment, subjects on average were willing to pay more to delay a kiss from a movie star of their choice by three days than for a kiss given immediately, in three hours, or in one day. Individuals were also willing to pay more to avoid a nonlethal 110-volt shock that was delayed for three hours or three days, and they were willing to pay substantially more to avoid a shock occurring in one year or three years. Both of these findings directly contradict the traditional rational choice discounted utility model and provide support for negative discount rates. In addition, Nagin and Pogarsky's (2001) discussion of the celerity effect assumed that people should have a positive discount rate; however, 21% of subjects in the sample had a negative discount rate, which challenged a key assumption in their model. When further probing time orientation, the authors found an indicator variable of negative discounting to be significant and, as expected, inversely related to the probability of drunk driving (Nagin and Pogarsky, 2001).

Findings that suggest that individuals have a negative time preference directly contradict and therefore cast doubt on the validity of Beccaria's celerity notion and alter policy implications. The classical (Beccarian) school of thought assumes that individuals have a positive discount rate and thus will be most effectively deterred through swift sanctions because for these individuals, future costs are devalued. By contrast, for those with negative discount rates, celerity carries an inverse weight in the model. These individuals would be deterred by sanctions that occur further in the future because they would face disutility not only from direct sanction costs (legal or extralegal) but also from the dread that results from waiting for the sanction to occur.

VIII. Hyperbolic Discounting

The positive and negative discount models previously discussed are both considered examples of exponential discounting. An important assumption of these models is that an individual's intertemporal preferences are consistent over time. When intertemporal preferences are time consistent, the preferred trade-off between period t and $t + 1$ is equivalent to the same choice when applied between period $t + 8$ and $t + 9$. The trade-off between any two future consecutive periods should always be equivalent. Economist R. H. Strotz (1955) first recognized that there might be instances in which individuals have time-inconsistent preferences and sought a discount function that was alternative to exponential discounting. Research from behavioral economics has drawn attention to Strotz's concern and explored instances in which the exponential model's assumption of consistent intertemporal preferences is violated. This model is referred to as hyperbolic time discounting.

O'Donoghue and Rabin (2000) provided an intuitive set of examples to make inconsistent time preferences more clear. First, suppose you must choose between (A) completing five hours of an unpleasant task today and (B) completing five and a half hours of the same unpleasant task tomorrow. Second, you must now choose between (C) completing five hours of the unpleasant task in 365 days and (D) completing five and a half hours of the unpleasant task in 366 days. If you prefer B to A, but also prefer C to D, you have demonstrated inconsistent time preferences. When looking a year into the future, individuals typically do not value single-day delays in having to complete an unpleasant task. However, people commonly put off unpleasant tasks until tomorrow when they could do them today. Although this example closely ties to problems of procrastination, it is also applicable to a wide range of behaviors for which individuals prefer to avoid actions that include immediate cost and delayed benefits (e.g., an unpleasant task or exercise) and overindulge in behavior that includes immediate benefits and delayed costs (e.g., crime, drug use, overeating, or general overconsumption) (O'Donoghue and Rabin 2000). Hyperbolic discounting takes into account that humans have a tendency toward immediate or short-term gratification and allow the discount function to decline hyperbolically instead of exponentially. The following is an example of a hyperbolic discount function:

$$\delta_t = \left(\frac{1}{1+rt} \right)$$

where, as in the previously defined models, r is an individual's discount rate, and t is a period of delay. Table 11.2 builds on the previous example established in table 11.1 and

Table 11.2 Applied Example Comparing Exponential to Hyperbolic Discounting

Expected Payment Period	Exponential Discounting		Hyperbolic Discounting	
	Discount Factor (δ_i)	Present Value of $1,000	Discount Factor (δ_i)	Present Value of $1,000
	$r = .10$		$r_i = .10$	
$t = 1$	.91	$910	.91	$910
$t = 2$	.83	$830	.83	$830
$t = 3$	.75	$750	.77	$770
$t = 10$	.39	$390	.50	$500
$t = 30$	.06	$60	.25	$250
$t = 50$	.01	$10	.17	$170

illustrates the comparative difference between exponential and hyperbolic discounting as periods increase, holding the discount rate constant. Note that although the hyperbolic discount model is also dependent on the values of r and t, this model differs from the exponential because the further into the future (as t increases), the delay will add increasingly less to the devaluation.

The key element of hyperbolic discounting, time inconsistency, suggests that at some point in time individuals may have a preference reversal. Whereas in the long term an individual may prefer not to steal from a store, in the short term when he or she is directly confronted with the opportunity, a theft may result. O'Donoguhe and Rabin (2000) believe this explains why individuals would "like" to behave one way but when the time comes they "choose" to behave another way. In hyperbolic discounting, individuals are thought to be patient when imagining future outcomes (thus having a low discount rate), but when considering immediate or short time delays, their discount rate becomes much larger, and they become impatient. For this reason, hyperbolic discounting has been considered "irrational" compared to exponential discounting.

Hyperbolic discounting has been equated with many aspects of human behavior, such as a lack of willpower or self-control and acting impulsively, but the differentiation or mechanism regarding these concepts is not always clear. For instance, Loewenstein (1999, p. 53) proposed that "willpower represents attempts to suppress viscerally motivated behaviors that conflict with higher level goals," where visceral factors include drives (hunger and sexual desire), emotions (anger and fear), and somatic sensations (pain). According to Loewenstein, individuals may overestimate their willpower because they underestimate the influence of visceral factors or because they may not recognize the potential for their willpower to be exerted or depleted from use.[6] This phenomenon has also been defined as impulsivity (Ainslie 1975) and a problem of self-control (O'Donoghue and Rabin 2000). O'Donoghue and Rabin (1999, 2000) further suggested that self-control problems can be improved or made worse, depending on an individual's sophistication or self-awareness regarding time-inconsistent preferences, whereas those who do not understand or foresee this tendency are referred to as naive. Although there are close inherent theoretical ties between hyperbolic discounting and Gottfredson and Hirschi's (1990) self-control, researchers should be hesitant or cautious about equating any of these concepts with discounting because there is relatively limited criminological literature on time preferences. In addition, Gottfredson and Hirschi consider self-control to be a relatively time-stable individual trait; this conceptualization is not consistent with hyperbolic time discounting because hyperbolic discounting allows the discount rate within an individual to vary over time and, as discussed later, can differ absolutely based on whether the outcome is a gain or a loss, whether it is large or small in magnitude, the type of good, and the framing of the outcome as either a delay or an acceleration.

Although criminology has historically ignored hyperbolic discounting, a study by Loughran, Paternoster, and Weiss (2012) closely examined this issue. They surveyed 478 university undergraduate students to determine if their willingness to drink and drive differed when different rewards and costs were introduced and said to occur at differing future points in time. The survey respondents were given the following scenario:

> Now, please imagine a hypothetical scenario in which you drove by yourself one night to meet some friends at a bar. The bar is located approximately 10 miles from your apartment. You have been casually drinking throughout the evening, and now you are ready to leave. You also remember that you have to be at work early the next morning, and your boss will have a fit if you are late. You can either drive home yourself or find another ride. However, if you find another ride tonight and leave your car, you will have to return early the next morning before work to pick it up. (p. 617)

In an effort to ensure respondents were not choosing to avoid drinking and driving because of personal safety, there was mention that their blood alcohol level, although higher than the legal limit, was only slightly higher. If pulled over by police, the penalty or cost associated with being caught drinking and driving was said to be three nights in jail and a fine. Loughran and colleagues then asked respondents to gauge their likelihood of driving home tonight (on a scale of 0–100) given that if they were pulled over, they would be forced to spend three nights in jail starting (a) tonight, (b) one week from now, (c) one month from now, (d) one year from now, and (e) ten years from now. This question allowed for the costs to be delayed into the future. Similarly, the authors then provided an additional incentive if the respondent were to decide to drink and drive:

> Now suppose that, as you are considering whether or not to drive yourself home and before you pay your tab, you run into your next-door neighbor who is also looking for a ride home. This person mentions that if you drive them home too, they will pay for your entire drink tab tonight. (p. 618)

Respondents were then asked their likelihood of driving home if their neighbor would pay their entire drink tab (a) tonight, (b) one week from now, (c) one month from now,

(d) one year from now, and (e) ten years from now. This question allowed for a time delay of the additional benefit. Through holding cost, benefit, and risk constant over time, Loughran et al. noted that the only reason an individual's willingness to drink and drive should have changed is due to the time discount factor δ_t. The authors were able to examine the possibility of hyperbolic discounting by comparing average effective weekly changes in reported willingness relative to the various time delays for the cost (three days in jail and fine) and the benefit (neighbor pays bar tab).

Loughran et al. (2012) also explored decision making using the concept of risk certainty. The respondent sample was randomly assigned into one of two groups: a high-risk group, with a 70 percent chance of getting pulled over, and a low-risk group, with a 10 percent chance of getting pulled over. Although a detailed discussion of risk certainty is outside the scope of this chapter, questions relating to risk allowed Loughran et al. to examine the interaction of time preferences and risk in an effort to determine if certainty of punishment (risk) trumps time preferences as much of the deterrence literature suggests. Results from the aforementioned study indicate that timing of rewards and costs influences respondents' willingness to drink and drive (Loughran et al., 2012). Specifically, with a one-week delay in reward (payment of bar tab), the mean willingness to drink and drive decreased by approximately 9 percent. When delaying the bar tab one month (three additional weekly delays), the mean willingness to drink and drive decreased only approximately 3.66 percent, which equates to approximately 1.22 percent per week. This finding was notable in that the change in mean willingness between the present and a one-week delay was much larger than the mean willingness change from week 1 to week 2 or from week 2 to week 3—a finding that is consistent with hyperbolic discounting in which short-term delays are discounted more heavily than long-term delays (Loughran et al. 2012). When examining costs delayed over time, the mean willingness to drive increased the further into the future the cost (jail time) was delayed, consistent with a celerity effect (Loughran et al. 2012). The average willing to drive increased each week at a decreasing rate, supporting the notion of a decreasing discount rate. In general support for deterrence theory, Loughran and colleagues found a significant main effect associated with risk and time delay, but the interaction between risk and time delay did not reach significant levels. Ultimately, this indicates that certainty (risk) and celerity (discount rate) are both independently significant deterrents, as would be expected based on classical Beccarian theory, and generally, hyperbolic discount rates are not sensitive to varying levels of risk certainty (Loughran et al. 2012).

An additional discount function, the quasi-hyperbolic discount function, was popularized by the economist David Laibson (1997). Although not implemented in the criminological literature, this model incorporates elements of exponential and hyperbolic discounting to emphasize human tendency toward *immediate* gratification. Using two parameters β and δ, this form of discounting allows for an immediacy effect. When $\beta = 1$, the model becomes standard exponential discounting. This means that an individual discounts the future consistently at all moments except the present.

IX. FURTHER ANOMALIES OF DISCOUNTING

The previous discussion provided a brief summary of time discounting; there are also many anomalies that have been observed that warrant discussion. For instance, referring to table 11.1, this example showed the discounted value of a present $1,000, where theoretically the $1,000 could have been a thousand-dollar reward or a thousand-dollar ticket (cost) and the value would have been discounted as shown in the table. This example followed an assumption of the DU model that the discount rate is the same for all goods. However, research has indicated that gains tend to be discounted more than losses. For instance, Thaler (1981) found that individuals' discount rates for paying a traffic ticket were lower than discount rates from a comparable question about a monetary gain. Similarly, Loughran et al. (2012) found the change in willingness to drive drunk each week was much smaller for costs than it was for rewards. This gave reason to believe costs and benefits may be valued differently (Loughran et al. 2012). These results suggest there might be asymmetry in choice preferences when comparing gains and losses, a finding that is consistent with prospect theory (Kahneman and Tversky 1979).

The example in table 11.1 and our review thus far also make no mention of another discounting anomaly, often referred to as the "magnitude effect." This implies that individuals may discount $1,000 in one manner and then discount $100 differently, and possibly even $10 using a different discount rate. Generally, research has indicated that smaller outcomes are discounted more than larger ones. Thaler (1981) found that as the magnitude of outcome increased, the discount rate decreased. Furthermore, Fredrick and Read (2002) found that the magnitude effect is enhanced when individuals consider small outcomes ($10) and large outcomes ($1,000) one after another rather than when considering these outcomes separately.

Given that discounting has been found to be different for costs and rewards, and across different magnitudes, it is not surprising that discounting may vary across *types* of goods (Frederick et al. 2002; McClure et al. 2007). The majority of discounting studies implement monetary costs and benefits (for a detailed overview of a good(s) included in discount rate studies, see Frederick et al. 2002, p. 377). Although at times monetary costs such as fines may be of interest to criminologists, quite often the costs of crime may include nonmonetary costs, such as days of incarceration, or even extralegal sanctions, such as embarrassment and the loss of attachments such as friends, family members, a spouse, or employment (Toby 1957; Zimring and Hawkins 1973; Grasmick and Bursik 1990).[7] In a similar manner, benefits of crime may not always be monetary. The potential for discounting to differ across different types of goods is worth careful consideration and requires further evaluation.

Discounting can also be influenced by whether or not an outcome is framed as a delivery acceleration or delay (Frederick et al. 2002). Lowenstein (1988) illustrated that respondents who believed that they would receive a good immediately would require two to four times more money on average to delay receiving the good compared to respondents who believed they would be receiving the item in a year and were offered the opportunity to pay to receive it immediately (an acceleration). This anomaly may have direct implications for criminals who have some preconceived notion regarding a typical celerity of punishment within the criminal justice system and frame their discounting around this expectation.

Although these DU anomalies are just a few among the increasing list of examples found in the field of behavioral economics, they highlight the importance of closely considering the generalizability of findings to situations because, as Frederick et al. (2002) note, "Virtually every assumption underlying the DU model has been tested and found to be descriptively invalid in at least some situations" (p. 252). Behavioral economics and, recently, criminology have been continuously recognizing DU anomalies and incorporating them, or at least considering them, in deterrence and rational choice theories.

X. Conclusion

Deterrence research has historically tended to focus on the certainty and severity components of deterrence while paying little, if any, attention to celerity. As discussed in this chapter, the notion of celerity appears to have consequences which directly affect intertemporal decision making because the celerity principle concludes that there is higher deterrent value in more immediate punishments. Correspondingly, the celerity principle also suggests that punishments delivered further into the future will be decreased in value. Therefore, the policy implication corresponding to the celerity principle is to increase the immediacy of sanctions in order to increase the cost associated with crime. Advances in behavioral economics have provided insight for criminological scholarship, highlighted that there may be inconsistencies within the traditional discounting utility model, and provided both cause and method for deeper examination. For instance, the acknowledgment of the potential for a negative discount rate (Loewenstein 1987) directly contradicts the celerity principle. If individuals have a negative discount rate, and thus derive utility from punishment occurring in the short term, increasing the speed of punishment could have the unwelcomed consequence of making crime less costly. In addition, research suggesting that a single individual's discount rate can vary across time (hyperbolic discounting), can be high when considering one type of "good" and low when considering another, or can even change absolutely needs further discussion in order to best inform policy decisions. Integrating research from behavioral economics into the study of crime may provide greater understanding of the ways in which individuals deviate from what traditionally has been considered "rational" behavior and allow for more accurate predictions regarding these deviations. Research must carefully examine under which conditions sanctions most effectively deter and how the timing of sanctions affects individuals with varying characteristics such as time preference.

Although evidence has been provided that discounting and impulsivity are two distinct theoretical constructs (Nagin and Pogarsky 2004), there is room for clarification on this topic and discussion as to where Gottfredson and Hirschi's (1990) element of self-control fits into the present research.

Discounting research can also be advanced within criminology through incorporating insights from developmental neuroscience. In an attempt to explain the disproportionately high prevalence of adolescent risk-taking behavior, Albert and Steinberg (2011) suggest that although adolescents may be no different in logic competency compared to adults, they may differ in their susceptibility or ability to handle immediate rewards. Although adolescents may evaluate cost similarly to adults, their immature cognitive control system makes them more sensitive to emotionally arousing immediacy of rewards; therefore, adolescents discount delayed rewards to a greater extent than do adults (Steinberg 2007, Steinberg et al. 2009). This raises interesting questions for future research to link age and discounting and as a possible explanation for the overrepresentation of adolescents in crime statistics. This also highlights interesting implications for methodology such that studying people using hypothetical scenarios may not be accurately assessing decision making in cases such as crime, in which emotional impacts of immediate rewards are likely (Steinberg 2005). Integrating research from neuroscience (Trepel, Fox, and Poldrack 2005; Steinberg 2007) will aid in deeper understanding of the neural pathways and physiological functioning associated with these discounting findings. Determining how the brain considers, processes, and weights rewards and risks will be important as the field becomes better adept at understanding the decision-making process of persons and offenders across the wide range of situations in which persons find themselves.

NOTES

1. "One of the greatest curbs on crime is not the cruelty of punishments, but their infallibility, and, consequently, the vigilance of magistrates, and that severity of an inexorable judge which, to be a useful virtue, must be accompanied by a mild legislation. The certainty of a punishment, even if it be moderate, will always make a stronger impression than the fear of another which is more terrible but combined with the hope of impunity even the least evils, when they are certain, always terrify men's minds" (Beccaria 1764/1985, p. 58). That is why Beccaria argued for prioritizing the perceived certainty of punishment over all else: "Do you want to prevent crimes? See to it that the laws are clear and simple. . . . See to it that men fear the laws and only the laws" (p. 94).

2. Nagin and Pogarsky (2001) noted that this equation assumes that benefits do not rely on the offender avoiding detection and is most likely ideal for crimes such as physical victimization, vandalism, or drunk driving. For crimes for which benefits are directly related to avoiding detection, such as property crime and embezzlement, the following may be a more appropriate equation: Commit crime if $1 - pU(\text{benefits}) > pU(\text{costs})$.

3. The high discounting scale included two questions: "What do you think are the chances that you will live to age 35?" and "How often during the past week did you feel hopeful about the future?"

4. The poor impulse scale included two items: "If you wanted to use birth control, how sure are you that you could stop yourself and use birth control once you were highly aroused or turned on?" and "When making decisions, you usually go with your gut feeling without thinking too much about the consequence of each alternative."

5. One period t can be defined as any length of time. In this example, it is 30 days, but it could have also been a week, a year, or any length of time depending on one's question of interest.

6. A similar conceptualization of willpower is found in Baumeister and Tierney's (2011) *Willpower: Rediscovering the Greatest Human Strength*, in which willpower is thought of as a muscle that can be strengthened or fatigued.

7. Albeit, it could be argued that many of these "nonmonetary" costs do carry some monetary burden, such as lost wages or professional networking opportunities.

REFERENCES

Ainslie, G. 1975. "Specious Reward: A Behavioral Theory of Impulsiveness and Impulse Control." *Psychological Bulletin* 82(4): 463–96.

Albert, D., and L. Steinberg. 2011. "Judgment and Decision Making in Adolescence." *Journal of Research on Adolescence* 21(1): 211–24.

Bachman, R., R. Paternoster, and S. Ward. 1992. "The Rationality of Sexual Offending: Testing a Deterrence/Rational Choice Conception of Sexual Assault." *Law and Society Review* 26:343–72.

Baumeister, R. F., and J. Tierney. 2011. *Willpower: Rediscovering the Greatest Human Strength*. New York: Penguin.

Beccaria, C. 1985. Essay *on Crimes and Punishments*, translated by H. Paolucci. New York: Macmillan. (Originally published 1764.)

Becker, G. 1968. "Crime and Punishment: An Economic Approach." *Journal of Political Economy* 76:169–217.

Bentham, J. 1988. *An Introduction to the Principles of Morals and Legislation*. Amherst, NY: Prometheus. (Originally published 1789.)

Chiricos, T. G., and G. P. Waldo. 1970. "Punishment and Crime: An Examination of Some Empirical Evidence." *Social Problems* 18:200–17.

Cornish, D. B., and R. V. G. Clarke. 1986. *The Reasoning Criminal: Rational Choice Perspectives on Offending*. New York: Springer-Verlag.

Frederick, S., and D. Read. 2002. "The Empirical and Normative Status of Hyperbolic Discounting and Other DU Anomalies." Working paper. Cambridge, MA/London: MIT/London School of Economics.

Frederick, S., G. Loewenstein, and T. O'Donoghue. 2002. "Time Discounting and TIME preference: A Critical Review." *Journal of Economic Literature* 40(2): 351–401.

Geerken, M. R., and W. R. Gove. 1975. "Deterrence: Some Theoretical Considerations." *Law and Society Review* 9(3): 497–513.

Gibbs, J. 1968. "Crime, Punishment, and Deterrence." *Southwestern Social Science Quarterly* 48: 515–30.

Gibbs, J. P. 1975. *Crime, Punishment, and Deterrence*. New York: Elsevier.

Gottfredson, M. R., and T. Hirschi. 1990. *A General Theory of Crime*. Stanford, CA: Stanford University Press.

Grasmick, H. G., and R. J. Bursik Jr. 1990. "Conscience, Significant Others, and Rational Choice: Extending the Deterrence Model." *Law and Society Review* 24(3): 837–61.

Grasmick, H. G., C. R. Tittle, R. J. Bursik, and B. J. Arneklev. 1993. "Testing the Core Empirical Implications of Gottfredson and Hirschi's General Theory of Crime." *Journal of Research in Crime and Delinquency* 30(1): 5–29.

Kahneman, D., and A. Tversky. 1979. "Prospect Theory: An Analysis of Decision Under Risk." *Econometrica: Journal of the Econometric Society* 47(2): 263–91.

Laibson, D. 1997. "Golden Eggs and Hyperbolic Discounting." *Quarterly Journal of Economics* 112(2): 443–77.

Levitt, S. D. 1996. "The Effect of Prison Population Size on Crime Rates: Evidence from Prison Overcrowding Litigation." *Quarterly Journal of Economics* 111(2): 319–52.

Loewenstein, G. 1987. "Anticipation and the Valuation of Delayed Consumption." *Economic Journal* 97:666–84.

Loewenstein, G. F. 1988. "Frames of Mind in Intertemporal Choice." *Management Science* 34(2): 200–14.

Loewenstein, G. 1999. "Experimental Economics from the Vantage-Point of Behavioural Economics." *Economic Journal* 109(453): 25–34.

Loughran, T. A., R. Paternoster, and D. Weiss. 2012. "Hyperbolic Time Discounting, Offender Time Preferences and Deterrence." *Journal of Quantitative Criminology* 28(4): 607–28.

McClure, S. M., K. M. Ericson, D. I. Laibson, G. Loewenstein, and J. D. Cohen. 2007. "Time Discounting for Primary Rewards." *Journal of Neuroscience* 27(21): 5796–5804.

Nagin, D. S. 1998. "Criminal Deterrence Research at the Outset of the Twenty-First Century." *Crime and Justice* 23:1–42.

Nagin, D. S. 2013. "Deterrence: A Review of the Evidence by a Criminologist for Economists." *Annual Review of Economics* 5:83–105.

Nagin, D. S., and R. Paternoster. 1991. "The Preventive Effects of the Perceived Risk of Arrest: Testing an Expanded Conception of Deterrence." *Criminology* 29(4): 561–87.

Nagin, D. S., and G. Pogarsky. 2001. "Integrating Celerity, Impulsivity, and Extralegal Sanction Threats into a Model of General Deterrence: Theory and Evidence." *Criminology* 39(4): 865–92.

Nagin, D. S., and G. Pogarsky. 2004. "Time and Punishment: Delayed Consequences and Criminal Behavior." *Journal of Quantitative Criminology* 20(4): 295–317.

O'Donoghue, T., and M. Rabin. 1999. "Doing It Now or Later." *American Economic Review* 89(1): 103–24.

O'Donoghue, T., and M. Rabin. 2000. "The Economics of Immediate Gratification." *Journal of Behavioral Decision Making* 13(2): 233–50.

Paternoster, R. 2010. "How Much Do We Really Know About Criminal Deterrence." *Journal of Criminal Law and Criminology* 100:765–823.

Piquero, A. R., R. Paternoster, G. Pogarsky, and T. Loughran. 2011. "Elaborating the Individual Difference Component in Deterrence Theory." *Annual Review of Law and Social Sciences* 7:335–60.

Piquero, A., and S. Tibbetts. 1996. "Specifying the Direct and Indirect Effects of Low Self-Control and Situational Factors in Offenders' Decision Making: Toward a More Complete Model of Rational Offending." *Justice Quarterly* 13:481–510.

Pratt, T. C., F. T. Cullen, K. R. Blevins, L. E. Daigle, and T. D. Madensen. 2006. "The Empirical Status of Deterrence Theory: A Meta-Analysis." In *Taking Stock: The Status of Criminological Theory*, edited by F. T. Cullen, J. P. and Wright, K. R. Blevins, pp. 367–96. New Brunswick, NJ: Transaction.

Ramsey, Frank P. 1931. *The Foundations of Mathematics and Other Logical Essays*. London: Kegan Paul, Trench, Trubner.

Savage, Leonard J. 1954. *The Foundation of Statistics*. New York: Wiley.

Schoemaker, Paul J. H. 1982. "The Expected Utility Model: Its Variants, Purposes, Evidence and Limitations." *Journal of Economic Literature* 20:529–63.

Sellin, T. 1959. *The Death Penalty*. Philadelphia: American Law Institute.

Sherman, L. W. 1990. "Police Crackdowns: Initial and Residual Deterrence." In *Crime and Justice: A Review of Research*, vol. 12, edited by M. Tonry and N. Morris, pp.1–48. Chicago: University of Chicago Press.

Sherman, L. W., and D. Weisburd. 1995. "General Deterrent Effects of Police Patrol in Crime "Hot Spots": A Randomized, Controlled Trial." *Justice Quarterly* 12(4): 625–48.

Simon, H. A. 1957. *Models of Man: Social and Rational*. New York: Wiley.

Steinberg, L. 2005. "Cognitive and Affective Development in Adolescence." *Trends in Cognitive Sciences* 9(2): 69–74.

Steinberg, L. 2007. "Risk Taking in Adolescence: New Perspectives from Brain and Behavioral Science." *Current Directions in Psychological Science* 16:55–59.

Steinberg, L., S. Graham, L. O'Brien, J. Woolard, E. Cauffman, and M. Banich. 2009. "Age Differences in Future Orientation and Delay Discounting." *Child Development* 80(1): 28–44.

Strotz, R. H. 1955. "Myopia and Inconsistency in Dynamic Utility Maximization." *Review of Economic Studies* 23(3): 165–80.

Thaler, R. 1981. "Some Empirical Evidence on Dynamic Inconsistency." *Economics Letters* 8(3): 201–7.

Tittle, C. 1969. "Crime Rates and Legal Sanctions." *Social Problems* 16:409–23.

Toby, J. 1957. "Social Disorganization and Stake in Conformity: Complementary Factors in the Predatory Behavior of Hoodlums." *Journal of Criminal Law* 48:12–17.

Trepel, C., C. R. Fox, and R. A. Poldrack. 2005. "Prospect Theory on the Brain? Toward a Cognitive Neuroscience of Decision Under Risk." *Cognitive Brain Research* 23:34–50.

Waldo, G. P., and T. G. Chiricos. 1972. "Perceived Penal Sanction and Self-Reported Criminality: A Neglected Approach to Deterrence Research." *Social Problems* 19:522–40.

Warren, Howard C. 1916. "Mental Association from Plato to Hume." *Psychological Review* 23:108–230.

Wilson, J. Q., and R. Herrnstein. 1985. *Crime and Human Nature*. New York: Free Press.

Zimring, F. E., and G. J. Hawkins. 1973. *Deterrence: The Legal Threat in Crime Control*. Chicago: University of Chicago Press.

Zimring, F. E., and G. J. Hawkins. 1995. *Incapacitation: Penal Confinement and the Restraint of Crime*. New York: Oxford University Press.

CHAPTER 12

THE ROLE OF MORAL BELIEFS, SHAME, AND GUILT IN CRIMINAL DECISION MAKING

An Overview of Theoretical Frameworks and Empirical Results

ROBERT SVENSSON, LIEVEN J. R. PAUWELS, AND FRANK M. WEERMAN

MORALITY can be regarded as a central cause of crime (Wikström 2010; Messner 2012). People who do not accept moral rules prescribed in laws are generally more inclined to break such rules than people who care about moral rules (prescribed in law). Moral beliefs, or beliefs about whether a certain behavior is right or wrong, have, under different denominators, played a major role in many theories of offending, such as social control theory (Hirschi 1969), differential association theory (Sutherland 1947), and situational action theory (Wikström 2010; Wikström et al. 2012). Sometimes morality is formulated in a conventional direction (prosocial belief in the moral validity of norms reflected in the law), and sometimes it is formulated in an antisocial direction (deviant definitions or subcultural acceptance of rule-breaking). Traditionally, the emphasis has been on convictions about what is right and wrong to do. However, moral belief systems are complex and deal with much more than cognitive processes: They also include vital behavioral, sensory, motivational, and affective features (Walters 2002).

Consequently, emotions, in their role as linchpins of human evolution, are instrumental in shaping and promoting the belief systems that support a person's actions, including crime. Only recently have moral emotions been included in theories and studies of offending. In particular, it has been assumed that the moral emotions of shame and guilt may play an important role in restraining people from committing crimes (Tibbetts

2003, 2014; Rebellon et al. 2010). Scholars have argued that people do everything they can to avoid the painful feeling of these two emotions (Elster 1999; Tangney, Stuewig, and Mashek 2007), and therefore they may have a powerful influence on criminal decision making.

The study of criminal decision making usually subsumes under the heading of rational choice theorizing or is nearly automatically linked to the perspective of rational choice. Does morality, particularly moral emotions as influence on criminal decision making, fit in such a perspective? Some scholars have argued that moral emotions are incompatible with the rational choice theory, and especially the narrow versions of rational choice theory that view all action as a consequence of a (suboptimal) decision guided by the principles of pleasure and pain, or the famous cost–benefit analysis (Etzioni 2010). Wider versions of rational choice theory do not share this view, and it is argued that there is no reason why moral beliefs could not be viewed as additional elements that affect processes of deliberation (Opp 2001). This seeming contradiction is one of the reasons why the rational choice approach has been heavily debated within criminology (Wikström and Treiber 2016). More generally, the rational choice perspective is a rather controversial theoretical approach in the social sciences (Kroneberg and Kalter 2012).

It is important to realize that the rational choice school of thought is not a homogeneous family of theories. Many scholars within the rational choice paradigm favor wide rational choice models, allowing the inclusion of social and moral incentives as well as nonmaterial and subjective constraints and opportunities: This approach paved the way for studies that include moral beliefs as a key part in rational choice models. Wide rational choice models stretch the core idea of "rationality" to what Boudon (2010) initially called relative rationality or cognitive rationality—that is, the assumption that humans can deliberate and thus have agency. It is within this wide framework of theories of cognitive rationality that the role of morals can fruitfully be studied. Criticism of this "wide" approach of rational choice thinking concerns the apparent ad hoc tendency as well as the nonfalsifiability of models that include an all-inclusive variety of motives and constraints in decision making (Finkel 2008).

Therefore, an increasing number of scholars have tried to make rational choice theories more explicit by formulating perceived preferences and perceived constraints of individuals, including a wide range of benefits, rewards, and motivations. In this line of reasoning, altruistic values, feelings of moral duty, social solidarity, moral approval and moral support for the law, internal norms, and moral emotions such as anticipated shame and anticipated guilt are not impossible features anymore.

In this chapter, we provide an overview of the role of moral beliefs and moral emotions in criminal decision making and discuss current findings from the empirical literature on the causes of offending. We argue that moral values cannot be studied without taking moral emotions such as anticipated shame and guilt into account. We therefore theoretically discuss morality in general and carefully describe the specific and often forgotten components of shame and guilt, and we present empirical findings and implications for theories of crime and criminal decision making and crime prevention.

We first give a sketch of the background of rational choice theories in criminology and the role of (moral) emotions within rational choice theory. After this general description, we address theorizing about morality in different disciplines and then provide a discussion of moral emotions and their role in decision making. We then focus on the moral emotions of shame and guilt and the role they play in individual decision making. Finally, we discuss the role of shame and guilt in criminological theories and address empirical findings reported in studies on the link between moral emotions and offending.

I. Moral Decision Making in Rational Choice Schools of Thought

Decision making has been considered a key element in explaining crimes for a long time. Beccaria and Bentham laid the foundations of what is now known as classicism, a collection of hypotheses regarding choice processes in the commitment of acts of crime. According to Beccaria and other classicists, people deliberately choose to engage in offending when they evaluate the potential costs and benefits. Classicism laid the foundations of rational choice theory (Cullen and Agnew 2003).

Cornish and Clarke (1986) reintroduced rational choice thinking in the field of criminology. The main ideas for the reasoning criminal and decision making derive from previous research in the field of psychology and mainly from cognitive psychology (Clarke and Cornish 1985). Clarke and Cornish were in need of a broad theoretical heuristic that could guide research and policy advice on situational crime prevention. Obviously, a rational choice perspective provided situational crime prevention analysts with a useful framework. By analyzing crime as if it involved rational decisions, scholars examined situational clues that could negatively affect perceived costs and benefits of crime as determinants of target selection and why some decide to commit a crime. These ideas of the rational choice models have a major impact for guiding policymakers with a special focus on situational crime prevention. The original premises of the "reasoning criminal" were strongly related to the key ideas of the classicist school.

Clarke and Cornish (1985) argued that the commission of acts of crime is the result of the following: first, the decision to become involved in crime (the initial involvement model) and, subsequently, the role of situational characteristics that affect processes of actually committing acts of crime (the criminal event model). Whereas the initial involvement model borrowed concepts from typical theoretical traditions of mainstream etiology, the criminal event model focused on situational triggers that triggered individuals who were ready to offend as a consequence of their psychological, social, and biological makeup. However, the link between the initial involvement model and the situational model was not fully developed and not addressed in detail (Wikström and Treiber 2016).

Furthermore, rational choice theories have had a major impact on the social sciences, particularly in the fields of economics, political science, and law. The theory also has a long tradition within sociology and constitutes an important approach within the theorizing of sociology (for a discussion of the evolution of rational choice sociology, see Kroneberg and Kalter 2012). Also, it is clear that rational choice sociology was influenced by economic theory (Coleman 1993). In sociological theorizing, rational choice theory was an influential framework in the development of action theories, and the theory refreshed thinking about macro–micro questions by developing bridging assumptions about how context affects decision making. Although the theory had a major impact on sociology, it has often been debated and criticized and even "declared dead by its critics" (Kroneberg and Kalter 2012, p. 86).

It is surprising that the sociological evolution in thinking and the development of action theories have not been noticed by theorists in the field of criminology. In sociology, rational choice theory is a theory about action that aims to explain human behavior in general, which helps us understand why some people act in a certain way and how aspects of the situation may have an impact on the choices and the actions that individuals take (Elster 1989; Coleman 1990). Critics of the rational choice perspective struggle with the term "choice" and their implicit dislike of the classicist image of individuals that act free and primarily in self-interest (Opp 2001).

In rational choice theory, the choices individuals make are merely deliberations aimed at optimizing outcomes in relation to individuals' preferences. Hedström (2005, p. 61) argued that rational choice theory is at its most fundamental level an explanation that assumes that actors, when confronted with action alternatives, choose the course of action that is optimal with respect to their personal preferences or desires. Some theorists who have their roots in sociological rational choice theory (i.e., the wide versions of rational choice theory) have posited that *emotions* may have an important role in the choices individuals make. In particular, Elster (2009) argued that emotions have an important role in the explanation of behavior.

Rational choice theories within criminology seem to have ignored the importance of individual differences in crime propensity for a long time (Nagin and Paternoster 1993). However, in relatively recent versions of rational choice models, some criminologists have included the concept of shame in integrated models of rational choice and deterrence (Grasmick and Bursik 1990; Nagin and Paternoster 1993; Tibbetts 1997). In these models, shame is included as a deterrence mechanism that is assumed to have an impact on people's decision making. One of Grasmick and Bursik's (1990) main arguments for including shame in their model is that

> shame can be considered a form of potential self-imposed, or reflective, punishment. Like the threat of state-imposed legal sanctions, the threat of self-imposed shame can be viewed as more or less certain and more or less severe. The greater the perceived threat of shame, the lower the expected utility of crime, and the less the likelihood that crime will occur. (p. 840)

Relatedly, Tibbetts (1997) suggested that shame should be viewed as a source of internal punishment that can be an important cost mechanism in subjective evaluations of offending utility. The mere idea of experiencing internal devastating feelings can be very powerful in restraining individuals to abide by the law.

More generally, Clarke (2014) argued in an elaboration of the rational choice perspective that we know much more about affect and criminal decision making nowadays than when the rational choice perspective was initially developed. He also suggested that knowledge about emotions and the importance of emotions regarding decision making could help in the development of a better explanatory and predictive power of the rational choice perspective. Therefore, developing a proper way to include affect and emotion in the rational choice perspective is an important and difficult challenge. In addition, van Gelder et al. (2014a) argued that there is a strong need for including emotions in the criminal decision-making framework and that this "will lead to a more encompassing picture of criminal decision processes" (p. 11). Although this will be a challenge for the rational choice theory within criminology, some theories already include the moral emotions in their theories of crime causation (see section V).

II. Morality in Context

Before addressing the question of morality and moral emotions in decision making, it is important to distinguish different concepts and to sketch the development of thinking about morality in various disciplines. First, there is a distinction between *norms* and *values*. A norm is a rule or a standard that states how individuals are expected to act in certain specific circumstances (Williams 1968; Homans 1974, p. 96). In contrast with norms, which are viewed as specific and concrete guidelines about right and wrong, values may instead be described as more general and abstract conceptions about right and wrong (Marini 2000).

Morality is often defined as what is right or wrong, or good or bad, to do in a given situation (Turiel 2002; Stets and Carter 2012). The question of what constitutes morally correct and incorrect behavior has never been an easy one to answer, and this question has occupied moral philosophers for centuries. Two well-known examples of the perspectives that have emerged within the field of moral philosophy are the Kantian approach, which emphasizes that we should act unto others as we would like them to act unto us and that people should not be treated merely as a means toward one's own ends, and the utilitarian view, which regards the moral status of an act as being dependent on the worth of its consequences. The study of morality also has a long tradition within other disciplines, such as sociology and psychology.

Within the field of sociology, morality has been discussed for a long time, but the study of morality has had a recent resurgence within the discipline (Hitlin and Vaisey 2013). Traditionally, it has been argued that morality is the cement that ties the individual to society through a common system of rules during interactions that in turn produce solidarity (Durkheim 1925/1961). Within society, relations to social groups are of major importance for the development of morality, and an individual's moral development "begins, accordingly, only in so far as we belong to a human group" (Durkheim 1925/ 1961, p. 80). In the group, the individual partakes in the norms of the group and internalizes them, and thus they become a part of the individual, morally binding him or her to the group's norms. Whether or not an individual is morally bonded to the norms of the group is decisive in determining whether the individual will choose to follow group norms (Durkheim 1897/1951; see also Hirschi 1969).

In psychology, scholars have addressed the question of how moral reasoning is related to moral behavior (Piaget 1932/1965; Kohlberg 1969). *Cognitive–developmental theory* views moral development as a result of socialization (Piaget 1932/1965). Kohlberg developed Piaget's ideas and created a scheme for conceptualizing and measuring moral development as a form of cognitive development. Kohlberg's theory holds that moral reasoning, the basis for ethical behavior, has a stage-like progression. The *preconventional level* of moral reasoning is typically observed in children and is mainly focused on concrete and fixed rules of what is right or wrong and how it is related to the self. The *conventional level* of moral reasoning is typical of adolescents and adults. At this stage, the arguments become more complex and less egocentric, and people judge their actions with general rules of society. The *postconventional level* is characterized by a growing realization that individuals go beyond society and that rules are justified from their own perspective—for example, with reference to universal principles of justice.

Although Piaget and Kohlberg laid the foundation, other scholars have also developed the perspective, including Nucci (2001) and Turiel (2002). Moral psychology has also been developed within the perspective of the *social–cognitive theory* (Bandura 1991, 1999; Bandura et al. 1996). Bandura attempted to explain how people rationalize unmoral actions—that is, how "good" people can behave "badly" without any feelings of remorse and guilt (Bandura et al. 1996; Bandura 1999).[1] For a brief review of moral psychology in a historical context, see Haidt (2008).

Morality also has an important role within criminological theory, and it has been stated that "if they are to be true to their calling, all criminologists have to be interested in morality" (Bottoms 2002, p. 24). For example, within the perspective of control theories, morality had an important role in containment theory through inner and outer containment (Reckless 1967). It also had a major role in Sykes and Matzas' (1957) discussion of techniques of neutralization and in social control or bonding theory in terms of belief in the moral validity of the law (Hirschi 1969). In addition, morality has an important role in differential association theory in terms of definitions favorable toward criminal behavior (Sutherland 1947; see also Akers 1998). Integrated theories also consider the causes and consequences of morality by stating which variables affect morality and how morality affects offending (Thornberry 1987; Catalano and Hawkins 1996). One theory that explicitly focuses on the importance of morality in crime involvement is situational action theory (Wikström 2010). Wikström argues that individuals vary in whether they have high or low levels of *moral values*, and the level of moral values determines whether an individual views crime as an option or not. Numerous studies in criminology, with different definitions of moral values, have shown that strong conventional moral values are negatively related to offending (Stams et al., 2006; Antonaccio and Tittle, 2008; Svensson, Pauwels, and Weerman 2010).

Although the importance of morality in the study of crime has been stressed in many empirical studies, relatively few studies have focused on the importance of moral emotions with regard to criminal decisions and offending. In the next section, we first discuss emotions in general and then moral emotions in particular, after which we focus on the relevance of these emotions to the decision to commit crime.

III. MORAL EMOTIONS

Emotions play an important role in everyday life. Jon Elster (1989) commented that "we do not choose to have them; rather, we are in their grip" (p. 61). He also stated that "emotions are the most important bond or glue that links us to others" (Elster 1999, p. 403). Emotions not only link us to other people but also are a major source of motivation, and it has been noted that "emotions are intimately related to action. They are among the main direct causes of action" (Frijda 2010, p. 570).[2] In the research literature, different emotions are discussed, including sadness, joy, anger, fear, surprise, and disgust; some of these are called "basic" emotions (for a discussion of emotions, see Frijda 1986; Kemper 1987; Ekman 1999; Elster 1999).

Some emotions are triggered by acts that violate moral rules of behavior. These emotions are moral emotions. *Moral emotions* play a central role in guiding people's choice of behavior, and they are closely linked to moral behaviors (Lewis 1992; Tangney and Dearing 2002; Sheikh and Janoff-Bulman 2010*a*). It has been suggested that: "moral behavior is ultimately motivated by emotions" (Blasi 1999, p. 16). It has also been posited that "moral emotions provide the motivational force—the power and energy—to do good and to avoid doing bad" (Tangney et al. 2007, p. 347). In general, emotions play an important role in moral judgment and moral motivation (Prinz and Nichols 2010). Turner and Stets (2007) stated that individuals need to feel the emotion of shame and guilt to be moral and to experience the emotions so that they can adjust behaviors and follow the norms of society. When individuals do not have the capability to experience the emotions of shame and guilt, they lack the power to develop feelings of empathy. According to biosocial criminologists, this is one of the strongest predictors of developing an antisocial personality disorder (Raine 2002, 2013).

A number of different moral emotions have been discussed in the literature, including empathy, shame, guilt, sympathy, concern, and compassion (Tangney and Dearing 2002; Turner and Stets 2007; Prinz and Nichols 2010). Many scholars believe that these moral emotions have evolutionary roots and that they are genetically transmitted because of the reproductive success of moral emotions for cooperation (vs. cheating) (Trivers 1971; Gintis 2003).[3] Haidt (2003) argued that there are four families of moral emotions: (1) the other-condemning family (contempt, anger, and disgust), (2) the self-conscious family (shame, guilt, and embarrassment), (3) the other-suffering family (empathy and compassion), and (4) the other-praising family (gratitude and fear). Two of the most studied moral emotions are shame and guilt (Elster 1999; Tangney and Dearing 2002; Tangney et al. 2007; Turner and Stets 2007).

IV. The Concepts of Shame and Guilt

Shame and guilt are not only moral emotions but also *self-conscious emotions*, which means that they "involve the self evaluating the self" (Tangey and Dearing 2002, p. 2). They are built on reciprocal evaluation and judgment. This means, for example, that "people are ashamed or guilty because they assume that someone (self and/or other) is making a negative judgment about some activity or characteristics of theirs" (Fisher and Tangney 1995, p. 4). The two emotions are also *social emotions*, which means that they are "triggered only by beliefs that make a reference to other people" (Elster 1999, p. 139). Turner (2014) contended that shame and guilt are second-order emotions because they involve the negative emotions of anger, fear, and sadness, in different ordering. For shame, the dominant emotion is sadness, followed by anger and then fear of the consequences for one's action. For guilt, the dominant emotion is also sadness, followed by fear about consequences for the action and then anger.

Shame and guilt are negative emotions that emerge in response to personal failure when there is an important moral dimension to the behavior involved in this failure. These emotions play a decisive role in whether an individual will act in one way or another, and they "play crucial roles in a person's motivation to avoid doing what is regarded as morally wrong" (Pestana 1995, p. 363).[4] It is not necessary that the individual would have committed a particular act; most important is whether the individual would feel ashamed or feel guilty about it. This would be a strong indication of his or her level of morality. Shame and guilt can be viewed as consequences of an individual's morality, and Wikström et al. (2012) argue that these emotions are strong indicators of an individual's morality (see also Tangney et al. 2007).

According to Tangney and Dearing (2002), moral emotions have an important role in moral decisions. They argue that moral decisions, such as the decision to commit a crime or break a rule, and moral behavior are guided by three main factors: moral standards (an individual's knowledge of moral norms), moral reasoning, and moral emotions. Both moral reasoning and moral emotions influence people's actual moral choice and behavior, but people's capacity for moral emotions is regarded as more important. Tangney and Dearing argue that "moral emotions provide immediate punishment (or reinforcement) of behavior. Moreover, people can *anticipate* their likely emotional reactions (e.g., guilt) as they consider behavioral alternatives" (p. 133). Furthermore, they note that it may be that the ability to experience moral emotions should be more directly linked to behavior than the level of moral reasoning.

The moral emotions of shame and guilt emerge during the process of primary socialization, and the family is essential for the development of these emotions (Lewis 1992;

Barrett 1995; Sheikh and Janoff-Bulman 2010*b*). Individuals who receive strong parental support and are subjected to love-oriented techniques of parental control internalize norms and learn moral values better than others, and they will experience higher levels of shame and guilt when they violate rules (Abell and Gecas 1997; Tangney and Dearing 2002; Grusec 2011). The school is probably the most important institution of secondary socialization for the development of these emotions, but the peer group also has been found to be important in the development of shame and guilt (Hart and Carlo 2005; Hart and Mueller 2013; Byungbae, Pratt, and Wallace 2014).

When the socialization process is completed, norms will be internalized and the individual will develop a moral sense of what is right or wrong. This leads the individual to feel ashamed in relation to significant others and feel guilt if he or she commits a particular type of crime. In other words, internalization of moral norms may lead to moral emotions of shame and guilt, both of which are assumed to restrain individuals from delinquency. On the other hand, if the socialization process is poor, internalization of norms and moral development will be adversely affected. This means that the individual will not feel shame or guilt when committing a crime. In this respect, the individual is then "free to deviate" (Hirschi 1969, p. 18). Svensson (2004*a*) stated that shame and guilt can be viewed as "*social control mechanisms* that restrain us from committing acts which violate internalised norms. Social control is thus manifested by means of an *inner control* that acts to constrain our behavioural choices via the effects of shame and guilt" (p. 18).

Of the two moral emotions, shame has been of interest to social scientists for a longer period of time (Elster 1999; Mischeva 2000), and it has been defined as one of the most important, painful, and intensive of all emotions (Tangney 1995; Elster 1999). It has been referred to both as the "master-emotion" (Scheff 1997, p. 12) and as "one of the quintessential human emotions" (Lewis 1992, p. 1). Shame emerges when an individual commits an act that violates internalized norms and believes that he or she has failed to live up to the norms of the group (Elster 1999). It is not the act itself that is important but, rather, the fact that the individual as a person has committed the act, thereby eliciting the disapproval of others (Tangney et al. 2007). The individual feels ashamed in front of other people, and he or she does not want to commit acts that are in breach of the norms and values of the group and that therefore affect the bonds that have been built up: "Shame signals threat to the bond" (Scheff 1997, p. 102). These others need not be physically present, however; it is sufficient that the individual feels that he or she has failed to live up to the norms and standards of others (Lewis 1992; Tangney and Dearing 2002).

Because shame is an emotion that focuses on an evaluation of the global self, individuals who feel shame often also feel small, worthless, and powerless. This may lead the individuals to hide, escape, or strike back. Because shame is related to the global self, it has also been noted to be related to people's self-esteem (Elster 1999).[5] Turner and Stets (2007) argue that "shame impairs self because it is so painful, increasing the probability that persons will activate defense mechanisms to protect self. As a result, shame often leads individuals to transmute their shame into anger and direct this anger at others" (p. 551). Elster noted that because shame is such an "ugly" feeling and cannot be easily avoided by self-deceptive maneuvers, "we often do everything we can to avoid the feeling of shame. . . . the anticipation of shame acts as a powerful regulator of behavior" (p. 154).

Guilt, on the other hand, is the emotional state that emerges when an individual commits a *specific act* that violates prevailing norms and values and then judges the violation of the norm as a morally wrong act (Elster 1999). This may lead to a belief that the individual has failed to live up to his or her own internalized moral code. In such instances, the question posed is one of moral adequacy. To feel guilt thus means that an individual has a conscience and a self with the capacity to differentiate between what is morally right and morally wrong (Barett 1995; Gecas 2001). Guilt is related to the specific act and not, as is the case with shame, an individual's core identity or self-concept (Tangney and Dearing 2002) or, as Elster argued, the individual's perception of self through the eyes of others and of these others' disapproval. At the same time, guilt is regarded as a painful emotion, although the emotion of guilt is considered to be less painful and less intense than the feeling of shame. If an individual feels guilty about doing a bad act, he or she feels a tension of remorse and regret and a willingness to confess, apologize, or repair the damage caused by the act and to undo the wrongdoing (Barrett 1995, Tangney and Dearing 2002).

Although guilt is less intensive than shame, when it is experienced, people want to eliminate it in various ways, including by confession, reparation, self-criticism, and punishment. Although some scholars argue that the feelings of guilt may keep people from doing things when they anticipate those feelings (Prinz and Nichols 2010), others argue that "guilt is less important than shame in the regulation of behavior" because it is less painful than shame (Elster 1999, p. 154).

V. Shame and Guilt in Contemporary Theories of Crime Causation

Because both shame and guilt are moral emotions, related to (im)moral behavior such as crime, it is rather surprising that the two emotions have received rather minor attention within the field of criminology. Currently, there are two major theories within the field of criminology that explicitly mention the role of moral emotions: the reintegrative shaming theory (Braithwaite 1989) and the situational action theory (Wikström 2010; Wikström et al. 2012). Braithwaite focused on the effect of shaming as a consequence when an individual has committed a crime. His theorizing suggests that shaming the offender for what he or she has done in an integrative way may decrease future offending. Shaming in a stigmatizing way, however, may enhance continuation of offending. The key is that an offender should be ashamed about his or her acts but not believe that he or she is an intrinsically bad person.

Situational action theory focuses on morality and the moral emotions of shame and guilt in crime causation (Wikström 2010; Wikström et al. 2012). Within the framework of this theory, Wikström argues that moral values and moral emotions such as shame and guilt are the most important elements of morality, and they are viewed as essential dimensions of "the moral filter." With this concept, he meant that motivations to break rules emerge from person–environment interactions. The decision to view crime as an action alternative and the choice to act and thus break a moral rule, prescribed in laws, are triggered by environmental cues such as provocation or temptation, in the absence of deterrents such as (in)formal control. Also, the context is important through the principle of moral congruence: When personal morality is low and the morality of the setting is crime-prone, the likelihood of offending is seriously increased. Wikström argues that individuals with a law-conforming morality do not tend to view crime as an action alternative, whereas individuals with a nonconforming morality may view crime as an action alternative and deliberately or habitually offend (Wikström et al. 2012).

In addition to these two major theories, the moral emotion of shame has also been incorporated in integrative models of rational choice and deterrence, as indicated previously (Grasmick and Bursik 1990; Nagin and Paternoster 1993; Tibbetts 1997). In these models, shame is included as an internally functioning deterrence mechanism, and the anticipated feeling of shame acts as a potential cost that is considered in the decision to break the law.

VI. Previous Research on the Association Between Shame, Guilt, and Offending

In crime causation studies, shame is often found to be negatively related to offending (Wikström and Svensson 2008; Svensson et al. 2013). In some of these studies, the measure of shame is more or less a measure of guilt, measuring whether a person would feel "guilty" if he or she committed an offense (Grasmick and Bursik 1990), guilt combined with remorse or personal discomfort (Byungbae et al. 2014), shame combined with embarrassment (Rebellon et al. 2010), or a measure of self-esteem (Piquero and Tibbetts 1996; Tibbetts 1997, 2014).

In other studies, shame is more explicitly measured by asking respondents if they would feel ashamed in front of significant others (parents, friends, and teachers) if they got caught committing different acts of crime (e.g., shoplifting and breaking into a car) (Wikström and Butterworth 2006; Svensson et al. 2013). In one of these studies, it was found that the predictor of feeling ashamed in the face of friends was the most important of the three predictors (Svensson 2004b). In most of these studies, the measure of shame is defined as *anticipated* and *situational-dependent* by asking respondents whether they would feel ashamed or guilty if caught committing certain criminal offenses (Rebellon et al. 2010; Svensson et al. 2013).

It is very uncommon that criminological studies also include the measure of guilt. Two studies included measures of both shame and guilt. Svensson et al. (2013) measured guilt by asking respondents whether they would feel guilty if they got caught committing certain criminal offenses. The results of this study showed that guilt, like shame, is negatively related to offending. Tibbetts (2014) also included both shame and guilt in his study. He found both anticipated shame and guilt to be significantly related to intentions to offend.

In other studies, often from a psychological perspective, shame has been defined as *shame-proneness* and guilt as *guilt-proneness* (i.e., a stable trait of the individual; see Tibbetts 1997). In some of these studies, shame has been found to be positively related or unrelated to both actual offending and intentions to offend (Tibbetts 1997, 2003; Stuewig and McCloskey 2005; Tangney et al. 2007; Hosser, Windzio, and Greve 2008; Tangney et al. 2011). In most of these studies, guilt was also included in the analysis, and feelings of guilt seemed to be negatively related to offending (Tibbetts 2003; Stuewig and McCloskey 2005; Hosser et al. 2008; Tangney et al. 2011).

A small number of studies have examined the relationship between shame and/or guilt and offending while controlling for other theoretically relevant variables. For example, Svensson (2004b) found that the relationship between family relation and offending is completely mediated by anticipated shame for girls and partially mediated by anticipated shame for boys. Rebellon et al. (2010) found only partial empirical evidence that the relationship between strain, delinquent friends, self-control, and intentions to steal is mediated by anticipated shaming. However, anticipated shaming mediated the entire relationship between perceived risk of getting caught and was negatively associated with intentions to steal. Piquero and Tibbetts (1996) found that the relationship between moral beliefs and intentions to drive drunk and intentions to shoplift is substantially mediated by anticipated shaming. Svensson et al. (2013) found that the relationship between parental monitoring, deviant peers, moral values, and offending is substantially mediated by anticipated shame and guilt. Pauwels and Svensson (2015) reported that the moral emotions of guilt and shame also predicted offending in children: Shame and guilt mediated the effects of social bonds, and when moral beliefs were added, guilt, but not shame, had an independent effect on child offending.

Tibbetts (2014) found shame and guilt to be related to intentions to offend when control was held for a number of variables, such as prior offending, deterrence, and background variables. It is important to note that the effect of perceived certainty/severity of being caught was no longer related to intentions to offend when all the emotional and control variables were included in the analysis. According to Tibbetts, this means that "the emotional traits and states of individuals may be more important factors than those of traditional deterrence/rational choice factors in making decisions to commit criminal acts" (p. 234). Also, van Gelder et al. (2014b) suggest that these "informal" moral costs of shame may be a stronger deterrent of crime than more "formal" ones.

VII. Discussion and Conclusion

This chapter demonstrated that the moral emotions of both shame and guilt are important in criminal decision making (in the process of deliberation) and that moral emotions have an important role in explaining criminal behavior. To improve our understanding of moral emotions from a theoretical standpoint, it is important to develop an interdisciplinary paradigm in which morality and emotions can be studied in relation to crime. This implies that criminologists are willing to learn the terminology from other fields (and vice versa). In an interdisciplinary approach, there is room for genuine discussion about the biological, psychological, and sociological roots of morality.

Increasing our knowledge about moral emotions is also important for crime prevention. Because the process of socialization has a central role in developing moral emotions, the focus should be on strengthening conventional social bonds and optimizing parenting practices that lead to the development of moral emotions that prevent crime before it happens (Tibbetts 2014).

Despite the empirical evidence of a link between moral emotions and criminal decision making, more research is needed that goes beyond the traditional survey methodology. Most studies have used self-reported offending as a dependent variable; however, self-reported offending studies, like intention to offend studies, are not necessarily the best measures of decision processes. One way to attempt to capture the processes of decision making is to make use of randomized scenario studies (Haar and Wikström 2010). The randomized scenario approach is vital for several reasons. First, it avoids problems of time order (self-reported offending often refers to past-year behavior, whereas measures of moral beliefs and emotions refer to one point in time). Second, randomized scenario studies allow for measuring the processes of choice, the role of moral emotions and beliefs, and situational triggers directly at the situational level (for an example, see Wikström et al. 2012).

Furthermore, it is important that we continue to develop the measurement of moral emotions because studies have used widely differing measures, particularly for shame. This makes the conclusions from studies of shame less clear. It is also important that we extend our knowledge about how and in what way moral emotions have an impact on deterrence. Shame and guilt can be viewed as an internal control (inner punishment), but how they are related with external controls and deterrence (severity and certainty) is still underresearched. In summary, there are many reasons to continue the study of morality and moral emotions and also to continue to integrate this research with that on criminal decision making.

Notes

1. Somewhat comparable to Sykes and Matza's (1957) theory of neutralization techniques.
2. A number of philosophers have discussed the importance of emotions over time. Aristotle contributed with an influential discussion of emotions. For a thorough discussion

regarding Aristotle's view on the importance of emotions, see Elster (1999, pp. 48–75). Other philosophers who addressed the importance of emotions are David Hume and Adam Smith.

3. It is worth noting that although the focus of this chapter is micro-level decision making, evolutionary psychologists argue that moral emotions played an important role in the decline of conflicts and violence in the past century (Pinker 2011). For a broader discussion of macro-level historical and evolutionary perspectives on the evolution of violence throughout human history and evolution, see Pinker (2011). Evolutionary macro-level explanations are not incompatible with micro-level social psychological perspectives (Heylen and Pauwels 2015).

4. For a discussion of moral emotions such as shame and guilt and their link to the criminal justice system, see Karstedt (2002).

5. Although self-esteem and shame are linked to the self, Tangney and Dearing (2002) argue that self-esteem and shame are distinct constructs: "Global self-esteem is a stable trait involving one's general evaluation of the self, largely independent of specific situations. . . . Shame on the other hand, is an emotion—an affective state. The *feeling* of shame involves a negative evaluation of the global self" (pp. 56–57). They also conclude that self-esteem seems to increase the probability of feeling shame.

References

Abell, E., and V. Gecas. 1997. "Guilt, Shame, and Family Socialization." *Journal of Family Issues* 18:99–123.

Akers, R. L. 1998. *Social Learning and Social Structure: A General Theory of Crime and Deviance.* Boston: Northeastern University Press.

Antonaccio, O., and C. R. Tittle. 2008. "Morality, Self-Control, and Crime." *Criminology* 46:479–510.

Bandura, A. 1991. "Social Cognitive Theory of Moral Thought and Action." In *Handbook of Moral Behavior and Development: Theory, Research and Applications*, vol. 1, edited by W. M. Kurtines and J. L. Gewirtz, pp. 71–129. Hillsdale, NJ: Erlbaum.

Bandura, A. 1999. "Moral Disengagement in the Perpetration of Inhumanities." *Personality and Social Psychology Review* 3:193–209.

Bandura, A., C. Barbaranelli, G. V. Caprara, and C. Pastorelli. 1996. "Mechanisms of Moral Disengagement in the Exercise of Moral Agency." *Journal of Personality and Social Psychology* 71:364–74.

Barrett, K. C. 1995. "A Functionalist Approach to Shame and Guilt." In *Self-Conscious Emotions: The Psychology of Shame, Guilt, Embarrassment, and Pride*, edited by J. P. Tangney and K. W. Fischer, pp. 25–63. New York: Guilford.

Blasi, A. 1999. "Emotions and Moral Emotions." *Journal for the Theory of Social Behaviour* 29:1–19.

Bottoms, A. 2002. "Morality, Crime, Compliance and Public Policy." In *Ideology, Crime and Criminal Justice: A Symposium in Honour of Sir Leon Radzinowicz*, edited by A. Bottoms and M. Tonry, pp. 20–51. Devon, UK: Willan.

Boudon, R. 2010. "The Cognitive Approach to Morality." In *Handbook of the Sociology of Morality*, edited by S. Hitlin and S. Vaisey, pp. 15–33. New York: Springer.

Braithwaite, J. 1989. *Crime, Shame and Reintegration.* Cambridge: Cambridge University Press.

Byungbae, K., T. C. Pratt, and D. Wallace. 2014. "Adverse Neighborhood Conditions and Sanction Risk Perceptions: Using SEM to Examine Direct and Indirect Effects." *Journal of Quantitative Criminology* 30:505–26.

Catalano, R. F., and J. D. Hawkins. 1996. "The Social Development Model: A Theory of Antisocial Behavior." In *Delinquency and Crime: Current Theories*, edited by J. D. Hawkins, pp. 149–97. Cambridge: Cambridge University Press.

Clarke, R. V. 2014. "Affect and the Reasoning Criminal: Past and Future." In *Affect and Cognition in Criminal Decision Making*, edited by J.-L. van Gelder, H. Elffers, D. Reynald, and D. Nagin, pp. 20–41. New York: Routledge.

Clarke, R. V., and D. B. Cornish. 1985. "Modeling Offenders' Decisions: A Framework for Research and Policy." In *Crime and Justice: An Annual Review of Research*, vol. 6, edited by M. Tonry and N. Morris, pp. 147–85. Chicago: University of Chicago.

Coleman, J. S. 1990. *Foundations of Social Theory*. Cambridge, MA: Harvard University Press.

Coleman, J. S. 1993. "The Impact of Gary Becker's Work on Sociology." *Acta Sociologica* 36:169–78.

Cornish, D. B., and R. V. Clarke. 1986. *The Reasoning Criminal: Rational Choice Perspectives on Offending*. New York: Springer-Verlag.

Cullen, F. T., and R. Agnew. 2003. *Criminological Theory: Past to Present*. Oxford: Oxford University Press.

Durkheim, E. 1951. *Suicide*. New York: Free Press. (Originally published 1897.)

Durkheim, E. 1961. *Moral Education*. New York: Free Press. (Originally published 1925.)

Ekman, P. 1999. "Basic Emotions." In *Handbook of Cognition and Emotion*, edited by T. Dalgleish and M. Power, pp. 45–60. New York: Wiley.

Elster, J. 1989. *Nuts and Bolts for the Social Sciences*. Cambridge: Cambridge University Press.

Elster, J. 1999. *Alchemies of the Mind: Rationality and the Emotions*. Cambridge: Cambridge University Press.

Elster, J. 2009. "Emotions." In *The Oxford Handbook of Analytical Sociology*, edited by P. Hedström and P. Bearman, pp. 51–71. Oxford: Oxford University Press.

Etzioni, A. 2010. *Moral Dimension: Toward a New Economics*. New York: Simon and Schuster.

Finkel, S. E. 2008. "In Defense of the 'Wide' Rational Choice Model of Collective Political Action." In *Rational Choice: Theoretische Analysen und Empirische Resultate*, edited by A. Diekmann, K. Eichner, P. Schmidt, and T. Voss, pp. 23–35. Wiesbaden: Verlag für Sozialwissenschaften.

Fisher, K. W., and J. P. Tangney. 1995. "Self-Conscious Emotions and the Affect Revolution: Framework and Overview." In *Self-Conscious Emotions: The Psychology of Shame, Guilt, Embarrassment, and Pride*, edited by J. P. Tangney and K. W. Fischer, pp. 3–22. New York: Guilford.

Frijda, N. H. 1986. *The Emotions*. Cambridge: Cambridge University Press.

Frijda, N. H. 2010. "Impulsive Action and Motivation." *Biological Psychology* 84:570–79.

Gecas, V. 2001. "The Self as a Social Force." In *Extending Self-Esteem Theory and Research*, edited by T. J. Owens, S. Stryker, and N. Goodman, pp. 85–100. Cambridge: Cambridge University Press.

Gintis, H. 2003. "The Hitchhiker's Guide to Altruism: Gene–Culture Coevolution, and the Internalization of Norms." *Journal of Theoretical Biology* 220:407–18.

Grasmick, H. G., and R. J. Bursik Jr. 1990. "Conscience, Significant Others, and Rational Choice: Extending the Deterrence Model." *Law and Society Review* 24:837–61.

Grusec, J. E. 2011. "Socialization Processes in the Family: Social and Emotional Development." *Annual Review of Psychology* 62:243–69.

Haar, D. H., and Wikström, P.-O. H. 2010. "Crime Propensity, Criminogenic Exposure and Violent Scenario Responses: Testing Situational Action Theory in Regression and Rasch Models." *European Journal of Applied Mathematics* 21:307–23.

Haidt, J. 2003. "Moral Emotions." In *Handbook of Affective Sciences*, edited by R. J. Davidson, K. R. Scherer, and H. H. Goldsmith, pp. 852–70. Oxford: Oxford University Press.

Haidt, J. 2008. "Morality." *Perspectives on Psychological Science* 3:65–72.

Harris, N. 2011. "Shame, Ethical Identity and Conformity: Lessons from Research on the Psychology of Social Influences." In *Emotions, Crime and Justice*, edited by S. Karstedt, I. Loader, and H. Strang, pp. 193–210. Oxford: Hart Publishing.

Hart, C. O., and C. E. Mueller. 2013. "School Delinquency and Social Bond Factors: Exploring Gender Differences Among a National Sample of 10th Graders." *Psychology in the Schools* 50:116–33.

Hart, D., and G. Carlo. 2005. "Moral Development in Adolescence." *Journal of Research on Adolescence* 15:223–33.

Hedström, P. 2005. *Dissecting the Social: On the Principles of Analytical Sociology*. Cambridge: Cambridge University Press.

Heylen, B., and L. J. R. Pauwels. 2015. "The Social Roots of Contemporary Prejudice." *International Journal of Criminology and Sociology* 4:28–35.

Hirschi, T. 1969. *Causes of Delinquency*. Berkeley: University of California Press.

Hitlin, S., and S. Vaisey. 2013. "The New Sociology of Morality." *Annual Review of Sociology* 39:51–68.

Homans, G. C. 1974. *Social Behavior: Its Elementary Forms*. Oxford: Harcourt Brace Jovanovich.

Hosser, D., M. Windzio, and W. Greve. 2008. "Guilt and Shame as Predictors of Recidivism: A Longitudinal Study with Young Prisoners." *Criminal Justice and Behavior* 35:138–52.

Karstedt, S. 2002. "Emotions and Criminal Justice." *Theoretical Criminology* 6:299–317.

Kemper, T. D. 1987. "How Many Emotions Are There? Wedding the Social and the Autonomic Components." *American Journal of Sociology* 93:263–89.

Kohlberg, L. 1969. "Stage and Sequence: The Cognitive–Developmental Approach to Socialization." In *Handbook of Socialization Theory and Research*, edited by D. A. Goslin, pp. 347–480. Chicago: Rand McNally.

Kroneberg, C., and F. Kalter. 2012. "Rational Choice Theory and Empirical Research: Methodological and Theoretical Contributions in Europe." *Annual Review of Sociology* 38:73–92.

Lewis, M. 1992. *Shame: The Exposed Self*. New York: Free Press.

Marini, M. M. 2000. "Social Values and Norms." In *Encyclopedia of Sociology*, vol. 4, edited by E. F. Borgatta and R. J. V. Montgomery, pp. 2828–40. New York: Macmillan.

Messner, S. F. 2012. "Morality, Markets, and the ASC: 2011 Presidential Address to the American Society of Criminology." *Criminology* 50:5–25.

Mischeva, V. I. 2000. *Shame and Guilt*. Uppsala, Sweden: Uppsala University, Department of Sociology.

Nagin, D., and R. Paternoster. 1993. "Enduring Individual Differences and Rational Choice Theories of Crime." *Law and Society Review* 27:467–96.

Nucci, L. P. 2001. *Education in the Moral Domain*. Cambridge: Cambridge University Press.

Opp, K. D. 2001. "How Do Norms Emerge? An Outline of a Theory." *Mind and Society* 2:101–28.

Pauwels, L. J. R., and R. Svensson. 2015. "Schools and Child Antisocial Behavior: In Search for Mediator Effects of School-Level Disadvantage." *Sage Open* 5(2): 1–13.

Pestana, M. S. 1995. "Guilt and Shame." In *International Encyclopedia of Ethics*, edited by J. K. Roth, pp. 363–64. London: Fitzroy Dearborn.

Piaget, J. 1965. *The Moral Judgement of the Child*. New York: Free Press. (Originally published 1932.)

Pinker, S. 2011. *The Better Angels of Our Nature*. New York: Viking.

Piquero, A., and S. Tibbetts. 1996. "Specifying the Direct and Indirect Effects of Low Self Control and Situational Factors in Offenders' Decision Making: Toward a More Complete Model of Rational Offending." *Justice Quarterly* 13:481–510.

Prinz, J. J., and S. Nichols. 2010. "Moral Emotions." In *The Moral Psychology Handbook*, edited by J. M. Doris, pp. 111–46. Oxford: Oxford University Press.

Raine, A. 2002. "Biosocial Studies of Antisocial and Violent Behavior in Children and Adults: A Review." *Journal of Abnormal Child Psychology* 30:311–26.

Raine, A. 2013. *The Anatomy of Violence: The Biological Roots of Crime*. New York: Vintage.

Rebellon, C. J., N. L. Piquero, A. R. Piquero, and S. G. Tibbetts. 2010. "Anticipated Shaming and Criminal Offending." *Journal of Criminal Justice* 38:988–97.

Reckless, W. C. 1967. *The Crime Problem*. New York: Appleton–Century–Crofts.

Scheff, T. J. 1997. *Emotions, the Social Bond, and Human Reality*. Cambridge: Cambridge University Press.

Sheikh, S., and R. Janoff-Bulman. 2010a. "The 'Shoulds' and 'Should Nots' of Moral Emotions: A Self-Regulatory Perspective on Shame and Guilt." *Personality and Social Psychology Bulletin* 36:213–24.

Sheikh, S., and R. Janoff-Bulman. 2010b. "Tracing the Self-Regulatory Bases of Moral Emotions." *Emotion Review* 2:386–96.

Stams, G. J., D. Brugman, M. Dekovic, L. van Rosmalen, P. van der Laan, and J. C. Gibbs. 2006. "The Moral Judgment of Juvenile Delinquents: A Meta-Analysis." *Journal of Abnormal Child Psychology* 34:697–713.

Stets, J. E., and M. J. Carter. 2012. "A Theory of the Self for the Sociology of Morality." *American Sociological Review* 77:120–40.

Stuewig, J., and L. A. McCloskey. 2005. "The Relation of Child Maltreatment to Shame and Guilt Among Adolescents: Psychological Routes to Depression and Delinquency." *Child Maltreatment* 10:324–36.

Sutherland, E. H. 1947. *Principles of Criminology*. Philadelphia: Lippincott.

Svensson, R. 2004a. *Social Control and Socialisation: The Role of Morality as a Social Mechanism in Adolescent Deviant Behaviour*. Stockholm: Almqvist and Wiksell.

Svensson, R. 2004b. "Shame as a Consequence of the Parent–Child Relationship: A Study of Gender Differences in Juvenile Delinquency." *European Journal of Criminology* 1: 477–504.

Svensson, R., L. Pauwels, and F. M. Weerman. 2010. "Does the Effect of Self-Control on Adolescent Offending Vary by Level of Morality? A Test in Three Countries." *Criminal Justice and Behavior* 37:732–43.

Svensson, R., F. M. Weerman, L. J. R. Pauwels, G. J. N. Bruinsma, and W. Bernasco. 2013. "Moral Emotions and Offending: Do Feelings of Anticipated Shame and Guilt Mediate the Effect of Socialization on Offending?" *European Journal of Criminology* 10:22–39.

Sykes, G. M., and D. Matza. 1957. "Techniques of Neutralization: A Theory of Delinquency." *American Sociological Review* 22:664–70.

Tangney, J. P. 1995. "Shame and Guilt in Interpersonal Relationships." In *Self-Conscious Emotions: The Psychology of Shame, Guilt, Embarrassment, and Pride*, edited by J. P. Tangney and K. W. Fischer, pp. 114–39. New York: Guilford.

Tangney, J. P., and R. L. Dearing. 2002. *Shame and Guilt*. New York: Guilford.

Tangney, J. P., J. Stuewig, and D. J. Mashek. 2007. "Moral Emotions and Moral Behavior." *Annual Review of Psychology* 58:345–72.

Tangney, J. P., J. Stuewig, D. Mashek, and M. Hastings. 2011. "Assessing Jail Inmates' Proneness to Shame and Guilt: Feeling Bad About the Behavior of the Self?" *Criminal Justice and Behavior* 38:710–34.

Thornberry, T. P. 1987. "Toward an Interactional Theory of Delinquency." *Criminology* 25: 863–92.

Tibbetts, S. G. 1997. "Shame and Rational Choice in Offending Decisions." *Criminal Justice and Behavior* 24:234–55.

Tibbetts, S. G. 2003 "Self-Conscious Emotions and Criminal Offending." *Psychological Reports* 93:101–26.

Tibbetts, S. G. 2014. "Traits and States of Self-Conscious Emotions in Criminal Decision Making." In *Affect and Cognition in Criminal Decision Making*, edited by J.-L. van Gelder, H. Elffers, D. Reynald, and D. Nagin, pp. 221–38. New York: Routledge.

Trivers, R. L. 1971. "The Evolution of Reciprocal Altruism." *Quarterly Review of Biology* 46:35–57.

Turiel, E. 2002. *The Culture of Morality: Social Development, Context, and Conflict*. New York: Cambridge University Press.

Turner, J. H. 2014. "The Evaluation of Human Emotions." In *Handbook of the Sociology of Emotions*, vol. 2, edited by J. E. Stets and J. H. Turner, pp. 11–31. New York: Springer.

Turner, J. H., and J. E. Stets. 2007. "Moral Emotions." In *Handbook of the Sociology of Emotions*, edited by J. E. Stets and J. H. Turner, pp. 544–66. New York: Springer.

van Gelder, J.-L., H. Elffers, D. Reynald, and D. Nagin. 2014a. "Affect and Cognition in Criminal Decision Making: Between Rational Choices and Lapses of Self-Control." In *Affect and Cognition in Criminal Decision Making*, edited by J.-L. van Gelder, H. Elffers, D. Reynald, and D. Nagin, pp. 1–19. New York: Routledge.

van Gelder, J.-L., D. Reynald, H. Elffers, and D. Nagin. 2014b. "Anticipated Emotions and Immediate Affect in Criminal Decision Making: From Shame to Anger." In *Affect and Cognition in Criminal Decision Making*, edited by J.-L. van Gelder, H. Elffers, D. Reynald, and D. Nagin, pp. 161–78. New York: Routledge.

Walters, G. D. 2002. *The Criminal Lifestyle*. Thousand Oaks, CA: Sage.

Wikström, P.-O. H. 2010. "Explaining Crime as Moral Actions." In *Handbook of the Sociology of Morality*, edited by S. Hitlin and S. Vaisey, pp. 211–40. New York: Springer-Verlag.

Wikström. P.-O. H., and D. A. Butterworth. 2006. *Adolescent Crime: Individual Differences and Lifestyles*. Cullompton, UK: Willan.

Wikström, P.-O. H., D. Oberwittler, K. Treiber, and B. Hardie. 2012. *Breaking Rules: The Social and Situational Dynamics of Young People's Urban Crime*. Oxford: Oxford University Press.

Wikström, P.-O. H., and R. Svensson. 2008. "Why Are English Youths More Violent Than Swedish Youths? A Comparative Study of the Role of Crime Propensity, Lifestyles and Their Interactions." *European Journal of Criminology* 5:309–30.

Wikström, P.-O. H., and K. Treiber. 2016. "Situational Theory: The Importance of Interactions and Action Mechanisms in the Explanation of Crime." In *Handbook of Criminological Theory*, edited by A. R. Piquero, pp. 415–44. New York: Wiley.

Williams, R. M. Jr. 1968. "The Concept of Norms." In *International Encyclopedia of the Social Sciences*, vol. 11, edited by D. L. Sills, pp. 204–8. New York: Macmillan.

CHAPTER 13

NEURAL MECHANISMS OF CRIMINAL DECISION MAKING IN ADOLESCENCE

The Roles of Executive Functioning and Empathy

EDUARD T. KLAPWIJK, WOUTER VAN DEN BOS, AND BERNA GÜROĞLU

THE prevalence of criminal behavior tends to increase during adolescence, peak in late adolescence, and then decrease in adulthood—a phenomenon referred to as the "age–crime curve" (figure 13.1) (Hirschi and Gottfredson 1983; Loeber and Farrington 2014). It is possible that criminal behavior mostly results from a combination of different factors (e.g., genetic and environmental) that influence decision-making processes (Moffitt 2005). For example, biological dispositions may place certain children at risk for antisocial behavior, but this risk might increase or decrease as a result of life experiences, particularly in interactions with parents and peers (Dodge and Pettit 2003). This chapter focuses on the underlying neurocognitive mechanisms in criminal decision making in adolescents. Understanding the decision-making processes and the possible differences between adolescents and adults may be crucial for gaining insight into the age–crime curve. The chapter first provides a general overview of the neural basis of decision making in typically developing adolescents. Then, studies that examine these processes in delinquent and antisocial adolescents are discussed.

Several cognitive processes may be involved in decisions that result in a person breaking the law (i.e., criminal decision making). This chapter focuses on two of these processes and their underlying neural circuitry: executive functioning and empathic skills. Executive functioning is an umbrella term that refers to domain general regulatory and control functions, including inhibition, self-regulation, planning, and organization. Poor executive functioning involves an inability to control behavior and may lead to increased impulsive risk-taking and difficulties in considering the future implications

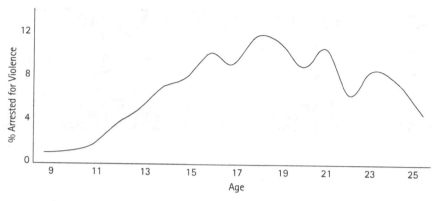

FIGURE 13.1 Age–crime curve, based on longitudinal data from the Pittsburgh Youth Study and using self-reported delinquency and official records of offending.

Source: Reprinted from Loeber and Farrington (2014).

of one's acts. Indeed, poorer executive functioning is generally observed in antisocial compared to typically developing individuals (Morgan and Lilienfeld 2000). Hence, juveniles with executive functioning deficits are at increased risk of criminal behavior, especially when their environment provokes or fosters such behavior (Moffitt and Henry 1989). When criminal acts directly involve victims, offender decision making might be influenced by a lack of empathic feelings. Empathy is the ability to share and understand the feelings of others and is usually divided into affective (e.g., shared affect and emotional resonance) and cognitive (e.g., emotion recognition, perspective-taking, and self–other distinction) aspects (Decety and Jackson 2004; Shamay-Tsoory, Aharon-Peretz, and Perry 2009). Realizing and feeling that the victim will suffer are thought to motivate individuals to inhibit harmful behavior. Many studies have indeed found a negative relationship between empathy and aggression (Lovett and Sheffield 2007). Together, research in the domain of executive functioning and that in the domain of empathy provide insight into how adolescents make decisions that have detrimental consequences for the self (e.g., problems in considering the implications of being arrested) and for others (e.g., lack of empathy for suffering victims of crime).

I. DEVELOPMENT OF BRAIN NETWORKS IN ADOLESCENCE

One of the plausible explanations for the increase in offending during adolescence is the increase in risk-taking and impulsive behavior during this age period (Steinberg 2008). In general, decision making by adolescents involves more risky and impulsive choices in comparison with that by adults (Blakemore and Robbins 2012). This developmental

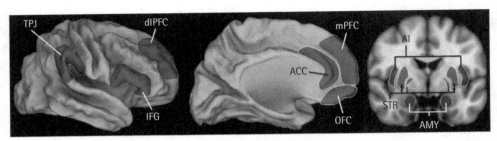

FIGURE 13.2 Schematic representation of brain networks involved in affective empathy (IFG, inferior frontal gyrus; ACC, anterior cingulate cortex; AI, anterior insula; AMY, amygdalae), cognitive empathy/mentalizing (mPFC, medial prefrontal cortex; TPJ, temporoparietal junction), regulation and reward processing (dlPFC, dorsolateral prefrontal cortex; OFC, orbitofrontal cortex; STR, striatum).

pattern is often associated with the finding that executive functioning, which relies heavily on frontal lobe functioning, is still improving during this period (Blakemore and Choudhury 2006). Several landmark studies have shown prolonged brain development during adolescence, especially in the frontal lobes (Giedd et al. 1999; Gogtay et al. 2004). Furthermore, experimental studies have found increasing activation of the dorsolateral prefrontal cortex (dlPFC; for an overview of brain regions discussed in this chapter, see figure 13.2) from childhood toward adulthood, which has been linked to increasing regulation and control with age (Luna et al. 2001; van Leijenhorst et al. 2010; Güroğlu et al. 2011; Steinbeis, Bernhardt, and Singer 2012). In addition to the gradual development of control-related brain areas across adolescence, neuroimaging studies have also shown a specific adolescence-related change in the affective system of subcortical areas, including the amygdala and striatum (Ernst et al. 2005; Hare et al. 2008). In contrast to the prolonged developmental trajectory of the control system, the affective system seems to mature rather early in adolescence (Nelson et al. 2005). This combination of findings has inspired neurodevelopmental theories that explain risky and impulsive adolescent behavior as a result of a developmental mismatch between affective and cognitive control systems in the brain (figure 13.3) (Steinberg 2008; Somerville, Jones, and Casey 2010). These theories hold that faster maturation of the affective subcortical brain areas in comparison to the slower maturation of cortical frontal areas leads to more emotionally driven and risky decisions in adolescence. This maturation mismatch suggests that the strong incentive-seeking behavior typically observed in adolescence is driven by the affective system, whereas the frontal control system is not yet mature enough to properly control this increase in impulses. As a result, adolescent risk-taking might be especially sensitive to "hot" contexts in which emotions play a role, whereas adolescents might show no increased risk-taking in "cold" situations compared to adults (Figner et al. 2009; Crone and Dahl 2012).

In addition to the changes in the affective and control systems, adolescence is also characterized by a process of social reorientation marked by an increased focus on peer relationships (Steinberg and Morris 2001). These changes in social behavior are also reflected

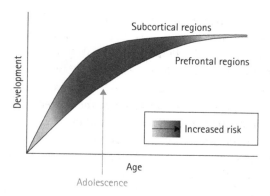

FIGURE 13.3 Schematic representation of the developmental mismatch model. Subcortical regions such as the amygdala and ventrial striatum (top line) mature earlier compared to prefrontal cortical regions (bottom line), leading to more emotionally driven behavior during adolescence.

Source: Reprinted from Somerville et al. (2010).

in an improvement in taking the perspective of others during adolescence (Güroğlu, van den Bos, and Crone 2009; Dumontheil, Apperly, and Blakemore 2010; Vetter et al. 2013). Neuroimaging studies have focused on understanding the neural underpinnings of these social changes by examining specific social processes, such as affective and cognitive empathy (Burnett et al. 2011; Crone and Dahl 2012). Affective empathy (i.e., sharing other's emotions) is often studied using experimental paradigms in which participants observe others in pain. The rationale behind this method is that vicariously experiencing the pain of others partly activates the neural networks involved in feeling pain ourselves (Singer and Lamm 2009). From childhood on, in typically developing populations, a network comprising the anterior insula and anterior cingulate cortex (ACC) is activated when experiencing pain firsthand as well as when observing someone else in pain (Decety, Michalska, and Akitsuki 2008; Bernhardt and Singer 2012). Other brain regions involved in empathy for pain, such as the amygdala, show a decrease in activation from childhood to adulthood, suggesting a reduction in arousal caused by other's distress with increasing age (Guyer et al. 2008; Decety and Michalska 2010). Possibly this reduction in spontaneous arousal or resonance with the feelings of others might be related to or result from increased regulation of emotions. This notion is supported by evidence showing an increase in activation in prefrontal regions involved in cognitive control and affect regulation, such as the dlPFC, with increasing age (Decety and Michalska 2010). These findings suggest that across adolescence, individuals become better at regulating emotions caused by seeing others in pain. According to some theoretical models of the development of empathy, this regulation is necessary to translate the personal stress caused by observing others in pain into positive action (i.e., prosocial behavior such as helping) (Eisenberg and Fabes 1990; Decety and Meyer 2008).

Cognitive empathy (i.e., attributing mental states to others) has been studied using a variety of tasks in adolescents, ranging from reflecting on other's thoughts and preferences (Burnett et al. 2009; Pfeifer et al. 2009) to strategic use of mental state information in social interaction games (Güroğlu et al. 2011; van den Bos et al. 2011). One specific example is a task used by Dumontheil et al. (2010) in which participants are instructed by a "director" to move objects between a set of shelves. Because the director can see only the contents of some of the shelves, participants have to take into account the director's visual perspective in order to move the correct objects and ignore those objects that the director cannot see. In this task and other cognitive empathy (or mentalizing) tasks, participants are critically required to represent the mental states and perspectives of other persons (Frith and Frith 2003). "Social brain regions" implicated in cognitive empathy are the temporoparietal junction (TPJ) and the medial prefrontal cortex (mPFC) (see figure 13.2). Several studies have shown that activation in the TPJ tends to increase with age across adolescence, accompanied by an increase in perspective-taking abilities (Blakemore et al. 2007; Güroğlu et al. 2011; van den Bos et al. 2011). In addition, activation in the mPFC decreases with age across adolescence, suggesting a shift in orientation from self to others (Burnett et al. 2009; Pfeifer et al. 2009; Gunther Moor et al. 2011; van den Bos et al., 2011).

Risk-taking in adolescence is also influenced by social changes during this life period. Accordingly, compared to adults, adolescents are more susceptible to the influence of peers on risk-taking behavior. In one study, participants played a video game in which they drove a car on a road with intersections and traffic lights. In this task, more points could be earned by driving fast and without stopping—for example, by driving through yellow traffic lights—but points were lost if the car crashed by hitting another car at an intersection. It was shown that when adolescents played this game in the presence of their peers, they showed an increase in risky decisions (as assessed by a higher number of car crashes), whereas children and adults did not show this increase (Gardner and Steinberg 2005). This study was followed up by a functional magnetic resonance imaging (fMRI) study that used the same experimental design in which participants performed the driving task both alone and with peers observing. During both conditions, compared to adults, adolescents showed less activation in the lateral prefrontal cortex, a brain region important for cognitive control. During peer observation specifically, compared to adults, adolescents showed greater activation in reward-related brain regions, including the ventral striatum. In addition, activity in these regions predicted subsequent risk-taking (Chein et al. 2011). These findings suggest that the presence of peers increases adolescent risk-taking, possibly due to the increased reward associated with risk-taking in a social context.

In summary, research has demonstrated important changes in brain regions implicated in control, affect, and social processes during typical adolescent development. During this life period, the affective brain areas mature relatively fast compared to the more gradual maturation of cortical frontal brain areas involved in control processes. This developmental mismatch between affective and control regions leads to an increase in sensation seeking in the absence of a sufficiently mature control system. In addition, the increased involvement of social brain regions with age, such as the TPJ, is associated with increased sensitivity to the perspective of others that might also heighten peer influence during adolescence. Together, these changes may underlie an increase in risk-taking during adolescence, especially when emotions play a role, such as in a social context with peers. This increase in risk-taking might be an important factor that can explain the age–crime curve. In addition, our understanding of the normative development can serve as a framework to interpret deviant developmental patterns in antisocial youth.

II. Deviating Patterns of Development in Adolescence

The normative adolescent increase in risk-taking, associated with the discrepancies between affective and cognitive systems, may partially explain why there is an increase in criminal behavior rates in adolescence. However, it does not explain the frequent and persistent antisocial behavior that is associated with disruptive behavior disorders, particularly conduct disorder (CD). Conduct disorder is characterized by a repetitive and persistent pattern of antisocial behavior in which the basic rights of others or major age-appropriate societal norms are violated (American Psychiatric Association 2013). Recent studies have estimated the lifetime prevalence of CD to be approximately 6.8 or 9.5 percent (Nock et al. 2006; Merikangas et al. 2010), whereas almost half of all incarcerated and detained adolescents fulfill criteria for CD, making it the most frequently occurring psychiatric disorder in this group (Colins et al. 2010). In addition, many symptoms of CD are also delinquent acts (e.g., stealing, raping, fire setting, and weapons use) (Loeber et al. 2000). An important distinction has been made between a relatively infrequent form of CD that begins in childhood and persists into antisocial behavior in adulthood (early onset CD) and a relatively common form of CD that begins in adolescence and mostly desists thereafter (Moffitt et al. 2002). It is hypothesized that CD is related to impairments in brain regions implicated in moral cognition, emotion, and executive functions, resulting in the inability to follow moral guidelines (Raine and Yang 2006). Indeed, difficulties in emotion processing have been found in CD (Herpertz et al. 2005), as well as impairments in executive functioning (Oosterlaan, Logan, and Sergeant 1998; Morgan and Lilienfeld 2000) that are already present in preschool children with CD symptoms (Schoemaker et al. 2012).

Another subgroup of antisocial and aggressive youths that has received increasing attention from researchers in recent years comprises those with conduct problems and high psychopathic traits. This research is focused mostly on a specific component of psychopathy, namely callous-unemotional (CU) traits (e.g., lack of guilt and empathy and callous use of others for one's own gain). Antisocial adolescents with high CU traits are thought to represent a specific group within antisocial and CD youth with a distinct neurocognitive profile characterized by low levels of fear and anxiety, blunted emotional reactivity, and insensitivity to punishment (Blair 2013; Frick et al. 2014). Moreover, it is suggested that antisocial individuals with high levels of CU traits exhibit a pattern of more severe and chronic antisocial behavior than those with low levels of these traits (Frick et al. 2005).

Next, this chapter focuses on studies of decision making in adolescent offenders recruited in forensic settings as well as studies that include antisocial adolescents with a diagnosis of CD (with high or low CU traits). This overview specifically focuses on executive functioning and empathic processes that are related to the antisocial behaviors displayed by these groups.

III. Executive Functioning in Antisocial Adolescents

Multiple studies provide converging lines of evidence that poor self-control is an important risk factor for criminal behavior (Pratt and Cullen 2000). Developmental neuroscience models suggest that risky behavior in adolescence results from slower maturation of cognitive control compared to affective systems in the brain. Accordingly, there is evidence that young offenders represent a subgroup of adolescents with particularly poor executive functioning skills, which are associated with risky decision making. For example, adolescents aged fourteen to eighteen years old with either early or adolescence-onset CD completed a task in which they could make risky decisions involving gains and losses (Fairchild et al. 2009). Participants could choose one of two roulette wheels: One wheel showed equal chances of gaining and losing money, and one wheel displayed various probabilities of gains and losses. Both CD groups exhibited more risky decision making compared to typically developing controls across a range of choices that varied in probability and size of the potential gains and losses. Importantly, these groups did not differ from typically developing controls in performance on the Wisconsin Card Sorting Test, an established measure of global "cold" (i.e., cognitive) executive functioning. This suggests that antisocial youth have specific deficits in affective and not cognitive control because they make more risky choices in a "hot" (i.e., affective) context independent of cognitive executive functioning deficits (Fairchild et al. 2009). In another study of a group of young offenders (aged twelve to eighteen years old) that used a similar roulette wheel task to measure risky choices, young offenders also made more risky decisions compared to typically developing controls (Syngelaki et al. 2009). In addition, compared to control participants, young offenders gambled more just after they had received a small compared to a large win, suggesting again that offenders make more risky decisions in an affective context.

A key function implicated in reward-based decision making is affect regulation. This involves regulatory processes in the orbitofrontal cortex (see figure 13.2) that generate and adjust the emotional responses that are used to assess risks (Ochsner and Gross 2005). For example, neurological patients with damage to the orbitofrontal cortex show impaired decision making under risk, which has been argued to be the result of an inability to optimally learn from rewards and punishments (Bechara 2004). Structural MRI studies have shown that youths with CD have reduced gray matter volume and cortical thickness in the orbitofrontal cortex, suggesting problems with affect regulation (Huebner et al. 2008; Fairchild et al. 2011; Hyatt, Haney-Caron, and Stevens 2012). Possible differences in affect regulation might also manifest themselves in aberrant reward processing in antisocial youth. For instance, in passive avoidance tasks, in which participants learn to respond to rewarding stimuli and to refrain from responding to stimuli that generate punishment, altered neural responses in the orbitofrontal cortex in participants with CD have been shown. In such passive avoidance tasks, youth with CD show reduced activity in both the orbitofrontal cortex and the caudate in response to reward and punishment outcomes (Finger et al. 2011; White et al. 2013). Similarly, in a study in which participants had to respond to target letters only and had to ignore non-target letters in order to receive rewards, a reward-related dysfunction in the orbitofrontal cortex in boys with CD was found (Rubia et al. 2009).

Impulsivity and self-control are often measured using a "temporal discounting task," in which temporal discounting refers to the decreasing value of rewards over time. In such a task, participants are asked to make a series of choices between an immediate small reward and a delayed reward of greater value. In one study, adolescents with CD (mean age, 15.7 years) more often preferred smaller immediate rewards over larger delayed rewards compared to typically developing controls (White et al. 2014). This may reflect a similar discounting in real life: The immediate rewards of criminal acts (e.g., gaining money by stealing) outweigh the temporally distant consequences of crime, such as jail or a criminal record (Petry 2002). As a result, individuals high on impulsivity and low on self-control seem to be more prone to choosing immediate high rewards associated with acts of crime. Furthermore, neuroimaging studies with CD youth suggest that they exhibit reduced activation in response to future rewards and punishments in the striatum and the orbitofrontal cortex during reversal learning (Finger et al. 2008). These impairments in reward representations might also further contribute to the preference for immediate rewards seen in youth with CD (White et al. 2014). This preference might lead to a focus on the short-term gains of crime. In addition, committing the crime may then seem appealing when the risk of getting caught and the impact of the possible punishment are also discounted (and hence probably underestimated).

Taken together, antisocial youth such as offenders and individuals with CD mainly show executive functioning difficulties in affective contexts and when rewards are at stake. These alterations in decision making in affective contexts may be partly explained by structural differences as well as reduced functional activity in brain regions related to the regulation of affect and reward processing, such as the orbitofrontal cortex. The impairments in affect regulation likely lead antisocial youth to make more risky choices. In addition, a heightened preference for immediate versus long-term rewards combined with impairments in predicting future rewards and punishments might make the law-breaking choices seem much more appealing to adolescent offenders than to their typically developing peers.

IV. EMPATHY IN ANTISOCIAL ADOLESCENTS

Diminished empathy is one of the main characteristics of aggressive, antisocial groups such as adolescents with CD and especially those with high CU traits (Decety and Moriguchi 2007). It is hypothesized that impairments in affective empathy (i.e., sharing other's emotions) play a more important role than impairments in cognitive empathy (i.e., understanding other's mental states) in antisocial and delinquent populations, particularly those with high CU traits (Blair 2005; but see van den Bos et al. 2014). This is in line with the idea that feeling an aversive emotional signal in reaction to another person in distress helps to inhibit aggressive and violent behavior (Miller and Eisenberg, 1988; Blair 1995). The lack of empathy that is part of high CU traits might be associated with less compassion for suffering of others, resulting in the lack of a barrier to use violence and to commit crimes that result in harm to others.

Several studies have found aberrant neural responses in young offenders and adolescents with CD when they observe photographs or film clips of other persons in distress. For example, brain activation as measured with electroencephalogram (EEG) showed that young offenders (aged fifteen to eighteen years old) have a reduced early response to pictures of others in pain compared to controls in a specific EEG component (the frontal N120 component) that is associated with an automatic aversive reaction to negative stimuli (Cheng, Hung, and Decety 2012). This suggests that offenders show less arousal in response to others in distress compared to controls. Two fMRI studies that used similar photographs of other persons in pain found reduced activation in youths with CD and high CU traits (aged ten to seventeen years old) in the anterior insula–ACC "pain network" and in other brain regions linked to empathy, such as the amygdala and inferior frontal gyrus (Lockwood et al. 2013; Marsh et al. 2013). Using emotional film clips and measures of vicarious responses, such as heart rate activity, studies have shown reduced responses to other's distress in groups of CD youth with CU traits compared to typically developing controls (Anastassiou-Hadjicharalambous and Warden 2008; de Wied et al. 2012). Thus, converging lines of evidence obtained using different techniques show that affective reactions toward others in distress are reduced in offenders and CD youth.

Another frequently used method within cognitive neuroscience to probe affective empathy is to present facial emotions of distress cues such as fear and sadness and assess spontaneous neural activity to these emotional expressions. Facial expressions of emotions have a communicatory function and can serve as aversive stimuli that can potentially change the behavior of the perceiver (Blair 2003). The amygdala is an important brain structure in processing of aversive stimuli and has been shown to be particularly sensitive to facial stimuli (Sergerie, Chochol, and Armony 2008). Adolescents with CD and psychopathic traits show reduced amygdala responses to fearful facial expressions compared to typically developing peers (Jones et al. 2009; White et al. 2012), as well as reduced coupling between the amygdala and the orbitofrontal cortex (Marsh et al.

2008). A reduced response in the amygdala was also found when fearful faces were presented below conscious awareness (masked by neutral, calm faces) in youth with CD and high CU traits (aged ten to sixteen years old). However, in this study, an increased amygdala response was found for the CD youth with low levels of CU traits compared to those with high CU traits and to controls (Viding et al. 2012). This suggests that affective empathy deficits as displayed by reduced responses to others in distress might not be omnipresent in all CD and antisocial youth but, rather, specific for those with high levels of CU traits. In contrast, antisocial individuals with low CU traits may show more reactive, impulsive aggression resulting from an increased sensitivity to negative emotions of others in comparison to proactive, premeditated aggression that is associated with high CU traits (Dodge et al. 1997).

Further differences in amygdala activation between CD with low and high CU traits were highlighted in a study by Sebastian et al. (2012). In this study, participants had to choose the appropriate ending of a short cartoon story that required them to understand the intentions of one story character (cognitive condition) or to infer how one story character would react to another character's emotional state (affective condition). In the affective condition, reduced activation was found in the amygdala and the anterior insula in the CD group compared to typically developing youth. In addition, a closer examination of amygdala activation within the CD group revealed that CU traits were negatively related to amygdala activation after controlling for the number of CD symptoms, whereas the number of CD symptoms was positively related to amygdala activation after controlling for CU traits (Sebastian et al. 2012). This latter finding might explain the heterogeneity that is often found in affective functioning in CD. For example, one study found increased amygdala activation in a small group of boys with CD when they watched others in pain (Decety et al. 2009), whereas most of the aforementioned studies revealed a reduced amygdala response specifically in relation to CU traits. Other studies also found reduced amygdala activation in response to sad faces in youths with CD regardless of CU traits (Passamonti et al. 2010). Hence, recent studies suggest that especially youths with antisocial behavior and high CU traits are impaired in the affective aspects of empathy. In other words, only a portion of young offenders and antisocial youth may show deficits in affective empathy.

Although most studies report problems with affective empathy in antisocial youth, the role of cognitive empathy and perspective-taking in antisocial behavior is less clear. Some studies suggest that cognitive empathy does not seem to be affected in antisocial populations (Dolan and Fullam 2004; Jones et al. 2010; Schwenck et al. 2012), whereas other studies suggest that there are also difficulties in the cognitive domain of empathy in CD and in detained youth (Happe and Frith 1996; Pardini, Lochman, and Frick 2003). For example, in our recent study (van den Bos et al. 2014), we investigated the role of perspective-taking, a cognitive aspect of empathy, in the context of the mini-ultimatum game (mini-UG). The UG is an interactive economic game with two players—a proposer and a responder (figure 13.4). The game starts with the proposer making a choice on how to split a sum of money, which the responder can decide to accept or reject.

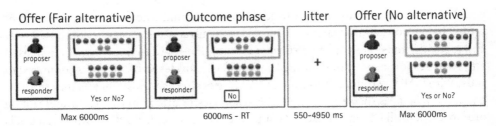

FIGURE 13.4 Trials from the mini-ultimatum game as used in van den Bos et al. (2014). Two offers each containing dark and light grey coins indicate the share for the proposer (dark grey coins) and the responder (light grey coins), and the offer made by the proposer is encircled in grey (here, eight and two coins, respectively). The responder was given five seconds to select "Yes" or "No" to accept or reject the offer. Upon response, the feedback screen displayed the given response (here, "No") until six seconds after the start of the trial. Both the "fair alternative" and the "no alternative" condition are displayed.

Source: Reprinted with permission from van den Bos et al. (2014).

When the responder accepts, both players get their share as proposed. When the responder rejects, none of the players get any money. The mini-UG is a modification of the UG and includes experimental manipulations enabling researchers to study intentionality considerations. Most important, it includes trials in which the proposer has a choice to be fair (i.e., fair alternative condition; the proposer has a choice between a fair and an unfair split of money) and trials in which the proposer is forced to make an unfair offer (i.e., no alternative condition; the proposer is given the same two unfair splits of money from which to choose). In our study, a group of adolescent delinquents and a matched control group played the role of the responder while in the MRI scanner. All participants rejected unfair offers significantly less when the other player had no alternative compared to when he or she had a fair alternative. However, the delinquents more often rejected offers when the other player had no alternative compared to typically developing controls, suggesting they were more focused on the unfairness of the offer and less influenced by the perspective of the proposer. The neuroimaging results showed that this behavior was associated with less activation in the TPJ, a region crucial for perspective-taking, but there were no differences in brain regions associated with emotional responses to unfairness (e.g., insula and ACC). This pattern of results suggests a cognitive rather than an affective impairment in situations in which young delinquents are confronted with unfairness. Interestingly, the pattern of both behavior and brain activity of the delinquent group shows striking similarities with that of the younger children reported in a developmental study with the same task (Güroğlu et al. 2011), suggesting that there might be a developmental delay in perspective-taking abilities in the adolescent offenders. However, longitudinal studies are needed to test this hypothesis in order to better characterize possible developmental differences.

In summary, there is clear evidence for impairments in affective empathy in antisocial youth, especially in individuals with high CU traits. Neural responses in reaction to other persons in distress are diminished in the anterior insula and ACC in youth with

CD, a brain network that is already involved in these processes in younger typically developing children. In addition, amygdala hypoactivation during affective empathy is mainly found in youth with high CU traits. There is also evidence for deficits in cognitive aspects of empathy such as perspective-taking, although this might be especially the case during social interactions.

V. Concluding Remarks
and Suggestions for Future Research

This chapter focused on two important mechanisms of criminal decision making in juveniles, namely executive functioning and empathy. Executive functioning in young offenders and adolescents with CD is particularly weaker in affective contexts, resulting in discounting of risks and deficits in predicting future rewards. As a result, when considering the short-term gains of crime, both the risk of getting caught and the impact of the possible punishment are discounted (and underestimated). Therefore, committing the crime may seem much more appealing to the delinquent than to the typically developing adolescent. In addition, difficulties in affective functioning are also apparent in studies of empathic functioning of young offenders and adolescents with CD. Reduced responses to other's distress are found in many studies, especially in adolescents with high CU traits, which might explain why some adolescents do not renounce to hurt others with threats or violence. Consequently, not only outcomes for the future self but also outcomes for others are discounted. Offending adolescents seem to combine a lack of care for what happens to others as a consequence of their criminal behavior with misperceptions about what the consequences of crime might be for themselves and possibly a lack of care for one's own future as well. Hence, we propose that when considering psychological mechanisms, affective deficits are one of the major processes contributing to altered decision making in delinquent and antisocial adolescents. These affective deficits manifest themselves in risky and impulsive decisions caused by problems in affect regulation and by an impaired responsiveness to the distress and perspective of other people, especially in seriously antisocial adolescents such as those with CD.

Another factor that is important in the context of adolescent risk-taking and offending is that adolescents seem to be more sensitive to peer influence compared to children and adults. As studies in typically developing peers have shown, risk-taking and neural processes are changed by the mere presence of peers (Gardner and Steinberg 2005; Chein et al. 2011). Studies have further shown that affiliation with deviant friends is strongly associated with juvenile delinquency (Simons et al. 1994; Laird et al. 1999; Heinze, Toro, and Urberg 2004) and that compared to adults, adolescents are more likely to commit crimes with others (Reiss and Farrington, 1991; Conway and McCord 2002). Indeed, a longitudinal study suggested that the peak in the age–crime curve can be explained in large part by the influence of antisocial peers (Sweeten, Piquero, and Steinberg 2013). When adolescents become older and more resistant to peer influence, engagement in antisocial behavior tends to decline (Monahan, Steinberg, and Cauffman 2009). Moreover, adolescents with poorer executive functioning skills such as self-regulation and greater sensitivity to reward versus punishment are more vulnerable to the influence of deviant peers on antisocial behavior (Goodnight et al. 2006; Gardner, Dishion, and Connell 2008). It would be of great interest to initiate experimental studies to investigate peer influence specifically in antisocial and offending youth. The heightened reward-related brain activity caused by the mere presence of peers in the Chein et al. (2011) study suggests that it is not necessarily the explicit encouragement of peers that influences risk-taking. Using similar paradigms in young offenders or CD youth, it could be investigated how brain and behavior are differentially influenced by deviant and nondeviant peers and whether activation in affective and cognitive brain regions could predict peer influence on later antisocial behavior.

Previous studies have shown that so-called "deviancy training," in which deviant peers react more positively to each other when discussing rule-breaking compared to more general topics, is linked to increases in violent and delinquent behavior (Dishion et al. 1996, 1997). The use of neuroscience methods in combination with peer influence paradigms has the advantage that more of the underlying processes of the social influences on risk-taking can be disclosed. Another advantage of such experimental studies on peer influence is that they could feature the use of real social interactions by using interactive games such as that used in our recent study (van den Bos et al. 2014). This could help to evade one important limitation of many of the previous studies on empathic functioning in antisocial youth, which are based mostly on passive (viewing) and self-report tasks instead of interactions with others (Dodge 2011). The neurocognitive mechanisms underlying real social interactions probably differ greatly from the mechanisms in merely observing others (Schilbach et al. 2013). In addition, it has been argued that individual differences in empathy become apparent mainly when people are required to act in a situation in which someone else is harmed as opposed to merely observing such a situation (Will and Klapwijk 2014).

The studies discussed in this chapter included offenders recruited in forensic settings as well as participants with CD (with low and high CU traits), meaning that some of the processes that were considered, such as diminished affective empathy, hold only for a particular subgroup of offenders with high CU traits. Therefore, it would be premature to conclude that all adolescent offenders show this affective deficit in executive functioning and empathy. Further comparisons of adolescent offenders and CD youths with low and high CU traits are warranted to characterize the specific pathways that lead to antisocial behavior in different groups. This reveals one of the important difficulties in the scientific study of adolescent criminal decision making: Criminal behavior is conducted by a variety of individuals, and disciplines such as criminology, psychology, and psychiatry study different groups using different labels. Although both offenders and individuals with CD show similar behaviors, such as stealing, aggression, and rule violations, offending and CD are related but not synonymous concepts. Despite these behavioral similarities, it is crucial to distinguish between subgroups of criminal adolescents because it is unlikely that the same intervention or treatment is adequate for such a diverse group (Frick and Ellis 1999). Recent attempts to distinguish a group of adolescents with high CU traits among youths with CD are promising, suggesting that this group differs on a range of genetic, neurocognitive, and personality characteristics from other youths with CD (for reviews, see Blair 2013; Frick et al. 2014). Crucially, neuroscience methods can serve as an important tool in establishing differences between subgroups and in identifying possible new subgroups within CD and antisocial populations. Quantitative measures of well-defined neurocognitive processes that are associated with discrete deficits would help to provide more insight into the differences and areas of overlap between subgroups. For example, efforts have been made to apply this approach to the concepts of impulsivity and compulsivity in a range of overlapping psychiatric disorders, such as attention deficit hyperactivity disorder (ADHD), substance dependence, and obsessive–compulsive disorder (Robbins et al. 2012). A similar approach aimed at underlying mechanisms that cross several of the current diagnostic categories (see also Insel et al. 2010) can be considered for the concept of impulsivity in ADHD, offenders and CD, or for affective and cognitive aspects of empathy in disorders associated with social deficits, such as autism and schizophrenia, in comparison to CD and offenders.

Another major challenge when focusing on the psychological mechanisms involved in adolescent criminal decision making is to integrate research on neurocognitive factors with knowledge about the influence of environmental factors. This chapter focused on the decision maker and on underlying neurocognitive processes of decision making. However, the role of environmental factors in decision making cannot be omitted if one wants to understand criminal behavior of adolescents. One contextual factor highlighted in this chapter is the peer environment, which seems to be of specific importance for decision making in adolescence. Other important contextual factors of antisocial behavior that are often mentioned are the influence of parenting style and neighborhood problems (Rhee and Waldman 2002). It remains an empirical question whether criminal decision making is more influenced by innate neurocognitive deficits than by contextual factors that may lead to crime either by direct influence on behavior or by an indirect influence on neurocognitive abilities. For example, genetic twin studies and longitudinal studies have shown that executive functioning is very highly heritable (Friedman et al. 2008) but also that genetic influences on antisocial behavior are stronger in socioeconomically advantaged compared to disadvantaged environments (Tuvblad, Grann, and Lichtenstein 2006). Likewise, it is also important to take into account the possible harmful effects of incarceration during such an important developmental period as adolescence. Most adolescent offenders already lack certain social and executive functioning skills before being arrested; the stress of incarceration and the separation from their families and neighborhoods might not be helpful in further developing such skills.

In conclusion, the neuroscience of adolescent decision making is a blossoming field, and much can be learned about adolescent-specific behavior from studies of population samples. However, although the prevalence of offending is significantly higher in adolescence, only a minority of adolescents engage in criminal behavior. Hence, if one wants to learn more about criminal decision making in adolescents, one must study groups of adolescents that show deviant behavior. Nevertheless, one should bear in mind that antisocial populations are notoriously difficult to study. Youth who are affiliated with correctional facilities might be suspicious about the agenda of the researchers, whereas antisocial youth outside a judicial setting are difficult to contact and to enroll and keep engaged in a study. However, we believe it is worth the effort to find ways to reach these adolescents and to design suitable paradigms aimed at elucidating the decision-making processes in delinquent and antisocial youth. More fine-grained knowledge about when (e.g., in affective vs. cognitive contexts) and which subtypes (e.g., low vs. high CU traits) of adolescent offenders make adverse decisions that result in crime may eventually help researchers design interventions that support at-risk adolescents to stay at the right path.

ACKNOWLEDGMENTS

The authors thank Geert-Jan Will for helpful comments on a previous version of this chapter.

REFERENCES

American Psychiatric Association. 2013. *Diagnostic and Statistical Manual of Mental Disorders*, 5th ed. Arlington, VA: American Psychiatric Publishing.
Anastassiou-Hadjicharalambous, X., and D. Warden. 2008. "Physiologically-Indexed and Self-Perceived Affective Empathy in Conduct-Disordered Children High and Low on Callous-Unemotional Traits." *Child Psychiatry and Human Development* 39(4): 503–17.
Bechara, A. 2004. "The Role of Emotion in Decision-Making: Evidence from Neurological Patients with Orbitofrontal Damage." *Brain and Cognition* 55(1): 30–40.
Bernhardt, B. C., and T. Singer. 2012. "The Neural Basis of Empathy." *Annual Review of Neuroscience* 35(1): 1–23.
Blair, R. J. R. 1995. "A Cognitive Developmental Approach to Morality: Investigating the Psychopath." *Cognition,* 57(1): 1–29.
Blair, R. J. R. 2003. "Facial Expressions, Their Communicatory Functions and Neuro-cognitive Substrates." *Philosophical Transactions of the Royal Society B: Biological Sciences* 358(1431): 561–72.
Blair, R. J. R. 2005. "Responding to the Emotions of Others: Dissociating Forms of Empathy Through the Study of Typical and Psychiatric Populations." *Consciousness and Cognition* 14(4): 698–718.
Blair, R. J. 2013. "The Neurobiology of Psychopathic Traits in Youths." *Nature Reviews Neuroscience* 14(11): 786–99.
Blakemore, S. J., and S. Choudhury. 2006. "Development of the Adolescent Brain: Implications for Executive Function and Social Cognition." *Journal of Child Psychology and Psychiatry and Allied Disciplines* 47(3-4): 296–312.

Blakemore, S. J., H. den Ouden, S. Choudhury, and C. Frith. 2007. "Adolescent Development of the Neural Circuitry for Thinking About Intentions." *Social Cognitive and Affective Neuroscience* 2(2): 130–39.

Blakemore, S. J., and T. W. Robbins. 2012. "Decision-Making in the Adolescent Brain." *Nature Neuroscience* 15(9): 1184–91.

Burnett, S., G. Bird, J. Moll, C. Frith, and S. J. Blakemore. 2009. "Development During Adolescence of the Neural Processing of Social Emotion." *Journal of Cognitive Neuroscience* 21(9): 1736–50.

Burnett, S., C. Sebastian, K. Cohen Kadosh, and S. J. Blakemore. 2011. "The Social Brain in Adolescence: Evidence from Functional Magnetic Resonance Imaging and Behavioural Studies." *Neuroscience and Biobehavioral Reviews* 35(8): 1654–64.

Chein, J., D. Albert, L. O'Brien, K. Uckert, and L. Steinberg. 2011. "Peers Increase Adolescent Risk Taking by Enhancing Activity in the Brain's Reward Circuitry." *Developmental Science* 14(2): F1–10.

Cheng, Y., A.-Y. Hung, and J. Decety. 2012. "Dissociation Between Affective Sharing and Emotion Understanding in Juvenile Psychopaths." *Development and Psychopathology* 24(2): 623–36.

Colins, O., R. Vermeiren, C. Vreugdenhil, W. van den Brink, T. Doreleijers, and E. Broekaert. 2010. "Psychiatric Disorders in Detained Male Adolescents: A Systematic Literature Review." *Canadian Journal of Psychiatry* 55(4): 255–63.

Conway, K. P., and J. McCord. 2002. "A Longitudinal Examination of the Relation Between Co-offending with Violent Accomplices and Violent Crime." *Aggressive Behavior* 28(2): 97–108.

Crone, E. A., and R. E. Dahl. 2012. "Understanding Adolescence as a Period of Social–Affective Engagement and Goal Flexibility." *Nature Reviews Neuroscience* 13(9): 636–50.

de Wied, M., A. van Boxtel, W. Matthys, and W. Meeus. 2012. "Verbal, Facial and Autonomic Responses to Empathy-Eliciting Film Clips by Disruptive Male Adolescents with High Versus Low Callous-Unemotional Traits." *Journal of Abnormal Child Psychology* 40(2): 211–23.

Decety, J., and P. L. Jackson. 2004. "The Functional Architecture of Human Empathy." *Behavioral and Cognitive Neuroscience Reviews* 3(2): 71–100.

Decety, J., and M. Meyer. 2008. "From Emotion Resonance to Empathic Understanding: A Social Developmental Neuroscience Account." *Development and Psychopathology* 20(4): 1053–80.

Decety, J., and K. J. Michalska. 2010. "Neurodevelopmental Changes in the Circuits Underlying Empathy and Sympathy from Childhood to Adulthood." *Developmental Science* 13(6): 886–99.

Decety, J., K. J. Michalska, and Y. Akitsuki. 2008. "Who Caused the Pain? An fMRI Investigation of Empathy and Intentionality in Children." *Neuropsychologia* 46(11): 2607–14.

Decety, J., K. J. Michalska, Y. Akitsuki, and B. B. Lahey. 2009. "Atypical Empathic Responses in Adolescents with Aggressive Conduct Disorder: A Functional MRI Investigation." *Biological Psychology* 80(2): 203–11.

Decety, J., and Y. Moriguchi. 2007. "The Empathic Brain and Its Dysfunction in Psychiatric Populations: Implications for Intervention Across Different Clinical Conditions." *Biopsychosocial Medicine* 1(1): 22.

Dishion, T. J., J. M. Eddy, E. Haas, F. Li, and K. Spracklen. 1997. "Friendships and Violent Behavior During Adolescence." *Social Development* 6(2): 207–23.

Dishion, T. J., K. M. Spracklen, D. W. Andrews, and G. R. Patterson. 1996. "Deviancy Training in Male Adolescent Friendships." *Behavior Therapy* 27(3): 373–90.

Dodge, K. A. 2011. "Social Information Processing Patterns as Mediators of the Interaction Between Genetic Factors and Life Experiences in the Development of Aggressive Behavior." In *Human Aggression and Violence: Causes, Manifestations, and Consequences*, edited by P. R. Shaver and M. Mikulincer, pp. 165–85. *Herzilya Series on Personality and Social Psychology*. Washington, DC: American Psychological Association.

Dodge, K. A., J. E. Lochman, J. D. Harnish, J. E. Bates, and G. S. Pettit. 1997. "Reactive and Proactive Aggression in School Children and Psychiatrically Impaired Chronically Assaultive Youth." *Journal of Abnormal Psychology* 106(1): 37–51.

Dodge, K. A., and G. S. Pettit. 2003. "A Biopsychosocial Model of the Development of Chronic Conduct Problems in Adolescence." *Developmental Psychology* 39(2): 349–71.

Dolan, M., and R. Fullam. 2004. "Theory of Mind and Mentalizing Ability in Antisocial Personality Disorders with and Without Psychopathy." *Psychological Medicine* 34(6): 1093–1102.

Dumontheil, I., I. A. Apperly, and S. J. Blakemore. 2010. "Online Usage of Theory of Mind Continues to Develop in Late Adolescence." *Developmental Science* 13(2): 331–38.

Eisenberg, N., and R. A. Fabes. 1990. "Empathy—Conceptualization, Measurement, and Relation to Prosocial Behavior." *Motivation and Emotion* 14(2): 131–49.

Ernst, M., E. E. Nelson, S. Jazbec, E. B. McClure, C. S. Monk, E. Leibenluft, . . . D. S. Pine. 2005. "Amygdala and Nucleus Accumbens in Responses to Receipt and Omission of Gains in Adults and Adolescents." *Neuroimage* 25(4): 1279–91.

Fairchild, G., L. Passamonti, G. Hurford, C. C. Hagan, E. A. H. von dem Hagen, S. H. M. van Goozen, . . . A. J. Calder. 2011. "Brain Structure Abnormalities in Early-Onset and Adolescent-Onset Conduct Disorder." *American Journal of Psychiatry* 168(6): 624–33.

Fairchild, G., S. H. M. van Goozen, S. J. Stollery, M. R. F. Aitken, J. Savage, S. C. Moore, and I. M. Goodyer. 2009. "Decision Making and Executive Function in Male Adolescents with Early-Onset or Adolescence-Onset Conduct Disorder and Control Subjects." *Biological Psychiatry* 66(2): 162–68.

Figner, B., R. J. Mackinlay, F. Wilkening, and E. U. Weber. 2009. "Affective and Deliberative Processes in Risky Choice: Age Differences in Risk Taking in the Columbia Card Task." *Journal of Experimental Psychology: Learning, Memory and Cognition* 35(3): 709–30.

Finger, E. C., A. A. Marsh, K. S. Blair, M. E. Reid, C. Sims, P. Ng, . . . R. J. R. Blair. 2011. "Disrupted Reinforcement Signaling in the Orbitofrontal Cortex and Caudate in Youths with Conduct Disorder or Oppositional Defiant Disorder and a High Level of Psychopathic Traits." *American Journal of Psychiatry* 168(2): 152–62.

Finger, E. C., A. A. Marsh, D. G. Mitchell, M. E. Reid, C. Sims, S. Budhani, . . . J. R. Blair. 2008. "Abnormal Ventromedial Prefrontal Cortex Function in Children with Psychopathic Traits During Reversal Learning." *Archives of General Psychiatry* 65(5): 586–94.

Frick, P. J., and M. Ellis. 1999. "Callous-Unemotional Traits and Subtypes of Conduct Disorder." *Clinical Child and Family Psychology Review* 2(3): 149–68.

Frick, P. J., J. V. Ray, L. C. Thornton, and R. E. Kahn. 2014. "Can Callous-Unemotional Traits Enhance the Understanding, Diagnosis, and Treatment of Serious Conduct Problems in Children and Adolescents? A Comprehensive Review." *Psychological Bulletin* 140(1): 1–57.

Frick, P. J., T. R. Stickle, D. M. Dandreaux, J. M. Farrell, and E. R. Kimonis. 2005. "Callous-Unemotional Traits in Predicting the Severity and Stability of Conduct Problems and Delinquency." *Journal of Abnormal Child Psychology* 33(4): 471–87.

Friedman, N. P., A. Miyake, S. E. Young, J. C. Defries, R. P. Corley, and J. K. Hewitt. 2008. "Individual Differences in Executive Functions Are Almost Entirely Genetic in Origin." *Journal of Experimental Psychology: General* 137(2): 201–25.

Frith, U., and C. D. Frith. 2003. "Development and Neurophysiology of Mentalizing." *Philosophical Transactions of the Royal Society B: Biological Sciences* 358(1431): 459–73.

Gardner, M., and L. Steinberg. 2005. "Peer Influence on Risk Taking, Risk Preference, and Risky Decision Making in Adolescence and Adulthood: An Experimental Study." *Developmental Psychology* 41(4): 625–35.

Gardner, T. W., T. J. Dishion, and A. M. Connell. 2008. "Adolescent Self-Regulation as Resilience: Resistance to Antisocial Behavior Within the Deviant Peer Context." *Journal of Abnormal Child Psychology* 36(2): 273–84.

Giedd, J. N., J. Blumenthal, N. O. Jeffries, F. X. Castellanos, H. Liu, A. Zijdenbos, ... J. L. Rapoport. 1999. "Brain Development During Childhood and Adolescence: A Longitudinal MRI Study." *Nature Neuroscience* 2(10): 861–63.

Gogtay, N., J. N. Giedd, L. Lusk, K. M. Hayashi, D. Greenstein, A. C. Vaituzis, ... P. M. Thompson. 2004. "Dynamic Mapping of Human Cortical Development During Childhood Through Early Adulthood." *Proceedings of the National Academy of Sciences of the United States of America* 101(21): 8174–79.

Goodnight, J. A., J. E. Bates, J. P. Newman, K. A. Dodge, and G. S. Pettit. 2006. "The Interactive Influences of Friend Deviance and Reward Dominance on the Development of Externalizing Behavior During Middle Adolescence." *Journal of Abnormal Child Psychology* 34(5): 573–83.

Gunther Moor, B., Z. A. Op de Macks, B. Guroglu, S. A. R. B. Rombouts, M. W. van der Molen, and E. A. Crone. 2011. "Neurodevelopmental Changes of Reading the Mind in the Eyes." *Social Cognitive and Affective Neuroscience* 7(1): 44–52.

Güroğlu, B., W. van den Bos, and E. A. Crone. 2009. "Fairness Considerations: Increasing Understanding of Intentionality During Adolescence." *Journal of Experimental Child Psychology* 104(4): 398–409.

Güroğlu, B., W. van den Bos, E. van Dijk, S. A. Rombouts, and E. A. Crone. 2011. "Dissociable Brain Networks Involved in Development of Fairness Considerations: Understanding Intentionality Behind Unfairness." *Neuroimage* 57(2): 634–41.

Guyer, A. E., C. S. Monk, E. B. McClure-Tone, E. E. Nelson, R. Roberson-Nay, A. D. Adler, ... M. Ernst. 2008. "A Developmental Examination of Amygdala Response to Facial Expressions." *Journal of Cognitive Neuroscience* 20(9): 1565–82.

Happe, F., and U. Frith. 1996. "Theory of Mind and Social Impairment in Children with Conduct Disorder." *British Journal of Developmental Psychology* 14:385–98.

Hare, T. A., N. Tottenham, A. Galvan, H. U. Voss, G. H. Glover, and B. J. Casey. 2008. "Biological Substrates of Emotional Reactivity and Regulation in Adolescence During an Emotional Go–Nogo Task." *Biological Psychiatry* 63(10): 927–34.

Heinze, H. J., P. A. Toro, and K. A. Urberg. 2004. "Antisocial Behavior and Affiliation with Deviant Peers." *Journal of Clinical Child and Adolescent Psychology* 33(2): 336–46.

Herpertz, S. C., B. Mueller, M. Qunaibi, C. Lichterfeld, K. Konrad, and B. Herpertz-Dahlmann. 2005. "Response to Emotional Stimuli in Boys with Conduct Disorder." *American Journal of Psychiatry* 162(6): 1100–1107.

Hirschi, T., and M. Gottfredson. 1983. "Age and the Explanation of Crime." *American Journal of Sociology* 89(3): 552–84.

Huebner, T., T. D. Vloet, I. Marx, K. Konrad, G. R. Fink, S. C. Herpertz, and B. Herpertz-Dahlmann. 2008. "Morphometric Brain Abnormalities in Boys with Conduct Disorder." *Journal of the American Academy of Child and Adolescent Psychiatry* 47(5): 540–47.

Hyatt, C. J., E. Haney-Caron, and M. C. Stevens. 2012. "Cortical Thickness and Folding Deficits in Conduct-Disordered Adolescents." *Biological Psychiatry* 72(3): 207–14.

Insel, T., B. Cuthbert, M. Garvey, R. Heinssen, D. S. Pine, K. Quinn, . . . P. Wang. 2010. "Research Domain Criteria (RDoC): Toward a New Classification Framework for Research on Mental Disorders." *American Journal of Psychiatry* 167(7): 748–51.

Jones, A. P., F. G. Happe, F. Gilbert, S. Burnett, and E. Viding. 2010. "Feeling, Caring, Knowing: Different Types of Empathy Deficit in Boys with Psychopathic Tendencies and Autism Spectrum Disorder." *Journal of Child Psychology and Psychiatry and Allied Disciplines* 51(11): 1188–97.

Jones, A. P., K. R. Laurens, C. M. Herba, G. J. Barker, and E. Viding. 2009. "Amygdala Hypoactivity to Fearful Faces in Boys with Conduct Problems and Callous-Unemotional Traits." *American Journal of Psychiatry* 166(1): 95–102.

Laird, R. D., G. S. Pettit, K. A. Dodge, and J. E. Bates. 1999. "Best Friendships, Group Relationships, and Antisocial Behavior in Early Adolescence." *Journal of Early Adolescence* 19(4): 413–37.

Lockwood, P. L., C. L. Sebastian, E. J. McCrory, Z. H. Hyde, X. Gu, S. A. De Brito, and E. Viding. 2013. "Association of Callous Traits with Reduced Neural Response to Others' Pain in Children with Conduct Problems." *Current Biology* 23(10): 901–5.

Loeber, R., J. D. Burke, B. B. Lahey, A. Winters, and M. Zera. 2000. "Oppositional Defiant and Conduct Disorder: A Review of the Past 10 Years, Part I." *Journal of the American Academy of Child and Adolescent Psychiatry* 39(12): 1468–84.

Loeber, R., and D. Farrington. 2014. "Age–Crime Curve. In *Encyclopedia of Criminology and Criminal Justice*, edited by G. Bruinsma and D. Weisburd, pp. 12–18. New York: Springer.

Lovett, B., and R. Sheffield. 2007. "Affective Empathy Deficits in Aggressive Children and Adolescents: A Critical Review." *Clinical Psychology Review* 27(1): 1–13.

Luna, B., K. R. Thulborn, D. P. Munoz, E. P. Merriam, K. E. Garver, N. J. Minshew, . . . J. A. Sweeney. 2001. "Maturation of Widely Distributed Brain Function Subserves Cognitive Development." *Neuroimage* 13(5): 786–93.

Marsh, A. A., E. C. Finger, K. A. Fowler, C. J. Adalio, I. T. Jurkowitz, J. C. Schechter, . . . R. J. Blair. 2013. "Empathic Responsiveness in Amygdala and Anterior Cingulate Cortex in Youths with Psychopathic Traits." *Journal of Child Psychology and Psychiatry and Allied Disciplines* 54(8): 900–10.

Marsh, A. A., E. C. Finger, D. G. V. Mitchell, M. E. Reid, C. Sims, D. S. Kosson, . . . R. J. R. Blair. 2008. "Reduced Amygdala Response to Fearful Expressions in Children and Adolescents with Callous-Unemotional Traits and Disruptive Behavior Disorders." *American Journal of Psychiatry* 165(6): 712–20.

Merikangas, K. R., J. P. He, M. Burstein, S. A. Swanson, S. Avenevoli, L. H. Cui, . . . J. Swendsen. 2010. "Lifetime Prevalence of Mental Disorders in U.S. Adolescents: Results from the National Comorbidity Survey Replication–Adolescent Supplement (NCS-A)." *Journal of the American Academy of Child and Adolescent Psychiatry* 49(10): 980–89.

Miller, P. A., and N. Eisenberg. 1988. "The Relation of Empathy to Aggressive and Externalizing/Antisocial Behavior." *Psychological Bulletin* 103(3): 324–44.

Moffitt, T. E. 2005. "The New Look of Behavioral Genetics in Developmental Psychopathology: Gene–Environment Interplay in Antisocial Behaviors." *Psychological Bulletin* 131(4): 533–54.

Moffitt, T. E., A. Caspi, H. Harrington, and B. J. Milne. 2002. "Males on the Life-Course-Persistent and Adolescence-Limited Antisocial Pathways: Follow-Up at Age 26 Years." *Development and Psychopathology* 14(1): 179–207.

Moffitt, T. E., and B. Henry. 1989. "Neuropsychological Assessment of Executive Functions in Self-Reported Delinquents." *Development and Psychopathology* 1(2): 105–18.

Monahan, K. C., L. Steinberg, and E. Cauffman. 2009. "Affiliation with Antisocial Peers, Susceptibility to Peer Influence, and Antisocial Behavior During the Transition to Adulthood." *Developmental Psychology* 45(6): 1520–30.

Morgan, A. B., and S. O. Lilienfeld. 2000. "A Meta-Analytic Review of the Relation Between Antisocial Behavior and Neuropsychological Measures of Executive Function." *Clinical Psychology Review* 20(1): 113–36.

Nelson, E. E., E. Leibenluft, E. B. McClure, and D. S. Pine. 2005. "The Social Re-orientation of Adolescence: A Neuroscience Perspective on the Process and Its Relation to Psychopathology." *Psychological Medicine* 35(2): 163–74.

Nock, M. K., A. E. Kazdin, E. Hiripi, and R. C. Kessler. 2006. "Prevalence, Subtypes, and Correlates of DSM-IV Conduct Disorder in the National Comorbidity Survey Replication." *Psychological Medicine* 36(5): 699–710.

Ochsner, K. N., and J. J. Gross. 2005. "The Cognitive Control of Emotion." *Trends in Cognitive Sciences* 9(5): 242–49.

Oosterlaan, J., G. D. Logan, and J. A. Sergeant. 1998. "Response Inhibition in AD/HD, CD, Comorbid AD/HD + CD, Anxious, and Control Children: A Meta-Analysis of Studies with the Stop Task." *Journal of Child Psychology and Psychiatry and Allied Disciplines* 39(3): 411–25.

Pardini, D. A., J. E. Lochman, and P. J. Frick. 2003. "Callous/Unemotional Traits and Social–Cognitive Processes in Adjudicated Youths." *Journal of the American Academy of Child and Adolescent Psychiatry* 42(3): 364–71.

Passamonti, L., G. Fairchild, I. M. Goodyer, G. Hurford, C. C. Hagan, J. B. Rowe, and A. J. Calder. 2010. "Neural Abnormalities in Early-Onset and Adolescence-Onset Conduct Disorder." *Archives of General Psychiatry* 67(7): 729–38.

Petry, N. M. 2002. "Discounting of Delayed Rewards in Substance Abusers: Relationship to Antisocial Personality Disorder." *Psychopharmacology* 162(4): 425–32.

Pfeifer, J. H., C. L. Masten, L. A. Borofsky, M. Dapretto, A. J. Fuligni, and M. D. Lieberman. 2009. "Neural Correlates of Direct and Reflected Self-Appraisals in Adolescents and Adults: When Social Perspective-Taking Informs Self-Perception." *Child Development* 80(4): 1016–38.

Pratt, T. C., and F. T. Cullen. 2000. "The Empirical Status of Gottfredson and Hirschi's General Theory of Crime: A Meta-Analysis." *Criminology* 38(3): 931–64.

Raine, A., and Y. Yang. 2006. "Neural Foundations to Moral Reasoning and Antisocial Behavior." *Social Cognitive and Affective Neuroscience* 1(3): 203–13.

Reiss, A. J., and D. P. Farrington. 1991. "Advancing Knowledge About Co-offending—Results from a Prospective Longitudinal Survey of London Males." *Journal of Criminal Law and Criminology* 82(2): 360–95.

Rhee, S. H., and I. D. Waldman. 2002. "Genetic and Environmental Influences on Antisocial Behavior: A Meta-Analysis of Twin and Adoption Studies." *Psychological Bulletin* 128(3): 490–529.

Robbins, T. W., C. M. Gillan, D. G. Smith, S. de Wit, and K. D. Ersche. 2012. "Neurocognitive Endophenotypes of Impulsivity and Compulsivity: Towards Dimensional Psychiatry." *Trends in Cognitive Sciences* 16(1): 81–91.

Rubia, K., A. B. Smith, R. Halari, F. Matsukura, M. Mohammad, E. Taylor, and M. J. Brammer. 2009. "Disorder-Specific Dissociation of Orbitofrontal Dysfunction in Boys with Pure Conduct Disorder During Reward and Ventrolateral Prefrontal Dysfunction in Boys with Pure ADHD During Sustained Attention." *American Journal of Psychiatry* 166(1): 83–94.

Schilbach, L., B. Timmermans, V. Reddy, A. Costall, G. Bente, T. Schlicht, and K. Vogeley. 2013. "Toward a Second-Person Neuroscience." *Behavioral and Brain Sciences* 36(4): 393–414.

Schoemaker, K., T. Bunte, S. A. Wiebe, K. A. Espy, M. Dekovic, and W. Matthys. 2012. "Executive Function Deficits in Preschool Children with ADHD and DBD." *Journal of Child Psychology and Psychiatry and Allied Disciplines* 53(2): 111–19.

Schwenck, C., J. Mergenthaler, K. Keller, J. Zech, S. Salehi, R. Taurines, . . . C. M. Freitag. 2012. "Empathy in Children with Autism and Conduct Disorder: Group-Specific Profiles and Developmental Aspects." *Journal of Child Psychology and Psychiatry and Allied Disciplines* 53(6): 651–59.

Sebastian, C. L., E. J. P. McCrory, C. A. M. Cecil, P. L. Lockwood, S. A. De Brito, N. M. G. Fontaine, and E. Viding. 2012. "Neural Responses to Affective and Cognitive Theory of Mind in Children with Conduct Problems and Varying Levels of Callous-Unemotional Traits." *Archives of General Psychiatry* 69(8): 814–22.

Sergerie, K., C. Chochol, and J. L. Armony. 2008. "The Role of the Amygdala in Emotional Processing: A Quantitative Meta-Analysis of Functional Neuroimaging Studies." *Neuroscience and Biobehavioral Reviews* 32(4): 811–30.

Shamay-Tsoory, S. G., J. Aharon-Peretz, and D. Perry. 2009. "Two Systems for Empathy: A Double Dissociation Between Emotional and Cognitive Empathy in Inferior Frontal Gyrus Versus Ventromedial Prefrontal Lesions." *Brain* 132(3): 617–27.

Simons, R. L., C.-I. Wu, R. D. Conger, and F. O. Lorenz. 1994. "Two Routes to Delinquency: Differences Between Early and Late Starters in the Impact of Parenting and Deviant Peers." *Criminology* 32(2): 247–76.

Singer, T., and C. Lamm. 2009. "The Social Neuroscience of Empathy." *Annals of the New York Academy of Sciences* 1156(1): 81–96.

Somerville, L. H., R. M. Jones, and B. J. Casey. 2010. "A Time of Change: Behavioral and Neural Correlates of Adolescent Sensitivity to Appetitive and Aversive Environmental Cues." *Brain and Cognition* 72(1): 124–33.

Steinbeis, N., B. C. Bernhardt, and T. Singer. 2012. "Impulse Control and Underlying Functions of the Left dLPFC Mediate Age-Related and Age-Independent Individual Differences in Strategic Social Behavior." *Neuron* 73(5): 1040–51.

Steinberg, L. 2008. "A Social Neuroscience Perspective on Adolescent Risk-Taking." *Developmental Review* 28(1): 78–106.

Steinberg, L., and A. S. Morris. 2001. "Adolescent Development." *Annual Review of Psychology* 52:83–110.

Sweeten, G., A. R. Piquero, and L. Steinberg. 2013. "Age and the Explanation of Crime, Revisited." *Journal of Youth and Adolescence* 42(6): 921–38.

Syngelaki, E. M., S. C. Moore, J. C. Savage, G. Fairchild, and S. H. M. van Goozen. 2009. "Executive Functioning and Risky Decision Making in Young Male Offenders." *Criminal Justice and Behavior* 36(11): 1213–27.

Tuvblad, C., M. Grann, and P. Lichtenstein. 2006. "Heritability for Adolescent Antisocial Behavior Differs with Socioeconomic Status: Gene–Environment Interaction. *Journal of Child Psychology and Psychiatry and Allied Disciplines* 47(7): 734–43.

van den Bos, W., P. Vahl, B. Güroğlu, F. van Nunspeet, O. Colins, M. Markus, . . . E. A. Crone. 2014. "Neural Correlates of Social Decision-Making in Severely Antisocial Adolescents." *Social Cognitive and Affective Neuroscience* 9(12): 2059–66.

van den Bos, W., E. van Dijk, M. Westenberg, S. A. Rombouts, and E. A. Crone. 2011. "Changing Brains, Changing Perspectives: The Neurocognitive Development of Reciprocity." *Psychological Science* 22(1): 60–70.

van Leijenhorst, L., B. Gunther Moor, Z. A. Op de Macks, S. A. Rombouts, P. M. Westenberg, and E. A. Crone. 2010. "Adolescent Risky Decision-Making: Neurocognitive Development of Reward and Control Regions." *Neuroimage* 51(1): 345–55.

Vetter, N. C., K. Leipold, M. Kliegel, L. H. Phillips, and M. Altgassen. 2013. "Ongoing Development of Social Cognition in Adolescence." *Child Neuropsychology* 19(6): 615–29.

Viding, E., C. L. Sebastian, M. R. Dadds, P. L. Lockwood, C. A. M. Cecil, S. A. De Brito, and E. J. McCrory. 2012. "Amygdala Response to Preattentive Masked Fear in Children with Conduct Problems: The Role of Callous-Unemotional Traits." *American Journal of Psychiatry* 169(10): 1109–16.

White, S. F., R. Clanton, S. J. Brislin, H. Meffert, S. Hwang, S. Sinclair, and R. J. Blair. 2014. "Reward: Empirical Contribution—Temporal Discounting and Conduct Disorder in Adolescents." *Journal of Personality Disorders* 28(1): 5–18.

White, S. F., A. A. Marsh, K. A. Fowler, J. C. Schechter, C. Adalio, K. Pope, . . . R. J. R. Blair. 2012. "Reduced Amygdala Response in Youths with Disruptive Behavior Disorders and Psychopathic Traits: Decreased Emotional Response Versus Increased Top-Down Attention to Nonemotional Features." *American Journal of Psychiatry* 169(7): 750–58.

White, S. F., K. Pope, S. Sinclair, K. A. Fowler, S. J. Brislin, W. C. Williams, . . . R. J. R. Blair. 2013. "Disrupted Expected Value and Prediction Error Signaling in Youths with Disruptive Behavior Disorders During a Passive Avoidance Task." *American Journal of Psychiatry* 170(3): 315–23.

Will, G. J., and E. T. Klapwijk. 2014. "Neural Systems Involved in Moral Judgment and Moral Action." *Journal of Neuroscience* 34(32): 10459–61.

CHAPTER 14

··

SOCIAL LEARNER DECISION MAKING

Matching Theory as a Unifying Framework for Recasting a General Theory

··

CARTER REES AND L. THOMAS WINFREE JR.

I. INTRODUCTION

THE objective of this chapter is to demonstrate the importance of the behavioral sciences literature regarding Herrnstein's (1961) matching law of behavior and reinforcement for Akers' (1973, 1985, 1998) social learning theory of crime and delinquency. Akers' variant of social learning theory is one of criminology's most widely embraced (Walsh and Ellis 1999; Ellis, Cooper, and Walsh 2008; Cooper, Walsh, and Ellis 2010), most often tested (Stitt and Giacopassi 1992), and empirically sound (Pratt et al. 2010) theories of crime and delinquency. Akers' social learning theory explains the mechanisms by which one learns to be a criminal or delinquent, which include both social and nonsocial forces, as well as ones with strong ties to operant conditioning. For its part, Herrnstein's matching law of behavior and reinforcement simply and elegantly states that there is a correlation between behavior and the environment. It contains a critical piece of the learning puzzle that is missing from current discussions of what is learned and what is not learned by criminals and delinquents, and it can further inform a significant decision-making process—that undertaken by offenders.

We propose that criminological social learning theory accommodates the theoretical propositions of human choice and decision making. Specifically, in this chapter, we argue the following: (1) The empirical and theoretical propositions of the matching law are embedded in social learning theory; (2) matching law is a vibrant area of research outside of criminology that has implications for offender decision-making processes; (3) these two observations argue for the inclusion of choice and decision-making principles as part of social learning theory; and (4) these ideas are testable using well-developed econometric models of human updating that account for the structure of social environments (i.e., social networks) while not inherently viewing humans simply as rational choice utility maximizers but, rather, as myopic or local suboptimal decision makers with the ability to maximize long-term utility.

II. Social Learning Theory

As a type of explanation for human social behavior, social learning theories collectively claim that humans can acquire valuable life skills and knowledge by copying what others say and do; moreover, such theories recognize that individuals rarely make choices and decisions in social isolation (Hoppitt and Laland 2013). Learning theories' conceptual approach to behavior casts the decision-making processes of agents as based partially on their direct and indirect experiences in the immediate social environment. As humans, we rely for guidance on information from others who share our social environment during the decision-making process. This theoretical claim makes it important to understand how people share information and learn from one another as individuals or members of social groups. That is, the observation of or interaction with other individuals or their verbal and behavioral products should facilitate our insights into behavior decisions and corresponding consequences (Hoppitt and Laland 2013). Viewing the social environment in this way equates to a learning environment wherein an agent's level of embeddedness in the social structure defines the social vantage point for observing behaviors of others along with the consequences of those behaviors.

Several variants of social learning theory may initially seem relevant to the current work, including ones that are strongly rooted in operant conditioning, such as that of Skinner (1955, 1963), and others, such as those of Rotter (1954) and Bandura (1963, 1977, 2001), that allow for the influence of other social psychological forces in the learning process. Each of these theories has a slightly different take on the mechanisms that serve to shape human decision making. For example, Skinner's (1954) approach is straightforward behaviorism, following the principles of operant conditioning. That is, learned behavior flows from conditioning; consequently, the task for the behaviorist is to establish patterns of stimulus, reward, or reinforcement that can modify animal behavior, including the behavior of humans. Rotter (1954) viewed learning in less rigidly behaviorist terms, allowing for the influence of social–environmental factors. He believed that the expected outcome guides behavior, suggesting the subject's engagement in cognitive processing. Finally, Bandura's theory, first called social learning theory (Bandura 1969, 1977), viewed learning as a straightforward process of imitation, an assertion grounded in his studies of aggression. Bandura later modified, expanded, and rebranded social learning theory as social cognitive theory (Bandura 1985, 1989), emphasizing that learning takes place in a holistic context wherein both human cognition and decision making are influenced by a host of factors, including, but not limited to, social interactions, social experiences, and media influences. None of these theories, however, was specifically constructed with the intent of providing insights into miscreant conduct and the errant decisions of law-offending persons (Sellers, Winfree, and Akers 2012; Akers and Sellers 2013; Winfree and Abadinsky 2017). There is one theory that does include psychological conditioning, sociological forces, and learning as part of a conceptual framework by which to understand better crime and delinquency—a theory referred to in this chapter as Akers' social learning theory (A-SLT).

Indeed, A-SLT has its origins in the work of Burgess and Akers (1966), who called their contribution a differential association/reinforcement theory of criminal behavior due to its merger of Sutherland's theory of differential association with elements of operant conditioning. Akers later recast it as social learning theory in his 1973 book of the same title. Akers (1985, pp. 52–55) viewed social learning theory as having four component parts. The first, *differential association*, refers to direct social interaction with members of a primary group and less concrete but no less important identifications with more distal groups, the latter also serving as sources of learning. These are not simply peer associations but, rather, the sum total of all social influences, which include one's family, schoolteachers, and other public officials, neighbors, and religious figures with whom an individual has contact. The second mechanism is *imitation*, which is said to occur when an individual copies the behavior of others, perhaps not completely understanding why the behavior is important or in what ways or even when it might be rewarding. As the most elementary form of learning, imitation boils down to a case of "monkey see, monkey do," much as Bandura's experiments on aggression in children revealed (Bandura, Ross, and Ross 1961). *Definitions*, the third element, serve as guideposts for behavior—good and bad, rewarding and punishing. *Differential reinforcement*, the final element, exists in both social and nonsocial forms. For example, one can anticipate gaining social rewards from one's peers for acting in what the latter view as an appropriate manner, or the action itself may result in physical or even physiological outcomes that one views as rewarding, such as the use of a psychoactive substance in a social setting. These reinforcements are either anticipatory or prospective in nature, suggesting to the actor whether the behavior guided by those definitions is likely to be rewarded or punished, even if that reward is only physiological in nature.

In essence, then, Akers' recasting of Sutherland's theory in the language of operant conditioning provided a detailed explanation of the mechanisms by which certain definitions become an integral part of a person's decision-making processes. Some sociologists viewed Akers' use of psychological behaviorism's operant conditioning, with its roots in the work of Skinner and Bandura, as making A-SLT less sociological and more psychological (Adams 1974). Akers (2011) noted that Sutherland's student and coauthor, Donald Cressey, was in the audience when Burgess and he first presented their theory in 1966. As Akers (2011) observed, Cressey was "very encouraging and expressed the opinion that, had Sutherland lived, he would have approved of our efforts" (p. 362).

Sutherland's theory references the rather vague "principle of differential association," an idea we interpret to mean that law-violating behavior ensues when the definitions favorable to criminal conduct overwhelm those definitions favoring lawful conduct. For

Sutherland (1947), people turned to crime "because of contacts with criminal patterns and also because of isolation from anti-criminal patterns" (p. 8). Akers viewed it differently, specifying that differential reinforcements provided the discriminative stimuli at the core of which definitions were to dominate a person's decisions to engage in deviant behavior, including delinquency. Such definitions conveyed unique normative meanings, which, as Akers (1985) noted, reinforced rulebreaking conduct by specifying which actions are right and which ones are wrong, condemning some and approving others. According to Akers, then,

> Discriminative stimuli are stimuli which become associated with reinforcement. In addition to the reinforcers, other stimuli are ordinarily present when behavior is reinforcers—the physical surroundings, one's own feelings, others' behavior, one's own and others' spoken words and so on. Those that customarily accompany reinforcement (or punishment) come to be associated with it; they set the stage or provide the *cues* for the reinforcement. In a sense discriminative stimuli signal the act that when they are present he can expect reinforcement. (p. 54, emphasis in original)

Only when the definitions become part of the class of stimuli Akers identifies as discriminative stimuli do they potentiate miscreant behavior. For A-SLT, then, it is not simply a question of "good" definitions overwhelming "bad" ones.

Akers' latter ideas, but especially the notion of the discriminative stimuli and their operant conditioning origins, build on Herrnstein's (1961) matching law. Response rates, in this case various forms of human behavior, tend to be proportionate to the amount and duration of reinforcements delivered. Humans are inclined to select those behaviors or responses most likely to be reinforced immediately (molecular maximizing) when faced with alternative courses of action and behaviors. This characteristic does not preclude the selected behaviors from maximizing the reinforcements received over time (molar maximizing). Finally, as the process moves in the direction of producing what Akers calls the behavior-directing discriminative stimuli, humans increasingly select the one of two alternative behaviors that produces the best local rates of reinforcements—until, that is, the response ratios equal the reinforcement ratios for each alternative choice or behavior (i.e., matching). Importantly, Herrnstein and Prelec (1991) suggested that the matching law could be explained by what they termed melioration or the choosing of higher immediate rewards when the alternative choice had a lower immediate payoff but would optimize overall future rewards. This idea was in contrast to the rational choice perspective that was also used to explain matching behavior. We return to this point later.

Both Akers and Herrnstein emphasized the significance of the immediate environment in which these operant conditioning processes take place for the observed outcomes (i.e., crime and matching); however, it is arguable that the larger social environment exerts far more influence over Akers' discriminative stimuli than is the case for Herrnstein's matching law, whose origins are traced to a more controlled, experimental state (Akers 1998). For A-SLT, the processes that generate the discriminative stimuli may be far more prone to the influence of "random" social influences than is the case for the operation of Herrnstein's matching law. This comment derives from the observation that whereas Akers (and Sutherland before him) sited learning processes within the social context of criminal or deviant behavior, matching law owes its origins to the observed behavior of pigeons in an experimental situation. Importantly, others, including Snyder and Patterson (1995), have examined the generalized matching equation in the "natural environment" and have found it to operate much as Herrnstein conceptualized it in his experiments.

Finally, we contend that the actor's social network influences both the creation of discriminative stimuli and the actions of the matching law. The significance of the social networks for human decision making is also integral to the rational choice perspective. Social networks represent the social environments individuals use to determine appropriate and normative behavior that may result in reinforcement. Social networks, then, are central to any test of whether humans are long-term utility maximizers or short-term myopic reward seekers.

III. CHOICE, AGENCY, AND CRIMINAL OFFENDER DECISION MAKING

Behavioral scientists define choice as the allocation of time among activities; all behavior is choice behavior because every situation permits more than one activity (Baum 1994). Specifically, choice is the distribution of a subject's behavior relative to reinforcement alternatives (Fisher and Mazur 1997). Behavioral (i.e., operant) responses represent a subject's choice to engage in a given behavior in lieu of one or more others at a particular time conditional upon positive or negative reinforcement (Herrnstein 1970; Reed and Kaplan 2011). At that exact moment, the person making the choice does not know precisely what will happen but is making an estimation of a preferential outcome. This estimation is based in part on a specific course of action, past choices of a similar nature, and past rewards. Behavioral scientists, then, equate this relative preference to choice and understand it "by examining the relative rates of reinforcement associated with each option" (Reed and Kaplan 2011, p. 15). This sequence of events is the essence of the "matching law" proposed by Herrnstein (1961), which can be expressed as a mathematical statement describing the relationship between the rate of behavioral response and the rate of reward. In summary, behavior matches reinforcement schedules (Reed and Kaplan 2011).

The matching law formula is relatively simple:

$$\frac{B_1}{B_1 + B_2} = \frac{R_1}{R_1 + R_2}$$

The formula suggests that a subject manifests real-world behavior first by choosing between, for example, two alternative behaviors B_1 and B_2 (i.e., total responses of each) at a rate equal to that to which he or she is relatively reinforced for either behavior as indicated by R_1 and R_2. The matching law formula indicates a perfect correlation between a subject's choices of behavior as a response to a reinforcing consequence. That is, proportional increases in reinforcers lead to proportional increases in behavior. For example, a person is given two buttons, numbered 1 and 2, to push, with each button having a different reinforcement schedule. These schedules allow responses (i.e., button pushing) to operate a reinforcement dispenser that might dole out food, cigarettes, cash, or drugs. In this type of setting, a subject faces two alternative ways of obtaining the same resource. The matching law would state that the ratio of responses would track the reinforcement ratio at the two alternatives. Thus, if there are five times as many reinforcers delivered by button 1, then pressing that button would occur roughly five times more than pushing button 2. Similarly, if one switched reinforcement schedules so that button 2 delivered three times the payoffs, a person's behavior would switch accordingly and he or she would press button 2 approximately three times more than button 1. Ultimately, the ratio of behavior tends to equal the ratio of reinforcement.

The original matching law equation has generated an abundance of research in the field of behavior analysis, including the extent to which the matching law holds under various reinforcement conditions (McDowall 2005). Most important for the current discussion is Baum's (1974, 1979) update to the matching formula, providing evidence that behavior matching is not as strict as Herrnstein's original formula indicates. According to Baum, subject behavior consistently and systematically differs from a linear relationship in three ways: undermatching, overmatching, and bias. These deviations can be quantified by the following formula, which is referred to as the generalized matching law:

$$\frac{B_1}{B_2} = b\left(\frac{r^1}{r^2}\right)^a$$

where parameter b represents bias, which varies from unity when choice is asymmetrical—for example, when the behaviors that constitute the two alternatives require different amounts of effort or cost. Davidson and McCarthy (1988) refer to exponent a as sensitivity, an idea that captures the magnitude and direction of deviating from strict one-to-one linear matching. For example, $a < 1$ represents undermatching, in which a subject's behavioral allocation is less than what is predicted by the original matching law—that is, when a subject's response is less than predicted on the behavioral alternative that consistently provides the highest reinforcement. Values of $a > 1$ represent overmatching, where subjects exhibit a higher rate of responding to the higher reinforcing alternative or when it is too costly to switch to the less preferred response. Last, bias occurs when the subject prefers or has a special affinity for one of the choices (for a review, see McDowell 1989, 2005).

McDowell (2013) reviews the current state of the behavioral literature regarding the matching law and the corresponding generalization equation, concluding that both "equations are widely accepted as accurate descriptions of individual-subject behavior in single and multivariate environments" (p. 1001). However, McDowell contends that the latter is favored due to generalizability across disciplines and reinforcement schedules. After all, human conduct that is rewarded will show bias because the individual is likely to express this special affinity in his or her choice behavior. For example, although certain crimes have serious and increasingly severe penalties associated with being caught on successive occasions, the repeat offender may simply enjoy the conduct so much that the risk of punishment is negated by this bias.

IV. Myopic or Long-Term Maximizers?

Akers (1973, 1985, 1998) implicitly includes the principles of the matching law in his updated conception of Sutherland's (1947; see also Sutherland and Cressey 1974) differential association theory. A-LST provides criminologists with a clear starting point to discuss choice in offender decision making, as the previous example suggests. Choice is an integral part of the operant conditioning tradition within the behavioral sciences and consequently is part of the theoretical foundation of A-SLT. For example, an adolescent will distribute his or her law-abiding or lawbreaking behaviors as a function of the relative rates of reinforcement for each behavior from, alternatively, the deviant peer group or the pro-social school authorities. However, although the matching law rests on firm mathematical evidence, its nature remains descriptive. That is, although the matching law accurately predicts patterns of reinforced behavior over time, it does not explain how or why a subject behaves in the manner in which he or she behaves (Bordens and Abbott 2011). The strategy of allocating responses according to the rate of reinforcement is a question of theoretical optimality in decision making and determining the mechanism by which this takes place.

Criminologists most often associate the notions of response allocation strategy, long-term optimality, utility maximization, and assumptions of human choice with the rational choice perspective. Alternatively, Herrnstein and Vaughan (1980) offer an explanation called melioration theory, claiming human behavior is governed by short-term tendencies toward choice alternatives with higher local rates of rewards (see also Herrnstein 1982; Herrnstein and Prelec 1991). What distinguishes these two perspectives of behavior, consequences, and choice is whether humans make choices based on immediate or delayed reinforcement.

V. Rational Choice

The rational choice model assumes (1) people respond to incentives, (2) changing incentives can change behavior, and (3) human behavior is not random. Rationality is reflected in the "consistency between a person's preferences and choices" (McCarthy 2002, p. 423). Economics defines expected utility as a subjective value placed on some good or action. Individuals maximize expected utility or an optimal mix of consequences by repeatedly weighing their actions' costs and benefits (Becker 1968; Baum 1981). In other words, human behavior is guided by evaluating alternatives, which consists of assigning each a probability that it will lead to a global maximization of the expected utility of desired outcomes based on an individual's subjective preferences. Rational individuals are thus future-oriented decision makers who use information from past behavioral decisions as data in the calculation of future payoffs from all possible choice alternatives and implement the decisions that maximize expected utility or the highest net payoff (Dawes 1988; Rachlin and Laibson 1997; Almy and Krueger 2013).

For example, imagine you have $1,000 to spend on food and recreation for the month. The question faced by the consumer in this example is how to spend the money? Consumers are rational in the sense that they choose a course of action that maximizes the utility of the market basket, which is a combination of goods (e.g., the combination of spending 30 percent for food and 70 percent for recreation). Utility is subjective and defined by the consumer subject to the constraints imposed by income and prices. Importantly, consumers cannot choose just any market basket combination. Instead, they actively engage in comparing different combinations of food and recreation in order to land on the combination that maximizes the subjective utility of the market basket (Salvatore 2008). This active engagement and comparison process involves the search for and processing of information gleaned from the social environment in order to make an informed rational decision based on individual preferences for outcome. Rational choice is a framework for understanding a variety of micro- and macrosocial behaviors (Hechter and Kanazawa 1997), including crime and delinquency, from an economic market-basket standpoint.

Choices and decision making are not static; actors are aware of and respond to decisions of other's in the social environment, updating information on different combinations and the resulting utilities until equilibrium is reached. This equilibrium is realized when actors are positioned so that expected utility is maximized and no additional benefits are possible. Economic rational choice views maximized utility as an irresistible conclusion; doing otherwise is nonsensical because redistribution (e.g., 40 percent for food and 60 percent for recreation) would lead to a decrease in total utility. This "narrow model" (Opp 1997) is associated with neoclassical economic theory (Becker 1968), whereby actors behave in predictable ways based on the assumed ability to recognize all possible courses of action (Brezina 2002).

This view is normative in that it sets a baseline of how actors *should* behave as they perform the required cognitive calculations in order to maximize expected utility (Camerer 2003; Davidson 2004; Hausman and McPherson 2006). Importantly, neoclassical models of rational choice make no assumptions about the characteristics of the individual nor are there attempts to explain the decision-making *process*. Again, the rational actor is someone who makes consistent choices in reference to subjective preferences and the value placed on goods. This perspective begins with outcomes of behavioral choices and views them "as if" they were generated by an expected utility maximization function (McFadden 2001; Moscati and Tubaro 2011). This is an exercise in deduction, given that one begins with the set of rational choice axioms and demonstrates that observed consequences stem from those assumptions. The actions a person engages in are those that will maximize expected utility, and this does not imply those actions will appear as rational, reasonable, thoughtful, reflective, selfish, or intelligent to another person.

The rational choice perspective, then, explains why and how potential offenders commit crime. Generally, offenders are said to be rational in making choices when the resulting actions and decisions are expected to maximize perceived potential benefits from illegal behavior (Cornish and Clarke 2014; but see McCarthy 2002). A core assumption of the rational choice perspective is that offenders are "goal oriented and seek to benefit themselves by their behavior" (Brezina 2002, p. 241). Cost–benefit analysis in offender decision making is often tested within the framework of deterrence theory and the ability of legal sanctions to increase risk and cost perceptions, thereby reducing crime (Cornish and Clarke 2014; for a review, see Pogarsky 2009; Piquero et al. 2011). The costs of offending include informal social sanctions from family and friends along with formal sanctions such as fines and incarceration (Tittle 1980; Williams and Hawkins 1986). These costs are weighed against the benefits or rewards of offending. Benefits can be intangible returns such as status among peers, emotional thrill-seeking behavior, or the basic immediate benefit of monetary gains (Nagin and Paternoster 1993, 1994).

Rational choice and deterrence theory continue to be active areas of research in the field of criminology, with recent work focusing on offender characteristics such as averseness to ambiguity and overconfidence in risk perception (Loughran et al. 2011, Loughran, Paternoster, and Weiss 2012; Loughran and Piquero 2013). The consideration of offender characteristics in the decision-making process is consistent with the bounded "wider view" of the rational actors and differs in many respects from neoclassical rationality (Opp 1997). The wider view recognizes that individuals do not always make decisions under optimal conditions, may be subject to limited availability of information, may not use the information efficiently, or are biased when making decisions regarding risk (Simon 1955, 1956; Kahneman and Tversky 1979; Smith 2003). The combination of these limitations also suggests that an individual is not always an expected utility optimizer. If so, the "as if" assumption no longer holds, and the theoretical perspective shifts to the decision-making process and why particular choices are made, along with the outcome of those choices (Hastie 2001). For example, a criminal offender may resort to using "cognitive shortcuts" to simplify otherwise complex information related to the probability of apprehension for committing a certain crime, thereby artificially limiting or even eliminating the number of possible outcomes to be considered for a certain course of action (Brezina 2002). The consideration of the role of offender characteristics in decision making moves rational-choice criminologists closer into the realm of behavioral economists, who value psychology and what it offers economics. Indeed, individual differences in studies of offender decision making are consistent enough that some criminologists consider deterrence theory a theory of social psychology (Piquero et al. 2011).

VI. Melioration and the Matching Law

Proponents of the rational choice perspective claim that humans conduct themselves with the goal of maximizing total utility or payoff, and that process is free of human assumptions and motivations. This contention greatly simplifies the equation of human behavior; preferences and subjective expectations are sufficient to produce observable behavior. The impetus behind human actions is to seek betterment as each individual has defined it, and importantly, the consequences of the current course of action matter (Sims et al. 2013). That is, rational human beings learn from the immediate consequences of their choices, but they also consider the delayed effect of those consequences on total or global utility maximization.

The absolute parsimony of the rational choice equation is appealing. However, the real-world complexities of the social and decision-making environment sometimes cause behavioral preferences that lead to what might appear as objectively irrational outcomes. A rational subject's aggregation of choices should appear to be made as if the subject had perfect knowledge of the social and decision-making environment; this "perfect knowledge" eventually translates into forgoing choices leading to instantaneous rewards in favor of those leading to overall utility maximization (Nau 1999). Therefore, the rational actor is a Bayesian maximizer in the truest sense with "unlimited cognitive abilities," reaching "mythical hero" status in terms of mathematical prowess (Selten 2001, p. 14).

Evidence suggests, however, that this scenario is not always true; human behavior can and does deviate from the standard of global utility maximization (for a review, see Shafir and LeBoeuf 2002). The result can be suboptimal decision making manifested in the selection of the immediate higher reward or myopic utility at the expense of expected global or total utility (Sims et al. 2013). Such suboptimal choices, failing to account for "the effect of current choices on future yields," comport well with what Herrnstein et al. (1993, p. 150) calls "melioration," which is the centerpiece of his proposed dynamic theory of choice underlying the matching law. Melioration is Herrnstein's explanation of why the matching law occurs.

Herrnstein's theory is founded on three central constructs: the matching law, hyperbolic discounting, and melioration. The matching law and melioration remain foundational to the study of human choice in the field of experimental psychology and continue to generate a notable body of research with animal and human subjects (McDowell 2013). The matching law proposed by Herrnstein (1961) equates the relative frequency of responding to the obtained relative frequency of reinforcement. As previously mentioned, the matching law was born from experiments with pigeons being reinforced or not reinforced for pecking on keys. Researchers conducted these experiments in the Skinnerian behaviorist tradition: Law-like human behaviors provide evidence of determinism and an absence of free will (Skinner 1953, 1974). However, Herrnstein (1974) does not adhere to Skinner's version of human behavior, noting instead the following:

> In contrast to R_1 we rarely if ever know the true value of the denominator [the sum of all possible reinforcers], even in experiments in which extraneous sources of reinforcements have been screened out. . . . Animals find unanticipated reinforcement in virtually any environment, no matter how hard the experimenter has tried to make it barren. (p. 159)

These unanticipated reinforcements can be viewed as unobservable reinforcements and importantly have an effect on behavior. This interpretation opens the possibility that reinforcers could be both extrinsic and intrinsic, inclusive of the person's mental states. Reinforcers need not be observable to have influence and value.

Hyperbolic discounting posits that humans tend to make impulsive choices in favor of immediate rewards and payoffs despite a previously held preference for the larger but delayed payoffs. Hyperbolic discounting stands in contrast to the rational actor's consistent intertemporal preference for a larger delayed payoff consistent with exponential functions (Loewenstein and Prelec 1992). That is, the rational actor is time consistent in his or her preferences (Listokin 2007; Loughran, Paternoster, and Weiss 2012). The hyperbolic discount function suggests a person negatively discounts the preference for delayed, larger rewards over time at a decreasing rate to the point at which a smaller, more immediate payoff is obtained (O'Donoghue and Rabin 2001; Loughran, Paternoster, and Weiss 2012). This is a direct challenge to rational choice because it suggests that a person's behavior may reflect choosing the local and immediate reward, even if the person has a full understanding about the long-term benefits of delayed payoffs and his or her own personal preferences (Camerer 1999). As will soon become clear, this apparent myopia makes hyperbolic discounting an important ingredient of melioration, especially for those making "bad choices," such as criminals (Nagin and Pogarsky 2004; Klochko 2006).

Melioration is the idea that an individual chooses at each point in time the alternative with the highest perceived immediate payoff regardless of how the specific choice affects expected utility. According to this interpretation, melioration functions as a *dynamic* theory of choice underlying the matching law in that behavioral choices are made from moment to moment based on probabilities of immediate reinforcement, behavior reinforcement, and utility (Herrnstein 1990). As noted in Herrnstein's theory, individuals may appear to choose rationally or irrationally depending on how present choices affect future payoffs. The neoclassical rational actor prefers and eventually continues to make choices over time that maximize future payoffs. Rationality requires this process to continue until the actor reaches a state of equilibrium at which time further decisions no longer improve total expected utility (Macy 2006).

Melioration, when applied to human choice, is understood as subsequently choosing the alternative action that appears to provide the most immediate reward while ignoring the negative impact of that choice on future expected utility. Importantly, the alternative does not have the highest immediate reward but would result in a higher global expected utility. Melioration assumes that individuals have the capacity to switch from being long-term utility optimizers to making choices that have a higher immediate but do not necessarily maximize the long-term payoff or utility (Herrnstein and Vaughan 1980). In other words, an individual could switch from choosing the local, less rewarding alternative that maximizes the long-term expected utility to choosing the local, more rewarding alternative. Switching does not necessarily preclude melioration from equating to utility maximization. If hyperbolic discounting does not take place, the outcome is that of maximum optimization; melioration can lead to maximizing expected utility proposed by neoclassical rational choice models of behavior (Tunney and Shanks 2002; Sims et al. 2013). That is, both often produce the same globally maximized result.

This last contention directly challenges rational choice theory's view of the ties between choice and human behavior. Achieving the highest immediate payoff or reinforcement in a decision situation is understandable and arguably rational, but not when the pursuit of that immediate reward is detrimental to overall expected utility (Shanks, Tunney, and McCarthy 2002). Criminologists will correctly surmise that the behaviorist notion of melioration and preference for immediate reward is related to an individual's level of self-control. In fact, self-control is suggested to be a product of melioration (Herrnstein and Vaughan 1980) and is an active area of research within the behaviorist tradition (Ainslie 1975; Herrnstein and Prelec 1992; Schelling 1992; Loewenstein 1996; Metcalfe and Mischel 1999; Trope and Fishbach 2000; Fujita et al. 2006).

Akers (1990, p. 654) contends that the rational choice perspective offers "no new general theoretical concepts or propositions . . . to criminological theory" and is subsumed by social learning theory. The intellectual history of A-SLT allows for a broader range of human decision making inclusive of behaviors such as self-control, which is often pitted against social learning theory as a separate rival explanation of crime and delinquency (Hirschi 1989; Gottfredson and Hirschi 1990). The ability to integrate these varying theoretical perspectives is still open to debate (Akers 1991; McCarthy 2002), but both social learning and rational choice are in agreement on the prominence of the social environment for the explanation of human behavior. The social network literature from sociology and economics is of particular importance, offering a tractable way to theorize and model an individual's social world.

VII. SOCIAL NETWORKS AND EMPIRICAL MODELS OF CHOICE

Various types of relational ties that are embedded within society often bind individuals together (Granovetter 1985, 1992). A set of relations and the corresponding set of entities or nodes (e.g., persons or corporations) constitute a social network (Young and Rees 2012). Social networks are inherently hierarchical; two nodes form a dyad, egocentric networks are the direct ties that a node has to other nodes, and all ties among all nodes represent a complete social network (Borgatti, Everett, and Johnson 2013). Social networks can consist of relationships between coworkers, high school peer groups, family members, or even macro entities such as corporations.

The system of relations tying nodes together represents the structure of the network and the social environment from which and individual (e.g., node) gathers and processes information concerning behavioral rules and norms. The empirical focus of social network analysis is to determine if this structure affects behavior (Wasserman and Faust 1994). In social network analysis of crime and delinquency, the node most often represents an individual in an attempt to understand how network structure affects various criminal outcomes (for a review, see Carrington 2011).

Network ties also serve as conduits through which behavioral information flows from the social environment to the individual and vice versa (Friedkin 1982). Transmission of information can occur from direct communication with other network members or by simple observation of their behavior—ideas consistent with A-SLT. The social network perspective provides mature theoretical and mathematical guidance on quantifying the structure of the social environment and how it affects human decision making and behavior. For example, a network's structural characteristics reveal who is connected to whom and whether or not it is possible to pass information directly from one person to another (Wasserman and Faust 1994). Alternatively, it is possible that such information must pass through and be processed by others before it reaches its final destination in the network. In this sense, network structure can affect a person's access to information, whether or not it is available, as well as the quality of the information. The structural position of an individual in the network is important, as are the positions of other network members in terms of how information is dispersed throughout the network (Granovetter 1973, 1985).

For example, consider a person with few or no ties or who may have little interaction with other network members. The isolated actor can observe very little of the network. The social information he or she receives may be different in quality and quantity compared to that received by a popular person in the network. Popularity, defined as having many incoming network ties, increases the probability of information passing through that person. The popular network member directly observes a larger portion of the network, making informed decisions and behavioral choices far easier.

Networks are natural tools for understanding information flows and behavioral outcomes in many social and economic contexts (Conley and Udry 2001; Jackson 2007). The social network represents the context in which an individual updates currently held beliefs and opinions that are a consequence of that person's own experiences. Learning from others in a network is fundamental to melioration theory, just as observation of the network as a source of data is fundamental to rational choice theory: Each assumes individuals account for the actions and choices of others during the decision-making process. This inclusion of others makes learning social in nature as opposed to purely individual trial-and-error learning such as that found in an operant conditioning chamber like Skinner's box (Laland 2001). As a result, there is a strong parallel between rational choice and melioration in terms of the importance of the social network as a source of behavioral information. A key difference is the process by which an individual updates his or her beliefs, opinions, and preferences. Scholars generally focus on two statistical models when testing these hypotheses. Bayesian learning models are consistently associated with the rational choice perspective (Kahneman and Tversky 1972, 1973), whereas, as the next section makes clear, the non-Bayesian local weighted averaging model by DeGroot (1974; see also Golub and Jackson 2010) is representative of non-optimizing choices consistent with melioration theory.

VIII. Bayesian Learning and Rational Choice

The empirical counterpart to the rational choice perspective is Bayes' rule or theorem and associated statistical models of learning (Bayes and Price 1763). Bayesian learning models assume individuals are rational in that they update beliefs and opinions in a statistically optimal way in order to maximize total expected utility (Acemoglu and Ozdaglar 2010). The individual starts with a certain probabilistic belief or view that a certain behavior will maximize expected utility, which is called a prior or prior probability (for a mathematical discussion of Bayesian learning, see Jackson 2008). The individual then interacts with the social environment by observing other individuals' behaviors and outcomes while also engaging in his or her own behaviors. This process is repeated over time and represents a feedback process in which a value is given to each experience in order to find the optimal utility. Consistent with tenets of neoclassical rational choice, rational actors update their prior beliefs, opinions, and experiences with the information received from observing the social environment using a weighted function of the prior belief and this new information. The updating process results in posterior probability, which is a newly updated view of the world expressed as a probability that a behavior or action would result in a reward. Bayes' rule dictates that over repeated trials, each individual will engage in behavior that maximizes the expected total utility conditional upon prior knowledge and each individual's current understanding of the social environment. This is consistent with the rational choice perspective: Actors are rational, conscious, and future-oriented decision makers (McCarthy 2002).

Bayesian models of learning view an individual's social network as an information repository and nothing more. That is, although the individual extracts behavioral information from the social environment, the structure of the environment does not govern the actions of the individual (Jackson 2008). Instead, Bayesian learners are optimal decision makers in the fullest sense guided by their own cost–benefit analyses and remain ungoverned by external unseen influences such as network structure (Corazzini et al. 2012). Of course, an individual's ability to maximize the expected payoff or utility is gradually improved by observing other network members. However, this information is gathered before the individual makes his or her own behavioral decision. The actions or behaviors of other network members are viewed as revealing something about their private beliefs and desires, and this information is used to benefit one's own decision process. This sequencing of events means behavior does not depend directly on the actions of others because those actions are used as a signal of how to improve one's own position and possibly at the expense of other network members (Gale and Kariv 2003). This is the very definition of an externality in the economics literature, whereby one agent's choice imposes a cost or benefit upon another agent who did not choose either one (Gale 2003; Jackson 2008).

Bayesian learning from a rational choice perspective has been applied to and empirically supported by a variety of disciplines inclusive of economics, negotiations, delinquency, policy, technology adoption, gender, politics, and criminology literatures (Leathers and Smale 1991; Sugden 1991; Macy and Flache 1995; Zeng and Sycara 1998; Breen and García-Peñalosa 2002; Grynaviski 2006; Matsueda, Kreager, and Huizinga 2006; Meseguer 2006; Piquero et al. 2011). Furthermore, a strong parallel exists between the theoretical and empirical studies of rational choice and social learning. Pioneering work by Banerjee (1992) found that a sequence of Bayesian rational actors who learn behavior via observation would ultimately form a consensus, with each member arriving at the same decision and behaviors. This type of consensus behavior is described as herding, whereby an individual potentially ignores his or her own signal in order to go along with the group (Choi, Gale, and Kariv 2012). Bikhchandani, Hirshleifer, and Welch (1992) reported similar findings using the term informational cascades, which "occur when it is optimal for an individual, having observed the actions of those ahead of him, to follow the behavior of the preceding individual without regard to his own information" (p. 994).

Imitation is the learning mechanism said to explain both herding and informational cascades, and it occurs when individuals are uncertain about the outcome of their next action (Çelen and Kariv 2004). The learning mechanism of imitation is precisely the same as theorized in A-SLT. Thus, herding and informational cascades can be explained from a rational choice perspective, but this statement does not preclude other psychological and sociological explanations. Classic studies of social psychology, learning, and influence could also account for this type of imitative behavior in the face of uncertainty (Baddeley 2010).

A criticism of Bayesian learning and rational choice is that there are two central assumptions each model makes about individuals' cognitive capabilities and how much direct access they have to information in their social network. First, individuals are assumed to have a perfect knowledge of the current state of the social environment and the corresponding ability to make a probabilistic statement about each possible outcome event given the current state (Corazzini et al. 2012). In other words, individuals have a complete set of prior probabilities, which sum to 1 (Acemoglu et al. 2011). Second, and by implication, each individual can directly observe the decisions of all members of the network, and there is no cost associated with gathering information used in the updating of prior probabilities. This latter activity requires a direct connection to each member in a network, resulting in an implausible and complex worldview. Choi et al. (2012, p. 7) noted that "in other words, it is a game of perfect information," whereby the players need not search for information. The difficulty arises when networks become large: Because the cognitive effort necessary to have a "reliable model of the world" is equally expanded, probability updating is nearly impossible (Acemoglu and Ozdaglar 2010, p. 5).

Scholars often draw upon the classic work of Simon (1955) in an attempt to address these issues. He proposed a bounded rationality in which individuals face cognitive, outcome, and behavioral constraints. The rational individual is lacking unlimited cognition while operating within the structure of the social environment and is thereby constrained by the costs of gathering information from others in the network (Gigerenzer and Selten 2001). Individuals are constrained in the sense that the benefit of gathering more information from the social environment must be weighed against the cost of doing so (Bala and Goyal 1998; Gigerenzer and Selten 2001; Jackson 2008). The non-bounded rational actor did not have this constraint because information, under that interpretation, was assumed to be freely available at all times and without cost. These new constraints, however, meant the possibility of not having full information and no longer assumed the individual was an optimizer.

Scholars have incorporated bounded rationality into the science of decision making in rather different terms, however. That is, individuals are still viewed as prototypic optimizers, albeit under cost constraints. Optimization still drives behavior in the neoclassical sense, resulting in a simplification of the cognitive load faced by the rational actor (Gigerenzer 2004). For example, assume an adolescent wants to become popular after moving to a new school. Neoclassical rational choice would assume there is no opportunity cost to making friends with all members of the school and gathering the necessary information to maximize expected utility. A more realistic view, then, would assume that the development and maintenance of friendships takes time; moreover, the neglect of one friendship for another can damage or end a relationship. In other words, there is opportunity cost to having friends and maintaining friendships. A bounded view of this social reality may be that the student attempts to develop friendships with other students who themselves have many friends. This interpretation leaves open the possibility of developing future friendships with friends of friends as long as the costs of doing so do not outweigh the benefits. The issue of optimization under constraints with individuals still acting "as if" they were optimizers in the neoclassical sense is avoided (Gigerenzer 2004).

In summary, there are empirical and theoretical advantages and disadvantages to viewing individuals as fully rational Bayesian learners. This is not a new issue in economics (Frongillo, Schoenebeck, and Tamuz 2011), and scholars continue to advocate revisiting the simplified view of the "rational man" with his self-regarding preferences but paradoxically complex assumptions regarding his cognitive abilities (Camerer 1999; Kahneman 2003; Camerer, Loewenstein, and Prelec 2004). We suggest that non-Bayesian models of social learning offer a more tractable theoretical and mathematical view of the decision-making process and are consistent with the theoretical assumptions of melioration theory. Specifically, DeGroot's (1974) model, considered seminal in the area of non-Bayesian models of information transmission, has revitalized recent thinking in the field of human choice and decision making (Demarzo, Vayanos, and Zwiebel 2003; Jackson 2008; Golub and Jackson 2010).

IX. Melioration and Non-Bayesian Decision Makers: The DeGroot Model

Non-Bayesian heuristic or "rule of thumb" learning refers to a class of opinion formation and consensus models that assume individuals gather information from their social network via observational learning or communication with other network members (Friedkin 1991). DeGroot (1974) proposed a non-Bayesian model of learning in which each individual in a social network begins with a belief about the state of the world. Individuals then construct weights based on the level of trust the individual has for each of these friends to which he or she is directly tied. An individual's beliefs are then updated in an iterative and linear manner through observation and communication with other network members by constructing a weighted average of their own and their neighbors' previous decisions (Jackson 2008). Therefore, unlike the Bayesian models, these weights explicitly account for characteristics of the relationship between network members, but they offer a less complicated or naive model of opinion formation compared to the difficult complexities of the rational actor. DeGroot's model also indicates that the structure of the network matters in terms of how much an individual is exposed to the information proffered (Flores et al. 2012). Similar to Bayesian models of herding and information cascades, imitation of behavior is a common mechanism used to explain how some learning takes place in the non-Bayesian framework (Acemoglu and Ozdaglar 2010).

An important aspect of the DeGroot model is that individuals should switch their behaviors toward the actions of others that have been more successful (Brenner 2006). This switching is consistent with melioration's view of selecting the action with the highest immediate reward. The melioration learning process is built on averaging one's own past experiences with those of people with whom he or she is directly tied. It is natural to retain the knowledge of reinforcement and reapply that knowledge in a similar situation (Brenner and Witt 2003). Therefore, an individual will experience a gradual but not necessarily immediate switch to new behavior or increase behavior that leads to a better result (i.e., more reinforcing). Switching also entails positively reweighting the more rewarding behavior while decreasing the selection of the alternative (Macy and Flache 1995). Melioration and choice behavior can and often does lead to expected utility or molar maximization consistent with modeling the behavior of others who may not necessarily be maximizing their own rewards.

Generally, tests of melioration and the matching law indicate that each represents a viable explanation of human choice, decision making, and behavior, along with non-Bayesian models of social learning (Jackson 2010; McDowell 2013). We expect that scholars will continue to try to reconcile the rational man with melioration theory's view of human decision making, as evidenced by the growing popularity of behavioral and neurological economics (Camerer 1999, 2007; Brenner and Witt 2003; Camerer and Loewenstein 2004). Some scholars have suggested that melioration and a preference for immediate rewards may provide a better understanding of choice behavior than expected utility (Shanks et al. 2002; Neth, Sims, and Gray 2006) or that melioration can equate to utility maximization (Sakai and Fukai 2008). Furthermore, it may be that melioration is not evident across all social and cognitive situations (Tunney and Shanks 2002; Sims et al. 2013; Chandrasekhar et al. 2014).

Last, DeGroot models allow for the incorporation of network structure into the learning process. This richer model also leads to a more complex description of the social environment, meaning that additional mathematical and cognitive assumptions must be considered. Repeated averaging and weighting of the information collected from other network members potentially introduces a redundant accounting of information flowing through network ties, leading to persuasion bias during the process of opinion formation (DeMarzo et al. 2003). Relatedly, social networks are not static entities; ties between actors can be made and broken, such as occurs with friendship ties during adolescence (Cairns and Cairns 1994). The principle of triadic closure, first introduced by Simmel (1908), suggests that a friend of a friend is likely to become a friend (Heider 1958; Granovetter 1973). This eventuality not only adds more structure to a network but also becomes another decision-making process that must be included in the final model (Bala and Goyal 2000; Jackson and Watts 2002). A rational actor might envision adding an additional link or friendship tie as beneficial to expected utility resulting in yet another link due to triadic closure. The same can be said of severing ties with others, along with the possibility that individuals do this in a myopic non-optimizing manner (Watts 2002). The co-evolution of network structure may parallel choosing actions based on the understanding of the current network structure. The economic principle of no free lunch applies: There is an opportunity cost when including network structure in a model, just as there is a cost to ignoring structure when modeling human decision making and choice.

X. Discussion

We began this chapter with the claim that matching theory provides a unifying framework for a recasting of Akers' variant of social learning theory. In fact, we find that Akers' theory, unlike rational choice theory, includes an appreciation for the theoretical implications of matching theory, especially the revised generalized matching law. To wit, we explored how Akers' social learning theory implicitly includes the fundamental operations of matching law but that the updated, revised version reflects more accurately the processes behind such decisions. Moreover, although both A-SLT and matching law include the operation of the larger social environment, our work advances the idea that social network analysis should enhance understanding of these processes. For example, five decades ago, Cressey (1965) acknowledged that their social networks, which must change as well, limit the extent to which we can achieve prosocial changes among ex-offenders, moving them into life situations that promote lawful conduct. Moreover, an important element in this inclusion of matching law in a social learning framework is the acknowledgment that most people, but certainly offenders, tend to be myopic decision makers, engaged in high levels of hyperbolic discounting.

We argue that the statistical modeling associated with social learning is best viewed as the engagement of a non-Bayesian model—one wherein the members have less-than-perfect insights into the options and behaviors of the members of their social network. Ultimately, actors switch their behavior to be consistent with those individuals believed to be more successful in the attainment of desired outcomes, particularly those with the highest immediate rewards and not necessarily to the detriment of long-term utility. Furthermore, this view accommodates cognitive and network structural heterogeneity across actors, thereby moving away from axiomatic deduction and toward an inductive process of empirical discovery of patterns of behavior. This model is also consistent with some rational choice theorists moving away from strictly instrumental motivations to what Simon (1956) calls "satisficing solutions," which are solutions that are "good enough" when optimality cannot be obtained. Furthermore, mounting evidence suggests that strict coherence to the neoclassical view of rational choice is unrealistic in all situations (Mueller-Frank 2013; Sims et al. 2013).

However, this does not constitute a death knell for the utility maximizer. Often, theories are pitted against one another in an effort to discover a single general theory of crime and criminality. In our view, A-SLT accommodates utility maximization and decision making along with the myopic meliorative tendencies of humans. It could be argued that this is closer to the intended meaning of rational choice, which defines the prototypical self-interested man as one who is present-aimed and engages in

> those activities that reflect the consideration of costs and benefits for whatever objectives the individual has at the moment a choice is made. It assumes a richer set of interests and argues that behaviors are rational if they attempt to meet an individual's ordered preferences. Thus, it allows for diverse interests (cultural, social, psychological, or emotional) that help explain such individually, and often materially, costly preferences (and resulting actions) as philanthropy altruism, and fidelity to a principle. (McCarthy 2002, p. 422)

There is, of course, a trade-off when incorporating cognition and network structure into the study of human decision making. Parsimony is considered a hallmark of rational choice theory and is even more attractive when coupled with its "elegant explanation" and "considerable predictive power" (McCarthy 2002, p. 422). This sentiment echoes Friedman's (1953) endorsement of rational choice because "theory is to be judged by its predictive power for the class of phenomena which it is intended to explain" (p. 5). However, Jones (1999, p. 305) suggests this approach results in "a laundry list of [empirical] problems" inclusive of the nature of the decision maker, the environment in which he or she acts, the cost of information, and the processing of information. The development of a "serious empirical theory of choice" would view human cognition as bounded and therefore adaptive, with recognition given to the "fundamental complexity of the environment" (Jones 1999, p. 305).

The art of scientific inquiry is in finding the balance between model complexity and parsimony. The principles of matching law and expected utility are based on the basic idea of a singular individual engaging in repeated trials in an effort to achieve a desired outcome. Information gathering from either perspective is not a singular event but, rather, one that for each individual occurs over time, on more than one occasion, and not in a social vacuum. That is, decision making is a dynamic microprocess indicative of the complexities of human interactions rendering their decisions and cognitions interdependent (Macy and Willer 2002). Parsimony gives way to complexity, resulting in potential black box psychological explanations of human behavior (Boudon 2003). Even the most sophisticated equation-based stochastic models of human behavior ultimately rely on parameterized point estimates based on population averages, thereby greatly simplifying each individual's decision-making process for the purposes of solvability. Fortunately, the complexity of human interaction and cognitions can be understood theoretically beginning with complex systems theory (complexity science) and empirically with agent-based modeling (ABM). We next discuss complexity and ABM because they form the basis for a promising research agenda that should prove capable of capturing the complexities of individual decision-making processes, interdependent human relationships, and the interplay between aggregate social phenomena and individual actions of autonomous agents.

A. Complexity

Complexity and complex systems theory is the "study of many actors and their actions" (Axelrod 1997, p. 3). Mitchell (2009) offers a more formal definition, viewing complex systems as "an interdisciplinary field of research that seeks to explain how large numbers of relatively simple entities organize themselves, without the benefit of any central controller, into a collective whole that creates patterns, uses information, and, in some cases, evolves and learns" (p. 3). This definition is consistent with Simon's (1962) informal definition of complex systems as "being made up of parts that interact in a nonsimple way . . . the whole [being] more than the sum of the parts" (p. 468). The science of complexity consists of computational and conceptual tools to describe accurately the interdependencies of such data, feedback processes, and how system-level behavior emerges from local interactions. The concept of emergence is of particular importance and refers to the development of system-level dynamics (i.e., macrodynamics) such as social norms and institutions, social conformity, and compliance stemming from microprocesses such as agents interacting with each other and their environment (Railsback and Grimm 2011; Squazzoni 2012).[1]

Complexity is a bottom-up approach to theorizing and analyzing human behavior. That is, complexity emphasizes how small microinteractions can lead to much larger and possibly unanticipated or unpredictable consequences at the systemic level (Mitchell 2009). Criminologists will be most familiar with complex-type thinking through Schelling's (1971, 1978) racial segregation model. Schelling showed that even a small preference for one's neighbors to be of the same race could lead to total racial segregation at the macro-level. His model assumed that individuals in a neighborhood varied in their threshold or tolerance for racial mixing in the neighborhood. Once an individual's threshold had been met (e.g., >30 percent of houses were occupied by families of a different race), then that individual would move to a neighborhood in which the percentage of houses occupied by another race was within his or her personal threshold (e.g., ≤30 percent). Schelling's results suggested that the consequences of individual actions within the complex system of social ties among neighbors could lead to high levels of systemic segregation. The unanticipated result was that a person did not necessarily want to live in complete segregation nor even live in a neighborhood in which his or her own race was in the majority (Schelling 1971). However, the interdependence of individual decisions or preferences within a neighborhood led to segregated neighborhoods in which racial mixing was not reflective of individual intrapersonal preferences. Schelling's segregation model, along with Sakoda's (1971) work, is considered foundational to the maturation of computational social science through its application of cellular automata, a construct commonly used in the biological sciences (for a review, see Alber et al. 2003). For sociological questions, this application aids in the development of agent-based models of human behavior (Macal and North 2010).

B. Agent-Based Models

Agent-based models are part of the computational science tradition and draw upon research from game theory, complexity science, and distributed artificial intelligence (Gilbert 2008; Elsenbroich and Gilbert 2014). In this context, computation refers to building quantitative or mathematical models to study processes of, for example, real-life social phenomena such as crime via computer programming and simulation. The resulting models are utilized to understand dynamic complex systems and to make predictions about the micro and macro processes and behaviors contained therein (Yasar and Landau 2003).

Agent-based models consist of heterogeneous, autonomous yet interdependent agents, ones that act and interact with other agents in time and space, often within the theoretical framework of bounded rationality (Epstein 2006). Agents refer to units represented in the computation model who follow behavioral rules derived from empirical and theoretical insights of the topic under study (Macy et al. 2011). They are autonomous in that agents "have control over their own goals, behaviors, and internal states and take the initiative to change aspects of their environment to attain those goals" (Macy et al. 2011, p. 251). Unseen macrosocial forces do not control agents; instead, agents are involved in feedback loops leading to the co-evolution of micro- and macrosocial processes (Epstein 2006). Interdependence refers to agents being sources and receivers of behavioral influence from other agents to which they may have relational ties. Last, heterogeneity "relaxes the assumption in system dynamics models (and many game theoretic models as well) that populations are composed of representative agents" (Macy et al. 2011, p. 251). That is, individuals are allowed to differ in time and space across, for example, demographics, cognitive capabilities, and network position (Epstein 2006). In summary, agents can be programmed to perceive their environment, move in that environment, communicate with other agents and perform actions (e.g., stealing a weapon), and have memories of each of these experiences (Gilbert 2008).

The potential for multiple moving parts means that ABMs range from simple to complex representations of social realities, ranging from panic behavior in human collectives (Helbing et al. 2000) to neighborhood regeneration and individual burglary risk (Malleson et al. 2013). This flexibility aids ABMs' ability to answer the generativist's question: "How could the decentralized local interactions of heterogeneous autonomous agents generate the given regularity?" (Epstein 2006, p. 5). That is, how do individual actions and behaviors based on rules and personal preferences lead to the emergence of macro-level consistencies such as social norms? Herein lies one of the greatest strengths and reasons to use an ABM in the course of a research project as opposed to more familiar statistical models such as ordinary least squares regression or some form of differential equation. Mapping macro-level regularities to individual-level behaviors allows the researcher to discover the mechanisms by which the social phenomena can be explained (Epstein 2006; Macy et al. 2011). That is, not only can we ask the theoretical question of "why" we see criminal behavior but also we can show empirically "how" it comes about (Hedström 2005).

These features may advance the research program of A-SLT by helping to improve theory building on melioration and maximization through the development and testing of specific explanations for patterns of behavior through computational simulation, which can be compared to existing empirical data (Epstein 2006). This claim is particularly true for adaptive learning theories of decision making that include a temporal component such as bounded rationality (Gilbert 2008). As with a basic least-squares regression, ABMs are only as good as the researcher's theoretical understanding of the phenomena under examination. Both methods become intractable when unguided by sound theory, resulting in an overloaded uninterpretable model or inadequate representation of the social fact(s) under study. Emergent systemic properties will result only if relevant theory is clear and precise enough to program interacting agents reflective of those found in the real world. Failure to specify correctly the behavioral and interaction rules at the micro level will result in nonemergence and failure of the proposed model.

We next discuss the work of Elsenbroich and Gilbert (2014), which provides an example of a clearly defined research question related to juvenile delinquency, social norms, and social networks. The purpose of the study was to build an ABM of the phenomena of adolescent network clustering associated with personal delinquency. The study is grounded in theoretical and empirical work related to juvenile delinquency, social networks, social influence, and opinion dynamics. Elsenbroich and Gilbert (2014) draw upon the socialization and selection arguments posited by differential association theory (Sutherland 1947) and social bond theory (Hirschi 1969). Clustering of delinquent youth can be modeled to determine if it should be attributed to friends influencing friends or if it is due to delinquents selecting delinquents as friends. Importantly, the authors build in precise mechanisms to account for potential clustering due to influence or selection. The influence mechanism is based on research on opinion dynamics, which suggests that change in opinion to or away from another person's opinion is not absolute. This change can happen in two ways. First, influence (e.g., change) happens when two people already share similar but not exact opinions. Second, change may occur when one person has an opinion but is not confident of its correctness, whereas another (e.g., a friend) has an opposite or more divergent opinion from that of his or her counterpart but is also confident in being correct. Elsenbroich and Gilbert (2014) use these concepts to assign agents in the model different levels of propensity to commit crime (i.e., criminality), and simulate the effect of criminal propensity on criminal outcomes across varying levels of susceptibility to social influence.

One of the major strengths of ABMs and simulation is the ability to generate social networks through the interaction and movement of agents who have initial behavioral rules to follow but are adaptive learners as they move and interact with their environment inclusive of other agents. Elsenbroich and Gilbert (2014) added a network component by incorporating a social circle networks model (Hamill and Gilbert 2009; Hamill 2010), whereby networks were generated by agent interaction, and importantly those interactions and resulting influence could be accidental, purposeful, or from time spent together. Furthermore, network structural characteristics such as size, density, and transitivity were easily incorporated into the model in order to replicate real adolescent social networks.

The networks become dynamic with the addition of different movement rules. Elsenbroich and Gilbert (2014) stipulated that agents could move toward the agent who is most behaviorally similar or susceptible relative to themselves (i.e., selection) or toward the agent's group geometric centroid indicative of the notion of the peer group in theories of socialization. Importantly, the model also captures the nuance of adolescent friendship networks by also allowing agents to have the option to move away from others who are similar to themselves. The authors cite Simmel's (1957) description of the human need to be social and also unique and identifiable as an individual. This particular detail is an exemplar of the advantages of ABMs over their equation-based counterparts. In summary, this particular model captures specific individual-level social mechanisms related to movement in networks, behavioral change, selection effects, and social structure in an effort to account for clusters of delinquent youth in social networks.

Elsenbroich and Gilbert (2014) found that both socialization and selection account for delinquent clustering in social networks. This finding is not new to criminologists (Kandel 1978). However, the authors present further insight into their findings that highlights another strength of ABMs: the ability to turn the implemented theoretical mechanisms on and off at the micro-agent level in order to see the resulting effect on the networks' macrostructure. Elsenbroich and Gilbert summarize these ideas as follows:

> The initial research question for this model was to see whether we can replicate the clustering of delinquent agents through some simple mechanisms. . . . The model allows a theoretical exploration of criminological theories. If we run the model with maximal criminals moving away from their social circle, the selective movement, and the opinion dynamics turned off we obtain a high correlation between transience and criminality. If the movement is centroidal, the correlation persists but is weakened. On the other hand, if we turn the opinion dynamics on, i.e. run it as a social influence model, there is almost no correlation. (pp. 158–159)

In other words, the making and breaking of friendship ties suggested by Hirschi (1969), who stated that delinquent friendships tend to be "cold and brittle," is meaningful for network structure, as are other predictions from differential association. According to Elsenbroich and Gilbert,

> The implementations differ when it comes to the social abilities of criminals and non-criminals. The results concerning the correlation of criminality and transience of relationships correspond with Hirschi's prediction of higher transience of friendships for delinquents. The non-centroidal selection is meant to mirror Hirschi's theory and is the movement producing a strong correlation. That the correlation does not persist for the case of social influence fits well with Sutherland's differential association theory where criminal networks are the same as non-criminal networks. It is not the structures that differ but the moral values transmitted within those structures. (p. 159)

XI. Summary and Conclusion

Agent-based modeling does not completely absolve criminologists from finding a balance between parsimonious and realistic models of human behavior. Nor is ABM without its critics (for a succinct discussion, see Epstein 2006), but it does provide a new method that may help advance the development of melioration/maximization research as it applies to criminal behavior and corresponding applications to policy. ABM is flexible enough to prove useful to criminological theorists because agents can be designed to reflect micro-level decision-making processes inclusive of rational, boundedly rational, or A-SLT frameworks of crime and delinquency. The programing of microprocesses, of course, does not equate to dictating the macro-level outcomes of the model. ABM offers an established empirical and descriptive tool to criminologists for testing theories from the ground up instead of the top down, and mapping microbehaviors to macrosocial realities can be surprising and unpredictable (Axelrod 1997). This final observation is important given the many untested assumptions our equation-based models make in regard to the theoretical ties between various personal-level cognitions, emotions, attitudes, and other dynamic variables and both crime and criminality.

In conclusion, this work does not represent an update or even a major expansion of social learning theory. Rather, our purpose was to demonstrate that a theory used to examine how people learn to become deviant, delinquent, and criminal could provide insights into the decision-making process that leads them in one direction over another. However, in order to achieve these insights, criminologists must develop a better understanding of the influence of matching theory on choices made by offenders and ex-offenders. To effect changes in conduct, then, criminologists must understand the complex nature of the amelioration learning process that is occurring within the subject's social network. Consider, too, that Akers' (1998) social learning/social structure theory added a macro-level construct, the social structure most conducive to deviant learning. We examined what is in this context a meso-level construct, the actor's social network. Thus, we further contend that A-SLT's ability to provide insights into the creation of discriminative stimuli that guide conduct is enhanced when we simultaneously consider Hernnstein's matching law and note the significant role played by social networks in making decision. Whenever criminologists tinker with a major theory, one foreseeable outcome is the approbation of some of that theory's stakeholders and adherents. We suspect that our work will elicit similar responses, both from sociologically oriented criminologists who already disavow A-SLT operant conditioning roots and from psychologically oriented criminologist who view A-SLT as oversimplifying the processes at work. If we do nothing more than cause these groups to explore further our contentions, we will have achieved our goal.

NOTE

1. Not to be confused with the study of system dynamics (Ogata 2003) via macrosimulation techniques.

REFERENCES

Acemoglu, D., M. A. Dahleh, I. Lobel, and A. Ozdaglar. 2011. "Bayesian Learning in Social Networks." *Review of Economic Studies* 78(4): 1201–36.

Acemoglu, D., and A. Ozdaglar. 2010. "Opinion Dynamics and Learning in Social Networks." *Dynamic Games and Applications* 1(1): 3–49.

Adams, R. 1974. "The Adequacy of Differential Association Theory." *Journal of Research in Crime and Delinquency* 11(1): 1–8.

Ainslie, G. 1975. "Specious Reward: A Behavioral Theory of Impulsiveness and Impulse Control." *Psychological Bulletin* 82(4): 463.

Akers, R. L. 1973. *Deviant Behavior: A Social Learning Approach*. Belmont, CA: Wadsworth.

Akers, R. L. 1985. *Deviant Behavior: A Social Learning Approach*, 3rd ed. Belmont, CA: Wadsworth.

Akers, R. L. 1990. "Rational Choice, Deterrence, and Social Learning Theory in Criminology: The Path Not Taken." *Journal of Criminal Law and Criminology* 81(3): 653–76.

Akers, R. L. 1991. "Self-control as a General Theory of Crime." *Journal of Quantitative Criminology* 7(2): 201–11.

Akers, R. L. 1998. *Social Learning and Social Structure: A General Theory of Crime and Deviance*. Boston: Northeastern University Press.

Akers, R. L. 2011. "The Origins of Me and of Social Learning Theory: Personal and Professional Recollections and Reflections." In *The Origins of American Criminology, Advances in Criminology Theory*, edited by T. Cullen, C. Lero Jonson, A. J. Myer, and F. Adler, vol. 16, pp. 347–66. New Brunswick, NJ: Transaction Publishers.

Akers, R. L., and C. Sellers. 2013. *Criminological Theories: Introduction, Evaluation, and Application*, 5th ed. New York: Oxford University Press.

Alber, M. S., M. A. Kiskowski, J. A. Glazier, and Y. Jiang. 2003. "On Cellular Automaton Approaches to Modeling Biological Cells. In *Mathematical Systems Theory in Biology,*

Communication, and Finance, IMA vol. 134, edited by J. Rosenthal and D. S. Gilliam, pp. 1–39. New York: Springer.

Almy, B., and J. I. Krueger. 2013. "Game Interrupted: The Rationality of Considering the Future." *Judgment and Decision Making* 8(5): 521–26.

Axelrod, R. M. 1997. *The Complexity of Cooperation: Agent-Based Models of Competition and Collaboration*. Princeton, NJ: Princeton University Press.

Baddeley, M. 2010. "Herding, Social Influence and Economic Decision-Making: Socio-Psychological and Neuroscientific Analyses." *Philosophical Transactions of the Royal Society B: Biological Sciences* 365(1538): 281–90.

Bala, V., and S. Goyal. 1998. "Learning from Neighbours." *The Review of Economic Studies* 65(3): 595–621.

Bala, V., and S. Goyal. 2000. "A Noncooperative Model of Network Formation." *Econometrica* 68(5): 1181–1229.

Bandura, A. 1969. "Social-Learning Theory of Identificatory Processes." In *Handbook of Socialization Theory and Research*, edited by D. A. Goslin, pp. 213–62. Chicago: Rand McNally.

Bandura, A. 1977. *Social Learning Theory*. Englewood Cliffs, NJ: Prentice Hall.

Bandura, A. 1985. *Social Foundations of Thought and Action: A Social Cognitive Theory*. Englewood Cliffs, NJ: Prentice Hall.

Bandura, A. 1989. "Human Agency in Social Cognitive Theory." *American Psychologist* 44(9): 1175–84.

Bandura, A. 2001. "Social Cognitive Theory: An Agentic Perspective." *Annual Review of Psychology* 52:1–26.

Bandura, A., D. Ross, and S. Ross. 1961. "Transmission of Aggression Through Imitation of Aggressive Models." *Journal of Abnormal and Social Psychology* 63(3): 575–82.

Bandura, A., and R. H. Walters.1963. *Social Learning and Personality Development*, vol. 14. New York: Holt, Rinehart and Winston.

Banerjee, A. 1992. "A Simple Model of Herd Behavior." *Quarterly Journal of Economics* 107(3): 797–817.

Baum, W. M. 1974. "On Two Types of Deviation from the Matching Law: Bias and Undermatching." *Journal of the Experimental Analysis of Behavior* 22(1): 231–42.

Baum, W. M. 1979. "Matching, Undermatching, and Overmatching in Studies of Choice." *Journal of the Experimental Analysis of Behavior* 32: 269–81.

Baum, W. M. 1981. "Optimization and the Matching Law as Accounts of Instrumental Behavior." *Journal of the Experimental Analysis of Behavior* 36(3): 387–403.

Baum, W. M. 1994. *Understanding Behaviorism: Science, Behavior, and Culture*. New York: Harper Collins.

Bayes, Mr., and Mr. Price. 1763. "An Essay Towards Solving a Problem in the Doctrine of Chances. By the Late Rev. Mr. Bayes, FRS communicated by Mr. Price, in a Letter to John Canton, AMFRS." *Philosophical Transactions (1683–1775)* 53:370–418.

Becker, G. 1968. "Crime and Punishment: An Economic Approach." *Journal of Political Economy* 76(2): 169–217.

Bikhchandani, S., D. Hirshleifer, and I. Welch. 1992. "A Theory of Fads, Fashion, Custom, and Cultural Change as Informational Cascades." *Journal of Political Economy*, 100(5): 992–1026.

Bordens, K. S., and B. A. Abbott. 2011. *A Process Approach to Research Design and Methods*. New York: McGraw-Hill.

Borgatti, S. P., M. G. Everett, and J. C. Johnson. 2013. *Analyzing Social Networks*. Thousand Oaks, CA: Sage.

Boudon, R. 2003. "Beyond Rational Choice Theory." *Annual Review of Sociology* 29(1): 1–21.

Breen, R., and C. García-Peñalosa. 2002. "Bayesian Learning and Gender Segregation." *Journal of Labor Economics* 20(4): 899–922.

Brenner, T. 2006. "Agent Learning Representation: Advice on Modelling Economic Learning". In *Handbook of Computational Economics*, vol. 2, edited by L. Tesfatsion and K. Judd, pp. 895–948. New York: Springer-Verlag.

Brenner, T., and U. Witt. 2003. "Melioration Learning in Games with Constant and Frequency-Dependent Pay-Offs." *Journal of Economic Behavior and Organization* 50(4): 429–48.

Brezina, T. 2002. "Assessing the Rationality of Criminal and Delinquent Behavior: A Focus on Actual Utility." In *Rational Choice and Criminal Behavior*, edited by A. Piquero and S. Tibbetts, pp. 244–64. New York: Routledge.

Burgess, R., and R. Akers. 1966. "A Differential Association-Reinforcement Theory of Criminal Behavior. *Social Problems* 14(2): 128–47.

Cairns, R., and B. Cairns. 1994. *Lifelines and Risks: Pathways of Youth in Our Time.* New York: Cambridge University Press.

Camerer, C. 1999. "Behavioral Economics: Reunifying Psychology and Economics." *Proceedings of the National Academy of Sciences of the USA* 96(19): 10575–577.

Camerer, C. 2003. "The Behavioral Challenge to Economics: Understanding Normal People." Paper presented at the Federal Reserve Bank of Boston 48th Economic Conference on How Humans Behave: Implications for Economics and Policy, June.

Camerer, C. 2007. "Neuroeconomics: Using Neuroscience to Make Economic Predictions." *Economic Journal* 117(519): C26–C42.

Camerer, C., and G. Loewenstein. 2004. "Behavioral Economics: Past, Present, Future." In *Advances in Behavioral Economics*, edited by C. Camerer, G. Loewenstein, and M. Rabin, pp. 3–51. Princeton, NJ: Princeton University Press.

Camerer, C., G. Loewenstein, and D. Prelec. 2004. "Neuroeconomics: Why Economics Needs Brains." *Scandinavian Journal of Economics* 106(3): 555–79.

Carrington, P. 2011. "Crime and Social Network Analysis." In *The Sage Handbook of Social Network Analysis*, edited by J. Scott and P. Carrington, pp. 236–255. London: Sage.

Çelen, B., and S. Kariv. 2004. "Distinguishing Informational Cascades from Herd Behavior in the Laboratory." *American Economic Review* 94(3): 484–98.

Chandrasekhar, A. G., C. Kinnan, and H. Larreguy. 2014. *Social Networks as Contract Enforcement: Evidence from a Lab Experiment in the Field*, no. w20259. Cambridge, MA: National Bureau of Economic Research.

Choi, S., D. Gale, and S. Kariv. 2012. "Social Learning in Networks: A Quantal Response Equilibrium Analysis of Experimental Data." *Review of Economic Design* 16(2-3): 135–57.

Conley, T., and C. Udry. 2001. "Social Learning Through Networks: The Adoption of New Agricultural Technologies in Ghana." *American Journal of Agricultural Economics* 83(3): 668–73.

Cooper, J., A. Walsh, and L. Ellis. 2010. "Is Criminology Moving Toward a Paradigm Shift? Evidence from a Survey of the American Society of Criminology." *Journal of Criminal Justice Education* 21(3): 332–47.

Corazzini, L., F. Pavesi, B. Petrovich, and L. Stanca. 2012. "Influential Listeners: An Experiment on Persuasion Bias in Social Networks." *European Economic Review* 56(6): 1276–88.

Cornish, D. B., and R. V. Clarke, eds. 2014. *The Reasoning Criminal: Rational Choice Perspectives on Offending*. Herndon, VA: Transaction Publishers.

Cressey, D. R. 1965. "Social Psychological Foundations for Using Criminals in the Rehabilitation of Criminals." *Journal of Research in Crime and Delinquency* 2(2): 49–59.

Davidson, D. 2004. *Problems of Rationality*, vol. 4. Oxford: Oxford University Press.

Davidson, M., and D. McCarthy. 1988. *The Matching Law*. Hillsdale, NJ: Erlbaum.

Dawes, R. M. 1988. *Rational Choice in an Uncertain World*. San Diego, CA: Harcourt Brace.

DeGroot, M. 1974. "Reaching a Consensus." *Journal of the American Statistical Association* 69(345): 118–21.

Demarzo, P., D. Vayanos, and J. Zwiebel. 2003. "Persuasion Bias, Social Influence, and Unidimensional Opinions." *Quarterly Journal of Economics* 118(3): 909–68.

Ellis, L., and A. Cooper. 1999. "Criminologists' Opinions About the Causes and Theories of Crime and Delinquency." *The Criminologist* 24(4): 1, 14, 26–27.

Ellis, L., Jonathon A. Cooper, and A. Walsh. 2008. "Criminologists' Opinions about Causes and Theories of Crime and Delinquency: A Follow-Up." The Criminologist. Available at: http://works.bepress.com/anthony_walsh/47/

Elsenbroich, C., and N. Gilbert. 2014. *Modelling Norms*. Dordrecht, the Netherlands: Springer.

Epstein, J. M. 2006. *Generative Social Science: Studies in Agent-Based Computational Modeling*. Princeton, NJ: Princeton University Press.

Fisher, W., and J. Mazur. 1997. "Basic and Applied Research on Choice Responding." *Journal of Applied Behavior Analysis* 30(3): 387–410.

Flores, R., M. Koster, I. Lindner, and E. Molina. 2012. "Networks and Collective Action." *Social Networks* 34(4): 570–84.

Friedkin, N. 1982. "Information Flow Through Strong and Weak Ties in Intraorganizational Social Networks." *Social Networks* 3(4): 273–85.

Friedkin, N. 1991. "Theoretical Foundations for Centrality Measures." *American Journal of Sociology* 96(6): 1478–1504.

Friedman, M. 1953. *Essays in Positive Economics. Part I - The Methodology of Positive Economics*. Chicago: University of Chicago Press.

Frongillo, R. M., G. Schoenebeck, and O. Tamuz. 2011. "Social Learning in a Changing World." *Internet and Network Economics* 7090:146–57.

Fujita, K., Y. Trope, N. Liberman, and M. Levin-Sagi. 2006. "Construal Levels and Self-Control." *Journal of Personality and Social Psychology* 90(3): 351–67.

Gale, D., and S. Kariv. 2003. "Bayesian Learning in Social Networks." *Games and Economic Behavior* 45(2): 329–46.

Gigerenzer, G. 2004. "Striking a Blow for Sanity in Theories of Rationality." In *Models of a Man: Essays in Memory of Herbert A. Simon*, edited by M. Augier and J. G. March, pp. 389–409. Cambridge, MA: MIT Press.

Gigerenzer, G., and R. Selten, eds. 2001. *Bounded Rationality: The Adaptive Toolbox*. Cambridge, MA: MIT Press.

Gilbert, G. N. 2008. *Agent-Based Models*, no. 153. Thousand Oaks, CA: Sage.

Golub, B., and M. Jackson. 2010. "Naïve Learning in Social Networks and the Wisdom of Crowds." *American Economic Journal: Microeconomics* 2(1): 112–49.

Gottfredson, M., and T. Hirschi. 1990. *A General Theory of Crime*. Stanford, CA: Stanford University Press.

Granovetter, M. 1973. "The Strength of Weak Ties." *American Journal of Sociology* 78(6): 1360–80.

Granovetter, M. 1985. "Economic Action and Social Structure: The Problem of Embeddedness." *American Journal of Sociology* 91(3): 481–510.

Granovetter, M. 1992. "Problems of Explanation in Economic Sociology." *Networks and Organizations: Structure, Form, and Action* 25: 56.

Grynaviski, J. 2006. "A Bayesian Learning Model with Applications to Party Identification." *Journal of Theoretical Politics* 18(3): 323–46.

Hamill, L. 2010. "Agent-Based Modelling: The Next 15 Years." *Journal of Artificial Societies and Social Simulation* 13(4): 7.

Hamill, L., and N. Gilbert. 2009. "Social Circles: A Simple Structure for Agent-Based Social Network Models." *Journal of Artificial Societies and Social Simulation* 12(2): 3.

Hastie, R. 2001. "Problems for Judgment and Decision Making." *Annual Review of Psychology* 52(1): 653–83.

Hausman, D., and M. McPherson. 2006. *Economic Analysis and Moral Philosophy*, 2nd ed. Cambridge: Cambridge University Press.

Hechter, M., and S. Kanazawa. 1997. "Sociological Rational Choice Theory." *Annual Review of Sociology* 23:191–214.

Hedström, P. 2005. *Dissecting the Social: On the Principles of Analytical Sociology*. Cambridge: Cambridge University Press.

Heider, F. 1958. *The Psychology of Interpersonal Relations*. New York: Wiley.

Herrnstein, R. J. 1961. "Relative and Absolute Strength of Response as a Function of Frequency of Reinforcement." *Journal of the Experimental Analysis of Behavior* 4(3): 267–72.

Herrnstein, R. J. 1970. "On the Law of Effect." *Journal of the Experimental Analysis of Behavior* 13: 243–66.

Herrnstein, R. J. 1974. "Formal Properties of the Matching Law." *Journal of the Experimental Analysis of Behavior* 21(1): 159–64.

Herrnstein, R. J. 1982. "Melioration as Behavior Dynamics." In *Quantitative Analysis of Behavior, Vol. II: Matching and Maxizing Accounts*, edited by R. L. Commons, R. J. Herrnstein, and H. Rachlin, pp. 433–58. Cambridge, MA: Ballinger Publishing.

Herrnstein, R. J. 1990. "Behavior, Reinforcement and Utility." *Psychological Science* 1(4): 217–24.

Herrnstein, R. J., G. Loewenstein, D. Prelec, and W. Vaughan. 1993. "Utility Maximization and Melioration: Internalities in Individual Choice." *Journal of Behavioral Decision Making* 6(3): 149–85.

Herrnstein, R. J., and D. Prelec. 1991. "Melioration: A Theory of Distributed Choice." *Journal of Economic Perspectives* 5(3): 137–56.

Herrnstein, R. J., and D. Prelec. 1992. *Melioration*. New York: Russell Sage Foundation.

Herrnstein, R. J., H. Rachlin, and D. I. Laibson. 1997. *The Matching Law: Papers in Psychology and Economics*. New York: Russell Sage Foundation.

Herrnstein, R. J., and W. Vaughan. 1980. "Melioration and Behavioral Allocation." In *Limits to Action: The Allocation of Individual Behavior*, edited by J. E. R. Staddon, pp. 143–76. New York: Academic Press.

Hirschi, T. 1969. *Causes of Delinquency*. Berkeley: University of California Press.

Hirschi, T. 1989. "Exploring Alternatives to Integrated Theory." In *Theoretical Integration in the Study of Deviance and Crime: Problems and Prospects*, edited by S. Messner, M. Krohn, and A. Liska, pp. 37–49. Albany: State University of New York Press.

Hoppitt, W., and K. Laland. 2013. *Social Learning: An Introduction to Mechanisms, Methods, and Models*. Princeton, NJ: Princeton University Press.

Jackson, M. 2007. "*Literature Review:* The Study of Social Networks in Economics." In *The Missing Links: Formation and Decay of Economic Networks*, edited by J. Rauch, pp. 19–43. New York: Russell Sage Foundation.

Jackson, M. 2008. *Social and Economic Networks*. Princeton, NJ: Princeton University Press.

Jackson, M., and A. Watts. 2002. "The Evolution of Social and Economic Networks." *Journal of Economic Theory* 106(2): 265–95.

Jones, B. D. 1999. "Bounded Rationality." *Annual Review of Political Science* 2(1): 297–321.

Kahneman, D. 2003. "A Perspective on Judgment and Choice: Mapping Bounded Rationality." *American Psychologist* 58(9): 697–720.

Kahneman, D., and A. Tversky. 1972. "Subjective Probability: A Judgment of Representativeness." *Cognitive Psychology* 3(3): 430–54.

Kahneman, D., and A. Tversky. 1973. "On the Psychology of Prediction." *Psychological Review* 80(4): 237.

Kahneman, D., and A. Tversky. 1979. "Prospect Theory: An Analysis of Decision Under Risk." *Econometrica* 47(2): 263–92.

Kandel, D. B. 1978. "Homophily, Selection, and Socialization in Adolescent Friendships." *American Journal of Sociology* 84(2): 427–36.

Klochko, M. 2006. "Time Preference and Learning Versus Selection: A Case Study of Ukrainian Students." *Rationality and Society* 18(3): 305–31.

Laland, K. 2001. "Imitation, Social Learning, and Preparedness as Mechanisms of Bounded Rationality." In *Bounded Rationality: The Adaptive Toolbox*, edited by G. Gigerenzer and R. Selten, pp. 233–247. Cambridge, MA: MIT Press.

Leathers, H., and M. Smale. 1991. "A Bayesian Approach to Explaining Sequential Adoption of Components of a Technological Package." *American Journal of Agricultural Economics* 73(3): 734–42.

Listokin, Y. 2007. "Crime and (with a Lag) Punishment: Equitable Sentencing and the Implications of Discounting. *SSRN Electronic Journal*.

Loewenstein, G. 1996. "Out of Control: Visceral Influences on Behavior." *Organizational Behavior and Human Decision Processes* 65(3): 272–92.

Loewenstein, G., and D. Prelec. 1992. "Anomalies in intertemporal choice: Evidence and an interpretation." *Quarterly Journal of Economics* 107(2): 573–97.

Loughran, T., R. Paternoster, A. Piquero, and J. Fagan. 2012. "A Good Man Always Knows His Limitations: The Role of Overconfidence in Criminal Offending." *Journal of Research in Crime and Delinquency* 50(3): 327–58.

Loughran, T., R. Paternoster, A. R. Piquero, and G. Pogarsky. 2011. "On Ambiguity in Perceptions of Risk: Implications for Criminal Decision-Making and Deterrence." *Criminology* 49: 1029–61.

Loughran, T., R. Paternoster, and D. Weiss. 2012. "Hyperbolic Time Discounting, Offender Time Preferences and Deterrence." *Journal of Quantitative Criminology* 28(4): 607–28.

Loughran, T., and R. Piquero. 2013. "Individual Differences and Deterrence." Paper presented at the American Society of Criminology. Atlanta, GA.

Loughran, T., G. Pogarsky, A. Piquero, and R. Paternoster. 2012. "Re-Examining the Functional Form of the Certainty Effect in Deterrence Theory." *Justice Quarterly* 29(5): 712–41.

Macal, C. M., and M. J. North. 2010. "Tutorial on Agent-Based Modelling and Simulation." *Journal of Simulation* 4(3): 151–62.

Macy, M. W., 2006. "Rational Choice." In *Contemporary Social Psychological Theories*, edited by P. Burke, pp. 70–87. Stanford, CA: Stanford University Press.

Macy, M. W., D. Centola, A. Flache, and R. Willer. 2011. "Social Mechanisms and Generative Explanations: Computational Models with Double Agents." In *Analytical Sociology and Social Mechanisms*, edited by P. Demeulenaere, pp. 250–65. Cambridge: Cambridge University Press.

Macy, M. W., and A. Flache. 1995. "Beyond Rationality in Models of Choice." *Annual Review of Sociology* 21(1): 73–91.

Macy, M. W., and R. Willer. 2002. "From Factors to Actors: Computational Sociology and Agent-Based Modeling." *Annual Review of Sociology* 28:143–66.

Matsueda, R., D. Kreager, and D. Huizinga. 2006. "Deterring Delinquents: A Rational Choice Model of Theft and Violence." *American Sociological Review* 71(1): 95–122.

McCarthy, B. 2002. "New Economics of Sociological Criminology." *Annual Review of Sociology* 28:417–42.

McDowell, J. J. 1989. "Two Modern Developments in Matching Theory. *The Behavior Analyst* 12(2): 153.

McDowell, J. J. 2005. "On the Classic and Modern Theories of Matching." *Journal of the Experimental Analysis of Behavior* 84(1): 111–27.

McDowell, J. J. 2013. "On the Theoretical and Empirical Status of the Matching Law and Matching Theory." *Psychological Bulletin* 139:1000–28.

McFadden, D. 2001. "Economic Choices." *American Economic Review* 91(3): 351–78.

Meseguer, C. 2006. "Rational Learning and Bounded Learning in the Diffusion of Policy Innovations." *Rationality and Society* 18(1): 35–66.

Metcalfe, J., and W. Mischel. 1999. "A Hot/Cool-System Analysis of Delay of Gratification: Dynamics of Willpower." *Psychological Review* 106(1): 3–19.

Moscati, I., and P. Tubaro. 2011. "Becker Random Behavior and the As-If Defense of Rational Choice Theory in Demand Analysis. *Journal of Economic Methodology* 18(2): 107–28.

Mitchell, M. 2009. *Complexity: A Guided Tour*. New York: Oxford University Press.

Nagin, D. S., and R. Paternoster. 1993. "Enduring Individual Differences and Rational Choice Theories of Crime." *Law and Society Review* 27(3): 467–96.

Nagin, D. S., and R. Paternoster. 1994. "Personal Capital and Social Control: The Deterrence Implications of a Theory of Individual Differences in Criminal Offending." *Criminology* 32(4): 581–606.

Nagin, D. S., and G. Pogarsky. 2004. "Time and Punishment: Delayed Consequences and Criminal Behavior." *Journal of Quantitative Criminology* 20(4): 295–317.

Nau, R. 1999. "Arbitrage, Incomplete Models, and Other People's Brains." In *Beliefs, Interactions and Preferences in Decision Making*, edited by M. J. Machina and B. Munier, pp. 217–36. New York: Springer.

Neth, H., C. R. Sims, and W. D. Gray. 2006. "Melioration Dominates Maximization: Stable Suboptimal Performance Despite Global Feedback. In *Proceedings of the 28th Annual Meeting of the Cognitive Science Society*, pp. 627–32. Hove, UK: Psychology Press.

O'Donoghue, T., and M. Rabin. 2001. "Choice and Procrastination." *Quarterly Journal of Economics* 116(1): 121–60.

Ogata, K. 2003. *System Dynamics*. Upper Saddle River, NJ: Prentice Hall.

Opp, K.-D. 1997. "'Limited Rationality' and Crime." In *Rational Choice and Situational Crime Prevention*, edited by G. Newman, R. Clarke, and S. Shoham, pp. 47–63. Brookfield, VT: Ashgate.

Piquero, A., R. Paternoster, G. Pogarsky, and T. Loughran. 2011. "Elaborating the Individual Difference Component in Deterrence Theory." *Annual Review of Law and Social Science* 7(1): 335–60.

Pogarsky, G. 2009. "Deterrence and Decision Making: Research Questions and Theoretical Refinements." In *Handbook on Crime and Deviance*, edited by M. D. Krohn, A. J. Lizotte, and G. P. Hall, pp. 241–58. New York: Springer.

Pratt, T. C., F. T. Cullen, C. S. Sellers, L. T. Winfree Jr., T. D. Madensen, L. E. Daigle, and J. M. Gau. 2010. "The Empirical Status of Social Learning Theory: A Meta-Analysis." *Justice Quarterly* 27(6): 765–802.

Railsback, S. F., and V. Grimm. 2011. *Agent-Based and Individual-Based Modeling: A Practical Introduction*. Princeton, NJ: Princeton University Press.

Reed, D. D., and B. A. Kaplan. 2011. "The Matching Law: A Tutorial for Practitioners." *Behavior Analysis in Practice* 4(2): 15–24.

Rotter, J. 1954. *Social Learning and Clinical Psychology*. New York: Prentice Hall.

Sakai, Y., and T. Fukai. 2008. "The Actor–Critic Learning Is Behind the Matching Law: Matching Versus Optimal Behaviors." *Neural Computation* 20(1): 227–51.

Sakoda, J. M. 1971. "The Checkerboard Model of Social Interaction." *Journal of Mathematical Sociology* 1(1): 119–32.

Salvatore, D. 2008. *Microeconomics: Theory and Applications*, 5th ed. New York: Oxford University Press.

Schelling, T. C. 1971. "Dynamic Models of Segregation." *Journal of Mathematical Sociology* 1(2): 143–86.

Schelling, T. C. 1978. *Micromotives and Macrobehavior*. New York: Norton.

Schelling, T. C. 1992. "Addictive Drugs: The Cigarette Experience." *Science* 255(5043): 430–33.

Sellers, C. S., L. T. Winfree Jr., and R. L. Akers. 2012. *Social Learning Theories of Crime*. Burlington, VT: Ashgate.

Selten, R. 2001. "What Is Bounded Rationality." In *Bounded Rationality: The Adaptive Toolbox*, edited by G. Gigerenzer, and R. Selten. Cambridge, MA: MIT Press.

Shafir, E., and R. A. LeBoeuf. 2002. "Rationality." *Annual Review of Psychology* 53(1): 491–517.

Shanks, D., R. Tunney, and J. McCarthy. 2002. "A Re-examination of Probability Matching and Rational Choice." *Journal of Behavioral Decision Making* 15(3): 233–50.

Simmel, G. 1908. *Soziologie: Untersuchungen über die Formen der Vergesellschaftung*. Leipzig: Duncker & Humblot.

Simmel, G. 1957. "Fashion." *American Journal of Sociology* 62(6): 541–58.

Simon, H. A. 1955. "A Behavioral Model of Rational Choice." *Quarterly Journal of Economics* 69(1): 99–118.

Simon, H. A. 1956. "Rational Choice and the Structure of the Environment." *Psychological Review* 63(2): 129–38.

Simon, H. A. 1962. "The Architecture of Complexity." *Proceedings of the American Philosophical Society* 106(6): 467–82.

Sims, C., H. Neth, R. Jacobs, and W. Gray. 2013. "Melioration as Rational Choice: Sequential Decision Making in Uncertain Environments." *Psychological Review* 120(1): 139–54.

Skinner, B. F. 1955. "Freedom and the Control of Men." *The American Scholar* 25: 47–65.

Skinner, B. F. 1963. "Behaviorism at Fifty: The Rapid Growth of a Scientific Analysis of Behavior Calls for a Restatement of the Philosophy of Psychology." *Science* 140(3570): 951–58.

Skinner, B. F. 1974. "Behavior Modification." *Science* 185(4154): 813.

Smith, V. L. 2003. "Constructivist and Ecological Rationality in Economics." *American Economic Review* 93(3): 465–508.

Snyder, J. J., and G. R. Patterson. 1995. "Individual Differences in Social Aggression: A Test of a Reinforcement Model of Socialization in the Natural Environment." *Behavior Therapy* 26(2): 371–91.

Squazzoni, F. 2012. *Agent-Based Computational Sociology*. New York: Wiley.

Stitt, B. G., and D. J. Giacopassi. 1992. "Trends in the Connectivity of Theory and Research in Criminology?" *The Criminologist* 17:1, 3–6.

Sugden, R. 1991. "Rational Choice: A Survey of Contributions from Economics and Philosophy." *Economic Journal* 101(407): 751–85.

Sutherland, E. H. 1947. *Principles of Criminology*, 4th ed. Philadelphia: Lippincott.

Sutherland, E. H., and D. R. Cressey. 1974. *Criminology*, 9th ed. Philadelphia: Lippincott.

Tittle, C. 1980. *Sanctions and Social Deviance: The Question of Deterrence*. New York: Praeger.

Trope, Y., and A. Fishbach. 2000. "Counteractive Self-Control in Overcoming Temptation." *Journal of Personality and Social Psychology* 79(4): 493–506.

Tunney, R., and D. Shanks. 2002. "A Re-examination of Melioration and Rational Choice." *Journal of Behavioral Decision Making* 15(4): 291–311.

Walsh, A., and L. Ellis. 1999. "Political Ideology and American Criminologists' Explanations for Criminal Behavior." *Criminologist* 24:1, 14.

Wasserman, S., and K. Faust. 1994. *Social Network Analysis: Methods and Applications*. Cambridge: Cambridge University Press.

Watts, D. 2002. "A Simple Model of Global Cascades on Random Networks." *Proceedings of the National Academy of Sciences of the USA* 99(9): 5766–71.

Williams, K., and R. Hawkins. 1986. "Perceptual Research on General Deterrence: A Critical Review." *Law and Society Review* 20(4): 545–72.

Winfree, L. T., Jr., and H. Abadinsky. 2017. *Essentials of Criminological Theory*, 4th ed. Long Grove, IL: Waveland Press.

Yasar, O., and R. H. Landau. 2003. "Elements of Computational Science and Engineering Education." *SIAM Review* 45(4): 787–805.

Young, J., and C. Rees. 2012. "Social Networks and Delinquency in Adolescence: Implications for Life-Course Criminology." In *Handbook of Life-Course Criminology*, edited by C. L. Gibson and M. D. Krohn, pp. 159–80. New York: Springer.

Zeng, D., and K. Sycara. 1998. "Bayesian Learning in Negotiation." *International Journal of Human-Computer Studies* 48(1): 125–41.

CHAPTER 15

....

VICTIM SELECTION

....

MARGIT AVERDIJK

I. INTRODUCTION

....

WHY do offenders select particular people to be the victims of crime? Why do they not pick others? As a topic of both theoretical and practical interest, the etiology of victimization has gained considerable research attention in the past four decades. Not only have victimization studies emerged as "an indispensable core of criminological research" (Lauritsen 2010, p. 501) but risk factors for victimization have been studied in the fields of psychology, sociology, social work, public health, and developmental science. In addition, studies on offending have contributed to our knowledge of victimization because they sometimes provide information about offenders' take on the role of victim characteristics and behavior in the occurrence of crime.

Together, this body of research has produced knowledge about key correlates of victimization and the question of who is most at risk. However, due to the vastness of the literature, the diversity of the involved scientific disciplines, and data limitations, it is not easy to provide a clear-cut answer to the question of why some individuals are selected to be the victims of crime and others are not. This chapter aims to answer this question by reviewing the literature on the role of victim characteristics, the victim–offender relationship, and victim behavior in offender decision making.

For some, the topic of victim selection has the unmistakable connotation of victim blaming because it focuses on the causal role of victim characteristics in the occurrence of crime. However, cause and blame should never be confused, and because the goal of a scientific study of crime is to better understand how crime and victimization come about, blameworthiness is irrelevant (Felson 1993). Moreover, knowledge about which particular characteristics increase victimization risk can inform us about the usefulness and most promising application of prevention techniques.

This chapter comprises four sections. The first section discusses the conceptual framework. The second section introduces data sources that have been used to investigate victim selection. The next section presents an overview of empirical findings. The final section concludes by discussing several research gaps and potential future directions in the field. Because this handbook focuses on crime, this chapter concentrates on criminal victimization. Furthermore, it focuses on human victims only and does not consider how characteristics of organizations or objects, such as houses, cars, and bicycles, affect offender decision making.

II. Theoretical Perspectives on Victim Selection

Several theoretical perspectives have been proposed to better understand how offenders select victims. The most often used is opportunity theory, which has given rise to the structural–choice theory of victim selection. The second is social interactionism, which has been proposed to better understand dispute-related violence. The third is the concept of target congruence, which combines certain aspects of the previous two perspectives but has received less criminological attention.

A. The Structural–Choice Model of Victim Selection

The structural–choice model of victim selection (Miethe and Meier 1990) is grounded in the dominant criminological victimization theories, namely lifestyle and routine activities theories (Hindelang, Gottfredson, and Garofalo 1978; Cohen and Felson 1979; van Dijk and Steinmetz 1980; Gottfredson 1984; Hough 1987), which have been united into an opportunity theory of predatory victimization (Cohen, Kluegel, and Land 1981). The theory is compatible with rational choice theory (Cornish and Clarke 2008) in the sense that offenders are not assumed to pick their victims randomly but, rather, to base their targeting decisions on cues about expected rewards and resistance.

According to the structural–choice model, the victim selection process consists of two steps (Miethe and Meier 1990). First, a potential victim must come into contact with an offender. The likelihood with which this is the case is determined by an individual's level of proximity (physical closeness) and exposure (physical visibility and accessibility) to a potential offender (Cohen et al. 1981). Second, given that an individual comes into contact with an offender, the offender has to select him or her as the victim. In this step, the offender assesses the "value" of a potential victim ("target attractiveness") and the level of guardianship in the particular situation to decide whether or not to commit the crime.

The elements of the first step, proximity and exposure, make up the structural part of the model because they predispose certain individuals (those who are physically close to offenders and those with risky lifestyles) to elevated victimization risk. Factors influencing proximity and exposure include people's location of residence and geographic area and their everyday activities, both of which have received much attention in the victimization literature. Rather than directly informing offender decision making, however, high proximity and exposure can be viewed as forming a precondition for victim selection because they bring victim and offender into contact. Therefore, these aspects are not considered further here; readers are referred to prior research that has demonstrated that exposure and proximity are both linked to increased victimization risk (Spano and Freilich 2009; Averdijk and Bernasco 2015).

Target attractiveness and guardianship comprise the choice part of the model and thus directly inform the topic of this chapter. Because empirical research and theory development on guardianship are discussed in other chapters in this handbook, this chapter focuses on target attractiveness, which refers to the instrumental or symbolic value of a target and its perceived inertia, including its weight, size, and potential to resist (Cohen et al. 1981).

The effect of target attractiveness on crime occurrence varies as a function of crime type (Cohen et al. 1981; Cornish and Clarke 2008). According to Cohen et al., the effects of victim characteristics on mostly instrumental crimes, such as burglary and larceny, are larger than those on mostly expressive crimes, such as assault; in fact, these authors equated the effect of target attractiveness on assault to zero. One important reason underlying this assumed null effect is the operationalization of target attractiveness in opportunity approaches; these approaches usually focus on a person's economic value, such as income and socioeconomic status, which are less important for victim selection in mostly expressive crimes. However, it can be argued that for the latter type of crimes, other types of victim characteristics besides economic value play an important role in victim selection, and these are of central focus in social interactionism.

B. Social Interactionism

The structural–choice theory of victim selection is most applicable to predatory stranger crimes, for which the routine activity approach was initially designed. In these crimes, offenders are opportunistic and victims are substitutable as long as certain criteria are fulfilled (Felson 1993; Dugan and Apel 2005). Victims and offenders are generally unknown to each other, there is no prior dispute, and offender motivation is treated as given.

On the other end of the spectrum, however, are the purely deliberate targeting strategies, in which offenders purposely select a specific victim. If this victim is not available, the occurrence of crime is unlikely. Here, victim selection is based on a prior victim–offender relationship or interaction, which often (but not always) includes disputes that involve provocation and retaliation. In these cases, it is difficult to separate the role of offender motivation from victim characteristics in victim selection. In order to explain victim selection in deliberate targeting strategies, situated transaction (Luckenbill 1977) or social interactionist (Felson 1993) theories have been offered. These explain violence as social behavior and analyze chains of interactions between the victim and the offender. A typical chain begins with an insult of one antagonist on the other, who then responds with violence, in turn leading to escalation. Due to the reciprocal nature of these incidents, victims and offenders are not easily distinguished.

Dispute-related violence can be viewed as the consequence of individuals feeling aggrieved over a perceived wrongdoing and their legitimate and justifiable response (Felson 1993). The response consists of punishment with the purpose of either deterring the wrongdoer and others from a repeat offense or doing justice. Thus, deterrence, retribution, and defensive self-representations to "save face" are the central motivations underlying dispute-related violence. Social interactionism is compatible with routine activities theory because both center on situations and consider the victim's role important in understanding crime (Felson 1993).

C. Target Congruence

An alternative interpretation of target attractiveness has been offered by Finkelhor (2008; Finkelhor and Asdigian 1996), who proposed the term "target congruence" to cover the match between an offender's needs or psychological vulnerabilities and a victim's characteristics. Target congruence has three subcategories, which include elements of opportunity theory and social interactionism. The first, target gratifiability, refers to a person's qualities, possessions, skills, or attributes that increase his or her value in the eyes of an offender. Examples include possessing valuables or demographic characteristics such as gender and age because the latter two may converge with an offender's sexual orientation.

Second, target antagonism refers to particular personal characteristics that arouse aggressive reactions in offenders. These include a person's ethnicity and sexual orientation in relation to hate crime and a child's impairment or defiance in relation to frustrated parental violence.

Third, target vulnerability refers to a person's lowered capacity to resist or deter victimization. Examples include small physical stature, having physical limitations, psychological distress, low social competence, and young age (Finkelhor and Asdigian 1996).

Like target attractiveness in the structural–choice model of victim selection, target congruence characteristics vary by crime type. For example, females may be more gratifiable targets for sexual assaults, but males may have more target antagonism for gay bashings (Finkelhor and Asdigian 1996).

III. Sources

Past studies have generally used one of three data sources to investigate victim selection. First, official data, most notably police reports, provide information about crime and often include basic victim characteristics such as gender and age. Second, victimization surveys assess the prevalence of victimization in particular populations and provide information about risk factors for victimization. Third, interviews with offenders sometimes include information not only about criminal careers and backgrounds but also about offenders' motivation to target particular victims.

A. Police Reports

Police reports have long been the most often used data source for crime measurement. They have many important and valuable applications, such as providing information about long-term trends in crime and the option to measure victim–offender dyads, but they also have a number of pitfalls. Probably the most important is that they include only crimes that are reported to the police, which are not a random selection of all crimes (Goudriaan 2006). In addition, they lack detailed information about victims, offenders, and the crime context, limiting their usefulness for studying victim selection. Nevertheless, police reports can be and have been used to study how basic demographic characteristics, such as gender and ethnicity, are related to victimization.

B. Victimization Surveys

Primarily due to the police data's inability to measure unreported crime, researchers started conducting victimization surveys in the 1970s. Ever since, such surveys have been used to gather information on nonlethal victimization among population samples and have been carried out in many countries (van Dijk et al. 2007). Although, unlike police records, surveys provide information on the "dark number of crime," the most victimized people are probably underrepresented because they are the least likely to participate (Lohr and Sun 1998). In addition to basic information about crime prevalence, surveys provide information about the crime context and victim's background characteristics and thereby about the types of people offenders target, although there is large variation among surveys in the extent to which they do so. Whereas national and local (regional or city) surveys often contain only basic demographic risk factors, (school) surveys among adolescents typically include more information. Furthermore, some surveys include information about the crime context and the development of events, thereby providing information about how disputes evolve and escalate, at least from the victim's point of view.

A disadvantage of victimization surveys for this chapter's purpose is that most do not contain data on the offenders, which makes it impossible to investigate differences between offenders in victim selection. Furthermore, many of the variables that are measured in the surveys confound exposure, proximity, target attractiveness, and guardianship, making it very challenging, if not impossible, to isolate the characteristics influencing target attractiveness (Cohen et al. 1981). For example, most surveys include some measure for income or socioeconomic status. Income is likely related to target attractiveness (because higher income often means more valuables) but also to lower exposure (because higher income is linked to less risky lifestyles), lower proximity (because richer people live in lower crime neighborhoods), and higher guardianship (richer people buy more security devices). The bivariate effect of income on victimization does not separate these effects, making it difficult to isolate the effect of income on target attractiveness. This is problematic not only for measures of income but also for other demographic characteristics, although other types of measures, such as psychological and physical characteristics, are less affected.

C. Offender Interviews

Finally, information collected among offenders is the most direct way of studying victim selection because it allows offenders to directly relate the criteria they use when selecting victims. This information is obtained in two ways, namely quantitatively (in the form of standardized surveys) and qualitatively (in the form of semistructured or open interviews). Like victimization surveys, offender interviews provide the opportunity to directly ask the participants in crime events (in this case, the offenders) about the development of incidents.

The disadvantages of offender interviews, however, include the fact that offenders may give inaccurate information because victim selection may have occurred under the influence of alcohol and drugs, impulsively, or in the distant past (Hough 1987). In addition, most offender studies have focused on more serious crimes because they have used prison samples or violent subcultures and thus have underrepresented minor "everyday" offenses. Furthermore, offenders probably, consciously or unconsciously, present their information in the best light so as to excuse them from culpability (Indermaur 1995). Finally, individuals are not always aware of the motivations for their actions (Nisbett and Wilson 1977), and human actions are often not well thought out or planned but, rather, automatic (Bourdieu and Wacquant 1992). Therefore, research utilizing offender interviews relies on *perceived* motivations for victim selection. This may result in post hoc rationalized accounts of decisions that were rather impulsive when made. Nevertheless, asking offenders about their motivations for targeting choices reveals information that is impossible to obtain through other data sources.

IV. FINDINGS

This section reviews empirical findings on victim selection. To cover the vast existing literature, the section is organized into nine subsections, including victims' demographic characteristics, psychological characteristics, physical characteristics, behavior, biological characteristics, prior victimization, and relationship to the offender. In addition, the effects of victim behavior *during* the offense and the role of randomness are discussed. Some of the mentioned characteristics are observable and play a direct role in victim selection, whereas others are less or not observable and affect victim selection indirectly. Note that the subsections overlap to a certain extent. For example, victims' demographic and psychological profile affects their behavior, which in turn affects victim selection. Nevertheless, it is hoped that these subsections facilitate the organization of the findings.

A. Demographic Characteristics

1. *Gender*

Gender is one of the most often studied predictors of victimization. Across countries, most victimization surveys have found that males are at higher risk for homicide, physical assault, threats, robbery, investor fraud, and Internet crimes (the latter at least for adults), and females are at higher risk for sexual violence and violence by intimate partners; the evidence is mixed for personal theft and consumer fraud (van Wyk and Mason 2001; van Wilsem, De Graaf, and Wittebrood 2002; Baker and Faulkner 2003; Ammermüller 2007; Lauritsen and Heimer 2008; Schoepfer and Piquero 2009; Perreault and Brennan 2010; Killias et al. 2011; van Wilsem 2013). Interpreting these findings is not necessarily straightforward, however, because, as discussed previously, victimization surveys confound exposure, proximity, target attractiveness, and guardianship. In other words, these patterns could be due both to the structural part (e.g., males may have riskier everyday activities, increasing their victimization risk) and to the choice part (e.g., males may have higher target attractiveness for some crimes, increasing their victimization risk) of the structural–choice theory of victim selection (Miethe and Meier 1990). In addition, structural factors and target attractiveness could be pulling in opposite directions (e.g., when males may have higher exposure but females higher subjective value for some crimes, such as sex crimes).

In order to disentangle the effects of target attractiveness from structural factors in victimization surveys, it is necessary to statistically control for risky lifestyles and proximity to offenders. Studies that have done so have shown that females still have a higher risk for sexual victimization and males for physical assault after these control variables have been added, although the evidence for theft remains mixed (Lauritsen, Sampson, and Laub 1991; Mustaine and Tewkesbury 1998; Averdijk, Müller-Johnson, and Eisner 2012). This suggests that gender plays a role in offenders' targeting choices beyond structural factors.

Research also suggests that the role of gender in victim selection is best understood in relation to the offender's gender. For sex crimes, females are probably considered to have a higher subjective value compared to males given that most sex offenders are males and most males are heterosexual. For assaults, beating up a male may yield greater reputational gains than beating up a female to the extent that physical assaults are associated with males' competition for dominance (Finkelhor and Asdigian 1996). Similarly, although both male and female robbers consider females to be easier targets because they are physically weaker, more easily intimidated, and less likely to resist (Wright and Decker 1997; Miller 1998), most males target male victims because robbing or assaulting females undermines masculinity (Miller 1998; Mullins, Wright, and Jacobs 2004) and transgresses moral rules (Brookman et al. 2007; Bernasco, Lindegaard, and Jacques 2013), which may explain why males have a higher risk of robbery victimization. Findings for female offenders are more mixed. Whereas female robbers mostly targeted females in St. Louis, Missouri (Miller 1998), they were just as likely to rob males in New York (Sommers and Baskin 1993) and the United Kingdom (Brookman et al. 2007). The UK study explained that robbery victims and offenders are often strangers in the United Kingdom and that strangers are easily intimidated, regardless of the offender's sex (Brookman et al. 2007). Some female robbers, car thieves, and burglars prefer male targets because they can use sex to create opportunities for crime (Wright and Decker 1997; Miller 1998; Mullins and Wright 2003; Mullins and Cherbonneau 2011). Also, males may be too ashamed of having been robbed by a woman to report the crime to the police (Brookman et al. 2007).

Findings are somewhat different for dispute-related violence, for which both male and female offenders either prefer female victims or are equally likely to choose male and female victims. In a quantitative US study, both male and female offenders of (unarmed) violence preferred female victims because they are smaller and weaker (Felson 1996). A qualitative study found that males retaliate against females for provocations similar to those leading to retaliation against males (Mullins et al. 2004). For intimate partner violence, males are more likely to physically retaliate against their female partners than vice versa (Felson 1996).

2. *Age*

The age–victimization curve for crimes such as physical assault, sexual assault, robbery, online and offline fraud, and personal theft trails off as people get older (van Wyk and Mason 2001; van Wilsem 2013; Australian Institute of Criminology 2014; Centraal Bureau voor de Statistiek 2014; Truman and Langton 2014). Although peak ages for economic crimes such as investor fraud are much higher in the mid-forties to fifties age range (Baker and Faulkner 2003; Trahan, Marquart, and Mullings 2005), victimization risk for most crime types peaks in adolescence and young adulthood. However, because most victimization surveys exclude people younger than age twelve and police data underrepresent child victims (Finkelhor and Ormrod 1999), it has been debated whether this peak is real or a data artifact. A US survey among ten- to seventeen-year-olds as well as the caregivers of two- to nine-year-olds showed that although property and sexual crimes increased during this developmental period, assault rates were fairly stable (Finkelhor et al. 2005). Furthermore, children are at increased risk for neglect and maltreatment, and infants for homicide (Finkelhor 2008; Hartjen and Priyadarsini 2012).

Although many offenders express moral objections against victimizing children and elderly people (Hearnden and Magill 2004; Brookman et al. 2007; Bernasco et al. 2013), research suggests that target attractiveness is age-graded and that both children and elderly have high subjective value for offenders. First, children are easy targets because they trust others (including potential offenders) easily, do not have the physical capabilities to resist or retaliate, and cannot or will not go to the police. Second, primarily for sex crimes, the physical attractiveness of teenagers likely drives their increased victimization risk (Felson and Krohn 1990; Felson and Cundiff 2014). Third, young people may also, willingly or unwillingly, "provoke" others into violence. For example, caregivers' frustration or stress over children's dependence, crying, or disobedience increases target antagonism (Finkelhor and Asdigian 1996), and the high victimization rates among adolescents are likely in part driven by their increased tendency for provocative behavior.

On the other end of the age spectrum, the assumed mental and physical frailty of elderly people may increase their risk of being targeted for crime (Jeary 2005). For example, some robbers and burglars have noted that elderly people are unlikely to resist or run after them (Miller 1998; Jeary 2005), especially if the victims are also female and white (Wright and Decker 1997). Some burglars have noted that elderly often have valuables, such as cash, at home (Decker et al. 1993; Jeary 2005). Furthermore, some sex offenders target elderly women to test their sexual performance with a victim perceived to be unlikely to resist, mock, or report it (Jeary 2005). Nonetheless, however, victimization surveys have shown that relatively few elderly are the victims of crime (Akers et al. 1987; Studer 2014). Again, this may in part be explained by the fact that victimization surveys confound the structural and the choice parts of the structural–choice model, which may pull in opposite directions. Although the elderly may, all else being equal, be attractive targets, they generally have few risky activities and therefore have relatively low exposure to perpetrators. However, whereas the elderly have a low risk of victimization of classic crime types, they are at risk for several types of abuse, including financial exploitation as well as neglect and abuse by caregivers (Teaster and Roberto 2004; Acierno et al. 2010; Naughton et al. 2012; for reviews, see Cooper, Selwood, and Livingston 2008; Daly, Merchant, and Jogerst 2011). Crimes involving fraud capitalize on the perceived gullibility and potential cognitive limitations of elderly people. Some studies have shown that caregiver stress contributes to the mistreatment of elderly, but others have not found the same result (Burnight and Mosqueda 2011). For these types of abuse, the elderly have both a high degree of exposure (because they are often surrounded by caregivers) and a high degree of target attractiveness, leading to increased victimization risk.

3. *Race and Ethnicity*

Victimization surveys have shown that ethnic minorities are at increased risk for property crimes, (serious) violence, and sexual victimization (Lauritsen and Heimer 2010; Averdijk et al. 2012; Centraal Bureau voor de Statistiek 2014). These findings are likely in part driven by the mediating effects of exposure and proximity to risky social settings (Berg 2014). For example, ethnic background and migration status are often associated with constraints and limited options of employment, housing, and transport, in turn influencing victimization risk (Hindelang et al. 1978; Larsen, Payne, and Tomison

2011). Beyond shaping structural constraints, however, it is likely that race and ethnicity play a direct role in offender's targeting choices as well. First, some offenders hold negative views of people of other races and ethnicities, which motivates them for so-called hate crimes. These are often committed against minority groups by majority groups, but they may also be committed by minorities against majority groups, and include various crime types, such as vandalism, threats, arson, assault, and homicide (van Donselaar and Rodrigues 2008; Wilson 2014). In England and Wales, 1.3 percent of non-white and 0.1 percent of white adults have been victims of racially motivated hate crimes (Home Office, 2013).

Second, some offenders use people's race as an indicator for their (unknown) behavior and yield. This evidence derives from Wright and Decker's (1997) study among armed robbers. They found that robbers had a preference for white victims because they are thought to offer less resistance than black people. In turn, black people are especially at risk for violent victimization involving weapons, probably because offenders utilize these to prevent or overcome (expected) resistance (Berg 2014). Furthermore, robbers use race to select those people who carry around the most cash, although robbers disagree about whether whites or blacks carry around more (Wright and Decker 1997). Finally, one robber in Wright and Decker's study stated that he targeted white drug users in high-crime black areas because they would be unlikely to go to the police due to the fact that they would have difficulty explaining why they were present in the area.

In some contexts, the effects of interracial hatred and perceived weakness combine and produce an extra high risk for members of certain ethnicities and races. This has most often been studied in US prisons, in which interracial sexual abuse is common for offense constellations involving white non-Hispanic victims and African American or Hispanic offenders (Davis 1971; Human Rights Watch 2001; Hensley, Tewksbury, and Castle 2003; Beck et al. 2013). On the one hand, these black on white sexual offenses have been viewed as forms of revenge for the domination of whites outside of prison. On the other hand, black inmates have reported that whites are viewed as weaker and unable or unwilling to fight, contributing to their image as easy victims (Human Rights Watch 2001).

4. *Income and Valuables*

Compared to people with higher incomes, people with lower incomes are more often the victims of violence (Lauritsen 2001; Wittebrood 2006; Perrault and Brennan 2010). The findings for theft and fraud are mixed, with some studies showing higher rates for low-income groups, others showing higher rates for high-income groups, and still others showing high rates for both or neither (Mustaine and Tewksbury 1998; van Wyk and Mason 2001; Wittebrood 2006; Perrault and Brennan 2010; van Wilsem 2013). This may be due to the type of analyses used; data limitations; and confounding effects of exposure, proximity, target attractiveness, and guardianship, which may pull in opposite directions. For example, people with low income may live in high-crime neighborhoods and therefore have a high proximity to offenders of both violent and property crime. People with high income, on the other hand, usually have more valuables, leading to high target attractiveness for property crime. As discussed previously, this chapter is focused on the effects of target attractiveness. In that respect, it has been argued that income plays a role in targeting choices for property crime, but not assault, because wealthier people have more valuables (Cohen et al. 1981).

The findings of qualitative research suggest that greater wealth is indeed related to increased target attractiveness for property crimes and robberies. In order to play a role in victim selection, wealth or income has to be observed. The extent to which wealth or income can be observed varies. Sometimes, income is not observed at all, such as in cases of online consumer fraud, which may explain why some studies have shown a null relation between income and victimization (van Wyk and Mason 2001; van Wilsem 2013). In many other cases, however, wealth or cues thereof play an important role in target selection. Some offenders, including some (identity) thieves and fraud perpetrators, have direct access to fairly robust indicators of wealth, such as credit card accounts or commercially available lists of affluent people and consumers of expensive goods, which are used to guide target selection (Baker and Faulkner 2003; Copes and Vieraitis 2012). Other offenders rely on cues to determine whether someone is wealthy enough to target. Research has shown that victim selection by street robbers and burglars is first and foremost determined by cues that people have valuables (Decker et al. 1993; Wright and Decker 1997; Hearnden and Magill 2004). Such cues can be direct or indirect (Brookman et al. 2007). Direct cues for robbers include visible valuables, such as jewelry, cell phones, and cash (Miller 1998). For burglars, observing valuables in someone's house prior to the crime facilitates victim selection (Wright and Decker 1994; Hearnden and Magill 2004).

In other cases, offenders rely on indirect cues to estimate the availability of valuables. Many burglars rely on a "belief" that valuables are present, and inferences about the occupants, rather than features of the properties, inform such beliefs (Hearnden and Magill 2004). These include people's appearance, including their clothing and jewelry (Wright and Decker 1994). As an indirect cue for street robbery, a robber in Brookman et al.'s (2007) study stated of her victim, "She looked like she was going out, so therefore she had money, she was dressed up to go out . . . 'dolled up' to go out" (pp. 877–878). Judging the yield is more difficult in robberies than in burglaries. Most houses contain a predictable range of valuable goods, but there is a large variance in the amount of valuables people carry with them (Wright and Decker 1997).

Although the most obvious link between income and victimization exists for property offenses and robberies, there is evidence that low income may be linked to sex crimes. Most studies have not found a relation between income or socioeconomic status and sexual victimization (Averdijk et al. 2012), but Beauregard, Rossmo, and Proulx's (2007) interview study with serial sex offenders showed that individuals with problematic backgrounds are sometimes targeted because they can be offered things in return.

B. Psychological Characteristics

1. *Low Self-Control*

The most often studied psychological characteristic in relation to criminal victimization is low self-control. At the core of self-control theory is the hypothesis that those who have low levels of it tend to disregard the longer term consequences of their behavior, which places them at risk for a variety of maladaptive experiences, including crime perpetration (Gottfredson and Hirschi 1990). Schreck (1999) adapted self-control theory to also account for criminal victimization. For example, a low level of self-control makes it less likely that people will take precautions against victimization and more likely that they provoke others and respond to provocations, in turn increasing the risk of violent and property victimization. Although studies initially focused on predatory contact crimes, low self-control also predicts fraud and online victimization (Holtfreter, Reisig, and Pratt 2008; van Wilsem 2013). Related to this literature are studies that have found that impulsivity increases victimization risk (Wilcox, Tillyer, and Fisher 2009). A meta-analysis of 66 studies concluded that low self-control is a modest but consistent predictor of victimization (Pratt et al. 2014). Although research has begun to investigate the link between self-control, sexual assault, and intimate partner violence victimization (Kerley, Xu, and Sirisunyaluck 2008), Pratt and colleagues (2014) note that studies linking low self-control with violence against women, family violence, and child abuse are currently absent, thereby limiting the theory's generalizability.

2. *Internalizing Problems*

Other psychological characteristics related to victimization include internalizing problems, although criminological research has been limited (von Hentig 1948). Most existing studies in this area have assessed the link between severe mental disorders and victimization and found much higher rates of sexual assault, robbery, and assault in the mentally disordered in adult psychiatric, prison, and community samples (Silver 2002; Silver et al. 2005; Teplin et al. 2005; Maniglio 2009; Pare and Logan 2011). This seems to be at least partly explained by mentally ill persons' provocative behavior and involvement in conflictive social relationships (Silver 2002; Pare and Logan 2011). Few studies have examined the impact of more general measures of psychological distress. Those that have found that psychological distress among adolescents increases their subsequent risk of violent and sexual victimization (Finkelhor and Asdigian 1996; see also Boney-McCoy and Finkelhor 1996; van Gelder et al. 2015). The withdrawal, social avoidance, poor assertiveness, and social isolation associated with psychological problems may disturb interpersonal relations and result in a person being labeled an "easy target" (Egan and Perry 1998; Storch et al. 2005). Furthermore, those who suffer from psychological distress may be more likely to seek assurance and affection from outsiders and more vulnerable to manipulative psychological tricks used by (sex) offenders. Especially in high-risk environments, notably prisons, a lack of assertiveness and being unaggressive, shy, intellectual, timid, fearful, not street smart, or "passive" are linked to an increased risk of sexual and physical assault (Chonco 1989; Human Rights Watch 2001).

3. *Control Imbalances*

Partly related to the previously discussed literature on internalizing problems, Piquero and Hickman (2003) extended Tittle's control balance theory to victimization, arguing that "the amount of control to which a person is subject relative to the amount of control they exercise" (p. 283), such as in relation to school, recreation, work, significant others, and society, is nonlinearly related to victimization. Individuals with control deficits display a sense of weakness and helplessness and a lack of confidence or skills to resist victimization, whereas individuals with control surpluses harbor feelings of invulnerability, which may provoke others into victimizing them. In a sample of university students, both control deficits and surpluses were found to increase the risk of on-campus victimization (assault, theft, or vandalism). Two other college student samples found that control imbalances did not account for stalking victimization, although control deficits in relationships specifically did so for women but not for men (Nobles and Fox 2013; Fox, Nobles, and Fisher 2016). These findings are reminiscent of developmental findings that have shown that children displaying submissive and nonassertive behaviors are at risk for peer victimization (Schwartz, Dodge, and Coie 1993).

4. *Externalizing Problem Behavior*

People who display externalizing problem behavior, such as aggression, attention deficit hyperactivity disorder (ADHD), oppositional defiant disorder (ODD), and nonaggressive conduct disorder, are at increased risk for victimization (Sentenac et al. 2011). The link between aggression and victimization is well established (Chan and Wong 2015), but fewer studies exist on the link between other types of externalizing behavior and victimization, especially beyond childhood and adolescence. In one study among a sample of adult mental health patients, conduct disorder prior to age fifteen was associated with an increased risk of assault victimization (Hodgins et al. 2008). In addition, children and adolescents with ADHD symptoms (Wiener and Mak 2009; but see Redmond, 2011) and ODD (Fite et al. 2014) reported more physical victimization by peers compared to those without. Furthermore, childhood ADHD symptoms were associated with increased sexual victimization risk in a sample of college women (White and Buehler 2012) and with intimate partner violence in young adult women (Guendelman et al. 2016). ADHD has been hypothesized to affect victimization risk because it is associated with reduced self-esteem, inadequate interpersonal relationships, decreased information processing, impaired regulatory behavior, and emotional reactivity (White and Buehler 2012). It seems that the links between externalizing problems and victimization are stronger in youths who associate with delinquent peers (Fite et al. 2014).

5. *Other*

Findings from offender interviews also suggest that the victim's personality is an important determinant for victim selection. For example, Beauregard et al. (2007) found that 22 percent of interviewed sex offenders chose their victims at least in part for their (perceived) favorable personality characteristics, including "easy girls," "caring, affectionate, and extraverted victims willing to smile," and naive people (see also Stevens 1995). In their interview study of drug robbers, Jacobs, Topalli, and Wright (2000) found that "soft" dealers, meaning those who were easily intimidated and unlikely to retaliate, were preferred targets.

Related to psychological processes, a small literature has found that religiosity is associated with decreased risk for intimate partner violence (Cunradi, Caetano, and Schafer 2002; Howard, Qui, and Boekeloo 2003). It has been argued that this is partly the case because religiosity lowers target attractiveness since religious people are less likely to engage in delinquency, retaliation, and disputes, in turn leading to lower victimization risk (Schreck, Burek, and Clark-Miller 2007). A test of this hypothesis in the Add Health data showed that although religiosity was not found to directly affect violent victimization among adolescents, there was a significant indirect effect, whereby religiosity reduced violent victimization through its effect on lower delinquency (Schreck et al. 2007).

C. Physical Characteristics

1. *Disabilities*

Although prior empirical research utilized widely differing definitions of "disability" and "violence" (Govindshenoy and Spencer 2007; Hibbard et al. 2007; Jones et al. 2012), findings among children, adolescents, and adults throughout the world have shown that physical, intellectual, or sensory disabilities are associated with an increased risk of physical violence, sexual violence, robbery, child maltreatment, intimate partner violence, hate crime, and murder (Petersilia 2001; Quarmby 2008; Chatzitheochari, Parasons, and Platt 2014; Hahn et al. 2014; Harrell 2014; Mikton and Shakespeare 2014; Scherer, Snyder, and Fisher 2014; Olofsson, Lindqvist, and Danielsson 2015; Chan, Emery, and Ip 2016). For example, a meta-analysis showed that the odds of experiencing physical and sexual violence were respectively 3.56 and 2.88 higher for children with disabilities compared to those without. Especially children and adults with mental illnesses or intellectual disabilities were at increased risk for violence (Hughes et al. 2012; Jones et al. 2012). However, almost all studies failed to measure disabilities before the occurrence of violence, which is important because violence may actually lead to disabilities (Pare and Logan 2011). Furthermore, many studies have not accounted for a full range of potential confounders (Govindshenoy and Spencer 2007).

Explanations for the association between disabilities and victimization are twofold (Finkelhor and Asdigian 1996). First, disabilities can limit an individual's capacity to resist an attack. Second, people with disabilities may be perceived as displaying provocative behavior and/or to be a burden to others, particularly caretakers, thereby increasing the risk of frustrated violence.

2. *Obesity*

Although findings are somewhat mixed (Finkelhor and Asdigian 1996), most evidence indicates that obese adolescents (measured by self-reported weight and height converted to body mass index [BMI] scores) are at higher risk of physical aggression compared to non-obese youth (Janssen et al. 2004; Fox and Farrow 2009). There is evidence of gendered effects, with the effects existing solely for girls (Janssen et al. 2004). However, this is not consistent (Fox and Farrow 2009), perhaps because boys with high BMI due to muscle mass, who may have lower victimization rates, confound these findings (Janssen et al. 2004). On the other hand, obese people are at similar or lower risk for sexual victimization (Janssen et al. 2004; Beck et al. 2013). Evidence among adults is less clear because these studies have focused mostly on the pathway from victimization to obesity and not vice versa, even though many are cross-sectional.

Explanations for the obesity–victimization link have focused on the influence of physical appearances on social reactions (Lerner 1978) because being overweight is related to negative stereotypes such as a lack of self-discipline, low self-control, laziness, low competence, unattractiveness, moral and emotional impairments, unpopularity, low intelligence, low life success, and unhappiness (Tiggemann and Anesbury 2000; Rudolph et al. 2009). Overweight individuals may internalize some of these beliefs and act accordingly (Janssen et al. 2004), thus communicating their vulnerability for victimization. A British cross-sectional study among eleven- to fourteen-year-olds suggested support for these hypotheses by showing that the obesity–victimization path was mediated by decreased self-worth, self-esteem, and body dissatisfaction (Fox and Farrow 2009). Qualitative findings suggest that adolescent obese victims of peer aggression display low self-confidence, body dissatisfaction, low social competence, and depressed feelings, with some internalizing feelings of social worthlessness (Griffiths and Page 2008).

Due to the potentially reciprocal relations between obesity and victimization, in which obesity may be both a cause and a consequence of victimization (Midei and Matthews 2011), longitudinal studies are needed. In fact, for sexual abuse, the hypothesis that abused women may gain weight as an adaptive strategy to reduce their attractiveness to offenders has been put forward (Wiederman, Sansone, and Sansone 1999).

3. *Physical Size and Strength*

Although not all studies are in agreement (Finkelhor and Asdigian 1996), greater physical size and strength seem to lower victimization risk. In probably the best known criminological study in this field, respondents from a US sample of ex-offenders, ex-mental health patients, and the general population were questioned about involvement in violent incidents (Felson 1996). People who said they were smaller and weaker than their antagonist were much more likely to get attacked and injured in unarmed violence compared to people who were larger and stronger. There was no effect of physical size and strength in armed incidents, suggesting that larger and stronger people no longer have an advantage when weapons are present. In line with these findings, most, but not all (Hensley et al. 2003), research among inmates has shown that victims look weaker, smaller, less athletic, and less physically coordinated than aggressors and other inmates (Davis 1971; Human Rights Watch 2001). Interviews with street robbers and sex offenders have also found that people who look fragile or physically weak are more likely to be targeted (Beauregard et al. 2007; Brookman et al. 2007).

The relation between small physical size and victimization seems to be primarily due to the lower perceived costs associated with attacking a small person versus a large person and not to confounding variables such as a potentially greater likelihood of small persons to provoke others in order to compensate for their small stature. In a study among US inmates, Pare and Logan (2011) found that smaller and average inmates (measured by weight, potentially overlapping with obesity) were more likely to be the victim of minor (but not serious) assault compared to larger inmates and that this effect was not due to a tendency of smaller inmates for provocative behaviors.

4. *Physical Attractiveness*

Beauty and physical attractiveness are important determinants for victim selection among sex offenders. Incarcerated sex offenders who had committed their crimes against strangers chose their victims because they were beautiful, sexy, and wore revealing clothes (Beauregard et al. 2007). Similarly, in studies of male-on-male sexual assaults in prison, victims were found to be pretty and "better looking"; especially feminine features in males, such as high-pitched voices or long hair, were associated with high sexual assault risk because they were related to both sexual attractiveness and perceived weakness (Davis 1971; Chonco 1989; Human Rights Watch 2001). In a victimization survey among female college students, self-reported attractiveness did not affect sexual victimization, but sexy dress did (Synovitz and Byrne 1998), which may be perceived as an expression of a victim's sexual interest by offenders despite the victim's intention (Abbey et al. 1987) or increase sexual arousal in sex offenders.

In one study, the beauty–victimization link was extended to theft and robbery victimization (Kaiser 2013). Because facially attractive people are often perceived to be more intelligent, more successful in life and work, wealthier, more likeable, more trustworthy, and more likely to be employed than others (Langlois et al. 2000; Kaiser 2013), it was hypothesized that attractive individuals are perceived to carry more valuables and be less likely to resist. Presented with photographs of attractive, average, and unattractive Caucasian young males, respondents from a community sample were asked how likely they would be to pick each type as a victim. Facially attractive males were not more likely to be victimized than the other two types. However, the sample was generally unwilling to victimize any of the potential targets.

5. *Other*

In addition to playing a role in victim selection per se, for some crime types it is the combination between victims' and offenders' physical appearances that facilitates victim selection. This is most obviously the case in identity theft, in which successful crimes require that offenders look like the victims (Copes and Vieraitis 2012).

Furthermore, although expensive dress can increase victimization risk by showing that one has valuables (discussed previously), it can also prevent victimization in certain contexts. Anderson (1994) noted that in poor inner-city US neighborhoods, physical appearance, including clothing and demeanor, communicates respect and a sense of being able to take care of oneself, which in turn can prevent victimization.

In addition, people who look "out of place" in cities, such as tourists, suburbanites, and county residents, are sometimes considered to be easy victims because they are both easily intimidated in an unknown environment and assumed to carry significant amounts of cash or other valuables (Wright and Decker 1997; Brookman et al. 2007).

Finally, a small literature has examined the link between pubertal development and victimization. Research using the US Add Health data has shown that early pubertal development increased violent victimization (Haynie and Piquero 2006). According to Haynie and Piquero, early pubertal development may increase victimization risk due to increased social exclusion by peers and reduced protection by parents and also due to increased stress, which in turn may be associated with provocative behavior.

D. Victim Behavior

1. *Criminal Behavior*

One of the most consistent and important predictors of victimization is offending (Jennings, Piquero, and Reingle 2012). In their interview study of active armed robbers, Wright and Decker (1997) found that six of every ten robbers usually targeted other offenders. Offenders make attractive victims for several reasons. First, they often have attractive valuables, such as cars, cash, and drugs (Jacobs, 2000; Topalli and Wright, 2004; Wright and Decker, 1994).

Second, some offenders mention having less moral objections when targeting fellow offenders. In their study of armed robbers, Wright and Decker (1997) found that some robbers targeting drug dealers justified their offenses by referring to the problems drug dealers were causing to families and neighborhoods.

Third, offenders are unlikely to report victimization to the police (Wright and Decker 1997). The reasons for this are threefold: Offenders may be afraid of exposing their own criminal behavior; they may not be taken seriously by officials; and "snitching" to the police is considered to be a sign of weakness, breaks street codes, and can lead to informal sanctions, including social isolation and violent retaliation (Topalli, Wright, and Fornango 2002; De Jong 2007). Indeed, compared to other victims, victimized offenders are less likely to go to the police (Berg, Slocum, and Loeber 2013).

Finally, particular types of criminal behavior increase target antagonism and therefore increase victimization. Sex offenders, especially child molesters, and domestic violence perpetrators have been reported to be at increased victimization risk, especially in prison (Beck et al. 2013).

However, there are also cases in which fellow offenders are considered to be unattractive targets. First, offenders are relatively likely to resist and retaliate (discussed later), meaning that considerable risks are involved (Wright and Decker, 1997). Furthermore, some crimes require "clean" victims. This is the case for identity theft, in which choosing fellow offenders means that the identity thieves might be confused with their criminal victims and chased by officials (Copes and Vieraitis 2012).

2. Expected Lack of Resistance and Retaliation

The expected likelihood that a victim will resist and retaliate is an important determinant of victim selection (Jacobs 2000). Whether or not a person will resist is not clear before a crime is committed and thus has to be inferred from other sources of information, including a victim's demographic, physical, and psychological profile. In other cases, the offender may have observed or experienced victims' prior response to victimization, which can be used to derive their resistance potential. A combination of these aspects has been referred to as a person's "street credibility" or his or her willingness and ability to use violence (Anderson 1994; Mullins 2006).

All else being equal, less street-credible persons are considered to be more attractive targets than more street-credible persons. However, because highly street-credible persons (e.g., offenders; discussed previously) are also often attractive targets, offenders must decide which they consider to be more important—lack of resistance or high payoff. Some offenders prefer to have some of both, which is why they target fellow offenders with little status who are least likely to retaliate (Wright and Decker 1994). Others "nip resistance in the butt" and coerce street-credible victims into compliance by using a high amount of violence from the crime's onset. In their study of robbers in Amsterdam, Lindegaard, Bernasco, and Jacques (2015) found that the robbers' likelihood of using violence increased threefold for street-credible victims (as measured by their looks, clothing, gestures, behavior, and observable demographics) compared to non-street-credible victims. Offenders with the most money or drugs are targeted by only the most fearless, who are willing to deal with the increased dangers of resistance and gun use (Wright and Decker 1994; Jacobs 2000).

3. Provocation

Many crimes are best understood as (violent) social interactions involving disputes. Such disputes are often started through the (later) victim's acts that are, intended or not, perceived as provocations by the (later) offender. Provocations may include crimes against the later offender or his or her family, friends, or neighbors; humiliating acts or severe challenges to status in social hierarchies, such as assaults in public; and also incidents or transgressions that may seem minor to outsiders or middle-class observers, such as accidentally bumping into someone, speaking down to someone, staring, and eye rolling (Feeney 1986; Topalli et al. 2002; Mullins, Wright, and Jacobs 2004; Jeary 2005; Wright, Brookman, and Bennett 2006; Brookman et al. 2007; Mullins and Miller 2008). In some cases, attacks are committed out of jealousy as a form of punishment for having more material possessions or more success in life than the offender (Jacobs, Topalli, and Wright 2002; St. Jean 2007). For example, one of the rapists in Hale's (1997) study said "nothing seemed to be going my way. And then, out in the bar, I saw this girl who seemed to have it all together, who seemed to have a lot. I decided right then I was going to show her before the night was over what it was like to lose something . . . what it felt like to hurt." In other cases, crimes are not directed against the provoking person but, rather, against persons who remind the offenders of the provoking person—for example, because they share demographic characteristics with the initial offender (Hale 1997; Jeary 2005). Possible reactions to provocations include robbery, assault, vandalism, carjacking, rape, burglary, identity theft, and murder (Wolfgang 1958; Brownstein et al. 1995; Indermaur 1995; Topalli and Wright 2004; Copes and Vieraitis 2012; Ganpat, van der Leun, and Nieuwbeerta 2013).

Provocations are especially risky in social venues in which reputations and masculinity statuses are established in the presence of bystanders, such as nightclubs and bars (Mullins, Wright, and Jacobs 2004), and in environments that emphasize masculinity, strength, and respect (Mullins, Wright, and Jacobs 2004), such as prisons and poor, inner-city "street cultures" (Anderson 1994; Topalli and Wright 2004; Pare and Logan 2011; Berg et al. 2012). As Jacobs et al. (2002) explain, "On the street, where one's honour must be protected at all cost, no affront is trivial" (p. 681). Note that although the term "masculinity" implies males, issues of "masculinity" also apply to females, at least in street cultures. However, provocations among females more often concern domestic matters and are typically followed by less violence than those among males (Mullins et al. 2004).

In a completely different context, parental violence against their children has partly been explained by caregivers' frustration over their children's perceived provocative behavior. Finkelhor and Asdigian (1996) hypothesized that disobedience in children and adolescents increases their target antagonism for parental assault. In their sample of US adolescents, they found that risky behaviors (running away from home, stealing, getting drunk, or carrying a weapon to school) increased the subsequent risk of parental assaults. Corporal punishment by parents, which is illegal in several jurisdictions, has been found to be preceded by children's conduct problems (Pardini, Fite, and Burke 2008; Topçuoğlu 2011), although this evidence is not consistent (Burke, Pardini, and Loeber 2008).

4. *Alcohol and Drug Use*

Alcohol and drug use has been linked to victimization of various crime types, including robbery, assault, and sexual violence. In several interview studies, offenders such as street robbers noted that they chose victims who seemed drunk (Miller 1998; Brookman et al. 2007). Although most quantitative studies on the link between victimization and alcohol and drug use have been restricted to correlational findings, two have demonstrated a causal and situational link. One of these used US data on adults to show that alcohol consumption affected victimization risk while drinking but not while sober (Felson and Burchfield 2004). The other used Dutch data on adolescents to show that victimization was related to alcohol consumption in the same hour, although this effect disappeared when respondents' delinquent behavior in the same hour was controlled for (Averdijk and Bernasco 2015). The latter study also found that cannabis use was unrelated to victimization, but other drugs could not be analyzed because they were absent in the sample.

Persons who are under the influence of drugs or alcohol are attractive targets because their physical condition makes them less capable of defending themselves, they are not alert about their surroundings and victimization risk, and they are relatively likely to lose their self-control and provoke others (Wright and Decker 1997). Women who consume alcohol may be especially vulnerable for victimization because experiments and focus groups have shown that women are rated as more sexually available after they have consumed alcohol (George, Gournic, and McAfee 1988; George et al. 1995; Lindgren et al. 2009), which may lead to misperceptions and sexual victimization.

5. *Other*

Other risky activities that increase victimization risk include engaging in prostitution or visiting a prostitute. Clients of prostitutes find themselves in a compromising position, making them easy targets of prostitute offenders or their affiliates (Wright and Decker 1994; Miller 1998; Brookman et al. 2007; Copes and Vieraitis 2012). Prostitutes are also at high risk of victimization of sexual and physical violence (Farley et al. 2004; Decker et al. 2010), which is likely in part due to the illegality and secrecy of their work.

E. Biological Characteristics

A small but emerging literature has begun to examine the influence of genotype on victimization risk. Although genotype is obviously unobservable for offenders, it may facilitate victim selection through its effect on self-control, which in turn affects the likelihood of provocative behavior and offending. Analyses using an adolescent sample of the US Add Health data found that genes were associated with serious violent victimization, but only for white males in low-risk environments (who were not surrounded by delinquent peers) (Beaver et al. 2007). In total, 63 percent of the shared variance between victimization and low self-control was explained by genetic factors (Boutwell et al. 2013), and 51–98 percent of the association between victimization and offending was (Barnes and Beaver 2012).

Sexual orientation has also been linked to victimization. Although there is debate on the origins of sexual orientation, it is at least partly driven by genetic factors (Långström et al. 2010), which is why it is discussed in this section. Research has shown that non-heterosexuals are at increased risk for victimization. For example, the Dutch national victimization survey found that gay, lesbian, and bisexual respondents reported more violence, property crimes, and vandalism compared to heterosexual respondents (Centraal Bureau voor de Statistiek 2014). Non-heterosexuals can be the target of hate crimes (Home Office 2013; Wilson 2014). In particular environments, such as prisons, they are specifically targeted (Human Rights Watch, 2001; Beck et al. 2013; Hensley et al. 2003).

F. Prior Victimization

Victims of crime are at increased risk to be victimized again (Pease 1998). For example, data from the British Crime Survey showed that substantial percentages of both property (e.g., theft from vehicles, vandalism, burglary, and theft) and violent crimes (assaults and threats) were "series crimes" that were very similar to one another and attributed to the same offender (Ashton et al. 1998). In a study among burglars on probation in England, Ashton et al. found that half of the sample stated they had committed repeated offenses against the same target. Most of the repeat offenses were repeated burglaries, followed by violence.

Repeat victimization has been explained by two mechanisms (Nagin and Paternoster 2000; Tseloni and Pease 2003). The first is that the victim has high-stable risk factors, such as immersion in a high-risk environment (Hindelang et al. 1978) or any of the characteristics of target attractiveness discussed in this chapter, which affect the choices of varied offenders and make the relation between prior and later victimization non-causal. The second is that victimization sets processes in motion that increase later victimization risk (Lauritsen and Davis Quinet 1995). Several explanations have been proposed for this phenomenon. In general, if an offender has found an attractive target, repeat offenses against the same target involve less costs (i.e., less effort and risk) and as many benefits as offenses against a new target (Farrell, Phillips, and Pease 1995). Prior victimization can also lead to maladaptive coping in victims, such as substance use, low assertiveness, internalizing problems, and social–psychological deficits (Ruback, Clark, and Warner 2014), which may in turn increase the risk of repeat victimization.

For violent victimization specifically, a victim labeling approach has been suggested in which the label of being a deserving victim may become known across peer networks, increasing the risk of further victimization (Lauritsen and Davis Quinet 1995). In addition, victimization may lead to submissive behavior, which may establish one as an "easy target," leading to further victimization. For example, the victim may realize that he or she is powerless and will stop resisting (Farrell et al. 1995). Prior victimization may especially increase future victimization in street cultures because it labels one as weak and an easy target, particularly when one fails to respond through retaliation (Anderson 1994; Mullins 2006).

The main reasons for repeat burglary include that the burglars know that there are more valuables to be taken (because others told them so, they saw new valuables being delivered or empty boxes being discarded, or they left behind valuables the previous time) and/or that they bore a grudge against the victim (Ashton et al. 1998; Hearnden and Magill 2004).

Although the evidence on repeat victimization is quite consistent, one exception has been reported. In their interview study with 25 drug robbers, Jacobs et al. (2000) found that robbers stayed away from dealers they had previously victimized because this would increase the risk of recognition and thus retaliation.

G. Relationship to the Offender

Many violent offenses occur between victims and offenders who had a prior relationship (Wolfgang, 1958; Amir 1971). For example, most homicides occur between spouses or ex-spouses, other family members, or individuals who are otherwise known to each other (Brookman 2005). In the British Crime Survey, victims of personal contact crime were almost always able to report some information about the offender (Gottfredson 1984). However, with the exception of theft, findings suggested that there had also been a prior relationship between victims and offenders in property crime: In one-third of burglaries, more than one-fourth of vandalism cases, and one in five motor vehicle thefts, the victims could give some information about the offenders (Gottfredson 1984). Interview studies with burglars have revealed similar findings. In southern England, more than half of the interviewed burglars had burgled houses whose occupants they knew, most likely friends, associates in crime, or neighbors (Hearnden and Magill 2004). In the United States, more than one in five burglars chose victims they knew (Wright and Decker 1994). This usually did not concern relatives or close friends but, rather, casual acquaintance, often neighborhood residents.

Crimes against known victims are often related to disputes involving provocation and retaliation (Felson 1993). Knowing the victim also increases the accuracy with which the likelihood of resistance and the reward can be estimated, thereby facilitating victim selection (Jacobs 2000). For example, having visited someone's house means that the presence of valuables can be observed (Wright and Decker 1994).

Of all violent crimes, robbery seems to be the most frequent stranger crime (Feeney 1986; Sommers and Baskin 1993; Brookman et al. 2007). When street robbers do target known victims, the victims and offenders are vaguely acquainted at best (Bernasco et al. 2013), or there is some preexisting dispute leading up to the incident (Brookman et al. 2007). In their interview study of drug robbers, Jacobs et al. (2000) found that most of the robbers did not target victims with whom they were overly familiar in order to reduce the likelihood of recognition and retaliation. Only for those with the most pressing needs were familiar targets attractive. Some robbers expressed that robbing a friend violates basic loyalties and moral rules, although such loyalties are fairly weak in street cultures (Jacobs 2000).

H. Effects of Victim Characteristics and Behavior on Offender Decision Making During Crimes

Many crimes can be understood as situated transactions in which the (perceived) actions of one party lead to reactions by the other. Hence, criminal decision making has multiple stages as criminal events unfold (Cornish and Clarke 2008). Little is currently known about the factors that affect offenders' decisions about proceeding with or aborting a planned crime in the very early stages of the crime. A study of robbers found that they sometimes decide to abandon a planned robbery because they are afraid that the chosen victim may resist (Bernasco et al. 2013). Among sex offenders, unexpected events or victim behavior, led offenders to abandon the planned assault (Beauregard et al. 2007).

Somewhat more is known about offender decision making in the later stages of a crime. Most research in this regard has been done on the effects of victim resistance on offenders' behavior. Although findings are somewhat mixed (Tark and Kleck 2004), the weight of the evidence suggests that victim resistance increases the likelihood that robbers and other violent offenders proceed with violence (Sommers and Baskin 1993; Brookman et al. 2007; Ganpat et al. 2013). For example, in a study of violent property crime among mostly male, adult prisoners in Western Australia, Indermaur (1995) reported that in half of the cases, violence was used in response to victim resistance. In their sample of robbers in Amsterdam, Lindegaard et al. (2015) found that the odds of using violence increased almost 50-fold when the victim resisted. In fact, victim resistance was the best predictor of offender violence during the robbery. In such cases, the use of violence is usually described as a way of forcing the victim into compliance. One robber in St. Jean's (2007) study stated, "If they resist, you must show you mean business" (p. 151).

The effects of victim resistance have also been studied in relation to sex crimes. In a sample of 22 female sex offenders from England, Gannon, Rose, and Ward (2008) found that victim resistance exacerbated the level of force and intrusiveness of the assault, especially among adult victims. In a study among male adolescent sex offenders against children in treatment centers, it was found that the intrusiveness of the sexual behavior, victim participation, and offender modus operandi were contingent on each other (Leclerc and Tremblay 2007). In a study among male offenders who had committed sex offenses against strangers, 35 percent said they had used more force than necessary to overcome the victim's resistance (Beauregard and Leclerc 2007).

I. The Role of Randomness

The previous sections discussed various victim characteristics that play a role in victim selection. Notwithstanding these findings, however, several authors have noted that some crimes have a significant element of randomness and spontaneous opportunities, meaning that in these cases, the risk of victimization is primarily determined by a victim's exposure to a motivated offender. This has been noted in studies on various crime types, including robberies, identity theft, and sex crimes (Stevens 1995; Wright and Decker 1997; Beauregard et al. 2007; St. Jean 2007; Copes and Vieraitis 2012). This evidence might be extended to some family crimes, for which one of the answers to the question of why family members commit violence against each other is that "they are there," which is an issue of proximity and offender motivation more than target attractiveness. Perhaps this is one of the reasons why victimization is usually less well statistically predicted than offending (i.e., the amount of variance explained is lower).

The role of randomness in victim selection seems to depend on the needs of the offenders: If offenders have particularly pressing needs, the importance of victim characteristics in victim selection decreases. In these cases, targets simply need to meet the minimal subjective criteria for an acceptable victim instead of being the best objectively available target (Wright and Decker 1997). As one of the robbers in St. Jean's (2007,) study stated, "If I want it now and it is here, I have it" (p. 156). In addition, in cases in which selection based on favorable victim characteristics is laborious and costly, offenders are more likely to operate randomly. In their interview study of identity thieves, Copes and Vieraitis (2012) reported that the majority of thieves were not selective because "it was easier to prey on any available target than to sift through potential candidates, looking for ideal victims" (p. 105).

In other words, although the "ideal victim" may exist, cost–benefit considerations as well as the constraints imposed by everyday life lead some offenders to settle for "good enough." In their study of armed robbers, Wright and Decker (1997) wrote, "Although these offenders had little difficulty identifying the characteristics of a perfect victim, it is important to remember that they were expressing preferences, not precise selection criteria" (p. 70).

V. Future Research

As discussed in this chapter, a vast literature on the question of who is most likely to be selected as the victim of crime has been produced during the past several decades. Despite the quantity of research reports on this issue, there is still considerable room for more studies. This section highlights several fruitful areas for future research.

In several of the subtopics discussed previously, more research would be welcomed because many of the findings are based on few studies. For example, further victimization research in the areas of internalizing problems and physical size and strength is desirable. In addition, an emphasis on theoretical explanations and mediators for found associations is necessary. For example, although it is clear that provocations and criminal behaviors are related to victimization risk, the precise underlying mechanisms are still elusive. One way in which to move forward is to provide detailed analyses of the interactions between victims and offenders and how these lead to escalation. In addition, although this chapter discussed the influence of several types of victim characteristics mainly in isolation, it is likely that interactions between the different components are of importance. For example, Wright and Decker (1997) noted that signs of wealth were insufficient for victim selection in robbery; instead, potential victims had to be judged as low risk, meaning that criminals preferred victims who would not resist.

A second potentially important area of future research is cross-cultural in nature. As is clear from the empirical findings described previously, the bulk of research derives from the United States. Although some basic mechanisms underlying victim selection, such as the role of expected rewards and resistance in targeting decisions, may be universal, it is possible that particular aspects, such as the types of cues that offenders use to estimate the likely rewards and resistance, differ across cultural and environmental contexts. However, the extent to which this is indeed the case is currently an open question. Some prior work suggests that this may be a fruitful area for future research because even between contexts such as the United Kingdom, the Netherlands, and the United States, which are all Western, industrialized countries, there appear to be differences in the circumstances surrounding victimization, such as the crime location and the victim–offender relationship (Stein 2009) and the types of victims who are considered to be easy targets (Brookman et al. 2007).

A third area in which further research is encouraged is methodological. Unlike research in other fields such as psychology and developmental science, most of the criminological research on criminal motivation is based on self-reports, which have important disadvantages (discussed previously). Information from alternative data sources could be used to compare findings from self-reported methods as well as provide additional information. Such alternative data could derive from at least three sources. First, for situational studies, data from third parties in crime events can provide information on how crimes and interactions develop. Such parties may include human observers such as guardians and bystanders, but also technological observers such as cameras and photographs (Collins 2009; Lindegaard et al. 2015). Second, for more disposition-oriented studies, people who have knowledge about the persons involved in crimes (both victims and offenders) and their backgrounds such as their psychological and physical profiles can be interviewed without the biases inherent in self-reports. Although it is clear that multiple informants likely provide divergent information about the same variables (Achenbach, McConaughy, and Howell 1987; Averdijk, Eisner, and Ribeaud 2013), it is currently unclear to what extent this plays a role in victim selection and thus further knowledge is desirable. Third, to further examine both the validity of self-reports and the probably differential ways in which different participants in crime events view the same event, the stories of both parties involved in the same event could be compared and studied. In addition to information from other sources, the previous discussion has also shown that there is considerable unclarity in various domains about the time sequences of (assumed) causes and effects. Short- and long-term longitudinal studies, detailed situational analyses, experiments, and mixed-method strategies provide opportunities to better approach causality.

Another interesting area for further research would be to study the interaction between victim characteristics and offender characteristics in victim selection. In other words, do different types of offenders select different types of victims, and for what reason? Relatedly, some have argued that motivation, victim selection, and commission of the offense merge into one continuous process (Jacobs et al. 2003), raising the question to what extent victim selection can be isolated from other aspects of criminal decision making. An interesting subquestion is whether and how victim selection techniques change over the course of criminal careers.

Finally, a largely open question concerns the extent to which mechanisms operate uniformly across crime types and subpopulations. Although this chapter has made several references to how mechanisms may operate for different subpopulations (e.g., by age and gender), a systematic overview of which mechanisms are empirically related to which crime types and which subpopulations was beyond the scope of this chapter and is currently challenging to provide due to gaps in our knowledge. Whereas some perspectives, including self-control theory, emphasize the generality of encountering unfortunate circumstances and life events and call claims of specificity by crime type into question, other perspectives stress the importance of distinguishing crime types. In particular, according to opportunity approaches, the effect of target attractiveness on crime varies as a function of crime type, and the definitional properties of specific crimes are important to understand the social distribution of crime victimization (Cohen et al. 1981; Cornish and Clarke 2008). Although this applies to more traditional types of crime such as burglary and assault, an interesting additional question is to what extent victim selection characteristics are associated with less studied or newer forms of crime, particularly fraud and Internet crimes, beyond the influence of structural characteristics such as everyday online activities. A recent review concluded that for some Internet crimes such as hacking, victim characteristics may play a minor role only because perpetrators are less interested in specific individuals (Holt and Bossler 2014). However, the effect of victim characteristics beyond routine activities on other types of Internet crimes is largely unknown. The question of whether target attractiveness varies by crime type and subpopulation has not received much attention in theory development and hypothesis testing, and it should be addressed in future victimization research.

At the outset of this chapter, it was noted that the etiology of victimization has received considerable research attention during the past four decades. This chapter discussed various factors that have been found to play a role in offenders' targeting decisions. Despite this growing body of research, however, much remains to be learned. Research that uses various complementary methodologies to study the factors influencing target attractiveness, that promotes interdisciplinary integration, and that places a strong focus on theoretical interpretation has the potential to not only advance our understanding of the factors influencing perpetrators' targeting decisions but also advance its usefulness for prevention purposes.

ACKNOWLEDGMENT

The author's research reported in this chapter was financially supported by the Swiss National Science Foundation.

REFERENCES

Abbey, A., C. Cozzarelli, K. McLaughlin, and R. J. Harnish. 1987. "The Effects of Clothing and Dyad Sex Composition on Perceptions of Sexual Intent: Do Women and Men Evaluate These Cues Differently?" *Journal of Applied Social Psychology* 17(2): 108–26.

Achenbach, T. M., S. H. McConaughy, and C. T. Howell. 1987. "Child/Adolescent Behavioral and Emotional Problems: Implications of Cross-Informant Correlations for Situational Specificity." *Psychological Bulletin* 101(2): 213.

Acierno, R., M. A. Hernandez, A. B. Amstadter, H. S. Resnick, K. Steve, W. Muzzy, and D. G. Kilpatrick. 2010. "Prevalence and Correlates of Emotional, Physical, Sexual, and Financial Abuse and Potential Neglect in the United States: The National Elder Mistreatment Study." *American Journal of Public Health* 100: 292.

Akers, R. L., A. J. La Greca, C. Sellers, and J. Cochran. 1987. "Fear of Crime and Victimization Among the Elderly in Different Types of Communities." *Criminology* 25:487–506.

Amir, M. 1971. *Patterns in Forcible Rape*. Chicago: University of Chicago Press.

Ammermüller, A. 2007. "Violence in European Schools: Victimization and Consequences." Discussion paper no. 07-004. Manheim, Germany: Centre for European Economic Research.

Anderson, E. 1994. "The Code of the Streets." *Atlantic Monthly* 273:80–94.

Ashton, J., I. Brown, B. Senior, and K. Pease. 1998. "Repeat Victimisation: Offender Accounts." *International Journal of Risk, Security and Crime Prevention* 3:269–79.

Averdijk, M., and W. Bernasco. 2015. "Testing the Situational Explanation of Victimization Among Adolescents." *Journal of Research in Crime and Delinquency* 52(2):151–80.

Averdijk, M., M. Eisner, and D. Ribeaud. 2013. "Method Effects in Survey Questions About Peer Victimization." In *Eenvoud and Verscheidenheid. Liber Amicorum voor Henk Elffers* [*Simplicity and Diversity. Festschrift for Henk Elffers*], edited by S. Ruiter, W. Bernasco, W. Huisman, and G. J. N. Bruinsma, pp. 425–40. Amsterdam: NSCR and Afdeling Criminologie Vrije Universiteit Amsterdam.

Averdijk, M., K. Mueller-Johnson, and M. Eisner. 2012. *Sexual Victimization of Children and Adolescents in Switzerland*. Zurich, Switzerland: UBS Optimus Foundation.

Australian Institute of Criminology. 2014. *Australian Crime: Facts and Figures*. Canberra: Australian Institute of Criminology.

Baker, W. E., and R. R. Faulkner. 2003. "Diffusion of Fraud: Intermediate Economic Crime and Investor Dynamics." *Criminology* 41:1173–1206.

Barnes, J. C., and K. M. Beaver. 2012. "Extending Research on the Victim–Offender Overlap: Evidence from a Genetically Informative Analysis." *Journal of Interpersonal Violence* 27(16): 3299–321.

Beauregard, E., and B. Leclerc. 2007. "An Application of the Rational Choice Approach to the Offending Process of Sex Offenders: A Closer Look at the Decision-Making." *Sexual Abuse* 19:115–33.

Beauregard, E., D. K. Rossmo, and J. Proulx. 2007. "A Descriptive Model of the Hunting Process of Serial Sex Offenders: A Rational Choice Perspective." *Journal of Family Violence* 22:449–63.

Beaver, K. M., J. P. Wright, M. DeLisi, L. E. Daigle, M. L. Swatt, and C. L. Gibson. 2007. "Evidence of a Gene × Environment Interaction in the Creation of Victimization Results from a Longitudinal Sample of Adolescents." *International Journal of Offender Therapy and Comparative Criminology* 51(6): 620–45.

Beck, A. J., M. Berzofsky, R. Caspar, and C. Krebs. 2013. "Sexual Victimization in Prisons and Jails Reported by Inmates, 2011–12." National Inmate Survey, 2011–12, NCJ 241399. Washington, DC: U.S. Department of Justice.

Berg, M. T. 2014. "Accounting for Racial Disparities in the Nature of Violent Victimization." *Journal of Quantitative Criminology* 30:629–50.

Berg, M. T., L. A. Slocum, and R. Loeber. 2013. "Illegal Behavior, Neighborhood Context, and Police Reporting by Victims of Violence." *Journal of Research in Crime and Delinquency* 50:75–103.

Berg, M. T., E. A. Stewart, C. J. Schreck, and R. L. Simons. 2012. "The Victim–Offender Overlap in Context: Examining the Role of Neighborhood Street Culture." *Criminology* 50:1–31.

Bernasco, W., M. R. Lindegaard, and S. Jacques. 2013. *Overvallen uit daderperspectief. Situationele aspecten van gewelddadige, niet-gewelddadige en afgeblazen overvallen*. Amsterdam: Politie and Wetenschap.

Boney-McCoy, S., and D. Finkelhor. 1996. "Is Youth Victimization Related to Trauma Symptoms and Depression After Controlling for Prior Symptoms and Family Relationships? A Longitudinal, Prospective Study." *Journal of Consulting and Clinical Psychology* 64(6): 1406.

Bourdieu, P., and L. J. D. Wacquant. 1992. *An Invitation to Reflective Sociology*. Chicago: University of Chicago Press.

Boutwell, B. B., C. A. Franklin, J. C. Barnes, A. K. Tamplin, K. M. Beaver, and M. Petkovsek. 2013. "Unraveling the Covariation of Low Self-Control and Victimization: A Behavior Genetic Approach." *Journal of Adolescence* 36(4): 657–66.

Brookman, F. 2005. *Understanding Homicide*. London: Sage.

Brookman, F., C. Mullins, T. Bennett, and R. Wright. 2007. "Gender, Motivation and the Accomplishment of Street Robbery in the United Kingdom." *British Journal of Criminology* 47:861–84.

Brownstein, H. H., B. J. Spunt, S. M. Crimmins, and S. C. Langley. 1995. "Women Who Kill in Drug Market Situations." *Justice Quarterly* 12:473–97.

Burke, J. D., D. A. Pardini, and R. Loeber. 2008. "Reciprocal Relationships Between Parenting Behavior and Disruptive Psychopathology from Childhood Through Adolescence." *Journal of Abnormal Child Psychology* 36(5): 679–92.

Burnight, K., and L. Mosqueda. 2011. *Theoretical Model Development in Elder Mistreatment*. Irvine: University of California Press.

Centraal Bureau voor de Statistiek. 2014. *Veiligheidsmonitor 2013*. Den Haag, the Netherlands: Centraal Bureau voor de Statistiek.

Chan, H. C. O., and D. S. Wong. 2015. "The Overlap Between School Bullying Perpetration and Victimization: Assessing the Psychological, Familial, and School Factors of Chinese Adolescents in Hong Kong." *Journal of Child and Family Studies* 24:3224.

Chan, K. L., C. R. Emery, and P. Ip. 2016. "Children with Disability Are More at Risk of Violence Victimization: Evidence from a Study of School-Aged Chinese Children." *Journal of Interpersonal Violence* 31(6): 1026–46.

Chatzitheochari, S., S. Parasons, and L. Platt. 2014. "Bullying Experiences Among Disabled Children and Young People in England: Evidence from Two Longitudinal Studies." Working Paper no. 14–11. London: University of London.

Chonco, N. R. 1989. "Sexual Assaults Among Male Inmates: A Descriptive Study." *Prison Journal* 69(1): 72–82.

Cohen, L. E., and M. Felson. 1979. "Social Change and Crime Rate Trends: A Routine Activity Approach." *American Sociological Review* 44:588–608.

Cohen, L. E., J. R. Kluegel, and K. C. Land. 1981. "Social Inequality and Predatory Criminal Victimization: An Exposition and Test of a Formal Theory." *American Sociological Review* 46:505–24.

Collins, R. 2009. *Violence: A Micro-sociological Theory*. Princeton, NJ: Princeton University Press.

Cooper, C., A. Selwood, and G. Livingston. 2008. "The Prevalence of Elder Abuse and Neglect: A Systematic Review." *Age and Ageing* 37(2): 151–60.

Copes, H., and L. Vieraitis. 2012. *Identity Thieves. Motives and Methods*. Boston: Northeastern University Press.

Cornish, D. B., and R. V. Clarke. 2008. "The Rational Choice Perspective." In *Environmental Criminology and Crime Analysis*, edited by R. Wortley and L. Mazerolle, pp. 21–47. Cullompton, UK: Willan.

Cunradi, C. B., R. Caetano, and J. Schafer. 2002. "Religious Affiliation, Denominational Homogamy, and Intimate Partner Violence Among U.S. Couples." *Journal for the Scientific Study of Religion* 41:139–51.

Daly, J. M., M. L. Merchant, and G. J. Jogerst. 2011. "Elder Abuse Research: A Systematic Review." *Journal of Elder Abuse and Neglect* 23(4): 348–65.

Davis, A. J. 1971. "Sexual Assaults in the Philadelphia Prison System." In *Total Institutions*, edited by S. E. Wallace, pp. 25–42. New Brunswick, NJ: Transaction Publishers.

De Jong, J. D. 2007. *Kapot moeilijk. Een ethnografisch onderzoek naar opvallend delinquent groepsgedrag van "Marokkaanse" jongens*. Amsterdam: Aksant.

Decker, M. R., H. L. McCauley, D. Phuengsamran, S. Janyam, G. R. Seage III, and J. G. Silverman. 2010. "Violence Victimization, Sexual Risk and STI Symptoms Among a National Sample of FSWs in Thailand." *Sexually Transmitted Infections* 86(3): 236.

Decker, S., R. Wright, A. Redfern, and D. Smith. 1993. "A Woman's Place is in the Home: Females and Residential Burglary. *Justice Quarterly* 10(1): 143–62.

Dugan, L., and R. Apel. 2005. "The Differential Risk of Retaliation by Relational Distance: A More General Model of Violent Victimization." *Criminology* 43(3): 697–730.

Egan, S. K., and D. G. Perry. 1998. "Does Low Self-Regard Invite Victimization?" *Developmental Psychology* 34:299–309.

Farley, M., A. Cotton, J. Lynne, S. Zumbeck, F. Spiwak, M. E. Reyes, and U. Sezgin. 2004. "Prostitution and Trafficking in Nine Countries: An Update on Violence and Posttraumatic Stress Disorder." *Journal of Trauma Practice* 2(3-4): 33–74.

Farrell, G., C. Phillips, and K. Pease. 1995. "Like Taking Candy: Why Does Repeat Victimization Occur?" *British Journal of Criminology* 35:384–99.

Feeney, F. 1986. "Robbers as Decision Makers." In *The Reasoning Criminal: Rational Choice Perspectives on Offending*, edited by D. B. Cornish and R. V. Clarke, pp. 53–71. New York: Springer.

Felson, R. B. 1993. "Predatory and Dispute-Related Violence: A Social Interactionist Approach." In *Routine Activity and Rational Choice*, edited by R. Clarke and M. Felson, pp. 103–25. New Brunswick, NJ: Transaction Publishers.

Felson, R. B. 1996. "Big People Hit Little People: Sex Differences in Physical Power and Interpersonal Violence." *Criminology* 34:433–52.

Felson, R. B., and K. B. Burchfield. 2004. "Alcohol and the Risk of Physical and Sexual Assault Victimization." *Criminology* 42:837–59.

Felson, R. B., and P. R. Cundiff. 2014. "Sexual Assault as a Crime Against Young People." *Archives of Sexual Behavior* 43(2): 273–84.

Felson, R. B., and M. Krohn. 1990. "Motives for Rape." *Journal of Research in Crime and Delinquency* 27(3): 222–42.

Finkelhor, D. 2008. *Childhood Victimization: Violence, Crime, and Abuse in the Lives of Young People*. Oxford: Oxford University Press.

Finkelhor, D., and N. A. Asdigian. 1996. "Risk Factors for Youth Victimization: Beyond a Lifestyle/Routine Activities Theory Approach." *Violence and Victims* 11:3–19.

Finkelhor, D., and R. Ormrod. 1999. "Reporting Crimes Against Juveniles." Juvenile Justice Bulletin. Washington, DC: U.S. Department of Justice.

Finkelhor, D., R. Ormrod, H. Turner, and S. L. Hamby. 2005. "The Victimization of Children and Youth: A Comprehensive, National Survey." *Child Maltreatment* 10(1): 5–25.

Fite, P. J., S. C. Evans, J. L. Cooley, and S. L. Rubens. 2014. "Further Evaluation of Associations Between Attention-Deficit/Hyperactivity and Oppositional Defiant Disorder Symptoms and Bullying-Victimization in Adolescence." *Child Psychiatry and Human Development* 45(1): 32–41.

Fox, C. L., and C. V. Farrow. 2009. "Global and Physical Self-Esteem and Body Dissatisfaction as Mediators of the Relationship Between Weight Status and Being a Victim of Bullying." *Journal of Adolescence* 32(5): 1287–1301.

Fox, K. A., M. R. Nobles, and B. S. Fisher. 2016. "A Multi-theoretical Framework to Assess Gendered Stalking Victimization: The Utility of Self-Control, Social Learning, and Control Balance Theories." *Justice Quarterly* 33:319–47.

Gannon, T. A., M. R. Rose, and T. Ward. 2008. "A Descriptive Model of the Offense Process for Female Sexual Offenders." *Sexual Abuse* 20:352–74.

Ganpat, S. M., J. van der Leun, and P. Nieuwbeerta. 2013. "The Influence of Event Characteristics and Actors' Behaviour on the Outcome of Violent Events Comparing Lethal with Non-Lethal Events." *British Journal of Criminology* 53(4): 685–704.

George, W. H., K. L. Cue, P. A. Lopez, L. C. Crowe, and J. Norris. 1995. "Self-Reported Alcohol Expectancies and Postdrinking Sexual Inferences About Women." *Journal of Applied Social Psychology* 25(2): 164–86.

George, W. H., S. J. Gournic, and M. P. McAfee. 1988. "Perceptions of Postdrinking Female Sexuality: Effects of Gender, Beverage Choice, and Drink Payment." *Journal of Applied Social Psychology* 18(15): 1295–1316.

Gottfredson, M. R. 1984. "Victims of Crime: The Dimensions of Risk." Home Office Research Study no. 81. London: H. M. Stationery Office.

Gottfredson, M. R., and T. Hirschi. 1990. *A General Theory of Crime*. Palo Alto, CA: Stanford University Press.

Goudriaan, H. 2006. "Reporting Crime: Effects of Social Context on the Decision of Victims to Notify the Police." Doctoral dissertation, University of Leiden.

Govindshenoy, M., and N. Spencer. 2007. "Abuse of the Disabled Child: A Systematic Review of Population-Based Studies." *Child: Care, Health and Development* 33:552–58.

Griffiths, L. J., and A. S. Page. 2008. "The Impact of Weight Related Victimization on Peer Relationships: The Female Adolescent Perspective." *Obesity* 16:39–45.

Guendelman, M. D., S. Ahmad, J. I. Meza, E. B. Owens, and S. P. Hinshaw. 2016. "Childhood Attention-Deficit/Hyperactivity Disorder Predicts Intimate Partner Victimization in Young Women." *Journal of Abnormal Child Psychology* 44:155–66.

Hahn, J. W., M. C. McCormick, J. G. Silverman, E. B. Robinson, and K. C. Koenen. 2014. "Examining the Impact of Disability Status on Intimate Partner Violence Victimization in a Population Sample." *Journal of Interpersonal Violence* 29(17):2063–85.

Hale, R. 1997. "Motives of Reward Among Men Who Rape." *American Journal of Criminal Justice* 22:101–19.

Harrell, E. 2014. "Crime Against Persons with Disabilities, 2009–2012—Statistical Tables." Washington, DC: U.S. Department of Justice.

Hartjen, C. A., and S. Priyadarsini. 2012. *The Global Victimization of Children: Problems and Solutions*. New York: Springer.

Haynie, D. L., and A. R. Piquero. 2006. "Pubertal Development and Physical Victimization in Adolescence." *Journal of Research in Crime and Delinquency* 43(1): 3–35.

Hearnden, I., and C. Magill. 2004. "Decision-Making by House Burglars: Offenders' Perspectives." London: Home Office, Research, Development and Statistics Directorate.

Hensley, C., R. Tewksbury, and T. Castle. 2003. "Characteristics of Prison Sexual Assault Targets in Male Oklahoma Correctional Facilities." *Journal of Interpersonal Violence* 18(6): 595–606.

Hibbard, R. A., L. W. Desch, and the Committee on Child Abuse and Neglect and Council on Children with Disabilities. 2007. "Maltreatment of Children with Disabilities." *American Academy of Pediatrics* 119:1018–25.

Hindelang, M. J., M. R. Gottfredson, and J. Garofalo. 1978. *Victims of Personal Crime: An Empirical Foundation for a Theory of Personal Victimization*. Cambridge, MA: Ballinger.

Hodgins, S., A. Cree, J. Alderton, and T. Mak. 2008. "From Conduct Disorder to Severe Mental Illness: Associations with Aggressive Behaviour, Crime and Victimization." *Psychological Medicine* 38(7): 975–87.

Holt, T. J., and A. M. Bossler. 2014. "An Assessment of the Current State of Cybercrime Scholarship." *Deviant Behavior* 35:20–40.

Holtfreter, K., M. D. Reisig, and T. C. Pratt. 2008. "Low Self-Control, Routine Activities, and Fraud Victimization." *Criminology* 46:189–220.

Home Office. 2013. *An Overview of Hate Crime in England and Wales.* London: Home Office.

Hough, M. 1987. "Offenders' Choice of Target: Findings from Victim Surveys." *Journal of Quantitative Criminology* 3:355–69.

Howard, D., Y. Qiu, and B. Boekeloo. 2003. "Personal and Social Contextual Correlates of Adolescent Dating Violence." *Journal of Adolescent Health* 33:9–17.

Hughes, K., M. A. Bellis, L. Jones, S. Wood, G. Bates, L. Eckley, E. McCoy, C. Mikton, T. Shakespeare, and A. Officer. 2012. "Prevalence and Risk of Violence Against Adults with Disabilities: A Systematic Review and Meta-Analysis of Observational Studies." *Lancet* 379:1621–29.

Human Rights Watch. 2001. "No Escape: Male Rape in U.S. Prison." http://www.hrw.org/reports/2001/prison/report.html

Indermaur, D. 1995. *Violent Property Crime.* Annandale, NSW, Australia: Federation Press.

Jacobs, B. A. 2000. *Robbing Drug Dealers: Violence Beyond the Law.* New York: Aldine.

Jacobs, B. A., V. Topalli, and R. Wright. 2002. "Carjacking, Streetlife and Offender Motivation." *British Journal of Criminology* 43:673–88.

Janssen, I., W. M. Craig, W. F. Boyce, and W. Pickett. 2004. "Associations Between Overweight and Obesity with Bullying Behaviors in School-Aged Children." *Pediatrics* 113:1187–94.

Jeary, K. 2005. "Sexual Abuse and Sexual Offending Against Elderly People: A Focus on Perpetrators and Victims." *Journal of Forensic Psychiatry and Psychology* 16(2): 328–43.

Jennings, W. G., A. R. Piquero, and J. M. Reingle. 2012. "On the Overlap Between Victimization and Offending: A Review of the Literature." *Aggression and Violent Behavior* 17(1): 16–26.

Jones, L., M. A. Bellis, S. Wood, K. Hughes, E. McCoy, L. Eckley, G. Bates, C. Mikton, T. Shakespeare, and A. Officer. 2012. "Prevalence and Risk of Violence Against Children with Disabilities: A Systematic Review and Meta-Analysis of Observational Studies. *Lancet* 380(9845): 899–907.

Kaiser, S. 2013. "Is Facial Attractiveness a Factor in Victimization Involving Robbery/Theft?" Doctoral dissertation, Simon Fraser University.

Kerley, K. R., X. Xu, and B. Sirisunyaluck. 2008. "Self-Control, Intimate Partner Abuse, and Intimate Partner Victimization: Testing the General Theory of Crime in Thailand." *Deviant Behavior* 29(6): 503–32.

Killias, M., S. Staubli, L. Biberstein, M. Bänziger, and S. Iadanza. 2011. *Studie zur Kriminalität und Opfererfahrungen der Schweizer Bevölkerung. Analysen im Rahmen der schweizerischen Opferbefragung 2011.* Zürich, Switzerland: Rechtswissenschaftliches Institut.

Langlois, J. H., L. Kalakanis, A. J. Rubenstein, A. Larson, M. Hallam, and M. Smoot. 2000. "Maxims or Myths of Beauty? A Meta-Analytic and Theoretical Review." *Psychological Bulletin* 126(3): 390.

Långström, N., Q. Rahman, E. Carlström, and P. Lichtenstein. 2010. "Genetic and Environmental Effects on Same-Sex Sexual Behavior: A Population Study of Twins in Sweden." *Archives of Sexual Behavior* 39(1): 75–80.

Larsen, J. J., J. Payne, and A. Tomison. 2011. *Crimes Against International Students in Australia, 2005–09.* Canberra City, ACT: Australian Institute of Criminology.

Lauritsen, J. L. 2001. "The Social Ecology of Violent Victimization: Individual and Contextual Effects in the NCVS." *Journal of Quantitative Criminology* 17(1): 3–32.

Lauritsen, J. L. 2010. "Advances and Challenges in Empirical Studies of Victimization." *Journal of Quantitative Criminology* 26(4): 501–8.

Lauritsen, J. L., and K. F. Davis Quinet. 1995. "Repeat Victimization Among Adolescents and Young Adults." *Journal of Quantitative Criminology* 11(2): 143–66.

Lauritsen, J. L., and K. Heimer. 2008. "The Gender Gap in Violent Victimization, 1973–2004." *Journal of Quantitative Criminology* 24:125–47.

Lauritsen, J. L., and K. Heimer. 2010. "Violent Victimization Among Males and Economic Conditions." *Criminology and Public Policy* 9(4): 665–92.

Lauritsen, J. L., R. J. Sampson, and J. H. Laub. 1991. "Link Between Offending and Victimization Among Adolescents." *Criminology* 29(2): 265–91.

Leclerc, B., and P. Tremblay. 2007). "Strategic Behavior in Adolescent Sexual Offenses Against Children: Linking Modus Operandi to Sexual Behaviors." *Sexual Abuse* 19:23–41.

Lerner, R. M. 1978. "Nature, Nurture, and Dynamic Interactionism." *Human Development* 21:1–20.

Lindegaard, M. R., W. Bernasco, and S. Jacques. 2015. "Consequences of Expected and Observed Victim Resistance for Offender Violence During Robbery Events." *Journal of Research in Crime and Delinquency* 52(1): 32–61.

Lindgren, K. P., D. W. Pantalone, M. A. Lewis, and W. H. George. 2009. "College Students' Perceptions About Alcohol and Consensual Sexual Behavior: Alcohol Leads to Sex." *Journal of Drug Education* 39(1): 1–21.

Lohr, S., and S. Sun. 1998. "Probability of Victimization over Time: Results from the U.S. National Crime Victimization Survey." *Proceedings of Statistics Canada Symposium 98. Longitudinal Analysis for Complex Surveys*: 161–66.

Luckenbill, D. F. 1977. "Criminal Homicide as a Situated Transaction." *Social Problems* 25(2): 176–86.

Maniglio, R. 2009. "Severe Mental Illness and Criminal Victimization: A Systematic Review." *Acta Psychiatrica Scandinavica* 119(3): 180–91.

Midei, A. J., and K. A. Matthews. 2011. "Interpersonal Violence in Childhood as a Risk Factor for Obesity: A Systematic Review of the Literature and Proposed Pathways." *Obesity Review* 12:159–72.

Miethe, T. D., and R. F. Meier. 1990. "Opportunity, Choice, and Criminal Victimization: A Test of a Theoretical Model." *Journal of Research in Crime and Delinquency* 27:243–66.

Mikton, C., and T. Shakespeare, eds. 2014. "Violence Against People with Disability: Guest-Edited Special Issue." *Journal of Interpersonal Violence* 29(17).

Miller, J. 1998. "Up It Up: Gender and the Accomplishment of Street Robbery." *Criminology* 36(1): 37–66.

Mullins, C. W. 2006. *Holding Your Square. Masculinities, Streetlife and Violence.* Cullompton, UK: Willan.

Mullins, C. W., and M. G. Cherbonneau. 2011. "Establishing Connections: Gender, Motor Vehicle Theft, and Disposal Networks." *Justice Quarterly* 28:278–302.

Mullins, C. W., and J. Miller. 2008. "Temporal, Situational and Interactional Features of Women's Violent Conflicts." *Australian and New Zealand Journal of Criminology* 41:36–62.

Mullins, C. W., and R. Wright. 2003. "Gender, Social Networks, and Residential Burglary." *Criminology* 41(3): 813–40.

Mullins, C. W., R. Wright, and B. A. Jacobs. 2004. "Gender, Streetlife and Criminal Retaliation." *Criminology* 42:911–40.

Mustaine, E. E., and R. Tewksbury. 1998. "Predicting Risks of Larceny Theft Victimization: A Routine Activity Analysis Using Refined Lifestyle Measures." *Criminology* 36(4): 829–58.

Nagin, D., and R. Paternoster. 2000. "Population Heterogeneity and State Dependence: State of the Evidence and Directions for Future Research." *Journal of Quantitative Criminology* 16:117–44.

Naughton, C., J. Drennan, I. Lyons, A. Lafferty, M. Treacy, A. Phelan, A. O'Loughlin, and L. Delaney. 2012. "Elder Abuse and Neglect in Ireland: Results from a National Prevalence Survey." *Age and Ageing* 41:98–103.

Nisbett, R. E., and T. D. Wilson. 1977. "Telling More Than We Can Know: Verbal Reports on Mental Processes." *Psychological Review* 84(3): 231–59.

Nobles, M. R., and K. A. Fox. 2013. "Assessing Stalking Behaviors in a Control Balance Theory Framework." *Criminal Justice and Behavior* 40:737–62.

Olofsson, N., K. Lindqvist, and I. Danielsson. 2015. "Higher Risk of Violence Exposure in Men and Women with Physical or Sensory Disabilities: Results from a Public Health Survey." *Journal of Interpersonal Violence* 30(10): 1671–86.

Pardini, D. A., P. J. Fite, and J. D. Burke. 2008. "Bidirectional Associations Between Parenting Practices and Conduct Problems in Boys from Childhood to Adolescence: The Moderating Effect of Age and African-American Ethnicity." *Journal of Abnormal Child Psychology* 36(5): 647–62.

Pare, P. P., and M. W. Logan. 2011. "Risks of Minor and Serious Violent Victimization in Prison: The Impact of Inmates' Mental Disorders, Physical Disabilities, and Physical Size." *Society and Mental Health* 1:106–23.

Pease, K. 1998. *Repeat Victimisation: Taking Stock.* London: Home Office Police Research Group.

Perreault, S., and S. Brennan. 2010. "Criminal Victimization in Canada, 2009. Juristat. Statistics Canada, Canadian Centre for Justice Statistics. Catalogue no. 85-002-X. http://www.statcan.gc.ca/pub/85-002-x/2010002/article/11340-eng.htm

Petersilia, J. R. 2001. "Crime Victims with Developmental Disabilities: A Review Essay." *Criminal Justice and Behavior* 28(6): 655–94.

Piquero, A. R., and M. Hickman. 2003. "Extending Tittle's Control Balance Theory to Account for Victimization." *Criminal Justice and Behavior* 30(3): 282–301.

Pratt, T. C., J. J. Turanovic, K. A. Fox, and K. A. Wright. 2014. "Self-Control and Victimization: A Meta-Analysis." *Criminology* 52:87–116.

Quarmby, K. 2008. *Getting Away with Murder: Disabled People's Experiences of Hate Crime in the UK.* London: Scope.

Redmond, S. M. 2011. "Peer Victimization Among Students with Specific Language Impairment, Attention-Deficit/Hyperactivity Disorder, and Typical Development." *Language, Speech, and Hearing Services in Schools* 42(4): 520–35.

Ruback, R. B., V. A. Clark, and C. Warner. 2014. "Why Are Crime Victims at Risk of Being Victimized Again? Substance Use, Depression, and Offending as Mediators of the Victimization–Revictimization Link." *Journal of Interpersonal Violence* 29:157–85.

Rudolph, C. W., C. L. Wells, M. D. Weller, and B. B. Baltes. 2009. "A Meta-Analysis of Empirical Studies of Weight-Based Bias in the Workplace." *Journal of Vocational Behavior* 74:1–10.

Scherer, H. L., J. A. Snyder, and B. S. Fisher. 2014. "Intimate Partner Victimization Among College Students with and Without Disabilities: Prevalence of and Relationship to Emotional Well-Being." *Journal of Interpersonal Violence* 31(1)

Schoepfer, A., and N. L. Piquero. 2009. "Studying the Correlates of Fraud Victimization and Reporting." *Journal of Criminal Justice* 37:209–15.

Schreck, C. J. 1999. "Criminal Victimization and Low Self-Control: An Extension and Test of a General Theory of Crime." *Justice Quarterly* 16(3): 633–54.

Schreck, C. J., M. W. Burek, and J. Clark-Miller. 2007. "He Sends Rain Upon the Wicked: A Panel Study of the Influence of Religiosity on Violent Victimization. *Journal of Interpersonal Violence* 22(7): 872–93.

Schwartz, D., K. A. Dodge, and J. D. Coie. 1993. "The Emergence of Chronic Peer Victimization in Boys' Play Groups." *Child Development* 64:1755–72.

Sentenac, M., C. Arnaud, A. Gavin, M. Molcho, S. N. Gabhainn, and E. Godeau. 2011. "Peer Victimization Among School-Aged Children with Chronic Conditions." *Epidemiologic Reviews* 34(1): 120–28.

Silver, E. 2002. "Mental Disorder and Violent Victimization: The Mediating Role of Involvement in Conflicted Social Relationships." *Criminology* 40:191–212.

Silver, E., L. Arseneault, J. Langley, A. Caspi, and T. E. Moffitt. 2005. "Mental Disorder and Violent Victimization in a Total Birth Cohort." *American Journal of Public Health* 95(11): 2015.

Sommers, I., and D. R. Baskin. 1993. "The Situational Context of Violent Female Offending." *Journal of Research in Crime and Delinquency* 30:136–62.

Spano, R., and J. Freilich. 2009. "An Assessment of the Empirical Validity and Conceptualization of Individual Level Multivariate Studies of Lifestyle/Routine Activities Theory Published from 1995 to 2005. *Journal of Criminal Justice* 37:305–14.

St. Jean, P. K. B. 2007. *Pockets of Crime: Broken Windows, Collective Efficacy, and the Criminal Point of View*. Chicago: University of Chicago.

Stein, R. E. 2009. "Assault Victimization: A Comparative Analysis of the United States, the Netherlands, and England and Wales." *International Journal of Criminal Justice Sciences* 4:44–59.

Stevens, D. J. 1995. "Predatory Rapists and Victim Selection Techniques." *Social Science Journal* 31:421–33.

Storch, E. A., C. Masia-Warner, H. Crisp, and R. Klein. 2005. "Peer Victimization and Social Anxiety in Adolescence: A Prospective Study." *Aggressive Behavior* 31:437–52.

Studer, D. 2014. *Kriminalitätsfurcht und Viktimisierung im Alter: Ergebnisse einer nationalen Opferwerdungsbefragung unter österreichischen Seniorinnen und Senioren*. Zürich, Switzerland: Dike.

Synovitz, L. B., and T. J. Byrne. 1998. "Antecedents of Sexual Victimization: Factors Discriminating Victims from Nonvictims." *Journal of American College Health* 46(4): 151–58.

Tark, J., and G. Kleck. 2004. "Resisting Crime: The Effects of Victim Action on the Outcomes of Crimes." *Criminology* 42(4): 861–910.

Teaster, P. B., and K. A. Roberto. 2004. "Sexual Abuse of Older Adults: APS Cases and Outcomes." *The Gerontologist* 44(6): 788–96.

Teplin, L. A., G. M. McClelland, K. M. Abram, and D. A. Weiner. 2005. "Crime Victimization in Adults with Severe Mental Illness: Comparison with the National Crime Victimization Survey." *Archives of General Psychiatry* 62(8): 911–21.

Tiggemann, M., and T. Anesbury. 2000. "Negative Stereotyping of Obesity in Children: The Role of Controllability Beliefs." *Journal of Applied Social Psychology* 30:1977–93.

Topalli, V., and R. Wright. 2004. "Dubs and Dees, Beats and Rims: Carjackers and Urban Violence." In *Criminal Behaviors: A Text Reader*, edited by D. Dabney, pp. 149–69. Belmont, CA: Wadsworth.

Topalli, V., R. Wright, and R. Fornango. 2002. "Drug Dealers, Robbery and Retaliation: Vulnerability, Deterrence and the Contagion of Violence." *British Journal of Criminology* 42:337–51.

Topçuoğlu, T. 2011. "Parents' Use of Corporal Punishment and Children's Externalising Behaviour Problems: A Cross-Cultural Assessment." Doctoral dissertation, University of Cambridge.

Trahan, A., J. W. Marquart, and J. Mullings. 2005. "Fraud and the American Dream: Toward an Understanding of Fraud Victimization." *Deviant Behavior* 26:601–20.

Truman, J. L., and L. Langton. 2014. "Criminal Victimization, 2013." NCJ 247648. Washington, DC: U.S. Department of Justice.

Tseloni, A., and K. Pease. 2003. "Repeat Personal Victimization: 'Boosts' or 'Flags'?" *British Journal of Criminology* 43:196–212.

van Dijk, J., J. van Kesteren, P. Smit; Tilburg University, UNICRI, UNODC. 2007. "Criminal Victimisation in International Perspective: Key Findings from the 2004–2005 ICVS and EU ICS." The Hague, Ministry of Justice, WODC.

van Dijk, J. J. M., and C. H. D. Steinmetz. 1980. *The Burden of Crime on Dutch Society, 1973–1979.* Den Haag, the Netherlands: WODC.

van Donselaar, J., and P. R. Rodrigues., eds. 2008. *Monitor racisme and extremisme: Achtste rapportage.* Amsterdam: Pallas Publications.

van Gelder, J. L., M. Averdijk, M. Eisner, and D. Ribaud. 2015. "Unpacking the Victim–Offender Overlap: On Role Differentiation and Socio-psychological Characteristics." *Journal of Quantitative Criminology* 31(4): 653–75.

van Wilsem, J. 20131. "'Bought It, but Never Got It' Assessing Risk Factors for Online Consumer Fraud Victimization." *European Sociological Review* 29(2): 168–78.

van Wilsem, J., N. D. De Graaf, and K. Wittebrood. 2002. "Variations in Cross-National Victimization: The Impact of Composition and Context." In *Crime Victimization in Comparative Perspective: Results from the International Crime Victims Survey, 1989–2000,* edited by P. Nieuwbeerta, pp. 119–40. Den Haag, the Netherlands: Boom Juridische Uitgevers.

van Wyk, J., and K. A. Mason. 2001. "Investigating Vulnerability and Reporting Behavior for Consumer Fraud Victimization Opportunity as a Social Aspect of Age." *Journal of Contemporary Criminal Justice* 17:328–45.

von Hentig, H. 1948. *The Criminal and His Victim.* New Haven, CT: Yale University Press.

White, J. W., and C. Buehler. 2012. "Adolescent Sexual Victimization, ADHD Symptoms, and Risky Sexual Behavior." *Journal of Family Violence* 27(2): 123–32.

Wiederman, M. W., R. A. Sansone, and L. A. Sansone. 1999. "Obesity Among Sexually Abused Women: An Adaptive Function for Some?" *Women and Health* 29:89–100.

Wiener, J., and M. Mak. 2009. "Peer Victimization in Children with Attention-Deficit/Hyperactivity Disorder." *Psychology in the Schools* 46(2): 116–31.

Wilcox, P., M. S. Tillyer, and B. S. Fisher. 2009. "Gendered Opportunity? School-Based Adolescent Victimization." *Journal of Research in Crime and Delinquency* 46:245–69.

Wilson, M. M. 2014. "Hate Crime Victimization, 2004–2012—Statistical Tables." NCJ 244409. Washington, DC: U.S. Department of Justice.

Wittebrood, K. 2006. *Slachtoffers van criminaliteit: Feiten en achtergronden.* Den Haag, the Netherlands: Sociaal en Cultureel Planbureau.

Wolfgang, M. E. 1958. *Patterns in Criminal Homicide.* Philadelphia: University of Pennsylvania Press.

Wright, R., F. Brookman, and T. Bennett. 2006. "The Foreground Dynamics of Street Robbery in Britain." *British Journal of Criminology* 46:1–15.

Wright, R. T., and S. Decker. 1994. *Burglars on the Job: Streetlife and Residential Break-ins.* Boston: Northeastern University Press.

Wright, R. T., and S. Decker. 1997. *Armed Robbers in Action: Stickups and Street Culture.* Boston: Northeastern University Press.

CHAPTER 16

....

CO-OFFENDING AND
CO-OFFENDER SELECTION

....

SARAH B. VAN MASTRIGT

RESEARCH dating back to the early 1900s (Breckinridge and Abbott 1912; Shaw and McKay 1931) has demonstrated that co-offending—the act of committing crime together with one or more accomplices—is a common feature of many offenders' criminal behavior, particularly during youth.[1] Current evidence suggests that between 10 and 15 percent of all crimes measured across age and crime type involve multiple offenders, with considerably higher rates for youths and offenses such as burglary and robbery (for a review, see Carrington 2014). Although a minority of all *offenses* are committed in groups, a significant proportion of *offenders* are nonetheless involved in co-offending at some stage during their criminal career. In an analysis of youth co-offending in Philadelphia, for example, Conway and McCord (2002, p. 99) reported that more than 80 percent of the 400 juvenile court offenders examined in their study were linked to at least one recorded accomplice during the eighteen-year study period. Sarnecki (2001) similarly observed high official levels of youth co-offending in Stockholm, Sweden, between 1991 and 1995, during which 56 percent of youths were involved in at least one group crime. Even in studies encompassing a wider age range, co-offending is ubiquitous: based on UK police data, nearly one-third of all offenders between the ages of ten and seventy-four years followed over a three-year period had at least one official record of co-offending (van Mastrigt and Farrington 2009, 2011).

Although there is a substantial body of evidence establishing the importance of co-offending globally and describing its empirical regularities (Reiss 1988; Reiss and Farrington 1991; Sarnecki 2001; Carrington 2002; Warr 2002; Piquero, Farrington, and Blumstein 2007; Andresen and Felson 2012; Carrington and van Mastrigt 2013), curiously little attention has been dedicated to understanding how joint offending impacts criminal decision making. However, there is good reason to believe that individual decision making might be altered in the company of other offenders. A long history of research in the fields of social psychology and sociology demonstrates that small group dynamics can play a formidable role in shaping all manner of behaviors, via social processes that are also likely to occur in offending situations (for a review, see Viki and Abrams 2013). To date, only a handful of studies have explored the relationship between co-offending and criminal decision making, but the emerging evidence from these investigations suggests that groups do, in fact, "alter individual calculus in criminal decisions in many ways" (Hochstetler 2014, p. 571).

In this chapter, current theoretical and empirical knowledge regarding co-offending and (a) the decision to (co)-offend, (b) the selection of accomplices, and (c) choices shaping the characteristics of the criminal event (planning, target selection, and seriousness) is reviewed and discussed in relation to the development of future work. An underlying assumption made throughout is that "choice" and "decision making" in criminal contexts are highly bounded and sometimes operate outside the conscious awareness of the actors involved. Co-offending can thus involve both explicit and implicit reasoning. Modern dual-process theories in psychology and behavioral economics argue that in any given situation or decision-making context, thinking and reasoning can occur via one of two cognitive systems or, alternatively, on a continuum from conscious and controlled analysis—sometimes referred to as System 1 thinking—to relatively automatic and unconscious System 2 processing (Stanovich and West 2000; Kahneman 2003; Osman 2004;Dijksterhuis and Nordgren 2006). Both of these pathways are considered in this chapter.

Another important starting point for the following discussion is the assumption that co-offending can in some cases impact all decisional features of an offense, whereas in other cases it may impact only some aspects of decision making. For example, in some situations, the initial decision to offend may be made independently and precede later choices regarding whether to offend alone or in company, the selection of accomplices, and the nature of the offense. In other cases, the presence or absence of a particular accomplice may govern both the primary decision to offend and all subsequent decisions regarding the crime. In this sense, the existence of potential co-offenders can be treated as a causal antecedent driving the commission and characteristics of the crime or, alternatively, the characteristics of the (planned) crime can be treated as antecedent to the decision to co-offend and with whom.

Finally, note that although choices regarding whether to (co)-offend, who to select as accomplices, and how to carry out the crime can be treated as theoretically distinct, they are rarely separated in discussions of co-offending. While recognizing that these decisions are often highly interconnected in reality, for the current academic exercise they are considered separately.

I. The Decision to (Co)-Offend

As Weerman (2014, p. 5174) has noted, theorizing about why individuals offend with others has received far less attention than basic empirical descriptions of co-offending prevalence and characteristics. The existing theoretical proposals vary from highly instrumental accounts that emphasize a deliberate, rational decision to offend with others to perspectives that downplay intentionality in favor of less calculated social processes.

A. Co-offending as Rational Choice

Instrumental theories of co-offending represent the most clear-cut application of a traditional decision-making perspective. These accounts are inspired by the rational choice approach (Becker 1968; Cornish and Clarke 1986) and suggest that offenders engage in a conscious decision-making process that leads them to maximize benefits and minimize costs. Consistent with a view of explicit and controlled human reasoning, this perspective frames the decision to co-offend as a deliberate weighing of potential advantages and risks that will lead to joint action only if accomplices are perceived to make the commission of a crime easier or more rewarding than if offending alone (Tremblay 1993; McCarthy, Hagan, and Cohen 1998; Weerman 2003).

A number of studies have confirmed that offenders are well aware of the risks of co-offending: Accomplices may be incompetent, cheat, or divulge one's identify if caught by law enforcement, potentially increasing the risk of detection (Wright and Decker 1994; McCarthy et al. 1998; Tillyer and Tillyer 2015). Nonetheless, individuals often choose to cooperate. Scholars who adopt an instrumental perspective argue that this is because, despite their risks, accomplices can also offer important advantages, including specialized skills/knowledge or a division of labor that may be not only beneficial but in fact necessary for more organized and sophisticated crimes (Weerman 2003). In supporting their position, functional theorists often point to the fact that rates of co-offending are typically highest for robbery and burglary, two of the crime types most likely to benefit from the presence of multiple offenders (by providing a lookout, a getaway driver, etc.). Based on the traditional instrumental account, the requirements of the (planned) crime are thus viewed as antecedent, either inviting or discouraging criminal co-operation and the selection of particular accomplices.

The argument that co-offending is more rational (and thus more prevalent) for some crime types implies that the significance of accomplices for the primary decision to offend is also likely to vary across offending categories. In cases in which a co-offender is essential to the successful commission of a crime, the co-offender's presence will also be central to the initial decision to offend. In contrast, for crime types for which accomplices are not strictly necessary but still advantageous, or for which they have no obvious functional advantage, the decision to offend and to co-offend may be made separately. In all circumstances, however, the instrumental approach predicts that group offending will occur only if co-offending is perceived to have more advantages than risks overall.

This perspective is often criticized for overemphasizing the role of individual rationality in the offending process (De Haan and Voss 2003). However, as McCarthy and colleagues (1998) argue in their study of street youths in Toronto and Vancouver, Canada, the decision to co-offend may be best viewed not as primarily governed by individual rationality but, rather, in game theoretic/prisoner dilemma terms. Here, "collective rationality" becomes central, in that accomplices recognize that it is in both their individual and joint interests to cooperate and not cheat the other party. This process of interdependent, instrumental decision making is what underlies two of the most comprehensive functional theories of co-offending proposed to date: Weerman's (2003) Social Exchange Theory and McGloin and Rowan's (2015) Threshold Model.

1. *Social Exchange*

In 2003, noting the weaknesses of existing theoretical perspectives to explain known regularities of co-offending (its peak in adolescence, variations across crime type, and considerable between- and within-individual differences in the propensity to cooperate), Frank Weerman advanced an integrated Social Exchange Theory of co-offending. Rooted in classic sociological and psychological ideas regarding exchange and reciprocity in human relationships (Thibaut and Kelley 1959; Blau 1964), the thrust of his theory is that

> on each occasion when crimes are committed in the company of other offenders, goods are exchanged between offenders. These "exchanged goods" can be material, a share in the catch or a payment, but also immaterial, such as social approval and acceptance. (p. 404)

According to this model, both the decision to (co)-offend and the selection of co-offenders are, determined by assessments of the costs and returns of particular social exchanges. In this sense, it is, at its core, a rational choice model, but it departs from the more traditional economic models of co-offending by allowing for both implicit and explicit reasoning and by including not only material (catch and payment) and instrumental (service) exchanges in the decision to co-offend but also immaterial rewards (acceptance, appreciation, and information). According to Weerman, these different categories of exchanged goods can be traded in various combinations to produce different forms of co-offending designed to meet the individual needs and motivations of the parties involved. Although direct empirical tests of the theory are still needed, this account is considered in some detail here because it currently represents the most widely used decision-making framework for co-offending.

In his theory, Weerman identifies several forms of co-offending, each of which is driven by a different combination of exchanged goods and, by extension, a potentially varied decision-making process. In instrumental co-offending, for example, service is exchanged for catch or payment, whereas in strategic co-offending, information is exchanged in addition to/instead of catch. Quasi-instrumental forms of co-offending are also possible, in which individuals exchange a combination of material and immaterial goods—for example, information and appreciation. Finally, some forms of co-offending are purely expressive, meaning that only social rewards are exchanged, as might be the case for some non-economic crimes such as vandalism. Within each of the aforementioned forms, co-offending may additionally be equal, where both parties reap equivalent benefit, or unequal (this point is further discussed later with respect to insti-gation and recruitment). Ultimately, Weerman (2003, p. 404) suggests "the general moti-vation behind co-offending is that it provides desired material and immaterial rewards." Whereas instrumental, strategic, and quasi-instrumental forms of co-offending are primarily purported to provide material rewards, expressive and unequal forms of co-offending provide social rewards. The theory also recognizes the complexity of person–situation interactions in noting that both individual and situational conditions have to be met for co-offending to occur. Specifically, Weerman proposes that in order to reach and carry out a decision to co-offend, an offender must be *willing* to co-offend, potential co-offenders must be *present/available*, and those co-offenders must be viewed as *attractive* accomplices. He further argues that variations in these conditions may go quite some way in explaining why some offenders are more likely than others to choose co-offending and why the decision to (co)-offend appears to vary, even within individuals, across situations.

First, individuals' willingness to co-offend will vary depending on a number of fac-tors. For example, compared to offenders with material motivations, who might avoid co-offending because it requires a division of proceeds, the theory suggests that offend-ers seeking appreciation and acceptance might be more willing to co-offend because social rewards are nearly always plentiful in co-offending. This could possibly explain the high rates of group crime observed in youth, when such social concerns are para-mount. In addition to basic need satisfaction, age is also likely to play an important role in the willingness to co-offend because, as Nguyen and McGloin (2013) argued, "in addi-tion to different decision-making capacities (i.e., being more oriented toward risk than rewards when making behavioral choices), most adults have higher opportunity costs than adolescents, which could make the uncertainties attached to co-offending more salient" (p. 858). Regardless of age, willingness may also reflect fundamental between-individual differences in the degree of trust one is prepared to place in others (McCarthy et al. 1998, p. 161), or it may reflect related personality differences that restrict or ease the decision to (co)-offend. Unfortunately, little research on these individual factors exists (for a review of co-offending and offender attributes, see van Mastrigt 2014; for recent empirical work investigating the potential importance of moral beliefs and impulsivity, see McGloin and Rowan 2015).

The larger social context in which an individual's offending occurs is also likely to be relevant because some research suggests that particularly difficult life circumstances at the time of the criminal event may promote co-offending willingness. In one of the first studies to explicitly investigate the decision to co-offend, McCarthy and colleagues (1998) found that adversity (hunger and lack of shelter) significantly increased street youths' willingness to co-offend by limiting the salience of risks in favor of the potential for gains. However, in a later study designed to test whether adversity increased *actual* co-offending behavior in two samples of incarcerated adult felons in the United States, Nguyen and McGloin (2013) found that neither objective measures of financial adversity nor self-confessed financial motivations predicted actual co-offending. Net of controls, only drug-related adversity (reporting that one offended in order to obtain money for drugs) was associated with increased odds of co-offending. Although the inconsistent results obtained in these two studies may be a function of the age differences of the samples, they may also imply that willingness alone may not be sufficient to produce actual co-offending behavior.

This could be because, according to Weerman (2003), the decision to co-offend also requires that accomplices are available. Individuals undoubtedly vary in their level of access to co-offenders and convergence settings (Felson 2003). Whereas individuals embedded in large criminal or social networks may have plentiful opportunities to co-offend, offenders with restricted access to potential accomplices will be likely to offend alone or not at all (Tremblay 1993; Sarnecki 2001; McGloin and Piquero 2010). Some scholars propose that it is precisely this situational availability that underlies the age co-offending curve such that high levels of co-offending are produced at younger ages when peers spend a great deal of unstructured time socializing and testing boundaries together, but these decrease with age as job and family commitments decrease the available accomplice pool (Warr 1993). Although availability is purported to be an important factor for all decisions to (co)-offend, there is good reason to suspect that it would be more central to some individuals' decision to offend than to others' decision to do so. For example, to the extent that some individuals may have a stronger dispositional propensity for offending (e.g., those low in self-control), the availability of a co-offender may not play a crucial role in the decision to offend because these individuals do not require accomplices to persuade or support them, whereas for others with lower propensity, the decision to offend may be highly dependent on the availability and encouragement of accomplices (see the Threshold Model of co-offending described later).

The third and final requirement for the decision to co-offend identified by Weerman is that available accomplices are deemed attractive criminal partners—that is, individuals who are trustworthy, skilled, or otherwise rich in relevant material or immaterial goods for exchange; physical, human, and social/group capital (Weerman 2014, p. 5178; see Section II).

A comprehensive discussion of the strengths and weaknesses of Weerman's theory is beyond the scope of this chapter; however, it provides many interesting hypotheses regarding the person–situation interactions involved in the choice to co-offend and the various causal chains that might be involved (e.g., accomplices as antecedent or outcome). From a decision-making perspective, it may provide a particularly fruitful framework for understanding the complexities of group crime because it emphasizes the fact that offenders involved in the same offense can have quite different, but interacting, needs, motivations, and decision-making bases for committing the same crime. Even so, the direct empirical value of the theory remains to be shown because systematic mapping of the model's key features onto offenders' own accounts of their crimes and decision-making processes is still lacking. However, indirect support for the theory has emerged from a number of studies in which offenders provide a combination of social, functional, and opportunity-based rationales for co-offending (McCarthy and Hagan 2001; Alarid, Hochstetler, and Burton 2009; Nguyen and McGloin 2013).

2. *The Threshold Model*

Recently, a new instrumental model of co-offending has been proposed. Like previous perspectives, McGloin and Rowan's (2015) Threshold Model of collective crime points to the weighing of potential costs and benefits as central to the decision to co-offend, but differs in its emphasis on identifying "tipping points" or "thresholds" at which individuals who would not individually be motivated to engage in offending come to see collective crime as maximizing utility. Drawing on Granovetter's (1978) sociological threshold model, this perspective places particular focus on framing individual choice as conditional upon the actions of others and on exploring how variations in group size and composition impact individual decision making.

Initial empirical tests of the theory using hypothetical vignette methods suggest that it may provide a promising new approach to understanding the decision to (co)-offend. Studies with university students have so far revealed interesting variations in individual thresholds to join in hypothetical collective crime scenarios (McGloin and Rowan 2015), as well as changes in both the anticipated costs and rewards of participating in collective crime depending on group size (McGloin and Thomas 2016). These findings highlight the need to consider such factors in future theoretical and empirical work applying rational choice perspectives.

B. Other Perspectives

Although the instrumental accounts outlined previously suggest that the decision to (co)-offend is, at least to some extent, a conscious and controlled one, it is worth noting that other perspectives frame co-offending less as the product of a deliberate, rational decision-making process and more as an artefact of social selection or as the natural and relatively unconscious outgrowth of other social processes.

1. *Co-offending as Artefact*

Some scholars reject traditional "choice" models completely, pointing instead to mere social selection effects to explain co-offending (Glueck and Glueck 1950; Gottfredson and Hirschi 1990). These theorists posit that the presence and influence of others are exaggerated as causal factors in the decision to offend (although accomplices may still impact the form and process of offending). Here, criminal behavior is primarily viewed as the result of individual characteristics and dispositional traits (e.g., low self-control) that are established early in life, typically before interactions with potential co-offenders take place. According to this logic, co-offending is *incidental* and occurs only as a by-product of the fact that offenders are likely to associate with similarly criminal companions (Weerman 2003). This process has been famously characterized by the term "birds of a feather flock together" (Glueck and Glueck 1950). From a decision-making perspective, this view essentially suggests that no "decision" to co-offend takes place. Rather, co-offending emerges relatively spontaneously out of opportunities that arise when two or more individuals, each individually predisposed toward crime, unite.

As Reiss (1988) outlines, this occurs easily because "active delinquents are continually signalling their interest in locating others with whom they may engage in offending. Such signalling is readily picked up by others who are similarly searching" (p. 145). Felson (2003) defined this phenomenon as "offender convergence"—a process through which routine activities bring motivated offenders into contact at informal and unsupervised meeting places where criminal opportunities can be seized and plans hatched (see Section II). Such selection effects are supported by some offenders' own accounts of their co-offending motivations. In a study of convicted robbers, for example, one-third reported that they joined with accomplices relatively spontaneously when an attractive robbery opportunity arose (Alarid et al. 2009).

By rejecting the centrality of accomplices in providing the primary motivation to offend, the selection perspective allows for a clear delineation to be made between an initial decision to offend and whether or not one commits the crime alone or with others. In addition, in framing joint offending as a nondecision, this perspective provides an important counterbalance to traditional rational choice theories that are often criticized for overemphasizing the extent of criminal calculation and explicit decision-making involved in much (co)-offending (De Haan and Vos 2003). However, rejection of social influence and other social processes as potentially important factors in criminal decision making runs counter to a large body of literature on the likely social mechanisms underlying group crime.

2. *Co-offending and Implicit Social Reasoning*

Inspired by classic criminological theorists such as Shaw and McKay (1931), Sutherland (1947), and Akers (1998), scholars have long pointed to the social power yielded by peers in general and co-offenders in particular (Reiss 1988; Sarnecki 2001; Weerman 2003). As Warr (2002) discusses, varied social processes, including norm acquisition, modeling, tutelage, loyalty, fear of ridicule/sanction, status seeking, and peer pressure, may all facilitate a decision to (co)-offend, although likely in more subtle ways than standard rational choice frameworks might suggest. Although criminal actors may, in some cases, be consciously aware of the social psychological forces influencing their behaviors and explicitly include these in their decision calculi, social influence/process views on co-offending typically conceptualize group crime as the product of more implicit social dynamics and pressures that may operate outside of the conscious awareness and calculation of the actor. In this sense, they are primarily concerned with the subtle and heuristic aspects of dual-process reasoning, and they tend not to frame co-offending in traditional *rational* decision terms. However, because newer economic models such as Weerman (2003) and McGloin and Rowan's (2015) theories of co-offending highlight the importance of considering explicit *and* implicit aspects of decision making, and/or material and immaterial costs and rewards, functional and implicit social reasoning perspectives need not necessarily be viewed as contradictory. They may, in fact, be highly complementary. With this framing in mind, the term "decision making" is used loosely in the following section to refer to both explicit and implicit forms of social reasoning.

As noted previously, delinquent peers and potential accomplices may play influential roles in the decision to (co)-offend via any number of social mechanisms (Canter and Alison 2000; Viki and Abrams 2013), only some of which have been explored empirically in relation to co-offending. Existing qualitative investigations support the notion that expressions of loyalty (Hochstetler 2001), group identity (Shover 1996; Hochstetler 2014), and the desire to fit in or impress others (McCluskey and Wardle 2000) can all have significance (see also McGloin and Rowan 2015). In addition, accomplices may sometimes provide the direct instigating force needed for a crime to take place. As McGloin and Nguyen (2014, p. 20) have stated, "The decision to co-offend is not necessarily a democratic one based on equal levels of motivation and interest." In a classic study by Warr (1996), a single instigator who initially suggested the offense could be identified for the vast majority of crimes (between 60 and 100 percent, depending on offense type) reported to the 1967 National Surveys of Youth (NSY). These instigators tended to be the older and more experienced males in the group, perhaps because these characteristics confer status that others deferred to in decision making (see Section II). A number of investigations of women who co-offend in sex crimes, including child sexual abuse, similarly point to the potential importance of a dominant (male) co-offender in driving the decision to offend (Vandiver 2006; Muskens et al. 2011). In these cases, the presence of others may be viewed as antecedent, rendering the decision to offend and the decision to co-offend inseparable, as the accomplice plays a key role in the realization of otherwise uncertain criminal actions of the individual. Even in the absence of status differentials or direct pressure, confident co-offenders may play an important role; in a study of convicted robbers, for example, Alarid and colleagues (2009) found that in the context of uncertainty regarding whether to commit a crime, more than one-third of group offenders reported being influenced by the "quick and confident assurances of partners" (p. 6). Although it is difficult to clearly establish the impact of such social influences on the decision to (co)-offend, particularly when these are implicit, current empirical support is consistent with the basic proposition that "individuals who commit offenses together exert some form of influence over one another, and this influence has significance for their behavior" (Sarnecki 2001, p. 51).

Social psychological processes other than normative social influence and peer pressure may also affect the decision to (co)-offend, either explicitly or implicitly. For example, dynamics of deindividuation and diffusion of responsibility may enable one to shift at least part of the moral responsibility for one's criminal activity to co-offenders (Festinger, Pepitone, and Newcomb 1952; Deiner 1977; Hochstetler 2001; Warr 2002). In Zimring's (1981, p. 878) words, it may be that offenders "find courage in numbers" to engage in acts they would not otherwise commit. Research also suggests that accomplices may maximize the excitement associated with offending (Katz, 1988) and thereby magnify the salience of this individual motivation. In their study of convicted felons, Nguyen and McGloin (2013) found that the "predicted odds of co-offending for subjects who reported excitement as a motivation for crime were more than three times higher than that for subjects who did not report this as a motivation" (p. 856). In both cases, these immaterial rewards of co-offending may factor in to (implicit) decision-making processes promoting joint action (see McGloin and Thomas 2016).

To the extent that susceptibility to social influence, shared sensation seeking, and the overall salience of social concerns is believed to vary across the life course (Warr 1993), the social processes outlined previously may help provide a partial explanation for the consistent finding that co-offending is most common at younger ages, when peers are both highly influential and accessible. Although there is still theoretical debate regarding the underlying causes of the age–co-offending curve (Stolzenberg and D'Alessio 2008), the empirical fact that group crime is far more prevalent among youths implies that accomplices are likely to have more influence on the decision to (co)-offend (be it implicit or explicit) early in the criminal career as compared to later.

Summarizing current research on the role of accomplices in the decision to (co)-offend, Hochstetler (2014) stated that "the influence of crime groups in most cases is best understood as a moderately significant situational inducement" (p. 547). However, the literature reviewed above suggest that considerable individual and situational variations in (co)-offender decision making are likely to exist. Currently, the factors underlying these variations are poorly understood. However, it does seem clear that whether through direct persuasion, subtle influence, improved opportunities, or instrumental necessity, potential accomplices can and do have a role to play in the decision to (co)-offend for at least some crimes. In the following section, a second important aspect of decision making is considered—namely the selection of co-offenders.

II. THE SELECTION OF CO-OFFENDERS

Depending on the theoretical starting point adopted, the decision regarding *with whom* one offends can be viewed as either fundamental or secondary to the decision as to *whether* to (co)-offend. In situations in which a crime would not or could not have been committed in the absence of accomplices, the decision to offend and the selection of co-offenders may be highly interdependent. However, in at least some cases, in which an individual first decides to offend and then seeks out appropriate accomplices, these two aspects of criminal decision making can be viewed as distinct. As was the case for discussions regarding the decision to (co)-offend, theoretical propositions about the "selection" of accomplices range from those that view the process as incidental and often spontaneous to those that highlight rationality and an explicit pursuit to seek out attractive crime partners to meet the needs of a particular crime. Either way, solid explanations of co-offender selection must account for at least three empirical facts about offending groups: they tend to be small, often comprising only a pair of offenders; they are highly homogeneous with respect to age, gender, and criminal experience; and they are transitory, typically committing only a single crime (Warr 1996, 2002; Weerman 2003; McGloin et al. 2008; Carrington and van Mastrigt 2013).

In order to explain these patterns, many theoretical and empirical investigations suggest that a "search" for suitable co-offenders takes place. Although fundamentally a rational choice approach, it is widely recognized that co-offender selection typically occurs within the confines of one's immediate geographical and social environment and that truly free choice is thus limited by spatial constraints (Reiss and Farrington 1991; Schaefer 2012) and routine activities (Clarke and Felson 1993). In this sense, *bounded searching* (Clarke and Cornish 1985; De Haan and Voss 2003), which operates both explicitly and implicitly, is perhaps the best framework from which to consider processes of co-offender selection.

Tremblay (1993), one of the first scholars to theorize directly on the topic, characterized the search for co-offenders as a market phenomenon in which specific accomplices are chosen because they are trusted and offer tangible benefits to the actor. McCarthy and Hagan 2001; see also McCarthy et al. 1998) refer to these desirable resources as "criminal capital" and the cooperative pursuit of crime as "criminal capitalization." Further elaborating on these ideas in his social exchange theory of co-offending, Weerman (2003) identifies four forms of capital that determine the attractiveness of a potential accomplice: physical capital (e.g., strength and tools), human capital (knowledge, skills, and toughness), social capital (contacts), and group capital (status, shared background). Although these are all desirable assets, he argues that certain forms of capital will be more or less important in assessing attractiveness on a case-by-case basis depending on the nature of the specific criminal act for which a co-offender is sought. According to this view, the requirements of the crime in question may therefore be antecedent not only to the decision to (co)-offend, as discussed previously, but also to the selection of particular accomplices possessing attractive criminal capital.

From a criminal capital perspective, the fact that many crime groups are small, homogeneous, and transitory is logical because it would be expected that individuals would want to limit the risks of cooperation by joining together only with accomplices who are perceived to be both attractive and essential for a particular offense (Weerman 2003). Of course, the theoretically ideal co-offender (one who is willing, with whom an actor shares a high degree of trust/similarity, and who simultaneously possesses the requisite criminal capital for the crime in question) may be elusive. Individuals may thus be required to choose the most attractive option from among those readily available. In this case, contrary to the previous view, the availability of particular accomplices and the nature of their individual skills may determine the characteristics of the ensuing crime. Felson (2003) proposed that this availability is facilitated or limited by access to offender convergence settings—the informal spaces mentioned previously in which unstructured socializing allows potential co-offenders to assess and select one another as accomplices (see also Osgood and Anderson 2004). According to Felson, these assessments often develop over an extended period of time, during which noncriminal social interactions allow individuals to gradually build impressions of one another. Offender convergence settings are thus purported to be central to both the underlying implicit and ongoing processes of co-offender selection and the immediate and spontaneous selection of accomplices from among those present when a criminal opportunity arises.

This dual characterization of the process is attractive because it allows for some degree of criminal calculation in the selection of co-offenders while simultaneously being consistent with the finding reported by many scholars that the vast majority of crimes occur relatively spontaneously when opportunities present themselves and do not involve a lengthy process of deliberation and discussion. Applied to offender decision making, Felson's reasoning implies that spontaneous choices that appear on the surface to be impulsive may actually have been a long time in the making implicitly. In a detailed qualitative study of robbery and burglary groups conducted by Hochstetler (2001), this was precisely the reality reported by many offenders. Several noted that subtle nonverbal cues that developed over time signaled shared availability and willingness for co-offending and allowed for split-second decisions to be made at the time of the crime. Furthermore, many co-offenders were friends and individuals acting out a shared identity around a particular type of offending that did not need to be communicated at all.

The fact that co-offenders are typically identified as preexisting friends, family members, or acquaintances from the neighborhood (Reiss and Farrington 1991; Budd, Sharp, and Mayhew 2005) lends credence to the view that in the vast majority of cases, offending groups form within the context of more general social networks and routine activities. As Gould et al. (1965) stated, "excepting recruitment for more sophisticated crimes, which require a variety of highly specialized skills, the daily round suffices to select accomplices" (p. 25). This would explain, at least in part, why offending groups tend to be so homogeneous. A great deal of research in the fields of sociology and psychology has demonstrated the power of human preference for homophily across all manner of social relations, not least because it appears to maximize trust. Homophily refers to the tendency to associate with others deemed similar to oneself with respect to key characteristics such as age, sex, social/economic background, and social values and attitudes (McPherson, Smith-Lovin, and Cook 2001). If it is the case that accomplices are selected from within individuals' general social networks, then the homogeneity of crime groups would naturally be expected. Van Mastrigt and Carrington (2014) attempted to probe this issue statistically by exploring whether co-offending groups displayed greater sex and age homogeneity than that expected by chance based on the demographic composition of the general offending population. They found that crime groups of all sizes were, in fact, more homogeneous than expected, indicating a high degree of inbreeding homophily by age and sex. However, the preference for similar accomplices was most pronounced for females and youths, a finding which suggests that the selection of co-offenders may operate differently across offender subgroups (for an extension of this work, see Carrington 2015). Similar effects have been observed in recent research exploring neighborhood effects on group offending, in which youths were more likely to co-offend in contexts with more peers of their own race/ethnicity, less disadvantage, and greater residential stability—all factors that were purported to promote trust among neighbors (Schaefer, Rodriguez, and Decker 2014).

The general importance of social networks for co-offending and co-offender selection is receiving increasing recognition (Sarnecki 2001; McGloin and Piquero 2010; Carrington 2011; Schaefer 2012; McGloin and Nguyen 2014) because some types of network ties appear to be more useful than others in identifying accomplices for particular types of offending. Whereas the selection of co-offenders for low-level and familiar types of offending can likely be accomplished by drawing on strong ties from within one's immediate social network, new or highly organized offending types might require a wider search for accomplices with specialized skills that is best achieved via weak ties. Consistent with this reasoning, McGloin and Piquero found that offenders with less redundant networks demonstrate more versatility in their offending. Offending with individuals who have different skill sets or expertise may be particularly relevant for processes of criminal tutelage (Sutherland 1947; McCarthy 1996) and mentoring (Morselli, Tremblay, and McCarthy 2006) or in situations in which role differentiation and a division of labor are important. A number of studies on burglars and robbers have identified offending roles, including the planner/leader, heavy, driver, and apprentice (Donald and Wilson 2000; McCluskey and Wardle 2000). It is reasonable to expect that individuals to fill some of these roles might need to be sought out more planfully than others. Hence, even in the context of a single crime, multiple pathways to co-offender selection may be operating.

One particular co-offending role that has received considerable attention is that of instigator or recruiter. As mentioned previously, co-offending is not always equal with respect to the social exchanges involved, and this imbalance may also apply to the selection of co-offenders and the adoption of offending roles. A number of scholars have hypothesized that some offenders act as recruiters to younger and less experienced accomplices. Testing Reiss' (1988) initial hypothesis regarding the existence of this group, Reiss and Farrington (1991), and later van Mastrigt and Farrington (2011), were able to identify a small group of offenders who consistently fit the recruiter profile over time. These individuals were older and more criminally experienced than their accomplices, and they were typically involved in property offending. Whereas these studies suggest that some offenders may be stable in this offending role over time, other studies point to the flexibility in instigation/joining across situations. In Warr's (1996) NSY study, for example, the majority of individuals reported acting as instigators for some crimes and joining in others. Recent evidence on the topic suggests that there is both within-individual stability and variation in instigation across the criminal career. In a study of incarcerated offenders, McGloin and Nguyen (2012) found that perceived expertise at the offense type in question was the most consistent and strong predictor of instigation when keeping other covariates constant, but age of onset was also important. Thus, both individual characteristics and situational contexts likely factor into decisions regarding whom one co-offends with and in what role. What remains to be seen is how the characteristics of the actor and the situation interact at the moment of decision making to produce differential offending roles. Whatever the mechanisms, the fact that many crimes appear to involve differential initiative on the part of some offenders suggests that decision making regarding the selection of co-offenders may be considerably more active for these offenders than for their accomplices, who passively join. An interesting question for future work is whether the same individuals who initially suggest the offense or recruit others to take part are also the ones most likely to take a leadership role during the offense and to wield more influence over later decisions made in the group as well (see Porter and Alison 2006).

A final point regarding the selection of co-offenders is that accomplices are changed frequently, and it is rare that crime groups commit multiple offenses in the same composition (Reiss and Farrington 1991; Sarnecki 2001; Warr 2002; McGoin et al. 2008; van Mastrigt and Farrington 2009). As Warr (1996) stated, "The modal life expectancy of offending groups is one event" (p. 24). Whether the transitory nature of co-offending reflects changing compositions of the underlying opportunity pools from which co-offenders are selected (e.g., offender convergence settings and general social networks) or more calculated efforts to match unique accomplices to different crimes is uncertain. However, the implication for decision making is that although individual co-offenders may influence decision making in particular crimes, in most cases, it is unlikely that the *same* accomplices directly impact on repeated decisions *across* the criminal career. On the other hand, co-participation in even a single offense with a chosen co-offender may lead to an accumulation of criminal capital (e.g., skills, knowledge, and networks) that has an indirect effect on later offending by functioning to further embed offenders in criminal lifestyles and behaviors (McCord and Conway 2002).

In summary, decisions regarding with whom to offend, like the decision as to whether to (co)-offend at all, are likely to be driven by a combination of both explicit choices regarding potential accomplices' attractiveness and more implicit and subtle processes that operate outside the conscious awareness of the decision maker. Therefore, a dual-process decision-making framework likely also provides the best model of co-offender selection.

III. Co-offending and Characteristics of the Criminal Event

In addition to basic decisions as to whether to commit a co-offense and with whom, accomplice interactions also appear to shape the character of the criminal event itself. It has been well documented that co-offending is more common for some crime types than others, with the highest rates for burglary, robbery, and motor vehicle theft and the lowest rates for sex offending and other serious interpersonal crimes (Sarnecki 2001; Carrington 2002; van Mastrigt and Farrington 2009). However, even within crime type, an emerging line of research has uncovered a number of interesting variations in the features of lone versus group crimes that are consistent with much social psychological theorizing and research that has demonstrated that individuals often behave differently in groups compared to when they are alone (see Viki and Abrams 2013). Although co-offender interactions could impact on any number of decisions regarding the offense, the focus here is on the few areas in which research has provided some insights, namely with respect to planning, target selection, level of risk, and seriousness of the offense.

In this section, the existence of a criminal pair/group is primarily treated as antecedent to producing particular crime characteristics because this is the directionality typically assumed in the extant literature exploring lone and group offenses. However, it is worth noting that focus can also be reversed to consider how crimes with particular characteristics invite the participation (or not) of a set of given accomplices, in line with the functional arguments presented in the first and second sections of this chapter.

A. Planning, Target Selection, and Risk

Most of the available research indicates that limited thought goes into planning the vast majority of co-offenses. Rather, crimes are typically committed relatively spontaneously against immediately available targets and when attractive opportunities arise (Hochstetler 2001; Alarid et al. 2009). Acting out explicitly preformed motivations and plans is thus the exception rather than the rule. However, in the case of some acquisition crimes such as burglary and robbery, the selection of suitable targets and plans regarding a getaway may be crucial decisions impacting the success or failure of the offense. Given that co-offending requires at least some degree of coordination, one might expect that offense planning would be more pronounced in joint compared to lone offenses. Alarid and colleagues (2009, p. 7) tested this hypothesis in a sample of 30 incarcerated robbers. Although most respondents indicated that little planning was involved in their crimes, those with accomplices were significantly more likely to report planning than lone offenders, even when controlling for other possible covariates. A sense of control over the offense was also more prevalent among group offenders, primarily due to this greater level of planning.

One of the most crucial aspects to consider in planning an offense is target selection. There are many reasons to believe that target selection may differ for joint versus lone offenses, not only due to general tendencies toward more extreme decisions in groups—a phenomenon termed "group polarization" by psychologists (Moscovici and Zavalloni 1969)—but also because multiple offenders have the potential to expand the knowledge base regarding available targets beyond what any single offender might be aware of and to wield greater power against them. As a result, one might expect that strength in numbers would allow for the selection of larger or riskier targets when offending in groups compared to alone. However, the empirical evidence on this point is mixed. In one of the first studies to explore target selection as it relates to co-offending, Cromwell, Olson, and Avary (1991) asked a sample of active burglars to explain the rationale behind their selection of a series of hypothetical targets. Somewhat contrary to expectations, the presence of co-offenders in fact led to more cautious choices, in part because accomplices were able to identify additional risk factors of which respondents were not aware. This finding was not replicated, however, in a more recent study of convicted US robbers, in which offending groups were found to be neither more risky nor more cautious in their real-world selections of targets (Alarid et al. 2009). One possible explanation for this finding could be that conflicting considerations weighing toward caution (increased risk awareness), on the one hand, and daring (division of labor, level of intimidation, etc.), on the other hand, balance each other out when groups are involved. Alternatively, it may simply be the case that for crimes such as robbery and burglary, the essential characteristics that signal the attractiveness of a target are so well recognized by all parties that the group character of the crime has no effect. In a study of residential burglaries in the Hague, Bernasco (2006) explored several key features related to the attractiveness of potential targets, including affluence, accessibility, proximity to home/city center, and social disorganization, and compared these target characteristics for group and solo offenses. It was hypothesized that some of these characteristics would be more important for lone offenders than for group offenders (e.g., accessibility, due to the absence of a lookout), whereas others would be more relevant for co-offending groups (e.g., affluence of the target, due to the need to share proceeds). However, this did not appear to be the case because group and solo burglars ultimately selected similar targets, namely those that were physically accessible and close in proximity to the home of the offender(s).

B. Seriousness/Violence

Although current research does not suggest that groups select riskier targets overall, it has been consistently demonstrated that crimes committed in concert tend to be more serious than those committed alone. In his large-scale analysis of co-offending in Canada, for example, Carrington (2002) found that in comparison to lone offenses, group crimes were more likely to involve the use of a weapon, particularly firearms, and that the number of offenders was positively related to the amount of property damage/loss and serious injury or death. Analysis of robbery incidents recorded in the 2011 National Incident Based Reporting System confirmed these patterns; joint offenses resulted in higher monetary yields in total (although with lower proceeds on average per offender), and the use of weapons and injury to victims were also more prevalent for group offenses (Tillyer and Tillyer 2015). Overall, the presence of accomplices appears to increase the negative impacts on victims while increasing the overall criminal earnings for offending groups (see also McCarthy and Hagan 2001; Morselli et al. 2006).

Even when controlling for possible covariates, these findings are robust. Focusing on violence specifically, McGloin and Piquero (2009) demonstrated that in a youthful US sample, "the likelihood of a co-offence being violent increased with each additional accomplice present, independent of whether these co-offenders had a history of prior violence" (p. 347). Alarid and colleagues (2009) similarly observed a significant difference in the use of violence in group robberies (57 percent) compared to lone robberies (31 percent), which could not be explained by the number of victims involved. It does not seem likely that offending groups make explicit choices to engage in more serious offenses. Rather, McGloin and Piquero draw on the notion of more subtle tendencies toward collective behavior to explain these findings, pointing to a great deal of psychological research indicating that in the presence of others, it is easier to deindividuate and diffuse responsibility and thereby decrease moral prohibitions against criminal behaviors in which one might not otherwise engage (Festinger et al. 1952; Zimbardo, 1970; Deiner 1977). This moral disengagement may also interact with the opportunities that the group provides to express bravado, fearlessness, or to enhance status by demonstrating a willingness to take risks (Warr 2002; Alarid et al. 2009). Even so, it is important to note that it is difficult to disentangle selection and influence effects here because it is not clear whether it is the characteristics of the co-offending context or the characteristics of the offenders who gravitate toward group crime that underlie these findings.

Importantly, the relationship between violence and co-offending appears to extend beyond the immediate offense to impact future offending as well. In one of the few studies exploring longitudinal patterns of co-offending, Conway and McCord (2002) found that when individuals with no personal history of violent offending joined with a violent accomplice for their first co-offense (even for a nonviolent crime), those individuals were themselves significantly more likely than other co-offenders to engage in subsequent violence—a finding the authors attributed to some form of social learning.

Although the current literature provides relatively few insights regarding the specific decision-making processes that underlie the planning, target selection, and seriousness of group offenses, findings such as those discussed previously have led several scholars to argue that the impacts of co-offending for victims, offenders, and society at large are substantial and deserve more attention in future work (van Mastrigt and Farrington 2009; Andresen and Felson 2010a, 2010b).

IV. Next Steps

The fact that many crimes are committed in company raises fundamental questions regarding the significance of co-offending and co-offenders for offender decision making. Although the limited research and theory outlined previously provide an important framework for better understanding the impacts of criminal cooperation on key decisional aspects of offending, a solid body of empirical evidence on this topic is still lacking. This is likely due, in part, to offenders' considerable reluctance to discuss their accomplices' characteristics and roles, possibly "for fear of being labeled a 'snitch' and because accomplices may not have been arrested or convicted" (Alarid et al. 2009, p. 4; see also Morselli et al. 2006). Because the richest information about offender decision making must come from offenders themselves (Bernasco 2010), progress will require considerable effort on the part of researchers to gain the trust and cooperation of criminals who have acted in concert. Assuming this can be done, a number of avenues for future research are worth noting.

First, from a theoretical standpoint, there is a need for more "explicit attempts to empirically test theoretical notions about fundamental processes behind co-offending" (Weerman 2014, p. 5183) and to trace causal processes (e.g., exploring potential co-offenders vs. crime characteristics as antecedent). This will require collection of more comprehensive information regarding both stable individual characteristics that increase the willingness to co-offend and situational contexts that promote behavioral expression of this willingness. As Hochstetler (2014, p. 575) has emphasized, a true understanding of the decision to offend, the role of co-offending in that decision, and the character of the criminal event that results must take account of the preceding and immediate social context in which the offending is embedded. Simply stated, more attention to person–situation interactions implied in theories such as that of Weerman (2003) and McGloin and Rowan (2015) is needed, as is better recognition that the decisions of groups are "much more complex than a simple aggregate of the preferences of the individuals that compose them" (Hochstetler 2014, p. 571).

Future research would also benefit from drawing more consistently on established social psychological knowledge regarding small group dynamics, social influence, and social cognition. Although there are growing calls for more systematic applications of such concepts and theories to the study of crime (Canter and Alison 2000; Gadd and Jefferson 2007; Wood and Gannon 2013), solid cross-disciplinary applications are still relatively rare, even in the co-offending literature (for exceptions, see McGloin and Piquero 2009; McGloin and Thomas 2016). One obvious priority is the adoption of a more formal psychological and dual-process/continuum approach to studying co-offending. A number of sophisticated dual-process decision-making frameworks have been proposed, which could provide both useful theoretical insights and empirical hypotheses for investigations of the implicit and explicit processes involved in the various stages of co-offender decision making (Stanovich and West 2000; Kahneman 2003; Osman 2004; Dijksterhuis and Nordgren 2006). Testing the applicability of these general theories to specific co-offending contexts would be of benefit not only to criminology but also to the wider decision-making field.

A third important avenue for future work will be to investigate variations in co-offending decision making across crime types. Nearly all of the studies addressing co-offender decision making focus on robbery and burglary (Donald and Wilson 2000; McAndrew 2000; Hochstetler 2001; Mullins and Wright 2003; Alarid et al. 2009; Tillyer and Tillyer 2015). Although even these types of crimes appear to develop relatively opportunistically, they are arguably *relatively* more likely than some others (e.g., vandalism and petty theft) to involve degrees of organization and calculation. Exclusive focus on these crime types may thus lead to an overemphasis on these factors in the literature. Following the logic of theories such as that of Weerman (2003), these crimes are also disproportionately likely to meet instrumental needs and involve primarily material exchanges, which may similarly paint a skewed picture of the decision-making processes involved in other types of joint offenses.

Fourth, it would be interesting to explore changes in (co)-offender decision-making within individual criminal careers. Many offenders appear to shift from group crime early in their criminal careers to lone offending later on (Reiss and Farrington 1991; Piquero et al. 2007;). This suggests that accomplices are likely to have more direct impact on decision making during the early stages of criminal involvement. However, even early involvement in co-offending can increase the frequency, persistence, and seriousness of offending over time (Conway and McCord 2002; Piquero et al. 2007; Carrington

2009; McGloin and Piquero 2010) by expanding criminal networks and criminal capital/knowledge. If this is the case, involvement in co-offending may act as a snare that further embeds offenders in a criminal lifestyle or network that indirectly limits their decision frameworks as their legitimate opportunities decrease.

Finally, it would be valuable to identify aspects of co-offending decision making that could be targeted for intervention efforts and to test whether such interventions decrease group crime rates. A reasonable first step would be to focus on offender convergence settings. As Andresen and Felson (2010a) argue, given that these may be crucial to co-offender selection, they are potentially interesting geographic targets for situational crime prevention efforts. More general attempts to disrupt criminogenic social networks at the individual level may also hold promise. As Wood and Gannon (2013) highlight, whatever the focus, the most effective interventions are likely to be those that recognize and address essential social contexts of crime.

In conclusion, although an organized research agenda exploring co-offending and offender decision making is only starting to take root, some important first steps have been made and a number of theoretical hypotheses and empirical questions are ripe for testing. Future research addressing these and other issues will be crucial for a better understanding of how offenders navigate the decision to (co-)offend, with whom, and in what form.

NOTE

1. The definition of co-offending presented here requires that two or more individuals (referred to as accomplices or co-offenders) act together at the same time and place to commit a joint offence. Although some authors adopt a broader definitional scope including everyone upon whom an offender relies before, during, or after the offence (Tremblay 1993, p. 20), or a more restrictive focus limited only to street crimes (Hochstetler 2014, p. 571), the current definition mirrors that used in the majority of co-offending studies (Reiss 1988; Reiss and Farrington 1991; Sarnecki 2001).

REFERENCES

Akers, R. 1998. *Social Learning and Social Structure: A General Theory of Crime and Deviance.* Boston: Northeastern University Press.

Alarid, L. F., A. L. Hochstetler, and V. S. Burton. 2009. "Group and Solo Robberies: Do Accomplices Shape Criminal Form?" *Journal of Criminal Justice* 37:1–9.

Andresen, M. A., and M. Felson. 2010a. "Situational Crime Prevention and Co-offending." *Crime Patterns and Analysis* 3:3–13.

Andresen, M. A., and M. Felson. 2010b. "The Impact of Co-offending." *British Journal of Criminology* 50:66–81.

Andresen, M. A., and M. Felson. 2012. "An Investigation into the Fundamental Regularities of Co-offending for Violent and Property Crime Classifications." *Canadian Journal of Criminology and Criminal Justice* 54:101–15.

Becker, G. S. 1968. "Crime and Punishment: An Economic Approach." *Journal of Political Economy* 78:189–217.

Bernasco, W. 2006. "Co-offending and the Choice of Target Areas in Burglary." *Journal of Investigative Psychology and Offender Profiling* 3:139–155.

Bernasco, W., ed. 2010. *Offenders on Offending*. Cullompton, UK: Willan.

Breckinridge, S. P., and E. Abbot. 1912. *The Delinquent Child and the Home*. New York: Arno Press.

Blau, P. M. 1964. *Exchange and Power in Social Life*. New Brunswick, NJ: Transaction Books.

Budd, T., C. Sharp, and P. Mayhew. 2005. *Offending in England and Wales: First Results from the 2003 Crime and Justice Survey*. Home Office research study, vol. 275. London: Home Office.

Canter, D., and L. Alison. 2000. *The Social Psychology of Crime: Groups, Teams and Networks*. London: Ashgate.

Carrington, P. J. 2002. "Group Crime in Canada." *Canadian Journal of Criminology* 44:277–315.

Carrington, P. J. 2009. "Co-offending and the Development of the Delinquent Career." *Criminology* 47:1295–1329.

Carrington, P. J. 2011. "Crime and Social Networks." In *The Sage Handbook of Social Network Analysis*, edited by J. Scott and P. J. Carrington, pp. 236–55. London: Sage.

Carrington, P. J. 2014. "Co-offending. In *Encyclopedia of Criminology and Criminal Justice*, edited by G. Bruinsma and D. Weisburd, pp. 548–58. New York: Springer-Verlag.

Carrington, P. J. 2015. "The Structure of Age Homophily in Co-offending Groups." *Journal of Contemporary Criminal Justice* 31(3): 337–53.

Carrington P. J., and S. B. van Mastrigt. 2013. "Co-offending in Canada, England and the United States: A Cross National Comparison." *Global Crime* 14:123–40.

Clarke, R. V., and D. B. Cornish. 1985. "Modeling Offenders' Decisions: A Framework for Research and Policy." *Crime and Justice* 6:147–85.

Clarke, R. V., and M. Felson. eds. 1993. *Routine Activity and Rational Choice: Advances in Criminological Theory*, vol. 5. New Brunswick, NJ: Transaction Books.

Conway, K. P., and J. McCord. 2002. "A Longitudinal Examination of the Relation Between Co-offending with Violent Accomplices and Violent Crime." *Aggressive Behavior* 28:97–108.

Cornish, D. B., and R. V. Clarke. 1986. *The Reasoning Criminal: Rational Choice Perspectives on Offending*. New York: Springer-Verlag.

Cromwell, P. F., J. N. Olson, and D. W. Avary. 1991. *Breaking and Entering: An Ethnographic Analysis of Burglary*. Newbury Park: Sage.

De Haan, W., and J. Vos. 2003. "A Crying Shame: The Over-rationalized Conception of Man in the Rational Choice Perspective." *Theoretical Criminology* 7:29–54.

Deiner, E. 1977. "Deindividuation: Causes and Consequences." *Social Behavior and Personality* 5:143–55.

Dijksterhuis, A., and L. F. Nordgren. 2006. "A Theory of Unconscious Thought." *Perspectives on Psychological Science* 1:95–109.

Donald, I., and A. Wilson. 2000. "Ram Raiding: Criminals Working in Groups." In *The Social Psychology of Crime: Groups, Teams, and Networks*, edited by D. Canter and L. Alison, pp. 189–246. Aldershot, UK: Ashgate/Dartmouth.

Felson, M. 2003. "The Process of Co-offending." In *Theory for Practice in Situational Crime Prevention*, edited by M. J. Smith and D. B. Cornish, pp. 149–167. Vol. 16 of *Crime Prevention Studies*. Monsey, NY: Criminal Justice Press.

Festinger, L., A. Pepitone, and T. Newcomb. 1952. "Some Consequences of Deinvidividuation in a Group." *Journal of Abnormal and Social Psychology* 47:382–89.

Gadd, D., and T. Jefferson. 2007. *Psychosocial Criminology: An Introduction*. Thousand Oaks, CA: Sage.

Glueck, S., and E. Glueck. 1950. *Unraveling Juvenile Delinquency*. Cambridge, MA: Harvard University Press.

Gottfredson, M. R., and T. Hirschi. 1990. *A General Theory of Crime*. Stanford, CA: Stanford University Press.

Gould, L., E. Bittner, S. Chaneless, S. Messinger, K. Novak, and F. Powledge.; President's Commission on Law Enforcement and the Administration of Justice. 1965. *Crime as a Profession: A Report on Professional Criminals in Four American Cities.*. Washington, DC: US Government Printing Office.

Granovetter, M. 1978. "Threshold Models of Collective Behavior." *American Journal of Sociology* 83:1420–43.

Hochstetler, A. 2001. "Opportunities and Decisions: Interactional Dynamics in Robbery and Burglary Groups." *Criminology* 39:737–63.

Hochstetler, A. 2014. "Co-offending and Offender Decision-Making." In *Encyclopedia of Criminology and Criminal Justice*, edited by G. Bruinsma and D. Weisburd, pp. 570–81. New York: Springer-Verlag.

Kahneman, D. 2003. "A Perspective on Judgement and Choice." *American Psychologist* 58:697–720.

Katz, J. 1988. *Seductions of Crime: The Sensual and Moral Attractions of Doing Evil*. New York: Basic Books.

McAndrew, D. 2000. "The Structural Analysis of Criminal Networks." In *The Social Psychology of Crime: Groups, Teams and Networks*, edited by D. Canter and L. Alison, pp. 51–94. Aldershot, UK: Ashgate.

McCarthy, B. 1996. "The Attitudes and Actions of Others: Tutelage and Sutherland's Theory of Differential Association." *British Journal of Criminology* 36:135–47.

McCarthy, B., and J. Hagan. 2001. "When Crime Pays: Capital, Competency, and Criminal Success." *Social Forces* 79(3): 1035–59.

McCarthy, B., J. Hagan, and L. E. Cohen. 1998. "Uncertainty, Cooperation, and Crime: Understanding the Decision to Co-offend." *Social Forces* 77:155–84.

McCluskey, K., and S. Wardle. 2000. "The Social Structure of Robbery." In *The Social Psychology of Crime: Groups, Teams and Networks*, edited by D. Canter and L. Alison, pp. 247–85. Aldershot, UK: Ashgate/Dartmouth.

McCord, J., and K. P. Conway. 2002. "Patterns of Juvenile Delinquency and Co-offending." In *Crime and Social Organization*, edited by R. Waring and D. Weisburd, pp. 15–30. New Brunswick, NJ: Transaction Publishers.

McGloin, J. M., and H. Nguyen. 2012. "It Was My Idea: Considering the Instigation of Co-offending." *Criminology* 50(2): 463–94.

McGloin, J. M., and H. Nguyen. 2014. "The Importance of Studying Co-offending Networks for Criminological Theory and Policy." In *Crime and Networks*, edited by C. Morselli, pp. 13–27. New York: Routledge.

McGloin, J. M., and A. R. Piquero. 2009. "I Wasn't Alone: Collective Behaviour and Violent Delinquency." *Australian and New Zealand Journal of Criminology* 42(3): 336–53.

McGloin, J. M., and A. R. Piquero. 2010. "On the Relationship Between Co-offending Network Redundancy and Offending Versatility." *Journal of Research in Crime and Delinquency* 47:63–90.

McGloin, J. M., and Z. R. Rowan. 2015. "A Threshold Model of Collective Crime." *Criminology* 53(3): 484–512.

McGloin, J. M., C. J. Sullivan, A. R. Piquero, and S. Bacon. 2008. "Investigating the Stability of Co-offending and Co-offenders Among a Sample of Youthful Offenders." *Criminology* 46:155–88.

McGloin, J. M., and J. K. Thomas. 2016. "Incentives for Collective Deviance: Group Size and Changes in Perceived Risk, Cost, and Reward." *Criminology* 54(3): 459–86.

McPherson, M., L. Smith-Lovin, and J. M. Cook. 2001. "Birds of a Feather: Homophily in Social Networks." *Annual Review of Sociology* 27:415–44.

Morselli, C., P. Tremblay, and B. McCarthy. 2006. "Mentors and Criminal Achievement." *Criminology* 44(1): 17–43.

Moscovici, S., and M. Zavalloni. 1969. "The Group as a Polarizer of Attitudes." *Journal of Personality and Social Psychology* 12(2): 125–35.

Mullins, C.W., and R. Wright. 2003. "Gender, Social Networks, and Residential Burglary." *Criminology* 41(3): 813–83.

Muskens, M., S. Bogaerts, M. van Casteren, and S. Labrijn. 2011. "Adult Female Sexual Offending: A Comparison Between Co-offenders and Solo Offenders in a Dutch Sample." *Journal of Sexual Aggression* 17(1): 46–60.

Nguyen, H., and J. M. McGloin. 2013. "Does Economic Adversity Breed Criminal Cooperation? Considering the Motivation Behind Group Crime." *Criminology* 51:833–70.

Osman, M. 2004. "An Evaluation of Dual-Process Theories of Reasoning." *Psychonomic Bulletin and Review* 11(6): 988–1010.

Piquero, A. R., D. P. Farrington, and A. Blumstein. 2007. *Key Issues in Criminal Career Research: New Analyses of the Cambridge Study in Delinquent Development.* Cambridge: Cambridge University Press.

Porter, L. E., and L. J. Alison. 2006. "Leadership and Hierarchies in Criminal Groups: Scaling Degrees of Leadership Behaviour in Group Robbery." *Legal and Criminological Psychology* 11:245–65.

Reiss, A. J. 1988. "Co-offending and Criminal Careers." *Crime and Justice* 10:117–70.

Reiss, A. J., and D. P. Farrington. 1991. "Advancing Knowledge About Co-offending: Results from a Prospective Longitudinal Survey of London Males." *Journal of Criminal Law and Criminology* 82:360–95.

Sarnecki, J. 2001. *Delinquent Networks.* Cambridge: Cambridge University Press.

Schaefer. D. R. 2012. "Youth Co-offending Networks: An Investigation of Social and Spatial Effects." *Social Networks* 34:141–49.

Schaefer, D. R., N. Rodriguez, and S. H. Decker. 2014. "The Role of Neighborhood Context in Youth Co-offending." *Criminology* 52:117–39.

Shaw, C. R., and H. D. McKay. 1931. *Report on the Causes of Crime.* Washington, DC: US Government Printing Office.

Shover, N. 1996. *Great Pretenders: Pursuits and Careers of Persistent Thieves.* Boulder, CO: Westview.

Stanovich, K. E., and R. F. West. 2000. "Individual Difference in Reasoning: Implications for the Rationality Debate? *Behavioural and Brain Sciences* 23:645–726.

Stolzenberg, L., and S. J. D'Alessio. 2008. "Co-offending and the Age–Crime Curve." *Journal of Research in Crime and Delinquency* 45(1): 65–86.

Sutherland, E. 1947. *Principles of Criminology.* 4th ed. Philadelphia: Lippincott.

Thibaut, J. W., and H. H. Kelley. 1959. *The Social Psychology of Groups.* New York: Wiley.

Tillyer, M. S., and R. Tillyer. 2015. "Maybe I Should Do This Alone: A Comparison of Solo and Co-offending Robbery Outcomes." *Justice Quarterly* 32:1064–88.

Tremblay, P. 1993. "Search for Suitable Co-offenders." In *Routine Activity and Rational Choice: Advances in Criminological Theory*, vol. 5, edited by R. V. Clarke and M. Felson, pp.17–36. New Brunswick, NJ: Transaction Publishers.

van Mastrigt, S. B. 2014. "Co-offending and Offender Attributes." In *Encyclopedia of Criminology and Criminal Justice*, edited by G. Bruinsma and D. Weisburd, pp. 559–70. New York: Springer-Verlag.

van Mastrigt, S. B., and P. J. Carrington. 2014. "Sex and Age Homophily in Co-offending Networks: Opportunity or Preference?" In *Crime and Networks*, edited by C. Morselli, pp. 28–51. New York: Routledge.

van Mastrigt, S. B., and D. P. Farrington. 2009. "Co-offending, Age, Gender and Crime Type: Implications for Criminal Justice Policy. *British Journal of Criminology* 49:552–73.

van Mastrigt, S. B., and D. P. Farrington. 2011. "Prevalence and Characteristics of Co-offending Recruiters. *Justice Quarterly* 28:325–59.

Vandiver, D. M. 2006. "Female Sex Offenders: A Comparison of Solo Offenders and Co-offenders." *Violence and Victims* 21(3): 339–54.

Viki, G. T., and D. Abrams. 2013. "The Social Influence of Groups on Individuals." In *Crime and Crime Reduction: The Importance of Group Processes*, edited by J. L. Wood and T. L. Gannon, pp. 3–33. London: Routledge.

Warr, M. 1993. "Age, Peers, and Delinquency." *Criminology* 31(1): 17–40.

Warr, M. 1996. "Organization and Instigation in Delinquent Groups." *Criminology* 34(1): 11–37.

Warr, M. 2002. *Companions in Crime: The Social Aspects of Criminal Conduct*. Cambridge: Cambridge University Press.

Weerman, F. 2003. "Co-offending as Social Exchange: Explaining Characteristics of Co-offending." *British Journal of Criminology* 43:398–416.

Weerman, F. 2014. "Theories of Co-offending." In *Encyclopedia of Criminology and Criminal Justice*, edited by G. Bruinsma and D. Weisburd, pp. 5173–84. New York: Springer-Verlag.

Wikström, P.-O. H. 2006. "Individuals, Settings and Acts of Crime: Situational Mechanisms and the Explanation of Crime." In *The Explanation of Crime*, edited by P.-O. H. Wikström and R. J. Sampson, pp. 61–107. Cambridge: Cambridge University Press.

Wood, J. L., and T. L. Gannon, eds. 2013. *Crime and Crime Reduction: The Importance of Group Processes*. London: Routledge.

Wright, R. T., and S. Decker. 1994. *Burglars on the Job: Streetlife and Residential Break-ins*. Boston: Northeastern University Press.

Zimbardo, P. G. 1970. "The Human Choice: Individuation, Reason, and Order Versus Deindividuation, Impulse, and Chaos." In *Nebraska Symposium on Motivation, 1969*, edited by W. J. Arnold and D. Levine, pp. 237–307. Lincoln: University of Nebraska.

Zimring, F. E. 1981. "Kids, Groups, and Crime: Some Implications of a Well-Known Secret." *Journal of Criminal Law and Criminology* 73:867–85.

CHAPTER 17

....

INFORMAL GUARDIANS AND OFFENDER DECISION MAKING

....

DANIELLE M. REYNALD

I. INTRODUCTION

....

THIS chapter focuses on the ways in which informal guardians influence the situational chemistry for crime by shaping offender choices when faced with criminal opportunity. Research on informal guardianship within criminology is quite limited compared to research on offenders and victims (Reynald 2011b). The subset of research that focuses specifically on the offender's perspective on informal guardians is equally restricted. However, there is a healthy body of research focused on offender decision making that provides some insight into how offenders perceive guardians within the situational context of their offending choices. Core studies in this body of research are discussed in this chapter with a view to developing a better understanding of how informal guardians factor into the decision-making processes in the course of various types of offending. With this in mind, this chapter focuses only on aspects of offender decision making that relate explicitly to guardianship. The chapter first examines the concept of informal guardianship and its theoretical underpinnings. It then highlights the function that informal guardians serve as agents of crime control and how informal guardianship is applied as a key technique within the framework of situational crime prevention. Evidence from seminal work on offender decision making is presented to provide insight about how informal guardians factor into offenders' choices of crime locations and crime targets. Three types of offending are focused on due to the availability of data related to these particular offenders' perceptions of informal guardians: burglary, armed robbery, and sex offending. The chapter concludes by comparing and contrasting the ways in which informal guardians shape the choices that offenders make in these varying types of crime situations.

II. Informal Guardians

In the routine activity approach to understanding crime, Cohen and Felson (1979) explained that the chemistry for crime requires the convergence of offenders with suitable targets in the absence of capable guardians. Capable guardians have been defined as any person or thing that discourages crime from taking place (Cohen and Felson, 1979). According to Felson (1995), guardians "keep an eye on potential crime targets," serving "by simple presence to prevent crime, and by absence to make crime more likely" (p. 53). Within the crime event model put forward by the routine activity approach, the guardian is not a formal police officer or security guard but, rather, an informal person or ordinary citizen whose presence, during the course of their daily routines, provides security to potential targets/victims of crime (Felson, 1995):

> A retired person at home might well discourage daytime burglary of his or her own home or even the home next door. Conversely, someone working away from home during the day contributes by that absence to a greater risk of burglary. Two persons walking down the street might serve as effective guardians for one another against a mugging or other attack, while each individual servers as a guardian for his or her own immediate property. (pp. 53–54)

It is therefore informal guardians such as residents and passers-by who are more likely to be present to discourage crime than formal guardians such as police officers and security guards, "who are very unlikely to be on the spot when a crime occurs" (Felson and Boba 2010, p. 28). Who fulfills the role of an informal guardian is dependent on who is present when an offender comes into contact with a potential target/victim (Reynald 2011*b*).

Clarke (1980, 1992) reinforces the importance of informal guardians as crime controllers within the framework of situational crime prevention. Situational crime prevention is based on the premise that specific situational characteristics help generate opportunities for offenders to commit crime. In line with rational choice theory, the fundamental goal is to manipulate situations so that the costs of committing crime outweigh the benefits, thereby discouraging the offender from committing the criminal act. With this objective in mind, one of the central strategies of situational crime prevention is to *increase the risks* for offenders to get caught. The key techniques associated with this strategy revolve around facilitating informal guardianship. These techniques include extending or increasing guardianship and providing assistance for guardians or tools to encourage or extend surveillance, including improved street lighting and the use of closed-circuit television (CCTV) (Clarke 1997).

III. Discouraging Offenders Through Informal Guardianship

Research on guardianship has demonstrated that there are three fundamental dimensions to active informal guardianship: (1) the presence or availability of guardians; (2) supervision, monitoring, or surveillance by guardians; and (3) intervention by guardians when necessary (Reynald 2009, 2010, 2011a, 2011b; Hollis-Peel and Welsh 2014). High levels of guardianship— supervision (watching) (Lynch and Cantor 1992) or willingness to intervene (Sampson, Raudenbush, and Earls 1997)—are associated with low levels of crime. Across different contexts, consistent evidence has demonstrated that sex offenders (Tewksbury and Mustaine 2006), burglars (Bennett and Wright 1984), thieves, robbers (Wright and Decker 1997), and terrorists (Hirschfield 2010) are discouraged from criminal acts or prevented from committing crime through the supervision and/or intervention of regular citizens. Empirical evidence suggests that informal guardianship works as a form of crime control (Garofalo and Clark 1992; Reynald 2009, 2011a; Hollis-Peel and Welsh 2014).

Informal guardianship is defined by very simple routines and modes of action. Cohen and Felson's (1979) concept of guardianship for crime prevention rests on the notion that any individual can serve as a guardian against crime simply by being present at the scene of a potential crime event (Felson 1995). Routine activities that require a higher proportion of time spent at or around the home rather than away from home, for instance, help increase the likelihood that informal guardians will be available to protect their property against victimization. This is supported by empirical evidence demonstrating that household occupancy or frequency of time people spend at home is negatively associated with burglary victimization (Miethe and Meier 1990; Wilcox Rountree and Land 1996; Coupe and Blake 2006). Time spent away from home decreases informal guardianship at properties by leaving properties unattended (Miethe et al. 1987). In addition, ordinary citizens going about their daily routines help provide a sense of security simply by their presence (Felson and Boba 2010). Their presence is therefore the cornerstone of the spectrum of capability that informal guardians can draw on to protect against victimization by offenders (Reynald 2011b).

The capability to guard against offending can be enhanced by actual supervision or monitoring by informal guardians. Felson (2006) argues that the absence of actual supervision is what determines when and where crime occurs because offenders primarily seek targets and places that are not well attended to so they can escape supervision by informal guardians. This premise is supported by Lynch and Cantor's (1992, p. 353) conclusion that safe areas are characterized by "high levels of watching" because their findings suggest that high levels of surveillance are a feature of low crime areas that keeps crime levels low.

The capability to guard against offending can be further intensified when guardians take direct action to intervene upon observing untoward activities in their surroundings

(Reynald 2011b, 2014). Recent research has drawn associations between the intervention stage of guardianship and bystander intervention from social psychology (Reynald 2010; Hollis-Peel et al. 2011). Intervention can be any action taken to disrupt or prevent a crime event, and it can encompass a range of actions, including shouting out to perpetrators, calling the police, or physically intervening to stop a crime (Reynald 2014). Brown and Bentley (1993) suggest the importance of intervention as a form of informal guardianship by arguing that the risk of being seen is not always a sufficient deterrent because "burglars also need to know whether potential onlookers would care about their presence. . . . Burglars also may decide that some neighbors will intervene and others will not" (p. 52). Availability, monitoring/supervision, and intervention can therefore be viewed as the most basic elements that informal guardians can draw on to guard against offending.

A. Burglary and Informal Guardians

Burglars confirm the role that informal guardians play in their decision making with regard to choosing suitable targets. Research on burglary reveals that burglars are primarily concerned with two forms of informal guardianship, the first of which is home occupancy or the presence of guardians. Several studies have revealed that the majority of burglars prefer to target houses that have no signs of occupancy (Maguire 1988; Nee and Meenaghan 2006). The second form of informal guardianship that burglars reportedly try to avoid is being seen by neighbors or passers-by (Murray 1983; Homel, Macintyre, and Wortley 2014).

Bennett and Wright's (1984) seminal work on decision making by burglars investigated what factors informed convicted burglars' decisions about which households were the most suitable targets for burglary. They used a combination of five research techniques to elicit responses from burglars about how they made decisions regarding target selection and which situational cues played a significant role in this decision-making process. These research methods included the videotape method, two photograph methods, the semistructured interview, and the walkabout. The videotape method was employed to elicit the situational cues that offenders use in their choice of targets. Forty convicted burglars were shown a video recording of 36 household dwellings on eight street blocks. While watching the video, offenders were asked to think out loud, and their verbalized decision-making process was documented and analyzed using protocol analysis (Bennett and Wright, 1984).

The convicted burglars explained whether and why they would or would not choose certain targets. Analysis of their responses resulted in the extraction of six key statements related to target choice, three of which were directly related to informal guardianship or the risk of being seen or detected during the offense (Bennett and Wright 1984, p. 61):

1. No, it's overlooked by this one.
2. No, I don't like all this openness.
3. There's no bushes or anything like that.

In keeping with the principles of situational crime prevention outlined previously, further analysis of the concepts extracted from offenders' responses revealed three major issues that offenders are concerned with when choosing a suitable target: the risk of being seen, the rewards they would acquire, and the effort they would have to expend (Bennett and Wright 1984, p. 62). Specifically, offenders expressed particular concern about guardianship and the risk of being seen by guardians, which emerged in four subcategories in the analysis of their responses. The first was household occupancy. Although no occupants were visible on the videotapes, offenders still talked about looking out for any signs or cues that a dwelling was occupied, in which case the dwelling would be deemed "unsuitable for burglary" (Bennett and Wright 1984, p. 65). This highlights the importance of the presence of guardians in burglar decision making. Offenders were also concerned with the proximity of neighboring houses and the presence of neighbors who might act as guardians. One property in particular elicited concerns about this issue, which is illustrated in the following quotes from two offenders (Bennett and Wright 1984):

> I wouldn't do that, too close, they'd know one another and notice strangers.
> Too near other property. It's the sort of property where you've got people nearby.
> They are probably nosey neighbors anyway. (p. 63)

Bennett and Wright (1984) go on to draw the following conclusions from the information provided by offenders: "Implicit in these statements, and explicit in many others, is the fear that neighbors will know who is a stranger to the area, or to the occupants of the house, and will be more likely than passers-by to do something about it" (p. 63). This reinforces the point that offenders were discouraged not only by the presence of guardians in the form of neighbors, and their proximity to the potential target, but also by the capability of available guardians, in terms of whether neighbors would see them and whether neighbors would take action on noticing them during the offense (Reynald 2011b). This confirms the importance of the presence or availability of informal guardians, as well as being seen by guardians, and intervention by guardians once offenders are detected.

Closely related to this, offenders in the Bennett and Wright (1984) study also expressed being put off by dwellings that were overlooked by neighboring houses. They expressed concern about "being seen by someone familiar with the property who might intervene if something suspicious occurred" (Bennett and Wright 1984, p. 64). This apprehension over the presence of active informal guardians near the potential target was expressed by one offender, who explained, "I wouldn't do that one 'cos plenty of people in those houses could see into the back garden. They just look out of their bedroom window or something and see you standing there trying to smash a window. They'd phone the police and you'd be caught straight away" (p. 64).

MacDonald and Gifford (1989) reported similar findings in their study of burglar target selection. They presented 44 incarcerated male burglars with 50 photographs of single-family houses to determine how burglars perceived these targets and which specific environmental and property cues they used to make judgments about the perceived vulnerability of targets. They reported that unobstructed opportunities for surveillance of properties by residents and clear visibility from individual households to the public street and also to neighboring properties rendered these households the least vulnerable targets in the eyes of burglars (see also Brown and Altman 1983).

In their study of the offender's perspective on the process of committing residential burglaries, Wright and Decker (1994) took this line of research a step further by using a sample of active rather than incarcerated burglars. They interviewed 105 active offenders in St. Louis, Missouri, about their motivations and decisions about committing burglary. Focusing specifically on the process involved in selecting suitable targets for burglary, Wright and Decker explained,

> In theory, the supply of residential properties is so vast that finding a target would seem a simple matter. In practice, however, potential targets are fairly limited. The offenders, after all, typically are seeking to solve a pressing problem, financial or other, and feel under pressure to act quickly. At the same time, they are reluctant to break in to a place without first determining the potential risks and rewards. As offenders attempt to settle on a target, therefore, they are under the influence of two seemingly conflicting demands: one calling for immediate action, and the other counseling caution. How do they manage to reconcile these demands and select a specific dwelling? (p. 62)

Results from this study showed that one of the ways offenders reconcile these demands in order to select a suitable home as a target is by avoiding neighborhoods in which informal guardianship was high. Wright and Decker reported that

> most of the offenders wanted to steer clear of neighborhoods in which the residents appeared to be keeping an eye out for each other.
> "[Those neighborhoods] are just a hassle. You walk down the street and the police come get you cause somebody done looked out the window and saw you walkin'"
> [no. 016]. (p. 92)

For this reason, offenders in this study also avoided neighborhoods with a high proportion of elderly residents because these residents were "presumed to be especially vigilant and prone to reporting suspicious looking persons to the police" (p. 92):

> "The thing is, if you got a lot of elderly people on one block, that'll get you killed mostly. .... I wanted to do [a burglary] over here by the bakery shop, but that's a retired area. Almost everybody that live on that block is retired and they constantly lookin' out windows and watchin' [out] for each other. Ain't nothin' you can do about that" (James West—no. 044). (p. 92)

Related to the issue of being detected, offenders in this sample also reported being concerned about being heard by neighbors whose homes were nearby. A study by Coupe and Fox (2015) confirmed that guardianship provided by neighbors plays a significant role in explaining the chances that nonresidential burglars would be seen during an offense.

In assessing the risks associated with targets, offenders in the Wright and Decker (1994) study were most concerned with household occupancy or the presence of guardians, and they reported looking for cues or relying on their instincts, or a sense or "feeling" that potential targets were occupied (Wright and Decker 1994, p. 96). Following occupancy, offenders reported being most concerned with visibility when assessing the risks associated with potential targets: Wright and Decker noted that "they did not want to be observed while entering or leaving a residence and therefore were drawn to dwellings with access points that could be easily seen from the street or from surrounding buildings" (p. 97). Concern with home occupancy and passers-by were also reported as two of the critical features of a dwelling that make it unattractive to burglars in Homel et al.'s (2014) study of experienced burglars who were released from prison in Melbourne, Australia.

B. Armed Robbery and Informal Guardians

Like burglars, armed robbers have also reported that the presence of informal guardians and the likelihood of intervention affect their decisions about where to commit armed robberies and who they target. Wright and Dekker's (1997) seminal, field-based study of active armed robbers in St. Louis, Missouri, revealed that armed robbers are typically required to make two fundamental decisions about the offense location and the victim when seeking an opportunity to successfully commit a robbery. Results from this study revealed that the risk of getting caught by informal guardians played a significant role in choosing locations for their offenses. Based on interviews and fieldwork with a sample of 86 active robbers, they reported that the majority of offenders in their sample "took into account the risk of being seen by passers-by when choosing robbery locations. In an attempt to minimize this risk, most of them elected to commit stickups at night in poorly lit areas" (p. 80). Similarly, armed robbers in this study explained that the location choice for their offenses was also influenced by the likelihood that they would stand out as being suspicious, as well as the likelihood that potential guardians would take action to intervene. Armed robbers explained that residents in St. Louis County were much more likely than residents in the city to intervene by reporting suspicious behavior to the police. One offender explained,

> "People in the city, I don't know what it is, but they are not too apt to call the police too often, and then a lot of them don't seem too concerned about what they see. They be like, 'It ain't my business and don't make it yours cause you might get caught up in it.' In the county [though], it's all totally different" (Burle—no. 80, p. 75).

Wright and Decker concluded that the armed robbers who participated in their study took a very practical approach to their risk assessments of potential crime sites: "Did they stand a good chance of getting away? Were they likely to be seen by passers-by? If the answers to those questions were yes and no respectively, most of them appeared to spend little extra time worrying about less predictable and more remote hazards" (p. 81).

The study by Wright and Decker (1997) provides unique insights into the role of informal guardians in offender decision making involving violent offenses. Few studies have explored the function of guardianship in preventing or disrupting violent crimes such as armed robbery, homicide, and sexual assault from the offender's perspective. Other notable exceptions derive from research on offender decision making within the context of sexual offenses.

IV. Sex Offending and Informal Guardians

Fairly recent research on sex offending has revealed that offender choices related to these crime events are influenced to some extent by the presence of informal guardians. Beauregard and Leclerc (2007) found that the majority of sex offenders estimate the risks that they will get caught before committing their offenses. Their sample consisted of 69 incarcerated serial sex offenders who committed two or more sexual assaults or sex-related crimes, such as sexual homicide, against stranger victims of both genders and all ages. These offenders were incarcerated in a penitentiary of the Correctional Service of Canada in Quebec. Analysis of the interview data acquired from these offenders revealed that 71% of them estimated the risks of offending before committing the offense. One of the key factors offenders considered in assessing the risk of apprehension was the presence/absence of capable guardians. In this study, capable guardians were defined as "people or potential witnesses near the crime scene who may interfere" (p. 122). In 17 percent of cases, the offense was disrupted by intervention from a witness or because the victim screamed for help. It is important to note, however, that although offenders' assessment of the risks of apprehension played an important part in their planning of the crime, 39 percent of offenders still committed the offense even when they assessed the risks to be high (Beauregard and Leclerc 2007).

In a study that focused on the effect of guardianship on the severity of child sexual abuse, Leclerc, Smallbone, and Wortley (2015) found that the presence of a guardian reduced the risk of sexual penetration of victims by 86 percent. This study was based on a survey questionnaire completed by a sample of 87 adult male offenders who were incarcerated in Queensland, Australia, for committing a sexual offense against a child (younger than age sixteen years). The majority of offenders in the sample (>84 percent) were Australia born, non-aboriginal. The presence of a guardian was measured by asking offenders whether or not someone else was present during the abuse (yes/no). Offenders were then asked whether the person was a child or adult and whether the person was a relative, acquaintance, or stranger. The data revealed that the most common situation was one in which both an adult and a child related to the offender were present in the home (Leclerc et al. 2015). Results also revealed that the presence of a guardian was less likely during incidents that occurred outside the home. The severity of the abuse was measured by asking whether penetration occurred (yes/no) and whether the duration of the sexual contact spanned more than five minutes (yes/no). Results showed that, while controlling for victim and situational characteristics, the presence of a guardian was less likely when the duration of the abuse was long (more than five minutes) and when penetration was involved (Leclerc et al. 2015). Unlike the burglary and armed robbery situations, informal guardians in the context of sex offending situations are sometimes strangers or passers-by, but they are often relatives or individuals who are known to the offender, particularly in cases of child sexual abuse events that occur in the offender's home (Leclerc et al. 2015). A large proportion of child sex offenses occur when someone else is present (Underwood et al. 1999; Leclerc et al. 2015), and Leclerc et al. reported that this is the case whether the crime site is the offender's home or another location. These results indicate that offenders are "willing to take risks to obtain sexual contact with a child. On the other hand, these risks may be relatively easy to manage in a context where the victim is a child and the potential guardian is most likely to be a person related to the offender" (Leclerc et al. 2015, p. 17). In these situations, who serves as a potential guardian depends on who is available when the offense is being committed. Also, because the likely potential guardians are known to the offender, the risks of getting caught may be more easily manipulable under these circumstances.

V. Conclusion

Across all the studies reviewed, the common theme is that the largest threat informal guardians provide is that they enhance the risk of offenders being detected, thus elevating the risk that they will be apprehended. It is important to note that the presence of informal guardians is not a guarantee that an offense will not be committed. In the context of burglary, the evidence that burglars want to avoid guardians is overwhelming, both in terms of encountering home owners and in terms of being seen, particularly by neighbors. However, the risk of being seen by neighbors or other passers-by is not always sufficient to deter all burglars because some offenders are more concerned with what an available guardian might do or how he or she will react. Armed robbers, on the other hand, are particularly concerned with passers-by who could function as guardians if the robbers are spotted in the process of committing their crime or if they are spotted and seen to be suspicious. For sex offenders, particularly child sex offenders, although the presence of others does necessarily elevate the risk of apprehension significantly, it is often not sufficient to prevent offenders from committing their planned offense. However, the previously discussed research clearly shows that in child sex abuse cases, the presence of a guardian makes a significant contribution to reducing the severity of the offense.

Taken together, the evidence from all of these studies confirms the role that informal guardians play in both crime prevention and crime disruption. In terms of the pre-crime or planning phase of a crime event from the offender's perspective, the presence of guardians is often sufficient to discourage an offender from a particular crime opportunity, depending on the situational context of the crime event. The presence of others is most often a deterrent in the planning phases of burglary events, often in armed robbery events, and sometimes in sexual offenses. In the actual phase of the criminal event, the evidence reviewed suggests that the presence, witnessing, and intervention of others are disruptive factors in burglary, armed robbery, and sexual offenses. The presence of guardians is often sufficient to disrupt an offense that is in the process of being committed or to lessen the severity of the offense being committed. Offenders are most concerned with being seen, so natural surveillance, monitoring, or supervision by guardians as a means of watching over their surroundings are also discouraging to offenders. Perhaps most important is action taken by available guardians by reporting offenders to the police or by intervening directly when they see or hear a crime being committed. The presence of informal guardians and the action they take can be problematic for offenders in the post-offense phase because their escape or getaway may be foiled by guardians who take direct action to detain them or who take indirect action to call the police to the scene of the crime.

Offender decision making as it relates to guardianship is influenced by offenders' assessments of the level of guardianship available. It seems important to consider that these assessments in turn are influenced not only by offenders' perception of guardianship levels at the time of the decision but also importantly by previous experience and learning. In any given situation, offender perceptions of guardianship relate to what they can actually perceive about guardianship levels at the moment of the criminal decision, as well as any prior experience they may have had related to guardianship at the same location or with the same target or victim through previous victimization. Research that examines how offender perceptions of guardianship affect their criminal decision making is limited. This area of research could be developed by examining differences in the influence of guardianship on offender decision making considering variations in the type of crime, the situational context, and the offender's prior criminal experience.

It is also important to note that there are many other ways in which other types of behavior by guardians can have an effect on criminal decision making related to burglary in particular. In addition to actual presence, supervision, and intervention, research suggests that guardians can potentially discourage offenders from selecting targets for burglary in particular through manipulations to their physical environment. These behaviors can be as simple as controlling access and creating signs of ownership at properties via territorial reinforcement, creating clear unobstructed lines of sight between neighboring properties and public space, and keeping properties well maintained and managed (e.g., repairing broken lights and windows, removing litter and graffiti, and maintaining lawns and gardens) (Newman 1972; Wilson and Kelling 1982). Other types of manipulations that may discourage offenders from selecting targets for burglary include the installation of CCTV cameras and increasing lighting and visibility at properties. These can be considered additional techniques that guardians may use to reinforce guardianship at properties and discourage burglary. Further research is required to examine the extent to which various types of offenders are discouraged from committing crime at particular locations by these cues and whether they actually perceive these types of cues as indicators of the level of guardianship at particular locations.

REFERENCES

Beauregard, E., and B. Leclerc. 2007. "An Application of the Rational Choice Approach to the Offending Process of Sex Offenders: A Closer Look at the Decision Making." *Sex Abuse*19:115–33.

Bennett, T., and R. Wright. 1984. *Burglars on Burglary: Prevention and the Offender*. Aldershot, UK: Gower.

Brown, B. B., and I. Altman. 1983. "Territoriality, Defensible Space and Residential Burglary: An Environmental Analysis." *Journal of Environmental Psychology* 3:203–20.

Brown, B. B., and D. L. Bentley. 1993. "Residential Burglars Judge Risk: The Role of Territoriality." *Journal of Environmental Psychology* 13:51–61.

Clarke, R. V. 1980. "Situational Crime Prevention: Theory and Practice." *British Journal of Criminology* 20:136–47.

Clarke, R. V. 1992. *Situational Crime Prevention: Successful Case Studies*. Albany, NY: Harrow and Heston.

Clarke, R. V. 1997. *Situational Crime Prevention: Successful Case Studies*, 2nd ed. Albany, NY: Harrow and Heston.

Cohen, L. E., and M. Felson. 1979. "Social Change and Crime Rate Trends: A Routine Activity Approach." *American Sociological Review* 44(4): 588–608.

Coupe, T., and L. Blake. 2006. "Daylight and Darkness Targeting Strategies and the Risks of Being Seen at Residential Burglaries." *Criminology* 44(2): 431–64.

Coupe, T., and B. H. Fox. 2015. "A Risky Business: How Do Access, Exposure and Guardians Affect the Chances of Non-residential Burglars Being Seen?" *Security Journal* 28: 71–92.

Felson, M. 1995. "Those Who Discourage Crime." In *Crime and Place: Crime Prevention Studies*, vol. 4, edited by J. E. Eck and D. Weisburd, pp. 53–66. Monsey, NY: Criminal Justice Press.

Felson, M. 2006. *Crime and Nature*. Thousand Oaks, CA: Sage.

Felson, M., and R. Boba. 2010. *Crime and Everyday Life: Insight and Implications for Society*. Thousand Oaks, CA: Pine Forge Press.

Garofalo, J., and D. Clark. 1992. "Guardianship and Residential Burglary." *Justice Quarterly* 9(3): 443–63.

Hirschfield, A. 2010. "Exploring Guardianship and Broken Windows in the Context of Terrorism: How Far Are There Parallels with Crime?" Paper Presented at ECCA Brisbane: Environmental Criminology and Crime Analysis Symposium, 5–7 July 2010, Brisbane, Australia.

Hollis-Peel, M., D. M. Reynald, M. van Bavel, H. Elffers, and B. Welsh. 2011. "Guardianship for Crime Prevention: A Critical Review of the Literature." *Crime, Law and Social Change* 56:53–70.

Hollis-Peel, M. E., and B. C. Welsh. 2014. "What Makes a Guardian Capable? A Test of Guardianship in Action." *Security Journal* 27(3): 320–37.

Homel, R., S. Macintyre, and R. Wortley. 2014. "How House Burglars Decide on Targets: A Computer-Based Scenario Approach." In *Cognition and Crime: Offender Decision Making and Script Analyses*, edited by B. Leclerc and R. Wortley, pp. 26–47. Abingdon, UK: Routledge.

Leclerc, B., S. Smallbone, and R. Wortley. 2015. "Prevention Nearby: The Influence of the Presence of a Potential Guardian on the Severity of Child Sexual Abuse." *Sexual Abuse* 27(2): 189–204.

Lynch, J. P., and D. Cantor. 1992. "Ecological and Behavioral Influences on Property Victimization at Home: Implications for Opportunity Theory." *Journal of Research in Crime and Delinquency* 29(3): 335–62.

MacDonald, J. E., and R. Gifford. 1989. "Territorial Cues and Defensible Space Theory: The Burglar's Point of View." *Journal of Environmental Psychology* 9:193–205.

Maguire, M. 1988. "Searchers and Opportunists: Offender Behaviour and Burglary Prevention." *Journal of Security Administration* 11:70–76.

Miethe, T. D., and R. F. Meier. 1990. "Opportunity, Choice and Criminal Victimization: A Test of a Theoretical Model." *Journal of Research in Crime and Delinquency* 27:243–66.

Miethe, T. D., Stafford, M. C. and J. S. Long. 1987. "Social Differentiation in Criminal Victimization: A Test of Routine Activities/Lifestyles Theories." *American Sociological Review* 52(2): 184–94.

Murray, C. 1983. "The Physical Environment and Community Control of Crime." In *Crime and Public Policy*, edited by J. Wilson, pp. 107–22. San Francisco: ICS Press.

Nee, C., and A. Meenaghan. 2006. "Expert Decision Making in Burglars." *British Journal of Criminology* 46:935–49.

Newman, O. 1972. *Defensible Space: Crime Prevention Through Urban Design*. New York: Macmillan.

Reynald, D. M. 2009. "Guardianship in Action: Developing a New Tool for Measurement." *Crime Prevention and Community Safety* 11(1): 1–20.

Reynald, D. M. 2010. "Guardians on Guardianship: Factors Affecting the Willingness to Monitor, the Ability to Detect Potential Offenders and the Willingness to Intervene." *Journal of Research in Crime and Delinquency* 47(3): 358–90.

Reynald, D. M. 2011a. "Factors Associated with the Guardianship of Places: Assessing the Relative Importance of the Spatio-Physical and Socio-Demographic Contexts in Generating Opportunities for Capable Guardianship." *Journal of Research in Crime and Delinquency* 48(1): 110–42.

Reynald, D. M. 2011b. *Guarding Against Crime: Measuring Guardianship Within Routine Activity Theory*. Surrey, UK: Ashgate.

Reynald, D. M. 2014. "Informal Guardianship." In *Encyclopedia of Criminology and Criminal Justice*, pp. 2480–89. New York: Springer.

Sampson, R. J., S. W. Raudenbush, and F. Earls. 1997. "Neighbourhoods and Violent Crime: A Multilevel Study of Collective Efficacy." *Science* 277(5328): 918–24.

Tewksbury, R., and E. E. Mustaine. 2006. "Where to Find Sex Offenders: An Examination of Residential Locations and Neighborhood Conditions." *Criminal Justice Studies* 19(1): 61–75.

Underwood, R. C., P. C. Patch, G. G. Cappelletty, and R. W. Wolfe. 1999. "Do Sexual Offenders Molest When Other Persons are Present? A Preliminary Investigation." *Sexual Abuse: A Journal of Research and Treatment* 11:243–47.

Wilcox Rountree, P., and K. C. Land. 1996. "Burglary Victimization Perceptions of Crime Risk, and Routine Activities: A Multilevel Analysis Across Seattle Neighborhoods and Census Tracts." *Journal of Research in Crime and Delinquency* 33:146–80.

Wilson, J. Q., and G. Kelling. 1982. "Broken Windows: The Police and Neighborhood Safety." *Atlantic Monthly* 249:29–38.

Wright, R. T. and S. H. Decker. 1994. *Burglars on the Job: Streetlife and Residential Break-Ins.* Boston: Northeastern University Press.

Wright, R. T., and S. H. Decker. 1997. *Armed Robbers in Action: Stickups and Street Culture.* Boston: Northeastern University Press.

CHAPTER 18

···

POLICE AND
OFFENDER CHOICES

A Framework

···

JOHN E. ECK AND TAMARA D. MADENSEN

I. COPS AND ROBBERS

···

THERE is no longer any dispute about whether police can influence crime. Multiple systematic reviews of police practices have shown that they can (Braga 2001, 2006; Maxwell, Garner, and Fagan 2002; Sherman and Eck 2002; Weisburd and Eck 2004; Mazerolle and Ransley 2005; Weisburd et al. 2010; Braga and Weisburd 2012; Braga, Papachristos, and Hureau 2014). The evidence is so substantial that Durlauf and Nagin (2011) suggest that we could reduce crime significantly by shifting resources from prisons to police. If there were little or no evidence of police influence on crime, this chapter would be short. We would simply state that police do not influence offender decision making. The presence of this body of evidence makes it necessary to map out the ways police can influence how potential offenders choose crime or non-crime.

Most attention has been paid to the specific and general deterrent effects of police on crime through hot spots policing and related enforcement techniques (Durlauf and Nagin 2011). This obscures the evidence and theory that police have other ways of influencing offender choices (Mazerolle and Ransley 2005; Ayling, Grabosky, and Shearing 2009; Weisburd et al. 2010). Thus, any description of how police influence potential offenders must go far beyond the law enforcement function of policing.

Bernasco, Elffers, and van Gelder (chapter 1 in this volume) propose a simple framework for understanding offender choice. They suggest that all people come into situations and that the combination of personal preferences, experience, and other characteristics help interpret the characteristics of the situation. The actor's choice is thus an outgrowth of personal and situational characteristics. The choice leads to outcomes. This model is shown in figure 18.1, with the addition of two feedback channels.

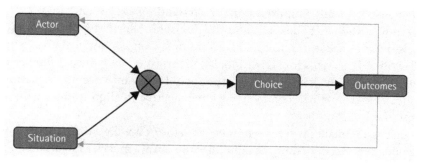

FIGURE 18.1 Elements of a decision-making situation (adapted from figure 1.1, this volume).

The outcome adds to the actor's experiences and thus alters how the actor will interpret future situations. The outcome can also alter a situation. A person enters a small park and notices some litter. She picks it up and puts it in the trash bin. This choice results in the outcome of a slightly cleaner park. The cleaner park is the situation the next actor will confront.

We use this model for two pragmatic reasons: It is simple, and it is useful. There are other, far more complex, frameworks that are possible to use. For example, Wikström et al. (2012) provide a related framework with numerous other elements, particularly moral rules. Ekblom's (2002) conjunction of criminal opportunities framework lists 11 elements at three temporal perspectives. The topic we are investigating—how police might influence offender decisions—is complex enough with the framework we have selected. Starting with a more detailed framework would divert attention from the points we are interested in making (and tax the readers' patience) without obvious increases in clarity or utility.

In constructing this chapter, we have drawn upon the dilemma facing cartographers. They cannot present all geographic details on their maps, and they too must distort some features. A road map for helping a reader drive from one place to another, for example, may not show hills and valleys (Monmonier 1993). To do so would make a map that is useless to its readers. Consequently, even the "best" map is a distortion of reality.

Consequently, we intentionally simplify the topic throughout this chapter. For example, usually we treat decisions by offenders (and others) as binary—commit crime/do not commit crime—when in most circumstances there are far more than two choices—commit crime A, commit crime B, delay committing a crime for some time, recruit a coconspirator, or do not engage in crime. We also do not spell out all the possible hypothetical feedback loops. Our synthesis of a set of interlocking literatures is complex enough for most readers. To include all the complexity in how police may influence offender decision making might achieve a higher level of accuracy, but it would probably be useless to researchers and practitioners.

We use this framework as the core of our examination of how police can influence a particular type of actor: potential offenders. Recognizing that offender choices are influenced by situations opens up a wide variety of considerations. Situations have become critically important in understanding crime and in preventing it (Clarke 1995). The basic idea is that individuals' propensity toward crime (or anything else) varies according to specific situations. Consequently, altering situations can alter offenders' behavior. Traditionally, theories of how police influence offenders naively focused on variations in deterrence. Taking into account situation shifts the police role from a narrow deterrence perspective to align it more with a broad prevention role.

Our discussion makes two main points. First, the police have multiple ways of influencing offenders. Second, how the police use these ways makes a major difference. We can think of the ways police can influence offenders as a set of pipes leading to the offender, and the offender's choice depending on the water temperature from all these pipes (with cold resulting in a crime and hot resulting in no crime). Our first point deals with the quantity of pipes delivering cold water. Our second point deals with quality: Each pipe has a valve that adjusts the temperature of the water. Even if the police have selected numerous pipes, if they cool down the water, they will have no impact. Worse yet, the police could help drive the potential offenders' choices in the wrong direction.

The organization of this chapter is simple. The next section describes the quantity of police influences on offenders. Figure 18.2 shows the three sets of influences police might have on potential offender decisions. One set of influences goes from police to the offender. These influences occur before the application of formal criminal justice sanctions and typically involve general or specific deterrence. Offenders can

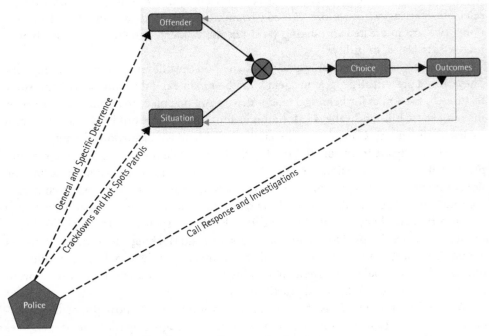

FIGURE 18.2 How we think police can influence offender choices.

anticipate the sanctions, so invoking the sanctions is not always necessary. Focused deterrence programs such as Boston's Cease Fire or the Cincinnati Initiative to Reduce Violence involve making explicit threats of future sanctions to specific individuals if these individuals engage in violence (Braga and Weisburd 2012). This set of influences corresponds, in part, to what Nagin (2013) has referred to as the "sentinel role" of police.

A second set of influences runs from police to outcomes and typically involves investigations, arrest, and prosecution mechanisms. This set corresponds to Nagin's (2013) "apprehension role" of police. These, too, invoke general or specific deterrence, but here the sanction (rather than its threat) influences future choices. Police arrest of domestic assaulters is an example of this form of influence (Maxwell et al. 2002). Many basic police anti-crime services are included in this set, including rapid response to calls (Spelman and Brown 1981) and follow-up investigations (Eck 1983). Although this set of influences is highly popular in the imagination of television and movie producers, as well as legislators, judging from the evidence cited here, these influences tend to be small or absent.

The third set of influences is from police to situation. This also falls within Nagin's (2013) "sentinel role." In some respects, we will be making the case that the sentinel role is a bundle of roles rather than a singular set of influences on offenders. What follows is an extension of this idea. Hot spots patrolling and crackdowns (Braga 2006) fall within this set of influences. These types of initiatives involve police finding small areas and discrete time periods with particularly high levels of crime or disorder and then allocating police officers to these places at the right time. The evidence suggests these influences are larger (Braga et al. 2014). The next section will show that although these pipes are large, there are other indirect pipe networks that might be larger.[1]

We show that police are not limited to enhancing deterrence or the use of criminal justice sanctions. The police can have a great many influences on situations, and many of these are only loosely connected to the role of policing within a criminal justice context. We conclude this section by noting that embedding policing and offender decision making within a "nodal governance" framework may be useful (Burris, Drahos, and Shearing 2005).

The third section of this chapter describes the quality of police decisions. Here, we discuss four attributes of how the police interact with people. This model was developed to explain how police can create peaceful crowd events or foster violent crowds, and it draws on literature dealing with crowds, legitimacy, and psychology. It has equal utility in many other circumstances. We focus on police interactions with potential offenders. At the end, we note that the same model applies to police encounters with all people: that how the police behave has important consequences for gaining cooperation or fostering resistance.

In our conclusions, the fourth section, we give a brief overview of our discussion and suggest implications for research on police and for police practice.

II. The Quantity of Police Influences on Offender Decisions

The standard explanation of police influence on offenders is similar to that depicted in figure 18.3. This is an expansion of the previous figure by showing that police impact on outcomes typically occurs through other entities. Here, the police influence parts of the criminal justice system and rehabilitation services—for example, through diverting offenders to drug treatment or other therapeutic interventions (Schaefer, Cullen, and Eck 2015). It is the justification for bundling the police within the criminal justice sanctioning process. It is shown here for that reason, despite its severe limitations.

The standard perspective is limited for two intertwined reasons. First, it is descriptively inadequate. There are numerous examples of police having influence—direct and indirect—on offender decision making for which this perspective cannot account. The evaluation literature on problem-oriented and third-party policing, for example, not only shows that other influences are possible but also shows that they have been used widely and that they often work (Mazerolle and Ransley 2005; Weisburd et al. 2010). Second, the standard perspective reinforces a law enforcement approach to influencing offenders. Hot spots policing, for example, can easily become a stop-and-frisk policy that imposes brutal costs on minority people living in poor communities (Gelman, Fagan, and Kiss 2007). By not making alternatives explicit, the standard perspective also stifles creativity in developing alternatives. The routine application of even evidence-based

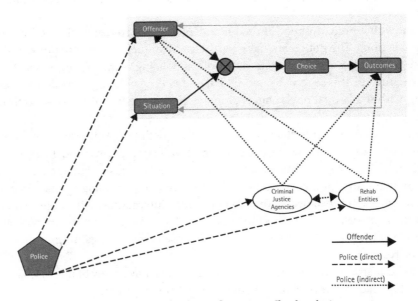

FIGURE 18.3 Common perspectives of police influencing offender choice.

interventions, such as hot spots policing, raises many concerns that could be addressed if alternatives are considered.

A. The Situation—The Exploded Version

What are these alternatives? To identify them, we must unbundle the term "situation." Clarke (1995) describes a situation as the immediate environment in which the offender makes a choice whether or not to commit a crime.[2] Like Clarke, we view the situation from the perspective of the offender. The offender needs to perceive the characteristics of the situation. This suggests two things. First, the situation will be relatively small and relatively short. Thus, situations will occur at small locations—places—and in short time intervals. We can now use routine activity theory (Cohen and Felson 1979; Felson 2008) as structure for describing the most salient features of the situation. To simplify maters, we use the crime triangle depiction of this theory (Eck 2003). At minimum, the situation, as seen by the offender, will contain the following elements:

1. The place and its various physical and social features
2. Evidence of active management of the place
3. Evidence of attractive targets
4. Evidence of the presence of guardians who might intervene
5. Evidence of handlers who might notice an offense

This is depicted in Figure 18.4. Because the situation is viewed from the offender's perspective, the offender has been left out of the description. These are the minimum elements. If offenders take into consideration other features, and if the police can exert some direct or indirect influence on these features, then the framework we are describing can be augmented accordingly.

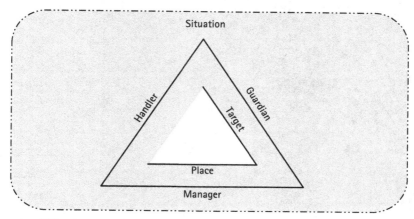

FIGURE 18.4 What is a situation?

B. Policing the Situation

Now we put this exploded view of the situation into the decision-making framework with which we have been working. This gives us figure 18.5. We now see that the police have multiple ways of influencing offender choices through manipulation of the situation elements. Some of these influences are direct, whereas others are indirect.[3]

1. *Offenders and Handlers*

We have already noted the influence of the police on offenders, so we need to say little more in this regard. Handlers are people who have some sort of emotional bond with offenders and who can influence offender involvement in crime. Offenders do not want handlers to know of their misbehavior, so handlers can exercise forms of informal social control. Parents are the most obvious examples, but so are spouses, other relatives, and, potentially, coaches, clergy, teachers, and even peers (Felson 1986). Police can develop programs to help such individuals keep potential offenders out of trouble. This can be extended to criminal handlers as well. Tillyer and Eck (2010) suggest that focused deterrence programs used to reduce gun violence can be viewed as efforts to get groups of offenders to regulate the conduct of their members.

Police mobilizing handlers becomes more obvious when we consider the police function as more than hard crime fighting. Crowd control is also an important police function, and recruitment of handlers is an important policing tool to keep calm crowds

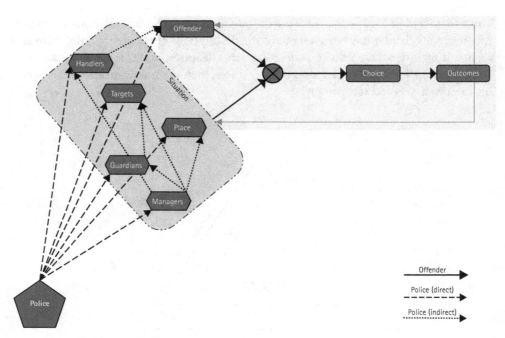

FIGURE 18.5 Police can influence situations in multiple ways.

calm and to dampen the potential for violence in antagonist crowds (Madensen and Knutsson 2011).

2. Targets and Guardians

For a crime to occur, not only must an offender be present but also that offender must have a target that is unprotected (Cohen and Felson 1979). Thus, it is not surprising that police engage in a great deal of crime prevention directed at potential targets of crime. They encourage people at risk of victimization to be aware of dangerous situations and how to develop countermeasures. Campaigns to get people to lock their doors and keep valuables hidden inside cars and programs to help college women avoid sexual assault are examples of this type of activity.

Police also attempt to promote guardianship: people protecting other people or the belongings of others. Effective guardianship has three components: The potential guardians must be observing the situation, they must have the ability to recognize potential trouble, and they must be prepared to intervene (Reynald 2010). Because we are interested in the offender's perception, effective guardianship is perceptual: The offender needs to have sufficient certainty that these conditions will not be met for the offender to choose crime. Thus, guardianship does not need to be perfect. Rather, the offender must have sufficient uncertainty[4] about the presence of effective guardianship that he or she avoids crime in the situation.

We have already noted that police hot spots patrol strategies are attempts to improve guardianship at high-crime locations. However, even before hot spots policing became popular, police tried to mobilize guardianship by members of their communities. Neighborhood and business watch programs are probably the most prominent examples. Police also make efforts to help special populations—for example, the elderly—avoid crime through disseminating information. Promoting guardianship may have an influence over targets as well. The homeowner attending a neighborhood watch program may be more likely to protect his or her own property and may also be more likely to encourage neighbors to take self-protective actions. This gives the police an indirect method of influencing potential victims.

3. Places and Managers

The direct influence of police on places is rather limited. It is putting police where they expect crime to occur. Although this could, in principle, influence the social characteristics of places, in most circumstances the police will not be present frequently enough to have a strong influence. And except in rare occasions, police have neither the capacity nor the legal authority to alter the physical characteristics of places. Place managers, on the other hand, have considerable influence over the social and physical characteristics of places (Madensen and Eck 2013). Place managers also can influence handling—for example, by encouraging the presence of parents at shopping venues (Rawe 2007). Place managers of bars can recruit patrons to handle their friends (Madensen 2007).

Place managers also have considerable influence over guardianship and targets at places (Madensen and Eck 2013).[5] Private security must be hired by place managers. But even much of what people think of as informal guardianship is stimulated through place managers: Training employees to be vigilant, signage asking patrons to watch their belongings, surveillance cameras, and the use of greeters at store entrances all influence guardianship and target vulnerability. The police can stimulate little of this unless they recruit place managers to do so. Virtually all situational crime prevention, defensible space, and crime prevention through environmental design at places are implemented by place managers. Police may be trained in these techniques, but they must implement them through place managers. Thus, probably the greatest influence police can have over situations is through their influence on place managers.

These are all direct influences on the situation that the offender encounters, so they indirectly influence offender decisions. The offender may not be aware of the police role. The standard conception of police influencing offenders through deterrence mechanisms, particularly the view held by economists who study the influence of police on crime (Becker 1968; Levitt 1997), ignores most of these mechanisms, but it is quite possible that these indirect influences might be more powerful in controlling crime and disorder than the deterrence mechanisms. Why economists miss these mechanisms is a mystery because the police influence on the offender involves manipulating the offender's perceptions of the relative costs and benefits of committing a crime at this place at this time.

One criticism of these indirect influences is that they require the cooperation of third parties, and this cooperation is far from ensured (Buerger 1994). If the police cannot persuade handlers, potential victims, guardians, and place managers to take precautionary measures, then the police have little influence.

C. Other Influence on the Situation

This concern brings us to another set of influence police can employ to impact offender decisions. Here, we draw on several intertwined perspectives that describe different aspects of the same underlying set of mechanisms: shifting and sharing responsibilities for problems (Scott 2004), third-party policing (Mazerolle and Ransley 2005), super controllers (Sampson, Eck, and Dunham 2009), and a regulatory approach to crime places (Eck and Eck 2012). Scott, building on unpublished work of Herman Goldstein, examines the ways police can persuade people and organizations that create situations that foster problems to alter their behavior to reduce problems. Mazerolle and Ransley specifically examine police collaborating with entities that have special legal authority in order to control problems. Sampson and colleagues are interested in explaining why guardianship, handling, and managing are not effective and how the police can motivate those who should be guarding, handling, and managing. Finally, Eck and Eck examine ways to reduce crime through regulations. Here, we use Sampson and colleagues' concept of super controllers because this is the broadest description and it fits neatly with routine activity theory.

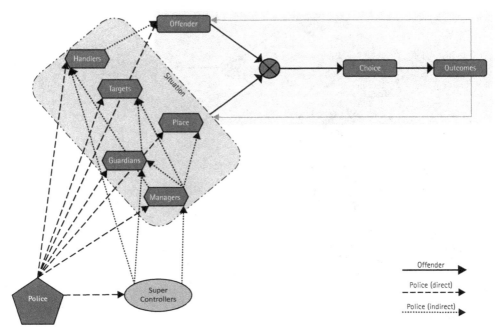

FIGURE 18.6 Police can influence those who control situations.

Sampson and colleagues (2009) suggest that controllers of situations—handlers, guardians, and managers—are embedded in a network of relationships: formal, informal, and personal. This network provides a set of incentives to handle, guard, or manage. Typically, this works. In particular instances, this network fails, and crime concentrations occur in and near situations the controller is supposed to be governing.

The members of these networks are called "super controllers." Figure 18.6 shows a simplified set of connections from super controllers to handlers, guardians, and managers. Sampson et al. (2009) propose that police can influence these super controllers to get reluctant and recalcitrant controllers to act in a way that makes the situation more crime resistant. Thus, we see an even more indirect set of mechanism for influencing offenders.

D. Policing and Nodal Governance

If we now add back in to our map of police influences the criminal justice and rehabilitation entities (figure 18.7), we see that police have a very dense network of influences on offenders. We have added paths between the criminal justice and rehabilitation entities to handlers as a reminder that handlers are sometimes attended to by these entities. We have, undoubtedly, omitted other paths that are possible, so this map may be much denser than depicted here. Consequently, although the number of lines of influence seems great, this is likely to be an underestimate rather than an exaggeration.

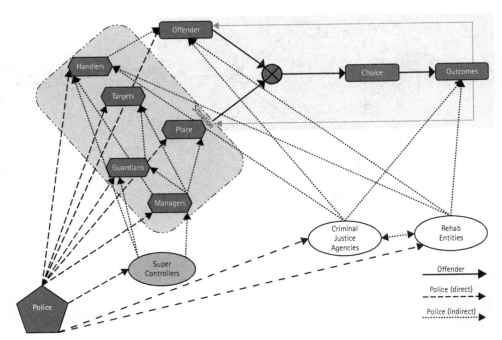

FIGURE 18.7 The web of police influence on offender choices.

A few of these paths are direct, but many more are indirect. There is no a priori reason to believe direct lines of influence are more powerful than indirect ones. Indeed, the third-party policing literature (Mazerolle and Ransley 2005) shows that very indirect policing can have fairly powerful impacts on offending. Also, although these lines of influence have received limited attention by academics interested in policing, there are numerous examples of their use (Scott 2004; Eck and Eck 2012).

Consequently, from a purely quantitative assessment (counting possible lines of influence), police have much more influence on offenders than one might believe based on the criminal justice perspective on policing. This conservative map of police influence reinforces a line of theorizing known as nodal governance. The idea behind nodal governance is that governance is not solely the function of government agencies but, rather, is the result of the interplay among a wide variety of networked individuals, organizations, and other entities (Burris et al. 2005). Because we have been explicitly police centric, we have not drawn all the other influences on the various entities depicted in figure 18.7. In particular, we have depicted police as if they had full control of their destiny, when in fact there are many lines of influence pointing at them. Similarly, place managers, guardians, handlers, potential victims, and offenders (not to mention the criminal justice and rehabilitation agencies) have numerous other influences affecting their behaviors.

Another limitation of our quantitative perspective is that it treats the influences between police and others as if they were governed by on–off switches. That is, we have implicitly assumed that it is largely a matter of the police choosing to use a particular path. In the next section, we consider this differently. We argue that how the police interact with others matters a great deal. Thus, there is an important qualitative component to police influence on offender decisions.

III. The Quality of Police Influences on Offender Decisions

We have established that police have multiple ways of influencing offenders. However, as noted by Henry David Thoreau, "It is not enough to be industrious; so are the ants. What are you industrious about?" Assuming that police are focused on preventing offenders from committing harm,[6] we have shown that industrious police officers can work to achieve this goal by interacting with the nine entities illustrated in figure 18.7: offenders, targets, places, handers, guardians, managers, super controllers, criminal justice agencies, and various rehabilitation services. We now address this chapter's second key thesis: how police go about leveraging the influence of these entities will determine the success of their efforts.

Police interventions do not guarantee that offenders will refrain from crime. Nor does police contact with the other eight entities guarantee that the entities will act in a way that could influence offenders in the desired way. We first focus on offenders, although much of what we have to say can be applied to the others with only minor changes to our argument. For example, victim cooperation or collaboration with place managers could be enhanced by the use of the framework we discuss. This is because much of the forthcoming discussion is based on research that is neither police nor offender specific: It describes people in general.

As noted previously, police efforts could have no impact or, worse, cause offending to escalate. The methods used by police to elicit responses from others determine much of the outcome, be it positive or negative. The potential negative impact of police intervention has been well documented in criminological theory and research. The point of this discussion is not to provide an exhaustive review of this literature.

We propose that there are four primary dimensions that determine the quality (i.e., success) of police interactions. Positive and voluntary cooperation from others is most likely to be elicited when police behave in a way that is perceived as (1) reasonable, (2) disarming, (3) focused, and (4) consistent. These factors make up the *RDFC interaction model*. Madensen, Heskett, and Lieberman (2012) first proposed this model to explain differential outcomes among police–crowd interactions. We demonstrate the universality of the RDFC dimensions for explaining the success (or failure) of all police attempts to influence offender decision making.

The four RDFC dimensions stem from others' ideas. They have been extracted from various theories that explain behavioral-control strategy failures. These theories include reactance theory (Brehm 1966), police legitimacy theory (Tyler 1990), defiance theory (Sherman 1993), the elaborated social identity model (Reicher 1996), differential coercion theory (Colvin, 2000), and situational crime prevention (Wortley 2001; Cornish and Clarke 2003), as well as other models and frameworks from which these theories were drawn. Those familiar with these theories will recognize the explicit connection between the model's four dimensions and previously established ideas. The RDFC interaction model synthesizes this diverse literature and emphasizes the most important qualities of police interactions in a way that makes immediate action possible. Police executives can use this model to formulate departmental policies, whereas individual line officers can use the model's basic principles to achieve more immediate goals.

A. Being Reasonable

To be reasonable, police must first ask, "*Why* am I asking others to do something?" In evaluating their answer to this question, police must consider two elements of their response. The first is whether their intervention is necessary (intervention necessity). The second is whether the police are actively concerned with protecting citizen rights during intervention (intervention objectives).

1. *Intervention Necessity*

Psychologists have established that people will naturally resist initial attempts to control their behaviors. People experience a form of "psychological arousal" that prompts resistance when their freedoms are threatened. This arousal is called "reactance."[7] Parents are familiar with this effect. If a child is suddenly told to stop playing and put on shoes, common initial responses include delaying cooperation by asking "Why?", openly ignoring the parental request, feigning forgetfulness of where shoes are kept, or actively resisting by removing additional items from the toy box.

Adults also display behaviors associated with reactance when interacting with police, particularly if police are attempting to restrict seemingly harmless behaviors. Consider an offender who frequently drives faster than the posted speed limit. In the first scenario, the offender is traveling 56 miles per hour (mph) along an abandoned stretch of road with a posted speed limit of 55 mph on a clear, sunny day. The second scenario involves the offender driving 56 mph along a busy road with a speed limit of 25 mph, in front of a school, with children present, during a heavy rainstorm. All else being equal, the degree of reactance by the offender to police intervention will be greater in the first scenario than in the second because the first involved a seemingly harmless behavior, whereas the second involved the threat of imminent and serious danger. In other words, the officer in the first scenario would be perceived as less reasonable than the officer in the second scenario and is more likely to elicit a negative response.

We also know that the larger the threat to harmless behavioral freedom, the more aggressive people will become in their attempt to challenge intervention. The driver traveling slightly faster than the speed limit will experience less reactance if pulled over and issued a warning than if pulled over and issued an expensive traffic ticket. Reactance also tends to be greater when police attempt to curtail highly valued freedoms. Should the traffic offender suspect that the loss of all driving privileges, which he needs to support his family, would occur as a result of a traffic stop, the threatened freedom suddenly becomes more valuable to the offender and resistance to police intervention is more likely to occur.

To be perceived as being reasonable, police must first understand that reactance is a normal psychological reaction among humans. Knowing that initial resistance to any intervention is common encourages police to more carefully re-examine their purpose for action and ask, "Is this intervention necessary?" A more defined and actionable question might be, "Will this intervention serve to prevent a greater and tangible harm?" Case studies throughout history have shown that police attempts to interfere with legitimate, harmless, and highly valued behaviors by groups of people (think peaceful protest marches) often produced collective violence and damaged police–community relations.[8]

Police ask drivers to adhere to posted speed limits to prevent traffic accidents and reduce injuries and fatalities. However, the perceived reasonableness of police response to traffic infractions will depend largely on whether drivers recognize the potential harm associated with their actions and whether police action is ultimately needed to prevent these behaviors and bring attention to the potential for harm. Clearly, context matters, as our examples illustrate.

2. *Intervention Objectives*

Police should treat the protection of citizen rights as a primary objective. This may seem obvious, but the current nature of police work and the previous argument that police should focus on preventing harm require us to briefly discuss the importance of this objective. Increased demand that police intervene in seemingly small, inconsequential events in an attempt to lower the risk of more serious crime has increased the likelihood that citizens will question police intentions when intervening in these contexts. The widespread use of officers as regulators of social behavior can encourage officer responses that appear unreasonable, particularly if not called on by citizens to intervene in the first place. If, in addition to preventing harm, officers convey their intention to defend individual rights, their presence and potential intervention during minor events are more likely to be perceived as being reasonable.

In addition, officer reactions to concerns about the dangers of police work can also blur the lines between what might be considered reasonable and unreasonable police action. Officers who, in the interest of officer safety, treat every interaction as life threatening run the risk of provoking normally law-abiding citizens. Placing every potential suspect in handcuffs, regardless of the person's characteristics and the circumstances surrounding the incident, would eventually violate departmental policies and individual constitutional rights. Equally important, such behavior would most likely serve to agitate previously composed individuals, especially when police are called to handle noncriminal and less serious offenses.[9] Likewise, cases involving officers who forced bystanders to stop using their cameras to film police action have resulted in much negative publicity and sanctions levied against officers and departments. Police in these cases did not protect citizens' rights to film in public spaces. Officers who do not actively focus on protecting, and explicitly acknowledge, individual rights are less likely to be perceived as being reasonable.

In summary, police reasonableness can be judged by the extent to which police act to (1) curtail only harmful behaviors and (2) protect citizen rights. Given the human inclination to resist interference, police must seek to restrict the fewest freedoms possible in their efforts to maintain public safety. A focus on preventing harm and protecting citizen rights, rather than strictly enforcing the law, can help police to achieve this goal and enhance perceptions of reasonableness.

B. Being Disarming

When police must act to prevent harm, it is important that police consider their style of intervention. Police are more likely to elicit calm, positive, and cooperative reactions if the officers behave in a disarming manner. To be disarming, police must ask and evaluate, "*How* am I asking others to do something?"

Research has found that as police increase displays of coercive power, target compliance decreases (McCluskey 2003). Consequently, police should search for ways to reduce psychological reactance—a motivational arousal created when their freedom is reduced or abolished (Pennebaker and Sanders 1976). When coerced, people experience social–psychological dynamics that result in the following:

1. Feelings of anger, which causes strain and weakens social bonds
2. Provoked unintended or heightened motivation to offend
3. Learned models of aggressive behavior that may be mimicked in the current situation or the future[10]

Consequently, overly aggressive police action reduces compliance now and in future police–citizen interactions. Being disarming involves avoiding any unnecessary use of force or coercion in an effort to increase positive reactions.

Evidence has long shown that the phrasing and source of specific requests for compliance determine levels of cooperation. Pennebaker and Sanders (1976) examined the effects of two different requests made to control graffiti. More graffiti was observed in locations where threatening messages were placed ("Do NOT write on the walls!" signed by "J. R. Buck, Chief of Security") compared to locations providing gentler messages ("Please do not write on these walls" signed by "J. R. Buck, Grounds Committeeman").

How does an officer learn to be disarming? This is not typically a subject that officers are encouraged to study and practice. The simple presence of an officer or the officer's style of dress—particularly if in riot gear (Stott et al. 2008)—can invoke feelings of coercion. However, many police departments provide less than passing remarks in police training about how to calm a potentially volatile situation without using displays of force.

To be disarming requires police to learn how to ask for compliance in creative ways. We find examples of how this learning might take place in texts aimed at teaching police the art of persuasion (Thompson and Jenkins 2013) and in the use of specialized police units such as the Dialogue Police within the Swedish National Police that open lines of communication between police commanders and outside groups (Holgersson and Knutsson 2011). However, widespread adoption of these techniques as common practice among all officers is lacking. This limits police ability to reduce negative offender decision making.

Mazerolle and colleagues (2013) provide an example and supporting empirical evidence regarding one disarming effort by Australian traffic officers. The officers conducted a traditional randomized breath testing operation. Half of these officers used an experimental script. This script prompted officers to (1) explain to drivers why they had been stopped (to reduce deaths), (2) describe how they were chosen to be stopped (randomly), (3) ask drivers for ideas and advice about problems in their communities, and (4) thank drivers for their time. Drivers who received these more time-consuming encounters (on average, four times longer) reported higher levels of compliance and satisfaction and were 1.24 times more likely to report changes in their views on drinking alcohol and driving.[11] The researchers concluded that "a little bit of being nice goes a long way" (Mazerolle et al. 2013, p. 55). The elements of the experimental script—to explain,[12] to listen, and to be kind—can be used as a blueprint for developing disarming tactics for a wide variety of common police–citizen encounters.

In summary, officer attempts at being disarming can be judged by the extent to which they employ noncoercive tactics to gain compliance. There is often a difference between what police *can* do (legally) and what they *should* do. Legally justified police shootings are not always the only or last option used by police.[13] Given the detrimental effects of coercive officer behavior, police should restrict the use of force, coercion, and intrusiveness to the lowest possible levels. An emphasis on, and demonstrations of, clever and creative responses that reduce stress in highly charged situations can help police to achieve this goal and increase perceptions of police as disarming.[14]

C. Being Focused

Not everyone poses a threat. Hence, broad police intervention is rarely justified. It is critical that police target their efforts, not only to conserve resources but also to limit the negative effects of any potentially necessary coercive intervention. To be focused, police must ask and evaluate the following: "To *whom* am I making this request?" In evaluating their answer to this question, police must consider whether this person is directly causing harm or has the capacity to stop someone else from causing harm.

The importance of a focused approach is best explained by describing the negative outcomes of unfocused police–crowd interactions. Crowds are complex. They consist of individuals and small groups of people who hold different opinions and agendas. When police report that a crowd has become violent, they likely observed a small minority of people in the crowd acting aggressively or harming others. Rarely does every person in a crowd act uniformly in a hostile and dangerous manner. Failure to distinguish between and act differentially in response to violent and nonviolent crowd members can produce disastrous results.

When police adopt the perspective that all crowd members are violent, this encourages the use of high-profile policing tactics: heavy presence of uniformed police, police in riot gear, the presence of police riot vehicles, and less communication and nonconfrontational activity between police and crowd members (Reicher et al. 2007). It may also encourage them to use force indiscriminately against all crowd members (e.g., throwing tear gas into a large crowd to attempt to disrupt a few agitators). This type of coercive police reaction serves to escalate the potential for violence in the crowd. Overly aggressive and unnecessary police tactics can cause initially peaceful crowd members to become more willing to engage in confrontation and more hostile toward police.[15]

When police choose to intervene, it is important that they first distinguish between those who are and those who are not causing harm. Failure to make this distinction will serve to frustrate and alienate law-abiding citizens from the police who purport to serve them. A lack of emphasis on routinized distinction might cause some police to view all members of a specific group as problematic.[16] This principle applies to all forms of police intervention. If police want to reduce burglaries by asking apartment owners to purchase reinforced security doors, they must first acknowledge that only a small percentage of complexes generate most of these crimes (Eck, Clarke, and Guerette 2007). Police must focus this request on owners of complexes with high burglary rates. An unfocused and sweeping approach[17] can harm previously positive owner–police relations, especially if the requested intervention is resource-intensive or fails to impact crime in most places.

In summary, police focus can be judged by the extent to which police limit their interventions to those who cause harm or allow harm to occur. Given that a small proportion of offenders and situations generate most of the crime, police must focus their attention toward these harm-producing behaviors and conditions. Stressing the importance of individualized assessment and treatment of people and problems can help police to achieve this goal and increase perceptions of police focus.

D. Being Consistent

It is not enough to be seen as reasonable, disarming, and focused if police actions do not regularly reflect these attributes. To be consistent, police must ask and evaluate the following: "*Where* and *when* do I treat others similarly?" The success of the RDFC interaction model depends on police ability to demonstrate consistency in being reasonable, disarming, and focused across similar situations and over time.

Predictability builds trust, and trust is necessary for police to elicit voluntary cooperation from the public (Tyler and Huo 2002). It is impossible for police to demonstrate predictability and build trust without a commitment to consistency in action. People must believe that police will *always* act reasonably,[18] use the least coercive tactics possible, and reserve intervention for those causing harm. Only then can police begin to build beneficial relationships with members of high-crime communities that require frequent police intervention.

When police behave erratically, particularly when using highly coercive tactics, this inspires defiant and hostile behavior toward authority. Erratic police intervention fosters feelings of helplessness. Negative events are then viewed as random occurrences and attributed to luck or fate rather than the consequences of individual behavior (Colvin 2000). Alternatively, predictable consequences enhance the credibility of authorities (Tyler and Jackson 2013) and are more likely to deter negative decision making by potential offenders.

In summary, police consistency can be judged by the extent to which police treat comparable behaviors and conditions similarly across time. Given that predictability fosters trust and cooperation, police must act in a consistent manner to successfully set and reinforce behavioral expectations. Steps taken to routinize reasonable, disarming, and focused officer actions can help police to achieve this goal and increase perceptions of police consistency.

E. Benefits of the RDFC Interaction Model

Tyler and Jackson (2013) note that the typical dynamics of offender deterrence strategies can stress and weaken police–community relationships. Together, the RDFC dimensions explain how police can influence offender decision making, and others who might also influence offenders, without sacrificing these relationships. As noted previously, there are substantially more indirect than direct paths used by police to influence offender decision making. The cooperation of those who fall along these paths thus appears critical for police efforts to maintain public safety. The RDFC interaction model provides one framework through which to improve the quality and success of exchanges with these indirect actors.

Although this chapter is focused on police influence (direct and indirect) on criminal offenders, it is worth noting that the regulatory compliance literature suggests approaches compatible with the RDFC interaction model. Ayres and Braithwaite (1992), for example, propose a regulatory pyramid—or graduated sanctioning framework—that enhances what we have been calling reasonableness and concentrates resources on the worst offenders, which corresponds to being focused. Valerie Braithwaite (2010) notes that inconsistency in criminal enforcement and a lack of focus through overuse of criminal enforcement can undermine regulatory efforts. Kirchler and Wahl (2008) provide a trust–power interaction framework to describe voluntary tax compliance. They raise many of the same concerns highlighted by the RDFC dimensions.

Table 18.1 RDFC Intervention Model Dimensions

Dimension	Goal	Perceptual Effects	Behavioral Outcomes
Reasonable	Restrict fewest freedoms possible	Autonomy is not threatened	Voluntary compliance
Disarming	Limit use of force, coercion, and intrusiveness	Implementation does not create duress, tension, or anxiety	Calm, positive reactions
Focused	Target only behaviors/ conditions causing harm	Intervention is acceptable and justified	Permit and support authority intervention
Consistent	Set and reinforce behavioral expectations	Responses are anticipated and predictable	Routine and instinctive compliance

Another of the model's salient benefits is its applicability to all levels of police work. Departmental training and policy grounded in the framework have the potential to improve aggregate perceptions of police. Still, we know that emergent properties cannot manifest in the absence of individual-level interactions. Every police encounter matters, and even brief interactions can shape an individual's generalized view of police (Mazerolle et al. 2013). Therefore, it is important that individual officers be able to judge their actions against clear criteria, understand how others perceive specific actions, and recognize desired behavioral outcomes (table 18.1). The RDFC interaction model was developed toward this aim.

IV. CONCLUSION

In this chapter, we set out to unify a variety of different literatures relevant to understanding how police can influence offender decisions. These literatures show that police have much more influence on offenders than a simple deterrence perspective suggests. We have made two major points in this chapter. The first is a point about quantity: The police have a multitude of ways of influencing offender actions, and most of these are indirect. This can be appreciated even though we have used a very simple framework. A more complex framework would, no doubt, reveal even more influences. The second is a point about quality: How the police interact with offenders and others will determine if their attempts to influence offenders will be successful. We have shown that there is a diverse literature, both within and outside police research, that supports these two points. Our goal has been to bring this rich literature together in a comprehensible framework that will support useful research and help guide productive police action.

As the reader can now appreciate, the relationship between police and offenders is rich and complex. It is complex even when we started with a very simple framework (see figure 18.1). Adding more complex frameworks, with more actors and relationships, can only reinforce our first major point. This has implications for those who study policing or offending. However, adding complexity to gain a modicum of descriptive improvement may not be worth the price if practitioners cannot discern actionable lessons. We have clearly sided with parsimony.

For those who study police and offending, the framework we provide describes a rich set of topics. Regarding the links between police action and offender behavior, each set of connections is worthy of research. Comparing the efficacy and side effects of sets of connections is another line of enquiry worth examining. This framework allows comparisons among different approaches to handling offenders. Thus, describing the way police address offender behavior in diverse settings and problems is possible. Regarding how the police behave when using a connection—where the RDFC interaction model plays a role—we have a set of hypotheses about what would reduce and what would increase conflict and resistance to police requests. By pulling together a diverse literature on the topic, we have provided a useful organizing framework.

For those whose interest is more toward action, both parts of our framework suggest ways in which police can become more effective. Systematically exploring the network of relationships connecting police to offenders can help police find more useful ways to reduce crime. At the same time, the RDFC interaction model provides guidance for how to improve the chances the police will achieve their desired outcomes with the least social disruption and conflict.

Of course, dividing the implications of this framework between research and practice ignores an important lesson of the past thirty years: Good practice and good research go hand-in-hand. We hope our framework enhances this sort of evidence-based practice.

NOTES

1. In this chapter, we ignore any incapacitation influences. This is because incapacitation removes the ability of the offender to make choices about crimes.
2. Wikström, in situational action theory, uses the term "situation" differently from the way we use this word. Rather, he uses the term "setting" much as we do the term situation: "A setting is defined as the part of the environment (the configuration of objects, persons, and events) that, at any given moment in time, is accessible to a person through his or her senses (including any media present). A situation is defined as the perception of action alternatives and process of choice, which emerges from the person–setting interaction" (Wikström et al. 2012, p. 15). In Figure 18.3, the circle with the "X" is roughly synonymous with Wikström's situation.
3. The police may influence elements of the situation for purposes other than prevention—for example, achieving justice. In this chapter, we are uninterested in these purposes. Thus, police promoting guardianship to encourage crime reporting to enhance criminal detection with the result that offenders are brought to court and given just sanctions is not of concern here.
4. We are making a distinction, standard in economics (Knight 1921; Ellsberg 1961), between risk and uncertainty. Risk is a quantifiable assessment of the chance of an outcome (here,

that there is a guardian observing the situation who will detect my misbehavior and take actions against me). Uncertainty, in contrast, is not quantifiable. Guerron-Quintana (2012) contrasts two situations: betting on the outcome of a fair coin flip (risk) and betting on the outcome of flipping an unfair coin (uncertainty). In the first case, a risk can be assigned (.5), whereas in the second, a quantifiable assessment of risk is impossible with the information at hand.

5. Not all guardianship is the result of place management. Some guardianship occurs without place manager prompting, particularly at locations where place management is weak, inattentive, or absent. How much guardianship is prompted by place management and how much is stimulated by other factors is an empirical question that has not been answered. Although often intertwined, guardianship and place management are different concepts (Madensen and Eck 2013).

6. This is an important assumption. If officers busy themselves with attempts to achieve traditional measures of police success, such as reducing response times and making arrests, then the discussion that follows is unimportant.

7. See Brehm (1966) and Brehm and Brehm (1981) for a more complete overview of this behavioral response.

8. Reicher et al. (2004) describe the elaborated social identity model. This model explains how collective conflict is instigated when groups believe that their legitimate actions are impeded by others.

9. Sherman's (1993) defiance theory explains how unjust police action can serve to increase the frequency or seriousness of future offending.

10. Colvin's (2000) differential coercion theory details these social–psychological dynamics.

11. This finding shows a change in declared opinions but does not describe whether offenders changed their behavior. Thus, it must be treated with some caution.

12. "The police clearly explain the reasons for their actions to the people they deal with" is a survey item commonly used to measure individual perceptions of procedural fairness (Tankebe 2013, p. 115).

13. This is not to suggest that police shootings are never justified. They are often necessary and the only option available to officers when offenders pose an immediate and significant risk to the safety of officers and others.

14. Coates (1972) provides an overview of how wit and humor have been used to reduce tension in crowds.

15. Reicher et al. (2004) describe how this process unfolds according to the elaborated social identity model.

16. This has long been a criticism of aggressive stop-and-frisk policies.

17. Eck and Eck (2012) further describe the related command-and-control approach and its potential benefits and drawbacks.

18. "When the police deal with people in my neighborhood, they *always* behave according to the law" (emphasis added) is a survey item commonly used to measure individual perceptions of police lawfulness (Tankebe 2013, p. 115).

References

Ayling, J., P. N. Grabosky, and C. D. Shearing. 2009. *Lengthening the Arm of the Law: Enhancing Police Resources in the Twenty-First Century*. New York: Cambridge University Press.

Ayres, I., and J. Braithwaite. 1992. *Responsive Regulation: Transcending the Deregulation Debate*. New York: Oxford University Press.

Becker, G. S. 1968. "Crime and Punishment: An Economic Approach." *Journal of Political Economy* 76:169–217.

Braga, A. 2001, November. "The Effects of Hot Spots Policing on Crime." *Annals of the American Academy of Political and Social Science* 578:104–25.

Braga, A. A. 2006. "Policing Crime Hot Spots." In *Preventing Crime: What Works for Children, Offenders, Victims, and Places*, edited by B. C. Welsh and D. P. Farrington, pp. 179–92. New York: Routledge.

Braga, A. A., A. V. Papachristos, and D. M. Hureau. 2014. "The Effects of Hot Spots Policing on Crime: An Updated Systematic Review and Meta-Analysis." *Justice Quarterly* 31(4): 633–63.

Braga, A. A., and D. L. Weisburd. 2012. "The Effects of 'Pulling Levers" Focused Deterrence Strategies on Crime." *Campbell Systematic Reviews* 2012:6.

Braithwaite, V. 2010. "Criminal Prosecution Within Responsive Regulatory Practice." *Criminology and Public Policy* 9(3): 515–23.

Brehm, J. W. 1966. *A Theory of Psychological Reactance*. New York: Academic Press.

Brehm, S. S., and J. W. Brehm. 1981. *Psychological Reactance: A Theory of Freedom and Control*. New York: Academic Press.

Buerger, M. E. 1994. "The Problems of Problem Solving." *American Journal of Police* 13(3): 1–36.

Burris, S., P. Drahos, and C. D. Shearing. 2005. "Nodal Governance." *Australian Journal of Legal Philosophy* 30(1): 30–58.

Clarke, R. V. 1995. "Situational Crime Prevention." In *Building a Safer Society: Strategic Approaches to Crime Prevention*, edited by M. Tonry and D. Farrington, pp. 91–150. Chicago: University of Chicago Press.

Coates, J. F. 1972. "Wit and Humor: A Neglected Aid in Crowd and Mob Control." *Crime and Delinquency* 18(2): 184–91.

Cohen, L. E., and M. Felson. 1979. "Social Change and Crime Rate Trends: A Routine Activity Approach." *American Sociological Review* 44(4): 588–608.

Colvin, M. 2000. *Crime and Coercion: An Integrated Theory of Chronic Criminality*. New York: St. Martin's Press.

Cornish, D. B., and R. V. Clarke. 2003. "Opportunities, Precipitators and Criminal Decisions." In *Theory for Practice in Situational Crime Prevention*, vol. 16, edited by M. Smith and D. Cornish. *Crime Prevention Studies*, pp.41–96. Monsey, NY: Criminal Justice Press.

Durlauf, S. N., and D. S. Nagin. 2011. "Imprisonment and Crime: Can Both Be Reduced?" *Criminology and Public Policy* 10(1): 13–54.

Eck, J. E. 1983. *Solving Crime: A Study of the Investigation of Burglary and Robbery*. Washington, DC: Police Executive Research Forum.

Eck, J. E. 2003. "Police Problems: The Complexity of Problem Theory, Research and Evaluation." In *Problem-Oriented Policing: From Innovation to Mainstream*, vol. 15, edited by J. Knutsson. *Crime Prevention Studies*, pp. 79–113. Monsey, NY: Criminal Justice Press.

Eck, J. E., R. V. Clarke, and R. T. Guerette. 2007. "Risky Facilities: Crime Concentration in Homogeneous Sets of Establishments and Facilities." In *Imagination for Crime Prevention: Essays in Honour of Ken Pease*, vol. 21, edited by G. Farrell, K. J. Bowers, S. D. Johnson, and M. Townsley. *Crime Prevention Studies*, pp. 225–64. Boulder, CO: Lynne Rienner.

Eck, J. E., and E. B. Eck. 2012. "Crime Place and Pollution: Expanding Crime Reduction Options Through a Regulatory Approach." *Criminology and Public Policy* 11(2): 281–316.

Ekblom, P. 2002. "From the Source to the Mainstream Is Uphill: The Challenge of Transferring Knowledge of Crime Prevention Through Replication, Innovation and Anticipation." In *Analysis for Crime Prevention*, vol. 13, edited by N. Tilley. *Crime Prevention Studies*, pp. 131–203. Monsey, NY: Criminal Justice Press.

Ellsberg, D. 1961. "Risk, Ambiguity, and the Savage Axioms." *Quarterly Journal of Economics* 75(4): 643–69.

Felson, M. 1986. "Routine Activities, Social Control, Rational Decisions, and Criminal Outcomes." In *The Reasoning Criminal*, edited by D. Cornish and R. V. G. Clarke, pp. 119–28. New York: Springer-Verlag.

Felson, M. 2008. "Routine Activity Approach." In *Environmental Criminology and Crime Analysis*, edited by L. G. Mazerolle and R. Wortley, pp. 70–77. Cullompton, UK: Willan.

Gelman, A., J. Fagan, and A. Kiss. 2007. "An Analysis of the New York City Police Department's 'Stop-and-Frisk' Policy in the Context of Claims of Racial Bias." *Journal of the American Statistical Association* 102(479): 813–23.

Guerron-Quintana, P. A. 2012. "Risk and Uncertainty." *Business Review* 95(1): 10–18.

Holgersson, S., and J. Knutsson. 2011. "Dialogue Policing: A Means for Less Crowd Violence?" In *Preventing Crowd Violence*, edited by T. D. Madensen and J. Knutsson, pp. 191–216. Boulder, CO: Lynne Rienner.

Kirchler, E. H., and I. Wahl. 2008. "Enforced Versus Voluntary Tax Compliance: The "Slippery Slope" Framework." *Journal of Economic Psychology* 29(2): 210–25.

Knight, F. H. 1921. *Risk, Uncertainty, and Profit.* New York: Houghton Mifflin.

Levitt, S. D. 1997. "Using Electoral Cycles in Police Hiring to Estimate the Effect of Police on Crime." *American Economic Review* 87(3): 270–90.

Madensen, T. D. 2007. *Bar Management and Crime: Toward a Dynamic Theory of Place Management and Crime Hotspots.* Cincinnati, OH: University of Cincinnati.

Madensen, T. D., and J. E. Eck. 2013. "Crime Places and Place Management." In *Oxford Handbook of Criminological Theory*, edited by F. T. Cullen and P. Wilcox, pp. 554–78. New York: Oxford University Press.

Madensen, T. D., C. L. Heskett, and J. D. Lieberman. 2012. "Predicting Crowd Behavior: A Response–Reaction Matrix." Paper presented at the International Seminar on Environmental Criminology and Crime Analysis (ECCA) 21st International Symposium, Stavern, Norway.

Madensen, T. D., and J. Knutsson. 2011. *Preventing Crowd Violence.* Boulder, CO: Lynne Reinner.

Maxwell, C. D., J. H. Garner, and J. A. Fagan. 2002. "The Preventive Effects of Arrest on Intimate Partner Violence: Research, Policy and Theory." *Criminology and Public Policy* 2(1): 51–80.

Mazerolle, L., E. Antrobus, S. Bennett, and T. R. Tyler. 2013. "Shaping Citizen Perceptions of Police Legitimacy: A Randomized Field Trial of Procedural Justice." *Criminology* 51(1): 33–63.

Mazerolle, L. G., and J. Ransley. 2005. *Third Party Policing.* New York: Cambridge University Press.

McCluskey, J. D. 2003. *Police Requests for Compliance: Coercive and Procedurally Just Tactics.* New York: LFB Scholarly.

Monmonier, M. 1993. *Mapping It Out: Expository Cartography for the Humanities and Social Sciences.* Chicago: University of Chicago Press.

Nagin, D. S. 2013. "Deterrence in the Twenty-First Century." In *Crime and Justice: A Review of Research*, vol. 42, edited by M. Tonry, pp. 199–263. Chicago: University of Chicago Press.

Pennebaker, J. W., and D. Y. Sanders. 1976. "American Graffiti: Effects of Authority and Reactance Arousal." *Personality and Social Psychology Bulletin* 2(3): 264–67.

Rawe, J. 2007. "Bye-Bye, Mall Rats: At Many Teen-Choked Shopping Centers, Managers Have Started Booting Kids Unless They're with a Parent." *Time.* http://content.time.com/time/magazine/article/0,9171,1638449,00.html

Reicher, S. D. 1996. "'The Battle of Westminster'": Developing the Social Identity Model of Crowd Behaviour in Order to Explain the Initiation and Development of Collective Conflict." *European Journal of Social Psychology* 26(1): 115–34.

Reicher, S. D, C. Stott, P. Cronin, and O. Adang. 2004. "An Integrated Approach to Crowd Psychology and Public Order Policing." *Policing* 27(4): 558–72.

Reicher, S. D., C. Stott, J. Drury, O. Adang, P. Cronin, and A. Livingstone. 2007. "Knowledge-Based Public Order Policing: Principles and Practice." *Policing* 1(4): 403–15.

Reynald, D. M. 2010. "Guardians on Guardianship: Factors Affecting the Willingness to Supervise, the Ability to Detect Potential Offenders, and the Willingness to Intervene. *Journal of Research in Crime and Delinquency* 47(3): 358–90.

Sampson, R., J. E. Eck, and J. Dunham. 2009. "Super Controllers and Crime Prevention: A Routine Activity Explanation of Crime Prevention Success and Failure." *Security Journal* 23(1): 37–51.

Schaefer, L., F. Cullen, and J. E. Eck. 2015. *Environmental Corrections: A New Paradigm for Supervising Offenders in the Community.* Thousand Oaks, CA: Sage.

Scott, M. S. 2004. "Shifting and Sharing Police Responsibility to Address Public Safety Problems." In *Handbook of Crime Prevention and Community Safety*, edited by N. Tilley, pp. 385–410. Cullompton, UK: Willan.

Sherman, L. W. 1993. "Defiance, Deterrence, and Irrelevance: A Theory of the Criminal Sanction." *Journal of Research in Crime and Delinquency* 30(4): 445–73.

Sherman, L. W., and J. E. Eck. 2002. "Policing for Crime Prevention." In *Evidence-Based Crime Prevention: What Works for Children, Offenders, Victims, and Places*, edited by L. W. Sherman, D. Farrington, B. Welsh, and D. MacKenzie, pp. 295–329. New York: Routledge.

Spelman, W., and D. Brown. 1981. *Calling the Police: A Replication of the Citizen Reporting Component of the Kansas City Response Time Analysis.* Washington, DC: Police Executive Research Forum.

Stott, C., O. Adang, A. Livingstone, and M. Schreiber. 2008. "Tackling Football Hooliganism: A Quantitative Study of Public Order, Policing and Crowd Psychology." *Psychology, Public Policy, and Law* 14(2): 115–41.

Tankebe, J. 2013. "Viewing Things Differently: The Dimensions of Public Perceptions of Police Legitimacy." *Criminology* 51(1): 103–35.

Thompson, G. J., and J. B. Jenkins. 2013. *Verbal Judo: The Gentle Art of Persuasion*, 2nd ed. New York: HarperCollins.

Tillyer, M. S., and J. E. Eck. 2010. "Getting a Handle on Crime : A Further Extension of Routine Activities Theory." *Security Journal* 24(2): 179–93.

Tyler, T. R. 1990. *Why People Obey the Law: Procedural Justice, Legitimacy, and Compliance.* New Haven, CT: Yale University Press.

Tyler, T. R., and Y. Huo. 2002. *Trust in the Law: Encouraging Public Cooperation with the Police and Courts.* New York: Russell Sage Foundation.

Tyler, T. R., and J. Jackson. 2013. "Future Challenges in the Study of Legitimacy and Criminal Justice." In *Legitimacy and Criminal Justice: An International Exploration*, edited by J. Tankebe and A. Liebling, pp. 83–104. Oxford: Oxford University Press.

Weisburd, D., and J. E. Eck. 2004, May. "What Can Police Do to Reduce Crime, Disorder, and Fear?" *Annals of the American Academy of Political and Social Science* 593:42–65.

Weisburd, D. L., C. W. Telep, J. Hinkle, and J. E. Eck. 2010. "Is Problem-Oriented Policing Effective in Reducing Crime and Disorder?" *Criminology and Public Policy* 9(1): 139–72.

Wikström, P.-O. H., D. Oberwittler, K. Treiber, and B. Hardie. 2012. *Breaking Rules: The Social and Situational Dynamics of Young People's Urban Crime.* New York: Oxford University Press.

Wortley, R. 2001. "A Classification of Techniques for Controlling Situational Precipitators of Crime." *Security Journal* 14(4): 63–82.

CHAPTER 19

···

CRIME LOCATION CHOICE
State of the Art and Avenues for Future Research

···

STIJN RUITER

I. OVERVIEW

···

OFFENDERS make numerous choices when they commit crimes. Geographical and environmental criminologists are mainly interested in those choices that affect the spatial and temporal patterns in crime. Studies on the uneven spatial distribution of crime abound. The study of seasonal patterns in crime also has a long tradition. Crime patterning by time of day and day of week has received far less attention, but clearly crime not only varies over space but also varies in cyclic patterns at different scales of temporal resolution (Andresen and Malleson 2013; Andresen and Malleson 2015). This chapter mainly discusses how offenders decide where to commit crime, but it also stresses the importance of more research into temporal aspects of target choice. Although the choices of potential victims and those of the people and agencies that try to prevent crime from happening will certainly have some impact on offenders' decisions on where and when to strike, it is ultimately the offender who decides on the location and time of the offense. Therefore, this chapter discusses the uneven spatial patterns in crime from an offender decision-making perspective. It describes the main theoretical perspectives and reviews empirical research with an emphasis on studies that use the discrete choice framework (Ben-Akiva and Lerman 1985) for analyzing individual crime location choices as introduced to the field of criminology by Bernasco and Nieuwbeerta (2003, 2005).

Before discussing the main environmental criminological theories for crime location choices and the often-ignored role of time, it is important to stress that this review mainly discusses these choices for crime types with a clear geography. The crimes should have specific geographical locations and should be committed at distinct times. So far, most crime location choice research has studied residential burglaries (Bernasco and Nieuwbeerta 2003, 2005; Bernasco 2006, 2010*a*, 2010*b*; Clare, Fernandez, and Morgan 2009; Bernasco, Johnson, and Ruiter 2015; Townsley et al. 2015; Vandeviver et al. 2015;

Townsley et al. 2016). However, the discrete choice framework has also been applied to street (Bernasco and Block 2009; Bernasco 2010*b*; Bernasco, Block, and Ruiter 2013) and commercial (Bernasco and Kooistra 2010) robberies, theft from vehicles (Bernasco 2010*b*; Johnson and Summers 2015), rioting (Baudains, Braithwaite, and Johnson 2013), assaults (Bernasco 2010*b*), drug dealing (Bernasco and Jacques 2015), and any type of crime (Lammers et al. 2015).

II. Environmental Criminological Theories

Research into the geography of crime has a long history in criminology, initially sparked by the moral statisticians of the early 1800s (Balbi and Guerry 1829) who already used maps to show that crimes were not uniformly distributed across the different regions of France. However, most criminological research addresses etiological questions about criminality. Criminal inclinations, the distinction between the people involved in criminal behavior and those who are not, and the conditions and interventions that affect onset and desistance from crime are key topics in this line of criminological research. There is a plethora of criminological theories aimed at understanding criminality. However, from the 1970s onward, several scholars shifted focus from the study of who commits crime and why to the study of criminal events. With their rational choice perspective (Clarke and Cornish 1985; Cornish and Clarke 1986), routine activity approach (Cohen and Felson 1979), and crime pattern theory (P. J. Brantingham and Brantingham 1978, 1984, 2008; P. L. Brantingham and Brantingham 1981, 1993), they shaped the field of environmental criminology with its strong emphasis on criminal opportunities and situational crime prevention (Clarke 1983). This field of criminology is primarily concerned with the circumstances in which crimes occur—when and where, how, and against what targets or victims—and in answering these questions, it generally treats criminal motivation as given.

Cohen and Felson (1979) provided a macro-level approach for analyzing how ordinary legal activities of people shape where and when crimes occur. When in the course of their daily routines, people who are motivated to commit crime converge with suitable victims or targets in the absence of capable guardians, crime is likely to happen. Because these convergence settings are not uniformly distributed over space and time, spatio-temporal crime clusters exist. The approach provides a framework for understanding such clustering, and it also predicts crime-level trends when macro-level shifts in daily routines occur. Its emphasis on the temporal aspects of people's routines proves highly valuable for understanding the often-ignored temporal patterning of crime. However, by emphasizing that crimes occur during the daily routines, it suggests that most crimes are opportunistic, and the routine activity approach cannot really account for the goal-oriented behavior of many offenders. The approach lacks an individual-level theory for offenders' crime location choices.

The rational choice perspective (Cornish and Clarke 1986) provides an informal rational choice theory for understanding offender behavior as goal-oriented decision making. Weighing the costs and benefits of different behavior alternatives, offenders would make those choices that are assumed to bring them closer to their goals. Clearly, the rational choice perspective is rather abstract, and it requires auxiliary assumptions and empirical regularities regarding the relevant goals and choice situations of offenders in order to arrive at testable hypotheses for understanding crime location choices. Because of the analogy between environmental criminological questions concerning the spatiotemporal aspects of target selection and questions regarding animals' choices of diet, foraging territory, and time spent in the territory, several authors have used optimal foraging theory from behavioral ecology as a supplement to the rational choice perspective (Johnson and Bowers 2004; Felson 2006; Morselli and Royer 2008; Bernasco 2009; Johnson, Summers, and Pease 2009; Pires and Clarke 2011; Johnson 2014). Both theories start from a neoclassical microeconomics concept of goal-oriented behavior and, as such, optimal foraging theory lends itself to arrive at testable hypotheses about crime specialization, the distance offenders are willing to travel, the choice of target area, the time spent during the commission of crime, and the profits obtained through crime (Bernasco 2009). For example, Morselli and Royer (2008) show that mobile offenders generally have higher financial earnings, which is in line with predictions from optimal foraging and rational choice theory because higher gains should offset the costs of further travel.

With their crime pattern theory, Brantingham and Brantingham (P. J. Brantingham and Brantingham 1978, 1984, 2008; P. L. Brantingham and Brantingham 1981, 1993) provided a comprehensive explanation of crime that combines insights from behavioral geography with the rational choice perspective and the routine activity approach. Their geometry of crime (P. L. Brantingham and Brantingham 1981) is central to their crime pattern theory, and it asserts that offenders search for suitable targets or victims at places that emit cues that fit their learned templates of the characteristics of a "good" crime site (P. L. Brantingham and Brantingham 1993, p. 5). Their search is not random in space and time, but it involves looking for targets or victims inside the offender's awareness space. All people, including offenders, have routine activities that shape their spatial knowledge. Activity spaces consist of the routine activity nodes, such as homes, workplaces, schools, shopping areas, and leisure locations, and the usual travel paths between these. P. J. Brantingham and Brantingham (2008, p. 84) define the awareness space as "the area normally within visual range of the activity space," and people will generally have limited knowledge of areas outside their awareness spaces. Crime pattern theory therefore asserts that crime occurs at locations where attractive opportunities for crime overlap with awareness spaces of individuals motivated to commit crime. Clearly, this does not predict that a particular offender will commit a burglary in exactly the same area as he or she would commit a robbery or any other type of crime because what is viewed as attractive opportunity varies by type of crime. This does not make crime pattern theory a crime-specific theory. On the contrary, it only stresses the importance of specifying what makes targets attractive for the specific type of crime under study.

III. The Discrete Choice Framework in Crime Location Choice Research

Before Bernasco and Nieuwbeerta (2003, 2005) introduced the discrete choice framework in the geography of crime, three other approaches to study crime location choices were used (Bernasco and Ruiter 2014). The offender-based approach as used in journey-to-crime research uses either offenders or offenses as units of analysis and studies the distribution of distances (Townsley and Sidebottom 2010) and directions in which the offenders traveled (Van Daele and Bernasco 2012) and how these vary with characteristics of the offender and the offense. The target-based approach uses potential targets as units of analysis and studies how victimization rates vary with characteristics of the targets (Haberman and Ratcliffe 2015). The mobility approach uses pairs of geographical locations—all potential areas of departure (home areas of offenders) in combination with all potential target areas—as the unit of analysis to study how the frequency of crime trips between these dyads varies with characteristics of the origin and the destination of the trips (Reynald et al. 2008). As described in much greater detail by Bernasco and Nieuwbeerta (2005) and Bernasco and Ruiter (2014), all three approaches have their own strengths and weaknesses, and the discrete choice framework improves upon all three approaches and thus provides the best approach to the study of crime location choices. It explicitly starts from a decision-making perspective and uses the outcome of a crime location choice, a particular target location out of a set of potential target location alternatives, as the dependent variable, and the unit of analysis is the individual decision maker.

Although relatively new in the geography of crime, the discrete choice framework has been used in many disciplines to theorize and statistically model individual choice behavior (Ben-Akiva and Lerman 1985). The framework is firmly rooted in the microeconomic random utility maximization (RUM) theory, a formal rational choice theory that adds a random component to the utility function. This random component only reflects incomplete information on the part of the analyst, not on the part of the decision maker. With some assumptions regarding the distribution of this random component, the statistical model can be directly derived from the theory (McFadden 1973). This tight connection between theory and model makes it easy for researchers to rigorously test new hypotheses. The discrete choice framework specifies four key elements to any choice situation:

1. Decision makers: These are the agents who make the choice.
2. Alternatives: Decision makers must choose one alternative from the choice set—a set of countable, mutually exclusive, and collectively exhaustive alternatives.
3. Attributes: All alternatives have characteristics that affect the utility a decision maker would derive from choosing the alternative. The decision maker evaluates the utilities of all alternatives. All decision makers have characteristics that potentially also affect the utility they derive from the alternatives.

4. Decision rule: RUM theory predicts that decision makers choose the alternative from which they expect to derive maximum utility. Utility can be any gain, profit, or satisfaction.

Following the notation of Bernasco and Nieuwbeerta (2005), the utility for decision maker i from choosing alternative j is given by the following equation:

$$U_{ij} = \beta' z_{ij} + e_{ij}$$

where z_{ij} is the matrix of attributes that vary across alternatives and possibly across decision makers; β is the vector of coefficients that need to be estimated empirically; and e_{ij} is the random error term, which contains all unmeasured aspects of the utility derived by decision maker i from choosing alternative j. These include unmeasured attributes that are actually relevant to the decision as well as measurement error.

When the discrete choice framework is applied to the study of crime location choices, it is obvious that offenders are the decision makers. The alternatives are all separate potential targets (generally target areas) in a study area. From the environmental criminological theories described previously, hypotheses regarding the relevant attributes of alternatives and offenders can be derived. The general decision rule translates into the prediction that offenders will target those areas where they expect to obtain highest rewards (RE) with least effort (EF) and minimal risks (RI). Entering these abstract choice criteria into the general utility function yields the following:

$$U_{ij} = \beta_{RE} RE + \beta_{EF} EF + \beta_{RI} RI + e_{ij}$$

where RE would be some variable that measures expected rewards, EF is a measure of effort, and RI is a variable that measures risk. Obviously, this linear function could be extended to include multiple measures for the three relevant choice criteria simply by adding another additive term. From the decision rule follows the expectation that β_{RE} should be positive because alternatives that yield higher rewards are more likely to be chosen, β_{EF} should be negative because alternatives that require more effort are less likely targeted, and β_{RE} should also be negative because offenders should favor less risky alternatives over more risky ones. A formal test of these expectations requires, of course, a translation of this formal model into a statistical model. McFadden (1973) shows that under specific assumptions, the formal theoretical model directly translates into the conditional logit model. In this statistical model, the probability that an offender i targets area j is given by the following formula:

$$\text{Prob}\left(Y_i = j\right) = \frac{e^{\beta' z_{ij}}}{\sum_{j=1}^{J} e^{\beta' z_{ij}}}$$

where Y_i is the choice actually made by offender i, and z_{ij} are all hypothesized attributes relevant to the decision. Conditional logit model estimates e^{β} are interpreted as multiplicative effects of a unit increase in the independent variable on the odds a target alternative is chosen. Although there is no room to discuss all assumptions underlying the conditional logit model here, in light of recent developments in crime location choice studies, it is important to discuss one specific assumption of the conditional logit model—that is, the assumption of the independence of irrelevant alternatives (IIA). This assumption states that adding or removing alternatives from the choice set will not change the relative odds associated with any existing alternatives. Bernasco (2010*a*) already argued that it is difficult to maintain the IIA assumption when modeling spatial decision making because nearby alternatives are generally very similar. That is why he used a different statistical model (the competing destinations model) that is consistent with RUM theory but does not rely on the overly restrictive IIA assumption. Nevertheless, most empirical crime location choice studies since then have used the conditional logit model (but see Townsley et al. 2016).

Although the discrete choice framework provides a superior approach to the study of crime location choices, it shows some statistical resemblance to the target-based approach. A target-based approach that uses a Poisson model to estimate how crime counts vary with target characteristics returns identical parameter estimates as a conditional logit model without offender-specific regressors and the same targets as choice set because the likelihood functions are equivalent (Guimarães, Figueirdo, and Woodward 2003). However, target-based approaches generally use all crimes reported to police, whereas the discrete spatial choice models purposefully use only the subsample of cleared crimes because that allows for the inclusion of offender-specific regressors such as distance. This obviously breaks the statistical equivalence. The question then arises which statistical model for crime location choice is to be preferred. Because distance is always one of the most important variables in the discrete crime location choice models (discussed later) and it could well be correlated with target characteristics, the gain of using more crime data in a Poisson model is probably offset by the possibility that its estimates will be biased. The degree of bias, however, could be assessed by comparing results from three different models: a Poisson model with all crimes, a Poisson model with cleared crimes only, and a conditional logit model with offender-specific regressors.

IV. Applications of the Discrete Choice Model

All 17 published crime location choice studies that used the discrete choice approach either implicitly or explicitly started from the general decision rule that offenders target those areas where they expect to obtain the highest rewards with least effort and minimal risks. The bulk of these studies analyzed burglaries, but the framework has also been applied to street and commercial robbery, theft from a vehicle, assault, rioting, drug dealing, and even any type of crime (table 19.1). In the remainder of this section, the main findings of all studies are discussed.

Table 19.1 Crime Location Choice Studies That Use the Discrete Choice Framework

Study	Crime Type(s)	Study Area(s)	Spatial Units	Main Findings (+/– for Positive/Negative Effects)
Bernasco and Nieuwbeerta (2003, 2005)	Residential burglary	The Hague, Netherlands	Neighborhoods	Proximity (+); number of residential units (+); proportion of single-family dwellings (+); ethnic heterogeneity (+) stronger for non-natives than for natives
Bernasco (2006)	Residential burglary	The Hague, Netherlands	Neighborhoods	Proximity (+); number of residential units (+); physical accessibility (+); choice criteria the same for solo burglars and co-offending groups
Clare et al. (2009)	Residential burglary	Perth, Australia	Suburbs	Proximity (+); number of residential units (+); river and major road between suburb and offender home (–); train connecting suburb with offender home area (+); ethnic heterogeneity, percentage indigenous (+) stronger for indigenous than for non-indigenous offenders; percentage rental properties (+)
Bernasco and Block (2009)	Street robbery	Chicago, IL	Census tracts	Proximity (+); population (+); racial and ethnic dissimilarity (–); gang territory dissimilarity (–); collective efficacy (–); illegal markets (drugs and prostitution) (+); retail employment levels (+); high school presence (+)
Bernasco (2010a)	Residential burglary	The Hague, Netherlands	Six-digit postal code areas	Proximity (+) more important for juveniles than for adults; number of properties (+); population aged 15–25 years (+); real estate values (+); population non-native (–) for native offenders
Bernasco (2010b)	Residential burglary, theft from vehicle, robbery, assault	Greater The Hague area, Netherlands	Four-digit postal code areas	Proximity (+); proximity to previous home location (+); lived in the area until recently (+); lived in the area for longer period of time (+)
Bernasco and Kooistra (2010)	Commercial robbery	Netherlands	Four-digit postal code areas	Proximity (+); proximity to previous home location (+); lived in the area until recently (+); lived in the area for longer period of time (+)
Bernasco et al. (2013)	Street robbery	Chicago, IL	Census blocks	Proximity (+); total population (+); connected by elevated train station or main street (+) also in adjacent block; legal cash economies (+), some also in adjacent blocks; illegal cash economies (+); high schools (+); ethnic group is majority (+)

Baudains et al. (2013)	Rioting	Greater London	Lower super output areas	Proximity (+) stronger for juveniles than for adults; presence of schools (+) stronger for juveniles than for adults; same side of river Thames (+); retail businesses (+); target area the previous days (+)
Johnson and Summers (2015)	Theft from vehicle	Dorset, UK	Lower super output areas	Proximity (+) stronger for juveniles than for adults; number of cars and vans (+); presence of school (+) only for juveniles; presence of train station (+) only for adults; contains major road (+) only for adults; population turnover (+); socioeconomic heterogeneity (+)
Townsley et al. (2015)	Residential burglary	The Hague, Netherlands; Birmingham, UK; Brisbane, Australia	Neighborhoods; super output areas; statistical local areas	Proximity (+) all three study areas, and juveniles more strongly affected in Birmingham and Brisbane; proportion accessible targets (+) all three study areas; number of potential targets (+) all three study areas
Townsley et al. (2015)	Residential burglary	Brisbane, Australia	Statistical local areas	Proximity (+); proximity to the city center (+); number of households (+); percentage single families (+); proximity effect strongest for juveniles, decreases until stabilizes in adulthood (+)
Lammers et al. (2015)	All crimes	Greater The Hague area, Netherlands	Four-digit postal code areas	Proximity (+); lived in the area until recently (+); lived in the area for longer period of time (+); previously targeted area (+) stronger effects for more recent offenses and same crime type; proximity to previous offense (+); number of prior offenses in same area (+); proportion of non-Western residents (+); number of employees in target area and number of several types of facilities (+)
Bernasco et al. (2015)	Residential burglary	West Midlands, UK	Lower super output areas	Proximity (+); previously targeted area (+) stronger effects for more recent offenses and closer to previous offenses; train stations (+); proximity to city center (+); number of households (+); mean house price (+); ethnic diversity (+); population turnover (+)
Vandeviver et al. (2015)	Residential burglary	East Flanders, Belgium	Individual properties	Proximity (+); semi-detached less likely than terraced (–); garage present (–); central heating or air conditioning present (–)
Bernasco and Jacques (2015)	Drug dealing	Amsterdam city center, Netherlands	Street segments	Tourist-attracting facilities (+); police activity (+); alleyways (+); public toilets (+)

In their groundbreaking burglary target choice study, Bernasco and Nieuwbeerta (2003, 2005) were the first to use the discrete choice framework in the geography of crime. They analyzed 548 burglaries committed by solitary offenders who lived in the city of The Hague, Netherlands. They used the conditional logit model to estimate why these burglars chose to commit their burglaries in one of the 89 potential neighborhoods of the city of The Hague. They hypothesized that burglars would favor affluent neighborhoods (measured by average property values), with many residential units, better accessible targets (measured by proportion of single-family dwellings), and in which it was less likely that they would be disturbed by the residents and other guardians (indicated by high residential mobility and high ethnic heterogeneity).

In line with both crime pattern theory and the rational choice approach, Bernasco and Nieuwbeerta (2003, 2005) also argued that burglars would prefer to target neighborhoods closer to home because they would be more familiar with these areas and committing offenses farther away would require more time and effort. Also for reasons of familiarity, they hypothesized that offenders would be more likely to target neighborhoods closer to the city center. They further acknowledged that choice criteria need not be equally applicable to all burglars. They reasoned that the proximity effect would be stronger for juveniles than for adults because juveniles are more constrained in their mobility and consequently have smaller awareness spaces. They also hypothesized that the effect of ethnic heterogeneity would be stronger for non-natives because non-natives would be more easily identified as outsiders in homogeneous (i.e., native white) neighborhoods than natives would in ethnically mixed neighborhoods. Their results showed that burglars indeed target areas that are closer to home, have more residential units, have more single-family dwellings, and are ethnically heterogeneous. Indeed, ethnic heterogeneity was more important for non-native than for native burglars, and although the different proximity effects did not statistically differ between juveniles and adults, the effects were in the expected direction. In a later study that used much smaller units of analysis and data that covered a longer period, Bernasco (2010a) also found statistical support for the hypothesized age-specific proximity effects.

Because the discrete choice model requires the researcher to define a single decision maker, in their original study, Bernasco and Nieuwbeerta (2003, 2005) simplified their analysis by excluding all multiple-offender burglaries. However, burglaries are clearly not always committed by solo offenders. Bernasco (2006) therefore extended the initial study by adding multiple-offender burglaries, and he tested whether the choice criteria were different for solo offenders and co-offending groups. The only difference he found was that solo offenders were more likely to target their own neighborhoods compared to co-offending groups.

In one of the few replication studies in criminology, Townsley et al. (2015) compared the original The Hague findings of Bernasco and Nieuwbeerta (2003, 2005) to the target choice criteria of burglars in Birmingham, United Kingdom, and Brisbane, Australia. The results showed consistent effects for proximity to the home of the offender, the proportion of easily accessible targets in the area, and the total number of targets available. Distance appeared to impede juveniles more than adults, although the difference only reached statistical significance in Birmingham and Brisbane. For two of the three consistent findings, the effects appeared to differ in size between the study areas. According to Townsley et al. (2015), the different proximity effects could be attributed to population density differences, although more replication studies are needed to test this more rigorously.

In a subsequent study using only the Brisbane burglary data, Townsley et al. (2016) used the mixed logit model, a generalization of the conditional logit model, to study the extent to which the choice criteria actually vary between burglars. The mixed logit model relaxes several overly restrictive assumptions of the conditional logit model, such as the IIA assumption, but also—and probably more important—the assumption that the choice criteria affect all offenders in the same way. The conditional logit model simply estimates a single parameter for each choice criterion for all offenders, and the only way to address the issue that effects might differ between offenders is by including different effects in the structural part of the model. The conditional logit model therefore implicitly assumes that all offenders weigh the costs and benefits equally. However, Bernasco and Nieuwbeerta (2005) already provided two examples of varying effects when they estimated age-specific proximity effects and separate effects of ethnic heterogeneity for natives and non-natives. The mixed logit model allows for the estimation of random effects or offender-specific parameters. This opens several new avenues for research because it allows the researcher further scrutiny of these random effects. Townsley et al. (2016) first show that the results from a conditional logit and a mixed logit model differ considerably. The effect of residential mobility even switches signs. They subsequently show that distance is much more important for juveniles than for adults, and the effect decreases until adulthood, during which it remains stable. These findings are in line with those from previous journey-to-crime research, but they also demonstrate that age explains only 3 percent of the variance in the proximity effect. Clearly, the mixed logit model provides new research opportunities. For instance, it enables studies on which offenders comply with the theorized effects, and it calls upon new theory to explain why some offenders weigh specific choice criteria more than others.

A recent burglary target choice study estimated how characteristics of individual houses affected their likelihood of being burglarized (Vandeviver et al. 2015). Using an unprecedentedly large choice set of more than 500,000 individual residences, the study showed that controlling for the distance from the home of the offender, burglars were less likely to target semidetached houses compared to terraced dwellings, and houses with garages and central heating were also less likely to be burglarized.

V. Barriers and Connectors

Although the finding that burglars prefer to target areas closer to home corroborated previous journey-to-crime research that consistently showed distance decay, Euclidean distance as used in the first discrete choice models actually provides a rather crude measure for the impedance people encounter when traveling. Clare et al. (2009) convincingly argued that travel in a city can be hampered by physical barriers such as major roads and rivers. They hypothesized that burglars will be less likely to cross such barriers when traveling to their burglary target area. Conversely, they argued that potential target areas that are connected by major rail tracks are more likely to be targeted. Their analysis of 1,761 burglaries committed in 292 suburbs of Perth, Australia, provided support for both hypotheses. They also showed that barriers have stronger effects the closer they are to the burglars' homes.

Although physical barriers clearly limit the possibilities of travel, Bernasco and Block (2009) argued that the same applies to social barriers. These barriers would deter offenders from committing crime in areas that are socially (economically, culturally, and ethnically) different from the areas in which offenders live. In their study of 12,872 robberies committed in the 844 census tracts of Chicago, Bernasco and Block showed that this indeed applies. Robbers are more likely to commit a robbery in a census tract in which the majority of the population is of their own ethnic background. This finding can be explained in two ways. First, it could be that they simply spend more time in those areas and consequently also commit their robberies there. If this is the case, their routine activities alone could explain this effect. Second, they could purposefully target those areas because they may be less conspicuous in those areas, which limits the risk of being identified as an outsider who is there to commit a crime. Distinguishing between these two explanations is difficult because it requires detailed information on offenders' routine activities. Bernasco and Block also identified a social barrier related to gang territory. Chicago robbers appeared to be less likely to commit a robbery in an area that had gang-related crime of a different gang than the gangs active in their home area. The same Chicago data were used to study in more detail how cash economies affect where street robberies are committed (Bernasco et al. 2013). The presence of both legal (a wide variety of small businesses) and illegal (drug, prostitution, and gambling areas) cash economies in a census block attracts street robbers, and some of these effects spill over into the adjacent census blocks, but not beyond. The social barrier effect was also tested more thoroughly, and the results showed that robbers of specific ethnic groups are much more likely to target census blocks in which their ethnic group is the majority, and Hispanic robbers are much less likely to target a census block with an African American majority. Furthermore, census blocks that were better connected by main streets and public transport were also more likely to be targeted.

Just like with robberies in Chicago, the presence of small businesses also attracts drug dealers to particular street segments in the Red Light District of the city of Amsterdam (Bernasco and Jacques 2015). Although their study was too small to statistically test for effects and to use a multivariate design, and because they did not include any offender-specific characteristics, their discrete choice model is similar to a target-based approach, their drug-dealing study is a unique crime location choice study because it did not use police-recorded data and it simultaneously studied multiple crime location choices of the same offenders. They studied where drug dealers solicit for customers separate from where they close the deal. The dealers were mainly attracted to street segments with the facilities that generally attract tourists (e.g., coffee shops, liquor stores, smartshops, tobacco shops, hotels and hostels, and clubs), and they were not at all deterred by police activity. On the contrary, they were much more likely to solicit for customers and to close the deal in street segments that were under some police surveillance. Alleyways and public toilets also stood out as drug dealer attractors.

VI. Awareness Space

Although some of the earlier crime location choice studies touched upon crime pattern theory's prediction that offenders mainly target areas within their awareness spaces, most crime location choice studies only include information about the home areas of offenders at the time they committed the offenses. However, the home is not the only reference point, of course. Many crimes are committed by homeless people, and they obviously have no home. Rengert (2004) argues that some of these people are homeless because of the addiction to drugs and their crimes are clustered about drug sales areas.

Canter and Larkin (1993) make a distinction between marauders and commuters—in other words, those who use the home base as a start of their crime journeys versus those who commit crimes outside their home range. They show that the marauder model best predicts the crime locations of their sample of serial rapists, which stresses the importance of the home base in crime location choice. Nevertheless, Costello and Wiles (2001) argue that the journey-to-crime distances are sometimes overestimated because it is almost always assumed that offenders started their crime journeys from their own homes, but it happens that they committed the crime when they were, for instance, staying with a friend.

Bernasco (2010*b*) and Bernasco and Kooistra (2010) were the first to explicitly theorize about the dynamics of awareness spaces in a discrete spatial choice framework. They tested whether offenders were more likely to target not only areas near their current homes but also areas close to where they used to live. This clearly was the case. They also showed that areas in which the offender had lived for a longer period of time and until more recently had stronger effects.

Obviously, other important nodes, such as where offenders went to school, their workplaces, the residential areas of family members and friends, as well as where they spend leisure time, could be included in crime location choice models in order to further test crime pattern theory. Information concerning these activity nodes is often missing and can only be collected using offender-based research designs (Bernasco 2013). Because crime location choice studies generally use police data, these studies simply do not contain systematically collected information concerning these other activity nodes of offenders. Baudains et al. (2013) and Johnson and Summers (2015) show, however, that it is not necessarily required to measure individual-level activity nodes to test predictions derived from crime pattern theory. Baudains et al. studied the crime location choices of 2,299 rioters during the 2011 London riots. In addition to a strong effect of proximity, they showed that rioters were more likely to target areas with schools, areas that were on the same side of the river Thames, and areas close to retail businesses. All these areas were of course more likely to be known to the offender than otherwise comparable areas. As predicted, the effects of school presence and distance appeared to be stronger for juveniles than for adults. They further showed that areas that were targeted the previous day (not necessarily by the same rioter) were more likely to be targeted again.

Johnson and Summers (2015) further scrutinized the age-specific effects for offenders who committed thefts from vehicles. Several findings were in line with crime pattern theory. Both juveniles and adults favored areas close to where they lived, but juvenile offenders committed their offenses closer to home compared to adult offenders, and only juveniles were also more likely to commit these offenses in areas where schools were located. The other variables included in their model again provide support for the idea that offenders prefer to commit crime where they are less likely to be disturbed by the residents and other guardians (indicated by population turnover and high socioeconomic heterogeneity).

Two recent studies (Bernasco et al. 2015; Lammers et al. 2015) used police data to test whether offenders also return to previously targeted areas, as was suggested in the literature on near repeat victimization (Bernasco 2008; Bowers and Johnson 2004). The effects of previous crime locations were more pronounced than those for previous residential areas. Offenders are very likely to return to areas of their previous offenses, especially when the time between a previous offense and a new one is short.

Although awareness spaces are defined to include both the area around activity nodes and the travel paths between these, research on the impact of the usual travel routes of offenders on their spatial decision making is virtually nonexistent. Rengert and Wasilchick (2000) showed that Philadelphia burglars were more likely to target homes that were along the routes to their workplaces and recreation sites, and Frank et al. (2011) showed directional consistency toward shopping malls in the city of Coquitlam, Canada. These findings suggest that offenders are indeed more likely to target areas that are along the paths between their activity nodes. It is not necessary to extensively measure the travel behavior of offenders in order to test for such effects in a discrete choice model. If some activity nodes are known, the likely routes between these can be estimated using metrics derived from graph theory (Davies and Johnson 2015), and their effects on crime location choices can subsequently be tested. The current approaches that use only distance from a particular activity node (e.g., distance from former home location) assume that the likelihood of targeting a particular area decays in a circular symmetric way around the activity node. However, it is more probable that the likelihood of targeting is especially increased in the direction of the offender's other activity nodes.

VII. Spatial Units of Analysis: Computational and Theoretical Challenges

In geographical criminology, there is a trend toward analyzing crime at increasingly smaller spatial units of analysis (Weisburd, Bernasco, and Bruinsma 2008). The crime location choice modeling literature has followed suit. It started with residential neighborhoods (Bernasco and Nieuwbeerta 2003, 2005) and census tracts (Bernasco and Block 2009) as spatial units of analysis, but it moved to smaller units such as postal code areas (Bernasco 2010a), census blocks (Bernasco et al. 2013), and lower super output areas (Baudains et al. 2013; Bernasco et al. 2015). This trend culminated in the recent burglary target choice study of Vandeviver et al. (2015), who used individual residences in East Flanders, Belgium. Although the studies at different scales of spatial resolution have not yet led to contradictory findings, it is unclear to what extent crime location studies are impacted by what geographers call the modifiable areal unit problem (Openshaw 1984). This is the problem that study results are often highly dependent on the size and shape of the spatial units of analysis. Although smaller spatial units of analysis seem to better fit the theoretical models of crime location choice, the trend toward smaller units also leads to computational and theoretical challenges.

The computational challenge is caused by the fact that the likelihood function needs to be computed for each offense-by-alternative combination during the iterative estimation procedure of the discrete choice model. For example, Bernasco and Block (2009) used a discrete choice model to study 12,872 street robberies in 844 census tracts of Chicago. For the estimation, they created a data set of more than 10 million rows (the number of robberies multiplied by the number of alternatives). Decreasing the size of the spatial unit of analysis increases the number of alternatives and thereby the computational complexity. This is immediately evident from the study of Bernasco et al. (2013), in which they analyzed the same data at the census block level. With 24,594 census blocks in Chicago, the required full data set would have contained more than 300 million rows. However, McFadden's (1978) sampling-of-alternatives method provides a solution to this computational problem because it yields consistent estimators for the parameters of the conditional logit model. This solution, however, entirely rests on the stringent IIA assumption, which is likely violated in crime location choice modeling (Bernasco 2010a; Townsley et al. 2016). Nevertheless, several studies have used this solution for estimating the models on very large data sets (Bernasco 2010a; Bernasco et al. 2013; Vandeviver et al. 2015). Sampling-of-alternatives methods for more complex models that relax the IIA assumption (e.g., nested logit and mixed logit models) have recently been developed (Guevara and Ben-Akiva 2013; von Haefen and Domanski 2013), but these have not yet been used in criminological research.

The theoretical challenge is twofold. The first relates to spatial spillover effects as recently discussed by Bernasco and Ruiter (2014) and empirically addressed by Bernasco et al. (2013). In general, the smaller the spatial units of analysis, the more likely it is that spatial spillover effects are in play, especially if these effects rapidly decay in space. For example, Bernasco et al. (2013) describe how a street robber might follow a customer from a store in a particular block to another block nearby that provides a better location for attack. Their empirical results provide evidence that the effects of robbery attractors indeed spill over to adjacent blocks (first-order spatial spillover) but not beyond (second-order spatial spillover effects were not statistically significant).

The fact that these spillover effects decay so rapidly shows that it is especially important to address spillover effects when using small spatial units of analysis. In analyses with larger units (e.g., neighborhoods or census tracts), these effects will probably be negligible because short-distance spillover occurs for the most part within the boundaries of the larger units. The second theoretical challenge is related to one of the core assumptions of RUM theory. The decision maker is assumed to have complete information about the alternatives—an assumption that becomes increasingly untenable when the number of alternatives increases into the hundreds or even thousands. No offenders will be able to determine the difference between all those alternatives, so how could they then weigh the costs and benefits in their crime location choice decision? They simply cannot. Nevertheless, by using the entire set of alternatives in the study area, all crime location choice studies so far have implicitly assumed that offenders can determine the difference. Before the discrete spatial choice approach gained traction in criminology, Elffers (2004) argued that "a sophisticated version of spatial rational choice theory does not assume that a prospective burglar evaluates all available targets in the same way as his information about some targets might be better than about others. . . . His evaluation of these [unknown] targets is nonexistent" (p. 189). Crime pattern theory actually provides such a sophisticated model because it predicts that offenders will commit their crimes in areas where their activity spaces overlap with attractive opportunities for crime. The challenge is how to translate this into empirical crime location choice research because it requires extensive data on offenders' activity spaces and possibly even the development of discrete spatial choice models with offender-specific choice sets.

VIII. Avenues for Future Research

Although the past decade has experienced a steady increase in interest in the discrete choice approach to study crime location choices, clearly more research is needed. This section discusses several potential avenues for future research, which can be summarized with the following questions:

- Crime location choice studies have so far focused on only the spatial aspects of criminal decision making, but how do temporal aspects affect these choices?
- In most crime location choice studies, only the home location of offenders was known, but are better data on awareness spaces and offenders' routine activities required?
- The discrete choice approach for crime location choices seems to be a model for planned crimes, but what to do with opportunistic crimes?
- Discrete choice models for crime location choice include only solved crimes, but can the findings be generalized to unsolved crimes? What about cybercrimes?

A. Temporal Aspects, Routine Activities, and Dynamic Awareness Spaces

Although most environmental criminological research is devoted to spatial patterns in crime and temporal aspects are often ignored, there are four reasons why future crime location choice studies should also consider temporal aspects of criminal decision making. First, offenders' daily routines directly affect where and when they are able to travel. Based on arguments from time geography (Hägerstrand 1970), Ratcliffe (2006) developed a temporal constraint theory for explaining the spatial patterns in opportunistic crimes. He argues that the nondiscretionary routine activities such as work and school strongly affect offenders' discretionary time, which limits the possibilities of travel and directly affects their awareness spaces. As such, the temporal constraints directly relate to the spatial constraints as already described in the geometry of crime (P. L. Brantingham and Brantingham, 1981). Because of the temporal constraints, Ratcliffe claims, offending patterns cluster around the activity nodes of offenders. When these temporal constraints are ignored, it is implicitly assumed that offenders are able to commit offenses at any time of the day and in all places—a clearly unrealistic assumption. Future crime location choice studies could incorporate these ideas by collecting data on the daily activities of offenders. Although many crimes are indeed opportunistic (Wiles and Costello 2000) and committed while offenders are on their way to regular legal activities, temporal considerations appear to be equally important for offenders who have much more discretionary time. In fact, Rengert and Wasilchick (2000) describe professional burglars who had purposefully quit their day jobs because the jobs did not allow them to burglarize homes when they were vacant during the day. This directly ties into the second reason why temporal aspects deserve more attention in crime location choice studies: Opportunities for crime are time specific, which leads to time-varying target attractiveness (Haberman and Ratcliffe 2015). For example, the best opportunities for burglary are when homes are unguarded. Rengert and Wasilchick argue that the burglars they interviewed knew when the properties were vacant because the spatial behavior of the homeowners is remarkably predictable. Although vacancy makes most suburban properties especially vulnerable during the daytime, Coupe and Blake (2006) stress the importance of studying what makes some properties attractive daytime targets and others good nighttime burglary opportunities. Haberman and Ratcliffe studied whether the effects of potentially criminogenic places for street robbery vary by time of day. Combining information on macro-level human activity patterns with information on the hours of operation of specific facilities in their target-based approach, they were able to show that certain types of facilities attract robberies only at specific times of the day, whereas others attract robbery all day. Although the arguments for such time-varying effects seem trivial from a routine activity perspective—because it is not known why retail businesses would attract robbers when they are closed—all crime location choice studies so far have treated the effects of crime attractors and generators as time stable.

The third reason why future crime location choice studies should address temporal aspects has to do with seasonal variation in routine activities. Andresen and Malleson (2013) show for the city of Vancouver that all crime types exhibit seasonal variation, but more important, the seasonal variation is different in different areas of the city. They argue that such seasonal variation is linked with changes in leisure activities throughout the year. Most cities show seasonal patterns in leisure activities, with more indoor activities in wintertime and outdoor activities during the summer. Although almost all crime location choice studies have used police-recorded crime data for a year or more, none of them have addressed seasonal variation in the characteristics of the alternative target areas. However, it seems reasonable to assume that just like with burglars who know the daily rhythm of home owners, offenders will incorporate seasonal variation with regard to where people spend their leisure activities into their decision on where to offend.

Finally, the dynamics of awareness spaces provide another reason to devote more attention to temporal aspects in crime location choice studies. Because most empirical environmental criminological research is cross-sectional, awareness spaces are generally operationalized as static. Often, only the home locations of the offenders are known. However, in reality, awareness spaces vary over time (Bernasco 2010b). P. L. Brantingham and Brantingham (1981) argued that it is more reasonable to conceptualize awareness spaces as dynamic. They claimed that novice offenders will generally start with relatively small awareness spaces developed through noncriminal activities, but as they continue to commit crimes, their awareness spaces will expand into areas adjacent to their pre-novice awareness spaces. Bernasco (2010b) and Lammers et al. (2015) generalized these claims about the dynamics of awareness spaces. Bernasco redefined awareness space as "a person's current activity space as well as his or her activity spaces in the recent past, including the area normally within visual range of these activity spaces" (p. 393). Wiles and Costello (2000) already provided evidence from their interviews with offenders that their awareness spaces were linked to where they had lived. Bernasco argued that although people's routine activities are quite stable across days, weeks, and months, their activity nodes eventually change. Consequently, not only do people acquire new activity nodes but also old activity nodes disappear. According to Bernasco, these old activity nodes gradually fade out of the dynamic awareness space because memory fades and the environments change. From this follows his recency hypothesis that offenders will be more likely to commit offenses in areas where they had activities more recently. Because people's image of particular areas will be more accurate if they have visited the areas over a longer period of time, Bernasco also hypothesized that the duration of exposure to a particular area is positively related to the likelihood that offenders target the area. Lammers et al. built on these claims, and they hypothesized that offenders are more likely to target areas they have visited more frequently. As already discussed, all three hypotheses concerning these dynamics of awareness spaces have been corroborated in research that used residential location histories (Bernasco 2010b; Bernasco and Kooistra 2010; Lammers et al. 2015) and crime location histories (Bernasco et al. 2015; Lammers et al. 2015) in the prediction of crime location choices. Although these crime location choice studies thus incorporated the dynamics of awareness spaces, these only concerned long-term changes in awareness spaces. However, awareness spaces develop during people's routine activities, and people generally spend specific times of the day and days of the week at some activity nodes (e.g., during office hours at workplaces), and only few activity nodes will be visited at many different times (e.g., the home). Why, then, would an offender have an accurate image of a particular area at a time of day during which he or she never visits the area? It seems more reasonable to assume that people in fact only have time-specific knowledge of their environment. If so, these short-term dynamics of awareness spaces would lead to time-specific predictions about where offenders commit crime. This again calls for crime location choice studies that address the different times at which offenses are committed and also for better measures of offenders' routine activities.

Using a discrete spatial choice model, Kitamura, Chen, and Narayanan (1998) showed how time of day can be incorporated into models of traveler destination choices. Bernasco and Nieuwbeerta (2003, 2005) introduced the discrete choice approach as it was developed by transportation researchers and economists to the field of criminology. It seems that criminologists should once again consider the more recent developments in those fields to learn about how to incorporate temporal aspects in the geography of crime.

B. A Framework Only for the Scientific Study of Crimes That Were Planned, Solved, and Have a Clear Geography?

Although none of the applications of the discrete choice framework have made the distinction between crimes that were committed after careful planning and opportunistic crimes, the name "crime location choice model" implicitly paints an image of an offender who rationally weighs the potential benefits against the effort and risks. RUM theory actually assumes that the decision maker evaluates the utilities of all alternatives and then chooses the alternative with the highest expected utility. Of course, RUM theory provides only an abstract model of human decision making. It nevertheless cannot be said that someone who is sufficiently motivated to commit crime and who happens upon an opportunity on his or her way to work really evaluates the utility of the other crime location alternatives. Crime journeys are often not driven by plans to offend but, rather, the opportunities for crime simply present themselves during normal routine activities (Bernasco 2014). For such opportunistic crimes, the only real decision offenders make is to seize the opportunity—a yes/no decision, not a location choice decision. However, if crime location choice studies do not differentiate between the two, their model results will reflect a combination of the two processes that lead offenders to commit crimes where they do. Suppose that half the offenders commit crimes while they encounter opportunities on their way to work and the other half of offenders make a rational crime location choice at home before they leave on their crime journeys. The results of a crime location choice model that combines the two will in large part reflect job location choice instead of crime location choice. Future crime location choice studies should therefore investigate the motives for the crime journeys and preferably only apply the discrete choice approach to those journeys with criminal intent.

Because the discrete choice approach allows for the simultaneous assessment of how potential target area characteristics as well as offender characteristics affect crime location choices, the approach is applied to solved crimes only. Although dark number issues are common to criminological research and recent research suggests that the spatial behavior of arrested offenders is remarkably similar to that of non-arrested offenders (Lammers 2014), it would be interesting to test whether the research findings concerning the effect of previous crime locations on subsequent crime location choices (Bernasco et al. 2015; Lammers et al. 2015) are identical for non-arrested offenders. In fact, the findings are somewhat counterintuitive because why would someone return to an area to commit an offense if he or she was unsuccessful (got arrested) the previous time? It is plausible to assume that offenders who were not arrested for a particular crime are much more likely to return to the same area. Obviously, this cannot be studied using police data and again calls for an offender-based research design.

Most crime location choice studies have examined burglary target choices, but as described in this chapter, the discrete choice framework has been applied to a wide variety of crimes. At the beginning of this chapter, it was argued that crime location choice studies apply to crime types with a clear geography. That is of course true for crime location choice studies, but it is not a requirement per se for crime target choice studies. The statement was only about the current state of affairs. The discrete choice framework does not require a geographical focus, and in fact, it would be interesting to apply it to cybercrimes such as DDoS attacks and malware. Tajalizadehkhoob et al. (2014) presented an innovative study on cybercrime target choice using the instruction files that were sent by the Zeus botnet to infected machines. Although it is largely a descriptive study that uses a target-based approach on cybercrime target choice, it shows how new ways of data collection could help address criminological research questions regarding target choice in cyberspace.

Although the discrete choice framework for crime location choice modeling has only been used with the scientific aim to test hypotheses from environmental criminological theories, environmental criminology itself is very much involved with practical questions of how to reduce crime. That is why this chapter concludes with a description of how crime location choice studies can also have practical value.

All crime location choice studies use observed preferences designs in which the behavioral decision-making model is derived from the actual choices made by offenders. This is a clearly observational design, and as such it lacks the possibility of experimental control. Although the research is firmly rooted in theory, it should be acknowledged that the research findings are mainly correlational, and it is difficult to make any causal claims, let alone predict change when implementing some crime reduction strategy based on the research findings. At best, the discrete choice approach allows for natural experiments—for instance, when a sudden external shock changed the opportunity structure or the connectivity of the street network and crime location choices before and after the shock can be compared. Unfortunately, no studies have used such natural experiments to test for truly causal effects. However, there is another way in which the discrete choice approach can potentially help to fight crime. It has the ability to improve geographic offender profiling techniques. Current techniques rely on several strong assumptions about the crime location choice mechanisms of offenders, such as circular symmetry and distance decay (van Koppen, Elffers, and Ruiter 2011). However, the crime location choice literature as described in this chapter clearly shows that target characteristics, which are generally not uniformly distributed, are very important in the decision where to offend. In a simulation study, Bernasco (2007) shows that a geographic profiling technique based on a reversal of the discrete choice model outperforms standard techniques that take only distance decay into account. Whether an improved geographic profiling technique based on the discrete choice framework also has practical value has yet to be evaluated in empirical research.

REFERENCES

Andresen, M. A., and N. Malleson. 2013. "Crime Seasonality and Its Variations Across Space." *Applied Geography* 43:25–35.

Andresen, M. A., and N. Malleson. 2015. "Intra-week Spatial–Temporal Patterns of Crime." *Crime Science* 4(1): 1–11.

Balbi, A., and A.-M. Guerry. 1829. *Statistique comparée de l'état de l'instruction et du nombre des crimes dans les divers arrondissements des Académies et des Cours Royales de France.* Paris: Jules Renouard.

Baudains, P., A. Braithwaite, and S. D. Johnson. 2013. "Target Choice During Extreme Events: A Discrete Spatial Choice Model of the 2011 London Riots." *Criminology* 51(2): 251–85.

Ben-Akiva, M. E., and S. R. Lerman. 1985. *Discrete Choice Analysis: Theory and Application to Travel Demand.* Cambridge, MA: MIT Press.

Bernasco, W. 2006. "Co-offending and the Choice of Target Areas in Burglary." *Journal of Investigative Psychology and Offender Profiling* 3(3): 139–55.

Bernasco, W. 2007. "The Usefulness of Measuring Spatial Opportunity Structures for Tracking Down Offenders: A Theoretical Analysis of Geographic Offender Profiling Using Simulation Studies." *Psychology, Crime and Law* 13(2): 155–71.

Bernasco, W. 2008. "Them Again? Same-Offender Involvement in Repeat and Near Repeat Burglaries." *European Journal of Criminology* 5(4): 411–31.

Bernasco, W. 2009. "Foraging Strategies of Homo Criminalis: Lessons from Behavioral Ecology." *Crime Patterns and Analysis* 2(1): 5–16.

Bernasco, W. 2010a. "Modeling Micro-Level Crime Location Choice: Application of the Discrete Choice Framework to Crime at Places." *Journal of Quantitative Criminology* 26(1): 113–38.

Bernasco, W. 2010b. "A Sentimental Journey to Crime: Effects of Residential History on Crime Location Choice." *Criminology* 48:389–416.

Bernasco, W. 2013. *Offenders on Offending: Learning About Crime from Criminals.* New York: Routledge.

Bernasco, W. 2014. "Crime Journeys: Patterns of Offender Mobility." In *Oxford Handbooks Online in Criminology and Criminal Justice*, edited by M. Tonry, pp. 1–31. Oxford: Oxford University Press.

Bernasco, W., and R. Block. 2009. "Where Offenders Choose to Attack: A Discrete Choice Model of Robberies in Chicago." *Criminology* 47(1): 93–130.

Bernasco, W., R. Block, and S. Ruiter. 2013. "Go Where the Money Is: Modeling Street Robbers' Location Choices." *Journal of Economic Geography* 13(1): 119–43.

Bernasco, W., and S. Jacques. 2015. "Where Do Dealers Solicit Customers and Sell Them Drugs? A Micro-Level Multiple Method Study." *Journal of Contemporary Criminal Justice* 31(4): 376–408.

Bernasco, W., S. D. Johnson, and S. Ruiter. 2015. "Learning Where to Offend: Effects of Past on Future Burglary Location." *Applied Geography* 60:120–29.

Bernasco, W., and T. Kooistra. 2010. "Effects of Residential History on Commercial Robbers' Crime Location Choices." *European Journal of Criminology* 7(4): 251–65.

Bernasco, W., and P. Nieuwbeerta. 2003. "Hoe kiezen inbrekers een pleegbuurt? Een nieuwe benadering voor de studie van criminele doelwitselectie." *Tijdschrift voor Criminologie* 45(3): 254–70.

Bernasco, W., and P. Nieuwbeerta. 2005. "How Do Residential Burglars Select Target Areas? A New Approach to the Analysis of Criminal Location Choice." *British Journal of Criminology* 45(3): 296–315.

Bernasco, W., and S. Ruiter. 2014. "Crime Location Choice." In *Encyclopedia of Criminology and Criminal Justice*, edited by G. Bruinsma and D. Weisburd, pp. 691–99. New York: Springer Verlag.

Bowers, K. J., and S. D. Johnson. 2004. "Who Commits Near Repeats? A Test of the Boost Explanation." *Western Criminology Review* 5(3): 12–24.

Brantingham, P. J., and P. L. Brantingham. 1978. "A Theoretical Model of Crime Site Selection." In *Crime, Law and Sanction*, edited by M. Krohn and R. L. Akers, pp. 105–18. Beverly Hills, CA: Sage.

Brantingham, P. J., and P. L. Brantingham. 1984. *Patterns in Crime*. New York: Macmillan.

Brantingham, P. J., and P. L. Brantingham. 2008. "Crime Pattern Theory." In *Environmental Criminology and Crime Analysis*, edited by R. Wortley and L. Mazarolle, pp. 78–93. Devon, UK: Willan.

Brantingham, P. L., and P. J. Brantingham. 1981. "Notes on the Geometry of Crime." In *Environmental Criminology*, edited by P. L. Brantingham and P. J. Brantingham, pp. 27–54. Beverly Hills, CA: Sage.

Brantingham, P. L., and P. J. Brantingham. 1993. "Nodes, Paths and Edges: Considerations on the Complexity of Crime and the Physical Environment." *Journal of Environmental Psychology* 13(1): 3–28.

Canter, D., and P. Larkin. 1993. "The Environmental Range of Serial Rapists." *Journal of Environmental Psychology* 13(1): 63–69.

Clare, J., J. Fernandez, and F. Morgan. 2009. "Formal Evaluation of the Impact of Barriers and Connectors on Residential Burglars' Macro-Level Offending Location Choices." *Australian and New Zealand Journal of Criminology* 42(2): 139–58.

Clarke, R. V. 1983. "Situational Crime Prevention: Its Theoretical Basis and Practical Scope." *Crime and Justice* 4:225–56.

Clarke, R. V., and D. B. Cornish. 1985. "Modelling Offenders' Decisions: A Framework for Research and Policy." *Crime and Justice* 6:147–85.

Cohen, L. E., and M. Felson. 1979. "Social Change and Crime Rate Trends: A Routine Activity Approach." *American Sociological Review* 44:588–608.

Cornish, D. B., and R. V. Clarke. 1986. *Reasoning Criminal: Rational Choice Perspectives on Offending.* New York: Springer-Verlag.

Costello, A., and P. Wiles. 2001. "GIS and the Journey to Crime: An Analysis of Patterns in South Yorkshire." In *Mapping and Analysing Crime Data: Lessons from Research and Practice,* edited by A. Hirschfield and K. J. Bowers, pp. 27–60. London: Taylor and Francis.

Coupe, T., and L. Blake. 2006. "Daylight and Darkness Targeting Strategies and the Risks of Being Seen at Residential Burglaries." *Criminology* 44(2): 431–64.

Davies, T., and S. D. Johnson. 2015. "Examining the Relationship Between Road Structure and Burglary Risk via Quantitative Network Analysis." *Journal of Quantitative Criminology* 31(3): 481–507.

Elffers, H. 2004. "Decision Models Underlying the Journey to Crime." In *Punishment, Places and Perpetrators: Developments in Criminology and Criminal Justice Research,* edited by G. Bruinsma, H. Elffers and J. De Keijser, pp. 182–97. Portland, OR: Willan.

Felson, M. 2006. *Crime and Nature.* Thousand Oaks, CA: Sage.

Frank, R., V. Dabbaghian, A. Reid, S. Singh, J. Cinnamon, and P. Brantingham. 2011. "Power of Criminal Attractors: Modeling the Pull of Activity Nodes." *Journal of Artificial Societies and Social Simulation* 14(1): 6.

Guevara, C. A., and M. E. Ben-Akiva. 2013. "Sampling of Alternatives in Multivariate Extreme Value (MEV) Models." *Transportation Research Part B: Methodological* 48:31–52.

Guimarães, P., O. Figueirdo, and D. Woodward. 2003. "A Tractable Approach to the Firm Location Decision Problem." *Review of Economics and Statistics* 85(1): 201–4.

Haberman, C. P., and J. H. Ratcliffe. 2015. "Testing for Temporally Differentiated Relationships Among Potentially Criminogenic Places and Census Block Street Robbery Counts." *Criminology* 53(3): 457–83.

Hägerstrand, T. 1970. "What About People in Regional Science?" *Papers of the Regional Science Association* 24:7–21.

Johnson, S. D. 2014. "How Do Offenders Choose Where to Offend? Perspectives from Animal Foraging." *Legal and Criminological Psychology* 19:193–210.

Johnson, S. D., and K. J. Bowers. 2004. "The Stability of Space–Time Clusters of Burglary. *British Journal of Criminology* 44(1): 55–65.

Johnson, S. D., and L. Summers. 2015. "Testing Ecological Theories of Offender Spatial Decision Making Using a Discrete Choice Model." *Crime and Delinquency* 61(3): 454–80.

Johnson, S. D., L. Summers, and K. Pease. 2009. "Offender as Forager? A Direct Test of the Boost Account of Victimization." *Journal of Quantitative Criminology* 25(2): 181–200.

Kitamura, R., C. Chen, and R. Narayanan. 1998. "Traveler Destination Choice Behavior: Effects of Time of Day, Activity Duration, and Home Location." *Transportation Research Record* 1645:76–81.

Lammers, M. 2014. "Catch Me if You Can: Using DNA Traces to Study the Influence of Offending Behaviour on the Probability of Arrest." Amsterdam: Vrije Universiteit.

Lammers, M., B. Menting, S. Ruiter, and W. I. M. Bernasco. 2015. "Biting Once, Twice: The Influence of Prior on Subsequent Crime Location Choice." *Criminology* 53(3): 309–29.

McFadden, D. 1973. "Conditional Logit Analysis of Qualitative Choice Behavior." In *Frontiers in Econometrics,* edited by P. Zarembka, pp. 105–42. New York: Academic Press.

McFadden, D. 1978. "Modeling the Choice of Residential Location." In *Spatial Interaction Theory and Planning Models*, edited by A. Karlkvist, L. Lundkvist, F. Snikars, and J. Weibull, pp. 75–96. Amsterdam: North Holland.

Morselli, C., and M.-N. Royer. 2008. "Criminal Mobility and Criminal Achievement." *Journal of Research in Crime and Delinquency* 45(1): 4–21.

Openshaw, S. 1984. *Concept and Techniques in Modern Geography, Number 38: The Modifiable Areal Unit Problem*. Norwich, CT: Geo Books.

Pires, S. F., and R. V. Clarke. 2011. "Sequential Foraging, Itinerant Fences and Parrot Poaching in Bolivia." *British Journal of Criminology* 51(2): 314–35.

Ratcliffe, J. H. 2006. "A Temporal Constraint Theory to Explain Opportunity-Based Spatial Offending Patterns." *Journal of Research in Crime and Delinquency* 43(3): 261–91.

Rengert, G. F. 2004. "The Journey to Crime. In *Punishment, Places and Perpetrators: Developments in Criminology and Criminal Justice Research*, edited by G. Bruinsma, H. Elffers, and J. De Keijser, pp. 169–81. Portland, OR: Willan.

Rengert, G. F., and J. Wasilchick. 2000. *Suburban Burglary: A Tale of Two Suburbs*. Springfield, IL: Charles C Thomas.

Reynald, D., M. Averdijk, H. Elffers, and W. Bernasco. 2008. "Do Social Barriers Affect Urban Crime Trips? The Effects of Ethnic and Economic Neighbourhood Compositions on the Flow of Crime in The Hague, The Netherlands." *Built Environment* 34(1): 21–31.

Tajalizadehkhoob, S., H. Asghari, C. Gañán, and M. van Eeten. 2014. "Why Them? Extracting Intelligence About Target Selection from Zeus Financial Malware." Paper presented at the Proceedings of the 13th Annual Workshop on the Economics of Information Security, WEIS 2014, State College, PA, June 23–24, 2014.

Townsley, M., D. Birks, W. Bernasco, S. Ruiter, S. D. Johnson, G. White, and S. Baum. 2015. "Burglar Target Selection. A Cross-national Comparison." *Journal of Research in Crime and Delinquency* 52(1): 3–31.

Townsley, M., D. Birks, S. Ruiter, W. Bernasco, and G. White. 2016. "Target Selection Models with Preference Variation Between Offenders." *Journal of Quantitative Criminology* 32:283.

Townsley, M., and A. Sidebottom. 2010. "All Offenders Are Equal, But Some Are More Equal than Others: Variation in Journeys to Crime Between Offenders." *Criminology* 48(3): 897–917.

van Daele, S., and W. Bernasco. 2012. "Exploring Directional Consistency in Offending: The Case of Residential Burglary in The Hague." *Journal of Investigative Psychology and Offender Profiling* 9(2): 135–48.

van Koppen, M. V., H. Elffers, and S. Ruiter. 2011. "When to Refrain from Using Likelihood Surface Methods for Geographic Offender Profiling: An Ex Ante Test of Assumptions." *Journal of Investigative Psychology and Offender Profiling* 8(3): 242–56.

Vandeviver, C., T. Neutens, S. van Daele, D. Geurts, and T. Vander Beken. 2015. "A Discrete Spatial Choice Model of Burglary Target Selection at the House-Level." *Applied Geography* 64:24–34.

von Haefen, R. H., and A. Domanski. 2013. "Estimating Mixed Logit Models with Large Choice Sets." Paper presented at the Third International Choice Modelling Conference, Sydney.

Weisburd, D., W. Bernasco, and G. Bruinsma. 2008. *Putting Crime in Its Place*. New York: Springer.

Wiles, P., and A. Costello. 2000. *The 'Road to Nowhere': The Evidence for Travelling Criminals*, vol. 207. London: Research, Development and Statistics Directorate, Home Office.

CHAPTER 20

HIGH STAKES

The Role of Weapons in Offender Decision Making

IAIN R. BRENNAN

WEAPONS are the tools of interpersonal violence, power, and control. The potential they have for causing serious injury gives them a contradictory power: They can be used to do serious violence or to reduce the likelihood of any violence; they can deescalate an altercation or prime aggressive behavior; and they can be essential mechanisms for self-protection while also being offensive and dangerous. These contradictions make weapon carrying and use fascinating but complicated areas to study, and this complexity can be seen both in public and in academic debate. Throughout this chapter, when considering offender decision making, it is important to recall the many overlapping and often contradictory functions that weapons fulfill for users. Binary interpretations of weapons as having purely offensive or defensive functions will limit our ability to understand offender decision making and should be avoided wherever possible. This chapter is divided into four main sections that relate to the decision to carry and use a weapon: (1) how we define and learn about weapon use in crime, (2) why and how weapons can affect the success of a crime, (3) why offenders choose to carry and use weapons, and (4) a discussion of how weapon use actually affects the success of a crime.

I. How We Define and Learn About Weapon Use in Crime

A. Definition

Any attempt to define weapons emphasizes the fractious nature of the concept. Dawson and Goodwill (2013) defined a weapon as "an object used to cause or threaten injury to another" (p. 20). This is a useful definition that covers most forms of violence with a weapon. However, it fails to specify the intentional nature of violence, overlooks the fact that not all violence results in injury, and does not acknowledge the potential use of weapons against oneself. Some minor amendments to their definition can accommodate these issues—"an object deliberately used to do or threaten violence." This definition would exclude fire and computer viruses among others, which some would regard as weapons, and it would include boots and a rope used in suicide, which many would not regard as weapons. The need to establish a watertight definition of weapon is not the aims of this chapter, and the majority of studies detailed here describe weapons in broad categories of firearm, sharp object, blunt object, and other weapon type.

Further difficulties emerge when we seek to define "weapon carrying" and "weapon use." Most of the studies that have explored weapon carrying and use have used binary categories to identify those who have and have not engaged in these behaviors, but this underestimates the many ways in which a person comes to be in possession of or use a weapon. At first glance, it might appear that weapon users must first be weapon carriers, but as can be seen from victimization surveys (Office for National Statistics 2013) and offender accounts (Feeney 1986), many violent incidents involve "environmental" or "situational" weapons such as beer glasses that were not carried on the user's person before use. For example, in England and Wales, 50 percent of intimate partner murders involve a weapon, but these weapons are usually kitchen knives and available blunt objects found at the scene rather than weapons brought to the scene for the purpose of violence (Home Office 2014). It should be remembered that the study of weapon use as a behavior is in its infancy, and the crude techniques currently used for categorizing these behaviors will be refined over time. Furthermore, just as with other types of crime, scaling weapon-related behavior is problematic. It is likely that combining the frequency and diversity of weapon-related behaviors will provide the best discrimination between low- and high-risk offenders (Sweeten 2012).

B. Measuring and Examining the Carrying and Use of Weapons

Most countries and districts have some legislation that regulates or prohibits the carrying and use of weapons. The illicit and deviant nature of weapon carrying (where it is prohibited) impairs the accurate measurement of this behavior. Furthermore, the contested and fleeting nature of what constitutes a weapon also impairs the accurate measurement of this behavior. If a person walking along a dark street at night pushes a set of keys in his pocket between his fingers to form a makeshift knuckleduster, is this a weapon? If so, if a person knows the keys in his pocket could become a weapon at short notice and is reassured by this knowledge, is the person a weapon carrier? Limiting the definition of weapon carrying to knives, firearms, and blunt objects may solve category errors, but it underestimates the diverse range of objects that people regard as weapons.

The measurement of weapon use is also difficult. Many offenders will be reluctant to admit to this serious violence. Victimization surveys and police reports are an alternative source of data on the prevalence of weapon use. However, for a number of reasons, many victims do not report their victimization, which results in a biased sample of police data or victimization survey data. Although victimization surveys suffer from underreporting, they are usually more reliable than police records. However, note that weapon use has been shown to almost double the likelihood of victim reporting of violence (Brennan 2011), suggesting that police data may not be a gross underestimation of weapon use prevalence but may result in an overestimation of the prevalence of weapon use relative to other violence.

With these limitations in mind, the Crime Survey for England and Wales found that in 2012 and 2013, weapons were used in approximately 20 percent of nonfatal violent incidents and more than half of homicides (Office for National Statistics 2014). Directly comparable statistics are not available for the United States, but in 2013, 73 percent of aggravated assaults involved weapons (Federal Bureau of Investigation [FBI] 2014a) and 94 percent of homicides involved weapons (FBI 2014b). Notably, two-thirds of US homicides involved a firearm.

In addition to measuring how much weapon carrying and weapon use occur, we may wish to know why they occur and in what circumstances. Again, sources of data are somewhat limited. Self-report surveys can suffer from unreliable reporting and weak sampling and question design, and their question design often overestimates the predictability of violent interactions. Crime reports can suffer from uneven reporting and inconsistencies in the way data are recorded. However, as in most offender decision making, prospective, controlled methods for studying the role of weapons in violence would be unethical in the real world and can lack ecological validity when explored in virtual or simulated environments. Qualitative studies—particularly if we are interested in learning about internal decision-making processes—can suffer from inaccurate responding as a result of social desirability, cognitive dissonance, and imperfect memories.

Despite their limitations, surveys and crime reports are a valuable source of data for understanding the outcomes of crime involving weapons. Every year, the details of thousands of criminal interactions are recorded and made available for analysis. However, these data provide only a "black box" understanding of the outcomes of these incidents. Summaries of incidents report what *went in* and what *came out*, but these crude outcomes, such as offender attacked/did not attack or victim injury/no injury, do not provide sufficient detail to thoroughly understand the psychological mechanisms and intentions of the weapon user. A contrary argument is that the crude quantification of violence into a set of binary outcomes is less prone to error or bias than the personal, retrospective accounts of offenders and victims. Both data sources have their strengths and weaknesses, which should be considered when drawing conclusions from the research literature.

Although qualitative research—both interviews and ethnographies—can address some of the gaps inherent in large-scale databases, the vast majority of this research is based on US samples and focuses almost exclusively on firearms. This is not particularly surprising given the high prevalence of firearm-related morbidity and mortality in the United States, but many of the features of firearms, such as their ability to cause serious harm from a distance, their highly lethal nature, and their varied legality, mean that the way in which they are used cannot be generalized to all weapons or populations outside the United States.

II. A RATIONAL INTERPRETATION OF WEAPON CARRYING AND USE

This section explores the behaviors of weapon carrying and weapon use from a rational perspective. Beginning with weapon carrying, the decision stages that lead to weapon use are presented and critically discussed.

A. The Decision-Making Stages of Weapon Use

Decision making about weapons is a multifaceted process. Assuming a logical pathway from weapon carrying to weapon use, the individual faces a range of choices, which are summarized in figure 20.1. First, there is the initial decision about whether to carry a weapon and the weapon(s) of choice, which later will be shown to be governed in part by community, availability, and a wide range of economic, dispositional, and social factors. The motivation to offend must then emerge. Some evidence suggests that the weapon itself can be instrumental in generating this motivation. When selecting a target, the presence of a weapon and the particular type of weapon carried can influence the pool of available victims and be a deciding factor in target selection of offense strategy. Upon making contact with the victim, the offender still faces the decision to make the victim aware of the presence of a weapon. The presentation of the weapon will prompt a quick escalating or de-escalating response from the victim, which in turn will affect the offender's decision on how to use his or her weapon. At each stage of this complex decision-making process, the weapon is not always a passive instrument but can actually determine the offender's and the victim's next moves. In attempting to understand these various stages, it is important to recognize that decision making in stressful situations is often not rational or measured, is often performed incompetently, and does not necessarily follow a logical pathway (Collins 2008; van Gelder 2013). Furthermore, it should be remembered that the decision-making pathway detailed in figure 20.1 is a simplified model of what in reality is a complex and nonlinear process. Much weapon use is not planned, and the eventual weapon user may not have carried a weapon to the interaction. Therefore, offenders can enter the decision-making tree of weapon use at almost any stage. Indeed, given the lethal potential of weapon use, a person who

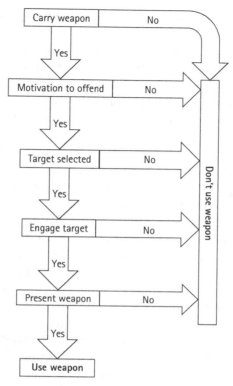

FIGURE 20.1 Decision stages of weapon use.

emerges as a perpetrator of violence may even have begun the interaction as a target for victimization.

B. The Decision to Use a Weapon: Rationality and Intentions

Although there has been considerable discussion since the 1950s regarding how and why offenders have selected particular weapons to facilitate their crimes, the literature that uses primary accounts of these decisions is small. Furthermore, because of this lack of first-hand account research, much of the conclusions drawn by researchers about offender intentions have been speculative and based on simple rational models despite the strong evidence that many offenders are prone to making decisions that appear irrational to the general public (Cornish and Clarke 1986). To date, no research has attempted to thoroughly interpret the decision to carry or use a weapon within a framework of "bounded" rationality that could more accurately reflect the decision-making styles of many offenders. However, research that has examined the factors influencing weapon carrying and use has shown these behaviors to be complex, often contradictory, and guided by much more than a rational calculation of utility.

To understand offenders' decision making, we need to gain insight into their intentions prior to an offense. We can start from the position that weapon selection broadly reflects the offensive intentions of the offender. To a large extent, the evidence supports this: During assaults, weapons greatly increase the severity of physical harm (Saltzman et al. 1992; Felson and Messner 1996; Brennan, Moore, and Shepherd 2006; Apel, Dugan, and Powers 2013) and psychological harm (Brewin et al. 1999), whereas in robbery they often reduce the likelihood of injury to a victim and facilitate easy execution and escape (Feeney 1986; Tillyer and Tillyer 2014). However, although weapons are capable of causing physical harm, they can also be a mechanism for protection. In fact, for most owners of legal firearms in the United States, protection against crime is the most cited reason for owning a gun (Cook and Ludwig 1997). In reality, because most gun owners will never use their firearms in the prevention of crime, the value of firearms is largely emotional rather than practical. The reasoning of gun owners—that widespread gun ownership deters potential criminals and that owning a gun can protect a person from an assailant—is a rational one. However, the effectiveness of gun ownership and gun carrying in protecting the owner has become hotly contested in the United States (Black and Nagin 1997; Hemenway 1997; Kleck 1999). Several of the articles cited in this chapter are disputed by different sides of the firearm debate in the United States, but this argument is not the focus of this chapter. Therefore, individual studies described in this chapter, particularly regarding the role of firearms in victim outcomes, should be interpreted with caution and as part of a larger discussion about the use of weapons in crime.

III. THE UTILITY OF WEAPONS

In order to understand how offenders might weigh the benefits and costs of weapon use, it is helpful to consider how weapons can be used in crime and to acknowledge the potential negative consequences of this behavior. It is also important to recognize that victims are not helpless targets in these interactions, and the calculations that an offender requires a victim to make are also discussed.

A. Benefits

In robbery, potential victims appreciate the harm that weapons permit and so may be more likely to hand over property without resistance. The avoidance of physical and verbal resistance to robbery can make it a faster and less conspicuous event, which reduces the likelihood of capable guardians intervening or the offense being detected by formal or natural surveillance (Cook 1991). For opportunistic robbers, carrying a weapon that can overpower even the strongest person greatly increases the pool of potential victims. Careful selection of weapons can also overcome guardians and target hardening measures in robbery. Finally, the ability to cause harm from distance can also allow an offender to control several victims simultaneously and to facilitate escape before victims seek help (Cook 1991).

During assaults, weapon use may make it easier to control the forensic evidence compared to a bodily assault because less physical contact will reduce the transfer of trace evidence. Also, the ability to remove the weapon from the crime scene and dispose of it effectively will complicate the subsequent criminal investigation. Violence with a weapon reduces the need for physical strength or skill, limits the potential for counterattack, facilitates surprise attacks and escape, and may reduce the uncertainty of the violent incident by making it faster and more lethal. Weapons can also overcome target hardening measures to protect against violence. For example, the right weapon can overcome body armor, armed resistance, and most physical barriers.

It should also be remembered that weapons do not have to be used to have value. Frequent weapon carrying by an offender can lead to a reputation for dangerousness or excessive or gratuitous violence. For some offenders, a reputation for disproportionality in violence or use of an incongruously lethal weapon such as a machete can have long-term benefits, such as protection from victim reporting, protection from counter-attack, and reduced future resistance from other victims (Levi and Maguire 2002).

B. Costs

Although weapons have many advantages over unarmed attacks, a number of potential costs prohibit their use. In general, the benefits of weapon use are seen during the commission of an incident, whereas the costs of weapon use are often incurred after the incident. The primary cost in an offender's decision to use a weapon is a legal one that affects both the likelihood of being apprehended and the severity of punishment.

The use of a weapon in violence is one of the strongest predictors of a victim regarding the incident as a crime (Brennan 2015), and it almost doubles the likelihood that the incident will be reported to the police (Brennan 2011). Cook et al. (2007) showed that the use of a gun in gang violence often brings unwanted attention from the police to a gang's activities, increasing ancillary costs to a drug business. These factors combined inevitably increase the likelihood of detection by police and the perceived costs of weapon use.

In most legal systems, weapons are regarded as "aggravating factors" in sentencing, resulting in more severe punishment (Cook 1987), and they can carry mandatory sentences that unarmed violence does not. Therefore, all things being equal, the punishment costs of weapon use are higher than those of unarmed violence.

In addition to legal costs, certain weapons can also have time and resource costs. Cook et al. (2007) provide a detailed discussion of the difficulties of sourcing reliable firearms in a "thin" market in Chicago. Firearms and ammunition on the black market sell for substantially more than their worth on the open market; they can be unreliable;

they may have been previously used in another crime; and they require considerable time, effort, and risk to acquire.

C. Victim Risk Calculus

The power of the weapon in victim management or coercion does not rest solely with the offender; the victim must also acknowledge the weapon and its potential for harm. Therefore, the success of weapon use, at least in robbery, is dependent on both the offender and the victim making rational calculations. An intended victim who shows no fear when faced with a weapon briefly retains his or her power in the conflict; obviously, this is a high-risk strategy. The offender must correctly make a judgment that the lethality of the weapon and the perceived probability that he or she will use it outweigh the financial or egotistical cost of the robbery for the victim. The offender's script for the incident relies on the victim being rational along with a shared valuation of the variables in the incident. For example, to protect a valuable item of property, a victim may be willing to take a chance against an offender with a knuckleduster but not against an offender with a knife. Similarly, to protect his masculine identity, a male victim may be willing to take his chances against a female with a club but not a female with a gun. Successful offenders must have accommodated these factors in their offense planning. The outcome of violence when risk has been miscalculated is a topic of interest to researchers, and as summarized later in this chapter, the effectiveness of victim resistance to weapon use is one of the most contested areas of this field (Cook 1986).

IV. WHY OFFENDERS CHOOSE TO CARRY AND USE WEAPONS

This section addresses some of the assumptions that have been made about weapon use in the public domain and in the research literature, specifically regarding the extent to which carrying and using particular weapons reflects the intentions of the user. After these issues are addressed, the chapter critically interprets weapon carrying and use from a variety of theoretical perspectives.

A. Weapons and Intentions

Retrospective, quantitative studies of offender decision making are often bound by the assumptions that offenders had stable, initial intentions, which they followed through on; that they were in control of the situation; and that they did not make any errors in their execution of the crime. Unfortunately, interviews with small samples of weapon users have shown that the success of offenders in executing their intentions can be over-estimated (Feeney 1986; Collins 2008); weapon availability, selection, and use are not always optimal (Cook et al. 2007); and crimes with weapons do not always go as planned (Phillips and Maume 2007). The following section discusses the evidence for and against the position that the outcomes of weapon use reflect the initial goals of the weapon user. This topic is explored through three main assumptions that underlie our ability to infer intentions from actions in weapon users: that the lethality of a weapon is constant, that an offender's weapon of choice is always available, and that offenders control the use of their weapons.

1. *Lethality, Incompetence, and the Uncertainty of Criminal Interactions*

Wolfgang (1958) proposed that the type of weapon carried or used by an offender reflects his or her intentions prior to the incident—that is, the more lethal the weapon, the more lethal the intent, and the harder the target of robbery, the more lethal the weapon. Although this perspective is rational, its universality is highly contested. Critics have argued that it underestimates the unpredictable nature of violent incidents and attributes too much control over the situation to the motivated offender (Zimring 1968, 2004; Wright and Decker 1997; Phillips and Maume 2007).

First, the relationship between weapons and harm is nonlinear. Newton and Zimring (1969), Apel et al. (2013), and the England and Wales Home Office (2012) have all found that weapon use tends to be associated with no injury or major injury; rarely do weapons cause minor injury. Second, illustrating that robberies—ideally quick, nonviolent interactions—can often go awry, Cook (1987) ranked the lethality of particular weapon types in robberies of unarmed targets, showing that despite their supposedly increased coercive power, gun robberies are three times more likely than robberies with knives to result in target fatality and twenty times more likely than unarmed robberies to result in fatality. Emphasizing the importance of weapon lethality in violent outcomes, Cook (1991) noted that "many homicides are not the result of a sustained, deliberate intent to kill but rather are etiologically indistinguishable from a larger set of assaults and robberies in which the victim does not die" (p. 4). When a criminal interaction has as much uncertainty as a robbery, the lethality of the weapon raises the stakes for offender and target considerably. Third, a common assumption about weapons is that when they are used in violence, they always inflict damage on the target. However, a range of sources suggest that this is not true. Kleck and McElrath (1991) cite National Crime Survey data that showed only 19 percent of gunshots actually hit their intended target and 55 percent of knife attacks resulted in a knife wound. Based on photographic and video evidence of conflict, Collins (2008) suggests that the stress of violent situations makes many motivated fighters incapable of or at least incompetent at completing violence.

Therefore, it is highly likely that the lethality of a weapon used in violence influences the outcome of that incident. However, to infer an offender's intentions from these few pieces of information underestimates the complexity and the unpredictability of the violent event.

2. *Decisions About Weapons of Choice*

Although Wolfgang's (1958) proposal that the lethality of the weapon used by an offender provides a retrospective insight into the offender's intent may be overly rational, there is convincing evidence that offenders do make some calculated decisions about their choice of weapon. A survey of 1,874 male prisoners in the United States found that offenders could generally provide rational reasons for their selection of a particular weapon type, including victim management and coercion, sentencing practices, legal constraints, and availability (J. D. Wright and Rossi 1986). R. T. Wright and Decker's (1997) study of armed robbers also provided valuable insight into offenders' weapon-related decision making. Although they reported that the presentation of weapons was instrumental in victim management, weapons were also often used against their victims to aid their escape, to dominate their victims, and to speed up the robbery. Feeney (1986) and Cook et al. (2007) have shown that offenders frequently carry and use firearms that are incapable of firing. Rationales for this include a desire to avoid injuring anyone, to maximize the chances of success while avoiding a harsher sentence that could come with robbery with an active firearm, and an awareness that much of the time simply showing a gun to a potential target is enough to de-escalate a situation.

Often, a weapon—specifically, the right type of weapon for the intended offense—is not available. As Wright and Rossi (1986) noted, offenders often have clear reasons for not using particular weapons in their offending. Offenders may realize the potential for excessive harm to victims that accompanies weapon use, the greater potential for their own harm if they lose control of the incident, a distaste for weapons (Harcourt 2006), the "challenge" of robbery or assault without a weapon, or a discord between their desired image and the use of weapons or particular weapon types. In "thin" markets, in which firearms are often expensive or difficult to source, potential offenders must compromise on the weapons they select (Cook et al. 2007). Currently, it is unknown how much offenders are willing to compromise on their weapon of choice. Questions to answer include the following: Can the choice of weapons available to an offender be so suboptimal as to prevent the crime being committed? When faced with a choice between more and less lethal alternatives, what is the more likely choice?

3. *"Weapon Instrumentality"*

It has long been hypothesized that the presence of a weapon, through its cultural association with violence, can increase the potential for aggressive behavior. This is known as the "weapons effect" or the "weapon instrumentality" hypothesis. Berkowitz and LePage (1967) produced the first experimental evidence for this effect, but several attempts at replication were inconclusive (Carlson, Marcus-Newhall, and Miller 1990), leading to a belief that the effect observed by Berkowitz and LePage was an artefact of the experimental procedure. However, a meta-analysis of "weapons effect" experiments (Carlson et al. 1990) found an overall effect of the presence of weapons on aggression. Later research found that weapons-associated words could also produce an enhanced aggressive response (Subra et al. 2010) and, particularly important in understanding the motivation to carry a weapon, that carrying a weapon increases the perception that other people are also carrying weapons (Witt and Brockmole 2012).

The implications of these findings for offender and victim decision making are considerable. An extension of these findings is that the presentation of a weapon—for example, in a robbery—could alter the aggressive intentions of the robber. Similarly, using a weapon to threaten someone could lead unexpectedly to violence (Feeney 1986). The "weapons effect" could also mean that the presentation of a weapon to a victim could increase the likelihood of the victim resisting aggressively. Whether this is true in reality is uncertain, and it is discussed in the later section on offender responses to victim resistance. Although the "weapons effect" may serve to prime the victim toward aggression, the stress of the situation and individual intent are likely to be more influential factors in their decision making (Phillips and Maume 2007).

Wells and Horney (2002) noted a difficulty of separating the harming effect of weapons from that of individual intent. Two conflicting possibilities are apparent: If a weapon is associated with increased harm, this may simply reflect the intention of the offender to cause more harm, or there may be an instrumentality effect of the weapon that influences the offender to cause more serious harm than originally intended. Using a novel within-individual case–control method, Wells and Horney compared offenders' use of weapons to comparable incidents of potential conflict that did not involve weapons. Their study found that, controlling for intention, when an offender possessed a weapon, he or she was more likely to attack an adversary. Interestingly, this finding contradicted that of Kleck and McElrath (1991), who found, based on victimization data, that when an offender possessed a weapon, he or she was less likely to attack the victim. The difference in these findings may be artefactual. Wells and Horney's study relied on offender accounts of weapon "possession," whereas Kleck and McElrath's study relied on victim accounts of weapon "presentation." These are not comparable stages of the weapon use pathway, and the latter reflects a more advanced stage of the offense process.

B. Theories of Weapon Carrying and Weapon Use

Relatively few studies have identified weapon users as psychologically distinct from other violent offenders (Brennan, Moore, and Shepherd 2010), but identifying any differences between weapon-using offenders and other violent offenders could provide valuable insight into the decision-making processes of weapon users. The research literature has not tended to view weapon violence as a distinct category of offending, and thus few comprehensive theories of weapon carrying or weapon use have been proposed. Three main approaches that have been employed to understand weapon-related behavior: Rational choice, dispositional theories, and differential association are presented later. Because weapon carriers and weapon users are often treated separately, particularly in the epidemiological literature, theories for these two overlapping behaviors are presented separately. Although the predominant focus is on weapon use, understanding weapon carrying can provide valuable insight into the precursory motivations of weapon users.

1. *Theories of Weapon Carrying*

Most theories of weapon carrying focus on three major motivations: self-protection/fear (Cook and Ludwig 1997; Harcourt 2006), self-presentation (Sheley and Wright 1993; Lizotte et al. 2000; Harcourt 2006), and utility (Wolfgang 1958; Feeney 1986). These motivations can exist simultaneously (Stretesky and Pogrebin 2007) and can often appear contradictory. Weapon carriers who are motivated by the first two factors may never actually use their weapons in anger. However, those motivated by the third factor carry weapons to facilitate more criminal goals and, most likely, represent more dangerous individuals. The uncertain and dynamic nature of violent incidents, particularly when weapons are available, means that weapon carriers can quickly become weapon users, regardless of their initial motivations for carrying a weapon.

Studies that have explored weapon carrying have focused predominantly on adolescents and have sought to identify predictors of this behavior rather than to establish a reliable prevalence rate. These studies have found that many of the factors that predict weapon carrying are also the factors that predict violent behavior more generally: male gender (Kodjo, Auinger, and Ryan 2003), late adolescence (Durant et al. 1999), social deprivation (Lizotte et al. 2000), substance misuse (Durant et al. 1995), and poor or deviant social support (Morrison, Furlong, and Smith 1994). Harcourt's (2006) detailed investigation into gun possession by juvenile offenders found a remarkably complex set of motivations for this behavior that included emotional regulation, a sense of entitlement to gun possession, group identity, and enacting masculine identities. Finally, important to bounded rational interpretations of weapon carrying is the evidence that the tendency to carry a weapon is influenced by the perception that one's peers also carry weapons (Bailey, Flewelling, and Rosenbaum 1997; Williams et al. 2002) and that individuals who carry weapons overestimate the prevalence of their peers' weapon carrying (Bailey and Hubbard 1991). The belief that members of one's peer group regularly carry weapons inevitably has a normalizing effect on attitudes toward weapons, which is likely to perpetuate the carrying of weapons within that group (Strodtbeck and Short 1964).

Interestingly, few studies have attempted to identify differences between weapon carriers and weapon users. In a school-based survey of Swiss adolescents, Thurnherr et al. (2009) found little difference between weapon carriers and weapon users. Compared to weapon carriers, male weapon users were more likely to be foreign born, to live in urban areas, to be undertaking an apprenticeship (as opposed to still being in school), to have poor school connectedness, to have engaged in unsafe sex, and to quarrel while under the influence of substances. Besides the usual predictors of offending behavior, there was little here to distinguish between the groups. There was no difference in history of victimization, family factors, or substance use involvement or diverse offending behavior, which are common predictors of violent behavior. The study found even fewer differences between female weapon carriers and users.

Dijkstra et al. (2012) tested three hypotheses regarding why adolescents carry weapons: to reflect their trait aggression, in response to perceived or actual threat of victimization, and in response to peer influence and peer behavior. In general, aggression and weapon carrying among peer networks predicted weapon carrying, whereas victimization did not. However, likelihood of weapon carrying did increase when aggression interacted with victimization. One explanation of this interaction effect is that it reflects the offender–victim overlap and weapon carrying is a normal part of a more aggressive lifestyle that involves victimization and offending. This is an important finding: One of the most commonly cited reasons among offenders for carrying a weapon is "self-defense" (Wright and Rossi 1986), but this fear of violence should be understood within the context of a risky lifestyle and living environment.

2. Theories of Weapon Use

a. Weapon Use as Rational

The first theory of weapon use is that the use of a weapon is a rational decision—that is, it maximizes benefits while minimizing costs to the user. Therefore, a weapon-using offender should be more likely to succeed with his or her intended crime and less likely to suffer the consequences of this crime in the form of detection, punishment, retaliation, or harm to self.

To begin assessing the rationality of weapon use, we can consider the circumstances in which weapon use is more likely than unarmed violence and assess this through a rational lens. Unfortunately, because it is gleaned from victimization surveys and police records, much of the event-level information is somewhat crude and considerable details are lost with regard to the psychological process of offending.

In terms of situational and contextual predictors of weapon use, Baumer et al. (2003) found that firearms were more likely to be used in assaults in disadvantaged neighborhoods. They argue that because weapon carrying is more prevalent in these areas, more lethality in the form of weapons is required to succeed in committing crime. Controlling for neighborhood disadvantage, Burgason, Thomas, and Burgason (2013) found that offender substance use, the incident taking place in a home, and victim age were all negatively related to the likelihood that a gun was presented. Guns were more likely to be presented in incidents in which the victim was male, black, and from outside the community. This study is limited by its binary focus on firearms. However, research by Rennison, Jacques, and Berg (2011) addressed this gap by including all weapons and placing them on a spectrum of lethality. Their study found that relational distance predicted weapon lethality. From these identifying factors, it is possible to surmise that availability of firearms played an important role in determining weapon use but that victim characteristics and victim–offender relational distance affect weapon choice and use. One rational explanation for this is that male, stranger victims represent greater uncertainty about their potential for resistance and retaliation that necessitates the use of a weapon.

A predominant feature of many lethal weapons is that they neutralize differences in physical power between two people. Therefore, one possible reason for weapon carrying and weapon use is that those with less physical power will be more inclined to use weapons against stronger physical opponents. Stretesky and Pogrebin (2007) describe an interview with an offender who, because of a reputation as an effective hand-to-hand fighter, was repeatedly subjected to surprise attacks with weapons. Ironically, this offender felt forced to carry a gun because of this ability to fight without one. A study of victims of unarmed and weapon-related violence by Felson and Messner (1996) found that weapon use mediated the effect of physical strength on injury to the victim, and Kleck and McElrath (1991) found that female murderers—less strong on average than males—were less likely to use guns against females than against males. Therefore, there is evidence to support the "equalizing" hypothesis of weapon use. An unfortunate extension of this logic is that belligerents will continuously address this imbalance by using increasingly more lethal weapons (Horowitz, 1983; Decker and van Winkle 1996; Brennan and Moore 2009).

As evidence that offenders choose to use weapons and select weapons to suit their offending purpose, Beauregard and Leclerc (2007) found that among a sample of 69 serial sexual offenders, when weapons were used, the primary reason for their use was to overcome victim resistance. This study indicates that this type of offender also frames his or her decision to use a weapon as part of a rational plan and that sexual offenders use weapons only when they believe that they have to do so or when the weapon plays a specific gratification-related role within the offense. In terms of offense characteristics, weapon users were less likely to use confidence approaches or vehicles and were more likely to attack outdoors and using surprise attacks. The weapon likely played an important part in permitting such crude tactics. The potential power of the weapon can neutralize the need for much planning, reduce the uncertainty and difficulty of confidence approaches, and increase the pool of potential victims. The similarities of sexual offenses using weapons and nonsexual offenses using weapons is striking. In both cases, weapons permit greater potential for opportunistic offending and reduce the uncertainty associated with these crimes.

As noted in the section on the costs of weapon use, this behavior is more likely to come to the attention of the police and likely to yield more severe punishment than unarmed violence. If offenders are rational decision makers, a consequence of enhanced punishment should be that weapon use decreases. Some of the juvenile offenders interviewed by Harcourt (2006) reported that the aggravating effect of firearms on sentencing influenced their decision to avoid using guns. However, focusing on firearm use, the US National Research Council found limited support for an effect of enhanced sentencing for firearm-related crimes on firearm-related offenses. When asked if they would use a gun to commit robbery again, 91 percent of *convicted* armed robbers surveyed in Western Australia stated that they would do so (Harding 1990). Recent evidence suggests that focused deterrence may have a greater effect on firearm-related reoffending (Braga and Weisburd 2015), but its US, firearm focus limits the generalizability of this phenomenon to this sample, whereas there is a dearth of rigorous evaluations of these policies from elsewhere in the world.

Despite the evidence that weapon use increases the likelihood of detection, Harding (1993) reported that a group of convicted armed robbers believed that the use of a weapon decreased the likelihood that they would be apprehended. It should be recalled that what appears rational to one person may not appear rational to the next (Cornish and Clarke 1986). A bounded rational interpretation of weapon use is that people who use weapons interpret and discount the risk of harm to victims in a different way from other individuals, which could be assessed through attitudes to risk, or that they care less about the potential harm to victims than others do. Furthermore, the aggravating component of weapon use on the severity of sentencing suggests that weapon users may be more inclined to discount the potential risks of weapon use. Following this logic, Brennan et al. (2010) found that compared to violent offenders who had not used weapons, weapon users took more risks on a gambling task. To date, this is the only evidence suggesting that weapon users think differently from other violent offenders. Because of the small sample employed by Brennan et al., until further supporting evidence is presented, any assumptions that weapon users calculate risk differently from other offenders must be made cautiously.

b. *Weapon Use Reflects a Violent Disposition*

There is growing evidence that in terms of length and diversity of criminal career, weapon-using violent offenders are simply more violent than other offenders and weapon use facilitates their desire to harm others.

Rothman et al. (2005) found that domestic abuse offenders who had previously used a knife to threaten or harm a partner were 8.8 times more likely to later use a gun to threaten a partner again, and Woodworth et al. (2013) showed that sadistic paraphilia is strongly predictive of weapon use by sexual offenders. Michie and Cooke (2006) found that the use of a weapon in violence was an indicator of a more seriously violent individual compared to offenders who committed violence without a weapon. Weapon use was also found to predict psychopathy (Cooke and Michie 2006) and trait anger (Brennan et al. 2006; Cooke and Michie 2006). Dawson, Goodwill, and Dixon's (2014) study of UK serious sexual offenses found nothing demographic to distinguish between weapon-using and non-weapon-using offenders. However, consistent with the findings of Michie and Cooke (2006) with non-sexual offenders, weapon users had more extensive offending histories.

Several studies have shown greatly increased prevalence of weapon carrying and weapon use among people with psychotic disorders (Swanson et al. 1990; Stueve and Link 1997; Lewis et al. 1998; Lewis and Bunce 2003). Although not condonable, weapon carrying and use among those experiencing psychotic episodes are understandable. The altered perception of reality, combined with extreme fear and confusion that these symptoms can produce, could easily make weapon use a reasonable action. As Lewis et al. (1998) noted, "the use of weapons by psychotic mothers was rarely related to punishment or frustration. Most frequently, it related to delusions involving the child being in danger or the child itself being dangerous" (p. 617).

Langevin and Curnoe's (2013) study of 1,533 sexual offenders in Canada who received psychiatric assessments found that weapon use was a statistically significant predictor of sadism, psychosis, suicide attempts, personality disorder, psychopathy, and attention deficit hyperactivity disorder. Furthermore, weapon use was also associated with alcohol and drug problems, and weapon users were more likely to be under the influence of some substance at the time of the offense. Weapon use was associated with lower intelligence and less advanced education. In terms of offending history, weapon use was associated with earlier age of first offense, longer criminal career, more violent offense convictions, more total convictions, and more court appearances. Again, many of these clinical, historical, and criminogenic characteristics are indicative of more diverse and serious offending potential, which Michie and Cooke (2006) demonstrated among non-sexual weapon-using offenders. This evidence lends support to Michie and Cooke's proposal that weapon use is a valuable indicator of more serious violence potential, suggesting that the reasons for weapon use are not fear related but instrumental in committing increasingly violent crime.

c. *Weapon Use as a Consequence of Differential Association*

Weapon use may reflect the level of availability and exposure to weapons in an individual's life or community. In a study of the increase in homicides in the United States in the late 1980s and early 1990s, Blumstein and Cork (1996) pointed to an increase in firearm use as a major cause. They surmised that the increasing prevalence and severity of violence caused by drug markets created a need for more accessible and more lethal weapons. From individuals involved in drug markets, access to firearms spread through peer networks to those not involved in drug markets. This, in turn, escalated the level of lethal violence outside drug markets, which perpetuated the need for access to firearms for self-defense.

Cook (1979) showed that the per capita availability of legal guns predicted rates of firearm use in robberies, and Cook and Ludwig (2004) found that teen gun carrying was related to the prevalence of gun ownership in the community. However, there was no relationship between carrying other types of weapons and community gun ownership. Harding (1990, 1993) suggested that it is not the prevalence or availability of weapons but, rather, the context in which a community uses weapons that influences the likelihood that they will be used in interpersonal violence. Harding (1993) found that the relationship between gun use and gun availability was mediated by the role of firearms as "utilitarian"—that is, for farming or practical purposes. In addition, the status of the individual who introduced the offender to guns was negatively related to the offender using a gun: Armed robbers who were introduced to firearms by a father or uncle were less likely to use a gun than were those introduced to guns by siblings, cousins, or peers. This suggests that the decision to carry a weapon is motivated by perceived need, but weapon of choice is dictated by culture and availability.

V. How Weapon Use Affects the Success of a Crime

A. Responding to Resistance: Offender Decision Making During Robbery

Particularly in robbery and sexual offending, overcoming victim resistance is the main purpose of weapon use. Therefore, from a decision-making perspective, it is valuable to understand how well weapons actually serve this function. Cook's work (Cook 1976, 1987) demonstrated that even in robbery, the lethality of a weapon predicts likelihood of victim fatality, but this work does not provide sufficient information about whether victims resisted the armed assailant. More recent, event-level studies have begun to collect this information.

Cook (1987) studied US National Crime Survey data (1973–1979) to determine the best course of action for victims to avoid injury when faced with a robber brandishing a weapon. This data set allowed a sequence of events from weapon presentation to weapon use to be constructed. When an offender experienced forceful resistance from the victim, 67 percent attacked compared to 29 percent when the victim offered no resistance and 30 percent when non-forceful resistance was experienced. From these data, it can be inferred that many offenders are willing to use weapons to do violence to as well as coerce their victims. Perhaps more surprising is that one in three offenders who faced forceful resistance from a victim chose not to use their weapon. As Cook noted, the crude event-level information in victimization surveys prohibited any further interpretation of the offender's motivations and decision making when facing forceful resistance. Perhaps victims were themselves carrying a weapon; perhaps the offender decided that the prize was no longer worth the risk; or perhaps the offender had never intended to use the weapon and, realizing that his or her bluff had been called, abandoned the robbery.

Baumer et al. (2003) found that during robberies, victims were less likely to resist when the offender had a gun, and their likelihood of resisting was not affected by the presentation of any other weapon type. Regarding assaults, Baumer et al. found that victims were less likely to resist physically when an offender had a gun. However, victims were more likely to resist both forcefully and nonforcefully when the offender had another weapon. Tillyer and Tillyer (2014) also found that victims were less likely to be injured if the offender presented a weapon during a robbery, suggesting that victims were more compliant when faced with a weapon. Tark and Kleck's (2004) study of victim resistance to offenders across a variety of crimes found no clear pattern in the effect of resistance with a weapon on victim injury.

Using data from the US National Crime Survey (1979–1985) and the FBI's Uniform Crime Reports (FBI 1982), Kleck and McElrath (1991) studied the role of weapons in the outcomes of violent incidents. They proposed that the possession of a weapon can play four roles in violent incidents: *facilitation* of an attack—for example, of a stronger person by a weaker person; *triggering* of an attack by priming the weapon carrier toward violence—the "weapon effect"; *inhibition* of an attack through "excessive lethality" (p. 673); and *redundancy*, wherein presentation of a weapon, with its ability to shift the balance of power to the possessor, negates the need to use it. They found that, in general, incidents of threat between strangers were less likely to escalate to attacks when guns or knives were presented but were more likely to escalate when other weapons, such as blunt objects and bottles, were involved. It is notable here that the weapons that are more likely to result in attacks are also more likely to be "opportunistic weapons" found at the scene of the incident. Whether the offender brought the weapon to the scene was not determinable through the data, so it is possible that the presentation of an "opportunistic weapon" reflects some other feature of the incident, such as an offender's lack of control over the situation, which could also influence his or her decision to attack. Kleck and McElrath (1991) also attempted to determine the likelihood of victim injury following attack. Their analysis found that firearms were less likely than other weapons to result in victim injury but that when victims were shot, they were more likely to die than if injured with another weapon type. In effect, these findings confirm the lethality of firearms, but they show an approximately nonlinear relationship between lethality and the hierarchy of victim injury (threat, attack, injury, and fatality).

In general, the more lethal the weapon, the less likely the victim is to react aggressively to the offender, but it is unclear how victim resistance affects the likelihood that an offender wielding a weapon will use the weapon. It is certain, however, that when the offender does use the weapon, the relationship between weapon lethality and victim injury is linear. Therefore, in terms of offending success, weapon use is a high-reward/high-cost activity: Although the use of a weapon makes offending success more likely, the consequences when things do not go as planned—for offender and victim—are greatly increased.

VI. Conclusion

Weapons are not a passive feature of crime. Just as sexual arousal is a driving factor in sexual assaults, the presence of a weapon in a potentially criminal incident is a driving factor in the outcome of that incident. In violence, the use of a weapon greatly increases the likelihood of severe injury for the victim. In robbery, the use of weapons and likelihood of injury are more complex, with weapons reducing the need for violence but greatly increasing the severity of that violence when it happens.

Decisions to carry and use weapons are complex and multifaceted. There is evidence that illegal weapon carrying is more a consequence of a risky lifestyle than solely a response to perceived risk. Weapon of choice appears to be highly influenced by cultural and community factors such as the prevalence of the weapon in the community and its use in neighborhood violence, but there is clear evidence among convicted offenders of some measured calculation based on the lethality of the weapon, its intended use, and the prospect of punitive consequences. There is also evidence that weapons use in violence can serve as a marker for being a high-risk offender.

The evidence from event-level studies of weapon use in robbery suggests that in general, victims are less likely to resist physically and less likely to be physically injured if an offender presents a weapon. Although weapon use increases the likelihood of a crime coming to the attention of police and generally comes with harsher penalties than unarmed crime, enhanced punishment does not appear to affect weapon-related offending, but the evidence is sparse.

Although weapon use can enhance the likelihood of successful offending, this success is dependent on the offender and victim having a common computation of the lethality of the weapon and the probability that the weapon will be used. When these calculations are mismatched, the potential for serious injury is high. There is conflicting evidence that victim resistance precipitates weapon use against victims, but there is clear evidence that, when used, weapons increase the likelihood of serious injury.

Although research has sought to plot the pathways to sexual offending (Hudson, Ward, and McCormack 1999), homicide (Cassar, Ward, and Thakker 2003), and drunk driving (Wilson, Ward, and Bakker 1998), this approach has not been followed with regard to weapon use. Understanding the role of the weapon from the perspective of the user is essential if we are to reduce the perceived value of weapons and to emphasize the costs and unpredictability that occur with weapon carrying. As currently constructed, crime reports and victimization surveys cannot provide the insight into the decision-making process that this complex behavior requires. Although qualitative studies by Cook et al. (2007) and Harcourt (2006) have provided valuable insight into the economics of access to guns and the motivations for gun carrying, respectively, there is a great need for further qualitative work in this area to inform the development of theories of weapon use and to guide the larger scale quantitative evaluations of weapons violence. In particular, given the dominance of firearms in the weapons-related literature, there is a need for this work to be undertaken outside the United States.

Finally, offender decisions and interactions with potential targets are situational phenomena, but they do not exist within a vacuum. In every weapon-related interaction between people, multilevel effects are in operation. Gang members must consider the effects of their actions for reprisals against their peers; police must consider how their use of deadly force might reflect on the institution of the police; and offenders may decide on weapon type within the bounds of what is culturally acceptable, and they must consider the impact of law and sentencing guidelines on their behavior and personal liberty. Most research on weapon use attempts to understand this behavior at only one or two levels of the social–ecological model, generally using a routine activities theory model with a rational choice framework. However, despite the methodological problems that it would impose, a full understanding of weapon use will only be gained by acknowledging the multileveled nature of decision making.

REFERENCES

Apel, R., L. Dugan, and R. Powers. 2013. "Gender and Injury Risk in Incidents of Assaultive Violence." *Justice Quarterly* 30:561–93.

Bailey, S. L., R. L. Flewelling, and D. Rosenbaum. 1997. "Characteristics of Students Who Bring Weapons to School." *Journal of Adolescent Health* 20:261–70.

Bailey, S. L., and R. L. Hubbard. 1991. "Developmental Changes in Peer Factors and the Influence on Marijuana Initiation Among Secondary School Students." *Journal of Youth and Adolescence* 20:339–60.

Baumer, E., J. Horney, R. Felson, and J. L. Lauritsen. 2003. "Neighborhood Disadvantage and the Nature of Violence." *Criminology* 41:39–71.

Beauregard, E., and B. Leclerc. 2007. "An Application of the Rational Choice Approach to the Offending Process of Sex Offenders: A Closer Look at the Decision-Making." *Sexual Abuse* 19:115–33.

Berkowitz, L., and A. LePage. 1967. "Weapons as Aggression-Eliciting Stimuli." *Journal of Personality and Social Psychology* 7:202–7.

Black, D. A., and N. D. Nagin. 1997. "Do Right-to-Carry Laws Deter Violent Crime?" *Journal of Legal Studies* 27:209–19.

Blumstein, A., and D. Cork. 1996. "Linking Gun Availability to Youth Gun Violence." *Law and Contemporary Problems* 59:5–24.

Braga, A. A., and D. Weisburd. 2015. "Focused Deterrence and the Prevention of Violent Gun Injuries: Practice, Theoretical Evidence and Scientific Evidence." *Annual Review of Public Health* 36:55–68.

Brennan, I. R. 2011. "In Vino Silentium? Individual, Situational, and Alcohol-Related Factors in Reporting Violence to the Police." *Violence and Victims* 26:191–207.

Brennan, I. R. 2016. "Victim Reponses to Violence: The Effect of Alcohol Context on Crime Labeling." *Journal of Interpersonal Violence* 31(6): 1116–40.

Brennan, I. R., and S. C. Moore. 2009. "Weapons and Violence: A Review of Theory and Research." *Aggression and Violent Behavior* 14:215–25.

Brennan, I. R., S. C. Moore, and J. P. Shepherd. 2006. "Non-firearm Weapon Use and Injury Severity: Priorities for Prevention." *Injury Prevention* 12:395–99.

Brennan, I. R., S. C. Moore, and J. P. Shepherd. 2010. "Aggression and Attitudes to Time and Risk in Weapon-Using Violent Offenders." *Psychiatry Research* 178:536–39.

Brewin, C. R., B. Andrews, S. Rose, and M. Kirk. 1999. "Acute Stress Disorder and Posttraumatic Stress Disorder in Victims of Violent Crime." *American Journal of Psychiatry* 156:360–66.

Burgason, K., S. Thomas, and E. R. Burgason. 2013. "Community Disadvantage, Incident Characteristics and the Nature of Violence: A Multi-level Analysis of Gun Use and Extent of Victim Injury." *Journal of Interpersonal Violence* 29:371–93.

Carlson, M., A. Marcus-Newhall, and N. Miller. 1990. "Effects of Situational Aggression Cues: A Quantitative Review." *Journal of Personality and Social Psychology* 58:622–33.

Cassar, E., T. Ward, and J. Thakker. 2003. "A Descriptive Model of the Homicide Process." *Behavior Change* 20:76–93.

Collins, R. 2008. *Violence: A Micro-Sociological Theory*. Princeton, NJ: Princeton University Press.

Cook, P. J. 1976. "A Strategic Choice Analysis of Robbery." In *Sample Surveys of the Victims of Crimes*, edited by W. Skogan, pp. 173–88. Cambridge, MA: Ballinger.

Cook, P. J. 1979. "The Effect of Gun Availability on Robbery and Robbery Murder: A Cross-section Study of Fifty States." In *Policy Studies Review Annual*, vol. 3, edited by R. H. Haveman and B. B. Zeller, pp. 743–81. London: Sage.

Cook, P. J. 1986. "The Relationship Between Victim Resistance and Injury in Noncommerical Robbery." *Journal of Legal Studies* 15:405–16.

Cook, P. J. 1987. "Robbery Violence." *Journal of Criminal Law and Criminology* 78:357–76.

Cook, P. J. 1991. "The Technology of Personal Violence." *Crime and Justice* 14:1–71.

Cook, P. J., and J. Ludwig. 1997. "Guns in America: National Survey on Private Ownership and Use of Firearms." Washington, DC: US Department of Justice.

Cook, P. J., and J. Ludwig. 2004. "Does Gun Prevalence Affect Teen Gun Carrying After All?" *Criminology* 42: 27–54.

Cook, P. J., J. Ludwig, S. Venkatesh, and A. A. Braga. 2007. "Underground Drug Markets." *Economic Journal* 117:F558–88.

Cooke, D. J., and C. Michie. 2006. "The Structure of Violent Behavior: A Hierarchical Model." *Criminal Justice and Behavior* 33:706–37.

Cornish, D., and R. Clarke. 1986. *The Reasoning Criminal: Rational Choice Perspectives of Offending.* New York: Springer-Verlag.

Dawson, P., and A. Goodwill. 2013. "A Review of Weapon Choice in Violent and Sexual Crime." *Beijing Law Review* 4:20–27.

Dawson, P., A. Goodwill, and L. Dixon. 2014. "Preliminary Insights and Analysis into Weapon Enabled Sexual Offenders." *Journal of Aggression, Conflict and Peace Research* 6:174–84.

Decker, S. H., and B. van Winkle. 1996. *Life in the Gang: Family, Friends and Violence.* New York: Cambridge University Press.

Dijkstra, J. K., S. D. Gest, S. Lindenberg, R. Veenstra, and A. H. N. Cillessen. 2012. "Testing Three Explanations of the Emergence of Weapon Carrying in Peer Context: The Roles of Aggression, Victimization, and the Social Network." *Journal of Adolescent Health* 50:371–76.

Durant, R. H., A. G. Getts, C. Cadenhead, and E. R. Woods. 1995. "The Association Between Weapon Carrying and the Use of Violence Among Adolescents Living in and Around Public Housing." *Journal of Adolescent Health* 17:376–80.

Durant, R. H., D. P. Krowchuk, S. Kreiter, S. H. Sinal, and C. R. Woods. 1999. "Weapon Carrying on School Property Among Middle School Students." *Archives of Pediatrics and Adolescent Medicine* 153:21–26.

Federal Bureau of Investigation. 2014a. "Crime in the United States, 2013—Aggravated Assault Table." https://www.fbi.gov/about-us/cjis/ucr/crime-in-the-u.s/2013/crime-in-the-u.s.-2013/violent-crime/aggravated-assault-topic-page/aggravated_assault_table_aggravated_assault_types_of_weapons_used_percent_distribution_by_region_2013.xls

Federal Bureau of Investigation. 2014b. "Crime in the United States, 2013—Expanded Homicide Data." https://www.fbi.gov/about-us/cjis/ucr/crime-in-the-u.s/2013/crime-in-the-u.s.-2013/offenses-known-to-law-enforcement/expanded-homicide/expanded_homicide_data_table_7_murder_types_of_weapons_used_percent_distribution_by_region_2013.xls

Feeney, F. 1986. "Robbers as Decision-Makers." In *The Reasoning Criminal: Rational Choice Perspectives on Offending,* edited by D. B. Cornish and R. V. Clarke, pp. 53–71. New York: Springer-Verlag.

Felson, R. B., and S. F. Messner. 1996. "To Kill or Not to Kill? Lethal Outcomes in Injurious Attacks." *Criminology* 34:519–45.

Harcourt, B. E. 2006. *Language of the Gun.* Chicago: University of Chicago Press.

Harding, R. W. 1990. "Rational-Choice Gun Use in Armed Robbery: The Likely Deterrent Effect on Gun Use of Mandatory Additional Imprisonment." *Criminal Law Forum* 1:427–50.

Harding, R. W. 1993. "Gun Use in Crime, Rational Choice and Social Learning Theory." In *Routine Activity and Rational Choice,* edited by R. V. Clarke and M. Felson, pp. 85–102. London: Transaction Publishers.

Hemenway, D. 1997. "Survey Research and Self-Defense Gun Use: An Explanation of Extreme Overestimates." *Journal of Criminal Law and Criminology* 87:1430–45.

Home Office. 2012. "Crime Statistics: Nature of Crime Tables, 2011/12—Violent Crime." http://www.ons.gov.uk/ons/rel/crime-stats/crime-statistics/nature-of-crime-tables--2011-12/rft-7-violence.xls

Home Office. 2014. "Focus on Violent Crime and Sexual Offences, 2012/13 Bulletin Tables." http://www.ons.gov.uk/ons/rel/crime-stats/crime-statistics/focus-on-violent-crime-and-sexual-offences--2012-13/rft-table-1.xls

Horowitz, R. 1983. *Honor and the American Dream: Culture and Identity in a Chicano Community.* New Brunswick, NJ: Rutgers University Press.

Hudson, S. M., T. Ward, and J. C. McCormack. 1999. "Offense Pathways in Sexual Offenders." *Journal of Interpersonal Violence* 14:779–98.

Kleck, G. 1999. "Degrading Scientific Standards to Get the Defensive Gun Use Estimate Down." *Journal on Firearms and Public Policy* 11:77–138.

Kleck, G., and K. McElrath. 1991. "The Effects of Weaponry on Human Violence." *Social Forces* 69:669–92.

Kodjo, C. M., P. Auinger, and S. A. Ryan. 2003. "Demographic, Intrinsic, and Extrinsic Factors Associated with Weapon Carrying at School." *Archives of Pediatrics and Adolescent Medicine* 157:96–103.

Langevin, R., and S. Curnoe. 2013. "Psychological Profile of Sex Offenders Using Weapons in Their Crimes." *Journal of Sexual Aggression* 20:55–68.

Levi, M., and M. Maguire. 2002. "Violent Crime." In *The Oxford Handbook of Criminology*, vol. 3, edited by M. Maguire, R. Morgan, and R. Reiner, pp. 795–843. Oxford: Oxford University Press.

Lewis, C. F., M. V. Baranoski, J. A. Buchanan, and E. P. Benedek. 1998. "Factors Associated with Weapon Use in Maternal Filicide." *Journal of Forensic Sciences* 43:613–18.

Lewis, C. F., and S. C. Bunce. 2003. "Filicidal Mothers and the Impact of Psychosis on Maternal Filicide." *Journal of the American Academy of Psychiatry and the Law* 31:459–70.

Lizotte, A. J., M. D. Krohn, J. C. Howell, K. Tobin, and G. J. Howard. 2000. "Factors Influencing Gun Carrying Among Young Urban Males over the Adolescent–Young Adult Life Course. *Criminology* 38:811–34.

Michie, C., and D. J. Cooke. 2006. "The Structure of Violent Behavior: A Hierarchical Model." *Criminal Justice and Behavior* 33:706–37.

Morrison, G. M., M. J. Furlong, and G. Smith. 1994. "Factors Associated with the Experience of School Violence Among General Education, Leadership Class, Opportunity Class and Special Day Class Pupils." *Education and Treatment of Children* 17:356–69.

Newton, G. D., and F. Zimring. 1969. "Firearms and Violence in American Life: A Staff Report to the National Commission on the Causes and Prevention of Violence." Washington, DC: US Government Printing Office.

Office for National Statistics. 2013. "Focus on Violent Crime and Sexual Offences, 2011/12." http://www.ons.gov.uk/ons/dcp171778_298904.pdf

Office for National Statistics. 2014. "Focus on Violent Crime and Sexual Offences, 2012/13." www.ons.gov.uk/ons/rel/crime-stats/crime-statistics/focus-on-violent-crime-and-sexual-offences--2012-13/rft-table-1.xls

Phillips, S., and M. O. Maume. 2007. "Have Gun Will Shoot? Weapon Instrumentality, Intent, and the Violent Escalation of Conflict." *Homicide Studies* 11:272–94.

Rennison, C. M., S. Jacques, and M. T. Berg. 2011. "Weapon Lethality and Social Distance: A National Test of a Social Structural Theory." *Justice Quarterly* 28:576–605.

Rothman, E. F., D. Hemenway, A. D. Miller, and D. Azrael. 2005. "Batterers' Use of Guns to Threaten Intimate Partners." *Journal of the American Medical Women's Association* 60:62–68.

Saltzman, L. E., J. A. Mercy, P. W. O'Carroll, M. L. Rosenberg, and P. H. Rhodes. 1992. "Weapon Involvement and Injury Outcomes in Family and Intimate Assaults." *Journal of the American Medical Association* 267:3043–47.

Sheley, J. F., and J. D. Wright. 1993. "Motivations for Gun Possession and Carrying Among Serious Juvenile-Offenders." *Behavioral Sciences and the Law* 11:375–88.

Stretesky, P. B., and M. Pogrebin. 2007. "Gang Related Gun Violence: Socialization, Identity, and Self." *Journal of Contemporary Ethnography* 36:85–114.

Strodtbeck, F. L., and J. F. Short. 1964. "An Explanation of Gang Action." *Social Problems* 12:127–40.

Stueve, A., and B. G. Link. 1997. "Violence and Psychiatric Disorders: Results from an Epidemiological Study of Young Adults in Israel." *Psychiatric Quarterly* 68:327–42.

Subra, B., D. Muller, L. Begue, B. Bushman, and F. Delmas. 2010. "Automatic Effects of Alcohol and Aggressive Cues on Aggressive Thoughts and Behaviors." *Personality and Social Psychology Bulletin* 36:1052–57.

Swanson, J. M., C. D. Hozer, V. K. Ganju, and R. T. Jono. 1990. "Violence and Psychiatric Disorder in the Community: Evidence from the Epidemiological Catchment Area Surveys." *Hospital and Community Psychiatry* 41:761–70.

Sweeten, G. 2012. "Scaling Criminal Offending." *Journal of Quantitative Criminology* 28:533–57.

Tark, J., and G. Kleck. 2004. "Resisting Crime: The Effects of Victim Action on the Outcomes of Crimes." *Criminology* 42:861–909.

Thurnherr, J., P. A. Michaud, A. Berchtold, C. Akré, and J. C. Suris. 2009. "Youths Carrying a Weapon or Using a Weapon in a Fight: What Makes the Difference?" *Health Education Research* 24:270–79.

Tillyer, M. S., and R. Tillyer. 2014. "Violence in Context: A Multilevel Analysis of Victim Injury in Robbery Incidents." *Justice Quarterly* 31:767–91.

van Gelder, J.-L. 2013. "Beyond Rational Choice: The Hot/Cool Perspective of Criminal Decision Making." *Psychology, Crime and Law* 19:745–63.

Wells, W., and J. Horney. 2002. "Weapon Effects and Individual Intent to Do Harm: Influences on the Escalation of Violence." *Criminology* 40:265–96.

Williams, S. S., P. F. Mulhall, J. S. Reis, and J. O. DeVille. 2002. "Adolescents Carrying Handguns and Taking Them to School: Psychosocial Correlates Among Public School Students in Illinois." *Journal of Adolescence* 25:551–67.

Wilson, L. A., T. Ward, and L. Bakker. 1998. "A Descriptive Model of the Relapse Process in Disqualified Drivers." *Behavior Change* 16:111–26.

Witt, J. K., and J. R. Brockmole. 2012. "Action Alters Object Identification: Wielding a Gun Increases the Bias to See Guns." *Journal of Experimental Psychology: Human Perception and Performance* 38:1159–67.

Wolfgang, M. E. 1958. *Patterns in Criminal Homicide*. Philadelphia: University of Pennsylvania Press.

Woodworth, M., T. Freimuth, E. L. Hutton, T. Carpenter, A. D. Agar, and M. Logan. 2013. "High-Risk Sexual Offenders: An Examination of Sexual Fantasy, Sexual Paraphilia, Psychopathy, and Offence Characteristics." *International Journal of Law and Psychiatry* 36:144–56.

Wright, J. D., and P. H. Rossi. 1986. *Armed and Considered Dangerous: A Survey of Felons and Their Firearms*. New York: Aldine.

Wright, R. T., and S. H. Decker. 1997. *Armed Robbers in Action: Stickups and Street Culture*. Boston: Northeastern University Press.

Zimring, F. E. 1968. "Is Gun Control Likely to Reduce Violent Killings?" *University of Chicago Law Review* 35:721–37.

Zimring, F. E. 2004. "Firearms, Violence, and the Potential Impact of Firearms Control." *Journal of Law, Medicine and Ethics* 32:34–37.

CHAPTER 21

THE EFFECT OF ALCOHOL AND AROUSAL ON CRIMINAL DECISION MAKING

M. LYN EXUM, LAUREN A. AUSTIN, AND JUSTIN D. FRANKLIN

DECISION making is the process of determining a response to an opportunity in which one can choose between two or more courses of action. *Criminal* decision making occurs when an individual has the opportunity to choose between an illegal course of action and some other response. When any of the consequences associated with a course of action is probabilistic, decision making is said to be completed under conditions of risk or uncertainty (Camerer and Loewenstein 2004). Given that the decision to commit a crime is not guaranteed to result in a punishment or a reward, criminal decision making is an example of an uncertain gamble.

Alcohol intoxication and intense emotional arousal commonly cloud the criminal decision-making process (Zimring and Hawkins 1973; Cook 1980; Nagin 2007). Epidemiological and ethnographic research seemingly bears this out. Approximately one-third of violent offenders in the United States and Canada, half of those in England and Wales, and two-thirds of those in Scotland are under the influence of alcohol at the time of their crimes (Brochu et al. 2001; Rand et al. 2010; Institute of Alcohol Studies 2013). More globally, in a study of homicide offenders across nine countries, Kuhns et al. (2014) found that 48 percent of murderers were under the influence of alcohol at the time of their crimes. In addition, interviews with both violent and property offenders reveal that powerful visceral/emotional states, such as rage, humiliation, fear, desperation, and drug cravings, frequently precipitate the decision to offend (Katz 1988, 1999; Wright and Decker 1994; de Haan and Vos 2003; Athens 2005; Cromwell, Parker, and Mobley 2006; Topalli and Wright 2006, 2014). Thus, in order to better understand why individuals choose to gamble on crime, criminologists must also understand how alcohol and arousal shape the criminal decision-making process.

In this chapter, we examine the impact of alcohol and arousal on decision making from a neuroeconomic perspective. First, we provide an overview of different theoretical models of decision making under risk/uncertainty and identify various neurological components relevant to decisional processing (see also chapter 6, this volume). Next, we discuss the neurological effects of acute alcohol consumption and heightened states of arousal on these decision-making structures and systems. Finally, we review the empirical evidence on alcohol and arousal as it relates to criminal/aggressive decision making, and we offer suggestions for future research.

I. THEORIES OF DECISION MAKING

Theories of decision making can be found in many disciplines, including economics, psychology, and criminology. Virtually all of these theories are rooted in the idea of consequentialism. Consequentialist theories assume that individuals make choices based on the consequences (good and bad) of the possible response options (Loewenstein et al. 2001). These consequences are assessed on such factors as how likely they are to occur and how desirable they are. Hedonistically, individuals choose the response that provides the most desirable outcome for themselves.

An example of a consequentialist theory is expected utility (EU) theory (von Neumann and Morgenstern 1947). Central to EU theory is the idea that each possible outcome's desirability—also known as its utility—is weighted by its probability of occurring. For example, if Prospect A offers a 50 percent chance to win $10 and a 50 percent chance to win nothing and Prospect B offers a 60 percent chance to win $10 and a 40 percent chance to win nothing, then EU theory endorses the selection of the latter gamble because it is the response that yields the larger expected value and, presumably, the greater utility for the decision maker.

In the previous illustration, the objective probability of each outcome (i.e., 50 percent chance of winning) was known to the decision maker; however, this condition is not true for many everyday decisions. For example, when choosing whether to drive to work or take the train, one does not necessarily know with certainty the odds of encountering a traffic-snarling accident on the roadway or a mechanical delay on the train. To account for this lack of known probabilities, EU theory was modified to allow individuals to impute their own subjective assessments of outcome probabilities. The resulting theory is known as subjective expected utility (SEU) theory (Savage 1954).

In the field of criminology, deterrence and rational choice theory are the dominant frameworks for studying the decision to offend. Both deterrence and rational choice are consequentialist theories; in fact, they can both be classified as SEU theories of criminal decision making (Braithwaite and Makkai 1991; Paternoster and Simpson 1996). Potential offenders are assumed to weight the consequences of a criminal act by their perceived certainties of occurring and by their perceived severity. Although seldom tested empirically (but see Yu and Williford 1995; Nagin and Pogarsky 2001), the swiftness with which these consequences occur is also thought to influence the subjective expected utility of crime. Note that punishments that occur over a long time horizon are subject to hyperbolic discounting; as a result, sanctions occurring in the distant future may not appear as severe as those occurring more immediately (Wilson and Herrnstein 1985; Frederick, Loewenstein, and O'Donoghue 2002; Nagin and Pogarsky 2004). From a consequentialist perspective, discounted punishments have less of a deterrent effect on criminal behavior.

As can be seen, traditional utility theories—and by extension, theories of deterrence and rational choice—offer a model of decision making that rests on a cognitive assessment of costs and benefits. Decision makers must estimate the probability of a set of consequences occurring and determine how desirable each outcome would be, conditioned in part by how quickly the outcome would occur. This hedonic calculus is the result of various neurological structures and cognitive systems working in concert. An overview of several of these structures/systems is provided next.

II. Neurological Foundations of Decision Making

From a reductionist perspective, decision making is the product of neurons that transmit signals to one another through an elaborate electrochemical network (Panskepp 1998; Toates 2006; Spear 2010). Activated nerve cells produce an electrical charge that triggers the release of neurotransmitters, which in turn bind with receptor sites of neighboring neurons. If *excitatory* neurotransmitters such as glutamate and norepinephrine bind with the neurons, then the neurons are stimulated in such a way that allows the electrical charge to continue to flow (Spear 2010). If *inhibitory* neurotransmitters such as gamma-aminobutyric acid (GABA) and serotonin bind with the neurons, then the neurons will cease to fire. Some neurotransmitters, such as dopamine, can be either excitatory or inhibitory depending on how they bind with the nearby neurons (Toates 2006; Spear 2010).

From a more holistic perspective, decision making is the product of two separate but interrelated cognitive systems, commonly referred to as System 1 and System 2 (Kahneman 2003, 2011). These systems process information in distinct ways. System 1 operates at an implicit (unconscious) level and makes decisions quickly, automatically, effortlessly, and instinctually (or based on mastery that comes from repeated practice). System 2 operates at an explicit (conscious) level and makes decisions more slowly, intentionally, arduously, and with human agency. This dual-process perspective of decision making offers a framework for understanding why individuals may sometimes make thoughtful choices that maximize their expected utility (System 2), whereas at other times they may rely on cognitive shortcuts in order to make decisions more impulsively and seemingly against their best interests (System 1). Although this idea of dual processing is not new (Shiffrin and Schneider 1977; Chaiken 1980; Petty and Cacioppo 1986), the application of a dual-process perspective to the study of criminal decision making is relatively recent (Reyna and Farley 2006; van Gelder and de Vries 2012, 2014; van Gelder 2013; Treiber 2014).

Reconciling these reductionist and holistic perspectives of decision making—and in turn, understanding how alcohol and arousal impact criminal decisions—requires an understanding of the organizational structure of the human brain. The largest component of the brain, the cerebrum, is enveloped by the cerebral cortex (Toates 2006). The cerebral cortex is categorized into four lobes: frontal, temporal, parietal, and occipital. Although they are not fully independent of one another, these lobes are generally associated with different cognitive and motor functions (Spear 2010). In this chapter, we focus on the frontal lobe, which relies heavily on working memory to regulate self-control and goal-directed behavior (Roberts, Robbins, and Weiskrantz 1998; Vartanian and Mandel 2012; Zayas, Mischel, and Pandey 2014).

A portion of the frontal lobe known as the prefrontal cortex (PFC) plays a central role in decision making under conditions of risk (Mohr, Biele, and Heekeren 2010; Vartanian and Mandel 2012; see also chapter 6, this volume) and in the regulation of aggressive behavior (Giancola and Zeichner 1994; Giancola et al. 1996). For example, the anticipation of costs and benefits, which is an essential element of consequential theories of decision making, is associated with greater dopamine activity in specific regions of the PFC, such as the ventromedial PFC and dorsolateral PFC. Increased activity in these regions is associated with lower levels of risk-taking (Reyna and Zayas 2014). In addition, damage to the ventromedial PFC impairs the ability to interpret physiological changes in body states (e.g., emotional/arousal states) that occur when anticipating rewards and punishments. This, in turn, can lead to more risky choices (Reyna and Zayas 2014). Note also that portions of the PFC have been shown to be associated with the hyperbolic discounting of delayed consequences (Kable and Glimcher 2007). As mentioned previously, such discounting can weaken the deterrent effect of a given punishment. In summary, the PFC (especially the ventromedial PFC) has the ability to anticipate future costs and benefits and also to utilize information stored in memory in order to regulate behavior. It provides a more deliberative and intentional process for making decisions, and it has been identified by some as the anatomical correlate of System 2 (Wood and Bechara 2014).

Beneath the cerebral cortex lie many other brain structures and systems that exchange information with the PFC. One such component is the limbic system. The limbic system is a conglomerate of individual brain structures/systems including the amygdala and the striatal system, which is itself a conglomerate of other structures including the nucleus accumbens (Spear 2010; Wood and Bechara 2014; see also chapter 6, this volume). The limbic system—and especially the amygdala and striatal system—is thought to play a role in the development of emotional and goal-directed responses. For example, the amygdala is involved in the emotional evaluation of rewards and losses, and within the striatal system, the release of dopamine in the nucleus accumbens produces a sensation of pleasure that accompanies a positive consequence (Becker, Rudick, and Jenkins

2001). Thus, these limbic structures/systems are important to the assessment of at least some forms of risky decisions. Such assessments are submitted to the PFC, where they can be evaluated in light of information gathered from elsewhere in the brain (Toates 2006; Dasgupta 2011; Wood and Bechara 2014). With its ability to process information impulsively and instinctively, the amygdala–striatal system is an anatomical correlate of System 1 (Wood and Bechara 2014).

Although additional neural structures may play a role in System 1 and System 2 processing (Kahneman 2011), for simplicity we limit our focus here to the amygdala–striatal system and PFC. In the remainder of this chapter, we discuss how the psychopharmacology of alcohol and the neurological effects of arousal can alter PFC and amygdala-striatal functioning and ultimately shape the decision to engage in crime.

III. THE PSYCHOPHARMACOLOGY OF ALCOHOL

Ethanol (ethyl alcohol) is the active form of alcohol in beer, wine, and distilled spirits. Because of its molecular properties and size, ethanol can dissolve across fatty membranes such as the blood–brain barrier—the protective lipid membrane designed to keep neurotoxins and other harmful macromolecules from reaching the brain (Braun 1996; Abbott et al. 2010;). Once inside this barrier, alcohol can flow largely unabated to almost any region of the brain and impact neurological functioning (Parrott et al. 2004; Dasgupta 2011).

Alcohol is a central nervous system depressant. It interferes with glutamate receptor sites and prevents this excitatory neurotransmitter from activating nearby neurons (Braun 1996). In addition, alcohol mimics the effects of the inhibitory neurotransmitter GABA, thereby further suppressing brain activity and even disrupting working memory in the PFC (Dasgupta 2011). For the purposes of our discussion, alcohol's GABA-related effects are especially noteworthy in that they can interrupt critical communication pathways between the subcortical areas of the brain (e.g., the amygdala–striatal system) and the cortex (including the PFC). Alcohol also impacts the reward center of the brain (Braun 1996; Parrott et al. 2004; Dasgupta 2011). It triggers an increase in the amount of dopamine in portions of the limbic system, which produces a sense of pleasure and reward. However, increased dopamine release can also alter an individual's anticipatory processing of cues that signal an upcoming reward. This, in turn, can promote impulsivity and risk-seeking, which are precursors for aggression (Heinz et al. 2011).

Collectively, the acute effects of alcohol consumption serve to slow down higher order cognitive processing while promoting euphoria and risk-seeking. Although individuals who drink alcohol are still able to attend to the immediate, central cues in the environment (a System 1 function), alcohol diminishes working memory's ability to take into consideration the more distal and peripheral cues (a System 2 function) (Steele and Josephs 1990). Under the influence of alcohol, individuals become more internally focused and less externally focused. They are more present oriented than future oriented. They see largely the short-term rewards and ignore the long-term consequences. Steele and Josephs refer to this condition as *alcohol myopia*, which can alter the drinker's ability to perceive and respond to conditions of risk/threat (see also Giancola et al. 2010). Consistent with this idea of alcohol myopia, laboratory studies that have examined the impact of alcohol on decisions under risk (i.e., gambling games) find that intoxicated participants show a greater preference for riskier responses relative to sober participants (Lane et al. 2004; George, Rogers, and Duka 2005; Euser et al. 2011; but see Breslin et al. 1999).

IV. THE NEUROLOGICAL EFFECTS OF AROUSAL

The term arousal can refer to a collection of physiological changes such as elevated heart rate, respiration, body temperature, hormonal activity, and/or nervous system activity (Hanoch and Vitouch 2004). Although often concomitant with an energizing emotion (e.g., anger and fear), arousal can also occur as the result of ordinary physical activity such as running or swimming, psychoactive substances such as caffeine or nicotine, and internal drive states such as drug cravings or sexual desire. Even so, arousal in the form of somatic changes (e.g., elevated blood pressure and increased sweat gland activity) does not necessarily require or result in increased neural activity in the brain (Frost, Burish and Holmes 1978); furthermore, when cortical arousal does occur, it is not necessarily uniform across all emotional states. In other words, the effect of arousal on the brain may be different depending on which emotion or other stimulus is triggering the arousal (Panskepp 1998). That being said, we provide a general overview of the cognitive effects of arousal. We focus on the effects of arousal on memory recall because the recollection of past attitudes and experiences from long-term memory helps individuals to identify and evaluate possible response options within their hedonic calculus (Exum and Zachowicz 2014).

Arousal has long been thought to be associated with memory recall (Yerkes and Dodson 1908); however, the research examining these relationships has been mixed. Some studies find that arousal impedes memory formation and recall, whereas other studies find that arousal facilitates it (Hanoch and Vitouch 2004; Murray and Kensinger 2012). Such differences may be due to the types of memories being recalled, with memories that are more central to the arousal state being more readily available while peripheral features remain unaffected or are suppressed in memory (Levin and Edelstein 2010). For example, fear may invoke a type of arousal that enhances the recall of memories that help us respond to the threat but simultaneously hinder the recollection of unrelated memories. This process of recalling selective memories has been referred to as *memory narrowing* (Levine and Edelstein 2010) and is largely identical to the *attention narrowing* process that Loewenstein (1996) argues takes place under conditions of heightened arousal. Exactly how arousal exerts these effects on memory/attention is not fully understood, but indirect evidence points to mechanisms related to System 1 and System 2 functioning.

Milliseconds before an individual becomes consciously aware of an emotionally charged stimulus, the human brain begins to process information about that stimulus quickly, implicitly, and instinctually (Levine and Edelstein 2010). These pre-attentive cognitions (System 1) can influence the individual's assessment of the stimulus and the surrounding situation, and they are more likely than non-emotionally charged cognitions to become a part of the PFC's working memory (System 2).[1] Such pre-attentive effects of arousal on memory may be traced in part to the amygdala, which increases in activity during heightened emotional arousal (Canli et al. 1998; Garavan et al. 2001; Hamann et al. 2002). Given that the amygdala–striatal system helps develop goal-directed responses (discussed previously), it appears that intense levels of arousal may operate indirectly through System 1 to narrow memory/attention in order to influence higher order processing.[2]

In addition to its impact on attention and memory, arousal can also impact individuals' estimates of how likely future consequences are to occur—although the effects can vary by the emotional valence associated with the arousal (Slovic et al. 2007). In general, individuals who are in a positively valenced arousal state perceive positive outcomes to be more likely, whereas those in a negatively valenced state believe negative outcomes are more likely (Johnson and Tversky 1983; Slovic et al. 2007; Blanchette and Richards 2010). Such effects of arousal on perceptions of certainty may be attributed to the availability heuristic, which is a cognitive shortcut associated with System 1 processing (Chaiken 1980). The availability heuristic states that the perceived probability of an outcome is positively related to how easily memories/attitudes about that outcome are retrieved from memory. Thus, to the extent that arousal can facilitate the recollection of events from memory (because of memory narrowing effects), these events should be viewed as more likely (because of the availability heuristic).

V. Alcohol, Arousal, and Criminal Decision Making

Having provided a neuroeconomic framework in which to understand the effects of acute alcohol consumption and heighted states of arousal on decision making more generally, we now turn to a review of the empirical research on the effects of alcohol and arousal on criminal/aggressive decision making. We focus largely on findings from experimental studies because they are best able to identify the causal impact of alcohol and/or arousal on the decision to offend.

A. Alcohol

Experimental studies of alcohol and aggression randomly assign participants to drink an alcoholic or inert beverage and then engage in a task designed to measure aggression. Most often, participants engage in a teaching task (Gustafson 1990) or a reaction-time task (Giancola and Parrott 2008) in which they can punish a fictitious opponent with an electric shock. The intensity and/or duration of the shock serves as the primary measure of aggression. In other studies, participants are given an opportunity to play a game in which they can deduct money from an opponent's allotment—a behavior that can also be viewed as an act of aggression (Dougherty et al. 1999).

Meta-analytic reviews of this experimental literature have shown that alcohol does indeed increase aggressive responding.[3] The global effect size estimate for alcohol is approximately .50 and constitutes a medium effect (Exum 2006). However, the effect of alcohol is not uniform and tends to vary across such factors as the drinker's sex, the type of alcohol consumed, and the amount of alcohol consumed. Specifically, the effect of alcohol on aggression appears to be stronger among males, when vodka or other distilled spirits are consumed, and when higher dosages of alcohol are consumed (Exum 2006). Other studies find that the effect of alcohol on aggressivity is stronger among individuals who already have difficult temperaments (Giancola 2004a) or aggressive dispositions (Giancola 2002).

Interestingly, alcohol's effect on aggressivity appears to be moderated by affective factors such as fear, provocation, and frustration. That is, alcohol's effect on aggressive responding is greater when participants are at risk for retaliation from their laboratory opponent, when participants are first provoked by their opponent, or when the opponent impedes the participant from achieving a desired goal (Exum 2006). These conditions of fear, provocation, and frustration introduce a heightened sense of arousal into the study, which in turn interacts with the alcohol effect. We further discuss these alcohol/arousal interactions later in the chapter.

Few studies examining the alcohol–aggression relationship have included a measure of participants' perceived risks and rewards of the act or of participants' neurological functioning; as a result, formal tests of the neuroeconomic properties of alcohol on criminal decision making are rare. However, in a quasi-experimental study of college partygoers, Lanza-Kaduce, Bishop, and Winner (1997) found that high levels of alcohol consumption were associated with a decrease in participants' perceived sanctioning risk and an increase in the perceived desirability of various criminal acts (including violent behavior). Given that individuals who consume a high dose of alcohol experience disruptions in cognitive functioning (Peterson et al. 1990) and that individuals with disrupted cognitive functioning—especially in the PFC—tend to be more aggressive (Hawkins and Trobst 2000; Paschall and Fishbein 2002), these results provide indirect evidence that the effect of alcohol on aggressivity is mediated through the PFC's calculations of risk and reward.

In a more direct test of the intoxicated aggression and PFC functioning relationship, Lau, Pihl, and Peterson (1995) classified participants into two groups—low and high functioners—based on neurological test scores. Participants in each of these groups were randomly assigned to drink an alcoholic or inert beverage, and then they took part in a competitive reaction time task that served as a measure of aggression. As expected, aggressive responding was higher among those who were intoxicated, who were provoked, and who were in the low cognitive functioning group. Although there was also a significant interaction between provocation and cognitive functioning (provocation had a larger effect on aggression among those with low neurological test scores), no interaction was found between alcohol and cognitive functioning.

In a subsequent study, Hoaken, Assaad, and Pihl (1998) administered a neurological test to assess participants' prefrontal functioning prior to consuming their assigned beverages and then after participants completed the aggression task. The results revealed that those who consumed alcohol experienced a significant decline in neurological functioning. In addition, those who consumed alcohol showed evidence of greater aggressivity; however, the overall relationship between PFC functioning, alcohol, and aggression was not as strong or straightforward as the researchers predicted. Hoaken et al. speculate that participants' baseline levels of cognitive functioning may have been strong enough to insulate them from alcohol's effects on aggressivity.

Using a more comprehensive battery of neurological assessments, Giancola (2004b) also examined the role of cognitive functioning in the alcohol–aggression relationship. After completing their neurological tests, participants were randomly assigned to drink an alcoholic or non-alcoholic beverage and then complete a competitive reaction time task in which the winner of the game could administer an electric shock to the loser. As predicted, alcohol consumption was associated with more aggressive responding, as was the level of provocation. More important, the results revealed that alcohol was more likely to be associated with aggressivity among males with lower levels of PFC functioning (no such relationship was found with female participants). This mediating effect of alcohol held true even after controlling for cognitive abilities in other lobes of the brain. As such, these findings underscore the impact that PFC functioning has on an individual's ability (at least in men) to curb the neuropsychological properties of alcohol that promote aggressive behaviors.

B. Arousal

As previously noted, crime is often concomitant with intense visceral/emotional states such as anger, fear, and drug cravings. Although these arousal-inducing conditions are thought to impact the subjective expected utility of the decision to offend, the research in this area has been mixed. For example, Carmichael and Piquero (2004) administered to participants a hypothetical bar fight scenario in which another patron in the bar becomes confrontational. Participants were asked to report how angry they would feel in this situation, how likely they would be to assault the provocateur, and the perceived costs and benefits associated with such an assault. Consistent with the notion of attention narrowing, participants who perceived high levels of anger were enticed to violence by the perceived thrills associated with the assault, but they were not deterred by informal sanctions and moral constraints.

Note that participants in Carmichael and Piquero's (2004) study were not necessarily experiencing high levels of anger at the time they completed their ratings. Instead, they had been asked to *predict* how angry they would feel if the hypothetical scenario were real. Only a few studies of criminal decision making have sought to manipulate participants' actual arousal levels, and most of these experimental studies have examined the impact of sexual arousal on sexually aggressive decisions.

For example, Ariely and Loewenstein (2006) examined how sexual arousal affected individuals' interests in various sexual acts, including some that were morally questionable and/or illegal. Male participants assigned to the arousal condition were instructed to masturbate to a pre-orgasmic state, whereas those in the non-aroused condition received no such instructions. Both groups then completed a questionnaire about their interest in engaging in a series of sexual activities. Compared to the non-aroused group, the aroused group expressed a greater willingness to take a date to an expensive restaurant and to tell a woman "I love you" in order to increase the likelihood of sex. More important to our discussion of *criminal* decision making, aroused men indicated they were more willing to persist in having sex with a woman after she says "no" and were more willing to secretly administer a drug to a woman in order to increase the likelihood of having sex. Taken at face value, these findings suggest that intense sexual arousal directs one's attention toward morally questionable/illegal behaviors that can satiate the sexual appetite, despite the negative consequences associated with those actions.

In a more direct test of this idea, Loewenstein, Nagin, and Paternoster (1997) administered a hypothetical date rape scenario to male participants immediately after they had viewed photographs of nude or fully clothed women. Participants indicated how likely they would be to respond to the scenario in a sexually aggressive manner; they also rated the certainty and severity/intensity of various costs/benefits associated with behaving that way. As predicted, participants in the aroused group reported a higher likelihood of engaging in sexually aggressive tactics. Contrary to expectation, however, there was no evidence that the groups differed on their assessments of the costs of sexual assault, and there was little evidence that the aroused group perceived greater benefits from the act.

In a similar study, Bouffard (2002) examined the effect of arousal on sexual aggression in men and, recently, in a sample of men and women (Bouffard 2014). Across the two studies, there were no significant group differences in aroused and non-aroused participants' self-reported likelihood to engage in sexually aggressive tactics, nor were there group differences in the estimates of the perceived certainty and severity/intensity of costs and benefits. However, in a series of non-experimental analyses, Bouffard (2002, 2014) found that higher levels of arousal were predictive of greater intentions to commit sexual aggression. Furthermore, arousal levels were found to be predictive of specific costs and benefits (especially for males), although not always in the expected direction. Collectively, the findings from the four previously discussed studies suggest that sexual arousal alters sexually aggressive decision making, but the results are not very strong or robust.

In light of these mixed findings, Exum and Zachowicz (2014) sought to examine the effect of sexual arousal on sexually aggressive decision making from a different perspective. Using a dual-process framework, these researchers focused on how quickly aroused and non-aroused participants could access the perceived consequences of sexual assault from memory (a System 1 function) rather than focus on participants' subjective estimates of the certainty and severity/utility of the act (a System 2 task). After viewing either a sexually explicit or a neutral video, participants were asked to read a date rape scenario and report their likelihood of engaging in various forms of sexual coercion. Next, participants were instructed to press their computer's spacebar each time they thought of a negative consequence they might face if they had sex with the woman in the scenario against her will. Subsequently, participants were asked to press the spacebar each time they identified a positive consequence associated with the act. The amount of time between spacebar presses (i.e., the response latency) represented the ease with which these consequences could be recalled from memory. Shorter response latencies represented greater accessibility.

Similar to prior research (Loewenstein et al. 1997; Bouffard 2002, 2014; Ariely and Loewenstein 2006), Exum and Zachowicz (2014) found evidence that aroused participants were more likely to endorse sexually coercive behaviors than were non-aroused participants. Contrary to the notion of attention narrowing, the *number* of spacebar presses for negative consequences did not differ significantly across the two groups; however, aroused participants identified a significantly greater number of benefits compared to the non-aroused group. Furthermore, there was evidence that aroused participants were also able to access their perceive benefits (but not costs) more quickly from memory.

In order to further examine this pattern of results, the response latencies for the most commonly identified cost associated with engaging in sexual aggression (legal repercussions) and the most commonly identified benefit (sexual gratification) were examined. This time, significant differences in response latencies were found not only for the benefit but also for the cost. Compared to their non-aroused counterparts, aroused participants were able to access the benefit of sexual assault more quickly and the cost more slowly (Exum and Zachowicz 2014). Thus, these findings suggest that heightened sexual arousal alters implicit System 1 functioning in order to narrow attention to the perceived benefits of an act and away from its possible costs.

C. Alcohol–Arousal Interactions

Recall that meta-analytic findings of the alcohol–aggression literature reveal that the effect of alcohol is greater under conditions of fear, provocation, and frustration. Each of these is an excitatory state and generates its own level of physiological arousal. Drawing from this interaction between alcohol and excitatory states, Exum (2002) used an experimental design to examine the effects of alcohol and anger (or angry arousal) on the decision to engage in physical assault.

In Exum's (2002) study, male participants were given an inert or alcoholic beverage to drink, the latter designed to elevate blood alcohol levels to approximately .08. After consuming their assigned drinks, half of the participants in each of these two groups were randomly assigned to an anger manipulation, and then all participants completed a bar fight scenario in which they were asked to report how likely they would be to assault the hypothetical provocateur (a measure of self-referent aggression). Given the potential for self-enhancing biases to spur participants to underreport their assaultive intentions, participants were also asked how likely the typical male would be to assault the provocateur (other-referent aggression). This served as an additional measure of aggressive intentions.

Although there were no significant effects for alcohol or arousal for the self-referent measure of aggression, an examination of the other-referent measure revealed a significant alcohol-by-anger interaction (Exum 2002). Anger had no impact on the aggressive intentions among sober participants, but it elevated the aggressive intentions among intoxicated individuals. Contrary to theoretical expectations—but not unlike the results from other empirical studies of arousal (Loewenstein et al. 1997; Bouffard 2002, 2014)—participants' perceptions of the certainty and severity of costs/benefits were largely unaffected by the experimental manipulations. However, additional analyses revealed that the way in which these perceptions influenced aggressive intentions varied across experimental conditions (Exum 2002). In other words, although everyone perceived the costs and benefits similarly, the degree to which these costs and benefits shaped aggressive intentions varied across groups, especially among the drunk and angry participants. This led Exum to conclude that normative decision-making processes begin to break down under conditions of intoxication and anger. Although the study did not include measures that are more closely related to System 1 and System 2, the findings from this study are consistent with the idea that alcohol and arousal change the decision-making process from one that is more cold and cognitive to one that is more hot and emotional.

VI. SUMMARY

Consequentialist theories assume crime is a choice that one undertakes after considering the severity and the timing of its probabilistic consequences (Loewenstein et al. 2001). In order to conduct this complex assessment, the human brain will take into account information that is processed automatically and instinctively (a System 1 activity) and then review this information in a more effortful and deliberative manner (System 2 activity; Kahneman 2011). However, under conditions of acute alcohol intoxication and/or heightened states of arousal, the neurological underpinnings of this process can become compromised.

Alcohol increases dopamine levels in the amygdala–striatal system (System 1), which produces a feeling of euphoria and makes risk-seeking activities seem more rewarding (Parrott et al. 2004; Dasgupta 2011). Furthermore, by mimicking the effects of GABA, alcohol suppresses higher order cognitive functioning in the PFC (System 2) (Dasgupta 2011). The end result is alcohol myopia—a cognitive perspective in which the immediate rewards of an act outweigh the more distal punishments (Steele and Josephs 1990). Although research shows that intoxicated persons tend to choose riskier gambles compared to sober individuals (Euser et al. 2011) and are also more aggressive (Exum 2006), little effort has been made to directly test the link between alcohol, altered System 1 and System 2 activity, and the consequentialist decision to offend. There is indirect evidence that the effect of alcohol on aggression is indeed mediated through its impact on PFC functioning (Giancola 2004*b*), but more research in this area is needed.

Heightened states of emotional/visceral arousal can also produce a type of cognitive myopia. Operating through the amygdala–striatal system, arousal can facilitate the recollection of certain memories and hinder that of others (Canli et al. 1998; Hanoch and Vitouch 2004; Murray and Kensinger 2012). This memory narrowing effect can alter the PFC appraisal of a criminal opportunity and/or the number of behavioral responses available from memory (Exum and Zachowicz 2014). Although aroused individuals (i.e., angry or sexually aroused) are more likely to endorse assaultive decisions, they do not necessarily view the costs/benefits of these decisions differently than their unaroused counterparts (Loewenstein et al. 1997; Bouffard 2002, 2014). Little research has sought to examine the neurological processes that may mediate the effect of arousal on aggressive decision making; however, there is evidence that arousal may indeed create a memory narrowing effect such that certain types of consequences are more easily accessed from memory than others (Exum and Zachowicz 2014). Tentative evidence also suggests that arousal can interact with alcohol to promote aggressive decision making (Exum 2002), but this process is not well understood. Again, more research is needed.

VII. Conclusion and Future Directions

In the late 1700s, the utilitarian philosopher Jeremy Bentham (1789/1970) outlined a consequentialist model of decision making: "Sum up all the values of all the pleasures on the one side, and those of all the pains on the other. The balance, if it be on the side of pleasure, will give the good tendency of the act upon the whole" (p. 40). More than two centuries later, consequentialist theories of decision making remain ever popular; however, given that the individuals who commit crime are often making decisions while under the influence of alcohol and/or heightened arousal (Topalli and Wright 2006, 2014; Rand et al. 2010), criminologists must broaden their study of decision making to focus on these altered states of mind.

This call to action is not new. In the dawn of modern-day deterrence research, Zimring and Hawkins (1973) noted,

> The threat of consequences would appear to be less effective when decisions about criminal conduct are made under the influence of drugs or alcohol. The

ineffectiveness of threat may in some cases be due to the increased affect and more uninhibited emotional expression resulting from drug or alcohol consumption. (p. 137)

Later, as Cook (1980) outlined a research agenda for the next decade of deterrence scholars, he challenged criminologists to examine "the extent to which such factors as age, emotional arousal, and inebriation are related to deterrability" (p. 259). However, the relative dearth of research in this area remained such that in his Sutherland address to the American Society of Criminology, Nagin (2007) was compelled to remind us that "decision making involves more than cognitive deliberation. It also involves emotion" (p. 262). He then called for more experimental studies on criminal decision making in which participants "could be randomly assigned to an alcohol consumption condition or . . . to conditions designed to arouse anger, frustration, sexual desire, and so on" (p. 264).

Gradually, progress in this area is being made. As this line of research continues to evolve, scholars should expand their focus beyond the traditional measures of the perceived costs and benefits of offending and also explore the neurological processes (e.g., Systems 1 and 2) that underlie intoxicated/aroused decision making. Functional neuroimaging studies such as those using single-photon emission computed tomography, positron emission tomography, and magnetic resonance imaging techniques have begun to identify areas of dysfunction in the brain among violent individuals. This research commonly finds impaired performance in the PFC and the amygdala (Bufkin and Luttrell 2005; Yang and Raine 2009). In some instances, aggression is characterized with lower PFC functioning relative to subcortical (e.g., amygdala) functioning (Raine et al. 1998). In other words, impulsive acts of aggression occurred when there was relatively more System 1 activity than System 2 activity.

To our knowledge, no experimental studies examining the effects of alcohol and/or arousal on an SEU model of criminal decision making have also utilized neuroimaging technology. That is, no study has bridged the gap between localized brain functioning, perceptions of costs and benefits, and intoxicated/aroused intentions to offend. Absent access to neuroimaging technology, researchers could utilize psychological assessments that have been shown to correlate with localized brain functioning, just as Hoaken and colleagues (1998) did in their study of intoxicated aggression. These assessments, along with the traditional measures of the perceived risks/rewards of offending, would provide a more complete picture of the neurological and economic processes that underlie criminal decision making. This research has important implications not only for the study of criminological theory but also for crime control policy and jurisprudence.

Illustratively, costly deterrence practices such as an increase in police presence and lengthier prison sentences may not effectively deter the emotional individual whose cognitive myopia has discounted future criminal justice sanctions. However, as researchers come to understand the role of emotions and decision making more fully, policymakers can take advantage of the power of emotions to help deter offenders more immediately by appealing to their sense of righteousness and morality. There is evidence of these effects in the literature. For example, the multibillion-dollar problem of tax evasion may be curbed by minimizing the public's anger toward paying taxes and instead emphasizing the societal benefits that derive from tax revenue (van Winden and Ash 2012). Additional acts of dishonesty and crime may also be curbed by invoking a sense of righteousness through the use honor codes or other moral/religious codes of conduct (McCabe and Trevino 1993; McCabe, Trevino, and Butterfield 2002; Murdock and Anderman 2006; Mazar, Amir, and Ariely 2008; Ariely 2013).

Finally, understanding the neuroeconomics of intoxicated/aroused decision making has important legal ramifications. Neuroimaging evidence of altered brain functioning has the potential to mitigate the court's impressions of a defendant's culpability and, ultimately, the corresponding punishment (Sapolsky 2004; Husted, Myers, and Lui 2008; Greene and Cahill 2012). As researchers learn more about the impact of acute alcohol intoxication and heightened arousal on otherwise "normal" neurological functioning, legal scholars will be required to further explore such fundamental questions as "Is there free will?" and "What constitutes *mens rea*?" (Burns and Bechara 2007; Moriarty 2008; Eagleman 2011; Palermo 2012; Merkel 2014).

NOTES

1. This process is similar to Damasio's (1994; Bechara and Damasio 2005) somatic marker hypothesis, which contends that the body's physiological reactions in the face of risk are evaluated by portions of the PFC in order to help determine the value of a response option. Individuals use these somatic markers to help determine the most advantageous decision.
2. Note that some scholars have used the Yerkes–Dodson law as a basic framework in which to explain attention/memory narrowing (Kaufman 1999; see also Gutnik et al. 2006). According to this perspective, if arousal levels are too low, then the scope of one's attention becomes too broad, and the individual cannot sort out relevant versus irrelevant information as it pertains to the decision at hand. However, if arousal levels are too high, then the scope of one's attention becomes too narrow, and information pertinent to the decision may be ignored. Thus, optimal levels of attention are under moderate states of arousal, which suggests that there is an inverted U-shaped relationship between arousal and attentional focus.
3. Nonexperimental studies also suggest that alcohol has a causal impact on crime, especially violent behavior (Felson et al. 2008, 2011; Felson and Staff 2010).

REFERENCES

Abbott, N. J., A. A. K. Patabendige, D. E. M. Dolman, S. R. Yusof, and D. J. Begley. 2010. "Structure and Function of the Blood–Brain Barrier." *Neurobiology of Disease* 37(1): 13–25.

Ariely, D. 2013. *The (Honest) Truth About Dishonesty.* New York: Harper Perennial.

Ariely, D., and G. Loewenstein. 2006. "The Heat of the Moment: The Effect of Sexual Arousal on Sexual Decision Making." *Journal of Behavioral Decision Making* 19(2): 87–98.

Athens, L. 2005. "Violent Encounters, Violent Engagements, and Tiffs." *Journal of Contemporary Ethnography* 34:631–78.

Bechara, A., and A. R. Damasio. 2005. "The Somatic Marker Hypothesis: A Neural Theory of Economic Decision." *Games and Economic Behavior* 52(2): 336–72.

Becker, J. B., C. N. Rudick, and W. J. Jenkins. 2001. "The Role of Dopamine in the Nucleus Accumbens and Striatum During Sexual Behavior in the Female Rat." *Journal of Neuroscience* 21(9): 3236–41.

Bentham, J. 1970. *An Introduction to the Principles of Morals and Legislation.* New York: Oxford University Press. (Originally published 1789.)

Blanchette, I., and A. Richards. 2010. "The Influence of Affect on Higher Level Cognition: A Review of Research on Interpretation, Judgment, Decision Making and Reasoning." In *Cognition and Emotion: Reviews of Current Research and Theories*, edited by J. D. Houwer and D. Hermans, pp. 276–324. New York: Psychology Press.

Bouffard, J. A. 2002. "The Influence of Emotion on Rational Decision Making in Sexual Aggression." *Journal of Criminal Justice* 30(2): 121–34.

Bouffard, J. A. 2014. "The Role of Sexual Arousal and Perceived Consequences in Men's and Women's Decisions to Engage in Sexually Coercive Behaviours." In *Affect and Cognition in Criminal Decision Making*, edited by J. L. van Gelder, K. Elffers, D. Reynald, and D. Nagin, pp. 77–96. Abingdon, UK: Routledge.

Braithwaite, J., and T. Makkai. 1991. "Testing an Expected Utility Model of Corporate Deterrence." *Law and Society Review* 25(1): 7–40.

Braun, S. 1996. *Buzz: The Science and Lore of Alcohol and Caffeine.* New York: Oxford University Press.

Breslin, F. C., M. B. Sobell, H. Cappell, S. Vakili, and C. X. Poulos. 1999. "The Effects of Alcohol, Gender and Sensation Seeking on the Gambling Choices of Social Drinkers." *Psychology of Addictive Behaviors* 13(3): 243–52.

Brochu, S., M. M. Cousineau, M. Gillet, L. G. Cournoyer, K. Pernanen, and L. Motiuk. 2001. "Drugs, Alcohol, and Criminal Behavior: A Profile of Inmates in Canadian Federal Institutions." *Forum on Corrections Research Focusing on Alcohol and Drugs* 13(3): 20–25.

Bufkin, J. L., and V. R. Luttrell. 2005. "Neuroimaging Studies of Aggressive and Violent Behavior: Current Findings and Implications for Criminology and Criminal Justice." *Trauma, Violence and Abuse* 6:176–91.

Burns, K., and A. Bechara. 2007. "Decision Making and Free Will: A Neuroscience Perspective." *Behavioral Sciences and the Law* 25:263–80.

Camerer, C. F., and G. Loewenstein. 2004. "Behavioral Economics: Past, Present, Future." In *Advances in Behavioral Economics*, edited by C. F. Camerer, G. Loewenstein, and M. Rabin, pp. 3–51. Princeton, NJ: Princeton University Press.

Canli, T., Z. Zhao, J. E. Desmond, E. Kang, J. Gross, and J. D. Gabrieli. 1998. "Hemispheric Asymmetry for Emotional Stimuli Detected with fMRI." *Neuroreport* 9(14): 3233–39.

Carmichael, S., and A. R. Piquero. 2004. "Sanctions, Perceived Anger, and Criminal Offending." *Journal of Quantitative Criminology* 20:371–93.

Chaiken, S. 1980. "Heuristic Versus Systematic Information Processing and the Use of Source Versus Message Cues in Persuasion." *Journal of Personality and Social Psychology* 39(5): 752–66.

Cook, P. J. 1980. "Research in Criminal Deterrence: Laying the Groundwork for the Second Decade." In *Crime and Justice: An Annual Review of Research*, vol. 2, edited by N. Morris and M. Tonry, pp. 211–68. Chicago: University of Chicago Press.

Cromwell, P., L. Parker, and S. Mobley. 2006. "The Five Finger Discount: An Analysis of Motivations for Shoplifting." In *In Their Own Words: Criminals on Crime*, edited by P. Cromwell, pp. 113–25. Los Angeles: Roxbury.

Damasio, A. R. 1994. *Descartes' Error: Emotion, Reason, and the Human Brain*. New York: Putnam.

Dasgupta, A. 2011. *The Science of Drinking: How Alcohol Affects Your Body and Mind*. Plymouth, UK: Rowman and Littlefield.

de Haan, W., and J. Vos. 2003. "A Crying Shame: The Over-rationalized Conception of Man in the Rational Choice Perspective." *Theoretical Criminology* 7:29–54.

Dougherty, D. M., J. M. Bjork, R. H. Bennett, and F. G. Moeller. 1999. "The Effects of a Cumulative Alcohol Dosing Procedure on Laboratory Aggression in Women and Men." *Journal of Studies on Alcohol and Drugs* 60(3): 322–29.

Eagleman, D. 2011. *Incognito: The Secret Live of the Brain*. New York: Pantheon.

Euser, A. S., C. S. van Meel, M. Snelleman, and I. H. A. Franken. 2011. "Acute Effects of Alcohol on Feedback Processing and Outcome Evaluation During Risky Decision-Making: An ERP Study." *Psychopharmacology* 271(1): 111–25.

Exum, M. L. 2002. "The Application and Robustness of the Rational Choice Perspective in the Study of Intoxicated and Angry Intentions to Aggress." *Criminology* 40(4): 933–66.

Exum, M. L. 2006. "Alcohol and Aggression: An Integration of Findings from Experimental Studies." *Journal of Criminal Justice* 34(2): 131–45.

Exum, M. L., and A. Zachowicz. 2014. "Sexual Arousal and the Ability to Access Sexually Aggressive Consequences from Memory." In *Affect and Cognition in Criminal Decision Making*, edited by J. L. van Gelder, K. Elffers, D. Reynald, and D. Nagin, pp. 97–118. Abingdon, UK: Routledge.

Felson, R., J. Savolainen, M. Aaltonen, and H. Moustgaard. 2008. "Is the Association Between Alcohol Use and Delinquency Causal or Spurious?" *Criminology* 46:785–808.

Felson, R. B., J. Savolainen, R. Bjarnason, A. Anderson, and I. T. Zohra. 2011. "The Cultural Context of Adolescent Drinking and Violence in 30 European Countries." *Criminology* 49:699–728.

Felson, R. B., and J. Staff. 2010. "The Effects of Alcohol Intoxication on Violent Versus Other Offending." *Criminal Justice and Behavior* 37:1343–60.

Frederick, S., G. Loewenstein, and T. O'Donoghue. 2002. "Time Discounting and Time Preference: A Critical Review." *Journal of Economic Literature* 40(2): 351–401.

Frost, R. O., T. G. Burish, and D. S. Holmes. 1978. "Stress and EEG-alpha." *Psychophysiology* 15(5): 394–97.

Garavan, H., J. C. Pendergrass, T. J. Ross, E. A. Stein, and R. C. Risinger. 2001. "Amygdala Response to Both Positive and Negative Valenced Stimuli." *Neuroreport* 12(12): 2779–83.

George, S., R. D. Rogers, and T. Duka. 2005. "The Acute Effect of Alcohol on Decision Making in Social Drinkers." *Psychopharmacology* 182(1): 160–69.

Giancola, P. R. 2002. "Alcohol-Related Aggression in Men and Women: The Influence of Dispositional Aggressivity." *Journal of Studies on Alcohol and Drugs* 63(6): 696–708.

Giancola, P. R. 2004a. "Difficult Temperament, Acute Alcohol Intoxication, and Aggressive Behavior." *Drug and Alcohol Dependence* 74(2): 135–45.

Giancola, P. R. 2004b. "Executive Functioning and Alcohol-Related Aggression." *Journal of Abnormal Psychology* 113:541–55.

Giancola, P. R., R. A. Josephs, D. J. Parrott, and A. A. Duke. 2010. "Alcohol Myopia Revisited: Clarifying Aggression and Other Acts of Disinhibition Through a Distorted Lens." *Perspectives on Psychological Science* 5(3): 265–78.

Giancola, P. R., C. S. Martin, R. E. Tarter, W. E. Pelham, and H. B. Moss. 1996. "Executive Cognitive Functioning and Aggressive Behavior in Preadolescent Boys at High Risk for Substance Abuse/Dependence." *Journal of Studies on Alcohol* 57(4): 352–59.

Giancola, P. R., and D. J. Parrott. 2008. "Further Evidence for the Validity of the Taylor Aggression Paradigm." *Aggressive Behavior* 34(2): 214–29.

Giancola, P. R., and A. Zeichner. 1994. "Neuropsychological Performance on Tests of Frontal-Lobe Functioning and Aggressive Behavior in Men." *Journal of Abnormal Psychology* 103(4): 832–35.

Green, E., and B. S. Cahill. 2012. "Effects of Neuroimaging Evidence on Mock Juror Decision Making. *Behavioral Sciences and the Law* 30:280–96.

Gustafson, R. 1990. "Wine and Male Physical Aggression." *Journal of Drug Issues* 20(1): 75–86.

Gutnik, L. A., A. F. Hakimzada, N. A. Yoskowitz, and V. L. Patel. 2006. "The Role of Emotion in Decision-Making: A Cognitive Neuroeconomic Approach Towards Understanding Sexual Risk Behavior." *Journal of Biomedical Informatics* 39(6): 720–36.

Hamann, S. B., T. D. Ely, J. M. Hoffman, and C. D. Kilts. 2002. "Ecstasy and Agony: Activation of the Human Amygdala in Positive and Negative Emotion." *Psychological Science* 13(2): 135–41.

Hanoch, Y., and O. Vitouch. 2004. "When Less Is More: Information, Emotional Arousal and the Ecological Reframing of the Yerkes–Dodson Law." *Theory and Psychology* 14(4): 427–52.

Hawkins, K., and K. Trobst. 2000. "Frontal Lobe Dysfunction and Aggression: Conceptual Issues and Research Findings." *Aggression and Violent Behavior* 5(2): 147–57.

Heinz, A. J., A. Beck, A. Meyer-Lindenberg, P. Sterzer, and A. Heinz. 2011. "Cognitive and Neurobiological Mechanisms of Alcohol-Related Aggression." *Neuroscience* 12(7): 400–13.

Hoaken, P. N., J. M. Assaad, and R. O. Pihl. 1998. "Cognitive Functioning and the Inhibition of Alcohol-Induced Aggression." *Journal of Studies on Alcohol* 59:599–607.

Husted, D. S., W. C. Myers, and Y. Lui. 2008. "The Limited Role of Neuroimaging in Determining Criminal Liability: An Overview and Case Report." *Forensic Science International* 179:e9–e15.

Institute of Alcohol Studies. 2013. "UK Alcohol-Related Crime Statistics." http://www.ias.org. uk/Alcohol-knowledge-centre/Crime-and-social-impacts/Factsheets/UK-alcohol-related-crime-statistics.aspx

Johnson, E. J., and A. Tversky. 1983. "Affect, Generalization, and the Perception of Risk." *Journal of Personality and Social Psychology* 45:20–31.

Kable, J. W., and P. W. Glimcher. 2007. "The Neural Correlates of Subjective Value During Intertemporal Choice." *Nature Neuroscience* 10(12): 1625–33.

Kahneman, D. 2003. "Maps of Bounded Rationality: Psychology for Behavioral Economics." *American Economic Review* 93(5): 1449–75.

Kahneman, D. 2011. *Thinking, Fast and Slow.* New York: Farrar, Straus and Giroux.

Katz, J. 1988. *Seductions of Crime: A Chilling Exploration of the Criminal Mind—From Juvenile Delinquency to Cold-Blooded Murder.* New York: Basic Books.

Katz, J. 1999. *How Emotions Work.* Chicago: University of Chicago Press.

Kaufman, B. E. 1999. "Emotional Arousal as a Source of Bounded Rationality." *Journal of Economic Behavior and Organization* 38(2): 135–44.

Kuhns, J. B., M. L. Exum, T. A. Clodfelter, and M. C. Bottia. 2014. "The Prevalence of Alcohol-Involved Homicide Offending: A Meta-Analytic Review." *Homicide Studies* 18(3): 251–70.

Lane, S. D., D. R. Cherek, C. J. Pietras, and O. V. Tcheremissine. 2004. "Alcohol Effects on Human Risk Taking." *Psychopharmacology* 172(1): 68–77.

Lanza-Kaduce, L., D. M. Bishop, and L. Winner. 1997. "Risk/Benefit Calculations, Moral Evaluations, and Alcohol Use: Exploring the Alcohol–Crime Connection." *Crime and Delinquency* 43:222–39.

Lau, M. A., R. O. Pihl, and J. B. Peterson. 1995. "Provocation, Acute Alcohol Intoxication, Cognitive Performance, and Aggression." *Journal of Abnormal Psychology* 104(1): 150–55.

Levine, L. J., and R. S. Edelstein. 2010. "Emotion and Memory Narrowing: A Review and Goal-Relevance Approach." In *Cognition and Emotion: Reviews of Current Research and Theories*, edited by J. D. Houwer and D. Hermans, pp. 168–210. New York: Psychology Press.

Loewenstein, G. F. 1996. "Out of Control: Visceral Influences on Behavior." *Organizational and Human Decision Making Processes* 65(3): 272–92.

Loewenstein, G. F., D. S. Nagin, and R. Paternoster. 1997. "The Effect of Sexual Arousal on Expectations of Sexual Forcefulness." *Journal of Research in Crime and Delinquency* 34(4): 443–73.

Loewenstein, G. F., E. U. Weber, C. K. Hsee, and N. Welch. 2001. "Risk as Feelings." *Psychological Bulletin* 127(2): 267–86.

Mazar, N., O. Amir, and D. Ariely. 2008. "The Dishonesty of Honest People: A Theory of Self-Concept Maintenance." *Journal of Marketing Research* 45:633–44.

McCabe, D. L., and L. K. Trevino. 1993. "Academic Dishonesty: Honor Codes and Other Contextual Influences." *Journal of Higher Education* 64:520–38.

McCabe, D. L., L. K. Trevino, and K. D. Butterfield. 2002. "Honor Codes and Other Contextual Influences on Academic Integrity: A Replication and Extension to Modified Honor Code Settings." *Research in Higher Education* 43(3): 357–78.

Merkel, R. 2014. "Neuroimaging and Criminal Law." In *Handbook of Neuroethics*, edited by J. Clausen and N. Levy, pp. 1335–62. Dordrecht, Netherlands: Springer.

Mohr, P. N. C., G. Biele, and H. R. Heekeren. 2010. "Neural Processing of Risk." *Journal of Neuroscience* 30(19): 6613–19.

Moriarty, J. C. 2008. "Flickering Admissibility: Neuroimaging Evidence in the US Courts." *Behavioral Sciences and the Law* 26:29–49.

Murdock, T. B., and E. M. Anderman. 2006. "Motivational Perspectives on Student Cheating: Toward an Integrated Model of Academic Dishonesty." *Educational Psychologist* 41(3): 129–45.

Murray, B. D., and E. A. Kensinger. 2012. "The Effects of Emotion and Encoding Strategy on Associative Memory." *Memory and Cognition* 40(7): 1056–69.

Nagin, D. S. 2007. "Moving Choice to the Center State in Criminological Research and Theory: The American Society of Criminology 2006 Sutherland Address." *Criminology* 45:259–72.

Nagin, D. S., and G. Pogarsky. 2001. "Integrating Celerity, Impulsivity, and Extralegal Sanction Threats into a Model of General Deterrence: Theory and Evidence." *Criminology* 39(4): 865–92.

Nagin, D. S., and G. Pogarsky. 2004. "Time and Punishment: Delayed Consequences and Criminal Behavior." *Journal of Quantitative Criminology* 20(4): 295–317.

Palermo, G. B. 2012. "Does Neuroimaging Have a Role in Assessing Criminal Culpability?" *International Journal of Offender Therapy and Comparative Criminology* 56:171–73.

Panskepp, J. 1998. *Affective Neuroscience: The Foundations of Human and Animal Emotions.* New York: Oxford University Press.

Parrott, A., A. Morinan, M. Moss, and A. Scholey. 2004. *Understanding Drugs and Behavior.* West Sussex, UK: Wiley.

Paschall, M., and D. Fishbein. 2002. "Executive Functioning and Aggression: A Public Health Perspective." *Aggression and Violent Behavior* 7(7): 215–35.

Paternoster, R., and S. Simpson. 1996. "Sanction Threats and Appeals to Morality: Testing a Rational Choice Model of Corporate Crime." *Law and Society Review* 30(3): 549–84.

Peterson, J. B., J. Rothfleisch, P. D. Zelazo, and R. O. Pihl. 1990. "Acute Alcohol Intoxication and Cognitive Functioning." *Journal of Studies on Alcohol* 51(2): 114–22.

Petty, R. E., and J. T. Cacioppo. 1986. *Communication and Persuasion: Central and Peripheral Routes to Attitude Change*. New York: Springer.

Raine, A., J. R. Meloy, S. Bihrle, J. Stoddard, L. Lacasse, and M. S. Buchsbaum. 1998. "Reduced Prefrontal and Increased Subcortical Brain Functioning Assessed Using Positron Emission Tomography in Predatory and Affective Murders." *Behavioral Sciences and the Law* 16:319–32.

Rand, M. R., W. J. Sabol, M. Sinclair, and H. N. Snyder. 2010. "Alcohol and Crime: Data from 2002 to 2008." Washington, DC: Bureau of Justice Statistics. http://www.bjs.gov/index.cfm?ty=pbdetail&iid=2313

Reyna, V. F., and F. Farley. 2006. "Risk and Rationality in Adolescent Decision Making: Implications for Theory, Practice, and Public Policy." *Psychological Science in the Public Interest* 7(1): 1–44.

Reyna, V. F., and V. Zayas. 2014. *The Neuroscience of Risky Decision Making*. Washington, DC: American Psychological Association.

Roberts, A. C., T. W. Robbins, and L. Weiskrantz. 1998. *The Prefrontal Cortex: Executive and Cognitive Functions*. New York: Oxford University Press.

Sapolsky, R. M. 2004. "The Frontal Cortex and the Criminal Justice System." *Philosophical Transactions of the Royal Society B: Biological Sciences* 359(1451): 1787–96.

Savage, L. J. 1954. *The Foundations of Statistics*. New York: Wiley.

Shiffrin, R. M., and W. Schneider. 1977. "Controlled and Automatic Human Information Processing II: Perceptual Learning, Automatic Attending, and a General Theory." *Psychological Review* 84(2): 127–90.

Slovic, P., M. L. Finucane, E. Peters, and D. G. MacGregor. 2007. "The Affect Heuristic." *European Journal of Operational Research* 177:1333–52.

Spear, L. P. 2010. *The Behavioral Neuroscience of Adolescence*. New York: Norton.

Steele, C. M., and R. A. Josephs. 1990. "Alcohol Myopia: Its Prized and Dangerous Effects." *American Psychologist* 45(8): 921–33.

Toates, F. 2006. *Biological Psychology*, 2nd ed. Harlow, UK: Pearson.

Topalli, V., and R. T. Wright. 2006. "Dubs and Dees, Beats and Rims: Carjackers and Urban Violence." In *In Their Own Words: Criminals on Crime*, edited by P. Cromwell, pp. 129–41. Los Angeles: Roxbury.

Topalli, V., and R. T. Wright. 2014. "Affect and the Dynamic Foreground of Predatory Street Crime." In *Affect and Cognition in Criminal Decision Making*, edited by J. L. van Gelder, K. Elffers, D. Reynald, and D. Nagin, pp. 42–57. Abingdon, UK: Routledge.

Treiber, K. 2014. "A Neuropsychological Test of Criminal Decision Making: Regional Prefrontal Influences in a Dual Process Model." In *Affect and Cognition in Criminal Decision Making*, edited by J. L. van Gelder, K. Elffers, D. Reynald, and D. Nagin, pp. 193–220. Abingdon, UK: Routledge.

van Gelder, J. L. 2013. "Beyond Rational Choice: The Hot/Cool Perspective of Criminal Decision Making. *Psychology, Crime and Law* 19(9): 745–63.

van Gelder, J. L., and R. E. de Vries. 2012. "Traits and States: Integrating Personality and Affect into a Model of Criminal Decision Making." *Criminology* 50(3): 637–71.

van Gelder, J. L., and R. E. de Vries. 2014. "Rational Misbehavior? Evaluating an Integrated Dual Process Model of Criminal Decision Making." *Journal of Quantitative Criminology* 30(1): 1–27.

van Winden, F., and E. Ash. 2012. "On the Behavioral Economics of Crime." *Review of Law and Economics* 8:181–213.

Vartanian, O., and D. R. Mandel. 2012. "Neural Bases of Judgment and Decision Making." In *Judgment and Decision Making as a Skill: Learning, Development and Evolution*, edited by

M. K. Dhami, A. Schlottmann, and M. R. Waldmann, pp. 29–52. Cambridge: Cambridge University Press.

von Neumann, J., and O. Morgenstern. 1947. *Theory of Games and Economic Behavior*, 2nd ed. Princeton, NJ: Princeton University Press.

Wilson, J. Q., and R. Herrnstein. 1985. *Crime and Human Nature: The Definitive Study of the Causes of Crime*. New York: Simon and Schuster.

Wood, S. M. W., and A. Bechara. 2014. "The Neuroscience of Dual (and Triple) Systems in Decision Making." In *The Neuroscience of Risky Decision Making*, edited by V. F. Reyna and V. Zayas, pp. 11–42. Washington, DC: American Psychological Association.

Wright, R. T., and S. H. Decker. 1994. *Burglars on the Job: Streetlife and Residential Burglary*. Boston: Northeastern University Press.

Yang, Y., and A. Raine. 2009. "Prefrontal Structural and Functional Brain Imaging Findings in Antisocial, Violent, and Psychopathic Individuals: A Meta-Analysis." *Psychiatry Research: Neuroimaging* 172:81–88.

Yerkes, R. M., and J. D. Dodson. 1908. "The Relation of Strength of Stimulus to Rapidity of Habit Formation." *Journal of Comparative Neurology and Psychology* 18(5): 459–82.

Yu, J., and W. R. Williford. 1995. "Drunk-Driving Recidivism: Predicting Factors from Arrest Context and Case Disposition." *Journal of Studies on Alcohol* 56(1): 60–66.

Zayas, V., W. Mischel, and G. Pandey. 2014. "Mind and Brain in Delay of Gratification." In *The Neuroscience of Risky Decision Making*, edited by V. F. Reyna and V. Zayas, pp. 145–76. Washington, DC: American Psychological Association.

Zimring, F. E., and G. J. Hawkins. 1973. *Deterrence: The Legal Threat in Crime Control*. Chicago: University of Chicago Press.

CHAPTER 22

....

EMOTIONS IN OFFENDER
DECISION MAKING

....

JEAN-LOUIS VAN GELDER

ALTHOUGH it has been contended that emotions have been incorporated into all the major theoretical perspectives in criminology (Benson and Livelsberger 2012), it is probably more accurate to argue that with some notable exceptions (Braithwaite 1989; Agnew 1992), emotional processes have failed to occupy a central position in criminological thought (Bouffard, Exum, and Paternoster 2000; Giordano, Schroeder, and Cernkovich 2007; Nagin 2007). As De Haan and Loader (2002) observe, many established modes of criminological thought pay little attention to or ignore entirely the impact of emotions on their subject matter.

Importantly, research and theorizing that has given a more prominent role to emotions has largely remained confined to narrative and interpretative studies or has treated them as enduring individual dispositions (Lofland 1969; Katz 1988, 1991; Braithwaite 1989; Agnew 1992; Shover 1996; Lopez and Emmer 2000; Athens 2005; Wikström 2006; Giordano et al. 2007). Very little attention has been given to the actual decision-making processes of offenders. This inattention to the choice process has diverted attention from issues that are fundamental to understanding crime as a phenomenon and also created a fundamental disconnect with criminal law and, therefore, important questions of public policy (Nagin 2007, p. 261).

As will be argued in more detail later, crime research examining emotions that did take a decision-making approach (Grasmick and Bursik 1990; Grasmick, Bursik, and Arneklev 1993; Nagin and Paternoster 1993; Piquero and Tibbetts 1996) has tended to examine emotions as predictions of *future* feeling states rather than of emotions actually experienced at the time of decision. Hence, these studies still modeled the decision process as a largely cognitive enterprise and did not fully acknowledge the role of emotions on offender decision making.

To begin, the next section provides some general observations and definitions regarding emotions drawing from criminology's sister disciplines in the social sciences. Then, criminological decision-making research that has addressed the role of emotions is discussed.

I. What Are Emotions?

Whereas the question as to what exactly are emotions is still the subject of lively debate among theorists (Keltner and Lerner 2010), many of their properties attract little disagreement among experts. Emotions are one type or manifestation of what is referred as "affect," which is a general term denoting the subjective experience of feelings, such as emotions, but also refers to moods and other visceral drive states, such as pain, drug craving, and sexual arousal (Loewenstein 1996). Often, these different feeling states are indiscriminately referred to as emotions in the criminological literature, but this is inaccurate. Moods and emotions are closely related but nonetheless distinct feeling states (Beedie, Terry and Lane 2005). Moods are low-intensity, diffuse (i.e., unfocused), and relatively enduring affective states without a clear antecedent cause and therefore have little cognitive content (e.g., feeling good or feeling bad) (Forgas 1995, p. 41). Emotions, on the other hand, are more intense than moods, more focused, short-lived, and usually do have a definite cause (e.g., being angry at, or fearful of, something) (Forgas 1995, p. 41).[1] Most definitions of emotion stress that they orient people to responding to events in their environment (Keltner and Lerner 2010). Frijda and Mesquita (1994, p. 51), for example, argue that emotions are principally modes of relating to the environment—that is, states of readiness for engaging or not engaging in interaction with that environment.

In the criminological literature, what is sometimes erroneously referred to as emotions in fact refers to a more enduring propensity to experience certain types of feelings, such as the tendency to experience negative feelings including anxiety and anger. This is the case, for example, in general strain theory (Agnew 1992), according to which the occurrence of negative life events and circumstances and the loss of positive stimuli are assumed to generate negative feelings, such as anger and frustration, that create a pressure for "corrective action," which can take the form of criminal conduct (Agnew 1992, 2001). As Nagin (2007, p. 261) observes, the idea of emotions as a social force or external agent that drives the individual toward or away from crime embedded in this type of theory lacks a sense of people making choices—what is sometimes referred to human agency. This chapter focuses on emotions as momentary and short-lived feelings with a clear antecedent cause, and their influence on the actual choice process, and not on individual dispositions or enduring feeling states. The next section discusses a class of emotions that have been dealt with in criminological research, and it is argued that these emotions in particular have properties that make them well suited for incorporation in rational choice frameworks. Later, it is argued that this does not apply to other types of emotions for which these frameworks are ill-equipped.

A. Shame and Guilt as Predictions of Future Feelings

One class of emotions that has attracted the attention of criminal decision making researchers is formed by those emotions that share a moral character, such as shame and guilt.[2] These emotions have historically also been pivotal in concepts of crime, justice, and culpability (Karstedt 2011). Moral emotions "function as an emotional moral barometer by providing immediate and salient feedback on our social and moral acceptability. That is, when we sin, transgress, or err, aversive feelings of shame, guilt, or embarrassment are likely to ensue" (Tangney, Stuewig, and Mashek 2007, p. 347). Shame and guilt are also referred to as self-conscious emotions in the sense that they involve self-reflection and evaluation (Lewis 2008).

The fact that guilt and shame have a negative hedonic value or, in psychological parlance, are negatively valenced means that people are motivated to avoid experiencing them and therefore have an intrinsic incentive to abide by social norms and to do the right thing while avoiding doing wrong (van Winden and Ash 2012). When values or norms are violated, they produce a sense of psychological discomfort, and the more serious the perceived violation, the more painful is this emotional experience (Tangney, Mashek, and Stuewig 2007). For example, whereas a speeding ticket might result in mild embarrassment, a drunk-driving arrest could activate intensely uncomfortable feelings of shame (van Winden and Ash 2012, p. 198).

In criminological decision-making research, self-conscious and moral emotions such as shame and guilt have tended to be modeled as anticipated costs to be taken into account by the decision maker (Grasmick and Bursik 1990; Grasmick, Bursik, and Kinsey 1991; Bachman, Paternoster, and Ward, 1992; Grasmick, Bursik, and Arneklev 1993; Nagin and Paternoster 1993; Paternoster and Simpson 1993, 1996; Piquero and Tibbetts 1996; Bouffard, Exum, and Paternoster 2000; Kamerdze, Loughran, and Paternoster 2013; Tibbetts 2013). These studies have generally attempted to fit emotions within rational choice and deterrence frameworks. For example, Grasmick et al. (1993, pp. 43–44) argue that the threat of shame and embarrassment function similarly to the threat of legal sanctions by reducing the expected utility of a contemplated behavior and by varying along the dimensions of subjective certainty and subjective severity. The desire to avoid feeling the pangs of their conscience is assumed to steer people away from committing crime. The difference with formal sanctions is that instead of the state, is that in the case of moral emotions the source of the threat of punishment is the self (Grasmick and Bursik 1990).

In these studies, shame and guilt are not experienced as feelings at the moment of decision making but are in fact cognitions about future feeling states; they are *predictions* of aversive feeling states that may emerge after a decision has been made (Frijda 1988; Loewenstein et al. 2001; Bouffard 2002; Loewenstein and Lerner 2003). Loewenstein et al. (2001) and Loewenstein and Lerner (2003) refer to these types of emotions as *anticipated emotions*, to be distinguished from emotions that are actually experienced at the time of decision, such as the fear of negative consequences following criminal conduct or the anger felt toward a wrongdoer. From a theoretical perspective, this distinction is relevant because even though anticipated emotions can be and have been incorporated in rational choice-based models, the decision process remains modeled as the implicitly cognitive task of predicting future emotions and weighing them in terms of their expected utility (Loewenstein et al. 2001).

B. The Immediate Emotions Fear and Anger

Like shame and guilt, fear and anger have a negative hedonic value and are negatively valenced. Different from shame and guilt, however, anger and fear are *immediate* rather than anticipated in nature. That is, in the decision-making context, fear and anger constitute immediate visceral reactions to an event, situation, individual, or prospect of sanction rather than feelings expected to be experienced sometime in the future (Loewenstein et al. 2001; Loewenstein and Lerner 2003). Specifically, immediate emotions "reflect the combined effects of emotions that arise from contemplating the consequences of the decision itself—what we call *anticipatory influences*—as well as emotions that arise from factors unrelated to the decision, which we call *incidental influences*" (Loewenstein and Lerner 2003, p. 620). For example, fear can be experienced in response to anticipated decision outcomes, such as the threat of punishment, but also toward an attacker.

The difference between anticipated affect and immediate affect is not only pivotal for our understanding of criminal decision making but also exposes an important limitation of the dominant models of criminal decision making, which are based on the idea of a reasoning or rational decision maker who weighs costs against benefits to arrive at a decision. Because the influence of emotions may go unnoticed to the decision maker, their influence on the criminal decision process is not necessarily consciously mediated. This makes them impossible to model as costs in ways similar to anticipated shame, regret, or guilt (van Gelder 2013). In other words, as far as the dominant models of criminal choice have addressed the role of emotions in crime causation, they have done so to a limited extent only. The next section further elaborates on differences between properties of the commonly used moral emotions and emotions such as fear and anger drawing from psychological appraisal perspectives on emotion.

II. Making Sense of Emotions in the Context of Criminal Decision Making: Drawing from Appraisal Theory

According to appraisal theorists, emotions are responses to the environment geared to help individuals respond to the challenges facing them (Smith and Ellsworth 1985; Frijda 1986, 1988; Ellsworth and Scherer 2003). The experience of an emotion is intimately related to the subjective appraisal of the circumstances in which it is experienced

(Smith and Ellsworth 1985). Emotions are furthermore adaptive in the sense that they set in motion psychological and physiological processes to ready the body for action, such as dealing with threat (Tooby and Cosmides 2008).

Emotion appraisals, at the most general level, involve evaluative judgments of whether an event is good or bad and whether people's current actions and environment correspond to their personal goals and expectations (Keltner and Lerner 2010). Dimensional approaches to appraisal argue that combinations of a limited set of core dimensions of appraisal—for example, the degree to which an individual is certain about what is going to happen, the extent to which an individual has control over the environment, and the degree to which others, the individual, or the situation are responsible for the events—give rise to specific emotions (Smith and Ellsworth 1985). For example, anger and guilt can be meaningfully distinguished with reference to these dimensions. In the face of a negative event, blaming others produces anger, whereas blaming oneself produces guilt (Keltner and Lerner 2010). Conversely, if the offense or frustration is viewed as caused by someone powerful who may commit further offenses in the future, then fear may be the emotional response (Frijda 1988, p. 350).

An appraisal generates an action tendency, which is a state of readiness to execute a given kind of action (Frijda 1986, p. 70). As mentioned previously, a perceived offense or frustration, for example, for which someone else is viewed as the cause and that could have been avoided, can trigger anger. The intensity of the anger inter alia will depend on the intentionality of the frustration, the proximity of the stimulus, and the stakes involved (van Winden and Ash 2012, p. 195).

According to appraisal theorists, the links between specific emotions and specific appraisals and choice propensities are relatively systematic (Frijda 1988; Loewenstein and Lerner 2003). In support of this assumption, Lerner and Keltner (2001) found that fearful and angry individuals (both dispositional and experimentally induced) differed in their risk assessments and risky choice behavior. Fearful individuals made more pessimistic risk assessments and risk-averse choices in comparison to angry individuals. This finding can be explained by the fact that anger is associated with appraisals of certainty and control, whereas fear is associated with appraisals of uncertainty and a lack of control (see also Smith and Ellsworth 1985; Lerner and Keltner 2000).

Appraisal frameworks, and their supportive empirical evidence, if taken seriously, have important repercussions for theorizing about the influence of emotions on criminal decision making because they show that rather than viewing them as irregular disruptions of sound decision making, emotions may serve adaptive functions and exert an influence on behavior that is systematic and therefore, to a certain extent, predictable. Note that the idea of emotions exerting a systematic influence on behavior runs counter to several fundamental assumptions underlying rational choice theory, which assumes that people are capable of making adequate probability and utility calculations, and while acknowledging that people can make mistakes in their calculations, these are assumed to be unsystematic (Gilovich and Griffin 2002). Next, empirical research on the effects of anger and fear on criminal decision making are discussed separately.

A. Anger

Anger is associated with a sense that the self or someone one cares about is offended or injured or that interests or goals are threatened or frustrated (Lazarus 1991; Lerner and Tiedens 2006). As mentioned previously, in terms of appraisal processes, anger is characterized by a sense of certainty over what has happened and a notion of control over the situation (Smith and Ellsworth 1985). In response to the anger-eliciting stimulus, the angry decision maker may be motivated to "set things straight" and to punish or retaliate in some way against the perceived cause(s) of his or her anger.

At high levels of intensity, anger may "take over" people's thoughts and guide their actions to the point of leading them to act directly contrary to their self-interest (Loewenstein 1996). Therefore, despite its adaptive function, if not regulated and properly expressed, anger runs the risk of incurring long-term costs (Lemerise and Dodge 2008). Concerning the interrelation between emotion and self-control, Baumeister and Heatherton (1996) note that an

> emotion increases the salience of whatever produces the emotion and so attention will tend to focus on whatever has prompted the emotion. Most commonly, something in the immediate situation is the cause and so emotion tends to have the effect of concentrating in the here and now, thereby thwarting transcendence and making self-regulation more difficult. (p. 5)

Loewenstein and Lerner (2003) add that

> the strength of immediate emotions is that they provide such amorphous, but often important, inputs into decision making. The pitfall of immediate emotions is that they often crowd out considerations of expected emotions altogether and cause people to make decisions that ignore or underweight important future consequences. Both types of emotions, therefore, are essential to decision making, but the wrong mix in the wrong situation can be destructive. (p. 621)

At lower levels of intensity, people seem able to overcome the influence of immediate emotions when they deem those emotions to be irrelevant to a decision at hand, but at higher levels of intensity, emotions can progressively assume control of behavior.

Furthermore, intense anger may "spill over" and be directed at other things besides the anger-eliciting stimulus. Subsequent decisions that are unrelated to the source of one's anger may still influence attributions of blame, lead to the perception of ambiguous behavior as hostile, and to discounting the role of uncontrollable factors (Loewenstein and Lerner, 2003). Incidental moods and emotions can therefore influence normatively unrelated judgments and decisions. Anger as a consequence of a conflict at work, for example, may facilitate road rage later on the way home.

Several criminological studies have examined the role of anger in a decision-making context (Broidy 2001; Capowich, Marerolle, and Piquero 2001; Exum 2002; Mazerolle,

Piquero, and Capowich 2003; Carmichael and Piquero 2004; Shalvi, van Gelder, and van der Schalk 2013; van Gelder, Reynald, and Elffers 2013). In one study, Exum (2002) experimentally examined the effect of anger (provoked by a false accusation by the experimenter) and alcohol intoxication on violent decision making using a "bar fight" scenario. It was found that participants who had been assigned to consume alcohol reported higher probability scores for other male-referent aggression in the anger-provoking condition compared to nonprovoked controls, although not for themselves. Furthermore, there was no independent effect of anger (or alcohol) on intentions to aggress. Perceived costs and benefits of violent decision making also remained unaffected under different levels of anger (Exum 2002).

Carmichael and Piquero (2004), also using a bar fight scenario and linking perceived anger (as opposed to actually induced anger such as in the study by Exum [2002]) to rational considerations, such as perceived formal and informal sanctions, did find a direct effect of perceived anger on intentions to aggress. In addition, they found that perceived anger was related to perceived thrill (of engaging in an assault) but not to either formal or informal sanctions. Finally, they found that the effect of informal and formal sanctions varied under different levels of perceived anger. Individuals perceiving little anger were more likely to be deterred than those perceiving high anger.

Schweitzer and Gibson (2008) and Shalvi et al. (2013) found that when people think that they are treated unfairly, they become angry at the person responsible for it and feel justified taking revenge on him or her. In the study by Shalvi et al., it was found that when people believe they are treated unfairly, they experience more anger and are also more prone to dishonestly disadvantage the person who evoked their anger in comparison to non-angered individuals. In their experiment, each participant wrote a short essay and subsequently evaluated an essay written by a student from another university (in reality, a computer) who simultaneously evaluated the participant's essay. In the experimental condition, the evaluation by the other student was overly harsh and critical. After the experiment, the (real) subjects engaged in a simple task that allowed them to anonymously determine their own as well as the other's monetary outcomes allegedly as part of the experiment. It was found that anger led to dishonestly disadvantaging the other (Shalvi et al. 2013).

Van Gelder, Reynald, and Elffers (2013) examined both moral emotions and anger in two experimental studies addressing the question of whether and to what extent feelings of anger influence the impact of moral emotions on decisions to offend. In the first study, anger operationalized as a consequence of being treated unfairly was shown to make people more prone to dishonestly disadvantage those who had treated them unfairly. Although moral emotions were negatively related to intentions to offend, this effect was muted and lost its deterrent potential under conditions of anger. In addition, the results of the second study revealed that *immediate* shame (i.e., experimentally induced shame), which was generated by means of a writing task in which subjects were asked to write about an event or situation that had led them to experience intense feelings of shame and that was therefore normatively unrelated to the situation and the decision outcomes, was also negatively associated with criminal choice. Therefore, immediate shame that is felt at the time of decision, and that is normatively unrelated to the decision at hand, was shown to influence criminal decisions negatively.

B. Fear

Karstedt (2002) notes that both popular wisdom and criminological theory have "established fear of sanctions as a cornerstone and powerful mechanism of the criminal justice system, the thing that makes it work" (p. 301). Indeed, fear was the foundational premise of the original deterrence model proposed by utilitarian philosophers Beccaria and Bentham. For example, in *Essay on Crimes and Punishments*, Beccaria (1764/1819) writes that "the laws are obeyed through fear of punishment" (p. 122). In a similar vein, Bentham (1830) writes, "It is the fear of punishment, in so far as it is known, which prevents the commission of crime" (p. 516). Over time, however, the idea of deterrence having an emotional basis was somewhat lost. The following passage from Loewenstein (2000) is worth quoting in extenso in this context:

> When Jeremy Bentham ... first proposed the construct of utility, emotions figured prominently in his theory. Because Bentham viewed utility as the net sum of positive over negative emotions, he devoted a substantial part of his treatise on utility to a discussion of the determinants and nature of emotions. When neoclassical economists later constructed their new approach to economics upon the foundation of utility, however, they rapidly became disillusioned with utility's psychological underpinnings and sought to expunge the utility construct of its emotional content. This process culminated in the development of ordinal utility and the theory of revealed preference which construed utility as an index of preference rather than of happiness. (p. 426)

In criminology, the essence of the deterrence model laid out by Beccaria and Bentham remained largely intact until economist Becker (1968) in his seminal article integrated utility ideas into the criminal decision-making process (Piquero et al. 2011, p. 337). According to Becker, the decision to offend is based on the same principles of cost–benefit analysis people use when selecting legal behaviors. In other words, the choice for crime is a purely rational one according to this view.

Becker's ideas resonated with crime researchers, and in the mid-1980s criminologists began to understand deterrence theory as a theory about the *perception* of sanction threats (Paternoster 2010). That is, most decision-making studies in criminology have operationalized deterrence as a function of the perceived probability of sanction and the perceived severity of sanction, possibly complemented with the perceived celerity of that sanction's imposition (Zimring and Hawkins 1973; Klepper and Nagin 1989; Bachman et al. 1992; Nagin and Paternoster 1993, 1994; Paternoster and Simpson 1996; Nagin and Pogarsky 2001).

Although the role of fear of sanction may be implicitly present in empirical studies on perceptual deterrence, little systematic research has attempted to directly measure it.[3] Most research essentially equates fear of punishment with perceived risk of sanction. However, as is argued in detail in chapter·9 of this volume, perceptions of sanction severity and probability incur in part different mental processes than does fear of punishment, and cognitions of sanction severity and probability are different from people's emotional reaction toward sanctions (van Gelder and de Vries 2012, 2014).

In support of the idea that fear of sanction as an *emotional experience* is different from the perceived risk of sanction as a *cognitive process*, van Gelder and de Vries (2012) examined both the negative feelings of fear, worry, and anxiety and the perceived risk of sanction, operationalized in line with deterrence theory as the product of the perceived probability of sanction and its perceived severity, as predictors of criminal choice alongside personality traits using a scenario design. They found that both negative affect and perceived risk of sanction predicted criminal choice, with the former being a stronger predictor than the latter. The difference between the emotional response to sanction (i.e., fear of punishment) and the cognitive response to it (i.e., perceived risk of sanction) was further demonstrated in a subsequent article (van Gelder and de Vries 2014) in which the authors used a priming task to show that having participants rely on their thinking strengthened the relation between perceived risk and criminal choice, whereas having them rely on their feelings strengthened the relation between negative affect and criminal choice. In other words, fear of crime and perceived sanction appear to belong to different mental modes of information processing—a "cool" cognitive mode versus a "hot" affective mode.[4]

III. CONCLUSION

This chapter provided an overview of research and theorizing on the role of emotions on offender decision making. It was argued that the treatment of emotions in the criminological literature on offender decision making has been limited, and research that has addressed emotions has tended to focus on a specific type of emotion (i.e., anticipated moral emotions) rather than emotions actually experienced at the time of decision.

The relative neglect of emotions in crime research has meant that dominant models of criminal decision making tend to draw from the rational choice paradigm and consider emotions to be largely irrelevant to the decision process or as unsystemic influences subverting sound decision making only. This is somewhat ironic given the fact that the architects of the rational choice paradigm in criminology argued that their perspective was based on psychological research: "[A] considerable body of recent psychological research on information processing and decision making has passed largely unnoticed by criminologists" (Clarke and Cornish 1985, p. 158; see also Cornish and Clarke 1986). Yet this work has received only sparse updating since. Consequently, insights from approximately three decades of research in the very same tradition that forms its basis have gone relatively unnoticed in criminal decision-making research (Van Gelder et al. 2013). This research has shown that emotions, and also other feeling states such as moods and visceral factors, play a fundamental role in human decision processes, alongside rational and cognitive considerations that commonly feature in theories of criminal decision making (van Gelder et al. 2013). In these three decades, research in all fields of psychology has led to a robust science of emotion that appears to represent a paradigm shift in thinking about human nature (Keltner and Lerner 2010, p. 317). This science may also prove vital to our understanding of crime. It is hoped that crime researchers will see the potential of this still largely open field in their discipline.

NOTES

1. For a more extensive discussion of the differences between moods, emotions, and visceral drive states such as sexual arousal and drug craving, see van Gelder et al. (2013) and van Gelder (2013).
2. A more extensive treatment of moral emotions is provided by in chapter 12 of this volume.
3. For an overview of work on perceptual deterrence, see chapter 7 in this volume.
4. For a discussion of dual process, see chapter 9 of this volume.

REFERENCES

Agnew, R. 1992. "Foundation for a General Strain Theory of Crime and Delinquency." *Criminology* 30:47–88.

Agnew, R. 2001. "Building on the Foundation of General Strain Theory: Specifying the Types of Strain Most Likely to Lead to Crime and Delinquency." *Journal of Research in Crime and Delinquency* 38:319–61.

Athens, L. 2005. "Violent Encounters, Violent Engagements, and Tiffs." *Journal of Contemporary Ethnography* 34:631–78.

Bachman, R., R. Paternoster, and S. Ward. 1992. "The Rationality of Sexual Offending: Testing a Deterrence/Rational Choice Conception of Sexual Assault." *Law and Society Review* 26: 343–72.

Baumeister, R. F., and T. F. Heatherton. 1996. "Self-Regulation Failure: An Overview." *Psychological inquiry* 7:1–15.

Beccaria, C. 1819. *Essay on Crimes and Punishments*. Philadelphia: Nicklin. (Originally published 1764.)

Becker, G. S. 1968. "Crime and Punishment: An Economic Approach." *Journal of Political Economy* 76:169–217.

Beedie, C., P. Terry, and A. Lane. 2005. "Distinctions Between Emotion and Mood." *Cognition and Emotion* 19: 847–78.

Benson, M. L., and T. Livelsberger. 2012. "Emotions, Choice and Crime." In *The Oxford Handbook of Criminological Theory*, edited by F. T. Cullen and P. Wilcox, pp. 494–512. Oxford: Oxford University Press.

Bentham, J. 1830. *The Rationale of Punishment*. London: Heward.

Bouffard, J. A. 2002. "The Influence of Emotion on Rational Decision Making in Sexual Aggression." *Journal of Criminal Justice* 30:121–34.

Bouffard, J. A., M. L. Exum, R. and Paternoster. 2000. "Whither the Beast? The Role of Emotions in a Rational Choice Theory of Crime." In *Of Crime and Criminality: The Use of Theory in Everyday Life*, edited by S. S. Simpson, pp. 159–78. Thousand Oaks, CA: Pine Forge Press.

Braithwaite, J. 1989. *Crime, Shame, and Reintegration*. Cambridge: Cambridge University Press.

Broidy, L. M. 2001. "A Test of General Strain Theory." *Criminology* 39: 9–36.

Cornish, D. B., and R. V. Clarke. 1986. *The Reasoning Criminal: Rational Choice Perspectives on Offending*. New York: Springer-Verlag.

Exum, M. 2002. "The Application and Robustness of the Rational Choice Perspective in the Study of Intoxicated and Angry Intentions to Aggress." *Criminology* 40:933–66.

Frijda, H. H. 1986. *The Emotions*. London: Cambridge University Press.

Frijda, N. H. 1988. "The Laws of Emotion." *American Psychologist* 43:349–58.

Frijda, N. H., and B. Mesquita. 1994. "The Social Roles and Functions of Emotions." In *Emotion and Culture: Empirical Studies of Mutual Influence*, edited by S. Kitayama and H. Markus, pp. 51–88. Washington, DC: American Psychological Association.

Giordano, P. C., R. D. Schroeder, and S. A. Cernkovich. 2007. "Emotions and Crime over the Life Course: A Neo-Meadian Perspective on Criminal Continuity and Change." *American Journal of Sociology* 112:1603–61.

Grasmick, H., and R. Bursik. 1990. "Conscience, Significant Others, and Rational Choice: Extending the Deterrence Model." *Law and Society Review* 24:837–61.

Grasmick, H., R. Bursik, and B. Arneklev. 1993. "Reduction in Drunk Driving as a Response to Increased Threats of Shame, Embarrassment, and Legal Sanctions." *Criminology* 31:41–67.

Grasmick, H., R. Bursik, and K. Kinsey. 1991. "Shame and Embarrassment as Deterrents to Noncompliance with the Law in the Case of an Antilittering Campaign." *Environment and Behavior* 23:233–51.

Haidt, J. 2003. "The Moral Emotions." In *Handbook of Affective Sciences*, edited by R. J. Davidson, K. R. Scherer, and H. H. Goldsmith, pp. 852–70. Oxford: Oxford University Press.

Kamerdze, A. S., T. Loughran, and R. Paternoster. 2013. "'I Would Have Been Sorry': Anticipated Regret and the Role of Expected Emotions in the Decision to Offend." In *Affect and Cognition in Criminal Decision Making*, edited by J. L. van Gelder, H. Elffers, D. Reynald, and D. S. Nagin, pp. 140–60. Abingdon, UK: Routledge.

Karstedt, S. 2002. "Emotions and Criminal Justice." *Theoretical Criminology* 6:299–317.

Karstedt, S. 2011. "Handle with Care: Emotions, Crime and Justice." In *Emotions, Crime and Justice: Onati International Series in Law and Society*, edited by S. Loader and H. Strang, pp. 1–19. Oxford: Hart.

Katz, J. 1988. *Seductions of Crime: Moral and Sensual Attractions in Doing Evil*. New York: Basic Books.

Katz, J. 1991. "The Motivation of the Persistent Offender." In *Crime and Justice: A Review of Research*, edited by M. Tonry, pp. 277–305. Chicago: University of Chicago Press.

Keltner, D., and J. S. Lerner. 2010. "Emotion." In *The Handbook of Social Psychology*, edited by D. T. Gilbert, S. T. Fiske, and G. Lindzey, pp. 317–52. New York: Wiley.

Klepper, S., and D. Nagin. 1989. "Tax Compliance and Perceptions of the Risks of Detection and Criminal Prosecution." *Law and Society Review* 23:209–40.

Lazarus, R. S. 1991. "Progress on a Cognitive-Motivational-Relational Theory of Emotion." *American Psychologist* 46 (8): 819–34.

Lemerise, E. A., and K. A. Dodge. 2008. "The Development of Anger and Hostile Interactions." In *Handbook of Emotions*, edited by M. Lewis, J. M. Haviland-Jones, and L. F. Barrett, pp. 730–41. New York: Guilford.

Lerner, J. S., and D. Keltner. 2000. "Beyond Valence: Toward a Model of Emotion-Specific Influences on Judgement and Choice." *Cognition and Emotion* 14: 473–93.

Lerner, J. S., and D. Keltner. 2001. "Fear, Anger, and Risk." *Journal of Personality and Social Psychology* 81:146–59.

Lerner, J. S., and L. Z. Tiedens. 2006. "Portrait of the Angry Decision Maker: How Appraisal Tendencies Shape Anger's Influence on Cognition." *Journal of Behavioral Decision Making* 19:115–37.

Lewis, M. 2008. "Self-Conscious Emotions: Embarrassment, Pride, Shame and Guilt." In *Handbook of Emotions*, edited by M. Lewis, J. M. Haviland-Jones, and L. F. Barrett, pp. 623–36. New York: Guilford.

Loewenstein, G. 1996. "Out of Control: Visceral Influences on Behavior." *Organizational Behavior and Human Decision Processes* 65:272–92.

Loewenstein, G. 2000. "Emotions in Economic Theory and Economic Behavior." *American Economic Review* 90:426–32.

Loewenstein, G., and J. Lerner. 2003. "The Role of Affect in Decision Making." In *Handbook of Affective Sciences*, edited by R. J. Davidson, K. R. Scherer, and H. H. Goldsmith, pp. 619–42. New York: Oxford University Press.

Loewenstein, G., E. Weber, C. Hsee, and N. Welch. 2001. "Risk as Feelings." *Psychological Bulletin* 127:267–86.

Lofland, J. 1969. *Deviance and Identity*. Englewood Cliffs, NJ: Prentice Hall.

Lopez, V. A., and E. T. Emmer. 2000. "Adolescent Male Offenders: A Grounded Theory Study of Cognition, Emotion, and Delinquent Crime Contexts. *Criminal Justice and Behavior* 27:292–311.

Mazerolle, P., A. R. Piquero, and G. E. Capowich. 2003. "Examining the Links Between Strain, Situational and Dispositional Anger, and Crime: Further Specifying and Testing General Strain Theory." *Youth & Society* 35: 131–57.

Nagin, D. S. 2007. "Moving Choice to Center Stage in Criminological Research and Theory: The American Society of Criminology 2006 Sutherland Address." *Criminology* 45:259–72.

Nagin, D. S., and R. Paternoster. 1993. "Enduring Individual Differences and Rational Choice Theories of Crime." *Law and Society Review* 27:467–96.

Nagin, D. S., and R. Paternoster. 1994. "Personal Capital and Social Control: The Deterrence Implications of a Theory of Individual Differences in Criminal Offending." *Criminology* 32: 581–606.

Nagin, D. S., and G. Pogarsky. 2001. "Integrating Celerity, Impulsivity, and Extralegal Sanction Threats into a Model of General Deterrence: Theory and Evidence." *Criminology* 39:865–91.

Paternoster, R. 2010. "How Much Do We Really Know About Criminal Deterrence?" *Journal of Criminal Law and Criminology* 100:765–824.

Paternoster, R., and S. Simpson. 1993. "A Rational Choice Theory of Corporate Crime." In *Advances in Criminological Theory*, vol. 5, edited by R. Clarke and M. Felson, pp. 36–58. New Brunswick, NJ: Transaction Press.

Paternoster, R., and S. Simpson. 1996. "Sanction Threats and Appeals to Morality: Testing a Rational Choice Model of Corporate Crime." *Law and Society Review* 30:378–99.

Piquero, A. R., R. Paternoster, G. Pogarsky, and T. Loughran. 2011. "Elaborating the Individual Difference Component in Deterrence Theory." *Annual Review of Law and Social Science* 7:335–60.

Piquero, A. R., and S. Tibbetts. 1996. "Specifying the Direct and Indirect Effects of Low Self Control and Situational Factors in Offenders' Decision Making: Toward a More Complete Model of Rational Offending." *Justice Quarterly* 13:481–510.

Schweitzer, M. E., and D. E. Gibson. 2008. "Fairness, Feelings, and Ethical Decision-Making: Consequences of Violating Community Standards of Fairness." *Journal of Business Ethics* 77:287–301.

Shalvi, S., J. L. van Gelder, and J. van der Schalk. 2013. "Emotional Justifications for Unethical Behavior." In *Affect and Cognition in Criminal Decision Making*, edited by J. L. van Gelder, H. Elffers, D. Reynald, and D. S. Nagin, pp. 179–92. Abingdon, UK: Routledge.

Shover, N. 1996. *Great Pretenders: Pursuits and Careers of Persistent Thieves*. Boulder, CO: Westview Press.

Smith, C. A., and P. C. Ellsworth. 1985. "Patterns of Cognitive Appraisal in Emotion." *Journal of Personality and Social Psychology* 48: 813–38.

Tangney, J. P., D. Mashek, and J. Stuewig. 2007. "Working at the Social–clinical Community–Criminology Interface: The George Mason University Inmate Study." *Journal of Social and Clinical Psychology* 26:1–21.

Tangney, J. P., J. Stuewig, and D. J. Mashek. 2007. "Moral Emotions and Moral Behavior." *Annual Review of Psychology* 58:345–72.

Tibbetts, S. 2013. "Traits and States of Self-Conscious Emotions in Criminal Decision Making." In *Affect and Cognition in Criminal Decision Making*, edited by J. L. van Gelder, H. Elffers, D. Reynald, and D. S. Nagin, pp. 221–37. Abingdon, UK: Routledge.

Tooby, J., and L. Cosmides. 2008. "The Evolutionary Psychology of the Emotions and Their Relationship to Internal Regulatory Variables." In *Handbook of Emotions*, edited by M. Lewis, J. M. Haviland-Jones, and L. F. Barrett, pp. 114–37. New York: Guilford.

van Gelder, J. L. 2013. "Beyond Rational Choice: The Hot/Cool Perspective of Criminal Decision Making." *Psychology, Crime and Law* 19:745–63.

van Gelder, J. L., and R. E. de Vries. 2012. "Traits and States: Integrating Personality and Affect into a Model of Criminal Decision Making." *Criminology* 50:637–71.

van Gelder, J. L., and R. E. de Vries. 2014. "Rational Misbehavior? Evaluating an Integrated Dual-Process Model of Criminal Decision Making." *Journal of Quantitative Criminology* 30:1–27.

van Gelder, J. L., H. Elffers, D. Reynald, and D. S. Nagin. 2013. "Affect and Cognition in Criminal Decision Making: Between Rational Choices and Lapses of Self-Control." In *Affect and Cognition in Criminal Decision Making*, edited by J. L. van Gelder, H. Elffers, D. Reynald, and D. S. Nagin, pp. 1–19. Abingdon, UK: Routledge.

van Gelder, J. L., D. Reynald, and H. Elffers. 2013. "Anticipated Emotions and Immediate Affect in Criminal Decision Making: From Anger to Shame." In *Affect and Cognition in Criminal Decision Making*, edited by J. L. van Gelder, H. Elffers, D. Reynald, and D. S. Nagin, pp. 161–78. Abingdon, UK: Routledge.

van Winden, F., and E. Ash. 2012. "On the Behavioral Economics of Crime." *Review of Law and Economics* 8:181–213.

Wikström, P.-O. 2006. "Individuals, Settings and Acts of Crime: Situational Mechanisms and the Explanation of Crime." In *The Explanation of Crime: Context, Mechanisms and Development*, edited by P.-O. Wikström and R. J. Sampson, pp. 61–107. Cambridge: Cambridge University Press.

Zimring, F. E., and G. Hawkins. 1973. *Deterrence: The Legal Threat in Crime Control*. Chicago, IL: University of Chicago Press.

....

CHAPTER 23

EXPERIMENTAL DESIGNS IN THE STUDY OF OFFENDER DECISION MAKING

....

JEFFREY A. BOUFFARD AND NICOLE NIEBUHR

CONSIDERATION of offender decision making traces its origin to the Enlightenment-era philosophers Cesar Beccaria (1764) and Jeremy Bentham (1789/1907), who wrote about the role of punishment in controlling crime. Their work became known as the Classical School of criminology and formed the foundation of deterrence theory, itself the central theoretical basis for most Western criminal justice systems. Formal specification of this model in the field of criminology waited several hundred years until Becker (1968), borrowing from economic theory, developed a model of deterrence theory focused on the individual's assessment of potential costs of crime, including the certainty and severity of punishment. Later, Clarke and colleagues (Clarke and Cornish 1985; Cornish and Clarke 1987; Clarke and Felson 1993) developed rational choice theory, expanding deterrence theory to include specific consideration of the benefits that also impact the offender's decision calculus.

I. DEVELOPMENT OF THE HYPOTHETICAL VIGNETTE METHOD

....

Several methodologies have been used to study these perceptual deterrence and rational choice models. Initial tests of deterrence examined how objective measures of punishment certainty and severity impacted aggregate crime rates (Gibbs 1968; Tittle 1969). Critics suggested, however, that researchers should consider the role of perceived, not objective, sanction risks (Waldo and Chiricos 1972; Piliavin et al. 1986). Subsequent cross-sectional studies and then longitudinal research attempted to link the perceived costs of crime to actual offending (for a review, see Klepper and Nagin 1989). Cross-sectional studies were criticized for often linking individuals' perceptions of consequences, measured in the past, to their current offending behaviors (Paternoster et al. 1983). Likewise, many longitudinal studies assumed stability in cost perceptions over time, often soliciting cost perceptions as much as one year before criminal behavior was measured (Grasmick and Bursik 1990).

Criticisms of these methods led to the use of hypothetical vignettes to examine would-be offenders' perceptions of the costs (and benefits) of crime in response to a specific, imagined offense situation (for discussion and criticisms of the use of hypothetical vignettes in the study of offender decision making, see Exum and Bouffard 2010). The hypothetical vignette methodology involves presenting research participants with what is typically a brief, written description of a fictional offending situation and then asking how likely it is that the participants would act in the same manner as the person in the story (e.g., "How likely is it that you would drive home drunk in this kind of situation?"). Participants are also often queried about what they think the consequences would be, with the researcher then linking these instantaneously generated consequence perceptions to each individual's offending intentions (Klepper and Nagin 1989; Nagin and Paternoster 1993, 1994; Bouffard 2002; Exum 2002; Pogarsky 2004; Piquero, Exum, and Simpson 2005).

Hypothetical vignettes have the benefit of providing uniform contextual information to all respondents, as opposed to asking a simple offending question in the absence of a detailed vignette (e.g., "What is the chance you would drive drunk?"). As such, each individual considers the same specific offending context rather than inferring a potentially unique situation to his or her decision (Klepper and Nagin 1989; Grasmick and Bursik 1990; Nagin and Paternoster 1994). The use of vignettes also allows researchers to correctly model the temporal order of the decision process, with consequences solicited at the same time as the individual's intention to offend, thus avoiding the assumption of temporally stable perceptions that plagued prior longitudinal research.

II. Combining Experimental Designs and Vignettes

A large body of research using the hypothetical scenario design has emerged in recent decades, although the method has also been subject to some criticisms (Bouffard 2002; Bouffard, Exum, and Collins 2010; Exum and Bouffard 2010; Exum, Turner, and Hartman 2011). Frequently, researchers have experimentally manipulated the situational characteristics presented within the vignette, especially the certainty and severity of a number of formal and informal costs and benefits (Nagin and Paternoster 1993; Pogarsky 2004; Piquero et al. 2005), as well as specific aspects of the survey setting, such as the participants' current emotional state (Weisman and Taylor 1994; Loewenstein,

Nagin, and Paternoster 1997; Exum 2002), to examine how these factors impact offender decision-making processes. Specifically, individuals in these studies are randomly assigned to various conditions (e.g., low vs. high arrest certainty and no vs. high emotional arousal at the time the decision is made) to make use of the strong internal validity provided by experimental designs (for a broader discussion of the use of experimental designs in testing criminological theories, see McGloin and Thomas 2013).

One of the central concerns regarding experimental designs is that although they are characterized by high levels of internal validity, in some cases the generalizability of their findings to real-world settings is potentially limited, particularly if the experimental setting is artificially created in order to control for internal design threats. Specifically, randomized experiments are well-suited to the precise control and manipulation of the independent variable (e.g., varied levels of arrest certainty presented to participants) and the control of many threats to internal validity (e.g., selection effects). Unfortunately, such strong internal control can also limit the generalizability of the results outside of similarly artificial circumstances. For instance, asking college students about hypothetical drunk driving while they are sober and sitting in a classroom may not represent how those students (or any group of participants) would behave in a similar, real-world setting. As such, a number of recent studies have attempted to manipulate these factors (alcohol intoxication and feelings of sexual arousal) not only to investigate their effects on decision making but also to make their experimental settings more realistic.

Another criticism related specifically to the use of hypothetical vignettes is that the dependent variable is not an actual behavior but, rather, the participants' estimation of what they would do in a similar situation. In response, a number of recent studies have utilized measures of actual misbehavior, usually minor forms of deviance such as cheating on a trivia test to earn more compensation, rather than hypothetical offending (Nagin and Pogarsky 2003; Mazar, Amir, and Ariely 2008; Gino, Ayal, and Ariely 2009; Mead et al. 2009; Shalvi et al. 2011; Fischbacher and Föllmi-Heusi 2013; van Gelder, Herschfield, and Nordgren 2013).

In the remainder of this chapter, the two common techniques for using experimental designs—those using hypothetical vignettes and those utilizing behavioral outcomes—are reviewed, along with some of the findings generated from these methods. The chapter concludes with a discussion of emerging research questions and ongoing issues related to the use of experimental designs in offender decision-making research.

III. Experimental Designs
Using Vignettes

Klepper and Nagin (1989) conducted one of the earliest criminological studies on offender decision making that used an experimental design and hypothetical vignettes. These authors examined how variations in the context of tax noncompliance might impact the individual's hypothetical decision to engage in such misbehavior. Students in a graduate business course considered one of several versions of a scenario varying the amount that a plumber underreported his self-employment income and overreported his charitable donations on his tax returns. Participants reported their hypothetical likelihood of engaging in each of several "gambles" related to misreporting this information on their own taxes. Participants also reported their perceptions of the likelihood of being caught by the Internal Revenue Service (IRS) and of being caught and criminally prosecuted if they cheated on their taxes. Results from this study generally supported deterrence theory and showed that perceptions of the risk of detection and the perceived risk of being criminally prosecuted significantly deterred hypothetical noncompliance. Likewise, as the size of the gamble randomly presented to the participant increased (larger percentages of income were not reported to the IRS), the likelihood of tax noncompliance declined because increased misrepresentation conceivably accompanied more risk of detection. These results are generally in agreement with those of earlier objective deterrence studies that found certainty of punishment to have a significant effect on offending. However, the authors conclude that unlike much prior cross-sectional and longitudinal research that had not used hypothetical vignettes, the severity (of being prosecuted) also significantly impacted offending likelihood.

IV. Manipulating Characteristics Within the Scenario

A number of studies have experimentally manipulated either the context of offending or the level of potential consequences (Bachman, Paternoster, and Ward 1992; Nagin and Paternoster 1993, 1994). Nagin and Paternoster (1993) utilized three different offense scenarios—theft, drunk driving, and sexual assault—varying three or four contextual aspects within each vignette. For instance, in their drunk driving scenario, the authors varied a number of formal risks, including factors related to the risk of formal apprehension such as the distance traveled to get home (e.g., 1 or 10 miles), how busy the road was (e.g., state highway or back roads), and the level of police enforcement activity (e.g., reduced due to budget cuts or enhanced due to DUI crackdowns). They also manipulated several informal costs related to how difficult it would be to return for the car if the respondent did not drive home drunk (e.g., roommate could give a ride, or the person would need to take a bus or walk). Despite the diverse set of hypothetical offenses and the experimental manipulation of several contextual characteristics, Nagin and Paternoster (1993) found few effects for these varied experimental conditions. Only one (informal) factor in the drunk driving scenario (the inconvenience of retrieving the car later) significantly reduced the likelihood of this offense; however, this result does support the notion that informal costs can also be important deterrents to offending behavior, along with formal risks.

Several other studies have also manipulated the risks presented to respondents (Decker, Wright, and Logie 1993; Paternoster and Simpson 1996; Pogarsky 2004; Piquero et al. 2005). For example, Decker and colleagues (1993) manipulated the levels of punishment certainty and severity, as well as the rewards, within hypothetical burglary scenarios. Using a group of active burglars and a group of matched, noncriminals, the authors randomized four levels of apprehension risk (from 10 percent, slim chance, to 90 percent, almost certain to be caught), four levels of punishment (from two years of probation up to five years in prison plus five more years on parole), and four levels of reward ($500 to $5,000 earned from the burglary). Among the non-offender sample, there was relatively little self-reported likelihood of engaging in burglary and, likewise, few significant predictors of such likelihood. Given this finding, the authors proceeded to provide results from the group of offenders and then also suggested that research on offender decision making involve the participation of actual criminals. Among the offender sample, the certainty of being caught, in interaction with the severity of the penalty, produced a strong negative effect on the willingness to offend. On the other hand, the interaction between a potential small penalty and a relatively large possible gain exhibited a positive influence on intentions to burglarize among the active criminals. Thus, the ratio of gains to risks appeared to influence offending decisions, whereas each of these factors alone had only minimal impact, such that offenders essentially assess whether the rewards are worth the risks, as Becker's (1968) economic model suggested.

Pogarsky (2004) conducted a novel study designed to not only investigate the role of cost perceptions on drunk driving intentions but also examine the link between hypothetical offending (i.e., drunk driving) and actual misbehavior in the research setting (i.e., cheating). Specifically, Pogarsky randomized risk levels within a hypothetical drunk driving vignette presented to college students (see also Nagin and Pogarsky 2003). Students were told they would receive $10 for completing the drunk driving scenario survey. In addition, in an effort to demonstrate the correspondence between hypothetical deviance (drunk driving intentions) and actual misbehavior (cheating), research participants were provided an opportunity to "cheat" on a very difficult trivia quiz. Specifically, a set of eight very obscure trivia questions were included at the end of the survey, and participants were told that answering six of them correctly (an extremely unlikely outcome) would yield an additional $10 payment. The participants were then told there was a copy of the trivia questions and answers on another page but that they were not to look at this until they had completed the trivia quiz.

Variations in the certainty and severity of punishment for cheating were also randomized, with participants in the low-certainty condition being told that the researcher would only make two brief visits during the one-hour survey session, whereas those in the high-certainty condition completed their surveys with a proctor present. Variations in punishment severity included some participants being told they would lose their $10 payment if they were caught cheating, whereas the low-severity condition included no such warning. Finally, in relation to the hypothetical drunk driving scenario, participants were allowed to report their own estimated probability of apprehension and conviction (using 0–100 percent scales), but they were randomly assigned to consider either one-month or twelve-month driver's license suspension (severity) if they were apprehended.

Results revealed that the estimated certainty of apprehension and conviction for drunk driving had more of an effect on such intentions than did the randomized severity of license suspension (i.e., one vs. twelve months). Similarly, the results of the cheating experiment revealed that the certainty of the punishment (i.e., the presence of a proctor) had a greater effect on cheating likelihood than did the punishment severity (i.e., potentially forfeiting the $10 participation payment). These results comport with prior research showing that certainty may have a larger deterrent effect than severity. Importantly for research that has employed hypothetical vignettes, Pogarsky (2004) also reported a significant relationship between actual cheating and intentions to drive drunk—a finding that has subsequently been used to validate the use of measures of hypothetical intentions to offend because they appear to relate to other forms of contemporaneous (within the laboratory setting) deviant behaviors.

Piquero et al. (2005) utilized this same research approach in a study of corporate crime, providing hypothetical vignettes to a sample of business executives and students in an MBA program. Each participant was presented with a survey including three corporate crime scenarios: price-fixing, bribery, and an Environmental Protection Agency (EPA) violation. The scenarios were each followed by questions related to the individual's perception of possible sanctions, the certainty and severity of punishments, and perceived benefits related to committing each specific act. In addition, the researchers randomly assigned nine different contextual aspects of the hypothetical offending scenario (e.g., the business was experiencing declining vs. growing sales/revenues and the company recently fired an employee who committed a similar act).

Piquero and colleagues (2005) found that four of their nine experimentally manipulated scenario conditions were related to the likelihood of individuals engaging in one of these corporate offenses: declining sales, losing ground to foreign competition, whether the act was perceived as commonly occurring in the industry, and whether the scenario depicted the employee being reprimanded for a similar act. In addition, a number of other individual-level factors (not experimentally manipulated) were found to be related to lower likelihood of corporate offending, including the perception of the acts as morally wrong, the potential for being publicly shamed, and the likelihood of being formally sanctioned. Finally, a number of perceived benefits, both long term (e.g., promotion) and short term (e.g., excitement), were related to significantly higher intentions to engage in corporate crimes. These findings serve as an example of the breadth of knowledge gained from the use of experimental designs coupled with hypothetical vignettes in that a number of formal and informal costs and benefits (including those internal to the individual, such as assessments of the behavior as immoral or exciting) were relevant predictors of corporate offending.

V. QUESTION FORM EFFECTS
IN DECISION-MAKING RESEARCH

In addition to using experimental designs and hypothetical vignettes to examine the perceived costs and benefits that influence criminal decision making, these methods have also been used to examine the techniques that researchers use to study offender decision making. For instance, a large body of psychological research on the cognitive aspects of survey methodology (for reviews, see Schwarz 1999, 2007) has demonstrated that the way questions are asked can have an impact on the answers that participants provide. Much of the research in criminology on offender decision making has presented a predetermined set of consequences for participants to consider when they engage in their hypothetical offending decision, without sufficient attention paid to whether those consequences actually would be relevant to the individuals being studied (Bouffard et al. 2010).

Bouffard and colleagues (2010) therefore asked a sample of university students to read a hypothetical shoplifting scenario and randomly assigned them to respond to the scenario using a set of researcher-derived consequences (RDCs; based on those used in prior rational choice research) or by generating their own set of potential costs and benefits (i.e., subject-generated consequences [SGCs]). The researchers included RDC cost items such as legal problems, emotional costs, family problems, social problems, school problems, immorality, and professional problems, which reflect those typically presented in existing rational choice research. Individuals in the SGC group were given seven blank lines for potential costs and seven more for potential benefits of taking batteries from a convenience store without paying. Participants in each condition then rated the certainty and severity of the consequences, using 0–100 percent scales.

Participants in the RDC group were more likely to view the consequences presented to them as possible outcomes than did those in the SGC group. For instance, 99 percent of RDC participants endorsed immorality as a possible consideration compared to 2.9 percent of the SGC group. Those in the SGC group also reported a number of novel items not previously examined by researchers, suggesting that the RDC method may not capture the full range of factors included in the decision calculus. Bouffard and colleagues (2010) also demonstrated that the RDC methodology yielded similar perceptions of the certainty and severity of costs but consistently lower perceptions of the certainty and value of benefits relative to the benefits that participants developed on their own in the SGC condition. Finally, Bouffard and colleagues found evidence that many of the novel consequences reported in the SGC condition had certainty and severity scores that were as large as, or larger than, those assigned to traditional RDCs, suggesting that the consequences not included in past rational choice tests may be just as impactful as those that are typically examined. The authors argue that researchers should pay more attention to how consequences are solicited from participants, to more accurately represent the content of their decision calculus, and to avoid possible biases in the certainty and severity ratings participants provide when asked about RDCs that were not actually relevant to their decision.

VI. MANIPULATING THE CONTEXT OF DECISION MAKING

As noted previously, a number of studies have experimentally manipulated the *content* presented within a hypothetical vignette (i.e., situational aspects of the offense and the certainty of apprehension: Bachman et al. 1992; Decker et al. 1993; Nagin and Paternoster 1993, 1994; Pogarsky 2004; Piquero et al. 2005). A number of studies have also utilized experimental designs to examine the various influences on the offender decision-making *process*, typically randomizing participants to either some form of heightened emotional (anger) or visceral (sexual arousal and drunkenness) state or to a control condition (Loewenstein et al. 1997; Bouffard 2002, 2011, 2013; Exum 2002; Topalli and O'Neal 2003; Ariely and Loewenstein 2006; Exum and Zachowicz 2013). Loewenstein (1996) outlined several ways in which such visceral and emotional states impact decision making—for instance, by shortening one's attention span, focusing on the self over others, and focusing attention on consequences that facilitate resolution of the current state (e.g., hunger leads to a focus on finding food, not on the costs of the food).

In one of the earliest such criminological studies, Loewenstein and colleagues (1997) randomly assigned male college students to an immediate sexual arousal condition ($n = 30$), a prior arousal condition (arousal was induced a day prior to completing the surveys; $n = 20$), or a control condition (no arousal; $n = 30$). Participants in the arousal conditions viewed sexually arousing materials (nude photographs from *Playboy* magazine) and those in the control group viewed neutral materials (fully clothed women from fashion magazines) prior to completing questions about the hypothetical sexual coercion scenario. After reading the scenario, all participants responded with their own self-reported likelihood of (1) coaxing the scenario female to remove her clothes and (2) having sex with her even if she protested, each using a 0–100 percent scale. Participants also responded to questions about "How much fun would it be to have sex with the woman in this situation?" as well as their perceptions of the certainty and severity of internally imposed (e.g., feelings of guilt and shame) and externally imposed (e.g., being arrested and being dismissed from the university) costs.

Derived from Loewenstein's (1996) work, Loewenstein and colleagues (1997) proposed that sexual arousal would increase sexual coercion likelihood and that it might do so by increasing the perceived benefits of being coercive, by decreasing the perceived costs of such behavior, and/or by desensitizing the individual to the influence of cost perceptions (i.e., making costs irrelevant to the decision). The experimental arousal manipulation did lead to increased likelihood of trying to coax the woman to remove her clothes; however, being in the arousal condition did not appear to alter the perception of costs or benefits. In light of the small sample size, and because of multicolinearity in their measures, the authors were unable to examine whether sexual arousal may have desensitized participants to the effect of perceived costs. In addition, the relatively low level of arousal reached by participants (average of 3.4 on a 10-point scale among those in the immediate arousal condition) may explain the lack of hypothesized relationships between group assignment and altered consequence perceptions.

Bouffard (2002) used a methodology very similar to that of Loewenstein and colleagues (1997) and again found that random assignment to either an arousal condition (e.g., viewed an erotic video clip) or to a no-arousal, control condition had no effect on the perceived costs or benefits of hypothetical sexual coercion, although, again, the manipulation produced only limited increases in arousal levels (approximately 57 percent arousal on a 0–100 percent aroused scale among those in the video condition). Bouffard did find that higher self-reported arousal levels (regardless of assigned condition) were related to higher perceptions that experiencing sexual pleasure was an important benefit considered within the decision.

In a re-examination of data from his 2002 study, Bouffard (2011) investigated the proposition that heightened arousal might desensitize individuals to their cost perceptions (following from Loewenstein et al. 1997). Specifically, Bouffard found that cost perceptions exhibited significant deterrent effects only among those who reported less sexual arousal, whereas among the more highly aroused, cost perceptions did not significantly deter sexual coercion intentions. Again, however, these results did not emerge when examining the impact of random assignment to arousal and control conditions. Utilizing a larger data set that included male and female university students, Bouffard (2013) again found that arousal level altered the perception of benefits (as more certain to occur and more valuable if they did occur) but had little impact on perception of the certainty or severity of costs related to sexual coercion among both sexes. Overall, this pattern of results supports Loewenstein's ideas about the attention-shifting effects of visceral states in that sexual arousal appeared to increase attention to the perceived benefits of sexual coercion while at the same time reducing the influence of cost perceptions (but not necessarily reducing the cost perceptions themselves).

Motivated partly by the failure of some prior studies of sexual arousal to find effects for random assignment to an arousal-inducing condition, Exum and Zachowicz (2013) used a novel methodology—that of measuring response latencies (the time it takes to respond to a question)—in order to further examine the impact of sexual arousal level on hypothetical sexual coercion. Speculating that participants might not be able to consciously report on the consequences they had considered in their decisions, these authors sought to measure the effect of heightened sexual arousal on the unconscious processing of such information. Among a sample of 202 male university students, Exum and Zachowicz found that participants randomly assigned to view an arousing video (average self-reported arousal level of approximately 6.9 on a 10-point scale) identified a greater number of potential benefits of engaging in sexual coercion, and identified these benefits more quickly, than did participants assigned to the control condition. In other words, these authors found that states of sexual arousal impacted the decision to engage in sexual aggression by making possible benefits more readily accessible from memory (i.e., more benefits were identified and in a shorter time frame). These results are largely in agreement with those of research using more traditional methodologies (Loewenstein et al. 1997; Bouffard 2002, 2013) that has found arousal "tips the scales" toward sexual coercion and aggression by making benefits, but not costs, more impactful—in this case, more readily recalled from memory—within the decision itself. Importantly, these authors were also able to produce a larger increase in arousal levels through the experimental manipulation than did either Bouffard (2002) or Loewenstein and colleagues (1997), which may account for the pronounced effects of arousal on perceived consequences.

Topalli and O'Neal (2003) used an experimental design to examine the impact of a different emotional state, anger, on decision making. Male college students were randomly assigned to be (1) either verbally provoked (by being accused of and ridiculed for being late and irresponsible) or not by the researcher and (2) offered an opportunity to retaliate (in the form of providing negative feedback to the supervisor) or not against the researcher who had angered them. Results revealed that individuals who were provoked and offered a chance to retaliate also scored higher on subsequent measures of hostility than did subjects assigned to the other three conditions. Controlling for experimental assignment, two dispositional measures (hostility and vengeance-seeking) also predicted attributing hostility to the researcher. They suggest that anger (from provocation) increased the likelihood of hostile attribution and that providing an opportunity to retaliate may have further increased such attributions. Thus, angered individuals focused on factors that facilitated retaliatory behavior, and they also reported higher feelings of hostility than un-angered participants. The authors also suggest that future research should examine whether provocation indirectly increases hostile attributions by fostering angry cognitions.

A number of additional studies have examined the impact of alcohol intoxication on aggression and specifically sexual aggression (Exum 2002; Davis et al. 2006; for a study of the effect of imagined alcohol intoxication, provocation, and social inhibition on aggression, see Cheong, Patock-Peckham, and Nagoshi 2001). Exum randomly assigned 84 male college students to one of four conditions based on the presence or absence of researcher-induced states of anger, as well as the presence or absence of alcohol intoxication. Although Exum's study is the only one in the field of criminology to utilize an experimental design to examine the role of anger and intoxication in aggression, considerable psychological research has examined the role of alcohol in physical aggression (e.g., see meta-analyses by Ito, Miller, and Pollock 1996; Lipsey et al. 1997). Specifically, Exum proposed that intoxication, anger, and/or their combination might impact participants' hypothetical likelihood of getting into a physical confrontation at a bar, at least partly by altering their perceptions of the costs and benefits. Exum also asked participants about what they thought other students at their university might do in the hypothetical situation (termed "other-referent" aggression; p. 944).

Although Exum (2002) did not find any independent or interactive effects of anger or intoxication on the participants' own hypothetical likelihood of getting into a fight, nor on the perception of costs or benefits, individuals who were angered and intoxicated did report higher likelihood that other males at the university would get in a fight if they were in the hypothetical situation presented to them. In a series of exploratory multivariate models, Exum also found that the rational choice model (based on the impact of perceived costs and benefits on offending) appeared to operate differently among individuals who were either angered or intoxicated relative to those who were neither. For instance, when either angered or intoxicated, perception of benefits had less influence on the hypothetical assault decision. At the same time, the influence of cost perceptions varied by cost type, such that perceived immorality of fighting had less influence among angry or intoxicated individuals, whereas the potential pain of the other person had more influence among these participants. In general, Exum concluded that the consideration of costs and benefits varied across conditions, such that there was some indication that the rational choice model of criminal decision making was not uniform across situational, visceral states.

Finally, Davis and colleagues (2006) examined the impact of sexual arousal and alcohol consumption on hypothetical sexual aggression among a sample of 84 male university students. Participants were randomly assigned to one of four conditions based on whether or not they consumed alcohol and whether the female in the hypothetical scenario was depicted as reacting to the male's sexual advances with pleasure or distress. Multivariate path model results revealed that both alcohol consumption and the presentation of the woman as experiencing pleasure led to higher levels of sexual arousal among the male participants and that having a higher level of sexual arousal was related to a significantly higher likelihood of sexual aggression. Importantly, alcohol consumption itself did not exhibit a direct effect on sexual aggression likelihood, operating instead indirectly through level of sexual arousal. Similar to the work in criminology that has examined the role of sexual arousal on the perception of costs and benefits of sexual coercion, these results suggest that alcohol intoxication focuses the individual on the current feelings of sexual arousal (e.g., benefits) and reduces attention to the potential costs (e.g., the woman's lack of sexual willingness), which then facilitate the offending behavior.

VII. EXPERIMENTAL DESIGNS WITH BEHAVIORAL OUTCOMES

Although this chapter has reviewed some studies that have measured actual forms of minor deviance (e.g., cheating) and related these behaviors to measures of hypothetical offending intentions, relatively few studies in the field of criminology have examined behavioral outcomes (Nagin and Pogarsky 2003; Pogarsky 2004). Despite the potential advantages to be gained by measuring actual misbehavior rather than intentions to offend, there are inherent ethical issues involved in allowing individuals to engage in real criminal behaviors, especially with regard to serious or violent offending. However, a number of studies have examined forms of minor deviance, such as cheating and lying, within the fields of psychology and human decision making (Mazar et al. 2008; Gino et al. 2009; Mead et al. 2009; Shalvi et al. 2011; Fischbacher and Föllmi-Heusi 2013; van Gelder et al. 2013). Often, these studies allow participants an opportunity to cheat on a trivia test or to lie about the number they rolled on a die, with these misrepresentations resulting in research participants receiving higher levels of compensation for their research involvement.

In one of the earlier studies of this type, Mazar and colleagues (2008) used a series of six experiments to examine whether one's likelihood of lying was influenced by the desire to maintain a positive self-concept. In particular, they suggested that many people will limit the extent of their lying so as to increase their gain while not severely damaging their self-concept. These authors' experiments all involved randomly assigning university students to conditions based on the provision of an opportunity to lie about how many math problems they correctly solved. Specifically, participants were instructed to search a matrix of numbers and find two three-digit numbers that sum to exactly 10.0, with their level of compensation determined by the number of correct solutions they were able to find.

In their first experiment, Mazar and colleagues (2008) randomly assigned 229 students to either make a list of ten books they had read in high school or list the Ten Commandments (i.e., a morality reminder condition). Participants were also randomly assigned to conditions based on their having an opportunity to cheat. Those who could cheat were allowed to report the number of math matrix problems they correctly solved without having to submit the actual worksheet to the researcher, whereas those with no chance to cheat had to submit their answers to the researcher for verification prior to being compensated. Results revealed that among those who could have cheated, none of those in the morality reminder condition actually cheated, whereas those who simply listed ten books they had read did have an increased likelihood of cheating when provided the opportunity to do so.

Subsequent variations of Mazar and colleagues' (2008) experiment examined the impact of reminding students about their university's honor code rather than the Ten Commandments; of providing students with tokens as compensation rather than real money; of providing students with social norm information in the form of data on the percentage of correct answers that other students provided; and of varied levels of the risk of being caught cheating. Results from these variations demonstrated that university honor code reminders deterred cheating and that compensating people with tokens rather than real money increased cheating behavior (possibly because participants were able to justify the cheating as not resulting in the loss of real money by the researcher). On the other hand, the provision of social norm data and increasing the certainty of apprehension did not impact cheating rates, which the authors' suggest means that the individuals were motivated to cheat by some internal standard (Mazar et al. 2008). Later research by Gino and colleagues (2009), using similar methodologies, further examined the impact of social norms by presenting participants with a confederate who cheated and was either like them (wore a plain T-shirt) or unlike them (wore a T-shirt from a rival university). Results revealed that cheating increased when the confederate who cheated was from the in-group (i.e., plain T-shirt) and was less likely when the cheating confederate appeared to be from the rival university.

Mead and colleagues (2009) utilized a similar cheating paradigm to examine the impact of depleting one's self-control resources. In their first experiment, 84 participants were randomly assigned to either a control condition in which they had to write a brief essay without using the letters X and Z (i.e., an easy task), or a self-control depletion condition in which they had the more difficult task of writing an essay without using the more common letters A and N. Participants were then given the same kind of number matrices task used by Mazar and colleagues (2008) and either had the researcher score their correct answers (no cheating opportunity) or could self-report the number of correct answers and destroy their worksheets (cheating opportunity). Among those who could have cheated, those who had their self-control depleted claimed approximately 25 percent more correct answers than did non-depleted participants whose answers were scored by the researcher. In addition, participants in the self-control depletion condition who could cheat claimed 104 percent more correct answers than did depleted participants who could not cheat (researcher-checked answers).

In Mead and colleagues' (2009) second experiment, university students were again randomly assigned to self-control depletion or control conditions and then presented with an opportunity to choose whether or not to cheat on a short test by choosing to use either a blank answer sheet or one that had the correct answers lightly marked on it. Outcomes measured in this experiment were the participants' choice of score sheet and the number of correct answers they claimed. Individuals with depleted self-control were significantly more likely (74 percent) to choose the score sheet with answers already marked on it than were non-depleted participants (40 percent). Depleted individuals who asked for the pre-marked score sheet also claimed more correct answers than non-depleted participants who chose the pre-marked sheet. The authors suggest that not only does self-control depletion increase the likelihood of dishonesty but also individuals may not be aware of the impact of such depletion on the choices they make, which can put them at increased risk for such dishonesty by having self-selected into risky situations.

Van Gelder and colleagues (2013) conducted a pair of experiments to examine the role of considering the "future self," under the assumption that delinquency is often the result of having failed to consider the long-term implications of such misbehavior. Their first study included a hypothetical behavior outcome measure and involved 114 young adults who were asked to write a letter to their future selves and were randomly assigned to either a distant-self condition (the self twenty years into the future) or a near-self condition (the self only three months into the future). Participants were then asked to rate their likelihood of engaging in each of five delinquent behaviors (i.e., buying a stolen laptop computer, two types of theft, insurance fraud, and illegal downloading). Results revealed that individuals who wrote letters to an imagined self more distant in the future reported significantly lower likelihood of engaging in each of the five delinquent behaviors. Only one of the theft measures and the illegal download outcome measure were significantly lower among those who had written to their distant self rather than to a nearer self.

In their second study, this time utilizing a behavior outcome (cheating), van Gelder and colleagues (2013) randomly assigned 67 university students to interact with a virtual reality version of themselves, either as they are now (control) or age-progressed to forty years old (experimental group). After interacting with their virtual self for several minutes, each group was then presented with an eight-item trivia quiz that represented their opportunity to cheat (as originally developed by Nagin and Pogarsky 2003). Results revealed that individuals who interacted with an age-progressed version of themselves were significantly less likely to cheat (6.1 percent) compared to those in the control group (23.5 percent), who had interacted with a current version of themselves. The authors suggest that by interacting with one's future self, the individual focuses on the longer term consequences of his or her actions, which then reduces the likelihood of delinquent behavior.

In a related set of experiments, using a different measure of cheating (based on work by Fischbacher and Föllmi-Heusi 2008, 2013), Shalvi and colleagues (2011) attempted to understand participants' willingness to lie to make a financial gain under varying conditions of possible self-justifications for the lies. In each study, participants rolled a six-sided die under a paper cup with a small hole cut in the top, such that only the participant could know what number had been rolled. Participants had been told that their compensation would be determined by the die roll. In the first experiment, participants were randomly assigned to roll the die either one time or once and then at least two more times "to verify the die" with specific instruction that only the number that appeared on the first roll would be used to determine their compensation. The authors hypothesized that when allowed to roll the die multiple times, individuals would be more likely to lie and overreport the value of their compensation by claiming the highest of the three rolls rather than the first roll. Specifically, seeing multiple rolls would increase chances that the person would observe a higher number somewhere in the three rolls, providing justification for the lie. Based on results from the first experiment, Shalvi and colleagues concluded that allowing participants the opportunity for a potential justification for the lie (i.e., multiple rolls) led to more dishonesty because the participants who rolled multiple times overreported 6's and underreported rolls of 1, 2, and 3 relative to what would be expected—that is, a uniform distribution of rolls for each number.

In a subsequent experiment, Shalvi and colleagues (2011) also found that when participants were provided with sets of die roles and asked what they would have reported to earn compensation (but did not actually receive compensation based on what they said they would have reported), there was considerably less overreporting. They also found, however, that the overreporting that did occur also represented what would have been "justified lies" (reporting one of the die rolls but not necessarily the first roll). In general, Shalvi and colleagues concluded from this set of experiments that individuals are more likely to lie in their own self-interest if they have available to them some form of justification (having at least seen the number they report) to make them feel more honest.

VIII. Conclusion

The use of experimental designs, often with hypothetical vignettes, has in many cases validated what has been learned about deterrence and rational choice theories from research using other methodologies, such as objective sanctions research using cross-sectional designs (Gibbs 1968; Tittle 1969) and perceptual deterrence tests based on longitudinal surveys. For instance, the perceived certainty and, to a lesser extent, severity of both formal and informal costs have been shown to influence offending likelihood, whereas perceived certainty and value of gains can increase it. At the same time, the use of experimental designs, coupled with hypothetical scenarios, has also produced a considerable volume of additional information about offender decision making, including the influence of various emotional and visceral states on the processing of information, especially the perception of consequences. In addition, this body of research has examined how a number of other situational and contextual features of the offending opportunity itself can alter offending likelihood and how various individual characteristics (e.g., self-control and aggressiveness) may interact with these opportunities. In recent years, researchers have also begun to use experimental designs with measures of actual, although usually minor, deviant behaviors. This research has not only validated the use of hypothetical scenario designs but also further investigated the situational and individual factors that influence decision making in relation to analogues of criminal behavior, such as lying and cheating.

Future research is needed on how various emotional and/or visceral states influence offenders' perceptions of sanction risks. Specifically, research should continue to utilize experimental designs to examine other states beyond anger, sexual arousal, and alcohol intoxication (e.g., fear, sadness, and fatigue), as well as the possible interaction of various states. Research has suggested that intoxication and anger may have synergistic effects in promoting violence, and indeed, other states may interact with one another to increase offending. However, it is also possible that certain states (e.g., fear) may be employed in attempts to counteract the effect of those states that predispose people to engage in crime (e.g., anger and sexual arousal). The investigation of possible tipping points at which these visceral states begin to impact decision making, as well as the duration of these attention-focusing effects, is also important. Likewise, additional research on how various individual characteristics (e.g., self-control) interact with contextual aspects of the offending situation (e.g., randomly assigned risks and rewards) is needed so that we can better understand how certain individuals may actively select into potential offending situations.

There continue to be a number of important challenges to the use of these methods. As McGloin and Thomas (2013) note, theories that focus on offender decision making (i.e., deterrence, rational choice, and routine activities) are especially well-suited to the use of experimental designs because their concepts are easily defined and experimentally manipulated. In some cases, however, these manipulations have not appeared to have their intended effects on hypothetical offending or consequence perceptions. In particular, a number of the studies of sexual arousal found no effects for arousal condition but some effects for level of arousal. Although these types of issues are amenable to study with experimental designs (e.g., manipulating levels of arousal or intoxication), there may be practical and ethical limitations on the "strength" of the manipulations to which participants can be exposed. Few of the sexual arousal studies, for instance, succeeded in creating very high levels of arousal in the laboratory setting. This issue again reflects the central limitation of experimental designs—their lack of external validity and the difficulty inherent in trying to simulate real-world situations in the research setting.

Researchers interested in accurately understanding offender decision making should also devote more attention to the role of the methodology. A number of studies in psychology have explored how question formats can impact participants' responses, and the experimental design is well-suited to continued use in this arena as well. Bouffard and colleagues (2010) demonstrated that the question format can influence the types of consequences reported, as well as the perceived certainty and severity that individuals assign to them. Future research should continue to investigate the hypothetical scenario design, as well as the possibility of other question form effects beyond those that accompany the use of open- versus closed-ended questions. In addition, this will be increasingly important as research using experimental designs and hypothetical vignettes begins to make more use of samples of known offenders. Likewise, current knowledge should be validated against that gained about offender decision making from other methodologies, including qualitative ethnographic research (Wright and Decker 1994, 1997), computer simulations (Sullivan 2013), and emerging neuropsychological research on the processing of information in the brain (Kahneman 2003, 2011).

Decision-making researchers should continue to use experimental designs to examine the influence of various individual and contextual factors on offender decision making, but they must begin to do so in ways that more closely approximate reality, recognizing that offender decision making is a highly individualized and context-dependent process (Clarke and Cornish 1985). Future research also needs to address decision making related to other, more serious, crime types and to investigate the decision-making processes of actual offenders. A number of crime types have been examined to date, including drunk driving, fighting, sexual coercion, burglary, and some corporate offending, but many other crime types, such as domestic violence, armed robbery, and drug use, have not been subject to empirical scrutiny using these methods. Likewise, many of the existing studies of *offender* decision making have examined samples of university students, and few, if any, have examined these acts of real (i.e., cheating) or hypothetical offending among samples of serious, known offenders. Of course, substantial ethical challenges exist in the examination of real and serious criminal behavior (e.g., burglary); however, researchers should strive to develop additional behavioral measurement strategies that move beyond hypothetical scenarios in the way that the research on cheating and lying has done so.

Our understanding of offender decision making has benefited immensely from the use of experimental designs, both with hypothetical vignettes and with behavioral analogs for minor deviance. As the preceding discussion outlined, however, a number of interesting and important questions about content and process of criminal decision making remain, as do a number of substantial methodological, ethical, and practical challenges to the use of experimental and hypothetical scenario methods. Nagin (2007) argued convincingly that criminologists need to pay more attention to the issue of choice in criminology, specifically suggesting that researchers look to research outside of criminology and to the role of emotions in decision making and that they should consider the development of offenders' decision making over time. This chapter outlined how use of the experimental design, often along with hypothetical vignettes, has generated a large volume of influential and informative research, both within and from outside the field of criminology. More research using these tools is needed if our understanding of crime, and how to prevent and control it, is to advance further.

REFERENCES

Ariely, D., and G. Loewenstein. 2006. "The Heat of the Moment: The Effect of Sexual Arousal on Sexual Decision-Making." *Journal of Behavioral Decision Making* 19:87–98.

Bachman, R., R. Paternoster, and S. Ward. 1992. "The Rationality of Sexual Offending: Testing a Deterrence/Rational Choice Conception of Sexual Assault." *Law and Society Review* 26(2): 343–72.

Beccaria, C. 1764. *On Crimes and Punishments.* Indianapolis, IN: Hackett.

Becker, G. 1968. "Crime and Punishment: An Economic Approach." *Journal of Political Economy* 76(2): 169–217.

Bentham, J. 1907. *An Introduction to the Principles of Morals and Legislation.* Oxford: Clarendon. (Originally published 1789.)

Bouffard, J. A. 2002. "Influence of Emotion on Rational Decision-Making in Sexual Aggression." *Journal of Criminal Justice* 30:121–34.

Bouffard, J. A. 2011. "In the Heat of the Moment? Mediating vs. Moderating Relationships Between Sexual Arousal and Perceived Sanctions." *Journal of Crime and Justice* 34(1): 24–44.

Bouffard, J. A. 2013. "The Role of Sexual Arousal and Perceived Consequences in Men's and Women's Decisions to Engage in Sexual Coercion." In *Affect and Cognition in Criminal Decision-Making,* edited by J. L. van Gelder, H. Elffers, D. Reynald, and D. S. Nagin, pp. 77–96. Abingdon, UK: Routledge.

Bouffard, J. A., M. L. Exum, and P. A. Collins. 2010. "Methodological Artifacts in Tests of Rational Choice Theory." *Journal of Criminal Justice* 38(4): 400–9.

Cheong, J., J. A. Patock-Peckham, and C. T. Nagoshi. 2001. "Effects of Alcoholic Beverage, Instigation, and Inhibition of Expectancies of Aggressive Behavior." *Violence and Victims* 16(2): 173–84.

Clarke, R., and D. Cornish. 1985. "Modeling Offenders' Decisions: A Framework for Policy and Research." In *Crime and Justice,* vol. 6, edited by M. Tonry and N. Morris, pp. 147–85. Chicago: University of Chicago Press.

Clarke, R. V., and M. Felson. 1993. "Introduction: Criminology, Routine Activity, and Rational Choice." In *Routine Activity and Rational Choice,* edited by R. V. Clarke and M. Felson, pp. 1–14. London: Transaction Publishers.

Cornish, D., and R. Clarke. 1987. "Understanding Crime Displacement." *Criminology* 25:933–47.

Davis, K. C., J. Norris, W. H. George, J. Martell, and J. R. Heiman. 2006. "Men's Likelihood of Sexual Aggression: The Influence of Alcohol, Sexual Arousal, and Violent Pornography." *Aggressive Behavior* 3:581–89.

Decker, S. H., R. Wright, and R. Logie. 1993. "Perceptual Deterrence Among Active Residential Burglars: A Research Note." *Criminology* 31:135–47.

Exum, M. L. 2002. "The Application and Robustness of the Rational Choice Perspective in the Study of Intoxicated and Angry Intentions to Aggress." *Criminology* 40:933–67.

Exum, M. L., and J. A. Bouffard. 2010. "Testing Theories of Criminal Decision Making: Some Empirical Questions About Hypothetical Scenarios." In *Handbook of Quantitative Criminology*, edited by A. R. Piquero and D. Weisburd, pp. 581–94. New York: Springer.

Exum, M. L., M. G. Turner, and J. L. Hartman. 2011. "Self-Reported Intentions to Offend: All Talk and No Action?" *American Journal of Criminal Justice* 37:523–43.

Exum, M. L., and A. Zachowicz. 2013. "Sexual Arousal and the Ability to Access Sexually Aggressive Consequences from Memory." In *Affect and Cognition in Criminal Decision-Making*, edited by J. L. van Gelder, H. Elffers, D. Reynald, and D. S. Nagin, pp. 97–118. Abingdon, UK: Routledge.

Fischbacher, U., and F. Föllmi-Heusi. 2008. "Lies in Disguise: An Experimental Study on Cheating." TWI working paper no. 40. Thurgau Institute of Economics, University of Konstanz.

Fischbacher, U., and F. Föllmi-Heusi. 2013. "Lies in Disguise: An Experimental Study on Cheating." *Journal of the European Economic Association* 11(3): 525–47.

Gibbs, J. P. 1968. "Crime, Punishment, and Deterrence." *Social Science Quarterly* 58:15–28.

Gino, F., S. Ayal, and D. Ariely. 2009. "Contagion and Differentiation in Unethical Behavior: The Effect of One Bad Apple on the Barrel." *Psychological Science* 20:393–98.

Grasmick, H. G., and R. J. Bursik. 1990. "Conscience, Significant Others and Rational Choice: Extending the Deterrence Model." *Law and Society Review* 24:837–61.

Ito, T. A., N. Miller, and V. E. Pollock. 1996. "Alcohol and Aggression: A Meta-Analysis on the Moderating Effects of Inhibitory Cues, Triggering Events, and Self-Focused Attention." *Psychological Bulletin* 120:60–82.

Kahneman, D. 2003. "Maps of Bounded Rationality: Psychology for Behavioral Economics." *American Economic Review* 93:1449–75.

Kahneman, D. 2011. *Thinking, Fast and Slow*. New York: Farrar, Straus and Giroux.

Klepper, S., and D. Nagin. 1989. "The Deterrent Effect of Perceived Certainty and Severity of Punishment Revisited." *Criminology* 27:721–46.

Lipsey, M. W., D. B. Wilson, M. A. Cohen, and J. H. Derzon. 1997. "Is There a Causal Relationship Between Alcohol Use and Violence? A Synthesis of Evidence." In *Recent Developments in Alcoholism, Vol. 13: Alcohol and Violence*, edited by M. Galanter, pp. 245–82. New York: Plenum.

Loewenstein, G. 1996. "Out of Control: Visceral Influences on Behavior." *Organizational Behavior and Human Decision Process* 65:272–92.

Loewenstein, G., D. Nagin, and R. Paternoster. 1997. "The Effect of Sexual Arousal on Predictions of Sexual Forcefulness." *Journal of Crime and Delinquency* 32:443–73.

Mazar, N., O. Amir, and D. Ariely. 2008. "The Dishonesty of Honest People: A Theory of Self-Concept Maintenance. *Journal of Marketing Research* 45:633–44.

McGloin, J. M., and K. J. Thomas. 2013. "Experimental Tests in Tests of Criminological Theory." In *Experimental Criminology: Prospects for Advancing Science and Public Policy*, edited by B. C. Welsh, A. A. Braga, and G. J. N. Bruinsma, pp. 15–42. New York: Cambridge University Press.

Mead, N. L., R. F. Baumeister, F. Gino, M. E. Schweitzer, and D. Ariely. 2009. "Too Tired to Tell the Truth: Self-Control Resource Depletion and Dishonesty." *Journal of Experimental Social Psychology* 45:594–97.

Nagin, D. S. 2007. "Moving Choice to Center Stage in Criminological Research and Theory: The American Society of Criminology 2006 Sutherland Address." *Criminology* 45(2): 259–72.

Nagin, D. S., and R. Paternoster. 1993. "Enduring Individual Differences and Rational Choice Theories of Crime." *Law and Society Review* 27:467–96.

Nagin, D. S., and R. Paternoster. 1994. "Personal Capital and Social Control: The Deterrence Implications of a Theory of Individual Differences in Criminal Offending." *Criminology* 32(4): 581–606.

Nagin, D. S., and G. Pogarsky. 2003. "An Experimental Investigation of Deterrence: Cheating, Self-Serving Bias, and Impulsivity." *Criminology* 41:167–94.

Paternoster, R., L. E. Saltzman, G. P. Waldo, and T. G. Chiricos. 1983. "Perceived Risk and Social Control." *Law and Society Review* 17:457–79.

Paternoster, R., and S. Simpson. 1996. "Sanction Threats and Appeals to Morality: Testing a Rational Choice Model of Corporate Crime." *Law and Society Review* 30(3): 549–83.

Piliavin, I., R. Gartner, C. Thornton, and R. L. Matsueda. 1986. "Crime, Deterrence, and Rational Choice." *American Sociological Review* 51:101–19.

Piquero, N. L., M. L. Exum, and S. S. Simpson. 2005. "Integrating the Desire-for-Control and Rational Choice in a Corporate Crime Context." *Justice Quarterly* 22(2): 252–80.

Pogarsky, G. 2004. "Projected Offending and Contemporaneous Rule-Violation: Implications for Heterotypic Continuity." *Criminology* 42:111–36.

Schwarz, N. 1999. "Self-Reports: How Questions Shape the Answers." *American Psychologist* 54:93–105.

Schwarz, N. 2007. "Cognitive Aspects of Survey Methodology." *Applied Cognitive Psychology* 21:277–87.

Shalvi, S., J. Dana, M. J. J. Handgraaf, and C. K. W. De Dreu. 2011. "Justified Ethicality: Observing Desired Counterfactuals Modifies Ethical Perceptions and Behavior." *Organizational Behavior and Human Decision Processes* 115:181–90.

Sullivan, C. J. 2013. "Computer Simulation Experiments and the Development of Criminological Theory." In *Experimental Criminology: Prospects for Advancing Science and Public Policy*, edited by B. C. Welsh, A. A. Braga, and G. J. N. Bruinsma, pp. 65–89. New York: Cambridge University Press.

Tittle, C. R. 1969. "Crime Rates and Legal Sanctions." *Social Problems* 16:409–23.

Topalli, V., and E. C. O'Neal. 2003. "Retaliatory Motivation Enhances Attributions of Hostility When People Process Ambiguous Social Stimuli." *Aggressive Behavior* 29:155–72.

van Gelder, J. L., H. E. Hershfield, and L. F. Nordgren. 2013. "Vividness of the Future Self Predicts Delinquency." *Psychological Science* 24(6): 974–80.

Waldo, G. P., and T. G. Chiricos. 1972. "Perceived Penal Sanctions and Self-Reported Criminality: A Neglected Approach to Deterrence Research." *Social Problems* 19:522–40.

Weisman, A. M., and T. P. Taylor. 1994. "Effect of Alcohol and Risk of Physical Harm on Human Physical Aggression." *Journal of General Psychology* 121:67–76.

Wright, R., and S. H. Decker. 1994. *Burglars on the Street: Streetlife and Residential Break-ins.* Boston: Northeastern University Press.

Wright, R., and S. H. Decker. 1997. *Armed Robbers in Action: Stickups and Street Culture.* Boston: Northeastern University Press.

CHAPTER 24

....

OBSERVATIONAL METHODS OF OFFENDER DECISION MAKING

....

MARIE ROSENKRANTZ LINDEGAARD AND HEITH COPES

PARTICIPANT observations were one of the cornerstones of criminology when the field developed out of the Chicago School in the early 1900s (Bennett 1981; Sampson 2002). Researchers in Chicago were interested not only in abstract variables but also in the sights, sounds, and feelings of the streets as the city was studied as a naturalistic experiment (Abbott 1997). Participant observation was an ideal tool to gain an insider understanding of the thieves, jackrollers, hobos, delinquents, and deviants who populated the city. This method privileged the voice of participants while still providing the theoretical and methodological rigor needed to explain the structural and cultural mechanisms and relationships found significant in statistical analyses. However, since the positivistic turn in the social sciences (and criminology specifically), studies using participant observation have become marginalized in criminology (Tewksbury, DeMichele, and Miller 2005; Maruna 2010; Tewksbury, Dabney, and Copes 2010). Furthermore, the increasing influence of ethical codes in international social sciences, including the imperative of informed consent, has made participant observations a distinct and complicated matter particularly among researchers of sensitive topics such as criminologists (Winlow et al. 2001).

Whereas qualitative researchers have taken on the challenge of increasing validity and developing transparency in the process of conducting and analyzing their data (Miller and Palacios 2015) and on fostering more qualitative research (Copes 2010), the potential of *observational data* has been largely neglected. This exclusion is illustrated by an analysis of research published in top criminology journals during the period from 2000 to 2009, which found that a mere 32 articles relied on fieldwork (13 percent of the ethnographic research and less than 1 percent of all research published in these journals)

(Copes, Brown, and Tewksbury 2011). Furthermore, the definition of ethnographic research in criminology does not necessarily focus exclusively on participant observations, even though this method is considered the cornerstone of ethnography in other disciplines (Atkinson and Hammersley 1994). In criminology, ethnographic research tends to include a wide range of research, including that which draws on any text-based data, regardless of how it was collected (Copes et al. 2011). We believe that this broad definition of the concept of ethnographic research underplays the strength of observational methods, which is to not only analyze what people *say* they do but also include attention to what they *do*. Therefore, in this chapter, we focus on studies of offender decision making that involve observational methods.

Our emphasis here is on describing knowledge gained about criminal decision making based on observational methodologies. Rather than limiting our focus to traditional participant observations, we include a range of different observational methods. That is, we include research that involves researchers interacting with people in real-life settings and research that involves video footage of real-life behaviors and interactions (even if researchers are not interacting with those being studied). We believe that recently emerging methods, derived from improved camera technologies, can play a crucial role in developing observational and qualitative research in criminology. Rather than excluding observational methods from the ethnographic toolbox due to the problems involved in conducting participant observations, we argue that camera observations offer new and exciting avenues for research on offender decision making and for ethnography more broadly (Piza and Sytsma 2016). We expect that observational methods (of all types) are going to take center stage in criminology again, as they did during the emergence of the field, by providing insights about what offenders do in addition to what they say they do.

I. Type of Information Gained from Observations

Independently of whether observations are carried out by a researcher, a camera, or a researcher with a camera, observations differ from narratives produced during interviews or in response to questionnaires by generating information about actions in real-life settings. Addressing the value of observations is an important step for understanding decision making. Buckle and Farrington (1984) described the potential of observational studies for criminology: "Our knowledge about the nature and incidence of offending would be increased greatly if more research projects were carried out in which offenses were observed as they occurred" (p. 63). By being a witness to actual events and actions, researchers are able to avoid the problems of retrospective studies, such as memory failure (Porter, Woodworth, and Douchette 2007) and social desirability biases. Such information is especially important for criminal decision-making research because there are accusations that people may present overly rational reconstructions of their behaviors when discussing them after the fact (Cromwell and Olson 2004).

By observing what people do, information gained from interviews or question-naires can be triangulated for the purpose of validity (Lindegaard 2010). By combin-ing observations with other methods, contradictory perspectives might emerge, which can provide understanding of the complexity of lived experiences. For example, gang members might claim to be indifferent toward peer pressure during interviews but real-world observations may reveal that they clearly adjust their behavior to impress their peers (Bucerius 2014). Robbers may say they carefully plan their crimes but observa-tions counter this by showing how some crimes are spontaneous events spawned by ser-endipitous events (Jacobs 2010). Such triangulation does not necessarily suggest that the observation-based perspective is more valid than the interview-based perspectives. Rather, it provides an understanding of how situations affect behavior outside of ideal beliefs. In addition, observations can be used to double-check factual information. For example, robbers might claim not to use a gun during a robbery, but closed-circuit tele-vision (CCTV) camera footage providing observations of the robbery shows that they do use a gun. Shoplifters may say they only steal low-cost items, but CCTV cameras may show otherwise (for the strength of using eye-tracking devices for understanding shop-lifting, see Jacques, Lasky, and Fisher 2015). It is clear that observational methods can provide tremendous insights into our understanding of crime.

II. Types of Observational Methods

Observational methods are typically categorized as either *structured* or *unstructured* (Muhall 2002). Structured observations refer to deductively driven research approaches. Typically, the researcher has developed a coding scheme based on existing research before conducting observations. The aim of structured observations is to record fac-tual aspects of behavior or conditions of a neighborhood to test existing hypotheses. For example, Sampson and Raudenbush (1999) videotaped neighborhoods to observe signs of social disorder based on concepts derived from their theory of collective efficacy. Unstructured observations refer to inductively driven research approaches in which the researcher develops a coding scheme after having conducted the observations. The aim of unstructured observations is to record the lived experiences of the people being observed to generate new theories and hypotheses. For example, Sandberg and Pedersen (2011) observed immigrant drug dealers in Oslo, Norway, and developed the idea of street capital to explain the behaviors of participants.

The distinction between structured and unstructured observations represents typical divisions between quantitative and qualitative research and positivistic and construc-tivist research paradigms. However, we believe that this distinction does not do justice to the potential analyses that are possible based on the variety of observations con-ducted by criminologists. These methods differ in terms of the degree of impact that the researcher has on the behavior observed and also in terms of the degree of systematic and detailed analysis that is possible to carry out based on the data generated.

Based on our review of observational studies of offender decision making, we distinguish between three key types: participant observations, researcher observations, and camera observations. These types of observations differ in terms of how much researchers disturb the object of study through their presence and how systematic the data produced can be analyzed. Participant observations have the greatest researcher influence and least systematic data, whereas camera observations have the least research influence and most systematic data.

A. Participant Observations

Participant observation research involves researchers interacting with and getting to know those under investigation. With this type of study, researchers take the time to observe people in their day-to-day lives. Alice Goffman's (2014) study of black men in Philadelphia exemplifies this approach (and the inherent ethical issues that arise when using this approach). It is true that some participant observation research involves observing crime as it occurs (Lindegaard 2009); however, most studies in this category simply involve observations in the everyday life of offenders and rarely include actual criminal events other than small-scale drug sells and purchases (Anderson 1999; Goffman 2014). Participant observation research differs from what we refer to as researcher observations by being carried out by a researcher who aims to directly interact with those being studied. Although researchers rarely need to become true "insiders" among those they study (because maintaining an outsider position is important for the ability to reflect on and be transparent about interpretations), the aim of the researcher is to avoid disturbing the object of study as much as possible. Ideally, the respondents get to know researchers as outsiders and then build long-term relationship with them so that they forget about the outsider position and perceive researchers as trusted insiders. This perceived insider position in principle provides the researcher with access to undisturbed behavior that may not be possible in non-observational studies.

Although some ethnographic researchers "go native" by becoming gang leaders (Venkatesh 2008), boxers (Waquant 2004), or driving people around to commit crimes (Goffman 2014), in practice researchers who do participant observations rarely get to observe undisturbed behavior because their presence tends to have some effect on those they are observing. The ability to reflect on their positionality or the ways researchers impact the people they study is therefore a crucial aspect of the analysis of observations (Huisman 2008). Because participant observations are unique, they are impossible to repeat for the purpose of validity and interreliability among researchers. Validity of this type of data is ensured through triangulating with other methods. Because the purpose with data produced through participant observations typically is to generate theories rather than test them, the most common type of analysis is inductively driven.

Compared to the more structured researcher observations, the analysis conducted on data from participant observations is less systematic.

B. Researcher Observations

Studies based on researcher observations are the most common in criminology, and they include observations of shoplifters (Buckle and Farrington 1994), drug dealers (Bernasco and Jacques 2015), and aggression inside bars (Graham et al. 2006) and outside bars (Townsley and Grimshaw 2013). Researcher observations differ from participant observations by being carried out by a researcher who remains at a distance from the object of study. In this role, the researcher remains an outsider and often is not even known among those being studied. The aim of the remote outsider position is to avoid disturbing the behaviors that are being observed. Ideally, the researcher is able to observe interactions without having an effect on the observed behavior. Whereas the participant observer tries not to stand out by claiming a position as "insider," the researcher observer aims to do the same but through the strategy of remaining at a distance. However, it is not always possible for the researcher to avoid disturbing the behavior observed. For example, Bernasco and Jacques (2015) describe how conducting researcher observations of rather neutral aspects of the environment of drug dealing areas of Amsterdam (e.g., the number of pedestrians) raised questions such as "What are you doing?" by the people being observed.

This style of observation lends itself to higher reliability because different researchers can compare their observations. By comparing observations of different researchers, it is possible to identify potential differences of interpretations. Typically, researcher observations are limited to predefined categories and concepts because this type of observational research is usually conducted to test existing theories in a deductively driven research approach. However, inductive research is also possible with this style. Researcher observations are typically quantified and included as variables for statistical analysis in ways similar to answers to questionnaires. The type of analysis carried out on these kinds of data is therefore more systematic than the analysis of participant observations, but it is much less detailed than what is possible based on camera observations.

C. Camera Observations

As in researcher observational research, in camera observations researchers try to remain distant from those under study. The difference between the two is in the use of video technology in recording the behaviors of those under study. The use of camera observations as a means to gain insights into criminal behavior is relatively new in criminology. Although body cameras (typically worn by law enforcement) have begun to emerge (Lum et al. 2015), studies of offender decision making have been limited to mobile camera devices and to CCTV surveillance cameras. Mobile camera devices have been used primarily for "systematic social observations" applied in the study of the impact of physical and social disorder on criminal behavior (Sampson and Raudenbush 1999; St. Jean 2007). CCTV cameras have recently been used to study how criminal events unfold, including street fights (Levine, Taylor, and Best 2011), violent demonstrations (Nassauer 2015), drug dealing (Moeller 2016), robberies (Lindegaard and Bernasco 2016), genocide (Kluseman 2012), shoplifting (Dabney, Hollinger, and Dugan 2004), and drug dealing (Piza and Sytsma 2016). Jacques and colleagues (Jacques et al. 2015; Lasky, Jacques, and Fisher 2015) have developed a particularly interesting methodology involving the use of eye-tracking devices to monitor the behavior of would-be shoplifters.

Mobile video devices tend to be carried by a researcher, who thereby may influence the object of study. CCTV cameras do not necessitate the presence of a researcher. Although it is known that people tend to change their behavior in the presence of a CCTV camera (van Bommel et al. 2014), observations carried out by CCTV cameras are likely to be less disturbed than those carried out by a researcher using body cameras or mobile devices. Compared to researcher-held camera observations, the disadvantage of CCTV cameras is that the footage is unrelated to the object of the study and may not be directed in the areas of most interest to the researcher. Furthermore, the camera is usually continuously on, which means it provides an endless amount of footage that requires time-intensive editing to select scenes relevant for the object of study. Nevertheless, this type of video footage can provide interesting results (Moeller 2016).

The main advantage of camera observations is the ability to repeat the footage and have multiple researchers code the same behaviors and interactions. Unlike participant and researcher observations, it is possible to watch the object of the study numerous times, which enables a highly detailed and systematic analysis. Furthermore, it is possible to take intercoder reliability into consideration. The validity of the study is thereby ensured through the possibility of systematic analysis. Unlike participant and researcher observations, camera observations are suitable for both generating and testing theories. Based on the footage, it is possible to conduct both an inductively driven approach involving open-ended coding and a deductively driven approach including closed-ended coding. Whereas qualitative research tends to be limited in the number of cases due to the time-consuming aspect of collecting the data, camera observations are capable of overcoming this limitation due to the relatively easy access to large numbers of cases. This possibility enables a combination of inductively driven coding on a subsample, which subsequently can be applied on larger samples.

III. Types of Offender Decision Making

The type of information that can be collected and analyzed from observational methods is nearly unlimited. Thus, before we provide an overview of the studies of offender decision making based on the three types of observational methods described previously, we explain the aspects of the decision-making process that we focus on. Our aim here is to discuss some of the types of information regarding criminal decision making obtained using observational methods. We focus on broad aspects of the decision-making process, including the choice to get involved in crime, characteristics of decision makers, conditions that enhance the likelihood that a criminal decision will be made, situational aspects of the criminal event in which decisions are made, and the way criminal decisions are carried out during the event (i.e., modus operandi).

In the criminological literature, these different aspects of the decision-making process tend to be divided into studies focusing on the structural conditions for crime involvement, and persistence and desistence from crime (i.e., life course studies), and studies focusing on the choice of committing specific types of crimes (i.e., rational choice). We do not reproduce this division here because we believe it is based on a normative construction of people as, on the one hand, being passive victims of (unfortunate) structural conditions rather than being driven by agency (intentional and aware choice) in their choice for crime involvement (Lindegaard and Jacques 2014) and, on the other hand, as carrying out their crimes as calculating individuals who focus on maximizing their personal benefits. By applying a broad definition of decision making, we emphasize the importance of acknowledging how all aspects of the criminal decision-making process are driven by both structure and agency to varying degrees.

In this chapter, we show how different types of observational methods provide valuable insights into different aspects of the criminal decision-making process. Studies based on participant observations have focused predominantly on the choice to get involved in and continue crime and on the personal characteristics of the criminal decision makers. Studies based on camera observations and researcher observations have primarily provided answers to questions relating to the conditions for the criminal decision, the situational characteristics of the criminal event, and the way crimes are enacted.

IV. INSIGHTS ABOUT OFFENDER DECISION MAKING

Here, we seek to provide a modest summary of the literature on observational research on offender decision making. Because the topics of inquiry vary from crack dealers in New York to genocide offenders in Rwanda and fraught offenders in the banking sector of London, we are reluctant to define common denominators of the findings presented. Instead, we highlight the potential gains that can be achieved with this style of research and provide supplementary evidence along the way.

A. Explanations for Criminal Decisions

Participant observation is a useful method to gain insights into the motivations (and potential constraints) for committing crime because it allows the researcher to become embedded into the lives of the people studied. Understanding the choices people make tends to be easier when researchers put themselves in the place of their participants. A range of studies have provided excellent insights into why people engage in crime (Willis 1977; Winlow et al. 2001; Wacquant 2004; Berenschot 2009; Bucerius 2014; Goffman 2014). This research suggests that motivations for crime are vast and vary based on the type of crime in question. Some crimes (e.g., burglary and fraud) are committed primarily for financial gain, whereas others (e.g., violence) may have more social reasons.

At the most basic level, most crimes are committed for financial gain. Sutherland (1937) was one of the first to use observational methods in the study of people who commit crimes. He focused on the life of a professional thief and showed the priority of money in instigating crime. Sutherland interviewed the same thief on different occasions and asked him to both observe the behavior of other thieves and to reflect on his own actions. The subject of the book made it clear that some thieves perceive theft like any other business: They steal to earn an income. Sutherland stated,

> A better description of a professional thief is that he seeks money not thrills. Every professional thief would pack in the racket tomorrow if he could get a legitimate job sufficiently remunerative to meet what he believed to be his necessary living costs. (pp. 141–142)

It is true that most crime is committed for financial reasons, but simply stating that criminals do it for the money does not provide the full picture of their motives. What they do with the proceeds of crime is important for a full understanding of criminal motives. Ethnographic research has shown that many persistent thieves use the money to maintain specific lifestyles. In his book on people who deal crack in El Barrio in New York, Bourgois (2003) described their motivations as related to being able to maintain a certain standard of living. His participants believed that they faced serious barriers to the legal labor market, and their legal employments were always short term. When his participants were fired from the low-wage employment they could get, they tended to narrate their dismissal as resistance toward mainstream society rather than the consequence of personal failure (p. 115). Dealing crack was explained through similar discourses of resistance. Bourgois described crack dealing as a way to establish upwardly social mobility. Like other groups involved in improving their status and living conditions, crack dealers tended to engage in conspicuous consumption so that they were constantly searching to obtain more cash. Such hustling spirits are common among observational research (Sandberg and Pedersen 2011).

Similar to the crack dealers in Bourgois' (2003) study, people in Lindegaard and Jacques's (2014) study in Cape Town, South Africa, described engaging in crime as a means for upward social mobility. In the post-apartheid era, with its promise of redistribution of resources from the white minority to the black and colored majority, young men living in township areas expected to experience improved living conditions. For those who did not trust that investments in education and legal jobs would pay off in the long term, criminal activities such as engaging in robberies and carjacking were viewed as a safer alternative. In addition to earning an income, crime provided a sense of belonging and an opportunity to become famous, even if only in their community.

It is undoubtedly true that the desire for cash is what most motivates offenders. However, participant observation research also informs us that motivations are complex. People have quite varied reasons for acting the way they do and for saying why they acted as they did (Mills 1940). In addition to money, people are motivated by the more expressive desires, including thrills and experiences, and these motivations should not be overlooked. These more sensual motives (Katz 1988) can lure those who do not fit the typical profile of offenders to dabble in crime. Through participation in a football hooligan group for more than eight years, Buford (1991) described how the thrill experienced when engaging in crowd violence was the driving force behind football-related violence:

> I had not expected the violence to be so pleasurable. I would have assumed, if I had thought to think about it, that the violence would be exciting—in the way that a traffic incident is exciting—but the pure elemental pleasure was of an intensity that was unlike anything I had foreseen or experienced before. (p. 219)

For young men who generally lived conventional lives with legal jobs and families to care for, attending football matches and getting involved in violence was a way to get out of the daily routine and feel alive.

Participant observations have also shown that offenders are motivated to engage in crime as a means to gain status among a certain group. Some youth engage in violence to show they adhere to the code of the street (Anderson 1999). Similarly, some sell or use drugs as a means to fit in better with their peers. Palacios and Fenwick (2002) participated in the nightlife scene for several months to observe Ecstasy users. They found that the search for a sense of belonging was an important motivation for engagement in crime. Among their participants, the main motivation for using drugs was to achieve a feeling of being able to connect with others (p. 278). Jacques and Wright (2015) found that young, suburban, white people considered dealing drugs as cool and made them worthy of friendship. For these suburban dealers, a place among peers was more important for their choice to deal than was the possible profit earned from their activities. Through drug dealing, one could offer cheap or free drugs and thereby claim a position as a generous type who was worth engaging.

Although the motivation to be considered cool was less at the forefront of the narratives of the participants in Sandberg and Pedersen's (2011) study of street dealers in Oslo, their participants described their involvement in dealing as a way of establishing status in the culture of the street (see also Sandberg 2008a, 2008b). Many of their participants were ethnic minority Norwegians who experienced extreme forms of marginalization. Through dealing, they gained a sense of belonging among people on the street—a sense they generally lacked in relation to mainstream society.

Anderson (1999) described a similar quest for status among the crime-involved participants in his study. Violent behavior was a way to gain status among people following what he referred to as "the code of the street." In the area where he conducted his study, people generally lacked conventional means for social status in mainstream society, such as education and reliable employment. The code of the street offered an alternative system for social status that could be acquired by engaging in crime and displaying willingness to use violence. Committing crime was a means for status in the social hierarchies of the street. Ness (2004) made similar conclusions in her study of fights among girls in Philadelphia. As she described, "When a fight is about to go down, everyone knows it. Go on the avenue. You run into so and so and fight. Even if you don't want to fight, to be popular you have to, so you just get it over with" (p. 39). Girls said they fought when they felt challenged by the way others looked at them on the street: "If a girl looks at me the wrong way, I may hit her. I ain't gonna listen to no shit for too long" (p. 40). Jealousy was also mentioned as an important reason to fight: "It's like, if another girl gets attention, she's taking it away from you. It's as if she's saying she's better than you. So you gonna knock her down a notch" (p. 40). Similarly, Garot (2010) found that gang members aggressively ask questions such as "Where you from?" to provoke fights to gain status.

By interacting with people in their worlds, we can see the various ways they make sense of their lives and crimes. Specifically, we can better understand how those who violate norms excuse and justify their acts. Sometimes this proximity shows that they do not define their deeds as criminal, regardless of how the law views these behaviors. Luyendijk (2015) studied bankers employed in the London financial world. Whereas the participants in Buford's (1991) study experienced their criminal acts as thrilling exactly because they were defined as illegal, participants in Luyendijk's study did not view their fraught practices as illegal. His observational research described how fraught practices were defined as a part of a gray zone of activities that were neither legal nor illegal. The motivation for carrying out such activities was to keep up a certain standard of living that despite being far above the average income in the country was defined as necessary for survival. Fraught practices were viewed by the offenders as a right rather than a risk, let alone a criminal act. This is remarkably similar to how more modest employee thieves make sense of their crime. For example, Ditton (1977) traveled with bread salesmen who stole bread and sold it on the side for personal profit. He found that these behaviors were defined as no big deal and were viewed as the perks of the job. In short, they did not define themselves as real thieves.

Participant observations also reveal that even those who commit horrible crimes can justify their actions. Based on participant observations among survivors of the Rwandan genocide, Fuji (2009) sought to understand what motivated and constrained killings of neighbors. Independent of ethnicity and whether her participants were "joiners" or "resisters," involvement in the killings was explained in situational ways. The general assumption was that no one would engage in killing practices without a particular reason. The reason for this was not explained through personal characteristics but, rather, through impact of the environment, as suggested by one of her participants: "Because of the war, people fled toward different areas and because of the different atmosphere [in each locale], the people, infected by their environment, picked up a new way of behaving. When they returned, people no longer got along like before" (p. 99). The reason people got involved in the killing was related to whether they got "infected" by others. Another "joiner" explained why he got involved:

> I didn't make a decision to participate in the genocide killing. I was only in the group because that day, I was right next to the road and when the people were screaming, I went to see what happened and it was the killing of [names victims] by the group, which included me.
>
> *Q. How did others decide to participate?*
> First, there was the mobilization by the authorities. The others were forced. The others entered into participating without knowing it, that is, without deciding to do it.
>
> *Q. Which category fits you?*
> I was in the last category, and it was why I wanted to speak the whole truth and to speak out about everything I saw. (p. 155)

To explain why some people resisted while others joined knowing that they potentially could get "infected" by group dynamics in similar ways, Fuji (2009) argued that "resisters" tended to believe in their own moral superiority; they did not allow any influence of others, and that aspect of their personality made them able to resist getting involved in the killings.

The described studies of the motivation to get involved in crime suggest that the reasons for crime involvement differ depending on whether people perceived themselves as included or excluded in mainstream society. Among people who considered themselves as included in mainstream society, crime was described as a way to get a thrill, to earn what one deserved, to avoid social exclusion, to gain a sense of belonging, and to be considered cool and socially likable. Among people who experienced being marginalized from mainstream society, crime was a way to earn an income, to become upwardly socially mobile, and to gain honor and status among other street-oriented people and thereby a sense of social belonging.

In summary, explanations for criminal decision making must be understood in the context of the offenders' lives. To understand decision making, it is necessary to know what makes sense to a person. Even if one can unravel the objective motive (e.g., money or revenge), it is still important (perhaps more so) to understand how the offender makes sense of his or her behaviors. Participant observations provide an ideal means of understanding how individuals make sense of their lives and crimes in the context of their social position.

B. Characteristics of the Criminal Decision Maker

One advantage of relying on observations when interested in the characteristics of criminal decision makers is that it is possible to take account of a range of people who offend, including those unknown to the authorities. As Buckle and Farrington (1984) noted, "Official statistics reflect the behavior of official agencies as well as that of offenders, and these two aspects are difficult to disentangle" (p. 63). Overall, this research has shown that relying solely on official statistics may distort our understanding of who commits crime. Observational research (especially camera observations) can provide some light into the dark figure of crime.

Dabney et al. (2006) used camera observations of shoppers' behaviors to identify what kinds of people were involved in shoplifting. Their findings suggested that contrary to official records of young people as the most common shoplifters, middle-aged shoppers (thirty-five to fifty-four years old) were the most likely to shoplift. Furthermore, Hispanic female shoppers were most likely to shoplift, whereas white females were least likely. These findings confirmed the results of Buckle and Farrington's (1984) study of shoplifting based on researcher observations in a department store in England. They found that shoppers who were older than age fifty-five years were more likely to steal than were younger shoppers and that men were more likely to steal than were women. When the same authors replicated their study in 1994, they confirmed official records suggesting that young people were more likely to shoplift than older people (Buckle and Farrington 1994). This suggests that determining who is most likely to offend is a difficult problem to address.

In a study of aggression, Graham and colleagues (2006, 2014) conducted researcher observations of occurrences of aggression that took place in bars and night clubs. Based on more than 1,000 incidences of aggression, they concluded that men were much more likely to be aggressors than were women. Women were more likely to slap others and less likely to push or kick their opponents compared to male aggressors; furthermore, women were more likely to engage in less severe forms of aggression than were men (Graham et al. 2006, p. 289). In an observational study of sexual aggression in bars, Graham et al. (2014) concluded that in 90 percent of the recorded incidences, the aggressors were male and the targets were female. Aggressors were more invasive when the target was intoxicated.

Studies based on participant observations rarely aimed at quantifying the likelihood that people with certain characteristics became involved in specific types of crimes. Findings from such research nevertheless suggest characteristics of people that made them at risk of crime involvement. As Anderson (1999) noted, not all people in high-crime areas commit crime. Despite living in the same communities, people he labeled decent abstained from predatory crimes and would code switch as a means of self-protection when interacting with those defined as street.

Much research based on participant observations has shown that the characteristics of offenders and non-offenders are often very similar. Humphreys' (1970) observations in tea rooms (public places men engage in casual sex) showed that the men who frequented these places had personal characteristics similar to those of the general population. Similarly, the joiners identified in Fuji's (2009) study of genocide were no different from the resisters in terms of personal characteristics. That is, joiners were ordinary members of the community, and most were married with children and were farmers who were born in the places where they resided at the time of the genocide.

Sutherland (1937) explained that his respondent started a working career in a legal job. Whereas amateur thieves tended to remain amateurs, professional thieves likely developed out of successful jobs in the legal sector. They simply changed one type of profession for another. Despite their success, they continuously doubted if they should quit stealing and get into legal businesses again. These findings are echoed by Steffensmeier's (1986) work on a professional fence (see also Steffensmeier and Ulmer 2005). Professional thieves were not fundamentally different from other kinds of people; they shared characteristics with people who were successful in legal businesses and, at least in the case of Steffensmeier's informant, viewed themselves as good people.

Participant observations have also shown that many offenders are relatively uncommitted to crime. They have little problem drifting back to conventionality due to their social capital. This clear separation of legal and illegal jobs in different life phases was found in Jacques and Wright's (2015) study of drug dealers in the suburbs of the United States. They described how any obstacles in their businesses (e.g., when being robbed or threatened) typically led to giving up on their illegal businesses and returning to investing in their educational lives and the prospects of getting a legal career in the future. Drug dealing provided the participants with respect and desirability and with the possibility of earning money without having to do lower class jobs. They generally tended to view themselves as too good for such jobs. The participants in Jacques and Wright (2015)'s study did not intend to make a career out of drug dealing. They simply wanted extra spending money in a life phase in which they could not yet capitalize on their middle-class positions. Drug dealing was therefore related to a short life phase of their middle-class existence because it enable them to live a middle-class life without yet being qualified for legal middle-class jobs.

This division between legal and illegal jobs in different life phases is not characteristic of all offenders, especially those from lower classes. For the offenders in Bourgois' (2003) study in El Barrio, it was common to combine legal work with drug dealing careers; in fact, drug dealing careers provided a type of continuity in income and status that dealers were unable to achieve through legal jobs. His participants were proud of their street culture identity that was defined as resisting mainstream society. MacLeod (1987) showed how even among the same housing project, those who commit crime take different paths in legitimate employment.

Sandberg and Pedersen (2011) described a similar combination of legal and illegal activities among street dealers in Oslo. Their participants belonged to the bottom of the hierarchy of mainstream society:

> In the legal economy they [their participants] were losers. Likely jobs for them in the white economy would be poorly paid, requiring few skills and be of low status. The River, however, offered them social rewards, a possibility of social status, money, and not least, respectability and admiration. (p. 21)

Their failure to get an education and become qualified for middle-class jobs was described as related to their foreign background and the difficulty in obtaining adequate education.

The previously described studies of characteristics of criminal decision makers suggest that little consistency exists in who tends to get involved in crime. Whereas the described studies potentially offer insights about offenders who are not necessarily deterred for the crimes they committed, the weakness of these findings is the nonrepresentative samples. To ensure generalizability, more observations and a more systematic approach are required. Nevertheless, this kind of research has shed light on the importance of context when determining characteristics of offenders and demonstrates why official statistics are insufficient in and of themselves.

V. Frequency of Criminal Decisions

Similar to the study of the characteristics of criminal decision makers, the advantage of relying on observations when studying the frequency of criminal decisions is to gain insights about those events that are not included in official crime statistics. Studies that have focused on the frequency of criminal decisions include camera and researcher observations. Both have provided insights into the way crimes are carried out and have described physical and social characteristics of neighborhoods known for high crime rates.

Due to the presence of security cameras in many large stores, shoplifting is an ideal crime for the study of crime prevalence. It is relatively easy to watch who enters a store and their behaviors once inside. Dabney et al.'s (2006) study of shoplifting based on recordings made in one store showed that 8.5 percent of shoppers were involved in shoplifting. Buckle and Farrington's (1984) study of shoplifting proposed that between 1 and 2 percent of the customers entering the shop were stealing. They estimated that in the particular shop of their study, approximately 500 shopliftings took place in 1 week—an estimation that was more than ten times the official figures for shoplifting.

The use of camera observations has also shed light on the amount and patterns of drug sales (Moeller 2016). Using police surveillance cameras, Moeller was able to provide information about the patterns and prevalence of cannabis sales in one area of Copenhagen (the open-air cannabis market in Christiana). Not only was he able to determine the prevalence of sales but also the cameras allowed him to determine the rhythm of sales, including variation in sales by time of day, day of week, and proximity to payday. In addition, Moeller and Pedersen (2014) found that buyers of cannabis prefer joints and to buy small amounts in individual purchases.

Observations based on camera recordings carried out by researchers are also useful for determining the prevalence of crime in public places, including street corners and neighborhoods. Through recorded observations of physical and social disorder in 23,816 face blocks of Chicago, Sampson and Raudenbush (1999) collected detailed information on physical conditions, housing characteristics, businesses, and social interactions. They were interested in understanding how social and physical disorder was related to different types of crimes. They defined social disorder as any threatening behavior, such as verbal harassment on the street, open solicitation for prostitution, public intoxication, and rowdy groups of young males. They defined physical disorder as the deterioration of urban landscapes (e.g., graffiti on buildings, abandoned cars, broken windows, and garbage in the streets). Based on an analysis of camera recordings of the street segments, they concluded that disorder was a moderate correlate with predatory but not violent crime. They found a significant albeit relatively modest association of disorder with officially measured robbery. According to their findings, offenders were likely to commit crime in areas characterized by structural disadvantage and attenuated collective efficacy.

St. Jean (2007) conducted an ethnographic study of neighborhood disorder in Chicago, combining interviews with both participant and researcher observations. Like Sampson and Raudenbush (1999), he was interested in understanding the relationship between neighborhoods and occurrences of crime. Based on his researcher observations, he concluded that collective efficacy reduced the risk of drug dealing and the amount of robberies in an area. Based on his participant observations, he suggested that what mattered for the likelihood that an offender would commit a crime was not collective efficacy (as defined by researchers) but, rather, subjective perceptions of solidarity among residents. He operationalized subjective solidarity as whether people perceived others on the block as being like them. Crimes occurred less often in areas where subjective solidarity was high. Apparently, offenders were less likely to commit crimes in places where people had a feeling of shared life experiences with their neighbors. In short, his participant observations in the community allowed him to uncover differing definitions of disorder, and his researcher observations enabled him to link this to its impact on crime. What outsiders (i.e., researchers) saw as disorder was not seen as such by residents.

VI. Situational Characteristics of Criminal Decision Making

All three types of observations of criminal events potentially provide insights into what kinds of situational factors influence the outcome of the events. Such factors include interactions between the parties involved, characteristics of the place, expression of emotions, and level of intoxication of the parties involved. Whereas camera observations potentially provide insights about sequences of actions during events, researcher observations typically focus on the number and type of people involved in criminals events and the physical structure of the places where the events occurred.

Based on camera observations, Levine et al. (2011) examined nightlife-related conflicts. They were interested in understanding how the presence of bystanders influenced the likelihood that conflicts would become physically aggressive. Their findings suggested that bystanders were more likely to take conciliatory actions than to escalate violence as the size of the group increased. In contrast to traditional psychological accounts of the role of groups and group size in violence, they found that the more bystanders present during a conflict, the more likely that someone would intervene in conciliatory ways.

In a study of sexual aggression in bar settings, Graham and colleagues (2014) observed how intoxication of victims and offenders influenced the likelihood that a conflict would become sexually aggressive. Based on researcher observations, they found that intoxication influenced the reaction of the victim when being exposed to sexual aggression, but it did not influence the likelihood that someone would become an offender of sexual aggression. Another study of aggression in bar settings found that, based on researcher observations, bystanders were more likely to intervene in conflicts that included the following characteristics: severe forms of aggression, aggression used by multiple people against each other, conflicts involving only men, and parties who were intoxicated (Parks et al. 2013). Bystanders were generally more likely to intervene in consolidating than escalating ways. Perceived danger of serious harm was an important factor for whether bystanders would intervene in aggressive situations.

Based on extensive hours of researcher observations in public spaces outside bars and night clubs, Townsley and Grimshaw (2013) analyzed acts of high- and low-level aggression. Their focus was situational characteristics of the places where these incidences occurred. They concluded that people were more likely to become aggressive in places with more cross-paths, with high levels of crowding, when more time was spent in queues, and when queues were managed in ineffective ways. In general, crowding made people significantly more likely to become aggressive. These results showed that aggression was more than just the product of the number of people on the street and how much alcohol they drink. Physical environment and the density of streets also played a role in the likelihood that someone would engage in violent acts.

In a study based on camera observations of demonstrations, Nassauer (2015) explained why some street protests remain peaceful, whereas others become violent. She suggested that certain patterns of the interaction emerge before violence occurs: First, a phase exists in which tension and fear build up, and then a phase evolves in which emotional dominance is established and tension is released into violence. These emotional phases precede the outbreak of violence in a period of one to three hours after the start of a protest. Furthermore, certain types of actions make violence more likely: the breaking up of police–protester lines and actors being outnumbered or falling down. The emotional dynamic between protesters and officers during a protest also influences the intensity of violence and how violent situations end.

Based on participant observations of male fights among young men in South Africa conducted as part of an ethnographic study, Lindegaard (2009) analyzed whether conflict situations developed in physically aggressive ways. Although a limited number of situations were analyzed, the details about each situation were extensive and included observations of the act while it took place and of the background characteristics and life histories and motivations of the people involved. Lindegaard concluded that conflicts tended to become violent when the social hierarchies between the young men interacting were unclear. An acknowledged dominator–dominated relationship made violence less likely to occur. Physical aggression was therefore closely related to the social positioning of the young men interacting. Male fights were more likely to occur in situations characterized by unclear social hierarchies.

A. Carrying out the Criminal Decision

Knowing how people carry out or enact their crimes is beneficial to theorists and social control agents. By observing offenders, it is possible to uncover the various ways they enact their crimes to increase profit and minimize risk. Whereas camera and researcher observations potentially provide details about how offenders commit their crimes, participant observations can be useful for understanding the way they experience committing their crimes. Here, we focus on the various insights that observations have provided for the ways offenders minimize the risks of doing crime—a branch of decision-making research that falls under restrictive deterrence (Jacobs 1996).

Observations have taught us much about the way offenders think about the risks of crime and how they overcome the risks. For instance, the professional thief in Sutherland's (1937) book described how stealing was a business, but one that never fully became routine:

> There is little thrill about it. When a job is being pulled off, there is a tense and emotional situation, and the work cannot be routine. From the start of the actual mechanics of taking off a score until it is completed, the thief is under a strain caused by suspicion, fear of a tumble (not an arrest), saying the right thing at the right time, thought of whether his partners will perform properly, retention of composure, appearance of nonchalance, hard thinking of other things. These are parts of series of actions which culminate in a touch being taken off or blowed. (p. 140)

Such insights suggest that offenders do not passively accept risk. Instead, they actively find ways to reduce it. The thief furthermore explained that the main challenge of stealing was the ability to manipulate the victim. Stealing from businesses typically involved a conversation with the victim to create distraction from co-offenders who would then steal the goods.

Offenders have different strategies for managing victims, depending on the crime in question. Sutherland's (1937) thief made a point of interacting with victims in stores to be better able to manipulate them. This way of carrying out the crime was quite different from the findings based on camera observations of shoplifting. Dabney et al. (2006) found that shoplifters tried to avoid workers by not buying anything. They would simply walk in, obtain the items, and walk out with as few interactions as possible. Another study of shoplifting based on researcher observations found that shoplifters tended to buy small, inexpensive items (Buckle and Farrington 1984). Shoplifters stole very expensive items while paying for low-cost objects presumably to present themselves as regular shoppers and allay suspicion, which is consistent with Sutherland's finding.

Similar to professional thieves, crack dealers in Bourgois' (2003) study emphasized that their business was very similar to legal ones. The only differences were the exceptional dangers, high profits, and the intensity of interacting with addicted customers. His participants described dealing crack under the ruse of a legitimate business, such as a game room, to act as a distraction for possible suspicion of law enforcement:

> A subtle touch of "normalcy" was added by the presence of Primo's adopted grandfather, Abraham, who was responsible for collecting the quarters from the video machines. Whenever potential undercover narcotic detectives entered the Game Room, this hopelessly alcoholic seventy-two-years-old man pretended to be senile. (p. 106)

Based on his participant observations among dealers, St. Jean (2007) also described how street dealers in his study searched for places to deal that were left undetected by local law enforcement. Places that were characterized by high levels of disorder were popular because dealers viewed the disorder as a sign that the city's government did not care about these places. St. Jean's participant observations furthermore showed that robbers searched for targets in places around businesses where people used cash frequently. When they were choosing a target, they would evaluate the vulnerability of the victim and the suitability of the escape route.

In a study based on researcher observations of the places where street dealers were doing business in Amsterdam, Bernasco and Jacques (2015) showed that they preferred to deal in places that were on crowded streets and around businesses. These places were heavily patrolled by formal social control such as CCTV and police. Participants were aware of the risks of getting caught but explained that the potential number of customers facilitated by these places were more important than the risk of getting caught. Dealers described encountering police officers ten to fifteen times per day while doing their business. To avoid getting caught, they developed a range of strategies, including walking rather than remaining stationary while interacting with customers.

Target selection is not simply about minimizing risk. Some targets are chosen based on the expressive gains they provide. Drug dealers target certain customers to reduce risk and for symbolic gain within the group. Jacques and Wright (2015) described dealers in the suburbs as living less risky lives by selling to people they knew beforehand. Most customers were friends or people they considered to be cool. The price offered depended on the relationship with the dealer. If a customer was viewed as important in terms of providing high levels of coolness for the dealer, that customer would get a better deal than people who were less important in terms of status. Disputes about trades were generally dealt with through the strategy of tolerating: Suburban dealers would rather accept being busted than get involved in a conflict. Retaliating violent victimization was also uncommon because they preferred to give up on their business rather than risk getting into legal trouble.

Sandberg's (2008) ethnographic study including participant observations of people involved in various types of hustling activities in Oslo suggested that dealers felt obligated to retaliate if they were robbed or attacked on the street (see also Anderson 1999). Participants in Sandberg's study would choose streetwise opponents for a fight to gain status in the hierarchies of the street. Target selection for fights was therefore heavily influenced by the logic of street culture with the aim of earning points to gain respect (Anderson 1999).

Based on participant observations as part of an ethnographic study of young men living in township areas of Cape Town, Lindegaard, Miller, and Reynald (2013) suggested that young men who behaved white, by speaking with a suburban accent and by greeting and dressing like people in the suburbs, were at risk in terms of harassment, fights, and robberies in the townships. These young men were seen as "coconuts" (black on the outside and white on the inside) who were trying to be better than the rest. Despite their avoidance of crime involvement, young men with a suburban cultural repertoire were victimized with similar frequencies as young men involved in crime. Offenders targeted not only young men who were involved in crime but also young men who were considered outsiders, challenged perceptions of blackness, and tried to be better than the rest by aspiring toward a life in the suburbs.

Studies based on different types of observations of shoplifting revealed the importance of tricking victims through conversations (Sutherland 1937), by buying low-cost items (Buckle and Farrington 1984), or by not buying anything (Dabney et al. 2006). Drug dealers were found to avoid suspicion from law enforcement by pretending to run legal businesses (Bourgois 2003), choosing areas they knew were considered unimportant by local authorities (St. Jean 2007), adapting their customer approach in ways that were considered not suspicious by the police (Jacques and Bernasco 2015), and choosing well-known customers (Jacques and Wright 2015). Studies of some dealers suggested they preferred to do business in quiet places (St. Jean 2007; Jacques and Wright 2015), whereas another emphasized that places around businesses and busy streets were popular due to their facilitation of customers (Jacques and Bernasco 2015). Target selections for violent crimes such as fights and robberies were found to at least partly be culturally embedded: Street-credible victims were chosen to gain status (Sandberg 2008b), and socially mobile young men were chosen as a means of maintaining hierarchies of class and race (Lindegaard et al. 2013). Retaliation among dealers was similarly found to be culturally embedded: Among low-class dealers, retaliation was considered necessary as a means to avoid future victimization (Sandberg 2008b), whereas among middle-class dealers, retaliation was considered too risky (Jacques and Wright 2015).

VII. Conclusion

Despite the potential for understanding "crime in the making," observations have been relatively rare in criminology. A push toward more feminist and humanist methods as well as recent technological developments might change this picture. Indeed, camera observations have the potential to play an important role in the currently ongoing discussion of validity in qualitative methodology and in better understanding and theorizing criminal decision making. Although there are limitations to observational research, their strength is the possibility of accessing and witnessing actual behavior as it occurs in real life. Such insights can offer important understandings about criminal behavior and those who commit it that cannot not be achieved when relying solely on retrospective perspectives.

Most studies that have included observations have been explorative and inductive. These studies used participant observations as a means of getting access to unexpected factors and mechanisms influencing offender decision making. Some studies have conducted systematic analysis of the social and physical environment in which crime tends to occur based on observations carried out by a researcher with or without mobile video devices. These studies used representative samples and deductive analytical methods to draw generalizable conclusions about offender decision making.

Regardless of whether one takes a deductive or inductive approach, observations are well suited for theorizing criminal decision making, perhaps more so than other methodological designs. The types of decision making one can examine are vast; thus, we chose to discuss a sampling of them. Specifically, we showed how observational research has provided insights about explanations for criminal decisions, characteristics of the criminal decision maker, frequency of criminal decisions, situational characteristics of criminal decision making, and carrying out the criminal decision.

Camera observations were conducted using CCTV cameras and mobile recording devices in streets outside night clubs and bars, during street protests, in shops, and in areas known for high or low frequencies of crime. Researcher observations were done by situating researchers trained in coding behavior while observing in shops, in bars, and on the street. Studies based on camera and researcher observations focused on the frequency of criminal decisions, situational characteristics of the criminal decision making, and carrying out the criminal decision. Participant observations were the most common type of observations in studies of offender decision making. Participant observations imply that researchers take part in the daily activities of respondents and immerse themselves into the lives of the group as much as possible. The most common types of decision making studied with this method were the explanations for criminal decisions and the characteristics of the criminal decision maker, including their sociocultural environments.

Future studies of offender decision making would benefit from drawing on observational methods (with or without the aid of video recording devices), particularly to gain insights about factors influencing crime as it unfolds. Camera observations provide unique opportunities for the researcher to become "a fly on the wall" and to conduct both inductively and deductively driven analyses. It is easier to gain access to representative samples of camera footage than to perform the more time-consuming practice of conducting observations on the spot while crime potentially takes place. (It is also easier to justify ethically.) It therefore offers the possibility of more deductively driven analysis and theory testing rather than just refinement and development. Furthermore, recorded observations provide exciting possibilities for developing ethnographic methods within criminology and possibly contributing to ongoing discussions about validity and transparency. Recorded observations allow researchers to observe behavior as crime unfolds, making it possible to triangulate what is done with what is said during interviews and what is experienced during participant observations. Camera observations offer insights into the way crimes are committed without compromising the safety and moral obligations of the researcher to intervene. Thereby, they replace the function of participant observations as a means of getting access to what people do rather than what they say they do. Nevertheless, participant observations are still important for the study of criminal decision making because they provide unique insights into the sociocultural circumstances of the people who engage in criminal activities and their experiences with carrying out crimes. Rather than excluding observational methods from the ethnographic toolbox, new types of camera-based observations are likely to take center stage in the analysis of offender decision making.

REFERENCES

Abbott, A. 1997. "Of Time and Space: The Contemporary Relevance of the Chicago School." *Social Forces* 75:1149–82.

Anderson, E. 1999. *Code of the Street*. New York: Norton.

Atkinson, P., and M. Hammersley. 1994. "Ethnography and Participant Observation." In *Handbook of Qualitative Research*, edited by N. K. Denzin and Y. S. Lincoln, pp. 105–17. Thousand Oaks, CA: Sage.

Bennett, J. 1981. *Oral History and Delinquency: The Rhetoric of Criminology*. Chicago: University of Chicago Press.

Berenschot, W. 2009. *Riot Politics: Hindu–Muslim Violence and the Indian State*. New York: Columbia University Press.

Bernasco, W., and S. Jacques. 2015. "Where Do Dealers Solicit Customers and Sell Them Drugs? A Micro-level Multiple Method Study." *Journal of Contemporary Criminal Justice* 31(4): 376–408.

Bourgois, P. 2003. *In Search of Respect: Selling Crack in El Barrio*, vol. 10. New York: Cambridge University Press.

Bucerius, S. 2014. *Unwanted: Muslim Immigrants, Dignity, and Drug Dealing*. New York: Oxford University Press.

Buckle, A., and D. P. Farrington. 1984. "An Observational Study of Shoplifting." *British Journal of Criminology* 24(1): 63–73.

Buckle, A., and D. P. Farrington. 1994. "Measuring Shoplifting by Systematic Observation: A Replication Study." *Psychology, Crime and Law* 1(2): 133–41.

Buford, B. 1991. *Among the Thugs*. London: Secker and Warburg.

Copes, H. 2010. "Advancing Qualitative Methods in Criminal Justice and Criminology." *Journal of Criminal Justice Education* 21:387–90.

Copes, H., A. Brown, and R. Tewksbury. 2011. "A Content Analysis of Ethnographic Research Published in Top Criminology and Criminal Justice Journals from 2000–2009." *Journal of Criminal Justice Education* 22:341–59.

Cromwell, P., and J. Olson. 2004. *Breaking and Entering: Burglars on Burglary.* Belmont, CA: Wadsworth.

Dabney, D., L. Dugan, V. Topalli, and R. C. Hollinger. 2006. "The Impact of Implicit Stereotyping on Offender Profiling Unexpected Results from an Observational Study of Shoplifting." *Criminal Justice and Behavior* 33 (5): 646–74.

Dabney, D., R. Hollinger, and L. Dugan. 2004. "Who Actually Steals? A Study of Covertly Observed Shoplifters." *Justice Quarterly* 21:693–728.

Ditton, J. 1977. "Perks, Pilferage, and the Fiddle: The Historical Structure of Invisible Wages." *Theory and Society* 4(1): 39–71.

Fuji, L. A. 2009. *Killing Neighbors: Webs of Violence in Rwanda.* Ithaca, NY: Cornell University Press.

Garot, R. 2010. *Who You Claim: Performing Gang Identity in School and on the Streets.* New York: New York University Press.

Goffman, A. 2014. *On the Run: Fugitive Life in an American City.* Chicago: University of Chicago Press.

Graham, K., S. Bernards, D. Wayne Osgood, A. Abbey, M. Parks, A. Flynn, T. Dumas, and S. Wells. 2014. "'Blurred Lines?' Sexual Aggression and Barroom Culture." *Alcoholism: Clinical and Experimental Research* 38:1416–24.

Graham, K., P. F. Tremblay, S. Wells, K. Pernanen, J. Purcell, and J. Jelly. 2006. "Harm, Intent, and the Nature of Aggressive Behavior: Measuring Naturally Occurring Aggression in Barroom Settings." *Assessment* 13:280–96.

Huisman, K. 2008. "Does This Mean You're Not Going to Come Visit Me Anymore? An Inquiry into an Ethics of Reciprocity and Positionality in Feminist Ethnographic Research." *Sociological Inquiry* 78(3): 372–96.

Humphreys, L. 1970. *Tearoom Trade: Impersonal Sex in Public Places.* Piscataway, NJ: Aldine Transaction.

Jacobs, B. A. 1996. "Crack Dealers and Restrictive Deterrence: Identifying Narcs." *Criminology* 34(3): 409–31.

Jacobs, B. A. 2010. "Serendipity in Robbery Target Selection." *British Journal of Criminology* 50(3): 514–29.

Jacques, S., N. Lasky, and B. S. Fisher. 2015. "Seeing the Offenders' Perspective Through the Eye-Tracking Device: Methodological Insights from a Study of Shoplifters." *Journal of Contemporary Criminal Justice* 31:449–67.

Jacques, S., and R. Wright. 2015. *Code of the Suburb: Inside the World of Young Middle-Class Drug Dealers.* Chicago: University of Chicago Press.

Katz, J. 1988. *Seductions of Crime: Moral and Sensual Attractions in Doing Evil.* New York: Basic Books.

Kluseman, S. 2012. "Massacres as Process: A Microsociological Theory of Internal Patterns of Mass Atrocities." *European Journal of Criminology* 9(5): 468–80.

Lasky, N., S. Jacques, and B. S. Fisher. 2015. "Glossing Over Shoplifting: How Thieves Act Normal." *Deviant Behavior* 36(4): 293–309.

Levine, M., P. J. Taylor, and R. Best. 2011. "Third Parties, Violence, and Conflict Resolution: The Role of Group Size and Collective Action in the Microregulation of Violence." *Psychological Science* 22(3): 406–12.

Lindegaard, M. R. 2009. *Coconuts, Gangsters and Rainbow Fighters: How Male Youngsters Navigate Situations of Violence in Cape Town, South Africa.* Amsterdam: University of Amsterdam.

Lindegaard, M. R. 2010. "Method, Actor and Context Triangulations: Knowing What Happened During Criminal Events and the Motivations for Getting Involved as Offender." In *Offenders on Offending*, edited by W. Bernasco, pp. 109–29. Cullompton, UK: Willian.

Lindegaard, M. R., and W. Bernasco. 2015. *Robbery in the Spotlight: Explanations of Violence and Failure*. Den Haag/Apeldoorn: Elsevier-Reed/Politie and Wetenschap.

Lindegaard, M. R., W. Bernasco, and T. de Vries. 2016. *Overvallen in beeld: Dader, slachtoffer en omstander gedrag*. Den Haag/Apeldoorn: Elsevier-Reed/Politie & Wetenschap.

Lindegaard, M. R., and S. Jacques. 2014. "Agency as a Cause of Crime." *Deviant Behavior* 35:85–100.

Lindegaard, M. R., J. Miller, and D. M. Reynald. 2013. "Transitory Mobility, Cultural Heterogeneity and Victimization Risk Among Young Men of Color: Insights from an Ethnographic Study in Cape Town, South Africa." *Criminology* 51(4): 1–42.

Lum, C., C. S. Koper, L. Merola, A. Scherer, and A. Rieoux. 2015. "Existing and Ongoing Body Worn Camera Research: Knowledge Gaps and Opportunities." Report for the Laura and John Arnold Foundation. Fairfax, VA: Center for Evidence-Based Crime Policy, George Mason University.

Luyendijk, J. 2015. *Dit kan niet waar zijn. onder bankiers*. Amsterdam: Atlas Contact.

MacLeod, J. 1987. *Ain't No Makin' It: Leveled Aspirations in a Low-Income Neighborhood*. Boulder, CO: Westview.

Maruna, S. 2010. "Mixed Method Research in Criminology: Why Not Go Both Ways?" In *Handbook of Quantitative Criminology*, edited by A. Piquero and S. Weisburd, pp. 123–40. New York: Springer.

Miller, J., and W. R. Palacios. 2015. "Introduction: The Value of Qualitative Research for Advancing Criminological Theory." *Advances in Criminological Theory* 20:3–14.

Mills, C. W. 1940. "Situated Actions and Vocabularies of Motive." *American Sociological Review* 5(6): 904–13.

Moeller, K. 2016. "Temporal Transaction Patterns in an Open-Air Cannabis Market." *Police Practice and Research* 17:37–50.

Moeller, K., and M. Pedersen. 2014. "Cannabis Retail Purchases in a Low-Risk Market: Purchase Size and Sex of Buyers." *Nordic Studies on Alcohol and Drugs* 31(2): 161–74.

Muhall, A. 2002. "In the Field: Notes on Observation in Qualitative Research." *Journal of Advanced Nursing* 41(3): 306–13.

Nassauer, A. 2015. "Effective Crowd Policing: Empirical Insights on Avoiding Protest Violence.: *Policing* 38(1): 3–23.

Ness, C. D. 2004. "Why Girls Fight: Female Youth Violence in the Inner City." *Annals of the American Academy of Political and Social Science* 595:32–48.

Palacios, W. R., and M. E. Fenwick. 2002. "E Is for Ecstasy: A Participant Observation Study of Ecstasy Use." In *In Their Own Words: Criminals on Crime*, edited by P. Cromwell, pp. 295–301. New York: Oxford University Press.

Parks, M. J., D. W. Osgood, R. B. Felson, S. Wells, and K. Graham. 2013. "Third Party Involvement in Barroom Conflicts." *Aggressive Behavior* 39:257–68.

Piza, E. L., and V. A. Sytsma. 2016. "Exploring the Defensive Actions of Drug Sellers in Open-Air Markets: A Systematic Social Observation." *Journal of Research in Crime and Delinquency* 53(1): 36–65.

Porter, S., M. Woodworth, and N. L. Douchette. 2007. "Memory for Murder: The Quality and Credibility of Homicide Narratives by Perpetrators." In *Offenders' Memories of Violent Crimes*, edited by S. A. Christianson, pp. 115–132. West Sussex, UK: Wiley.

Sampson, R. J. 2002. "Transcending Tradition: New Directions in Community Research, Chicago Style." *Criminology* 40(2): 213–30.

Sampson, R. J., and S. W. Raudenbush. 1999. "Systematic Social Observation of Public Spaces: A New Look at Disorder in Urban Neighborhoods." *American Journal of Sociology* 105:603–51.

Sandberg, S. 2008a. "Black Drug Dealers in a White Welfare State: Cannabis Dealing and Street Capital in Norway." *British Journal of Criminology* 48:604–19.

Sandberg, S. 2008b. "Street Capital: Ethnicity and Violence on the Streets of Oslo." *Theoretical Criminology* 12:153–71.

Sandberg, S., and W. Pedersen. 2011. *Street Capital: Black Cannabis Dealers in a White Welfare State*. Bristol, UK: Policy Press.

St. Jean, P. K. 2007. *Pockets of Crime: Broken Windows, Collective Efficacy, and the Criminal Point of View*. Chicago: University of Chicago Press.

Steffensmeier, D. 1986. *The Fence: In the Shadow of Two Worlds*. Savage, MD: Rowan and Littlefield.

Steffensmeier, D., and J. Ulmer. 2005. *Confessions of a Dying Thief: Understanding Criminal Careers and Illegal Enterprise*. New Brunswick, NJ: Transaction Press.

Sutherland, E. H. 1937. *The Professional Thief*. Chicago: University of Chicago Press.

Tewksbury, R., D. Dabney, and H. Copes. 2010. "The Prominence of Qualitative Research in Criminology and Criminal Justice Scholarship." *Journal of Criminal Justice Education* 21:391–411.

Tewksbury, R., M. T. DeMichele, and J. M. Miller. 2005. "Methodological Orientations of Articles Appearing in Criminal Justice's Top Journals: Who Publishes What and Where." *Journal of Criminal Justice Education* 16:265–79.

Townsley, M., and R. Grimshaw. 2013. "The Consequences of Queuing: Crowding, Situational Features and Aggression in Entertainment Precincts." *Crime Prevention and Community Safety* 15:23–47.

van Bommel, M., J. W. van Prooijen, H. Elffers, and P. A. van Lange. 2014. "Intervene to Be Seen: The Power of a Camera in Attenuating the Bystander Effect." *Social Psychological and Personality Science* 5:459–66.

Venkatesh, S. 2008. *Gang Leader for a Day*. New York: Penguin.

Wacquant, L. 2004. *Body and Soul: Notebooks of an Apprentice Boxer*. Oxford: Oxford University Press.

Willis, P. 1977. *Learning to Labor*. New York: Columbia University Press.

Winlow, S., D. Hobbs, S. Lister, and P. Hadfield. 2001. "Get Ready to Duck: Bouncers and the Realities of Ethnographic Research on Violent Groups." *British Journal of Criminology* 41(3): 536–48.

CHAPTER 25

....

UNDERSTANDING OFFENDER DECISION MAKING USING SURVEYS, INTERVIEWS, AND LIFE EVENT CALENDARS

....

RONET BACHMAN AND RAY PATERNOSTER

I. INTRODUCTION

....

As the chapters in this handbook vividly reveal, researchers have been quite creative in employing numerous research methods to explore the factors that impact an individual's decision to get involved in crime, stay involved in crime, or desist from criminal activity. As chapter 23 illuminated, vignette research has perhaps been the "go to" method among scholars to examine the likelihood that individuals from the general population, typically college students, would engage in the criminal conduct depicted in a fictional scenario. This research has provided a wealth of knowledge about both the factors that deter would-be offenders from committing offenses and the expected gains or benefits that would attract them to crime.

Although vignette studies have in the past been the data collection strategy of choice for criminological scholars interested in offender decision making, work by Loughran, Paternoster, and Thomas (2014) has questioned the validity of scenario studies' findings that would-be offenders are inhibited by sanction threats. Specifically, Loughran and colleagues found that when respondents were incentivized by a scoring strategy that encouraged accurate and thoughtful responses, evidence of deterrence declined dramatically. In the absence of incentives, respondents relied on quick intuition that inclined them to overemphasize the certainty of punishment and underreport their intentions to offend in response to a provided hypothetical scenario. Under conditions of no incentives, then, respondents answered in a way that appeared to produce a deterrent effect. Based on this recent finding, the importance of relying on multiple methods including surveys and interviews to investigate offender decision making appears especially important.

Although vignette research has been the reigning "methodology of the moment," researchers interested in more detailed information regarding perceptions and offending, such as the consequences of offending on perceptions, have often relied on surveys or interviews with offenders. In fact, researchers have increasingly utilized a mixed-methods approach to enhance recall by incorporating life events calendars (sometimes referred to life history calendars) into the survey or interview format (Giordano, Cernkovich, and Rudolph 2002; Laub and Sampson 2003; Bachman et al. 2013) or by including surveys as part of an experimental design (Nagin and Pogarsky 2003). This chapter explores how each of these methods has been used to understand offender decision making, along with the strengths and weaknesses of each.

II. Surveys

Survey research involves the collection of information from a sample of individuals through their responses to posed questions. The primary strengths of using surveys to understand offender decision making are their versatility, efficiency, and generalizability. Because surveys can collect information relatively quickly, they more often lend themselves to probability sampling (e.g., a random sample of some population), which enhances the extent to which findings can be generalized to a larger population. There are several benefits of using a survey methodology to explore offender decision making. First and most important is that survey methods are extremely versatile. A well-designed survey can enhance our understanding of just about any social issue and can often measure a range of theoretical constructs of interest. Surveys are also very efficient because data can be collected from many people at a relatively low cost relatively quickly. Moreover, many variables can be measured without substantially increasing the time or cost of data collection. Finally, as already noted, survey methods lend themselves to probability sampling from large populations. As such, when sample generalizability is a central research goal, survey methodology is often the only means available for developing a representative picture of a large population.

Surveys can be conducted in many ways, including being self-administered by respondents who obtain the survey through the mail, via the Internet, in person individually, or as part of a group. Surveys can be self-administered, or respondents can be asked questions directly by an interviewer via in-person surveys or over the telephone. Computer technology has greatly advanced the capacity to conduct surveys over the phone and in person, which has made surveys even more versatile. Computers have also made asking sensitive questions such as questions about offending behavior less invasive. The presence of an interviewer may cause respondents to have difficulty providing honest answers, especially about sensitive issues such as criminal offending or even intentions to commit criminal acts. Computers have helped to allay this through the use of computer-assisted personal interviewing (CAPI). In a CAPI interview, respondents can enter their answers directly into a computer or tablet without the interviewer knowing their responses. Surveys can be conducted exclusively via CAPI or only partially for sensitive questions (Bachman and Schutt 2015).

A. Surveys of Adolescents and Young Adults

Like all criminological research devoted to theoretical tests, a great deal of research examining offender decision making has utilized survey research. However, the vast majority of research in this area has relied on large samples of adolescents and college students and occasionally longitudinal studies that track adolescents through young adulthood. These studies have illuminated important relationships between variables intended to measure various constructs that pertain to offender decision making (e.g., the probability of experiencing formal sanctions, perceptions of risk, the perceived benefits of offending, and self-reported offending behavior). We begin our discussion of the literature focusing on research that has relied exclusively on survey methods to explore issues pertaining to offender decision making. Unfortunately, the majority of this research has examined adolescent or young adult populations, and the offenses that have been examined are relatively minor delinquent acts. As such, it is not known how well the results of these studies are generalizable to actual offending populations. Moreover, the majority of respondents in random samples of the general population have a very low base rate of self-reported offending, which makes it statistically difficult to examine explanatory models to predict the intricacies of decision making.

Two such general surveys of conventional youth that have been employed in the study of offender decision making are the National Youth Survey (NYS) and the National Longitudinal Survey of Youth (NLSY), both national probability samples. Lochner (2007) used both data sets in a study of the effect of risk perceptions on offending. Consistent with a deterrent effect, Lochner found that a ten percentage point increase in an individual's perception of the certainty of arrest was correlated with a three percentage point decrease in major thefts and a seven percentage point decrease in auto thefts in the NLSY data. Similar evidence of rational offender decision making was found in the NYS. A ten percentage point increase in the perceived risk of arrest for each of four different crime types (theft of something worth less than $5, theft of something worth more than $50, breaking and entering, and assault) resulted in a decrease in participation in the respective crime from 7 to 12 percent. If it is rational for offenders to be affected by the perceived risk of punishment, it is equally consistent with a rational actor model of offender decision making if these perceptions of risk are in turn influenced by information about what that risk might be. With the NLSY, Lochner found evidence of such rational updating: Those who reported stealing or selling drugs in one year (most of whom did so without getting caught) reported a lower perceived probability of getting arrested in the following year. Similarly, those who were arrested for theft in one year increased their perceived risk of arrest in the next year. As in the NLSY, respondents in the NYS who engaged in crime from 1984 to 1986 had lower perceived probabilities of arrest at the end of 1986. As highlighted later, these findings are consistent with a Bayesian learning model of change over time in perceived risk in response to new information.

In addition to surveys with the general population, there are several other survey studies that have been conducted with samples of offenders or with samples of individuals who have a higher risk of offending. One survey is particularly noteworthy because it relied on a sample of youth residing in high-risk neighborhoods, which increased the probability of obtaining data with enough variation in both the explanatory variables (e.g., perceptions of risk) and self-reported offending. Matsueda, Kreager, and Huizinga (2006) used the Denver Youth Survey (DYS) to examine how individuals' risk perceptions are formulated as well as the extent to which those perceptions are related to the decision to commit crimes (i.e., violence and theft). The DYS is a longitudinal study of delinquency and drug use that was conducted in high-risk neighborhoods in Denver, Colorado. After high-risk neighborhoods were identified based on such information as family structure, socioeconomic status, and police reports, a random sample of households was selected that included youth at the target ages. At the first annual survey, the birth cohorts were aged seven, nine, eleven, thirteen, and fifteen years (Esbensen and Huizinga 1993). The original sample included 1,527 youths at the first baseline survey. Respondents were surveyed annually for three more years to produce four waves of data. The sample included roughly equal numbers of males and females; however, respondents were primarily Hispanic (45 percent) or African American (33 percent). Consistent with measures of offending in research for similarly aged samples, the survey solicited information about engagement in delinquency and drug use only and not about engagement in more serious felony offending (Matsuead et al. 2006). In addition, the DYS measured several experienced sanctions, including the number of times individuals were ever arrested or questioned by police as well as the perceived costs and returns of offending. To measure the perceptual variables associated with rational choice theory, Matsueda and colleagues measured perceived risks and rewards of offending, perceived opportunities to offend, risk preferences, and opportunity costs. Their central explanatory variables were the perceived costs and returns for offending. They developed a variable to measure the costs of offending that calculated the perceived probability of arrest for committing a particular offense weighted by how good or bad an arrest would be for them. The perceived rewards of committing crime were similarly measured by asking respondents about the probability of "getting excitement" from a particular offense and the probability of "being seen as cool," each weighted by how good or bad these attributes were perceived.

Matsueda et al.'s (2006) research examined two rational choice-based research questions: (1) How are arrest experiences as a consequence of offending related to perceptions of arrest risk? and (2) What is the relationship between risk perceptions and offending? Regarding the first question, their results generally supported a learning process for the updating of perceived risks. That is, individuals began with a prior subjective probability of arrest based on all information they had accumulated to the present, but this probability was then updated/modified in response to new information. Specifically, they found that respondents' risk perceptions were updated in response to both their own arrest experiences and those of their peers. With respect to the second question, Matsueda et al. found that offending decisions were inversely related to the perceived cost of crime (the perceived risk of arrest) and positively related to the perceived benefits of offending (i.e., perceived excitement and "coolness" of crime) and the perception of opportunities to commit crimes. They concluded that "our results support a Bayesian learning model of perceived risk formation, a rational choice model of criminal behavior, and a deterrence hypothesis of perceive risk of arrest" (p. 116). Survey data from the DYS, then, provide evidence for the position that criminal offending is in large measure a matter of calculated choice and that decisions to offend are not static but, rather, dynamically changed in response to new information.

B. Surveying Adolescent and Young Adult Offenders

As mentioned previously, one limitation of survey research of the general population, even samples obtained from high-risk neighborhoods, is that findings cannot be generalized to more serious offending populations who have already been sanctioned by the criminal justice system, especially those offenders who have committed more serious offenses. Because of these generalizability issues, some researchers have begun to utilize survey methods to examine the decision-making processes of individuals who have already been formally sanctioned by the criminal justice system. Unfortunately, when attempting to understand the reasoning and decision making of offending populations who have already been sanctioned (i.e., arrested and incarcerated), harnessing the strength of surveys to question a large representative sample is usually not possible. This is primarily because it is virtually impossible to obtain a population list of offenders from which to sample, even offenders of a specific type, such as robbery or burglary offenders. As such, research using survey methodology with offenders most often relies on a convenience sample of offenders. Despite this limitation, surveys have still been used to understand offender decision making from a more serious offender's point of view.

One notable study is called the Pathways to Desistance study, which is a longitudinal sample of serious adolescent offenders who transitioned from adolescence to young adulthood in Maricopa County, Arizona, or Philadelphia, Pennsylvania (for a review of the study methods, see Mulvey et al. 2004; for a review of measurement issues, see Schubert et al. 2004). A total of 1,354 fourteen- to seventeen-year-old youth were interviewed at baseline with six consecutive 6-month follow-up interviews from November 2000 through January 2003. The Pathways sample is predominantly minority (41 percent African American and 34 percent Hispanic) and male (86 percent). The Pathways data have been exploited to great success in developing understandings of the decision-making processes of serious young criminal offenders.

One such Pathways-based study was done by Anwar and Loughran (2011), who, like Matsueda et al. (2006), examined the process of perceptual updating in assessments of risk. Consistent with an updating process, they found that individuals who committed one crime and were arrested for it increased their estimate of the perceived probability of arrest by 6.3 percent compared to those who had committed an offense but had not been arrested. Therefore, the signal that an arrest sends in this case is that the risk of crime is greater than previously thought—a rational response to getting arrested. Also consistent with a process of rational updating, they found that this signal is far less informative the more frequent the offending. In addition, they found that the process of updating was not crime specific; that is, even if an individual was arrested for crime A, there would be an updating of the perceived risk of arrest for crime B.

This Bayesian perceptions-updating model of Anwar and Loughran (2011) was revisited by Thomas, Loughran, and Piquero (2013), who also employed the Pathways to Desistance data. The question raised in this study was whether or not Anwar and Loughran's updating model varied across persons. Specifically, Thomas and colleagues tried to determine if the signal provided by new offending information was weighted differently depending on an individual's personal characteristics. The phenomena of differential deterrence (deterrence is more effective among those with strong informal bonds and weak moral beliefs) has been well documented, but the issue of differential updating had yet to be explored. Thomas et al. found that some psychological characteristics of individuals, such as their level of anxiety and their orientation to the future, had no effect on the weight that they placed on an arrest when updating their risk perceptions, but others, such as their verbal IQ and whether they had early behavioral problems, did have an effect. Specifically, individuals with higher verbal IQ scores placed less weight on the new information provided by an arrest than did those with lower verbal IQs. The high verbal IQ respondents did not update their perceptions of risk in response to a previous arrest. In addition, those who showed evidence of early behavior problems placed greater weight on the new signal provided by an arrest compared to those without such problems. It would appear, then, that corresponding to the process of differential deterrence, a new finding based on survey research in the literature is the notion of differential updating. Different people use information differently when making decisions either to offend or to learn from their past experiences.

Another study by Loughran and colleagues (2011) that relied on the Pathways data examined the ambiguity around perceptions of sanction threats and the effect of perceptual ambiguity of risk on deterrence. To measure perceived risk of sanctions, the survey asked individuals how likely they believed it was that they would be caught and arrested for seven specific crimes with response options ranging from 0 (no chance) to 10 (absolutely certain to be caught). To measure the perceived "ambiguity" of these risks, Loughran et al. computed the variance of perceived risk for both "no one around" crimes (i.e., property crimes) and "face-to-face" crimes (i.e., crimes of violence) for individuals at each time point. A detailed account of this research is beyond the scope of this chapter; however, one interesting finding that emerged was that for both types of crimes, perceived risk of being caught generally increased over time, but the average ambiguity of these risk perceptions generally decreased. Loughran et al. explained that "with time (and presumably more experience), individuals become less ambiguous about the subjective risk perceptions" (p. 1046). How did perceptions and ambiguity affect involvement in crime? Results indicated that there was a significant inverse relationship between perceived risk of arrest and self-reported crime. In addition, for "no one around" crimes, Loughran et al. found that ambiguity of risk had an independent deterrent effect at lower ranges of detection risk but encouraged offending for higher perceived detection probabilities. Ambiguity of risk at lower levels of perceived risk seemed to increase the perceived riskiness of crimes, leading to more deterrence, but ambiguity of risk at higher levels of risk moved toward lower levels of risk, leading to weakened deterrence. However, this was not the case for face-to-face crimes. The difference between these two crime types, the authors speculated, may result from the fact that the property crimes included in these "no one around" crimes are "more susceptible to deliberative decision making, and thus deterrence, than expressive (i.e., violent) crimes are" (p. 1055).

In a subsequent study using the Pathways data, Loughran et al. (2012) found a significant inverse effect between the perceived certainty of arrest for seven offenses (fighting, robbery with a gun, stabbing someone, breaking into a store or home, stealing clothes from a store, vandalism, and auto theft) and self-reported offending for a summary scale composed of 17 different criminal acts. However, this relationship did not exist across all levels of certainty; rather, there appeared to be boundary effects. At low levels of perceived certainty (below a probability of .30), there was no relationship with self-reported offending. At a mid-range of arrest probability, from .30 to .70, a 10 percent increase in the perceived probability of arrest was associated with a statistically significant average decrease of .5 offenses. However, beyond the .70 risk probability area, there was an inverse relationship between perceived risk and offending that was not significantly different from zero. Consistent with some research at the aggregate level, then, this study seemed to suggest that perceived certainty had to reach a certain threshold or "tipping point" before the threat was credible enough to create a deterrent effect. The finding of a nonlinear relationship between the perceived risk of arrest and self-reported offending was more consistent with prospect theory (Kahneman and Tversky 1979) than deterrence theory, but both are consistent with the idea that offenders make rational decisions.

C. Surveys with Adult Offenders

The literature discussed so far relied on survey data from adolescents or young adults. Other researchers have used survey methods to examine the decision-making process of adult offenders. To understand the factors related to incarcerated offenders' self-reported likelihood of future offending, Holliday, King, and Heilbrun (2013) sampled 88 male residents from a correctional treatment facility in New Jersey. The survey asked questions designed to measure several constructs, including assessments of factors related to offending behavior such as the Level of Service/Case Management Inventory (LS/CMI), which is designed to measure the risk of general recidivism among offenders sixteen years old or older (Andrews, Bonta, and Wormith 2006). They also asked inmates questions about their perceptions of general risk factors as well as factors related to their own risk of reoffending upon release. For example, one question asked, "Which of these factors do you think may increase the chance that a person will commit a crime in the future?" Inmates could select from a list of several factors, including criminal history, friends, mental illness, and so on. Also on the list were factors that have no empirical relationship to offending, such as athleticism and physical attractiveness. Inmates were then asked which of these factors they perceived would increase their own risk of committing a crime in the future. The authors called this the Risk and Need Perception Survey. Results from the LS/CMI indicated that inmates had a reasonably good understanding of the factors that increase the risk of offending based on the empirical literature. For example, the majority believed that criminal history was a good predictor of recidivism, whereas athleticism was not. Interestingly, however, inmates rated only five items as important for their own risk of offending upon release, including friends, how free time is spent, attitudes and thoughts, and financial difficulties. Andrews et al. concluded that "offenders recognize most factors that increase the risk of reoffending, but they are less inclined to regard these factors as personally applicable" (p. 1056). The authors concluded that these results raise questions about the ways in which an offender's understanding of personal risk factors may be improved through treatment.

A slightly larger survey of inmates to examine decision-making processes was obtained by Wood (2007). He sampled 726 male and female inmates in a state correctional facility in the southern United States. Wood's main goal was to examine the effects of prior punishments on adult criminal offenders' self-reported likelihood to reoffend after release. Inmates who volunteered to participate for the study filled out the questionnaires in groups in large rooms. Questions used to measure previous experiences with criminal justice sanctions included whether respondents had ever served time in a juvenile facility, whether they had served time in an adult jail or prison prior to their current incarceration, length of current sentence, and amount of current sentence served. To measure their perceptions of the likelihood of future criminal behavior and future punishments, they were asked the numbers of years they thought they would be given if released and subsequently arrested for committing a crime "like the one that put you here in prison" and the perceived likelihood of being arrested if they were to commit a similar crime. Inmates were also asked the following question: "Imagine someone like yourself will be released next week. . . . Please circle the likelihood that within three years that person will commit another crime" (p. 14). The purpose of asking about a person "like themselves" instead of directly asking about their own future behavior, similar to vignette research, was to increase the probability of inmates responding truthfully. Although it is not possible to determine the extent to which inmates answered truthfully, it is important to note that more than 55 percent of those in Wood's research reported a non-zero probability of someone like themselves committing another crime. Results were somewhat inconsistent, but the strongest correlations were negative and found between past punishment and future behavior. That is, those who had been in prison before were more, not less, likely to report that someone like them would reoffend in the future. A hypothesis based on specific deterrence would predict otherwise. Specifically, deterrence theory would predict that those who had previously served time in prison would be less likely to reoffend compared to those who had not. Inexplicable results such as these illuminate the problems inherent in measuring complex perceptual constructs with large-scale survey methodology.

Is it possible to measure perceptual constructs such as perceived risk of arrest in the future with a fixed-choice question? Are these questions validly measuring the complex perceptual processes that would occur during the commission of a crime, particularly within the varied contexts of real-life situations? Herein lies one of the weaknesses of survey research when investigating offender decision making. Survey research may illuminate that would-be offenders, and even offenders themselves, are less likely to self-report committing a crime when they perceive that detection is probable, but it is impossible to understand the intricate mechanisms of this process without asking respondents open-ended questions about exactly "how" they perceive a particular situation. Moreover, researchers investigating deterrence theory, which is a perceptual theory about how offenders think about, process, and respond to threats of both formal and informal sanctions, usually want more detailed accounts of these perceptual processes. For this reason, much of the research that has asked offenders directly about their offending behavior and decision making has relied on a more intensive interview techniques using open-ended questions. We turn to this method next.

III. Interviews

Two very different types of interviews can be used to examine offender decision making. The first is more like a survey, but instead of being self-administered by respondents, professional interviewers question respondents face-to-face and record their answers. In these cases, the survey design can accommodate more complexity and contain both open-ended and closed-ended questions (Giordano et al. 2002; Laub and Sampson 2003; Bachman et al. 2013, 2016Bachman and Schutt 2015). Moreover, respondents' interpretations of the questions along with their answers to the questions can be probed and clarified. When more detailed and extensive narratives are desired, researchers often use a more intensive, open-ended style of asking questions.

Intensive interviews, sometimes called depth interviews, are qualitative methods used for finding out about people's experiences, thoughts, and perceptions. Researchers employing intensive interviews are more often relying on inductive reasoning to inform their research. That is, they begin their research not seeking to test formulated hypotheses but, rather, to discover what people think, how they act, and why they act the way they do in some social situation. For offender decision making, researchers employing this methodology are more concerned with the meanings that people attach to events and to the holistic context within which decisions are or were made (Maruna 2001; Opsal 2012; Breen 2014). These interviews more often rely exclusively on open-ended questions. Like other qualitative research methods, they share a commitment to learning about people in depth, in their own words, and in the context of their environments and situations (Bachman and Schutt 2015). What distinguishes intensive interviewing from more structured forms of questions on surveys is that the goal is to develop a comprehensive picture of the respondent's perceptions and actions, in his or her own words.

When researchers use intensive interviews, they are clearly more engaged with respondents compared to when standard fixed-format surveys are used. As such, a great deal of training is necessary to teach interviewers how to actively listen, ask follow-up questions tailored to the preceding answers, and seek to learn about interrelated belief systems or personal approaches to things rather than measure a limited set of variables. Interviewers should actively probe understandings and engage respondents in a dialogue about what they mean by their comments. Clearly, researchers investigating offending populations must receive extensive training and even review their own feelings to avoid reacting to divulged information. As a result, intensive interviews are often much longer than surveys, sometimes several hours long. In reality, an intensive interview is more like a conversation between two people.

Typically, the intensive interview follows a preplanned outline of topics. It may begin with a few simple questions that gather background information while building rapport. These are often followed by a few general grand tour questions that are meant to elicit lengthy narratives. Some research may use more structure in its questioning—for example, by asking the same questions about prior events (e.g., the last time respondents committed an offense). More exploratory research, especially those projects aimed at understanding respondents' interpretations of events, may let each interview flow in a unique direction. Regardless of the structure, intensive interviewers must adapt nimbly throughout the interview, paying attention to nonverbal cues, expressions with symbolic value, and the ebb and flow of the respondent's feelings and interests (Bachman and Schutt 2015).

Because of the time element of intensive interviewing and the lack of standardized questions and answers, the generalizability of the findings for this type of research is often diminished compared to that of large surveys conducted with random samples. However, the depth of understanding and increased validity of the measured constructs are usually the goal of intensive interviews, not generalizability. Although random selection is rarely possible to select respondents for intensive interviews, how the sample is selected should still be carefully considered. If respondents are selected in a haphazard manner, such as by speaking only to those who happen to be available at the time, the findings are likely to be of less value than when a more purposive selection strategy is used. Although research using intensive interviews typically relies on smaller sample sizes compared to those of survey research, research using this methodology should continue to seek new respondents, if possible, until a saturation point is reached—typically when new interviews seem to yield little new information (Bachman and Schutt 2015).

Interviews have been extensively used in studies of offenders' decisions to quit crime or desist. An early use of detailed interviews with offenders in an attempt to discover their decision-making processes was Neal Shover's (1996) study of thieves. One of the most interesting findings from his interviews was the fact that their preferences changed over time away from the "party life" toward a greater emphasis on the value of time, family, and the escalating personal costs that additional arrests and incarcerations would present. Another one of Shover's (1983) findings from an earlier series of interviews with ordinary property offenders was evidence of "delayed deterrence" whereby it was only when offenders were older that the costs of crime had escalated in their minds to constitute a salient deterrent:

> At first glance, multirecidivists are living examples of the ineffectiveness of punishment. Yet there seems to be a relationship between the fear of punishment and the abandoning of crime. Men who for years could not be intimidated despite many severe punishments end by deciding to go straight mainly because they do not want to go back to prison. Delayed deterrence is the gradual wearing down of the criminal drive caused by the accumulation of punishments. In the long run, the succession of arrests and incarcerations do have their effect. They engender a pervasive fear, which over the years becomes acute and makes acting out more and more difficult. This delayed deterrence has four components: (a) a higher estimate of the cumulative probability of punishment, (b) the increasing difficulty of "doing time," (c) an awareness of the weight of previous convictions on the severity of the sentences, and (d) a spreading of fear. (p. 212)

One of the most highly cited relatively recent studies of desistance (Laub and Sampson 2003) consisted in large measure of intensive interviews with 52 men who had been in the original Glueck study and for whom Laub and Sampson had arrest records up to age seventy-two years. All of these men had been serious juvenile offenders, and throughout the years, some of them continued to persist in crime, others desisted, and still others "zigzagged" their way in and out of crime. The interviews provide detailed narratives describing the decision-making process that comprised these different life directions. A theme behind many of those who had quit crime was that throughout the years they had accumulated enough valuable and conventional social capital (good jobs and emotionally satisfying intimate relationships) that crime was now seen to be too costly. In a sense, they were experiencing the delayed deterrence found in Shover's (1983) property offenders. In addition, the more conventional lives of these desisters provided many fewer opportunities for crimes because they were experiencing greater social control.

Another interview study, called the Liverpool Desistance Study, relied on interviews with 55 men and 10 women, of whom 30 were considered to have desisted from crime and 20 were still persisting (Maruna 2001). Using these interview narratives, Maruna reported that a common theme among those who had desisted from crime was that individuals attempted to *recast* their old offender identities. In doing this, they "made good" by a "willful cognitive distortion" (p. 9) of their past so that it was aligned with their current views of themselves as law-abiding good people. The decision to quit crime, therefore, was a matter of personality persistence for these offenders whereby old offenses and misbehaviors were rationalized and explained in a way consistent with their conventional life though the creation of a "redemption script."

The Oxford Desistance Study is another interview-based data set consisting of 130 male property offenders who were interviewed when released from incarceration and again ten years later. They were interviewed with respect to both the subjective factors of release (feelings of hope/self-efficacy, regret and shame, stigma, and self-identity) and structural/social factors (housing, employment, relationships, and alcohol and drug use). LeBel et al. (2008) used these interview narratives to examine the decision to desist from crime, and they found that the risk of reconviction over a ten-year period was inversely related to the subjective factor of hopefulness and positively related to the subjective expectation of stigma as an offender and the existence of reentry problems. They also found that the risk of being reincarcerated was related to subjective factors such as feelings of hope, stigma, and the self-identity as a family man. LeBel et al.' study is an excellent illustration of the use of interview data in quantitative analyses of offender decision making. Similar findings from offender interviews about the importance of both objective/structural and subjective factors in decisions to desist from crime can be found in Opsal (2012) and Breen (2014).

A recent example of intensive interviewing of offenders is the study by Jacobs and Cherbonneau (2014). These researchers were interested in how a discrete sample of auto thieves manipulated and attempted to reduce their risk of apprehension. How does one find a sample of active auto thieves? Most research examining "active" offenders must rely on what is called a purposive sample, often combined with a snowball sample. This type of sample serves the purpose of the research question, but because it is not a random sample that is representative of some population, the generalizability of such studies is not known. Jacobs and Cherbonneau relied on a street-based fieldworker to recruit active offenders from a "large Midwestern US city" who was a "revered member of the criminal order in the area, where he maintained ties to persons involved in street culture and crime" (p. 348). The exact sampling procedure was a purposive snowball technique whereby each recruited respondent was asked to provide names of other active offenders. Jacobs and Cherbonneau explained the attempt to broaden the sample to include a heterogeneous sample of offenders:

> To expand the sample into new networks . . . the recruiter capitalized on referrals provided by initial recruits. In this way, some of the initial recruits served as "sampling seeds" which, in theory, reduced the likelihood of having a sample built entirely from one established network and also guards against having a sample comprised solely of atypical offenders. (p. 349)

To be a member of the sample, individuals had to have committed at least one auto theft in the prior month, have committed at least five auto thefts in their lifetimes, and consider themselves to be actively involved in auto theft at the time of the interview. The intensive interviews relied on open-ended questions focused on the circumstances of interviewees' initial involvement in motor vehicle theft and detailed descriptions of their most recent theft(s). Like most qualitative endeavors, Jacobs and Cherbonneau were careful to make respondents feel comfortable and trusting enough to divulge their thought processes. For example, the researchers noted, "The objective in the interview was to create a relaxed and unthreatening atmosphere. This style of interviewing seemed to put respondents at ease, and many were forthright in their conversations, even those who appeared skeptical at first" (p. 350). Typical of most research of this nature, both those who were interviewed and the recruiter were paid for their time (respondents received $50 and the recruiter received $75 for each successful interview).

The narratives from these respondents graphically illuminated how perceptions of sanction threats influenced behavior. Jacobs and Cherbonneau (2014) found that offenders engaged in specific tactics to reduce detection and/or arrest, including discretionary target selection, normalcy illusions related to appearance management once the stolen vehicle was under the offenders' possession, and defiance-involved flight (e.g., how and when to flee and under what circumstances). These tactics were made real by the narratives provided by the authors, which served to validate their assertions. For example, to underscore the nature of "normalcy illusions," many respondents talked about driving sensibly after a vehicle was stolen. One noted,

> The whole mission is to drive like you got some sense. If you driving like you got some sense, ain't nobody going to trip off you. But when you out here skirting off on lights and running stoplights and running stop signs, and shit like that, you looking for trouble. . . . [If the police get around me] I just get real nerdy. . . . The ten and two [on the steering wheel], seatbelt action . . . I'm minding my business. (p. 355)

The rich narratives examined in this research illuminated the more nuanced perceptual decision making engaged in by offenders. These insights would be virtually impossible to obtain in a fixed-format survey.

Jacobs and Cherbonneau (2014) were also diligent to note the limited generalizability of their findings:

> The precise relationship of our sample to larger populations of theoretical and substantive interest is unknown and unknowable because a sampling frame for auto thieves' representation in the general population does not exist. . . . Nevertheless, it clearly over-represents African Americans. This reflects the fact that the criminal underworld in the study site was strongly segregated along racial lines and our field recruiter, by virtue of his own racial background, only had ties to other African Americans. (p. 350)

As noted previously, limitations of generalizability are not uncommon with research employing an intensive interview design.

Copes and Vieraitis (2009) also used intensive interviews to explore the subjective assessments of risks and rewards that facilitated the decision to engage in identity theft for a sample of identity thieves serving time in a federal prison. To locate offenders, these researchers had a novel sampling strategy that utilized newspaper articles and press releases from US Attorney's websites. Their search found 470 individuals who had been sentenced to federal prison for identity theft, 297 of whom were housed in federal prisons. They then selected the prisons with the largest number of these inmates. The resulting sample was 65 people incarcerated for identity theft from 14 correctional facilities of various levels of security throughout the United States. This effort to obtain a diverse sample of identity thieves is noteworthy. Like most research utilizing intensive interview methodology, the goal for Copes and Vieraitis (2009 was "to have the participants tell their own stories" (p. 244).

Not surprisingly, money was the most commonly given reason for engaging in identity theft. More than half of those interviewed by Copes and Vieraitis (2009) did not contemplate the long-term consequences of their crimes. Many claimed that they pushed out thoughts of getting caught. In addition, most minimized the risks posed by getting caught by believing that their skills were advanced and law enforcement was incompetent. Still, slightly less than half of those interviewed believed they would eventually get caught but not necessarily go to prison. Many thought they may be fired from their jobs and possibly receive probation. Copes and Vieraitis explain,

> Such beliefs about sanctioning were based on stereotypes regarding the perceived lenient punishment of white-collar criminals who are more likely to be of high class status, have legitimate occupations, and may thus have greater resources brought to bear in their legal defense. . . . When identity thieves conducted a mental cost/benefit analysis of the crime, the belief that little harm would come to them coupled with the perceived high financial and intrinsic payoffs of the crime made it an attractive choice. (p. 252)

With the exception of the previously discussed longitudinal surveys that predicted future offending behavior based on past assessments of risk, the other cross-sectional surveys and/or interviews have asked respondents to contemplate past thoughts or behavior. Unfortunately, the validity of these recalled perceptions is often difficult to establish in research. One research tool that has increasingly been used in tandem with interview methodology is the event history calendar, which is discussed next.

IV. Adding Event History Calendars to Interviews

Event history calendars (EHCs), which are also called life event calendars, are increasingly being used in combination with interviews to facilitate recall of the past. These calendars typically contain several domains of questions and cues (e.g., living arrangements, employment, drug and alcohol use, and crime involvement) (Belli, Stafford, and Alwin 2009). The calendar instrument helps respondents recall events in their past by displaying each month (or other unit of time) along with key dates noted within the calendar, such as birthdays, arrests, and so on. Respondents are given a calendar that displays these key dates, typically called anchors, and then are asked to recall the events of interest, such as drug use and offending, which also occurred during the specified time frame. The use of a life calendar has been shown to improve respondent recall of events in the past compared to basic questions without a calendar. For example, using random assignment to either standard open-ended questions or questions along with EHC instruments, Belli, Shay, and Stafford (2001) found that the EHC elicited superior retrospective reports and that respondents found questions presented within the EHC easier to understand and answer.

EHC instruments have been used to collect both quantitative fixed-format data from offenders (Horney, Osgood, and Marshall 1995) and qualitative narrative data (Bachman et al. 2013). In fact, Laub and Sampson's (2003, pp. 66–70) groundbreaking study of decisions to desist or persist in crime within the Gluck subsample of interviewed men was premised on life history calendars. These life course interviews provided the grist for their detailed descriptions as to how offenders weighed the various costs and benefits of adult offending. This allowed Laub and Sampson to create a time stream in the narratives in which offenders could put the events into some kind of causal order for themselves. For example, for many, having a good marriage made crime too costly to contemplate: "The thing that changed me was marriage. That turned me right straight down the line" (p. 134). For many of those who persisted in crime, there were few conventional social bonds that could provide a costly counterweight for the pleasures of crime: "If I didn't get married at a young age, finished my high school. Who knows if I would have got a scholarship to college. See, this is it" (p. 176). In fact, Laub and Sampson credit the use of life history information for many of the unique and unexpected discoveries from the updated Glueck data: "One of the advantages of employing life history narratives is their ability to uncover new ideas and challenge conventional wisdom. We are struck by the surprises in our data, surprises that challenge not only the prevailing wisdom in criminology but also some of the themes in our prior work, *Crime in the Making*" (pp. 277–278).

Bachman and colleagues (2013, 2016) examined the mechanisms and process by which formally incarcerated drug-involved male and female offenders either desisted or persisted from crime during a twenty-year period. The sample of 304 respondents was part of a larger project designed to test the treatment alternatives for drug-involved offenders, and sample members were originally released from prison during the early 1990s. Bachman et al. (2013) obtained official arrest records for the original 1,250 people in the sample and performed trajectory models of offending from 1979 through 2008. Within each of the five trajectory groups that emerged, random samples of both African American and white male and female respondents were then selected for intensive interviews. To facilitate recall of criminal events, official arrest and incarceration dates were placed on event history calendars that spanned the years since their baseline release from prison. The EHC was primarily used in this research as a heuristic device to facilitate recall of respondents' memories of events and not to collect quantitative data points within each calendar year. The interviews were open-ended and were designed to uncover what Agnew (2006) called "storylines" in understanding criminal offending. A storyline is a "temporally limited, interrelated set of events and conditions that increase the likelihood that individuals will engage in crime" (p. 121). For each criminal and drug relapse event self-reported or obtained from official records, respondents were asked to re-create the event both perceptually and structurally, including perceptions related to their decision-making process at the time. Bachman et al. (2013) noted, "Unlike solely variable-driven research that predict models of recidivism and relapse, these narratives helped us understand the causal mechanisms through which background, situations factors, and identity affected both offending and desistance" (p. 43).

Bachman et al.'s (2013; see also Bachman et al. 2016) study was particularly concerned with respondents' narratives that revealed the cognitive decision-making processes at each criminal event or opportunity thereof. Results indicated that of those who had desisted from drugs and crime, more than 80 percent, regardless of race or gender, appeared to have made a cognitive identity transformation (for a discussion of desistance from heroin use, see Biernacki 1986). As such, the narratives were consistent with Paternoster and Bushway's identity theory of desistance (Paternoster and Bushway 2009; Bushway and Paternoster 2011, 2013), which contends that offenders will retain an "offender" working identity as long as they perceive it will net more benefits than costs. The process of changing an offender identity occurs when perceived failures and dissatisfactions within different domains of life become connected. They also assert that this linkage of failures is often coupled with a feared self. That is, offenders perceive that without making a behavioral change, their future is bleak and will only contain more pain and hardship.

The respondents in Bachman et al.'s (2013, 2016) study who made an identity transformation were also cognizant of this so-called "feared self," or someone they did not want to become. For many offenders, the self they feared was simply a generalized fear of being stuck where they were or, as many of them stated, "tired of being sick and tired." This was a common refrain, but when pressed to explain what they meant by "sick and tired," most offered more specific fears, such as dying in jail or ending up losing everything. Connecting past failures with future failures was also a salient process in the desistance process as revealed by the narratives. One respondent noted, "Like I said, you just get tired of it, you just don't want that life no more, at a point it's just over, you get the same results, you keep doing the same thing, you're gonna get the same results . . . and it's just not good . . . that's not worth it" (Bachman et al., 2013, p. 59).

As can be seen from the studies reviewed in this section, intensive interview methods, especially when coupled with EHC used as a heuristic devise for recall, can reveal many more details about offender decision making and the mechanisms that lead to both persistence and desistance from crime.

V. Conclusion

Survey research and interviews methods are exceptional ways to understand the decision-making processes of both offenders and would-be offenders. The strengths and limitations of each are complimentary and, as such, when possible, it may be worth pursuing a multiple method approach when investigating the complex cognitive mechanisms that are inherent in any decision-making process. For example, survey research could readily be supplemented with a subsample of respondents who are interviewed with less structured and open-ended response formats. In any case, researchers should always let the research question dictate the research method.

References

Agnew, R. 2006. "Storylines as a Neglected Cause of Crime." *Journal of Research in Crime and Delinquency* 43(2): 119–47.

Andrews, D. A., J. Bonta, and S. J. Wormith. 2006. "The Recent Past and Near Future of Risk and/or Need Assessment." *Crime and Delinquency* 52:7–27.

Anwar, Shamena, and Thomas A. Loughran. 2011. "Testing a Bayesian Learning Theory of Deterrence Among Serious Juvenile Offenders." *Criminology* 49:667–98.

Bachman, R., E. Kerrison, D. O'Connell, and R. Paternoster. 2013. "Roads Diverge: Long-Term Patterns of Relapse, Recidivism, and Desistance for a Cohort of Drug Involved Offenders." Final Report, Grant no. 2008-IJ-CX-0017. National Institute of Justice, Office of Justice Programs, US Department of Justice.

Bachman, R., E. Kerrison, R. Paternoster, D. O'Connell, and L. Smith. 2016. "Desistance for a Long-Term Drug-Involved Sample of Adult Offenders." *Criminal Justice and Behavior* 43(2): 164–86.

Bachman, R., and R. Schutt. 2015. *Fundamentals of Research in Criminology and Criminal Justice*, 3rd ed. Thousand Oaks, CA: Sage.

Belli, R. F., W. L. Shay, and F. P. Stafford. 2001. "Event History Calendars and Question List Surveys: A Direct Comparison of Interviewing Methods." *Public Opinion Quarterly* 65(1): 45–74.

Belli, R. F., F. P. Stafford, and D. F. Alwin. 2009. *Calendar and Time Diary: Methods in Life Course Research*. Thousand Oaks, CA: Sage.

Biernacki, P. 1986. *Pathways From Heroin Addiction: Recovery Without Treatment*. Philadelphia, PA: Temple University Press.

Breen, Andrea V. 2014. "Changing Behavior and Changing Personal Identity: The Case of Pregnant and Parenting Young Women and Antisocial Behavior." *Identity* 14:60–79.

Bushway, S. D., and R. Paternoster. 2011. "Understanding Desistance: Theory Testing with Formal Empirical Models." In *Measuring Crime and Criminality: Advances in Criminological Theory*, edited by J. MacDonald, pp. 299–333. New Brunswick, NJ: Transaction Publishers.

Busway, S. D. and R. Paternoster. 2013. "Desistance from Crime: A Review of Ideas for Moving Forward." In *Handbook of Life-Course Criminology*, edited by C. L. Gibson and M. D. Krohn, pp. 213–31. New York, NY: Springer.

Copes, H., & Vieraitis, L.M. 2009. "Bounded rationality of identity thieves: Using offender-based research to inform policy." *Criminology and Public Policy* 8:237–62.

Copes, H. and L. M. Vieraitis. 2012. *Identity Thieves: Motives and Methods*. Boston, MA: Northeastern University Press.

Esbensen, F. A., and D. Huizinga. 1993. "Gangs, Drugs, and Delinquency in a Survey of Urban Youth." *Criminology* 31(4): 565–89.

Giordano, Peggy C., Stephen A. Cernkovich, and Jennifer L. Rudolph. 2002. "Gender, Crime, and Desistance: Toward a Theory of Cognitive Transformation." *American Journal of Sociology* 107:990–1064.

Holliday, S. B., C. King, and K. Heilbrun. 2013. "Offenders' Perceptions of Risk Factors for Self and Others: Theoretical Importance and Some Empirical Data." *Criminal Justice and Behavior* 40:1044–61.

Horney, Julie, D. Wayne Osgood, and Ineke Haen Marshall. 1995. "Criminal Careers in the Short-Term: Intra-individual Variability in Crime and Its Relation to Local Life Circumstances." *American Sociological Review* 60:655–73.

Jacobs, B. A., and M. Cherbonneau. 2014. "Auto Theft and Restrictive Deterrence." *Justice Quarterly* 31(2): 344–67.

Kahneman, Daniel, and Amos Tversky. 1979. "Prospect Theory: An Analysis of Decision Under Risk." *Econometrica* 47:263–91.

Laub, John H., and Robert J. Sampson. 2003. *Shared Beginnings, Divergent Lives; Delinquent Boys to Age 70.* Cambridge, MA: Harvard University Press.

LeBel, Thomas P., Ros Burnett, Shadd Maruna, and Shawn Bushway. 2008. "The 'Chicken and Egg' of Subjective and Social Factors in Desistance from Crime." *European Journal of Criminology* 5:131–59.

Lochner, Lance. 2007. "Individual Perceptions of the Criminal Justice System." *American Economic Review* 97:444–60.

Loughran, Thomas A., Ray Paternoster, Alex R. Piquero, and Greg Pogarsky. 2011. "On Ambiguity in Perceptions of Risk: Implications for Criminal Decision-Making and Deterrence." *Criminology* 49(4): 1029–61.

Loughran, Thomas A., Ray Paternoster, and Kyle J. Thomas. 2014. "Incentivizing Responses to Self-Report Questions in Perceptual Deterrence Studies: An Investigation of the Validity of Deterrence Theory Using Bayesian Truth Serum." *Journal of Quantitative Criminology* 30:677–707.

Loughran, Thomas A., Greg Pogarsky, Alex R. Piquero, and Ray Paternoster. 2012. "Reassessing the Functional Form of the Certainty Effect in Deterrence Theory." *Justice Quarterly* 29:712–41.

Maruna, Shadd. 2001. *Making Good: How Ex-Convicts Reform and Rebuild Their Lives.* Washington, DC: American Psychological Association.

Matsueda, R. L., D. A. Kreager, and D. Huizinga. 2006. "Deterring Delinquents: A Rational Choice Model of Theft and Violence." *American Sociological Review* 71:95–122.

Mulvey, E. P., L. Steinberg, J. Fagan, E. Cauffman, A. R. Piquero, L. Chassin, G. P. Knight, R. Brame, C. Schubert, T. Hecker, and S. H. Losoya. 2004. "Theory and Research on Desistance from Antisocial Activity Among Serious Adolescent Offenders." *Youth Violence and Juvenile Justice* 2:213–36.

Nagin, Daniel S., and Greg Pogarsky. 2003. "An Experimental Investigation of Deterrence: Cheating, Self-Serving Bias, and Impulsivity." *Criminology* 41:167–94.

Opsal, Tara. 2012. "'Livin' on the Straights': Identity, Desistance, and Work Among Women Post-incarceration. *Sociological Inquiry* 82:378–403.

Paternoster, R. and S. Bushway. 2009. "Desistance and the 'Feared Self': Toward an Identity Theory of Criminal Desistance." *The Journal of Criminal Law and Criminology* 99(4): 1103–56.

Schubert, C. A., E. P. Mulvey, L. Steinberg, E. Cauffman, S. H. Losoya, T. Hecker, L. Chassin, and G. P. Knight. 2004. "Operational Lessons from the Pathways to Desistance Project." *Youth Violence and Juvenile Justice* 2:237–55.

Shover, Neal. 1983. "The Later Stages of Ordinary Property Offender Careers." *Social Problems* 31:209–18.

Shover, Neal. 1996. *Great Pretenders: Pursuits and Careers of Persistent Thieves.* Boulder, CO: Westview Press.

Thomas, Kyle J., Thomas A. Loughran, and Alex R. Piquero. 2013. "Do Individual Characteristics Explain Variation in Sanction Risk Updating Among Serious Juvenile Offenders?" *Law and Human Behavior* 37:10–21.

Wood, P. B. 2007. "Exploring the Positive Punishment Effect Among Incarcerated Adult Offenders." *American Journal of Criminal Justice* 31:8–22.

....

CHAPTER 26

SIMULATING CRIME EVENT DECISION MAKING

Agent-Based Social Simulations in Criminology

....

DANIEL BIRKS

CRIME is the result of numerous interconnected and interdependent crime event decisions made by potential offenders, victims, and crime preventers. The majority of these decisions go unobserved, and the situations within which they take place are difficult to control in support of traditional experimental studies. For these reasons, it can be difficult to identify causal links between individual behavior and observable crime phenomena and, in turn, to assess the veracity of proposed crime event decision calculi. This chapter discusses the application of agent-based modeling (ABM) in studying such crime event decision calculi. ABM can be used to develop formal models of crime event actors, the decisions they make, and the interactions that occur among them and the environment they inhabit. Acknowledging the diverse applications of ABM, the chapter concentrates on the approach of agent-based social simulation (ABSS)[1] (Epstein and Axtell 1996; Davidsson 2002) in support of exploring how crime event decisions give rise to observed crime events and patterns. ABSS allow researchers to construct simulated worlds and inhabit them with large numbers of heterogeneous autonomous goal-oriented decision makers whose behaviors are derived from theory or empirical observation. By manipulating the conditions of this artificial society and scrutinizing data collected about them, social simulations permit exploration of the emergent aggregate properties of individual-level behaviors (Epstein and Axtell 1996). This approach provides a means to assess if proposed decision calculi are viable explanations of commonly observed empirical regularities—linking the micro and the macro, the theoretical and the empirical, and providing a platform to prototype, test, and refine theoretical accounts of cognition, action, and interaction.

The chapter begins by describing the computational ABM approach and summarizing several of its strengths relative to other methods more commonly used to study complex social systems. Second, it outlines how ABSS provide a unique scientific instrument through which the explanatory sufficiency of proposed crime event decision calculi can be assessed. Third, it summarizes key processes involved in the design and development of ABM. Fourth, it provides an illustrative description of an ABSS of property victimization and several computational experiments carried out using it. The chapter concludes by summarizing key strengths and weaknesses associated with the construction of ABSSs for the purposes of better understanding crime event decision making.

I. COMPUTATIONAL MODELS

The practice of developing, testing, disputing, and refining models is core to the scientific enterprise. A model aims to capture key attributes of some target system at a manageable level of complexity, providing an appropriate analogue that is easier to study than the target itself. All theories are models, both in the minds of those who propose and utilize them and through their written and verbal description in academic manuscripts and conference proceedings. In the social sciences, statistical models often support written or verbal theoretical models. Statistical models aim to quantitatively measure the capacity of one or more independent factors in explaining hypothesized dependent outcomes as proposed by an underlying theoretical model. These models are the bedrock of social science, but they are not without their weaknesses. Written models typically lack formalization and, as a result, are often open to interpretation by readers. Moreover, the ramifications of hypotheses put forward in written form can often be difficult to envisage at higher orders than those initially described. In the social sciences, this is particularly problematic where the target of interest—society—is inherently complex. Conversely, although statistical models are considerably more formalized than their written equivalents, when dealing with complex social systems they are often forced to implement undesirable levels of abstraction in order to provide mathematical tractability (Epstein and Axtell 1996).

A third type of model is the computational model or simulation. Drawing from a number of interrelated fields, including mathematics, computer science, cognitive science, and artificial intelligence, computational models attempt to capture a target system by formalizing it in a computer program. The development of computational models requires researchers to formalize constituent elements of the target system as a series of interacting data structures and algorithms that collectively aim to characterize how the target system operates. Once such a computational model has been developed, it can then be used to carry out simulations. A simulation represents a specific instantiation of a given computational model whereby a particular model configuration is computed over repeated time steps and the behavior of the simulated system scrutinized and analyzed with the hope of providing insight into the target system.[2]

Computational models offer a number of unique strengths relative to both theoretical and statistical models when examining complex systems; for this reason, they have become increasingly popular in a range of natural, life, and social sciences. Primarily, computational models offer considerable scope for modeling complexity. The programming languages used to construct computational models—for example, Netlogo (Wilensky 1999), Repast (North et al. 2005), MASON (Luke et al. 2005), and Swarm (Minar et al. 1996)—are typically less abstract than their statistical counterparts. As such, they allow system elements to be decomposed into manageable subprocesses that are represented through appropriate software objects. This process, commonly referred to as hierarchical decomposition, facilitates the exploration of target systems at multiple levels of abstraction, initially implementing high orders of abstraction only to subsequently explore further complexity. This is particularly compelling in the study of complex systems because capturing all elements of a system at fine levels of granularity is likely initially overwhelming. Once an initial model has been built, lower orders of abstraction are then incrementally added to replace those initially devised higher order concepts, thus allowing effective management of model complexity (Jennings 2001).

II. Computational Agent-Based Models

One type of computational model that has received considerable attention from social scientists in recent years is the computational ABM. ABM provide the means to simulate the action and interaction of autonomous and often heterogeneous actors, with the aim of analyzing how the decentralized behavior of individual units impacts on the behavior of the system as a whole. These types of models are well suited to studying target systems characterized by unit heterogeneity (Bonabeau 2002), local interaction, individual-level adaptive behavior (Grimm 2008), and parallel processes that lack a defined order (Gilbert and Troitzsch 2005). Furthermore, the simulations that can be run using ABM are well suited to longitudinally study dynamical systems in which system properties, processes, and behaviors change over time as a result of feedback (Epstein 1999; Bonabeau 2002)—a key property of complex systems (Cilliers 2000). Capitalizing on these strengths, ABM are highly aligned to a number of social science research problems, allowing researchers to explicitly represent populations of individual actors and explore the emergent outcomes that result from their repeated interaction over time. ABM can be informed by both quantitative and qualitative research (Edmonds 2015), and they can be parameterized with and validated against empirical data (Hedström 2005). Advocates of the agent-based approach thus suggest that it offers a "natural" method for studying human systems (Axelrod 1997b; Epstein 1999; Bonabeau 2002; Hedström 2005).

A. Agent-Based Social Simulations

Although ABM can be constructed to explore a wide variety of research problems involving complex systems, as previously stated, this chapter predominantly discusses the use of ABM for the development of ABSS (Epstein and Axtell 1996; Epstein 1999). Broadly speaking, ABSS provide a platform to examine the emergent aggregate outcomes of numerous individual-level interactions occurring among a typically large population of individual actors. ABM (and thus ABSS) are composed of two key components: a population of one or more simulated actors—agents—and an environment in which these actors are situated, act, and interact with one another. An agent is a formal computational model of an autonomous decision-making entity. Within the social sciences, such agents typically represent human actors, although they may also be used to model groups of individuals, organizations, nations, and so on.

1. *Agent Characteristics*

Just like the members of a real population, agents can take on individual characteristics, thus allowing ABM to represent diverse populations of decision makers. To illustrate, agents might be characterized by age, gender, home location, and peer group (made up of a relational network of other agents).

2. *Agent Behaviors*

Agents also execute a variety of behaviors that govern how they perceive, reason, and act in particular situations. It is these behaviors that enable the formal modeling of actor decision making and through which agents interact with one another, observe, and analyze their environment and alter that environment or their internal state. Within the social sciences, such behaviors are typically inspired by the formalization of theory, such that algorithms, heuristics, and data structures are developed to reflect the decision calculi theory suggests are operating at the individual level.

A considerable number of frameworks exist for representing agent decision making. These range from collections of relatively simple condition–action rules to complex cognitive models inspired by psychology and neuroscience. Frameworks differ by approach, assumption, complexity, and ease of application, and although a thorough review is beyond the scope of this chapter, here we briefly discuss two popular frameworks previously applied by criminologists in developing ABSS—production systems and beliefs–desires–intentions (BDI) agents (for a more in-depth discussion of these and other models, see Balke and Gilbert 2014).

Originally conceived in the 1970s, production systems specify agent behavior as a reactive response to presented stimuli (Gilbert and Terna 2000). Production systems are made up of three key components: (1) a series of *condition–action rules* (i.e., *if A, then B*); (2) a *working memory* that enables an agent to store information pertaining to its current and previous states (which may include internal and perceived environmental states); and (3) a *rule interpreter* that specifies which rules apply given current stimuli and resolves any conflicts between multiple viable rules. Agents operating under production systems usually have no explicit means of evaluating multiple alternative methods of action to achieve a particular goal or, similarly, generating new or updating existing goals. As a result, their behavior is typically[3] less adaptive than that of other agent architectures. However, they are also often less computationally demanding than other more complex architectures, especially when large numbers of agents are to be modeled. Furthermore, production systems are typically more tractable than other approaches, such that the relationship between individual agent behavior and aggregate model outcome is more easily understood. For these reasons, the use of production systems remains relatively popular in the field of ABSS.

A production system is an example of a reactive agent architecture (Wooldridge and Jennings 1995), where an agent typically only reacts to current stimuli. By contrast, deliberative agent architectures are characterized by the ability to construct, manipulate, and utilize an internalized mental state. This mental state provides agents with a symbolic representation of the world in which they find themselves. Using this model, agents can reason about their current state and situation, and through the construction and evaluation of plans, they can implement complex action selection strategies for achieving particular goals. A popular deliberative agent architecture is the BDI framework (Rao and Georgeff 1991). BDI agents utilize three core data structures in defining their behavior. The first—*beliefs*—allows agents to represent their current beliefs about the state of the world around them. This likely reflects known characteristics of the environment an agent inhabits and other agents encountered within it. The second—*desires*—sets out a series of goals the agent wishes to accomplish. The third—*intentions*—represents both a selected desire and a series of actions or plans (selected from some set) through which an agent proposes to bring about that desire. The presence of these structures dictates that BDI agents can maintain persistent goals over time rather than reflexively acting based purely on current stimuli (as is typical through a production system). Goal persistence enables agents to react to immediate stimuli when required, but not at the cost of other goals. Thus, BDI agents can revisit previously unachievable goals as context changes, allowing them to more easily adapt to dynamic contexts. Key criticisms of the BDI framework relate to the underlying assumption that agents act in a (boundedly) rational manner in achieving their goals, and that learning, adaptation, and multi-agent behavior are not explicitly represented using the framework. A range of extensions to the BDI decision-making model have thus been explored. In an attempt to address the notion that human decision makers are not purely rational and instead are influenced by emotion, the eBDI (Jiang, Vidal, and Huhns 2007) framework seeks to integrate emotional states into the standardized BDI framework. Similarly, the BOID (beliefs, obligations, intentions, desires) architecture (Broersen et al. 2002) incorporates social norms into agent calculi by forcing agents to balance societal obligations with their own individual desires.

The debate regarding the appropriateness of these and other frameworks for modeling human (and thus crime event) decision making—and the trade-offs that exist between model approach, complexity, and utility—remains ongoing. As a result, no definitive "best" architecture for modeling crime event decision making exists. Here, it is suggested that like all social science methodology, the selection of agent framework should be driven by the research problem at hand, which in turn should result from identifying the calculus proposed by theory that is to be modeled and selecting an architecture that is sufficient to model it at an appropriate level of complexity. Moreover, it should be noted that the selection of one framework over another is unlikely to preclude the formalization of a particular calculi. More often than not, the choice of framework simply guides the researcher to decompose and formalize theoretical constructs in a particular manner, which is likely one of many viable approaches.

3. *Model Environment*

The second fundamental component of any ABM is a model environment within which agents will act and interact with one another. Although model environments may take on a wide variety of forms that reflect the goal of model development, agents must be situated in some explicit space, be it abstract or physical. To illustrate, in an ABM of social interaction, agents might interact in an abstract social space where proximity reflects the convergence of individual ideals, opinions, and social ties. Conversely, model environments may be developed to mirror real or imagined physical spaces around which agents navigate and interact with one another (e.g., a street network or the floor plan of a building). The primary requirement of any environment is to provide sufficient features from which agents and their associated behaviors can draw information.

III. AGENT-BASED MODELS OF CRIME EVENT DECISION MAKING

Recently within the field of environmental criminology, a number of scholars have begun to explore how ABM (and ABSS in particular) might provide insight into the mechanisms that underlie observed crime events and patterns (P. L. Brantingham and Brantingham 2004; P. L. Brantingham et al. 2005*a*, 2005*b*; Liu et al. 2005; Groff 2007*a*, 2007*b*, 2008; Birks, Donkin, and Wellsmith 2008; P. J. Brantingham and Tita 2008; L. Wang, Liu, and Eck 2008; Malleson and Brantingham 2009; Malleson, Evans, and Jenkins 2009; Bosse, Elffers, and Gerritsen 2010; Birks, Townsley, and Stewart 2012; Birks, Townsley, and Stewart 2014; X. Wang, Liu, and Eck 2014). More broadly, a number of other applications of ABM have also been undertaken to explore a range of other criminological research problems (Bosse, Gerritsen, and Treur 2009; Pontier, van Gelder, and de Vries, 2013; Bichler and Birks, 2015).

Concentrating here on the former, applications of ABSS within environmental criminology typically aim to better understand spatial, temporal, and functional distributions of criminal opportunities and also configurations of proximal circumstances that result in observed patterns of crime. In constructing these models, agents are designed to represent populations of potential offenders, victims, and, in some cases, crime preventers. The behavior of these agents is then designed to reflect decision calculi proposed by criminological theory. Typically, these agents are then situated in a spatial environment and simulations are run in which virtual offenders interact with virtual victims and commit virtual crimes. Subsequently, these crime data are analyzed and compared to commonly observed patterns of crime or, where data are unavailable, key predictions of theory.

To illustrate, both Groff (2007*a*) and Birks et al. (2014) present ABSS in which agents are designed to act based on formalizations of the routine activity approach (Cohen and Felson 1979). These models are used to (1) assess the validity of several key predictions proposed by theory and (2) examine the likely impacts of individual spatial activities on aggregate patterns of interpersonal victimization. Other ABSS within the field are also applied to conduct "What if?"-type simulations in which the downstream impacts of particular system manipulations are explored (e.g., varying policing strategies; Bosse, Elffers, and Gerritsen 2010). In using these models to study the likely impacts of crime event decision calculi or manipulations to them, the agent-based method offers a number of unique strengths relative to other analytical techniques previously applied in the study of crime events and patterns.

A. Heterogeneous Autonomous Actors

Agents are an ideal fit to represent the individual actors portrayed by a range of criminological perspectives. Agents can embody victims, offenders, formal and informal guardians, place managers, and so on and, in turn, the individual characteristics and behaviors exhibited by each. Importantly, these populations need not defer to representative agent methods commonplace in economic modeling (Epstein and Axtell 1996). Such heterogeneity can be applied to both individual characteristics (e.g., specifying agents with differing ages, criminal propensities, readiness, and configurations of routine activities) and behaviors through functionally different behaviors or parameterized behaviors that draw upon individual characteristics that differ between agents. To illustrate, a model of criminal foraging might represent three classes of offender agent that mimic the antisocial predator, mundane, and provoked offenders proposed by Cornish and Clarke (2003). The behavior of these agents could be represented by three distinct target selection behaviors or a single behavior parameterized by home range and persistence characteristics that differ by agent.

B. Explicit Space and Localized Interaction

ABM represent agents acting and interacting in some explicit space (abstract or real). Thus, agent perception, reason, action, and interaction are modeled as inherently situated processes (Epstein and Axtell 1996; Epstein 2006). Consequently, ABM allow researchers to explicitly represent localized interactions and, in turn, incorporate both individual and situational factors that influence decision making. For example, a model of direct contact predatory offending could bestow agents with an offending behavior that specifies the choice to offend as a function of an individual's propensity, current readiness, and—following routine activity depictions of crime—the current situation within which an agent finds him- or herself. This might include the presence of viable targets, the absence of capable guardians, and so on; such viability and capability would likely also be specified in terms of the respective individual's characteristics and situation.

C. Bounded Rationality

Statistical models of decision making often operate under the assumption that actors possess absolute knowledge of the world they inhabit and the courses of action available to them. This assumption aids in managing mathematical tractability but, in almost all cases, is unrealistic. Theories of decision making (and offender decision making) typically conceptualize actors as boundedly rational, such that real-world rationality is constrained by incomplete knowledge, restricted cognitive capacity, and finite timescales in which decisions must be made (Simon 1990). To mimic these depictions of the decision-making process, agents can be bestowed with decision calculi that draw only from localized and/or limited information (Axtell 2000; Epstein 2006). Thus, agent rationality is limited by the information available at the time a decision is made. Moreover, agent behaviors can be implemented to utilize limited computational resources (Epstein 1999), thus precluding agents from exhaustively searching all possible actions in order to determine optimal solutions to a given choice situation. Such representations of actor rationality are considerably more realistic than those that underlie a range of mathematical and statistical models.

D. Observation and Control

In addition to those characteristics that position ABM as pertinent tools in the formal modeling of crime event decision calculi, ABM also bestow distinct strengths in their ability to observe, control, and analyze the outcomes of these formalized theoretical constructs. In empirical study, a range of ethical and logistical impediments constrain our ability to observe crime event decision-making processes in representative ways. Moreover, if one aims to understand the impact of particular stimuli through experiment, it is often infeasible to control the vast number of variables that are constantly operating within the empirical world.

Conversely, ABM provide a platform for controlled simulation experimentation in which constraints on observation and manipulation of experimental conditions are limited only by the scope of the model (Epstein and Axtell 1996). Although such simulation experiments do not seek to replace traditional empirical studies, they provide a unique platform from which the simulation experimenter can investigate important fundamental questions free from the constraints of real-world experimentation. ABM thus provide a platform to undertake formalized thought experiments that explore the likely outcomes of a range of proposed real-world configurations, supporting existing theoretical and empirical endeavors.

To illustrate, in an ABM, the researcher is free to systematically manipulate the environment within which offender agents operate and also the characteristics and behaviors of those agents in order to observe the resulting impact on simulated crime. Thus, the potential impact of particular individual or environmental configurations can be explored in a systematic and rigorous manner. Furthermore, it is possible to scrutinize the internal structure of agents and identify, for instance, when, where, and how an offender agent's decision calculus is employed (Townsley and Birks 2008). Moreover, as is often the case if multiple interdependent decision calculi are proposed by theory, it is possible to systematically enable and disable these calculi with the hope of better understanding how they may interact with one another to produce particular outcomes (Birks et al. 2012).

IV. Explanatory Agent-Based Social Simulations

The word simulation often conjures up the notion of prediction; however, there are numerous other reasons one may wish to construct ABSS (for a compelling range, see Epstein 2008). Although prediction is undoubtedly possible through the agent-based method, the veracity of predicted outcomes is often reliant on the accuracy of a confluence of factors. In modeling crime event decision making, one should remain mindful that most models specify agent behavior from theory and not observation—indeed, it is the difficulties associated with observing such behavior that are often the very impetus around which models are built. Moreover, even if one were to be completely aware of the cognitive processes of those involved in the crime event, the production of actionable predictions would require specification of their relative configuration at a given point in time—that is, How many offenders are operating? Where are they located? What do their activity spaces look like? and so on. Detailed widespread data such as these are typically well beyond the realms of even the most well-designed empirical studies.

One particularly useful alternative application of the agent-based method is in the development of explanatory models. Explanatory models seek to identify mechanisms that are viable explanations for particular observed societal outcomes and under what circumstances such outcomes may arise. These explanatory ABSS provide researchers with a computational laboratory in which the fundamental propositions of theory can be formalized, imbued among an artificial society, and their likely outcomes estimated. This approach views the ABSS as a petri dish of sorts and is perhaps most compelling if one considers the ABSS as a tool to formally test the explanatory sufficiency of theoretical accounts of individual cognition and action.

By exploring the emergent outcomes of multiple interacting agents whose individual-level behaviors are derived from theory, ABSS can be used as a means to assess if those mechanisms proposed by theory are sufficient to explain commonly observed characteristics of crime. In taking this approach, the results of ABSS can be used to guide researchers toward those theoretical accounts that are likely to be most fruitful in terms of explanatory capacity, in turn supporting further theoretical refinement and empirical inquiry.

In the following section, the epistemological grounding associated with this approach is briefly discussed. Subsequently, key processes involved in designing and developing an ABSS that aims to test the explanatory capacity of proposed theoretical accounts of crime event decision making are set out.

V. Generative Accounts of Crime

Recent advances in the application of ABM within the social sciences have seen advocates propose that the social simulation permits a new "third way of doing science" alternate to traditional forms of inductive and deductive reasoning (Axelrod 2005, p. 5). This methodology views the ABM as a scientific instrument through which social macrostructures of interest can be "computed" (Epstein 1999, 2006; Hedström 2005). Focusing on mechanisms as explanations, this approach positions the ABSS as a means to systematically establish which individual-level mechanisms proposed by theory *can* and *cannot* be viable explanations for observed phenomena.

Following this approach, the veracity of theoretical accounts of social science phenomena is assessed by building ABM of hypothesized individual-level mechanisms and, through simulation, testing if such mechanisms are sufficient to produce observed regularities of the target. Such regularities represent characteristic patterns that are consistently observed in the empirical study of the target system—for instance, right-skewed wealth distributions, price equilibriums, segregation patterns, and, in the case of this handbook, common characteristics of crime events and patterns.

In contrast to statistical models that commonly operate in a top-down manner, such that identified associations among aggregate observations inform inferences about underlying mechanisms, this generative approach to social science operates from the bottom-up, identifying generative explanations as those hypothesized micro-level mechanisms that are sufficient to produce aggregate outcomes congruent with regularities of the target (Epstein 1999).

Mechanisms are thus deemed generatively sufficient if, when employed by a population of agents, they generate patterns that mimic those regularities observed in empirical study. Following one of the general principles of the scientific endeavor, the greater the number of empirical regularities a proposed mechanism is capable of generating, the greater the confidence in its validity. Importantly, where a proposed mechanism is not sufficient to generate a given regularity, confidence in it is reduced. Given sufficient contradictory evidence, this approach provides a means to eliminate potential explanations of observed phenomena and, in turn, falsify theory—a principal requirement of any scientific proposition (Popper 1963) that is often difficult to meet in the study of complex social systems.

Importantly, although this approach can be used to identify hypotheses that are causally sufficient to explain a given phenomenon, it cannot infer causal explanation (Epstein 1999; Hedström 2005). As such, whereas generative sufficiency is a prerequisite of causal explanation, the converse is not necessarily the case. Drawing parallels to Mackie's (1974) theory of causation, those mechanisms that give rise to an observed effect are sufficient but not necessary. This is a result of the equifinality principle (Bertalanffy 1968), such that in any open system there may be multiple distinct input states that are sufficient to produce a particular output state.

The primary task of those applying the generative method is thus to eliminate those hypotheses that are generatively insufficient, identifying generatively sufficient candidate explanations from a range of initial hypotheses. Having done so, each can be scrutinized in further detail and empirical studies devised to test for the presence of those generatively sufficient mechanisms (Epstein 1999; Hedström 2005). Thus, the development of ABM and the identification of generatively sufficient explanations guides further empirical observation of the target phenomena, which in turn may identify further potential explanations that can be assessed for generative sufficiency (Epstein 1999). Although this cyclical process of computational and empirical investigation is not guaranteed to produce a single viable explanation of a phenomenon, it can eliminate those that are insufficient, implausible, or have been falsified through empirical study.

A. Assessing the Veracity of Hypothesized Crime Event Decision Calculi Using Agent-Based Social Simulation

In undertaking this approach to study theories of crime event decision making, there are two necessary requirements: (1) an individual-level theoretical account of crime event decision making and (2) a series of empirically derived regularities of crime against which the sufficiency of proposed decision calculi are to be assessed. Fortunately, within criminology, both are commonplace.

With regard to individual-level accounts of crime event decision making, this handbook serves as an excellent exemplar to the broad range of theoretical depictions that exist within the criminological literature. With regard to the empirical regularities of crime, criminological research has identified a range of characteristics of crime that are consistently observed across multiple crime types, jurisdictions, contexts, and through a range of measurement instruments. For example, research consistently shows that crime is not uniformly distributed across space or time and instead typically concentrates in "hot" locations and at "hot" times. Similarly, victimization is not uniformly distributed among victims; instead, a small number of victims are subject to a disproportionate amount of "repeat victimization." Such concentrations do not only apply to the distributional properties of crime events. Empirical studies consistently show that a small number of "prolific" offenders are responsible for a disproportionate amount of offenses. Moreover, in examining patterns of life course criminal involvement, the oft cited "age–crime curve" consistently depicts rates of offending that peak in late adolescence and decline in early adulthood. These regularities represent the trace effects of whatever mechanisms are indeed operating at the individual level and thus provide the outcomes against which relevant individual-level accounts of crime can be assessed.

VI. Building an Explanatory Agent-Based Model of Crime

Having identified a theoretical account of crime event decision making of which one aims to assess the causal sufficiency, and a number of empirical regularities against which this account is to be assessed, the process of conceptualizing, implementing, verifying, and validating an ABM is now described. Although this section eschews complex implementation-specific descriptions of the modeling process, it is hoped that it will provide interested readers with an appropriate "recipe" outlining the significant steps involved in making use of this approach in the study of crime event decision calculi.

A. Model Conceptualization

The first step in the modeling process is model conceptualization. In undertaking this task, the researcher must specify key components derived from the theoretical account being studied. Such formalisms are designed to encompass the significant propositions of a given theoretical model, and in unison they represent a conceptualization of the model to be implemented. The development of a conceptual model involves extracting key propositions from the relevant literature and the iterative conversion of these written models into more formalized constructs—typically a logical diagram (e.g., flow chart) of processes/mechanisms and their relational structure. In taking a computational laboratory approach, model conceptualization can also involve the specification of submodels to support subsequent controlled simulation experimentation. This process involves designing a series of model variants that represent competing or counterfactual (e.g., the absence of a proposed mechanism; see section VII) explanations of observed phenomena. These counterfactual submodels then act as a series of experimental conditions in which the model can be placed, allowing us to assess the impact of our proposed behaviors on model outcomes.

B. Model Implementation

Once the conceptual model and any associated submodels have been adequately specified, they must be implemented using an appropriate software platform. This process involves the development of data structures, procedures, and algorithms designed to represent the conceptual model.[4] To illustrate, agent and environment models must be bestowed with appropriate variables to store their internal characteristics. Furthermore, agents' behaviors must be specified as procedures/functions that allow them to (if necessary) draw information from the environment model and/or other agents, operate on those data, and effect change internally and/or within the environment.

In addition to the formalization of agent and environment models and their characteristics and behaviors, a key model loop should also be devised. It is this loop that will set out how all the constituent elements of the model act in a given cycle and subsequently over multiple cycles. Although the structure of this loop will vary considerably dependent on model conceptualization, it will typically specify the order in which agents enact their behaviors,[5] any environment model updates in response to agent activity (or otherwise), and any recording (to data files) or output (to the model interface) that might take place.

In addition, model implementation will also involve the design and implementation of a range of housekeeping procedures that are run at the start, during, and end of a given simulation. These might include procedures that (a) create and distribute agent populations according to specified parameters; (b) document all selected parameters, values, and the associated model initial state in a data file; (c) create and assign appropriate output files in which key simulation events are recorded; (d) write data to that output file describing key events as and when they occur; and (e) export that data for further analysis on finalization of a given simulation.

C. Model Verification

The next stage in the modeling process is model verification, whereby the researcher assesses whether the developed model's components sufficiently represent the conceptual model from which they are derived. This process often takes place by examining the behavior of the model in a series of unit tests (Gilbert and Troitzsch 2005). Because even the simplest of models can produce relatively complex behavior (indeed, this represents the underlying rationale for building the model), such unit tests are devised with the hope of ensuring the model is producing expected/plausible outputs in simple scenarios.

Unit tests typically include scrutiny of key behaviors in a series of test scenarios from the simple (e.g., single agent and simple environment) to the more complex (e.g., multiple agents, non-uniform characteristics, and complex environment). In each unit test, one ensures through inspection that one's model is operating as conceptualized and in line with commonsense predictions. In addition, the aforementioned housekeeping procedures should be tested to ensure they are operating as designed.

Model verification is often a considerable enterprise. Unintentional errors in computer code can be difficult to identify, and within ABM their impact on model outcomes may be considerable (Galán et al. 2009). For this reason, a significant amount of resources should be allocated to the model verification phase of any ABM development.

D. Model Validation

After both conceptual and computational models have been assessed, the model should be validated. Whereas model verification seeks to ensure that the developed model is an appropriate formalization of the conceptual model, model validation seeks to assess if the developed model is an appropriate analogue of the real-world target system.

Model validation typically involves scrutinizing the outcomes of models at varying levels of abstraction and, in turn, assessing the sufficiency of modeled constructs in explaining known characteristics of the target system. This process of model validation is undertaken by comparing the output of models (i.e., simulated data) to specific empirical data, generalized distributional properties derived from empirical data, or, in the absence of appropriate data, outcomes predicted by theory.

In making such comparisons, it is obvious that various levels of equivalence between simulated and empirical data can be observed. These range from the model presenting a simple caricature of the target system as assessed via observation to qualitative equivalence of distributional properties and quantitative agreement with both micro and macro patterns of the target system (Axtell and Epstein 1994). Here, the most significant factor in determining at what level model–empirical equivalence should be considered as insightful is defined by the state of current knowledge in the field in which models are applied (Axtell and Epstein 1994). Furthermore, attainable levels of equivalence are also mediated by both model complexity and the accuracy of empirical data against which simulated data can be validated. Concerning the former, the goals of highly abstract models may not be to attain quantitative equivalence with empirical observation but, instead, qualitative equivalence with a broad range of target regularities. With regard to the latter, the limitations of empirical crime data are well acknowledged (Maguire 2007). Thus, in assessing equivalence of simulated and empirical data, researchers must interpret levels of correspondence carefully, acknowledging that quantitative model–empirical equivalence will likely require appropriate models of existing data collection practices—and their associated frailties (Eck and Liu 2008).

E. Model Replication and Sensitivity Analysis

Once simulation outcomes have been observed and analyzed, a number of methods should be employed in assessing their overall validity. These methods aim to ensure that the inferences drawn from a model are reliable and truly indicative of the mechanisms formalized in the model and, in turn, maximize insight into those hypotheses from which they are derived (Galán et al. 2009).

First, many ABM contain probabilistic elements and as such are nondeterministic, producing different outputs each time they are run (Axelrod 1997a). If this is the case, simulated experiments should be replicated such that outcomes are averaged over numerous "runs" using the same simulation model (Townsley and Birks 2008). Through this approach, the range and consistency of possible simulation outputs can be explored.

Second, ABM should be subjected to sensitivity analysis. When models are developed, it is commonplace for a number of significant parameters to be specified. These parameters may dictate the initial conditions of the agents, their behaviors, and the environment in which they reside. Although the results of a particular simulation are of interest, the mapping between these input parameters and output behavior should also be scrutinized (Axelrod 1997a; Gilbert and Troitzsch 2005). This is particularly important in the absence of empirical data from which these parameters can be readily derived. Model sensitivity analyses seek to examine the influence that these initial parameters have on model outcomes and involve manipulating model parameters in isolation (ideally reflecting both model initial conditions and behavioral parameters; Fung and Vemuri 2003), performing a number of simulation replications, and examining changes in model outcomes. The aim of this process is to (1) ensure that simulation outcomes are not overly sensitive to small perturbations of model parameters—thus assessing the robustness of model outcomes; and (2) to gain insight into the relative importance of varying mechanisms formalized in determining model outcomes—thus assessing the robustness of the modeled theoretical account.

VII. Simulating Residential Burglary: An Example Model

In order to provide the reader with an illustrative example, this section summarizes recent research undertaken by the author and colleagues to develop an ABSS of residential burglary (for a full discussion of the model summarized here, see Birks et al. 2012).

Constructing a computational laboratory that aims to explore the macroscopic impacts of several offender calculi proposed by the field of environmental criminology, this model is used to assess the generative sufficiency of key offender behaviors of target selection, learning, and movement in explaining three commonly observed regularities of crime, namely spatial clustering, repeat victimization, and the characteristic positively skewed journey-to-crime curve.

A. Model Description

The model simulates a population of residential burglars who navigate an urban environment, developing spatially referenced cognitive maps and, in turn, victimizing encountered residential properties of which they are both sufficiently aware and deem sufficiently attractive. Figure 26.1 provides a conceptual depiction of this system that is represented through (a) a population of offender agents who represent a pool of motivated burglars; (b) a population of target agents who represent residential properties that may be targeted by offender agents; and (c) a simple spatial environment in which a series

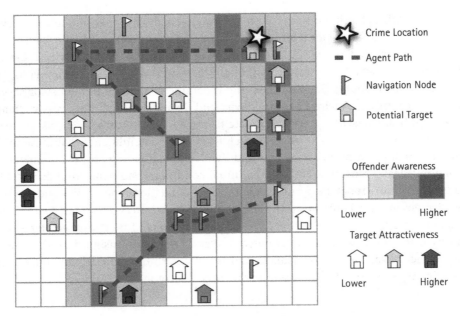

FIGURE 26.1 Conceptual depiction of the simulation system.

of navigation nodes mimic intersections on a hypothetical road network and through which offender agents navigate using a simple route-finding behavior (Birks et al. 2014).

In exploring their impact on patterns of crime, offender agents are bestowed with three key behaviors of movement, target selection, and learning, derived from selected propositions of the routine activity approach, rational choice perspective, and crime pattern theory. Following the computational laboratory approach discussed previously, for each of the proposed offender behaviors, a control and experimental condition are constructed, such that the experimental condition represents the presence of the behavior and the control condition its absence. These offender agent behaviors are briefly described next.

B. Offender Agent Behaviors

1. Movement Behavior

Both the routine activity approach and crime pattern theory propose that observed distributions of crime are a function of the routinized spatial and temporal activity patterns of potential offenders, victims, and crime preventers (P. L. Brantingham and Brantingham 1978, 1981; Cohen and Felson 1979). Offender agents are bestowed with a movement behavior that permits investigation of the impact that these activity patterns have on patterns of crime. In the *experimental model condition*, in which offenders operate according to the propositions of theory, offender agents are allocated a series of activity nodes comprising five randomly selected navigational nodes. These nodes are designed to represent an offender's home location and other commonly visited locations, such as a place of work or the home of a peer. Offender agents begin the simulation located at their home node. As the simulation progresses, offender agents select a destination from these activity nodes at random, and they travel to it via the transport network. Reflecting anchor-based accounts of human movement (Golledge and Spector 1978), once an activity node is reached, agents either return to their home node (with $p = 0.8$) or navigate to another one of their activity nodes ($p = 0.2$). By contrast, under the *control model condition*, offender agents are only allocated a home node and proceed to navigate to randomly selected navigational nodes throughout the environment. Figure 26.2 depicts illustrative movement paths of an agent operating under both control and experimental model conditions.

2. *Target Selection Behavior*

When potential target and offender converge, the rational choice perspective sets out an expected utility calculus employed by offenders in assessing the suitability of a given target (Cornish and Clarke 1986). The perspective proposes that in selecting targets, offenders aim to maximize reward while minimizing risk and effort. Consequently, a fundamental implication of the rational choice perspective is that some targets are more attractive than others. Investigating the impact of this target selection strategy, target agents are allocated an attractiveness characteristic (A) ranging from 0 to 1. This characteristic provides a combined measure of the risk, reward, and effort associated with a given target agent. As $A \to 1$, targets offer high rewards at low risk/effort. Conversely, as A

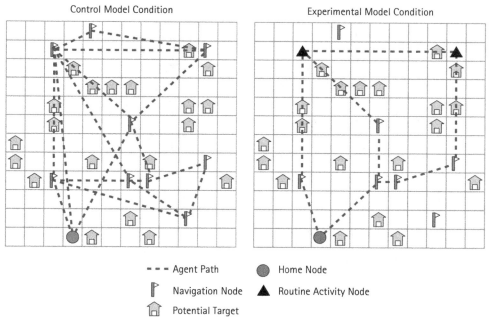

FIGURE 26.2 Illustrative agent movement paths under control and experimental model conditions.

→ 0, targets provide few rewards for high effort/risk. Under the experimental model condition, all target agents are randomly allocated an attractiveness from the uniform distribution $U(0,1)$, such that as theory suggests, some targets are more attractive than others. Under the control model condition, target attractiveness is homogeneous (default = 0.5), and offender agents consider all targets equally viable. Figure 26.3 depicts an example distribution of target attractiveness under both control and experimental model conditions.

3. *Learning Behavior*

A key proposition of crime pattern theory is that offenders are most likely to commit crime where cognitively known areas intersect with attractive targets (Brantingham and Brantingham 1993). Crime pattern theory suggests that as an offender spends more time in an area, awareness of it and the criminal opportunities found within it increases, which enables increases in the likelihood that suitable opportunities for crime can be found. Investigating the impact of this construct on patterns of crime, each agent is allocated a spatially referenced two-dimensional matrix of awareness values (normalized in the range 0–1) that map directly to the simulation environment. Under the experimental model condition, offender agents begin the simulation with no awareness of any locations in their environment. As they navigate the environment, their awareness of it increases following a common logistic function, such that as the time spent at a particular location increases, so does one's awareness of it. Conversely, under the control model condition, offender agents do not learn about their environment and instead are allocated a uniform awareness at simulation initialization that remains static throughout

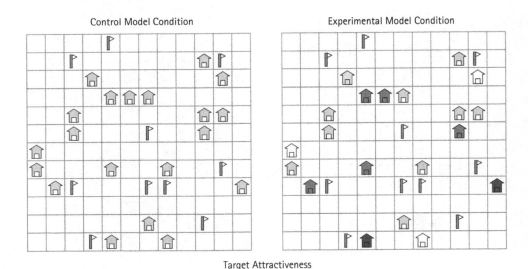

FIGURE 26.3 Illustrative distribution of target attractiveness under control and experimental model conditions.

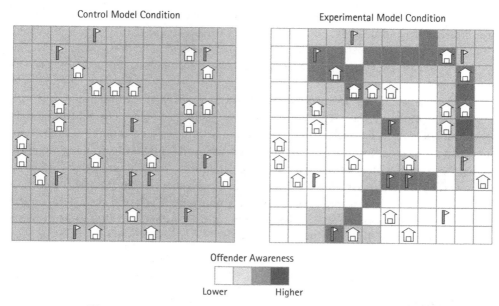

FIGURE 26.4 Illustrative awareness spaces of a single offender under control and experimental model conditions.

the simulation (default = 0.5). Figure 26.4 depicts illustrative awareness spaces of a single offender agent operating under both control and experimental model conditions.

4. *Offending Behavior*

In assessing the respective impacts of the three proposed mechanisms, offender agents are also bestowed with an offending behavior that allows them to choose to victimize target agents they encounter (through the movement behavior), are aware of (through the learning behavior), and deem attractive (through the target selection behavior). This behavior simply seeks to combine the impact of all three behaviors, and their respective condition, into a single probabilistic decision calculus. Thus, on encountering a target agent, the likelihood that it will be victimized is expressed as the product of the probabilities that (a) the offender is sufficiently motivated,[6] (b) the target is deemed suitably attractive, and (c) the location of the target is sufficiently well known to the offender. The likelihood that an offense p(offend) will occur is expressed as

$$p\left(\text{offend}\right)= p\left(\text{motivated}\right)\times p\left(\text{attractive}\right)\times p\left(\text{aware}\right) \tag{26.1}$$

C. Simulation Experiments

Following a traditional $2 \times 2 \times 2$ experimental design, we investigated patterns of crime that emerged under the eight distinct configurations of offender agent experimental and control behavioral conditions. In particular, simulated crimes were analyzed for the presence of three commonly observed empirical regularities of crime: (1) spatial clustering, measured via the nearest neighbor index; (2) repeat victimization, measured via the Gini coefficient; and (3) journey-to-crime curve skewness, measured via Pearson's coefficient of skewness.

In running a simulation, we create a world 100 × 100 cells in size and populate it with 25 offender agents, 2,500 targets, and 1,000 navigational nodes.[7] Due to the model's probabilistic nature, for each behavioral configuration, 500 simulation replications are performed, each using a different random number seed. This results in the simulation being populated with a unique population of offenders with unique activity nodes, a unique distribution of targets (and associated attractiveness under the target selection experimental condition), and a unique transport network. Each of these 4,000 simulations is run until 1,000 crimes have been committed. Subsequently, all simulated crime data are analyzed with respect to spatial clustering, repeat victimization, and journeys to crime.

D. Results

Table 26.1 summarizes the results of these experiments with respect to the eight model configurations and the three key output measures. Primarily, these results demonstrate that when offender agents operate according to modeled propositions of the routine

Table 26.1 Mean and Standard Deviation of Nearest Neighbor Index, Gini Coefficient, and Pearson's Coefficient of Skewness for Journey to Crime Curves by Model Configuration (n = 500 per Model Configuration)

Movement Behavior Condition	Target Selection Behavior Condition	Learning Behavior Condition	Nearest Neighbor Index (NNI)[a,*]	Gini Coefficient[b,*]	JTC Skewness[c,*]
Ctrl	Ctrl	Ctrl	0.51 (0.03)	0.27 (0.02)	0.31 (0.11)
Ctrl	Exp	Ctrl	0.48 (0.03)	0.30 (0.02)	0.31 (0.10)
Ctrl	Ctrl	Exp	0.27 (0.03)	0.41 (0.02)	0.32 (0.12)
Ctrl	Exp	Exp	0.26 (0.02)	0.45 (0.02)	0.31 (0.13)
Exp	Ctrl	Ctrl	0.19 (0.02)	0.39 (0.02)	0.75 (0.13)
Exp	Exp	Ctrl	0.18 (0.02)	0.42 (0.02)	0.75 (0.13)
Exp	Ctrl	Exp	0.13 (0.02)	0.43 (0.02)	0.89 (0.14)
Exp	Exp	Exp	0.13 (0.02)	0.47 (0.02)	0.91 (0.16)

[a]As NNI → 0, greater spatial clustering is observed.

[b]As Gini → 1, greater levels of repeat victimization are observed.

[c]As Pearson's coefficient increases, greater levels of positive skew are observed.

* Significant differences (p < .001) between one or more model configurations.

Ctrl, control; Exp, experimental.

activity approach, rational choice perspective, and crime pattern theory, simulated crime is consistently at its most spatially concentrated, the greatest levels of repeat victimization are observed, and the journey-to-crime curve is at its most positively skewed. These findings demonstrate that crime event decisions put forward by these theories provide a generatively sufficient explanation for why residential burglary tends to be spatially concentrated, disproportionately experienced by a small number of repeat victims, and why the journey-to-crime curve typically follows a characteristic distance decay.[8]

VIII. LIMITATIONS OF AGENT-BASED MODELS

Having summarized the ABM methodology, its application through ABSS, and described an illustrative ABSS pertinent to those who aim to study crime event decision making, this section summarizes a number of potential frailties of which those who aim to pursue this approach should be aware.

One of the primary concerns in developing ABM relates to the management of model complexity. As previously discussed, the agent-based method offers considerable flexibility in describing complex systems; however, such flexibility can be a mixed blessing. When developing ABM, researchers should be mindful that without appropriate restraint, developed models can rapidly become unwieldy and difficult to interpret, in turn limiting the inferences that can be reliably drawn from their outcomes. Of course, this is somewhat of a tautological frailty, in that complex systems lead to complex models. In managing these issues, model complexity should be incorporated incrementally, such that simple models precede more complex ones (Townsley and Birks 2008). This approach allows new model elements (or replacements for existing ones) to be adequately verified and validated by systematically examining, testing, and observing their impacts on model outcomes with respect to an original conceptual model. Furthermore, the development of simple initial models, and in turn their outcomes, can be used as further counterfactuals against which an incrementally developed model can be compared, thus allowing the impacts of new model elements to be quantified.

Second, ABM can be particularly sensitive to unintentional development decisions that unknowingly impact on the observed output behavior of the model (Galán et al. 2009). In complex models, these "ghosts in the machine" (Polhill, Izquierdo, and Gotts 2004) can rapidly become obfuscated from the researcher and, in turn, lead to inappropriate inferences relating microspecification and macrostructure. Attempts to minimize such problems rely on the incorporation of thorough and competent model verification in the development process, the logistics of which should not be overlooked. Gilbert and Troitzsch (2005), for instance, suggest that an equal amount of time to that spent developing the model should be spent verifying it. In the author's experience, this is not an overestimate.

Although these approaches of incremental model development and testing do not preclude such problems, they do minimize the risk of their occurrence and provide multiple points to identify, isolate, and remove potential threats to model utility.

A third point of note that is particularly pertinent to this volume relates to the holistic nature of the ABM approach. Throughout this chapter, the phrase "crime event decision calculi" has been purposefully used to refer to all purposive individual-level behaviors to be examined through the ABM. In applying the agent-based method to study offender decision making, all but the simplest models likely require formalization of not only offender decision making but also that of potential victims, crime preventers, and furthermore a range of other important constructs. Again, this is a reflection of our desire to model interconnected and interdependent systems as a single enterprise and is clearly advantageous in many respects. However, it does require that scholars have clear theories about how they propose particular outcomes come about, and thus it relies on sufficiently detailed and unambiguous conceptual models. Although this may initially seem daunting, once an initial model is developed, the approach does permit multiple candidate conceptual submodels to be assessed relative to one another, with the hope of identifying the most plausible.

Finally, although discussed previously, the limitations of ABM in establishing causal explanation should be reiterated. The computational ABM identifies sufficient but not necessary conditions for observed outcomes, and the results of simulation experiments must be interpreted with this in mind. Although this weakness may seem significant, in reality it applies equally well to all other analytical approaches in which there is clearly no limit on the number of potential explanations for observed phenomena one can hypothesize and test.

IX. CONCLUSION

Computational ABM and ABSS are new and insightful instruments for social science inquiry. They offer unique means to explore the explanatory capacity of individual-level mechanisms of cognition, action, and interaction proposed by theory in explaining commonly observed societal phenomena. In leveraging this method, agent-based crime simulations can support criminologists in the study of both accepted and proposed crime event decision calculi in a number of fundamental ways.

First, and most important, the construction of ABM promotes rigorous specification of crime event theory (Birks and Elffers 2014). The central enterprise of designing and developing ABM is the effective translation of hypotheses into appropriate model formalizations. This process of translating theoretical construct into computational equivalent forces researchers to be explicit, unambiguous, and logically consistent in describing the concepts, entities, and interactions by which they propose particular outcomes come about. Thus, the development of ABM can highlight ambiguity, inconsistency, and incompleteness in underlying theories that may otherwise go unnoticed in theoretical models or be suppressed for the sake of tractability in statistical models. Consequently, formalization serves well to highlight those theoretical accounts that lack adequate specification and require further refinement in order to support rigorous scientific inquiry. As Epstein (2006) well emphasizes, the modeling enterprise as a whole is most useful in that it "enforces a scientific habit of mind" (p. 1.16). This desire to make explicit, question, and expose all assumption to interrogation is undoubtedly necessary as we strive to increase understanding of complex societal phenomena.

Second, ABM and ABSS provide a new scientific instrument through which the divide between individual action and societal outcomes can be systematically explored. Although a wide range of research methods afford invaluable insight into both of the factors that influence individual crime event decision making and their outcomes—crime events and patterns—our ability to quantify the mechanisms through which the former are causally linked to the latter still remains fundamentally constrained. Such problems are not unique to the study of criminal events. The social sciences strive to characterize situated complex systems that interact in rich nonlinear ways that are difficult to observe and manipulate in support of experimental studies. Agent-based methods provide a platform for analyzing decision making in a complex systems context in which modeled decision makers are situated, influenced, and contextualized by an array of interconnected and interdependent individual, social, and situational factors. Although simulation experimentation cannot, and does not purport to, overcome all constraints of empirical investigation, it does provide means to explore whether observed crime phenomena can or cannot be explained by a particular proposed account of individual action. Within criminology, in which a vast array of such accounts exist, the ability to prototype and prioritize hypotheses in terms of their plausibility is undoubtedly desirable, especially at a vastly reduced logistical and ethical cost relative to many other approaches. The triangulation of theoretical, empirical, and computational studies has for some time supported inquiry in a range of other disciplines. Following this example, the ABM represents a new instrument in the criminologist's ever-expanding tool kit.

Third, the processes of designing, developing, and utilizing computational models of crime and criminal behavior act as a unifier across several dimensions of criminological inquiry (Birks 2017) as follows: (1) by encouraging the integration of research and researchers from a range of commonly disparate fields beyond criminology, including the computer and cognitive sciences, mathematics, psychology, economics, and geography; (2) as noted previously, in providing a bridge between the theoretical and the empirical and a means by which the veracity of the former in explaining the latter can be formally assessed; and (3) by producing instruments that can both inform (e.g., in the development of novel hypotheses) and be informed by qualitative (e.g., in the conceptualization of agent behaviors) and quantitative (e.g., in parameterization of those behaviors) methods of inquiry (Birks and Townsley, 2014).

Notwithstanding these strengths, it is also important to acknowledge that applications of agent-based methods within criminology are still in their infancy relative to many other analytical techniques applied to study crime events. As such, standards for model use, description, and analysis have not been widely recognized by criminologists. This lack of consensus has slowed progress such that model comprehension, comparison, and replication can sometimes be difficult tasks. These goals will undoubtedly be addressed as increasingly more researchers begin to explore the application of these methods to address problems within criminology. Broadly accepted standards for agent-based research dissemination exist in a range of other domains (Grimm et al. 2010), and it is likely from these that the field of computational criminology can learn a great deal.

In conclusion, it is hoped that this chapter will provide readers with both the impetus and the appropriate apparatus to begin exploring the application of ABM to address their own research problems in criminology. Currently, there remains considerable debate within the field of computational criminology as to how agent-based methods can best be applied in the study of crime and criminal behavior. These discussions will undoubtedly be sustained by those applying models to address meaningful research questions and through productive discourse and criticism by the wider discipline. I, for one, am excited that this process is underway.

Notes

1. Throughout this chapter, the terms agent-based model (ABM) and agent-based social simulation (ABSS) are used in a range of contexts. The reader is reminded that ABSS is simply an application of ABM with a particular focus on assessing the aggregate outcomes of individual-level behavior, most commonly among a large population of heterogeneous, spatially situated actors.
2. Note that whereas some computational models are deterministic in nature, such that a simulation run multiple times produces the same outcomes, many models contain probabilistic elements. In this case, running the same simulation multiple times results in different outcomes and necessitates that multiple simulation outcomes are examined for the purposes of understanding a particular system.
3. We purposively use the word "typically" here because the Turing-complete nature of production systems mean that they may in principle, given sufficient rules, encode any of the more complex behaviors subsequently discussed—for instance, incorporating learning, plan adaptation, and emotional states (Balke and Gilbert 2014). Note, however, that the required rules sets associated with such implementations would likely dictate unwieldy levels of complexity.
4. Although a thorough description of how such computer programs are constructed is well beyond the scope of this chapter, a range of software platforms exist in which ABM can be developed, including Netlogo (Wilensky 1999), Repast (North et al. 2005), MASON (Luke et al. 2005), and Swarm (Minar et al. 1996). For a review, readers are directed to Railsback, Lytinen, and Jackson (2006).
5. The scheduling of such actions should be scrutinized to ensure that the order of agents and actions within agents has no untoward effect on model outputs. Most commonly used agent-based modeling software platforms provide tools to perform such tests.

6. In Birks et al.'s 2012 study, offender motivation is held static across all offenders (default p(motivated) = 0.1) in order to investigate the impact of the proximal circumstances derived from the other behaviors.

7. A series of sensitivity analyses were also performed to assess the impact of manipulating several key parameters on model outcomes. Results of these analyses are presented in Birks et al 2012.

8. Birks et al. (2014) replicated this approach by studying the interactions of offenders and mobile, rather than static, targets (interpersonal victimization) and found similar results, further strengthening the plausibility of the decision calculi modeled as causal explanations for widely observed patterns of spatial concentration, repeat victimization, and skewed journeys to crime.

References

Axelrod, R. 2005. "Advancing the Art of Simulation in the Social Sciences." In *Handbook of Research on Nature-Inspired Computing for Economy and Management*, edited by J. Rennard. Hersey, PA: Idea Group.

Axelrod, R. 1997a. "Advancing the Art of Simulation in the Social Sciences." In *Simulating social phenomena*, edited by R. Conte, R. Hegselmann, and P. Terna, pp. 21–40. Berlin: Springer.

Axelrod, R. 1997b. *The Complexity of Cooperation: Agent-Based Models of Competition and Collaboration*. Princeton, NJ: Princeton University Press.

Axtell, R. 2000. "Why Agents? On the Varied Motivations for Agent Computing in the Social Sciences." Working Paper no. 17. Center on Social and Economic Dynamics. http://www.brookings.edu/~/media/research/files/reports/2000/11/technology-axtell/agents.pdf

Axtell, R., and J. Epstein. 1994. "Agent-Based Modeling: Understanding Our Creations." *Bulletin of the Santa Fe Institute* Winter:28–32.

Balke, T., and N. Gilbert. 2014. "How Do Agents Make Decisions? A Survey." *Journal of Artificial Societies and Social Simulation* 17(4): 13.

Bertalanffy, L. v. 1968. *General System Theory: Foundations, Development, Applications*. New York: Braziller.

Bichler, G., and D. Birks. 2015. "Exposed: Agent-Based Simulation of Military Weapons Transfers." Poster presented at the Center for Criminal Justice Research, California State University, San Bernardino.

Birks, D. J. 2017. "Formal Models of the Crime Event: Agent-Based Modelling in Support of Crime Prevention." In *Crime Prevention in the 21st Century*, edited by B. LeClerc and E. Savona, pp. 215–33. New York: Springer.

Birks, D. J., S. Donkin, and M. J. Wellsmith. 2008. "Synthesis over Analysis: Towards an Ontology of Volume Crime Simulation." In *Artificial Crime Analysis Systems: Using Computer Simulations and Geographic Information Systems*, edited by L. Liu and J. Eck, pp. 160–91. Hershey, PA: Idea Group.

Birks, D. J. and H. Elffers. 2014. "Agent-Based Assessments of Criminological Theory." In *Springer Encyclopedia of Criminology and Criminal Justice*, edited by G. Bruinsma and D. Weisburd, pp. 19–32. New York: Springer-Verlag.

Birks, D. J., and M. Townsley. 2014. "Making Crime Simulation Richer: 8 Steps on the Path to Criminology's Computational Enlightenment." In *Wis en waarachtig. Liber amicorum voor Henk Elffers*, edited by R. Ruiter, W. Bernasco, W. Huisman, and G. Bruinsma, pp. 477–90. Amsterdam: NSCR and Vrije Universiteit Amsterdam.

Birks, D. J., M. Townsley, and A. Stewart. 2012. "Generative Explanations of Crime: Using Simulation to Test Criminological Theory." *Criminology* 50(1): 221–54.

Birks, D. J., M. Townsley, and A. Stewart. 2014. "Emergent Patterns of Interpersonal Victimization—An Agent-Based Approach." *Journal of Research in Crime and Delinquency* 51:119–40.

Bonabeau, E. 2002. "Agent-Based Modeling: Methods and Techniques for Simulating Human Systems." *Proceedings of the National Academy of Sciences of the USA* 99(3), 7280–87.

Bosse, T., H. Elffers, and C. Gerritsen. 2010. "Simulating the Dynamical Interaction of Offenders, Targets and Guardians." *Crime Patterns and Analysis* 3(1): 51–66.

Bosse, T., C. Gerritsen, and J. Treur. 2009. "Towards Integration of Biological, Psychological, and Social Aspects in Agent-Based Simulation of Violent Offenders." *Simulation Journal* 85(10): 635–60.

Brantingham, P. J., and G. Tita. 2008. "Offender Mobility and Crime Pattern Formation from First Principles." In *Artificial Crime Analysis Systems: Using Computer Simulations and Geographic Information Systems*, edited by L. Liu and J. Eck, pp. 193–208. Hershey, PA: Idea Group.

Brantingham, P. L., and P. J. Brantingham. 1978. "A Theoretical Model of Crime Site Selection." In *Crime, Law and Sanctions*, edited by M. Krohn and R. Akers. New York: Sage.

Brantingham, P. L., and P. J. Brantingham. 1981. "Notes on the Geometry of Crime." In *Environmental Criminology*, edited by P. Brantingham and P. Brantingham, pp. 27–54. Beverly Hills, CA: Sage.

Brantingham, P. L., and P. J. Brantingham. 1993. "Nodes, Paths and Edges: Considerations on the Complexity of Crime and the Physical Environment." *Journal of Environmental Psychology* 13(1): 3–28.

Brantingham, P. L., and P. J. Brantingham. 2004. "Computer Simulation as a Tool for Environmental Criminologists." *Security Journal* 17(1): 21–30.

Brantingham, P. L., U. Glasser, B. Kinney, K. Singh, and M. Vajihollahi. 2005a. "A Computational Model for Simulating Spatial and Temporal Aspects of Crime in Urban Environments." *IEEE International Conference on Systems, Man, and Cybernetics* 4:3667–74.

Brantingham, P. L., U. Glasser, B. Kinney, K. Singh, and M. Vajihollahi. 2005b. "Modelling Urban Crime Patterns: Viewing Multi-agent Systems as Abstract State Machines." *Proceedings of the 12th International Workshop on Abstract State Machines*, 101–117.

Broersen, J., M. Dastani, J. Hulstijn, and L. van der Torre. 2002. "Goal Generation in the BOID Architecture." *Cognitive Science Quarterly* 2(3-4): 428–47.

Cilliers, P. 2000. "What Can We Learn from a Theory of Complexity?" Emergence 2(1): 23–33.

Cohen, L. E., and M. Felson. 1979. "Social Change and Crime Rate Trends: A Routine Activity Approach." *American Sociological Review* 44:588–608.

Cornish, D., and R. Clarke. 1986. *The Reasoning Criminal: Rational Choice Perspectives on Offending*. New York: Springer-Verlag.

Cornish, D. B., and R. V. Clarke. 2003. "Opportunities, Precipitators and Criminal Dispositions: A Reply to Wortley's Critique of Situational Crime Prevention." In *Theory for Practice in Situational Crime prevention*, edited by M. J. Smith and D. B. Cornish, pp. 41–96. *Crime Prevention Studies*, vol. 16. Monsey, NJ: Criminal Justice Press.

Davidsson, P., 2002. "Agent Based Social Simulation: A Computer Science View." *Journal of Artificial Societies and Social Simulation* 5(1). http://jasss.soc.surrey.ac.uk/5/1/7.html

Eck, J., and L. Liu. 2008. "Contrasting Simulated and Empirical Experiments in Crime Prevention." *Journal of Experimental Criminology* 4:195–213.

Edmonds, B. 2015. "Using Qualitative Evidence to Inform the Specification of Agent-Based Models." *Journal of Artificial Societies and Social Simulation* 18(1): 18. http://jasss.soc.surrey. ac.uk/18/1/18.html

Epstein, J. 1999. "Agent-Based Computational Models and Generative Social Science." *Complexity* 4(5): 41–60.

Epstein, J. 2006. *Generative Social Science: Studies in Agent-Based Computational Modeling.* Princeton, NJ: Princeton University Press.

Epstein, J. 2008. 'Why Model?' *Journal of Artificial Societies and Social Simulation* 11(4): 12. http://jasss.soc.surrey.ac.uk/11/4/12.html

Epstein, J., and R. Axtell. 1996. *Growing Artificial Societies: Social Science from the Bottom Up.* Cambridge, MA: MIT Press.

Fung, K., and S. Vemuri. 2003. "The Significance of Initial Conditions in Simulations." *Journal of Artificial Societies and Social Simulation* 6(3).

Galán, J. M., L. R. Izquierdo, S. S. Izquierdo, J. I. Santos, R. Del Olmo, A. López-Paredes, and B. Edmonds. 2009. "Errors and Artefacts in Agent-Based Modelling." *Journal of Artificial Societies and Social Simulation* 12(1): 1.

Gilbert, N., and P. Terna. 2000. "How to Build and Use Agent-Based Models in Social Science." *Mind and Society* 1(1): 57–72.

Gilbert, N., and K. Troitzsch. 2005. *Simulation for the Social Scientist,* 2nd ed. Maidenhead, UK: Open University Press.

Golledge, R., and A. Spector. 1978. "Comprehending the Urban Environment: Theory and Practice." *Geographical Analysis* 9:403–26.

Grimm, V. 2008. "Individual-Based Models." In *Reference Module in Earth Systems and Environmental Sciences Encyclopedia of Ecology,* edited by S. E. Jørgensen and B. D. Fath, pp. 1959–68. Amsterdam: Elsevier.

Grimm, V., U. Berger, D. L. DeAngelis, J. G. Polhill, J. Giske, and S. F. Railsback. 2010. "The ODD Protocol: A Review and First Update." *Ecological Modelling* 221(23): 2760–68.

Groff, E. 2007a. "Simulation for Theory Testing and Experimentation: An Example Using Routine Activity Theory and Street Robbery." *Journal of Quantitative Criminology* 23(2): 75–103.

Groff, E. 2007b. "'Situating' Simulation to Model Human Spatio-temporal Interactions: An Example Using Crime Events." *Transactions in GIS* 11(4): 507–30.

Groff, E. 2008. "Adding the Temporal and Spatial Aspects of Routine Activities: A Further Test of Routine Activity Theory." *Security Journal* 21(1-2): 95–116.

Hedström, P. 2005. *Dissecting the Social: On Principles of Analytical Sociology.* Cambridge: Cambridge University Press.

Jennings, N. 2001. "An Agent-Based Approach for Building Complex Software Systems: Why Agent-Oriented Approaches Are Well Suited for Developing Complex, Distributed Systems." *Communications of the ACM* 44(4): 35–41.

Jiang, H., J. M. Vidal, and M. N. Huhns. 2007. "EBDI: An Architecture for Emotional Agents." In *Proceedings of the 6th International Joint Conference on Autonomous Agents and Multiagent Systems,* p. 11. New York: ACM.

Liu, L., X. Wang, J. Eck, and J. Liang. 2005. "Simulating Crime Events and Crime Patterns in a RA/CA Model." In *Geographic Information Systems and Crime Analysis,* edited by F. Wang, pp. 197–213. Reading, PA: Idea.

Luke, S., C. Cioffi-Revilla, L. Panait, K. Sullivan, and G. Balan. 2005. "MASON: A Multiagent Simulation Environment." *Simulation* 81:517–27.

Mackie, J. L. 1974. *The Cement of the Universe*. New York: Oxford University Press.

Maguire, M. 2007. "Crime Data and Statistics." In *The Oxford Handbook of Criminology*, 4th ed., edited by M. Maguire, R. Reiner, and R. Morgan, pp. 241–301. New York: Oxford University Press.

Malleson, N., and P. L. Brantingham. 2009. "Prototype Burglary Simulations for Crime Reduction and Forecasting." *Crime Patterns and Analysis* 2(1): 47–65.

Malleson, N., A. Evans, and T. Jenkins. 2009. "An Agent-Based Model of Burglary." *Environment and Planning B: Planning and Design* 36:1103–23.

Minar, N., R. Burkhart, C. Langton, and M. Askenazi. 1996. The Swarm Simulation System: A Toolkit for Building Multi-agent Simulations." Report no. 96-06-042. Santa Fe, NM: Santa Fe Institute.

North, M., T. Howe, N. Collier, and J. Vos. 2005. "The Repast Simphony Runtime System." Proceedings of the Agent 2005 Conference, October 2005, pp. 151–58.

Polhill, G., L. Izquierdo, and N. Gotts. 2004. "The Ghost in the Model (and Other Effects of Floating Point Arithmetic)." *Journal of Artificial Societies and Social Simulation* 8(1).

Pontier, M. A., J.-L. van Gelder, and R. E. de Vries. 2013. "A Computational Model of Affective Moral Decision Making That Predicts Human Criminal Choices." In *PRIMA 2013: Principles and Practice of Multi-agent Systems*, edited by G. Boella, E. Elkind, B. T. R. Savarimuthu, F. Dignum, and M. K. Purvis. *Lecture Notes in Computer Science*, vol. 8291, pp. 502–09. Berlin: Springer-Verlag.

Popper, K. 1963. *Conjectures and Refutations: The Growth of Scientific Knowledge*. London: Routledge.

Railsback, S. F., S. L. Lytinen, and S. K. Jackson. 2006. "Agent-Based Simulation Platforms: Review and Development Recommendations." *Simulation* 82(9): 609–23.

Rao, A. S., and M. P. Georgeff. 1991. "Modeling Rational Agents Within a BDI Architecture." *KR* 91:473–84.

Simon, H. 1990. "Invariants of Human Behaviour." *Annual Review of Psychology* 41:1–19.

Townsley, M., and D. J. Birks. 2008. "Building Better Crime Simulations: Systematic Replication and the Introduction of Incremental Complexity." *Journal of Experimental Criminology* 4(3): 309–33.

Wang. N., L. Liu, and J. E. Eck. 2014. "Analyzing Crime Displacement with a Simulation Approach." *Environment and Planning B: Planning and Design* 41(2): 359–74.

Wang, X., L. Liu, and J. Eck. 2008. "Crime Simulation Using GIS and Artificial Intelligent Agents." In *Artificial Crime Analysis Systems: Using Computer Simulations and Geographic Information Systems*, edited by L. Liu and J. Eck, pp. 209–25. Hershey, PA: Idea Group.

Wilensky, U. 1999. *NetLogo*. Evanston, IL: Center for Connected Learning and Computer-Based Modeling, Northwestern University. http://ccl.northwestern.edu/netlogo

Wooldridge, M. J., and N. R. Jennings. 1995. "Agent Theories, Architectures, and Languages: A Survey." In *Intelligent Agents: ECAI-94 Workshop on Agent Theories, Architectures, and Languages*, edited by M. J. Wooldridge and N. R. Jennings, pp. 1–39. Berlin: Springer-Verlag.

CHAPTER 27

MODELING OFFENDER DECISION MAKING WITH SECONDARY DATA

WIM BERNASCO

As the contributions to this handbook testify, offenders make many types of decisions before and while committing crimes. Some examples of decisions are whether to offend in the first place, whether to offend alone or with others, with whom to offend, when to offend, where to offend and how to travel to the crime site, whether or not to carry and use a weapon, what other methods and tools to use, and what clothes to wear, to mention only a few salient decisions involved in offending.

There are various methods available to learn about offender decisions. The most straightforward strategy is to focus on the decision makers by asking them questions about their choices or by observing their choices in natural or experimental situations. These strategies all have their own drawbacks. Offenders may be unwilling or unable to describe their decision making, scientists can very seldom observe criminal behavior as it unfolds in the real world, and experimentation is limited by ethical concerns. As a result, many studies on offender decision making only observe and analyze the materialized result of offender decisions. They collect and statistically model decision outcomes by using secondary data—that is, data provided by law enforcement agencies, possibly combined with information from other registries.

Although the research questions that motivate this analytical strategy often apply to acts that individuals can willfully decide to commit (i.e., decisions), the questions are not always literally framed in terms of decision making. Rather, they are usually coined in statistical terms of "effects of attributes on outcomes." Although such phrasing may seem to ignore the agency of the individuals being studied, it could reflect the caution that many researchers exercise when drawing conclusions from data not originally designed for their research question, leading them to provide cautious interpretations of their findings.

This chapter takes the viewpoint that if the behavior being studied involves any choice at all, there is good reason to interpret and discuss the research outcomes in terms of decision making, irrespective of the particular research methodology being used. This viewpoint is inspired by microeconomics. Microeconomic theory is about how individual agents make decisions under a variety of constraints, and most (although certainly not all) of the empirical tests of the theory are based on the statistical analysis of secondary data.

This chapter is a review of this methodology in the study of offender decision making. Because of the great variety of data sources, data types, and analytical techniques that are used in research on crime and criminal justice, this chapter cannot cover any specific source, data type, or technique in detail and must thus refer to other materials for in-depth treatment. The chapter can neither be exhaustive in terms of the types of decisions being reviewed. It focuses on two types of decisions: whether to offend and where to offend.

The remainder of this chapter consists of four sections. The first section briefly describes some types of secondary data used in research on offender decision making, particularly data from law enforcement. The second section addresses the use of secondary data in the offender's decision on where to commit crime. The third section describes how secondary data have been used in studying whether to offend in the first place. The fourth section discusses advantages and disadvantages of secondary data analysis in the study of offender decision making.

I. SECONDARY DATA SOURCES

In this chapter, secondary data include all data that have been recorded and collected for other reasons than scientific research. They include records of agencies in the criminal justice system (courts, prisons, and police departments) but also the following: population registries; census data; registries of schools, firms, and companies; tax registries; Internet provider databases; and so on. The definition also includes the secondary analysis of observational qualitative data (e.g., police interrogation transcripts and closed-circuit TV [CCTV] footage of offending) that were collected for other than research purposes.

A. Criminal Justice Data

Police records are one of the most widely used types of data in criminological research. This is not surprising because police records include information on some of the main topics of interest to criminologists: criminal events and their perpetrators and victims. The police record information about crimes and their perpetrators for several reasons. The first reason is that detailed documentation about incidents and individuals is required for prosecution. The second reason is that the records can be used for solving future crimes. The third reason is that police records provide a measure of police productivity.

In the United States, the Federal Bureau of Investigation has since 1930 administered the Uniform Crime Reports (UCR) program, a national multi-agency program that collects and reports standardized data on crime from a large variety of law enforcement agencies. It has been used extensively in research on crime, including work focusing on individual decision making (Lochner 2004). Since 1988, the traditional Summary Reporting System (SRS), which contains aggregated data, has been supplemented with the National Incident-Based Reporting System (NIBRS), which goes into much greater detail and allows for analyzing data at the incident level. It includes, but is not limited to, a detailed classification of the type of crime; characteristics of the incident, such as date, time, and location type; characteristics of properties involved in the offense (including residences, offices, vehicles, and stolen items); and characteristics of victims, offenders, and arrestees, such as age, sex, ethnicity, and the type of weapon they carried, if any. Compared to aggregated summary reports, the incident-level data in the NIBRS have greatly increased the opportunities for scholarly research on crime and have been used extensively for that purpose (Thompson, Saltzman, and Bibel 1999; Tillyer and Tillyer 2015).

Nevertheless, some research questions require more or other details than the NIBRS offers, such as data on addresses of offenders and crime locations. Therefore, many studies utilize offense and offender samples from police records that contain more detailed information, typically of a single jurisdiction.

Most countries have databases in which DNA profiles are stored to support criminal investigations (Corte-Real 2004). They typically contain two types of DNA profiles. The first are DNA profiles of biological stains (typically blood, saliva, or semen) that have been secured at crime sites and are assumed to belong to a person involved in the crime. The second are DNA profiles of reference samples taken (usually by way of a buccal swab) from suspects or from convicted offenders. Although DNA databases have been designed for investigate purposes, some scholars in England (Leary and Pease 2003; Townsley, Smith, and Pease 2006), the Netherlands (Lammers 2014; Bernasco, Lammers, and van der Beek 2016), and Belgium (Jeuniaux et al. 2016) have used national DNA databases for the study of crime patterns. Because DNA databases contain information on criminal behavior of both identified and unidentified offenders (in particular, crime type, date, location, and links to other crimes), a particular advantage of these data is that they allow researchers to study geographic patterns and patterns of co-offending irrespective of whether the offenders are known to law enforcement agencies.

A relatively recent development is the usage of surveillance camera footage of illegal behavior for research purposes. CCTV cameras are usually installed for security reasons, but when crimes are committed in front of the cameras, the recorded footage is often used for investigative purposes and can also be useful for a detailed analysis of behavior. Examples are a study of the role of bystanders in public violence (Levine, Taylor, and Best 2011) and a study on drug sellers in open-air markets (Piza and Sytsma 2016).

B. Population Registries

As exemplified by the studies cited in section III of this chapter and as discussed extensively by Lyngstad and Skarðhamar (2011), the Nordic countries as well as some other countries (e.g., the Netherlands) have set up (digital) population registries that document basic demographic and administrative data about their citizens. These include gender, date of birth, nationality, address, and links to records of parents, children, and marital partners. Usually these files can be linked to other data files on education, employment, tax administration, social services, utilization of health services, and—of particular relevance in this chapter—law enforcement data. Address data can be further linked to area-based sociodemographic and land use data, which allows social-ecological research to be fully based on registry data.

C. Victimization Surveys

A substantial percentage of crime is never registered because the victims do not report it to the police or because the police do not record it. Unrecorded crime remains a "dark number" when only police statistics are available. To provide more valid and reliable crime statistics, the victimization survey was invented in the 1960s. By the end of the twentieth century, some industrialized countries had their own annual or bi-annual survey, such as the National Crime Victimization Survey (NCVS) in the United States and the British Crime Survey (BCS) in the United Kingdom. As a collaborative effort of academic researchers, the International Crime Victimization Survey (ICVS) has been underway for several decades.

In victimization surveys, random samples of the population are asked to report on how often they have been a victim of a variety of crimes during a reference period (usually twelve months). Because the outcomes of victimization surveys are used mostly for periodic evaluations of trends and developments in crime and victimization (and not to answer specific research questions), they are treated here as "secondary" data rather than as primary data. Because every crime victim is a target implicitly or explicitly chosen by an offender, victimization surveys may be helpful in answering questions about offender's target or victim selection. Do pickpockets prefer male or female victims? Do robbers select young or middle-aged victims? Do burglars select affluent or poor households? The advantage of victimization surveys compared to police records is that victimization surveys provide much more details about the geographic, demographic, social, and economic characteristics of victims than do police records. On the other hand, victimization surveys contain almost no information on offenders.

II. WHERE TO COMMIT CRIME

This section addresses a decision frequently studied in criminology—the decision of where to commit crime (for a detailed account see chapter 19).

The study of geographic variation in crime dates back to the nineteenth century. The classic works of Guerry and Quetelet as well as the studies of the Chicago School focused on regional and neighborhood variations in crime and delinquency. They documented variations in numbers of registered crimes or numbers of registered offenders across geographic areas. Because the geographic units of analysis were relatively large, and because individual geographic mobility was limited in the nineteenth and early twentieth centuries, these studies did not explicitly distinguish between where offenders lived and where they committed crimes. It was assumed (and the assumption was probably justified) that offenders would commit crimes in the district or neighborhood in which they lived. The interest in the "criminal commute" or "journey to crime" is more recent and was inspired by journey-to-work studies. It was based on the premise that for offenders, crime is a source of livelihood, and that like other workers they must travel from their homes to the crime target to earn their illegal income (Rengert 1992, p. 109).

Time and again it has been empirically verified that the frequency of crime decreases with the distance from home—a phenomenon referred to as distance decay—and that most crimes are perpetrated near the offenders' main anchor points (i.e., near their homes) (Levine and Lee 2013; Andresen, Frank, and Felson 2014; Vandeviver, van Daele, and Vander Beken 2015). This regularity has usually been interpreted in terms of travel cost minimization: Why travel far if the same can be achieved nearby?

However, the question *how far* offenders move away from home to commit crime is not necessarily a very good question. A more ambitious question is *where* they go to commit crime. The answer to the latter implies an answer to the former question, but it requires more precision. At one kilometer distance from an offender's home, there are numerous opportunities for crime, but only some of these places are potentially selected as crime sites, whereas others are not. Thus, travel cost minimization might provide an answer to the question how far offenders travel to commit crime, but it does usually not provide an adequate explanation of where offenders commit crime.

Several recent studies on the geography of crime address this question of crime location choice. A common theme is that distance is not the object of explanation but, rather, part of the explanation itself: It is one of the criteria that make a possible target more or less attractive to a prospective offender. This line of research is interesting to discuss in this chapter not just because it applies secondary data to analyze offender decisions, but in particular because the analytical framework that is used in these studies explicitly analyzes crime locations as the result of offenders' decisions.

Bernasco and Nieuwbeerta (2005) started this line of research by using random utility maximization theory and discrete choice modeling (Ben-Akiva and Lerman 1994) to answer crime location choice questions. They assumed that motivated offenders must choose a crime site from a limited set of alternatives. For example, they must choose a neighborhood from the set of all neighborhoods in a city. According to the version of rational choice theory that Bernasco and Nieuwbeerta formulated, offenders rate each potential target neighborhood in terms of rewards, costs, and risks. For example, neighborhood affluence may be used as an indicator of prospective burglary rewards, police patrol intensity in the neighborhood may be used as an indicator of apprehension risk, and distance from home may be used as a measure of transportation cost. Provided that offenders have information on all relevant neighborhood characteristics, they choose the neighborhood that offers the optimal mix of rewards, costs, and risks. If the alternatives and their attributes are known, and if it is observed where offenders decided to offend and where not, the model outcomes tell us how they value the measured neighborhood attributes. This analytical strategy is called "revealed preference" in economics, in which it was initially applied to consumer choices (Samuelson 1938; Varian 2006). It tells us what individuals find important based on observing what they do rather than what they say they find important or what they say they would do if given the choice.

The idea to learn about offender preferences by comparing attributes of targeted and not-targeted areas has been applied to burglary (Bernasco and Nieuwbeerta 2005; Clare, Fernandez, and Morgan 2009; Townsley et al. 2015), robbery (Bernasco and Block 2009; Bernasco, Block, and Ruiter 2013; Bernasco, Johnson, and Ruiter 2015), thefts from vehicles (Johnson and Summers 2015), and riot-related offenses in the 2011 London riots (Baudains, Braithwaite, and Johnson 2013). Each of these studies uses police records that link offenders (and the neighborhoods or city blocks where they live) to the crimes they have been charged with (and the neighborhoods or the city blocks where they committed these crimes). Each of these studies also combines the police recorded data with administrative and census or registry-based data on all neighborhoods and city blocks in the catchment area. A common finding across all studies is that offenders, when given a choice of identical target locations, prefer nearby locations over distant targets. The finding strengthens the ubiquity of the law of distance decay because it not merely confirms its validity but also demonstrates that the preference for nearby locations remains after controlling for other choice criteria.

Whereas the majority of crime location choice studies are based on the assumption that all offenders possess complete information on all alternatives (e.g., they know all relevant characteristics of all neighborhoods in the city), recent research on crime location choice has suggested that spatial decisions are heavily influenced by the awareness spaces of the offenders involved. Bernasco (2010) used police recorded data from The Hague on perpetrators of residential burglaries, thefts from vehicles, robberies and assaults, and street robberies and linked the data to a registry containing historic residential address data. The results demonstrated for all four crime types that offenders not only committed crimes nearby their current residences but also preferred committing crimes in former areas of residence, particularly if they had lived there a long time and until recently. Their findings were replicated in a nationwide study in the Netherlands on commercial robberies (Bernasco and Kooistra 2010).

Building on this evidence, Lammers et al. (2015) argued that in addition to prior areas of residence, prior crime locations might also be part of offenders' awareness spaces. Using police data on serial offenders in the greater The Hague area during the period from 2003 to 2009, combined with registry data on historic residential addresses, they assessed the tendency of offenders to return to their prior crime locations to commit new crimes. In line with findings in the literature on spatiotemporal risk clusters (Johnson et al. 2007) and offender behavioral consistency (Tonkin et al. 2011), they showed that offenders prefer to offend near their prior crime locations, especially if the prior crimes were committed recently and involved the same type of crime. These findings were confirmed in a study on burglars in the West Midlands in the United Kingdom (Bernasco et al. 2015).

With respect to decision-making mechanisms, the effects of offender awareness space on their location choices require further study. Research findings have thus far suggested that locations already have increased attraction value if only they are situated within the offender's awareness space. However, from a theoretical standpoint, it should be expected that awareness space does not directly affect attractiveness, but that it modifies other effects: One would expect that both negative attributes (indicating high risk or high cost) and positive attributes (indicating high rewards) would weigh more strongly for places within an offender's awareness space than for places outside the offender's awareness space.

In summary, empirical research on the geography of crime has extensively used police records, census data, and other secondary administrative data sources. Recent research on crime location choice has continued this tradition and has demonstrated how detailed registry data can be used to enrich the framework by testing effects of awareness space. Moreover, this work is a straightforward example of how mathematical offender decision-making models can be applied to secondary data.

III. Whether or Not to Offend

The type of decision most frequently studied in criminology is probably the decision whether or not to commit crime. In the field that studies this decision, developmental and life course criminology (Farrington 2003a), the involvement in crime is not commonly framed in terms of decision making. Rather, the literature identifies structural economic and social conditions and life events that determine whether individuals become involved in crime. Thus, it implicitly follows a medical "risk-factor" logic whereby criminal behavior is not explicitly chosen by individuals but, rather, induced by "criminogenic" circumstances. A possible exception in criminology is the age-graded theory of informal social control (Laub and Sampson 2003), which uses the concepts of "agentic action" and "situated choice" to emphasize that individuals make choices that are constrained but not determined by external factors, a perspective common in economics, in which crime (like all other behavior) is studied from a decision-making perspective (Becker 1968; Ehrlich 1973).

Nevertheless, the view that committing crime is a matter of choice between expected costs and benefits is fully compatible with empirical observations. Many of the conditions that generally appear to reduce criminal involvement in adolescents (parental monitoring, scholarly achievement, and nondelinquent friends) and those that appear to reduce it in adults (marriage, parenthood, and employment) can easily be interpreted as conditions that make crime a more costly and risky alternative than abstinence from crime, but not necessarily more rewarding. In other words, there seems to be no theoretical obstacle to analyzing the involvement in criminal activity as a decision, the outcome of which is affected by the perceived costs and benefits of each alternative, and where these perceived costs and benefits depend on external factors that are mostly outside the control of the individual.

Most US- and UK-based studies on criminal careers are panel studies among respondents who report their attitudes and behavior in questionnaires and interviews. In other words, they are primary data. Well-known examples are the Cambridge Study (Farrington 2003b; Farrington, Piquero, and Jennings 2013), the Rochester Youth Development Study (Thornberry, Lizotte, and Krohn 2003), the Denver Youth Survey (Huizinga, Wylie Weiher, and Espiritu 2003), the Pittsburgh Youth Study (Loeber, Farrington, and Stouthamer-Loeber 2003), the Peterborough Adolescent and Young Adults Development Study (Wikström et al. 2012), and, in economics, the National Longitudinal Survey of Youth (Grogger 1998; Lochner 2004). Although these studies provide rich data on many life domains, including deviance, criminal involvement, and victimization, they require enormous amounts of resources, are necessarily limited in size, and are affected by attrition issues despite the efforts of researchers to keep panel retention levels high.

Alternatively, various studies in the Nordic countries (Denmark, Norway, Sweden, and Finland) and in the Netherlands have used registration data to answer questions on criminal involvement—questions that are often similar to the questions answered in expensive self-report samples that are used elsewhere. These studies have utilized the existence of comprehensive registry data involving multiple life domains and that typically cover the full population of the respective countries. In these countries, registry data replace the censuses that are common in most other countries of the world.

All four Nordic countries (Norway, Sweden, Finland, and Denmark) have registry data systems that are normally used for a variety of administrative purposes but have also been used for purposes of producing official statistics and research, including criminological research (Lyngstad and Skarðhamar 2011).

In Denmark, registry data were used to study risk factors for first-time convictions for violent crime (Christoffersen, Francis, and Soothill 2003) and for drunk driving (Christoffersen, Soothill, and Francis 2008) among a cohort of men born in 1966 ($N = 43,403$). In both studies, the authors combined twelve registries that could be linked because they all included the subjects' personal identity numbers. Examples of registries that were used and of the information included in them are population statistics (gender, age, marital status, and address), fertility database (links to parents, siblings, and children), psychiatric registry (psychiatric diagnoses), employment statistics (unemployment), education statistics (grades, schooling, and vocational training), and crime statistics (violation, conviction, and imprisonment).

In another study based on registry data in Denmark (Soothill et al. 2010), first-time convictions for shoplifting, burglary, and violence were examined. The authors used data of a national cohort of men born in 1980 who were living in Denmark by January 1994. Again, all information on these individuals and their parents and siblings was obtained from national administrative registries based on contacts with public services, including law enforcement. Whereas the theoretical language of these studies was written in terms of "risk factors," and although criminal convictions do not translate one-on-one to crimes, each of the dependent variables in these studies can be interpreted as the decision to commit a crime, and each person involved in crime can be compared to a similar person in the data set who was not convicted. All three studies applied a discrete time survival analysis approach in which continuous time was split up in person-year units. Whereas this approach is helpful in identifying censored observations, incorporating in the analysis time-varying causal factors and taking into account repeated observations of the same individual, it does not fully utilize the main strength of panel data, which is controlling for unobserved stable between-person heterogeneity.

In Norway, population registry data of five entire birth cohorts were used to analyze the effect of parental income and parental education on the first-time involvement in crime of their adolescent children (Galloway and Skarðhamar 2010). It was found that high educational qualifications of parents, more than high income, reduced the risk of their adolescent children becoming involved in crime. The first-time involvement was analyzed using Cox proportional hazard survival models, where the variable to be explained is the instantaneous hazard of committing a crime at time t if one has not committing the crime before time t.

In another study on Norwegian registry data, Skarðhamar (2009) used registry data from the Norway 1982 birth cohort ($N = 49,975$) to explore the relation between parental relationship dissolution (separation and divorce) and children's adolescent delinquency between ages ten and twenty-two years. Using growth curve modeling, it was shown that although some of the effect of parental breakup is explained by socioeconomic conditions, there appears to be an independent and strong positive effect of family dissolution on children's delinquency.

Skarðhamar and Savolainen (2014) used Norwegian registry data to study the relation between employment and desistance from crime among a sample of 783 male recidivists. Applying smoothing spline regression techniques to model changes in criminal offending around the point of entry to stable employment, they concluded that the transition to employment is most likely a consequence rather than a cause of desistance.

A study in Finland (Savolainen 2009) used registry data from the central statistical agency of the Finnish government to test the applicability of Laub and Sampson's (2003) age-graded informal social control theory in a Nordic welfare state. Savolainen estimated the effects of work, parenthood, marriage, and unmarried cohabitation on desistance from crime among a national sample of 1,325 male felony offenders with a felony conviction in 1996 who had at least two prior felony convictions, who had never been married or lived in a cohabiting relationship, who had never had any children, and who had never had a job. The results demonstrated strong reductions in offending for those who were able to find employment and for those who formed a union in combination and became a father.

A large-scale analysis of the Finnish registry data is reported in a study of the effects of upward and downward social mobility on criminal involvement among a total birth cohort of 60,069 individuals born in Finland in 1987 (Savolainen et al. 2014). The authors combined available registry data on demographics, education, employment, income, and health of individuals and their parents. Their findings show that after controlling for a number of other characteristics, neither downward nor upward mobility is an important correlate of crime.

An example of the extended use of registry data in the Netherlands is the Criminal Career and Life-Course Study (CCLS) study, a large-scale longitudinal study on the life course of a representative sample of 4% of all cases of criminal offenses tried in the Netherlands in 1977 (Blokland, Nagin, and Nieuwbeerta 2005; Blokland and Nieuwbeerta 2005). After the researchers gained access to the original 1977 data set, they first linked it to extracts from the General Documentation Files (GDF) of the Criminal Record Office ("rap sheets") in order to reconstruct the entire criminal careers of the sampled individuals. Next, they enriched it by adding data from the Dutch national population registration records (BRP, formerly GBA). The BRP is a national electronic registration system that contains information on date of birth, date of death, gender, marriage, fertility, residential location, and parenthood for all Dutch inhabitants since 1938, linking individuals directly to their parents and children. This system partially replaces the census that was formally abolished in 1991 in the Netherlands (the last census took place in 1971). The resulting data set documents not only the complete criminal careers of the sample but also major life course events, including changes in marital status, parenthood, and residential relocation. Because the population registration records can be used to link individuals to their parents and to their offspring, the data have been further extended to include conviction information of parents, siblings, and children of the original sample. The CCLS data set has been used extensively in studies of the effects of life course events on offending behavior (van de Rakt, Nieuwbeerta, and de Graaf 2008; Bushway, Nieuwbeerta, and Blokland 2011; McGloin et al. 2011; van Schellen, Apel, and Nieuwbeerta 2012; van Schellen, Poortman, and Nieuwbeerta 2012).

In contrast to most longitudinal surveys in the United States and England that cover crime and delinquency, none of these Nordic and Dutch studies have included any offender interviews or other forms of primary data collection.[1] They fully rely on the advantages of secondary data to draw conclusions on offender decision making.

IV. ADVANTAGES AND DISADVANTAGES

Studying offender decision making by collecting and analyzing secondary data from registrations, including law enforcement records, has several advantages compared to alternative data sources and methods, but it is also saddled with limitations and caveats. This section addresses both the advantages and the disadvantages (for a comprehensive list of the uses of secondary data and for practical guidelines, see Argyrous 2009).

A. Advantages

A key advantage of criminal justice data and population registries (but not of victimization surveys) is that the subjects studied need not be recruited to measure their behavior, and their cooperation is not necessary to do the research. Recruiting participants to take part in surveys or experiments is a difficult and time-consuming task, and registry and criminal justice data free the researcher from the task of identifying a sample frame in the population, finding a relevant sample of subjects, and obtaining their cooperation. The latter is important if the topic of the research is sensitive. Offenders may not always be eager to be interviewed or complete surveys, particularly when the topic is crime and their own criminal behavior. Because the research does not involve the offenders personally, subject remuneration is not required.

A related advantage is that most secondary data have no non-response and panel attrition issues. Non-response refers to individuals who are sampled but decline the invitation to participate in the survey. Selective non-response is one of the drawbacks of survey research. It takes place if the participants willing to take part in the survey are not representative for the targeted population. Most contemporary surveys have response rates below 50%, depending on contact mode (e.g., face-to-face, telephone, paper mail, e-mail, web-based, and smartphone app), expected duration, and survey topics. In research based on registries, all subjects in the sample frame are included in the research, and none drop out.

Another advantage of secondary data is that typically it is not necessary to sample a limited number of subjects from the population. Registry and criminal justice data are population data, and once the researcher has access to these data, the full population at risk is normally included. There is no need to take a sample, to make power calculations, and to accept large standard errors. In fact, descriptive research based on population data does not require inferential statistics, although standard errors are still needed when causal estimates are required (Abadie et al. 2014). Occasionally, including the full population may create computational problems, but in these cases random sampling is an easy and acceptable solution.

A further advantage of many (but not all) criminal justice and registry data is that in contrast to census survey data, which are usually obtained at regular intervals (e.g., decennially), criminal justice and registry data are continuously updated and thus provide fine-grained temporal detail while still allowing the researcher to take "snapshots" that apply to a particular point in time. Related to this point is the advantage that the use of criminal justice and registry data avoids the danger of recall bias, such as telescoping (Christoffersen et al. 2008, p. 417). An example is recalling details of offending. Police records are typically entered directly upon arrest, usually on the day of the crime or within a few days of it. There is little risk that major mistakes are made when recording details such as date, time, place, or modus operandi. If an offender is interviewed about the event six months later in a retrospective offender interview, the risk of memory constraints biasing the account is much greater.

Data on sensitive issues or on socially less acceptable behaviors or experiences (crime is a case in point) may be difficult to obtain because many respondents are unwilling to report such experiences and behaviors. This certainly applies to the majority of offenders, who have broken moral rules and committed acts that are condemned by most people. Although the unwillingness of most people to report on their own offenses may also lead criminal justice or registry data to be incomplete (e.g., crimes undetected by the police will not be included), the data sources themselves do not lie, and the risk that criminal justice and registry data are systematically biased is arguably lower than the risk that respondent answers are biased.

National population registries can be very useful for exploring rare behaviors, events, or groups (Breslow and Day 1980) because it is often impossible or difficult to identify and find respondents. For example, if researchers are interested in the effects of adoption on deviance, registries containing such information can be ideal for sampling. In fact, although this is not a case of using registry data for secondary analysis, the registry itself might be used to sample subjects for face-to-face interviews.

Finally, although criminal justice and registry data are usually not open access in the sense of "publicly available," they are usually available for scientific research under certain conditions. Because they are not owned by a single researcher or research institute, they are potentially available for everyone—a situation that makes it possible to replicate any research performed on the data. The reality of most primary data sets is that they remain the property of the institutes and researchers who collected them, unless and until they are willing to share the data with others. The public nature of most secondary data ensures that replication is in principle possible. In the ideal situation, secondary data on crime are publicly accessible, but such data are often highly aggregated, which limits their usefulness.

B. Disadvantages

Secondary data are collected and stored for other purposes than scientific discovery. They are not tailored to answer specific research questions and may thus not cover the full population of interest. Also, they may contain measures that are less valid and less reliable than would have been the case if they were collected for research purposes. In addition, a point made by Christie (1997) and reiterated by Lyngstad and Skarðhamar (2011) is that researchers are forced to accept the definitions and interpretations of the designers of secondary data, often national or local government authorities. Criminal justice registries are based on strictly legal criteria that do not always align with the aims of academic researchers. For example, a researcher may be interested in domestic violence, but the available police records may not include this category according to the preferred definition.

An obvious implication of this disadvantage is that secondary data are not based on rigorous experimental designs and that, therefore, research based on secondary data cannot generate strong causal inferences. This disadvantage is not unique to secondary data, however, because most primary data collections record observational data only and thus suffer from the same problem. In defense of this approach, note that the issue is increasingly alleviated by the development of advanced statistical techniques that assist in assessing causality from observational data designs. The application of many of these techniques in research on crime and criminal justice is discussed in the *Handbook of Quantitative Criminology* (Piquero and Weisburd 2010), including instrumental variables (Bushway and Apel 2010), propensity score matching (Apel and Sweeten 2010), regression discontinuity (Berk 2010), and fixed effects regression (Dugan 2010). Furthermore, secondary data sometimes provide opportunities for designing natural experiments, in which random assignment to experimental conditions takes place although not planned and designed by researchers. An example is the use of the quasi-random assignment of judges to criminal cases in the United States, which has been used for assessing causal effects on imprisonment on subsequent life events (Kling 2006; Loeffler 2013).

Although the tenet of this chapter is that we do not necessarily need to have access to offender accounts of crime to learn about offender decision making, their knowledge, beliefs, attitudes, and arguments may be very helpful in understanding their decisions. Thus, the absence of the offenders' views on their own criminal conduct and decision making is a disadvantage in almost all secondary analyses of offender decision making (an exception may be the analysis of autobiographies; e.g., see Shover and Hunter 2010).

In the study of crime and criminal justice issues, secondary data contain only information on crime and related social problems that are known to the criminal justice system, including the police. This selection implies that crimes unknown to the police or other law enforcement agencies are by definition excluded from these data; this includes most consensual crimes (e.g., drug dealing), most "victimless" crimes (e.g., intoxicated driving), and crimes that victims do not report to the police. Moreover, when secondary data are used for studying offender decision making, researchers typically require data on arrested (or convicted) offenders. Because the police do not solve all crimes, arrested (and convicted) offenders comprise only a small subset of all offenders. For example, in most countries throughout the world, the detection rate for burglary is less than 10% (Bernasco 2014). Other registry data are also affected by biases. An example is the difficulty of measuring household composition in the Norwegian registry data (Lyngstad and Skarðhamar 2011). Whereas survey questionnaires have no difficulty assessing household composition and distinguishing married from unmarried cohabiting couples (unmarried consensual unions are fairly common in Norway), the identification of cohabiting couples with the Norwegian registry is difficult.

Registry data are usually context-poor. Hypotheses tested using context-poor data must often rely on simplifying assumptions because there are no options available for multiple measurement or other forms of triangulation. Too much reliance on such assumptions endangers the validity of the findings. An interesting account of such a situation is provided in a study on "defended community homicide" (Griffiths et al. 2008), defined as "homicides . . . perpetrated against nonresidents to protect the subjective and/or objective well-being of the perpetrator's neighborhood" (p. 233). The authors used police records and census data to regress two types of homicide on social disorganization variables, with the findings confirming the hypothesis that social organization had opposite effects on both types of homicide. A closer qualitative examination of case descriptions of 34 homicides labeled as "defended community homicides" revealed that in only 4 of the 34 cases could the circumstances suggest a "community defense" motivation, thereby effectively falsifying the hypothesis. Often, however, triangulation is not possible because secondary data do not include detailed case descriptions.

Possibly the most serious danger of secondary databases is that they may have the capacity to seduce researchers into formulating their research questions based on what they know is available in registry data rather than on what is interesting from a scientific standpoint (Christie 1997). In other words, the risk is that they let data availability dictate their substantive research questions.

Note

1. The CCLS study is currently interviewing the individuals in the sample for the first time.

References

Abadie, Alberto, Susan Athey, Guido W. Imbens, and Jeffrey M. Wooldridge. 2014. "Finite Population Causal Standard Errors." In *NBER Working Papers Series*, pp. 1–53 Cambridge, MA: National Bureau of Economic Research.

Andresen, Martin A., Richard Frank, and Marcus Felson. 2014. "Age and the Distance to Crime." *Criminology and Criminal Justice* 14:314–33.

Apel, Robert J., and Gary Sweeten. 2010. "Propensity Score Matching in Criminology and Criminal Justice." In *Handbook of Quantitative Criminology*, edited by A. Piquero and D. Weisburd, pp. 543–62. New York: Springer.

Argyrous, George. 2009. "Sources and Uses of Secondary Data." In *Evidence for Policy and Decision Making: A Practical Guide*, edited by G. Argyrous, pp. 162–74. Sydney, Australia: University of New South Wales Press.

Baudains, Peter, Alex Braithwaite, and Shane D. Johnson. 2013. "Target Choice During Extreme Events: A Discrete Spatial Choice Model of the 2011 London Riots." *Criminology* 51:251–85.

Becker, Gary S. 1968. "Crime and Punishment: An Economic Approach." *Journal of Political Economy* 76:169–217.

Ben-Akiva, Moshe E., and Steven R. Lerman. 1994. *Discrete Choice Analysis: Theory and Applications to Travel Demand.* Cambridge, MA: MIT Press.

Berk, Richard. 2010. "Recent Perspective on the Regression Discontinuity Design." In *Handbook of Quantitative Criminology*, edited by A. Piquero and D. Weisburd, pp. 563–80. New York: Springer.

Bernasco, Wim. 2010. "A Sentimental Journey to Crime: Effects of Residential History on Crime Location Choice." *Criminology* 48:389–416.

Bernasco, Wim. 2014. "Residential Burglary." In *Encyclopedia of Criminology and Criminal Justice*, edited by G. Bruinsma and D. Weisburd, pp. 4381–91. New York: Springer.

Bernasco, Wim, and Richard Block. 2009. "Where Offenders Choose to Attack: A Discrete Choice Model of Robberies in Chicago." *Criminology* 47:93–130.

Bernasco, Wim, Richard Block, and Stijn Ruiter. 2013. "Go Where the Money Is: Modeling Street Robbers' Location Choices." *Journal of Economic Geography* 13:119–43.

Bernasco, Wim, Shane D. Johnson, and Stijn Ruiter. 2015. "Learning Where to Offend: Effects of Past on Future Burglary Locations." *Applied Geography* 60:120–29.

Bernasco, Wim, and Thessa Kooistra. 2010. "Effects of Residential History on Commercial Robbers' Crime Location Choices." *European Journal of Criminology* 7:251–65.

Bernasco, Wim, Marre Lammers, and Kees van der Beek. 2016. "Cross-Border Crime Patterns Unveiled by Exchange of DNA Profiles in the European Union." *Security Journal* 29(4): 640–60.

Bernasco, Wim, and Paul Nieuwbeerta. 2005. "How Do Residential Burglars Select Target Areas? A New Approach to the Analysis of Criminal Location Choice." *British Journal of Criminology* 45:296–315.

Blokland, Arjan A. J., Daniel Nagin, and Paul Nieuwbeerta. 2005. "Life Span Offending Trajectories of a Dutch Conviction Cohort." *Criminology* 43:919–54.

Blokland, Arjan A. J., and Paul Nieuwbeerta. 2005. "The Effects of Life Circumstances on Longitudinal Trajectories of Offending." *Criminology* 43:1203–40.

Breslow, Norman E., and Nicholas E. Day. 1980. *Statistical Methods in Cancer Research. Volume 1: The Analysis of Case–Control Studies*. Lyon, France: International Agency for Research on Cancer.

Bushway, Shawn D., and Robert J. Apel. 2010. "Instrumental Variables in Criminology and Criminal Justice." In *Handbook of Quantitative Criminology*, edited by A. Piquero and D. Weisburd, pp. 595–614. New York: Springer.

Bushway, Shawn D., Paul Nieuwbeerta, and Arjan Blokland. 2011. "The Predictive Value of Criminal Background Checks: Do Age and Criminal History Affect the Time to Redemption?" *Criminology* 49:27–60.

Christie, Nils. 1997. "Four Blocks Against Insight: Notes on the Oversocialization of Criminologists." *Theoretical Criminology* 1:13–23.

Christoffersen, Mogens Nygaard, Brian Francis, and Keith Soothill. 2003. "An Upbringing to Violence? Identifying the Likelihood of Violent Crime Among the 1966 Birth Cohort in Denmark." *Journal of Forensic Psychiatry and Psychology* 14:367–81.

Christoffersen, Mogens Nygaard, Keith Soothill, and Brian Francis. 2008. "Risk Factors for a First-Time Drink-Driving Conviction Among Young Men: A Birth Cohort Study of all Men Born in Denmark in 1966." *Journal of Substance Abuse Treatment* 34:415–25.

Clare, Joseph, John Fernandez, and Frank Morgan. 2009. "Formal Evaluation of the Impact of Barriers and Connectors on Residential Burglars' Macro-Level Offending Location Choices." *Australian and New Zealand Journal of Criminology* 42:139–58.

Corte-Real, Francisco. 2004. "Forensic DNA databases." *Forensic Science International* 146(Suppl.):S143–44.

Dugan, Laura. 2010. "Estimating Effects over Time for Single and Multiple Units." In *Handbook of Quantitative Criminology*, edited by A. R. Piquero and D. Weisburd, pp. 741–63. New York: Springer.

Ehrlich, Isaac. 1973. "Participation in Illegitimate Activities: A Theoretical and Empirical Investigation." *Journal of Political Economy* 81:521–65.

Farrington, David P. 2003a. "Developmental and Life-Course Criminology: Key Theoretical and Empirical Issues—The 2002 Sutherland Award Address." *Criminology* 41:221–25.

Farrington, David P. 2003b. "Key Results from the First Forty Years of the Cambridge Study in Delinquent Development." In *Taking Stock of Delinquency: An Overview of Findings from Contemporary Longitudinal Studies*, edited by T. P. Thornberry and M. D. Krohn, pp. 137–75. New York: Springer.

Farrington, David P., Alex R. Piquero, and Wesley G. Jennings. 2013. *Offending from Childhood to Late Middle Age: Recent Results from the Cambridge Study in Delinquent Development*. New York: Springer.

Galloway, Taryn Ann, and Torbjørn Skarðhamar. 2010. "Does Parental Income Matter for Onset of Offending?" *European Journal of Criminology* 7:424–41.

Griffiths, Elizabeth, Robert D. Baller, Ryan E. Spohn, and Rosemary Gartner. 2008. "Is There Such a Thing as 'Defended Community Homicide'?: The Necessity of Methods Triangulation." *Victims and Offenders* 3:228–44.

Grogger, Jeff. 1998. "Market Wages and Youth Crime." *Journal of Labor Economics* 16:756–91.

Huizinga, David, Anne Wylie Weiher, and Rachele Espiritu. 2003. "Delinquency and Crime: Some Highlights from the Denver Youth Survey." In *Taking Stock of Delinquency: An Overview of Findings from Contemporary Longitudinal Studies*, edited by T. P. Thornberry and M. D. Krohn, pp. 47–92. New York: Springer.

Jeuniaux, Patrick P. J. M. H., Leen Duboccage, Bertrand Renard, Pierre Van Renterghem, and Vanessa Vanvooren. 2016. "Establishing Networks in a Forensic DNA Database to Gain Operational and Strategic Intelligence." *Security Journal* 29(4): 584–602.

Johnson, Shane D., Wim Bernasco, Kate J. Bowers, Henk Elffers, Jerry Ratcliffe, George Rengert, and Michael T. Townsley. 2007. "Space–Time Patterns of Risk: A Cross National Assessment of Residential Burglary Victimization." *Journal of Quantitative Criminology* 23:201–19.

Johnson, Shane D., and Lucia Summers. 2015a. "Testing Ecological Theories of Offender Spatial Decision Making Using a Discrete Choice Model." *Crime and Delinquency* 61(3): 454–80.

Kling, Jeffrey R. 2006. "Incarceration Length, Employment, and Earnings." *American Economic Review* 96:863–76.

Lammers, Marre. 2014. "Are Arrested and Non-Arrested Serial Offenders Different? A Test of Spatial Offending Patterns Using DNA Found at Crime Scenes." *Journal of Research in Crime and Delinquency* 51:143–67.

Lammers, Marre, Barbara Menting, Stijn Ruiter, and Wim Bernasco. 2015. "Biting Once, Twice: The Influence of Prior on Subsequent Crime Location Choice." *Criminology* 53(3):309–29.

Laub, John H., and Robert J. Sampson. 2003. *Shared Beginnings, Divergent Lives: Delinquent Boys Through Age 70*. Cambridge, MA: Harvard University Press.

Leary, Dick, and Ken Pease. 2003. "DNA and the Active Criminal Population." *Crime Prevention and Community Safety* 5:7–12.

Levine, Mark, Paul J. Taylor, and Rachel Best. 2011. "Third Parties, Violence, and Conflict Resolution: The Role of Group Size and Collective Action in the Microregulation of Violence." *Psychological Science* 22:406–12.

Levine, Ned, and Patsy Lee. 2013. "Journey-to-Crime by Gender and Age Group in Manchester, England." In *Crime Modeling and Mapping Using Geospatial Technologies*, vol. 8, *Geotechnologies and the Environment*, edited by M. Leitner, pp. 145–78. Dordrecht, Netherlands: Springer.

Lochner, Lance. 2004. "Education, Work, and Crime: A Human Capital Approach." *International Economic Review* 45:811–43.

Loeber, Rolf, David P. Farrington, and Magda Stouthamer-Loeber. 2003. "The Development of Male Offending: Key Findings from Fourteen Years of the Pittsburgh Youth Study." In *Taking Stock of Delinquency: An Overview of Findings from Contemporary Longitudinal Studies*, edited by T. P. Thornberry and M. D. Krohn, pp. 93–136. New York: Springer.

Loeffler, Charles E. 2013. "Does Imprisonment Alter the Life Course? Evidence on Crime and Employment from a Natural Experiment." *Criminology* 51:137–66.

Lyngstad, Torkild Hovde, and Torbjørn Skarðhamar. 2011. "Nordic Register Data and Their Untapped Potential for Criminological Knowledge." *Crime and Justice* 40:613–45.

McGloin, Jean Marie, Christopher J. Sullivan, Alex R. Piquero, Arjan Blokland, and Paul Nieuwbeerta. 2011. "Marriage and Offending Specialization: Expanding the Impact of Turning Points and the Process of Desistance." *European Journal of Criminology* 8: 361–76.

Piquero, Alex R., and D. Weisburd. 2010. *Handbook of Quantitative Criminology*. New York: Springer.

Piza, Eric L., and Victoria A. Sytsma. 2016. "Exploring the Defensive Actions of Drug Sellers in Open-Air Markets: A Systematic Social Observation." *Journal of Research in Crime and Delinquency* 53:36–65.

Rengert, George F. 1992. "The Journey to Crime: Conceptual Foundations and Policy Implications." In *Crime, Policing and Space: Essays in Environmental Criminology*, edited by D. J. Evans, N. R. Fyfe, and D. T. Herbert, pp. 109–17. London: Routledge.

Samuelson, P. A. 1938. "A Note on the Pure Theory of Consumer's Behaviour." *Economica* 5:61–71.

Savolainen, Jukka. 2009. "Work, Family and Criminal Desistance: Adult Social Bonds in a Nordic Welfare State." *British Journal of Criminology* 49:285–304.

Savolainen, Jukka, Mikko Aaltonen, Marko Merikukka, Reija Paananen, and Mika Gissler. 2014. "Social Mobility and Crime: Evidence from a Total Birth Cohort." *British Journal of Criminology* 55:164–83.

Shover, Neal, and Ben W. Hunter. 2010. "Blue-Collar, White-Collar: Crimes and Mistakes." In *Offenders on Offending: Learning About Crime from Criminals*, edited by W. Bernasco, pp. 205–27. Cullompton, UK: Willan.

Skarðhamar, Torbjørn, and Jukka Savolainen. 2014. "Changes in Criminal Offending Around the Time of Job Entry: A Study of Employment and Desistance." *Criminology* 52:263–91.

Skarðhamar, Torbjørn. 2009. "Family Dissolution and Children's Criminal Careers." *European Journal of Criminology* 6:203–23.

Soothill, Keith, Mogens N. Christoffersen, M. Azhar Hussain, and Brian Francis. 2010. "Exploring Paradigms of Crime Reduction: An Empirical Longitudinal Study." *British Journal of Criminology* 50:222–38.

Thompson, Martie P., Linda E. Saltzman, and Daniel Bibel. 1999. "Applying NIBRS Data to the Study of Intimate Partner Violence: Massachusetts as a Case Study." *Journal of Quantitative Criminology* 15:163–80.

Thornberry, Terence P., Alan J. Lizotte, and Marvin D. Krohn. 2003. "Causes and Consequences of Delinquency: Findings from the Rochester Youth Development Study." In *Taking Stock of Delinquency: An Overview of Findings from Contemporary Longitudinal Studies*, edited by T. P. Thornberry and M. D. Krohn, pp. 11–46. New York: Springer.

Tillyer, Marie Skubak, and Rob Tillyer. 2015. "Maybe I Should Do This Alone: A Comparison of Solo and Co-offending Robbery Outcomes." *Justice Quarterly* 32(6): 1064–88.

Tonkin, Matthew, Jessica Woodhams, Ray Bull, John W. Bond, and Emma J. Palmer. 2011. "Linking Different Types of Crime Using Geographical and Temporal Proximity." *Criminal Justice and Behavior* 38:1069–88.

Townsley, Michael, Daniel Birks, Wim Bernasco, Stijn Ruiter, Shane D. Johnson, Gentry White, and Scott Baum. 2015. "Burglar Target Selection: A Cross-National Comparison." *Journal of Research in Crime and Delinquency* 52:3–31.

Townsley, Michael T., Chloe Smith, and Ken Pease. 2006. "First Impressions Count: Serious Detections Arising from Criminal Justice Samples." *Genomics, Society and Policy* 2:28–40.

van de Rakt, Marieke, Paul Nieuwbeerta, and Nan Dirk de Graaf. 2008. "Like Father, Like Son: The Relationships Between Conviction Trajectories of Fathers and Their Sons and Daughters." *British Journal of Criminology* 48:538–56.

van Schellen, Marieke, Robert Apel, and Paul Nieuwbeerta. 2012. "'Because You're Mine, I Walk the Line'? Marriage, Spousal Criminality, and Criminal Offending over the Life Course." *Journal of Quantitative Criminology* 28:701–23.

van Schellen, Marieke, Anne-Rigt Poortman, and Paul Nieuwbeerta. 2012. "Partners in Crime? Criminal Offending, Marriage Formation, and Partner Selection." *Journal of Research in Crime and Delinquency* 49(4): 545–71.

Vandeviver, Christophe, Stijn van Daele, and Tom Vander Beken. 2015. "What Makes Long Crime Trips Worth Undertaking? Balancing Costs and Benefits in Burglars' Journey to Crime." *British Journal of Criminology* 55:399–420.

Varian, Hal R. 2006. "Revealed Preference." In *Samuelson Economics and the Twenty-First Century*, edited by M. Szenberg, pp. 99–115. Oxford: Oxford University Press.

Wikström, Per-Olof H., Dietrich Oberwittler, Kyle Treiber, and Beth Hardie. 2012. *Breaking Rules: The Social and Situational Dynamics of Young People's Urban Crime*. Oxford: Oxford University Press.

CHAPTER 28

....

"DECIDING" TO KILL
Understanding Homicide Offenders' Decision Making

....

FIONA BROOKMAN AND MICHELLE WRIGHT

I. INTRODUCTION

....

THERE is surprisingly little literature on decision making in relation to the crime of homicide. In fact, homicide has presented particular challenges to the most well-established decision-making perspective, the rational choice perspective (RCP), due to assertions that it is a highly emotional crime that lacks rationality. As Wortley (2014) explains, "One of the most persistent criticisms of RCP is that it cannot account for the decisions made by offenders who commit so-called expressive crimes (assault, murder, rape) when in a state of emotional arousal (anger, fear, jealousy, sexual excitation)" (p. 244). RCP views offending behavior as purposeful or goal-directed (Clarke and Cornish 1985; Cornish and Clarke 2008). Furthermore, RCP emphasizes the situational factors that facilitate (or inhibit) the perpetration of crime. Rather than being propelled toward crime by uncontrollable urges, the offender interacts with, and is influenced by, the immediate environment, weighing the potential risks and rewards. It is this appraisal of the benefits and risks that renders the offender "rational." RCP does make space for (seemingly) expressive crimes such as homicide through its acknowledgment of various cognitive and emotional bounds to rationality. Nevertheless, until recently, the bounded aspects of rationality received limited attention among the criminological research community. A notable example of this recent change is the introduction, to the criminological literature, of "dual-process models" of decision making that bring together an appreciation of both cognitive and affective contributions to offender decision-making processes (Treiber 2014; van Gelder and de Vries 2014). Bringing emotion more center stage is an important step forward in understanding homicides, which are often highly charged emotional events. Nevertheless, both approaches remain offender-centered and, as such, provide only a partial picture of lethal events. Given that homicide involves at least one other "actor" (the victim) and often third parties, it is important to understand offender decision making in the broader context of the situational and interactional dynamics that characterize most violent events. Research on homicide that takes into account situational characteristics is scarce (Ganpat, van der Leun, and Nieuwbeerta 2013). However, Wolfgang's (1958) homicide research in Philadelphia and particularly his finding that 26 percent of all homicides were victim precipitated as well as Luckenbill's (1977) research on "situated transactions" resulting in homicide clearly demonstrated the need to reorient homicide research beyond the offender (Athens 1997; Hull 2001; Polk 1994).

In this chapter, we pay particular attention to the cognitive, emotional, and micro-situational components of decision making in relation to homicide. We ask, What were killers thinking and feeling immediately prior to, during, and after homicide? How did these thoughts and feelings guide their actions? What situational factors influenced their decision making? Our overall aim is to bring together key elements of rational choice theory with theories of cognition, affect, and situated transaction theory. In this way, we hope, in some small way, to advance rational choice theory by a careful consideration of how so-called "rationality" is bounded by emotion (hot or cold) and inextricably tied to the microsituation within which violent encounters unfold.

In section II, we examine three bodies of research literature that we believe together provide a fuller understanding of homicide decision making than the rational choice perspective in isolation. First, we focus on theories of violence-related cognition followed by a review of research that highlights specifically the role of affect in the decision to commit lethal violence and, finally, we consider research on the interactional and situational dynamics of homicide that places decision making clearly in the phenomenological foreground. In section III, we bring some of the key findings from this body of research "to life" by considering a select number of case studies of homicide and sublethal violence, unpacking offenders' narratives of their thoughts and feelings before, during, and after acts of serious violence. These case studies reveal the complex interplay of cognitive, affective, and situational factors in lethal and sublethal events. In conclusion, we offer suggestions for avenues of future research on homicide and decision making based on what we perceive to be current gaps in knowledge.

A. A Methodological Note

Section III of this chapter draws upon four case studies—specifically, two cases of homicide and two cases of sublethal encounters (just short of homicide). We purposely selected both lethal and nonlethal outcomes to illustrate how the outcome of violent interactions is often dependent on small but significant events, feelings, and decisions in the phenomenological foreground. The case studies were compiled from data collected by the first author as part of her doctoral research on homicide (collected during 1998–9) and an Economic and Social Research Council qualitative study of street violence (collected during 2004–5). The first study specifically explored the nature and circumstances of homicide in England and Wales and, in order to understand the social reality of committing acts of serious violence, included interviews with men who had killed or seriously harmed other men. The second study explored street violence (e.g., robbery, carjacking, and retaliatory violence) and included both male and female offenders. Issues discussed during interviews included the fine details of one recent violent street offense—that is, how it happened, why it happened, whether any weapon(s) were used, whether it was typical of any other kinds of street violence perpetrated, and generally how the violent act began, evolved, and ended.

In both cases, semistructured in-depth interviews were conducted by the first author with offenders incarcerated in various prisons throughout Britain. Interviews took place in private rooms within the respective prisons with the informed consent of the interviewees. Interviewees were provided with information sheets and consent forms prior to agreeing to take part in the research. The information sheets outlined the aims of the study and the areas the interview would cover. Participants were assured that their identities would remain anonymous and that nothing of what they revealed during interviews would be passed on to the prison authorities, police, or any other agency or individual.[1] As part of the process of confidentiality and anonymity, interviewees were asked to create a pseudonym, and these are used throughout this chapter.

Interviews lasted on average eighty minutes. Each interview was recorded with the permission of the inmate and subsequently transcribed verbatim. The interview transcripts have been analyzed over the years for various publications and in different ways (sometimes thematically by hand and other times with the assistance of the qualitative software package NVivo). For the purposes of this chapter, each transcript was visited afresh and analyzed by hand.

II. Cognitive, Affective, and Situational Theories

We begin this section with a consideration of research most pertinent to developing an understanding of homicide offender decision making. We do not restrict ourselves to research exclusively concerned with homicide because (a) that literature is very sparse and (b) many offenders do not actually plan (or intend) to kill (Brookman 2005; Felson and Massoglia 2012) but, rather, to inflict some level of physical harm upon the victim. Therefore, it makes sense to draw upon the wider body of literature on violent offenders' cognition.

A. Killer Cognition: Schemas, Scripts, and Thinking Patterns

Felson (2014) asserts that "many acts of violence involve careless decisions and an offender's failure to consider the consequences." (p. 17). This statement exemplifies the backdrop to a body of research that has tasked itself with unraveling whether and how violent offenders have particular thinking patterns or cognitive distortions that influence their "decisions" to engage in (lethal) violence.

There is a fairly substantial body of work suggesting that cognitive distortions characterize the thinking processes of (some) violent offenders (Walker and Bright 2009). For example, research has found that violent offenders perceive and interpret information in a biased manner, making "hostile attributional biases" (Dodge and Coie 1987; Beck 1999; James and Seager 2006), more recently referred to as "provocation interpretational bias" (Fontaine 2009). These biases in thinking apparently lead some individuals to perceive and interpret hostility or provocation where none exists. Research has found that some violent offenders also have attitudes and beliefs that are supportive of aggression and violence; violence is viewed as a "normal" way of dealing with conflict and solving problems (Collie, Vess, and Murdoch 2007). Normative attitudes and beliefs influence how violent offenders process information (Anderson and Bushman 2002) and, it is argued, increase the likelihood of aggressive or violent behavior (Huesmann 1988; Bowes and McMurran 2013). Such cognitive biases, attitudes, and beliefs are said to stem from maladaptive schemas, also referred to as "hostile world schemas" (Seager 2005), developed from direct and observational learning and experience in which antagonistic behavior serves a functional purpose (Anderson and Huesmann 2003).

Schemas are regarded as the building blocks of cognition (Neisser 1976; Rumelhart 1980) and play a fundamental role in how individuals appraise, interpret, perceive, interact, and respond to situations. Three types of schemas relevant to violent offenders' cognition are (a) *self-schema* (which is synonymous with self-concept); (b) *relational schema* (guiding interaction with others); and (c) *event schemas*, also referred to as *scripts* (Huesmann 1988), which guide reactions and expectations of what will happen in certain situations (Schank and Abelson 1977). Schemas and scripts apparently operate via automatic processing and are activated by external situational cues or internal cues, such as thoughts and emotions (Anderson and Bushman 2002). Anderson and Bushman theorize that aggression is the result of the convergence of both personological (i.e., knowledge structures and personality traits) and situational factors: "The right situation can provoke most people to behave aggressively, but some people are much more likely to aggress than others" (p. 299). In terms of the enactment of violence, there is a growing body of research focusing on particular kinds of pro-violent cognition.

The term "implicit theory" (IT), rather than schema, has been advocated by Ward (2000) to refer to offenders' beliefs about the world and the desires and goals that guide their social and interpersonal behavior. From in-depth semistructured interviews with 28 sexual murderers in the United Kingdom, Beech, Fisher, and Ward (2005) identified five ITs: dangerous world, male sex drive uncontrollable, entitlement, women as sexual objects, and women as unknowable. These ITs were identical to those found in previous research with sex offenders (Polaschek, Calvert, and Gannon 2009; Polaschek and Ward 2002), suggesting that "rapists and sexual murderers think in the same way" (Beech et al. 2005, p. 1387). The two most common ITs identified were dangerous world (70 percent) and male sex drive uncontrollable (71 percent). The sexual murderers formed three distinct groups. Each group was motivated to offend according to their IT: (1) Murderers in the dangerous world plus male sex drive uncontrollable group were motivated by the urge to rape and murder and carry out their violent/sexual fantasies; (2) those in the dangerous world in the absence of male sex drive uncontrollable group were motivated by anger, grievance, and resentment directed toward women; and (3) those in the male sex drive uncontrollable in the absence of dangerous world group were motivated by sexual urges but prepared to kill to secure compliance or avoid detection. Interestingly, the method of killing and injuries inflicted on the victim differed across the three groups, suggesting that the offenders' ITs shaped the decisions that they made while committing sexual murder.

To explore the ITs of violent offenders, Polaschek et al. (2009) analyzed 20 offense process interviews with offenders who were currently in a prison rehabilitation program in New Zealand. The interviews focused on their index offenses, which were mostly for serious violent assaults, two of which included homicide. Four ITs were identified: (1) "beat or be beaten," which was subcategorized into self-enhancement and self-preservation; (2) "I am the law"; (3) "normalization of violence"; and (4) "I get out of control." The most common IT was "beat or be beaten" (57 percent), followed by "normalization of violence" (46 percent), "I am the law" (39 percent), and the least frequent "I get out of control" (12 percent). Like previous research, how violent offenders viewed themselves and others was a common theme across the ITs identified.

Toch's (1992) "inquiry into the psychology of violence" revealed two types of approaches that violent offenders adopt in violent situations: (1) "self-preserving strategies" related to defending or enhancing self-image and (2) "approaches that dehumanize others" related to attitudes that others' rights are not as important as their own. Maruna and Butler (2013) also identified the central importance of maintaining and defending self-image in their research on violent incidents in prison. Two key motivators for engaging in violent behavior were highlighted: "oversensitivity to being disrespected" and "threat to one's identity." A common theme running throughout each of these studies is the way in which violent offenders interpret and respond to perceived threats or hostility.

In addition to interviews with violent offenders or analysis of case file material, psychometric tests have also been used to assess social cognition. In a psychometric-based study examining the personality and cognition of 137 murderers, Holcomb and Adams (1983) found that these males had a greater introspective self-focus than problem-solving focus. In another study, Gauci and Hollin (2012) analyzed the results of six psychometric measures of social cognition administered to 78 violent and 78 non-violent offenders. Although no significant differences were found between violent and nonviolent offenders' social cognition, differences were evident in the problem-solving strategies and the thinking styles of violent offenders classified as high and low risk. High-risk violent offenders scored higher on the Psychological Inventory of Criminal Thinking Styles (PICTS), an 80-item self-report measure of thinking styles associated with criminal lifestyles, and they scored lower on positive and rational problem solving.

In summary, various cognitive distortions and maladaptive thinking patterns have been identified that are said to play a contributory role in how individuals appraise and respond to confrontation or conflict. However, the identification that violent offenders tend to have distorted cognitions, although helpful, does not tell us about the decision-making processes that offenders engaged in immediately prior to, during, or after committing a violent act. Other researchers have moved closer to understanding such processes by directly probing the thoughts, feelings, and actions of violent offenders and murderers, to which we now turn.

B. To Kill or Not to Kill: Inhibitors and Disinhibitors to (Lethal) Violence

In a pioneering study, Athens (1980, 1997), a symbolic interactionist, carried out in-depth interviews with 58 imprisoned violent offenders, 27 of whom had committed homicide. He carefully analyzed the accounts of the violent offenders, focusing on the interpretations they made of situations in which they (a) committed violent acts and (b) *almost* committed such acts, as well as the self-images that they held.

Athens discovered that individuals who had committed violent acts (including homicide) formed one of four possible interpretations of the situation (Athens 1997, pp. 33–41):

1. Physically defensive: The offender interprets the victim's gesture as foreshadowing or constituting a physical attack, generating a grave sense of fear for self or other.
2. Frustrative: The offender becomes angry at the victim's attempts to block a specific course of action by the offender.
3. Malefic: The offender judges the victim to be extremely evil or malicious, igniting hatred for the victim.
4. Frustrative–malefic: This combines features of the two prior types; the offender starts with frustrative interpretations and then hatred replaces anger.

When these same individuals *almost* resorted to violence, they formed a "restraining judgment," escaping the tunnel vision that characterized the violent events and redefining the situation as not requiring a violent response. There were various reasons for the change of interpretation and sentiments, such as perceiving that the attack would fail, fear of jeopardizing an important relationship, deference to the other person, or fear of legal sanctions. Finally, other individuals indicated that they re-evaluated the situation in light of a change in the course of action of the other person (e.g., the "opponent" conceded in some way or apologized). Notably, some of the decisions toward restraint were based on immediate or anticipated actions during the moment of the encounter (e.g., victim apologized), whereas others were based on perceived future outcomes (e.g., legal sanctions). For Athens, individuals form restraining judgments far more often than overriding judgments or fixed lines of indication and, therefore, far more violent acts are begun (or contemplated) than are ever completed.

In another notable work, Hull (2001) conducted in-depth interviews with twelve men who had planned to commit an act of workplace homicide (or serious violence[2]) but then decided against this course of action. She specifically explored the cognitive and affective processes in which these men engaged, in both deciding to commit the fatal/serious act of workplace violence and deciding to refrain from committing the planned act. Hull's work is particularly valuable in understanding decision making *before* the event.

Hull (2001) discerned five disinhibitor themes (i.e., cognitive or affective factors) that served to move the would-be perpetrators toward the decision to commit fatal or serious violence:

1. Closed-channel: A way of thinking that shuts out or distorts incoming information such that only the already formed view is validated; assumptions are not questioned.
2. Polarity: Extreme way of thinking; for example, a minor offense is viewed as degrading, and a criticism is viewed as an attack on their very sense of self.
3. Rush-seeking: The desire to seek an adrenalin rush.
4. Criminal pride: A belief system that promotes violence and in which the focus is on avoiding personal consequences. A significant amount of time is spent in planning the detail of the attack in order to prevent detection.
5. Victim stance/restorative revenge: Feelings of shame, disrespect, or embarrassment due to the provocateur's words or actions and a belief that the actions were intentional; a belief that the only way to restore a sense of power or respect is to avenge the individual.

This latter disinhibitor was the most frequently used by the twelve men, followed by criminal pride and closed-channel thinking. Five inhibitors were also identified:

1. Fear of consequences to self: Weigh the perceived consequences on their lives and report a shift away from the belief that they will not get caught.
2. Fear of consequences to others: Extend their consideration of consequences to how others will be hurt by their proposed actions—mainly family or friends.
3. Viewed self as better: After consideration, come to conclude that they were above or beyond such behavior—a moral engagement mechanism that allowed the individual to refrain from violence and still feel intact emotionally.

4. Found safer, lesser form of revenge: This lesser form of revenge still allowed them to know that they had taken action toward reinstating self-respect and power.

5. Forgave or reinterpreted: Actively decided not to take revenge or decided that the provocateur did not mean to be as insulting as previously assessed.

Although Hull (2001) does not specifically elaborate on the issue, a close reading of her data indicates that almost half of the men experienced a sense of relief having made the decision *not* to kill (or seriously harm) the "protagonist." This suggests that in addition to consideration of the consequences of their actions, they may have also experienced negative emotions when anticipating the homicide itself or its aftermath that prevented them from carrying out the lethal act.

In summary, violent offenders' cognition has been found to mediate violent behavior. However, this is only part of the picture, as Athens (1997) explains: "Violent criminal acts are products of people's interpretations of collective situations, and in constructing these interpretations individuals' emotions are every bit as important as their thoughts. In fact, thinking about their raw feelings creates their emotions" (p. 129). We next consider the role of affect in shaping homicide offender decision making.

C. The Role of Affect in Homicide

The saying "blinded by emotion" captures the theoretical notion that feelings can disrupt cognitive processing and lead to less than optimal decision making. The role of affect in decision making has received increasing attention since RCP was first proposed (Damasio 1994; Goleman 1995; Rusting 1998), and recently Clarke (2014) and van Gelder (2013) have advocated the development of RCP to incorporate the role of affect in offender decision making. For example, van Gelder proposed a new dual-process framework of offender decision making that incorporates both affective ("hot") and cognitive ("cool") perspectives. This model is reminiscent of Kahneman's (2011) two-system model of "fast" (System 1) and "slow" (System 2) thinking. System 1 involves heuristic, intuitive, and emotional processes and is fast, automatic, effortless, associative, and difficult to control or modify. In contrast, System 2 is deliberative, involving slower, effortful, controlled, and flexible processes. Van Gelder's model differs only in the explicit focus on the interaction of the processes underlying affect and cognition based on Metcalfe and Mischel's (1999) hot emotional "go" and cool cognitive "know" two-system framework underlying self-control. These developments are particularly important when considering homicide, given the emotionally charged contexts within which such violence usually occurs.

Various kinds of affect have been identified in the research literature, including six universally recognized primary emotions (anger, fear, disgust, sadness, surprise, and happiness) (Ekman and Friesen 1975; Damasio 1994) and a set of moral or social emotions (e.g., embarrassment, shame, compassion, guilt, and pride). These moral emotions are viewed as socially constructed and develop through socialization (Kemper 1987;

Tangney and Fischer 1995; Haidt 2003). Damasio has also identified "background emotions" (i.e., well-being or malaise and calm or tension), and two major dimensions of emotional experience—positive and negative affect—have been identified (Watson and Tellegen 1985). Affect can also be differentiated in terms of whether it is immediate or anticipated (Loewenstein and Lerner 2003).

So let us consider some of the emotions that seem to be operating (and therefore impacting upon decision- making) before, during, and after homicide.

Jacobs and Wright (2010) explored the bounded nature of rationality during retaliatory violence, paying particular attention to the emotion of anger and its potent relationship to retaliatory violence. Through their analysis of in-depth interview data with 52 active street criminals from St. Louis, Missouri, they discerned three prominent bounds that mediate retaliatory decision making: anger, uncertainty, and time pressure. To briefly elaborate on the first of these, they found that anger bounds retaliatory decision making either by encouraging offenders to "strike excessively relative to the affront" (an error of scale) or by causing aggrieved individuals to lash out at innocent victims (an error of target) (pp. 1746–47). Aggrieved individuals cannot always locate their primary target or may only suspect their involvement. This uncertainty leads to redirected strikes.

In addition to the primary emotion of anger, moral emotions such as shame and humiliation have been identified as predominant features in violent offenders' accounts of their behavior (Katz 1988; Walker and Bright 2009). For example, Gilligan (1996) found that homicide and violent offenders identified being "disrespected" or "ridiculed" as a key trigger for their violence because it engendered feelings of shame and humiliation. Gilligan, like Luckenbill (1977) and Athens (1997), explains how violence often stems from violent offenders' motivation to "save face." Shame has also been identified as the dominant emotion propelling offenders to commit familicide (Websdale 2010) and multiple homicide (Scheff 2011). For example, Scheff suggests that together with social isolation, shame, embarrassment, and humiliation result in a "social emotional equivalent of a chain reaction" that leads individuals to decide to commit multiple murder.

In Collins' (2008) microsociological theory of violence, "confrontational tension and fear" are the emotional states from which violence stems. Collins states, "Violence as it actually becomes visible in real-life situations is about the intertwining of human emotions of fear, anger, and excitement, in ways that run right against the conventional morality of normal situations" (p. 4). He notes that many existing criminological theories assume that violence is easy, whereas he takes the opposite view and argues that violence is in fact difficult: "No matter how motivated someone may be, if the situation does not unfold so that confrontational tension/fear is overcome, violence will not proceed" (p. 20). For Collins, emotional tension gets released into a violent attack only where there is a weak victim or where there is an audience, especially where audience members are well known to the protagonist, making it difficult to back down without losing one's reputation.

What is notable about most research on affect and homicide is the attention to negative emotional states (e.g., anger, humiliation, and fear) in either propelling the offender toward violence or, in the case of Collin's findings, holding him or her back. Rarely have researchers investigated the role of positive affect in homicide, despite some evidence that this may play an important role. Even Katz (1988), well known for his work on the seductions and pleasures of crime, reserves his discussion of pleasurable emotions ("sneaky thrills") to property offenses.

Equally, empirically based research on positive affect and violent crime is virtually nonexistent. Farrington (1987) found that violent offenders had lower resting heart rates than nonviolent offenders, from which it has been suggested that violent offenders are likely to be "thrill seekers attempting to relieve their boredom" (p. 13). Furthermore, research has found that psychopathic offenders are often motivated by external goals (e.g., monetary gain, revenge, or sadism) and are more likely than non-psychopathic offenders to engage in instrumental rather than reactive violence and commit instrumental/predatory homicide (Cleckley 1976; Williamson, Hare, and Wong 1987; Cornell et al. 1996; Woodworth and Porter 2002; Porter et al. 2003). Porter and Woodworth (2007) suggest that psychopathic offenders "may derive satisfaction from the process of planning and committing predatory violence" (p. 103).

In summary, the way in which violent offenders think and feel influences their decision making. However, we must also consider the immediate social context within which homicide occurs and the situational factors that facilitate (or inhibit) lethal violence.

D. Interactional and Situational Dynamics of Homicide

Since Wolfgang's (1958) classic study of homicide in Philadelphia, criminologists have developed increasingly sophisticated analyses of the processual development and interactional dynamics of violent situations. The major substantive approach that has guided such investigations derives from symbolic interactionism and stresses the role of situational identities or self-images in interaction (Becker 1962; Toch 1969; Luckenbill 1977; Athens 1997). Relatedly, criminological research on the microenvironment of crime (e.g., studies of the interactional dynamics of offenders, victims, and third parties and the lethality of situations dependent on the availability of weapons, temporal, and spatial factors) has provided some important clues as to the social–environmental triggers that can impact decision making (prior to and during the commission of crime). What the two approaches (interactionist and microsituational) acknowledge is that homicide is (often) a dynamic and evolving event in which the "actors" interpret and mold each other's decision making and behavior. It is because of this focus on the dynamic and evolving nature of homicide that it lends itself to an appreciation of decision making *in the moment*.

One particularly illuminating analysis of lethal interactions is Luckenbill's (1977) article, "Criminal Homicide as a Situated Transaction." Luckenbill's research, based on the content analysis of 70 homicides (excluding felony and contract murder) from various official documents, unraveled the dynamic interchange of moves and counter-moves between offenders, victims, and, often, bystanders of homicide. During these interactions, the key players develop lines of action shaped in part by the actions of each other and predominantly focused on saving or maintaining "face" and reputation and demonstrating character. Luckenbill identified the following six stages of interaction: (1) The victim affronts the offender with insults or noncompliance; (2) the offender interprets this as personally offensive; (3) in order to restore "face" and demonstrate strong character, the offender retaliates with a challenge or physical attack (in 14 percent of cases, the victim was killed at this stage); (4) the victim does not comply with the offender's challenge or command or else physically retaliates, and a "working agreement" that the situation is suited to violence emerges; (5) a commitment to battle is now forged (enhanced by the securing of/availability of weapons); and (6) the termination and aftermath (e.g., the offender flees the scene or awaits the police).

In a similar vein (although more quantitative in focus), Felson and Steadman (1983) compared the interactive processes leading to homicide and assault by examining the case files of 159 males incarcerated for convictions of assault, manslaughter, or murder. Felson and Steadman discovered that homicide victims were more likely to have displayed a weapon compared to victims of assault, "suggesting that offenders were more likely to kill the victim if the latter had a weapon" (p. 65). Their data also suggested that offenders were more likely to kill intoxicated victims. Finally, victims of homicide were found to be more aggressive than those who were assaulted but not killed; specifically, they were more likely to engage in identity attacks, physical attacks, and threats compared to victims of assault. Felson and Steadman further debated whether their homicide offenders retaliated for strategic reasons (e.g., to avoid being attacked/killed) or for the purpose of saving face. They suggested that both were relevant and concluded that the actions of offenders are not irrational; rather, "each participant's actions were a function of the other persons behavior and the implications of that behavior for defending one's well-being as well as one's honor" (p. 72).

The aforementioned research illustrates that in many forms of homicide, offenders and victims are cognizant of each other's intentions and potential to do harm—a theme that has been developed further in research on adversary and weapons effects. Adversary effects refer to "the threat posed by the person or persons with whom an individual is in conflict" (Felson and Painter-Davis 2012, p. 1241). For example, Stretesky and Pogrebin (2014) conducted in-depth interviews with inmates convicted of gang-related gun violence and discovered that all 22 viewed "the streets" as fraught with danger. This fear, combined with a desire to display power, ensured that they armed themselves and were willing to use their weapons. As one female respondent indicated, "I'd rather get caught with a gun than without" (p. 317). This statement illustrates the cost–benefit analysis undertaken by such young people who reason that it is riskier to go without a gun (it may result in death should they encounter an armed rival) than be caught with a gun by the police (and risk criminal justice sanctions). This "kill or be killed" sentiment is arguably more prevalent in communities in which people are quick to retaliate and prone to carrying and using weapons (Felson and Painter-Davis 2012). For example, Felson and Pare (2010) analyzed dispute-related homicides and assaults in order to explore the role of adversary effects in these violent encounters, and they found that offenders avoided assaulting blacks and southern whites unless the offenders had a gun. They suggested that this was due to the fact that members of these groups were perceived as a greater threat (i.e., more likely to be armed and/or prone to retaliation).

Despite this research, predicting how a person might respond to his or her perceptions of an adversary or a weapon is far from clear. As "game theory" reminds us, people confronted with such situations face the dilemma of whether to attack or retreat. Hence, adversaries who are armed and violent may or may not elicit a violent response (Myerson 1997; Felson and Pare 2010). Therefore, although there is research that seems to demonstrate that the presence of a weapon can make individuals behave more aggressively compared to situations without weapons (Carlson, Marcus-Newhall, and Miller 1990), equally there is research that suggests the reverse (Kleck and McElrath 1991).

Those caught up in violent confrontations do not simply focus on their adversary in deciding whether and how to respond; their "decisions" can also be influenced by the effects of third parties. Although not all homicides involve bystanders, those that do, it seems, evolve in ways that are dependent on whether and how the audience intervenes and the relationship between combatants and the audience. To elaborate, 70 percent of the homicides that Luckenbill (1977) examined were performed in front of an audience.[3] In more than half of the cases, interested members of the audience intervened in the interaction and actively encouraged the use of violence (e.g., by cheering one or other of the combatants toward violent action or providing a lethal weapon). In the remaining cases, members of the audience adopted a neutral role. Luckenbill suggests that such inaction "can be interpreted by the opponents as a move favoring violence" (p. 194). The audience also played a key role once the victim had fallen, adopting a supportive, hostile, or neutral role. Supportive audience members (almost 50 percent of cases) assisted the offender to escape, destroyed incriminating evidence, and failed to assist the police when initially questioned. In the hostile role (more than one-third of cases), bystanders tried to apprehend the offender, assist the victim, and notify the police. In the remaining cases, the audience was neutral, apparently shocked at having witnessed a homicide.

Collins (2008, p. 203) analyzed the role of the audience in 89 first-hand observations of "violence-threatening confrontations" and found strong parallels between the degree of encouragement or opposition by the audience and the amount of violence that occurred. For example, of those cases in which the audience encouraged the fight, 88 percent resulted in a serious fight, compared to 32 percent of the incidents in which the audience remained neutral. Collins also claims that the influence of the audience is "all the more powerful" when at least one of the combatants is well known to the audience because this gives the actor a stake in maintaining or losing his reputation (p. 368) (see also Phillips and Cooney 2005).

Finally, it is worth noting that alcohol and/or drug consumption permeates many situations in which homicide occurs (Brookman 2010). For example, Shaw et al. (2006) found that in 45 percent of 1,579 homicides they examined, the offender was intoxicated at the time of the killing, whereas Dobash et al. (2002) found that 38 percent of male homicide offenders were drunk or very drunk at the time of the offense and 14 percent were using illegal drugs. Although the links between drug/alcohol consumption and homicide are far from straightforward, there is evidence that alcohol decreases cognitive capacity and lowers self-control and can contribute to the "decision" to use violence because intoxicated individuals may fail to consider the costs (Felson 2014).

Research by Ganpat et al. (2013) considered a range of the factors discussed thus far. Their study compared several event characteristics (e.g., location and time of the event, alcohol consumption by offender or victim, and the presence and number of third parties) and actors' behavior (e.g., the offender or victim displaying/using a weapon and victim precipitation) in lethal versus nonlethal events and examined the extent to which these factors influenced the likelihood of a lethal outcome. In terms of event characteristics, they found that in lethal events it was more likely that offenders carried a firearm; that either no third parties were present or, if present, third parties had no ties with either offender or victim; and that victims were under the influence of alcohol. Alcohol use by offenders did not influence the likelihood of a lethal versus nonlethal outcome. In terms of actors' behavior, they discovered that offenders of lethal events were more likely to have displayed or used a firearm and that victims who died were more likely to have precipitated the event than those who survived.

In summary, research to date has revealed how the decision to resort to violence or, in relatively rare instances, to kill depends on how offenders perceive, interpret, and react both cognitively and affectively to elements of the microsituation, which is guided by their schemas, scripts, and implicit theories. In section III, we bring the research literature "to life" by presenting four case studies of homicide and sublethal violence, narrated by the offenders. These various case studies reveal the complex interplay of cognitive, affective, and situational factors in lethal and sublethal events.

III. Case Studies of Homicide and Sublethal Violence

In this section, we consider four case studies and in so doing elaborate upon, and in some cases problematize, existing research in the area of cognition, affect, and homicide. Each case study picks up a particular subtheme within the literature examined thus far and helps to demonstrate the complex cocktail of cognitive, affective, and situational forces that play a role in decision making and homicide.

A. The Case of Gavin: Adversary, Weapons, and Third-Party Effects on Decision Making

This case, which typifies the most common type of homicide in the United Kingdom and many other areas of the world, involves a male-on-male spontaneous confrontation in the context of a "night out." It illustrates adversary, weapons, and third-party effects in the unraveling of the violent exchange, as well as the violence-related cognitions (schemata) of young men.

Gavin was twenty-three years old at the time of interview and was serving a four-year prison sentence for a serious violent assault after being charged with attempted murder. Gavin had previous convictions for assault, theft, and burglary. He relates the following sequence of events that led up to a sublethal assault on a young male outside a nightclub:

> I just went out with the boys in my local area drinking, and it's guaranteed to have a fight up there. We were talking to this guy, he pulled a knife on my mate so him and my mate started arguing. We were talking tidy [politely] first of all and then he pulled a knife out and I thought "well I can't let my mate, you know" [get hurt] so then he turned the knife on me and I just took the knife off him and that.

Gavin and his friends launched a vicious assault upon the victim, who remained on a life support machine for four months and was ultimately brain damaged and partially paralyzed. Gavin explained his part in the assault as follows:

> I just felt angry cos he pulled a knife out and I felt if you have to fight you don't need weapons, if you do, you've got to be prepared to use it, so it just wound me up. If someone carries a knife well it's not there for show is it? It's there to be used. I did feel really bad about it and I do now, all the way through my sentence like, I've felt bad about it. What happened, it shouldn't have happened, but at the end of the day he shouldn't have pulled a knife out. If he hadn't pulled it out, nothing would have happened.

The situational "trigger" for Gavin's attack on the victim appears to be the appearance of the knife, and in this brief initial account, Gavin provides information about his beliefs (schemas) regarding the fair "rules" of fighting (i.e., knifes are not necessary) and his apparent emotional reaction to seeing the knife (i.e., anger, as opposed to fear).

As outlined previously, the precise role that weapons play in the cost–benefit calculations of would-be violent offenders is complex. On the one hand, there is research that suggests that aggressive stances and the carrying of weapons can deter adversaries from becoming aggressive and inhibit violence (Anderson 1999). On the other hand, there is also research that suggests that offenders are more likely to have lethal intent when they expect their victims to be armed and willing to retaliate (Felson and Messner 1996).

This case study reveals how the microdetail of violent encounters can affect decision making. In a slightly different scenario, in which the offender was not among friends, he may not have pushed forward with an attack in response to the "threat" of a knife. Perhaps, instead, he would have formed a "restraining judgment" based on the fear of consequences to himself (Athens 1980; Hull 2001).

Although Gavin states that "nothing would have happened" if the victim had not produced a knife, it is clear from his opening statement that violence was a common and expected feature of the night-time lifestyle in which he indulged. As such, his preexisting event schemas primed him to respond with violence to this kind of situation. Gavin's statements suggest that he may have held the implicit theory (IT) of "beat or be beaten" and "I am the law," discussed previously (Polaschek et al. 2009).

The fact that this group of friends enacted this violent assault in front of one another is also significant insofar as threats to their "masculine" identity were made publicly and so the pressure to respond and escalate the violence in order to "save face" (Luckenbill 1977; Polk 1994) may have also played an important role. Nevertheless, the presence of (one of) the third parties was also critical in helping to prevent a further (potentially lethal) escalation of violence:

> I was gonna use the knife, I did go back to pick it up to use it. I thought "well if he was gonna use it on me, I'm gonna use it on him so he'll never do it again." But one of my mates took it off me and said "don't be stupid," so just left it there then.

This exchange between friends was a key moment within the "heat" of the violent act, realigning Gavin's decision making and, ultimately, his decision not to use the knife.

B. The Case of Paul: The Role of Affect and Pleasurable Emotion in the Enactment of Lethal Violence

As outlined previously, most research on offender decision making has focused on negative affect. The following case, by contrast, illustrates how positive affect—pleasure—can play a role in propelling one toward the decision to kill.

Paul was twenty-six years old at the time of interview. He had served half of a fourteen-year prison sentence for the robbery and murder of an elderly man in his home. Paul had convictions for arson, criminal damage, vehicle theft, credit card fraud, and burglary. Paul describes the murder, which he states was orchestrated by his co-defendant's hatred of the victim whom, he claimed, was a pedophile. Paul had already explained that their intentions were to "get the victim drunk" and then rob him when he fell asleep. This plan had gone awry when the victim became uneasy and "sensed danger":

> My co-defendant said, "get upstairs then" and as he knew the bloke I thought, well I didn't know what he was gonna do, this is totally new to me, um, so they went upstairs, and I just started to ransack the place downstairs . . . and then there was movement upstairs, banging going on, as if furniture is being moved and I just went upstairs, 'cos it was getting louder and louder, and the bloke was tied up on the bed. The bedroom was smashed up, it was in total disarray. It seemed as if I stood there for about five minutes in shock, but it was only a few seconds, and he said, my co-d said, "grab this," so I grabbed this telephone cord and put it around his neck, literally five seconds, and then I said, "come on, let's get out of here." I could see blood over the top of his head and my co-defendant went out of the room, and I stood at the doorway

and looked back at the man and I could see he was still breathing, his head was moving from side to side and I thought "he'll be OK."

When pressed further to explain why he pulled the cord around the victim's neck, he explained:

> I looked at him and, um, I just felt, how can I put it, like a sensation run through me. Even though what I was doing was bad, I felt good, I don't know if you can understand that, um, I felt good and obviously afterwards, you know, I felt terrible about it, but at the time, when I was actually doing, the actual, putting everything else to one side, me, flex and him, um, the feeling for what I was doing, you know . . .

Aside from the immediate emotions highlighted by Paul (initial shock, followed by pleasure), he also indicated a more general experience of negative affect or "background emotion" (Damasio 1994) of tension and chaos:

> Once I started ransacking, it was as though, if you have a bottle of pop and you shake it and take the top off, it all comes out, that's what happened in the house to me and um it was as if someone had a video recorder and was flashing things from my past and it was all running round in my mind and it was haywire, just total confusion and such a horrible feeling, and I've never experienced it again, and I never want to.

This case also exemplifies the dynamic and evolving nature of violent events in that the change in mood and behavior of the victim as he "sensed danger" and became scared led the offenders to quickly change their plans. Clearly, it is not possible to understand homicide by focusing solely on the offender and his or her cognition and emotions because those of the victim and any third parties are also critical in understanding how such encounters evolve in situ.

C. The Case of Burt: The Role of Planning in a Premeditated Revenge Killing

Burt was thirty-six years old when interviewed and had served eleven years of a life sentence for murdering a man who, he claims, had sexually abused him as a teenager. Aged twenty-five years old at the time of the killing, he had previous convictions for armed and street robbery and various forms of assault. He and his brother were working together on a market stall when they spotted the abuser. Burt picks up the story:

> He walked off and Bill said, "I'm going after him," and I said, "no, no, you've got thousands of people on the streets, you kill him here and what's gonna happen, we'll follow him." So we followed him . . . to a club . . . and we sat there for about seven hours

and I said, "look he's either drunk, or he's gone out the back door or he owns the place. One of us is gonna have to go in there." I said, "I'm not going in there, cos you know we're panicking now." So I said, "we're gonna have to pull straws," and I pulled the short one. So I go in, disguised, actually gone in a shop and bought a hat and glasses . . . and he's behind the bar. So we got the address and went away, back to the stall, we know where he is now. We can talk about it later on. This is about four or five weeks before the actual murder took place.

Burt's account illustrates his initial "rational" decision to avoid attacking the victim in front of a street full of witnesses and his efforts to avoid being recognized by the victim. Burt and his brother followed the victim on several other occasions between the initial sighting and the murder, including to his home and several other clubs where he worked. Burt then made the decision to visit one of the clubs where he knew the victim was working and attack him:

Anyway so decided to go round and beat him up . . . I'm on me own, me brothers not there . . . and I just went for him, we started fighting and I actually beat him to death in the club, but I got my fair share, got a broken nose, black eye . . . for a sixty-year-old, he couldn't half go. I used a vodka bottle. He threw me across the fucking bar, I went behind the bar and come up chucking bottles. But even with the vodka bottle, it was half full, he's still coming at me. It took about twenty minutes.

When asked how he felt when he realized that he had killed the victim, he replied,

Relieved. But I just, you know afterwards I wished my brother had been here, cos he would have got the same pleasure.

Some five weeks of planning were involved in this event, which included following the victim on numerous occasions. Moreover, the actual murder took twenty minutes to complete—far from the quick event that some scholars (e.g., Collins 2008) suggest typifies most homicides. Despite the planning, the homicide itself was far from controlled. Burt was heavily intoxicated, and his fight with the victim was more difficult than he had anticipated. Finally, various emotions are described during this narrative, including panic (beforehand) and anger (during the attack), followed by both relief and pleasure (in the aftermath) when the victim lay dead.

D. The Case of Jane: Kidnap, Torture, and an Aborted Homicide

This final case study is included to illustrate (a) how the decision to commit a homicide can be made but then unmade, (b) the role of group dynamics in spiraling violence, and (c) the aftermath of violence. The story, as it unfolds, provides a compelling illustration of the value of combining elements of rational choice theory, situated transaction theory, and research on affect.

Aged twenty-eight years old at the time of interview, Jane had more than 40 criminal convictions, mostly for violent offenses such as assault, kidnapping, robbery, false imprisonment, and various weapons charges. Jane provides an account of the kidnap and prolonged torture of a young woman:

> JANE: A girl owed me 10 pound for drugs. I had three co-defendants and we took her in my house and against her will took some money off her and her jewelry and beat her up and kept her there for a few hours. They didn't like her anyway and she was passing down the road and that I just said I would call her in and see what she had to say. Nothing was planned it just went, you know what I mean, one thing after the other and it just got out of hand like. . . . I called her over to my house and I hit her and her eye come out really, really bad and I thought "I gone a bit far here so I can't let her go." Things then went from bad to worse like . . . it went on for hours. Do you know what I mean? Shaved her hair off and broke her ribs with a hammer, made her drink bleach. It was quite a big case, do you know what I mean?
>
> FIONA: Why did it spiral like that?
>
> JANE: Don't know. We were just, I don't know. We were out of control. I just don't know. I don't know. Obviously she owed me money but I would never have . . . things just got out of hand. I think people were showing off in front of people and she lost her sense of being a person like. I just went overboard. The four of us were, yeah, "bigging" ourselves up.
>
> FIONA: Did you think at any time, "we should stop this"?
>
> JANE: Yeah, from the beginning. I remember when I hit her and her eye really came up bad I just thought "I have gone too far."
>
> FIONA: Why didn't you stop then?
>
> JANE: I was frightened she would go to the police. My intention then was to kill her. Do you know what I mean? I just thought when I hit her and it come out huge I thought "I'm gonna go back to jail" and I thought "right, you can't go now."

This extract illustrates Jane making a cost–benefit calculation in keeping with the RCP. In order to avoid the pains of punishment, she made the decision to kill the victim. Although this may seem "irrational," Jane had already accrued several convictions and knew that even a relatively minor assault would result in her arrest and likely imprisonment. Nevertheless, whether by design or luck, the attack on the victim did not result in her death, and Jane ultimately made the decision to release the victim, as she explains:

> JANE: My friends had to go a couple of hours later, it was just me and her. They went and I was on my own with her. She was sitting in the chair and I said "just go and get out" and she ran out the back door like.
>
> FIONA: Why did you then let her go?
>
> JANE: I was on a come down like, do you know what I mean? I was left on my own and my baby was upstairs and I wanted it to end. I had sobered a bit and come down off the drugs, do you know what I mean?

FIONA: So she left and then what?
JANE: The police came and that was that.

This final part of Jane's account outlines her consequential thinking and also hints at the disinhibiting effects alcohol and drugs may have had on her thoughts, emotions, and actions prior to and during the attack on the victim and the inhibiting effect once the effects wore off. Jane must have known that she would be arrested and imprisoned for this vicious attack as she was making the decision to release the victim, yet she did so. She highlights four factors that prevented her from carrying through her original plan to kill the victim: (1) Her friends have left and she is alone with the victim, (2) an awareness that her baby is upstairs, (3) "coming down" from the effects of alcohol and drugs, and (4) wanting "it to end."

This case clearly illustrates how, in one event, a violent offender (or group of offenders) can move between various affective states and that these, in turn, can impact upon the extent to which "rational" or irrational decision making occurs. Relatedly, in keeping with the case of Burt, this case also illustrates how violent incidents are not necessarily the short-lived or quick events that some researchers (e.g., Collins 2008; Felson 2014) have suggested.

It is hoped that the case studies have helped to illustrate the dynamic nature of different types of homicide events and how cognitive, affective, and situational factors together precipitate violent actions. Homicide offender decision making takes place in a context that is often fast-paced, highly emotional, and often the offender, victim, or both have consumed alcohol (or drugs) that likely impairs "rational" decision making. Even in planned homicides, one cannot fully prepare (cognitively or emotionally) for every eventuality or anticipate fully one's own emotions or reactions in the moment.

IV. Conclusion

Understanding the decision-making processes of killers is a complex task. However, by synthesizing research from cognitive, affective, and situational perspectives, it is possible to more carefully untangle how and why violence generally, and lethal violence specifically, unfolds. Nevertheless, many questions remain. For example, in thinking about the role of emotion in homicide, van Gelder's (2013) "hot/cool" perspective provides a useful conceptual framework leading us to consider how the "hot" (affective) and "cool" (cognitive) systems function before, during, and after homicide. Does the "hot" system have a more dominant role in the "decision" to enact violence in the moment and the "cool" system in planning murder? We hypothesize that the reality is rather more complex. As we have seen from the case studies considered in this chapter, within one homicide event, an offender can move between various kinds of affect (e.g., from calm to agitated) and experience different emotions (e.g., anger and fear). We think it likely that different emotions are evoked in different homicide scenarios and that the emotions experienced by offenders will vary during the different stages of enactment and aftermath.

Similarly, questions remain regarding the precise role of affect in different types of homicide, and more research is warranted into the role of positive affect. For example, in relation to sexual homicide, is it anger, sadistic pleasure, or both that arouses the "decision" to kill? Is the action of taking items of the victim's belongings ("trophies") a way of cognitive and emotionally reliving and fantasizing about the killing? Does the method of killing influence the type of emotion experienced? How does it feel to fire a gun?

Homicide is an incredibly diverse offense, and we have only touched upon some of its manifestations in this chapter. Future research might consider distinguishing between homicides that fall at various points on the continuum of those planned ahead of time with a targeted victim or set of victims at one extreme (e.g., hit men and suicide bombers) to those for which death was not an intended outcome at all (e.g., some corporate homicide, gross negligence cases, and brief fist fights). In this way, we may be able to move closer to a more nuanced understanding of the various ways in which killers "decide" (consciously or subconsciously, with or without particular affect) to take a life.

Finally, future research could pay considerably more attention to the role of inhibitors to lethal violence, particularly among violent offenders who have stopped short of killing and especially among "competent" killers, such as contract killers or terrorists. Understanding how pathways to homicide can become blocked among those who are committed to murderous intent may be invaluable in helping to prevent or reduce lethal violence.

We hope this chapter has gone some way to unraveling homicide offenders' decision-making processes and look forward to further research that finds new and refined ways to understand the cognitive, affective, and situational factors that propel would-be killers toward, or away from, lethal action.

NOTES

1. Interviewees were aware that confidentiality would not apply if they (a) mentioned something that showed a significant and previously undetected risk to themselves or another or (b) provided specific and identifying details that could link them to a serious offense (e.g., murder) that had not previously been disclosed.
2. Workplace homicide/violence in this context referred to a planned act (although ultimately aborted) of lethal or serious violence against one or more individuals working at, or otherwise present at, the workplace of the offender. Generally, this referred to coworkers and managers.
3. However, this is an artefact of Luckenbill's selection processes for the homicides that he examined rather than a "good" measure of the usual proportion of homicides that take place in front of an audience.

REFERENCES

Anderson, C. A., and B. J. Bushman. 2002. "Human Aggression." *Annual Review of Psychology* 53:27–51.

Anderson, C. A., and L. R. Huesmann. 2003. "Human Aggression: A Social Cognitive View." In *The Sage Handbook of Social Psychology*, edited by M. A. Hogg and J. Cooper, pp. 296–323. Thousand Oaks, CA: Sage.

Anderson, E. 1999. *The Code of the Street: Decency, Violence and the Moral Life of the Inner City.* New York: Norton.

Athens, L. H. 1980. *Violent Criminal Acts and Actors: A Symbolic Interactionist Study.* London: Routledge and Kegan Paul.

Athens, L. H. 1997. *Violent Criminal Acts and Actors Revisited.* Chicago: University of Illinois Press.

Beck, A. T. 1999. *Prisoners of Hate: The Cognitive Biases of Anger, Hostility and Violence.* New York: HarperCollins.

Becker, E. 1962. "Anthropological Notes on the Concept of Aggression." *Psychiatry* 23:328–38.

Beech, A., D. Fisher, and T. Ward. 2005. "Sexual Murderers' Implicit Theories." *Journal of Interpersonal Violence* 20(11): 1366–89.

Bowes, N., and M. McMurran. 2013. "Cognitions Supportive of Violence and Violent Behavior." *Aggression and Violent Behavior* 18:660–65.

Brookman, F. 2005. *Understanding Homicide.* London: Sage.

Brookman, F. 2010. "Homicide." In *The Handbook on Crime*, edited by F. Brookman, M. Maguire, H. Pierpoint, and T. Bennett, pp. 217–44. Cullompton, UK: Willan.

Carlson, M., A. Marcus-Newhall, and N. Miller. 1990. "Effects of Situational Aggression Cues: A Quantitative Review." *Journal of Personality and Social Psychology* 58:622–33.

Clarke, R. V. 2014. "Affect and the Reasoning Criminal: Past and Future." In *Affect and Cognition in Criminal Decision Making*, edited by J. L. van Gelder, H. Elffers, D. Reynald, and D. Nagin, pp. 20–41. Abingdon, UK: Routledge.

Clarke, R. V., and D. B. Cornish. 1985. "Modeling Offenders' Decisions: A Framework for Research and Policy." *Crime and Justice* 6:147–85.

Cleckley, H. 1976. *The Mask of Sanity.* St. Louis, MO: Mosby.

Collie, R. M., J. Vess, and S. Murdoch. 2007. "Violence-Related Cognition: Current Research." In *Aggressive Offenders' Cognition: Theory, Research and Practice*, edited by T. A. Gannon, T. Ward, A. R. Beech, and D. Fisher, pp. 179–98. Chichester, UK: Wiley.

Collins, R. 2008. *Violence: A Micro-sociological Theory.* Princeton, NJ: Princeton University Press.

Cornell, D. G., J. Warren, G. Hawk, E. Stafford, G. Oram, and D. Pine. 1996. "Psychopathy in Instrumental and Reactive Violent Offenders." *Journal of Consulting and Clinical Psychology* 64(4): 783–90.

Cornish, D. B., and R. V. Clarke. 2008. "The Rational Choice Approach." In *Environmental Criminology and Crime Analysis*, edited by R. Wortley and L. Mazerolle, pp. 21–47. Cullompton, UK: Willan.

Damasio, R. 1994. *Descartes' Error: Emotion, Reason and the Human Brain.* London: Vintage.

Dobash, R. E., R. P. Dobash, K. Cavanagh, and R. Lewis. 2002. "Homicide in Britain: Risk Factors, Situational Contexts and Lethal Interventions (Focus on Male Offenders)." Research Bulletin no. 1. Department of Applied Social Science, DASS, University of Manchester.

Dodge, K. A., and J. D. Coie. 1987. "Social Information Processing Factors in Reactive and Proactive Aggression in Children's Peer Groups." *Journal of Personality and Social Psychology* 53:1146–58.

Ekman, P., and W. V. Friesen. 1975. *Unmasking the Face*. Englewood Cliffs, NJ: Prentice Hall.

Farrington, D. P. 1987. "Implications of Biological Findings for Criminological Research." In *The Causes of Crime: New Biological Approaches*, edited by S. A. Mednik, T. E. Moffit, and S. A. Stack, pp. 42–64. New York: Cambridge University Press.

Felson, R. B. 2014. "What Are Violent Offenders Thinking? In *Cognition and Crime: Offender Decision Making and Script Analysis*, edited by B. Leclerc and R. Wortley, pp. 12–25. Abingdon, UK: Routledge.

Felson, R. B., and M. Massoglia. 2012. "When Is Violence Planned?" *Journal of Interpersonal Violence* 27(4): 753–74.

Felson, R. B., and S. F. Messner. 1996. "To Kill or Not to Kill? Lethal Outcomes in Injurious Attacks." *Criminology* 34(4): 519–45.

Felson, R. B., and N. Painter-Davis. 2012. "Another Cost of Being a Young Black Male: Race, Weaponry and Lethal Outcomes in Assaults." *Social Science Research* 41(5): 1241–53.

Felson, R. B., and P. Pare. 2010. "Firearms and Fisticuffs: Religion, Race and Adversary Effects on Homicide and Assault." *Social Science Research* 39:272–84.

Felson, R. B., and H. J. Steadman. 1983. "Situational Factors in Disputes Leading to Criminal Violence." *Criminology* 21(1): 59–74.

Fontaine, R. G. 2009. "Reactive Cognition, Reactive Emotion: Toward a More Psychologically-Informed Understanding of Reactive Homicide." *Psychology, Public Policy and Law* 14(4): 243–61.

Ganpat, S. M., J. van der Leun, and P. Nieuwbeerta. 2013. "The Influence of Event Characteristics and Actors' Behaviour on the Outcome of Violent Events." *British Journal of Criminology* 53:685–704.

Gauci, A., and C. R. Hollin. 2012. "The Social Cognition of Violent Offenders." *Journal of Criminal Psychology* 2(2): 121–26.

Gilligan, J. 1996. *Violence: Our Deadly Epidemic and Its Causes*. New York: Vintage Books.

Goleman, D. 1995. *Emotional Intelligence. Why It Can Matter More Than IQ*. London: Bloomsbury.

Haidt, J. 2003. "The Moral Emotions." In *Handbook of Affective Sciences*, edited by R. J. Davidson, K. R. Scherer, and H. H. Goldsmith, pp. 852–70. Oxford: Oxford University Press.

Holcomb, W. R., and N. Adams. 1983. "The Inter-Domain Among Personality and Cognition Variables in People Who Commit Murder." *Journal of Personality Assessment* 47:524–30.

Huesmann, L. R. 1988. "An Information Processing Model for the Development of Aggression." *Aggressive Behaviour* 14:13–24.

Hull, J. 2001. "Identifying Cognitions That Influence Decisions to Engage in or Refrain from Acts of Workplace Homicide." PhD thesis, Walden University.

Jacobs, B. A., and R. Wright. 2010. "Bounded Rationality, Retaliation, and the Spread of Urban Violence." *Journal of Interpersonal Violence* 25(10): 1739–66.

James, M., and J. A. Seager. 2006. "Impulsivity and Schemas for a Hostile World: Postdictors of Violent Behaviour." *International Journal of Offender Therapy and Comparative Criminology* 50(1): 47–56.

Kahneman, D. 2011. *Thinking Fast and Slow*. London: Allen Lane.

Katz, J. 1988. *Seductions of Crime: Moral and Sensual Attractions in Doing Evil*. New York: Basic Books.

Kemper, T. D. 1987. "How Many Emotions Are There? Wedding the Social and Autonomic Components." *American Journal of Sociology* 93:263–89.

Kleck, G., and K. McElrath. 1991. "The Effects of Weaponry on Human Violence." *Social Forces* 69(3): 669–92.

Loewenstein, G., and J. S. Lerner. 2003. "The Role of Affect in Decision Making." In *Handbook of Affective Sciences*, edited by R. J. Davidson, K. R. Scherer, and H. H. Goldsmith, pp. 619–42. Oxford: Oxford University Press.

Luckenbill, D. F. 1977. "Criminal Homicide as a Situated Transaction." *Social Problems* 25(2): 176–86.

Maruna, S., and M. Butler. 2013. "Violent Self-Narratives and the Hostile Attribution Bias." In *Behavioural Analysis of Crime. Studies in David Canter's Investigative Psychology*, edited by D. Youngs, pp. 27–47. Aldershot, UK: Ashgate.

Metcalfe, J., and W. Mischel. 1999. "A Hot/Cool System Analysis of Delay of Gratification: Dynamics of Willpower." *Psychological Review* 106:3–19.

Myerson, R. B. 1997. *Game Theory: Analysis of Conflict.* Cambridge, MA: Harvard University Press.

Neisser, U. 1976. *Cognition and Reality.* San Francisco: Freeman.

Phillips, S., and M. Cooney. 2005. "Aiding Peace, Abetting Violence: Third Parties and the Management of Conflict." *American Sociological Review* 70(2): 334–54.

Polaschek, D. L. L., S. W. Calvert, and T. A. Gannon. 2009. "Linking Violent Thinking: Implicit Theory-Based Research with Violent Offenders." *Journal of Interpersonal Violence* 24(1): 5–96.

Polaschek, D. L. L., and T. Ward. 2002. "The Implicit Theories of Potential Rapists: What Our Questionnaires Tell Us." *Aggression and Violent Behavior* 7:385–406.

Polk, K. 1994. *When Men Kill: Scenarios of Masculinity Violence.* New York: Cambridge University Press.

Porter, S., and M. Woodworth. 2007. "'I'm Sorry I Did It . . . but He Started It': A Comparison of the Official and Self-Reported Homicide Descriptions of Psychopaths and Non-Psychopaths." *Law and Human Behaviour* 31:91–107.

Porter, S., M. Woodworth, J. Earle, J. Drugge, and D. Boer. 2003. "Characteristics of Sexual Homicides Committed by Psychopathic and Nonpsychopathic Offenders." *Law and Human Behavior* 27:459–70.

Rumelhart, D. E. 1980. "Schemata: The Building Blocks of Cognition." In *Theoretical Issues in Reading and Comprehension*, edited by R. J. Spiro, B. Bruce, and W. F. Brewer, pp. 33–58. Hillsdale, NJ: Erlbaum.

Rusting, C. L. 1998. "Personality, Mood, and Cognitive Processing of Emotional Information: Three Conceptual Frameworks." *Psychological Bulletin* 124(2): 165–96.

Schank, R. C., and R. P. Abelson. 1977. *Scripts, Plans Goals and Understanding.* Hillsdale, NJ: Erlbaum.

Scheff, T. J. 2011. "Social–Emotional Origins of Violence: A Theory of Multiple Killing." *Aggression and Violent Behavior* 16:453–60.

Seager, J. A. 2005. "Violent Men: The Importance of Impulsivity and Cognitive Schema." *Criminal Justice and Behaviour* 32:26–49.

Shaw, J., I. M. Hunt, S. Flynn, T. Amos, J. Meehan, J. Robinson, H. Bickley, R. Parsons, K. McCann, J. Burns, N. Kapur, and L. Appleby. 2006. "The Role of Alcohol and Drugs in Homicides in England and Wales." *Addiction* 101:1117–24.

Stretesky, P. B., and M. B. Pogrebin. 2014. "Gang-Related Gun Violence: Socialization, Identity, and Self." In *In Their Own Words: Criminals on Crime—An Anthology*, 6th ed., edited by P. Cromwell and M. L. Birzer, pp. 301–22. New York: Oxford University Press.

Tangney, J. P., and K. W. Fischer, eds. 1995. *Self-Conscious Emotions: The Psychology of Shame, Guilt, Embarrassment, and Pride.* New York: Guilford.

Toch, H. 1969. *Violent Men: An Inquiry into the Psychology of Violence.* Chicago: Aldine.

Toch, H. 1992. *Violent Men: An Inquiry into the Psychology of Violence.* Washington, DC: American Psychological Society.

Treiber, K. 2014. "A Neuropsychological Test of Criminal Decision Making. In *Affect and Cognition in Criminal Decision Making*, edited by J. L. van Gelder, H. Elffers, D. Reynald, and D. Nagin, pp. 193–220. Abingdon, UK: Routledge.

van Gelder, J. L. 2013. "Beyond Rational Choice: The Hot/Cool Perspective of Criminal Decision Making. *Psychology, Crime and Law* 19(9): 745–63.

van Gelder, J. L., and R. E. de Vries. 2014. "Rational Misbehavior? Evaluating an Integrated Dual-Process Model of Criminal Decision Making." *Journal of Quantitative Criminology* 30:1–27.

Walker, J. S., and J. A. Bright. 2009. "False Inflated Self-Esteem and Violence: A Systematic Review and Cognitive Model." *Journal of Forensic Psychiatry and Psychology* 20(1): 1–32.

Ward, T. 2000. "Sexual Offenders' Cognitive Distortions as Implicit Theories." *Aggression and Violent Behavior* 5:491–507.

Watson, D., and A. Tellegen. 1985. "Toward a Consensual Structure of Mood." *Psychological Bulletin* 98:219–35.

Websdale, N. 2010. *Familial Hearts: Emotional Styles of 211 Killers.* Oxford: Oxford University Press.

Williamson, S., R. D. Hare, and S. Wong. 1987. "Violence: Criminal Psychopaths and Their Victims." *Canadian Journal of Behavioral Science* 19:454–62.

Wolfgang, M. E. 1958. *Patterns in Criminal Homicide.* Philadelphia: University of Pennsylvania Press.

Woodworth, M., and S. Porter. 2002. "In Cold Blood: Characteristics of Criminal Homicides as a Function of Psychopathy." *Journal of Abnormal Psychology* 111:436–45.

Wortley, R. 2014. "Rational Choice and Offender Decision Making: Lessons from the Cognitive Sciences." In *Cognition and Crime: Offender Decision Making and Script Analysis*, edited by B. Leclerc and R. Wortley, pp. 236–52. Abingdon, UK: Routledge.

CHAPTER 29

COLD-BLOODED AND BADASS

A *"Hot/Cool" Approach to Understanding Carjackers' Decisions*

GABRIEL T CESAR AND SCOTT H. DECKER

CARJACKING is unpredictable and dangerous. This specialized form of robbery may target luxury vehicles, cars with valuable custom parts, or more average-looking vehicles that are easier to steal, conceal, and use. Media reports have noted carjackings throughout the world in places as diverse as England,[1] India,[2] Kenya,[3] and the Netherlands.[4] The most recent statistics from the United States indicate that between 1993 and 2002, approximately 34.000 carjackings occurred per year. However, the study of carjacking by social scientists has examined the phenomenon almost exclusively in urban America. Furthermore, even in the United States, official (national) statistics on carjacking are difficult to come by since the Uniform Crime Reporting (UCR) system does not differentiate carjacking from other crimes. As a result, similar carjacking events in different jurisdictions are routinely recorded as robberies, car thefts, or assaults, depending on local policy. The prevalence and distribution of carjacking in the United States and abroad are therefore at best loosely defined. This lack of systematic record-keeping limits the ability of criminologists and policymakers to analyze and account for carjacking.

Two common characteristics of carjacking events are the fear of imminent death or grave bodily injury imposed on victims by carjackers (Wright and Decker 1997a, 1997b; Jacobs 2013) and the difficult-to-avoid places such as red lights, parking lots, and driveways where carjacking often occurs. The resulting unpredictability of these crimes generalizes the fear of victimization to the public and presents problems for prevention. With regard to offender decision making, the fleeting nature of carjacking opportunities, the potential for serious violence, and the symbolic relevance of forcefully appropriating an automobile combine to suggest a visceral, spur-of-the moment decision. Consistent with previous research, we argue that the functional act of successfully removing a driver and driving off in a vehicle also involves a more rational series of perceptions and decisions. These factors—raw emotion and predictable steps—combine to generate a useful framework to examine the balance between emotion and rationality and to analyze the unique challenges to preventing carjacking (Miethe and Souza 2010).

To that end, attention has been paid to the psychosocial context or "phenomenological foreground" of carjacking in environments characterized by street culture (Jacobs, Topalli, and Wright 2003; Topalli and Wright 2011; Wright and Topalli 2013). Much of this work is based on connections between researchers and street-level criminals (Dickinson 2014; Decker and Smith 2015) and fieldwork with offenders in the neighborhoods where they live, hang out, and offend (Wright et al. 1992; Wright and Decker 1994, 1997a; Decker and Van Winkle 1996). Building on previous work with burglars, armed robbers, and gang members, researchers have considered carjackers as a specialized form of street criminal similar to armed robbers who specialize in victimizing drug dealers (i.e., high risk–high reward; Jacobs 2000). In short, ethnographic interviews with active American street criminals depict decision-making processes that are "encapsulated" in street culture (Lofland 1969; Topalli and Wright 2014) and aimed at addressing a pressing need for money with minimal planning. However, carjacking presents offenders with more complex and risky decisions compared to other forms of crime.

In particular, carjackers must perform reflexive and ongoing calculations in order to regulate emotions (e.g., anger, challenge, and fear) while accomplishing a predictable and necessary set of tasks, such as approaching drivers, removing victims, and escaping with a vehicle. Research examining this process with incarcerated offenders has characterized carjacking as a form of robbery associated with high levels of victim resistance relative to traditional robbery (i.e., robberies that do not involve taking cars; Copes, Hochstetler, and Cherbonneau 2012). This finding is consistent with those of studies of active offenders that suggest the roles of violence and fear are even more salient in carjackings than in traditional robbery (Jacobs 2012, 2013). Furthermore, in contrast to more conventional forms of street robbery, carjackings are likely to occur in public places as opposed to more discreet locations preferred by traditional robbers (Bernasco and Block 2009; Miethe and Souza 2010). Finally, carjacking has the potential to accomplish symbolic group process goals beyond securing money and/or drugs (Topalli and Wright 2011).

To better understand the decision making of carjackers, we synthesize the literature on street crime and carjacking events. We then integrate a dual-process approach (van Gelder 2013) to offender decision making in the enactment and accomplishment of these crimes. We argue that carjacking is a crime that requires carjackers to master and incorporate both hot (emotional) and cool (rational) decision-making processes. Furthermore, in the context of a carjacking event, the reflexive and evolving emotional processes, coupled with the predictable and necessary steps needed to complete a successful carjacking, make this crime ideal for exploring dual-process models of criminal decision making. We conclude with a discussion of the resulting difficulties associated with preventing carjacking. The broader goal is to demonstrate the utility of dual-process decision-making models in thinking about carjacking and other violent acquisitive crimes.

I. Street Crime, Status, and Technology

A common theme in active offender research is an emphasis on the phenomenological foreground of street offending (i.e., the psychosocial characteristics and emotional state of potential offenders) as a basis for the cost–benefit analyses conducted by offenders (Topalli and Wright 2014). This body of research suggests two driving forces in the lives of street offenders: a chronic need for money and persisting concerns about social status (e.g., "juice"; Shover and Honaker 1992; Wright and Decker 1994, 1997a; Anderson 1999). Maintaining status in street culture requires keeping up appearances through ostentatious displays of independence and conspicuous consumption. Topalli and Wright's (2011) interviews with active carjackers illustrate the social relevance of driving cars:

> Put it this way, you got people you know that's driving around. We just wanna know how it feels. We're young and we ain't doing shit else. So they see you driving the car, they gonna say "Hey there's C-Low!" . . . That makes us feel good 'cause we're riding, and then when we're done riding we wreck the car or give it to somebody else and let him ride. We took the car and drove around the hood, flossing everything.
>
> —C-Low (p. 57)

These interviews also illustrate the relevance of and wearing shoes and clothes:

> . . . not where I'm from. You try to walk up to a girl, boy, you got on some raggedy tore up, cut up shoes they're gonna spit on you or something. Look at you like you crazy. . . . Let's say you walking with me. I got on creased up pants, nice shoes, nice shirt and you looking like a bum. Got on old jeans. And that dude, that dude, he clean as a motherfucker and you look like a bum. . . . *You ain't gon' understand, you don't come from the projects.*
>
> —Corleone (pp. 58–59, emphasis added)

Street-level offenders also tend to have restricted access to legitimate means of obtaining resources. For instance, Wright and Topalli (2013, pp. 466–67) note that employment and borrowing prospects for street criminals are "slim and dim." Even for offenders who might consider working, low wages and delayed payment present barriers to requirements of status maintenance. As an active burglar told Wright and Decker (1994), "Even if I had a job, I betcha I couldn't find a job payin' me over minimum wage. Then they probably want to pay me every two weeks, so I would have to supplement that week that I didn't get paid something" (p. 48).

Another consistent theme in street offender research suggests that proceeds from street crime tend to be depleted quickly in dedicated pursuit of the intense consumption of drugs and alcohol, gambling, and sexual conquests (Shover and Honaker 1992; Wright and Decker 1994, 1997a; Jacobs 2000; Topalli and Wright 2014). The rapid depletion of cash and drugs leads street offenders into cycles of "desperate partying" that require constant replenishment of liquid resources:

> Just get high. I just blow money. Money is not something that is going to achieve for anybody, you know what I'm saying? So every day, there's not a promise that there'll be another so I just spend it. . . . At a job you've got to work a lot for it, you know what I'm saying? You got to punch the clock, do what somebody else tells you. I ain't got no time for that. Oh yeah, there ain't nothing like getting high on $5,000!
>
> —Mo (as quoted by Topalli and Wright 2011, p. 58)

A. Street Crime and Carjacking

Wright and Topalli (2013) hint at a likely distinction between carjackers and more traditional street criminals who focus on cash and liquid assets, stating "perhaps a little more surprisingly [the focus on cash applies to] carjacking too" (p. 463). Although cars represent enduring status symbols, their utility in generating liquid assets (i.e., cash and drugs) is less straightforward (for one innovative solution, see Copes, Forsyth, and Brunson [2007] for a discussion of "rock rentals"). To be sure, stolen cars can generate considerable income for offenders with connections to chop shops and/or the know-how to remove, sell, and repurpose stolen car parts (Copes 2003). At the same time, the US Bureau of Justice Statistics (BJS) has indicated that the median value of vehicles carjacked between 1987 and 1993 was approximately $7,300 in 2015 US dollars (adjusted for inflation; Rand 1994), suggesting that vehicles selected by carjackers are not necessarily the most luxurious or expensive. This underscores the instrumental element of carjacking as a means of producing a functional asset for transportation as well as a symbol of independence.

It is therefore plausible that carjacking is more effective in maintaining temporary arcs of social status and desperate partying than as a reliable source of fast cash. This is so because the act of carjacking combines the downside of burglary (the need to locate and liquidate valuable proceeds) with the negative aspects of robbery (face-to-face violent confrontation). For instance, the BJS reports that between 1993 and 2002, 67 percent of carjacking victims resisted the carjacker, resulting in injury to 24 percent of victims (Klaus 2004). Furthermore, in addition to the immediate risk of victim resistance and witness intervention, carjackers motivated by cash are faced with the procedural challenges of identifying and commandeering lucrative targets and selling stolen cars, parts, or the contents of the car.

The liquidation of cars and car parts for cash is certainly an option for offenders who have access to underground markets. Furthermore, carjacking can foster the extension of desperate and excessive partying by providing low-cost transportation. However, a somewhat unique component of the motivation for street-level offenders to engage in carjacking is the concept of "flossing" (Jacobs et al. 2003; Topalli and Wright 2011). Flossing refers to the act of purposefully flaunting flashy or expensive symbols of excess relevant to status in American street culture. Flamboyant, expensive jewelry and cars with unique paint jobs, custom wheels, and loud aftermarket stereo systems are potent symbols of independence, self-sufficiency, and dominance on the street. In other social contexts (e.g., suburban youth and emerging international consumer markets), simply having a private car for transportation may bring a level of prestige. Flossing implies emphatic or over-the-top flaunting that is intended as a dare or affront to others, especially peers. As Snake succinctly explained to Jacobs and colleagues, "You floss too much you get [carjacked]" (p. 681).

However, the line between demonstrating one's own prowess and impugning the prowess of others is highly subjective, and lightheartedly possessing these valued objects could be interpreted as flossing by people who are desperate, easily offended, or both:

> People out here with their windows down or whatever late at night. You know you got your little self on or you flossing. That's considered flossing . . . you know, you look at a certain person and one of them's like when we was walking, he looked at us. . . . But a look like, ha, they walking and I'm not [so we jacked him].
>
> —Playboy (as quoted by Jacobs et al. 2003, p. 681)

Against this backdrop, neighborhood rivals and unknown adversaries drive by and show off their symbols of power and status, presenting offenders who are encapsulated in street culture with a challenge to their own status, as well as an opportunity to establish and transcend their reputations and demonstrate that they are "badasses" (Katz 1988; Topalli, Wright, and Fornango 2002; Lyng, Matthews, and Miller 2009; Topalli and Wright 2011). Carjacking can therefore serve as a potent response to flossing, in addition to the pecuniary rewards associated with traditional street robbery. In the context of street culture, flossing represents a group process (Decker 1996) that plays a role in carjacking due to the perceived social implications of maintaining the appearance of financial and physical dominance and the enduring symbolic nature of cars as a demonstration of independence and success. As such, preventing carjacking may be more complex than crime control approaches and "tips" aimed at preventing other street crimes might suggest.

B. Carjacking and Technology

Regarding prevention, researchers who study traditional armed robbers and street crime have suggested that with the growing influence of technology in our everyday lives, street culture will be undermined and crime is likely to move "from the street to the suite" (Wright and Topalli 2013, p. 473; Wright et al. 2014). In contrast, carjacking represents a specific type of culture-driven crime that is likely to persist, even as preda-tory crimes increasingly involve advanced technology (e.g., the Internet; Titus 2001; Pyrooz, Decker, and Moule 2015). Cars will continue to provide status and private trans-portation, and they will still be composed of component parts that are easily removed and sold in second-hand markets (Mullins and Cherbonneau 2011). Indeed, advance-ments have been made in the use of on-board biometric systems, wireless Internet, and global positioning technology to identify drivers and control, disable, and locate vehi-cles (Reddy and Karunya 2014; Jadav, Wandra, and Dabhi 2015; Kiruthiga, Latha, and Thangasamy 2015; Punnoose and Kumar 2015; Swan 2015). Despite these advancements, emerging evidence suggests the carjacker of the future may have already moved to the suite via remote access (Miller and Valasek 2013), even from "unconstrained" distances (Woo, Jo, and Lee 2014, p. 995).

Stated simply, as long as there are cars and drivers, some forms of carjacking will per-sist. This is also due in part to the ubiquitous nature of automobile transportation in many countries. However, the research to date on carjacking is based on studies in only a hand-ful of US cities, conducted by relatively few researchers. How carjacking in the United States and elsewhere is affected by emerging technology remains to be determined. Regardless of the geographic location, in consumer-oriented social environments, par-ticularly where street culture is pervasive and "money talks and bullshit walks," interac-tions between people who have things that others want or need are likely to continue. At this fundamental level, another unique characteristic of carjacking emerges.

C. Carjacking and Cash

In the United States and other industrialized nations, the use of debit cards will likely continue, and cash may become rarer on the street (Wright et al. 2014). Nevertheless, the importance of liquid currency to underground commercial markets (e.g., illicit drug markets) is less likely to wane. Even in relation to emerging web-based markets for illicit drug sales (e.g., Silk Road; Van Hout and Bingham 2014) in which noncash currency is required, associated violent offending is likely to persist. For instance, Dickinson, (2014) notes that

> the anonymous nature of [illegal] transactions conducted through online markets may preclude grievants from committing *violent reflexive, calculated,* or *deferred* retaliation because it makes it virtually impossible to identify and locate those responsible for systemic violations. ... Nevertheless, systemic violence may not be completely eliminated from these markets, as buyers and sellers who have been defrauded may retaliate against others who are not associated with the exchange, thereby increasing rates of *wholly imperfect* retaliation. Consequently, while on its face the transactional nature of these markets may seem to reduce the likelihood of systemic violence, it may actually shift it from drug market participants onto persons outside of the market. (p. 81, emphasis added)

In the context of carjacking in a cashless society, the functional benefits of transportation and status maintenance serve to further insulate carjacking from preventive and deterrent effects that might influence rates of traditional robbery. If there is no cash to be had, taking cars or drugs by force represents a logical adaptation for individuals desperate to continue partying and augment their social standing. How these developments play out regarding the etiology of violence in both street and online contexts remains an area of developing inquiry (Dickinson 2014; Moule 2014). Regardless, people will continue to drive cars, stop at red lights, and possess drugs. As such, carjacking represents an ongoing opportunity for victimization that will not likely be diminished by a reduction in the use of cash.

II. Carjacking and Decision Making

Taken together, the existing research suggests that carjacking is a unique category of robbery that is characterized by less predictability, less anonymity, and more opportunity for violence and injury relative to traditional street robbery. Carjacking also offers potent benefits in the context of street culture, despite the inherent risks associated with removing a driver by force from his or her vehicle. The unique nature of this offense is illustrated by two broad points. First, carjacking is a risky street crime that affords perpetrators high levels of excitement and results in potent development and maintenance of status as a "badass" (Katz 1988; Jacobs and Wright 2006; Topalli and Wright 2011). Second, offenders who are willing and able to face down higher levels of danger and violence are able to use carjacking as an effective and inexpensive means to facilitate travel, desperate partying, and escape from problematic situations (e.g., impromptu dentist office shootouts; Jacobs et al. 2003, p. 680).

These characteristics make carjacking uniquely desirable for committed and capable street offenders because it places them on the top rung of bold street offenders who are adept at both reflexively interpreting social cues and selecting and employing the necessary levels of violence to effectively conduct their crimes. Still, given the unpredictable and relatively more risky nature of carjacking that emerges from active offender research, the rational link between an urgent need for money and the act of carjacking becomes somewhat attenuated (Wright, Topalli, and Jacques 2017). Stated simply, if fast cash is the primary goal of a street robbery, why rob someone inside what amounts to a mobile fortress? Even granting that a need for cash is a primary motivator for carjacking and other street crimes, what role might a sense of challenge (Lindegaard et al. 2014) or an existential desire for transcendence through "edgework" (Lyng 2004; Lyng et al. 2009) play in the decision to carjack someone? Questions such as these require a more detailed and systematic examination of the ways that offenders interact with the complex and dynamic nature of carjacking.

A. Carjacking Compared to Other Crimes

Traditional robbers and carjackers both commit robberies contingent on emerging opportunities. Robbers prefer predictable and lucrative areas near their homes (Bernasco and Block 2009; Bernasco, Block, and Ruiter 2013). They also tend to search for isolated or vulnerable victims, and they rely on direct threats of force and impending death to achieve submission (Wright and Decker 1997a). Ultimately, traditional robbers and carjackers are both involved in acquisitive violent crimes, but the nature of the transaction in a carjacking (e.g., removing victims from vehicles vs. removing items from pockets) makes coercing compliance more salient and complex (Copes et al. 2012; Jacobs 2013), and the mobile nature of cars makes opportunities to carjack more public and fleeting. Carjacking therefore demands that its perpetrators first establish co-presence either through approaching "normally" and perhaps asking for something (e.g., spare change or a cigarette) or "blitzing" so that victims are unable to react with resistance or defiance (Jacques 1994; Donald and Wilson 2000; Jacobs 2012).

A car can be used as a weapon, a shield, or a means of quick escape if a potential victim realizes what is happening too soon for the carjacker to firmly establish an "impending fear of death" (Wright and Decker 1997b; Jacobs 2012), and these risks persist throughout the process of carjacking. Navigating this ongoing and reflexive process requires that offenders determine and deploy necessary, but not excessive, levels of threat and violence. Stated simply, carjackers must scare victims enough to gain compliance but not so much that they become defiant or paralyzed with fear. Furthermore, evidence suggests that the parameters of this emotional/rational calculus evolve as the event progresses (Lindegaard, Bernasco, and Jacques 2015).

Successful carjacking is therefore a predatory act at the apex of violent criminality, where high-level emotional regulation intersects with high-level rational skills. As a means of generating income, carjackings are less predictable than burglaries, more risky than armed robberies, and opportunities are more serendipitous and fleeting. As such, it is likely that carjacking does not serve well as a "main line" occupation for street criminals but, rather, is a corollary crime that often serves symbolic but important purposes in the context of street life, such as status maintenance and retribution. Namely, the ubiquity of cars in many settings makes carjacking unique in its utility for seizing serendipitous opportunities to steal (i.e., alert opportunism; Topalli and Wright 2014), to exact potent symbolic retribution (e.g., for "flossing" or other affronts; Jacobs et al. 2003), and to facilitate the navigation of desperate partying and street crime as a lifestyle (e.g., to accomplish traveling goals and to escape danger; Topalli and Wright 2011, p. 680).

The ability and desire to carjack therefore depend heavily on the perceptions of offenders and their experiences with violence and crime. Along these lines, a growing body of research suggests that street criminals interpret opportunity and conflict in unique ways compared to non-offenders. As discussed in the sections that follow, these differences have important implications for the decision-making behaviors of carjackers.

B. Measuring the Skills of Active Offenders

Topalli (2005) integrated work with active offenders into psychological paradigms by examining the tendency to interpret situations as aggressive using a quasi-experimental design and a multidimensional sample. The experimental group consisted of 18 urban street robbers and carjackers and a "demographic control group" of 18 non-offender residents of the same neighborhood. The third group consisted of 18 college students. The criteria for inclusion as an offender was having "(1) committed one violent crime in the past three months and (2) committed at least three such offenses in the last year" (p. 274). Point light display (PLD) methodology (Topalli 2005, p. 277) involves creating scenes in which actors, dressed in all black and against an all-black backdrop, wear lights on key body parts (e.g., hands, feet, elbows, and knees) in order to illustrate human movements with very minimal social cueing, such as clothing or facial expression, and without overt indications of the racial, ethnic, or gender characteristics of the actors. Using PLD, Topalli constructed three experimental video vignettes in which one person approaches another and then moves away.

The analysis focused on the reactions and interpretations of the vignettes by respondents. The vignettes were displayed in three conditions: slow, medium, and fast velocities. The treatment conditions were randomly assigned across each research group, and respondents were then asked to interpret the interaction they had seen in the video. Ultimately, the authors presented evidence that perceptions of aggressiveness differed across research groups. Specifically, "aggressive or crime content was noted to be higher for offenders viewing *slow* and *medium* clips" as opposed to college students and demographic controls, who tended to perceive aggressive or crime content while viewing *faster* speeds[5] (Topalli 2005, p. 282, emphasis added). This bias in perceptions has important implications in the context of carjacking. Namely, Topalli's findings suggest that experienced offenders may be suspicious of attempts to establish co-presence (e.g., through portrayals of normalcy) and employ a state of "alert preventionism" similar to the "alert opportunism" discussed elsewhere.

Topalli's (2005) findings are consistent with research elsewhere that indicates that people perceive opportunity and deterrence differently based on experience with crime. Wright, Logie, and Decker (1995) conducted photo elicitation experiments with active burglars in a US city and a comparison group drawn from a local community center. Both groups were shown photographs of houses and asked a series of questions regarding the suitability of the houses for burglary. After a short survey about the deterrent abilities of burglary-relevant characteristics, participants were shown an altered set of pictures (e.g., adding or removing extra locks and alarms systems) of the same houses and asked to identify differences. The study generated two important results. First, whereas comparison group participants tended to view extra locks and alarm systems as deterrent, experienced burglars were less likely to view them as credible impediments. Second, active burglars were also better at remembering details from the photos and identifying changes, suggesting that offenders develop expertise with experience.

Wright and colleagues noted that in light of their results, and a growing body of active offender research,

> [the] contention that the criminal career is not characterized by the acquisition of skill and sophistication would appear to be ill-founded; as with those in other occupations, residential burglars clearly understand their trade in a way that outsiders fail to appreciate. (p. 52)

Building on this body of work, Topalli, Jacques, and Wright (2014) analyzed how offenders apply skills and expertise in conducting carjacking offenses. The authors acknowledge that carjackings do not occur in a vacuum, and they suggest that the necessary skills are deployed in a context of "prevailing dispositional and situational factors [which] enhance or mitigate the application of expertise in real-world settings" (p. 19). Specifically, Topalli et al. focus on the initial stages of carjacking events (i.e., deciding to commit an offense on a specific target) and find that these decisions are made predominately with offenders' perceptual skills. For example, carjackers scrutinize and target drivers and vehicles quickly, relying on visceral perceptions of victim characteristics. Research suggests urban carjackers search for "ducks" (victims they perceive to be least likely to resist; Copes et al. 2012) such as women, unsuspecting drivers, and Caucasians in cars they perceive as valuable or easy to steal.

C. Jacking a Car: "Hitting a Lick" or Getting Licked

Understanding the challenges and risks associated with carjacking discussed previously, offenders are tasked with continually "sizing up" their victims in order to properly allocate force throughout the initiation and all subsequent stages of the offense. If at any point carjacking victims are not intimidated enough, they may stall, employing "passive resistance" (Jacobs 2013):

> I ran up over there, put the gun to his head, asked him if he was going to get out or die . . . He was steady bullshitting, time was steady ticking. He bullshitting. Don't want to get out. Don't want to get out. I'm gonna make him get out.
>
> —Goldie (p. 534)

Which can spiral into fighting back with active resistance:

> [H]e tried to spin off with it so now I'm hustling with him and tussling with him. I dropped my gun on his lap. I had to pick the gun up, right? So we still tussling and everything. . . . So I grabbed the gun and put it to his throat. I asked him, you know, so what you gonna to do? Is you gonna die or give up this car? . . . He don't want to give up his car, right. So I cocked it one time, you know, just to let him know I wasn't playing, you dig? Shot him in the leg. . . . Boom. Shot him on his leg. . . . He got out the car, you know what I'm saying? . . . I opened the door and pushed him out. Drove off. Know what I'm saying? But before I drove off I backed up, ran over him I think

on the ankles like . . . I hear bones break, like all this down here [indicating] was just crushed.

—Goldie (p. 534)

At the other extreme, if carjacking victims become too scared, they could panic and be unable to respond or react. A panicked victim may also "speed off" despite threats or actual violence.

Successful carjackers therefore use perceptual skills to access and maintain (albeit briefly) a "sweet spot" of fear in victims that ensures unquestioned compliance but allows victims to successfully process and adhere to the demands of the carjacker (Jacobs 2013). Most traditional armed robbers report a desire to "get the drop" on unsuspecting targets and use no less than "the fear of impending death" on their victims (Wright and Decker 1997b). Carjackers, on the other hand, are required to remove their victims from cars and therefore must either remove them by force (e.g., yanking a driver through an open or broken-out window) or coerce physical compliance. Importantly, Topalli et al. (2014) found that although *targeting* decisions are predominantly perceptual in nature, the procedural skills necessary to effect a carjacking are also at play. This approach to the analysis of offender decision making distinguishes carjacking from armed robbery, and it brings into relief the interacting roles of perceptual (i.e., reactive) and procedural (i.e., proactive) skills in carjacking.

After a carjacker has decided on a target or one presents itself in a compelling manner, he or she must first achieve "co-presence" in the same activity frame with the victim (Copes et al. 2012; Jacobs 2012). This is generally done in one of two ways. "Portrayals of normalcy" involve a ruse, such as asking for change or the time as a means to get close to a victim without alerting the victim to the impending danger. A second common tactic to establish co-presence is "blitzing," which is similar to ram raiding (Jacques 1994; Copes et al. 2012; Jacobs 2012). Blitzing involves little subterfuge and a full assault without regard for the awareness of potential victims. Topalli and colleagues (2014) note that the goal of a blitz is to catch the victim by surprise, similar to normalcy techniques, but that blitzing "involves speed rather than cunning" (p. 5).

Blitzing is more likely to be employed given a serendipitous opportunity such as a vehicle approaching a nearby red light. In situations of perceived flossing, or where an offender in a state of "alert opportunism" (Topalli and Wright 2011, 2014) encounters an inattentive driver, the opportunity may prove attractive enough for motivated offenders to proceed with little caution (Jacobs 2010a):

> Unlike other forms of street robbery that emerge by chance, carjacking puts a particular premium on spontaneity. A "regular" robbery victim might be banked in a perceptual reservoir for future consideration . . . but a desirable car is there one minute and gone the next. Acting decisively can mean the difference between hitting a "lick," as offenders refer to it, or going home empty-handed. (p. 519)

Compared to traditional robberies, then, carjacking opportunities are likely to be more fleeting and unpredictable in nature, in no small part due to the timing of street lights, traffic patterns, and the relative ease of victim escape. The implication is that carjackers must make split-second decisions based on "gut feelings" and act quickly on those perceptions with functionally effective tactics.

The relative importance of perceptual skills and procedural skills shifts, however, as a carjacking offense continues into the *enactment* phase, which entails announcing the crime and removing victims. Topalli et al. (2014) found that during this phase of a carjacking offense, procedural skills become more salient to successful carjackings, although still interacting with perception. Indeed, although initial decisions are made largely in the context of offenders' visceral, emotional perceptions of vulnerable victims and amenable situations, removing drivers and escaping with vehicles calls for a more rational set of procedures. In other words, "You can know what car to take, but if you don't know how to take it, you will get your ass killed every time" (Pac, as quoted in Topalli et al. 2014, p. 22). Taken together, the findings presented by Topalli and colleagues suggest the need for successful carjackers to regulate their emotions (e.g., fear, challenge, and anger) effectively regarding target selection and interaction and to employ them in concert with rational strategies to accomplish high-stakes goals.

In the context of street culture, having the ability to employ these emotional and rational skills in concert places carjackers at the apex of violent acquisitive crime and allows offenders to develop expertise over time, as illustrated in figure 29.1.

Carjackers employ both emotional and rational skills throughout the carjacking process. As a carjacking event is initiated and progresses, offenders are required to perceptually assess the situation, select preliminary tactics, and interpret victims' reactions in order to select and tailor subsequent strategies. At the same time, offenders must employ procedural protocols or "scripts" in order to accomplish goals, often requiring some level of coerced cooperation from victims (Copes et al. 2012). Preformed scripts detailing how to act are particularly important in highly charged, high-stakes settings. Carjackers must make their calculations without hesitation or error, and the possible

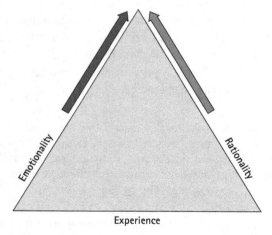

FIGURE 29.1 Apex of violent criminality.

consequences for failure at each turn are dire, including physical injury, arrest and incarceration, or death.

This point was underscored by an incarcerated carjacker to Hochstetler, Copes, and Williams (2010):

> I'm talking about to the bone I felt it hit. It hit my bone and like the pain . . . I want to bust her at this point in time; I want to pull this trigger. You, man, you trying to hurt me, so therefore I got to hurt you. But I don't know what made me not do it. That's something I don't know 'til this day, you know. I just took my lick on that one, you know. I couldn't even get out of the car man when she hit me, I'm talking about it like paralyzed that whole leg or something man. I'm trying and she just drove, I'm like "god," I said, "I can't believe it's a knife." Tip is still in me. It is still in me. She was just bolder than I was, you know.
>
> —Shawn (p. 508)

Stated clearly, successful carjackers must be adept at the simultaneous navigation of both emotional reactions to outside stimuli (e.g., victim resistance) and more proactive rational considerations (e.g., whether to kill in retaliation).

As such, carjacking offers a useful point of departure for examining the decision-making processes of violent offenders, in that it positions the emotions of offenders (e.g., fear, anger, and challenge) in relief against their more rational procedural calculations, generating important implications for research and the deterrence of carjackers. Carjacking also represents an area of importance in the development of a "hot/cool perspective of criminal decision making" (van Gelder 2013, p. 751). In particular, it is likely that in addition to the rational ("cool") decision-making processes highlighted in studies of burglars and traditional street robbers, the role of emotion-based ("hot") processes may be more readily apparent in the decision making of street offenders who ultimately commit carjackings.

D. Dual-Process Decision Making at the Apex of Street Crime

The interaction between perceptions and procedural skills that is required to successfully select and manipulate targets, victims, and situations has parallels with what Deutsch and Strack (2006) referred to generally as a "dual-process" model (for a more detailed discussion of the similarities and distinctions between *dual-process* and *dual-system* paradigms, see chapter 9, this volume). In brief, despite the numerous restrictions on rationality discussed previously, such as encapsulation in street life, excessive substance abuse, and a chronic need for cash, very little has been suggested regarding an alternative model that better accounts for observed offender decision making. Van Gelder (2013) adopted an interdisciplinary approach and integrated the dual-process model with criminological decision making, drawing on concepts from the fields of social psychology and neuroscience. The model that resulted is referred to as the "hot/cool perspective," wherein

> the cool, cognitive, mode is sensitive to considerations such as probabilities and extralegal costs such as anticipated guilt . . . [whereas] . . . the hot mode . . . evaluates in a more intuitive way and responds to different situational characteristics, such as the temporal and spatial immediacy of decision outcomes, their controllability, and the vividness with which they can be imagined, but remains largely unresponsive to probabilities and outcomes themselves. (p. 752)

In other words, "cool" processes refer to deliberate thinking such as weighing costs of potential actions against their benefits, whereas "hot" processes are more automatic and nonvolitional. The latter are triggered by external forces, such as anger caused by the resistance of a victim, or the pressure felt from co-offenders or threats to status (Collins 2009).

The dual-process approach is therefore compatible with findings such as those discussed by Topalli et al. (2014) regarding the decisions and behaviors of carjackers because it allows for both emotional and rational processes in the development of perceptual and procedural expertise, as well as the reflexive interaction between the hot and cool modes of offender decision making over time (Deutsch and Strack 2006, p. 167). Still, the applicability of the dual-process model to street crimes in general, and carjacking specifically, remains largely unexplored. For instance, van Gelder and de Vries (2014) found support for the dual-process model with a sample of undergraduate students regarding their hypothetical willingness to commit online and fraud crimes, but how the dual-process model functions for active violent offenders and their crimes is less well understood. Given the ability of the dual-process model to consider both "trait" and "state" characteristics (van Gelder and de Vries 2012), the model holds promise for research and policy. Table 29.1

Table 29.1 Hypothesized Configurations of Hot/Cool and Perceptual/Procedural Processes in Carjacking

Process	Hot (Emotional)	Cool (Rational)
Perceptual (selection)	Challenge/shame: As a would-be offender's emotional drive to overcome challenge outweighs the perceived shame of failure, carjackings become more likely to occur.	Benefit/cost: As a would-be offender's perception of the relative benefits (e.g., transportation, prestige, and cash) outweigh the costs, carjackings become more likely to occur.
Procedural (execution)	Anger/fear: Successful offenders must manage emotional states such as anger (e.g., to impose threats and conduct violence) and fear of resistance to "stomach" high-level violence.	Effectiveness/risk: Successful offenders must determine and employ tactics that quickly coerce compliance but do not induce resistance or debilitating fear, and they must be able to "think on their feet."

presents a simplified framework that integrates research on active carjackers with van Gelder's (2013) dual-process model.

It is important to note that the typologies presented in Table 29.1 are not meant to be comprehensive or mutually exclusive. Hot and cool processes do not operate in isolation, and perceptual and procedural skills reflexively inform each other. It stands to reason that these states, traits, and skills would become specialized over time, generating an increasing level of expertise. Table 29.1 is presented here as a heuristic to more systematically understand the development of carjacking as a phenomenon. Furthermore, the framework may apply more broadly to all crimes and indeed all human behavior, but it is presented here based on previous research with American carjackers.

In summary, empirical examination of hot/cool decision-making processes in the context of criminal decision making has been conducted by only a few studies, and the study of carjacking has been largely limited to a few researchers in a small number of US cities. Applying the hot/cool approach to carjacking therefore remains a promising and as yet unexplored direction for future research. This is especially true in light of the substantial theoretical overlap between the perceptual and procedural decisions made by carjackers (Topalli et al. 2014) and the hot and cool modes described by van Gelder (2013). Understanding how these factors interact to generate carjacking decisions in other social settings (e.g., in suburban areas, in emerging economies outside the United States, or with non-black offenders) and in the face of emerging security technology represents an important step in understanding offender decision making more broadly. Understanding carjacking as a dual-process phenomenon also has implications for interacting with carjackers.

III. Discussion

This review paints a picture of carjacking as a distinctive form of street robbery that requires its practitioners to accurately perceive external social cues and to select and accomplish predictable goals to achieve their end. Completing carjackings requires a substantial amount of raw guts, as well as specialized technical skill. Like residential burglary and more traditional forms of street robbery, carjacking is used by street offenders to get money, achieve status, and enact retribution. In the context of the code of the street (Anderson 1999), carjacking is a function of group processes that allow offenders to take what they do not have, to "right the moral order" (Katz 1988), and to respond rebelliously to "system colonization" (Lyng 2004). In many ways, however, carjacking most closely resembles ram raiding. Both are bold, confrontational, and risky. The group processes underlying such ventures enable and motivate individuals to do things and take risks that they might normally not do, and over time this interaction favors those who are best equipped emotionally and rationally.

A. Responding to Carjacking

These characteristics combine to make preventing and responding to carjacking difficult tasks. Indeed, typical policy recommendations appear to come up short in their ability to prevent this crime (Miethe and Souza 2010). The "hot" processes required of carjackers do not lend themselves well to deterrent processes (Jacobs 2010*b*; Jacobs and Cherbonneau 2012). For deterrence to be effective, the rational calculation of cost and benefit must be central to offenders' decisions. This is not likely the case for street-level carjackers. In fact, carjacking requires the opposite of such a calculus; "going for it" and "pedal to the metal" (literally) are key elements of committing to such an offense and being successful in its execution. Traditional forms of target hardening (e.g., firearm possession; Tark and Kleck 2004) are not likely to have much effect on reducing attempts to "jack" a car because such efforts require considerable diligence to be effective, and emerging epidemiological research indicates that guns may not be particularly effective at reducing injury or property loss (Hemenway and Solnick 2015).

Even for those disciplined enough to carry a firearm at the ready at all times, if a carjacker is allowed to establish co-presence, the chance to resist may have already passed (Copes et al. 2012):

> They never think it would happen to them. Right there at the red light? You would never think nobody rob nobody at the red light when you got cars over here, cars over there, especially in broad daylight I mean c'mon. . . . They had a gun on the passenger side of the seat. . . . They couldn't get to it.
>
> —Derrick (p. 257)

Faithfully practicing "alert preventionism" by maintaining constant awareness of one's surroundings may be the only way to reduce risk of being carjacked. The sudden, opportunistic nature of carjacking combined with the emotional ("hot") states and rational ("cool") traits of its perpetrators make standardized prevention tactics and devices much less likely to succeed relative to a crime such as residential burglary. Common crime-prevention admonitions such as suggestions to be wary and observant of one's surroundings (Miethe and Souza 2010) may be particularly unhelpful in preventing carjackings in which offenders establish co-presence with portrayals of normalcy. In other words, in order for hypervigilance to thwart this carjacker tactic, people determined to head off carjackers would have to refuse to converse with strangers at all times. Avoiding co-presence is a key to avoiding being a victim of this crime, which requires wariness of anybody one does not know and trust.

Furthermore, alert preventionists must be willing to refuse to accommodate any small request (e.g., for directions and for change) without hesitation or recalcitrance. Maintaining such a state of vigilance at all times is socially complex. Anderson's (1999) urban ethnography and Topalli's (2005) PLD experiments provide insight into the differential perceptions and behaviors of violent offenders and people who interact with the "code of the streets" that may prove useful in understanding this dynamic and the role it plays in preventing victimization. For instance, in street code environments, "running up on someone" (i.e., approaching quickly and without invitation) and "getting in someone's face" (i.e., encroaching on personal space) are considered threatening behaviors, calling for rebuke or retaliation. At the individual level, safeguarding one's self from carjacking requires keen perceptions of all approaching people, along with standing protocols for avoiding unwanted engagement with others. In short, preventing victimization by carjackers requires would-be targets to be "cold-blooded" and at least a bit "badass."

Regarding policy, the US Department of Justice Office of Community Policing has published a number of POP (problem-oriented policing) guides. These guides are intended for police departments and citizens to use in responding to and preventing a wide range of offenses. There is a useful POP guide for street robbery and one for thefts of cars from parking facilities but none for carjacking. This is because the kinds of measures that traditionally prevent or reduce the risks of victimization do not translate well to carjackings. As the previous discussion suggests, carjacking is an offense in which the "hot" considerations of a motivated offender can overwhelm the perceived impact of guardianship and generate viable opportunities where others see only deterrent factors. Technological target hardening, such as biometric driver identification, remote kill switches, and global positioning services, can help respond to completed carjackings (e.g., to disable or locate cars) after the fact but is not generally equipped to prevent attempts in the first place.

Wright and colleagues (2014) note that the current move toward a cashless society makes street robbery a less desirable offense for street offenders. Similarly, keyless entry and ignition, fingerprint recognition, and wireless technology make leaving with a stolen car more problematic. Despite these advances, a hallmark of technology is the adaptation it produces. As a consequence, hackers have already begun to generate workarounds to emerging security measures. It may be just a matter of time before determined carjackers catch up, adapt perceptually and procedurally, and execute their crimes in a new manner. For instance, carjackers motivated by anger, or those in desperate need for transportation, could elect to keep biometrically secured drivers in the vehicle during transport. Carjackers motivated by challenge or those interested in stealing cars for profit could move "to the suite" and hack into cars from long distances. In fact, there may already be "an app for that" when it comes to carjacking the car of the future (Woo et al. 2015).

B. The Takeaway for Future Research

Finally, carjacking is at the apex of street crime because it incorporates and requires both emotional ("hot") and rational ("cool") decision-making capabilities at a high level of performance and reflexivity (see figure 29.1). In practice, this requires well-developed perceptual skills, as well as specialized procedural skills (see Table 29.1). In other words, offenders who are successful at carjacking must be at the top of the food chain regarding their willingness to engage challenging targets, as well as their ability to successfully execute complicated tasks under constant risk of injury, apprehension, and death. As offenders operating at the apex of acquisitory violence, carjackers are required to exert extreme levels of force precisely: too aggressive, and their target may escape; not aggressive enough, and the victim may resist. Therefore, research that fails to examine carjacking in the context of hot and cool decision making does so at the risk of mischaracterizing the process. Following Topalli et al.'s (2014) work on the "perceptual and procedural" aspects of decision making in carjacking, researchers interested in the development of violent events and specialization would be well advised to consider the relative roles of hot and cool decision-making processes at all stages of carjacking events and careers.

However, active offenders who commit carjackings may not be likely to self-identify as carjackers or to derive income primarily from carjacking offenses. Researchers interested in the decision-making processes of active carjackers have therefore largely been left to derive and examine subsamples from existing groups of general offenders—on the street, incarcerated, and otherwise. The focus on American street-level offenders, however, may have artificially excluded important types of carjackings from examination, such as carjackings that occur outside street code-dominated environments[6] and those that occur outside the United States. Similarly, little is known about carjackers who do not adhere to the code of the streets (Anderson 1999) or who may be members of more highly organized groups. Inconsistencies in official reporting and the lack of classification in the UCR add to the confusion (Miethe and Souza 2010, p. 242). Developing an understanding of baseline offense rates and the geographical and social dispersion of carjacking is therefore difficult. As such, several questions remain unanswered, including the following:

1. How does carjacking vary by region? How does carjacking in the United States compare empirically with carjacking elsewhere in North America or in Europe, Asia, South America, or Africa?
2. How can the existential concept of edgework inform our developing understanding of criminal decision making? Is there some subset of people who are more likely to perceive carjackings as a desirable challenge precisely due to the risk of grave consequence and the resulting potential for transcendence of roles?
3. In the United States, outside of the target selection considerations of black, urban offenders, what role does race/ethnicity play in carjacking offenses? How do the decision-making processes of Latino, Asian, and Caucasian carjackers differ from those of blacks? How does "car culture" (e.g., lowrider, tuner, and donk car clubs and enthusiasts) shape carjacking across racial and ethnic groups?
4. How might increasingly prevalent technologies such as biometric identification and GPS shape carjacking in the future?
5. Does "flossing" help link street culture and carjacking offenses, despite the amorphous nature of carjackers as a group? Is flossing a group process confined to American street culture settings?

Our current understanding of the decision-making processes of carjackers and other violent criminals is therefore at best only loosely defined. To that end, the integration of fieldwork with active offenders and the dual-process approach to criminal decision making offers a more comprehensive and promising framework for researchers, policymakers, and citizens to better understand carjacking offenses, develop prevention techniques, and plan for criminal adaptation.

ACKNOWLEDGMENTS

The authors thank Richard Moule, Jean-Louis van Gelder, and three anonymous reviewers for their insightful comments on earlier versions of this chapter.

NOTES

1. "Arrest after Birmingham Carjack Footage Released." BBC News, February 4, 2015. http://www.bbc.com/news/uk-england-birmingham-31136475
2. "Stealing Tough, Carjackings Rise." *The Times of India*, April 20, 2015. http://timesofindia.indiatimes.com/city/delhi/Stealing-tough-carjackings-rise/articleshow/33978008.cms
3. "Kenyan Leader's Carjacked Motorcade Vehicle Found." BBC News, September 3, 2014. http://www.bbc.com/news/world-africa-29045106
4. "German Police Arrest Couple Wanted for Carjacking, Shooting." *Dutch News*, February 26, 2014. http://www.dutchnews.nl/news/archives/2014/02/german_police_arrest_couple_wa
5. Specifically, offenders viewed slow and medium speeds as threatening, college students viewed fast speeds as threatening, and the demographic control group viewed both fast and medium speeds as threatening.
6. "Shattered Routine: Great-Grandfather Dies in Carjacking." *The Detroit Free Press*, January 20, 2015. http://www.freep.com/story/news/local/michigan/oakland/2015/01/19/woman-arrested-fatal-waterford-carjacking/21986003

REFERENCES

Anderson, E. 1999. *Code of the Street*. New York: Norton.

Bernasco, W., and R. Block. 2009. "Where Offenders Choose to Attack: A Discrete Choice Model of Robberies in Chicago." *Criminology* 47(1): 93–130.

Bernasco, W., R. Block, and S. Ruiter, 2013. "Go Where the Money Is: Modeling Street Robbers' Location Choices." *Journal of Economic Geography* 13(1): 119–43.

Collins, R. 2009. *Violence: A Micro-sociological Theory*. Princeton, NJ: Princeton University Press.

Copes, H. 2003. "Streetlife and the Rewards of Auto Theft." *Deviant Behavior* 24(4): 309–32.

Copes, H., C. J. Forsyth, and R. K. Brunson. 2007. "Rock Rentals: The Social Organization and Interpersonal Dynamics of Crack-for-Cars Transactions in Louisiana, USA." *British Journal of Criminology* 47(6): 885–99.

Copes, H., A. Hochstetler, and M. Cherbonneau. 2012. "Getting the Upper Hand: Scripts for Managing Victim Resistance in Carjackings." *Journal of Research in Crime and Delinquency* 49(2): 249–68.

Decker, S. H. 1996. "Collective and Normative Features of Gang Violence." *Justice Quarterly* 13(2): 243–64.

Decker, S. H., and D. L. Smith. 2015. "A Conversation with Street Daddy: Pulling Back the Curtain on Twenty Years of Ethnography." In *Envisioning Criminology*, edited by M. Maltz and S. Rice, pp. 9–25. New York: Springer.

Decker, S. H., and B. Van Winkle. 1996. *Life in the Gang: Family, Friends and Violence.* New York: Cambridge University Press.

Deutsch, R., and F. Strack. 2006. "Duality Models in Social Psychology: From Dual Processes to Interacting Systems." *Psychological Inquiry* 17(3): 166–72.

Dickinson, T. 2014. "Exploring the Drugs/Violence Nexus Among Active Offenders: Contributions from the St. Louis School." *Criminal Justice Review* 40(1): 67–86.

Donald, I., and A. Wilson. 2000. "Ram Raiding: Criminals Working in Groups." In *The Social Psychology of Crime*, edited by D. Canter and L. Alison, pp. 191–246. Burlington, VT: Ashgate.

Hemenway, D., and S. J. Solnick. 2015. "The Epidemiology of Self-Defense Gun Use: Evidence from the National Crime Victimization Surveys 2007–2011." *Preventive Medicine* 79:22–27.

Hochstetler, A., H. Copes, and J. P. Williams. 2010. "'That's Not Who I Am': How Offenders Commit Violent Acts and Reject Authentically Violent Selves." *Justice Quarterly* 27(4): 492–516.

Jacobs, B. A. 2000. *Robbing Drug Dealers: Violence Beyond the Law.* New York: Transaction Books.

Jacobs, B. A. 2010a. "Serendipity in Robbery Target Selection." *British Journal of Criminology* 50(3): 514–29.

Jacobs, B. A. 2010b. "Deterrence and Deterrability." *Criminology* 48(2): 417–41.

Jacobs, B. A. 2012. "Carjacking and Copresence." *Journal of Research in Crime and Delinquency* 49(4): 471–88.

Jacobs, B. A. 2013. "The Manipulation of Fear in Carjacking." *Journal of Contemporary Ethnography* 42(5): 523–44.

Jacobs, B. A., and M. Cherbonneau. 2012. "Auto Theft and Restrictive Deterrence." *Justice Quarterly* 31(2): 344–67.

Jacobs, B. A., V. Topalli, and R. Wright. 2003. "Carjacking, Streetlife and Offender Motivation." *British Journal of Criminology* 43(4): 673–88.

Jacobs, B. A., and R. Wright. 2006. *Street Justice: Retaliation in the Criminal Underworld.* New York: Cambridge University Press.

Jacques, C. 1994. "Ram Raiding: The History, Incidence and Scope for Prevention." In *Crime at Work: Studies in Security and Crime Prevention*, edited by M. L. Gill, pp. 42–55. New York: Palgrave Macmillan.

Jadav, J. B., K. H. Wandra, and R. Dabhi. 2015. "Innovative Automobile Security System Using Various Security Modules." *International Journal of Scientific Progress and Research* 8(1): 24–27.

Katz, J. 1988. *Seductions of Crime: Moral and Sensual Attractions in Doing Evil.* New York: Basic Books.

Kiruthiga, N., L. Latha, and S. Thangasamy. 2015. "Real-Time Biometrics-Based Vehicle Security System with GPS and GSM Technology." *Procedia Computer Science* 47:471–79.

Klaus, P. A. 2004. "Carjacking, 1993–2002." Bureau of Justice Statistics, US Department of Justice, Office of Justice Programs.

Lindegaard, M. R., W. Bernasco, and S. Jacques. 2015. "Consequences of Expected and Observed Victim Resistance for Offender Violence During Robbery Events." *Journal of Research in Crime and Delinquency* 52(1): 32–61.

Lindegaard, M. R., W. Bernasco, S. Jacques, and B. Zevenbergen. 2014. "Posterior Gains and Immediate Pains: Offender Emotions Before, During and After Robberies." In *Affect and Cognition in Criminal Decision Making*, edited by J. L. van Gelder, H. Elffers, D. Reynald, and D. S. Nagin, pp. 58–76. New York: Routledge.

Lofland, J. 1969. *Deviance and Identity*. Englewood Cliffs, NJ: Prentice Hall.

Lyng, S. 2004. "Crime, Edgework and Corporeal Transaction." *Theoretical Criminology* 8(3): 359–75.

Lyng, S., R. Matthews, and W. J. Miller. 2009. "Existentialism, Edgework, and the Contingent Body: Exploring the Criminological Implications of Ultimate Fighting." In *Existentialist Criminology*, edited by R. Lippens and D. Crewe, pp. 94–126. New York: Routledge.

Miethe, T. D., and W. H. Sousa. 2010. "Carjacking and Its Consequences: A Situational Analysis of Risk Factors for Differential Outcomes." *Security Journal* 23(4): 241–58.

Miller, C., and C. Valasek. 2013. "Adventures in Automotive Networks and Control Units." http://illmatics.com/car_hacking.pdf

Moule, R. K. Jr. 2014. "A View from the Street: Active Offenders, the Life-Course, Technology, and Implications for Security." In *The Handbook of Security*, 2nd ed., edited by M. Gill, pp. 516–45. New York: Routledge.

Mullins, C. W., and M. G. Cherbonneau. 2011. "Establishing Connections: Gender, Motor Vehicle Theft, and Disposal Networks." *Justice Quarterly* 28(2): 278–302.

Punnoose, S., and J. S. J. Kumar. 2015. "Iris Recognition for Security and Safety of Automobiles." *International Journal of Innovative Science, Engineering and Technology* 2(4).

Pyrooz, D. C., S. H. Decker, and R. Moule Jr. 2015. "Criminal and Routine Activities in Online Settings: Gangs, Offenders and the Internet." *Justice Quarterly* 32(3): 471–99.

Rand, M. 1994. "Carjacking." Bureau of Justice Statistics, US Department of Justice, Office of Justice Programs.

Reddy, Y. S., and N. Karunya. 2014. "Multitudinous Anti-theft Security System Using Wireless Technology. *International Journal of Scientific Engineering and Technology Research* 3(32): 6357–60.

Shover, N., and D. Honaker. 1992. "The Socially Bounded Decision Making of Persistent Property Offenders." *Howard Journal of Criminal Justice* 31(4): 276–93.

Swan, M. 2015. "Connected Car: Quantified Self Becomes Quantified Car." *Journal of Sensor and Actuator Networks* 4(1): 2–29.

Tark, J., and G. Kleck. 2004. "Resisting Crime: The Effects of Victim Action on the Outcomes of Crimes." *Criminology* 42(4): 861–910.

Titus, R. 2001. "Personal Fraud and Its Victims." In *Crimes of Privilege: Readings in White-Collar Crime*, edited by N. Shover and J. P. Wright, pp. 57–66. Oxford: Oxford University Press.

Topalli, V. 2005. "Criminal Expertise and Offender Decision-Making: An Experimental Analysis of How Offenders and Non-offenders Differentially Perceive Social Stimuli." *British Journal of Criminology* 45(3): 269–95.

Topalli, V., S. Jacques, and R. Wright. 2014. "'It Takes Skills to Take a Car': Perceptual and Procedural Expertise in Carjacking." *Aggression and Violent Behavior* 20:19–25.

Topalli, V., and R. Wright. 2011. "Dubs and Dees, Beats and Rims." In *About Criminals: A View of the Offenders' World*, edited by M. Pogrebin, pp. 50–63. Thousand Oaks, CA: Sage. (Originally published 2004.)

Topalli, V., and R. Wright. 2014. "Affect and the Dynamic Foreground of Predatory Street Crime." In *Affect and Cognition in Criminal Decision Making*, edited by J. L. van Gelder, H. Elffers, D. Reynald, and D. S. Nagin, pp. 42–57. New York: Routledge.

Topalli, V., R. Wright, and R. Fornango. 2002. "Drug Dealers, Robbery and Retaliation: Vulnerability, Deterrence and the Contagion of Violence." *British Journal of Criminology* 42(2): 337–51.

van Gelder, J. L. 2013. "Beyond Rational Choice: The Hot/Cool Perspective of Criminal Decision Making." *Psychology, Crime and Law* 19(9): 745–63.

van Gelder, J. L., and R. E. de Vries. 2012. "Traits and States: Integrating Personality and Affect into a Model of Criminal Decision Making." *Criminology* 50(3): 637–71.

van Gelder, J. L., and R. E. de Vries. 2014. "Rational Misbehavior? Evaluating an Integrated Dual-Process Model of Criminal Decision Making." *Journal of Quantitative Criminology* 30(1): 1–27.

Van Hout, M. C., and T. Bingham. 2014. "Responsible Vendors, Intelligent Consumers: Silk Road, the Online Revolution in Drug Trading." *International Journal of Drug Policy* 25(2): 183–89.

Woo, S., H. J. Jo, and D. H. Lee. 2015. "A Practical Wireless Attack on the Connected Car and Security Protocol for In-Vehicle CAN." *IEEE Transactions on Intelligent Transportation Systems* 16(2): 993–1006.

Wright, R. T., and S. H. Decker. 1994. *Burglars on the Job: Streetlife and Residential Break-ins.* Boston: Northeastern University Press.

Wright, R. T., and S. H. Decker. 1997a. *Armed Robbers in Action: Stickups and Street Culture.* Boston: Northeastern University Press.

Wright, R. T., and S. H. Decker. 1997b. "Creating the Illusion of Impending Death: Armed Robbers in Action." *Harry Frank Guggenheim Review* 2:10–18.

Wright, R. T., S. H. Decker, A. K. Redfern, and D. L. Smith. 1992. "A Snowball's Chance in Hell: Doing Fieldwork with Active Residential Burglars." *Journal of Research in Crime and Delinquency* 29(2): 148–61.

Wright, R. T., R. Logie, and S. H. Decker. 1995. "Criminal Expertise and Offender Decision-Making: An Experimental Study of the Target Selection Process on Residential Burglary." *Journal of Research in Crime and Delinquency* 32(1): 39–53.

Wright, R. T., E. Tekin, V. Topalli, C. McClellan, T. Dickinson, and R. Rosenfeld. 2014. *Less Cash, Less Crime: Evidence from the Electronic Benefit Transfer Program*, no. w19996. Cambridge, MA: National Bureau of Economic Research.

Wright, R. T., and V. Topalli. 2013. "Choosing Street Crime." In *The Oxford Handbook of Criminological Theory*, edited by F. T. Cullen and P. Wilcox, pp. 461–74. New York: Oxford University Press.

Wright, R. T., V. Topalli, and S. Jacques. 2017. "Crime in Motion: Predation, Retaliation, and the Spread of Urban Violence." In *On Retaliation: Toward an Interdisciplinary Understanding of a Basic Human Condition*, edited by B. Turner and G. Schlee. Oxford: Berghahn Books.

CHAPTER 30

....

THE REASONING SEX OFFENDER

....

ERIC BEAUREGARD

OFTEN described as offenders suffering from mental disorders, there exists a long tradition of beliefs suggesting that sex offenders are mainly driven by an uncontrollable
impulse to sexually offend (Simon 2000). It is believed that because of their sexual
"urges" and deviant sexual fantasies, sex offenders are unable to control themselves and
thus act out on victims without any thought about the when, where, who, and how. This
assumption is not well supported by empirical evidence (Lussier, Proulx, and Leblanc
2005) because relatively recent studies have shown that sex offenders are much more
similar to other offenders than previously thought (Lussier, Leblanc, and Proulx 2005;
Lussier and Healey 2009). Despite accumulating evidence showing the versatility of sex
offenders (Lussier 2005), researchers have yet to examine sex offenders' decision making
similar to what has been done with robbers (Wright and Decker 1997), burglars (Bennett
and Wright 1984; Cromwell, Olson, and Avary 1991), shoplifters (Carroll and Weaver
1986), and car thieves (Cherbonneau and Copes 2006).

I. SEX OFFENDERS AS DECISION MAKERS

....

Decision making is crime specific (Cornish and Clarke 1986). Therefore, the decision-
making rationales identified for crimes such as burglary and robbery are of limited use
for sexual crimes. For each type of crime, choices and actions are shaped by a constel-
lation of specific external constraints, which Cornish and Clarke (1987) referred to as
the *choice-structuring properties* of a crime. In most sexual crimes, offenders face decisions before committing the crime (e.g., selecting the victim), during the crime (e.g., use
of a weapon), and following the crime (e.g., confessing to the police if apprehended).
The effect of these external constraints is not random but, rather, driven by an internal

logic that permits only a limited number of ways to commit a sexual crime (Proulx and Beauregard 2009).

Although *rationality* is the criterion for decision making, the rational choice perspective nonetheless recognizes that perfect rationality is unattainable and that rationality is limited or bounded (Cornish and Clarke 1986) for several reasons (e.g., limited information available and time-constrained decisions). Moreover, sex offenders' decision making is influenced by internal constraints, such as deviant sexual fantasies (Proulx, McKibben, and Lusignan 1996), disinhibition caused by alcohol and/or drugs, and a lack of self-control (Lussier, Proulx, et al. 2005). Even non-offending populations have been shown to systematically make irrational choices based on factors such as sexual arousal or anger (Loewenstein, Nagin, and Paternoster 1997; Carmichael and Piquero 2004; Bouffard 2011). Regarding the effect of sexual arousal on decision making specifically, Ariely and Loewenstein (2006) suggested that sexual arousal narrows the focus of motivation, similar to tunnel vision, so that goals other than sexual gratification are overshadowed by the motivation to have sex. Ariely (2008) has shown in several experiments that people tend to behave irrationally but in a predictable or systematic manner, with their decision making being influenced by previously understudied and misunderstood influences such as motivational drives (Loughran et al. 2011). The concentration on immediate sexual rewards is congruent with van Gelder's (2013) "hot/cool" model of criminal decision making.

However, in a study conducted on male college students, Bachman, Paternoster, and Ward (1992) found that the perceived risks of formal sanctions from hypothetical scenarios had a deterrent effect on the self-reported projection of committing a sexual assault. The authors rightfully acknowledged that such positive findings may have been possible due to the strong investment of the participants (college students) in a conventional life. This could well be the case. Pedneault (2015) examined the effect of positive and negative outcomes—or the costs and benefits—related to the commission of sexual crimes on the decision to persist or desist for these sex offenders. She found that when taking into account the costs and benefits altogether, the costs involved in sexual crimes (e.g., incarceration and a long sentence) had no effect on the decision to desist from committing sexual crimes, whereas the benefits (e.g., sexual touching, oral sex on victim, and penetration of victim) had a positive effect on persistence in sexual crimes.

A study by Pedneault et al. (2015) well illustrates the seemingly irrational, but systematic, decision making that takes place in cases of sexual burglary. The authors investigated reasoning in a sample of 224 individual incidents of residential burglary with apparent sexual motivations committed by 104 male offenders sent to the Massachusetts Treatment Center. Specifically, these authors analyzed the situational cues identified by sexual burglars in their target selection. Their findings indicated that most sexually motivated burglaries occurred in occupied residences with deficient physical guardianship (no male present) and when a female victim was alone and unlikely to resist because she was asleep. Violence, theft, penetration, and even fetishism—a behavior that is often described as ritualistic and compulsive—were found to be committed in circumstances that increased the benefits and lowered the risks (e.g., fetishistic behaviors were committed in unoccupied houses).

Moreover, Pedneault et al.'s (2015) results showed that sexual burglars are reasoning sex offenders who consider costs and benefits as they select residences that are easy to break into; therefore, these events should not be considered an "added bonus" in an otherwise nonsexual burglary. Instead, sexual burglars act opportunistically on situational cues that are markedly dissimilar to those of regular burglars. Specifically, sexual burglaries disproportionately (1) involve apartments (high-risk targets to gain entrance); (2) target occupied residences; (3) occur at night, between midnight and 3 a.m., a time period during which people are more likely to be at home; and (4) involve weapons from the onset, as if the burglars are prepared to find something different than empty residences. Finally, this study showed that despite the apparent lack of rationality, sexual burglars make decisions that are congruent with their motivation and their goal. The examination of specific behaviors associated with a particular form of crime allows for a better understanding of the decision making involved in such crime.

Different approaches have been used to examine decision making in sex offenders. For instance, Hudson, Ward, and McCormack (1999; see also Proulx et al. 2014) identified offense pathways in a sample of 72 child molesters. One of the strengths of their model was that it identified that positive affect could play a role in the offending process of sex offenders and influence how the crime would be committed. However, one of the main limitations associated with their model was that offender and victim behaviors during the offense (e.g., victim resistance, physical coercion, and humiliation) were minimally described (Proulx et al. 2014).

A different approach—the identification of scripts—was used by Leclerc, Wortley, and Smallbone (2011), who examined 221 child sex offenders incarcerated in Australia. According to the protoscript identified, before the sexual abuse occurs, offenders first encounter their victims in institutional, domestic, or public locations (Wortley and Smallbone 2006), although some offend against their own children. The offender must gain the victim's trust, which is often accomplished by giving love and attention (Smallbone and Wortley 2000). Once this is accomplished, offenders will often use strategies (e.g., promise rewards and money) to proceed to the location for sexual contact, or they may stay at the current location if they are already in their own home and/ or have established an intimate relationship with the victim. After selecting the crime location, offenders will exploit a set of circumstances (e.g., watching TV or taking bath with the victim) in which they can be alone with the victim and avoid being interrupted (Wortley and Smallbone 2006).

Once the victim is isolated, the offender will proceed to gain the victim's cooperation in sexual activity (e.g., talking about sex; Berliner and Conte 1990; Goldstein 1999). According to Leclerc et al. (2009), the strategies for gaining the victim's cooperation and the outcome of the crime are interrelated (see also Leclerc and Tremblay 2007). Leclerc et al. (2011) distinguish between two crime outcomes: proximate (i.e., time spent by the offender with the victim in sexual activity) and the terminal outcome (i.e., sexual behaviors performed by the offender and the victim). As illustrated by the protoscript of child sex offending, the terminal outcome is influenced by the offender's skills and by the victim's cooperation during the event. The offender also needs to take into account the nature of the interaction between him and the victim because in some cases it may be necessary to adopt strategies to prevent disclosure by the victim (e.g., threatening to withdraw love and attention; Smallbone and Wortley 2000).

This chapter presents a review of the literature on the decision making involved in sexual crimes. However, the decision making involved in the *decision* to first engage in a sexual crime is not discussed. The reason to first engage in a sexual crime is often not known—even by the offender—and thus is inferred by the researchers or clinicians working with these individuals. Instead, the focus is on the decision making involved at the different crime stages—that is, before, during, and following the crime. Therefore, the goal is to take the reader through the different decision points an offender has to go through when committing a sexual crime.

Despite being scarce, an attempt has been made to collect and discuss the majority of the studies examining—one way or another—the decision making that takes place once an offender has decided to commit a sexual crime. Based mainly on the rational choice perspective, these studies examine the entire sexual crime event. Each section in this chapter is organized so as to present two types of information pertaining to decision making. First, whenever possible, the decision-making rationales from the offenders are presented. A small group of studies have interviewed sex offenders and have recorded their responses on a number of questions pertaining to decision making at different crime stages (e.g., Why did you use a weapon?). The second type of information presented in this chapter derives from studies that have analyzed the behaviors of large samples of sex offenders. Despite not having direct access to the offenders, these studies allow for an examination of offenders' behaviors conditional on certain contingencies. The main arguments supporting this chapter are that (1) like other offenders, sex offenders consider costs and benefits even though they may make systematic errors/deviate from rationality at times (as do other offenders) and (2) understanding cost–benefit structures can help researchers understand the decision making of sex offenders.

II. Before the Crime

A. Planning of the Crime

Before actually getting into contact with the victim, sex offenders need to go through several stages to prepare for the crime. One of these stages is the planning of the crime. Beauregard and Leclerc (2007) analyzed the rationales provided by 72 repeat sex offenders who had committed at least two sexual crimes against a stranger. These authors showed that some offenders carefully plan their attack with a structured premeditation (i.e., have selected a victim, have selected a time and a place to commit the crime, and have groomed the parents to get access to the children; Leclerc, Proulx, and McKibben

2005), whereas others act impulsively without any forethought. Their analyses also revealed that some sex offenders are ready to act out when the right opportunity presents itself—a phenomenon referred to as premeditated opportunism (Rossmo 2000). In such cases, findings revealed that offenders were aware of the offending scenario that was in place, like in scripts (Cornish 1994), but were waiting to encounter the right situation and opportunity to act on it. Offenders explained that in cases of premeditated opportunism, it is the situational cues that trigger the acting out, similar to what Bennett and Wright (1984) found for burglars, the vast majority of whom identified a trigger that prompted the decision to offend.

B. Choice of Hunting Field

In a study that used the same sample as Beauregard and Leclerc (2007), Beauregard, Rossmo, and Proulx (2007) investigated specifically the decision making involved in the hunting patterns of serial sex offenders. One aspect of their hunting patterns that involve decision making is their choice of the hunting field, which is the type of area where offenders hunt for victims. More than half of the subjects interviewed reported hunting in specific public places to find a victim (e.g., a bar, park, and shopping mall). Offenders explained that this choice of hunting field was motivated by the fact that it is an easy way to find attractive targets, to gain access to them, and to estimate their vulnerability. Moreover, some of these places were also known by offenders to be both isolated and attractive to potential victims. Other offenders decided to search for victims through their own occupation (e.g., hockey coach and kindergarten teacher), explaining that it served as an effortless hunting field because the victims, most often children, came to them on their own. Furthermore, because of the offenders' positions, victims were in a vulnerable situation and could be easily manipulated, thus reducing the risk of the crime being reported.

Although choosing an appropriate hunting field to identify potential targets is important for sex offenders, it is not enough. Sex offenders must also choose a location where they will encounter their victim. Hewitt, Beauregard, and Davies (2012) examined temporal, hunting behavior, and modus operandi factors to determine those variables that influence the victim encounter and release locations in serial sexual crimes. Using generalized estimating equations on the sample used by Beauregard, Rossmo, et al. (2007), their findings showed that all these factors are significant predictors of both the victim encounter and release sites, but their importance varies depending on whether the location is in a residential land use area, a private site, inside location, or a site that is familiar to the offender. Specifically regarding the encounter site, their findings revealed that the encounter for sexual crimes involving stranger victims is less likely to occur in a private site and inside location compared to encounters in which the offender and victim are not strangers. This finding is consistent with prior studies that have found that non-stranger rapes are more likely to take place in the victim's home (Warr 1988). Moreover, their analyses showed that crimes that involve victims who are not selected at random or those for which there is a pattern to offenders' choices are less likely to take place in residential areas.

C. Target Selection

During the criminal event, most sex offenders have to decide who to select. Although victim selection may often appear to be random, most sex offenders use specific criteria when targeting a victim, even if this requires more searching on the offender's part compared to random victim selection. Furthermore, because offenders exercise some degree of reasoning, their selection of a particular target over another, within a sociospatial context, will be determined by the subjective value of the target. When considering the subjective value of targets, most empirical research examining target selection processes has been carried out on burglars. Although burglars and sex offenders have different types of targets (i.e., static vs. mobile), their target selection processes nonetheless share several similarities (Warr 1988). Both types of offenders decide to select one target over another based on intelligence gathered from making observations of specific targets (Nee and Meenaghan 2006) and/or based on a combination of different environmental cues that constitute "specialist knowledge" in target selection (Coupe and Blake 2006). Beauregard, Rossmo, et al. (2007) showed that the majority of offenders targeted a specific victim, and these offenders were able to identify the most important selection criteria, such as location/availability of the victim (e.g., easy victim access and geographic isolation) and the victim's vulnerability (e.g., young, alone, or alone with children).

With regard to the importance of location, Beauregard, Rebocho, and Rossmo (2010) tested the decision making in target selection for Canadian and Portuguese rapists. The results of the TwoStep cluster analysis of a mixed sample of 78 Canadian and Portuguese rapists indicated that these rapists exhibit different target-selection patterns, but their geographic decision making is congruent, and consistent, with the environment within which they operate. Similarly, using latent class analysis on the 72 repeat sex offenders from the study by Beauregard, Proulx, et al. (2007), Deslauriers-Varin and Beauregard (2010) identified scripts of target selection among sex offenders. The identified scripts showed that the target selection stage is highly influenced by the victim's routine activities (and the offender's routine activities; see Pedneault and Beauregard 2014) and the physical environment in which the crime takes place. As suggested by Beauregard, Proulx, et al. (2007), the type of location has a major impact on the types of strategies an offender will use to offend. The type of location where the offender and the victim meet can also trigger some strategies. If the victim is outside, the offender might have to act faster and use violence to control the victim and reduce the risk of apprehension (Beauregard, Proulx, et al., 2007).

However, sex offenders explained that in some cases, targeting a specific victim did not automatically lead to the attack of that same victim. In fact, sex offenders explained that sometimes they had to adapt their decision making due to the circumstances present at the time. Circumstances in which the situational factors were not right included the victim not being alone, the victim was not easily available, someone nearby might interfere, the location was too risky, or the victim's behavior made the offender change his mind (e.g., the offender lost his patience and left before the victim became available; Beauregard, Rossmo, et al., 2007).

D. Risk Assessment and Avoiding Detection

While planning a sexual assault, sex offenders also assess the risks associated with a particular crime, and some will even consider certain strategies to avoid detection at this stage. Congruent with the routine activity theory (Cohen and Felson 1979), Beauregard, Rossmo, et al. (2007) demonstrated that many sex offenders commit their crimes when the risks are estimated to be low and when certain conditions are present/absent: (1) presence/absence of a capable guardian (2) favorable/risky environment, and (3) easy/uneasy target. This shows that sex offenders are "situationally aware" and are capable, up to a certain point, of a costs–benefits evaluation before committing the crime. However, some sex offenders still commit their crimes when the risks are high (Beauregard, Rossmo, et al. 2007). As discussed previously, it could be that their personality, the severity of their sexual deviance, or a lack of self-control causes them to make "erroneous" decisions or decisions based on partial information (Simon and Zgoba 2006). In conformity with the work of Ariely and Loewenstein (2006) and Loewenstein et al. (1997), in some cases, the level of sexual arousal makes offenders careless about risk. However, it is also possible that an opportunity structure first evaluated as low risk may have suddenly changed due to unexpected events, such as a witness/bystander interfering with the crime, or some behavior from the victim (e.g., a victim resisting more vigorously than the offender expected).

Whether sex offenders commit their crimes when the risks are high or low, most, if not all of them, want to avoid being detected by the police. Some offenders will adapt their modus operandi (MO) or take precautions before, during, or post crime commission to decrease their risk of apprehension. Offenders who adapt their MO to thwart police investigative efforts may be said to be exhibiting investigative awareness (i.e., a knowledge or understanding of police investigative practice; Beauregard and Martineau 2012). Relatedly, "forensic awareness" (Davies 1992) is exhibited when an offender reveals knowledge or an understanding of the importance of forensic evidence (e.g., DNA) to a police investigation through the offender's behaviors or actions. Thus, forensic awareness is defined as the taking of additional steps and adapting the MO used in a crime to hide evidence in order to ultimately avoid apprehension (Davies 1992). The analysis of sex offenders' interviews by Beauregard and Leclerc (2007) revealed that approximately only one out of four offenders showed signs of forensic awareness while planning their crime. However, some offenders who had previous contacts with the criminal justice system (see also Davies, Wittebrood, and Jackson 1997) took special care either not to leave evidence at the crime scene (e.g., brought condoms and put on gloves) or to protect their identity and not be recognized while committing the crime (e.g., used a mask and changed their license plate while prowling for victims). Moreover, in a quantitative analysis of 222 rape events taken from the study by Beauregard, Rossmo, et al. (2007), Beauregard and Bouchard (2010) showed that the most common specific strategies used by offenders to avoid detection had to do with protecting their identity, whereas only a few offenders took precautions to destroy/remove forensic evidence at the crime scene. These behaviors suggest that offenders are capable of forensic awareness in the early stages of the crime-commission process (e.g., planning not to be recognized by the victim) but may become less careful after the actual rape. Importantly, the findings by Beauregard and Bouchard (2010) on the use of forensic awareness strategies to avoid detection in sexual assaults showed that the decision to use such strategies was heavily influenced by the situation. For example, offenders who were under the influence of drugs and/or alcohol were less forensically aware during the crime-commission process, in which these factors caused them to overlook specific details that were necessary to avoid detection. It can also be hypothesized that being in a "hot" or heightened state of sexual arousal makes sex offenders less concerned about risk and focused only on their target/benefits and not the costs or potential consequences of their decisions (Loewenstein et al. 1997; Ariely and Loewenstein 2006).

However, what may seem surprising is that even with the widely recognized importance of forensic evidence, the majority of sex offenders did not think about forensic precautions or simply did not care about them (Beauregard and Leclerc 2007). Beauregard and Bouchard (2010) examined the rationales as to why sex offenders would not take precautions to avoid being detected, and four distinct categories were found:

- They did not think about forensic awareness (e.g., crime was not planned).
- They were confused at the moment of the crime (e.g., being intoxicated).
- They showed "irrational thinking" (e.g., thought the victims consented).
- They used an alternative (e.g., use of manipulation or bribes).

As this discussion demonstrated, sex offenders are reasoning offenders who can consider costs and benefits in their decision making, especially when preparing to commit the crime. Some will carefully plan their crime, whereas others will simply act on the spur of the moment. In both cases, sex offenders make decisions that are influenced by several factors, many of which are shaped by the situation. In addition to the situation, offenders have to take into consideration another factor during the crime: the victim. The next section discusses the decision making of sex offenders during the crime and how factors such as the victim's behavior may influence the choices made by the offender.

III. During the Crime

A. Using Props to Commit the Crime

Once the offender and the victim have made contact, the next step of the criminal event begins. Despite having made several decisions in preparing for the crime, other choices are presented to the offender during the crime. Some of these choices concern the strategies used to commit the crime. Beauregard and Leclerc (2007) showed that in a minority of cases, sex offenders used a weapon (e.g., knife or gun) when committing the crime. The decision to use a weapon was based on the fact that a weapon constitutes an effective means to control, intimidate, or threaten the victim and to prevent him or her from resisting, but it could also be instrumental in facilitating breaking and entering into the victim's residence. However, most sex offenders decided not to use a weapon even if this could facilitate the commission of the crime. In these instances, the sex offenders explained that they decided not to use a weapon because the crime was not planned, it was not deemed necessary to commit the assault, or it was simply not compatible with the offenders' MO and deviant sexual fantasies. On the other hand, some offenders used a weapon for some of their crimes but not for others, and this decision was dependent on the availability of the weapon at the time of the crime.

In addition to a weapon, some sex offenders resort to the use of physical restraints (e.g., ropes and handcuffs). In Beauregard and Leclerc's (2007) study, only a minority of offenders chose to make use of restraints, most of the time to prevent victim resistance or victim escape. Offenders who did not use restraints explained that it was not necessary, they did not think about it, or it was simply not compatible with their MO.

B. Attack Methods

Once a victim has been targeted, sex offenders need to choose a method to approach him or her. Beauregard, Rossmo, et al. (2007) found that the preferred method to approach victims by sex offenders is the con approach. Offenders explained that using this type of approach allowed them to gain their victims' trust, avoid scaring or hurting them physically, and permitted offenders to get physically close to the victims and gain access to them.

However, some sex offenders are far more violent and will use physical violence from the start in their victim approach (Beauregard, Rossmo, et al. 2007). Sex offenders are faced with a decision to use violence or not during the crime, but they also have to decide how much violence they are willing to use. In the study by Beauregard and Leclerc (2007), sex offenders who did did not use any violence explained that they did not do so because the victim showed no resistance, it was not compatible with their fantasies (e.g., they did not want to physically hurt the victim), or they preferred alternative means to achieve their goals (e.g., using manipulation in cases involving child victims). However, some offenders reported using minimal force because it was the amount of force necessary to control the victim and to commit the crime (e.g., to commit and/or obtain certain sexual acts). In one-third of the cases, sex offenders explained that they used more force than was necessary mainly to overcome victim resistance, because it was part of their fantasies, to scare the victim, to make the victim suffer, and, in some extreme cases, to kill the victim. Some studies have shown a link between a negative emotional state prior to the crime and the infliction of injuries on the victim (Beauregard, Lussier, and Proulx, 2005).

For some offenders, violence helps surprise the victim and prevent him or her from resisting or escaping (Beauregard, Rossmo, et al. 2007). As such, violence can be used to make the victim lose consciousness so that the offender can do whatever he wants with the victim, whereas for others, violence is committed only for the thrill. Others resort to verbal violence, such as threats, to scare victims, to "freeze" them, to prevent them from alarming witnesses or resisting, and to make sure they will be completely submissive during the sexual assault.

Interestingly, Beauregard, Rossmo, et al. (2007) showed that the offender's choice of approach was largely influenced by the type of victim (i.e., child vs. adult). Findings indicated that three methods are used by sex offenders specifically against children: seduction/persuasion, money/gifts, and games. Offenders explained that these methods help them make contact with the victims slowly and gradually increase their chance of succeeding in getting victims involved in sexual activities. However, research also shows that sex offenders can use more than one method or they may switch methods during the crime (Beauregard, Rossmo, et al. 2007; Deslauriers-Varin and Beauregard 2010). Ouimet and Proulx's (1994) study illustrates the switch in methods used to approach victims. The authors argue that if child molesters are not able to find a suitable victim near their home, they may have to travel farther. As they journey farther distances, convincing children to return home with them becomes more difficult because few are willing to take a car trip with a stranger. The offender has to adapt his hunting strategies and use a more direct approach, such as a direct attack or an ambush, which in turn may lead to an increase in the level of violence used during the crime.

C. Reaction to Victim Resistance

The findings regarding the use of a weapon, restraints, and violence suggest that to fully understand the offending behaviors of the offender and the associated decision making, the person–situation interaction needs to be investigated as well (Leclerc and Tremblay 2007). One of the most important person–situation interactions during a sexual assault concerns the offender's reaction to victim resistance. Varying levels and types of resistance can have a range of effects on the offender's behavior. Upon encountering victim resistance during the commission of a sexual assault, an offender makes a decision as to how to react to the resistance, via the use of varying degrees of coercive or noncoercive tactics. It has been well documented that the victim's actions during the commission of the crime affect the offender's behavior, just as the offender's actions will affect those of the victim (Block 1981). In their study investigating the offender's reaction to victim resistance in 624 sexual assault cases, Balemba and Beauregard (2012) found that with an adult victim, an offender is more likely to resort to violence according to the resistance level of the victim. Although this finding is in opposition to those of studies conducted by Ullman (e.g., Ullman 1998), it is important to stress the fact that

Ullman's studies failed to distinguish a temporal sequence in the event. If, for example, the offender begins with a violent offense strategy and the victim reacts physically, this is a much different scenario than if an offender reacts violently to a victim's physical resistance. Specifically considering the offender's reaction to victim resistance allowed for a consideration of this temporal sequence, which is very important for understanding the offender's decision making. However, there appears to be a completely different social environment surrounding a sexual assault of a child. Balemba and Beauregard (2012) found that assaults involving children seem to be premeditated to a greater extent in an attempt to circumvent the use of expressive violence to complete the assault. Offenders against children are prepared with regard to the surrounding setup and physical environment, and they are aware of the amount of force they are likely and willing to use prior to the commencement of the assault. As discussed previously, this planning often involves an assessment of victim vulnerability and risks of apprehension (Leclerc and Tremblay 2007).

In a subsequent study using the same sample as in Balemba and Beauregard (2012), Balemba, Beauregard, and Mieczkowski (2012) showed that specific variables and interactions among variables (e.g., strategy used by the offender to commit the crime and use of a weapon) increase the risk of sexual assault victims experiencing a violent reaction to their resistance. For instance, an offender who brandishes a weapon potentially has a different range of coercive possibilities than does an offender who does not use a weapon (Coker, Walls, and Johnson 1998). Also, if an offender possesses a weapon during the commission of a sexual assault, deciding to use that weapon could be viewed as a much easier solution than physically restraining the victim or using threats to control him or her (Mieczkowski and Beauregard 2010). Last, victims may be more evenly matched to an attacker without a weapon and thus are more likely to physically resist.

D. Attack Location Choice

Similar to the pre-crime phase in which they decide where to hunt for victims, sex offenders also need to choose where they will attack their victims, which is often different from where they have targeted them. Beauregard, Rossmo, et al. (2007) showed that for some offenders, the location was chosen only because the victim was there (as with the rape of an acquaintance), explaining that no situational nor environmental cues were taken into consideration when they decided to attack the victim. Others mentioned that they had no choice but to attack the victim at that particular location because he or she was going to escape or no longer be available (as in the case of the rape of a stranger). However, some offenders were more selective in their choice of attack location. These offenders specifically chose an isolated area (e.g., offender's home) to attack the victim in order to prevent being seen or disturbed by witnesses and to have some time alone with the victim. Ouimet and Proulx (1994) observed that in the case of child molesters, the offender's home appears to be the best possible location to commit an offense because it offers several advantages compared to competing locations (e.g., the child might feel more secure and more willing to participate in sexual contact; see also Leclerc, Beauregard, and Proulx, 2008). Other offenders revealed that their choice of attack location was motivated mainly by places known to be frequented by victims (e.g., red light district for prostitutes) or by the availability/accessibility of the victims. These offenders explained that they engaged in their offending process not only because the victims were there but also because they could have easy access to them.

E. Criminal Mobility

Sometimes offenders need to change locations during the criminal event. For instance, some sex offenders choose to be mobile during the criminal event because they are influenced by the context of crime (e.g., the presence of witnesses). However, other offenders may not be mobile at all because of the situation. For instance, a sex offender overwhelmed by deviant sexual fantasies could decide to sexually assault a victim even if witnesses are present, being unable to assess the potential risks associated with such a decision. The decision to move or change location during the criminal event should be considered a goal-oriented action (Clarke and Cornish 2001). Studies have shown that traveling farther or changing location during the crime was associated with greater rewards (Morselli and Royer 2008) and may also serve the purpose of successfully completing the crime and avoiding detection.

Very few studies have specifically examined the decision of offenders to move during the criminal event. A study of 77 child sex offenders from Australia by Leclerc, Wortley, and Smallbone (2010) provided an alternative to the measure of journey to crime by conceptualizing geographic mobility as the use of multiple locations for the purpose of repetitive sexual contact with the same victim. Specifically, the authors set out to examine whether offending differences existed between perpetrators who used multiple locations for sexual contact and those who used a single location for the entire crime-commission process. Overall, the results demonstrate that mobile offenders are more likely to isolate their victims, use violence, involve the victim in several sexual episodes, abuse the victim for more than a one-year period, and make the victim participate in and perform sexual acts on them during sexual episodes.

In a similar study, Beauregard and Busina (2013) examined situational and MO factors that could influence the criminal mobility of 72 repeat sex offenders, but mobility was defined this time as the number of changes of location during the criminal event (i.e., during encounter, attack, crime, and victim release). Their findings revealed that sex offenders are concerned about the risks of detection present in the situation. Thus, committing a sexual assault when the victim resists entails higher risks of being seen or being interfered with by witnesses or bystanders (Beauregard and Leclerc 2007). This suggests that some sex offenders choose to change location with their victim to find a safe place to commit the crime (e.g., where people will not be able to see or hear anything).

However, when Beauregard and Busina (2013) included the MO used by sex offenders, results demonstrated that the situation was no longer important in explaining criminal mobility patterns. The choices made by these offenders as to how to commit their crime dictate their criminal mobility patterns. For instance, sex offenders who exhibit sophistication in the crime, such as taking various precautions to protect their identity (i.e., forensic awareness) and displaying a greater degree of planning and organization, show greater mobility during the criminal event. However, although sex offenders try to minimize the risks of detection, they also want to maximize the rewards associated with their crime. One way to accomplish this is to move the victim to a location where both actors will be alone. As suggested by Leclerc et al. (2010), being alone with the victim not only reduces risks of interruption or apprehension by a capable guardian but also provides a better opportunity to successfully complete the sexual assault. Thus, sexual assault events involving victim resistance and sexual penetration are more likely to exhibit criminal mobility on the offender's part. Whatever the criminal mobility pattern, Deslauriers-Varin and Beauregard (2013) showed that it was highly inconsistent in a sample of 72 repeat sex offenders, meaning that sex offenders are likely to change their decision to move or not during the event, from one crime to the next. Although all these behaviors related to the crime are important, especially in relation to sex offenders' decision making, very few studies have examined what happens next, as if the criminal event was over. However, sex offenders still need to make important decisions after having committed the crime, whether it be what to do with the victim, how to avoid detection, or, if apprehended, whether to confess or not their crime to the police.

IV. After the Crime

A. Victim Release Location Choice

In the study by Beauregard and Leclerc (2007), sex offenders were asked about what caused the criminal event to end. In almost three out of four cases, the sexual assault was successfully completed before the offender left the crime scene. In some cases, however, the crime was interrupted by the intervention of a witness because the victim was able to scream for help. It was also the case that the victim was able to escape from the offender by her- or himself, again highlighting the importance of situational factors when examining the entire offending process.

Most offenders decided to leave their victims at the crime scene after the sexual assault was completed (Beauregard and Leclerc 2007). Few offenders, however, were careful in their choice of victim release site location. Some offenders took special care to release the victim in a remote area in order to not be associated with the victim or so the victim would not recognize the offender's residence or neighborhood (Beauregard, Rossmo, et al. 2007). Hewitt and colleagues (2012) showed that the victim release site for crimes taking place during the day is less likely to be in a residential area and private site than for those events that occur during the night. Because most people are awake and active during the day, releasing the victim in a residential area during this time may be risky for the offender due to the fact that there is a greater possibility that he will be seen (Brantingham and Brantingham 1984). To avoid apprehension, rapists may be more inclined to release victims during the night. Similarly, victims are more likely to be released at sites that are familiar to the offender if the rape takes place during the day and on the weekend. Because offenders face an increased risk of being apprehended during daylight hours and on the weekend when people are more visible and mobile throughout the environment, sexual offenders will try to minimize their risk by releasing victims in areas where they know it will be safe for them to do so.

However, in some extreme cases, sex offenders end the criminal event by killing their victims. Even when the victim is dead, sex offenders have to make a decision regarding body disposal: leaving the body at the crime scene or moving the body to another location. Again, the decision of whether to move the victim's body is largely influenced by situational factors. A study of 85 sexual murderers from Canada by Beauregard and Field (2008) showed that sexual murderers who had a conflict with the victim within 48 hours prior to the crime were more likely to leave the victim's body at the crime scene. In addition, the findings revealed that older victims are more likely to be left at the crime scene after the murder, whereas younger victims are more readily transportable from the crime scene to the disposal site. Furthermore, they are easier to hide because they are smaller and easier to control. The decision to move the victim's body to a different location is related to precautions taken by some offenders at this stage to avoid detection.

B. Avoiding Detection

It was previously discussed that some offenders, while planning the crime, will adopt certain strategies in order to avoid being detected by the police. Although this is true in the planning stage of the crime, it is also true when the sexual assault is completed. Some sex offenders are conscious that if they do not act, they will be easy to apprehend by the police. In a study that examined the "successful" sex offender, Lussier, Bouchard, and Beauregard (2011) found that in a sample of 373 Canadian sex offenders, those who were more successful at delaying detection had chosen victims (i.e., children) who may not have understood that a crime had been perpetrated against them. Therefore, they were less likely to verbally and physically resist, as well as to disclose the offense to someone. In addition, sex offenders who managed to escape apprehension the longest were the most specialized in sex crimes, suggesting that they possessed the necessary skills and knowledge to complete the crimes. As such, more successful offenders may have opted against using physical violence to increase victim participation, minimize physical resistance, and decrease the risk of the victim reporting the offense (Leclerc et al. 2009). Instead, these offenders may have opted for nonviolent strategies such as manipulation (e.g., gifts and money), deception (e.g., lies and alcohol/drugs), and/or persuasion (e.g., convincing the victim that it is okay for children to have sex with an adult) to force a victim to have sex and to maintain secrecy about it.

Sex offenders do adopt certain strategies to avoid police detection. In cases of sexual homicide, for instance, it has been shown that some offenders consider costs and benefits in targeting certain types of victims (e.g., sex trade workers) and in adopting certain strategies in order to delay body recovery and complicate the police investigation (e.g., concealing the body). In their study of 350 sexual murderers from a national police database, Beauregard and Martineau (2014) found that when sexual murderers choose to conceal the victim's body post murder, it takes longer to recover the victim's body. This does not necessarily mean that the police will never apprehend the offender. However, delaying body recovery increases the chance of forensic evidence being lost and decreases the likelihood of the offender being connected to the crime.

In a related study conducted on the same sample, Balemba, Beauregard, and Martineau (2014) identified characteristics associated with avoiding detection in sexual homicide using latent class analysis. The profile was characterized by the absence of vaginal intercourse and semen, and the offenders typically did not steal items and were the least likely to resort to physically beating, strangling, or mutilating the victims. The authors concluded that these types of crimes involve behavior that is more focused on avoiding apprehension (whether intentionally for that purpose or not) and do not involve behaviors that typically supply investigators with DNA or trace evidence.

V. Decision Making and Criminal Outcome

The studies discussed thus far have clearly shown that sex offenders are reasoning offenders capable of performing, at least to a certain point, a cost–benefit analysis. However, one issue that has been overlooked in the studies on decision making in the field of criminology is whether the offender's decisions are actually related to the "best" or the desired outcome. Bouchard, Beauregard, and Kalacska (2013) noted,

> Offenders may show much deliberation and thinking but still come up short—at least shorter than they could have been if they had made a "better decision." In other words, a rational choice approach should recognize that while most to all offenders show thinking and deliberation prior to offending, not all of them are as successful in their endeavors. (p. 35)

Whereas the relationship between the decisions and the outcomes may appear relatively easy to measure for property crimes (e.g., number and value of items or money stolen), this is very different in sexual crimes. The example of sexual burglary presented at the beginning of the chapter was used to illustrate how the decisions need to be tied to the results. For instance, sexual burglaries were more likely to occur in occupied residences with no male present but with a female victim alone who was unlikely to resist because she was asleep (Pedneault et al. 2015). These findings indicate that not only are sex offenders decision makers but also they consider what it is that they need to achieve when committing the crimes. As mentioned previously, trying to commit a sexual burglary when the victim is absent not only will be unsuccessful but also defeats the purpose as to why the offender wanted to commit the crime in the first place. Although rational choice theorists emphasize that the decisions made by the offender do not need to be "good," it is necessary to increasingly consider the outcomes we think are desired by the offenders when they choose to act a certain way. In doing so, a better understanding of the decision-making process of all types of criminals will be obtained.

Despite the limited number of studies that have examined the issue of decision making and the related outcomes, sex offender research has started to investigate whether the decisions made by the offender during the crime were actually related to a desired outcome. Probably the first study to take into account the outcomes related to decision making in sexual crimes, Hewitt and Beauregard (2014) used both contextual factors and MO strategies to predict whether the rape was completed, the offender forced the victim to commit sexual acts, the offender's reaction to victim resistance, and the level of physical force used on the victim by the offender. Their findings suggested that sex offenders are reasoning offenders who consider costs and benefits. For example, if the offense takes places during the week or outdoors, the rape is less likely to be completed, and this factor might be related to people's routine activities (Cohen and Felson 1979). However, crime events perpetrated by an offender who is forensically aware and uses a coercive strategy during the rape are more likely to be completed. Thus, if the offender has chosen to commit the sexual assault in a location that would reduce his likelihood of identification and/or apprehension while allowing him to spend a greater amount of time with the victim, there is a greater chance that he will achieve his desired outcome. Interestingly, there are certain situations in which offenders are less capable of reasoning due in part to the fact that the context of the offense is more deterministic of the outcome than is the offender and his behavior. Specifically, whether or not the victim is forced to commit sexual acts differs from the other outcome measures in that the offender wants the victim to actively participate in the sexual assault by pleasuring him, but ultimately the victim may decide not to cooperate. Forcing himself on the victim is arguably easier for an offender than to force the victim to perform certain actions.

VI. Conclusion

Despite being a personal crime, sexual assaults are often committed by individuals who are capable of reasoning. Although these decisions may sometimes appear "irrational," the studies reviewed in this chapter reveal that sex offenders make decisions that help them to achieve their goals. Whether or not these goals are rational is a different issue that lies outside this chapter.

The "reasoning" sex offender makes decisions throughout the criminal event, from the early planning stages to the commission of the acts and the strategies to avoid police detection. These findings are important not only for research on decision making but also for research in criminology in general. Too often in our field, sex offenders have been treated differently or have simply been ignored by researchers. However, findings from the sex offender decision-making literature seem to suggest that these offenders may not be very different and may actually think in a similar way as those who perpetrate other types of crimes. Sex offenders are capable of explaining why they selected a specific victim in the same way a burglar can explain why he chose a particular house. Moreover, the studies reviewed in this chapter indicate that sex offenders, similar to other criminals, respond to contingencies. Most studies show that sex offenders are influenced by the contextual factors and the reactions of the victims. Some offenders seem willing to take more risks while simultaneously ignoring the risks already present in the particular situation. However, it is important to mention that most of the research included in this chapter concerns the more serious sex offenders. Sex offenders constitute a very heterogeneous group (Knight and Prentky 1990), and it is crucial to determine whether the findings also apply to different groups of sex offenders, such as juveniles, group offenders, and persons involved in cybersex offending. Also, most of the studies reviewed here are based on a handful of different samples of sex offenders, which could raise issues regarding the generalization of the findings. New samples from different countries will be needed in order to replicate some of these findings. Moreover, it is important to keep in mind that only a minority of sex offenders get caught. There is a real possibility that sex offenders who get caught present characteristics that would make them easier to apprehend by the police (e.g., impulsivity) compared to offenders who are capable of better reasoning, as suggested by the differential detection hypothesis.

Despite these limitations, the findings reviewed in this chapter have some implications for policy. First, based on Pedneault's (2015) study, it seems increasingly more evident that sex offenders do not respond well to the different policies put in place to prevent sexual recidivism. In fact, her findings have shown that despite the costs involved in committing sexual crimes (e.g., incarceration and long sentences), sex offenders will continue offending because of the benefits they get from their offending (e.g., penetration of the victim). Moreover, as attempted to show in this chapter, the different studies on the decision making of sex offenders seem to suggest that they "reason" as other criminals, such as burglars and robbers. Therefore, the notion that sex offenders require specific legislation to control them (e.g., residence restriction and community notification) needs to be revisited.

Second, the different findings reviewed in this chapter suggest that sex offenders generally react to the immediate costs and benefits related to the crime and not so much to the more distant costs such as incarceration. It is thus important to develop ways to make the commission of sexual assault less attractive and more difficult to complete, as suggested by Cohen and Felson (1979). Although situational crime prevention may represent an interesting avenue to accomplish such a task, Pedneault (2015) advocates for the adoption of a public health approach to prevention, which focuses on the "time–person–place" dimensions. One specific way that the public health model of prevention can help increase the costs associated with sexual offending is by increasing guardianship—making the potential victims, parents, or others with supervisor roles, as well as place managers, more aware and provide them with education and different means to detect and increase surveillance in different settings.

Future studies need to continue investigating the decision making of sex offenders. To do so, one area of study that clearly deserves more attention is the relationship between the characteristics of the sex offenders and their decision-making process. It is important to assess how personality characteristics (e.g., low self-control), or even experience and knowledge, may impact the evaluation of the situation and the choices that are offered to the offender. Pedneault (2015) showed that impulsivity as well as psychopathy influence sex offenders' decision making both during the crime and when contemplating the decision to continue or desist from offending. Moreover, it is suggested that researchers take the time to ask offenders about the real "why"—not why did they commit the crime, but why did they do it the way they did. Another promising avenue for research on the decision making of sex offenders would be to conduct experimental studies such as those conducted by Bouffard and colleagues as well as Ariely and colleagues on sex offender populations. Despite the challenges involved in conducting such research in prison settings, it would significantly increase our understanding of the decision making of sex offenders and improve the different methods used to prevent such crimes. Only then will we have a true picture of the *reasoning* sex offender decision-making process.

REFERENCES

Ariely, D. 2008. *Predictably Irrational: The Hidden Forces That Shape Our Decisions.* New York: HarperCollins.

Ariely, D., and G. Loewenstein. 2006. "The Heat of the Moment: The Effect of Sexual Arousal on Sexual Decision Making." *Journal of Behavioral Decision Making* 19(2): 87–98.

Bachman, R., R. Paternoster, and S. Ward. 1992. "The Rationality of Sexual Offending: Testing a Deterrence/Rational Choice Conception of Sexual Assault." *Law and Society Review* 26:343–72.

Balemba, S., and E. Beauregard. 2012. "Reactions to Resistance: The Role of Contextual Factors on Sex Offending." *Violence and Victims* 27:148–65.

Balemba, S., E. Beauregard, and M. Martineau. 2014. "Getting Away with Murder: A Thematic Approach to Solved and Unsolved Sexual Homicide Using Crime Scene Factors." *Police Practice and Research* 15:221–33.

Balemba, S., E. Beauregard, and T. Mieczkowski. 2012. "To Resist or Not to Resist? The Effect of Context and Crime Characteristics on Sex Offenders' Reaction to Victim Resistance." *Crime and Delinquency* 58:588–611.

Beauregard, E., and M. Bouchard. 2010. "Cleaning Up Your Act: Forensic Awareness as a Detection Avoidance Strategy." *Journal of Criminal Justice* 38:1160–66.

Beauregard, E., and I. Busina. 2013. "Journey 'During' Crime: Predicting Criminal Mobility Patterns in Sexual Assaults." *Journal of Interpersonal Violence* 28:2052–67.

Beauregard, E., and J. Field. 2008. "Body Disposal Patterns of Sexual Murderers: Implications for Offender Profiling." *Journal of Police and Criminal Psychology* 23:81–89.

Beauregard, E., and B. Leclerc. 2007. "An Application of the Rational Choice Approach to the Offending Process of Sex Offenders: A Closer Look at the Decision-Making." *Sexual Abuse* 19:115–33.

Beauregard, E., P. Lussier, and J. Proulx. 2005. "The Role of Sexual Interests and Situational Factors on Rapists' Modus Operandi: Implications for Offender Profiling." *Legal and Criminological Psychology* 10:265–78.

Beauregard, E., and M. Martineau. 2012. "A Descriptive Study of Sexual Homicide in Canada: Implications for Police Investigation." *International Journal of Offender Therapy and Comparative Criminology* 57:1454–76.

Beauregard, E., and M. Martineau. 2014. "No Body, No Crime? The Role of Forensic Awareness in Avoiding Police Detection in Cases of Sexual Homicide." *Journal of Criminal Justice* 42:213–20.

Beauregard, E., J. Proulx, K. Rossmo, B. Leclerc, and J.-F. Allaire. 2007. "Script Analysis of Hunting Process in Serial Sex Offenders." *Criminal Justice and Behavior* 34:1069–84.

Beauregard, E., M. F. Rebocho, and K. Rossmo. 2010. "Target Selection Patterns in Rape." *Journal of Investigative Psychology and Offender Profiling* 7:137–52.

Beauregard, E., K. Rossmo, and J. Proulx. 2007. "A Descriptive Model of the Hunting Process of Serial Sex Offenders: A Rational Choice Approach." *Journal of Family Violence* 22:449–63.

Bennett, T., and R. Wright. 1984. *Burglars on Burglary: Prevention and the Offender.* Aldershot, UK: Gower.

Berliner, L., and J. R. Conte. 1990. "The Process of Victimization: The Victim's Perspective." *Child Abuse and Neglect* 14:29–40.

Block, R. 1981. "Victim–Offender Dynamics in Violent Crime." *Journal of Criminal Law and Criminology* 72(2): 743–61.

Bouchard, M., E. Beauregard, and M. Kalacska. 2013. "Journey to Grow: Linking Process to Outcome in Target Site Selection for Cannabis Cultivation." *Journal of Research in Crime and Delinquency* 50(1): 33–52.

Bouffard, J. 2011. "'In the Heat of the Moment': Mediating Versus Moderating Relationships Between Sexual Arousal and Perceived Sanctions." *Journal of Crime and Justice* 34(1): 24–44.

Brantingham, P. J., and P. L. Brantingham. 1984. *Patterns in Crime.* New York: Macmillan.

Carmichael, S., and A. R. Piquero. 2004. "Sanctions, Perceived Anger, and Criminal Offending." *Journal of Quantitative Criminology* 20(4): 371–93.

Carroll, J., and F. Weaver. 1986. "Shoplifters' Perceptions of Crime Opportunities: A Process-Tracing Study." In *The Reasoning Criminal: Rational Choice Perspectives on Offending*, edited by D. B. Cornish and R. V. Clarke, pp. 19–38. New York: Springer-Verlag.

Cherbonneau, M., and H. Copes. 2006. "'Drive It Like You Stole It': Auto Theft and the Illusion of Normalcy." *British Journal of Criminology* 46:193–211.

Clarke, R. V., and D. B. Cornish. 2001. "Rational Choice." In *Explaining Criminals and Crime: Essays in Contemporary Criminological Theory*, edited by R. Paternoster and R. Bachman, pp. 23–42. Oxford: Oxford University Press.

Cohen, L., and M. Felson. 1979. "Social Change and Crime Rate Trends: A Routine Activity Approach." *American Sociological Reviews* 44:588–608.

Coker, A. L., L. G. Walls, and J. E. Johnson. 1998. "Risk Factors for Traumatic Physical Injury During Sexual Assaults for Male and Female Victims." *Journal of Interpersonal Violence* 13(5): 605–20.

Cornish, D. B. 1994. "Crime as Scripts." In *Proceedings of the International Seminar on Environmental Criminology and Crime Analysis, University of Miami, Coral Gables, Florida, 1993*, edited by D. Zahm and P. Cromwell. Tallahassee: Florida Statistical Analysis Center, Florida Criminal Justice Executive Institute, Florida Department of Law Enforcement.

Cornish, D., and R. V. Clarke. 1986. "Introduction." In *The Reasoning Criminal*, edited by D. Cornish and R. V. Clarke, pp. 1–16. New York: Springer-Verlag.

Cornish, D. B., and R. V. Clarke. 1987. "Understanding Crime Displacement: An Application of Rational Choice Theory." *Criminology* 25:901–16.

Coupe, T., and L. Blake. 2006. "Daylight and Darkness Targeting Strategies and the Risks of Being Seen at Residential Burglaries." *Criminology* 44:431–64.

Cromwell, P., J. Olson, and D. A. W. Avary. 1991. *Breaking and Entering: An Ethnographic Analysis of Burglary*. Newbury Park, CA: Sage.

Davies, A. 1992. "Rapists' Behaviour: A Three Aspect Model as a Basis for Analysis and the Identification of Serial Crime." *Forensic Science International* 55:173–94.

Davies, A., K. Wittebrood, and J. L. Jackson. 1997. "Predicting the Criminal Antecedents of a Stranger Rapist from His Offence Behaviour." *Science and Justice* 37:161–70.

Deslauriers-Varin, N., and E. Beauregard. 2010. "Victims' Routine Activities and Sex Offenders' Target Selection Scripts: A Latent Class Analysis." *Sexual Abuse* 22:315–42.

Deslauriers-Varin, N., and E. Beauregard. 2013. "Investigating Offending Consistency of Geographic and Environmental Factors Among Serial Sex Offenders: A Comparison of Multiple Analytical Strategies." *Criminal Justice and Behavior* 40:156–79.

Goldstein, S. L. 1999. *The Sexual Exploitation of Children: A Practical Guide of Assessment, Investigation and Intervention*. Boca Raton, FL: CRC Press.

Hewitt, A., and E. Beauregard. 2014. "Sexual Crime and Place: The Impact of Environmental Context on Sexual Assault Outcomes." *Journal of Criminal Justice* 42:375–83.

Hewitt, A., E. Beauregard, and G. Davies. 2012. "'Catch and Release': Predicting Encounter and Victim Release Location Choice in Serial Rape Events." *Policing* 35:835–56.

Hudson, S. M., T. Ward, and J. C. McCormack. 1999. "Offense Pathways in Sexual Offenders." *Journal of Interpersonal Violence* 14:779–98.

Knight, R. A., and R. A. Prentky. 1990. "Classifying Sexual Offenders: The Development and Corroboration of Taxonomic Models." In *Handbook of Sexual Assault: Issues, Theories and Treatment of the Offender*, edited by W. L. Marshall, D. R. Laws, and H. E. Barbaree, pp. 23–54. New York: Plenum.

Leclerc, B., E. Beauregard, and J. Proulx. 2008. "Modus Operandi and Situational Aspects in Adolescent Sexual Offenses Against Children." *International Journal of Offender Therapy and Comparative Criminology* 52:46–61.

Leclerc, B., J. Proulx, P. Lussier, and J.-F. Allaire. 2009. "Offender–Victim Interaction and Crime Event Outcomes: Modus Operandi and Victim Effects on the Risk of Intrusive Sexual Offenses Against Children." *Criminology* 47:595–618.

Leclerc, B., J. Proulx, and A. McKibben. 2005. "Modus Operandi of Sexual Offenders Working or Doing Voluntary Work with Children and Adolescents." *Journal of Sexual Aggression* 11:187–95.

Leclerc, B., R. Wortley, and S. Smallbone. 2010. "Investigating Mobility Patterns for Repetitive Sexual Contact in Adult Child Sex Offending." *Journal of Criminal Justice* 38:648–56.

Leclerc, B., R. Wortley, and S. Smallbone. 2011. "Getting into the Script of Adult Child Sex Offenders and Mapping out Situational Prevention Measures." *Journal of Research in Crime and Delinquency* 48:209–37.

Leclerc, B., and P. Tremblay. 2007. "Strategic Behavior in Adolescent Sexual Offenses Against Children: Linking Modus Operandi to Sexual Behaviors." *Sexual Abuse* 19:23–41.

Loewenstein, G., D. S. Nagin, and R. Paternoster. 1997. "The Effect of Sexual Arousal on Expectations of Sexual Forcefulness." *Journal of Research in Crime and Delinquency* 34(4): 443–73.

Loughran, T. A., R. Paternoster, A. R. Piquero, and G. Pogarsky. 2011. "On Ambiguity in Perceptions of Risk: Implications for Criminal Decision Making and Deterrence." *Criminology* 49(4): 1029–61.

Lussier, P. 2005. "The Criminal Activity of Sexual Offenders in Adulthood: Revisiting the Specialization Debate." *Sexual Abuse* 17:269–92.

Lussier, P., M. Bouchard, and E. Beauregard. 2011. "Patterns in Criminal Achievement in Sexual Offending: Unravelling the Successful Sex Offender." *Journal of Criminal Justice* 39:433–44.

Lussier, P., M. Leblanc, and J. Proulx. 2005. "The Generality of Criminal Behavior: A Confirmatory Factor Analysis of the Criminal Activity of Sex Offenders in Adulthood." *Journal of Criminal Justice* 33:177–89.

Lussier, P., and J. Healey. 2009. "Rediscovering Quetelet, Again: The 'Aging' Offender and the Prediction of Reoffending in a Sample of Adult Sex Offenders." *Justice Quarterly* 26: 827–56.

Lussier, P., J. Proulx, and M. Leblanc. 2005. "Criminal Propensity, Deviant Sexual Interests and Criminal Activity of Sexual Aggressors Against Women: A Comparison of Explanatory Models." *Criminology* 43:249–81.

Morselli, C., and M.-N. Royer. 2008. "Criminal Mobility and Criminal Achievement." *Journal of Research in Crime and Delinquency* 45:4–21.

Mieczkowski, T., and E. Beauregard. 2010. "Lethal Outcome in Sexual Assault Events: A Conjunctive Analysis." *Justice Quarterly* 27:332–61.

Nee, C., and A. Meenaghan. 2006. "Expert Decision Making in Burglars." *British Journal of Criminology* 46:935–49.

Ouimet, M. and J. Proulx. 1994. "Spatial and Temporal Behavior of Pedophiles: Their Clinical Usefulness as to the Relapse Prevention Model." Paper presented at the Meeting of the American Society of Criminology, Miami, Florida.

Pedneault, A. 2015. "An Analysis of Decision Making and Criminal Outcomes in Sexual Offenders." Unpublished doctoral dissertation, Simon Fraser University, Burnaby, Canada.

Pedneault, A., and E. Beauregard. 2014. "Routine Activities and Time Use: A Latent Profile Approach to Sexual Offenders' Lifestyle." *Sexual Abuse* 26:34–57.

Pedneault, A., E. Beauregard, D. A. Harris, and R. A. Knight. 2015. "Rationally Irrational: The Case of Sexual Burglary." *Sexual Abuse* 27(4): 376–97.

Proulx, J., and E. Beauregard. 2009. "Decision Making During the Offending Process: An Assessment Among Subtypes of Sexual Aggressors of Women." In *Assessment and Treatment of Sex Offenders: A Handbook*, edited by A. R. Beech, L. A. Craig, and K. D. Brown, pp. 181–99. Winchester, UK: Wiley.

Proulx, J., E. Beauregard, P. Lussier, and B. Leclerc. 2014. *Pathways to Sexual Aggression*. Abingdon, UK: Routledge.

Proulx, J., A. McKibben, and R. Lusignan. 1996. "Relationships Between Affective Components and Sexual Behaviors in Sexual Aggressors." *Sexual Abuse* 8:279–89.

Rossmo, K. 2000. *Geographic Profiling*. Boca Raton, FL: CRC Press.

Simon, L. M. J. 2000. "An Examination of the Assumptions of Specialization, Mental Disorder, and Dangerousness in Sex Offenders." *Behavioral Sciences and the Law* 18:275–308.

Simon, L. M. J., and K. Zgoba. 2006. "Sex Crimes Against Children: Legislation, Prevention and Investigation." In *Situational Prevention of Child Sexual Abuse,* edited by R. Wortley and S. Smallbone. *Crime Prevention Studies,* vol. 19, pp. 65–100. Monsey, NY: Criminal Justice Press.

Smallbone, S., and R. Wortley. 2000. "Child Sexual Abuse in Queensland: Offender Characteristics and Modus Operandi." Full report. Queensland Crime Commission, Brisbane, Australia.

Ullman, S. E. 1998. "Does Offender Violence Escalate When Rape Victims Fight Back?" *Journal of Interpersonal Violence* 13(2): 179–92.

van Gelder, J.-L. 2013. "Beyond Rational Choice: The Hot/Cool Perspective of Criminal Decision Making." *Psychology, Crime, and Law* 19:745–63.

Warr, M. 1988. "Rape, Burglary, and Opportunity." *Journal of Quantitative Criminology* 4: 275–88.

Wortley, R., and S. Smallbone. 2006. "Applying Situational Principles to Sexual Offenses Against Children." In *Situational Prevention of Child Sexual Abuse*, edited by R. Wortley and S. Smallbone, pp. 7–35. *Crime Prevention Studies*, vol. 19. Monsey, NY: Criminal Justice Press.

Wright, R., and S. Decker. 1997. *Armed Robbers in Action: Stickups and Street Culture*. Boston: Northeastern University Press.

CHAPTER 31

....

BURGLARY DECISIONS

....

TIMOTHY COUPE

BURGLARS make decisions leading up to, during, and following the criminal event. They also make decisions about the frequency of burglary commission, the start and finish of their burglary careers, and, for some, whether they commit burglary or other offenses. The emphasis in this chapter is on event decisions, of which the most important concerns target selection, which shapes as well as reflects the journey to crime, access to premises, and goods thought to be available to steal. There are also decisions about whether or not to commit the offense alone or with others, premises entry and exit points, when to undertake the burglary, how many rooms to visit, how long to stay at the scene, and how to dispose of stolen property. Outcomes of burglary decisions include event and target characteristics; offender sightings and arrests; and effects on victims, including loss of well-being, property loss, and damage to premises. These characteristics enable inferences to be drawn about the types of property offenders decide to burgle and where and when this occurs. They provide behavioral evidence from which the principal factors affecting decisions may be better understood and the different theories evaluated. These are considered selectively, only insofar as they improve understanding of burglars' decisions. The success of burglary decisions may be judged on the basis of gains made from the crime and whether burglars are able to avoid being seen and arrested.

Knowledge of the decisions involved in burglary commission relies on two types of study. In the first type, inferences may be drawn about decisions from targeting patterns and target characteristics. The other type uses evidence from interviews and experimental research with imprisoned offenders and, less commonly, active burglars on target preferences, target selection processes, and decisions made at burglary scenes. Offender studies enable valuable insights into decision processes, but due to low burglary arrest rates, findings about their relative importance are less certain. Equally, although studies of target or event characteristics can help establish the importance of different types of burglar behavior, there are limits on the inferences about target search and selection decisions and processes that may be drawn from them. By linking findings from different types of studies, this chapter presents a coherent portrayal of burglary decisions.

The chapter reviews evidence on burglar decision making and the burglary characteristics that provide insight into decisions; highlights gaps in knowledge, methodologies, and aspects of theory; and discusses potential avenues for additional research. The chapter is ordered to consider key theories; targeting strategies and selection decisions; decisions at the scene relating to entering, while inside, and leaving premises; decisions about which goods to steal and their disposal; and the evaluation of successful and unsuccessful decisions. The extent to which different theories help explain key decisions is critically assessed.

I. Theories and Burglary Decisions

Rational choice theory (Becker 1968; Cornish and Clarke 1986) and routine activity theory (Cohen and Felson 1979) and its extension to opportunity theory (Cohen, Kluegel, and Land 1981) are the criminal event theories that have been most commonly used to explain and predict burglary decisions, actions, and outcomes. Other important theories and concepts relevant to decisions about burglary target search strategy are the burglar's activity and awareness space; the two-stage and three-stage, hierarchical target selection models; the "optimal foraging" search model; and concepts associated with near-repeat and repeat burglary.

A. Rational Choice Theory

The rational choice approach is focused on decisions made at the point of action in response to varying opportunities (Cornish and Clarke 1986). It assumes offenders are in a state of readiness with "standing decisions" to undertake particular offenses (Wikstrom and Treiber 2016). Self-interest is the principal motivation, with rules and moral issues being dealt with prior to the event decision. Like routine activity theory applications, it is less concerned with different sorts of offenders (Wikstrom and Treiber 2016), although targeting decisions for aggravated burglary and those involving theft or excitement would involve marked contrasts in target circumstances and offender propensities, motives, and behavior. Even for burglary decisions driven by material gain, different offenders would place different values on benefits and costs.

Applications of rational choice theory search for whatever rationality exists (Wortley 2012), even though event decisions may reflect automatic procedures (Wright and Decker 1994) or habitual decisions guided by rules reflecting biases as well as rational and reflective thought processes (Wikstrom and Treiber 2016). Other theoretical perspectives point to a mixture of rational and other mental processes on criminal decisions. Heuristics are mental shortcuts that use limited facets of complex decisions and involve cognitive biases as well as rational consideration (Kahneman and Tversky 1979), which may help describe burglars' decisions. Risk and gain cues at burglary events would be rapidly assessed to provide "instinctive" decisions and actions. Equally, "cool" cognitive evaluation of costs and benefits combines with "hot" feelings to influence criminal decisions (van Gelder 2013; van Gelder and de Vries 2014), improving explanations of criminal behavior based solely on rational consideration. Both cognitive biases and irrational feelings, as well as rational consideration, are likely to play a role in burglary decisions, deployed in an "automatic" way (Nee and Taylor 2000; Wortley 2012; Leclerc and Wortley 2014), drawing on experience of past burglaries. Situational action theory goes further in viewing the offender as rule-guided, with habitual influences rather than rational deliberation dominating decision making (Wikstrom and Treiber 2016). The balance of rational deliberation and deviation from it due to cognitive bias, "hot" feelings, and habitual rules in burglary decisions is likely to depend on offender characteristics and environmental circumstances while on burglary journeys.

B. Routine Activity Theory

Routine activity theory describes the necessary conditions that create burglary opportunities to which burglars would implicitly respond with decisions and actions (Cohen and Felson 1979). Its key concepts—guardianship, motivated offender, and suitable target—are not precisely specified (Wikstrom and Trieber 2016), nor is the decision process made explicit (Felson 2008). Few, if any, studies examining burglary decisions, actions, or outcomes have measured all three routine activity concepts and systematically linked offender characteristics and incident circumstances, so there has been no complete test of the theory (Akers and Sellers 2009). Routine activity theory has been subsequently formalized as "opportunity theory" (Cohen et al. 1981), which involves the concepts of guardianship, target exposure, offender proximity, and target attractiveness and incorporates rational choice and crime pattern theory (Felson and Clarke 1998).

Marked differences in the operational measures used to measure routine activity concepts are liable to result in inconsistent findings. In burglary studies, there is reliance on using distances between offenders' homes and targets to measure the motivated offender concept. Equally, measures of guardianship are often limited to premises occupancy, although some studies include measures of neighbor and passer-by guardianship. The definition and measurement of guardianship objects, such as alarms, closed-circuit TV (CCTV), locks, and security lighting, also tend to differ.

Other differences in operational measures reflect data constraints as in studies reliant on secondary census data or national household surveys, which are not designed to specifically evaluate burglary theories or decisions. These rarely take account of, for instance, vegetative cover and building disposition—factors that control intervisibility between targets and neighbors and passers-by and that modify guardianship effectiveness (Coupe and Fox 2015). Equally, samples not tailored to burglary study rarely contain data on the nature, weight, or value of stolen goods or occupancy at the time of burglary. With census data aggregated by area, indicators such as dwelling size or age, number of occupants, or the socioeconomic status of people in an area can be used instead. These can be ambiguous, with house size, for instance, indicating value of goods to steal as well as guardianship.

C. Discussion

Routine activity and rational choice theory view deterrent factors as preventing burglary events by exerting controls that affect the choice process by creating fear of consequences. Guardianship stems from heightened risk of being seen during the event. In routine activity theory (Cohen and Felson 1979), the decision process is implied and is aligned with that of rational choice theory, involving benefits and costs. Benefits most often involve stolen property, and costs reflect sighting risks, liable to result in arrest and punishment. Perceived risks deter and reduce burglary odds. Risk-averse burglars may avoid higher risk situations, despite the promise of additional gains, although more skillful and experienced offenders may deal with riskier situations in a way that enables them to avoid capture.

D. "Awareness Space" and "activity space"

The domain of "candidate" areas in which burglars decide to search for targets may be conceptualized as being delineated by their cognitively known "awareness space" (P. L. Brantingham and Brantingham 1984). This is the spatial area with which burglars are familiar, and it is delineated by offenders' activity patterns and travel that connect activity nodes (Morgan 2000), such as offenders' homes, friends' homes, shopping centers, public houses, workplaces, and schools. Burglary activities extend awareness space. Burglary incidence should be highest in neighborhoods in which awareness space coincides with burglary opportunities (P. L. Brantingham and Brantingham 1984).

Awareness and activity space depend on burglar mobility, being smaller for those without their own transport. Every burglary selection strategy is limited by offender mobility and shaped by awareness space. Journeys to crime connect burglars' activity nodes with targets (Morgan 2000). The limits of the most distant journeys define the boundary of each burglar's activity space, and temporospatial journey frequencies reveal preferred target areas and times.

E. Target Search Models

Target search models attempt to explain burglary journeys, targeting strategy, and target choice. They do not help explain decisions and behavior for planned burglaries because these do not involve active real-time searching to evaluate different areas or compare candidate properties. Their choice may be informed by searches on previous burglary trips or by other criminal or noncriminal activities, and they may involve mental evaluation that mirrors active searching. Burglary search models fit with and complement routine activity, opportunity, and rational choice theories. They describe how burglars locate the targets whose selection depends on factors identified in criminal event theories and define the geographical areas in which burglars operate.

Burglary targeting has been described both as a *two-stage, hierarchical process*, with burglars first selecting a neighborhood and then deciding to burgle a particular premises (P. J. Brantingham and Brantingham 1991; P. L. Brantingham and Brantingham 1984, 1995), and as a *three-stage model*, with sequenced evaluation of neighborhood, street, and then the property (Bennett and Wright 1984). These models imply that consideration of alternative areas, streets, and specific target premises in terms of rewards, risks, and effort in order to identify a suitable target is a critical part of the decision-making process.

Search strategies have been conceived as a process of *optimal foraging*, or hunting for suitable targets with superior gains at minimum inconvenience, effort, and risk (Bernasco 2003; Johnson and Bowers 2004). *Near-repeat burglaries*, occurring close to and soon after initial incidents, often involve the same type and layout of dwelling, often on the same street. These improve target and crime journey familiarity, reduce unpredictability, and minimize search effort, and they may be viewed as an example of optimal foraging.

Repeat burglary is a burglary at a property that has been previously burgled, particularly if it occurs within six months to one year after the first incident. It capitalizes on prior knowledge to minimize effort, but it does not involve searching. To the extent that they involve the same offenders returning, repeat burglary decisions are likely to reflect "event dependency" (Johnson, Summers, and Pease 2009), whereby knowledge of premises, neighbors, means of entering and exiting, and goods to be stolen enables a more precise appreciation of risks and likely gains. This "boosts" the odds of repeat targeting decisions. Repeat target selection may also reflect low risks at properties that help "flag" (Tseloni and Pease 2003) and explain initial and further victimization (Tseloni and Pease 2004).

The usefulness of these theories and models for explaining burglary decisions is critically evaluated, selectively, in the following sections.

II. Principal Target Selection Strategies

This section considers burglars' activity and awareness space and trip decisions; search strategies, specifically methodological critique, an evaluation of target search and planning evidence, the two-stage and three-stage hierarchical models, and the optimal foraging process; "acquaintance" and "stranger" burglaries; and near-repeat and repeat targeting decisions. In addition, decisions with regard to burglary timing and burgled areas are examined.

A. Awareness Space, Activity Space, and Burglary Journeys

Every burglary selection strategy is limited by offender mobility, which controls awareness and activity space size. As a result, the quantity of targets and areas in which burglaries are committed are related to accessibility and proximity to offenders' homes (Bernasco 2003; Townsley et al. 2015). Burglars younger than legal driving age are less mobile, have smaller awareness space, and make shorter burglary journeys compared to adults in England (Wright, 2013) and young adults in Canada, where travel distances decrease after burglars reach their thirties (Andersen et al. 2014). Activity space is also modified by offenders' residential histories, co-offending decisions, physical barriers, and connectors such as public transport routes (Reynald et al. 2008; Clare, Fernandez, and Morgan 2009).

Co-offending also modifies targeting strategy decisions (Bernasco 2006) by pooling the awareness spaces of a number of burglars. Co-offenders' combined knowledge enlarges the number of "candidate" neighborhoods and potential targets and increases the ethnicity, age, offending skills, and experience factors affecting targeting decisions to an extent that matches the differences between co-offenders. Most burglars decide to co-offend at some time (Reiss 1988), even if burglar populations have fewer co-offenders. Little more than one-third of UK residential burglars, for instance, are co-offenders (Budd 1999). Because co-offenders tend to be younger (Carrington 2009; van Mastrigt and Farrington 2009), a wider pool of candidate target areas of the types favored by youthful burglars is likely to be considered compared to that considered by a lone burglar of similar age, reliant on only his or her own territorial knowledge.

B. Journey to Burglary Decisions

The combination of burglars' targeting decisions describes a density decay of burglary with increasing distance from their homes so that short crime journeys, within two miles of offenders' homes, predominate (P. L. Brantingham and Brantingham 1984; Rengert, Piquero, and Jones 1999; Sorensen 2005). For every additional kilometer from the offender's home, the probability of a burglary decreases by 26 percent in The Hague, the Netherlands (Bernasco 2009). This is partly due to accessibility and mobility constraints. It also reflects decisions to remain in familiar areas (P. J. Brantingham and Brantingham 1991), a supply of sufficiently attractive targets (Townsley et al. 2015), avoidance of risks of traveling farther (P. J. Brantingham and Brantingham 1991), and effort minimization (Zipf 1949)—factors indicative of optimal foraging. It may also reflect ethnic characteristics, which may deter offending in areas where the ethnic status of residents differs from that of the burglar (Pettiway 1982; Reynald et al. 2008). Longer trips are made by offenders who burgle near former homes (Bernasco 2010) or in co-offenders' neighborhoods and also by older burglars (Nichols 1980; Rengert et al. 1999) and others with their own transportation.

C. Burglar "Buffer Zones"

Many burglars avoid areas where they can be easily recognized. There are "buffer zones" of low burglary incidence close to offenders' homes where recognition risks raise guardianship effectiveness (Rengert et al. 1999; Sorensen 2005). There are exceptions. The limited physical extent of villages and small towns eliminates "buffer zones" close to the homes of "low-mobility" resident offenders. Rural burglars without transportation often commit burglaries in their own villages and towns due to difficulties of traveling elsewhere, and these settlements can be encapsulated within the buffer zones of burglars on foot. Offenders from the same village commit almost half of remote village burglaries (Shapland and Vagg 1985). Burglary also occurs in buffer zones in high-density central city neighborhoods with apartments (Sorensen 2005), where greater anonymity and lower local recognition are likely to weaken guardianship and encourage burglary of immediate neighbors.

D. Burglary Search Strategies

Offender studies question burglars less about search models than about the selection and evaluation of specific target properties, but they do establish whether burglars search, plan, or are opportunist. Temporospatial relationships between burglaries, particularly those involving near-repeat and repeat burglaries, and other characteristics provide further insights into search strategies.

Offender studies are indispensable to understanding burglary decisions, including search processes, but findings about their relative importance are less certain, even when a number of studies are in agreement. This is because few burglaries are solved, with only 13 or 14 percent of cases cleared, respectively, in England and Wales (Taylor and Bond 2012) and the United States (FBI 2011). Therefore, inferences about unsolved offenses must be drawn from offender responses relating to solved offenses, whose decisions may differ from those of offenders who are not arrested or charged. For example, convicted burglars tend to be more prolific (Ahlberg and Knutsson 1990) and less geographically mobile (Lammers and Bernasco 2013), and many are young co-offenders (Coupe and Blake 2006) likely to be less skillful. Studies of burglary characteristics provide information on areas, properties, stolen property, crime trips, and offender numbers, but they provide only circumstantial evidence about planning and search decisions. No studies with large, representative samples combine the two approaches, systematically linking offenders' statements about burglary decisions to specific burglaries so as to reveal how offender characteristics, decisions, and attitudes about risk and gain fit with empirical targeting outcomes and characteristics of the burglary event, property, and its environment. Evidence from both types of studies is used to present a balanced portrayal of targeting decisions.

E. Searching, Planning, and Evaluating Hierarchical Models

Actively searching and evaluating the built environment on burglary trips to identify a suitable neighborhood is likely to be exercised selectively according to the type of burglary and the burglar's expertise, knowledge, and motivation. A neighborhood search would occur if burglars had recently moved to an unfamiliar area, just started burglary offending, or were evaluating newly built property. In addition, more mobile burglars and those who use a vehicle or use one for the first time may occasionally extend their activity spaces. This includes older burglars who commit rural burglary and who travel large distances from towns and cities or other rural districts (Wright 2013). "Car key" (Carden 2012) and distraction burglars (Pearson 2012) also search over wide areas. Car key burglary is breaking into properties in order to steal car keys and cars, whereas distraction burglars gain entry to dwellings by deceiving incapable guardians, particularly the elderly. In these cases, searching appears to fit hierarchical decision steps: searching for promising neighborhoods, locating suitable streets or estates, and then identifying dwellings with the right types of cars in the driveways or properties with telltale cues to aged and vulnerable occupants, including handrails for impaired locomotion or public-sector elderly persons' bungalows.

On the other hand, many burglars will be experienced and know their activity spaces well, given lengthier burglary careers that, for instance, span an average of 10 years in Adelaide, Australia (Killmier 2014). By drawing on accumulated knowledge, they can aim directly for a street, a row of houses, or an estate (Nee and Taylor 2000; Nee and Meenaghan 2006), eliminating neighborhood searching. Exploration of new neighborhoods is not common, and unpromising areas in terms of risks and gains are screened out (P. L. Brantingham and Brantingham 1984; Cromwell, Olson, and Avery 1991; Rengert and Wasilchick 2000), especially if offenders have been disturbed at the scene or nearly caught there on previous trips. Most burglars routinely scan environments for suitable targets or undertake "scouting" trips to identify promising targets, "casing" potential properties while going about their daily business in advance of crimes (Bennett and Wright 1984; Shover 1991; Wright and Decker 1994). Some burglars decide to burgle properties they notice while traveling between activity nodes, such as home, school, or work (Cromwell et al. 1991; Rengert and Wasilchick 2000). This helps maintain up-to-date targeting knowledge and reduces active searching on burglary journeys.

Burglars who plan to target specific properties before setting out to burgle perform little active searching on the crime trip itself unless circumstances at the scene frustrate intentions and alternative targets are sought (Bennett and Wright 1984; Wright and Decker 1994). "Planners" are likely to include some repeat burglars; those targeting the homes of friends, acquaintances, and family (Budd 1999); or employees and prior employees and their partners targeting nonresidential workplaces.

Offender studies classify most dwelling burglars as "searchers" and few as opportunists, making "on the spot" targeting decisions, or planners who set out with a specific target in mind (Bennett and Wright 1984; Cromwell et al. 1991; Nee and Taylor 2000). It is possible that arrestee samples may undervalue the importance of planners because two-thirds of Wright and Decker's (1994) active burglars were identified as planners who had in mind, when setting out, a single target they had been previously watching. However, the representativeness of their "snowball" sample compiled using referral recruitment is unknown (Wright and Decker 1994). Although not planning trips to individual targets, many burglars plan to start their search at specific streets or street segments (Nee and Taylor 2000; Nee and Meenaghan 2006), where burglaries may be committed.

Equating to hierarchical models' later stages, on arrival in an area, estate, or street, burglars use "optimal foraging" to search for and evaluate potential burglary targets, seeking those with superior gains for lower risk and effort (Bernasco 2003; Johnson et al. 2009). Journeys to planned single burglaries that were successfully implemented would not involve local search. Burglary trips with a target or alternative targets in mind may sometimes be modified by opportunities en route (Elffers et al. 2008). Also, immediate circumstances on arrival at the scene of planned targets that prove too risky or result in failure to gain entry and steal property may cause burglars to search for alternatives. Final selected targets are often different from the ones initially considered (Palmer, Holmes, and Hollin 2002; Hearnden and Magill 2004).

The fact that offenders often know victims—for instance, offenders know their victims in half of domestic burglaries in England and Wales (Budd 1999)—indicates that extensive target search is unlikely to be undertaken at many burglaries. This includes "acquaintance burglary" incidents that involve personal or family matters (Maguire and Bennett 1982; Wright and Decker 1994) involving anger, dispute, and revenge (Ericsson 1995; Killmier 2014). These offenders focus on particular known targets, which are more likely to be in home neighborhoods or properties where friends and family live. Therefore, more "stranger" burglaries than "acquaintance" burglaries may result from search processes that align with elements of hierarchical models, whereas fewer stranger burglaries may occur in "buffer zones" close to burglars' current and former homes.

F. Near-Repeat and Repeat Burglary Decisions and Targeting Strategies

Subsequent activities differ once a burglary has occurred on a particular street. Some burglars target a single property but then decide to switch to another street or neighborhood on subsequent burglary trips. In contrast, others return, generally within three months but more often sooner, to selectively repeat burgle properties. Yet others commit near-repeat burglaries at properties close to the initial target, especially within five to ten dwellings of it on the same street (Everson and Pease 2003; Bowers and Johnson 2005).

After a few days of additional burglaries, near-repeat burglars decide to switch to targets elsewhere within activity spaces that could be up to several miles away for offenders on foot and even more distant for those in automobiles (Coupe and Blake 2006).

Near-repeat incidence varies considerably. It accounts for half the burglaries in Merseyside, UK (Bowers, Johnson, and Pease 2005), but only 6 percent of those in Perth, Western Australia (Zanetti 2015). Repeat burglary is particularly important for nonresidential decisions. In England and Wales, for example, half of all nonresidential burglaries (Mirrlees-Black and Ross 1995) and approximately 15 percent of domestic burglaries (Budd 1999; Townsley, Homel, and Chaseling 2000) are repeat incidents.

Repeat and near-repeat burglaries provide important clues about targeting strategies. Nine out of ten repeat domestic burglaries occurring within three months and greater than three-fourths of burglaries committed within two weeks and 100 meters of initial targets are committed by the same offenders (Bernasco 2008; Johnson et al. 2009). Same-offender knowledge about repeat targets virtually eliminates the need for search. Some will involve planning, with the dwelling to be burgled known when setting out on a burglary journey, either as the single target or as an option. Other repeat burglaries are not the result of planned trips and are targeted following fruitless searches for alternatives (Bennett and Wright 1984; Forrester et al. 1988). Such repeats are neither the result of planning nor require any search; rather, they are the products of prior knowledge and by-products of circumstances on specific burglary journeys.

An unfavorable risk evaluation of repeat premises on arrival at the scene displacing offenders to nearby properties is a less common explanation for near-repeat burglaries. This is because their timing often precedes the replacement of stolen property at initial targets (Bowers and Johnson 2005), although some might involve offenders returning for property that could not be removed during the first visit. Near-repeats are more likely to have been spotted on prior trips to initial targets and incorporated on subsequent crime journeys as possible or planned targets. Optimal foraging behavior characterizes near-repeat burglary (Townsley, Homel, and Chaseling 2003; Johnson et al. 2009). Targeting nearby dwellings, often of similar design, is likely to involve less effort and risk because offenders possess knowledge about site access, break-in points and room layouts, and possibly neighbor guardianship.

Motivations for repeat burglary include familiarity with premises and neighbors and knowledge of goods left behind or probably replaced, which enable quicker search and escape (Ericsson 1995), infrequently facilitated by key theft if locks remain unchanged (Budd 1999). These enable a more precise appreciation of risks and likely gains and "boost" the odds of repeat targeting decisions (Tseloni and Pease 2004). Burglars can have "event-dependent" knowledge of occupancy or routines of security staff or private patrols at nonresidential sites so that risks are lower, unless security has been upgraded (Bowers et al. 2005). Little is known about guardianship and intervisibility at repeat domestic burglaries, let alone nonresidential incidents, so that the extent to which low, heterogeneous risk helps explain initial and repeat incidents has yet to be established.

Because prior knowledge makes neighborhood search redundant for near-repeat and repeat burglaries, and local search is also unnecessary for repeats, neither matches hierarchical search models. Taken together, the incidences of repeat burglary and "acquaintance" burglary suggest that hardly any search is undertaken for many burglaries. Given the far higher number of repeat nonresidential burglaries, it would be expected that searching would play a far smaller role and planning a greater one than in domestic burglary targeting.

G. Further Research Needs

Often, offender studies focus on the selection of "stranger" burglary targets by lone offenders, whereas studies of burglary characteristics can be insufficiently discriminating with regard to the different types of burglaries. There is insufficient information about targeting decisions and search processes for acquaintance burglary (half of domestic incidents), aggravated burglary (one-fifth of domestic incidents), burglary carried out by co-offenders (one-third of domestic incidents), and burglary carried out by those who knowingly target occupied dwellings. In addition, there is a dearth of knowledge about multiple burglary offenses that occur on the same burglary journeys and the commission of other offenses, such as theft from vehicles, shoplifting, or robbery, that probably occur on some burglary journeys, given burglars' high offending versatility (Blumstein et al. 1988; Shover 1996).

H. Seasonal and Timing Decisions

Examination of the combined outcomes of burglars' decisions, in terms of daily and seasonal timing and types of households victimized, indicates that guardianship and visibility, key aspects of routine activity theory, are important factors in shaping those decisions.

Rather more domestic burglary decisions are taken in daylight (Budd 1999), with successful entry to premises peaking during weekday mornings and afternoons (Ratcliffe 2001; Sagovsky and Johnson 2007; Killmier 2014), whereas more nonresidential burglaries take place outside the work week and after dark (Ratcliffe 2001), reflecting times when many premises are routinely unoccupied (Cohen and Felson 1979). Aggregated burglary timings point to decisions shaped by low premises occupancy and weaker guardianship.

In addition, more residential burglary occurs outside summer months, whereas nonresidential burglary peaks during summer in temperate climates (Farrell and Pease 1994). In Harrow, UK, November domestic burglary incidence is 38 percent higher than the average, whereas the incidence in July is 28 percent lower (Hird and Ruparel 2007). It appears likely that residential burglary is displaced to nonresidential targets during summer, and the converse occurs during winter months. Fewer hours of darkness in the summer results in improved visibility in residential areas so that targets there are riskier outside the working day than at nonresidential properties situated outside residential areas, where guardianship is poorer (Coupe and Fox 2015).

I. Area Status, Deprivation, and Decisions

Fewer offenders decide to commit rural burglary, and burglary rates in or near villages and small towns in urbanized lowland England are approximately half those in large urban areas, given the distances that urban burglars, who are responsible for most rural burglaries, must travel (Wright 2013). In rural areas, nonresidential burglary incidence is higher than residential burglary incidence, which is the opposite of urban areas (Wright 2013). This is likely a reflection of the poorer guardianship at isolated farms and industrial premises in the countryside.

Burglary patterns within cities reflect the opportunities accessible from the activity nodes of burglars. Affluent suburbs are burgled less in the United States than in the United Kingdom (Tseloni et al. 2004), where distances between poorer and richer areas are shorter and affluent districts lie within burglars' activity spaces. In addition to poor inner-city neighborhoods, social housing estates are located in UK suburbs and also prosperous areas near poorer neighborhoods experience burglary disproportionately more than other prosperous neighborhoods (Baldwin and Bottoms 1976).

However, even in England and Wales, poorer urban neighborhoods with social and privately rented housing experience more burglary (Baldwin and Bottoms 1976; Budd 1999) because this is where most burglars live. Accessibility is also one of the keys to area burglary rates (Bernasco and Luykx 2003; Bernasco and Nieuwbeerta 2005): Poor areas situated well within burglars' activity spaces experience the highest rates of burglary (Budd 1999). The most deprived areas in Merseyside, UK, experience twice the domestic burglary prevalence rates and triple the repeat burglary rates of the least deprived areas (Bowers et al. 2005).

Burglars target more ethnically diverse areas (Bernasco and Nieuwbeerta 2005) and those with family dwellings (Hakim, Rengert, and Shachmurove 2001; Bernasco and Nieuwbeerta 2005). Burglary rates are higher in street segments with weaker guardianship (Reynald 2011a) and at properties that are more frequently empty (Tseloni et al. 2004) or occupied by single adults or that do not have children (Budd 1999; Tseloni et al. 2004)—groups likely to provide longer "time windows" of absence.

J. Summary of Targeting Strategies

Targeting strategy decisions reflect burglars' mobility and activity spaces. These define the sizes and limits of potential search areas, within which different targeting strategies are pursued. Most seek empty properties, but some target properties likely to be occupied, and others specifically search for occupied properties with elderly, incapable guardians or those with expensive vehicles. Some consider strangers' properties, and others target properties of acquaintances or those in which the offenders currently work or formerly worked. "Inside knowledge" of premises is far more significant than indicated by burglars' responses to questionnaire surveys, as are "acquaintance" burglaries and those aggravated by offenders deciding to use weapons to threaten or harm (Budd 1999).

Burglary trip distances vary, with older mobile, car key, and distraction burglars undertaking longer journeys, but with co-offending and burglary near offenders' former homes enlarging activity spaces. Burglary incidence declines as distance from burglars' homes increases, but recognition risk deters burglary in the immediate vicinity of offenders' homes, except in anonymous central city areas and in small towns and villages with limited built-up areas. Seasonal timings confirm the effects of opportunity relating to variations in daylight visibility on guardianship and burglary decisions. Targets with weak guardianship in poor areas closer to burglars' homes have the highest burglary rates, and accessible wealthier areas are more heavily targeted than inaccessible ones. Many targeting characteristics are in alignment with the elements of routine activity and rational choice theories, and most burglaries in the United Kingdom, United States, and Australia are motivated by offending opportunities that relate to financial gain (Maguire and Bennett 1982; Wright and Decker 1994; Killmier 2014). Target selection involves assessing the risks of being seen and potential rewards, whereas optimal foraging draws on these but utilizes effort minimization as an additional factor in shaping targeting tactics.

Hierarchical search models appear to make an important contribution to explaining certain types of burglaries, including offenders who explore new activity space, more mobile offenders who travel more widely to reduce the odds of capture (Lammers and Bernasco 2013), and car key and distraction burglars. On some trips, their targeting activities may fully match the models. Good knowledge of property stocks in different areas of activity spaces is likely to make neighborhood-level searching redundant so that other burglars travel directly to streets or estates where local searches for individual targets that fit the lower levels of hierarchical models are undertaken. Some switch to distant streets to search for fresh targets, whereas others return over the following few days to commit burglaries in nearby properties. There are few, if any, targets that need not be risk-assessed for approval or rejection as unsafe, immediately prior to entry.

The numbers of repeat, sometimes near-repeat, and "acquaintance" compared with "stranger" burglaries confirm that search may often be either absent or rudimentary. They also suggest that existing research may undervalue the role of planning in targeting decisions. Some burglars plan to burgle specific targets that have been seen or monitored or previously burgled, whereas others plan to start searches at specific streets or street segments. The fact that the final targets selected on many burglary journeys are often not the original targets indicates that initial plans are frequently frustrated and displaced to searches for alternatives, sometimes to repeat and possibly some near-repeat targets.

In summary, hierarchical models apply fully to certain burglaries with evidence of some neighborhood search. Street clusters and estates, rather than neighborhoods, may frame many burglars' mental maps of urban burglary activity space so that target search and burglary journeys are often driven by comparison of spatial units at the middle to lower levels of hierarchical models rather than by selecting neighborhoods and then streets within them. Wider search would therefore involve travel that connects different street clusters. Local search plays an important role in identifying individual targets following arrival at streets or estates, and it frequently follows optimal foraging principles, although this may be limited at near-repeat burglaries and will be more in evidence in "stranger" rather than "acquaintance" burglaries. Repeat and near-repeat incidents, however, reflect effort minimization. The "sizing" of the diverse alternative models of burglary targeting identified in this chapter needs further work.

III. TARGET SELECTION DECISIONS AT BURGLARY SCENES

This section considers decisions made at targets. It includes an examination of risk–gain assessment and an evaluation of the characteristics of risky versus vulnerable targets, from which inferences about the property and environmental factors affecting decisions may be drawn. This complements understanding of decisions about risks and gains and burglary target selection drawn from research involving interviews, simulations, and experiments with incarcerated and recruited active burglars, sometimes contrasted with non-burglars.

A. Risk–Gain Assessment

Assessment of sighting and arrest risk underpins most searching and target selection (Wright and Decker 1994; Cromwell and Olson 2003). Perceptions of potential rewards also make some targets more attractive than others. Although some burglars are motivated by a wish to damage property or commit a violent offense, the majority of burglars enter private premises with the intention of stealing goods and the majority of completed burglaries involve theft (Mirrlees-Black and Ross 1995; Budd 1999). Studies indicate the existence of bounded rational decision making that involves the evaluation of risks and rewards at candidate targets undertaken by reasoning criminals (Cornish and Clarke 1986; Hakim et al. 2001). This may involve only partial assessment of risks and gains (Cromwell et al. 1991) or the use of heuristics (Garcia-Retamero and Dhami 2009) rather than calculations based on "expected utility functions," as suggested in the rational choice model (Becker 1968). Feelings are likely to modify decisions (van Gelder 2013).

For virtually all burglars, risk–gain assessment drives final selection of specific targets in the lowest levels of the hierarchical search models because there are few targets, even "repeat" ones, that need not be examined for security changes, occupancy, and the presence of neighbors or passers-by before being burgled. Experienced burglars with sound knowledge of property stocks will filter out higher risk targets and streets (P. L. Brantingham and Brantingham 1984), especially those where capture has been narrowly avoided. Assessment of risk and gains (Cornish and Clarke 1986) drawing on knowledge and experience is likely to be a precondition for "screening in" unprotected candidate targets.

Some studies, often based on offender interviews, indicate that gains are of greater concern to burglars in selecting targets (Piquero and Rengert 1999; Hearnden and Magill 2005), whereas studies that draw inferences from target patterns and characteristics suggest that risks, especially that of being recognized, are more important than gains (Hakim et al. 2001; Coupe and Fox 2015). Although targets must meet both criteria, as long as burglars remain free, they can break into other properties, so mistakes about goods available to steal appear less critical than those that can result in arrest. Very risky targets with reasonable gains appear to be at least as unattractive as safe ones with poor prospects for gain.

Being seen by informal guardians, who summon formal guardians, poses a threat of arrest. This involves risks not only while at targets but also when approaching them and leaving them with stolen goods. The risk of being recognized when approaching targets is heightened in "buffer zones" close to burglars' homes (Rengert et al. 1999) or in neighborhoods in which residents differ markedly in appearance (Reynald et al. 2008), dress, or other characteristics, such as being on foot or using a dated car or bicycle (Nee et al. 2015). Burglars avoid such areas more. Some decide to mitigate obtrusiveness by simulating behaviors that make them appear less out of place, including jogging, walking a dog, or pretending to deliver leaflets. There is also the risk of interception during the crime journey when many offenders, including one-third of those in Adelaide, carry break-in tools (Killmier 2014) and especially during the return leg when offenders are carrying stolen goods. Thus, informal guardianship by residents and passers-by helps protect properties in some areas via deterrence attributable to risks due to differences in appearance or unusual behavior.

B. Decisions at Targets

On arrival at burglary scenes, burglars use their superior recognition memory and specialized awareness of visual cues to rapidly assess risks and probable gains before breaking in, making instant responses to environmental stimuli with "domain-specific" expertise (Clare 2011; Nee and Meenaghan 2006) that outclasses non-burglars' and police officers' reactions (Taylor and Nee 1988). In simulated tests, burglars quickly assess security weaknesses such as open windows, ease of rear escape, and a corner position less visible to neighbors, as well as taking distinctive and systematic routes to access properties, with twice as many exploring the rear first and a majority taking routes that no non-burglars used (Taylor and Nee 1988). This indicates homogeneity in burglars' perceptions and likely behavior. It suggests prior learning underpins their expertise and is applied to decisions supported by quasi-rational evaluation.

Visual site features that influence decisions are layout cues, affecting surveillability, access and escape routes, security cues, and wealth cues (Taylor and Nee 1988) such as upkeep and decor, visible items of value, and vehicle type (Nee and Meenaghan 2006). Guardianship objects may have a deterrent effect. Bars on windows and alarms deter burglars, but better locks are less effective deterrents (Maguire and Bennett 1982; Wright and Logie 1988).

Occupancy cues feature prominently in decision making. A car in the driveway (Taylor and Nee 1988), a television that is on, lights on at night, or security personnel at nonresidential premises can indicate that target and neighboring properties are occupied (Hakim et al. 2001; Taylor and Lee 1988).On the other hand, uncollected newspapers and mail, closed windows in summer, or open bedroom curtains at night can signal an empty property. Lights inside properties after dark or cars in driveways are used to flag occupancy and deter even when a property is empty, capitalizing on expectancy effects (Wortley 1998). Many burglars test occupancy by ringing doorbells or knocking on doors (Nee and Taylor 1988). At commercial premises, burglars often break a door or window, delaying entry to see if a police patrol unit attends in response to the triggering of a silent or delayed audible alarm system, a cause of some apparently false alarms (Cahalane 2001).

Studies of offenders' views about the decisions they make when selecting targets indicate the use of specialized expertise to rationally prioritize features affecting sighting risks (Nee and Taylor 1988; Nee and Meenaghan 2006; Clare 2011). These fit key concepts of routine activity theory and particularly concern burglars evaluating safety with regard to guardianship from occupants, neighbors, and passers-by. Even if instinctive and "automatic," "testing" targets to check occupancy indicates rational consideration and behavior. Security is a less important issue because there are plentiful properties, many of which are not strongly protected. If targets are not overlooked and out of earshot, there are few security measures that cannot be overcome.

C. Characteristics of Risky Versus Vulnerable Targets and Environments

The principal risks for burglars are being seen while committing an offense or triggering an alarm. These often lead to an immediate patrol response and to on-scene capture or eyewitness descriptions of suspects that can subsequently result in arrest (Hakim et al. 2001; Burrows et al. 2005). With the exception of car key burglary and distraction burglary, most burglars prefer an empty property (Repetto 1974; Maguire and Bennett 1982; Carden 2012; Pearson 2012). Only for a minority of burglars, who break in while occupants are sleeping, is occupancy less of a deterrent (Nee and Taylor 1988). Decisions to avoid risk mean the that probability of burglary is far higher at "non-alarmed" than at comparable "alarmed" premises; for example, this risk is 4.6 times higher in Philadelphia (Hakim and Shachmurove 1996).

D. Guardianship and Occupancy Risks

Properties that are unoccupied and those less surveillable with poorer site access, fewer visible break-in points, and few passers-by have weaker guardianship and lower risks

(Wright and Logie 1988; Reynald 2011a, 2011b). Larger households have shorter and less predictable time periods during which occupants are absent compared with single adult households, which are easier to monitor. Shops, especially larger ones, are burgled more frequently than warehouses, offices, or factories (Mirrlees-Black and Ross 1995). Smaller shops are often situated close to residential properties, indicating the effects of guardianship on burglary decisions.

Neighbor guardianship hinges on intervisibility between targets and neighboring premises, and sighting risks are lower where properties are more separated and fewer have sight of targets and where the disposition of buildings and vegetative cover obstructs a view of break-in points (Coupe and Fox 2015). Visibility of targets from neighboring properties is far poorer after dark, particularly on poorly lit streets (Hakim et al. 2001). Audibility is an important element of neighbor guardianship after dark. In addition, for risks at night to be comparable to those during daylight, premises must be closer together and there must be more of them, especially with an upstairs view of targets (Coupe and Fox 2015). This makes nighttime burglary even safer for burglars.

E. Target Site Risks

Positioning of targets in terms of roads and land use adjacent to targets modifies risks and selectively directs burglary decisions at certain types of premises. Visibility and risk to burglars are enhanced by crescent-shaped streets and cul-de-sacs, where there are lateral and longitudinal views of targets (Maguire and Bennett, 1982; Johnson and Bowers 2010), but these are reduced at street corner premises (Poyner and Webb 1991; Hakim and Shachmurove 1996). Domestic properties on main or nearby roads are less risky for burglars during the workday than those on housing estates, whereas nonresidential premises close to main roads are more risky than those on industrial estates, especially outside the workweek (Maguire and Bennett 1982; Hakim and Shachmurove 1996; Rengert and Wasilchick 2000). Nondwelling burglary is more risky where break-in points are visible to residential neighbors or passers-by (Hillier and Shu 1999); where premises back onto parks, or other open spaces (Repetto 1974; Hakim and Shachmurove 1996); and where more access paths and roads lead to and from premises (Coupe and Fox 2015). These characteristics suggest that easier access and low target visibility create low-risk opportunities that elevate burglary rates. Alleys at the sides of targets, however, reduce daylight sighting risks (Coupe and Fox 2015).

Mixtures of certain land uses near burglary sites modify burglary risks at different times of day, selectively deterring and facilitating burglary. Mixed residential–commercial areas are less risky for domestic and nonresidential burglars during the workday, but they are riskier for commercial burglars outside the workday (Maguire and Bennett 1982; Rengert and Wasilchick 1985; Hakim and Shachmurove 1996). Burglary timing decisions also vary by residential property environment. More detached properties, which have better vegetative cover, are targeted in daylight. Terraced dwellings are burgled in darkness, given limited vegetative cover and higher density that result in high daylight exposure to more and closer neighbors and more passers-by providing guardianship (Coupe and Blake 2006). Residential environments with more retired or unemployed households have superior daytime neighbor and occupant guardianship that deters daylight burglars (D'Alessio et al. 2012).

F. Risk at Affluent-Appearing Properties

In addition to accessible affluent areas, individual dwellings with an appearance of prosperity also attract burglars. Burglars target seven times as many detached and three times as many semi-detached houses in the poorest areas compared to such houses in the richest areas in Merseyside, England (Bowers et al. 2005). Burglars base assessments of likely gains on dwelling appearance and prosperity "flags," selecting better maintained properties (Winchester and Jackson 1982). This tends to indicate purposeful, selective target selection decisions related to stolen property gains. Value of goods available to steal appears to be a factor making shops and particularly large shops more attractive to burglars than warehouses, offices, or factories (Mirrlees-Black and Ross 1995).

G. Summary

Burglary targets are selected using burglars' superior recognition and awareness of visual cues that form the bases of burglars' learned expertise. These are applied to rapid quasi-rational or heuristically based evaluations that are automatically applied to gauge risks and gains. Risks concern occupancy and neighbor and passer-by guardianship. Guardianship risk also relates to visibility of break-in points, access to sites, and while approaching potential targets on the street.

Riskier target environments depend on differences in target sites, positioning on roads, and surrounding land uses. Visibility and risk are higher on crescent streets and cul-de-sacs but lower at street corner premises. Mixed residential–commercial areas make domestic burglary less risky for burglars during the workday, but commercial burglary is more risky outside the workday. Domestic properties on main roads are less risky for burglars during the workday than those on housing estates, whereas nonresidential premises close to main roads are more risky than those on industrial estates. Burglars are attracted to affluent-looking targets rather than poor-appearing targets. Examining burglary characteristics affords an understanding of the ways environmental circumstances affect decision risks and increases understanding of the decision situation by placing environmental cues in the context of the positioning of burglary sites and contiguous road and land uses.

Evidence from questionnaires and the examination of target characteristics confirms the importance of occupant, neighbor, and passer-by guardianship but also places it in the context of daily routine activities and wider environmental circumstances. It highlights the systematic effects of visibility due to vegetative cover, darkness, and neighboring site land uses that enable unobserved access to burglary scenes and entry points—factors that have a systematic effect on burglars' decisions. The importance of routine activity concepts regarding guardianship, visibility, access, and stolen property gain is highlighted by decisions taken at the scene with regard to specific target selection.

IV. Decisions During the Burglary Event

The principal decisions during the burglary event concern where to enter and exit premises, the method of entry, how many rooms to visit, the order and manner in which they are searched, and how long to stay on the premises.

A. Burglar Decisions While Entering Premises

Apart from apartments, burglars most often decide to enter at the rear of properties (Nee and Meenaghan 2006; Killmier 2014), which is generally less visible to neighbors and passers-by. Doors are used more often than windows, although more varied access points are used at detached and semi-detached properties, including patio doors, skylights, and side windows (Budd 1999; Bowers et al. 2005). "Daylight burglars" break into upscale dwellings with better vegetative cover via front windows and doors, whereas burglars enter exposed terraced properties via rear doors under cover of darkness (Coupe and Blake 2006).

Burglars commonly gain entry by levering open doors and windows—also common during "attempts" in which offenders fail to enter premises-, using screwdrivers and small crowbars (Nee and Taylor 1988; Hearnden and Magill 2004) or sometimes by removing window glass or door panels (Budd 1999). In more than one-fifth of burglaries, entry is through open windows or unlocked doors. It was reported that in only a minority of instances did burglars have a key; in one-tenth of cases, burglars pushed past or used deception to gain entry (Budd 1999). Car key burglars not only quietly remove glazing but also sometimes use a hook-ended pole through letter boxes to steal keys (Carden 2012).

During many dwelling burglaries—almost half of those in the United Kingdom—someone was at home, although half were unaware they were being burgled and did not see the burglar, whereas others heard the burglar (Budd 1999). Some offenders risk encountering occupants by deliberately targeting properties unlikely to be empty, although some aggravated burglaries may result from householders or employees attempting to thwart burglars (Wortley 1998).

Behavior and decisions about entering properties are framed in most cases to minimize visibility, audibility, and the risk of being seen by capable informal guardians using vegetative cover and cover of darkness and by first checking occupancy (Cohen and Felson 1979). Although many cases of aggravated burglary arise from occupancy misjudgments, some appear attributable to burglars knowingly targeting occupied premises with the intention of using a weapon if they are challenged. Few guardians are sufficiently capable to deal with this sort of offender, whom guardian presence fails to deter.

B. Burglar Decisions Inside Premises

Once inside premises, if the dwelling is empty, burglars often decide to lock or bolt front doors to prevent occupants entering (Nee and Meenaghan 2006). Burglars used violence in less than one-fifth of UK dwelling burglaries, particularly when premises were entered (Budd 1999). Three-fourths of burglars in the United States have committed other violent offenses, although this decreases with age (Blumstein et al. 1988). Interview studies place less emphasis on aggravated burglaries in which victims experience violence or threats, possibly suggesting that fewer violent burglars are arrested or recruited in these samples or that they have less often been asked about circumstances in which they are violent. Most interview studies suggest burglars try to avoid targets with capable guardians, but fewer explore what happens when these are encountered.

While searching premises, burglars listen for noises in case of being disturbed, and search methods based on instinct and experience are employed irrespective of whether the burglary was planned or opportunistic and also irrespective of offender age or indexed offense (Nee and Meenaghan 2006). Most burglars utilize the same search pattern, which commonly involves a sequence of master bedroom, other adult bedrooms, living room, dining room, study, and the kitchen. The search order of bedrooms and living areas is occasionally reversed and kitchens, the least promising, are inevitably last or, like children's bedrooms, disregarded (Nee and Meenaghan 2006). More time is devoted to rooms containing high-value items (Nee et al. 2015). Burglars decide to visit every room in approximately half of burglaries in which premises are entered, between one and three rooms in the other half in incidents in Adelaide (Killmier 2014), and more rooms are visited when co-offenders burgle larger dwellings (Coupe and Blake 2006). Three-fourths of burglary scenes are left "tidy," confirming organized approaches to searching; younger offenders and co-offenders leave scenes untidy (Killmier 2014). Most offenders stay inside properties for less than twenty minutes (Nee and Meenaghan 2006), and they remain for far shorter periods if disturbed by occupants or neighbors, when burglars normally flee the scene.

C. Stolen Property Decisions

Criteria likely to influence decisions as to which items to steal are value, particularly convertibility into cash, and weight and size (Cohen and Felson 1979). These affect portability, which is related to burglars' transport mode.

Burglar's decisions as to what to steal confirm routine activity theory's specification of a suitable target with regard to property theft. Items that are easy to carry, including cash, jewelry, and documents such as passports or credit cards, are most commonly stolen during domestic burglaries (Budd 1999; Nee and Meenaghan 2006). More portable electrical goods such as laptops, mobile phones, digital cameras, and TVs are also popular. The theft of fewer but more valuable items reflects burglars' specialist expertise (Nee et al. 2015). Theft of electrical goods is linked to ownership, value, and the age of the goods (Sutton 1995; Johnson, Bowers, and Hirschfield 1997). Distinctive items, including antiques, paintings, and silver, are less often stolen because they are more easily identifiable and may tie burglars or receivers to the crimes (Maguire and Bennett 1982). More burglars in Ireland than in England use receivers (Nee and Taylor 1988). They include pawnbrokers, second-hand goods shops, acquaintances, and family members (Wright and Decker 1994), but items may also be disposed of at car-boot sales. Stolen goods commonly sell for only one-third of their market value (Clare 2011).

V. Success of Burglary Decisions

The success of burglary decisions, from a burglar's perspective, may be assessed in terms of the value of the reward gained and the rate at which burglars are seen and arrested.

Police records indicate that property is stolen in three-fourths of domestic burglaries (Coupe and Griffiths 1996; Killmier 2014), whereas only two-fifths of British Crime Survey burglary victims report property loss (Budd 1999), partly because upon entering some premises, burglars find little portable property worth stealing, and fewer burglary "attempts" are reported to the police. It seems likely that less than half of incidents can be rated as successful in terms of gain.

Most burglary decisions are successful, in that less than 17 percent of offenders are seen and reported while the burglary is in progress, and few are arrested at the scene or subsequently (Tilley, Robinson, and Burrows 2007). Only one-seventh of burglaries are solved and burglars arrested in the United States and England and Wales (FBI 2011; Taylor and Bond 2012). Arrest rates are less than 5 percent of attempted incidents in the Thames Valley Police jurisdiction in England (Paine and Ariel 2013), so most offenders are able to subsequently target other premises.

The fact that burglary remains one of the least solved crimes reflects low solvability, underresourced investigations, and imperfectly targeted resources (Coupe 2014, 2016). Solvability is the ease with which burglaries may be solved or whether or not they can be solved. It depends on evidence that, in turn, reflects burglary event characteristics, which ultimately derive from the interaction of offender and environmental circumstances (Coupe 2016). It is the burglary decisions examined previously that influence whether burglars are seen, trigger alarms, filmed on CCTV, or leave forensic clues, and these affect burglary incident solvability (Coupe 2014).

Additional resources directed at highly solvable cases would improve arrest rates. Part of the success of burglars' decisions, therefore, is due to insufficient and poorly targeted police resources. These are almost a third as important as low solvability (Coupe 2014).

Targeting decisions are inherently less safe and successful for youths. By deciding to co-offend in daylight and enter property via the front, they are more conspicuous, and twice as many are arrested compared with older adult burglars who make safer and more successful decisions, offending alone after dark and entering properties via the rear (Coupe and Blake 2006). Prolific burglary decisions result in greater probability of arrest; for example, a Swedish offender who has committed 90 incidents has an approximately 86 percent probability of being arrested (Ahlberg and Knutsson 1990).

In summary, although less than half of burglary decisions are successful in terms of gain, most are successful in that they do not lead to arrest. Success is attributable to selecting low-risk, low-solvability targets combined with insufficient or misdirected police resources. Younger and more prolific burglars make targeting decisions that result in less successful outcomes in terms of sighting and arrest.

VI. Conclusion

Burglars' decisions involve seeking out favorable risk–gain target opportunities within their activity spaces. Offenders on foot dominate so that poorer areas nearer to burglars' homes suffer the brunt of burglary decisions, particularly more affluent properties within them. Offenders often avoid their immediate neighborhoods, where there can be a high risk of recognition that boosts guardianship. As nondesisting burglars age, activity space may be enlarged as mobility is extended and they access more varied targets in affluent urban neighborhoods and rural villages with safer burglary opportunities. Lengthier burglary journeys may also result from co-offending and offending near burglars' former homes.

Within activity spaces, findings from offender studies and those that measure burglary characteristics are consistent with bounded rational consideration of alternatives using concepts embodied in routine activity theory, while often optimally foraging to also minimize effort. Evaluating probable gains and avoiding risk are significant parts of burglary decision-making processes. Burglars cite prosperity cues at targets as factors influencing decisions. Burglars mainly avoid occupied premises and those with strong neighbor and passer-by guardianship, seeking those that can be more easily reached unobserved, entering and leaving at less visible points or, if exposed, during darkness. A majority of burglars have committed violent offenses when younger, and violence or threats can sometimes be used when occupants are encountered during dwelling burglaries. The targets that most attract burglars have weaker guardianship; are less visible due to building disposition, road layout, vegetation, or street lighting; and may be approached covertly using adjacent sites or side or rear alleys.

Burglars possess considerable learned expertise that enables rapid evaluation of potential targets so that decisions at the scene are often "automatic," involving heuristics or bounded rational consideration. A number of mental processes operate, involving differing degrees of cognitive biases and rationality. Burglars follow well-practised procedures to enter properties and search inside them. Property stolen tends to be portable because many burglars are on foot, and cash or valuable goods that are easily converted into cash are most frequently taken, indicating alignment with routine activity theory's target suitability concept. Although as many burglars leave domestic incidents empty-handed as those carrying stolen property, burglary decisions are enormously successful from an offender perspective, with low arrest rates that decline as offenders age, travel farther afield, or switch to nighttime burglary.

Burglars also have knowledge of property stocks with burglary potential in their activity spaces, filtering out unpromising areas. Rather than first searching for a suitable neighborhood, many journey directly to estates, streets, and rows of houses, and search journeys may connect these with local foraging for suitable targets. Older and more mobile burglars who burgle more widely in urban and accessible rural areas and burglars who are exploring new activity space may use targeting strategies that fit hierarchical models and include neighborhood searching. Others with considerable knowledge of burglary opportunities directly target streets or estates, and interconnections between spatial units at this scale may be the basis of mental maps of activity spaces and help shape burglary travel. Burglars carry out local searches to identify suitable targets, particularly "stranger" burglaries, although if these are near-repeat burglaries, searching may be more limited than that for burglars who switch streets, estates, or areas after a single offense. High numbers of "acquaintance" and repeat burglaries indicate that prior knowledge and planning often have a significant role in targeting strategy, even if some repeat burglaries do not result from planned trips, and some of those that do may be thwarted by circumstances and displaced to nearby properties. The sizing of these models of burglary targeting and the roles of searching and planning need further work.

Low detection rates mean that known burglar populations are skewed toward those who make unsuccessful decisions; thus, improving detection rates and gaining access to police and offender data are keys to improving understanding of burglary decision making. Unfortunately, the inherent nature of the offense, the plentiful supply of territorially diffuse and lightly guarded targets, offenders with pertinent knowledge and expertise, and insufficient policing resources make this challenging. However, a picture may be pieced together from methodologically disparate studies, and these will continue to advance our understanding. It is hoped that additional effort will be directed at improving knowledge of nonresidential burglary decision making and highlighting similarities and differences in burglary decisions and circumstances in different countries and in rural situations.

REFERENCES

Ahlberg, J., and J. Knutsson. 1990. "The Risk of Detection." *Journal of Quantitative Criminology* 6(1): 117–30.

Akers, R. L., and C. S. Sellers. 2009. *Criminological Theories: Introduction, Evaluation and Application*, 5th ed. Oxford: Oxford University Press.

Andersen, M., R. Frank, and M. Felson. 2014. "Age and the Distance to Crime." *Criminology and Criminal Justice* 14(3): 314–33.

Baldwin, J., and A. E. Bottoms. 1976. *The Urban Criminal: A Study in Sheffield*. London: Tavistock.

Becker, G. S. 1968. "Crime and Punishment: An Economic Approach." *Journal of Political Economy* 76:169–217.

Bennett, T., and R. Wright. 1984. *Burglars on Burglary*. Aldershot, UK: Gower.

Bernasco, W. 2006. "Co-offending and the Choice of Target Areas in Burglary." *Journal of Investigative Pyschology and Offender Profiling* 3:139–55.

Bernasco, W. 2008. "Them Again: Same-Offender Involvement in Repeat and Near-Repeat Burglaries." *European Journal of Criminology* 5:411–31.

Bernasco, W. 2009. "Burglary." In *The Oxford Handbook of Crime and Public Policy*, edited by M. Tonry, pp. 165–90. Oxford: Oxford University Press.

Bernasco, W. 2010. "Modeling Micro-level Crime Location Choice: Application of the Discrete Choice Framework to Crime at Places." *Journal Quantitative Criminology* 26:113–38.

Bernasco, W. and F. Luykx. 2003. "Effects of Attractiveness, Opportunity and Accessibility to Burglars on Residential Burglary Rates of Urban Neighbourhoods." *Criminology* 41(3): 981–1001.

Bernasco, W., and P. Nieuwbeerta. 2005. "A New Approach to the Analysis of Criminal Location Choice." *British Journal of Criminology* 44:296–315.

Blumstein, A., J. Cohen, S. Das, and D. Miotra. 1988. "Specialization and Seriousness During Adult Criminal Careers." *Journal of Quantitative Criminology* 4(4): 303–45.

Bowers, K. J., and S. D. Johnson. 2005. "Domestic Burglary Repeats and Space–Time Clusters: The Dimensions of Risk." *European Journal of Criminology* 2:67–92.

Bowers, K. J., S. D. Johnson, and K. Pease. 2005. "Victimisation and Re-victimisation Risk, Housing Type and Area: A Study of Interactions." *Crime Prevention and Community Safety* 7(1): 7–17.

Brantingham, P. J., and P. L. Brantingham. 1991. *Environmental Criminology*. Prospect Heights, IL: Waveland Press.

Brantingham, P. L., and P. J. Brantingham. 1984. *Patterns in Crime*. New York: Macmillan.

Brantingham, P. L., and P. J. Brantingham. 1995. "Location Quotients and Crime Hotspots in the City." Chapter 10, 129–150, in *Crime Analysis Through Computer Mapping*, edited by C. R. Block, M. Dabdoub, and S. Fregly. Washington, DC: Police Executive Research Forum.

Budd, T. 1999. *Burglary of Domestic Dwellings: Findings from the British Crime Survey*. Issue 4/99. London: Home Office.

Burrows, J., M. Hopkins, R. Hubbard, A. Robinson, M. Speed, and N. Tilley. 2005. *Understanding the Attrition Process in Volume Crime Investigations*. Home Office Research Study 295. London: Home Office Research, Development and Statistics Directorate.

Cahalane, M. 2001. "Reducing False Alarms Has a Price—So Does Response: Is the Real Price Worth Paying?" *Security Journal* 14(1): 31–53.

Carden, R. 2012. "Car Key Burglaries: An Exploratory Analysis." Paper presented at the fifth Cambridge Evidence-Based Policing Conference, 2012.

Carrington, P. J. 2009. "Co-offending and the Development of the Delinquent Career." *Criminology* 47(4): 1295–1329.

Clare, J. 2011. "Examination of Systematic Variations in Burglars' Domain-Specific Perceptual and Procedural Skills." *Psychology, Crime and Law* 17(3): 199–214.

Clare, J., J. Fernandez, and F. Morgan. 2009. "Formal Evaluation of the Impact of Barriers and Connectors on Residential Burglars' Macro-level Offending Location Choices." *Australian and New Zealand Journal of Criminology* 42(2): 139–58.

Cohen, L. E., and M. Felson. 1979. "Social Change and Crime Rate Trends: A Routine Activities Approach." *American Sociological Review* 44: 588–608.

Cohen, L. E., J. R. Kluegel, and K. C. Land. 1981. "Social Inequality and Predatory Criminal Victimization: An Exposition and Test of a Formal Theory." *American Sociological Review* 46:505–24.

Cornish, D. B., and R. V. Clarke. 1986. *The Reasoning Criminal: Rational Choice Perspectives on Offending.* New York: Springer-Verlag.

Coupe, R. T. 2014. "An Evaluation of the Effects of Police Resources and Incident Solvability on Crime Detection." Paper no. 46/2014, August 2014, Legal Studies Research Paper Series, Faculty of Law, University of Cambridge.

Coupe, R. T. 2016. "Evaluating the Effects of Resources and Solvability on Burglary Detection." *Policing and Society* 26(5): 563–87.

Coupe, R. T., and L. Blake. 2006. "Daylight and Darkness Targeting Strategies and the Risks of Being Seen at Residential Burglaries." *Criminology* 44(2): 431–64.

Coupe, R. T., and B. H. Fox. 2015. "A Risky Business: How Do Access, Exposure and Guardians Affect the Chances of Non-residential Burglars Being Seen?" *Security Journal* 28:71–92.

Coupe, R. T., and M. Griffiths. 1996. *Solving Residential Burglary.* Crime Detection and Prevention Series Paper 77. London: Home Office.

Cromwell, P. F., and J. N. Olson. 2003. *Breaking and Entering: Burglars on Burglary.* Belmont, CA: Wadsworth.

Cromwell, P. F., J. N. Olson, and D. W. Avery. 1991. *Breaking and Entering. An Ethnographic Analysis of Burglary.* Newbury Park, CA: Sage.

D'Alessio, S. J., D. Eitle, and L. Stolzenberg. 2012. "Unemployment, Guardianship and Weekday Residential Burglary." *Justice Quarterly* 29(6): 919–32.

Elffers, H., D. Reynald, M. Averdijk, W. Bernasco, and R. Block. 2008. "Modelling Crime Flow Between Neighbourhoods in Terms of Distance and of Intervening Opportunities." *Crime Prevention and Community Safety* 10(2): 85–96.

Ericsson, U. 1995. "Straight from the Horse's Mouth." *Forensic Update* 43:23–25.

Everson, S., and K. Pease. 2003 "Crime Against the Same Person and Place: Detection Opportunity and Offender Targeting." *Crime Prevention Studies* 12:199–220.

Farrell, G., and K. Pease. 1994. "Crime Seasonality: Domestic Disputes and Residential Burglary in Merseyside 1988–90." *British Journal of Criminology* 34(4): 487–97.

Federal Bureau of Investigations. 2011. "Offenses Cleared." *Uniform Crime Report: Crime in the United States, 2010.* U.S. Department of Justice. https://ucr.fbi.gov/crime-in-the-u.s/2010/crime-in-the-u.s.-2010/clearancetopic.pdf

Felson, M. 2008. "Routine Activity Approach." In *Environmental Criminology and Crime Analysis,* edited by R. Wortley and L. Mazerolle, pp. 70–77. Oxon: Routledge.

Felson, M., and R. V. Clarke. 1998. *Opportunity Makes the Thief: Practical Theory for Crime Prevention*. London: Home Office, Policing and Reducing Crime Unit, Research, Development and Statistics Directorate.

Forrester, D., M. Chatterton, and K. Pease. 1988. *The Kirkholt Burglary Prevention Project, Rochdale*. Crime Prevention Unit Paper 13. London: Home Office.

Garcia-Retamero, R., and M. Dhami. 2009. "Take-the-Best in Expert–Novice Decision Strategies for Residential Burglary." *Pyschonomic Bulletin and Review* 16(1): 163–69.

Hakim, S., G. F. Rengert, and Y. Shachmurove. 2001. "Target Search of Burglars: A Revised Economic Model." *Papers in Regional Science* 80:121–37.

Hakim, S., and Y. Shachmurove. 1996. "Spatial and Temporal Patterns of Commercial Burglaries." *American Journal of Economics and Sociology* 55(4): 443–56.

Hearnden, I., and C. Magill. 2004. *Decision-Making by House Burglars: Offenders' Perspectives*. Home Office Research Findings no. 249. London: Home Office.

Hillier, B., and S. Shu. 1999. "Design for Secure Space." *Planning in London* 29:36–38.

Hird, C., and C. Ruparel. 2007. "Seasonality in Recorded Crime: Preliminary Findings." Home Office online report 02/07.

Johnson, S. D., and K. J. Bowers. 2004. "The Burglary as Clue to the Future—The Beginnings of Prospective Hot-Spotting." *European Journal of Criminology* 1:237–55.

Johnson, S. D., and K. J. Bowers. 2010. "Permeability and Burglary Risk: Are Cul de Sacs Safer?" *Quantitative Journal of Criminology* 26(1): 89–111.

Johnson, S. D., K. J. Bowers, and A. Hirschfield. 1997. "New Insights into the Spatial and Temporal Distribution of Repeat Victimisation." *British Journal of Criminology* 37(2): 224–41.

Johnson, S. D., L. Summers, and K. Pease. 2009. "Offender as Forager? A Direct Test of the Boost Account of Victimisation." *Journal of Quantitative Criminology* 25(2):181–200.

Kahneman, D., and A. Tversky. 1979. "Prospect Theory: An Analysis of Decision Under Risk." *Econometrica* 47(2): 263–92.

Killmier, B. 2014. "Offenders and Their Offences: Convicted Burglars in Adelaide." PhD thesis, Cambridge University.

Lammers, M., and W. Bernasco. 2013. "Are Mobile Offenders Less Likely to Be Caught? The Influence of the Geographical Dispersion of Serial Offenders' Crime Locations on Their Probability of Arrest." *European Journal of Criminology* 10:168–86.

Leclerc, B., and R. Wortley, eds. 2014. Cognition and Crime: Offender Decision-Making and Script Analyses. New York: Routledge.

Maguire, M., and T. Bennett. 1982. *Burglary in a Dwelling: The Offence, the Offender and the Victim*. London: Heinemann.

Mirrlees-Black, C., and A. Ross. 1995. *Crime Against Retail and Manufacturing Premises: Findings from the 1994 Commercial Victimisation Survey*. Home Office Research Study 146. London: Home Office Research and Statistics Department.

Morgan, F. 2000. "Repeat Burglary in a Perth Suburb: Indicator of Short-Term or Long-Term Risk." In *Repeat Victimisation*, edited by G. Farrell and K. Pease. Vol. 12 of the *Crime Prevention Studies*, pp. 83–118. Monsey, NY: Criminal Justice Press.

Nee, C., and A. Meenaghan. 2006. "Expert Decision-Making in Burglars." *British Journal of Criminology* 46:935–49.

Nee, C., and M. Taylor. 1988. "Residential Burglary in the Republic of Ireland: A Situational Perspective." *Howard Journal of Criminal Justice* 27(2): 105–16.

Nee, C., and M. Taylor. 2000. "Examining Burglars' Target Selection: Interview, Experiment or Ethnomethodology?" *Psychology, Crime and Law* 6:45–59.

Nee, C., M. White, K. Woolford, T. Pascu, L. Barker, and L. Wainwright. 2015. "New Methods for Examining Expertise in Burglars in Natural and Simulated Environments: Preliminary Findings." *Psychology, Crime and Law* 21(5): 507–13.

Nichols, W. W. 1980. "Mental Maps, Social Characteristics and Criminal Mobility." In *Crime: A Spatial Perspective*, edited by D. E. Georges-Abeyie and K. D. Harries, pp. 156–66. New York: Columbia University Press.

Paine, C., and B. Ariel. 2013. "Solvability Analysis: Increasing the Likelihood of Detection in Completed, Attempted and In-progress Burglaries." Paper presented at the Sixth Cambridge Evidence-Based Policing Conference, 2013.

Palmer, E. J., A. Holmes, and C. R. Hollin. 2002. "Investigating Burglars' Decisions: Factors Influencing Target Choice, Method of Entry, Reasons for Offending, Repeat Victimisation of a Property and Victim Awareness." *Security Journal* 15(1): 7–18.

Pearson, A. 2012. "An Exploratory Study of Distraction Burglary in Thames Valley Police Jurisdiction 2003–2011." Unpublished thesis, University of Cambridge.

Pettiway, L. E. 1982. "Mobility of Robbery and Burglary Offenders: Ghetto and Nonghetto Spaces." *Urban Affairs Quarterly* 18:255–70.

Piquero, A., and G. F. Rengert. 1999. "Studying Deterrence with Active Residential Burglars." *Justice Quarterly* 16(2): 451–71.

Poyner, B., and B. Webb. 1991. *Crime Free Housing*. Oxford: Butterworth.

Ratcliffe, J. 2001. *Policing Urban Burglary*. Trends and Issues in Crime and Criminal Justice, no. 213. Canberra: Australian Institute of Criminology.

Reiss, A. J. 1988. "Co-offending and Criminal Careers." In *Crime and Justice: A Review of Research*, vol. 10, 117–170, edited by M. Tonry and N. Morris. Chicago: University of Chicago Press.

Rengert, G. F., A. R. Piquero, and P. R. Jones. 1999. "Distance Decay Re-examined." *Criminology* 37(2): 427–45.

Rengert, G. F., and J. Wasilchick. 2000. *Suburban Burglary: A Tale of Two Suburbs*. Springfield, IL: Charles C Thomas.

Repetto, T. 1974. *Residential Crime*. Cambridge, MA: Ballinger.

Reynald, D. M. 2011a. "Factors Associated with the Guardianship of Places: Assessing the Relative Importance of the Spatio-physical and Sociodemographic Contexts in Generating Opportunities for Capable Guardianship." *Journal of Research in Crime and Delinquency* 48(1): 110–42.

Reynald, D. M. 2011b. *Guarding Against Crime: Measuring Guardianship with Routine Activity Theory*. Farnham, UK: Ashgate.

Reynald, D. M., M. Averdijk, H. Elffers, and W. Bernasco. 2008. "Do Social Barriers Affect Urban Crime Trips? The Effects of Ethnic and Economic Neighbourhood Compositions on the Flow of Crime in The Hague, the Netherlands." *Built Environment* 34:21–31.

Sagovsky, A., and Johnson, S. D. 2007. "When Does Repeat Victimisation Occur?" *Australian and New Zealand Journal of Criminology* 40:1–26.

Shapland, J., and J. Vagg. 1985. *Social Control and Policing in Rural and Urban Areas: A Final Report to the Home Office*. London: Home Office.

Shover, N. 1991. "Burglary." In *Crime and Justice: An Annual Review of Research*, edited by M. Tonry and N. Morris, pp. 73–113. Chicago: University of Chicago Press.

Shover, N. 1996. *Great Pretenders: Pursuits and Careers of Persistent Thieves*. Boulder, CO: Westview.

Sorensen, D. W. M. 2005. *The Journey to Danish Residential Burglary: Distributions and Correlates of Crime Trips Made by Convicted Danish offenders*. Research Department III,

Faculty of Law, University of Copenhagen. Report prepared for Denmark's Ministry of Justice.

Sutton, M. 1995. "Supply by Theft: Does the Market for Second-hand Goods Play a Role in Keeping Crime Figures High?" *British Journal of Criminology* 38(3): 352–65.

Taylor, P., and S. Bond. 2012. *Crimes Detected in England and Wales 2011/12*. Statistical Bulletin, 08/12. London: Home Office.

Taylor, P., and C. Nee. 1988. "The Role of Cues in Simulated Residential Burglary: A Preliminary Investigation." *British Journal of Criminology* 28:396–401.

Tilley, N., A. Robinson, and J. Burrows. 2007. "The Investigation of High Volume Crime." In *Handbook of Criminal Investigation*, edited by T. Newburn, T. Williamson, and A. Wright, pp. 226–54. Cullompton, UK: Willan.

Townsley, M., D. Birks, W. Bernasco, S. Ruiter, S. Johnson, G. White, and S. Baum. 2015. "Burglar Target Selection: A Cross-National Comparison." *Journal of Research in Crime and Delinquency* 52:3–31.

Townsley, M., R. Homel, and J. Chaseling. 2000. "Repeat Burglary Victimisation: Spatial and Temporal Patterns." *Australian and New Zealand Journal of Criminology* 33(1): 37–63.

Townsley, M., R. Homel, and J. Chaseling. 2003. "Infectious Burglaries: A Test of the Near Repeat Hypothesis." *British Journal of Criminology* 43:615–33.

Tseloni, A. K., and K. Pease. 2003. "Repeat Personal Victimisation: 'Boosts' or 'Flags'?" *British Journal of Criminology* 43:196–212.

Tseloni, A. K., and K. Pease. 2004. "Repeat Personal Victimisation: Random Effects, Event Dependence and Unexplained Heterogeneity." *British Journal of Criminology* 44:931–45.

Tseloni, A., K. Wittebrood, G. Farrell, and K. Pease. 2004. "Burglary Victimisation in England and Wales, the United States and the Netherlands: A Cross-National Comparative Test of Routine Activities and Life-style Theories." *British Journal of Criminology* 44:66–91.

van Gelder, J.-L. 2013. "Beyond Rational Choice: The Hot/Cool Perspective of Criminal Decision Making. *Psychology, Crime and Law* 19(9): 745–63.

van Gelder, J.-L., and R. E. de Vries. 2014. "Rational Misbehavior? Evaluating an Integrated Dual-Process Model of Criminal Decision Making." *Journal of Quantitative Criminology* 30:1–27.

van Mastrigt, S. B., and D. P. Farrington. 2009. "Co-offending, Age, Gender and Crime Type: Implications for Criminal Justice Policy." *British Journal of Criminology* 49(4): 552–73.

Wikstrom, P.-O. H., and K. Treiber. 2016. "Situational Theory: The Importance of Interactions and Action Mechanisms in the Explanation of Crime." Chapter 22, 415–444, in *Handbook of Criminological Theory*, edited by A. Piquero. Chichester UK: John Wiley.

Winchester, S., and H. Jackson. 1982. *Residential Burglary: The Limits of Prevention*. Home Office Research and Planning Unit Report. London: HMSO.

Wortley, R. 1998. "A Two-Stage Model of Situational Crime Prevention." *Studies on Crime and Crime Prevention* 7:173–88.

Wortley, R. 2012. "Exploring the Person–Situation Interaction in Situational Crime Prevention." In *The Reasoning Criminologist: Essays in Honour of Ronald V. Clarke*, edited by N. Tilley and G. Farrell, pp. 184–93. London: Routledge.

Wright, O. 2013. "Urban to Rural: An Exploratory Analysis of Burglary and Vehicle Crime with a Rural Context." Unpublished thesis, University of Cambridge.

Wright, R., and S. H. Decker. 1994. *Burglars on the Job: Street-life and Residential Break-ins*. Boston: Northeastern University Press.

Wright, R., and R. H. Logie. 1988. "How Young House Burglars Choose Targets." *Howard Journal of Criminal Justice* 27:92–104.

Zanetti, P. 2015. Personal communication with Asst. Commissioner, Western Australia Police Service.

Zipf, G. 1949. *Human Behavior and the Principle of Least Effort: An Introduction to Human Ecology*. Cambridge, MA: Addison-Wesley.

CHAPTER 32

....

OFFENDER DECISION MAKING IN CORPORATE AND WHITE-COLLAR CRIME

....

WIM HUISMAN

I. INTRODUCTION

....

TRADING stocks with insider information, providing false information on profits to avoid taxes, saving money by not taking legally prescribed safety measures, fixing prices with competitors to neutralize competition and to inflate prices, and filing insurance claims for costs that were never incurred are crimes that are all outcomes of decision making by managers or other professionals acting in an occupational or business-related context. White-collar crime and corporate crime are generally viewed as purposive action and as the outcome of rational decision-making processes. Due to the goal-oriented nature of corporations, the context of doing business, and the intellectual capabilities of corporate officials, white-collar and corporate crimes are generally viewed as being more planned and more based on conscious decision making than most "ordinary" street crimes (Shover and Hochstetler 2006; Benson and Simpson 2009). The term "white-collar crime" was coined by Edwin Sutherland in the 1930s, and he referred to it as "crime committed by a person of respectability and a high social status in the course of his occupation" (Sutherland 1949, p. 9). Although the term white-collar crime is deeply embedded in daily speech and has a strong symbolic meaning, the term and its definition have also been heavily criticized in academia for being an umbrella concept or a "plastic phrase that means many things in many contexts" (Tonry and Reiss 1993, p. vii). The term has been especially criticized for not differentiating between crimes that managers or professionals commit for the benefit of the corporation and crimes they commit for their personal benefit (and not seldom to the detriment of their organization) (Clinard and Quinney 1973). Most criminological studies of white-collar crime distinguish *corporate crime*, those offenses that employees commit while acting in the interest of their company, from other white-collar crimes that offenders with a white-collar status commit for personal benefit (Friedrichs 2009, pp. 6–7). However, the boundary between these two types can be blurred in reality—for example, when personal bonuses are attached to achieving corporate goals or when the owner of a small or mid-sized company is committing crimes. Therefore, this chapter mostly refers to "white-collar and corporate crime" and explicitly differentiates between these two when it is relevant to understanding criminal decision making. This is especially important because although all corporate crime is a form of white-collar crime, not all white-collar crime is also corporate crime. It should be acknowledged, therefore, that this chapter mainly aims at those forms of white-collar crime that are closest to the ideal type envisioned by Sutherland: actors with high social statuses, acting from corporate contexts, committing crimes that are typified by legal and moral ambiguities, partly due to the lack of clear and direct victimization (Geis 2007).

This chapter follows the main assumptions of this handbook. Offender decision making is viewed as a process that links an offender to the characteristics of a situation in which the offender makes a choice among two or more alternatives. That choice results in an outcome that is in violation of the law. Criminal decision making requires that the actor perceives at least two behavioral alternatives from which to choose, with at least one of them involving a criminal act. The outcome of the choice depends on a number of elements, including characteristics of the decision maker, characteristics of the situation, the perception and evaluation of choice alternatives, and potentially also changes in one or more of these elements that take place once a choice has been made and the decision maker has instigated a certain course of action.

This chapter is structured as follows. Section II focuses on the characteristics of the *decision maker*. Especially for corporate crime, a central issue is who should be viewed as the *actor*, making criminal decisions: individual managers acting on behalf of the corporation or the corporation itself. Both the characteristics of individual managers and organizational characteristics of the corporation can influence decision making that leads to white-collar and corporate crime. Section III focuses on the characteristics of the *situations* in which white-collar offenders decide to commit white-collar crime. These situations can provide the opportunity to commit crime as well as influence the motivations to do so. Section IV discusses research on the *perception* and *evaluation of choice* in the setting of white-collar and corporate crime.

II. Characteristics of the Actor

The characteristics of a decision maker influences the outcome of choices made by that decision maker. Some have more insight than others in the likely consequences of their choices, and some people have a longer temporal horizon than others; there may also be differences in personality. This is as true for perpetrators of street crime as it is for perpetrators of white-collar and corporate crime. However, it is generally assumed that those who commit white-collar crime have more insight into the consequences of their actions and have a longer temporal horizon than offenders of street crime because these traits enabled them to get into the white-collar position from which they commit these crimes and the complexity of their crimes requires these traits. For understanding decision making that leads to white-collar or corporate crime, the following are crucial questions: Whose decision is this? Which actor do we see at the decision-making unit: an individual manager or the organization?

A. Organizational Properties and Dynamics

In organizational sciences, a corporation is viewed as an independent actor possessing behavior that may be appropriately studied. In this view, corporations have a "life" that is independent from the lives of the individuals who make up the organization, just like the life of the human body is independent from the life span of the individual cells that form the human body (Morgan 2006). Organizations can act to achieve organizational goals and can therefore be held accountable for the consequences of these actions. This is also in line with legal systems in which corporations are viewed as legal entities that can be held (criminally) liable for their actions (Wells 2001). Corporate or organizational decision making is a well-established field of academic study (Loasby 2008).

In understanding corporate crime, many criminologists follow this anthropomorphic approach (Huisman 2016). This is also reflected in leading definitions of corporate crime: "Any act committed *by corporations* that is punished by the state, regardless of whether it is punished under administrative, civil, or criminal law" (Clinard and Yeager 1980, p. 16). Even Sutherland, who coined the term "white-collar crime" regarding the individual manager's wardrobe, anthropomorphized the corporation by attributing human capacities and stating that "corporations have committed crimes" and speaking of "the criminality of corporations" (Sutherland 1983, p. 217). In explaining corporate crime, Braitwaite and Fisse (1990) stated that "the products of organization are more than the sum of the products of individual actions" (p. 20).

In this anthropomorphic approach, a corporation is not only viewed as an actor but also viewed as a *rational* actor. A high level of rationality is attributed to corporations that are designed in economically efficient ways to achieve set corporate goals. Corporate crime can then be seen as a choice by the corporation in furthering these goals and the outcome of corporate decision making.

1. *Bounded Rationality*

Both assumptions—corporations being actors and being rational—have also been criticized. First, the rationality of corporate decision making has been questioned. According to March and Simon (1958), it is at best a *bounded rationality* because the rationality of corporate decision making is bounded by a variety of individual and situational factors that affect how information is comprehended and processed. Also, the empirical analysis of landmark cases of corporate harm, particularly the unsafe Ford Pinto automobile in the 1970s and the explosion of the NASA *Challenger* space shuttle in 1986, challenged the rationality of the corporate decision making that led to these tragedies. According to the initial readings of the Pinto case, Ford did not fix the defect of the fuel tank of the Pinto for eight years "because its internal 'cost–benefit analysis' that places a dollar value on human life, said it wasn't profitable to make changes sooner" (Dowie 1977, as quoted in Lee and Ermann 2002, p. 278). According to Lee and Ermann, the Pinto case was taught to students of organizational deviance as the "most notorious" example of a corporation "willfully" marketing a product "known to be dangerous" (Lee and Ermann 2002, p. 279). However, after re-analyzing the facts of the case, Lee and Ermann conclude that Ford employees' perceptions and behaviors were shaped by organizational, industry, and regulatory contexts. Their reading of the case suggests that the defining characteristic of the Pinto narrative is its misplaced emphasis on amoral calculation. Instead, they argue that institutionalized norms and conventional modes of communication at the organizational and network level better explain the available data: "What appeared from a distance as decisions made by rational, coordinated, profit-driven actors with fairly complete knowledge acting on an essentially economic pleasure/pain calculus, are better understood as non-rational outcomes of distinct subunit acts, based on doubtful information" (Lee and Ermann 2002, p. 293). A similar revisionist account was given to the NASA *Challenger* disaster by Vaughan (2002*a*). Initially, the official reading was that it was a rational decision to go ahead with the launch, although it was known that there was a technical problem with a rubber-like O ring that lay in a joint of the left solid rocket booster. According to a presidential committee, NASA managers, who were experiencing production pressure because the launch was essential to the future of the space program, ignored the advice of engineers and went forward with the launch, violating rules about reporting problems up the hierarchy in the process. After re-examining the facts, Vaughan came to the conclusion that "the cause of the *Challenger* disaster was not amorally calculating managers." Instead, "The causes of the tragedy lay in the generic structures and processes of organizations and their institutional environments" (p. 325).

In these case studies, as in other industrial disasters, organizational deviance is viewed not as the outcome of well-informed choice but, rather, as the result of organizational processes characteristics. Vaughan views organizational deviance as an unanticipated suboptimal outcome and a routine by-product of the characteristic of the system. She views the systematic production of organizational deviance as the inevitable outcome of all socially organized systems: "It follows that the same characteristics of a system that produce the bright side will regularly provoke the dark side from time to time" (Vaughan 1999, p. 274). Especially the use of technology—common in every contemporary corporation—and a certain level of uncertainty and imperfect knowledge that accompanies the use of technology produce unanticipated outcomes (Vaughan 1999). This is even more the case with innovative, risky technology (Vaughan 2002*b*). It is well established that regulated firms vary in relation to economic recourses, technical know-how, knowledge about the law, managerial capacity and oversight, and other recourses, and that these differences to a large degree explain differences in compliance behavior (Parker and Nielsen 2011, p. 15).

According to Simpson, Leeper-Piquero, and Paternoster (2002), firm size and complexity affect the rationality in strategic decision making: "As firms grow, they shift into a planning mode which requires a more detailed strategic process—more data, more analysis, and strategizing. Similarly, as firms stop growing, comprehensiveness decreases" (p. 31). Nonstrategic, routine day-to-day decisions are facilitated by the corporate structure. Along the lines of the division of tasks, these decision types are formally guided by so-called "standard operation procedures" (SOPs). These SOPs are rational for preventing time-consuming decision-making processes over routine activities, but they might be a poor fit for new problems and may result in economically irrational behavior. When environmental conditions change—such as regulatory requirements over business practices—adjustment of SOPs might be constrained by organizational structure, a phenomenon termed by Simpson et al. (2002, p. 32) as "creeping rationality." This creeping rationality might also contribute to the normalization of routine nonconformity (Vaughan 1999). It produces a decision framework in which "risky" decisions fall within the parameters of acceptable and normative behavior. Then, illegality and the belief that what one is doing is breaking the law are "not even on the radar screen" (Simpson et al. 2002, p. 29).

Furthermore, literature on corporate misconduct is full of examples of extraordinary situations that require extraordinary measures (Passas 1990, p. 173; Vandivier 2002; Vaughan 2002a). Extraordinary circumstances can justify a one-time deviation from the norm or the lowering of an ethical standard, after which the normal standard is put back in place. However, if the extraordinary situation continues or recurs, the deviation can become normalized. If the problem recurs, the deviation from the norm can be accepted again and again, and the deviation then becomes the new norm. This new norm will in turn also be used in situations in which the original justification does not apply. In this way, deviant behavior becomes the standard operating procedure instead of the outcome of rational decision making (Huisman 2010).

Organizational flaws and the normalization of deviance offer an alternative account to the rational choice explanation of white-collar crime and show that organizational factors can limit the rationality of decision making that has lawbreaking as an outcome. This perspective has been used not only in the United States to analyze cases of corporate crime but also in Australia and Europe (Braithwaite 1989; Van de Bunt and Huisman 2007; van Erp, Huisman, and Vande Walle 2015). However, the normalization of deviance may account for some instances of corporate malfeasance, but it might not apply in other cases of corporate or white-collar crime. For example, Calavita and Pontell's (1990) study of fraud committed in the savings and loans scandal of the 1980s, the analyses of Enron and other accounting scandals of the 1990s and 2000s (Friedrichs 2009), and examinations of mortgage fraud of the mid-2000s (Nguyen and Pontell 2010; Simpson 2011), as well work on fraud in the health care industry (Benson, Madensen, and Eck 2009), have found important explanations in amoral profit-seeking. It seems that in cases of industrial accidents, lawbreaking may be the unwanted outcome of organizational processes, whereas cases of financial fraud—committed for corporate or personal benefit—are the outcome of deliberate choice, albeit influenced by organizational factors. In a comparative analysis of US and European corporate fraud cases, Soltani (2014) identified significant similarities in ineffective boards, inefficient corporate governance and control mechanisms, distorted incentive schemes, accounting irregularities, failure of auditors, dominant CEOs, dysfunctional management behavior, and the lack of a sound ethical tone at the top.

2. *Individual or Corporate Actors?*

In addition to the rationality of corporate decision making, the anthropomorphic idea of a corporation being an actor has also been criticized. Chief among the proponents of the anthropomorphic view was Cressey—a student of Sutherland well known for his work on embezzlers (Cressey 1973)—who argued that the idea of corporations committing crimes is merely a legal fiction (Geis 1991). Cressey insisted that corporate crime involves acts committed by executives in these organizations and not by the organizations (Cressey 1989). Cressey maintained that the study of the corporation as a law-breaking actor is "self-defeating because it is based on the erroneous assumption that organizations think and act, thus saddling theoretical criminologists with the impossible task of finding the cause of crimes committed by fictious persons" (Cressey 1989, p. 32). Cressey's position, for his part, was criticized by Braithwaite and Fisse (1990), who argued that sound scientific theories can be based on a foundation of corporate action (Geis 1991, p. 21). Braithwaite and Fisse remonstrate Cressey that

> the notion that individuals are real, observable, flesh and blood, while corporations are legal fictions, is false. Plainly, many features of corporations are observable (their assets, factories, decision-making procedures), while many features of individuals are not (for example, personality, intention, unconscious minds). (p. 15)

Contemporary criminologists studying white-collar and corporate crime have tried to integrate organizational properties and dynamics with a rational choice model of corporate offending (Paternoster and Simpson 1996; Simpson et al. 2002; Simpson and Rorie 2011). On the one hand, and unlike perpetrators of street crime, white-collar offenders, acting in a business context, are generally viewed as more purposive and rational. Although some white-collar crimes might be committed without clear criminal intent (Levi 2008), offenders are assumed to be sensitive to changes in their environment that influence costs and benefits, more so than street criminals. White-collar offenders have a higher education and intellectual capabilities that have brought them into a white-collar position and that enable rational decision making. Also, they do not experience the low self-control that causes common offenders commit impulsive and seemingly irrational criminal behavior.

On the other hand, this process of decision making and the outcomes are strongly influenced by the organizational properties and dynamics of the corporation (Huisman 2016). Agency theory helps explain how the structural properties of agency relationships facilitate misconduct and confound systems of social control. In agency theory, organizations can be seen as principals and the employees as the agents carrying out the principals' actions (Shapiro 2005). Note, however, that organizational properties and dynamics that shape principal/agent-related actions are in turn shaped by factors external to the corporation. Literature often distinguishes among the sources of economic constraints (intraorganizational vs. external). However, beginning with Clinard and Yeager (1980), research is inconsistent regarding which matters, or which matters more. Most authors do agree that an integrated explanation of corporate crime should include micro-, meso-, and macro-levels in a multilevel approach (Shover and Bryant 1993; Vaughan 2002b).

Although this issue is outside the scope of this chapter, which focuses on white-collar offender decision making, it is briefly noted that the corporate environment can be divided into horizontal and vertical axes. On the horizontal axis is the branch of industry. Companies and people working in criminogenic branches of industry—that share relevant characteristics with other companies in the same branch of industry—commit more offenses than companies and people in other branches of industry. On the vertical axis is the supply chain. Industry actors operate autonomously on the market and are interdependent of suppliers and customers in the supply chain at the same time. Structural power rests primarily at the top of the supply chain, as was shown in research on various supply chains (Simpson 2011). Consequently, pressures and constraints mainly are pushed downward along the chain. This process, whereby pressures at one structural level affect others, is known as a "criminogenic tier" (Simpson 2011). According to Simpson, "A criminogenic tier approach has the utility to link individual and organization actors in a network of interdependent relationships" (p. 502).

No matter whether corporate crime is viewed as the outcome of decision making by the corporation or by individuals acting on behalf of the corporation, the process of decision making as well as its outcome are strongly influenced by organizational properties and dynamics. In the anthropomorphic view, corporations are often portrayed as having a *body* and a *mind*. Body refers to the corporate structure, and mind refers to the corporate culture. Another metaphor used is the *hardware* and the *software* of the corporation.

3. *Organizational Structure*

Structure refers to the way the corporation is organized and the division of tasks and responsibilities between the organizational members. Organizational structure influences decision-making processes, of which lawbreaking could be the outcome. Slapper and Tombs (1999) noted, "There is no doubt that corporate crime needs to be partially understood with respect to the organizational characteristics of different corporations, and any full-blown theory of corporate crime needs to take account of various aspects of organizational form and structure" (p. 126).

In the age of industrialization, the bureaucratic type of structure, which resembles a pyramid with integrated levels of management, was seen as the ideal type for modern corporations (Chandler 1962). In a centralized structure, decision-making power is concentrated in the top layer of management, and tight control is exercised over departments and divisions. Efficiency is achieved by a fixed division of tasks and a limited autonomy of the execution of these tasks, while being guided by hierarchical supervisions and detailed rules and regulations. This has also been linked to the causation of corporate crime. The many hierarchical layers in a bureaucratic structure might lead to information loss as commands and data are communicated up and down the hierarchy. This can prevent crucial information from reaching the top—strategic decision-making—level. Multiple hierarchical levels and divisionalized structures can create barriers to the discovery or reporting of illegal activity (Szwajkowski 1985; Dugan and Gibbs 2009). Furthermore, the long lines between the shop floor and executive offices might provide the opportunity to diffuse responsibilities for rule-breaking. This can create a de facto immunity for highly placed managers, who can remain at a safe distance from criminal acts performed lower in the corporate hierarchy (Kramer 1984, p. 70).

With growth and globalization in the second half of the twentieth century, multinational corporations faced higher degrees of external and internal uncertainty. Therefore, many corporations shifted to a more decentralized, independent structure referred to as the corporate multidivisional form (Chandler 1962; Dugan and Gibbs 2009). In a decentralized structure, decision-making power is distributed, and the departments and divisions have varying degrees of autonomy. In these "loosely coupled systems," the number of hierarchical levels is decreased, and subunits are permitted more autonomy (Keane 1995). Loose coupling might enable corporations to respond better to changes in the regulatory environment and, therefore, might be positively related to corporate compliance (Vaughan 1999). Nevertheless, several dysfunctions of loose coupling may be associated with illegal behavior as well. A parent company might not be attentive to disreputable practices of distant subsidiaries (Keane 1995). According to Tombs (1995, p. 141), decentralization and autonomy create an institutionalized "willful blindness" and mobilize techniques of distancing and neutralization, making corporate crimes more possible and more likely.

4. *Corporate Culture*

Culture refers to the set of beliefs, values, and norms that represents the unique character of an organization and provides the context for action in it and by it (Morgan 2006). In criminology, a strong explanatory power is attributed to corporate culture in the causation of white-collar and corporate crime. Corporate culture influences the perception of the attractiveness or the reprehensibility of alternative courses of action, and it influences the perception of the costs and benefits attached to those alternatives. Criminogenic corporate cultures can be typified by placing a high value on making profit and attaining ambitious financial goals, stimulating internal competition to achieve such goals, attaching much less (or no) value to the means by which these are achieved, showing a moral ambivalence to lawbreaking, strong individualization of moral responsibility and management behavior, and reward structures that enforce these elements (Clinard and Yeager 1980; Cohen 1995). Cohen noted that "these dimensions of corporate culture are seen as replacing the individual decision-making process with organizationally devised decision-making procedures, especially in relation to choices about violating the law or engaging in unethical business practices"(p. 188). A limitation is that such theorizing in the influence of corporate culture on criminal decision making in organizations is often based on case studies that post hoc reconstruct a corporate culture and thereafter ascribe criminal conduct. These cases are often high profile—in terms of both the seriousness of the crimes and the reputation of the offenders or the corporation—becoming landmark narratives of scholarship on organizational crime (Shover and Hochstetler 2002, p. 9). Fortunately, more robust research designs in the field of business ethics have validated the relationship between such unethical corporate cultures and unethical conduct, such as white-collar and corporate crime (Kaptein 2008, 2010).

B. Individual Characteristics

For a long time, the anthropomorphic view dominated corporate crime criminology. Even if corporate crime was viewed as the actions of individual agents, the explanation was situational because their actions were assumed to be influenced or even determined by the nature of corporations and the capitalist culture of competition in which corporations operate and that make these agents commit criminal actions to further corporate goals. Kramer (1984) noted that "the task for criminologists is to identify and examine the organizational factors that account for the illegal and/or socially harmful acts of individuals within corporations on behalf of the corporations themselves" (pp. 79–80). Braithwaite (1984) stated that most cases of corporate crime cannot be explained by "the perverse personalities of their perpetrators. . . . Rather than think of corporate actors as individual personalities, they should be viewed as actors who assume certain roles. The requirements of these roles are defined by the organization, not by the actor's personality" (p. 2). In trying to understand and explain white-collar crime, Coleman (1987, 2002, p. 409) spoke of the "irrelevance" of persons . According to Coleman, although some attention has been given to the psychological makeup of white-collar offenders, "this line of investigation has proved no more rewarding." He cited Sutherland (1949, 1983) in arguing strongly for the psychological normality of white-collar criminals, and he referred to various studies of different groups of white-collar offenders to support this conclusion (Spelling 1944; Bromberg 1965; Spencer 1965; Blum 1972).

1. *Sociodemographic Characteristics of White-Collar Offenders*

In this tradition, there is no use for any interest in sociodemographic characteristics of white-collar offenders. In addition, in the so-called "offender-based" approach in white-collar crime research, the sociodemographics are given by the white-collar people in occupational leadership positions and therefore of at least middle-class social status, white (at least in the Anglo-American world and Europe), middle-aged, and mostly male. Because of this circular argument and the problematic operationalization of high social status for empirical research, critics suggested that white-collar crime should not be typified by the profile of the offender but, rather, by the characteristics of the crime, being nonviolent property crimes (Edelhertz 1970). Using this approach, criminologists started gathering data on relatively large samples of officially registered white-collar offenders, including their sociodemographic characteristics (Wheeler et al. 1988; Weisburd, Chayet, and Waring 1990; Benson and Moore 1992; Benson and Kerley 2001; Weisburd and Waring 2001).

Although proponents of the offender-based tradition challenge that registered offences represent true white-collar crime, offense-based studies have produced considerable knowledge of the sociodemographics of perpetrators of white-collar crimes. To a large extent, this confirms the traditional profile of the white-collar offender. Compared to ordinary street criminals, the percentage of offenders of white-collar crimes who are Caucasian is much higher. In addition, offenders of white-collar crimes are even more predominantly male, older, have more stable relationships, and earn higher salaries and own more assets. These studies also demonstrated that white-collar offenders have a distinct criminal development from that of general offender populations: They start offending at an older age, the duration of their criminal career is relatively long, the frequency of offending is rather low, and they age out of crime much later in life. Recent research shows that these profiles and criminal careers are typical not only for American samples of white-collar offenders but also for European samples (van Onna et al. 2014). However, not all offenders are as stereotypical as one would expect because not all offenders of white-collar crimes fit the high-status profile, and these offense-based studies also identify smaller groups of highly active criminals who do not limit themselves to white-collar crimes and whose sociodemographic profiles are closer to those of ordinary criminals (Benson and Moore 1992; Benson and Kerley 2001; Weisburd and Waring 2001; van Onna et al. 2014). Proponents of the offender-based tradition, however, criticize that this is the result of the bias of selecting samples on convictions: Real white-collar crimes are not that easily criminalized, and real white-collar criminals escape criminal prosecution and conviction because of their socioeconomic status.

The most important sociodemographic factor in understanding individual differences in criminal behavior is gender. In general, men commit much more crime than women. However, for white-collar crime, this gender gap is even larger (Dodge 2009). There are two possible explanations for this difference. First, men may be more *exposed* to risk factors for committing white-collar crime because these are associated with the professional and managerial positions in business and organizations that are occupied mostly by men. This explanation is most in line with dominant criminological theories of white-collar crime that attribute criminal decision making to criminogenic business settings and organizational characteristics. When women do well at the higher levels of the labor market and enter management positions, this has no effect on the prevalence of white-collar crime because they will be exposed to the same risk factors as their male colleagues and therefore will show the same type of behavior. A second alternative explanation is that women are less *vulnerable* to such criminogenic factors and are less inclined to commit white-collar crime than their male colleagues. When women do well in the labor market and replace men in management positions, this should be good news because there will be less white-collar crime. Research on gender differences in the prevalence of white-collar crime and criminal decision making in business settings is too scarce to verify either of these contradicting explanations. Dodge elaborates the difficulties of unraveling the gender gap in white-collar crime: Gender differences are socially constructed, and the gender gap is influenced by gender biases in law enforcement.

However, recent studies on gender differences show different outcomes. Steffenmeister et al. (2013) focused on female involvement in 83 cases of corporate fraud involving 436 defendants. Their results seem to support the exposure hypothesis. Women were mostly not part of conspiracy groups; when women were involved, they had more minor roles and made less profit than their male co-conspirators. Female involvement was mostly due to close personal relationships with a main male co-conspirator or was related to typical female, mid-level, easily monitored positions, such as in compliance and accounting, in which they collected and reported financial data that, in turn, made them useful tools for the prosecution to gain evidence and to turn state's witness against co-conspirators (Steffenmeister et al. 2013). Using data obtained from a sample of adult MBA students, Piquero et al. (2013) explored the interplay between ethics, gender, and corporate offending decisions. Results are more in line with the vulnerability hypothesis. They show that women are more likely to believe that corporations need regulation (i.e., women are more ethical) and that they are less likely to report affirmative offending intentions. In addition, women are more than twice as likely than men to report lower offending intentions and higher ethics (Piquero et al. 2013).

Recent studies have also examined how male and female white-collar offenders neutralize their crimes. Outcomes are also unequivocal. Klenowski, Copes, and Mullins (2011) found that female and male white-collar offenders differ in the frequency with which they call forth specific accounts and in the rhetorical nature of these accounts. Klenowski et al. observed that when accounting for their crime, white-collar offenders draw on gendered themes to align their actions with cultural expectations of masculinity and femininity. They concluded that gender does constrain the accounts that are available to white-collar offenders. On the contrary, Viraitis et al. (2012) did not find such differences in the use of neutralization techniques between male and female white-collar offenders. With regard to the selection of techniques to neutralize their intentions to commit corporate crime, Viraitis et al. found more similarities than differences between men and women. They concluded that these results support the view that neutralization theory tends to operate in a gender-neutral way with respect to corporate offending intentions, at least in their sample.

2. Psychological Characteristics of White-Collar Offenders

Challenges to the leading organizational paradigm in the causation of corporate and white-collar crime have been made by recent research on the psychological and even biological characteristics of offenders of white-collar and corporate crimes. This research has revealed increasing evidence of particular personality traits and psychological disorders among white-collar offenders, just as research has documented among street offenders (Blickle et al. 2006; Bucy et al. 2008; Piquero, Schoepfer, and Langton

2010; Ragatz and Fremouw 2010). Biomedical research has even linked taking risks in the financial market to masculine hormones (Coates and Herbert 2010). In a study on neurobiological characteristics of white-collar criminals, Raine et al. (2011) found that compared to blue-collar offenders, white-collar criminals have better executive functioning, enhanced information processing, and structural brain superiorities that give them an advantage in perpetrating criminal offenses in occupational settings.

This research is very relevant to the rational choice perspective because it implies that decisions are influenced by psychological or even biological factors as these influence how individuals perceive and weigh the various costs and benefits associated with different potential courses of actions.

Several overview studies have been published that summarize personality traits of white-collar offenders.[1] According to Perri (2011), personalities of white-collar criminals have largely been ignored, and the modern approach to studying this type of crime incorporates personality traits as a factor in the decision to commit a crime. He further elaborates on three personality traits that are displayed both by white-collar criminals and by street-level offenders: antisocial personality disorder, narcissism, and psychopathy. Ragatz and Fremouw (2010) observe that available studies use different definitions of white-collar crime, different measures of white-collar crime, different measures of personality traits, and different research methodologies, making it difficult to generalize the findings. However, they find that compared to white-collar professionals, white-collar offenders tend to be lower in conscientiousness, agreeableness, and behavioral self-control. In addition, white-collar offenders report higher levels of anxiety and extroversion compared to white-collar professionals (Collins and Schmidt 1993; Kolz 1999; Alalehto 2003; Blickle et al. 2006).

In an overview study, Bucy et al. (2008) derive eight personality traits that are related to white-collar crime: a need for control, charisma, bullying, company ambitions, fear of falling, narcissism, a lack of social conscience, and a lack of integrity. Bucy et al. also interviewed 45 experts who had professional experience in working with white-collar criminals (lawyers and forensic accountants). These experts made a distinction between two types of white-collar criminals: leaders and followers. Leaders are described as possessing the following personality traits: intelligent, arrogant, greedy, successful, cunning, narcissistic, charismatic, determined, aggressive, and prone to take risks (Bucy et al. 2008). Only approximately half of the participants in this study reported specific personality traits of followers, but they were consistent: less aggressive, less confident, passive, gullible, prone to blindly follow others, subservient, dominated, less ambitious, and less likely to accept responsibility for their own actions (Bucy et al. 2008).

Blickle et al. (2006) present the results of the first cross-sectional study in Europe examining personality correlates of white-collar crime in business. They found that white-collar criminals were more hedonistic than noncriminal managers, meaning that material things and enjoyment are more strongly valued by white-collar criminals. Second, they found stronger narcissistic tendencies in white-collar criminals than in noncriminal managers. Third, self-control was lower in white-collar criminals than in their noncriminal counterparts. Finally, they found that white-collar criminals had a higher degree of conscientiousness compared to noncriminal managers (Blickle et al. 2006).

From the research on the psychological profiles of white-collar offenders, three categories of personality traits that are related to white-collar crimes can be deduced: risk-taking, narcissism, and psychopathy.

3. Risk-Taking and Self-Control

Between-individual differences in offending are related to a disposition toward (high) risk-taking and recklessness among white-collar offenders (Wheeler 1992). In this view, white-collar offenders are (more than others) willing to take high risks and manipulate the circumstances to their benefit. Research has shown white-collar offenders to be more risk-taking than their business peers (Collins and Schmidt 1993; Blickle et al. 2006). However, because risk-taking is also associated with legitimate business success (Brockhaus and Horwitz 1986; Friedrichs 2009), by itself it cannot account for white-collar offending. Other studies therefore suggest that white-collar offenders not only have a tendency to take risks but also do so in a calculative, aggressive, highly self-controlled manner (Benson and Moore 1992), and they also have a "desire for control"— a tendency that makes them decisive and active and prefer to avoid unpleasant situations or failure and manipulate events to ensure a desired event, thus leading to unethical behavior (Piquero, Exum, and Simpson 2005; Piquero, Schoepfer, and Langton 2010).

4. Narcissism

Perri (2011) describes narcissism as "a pervasive pattern of grandiosity, a need for admiration, a lack of empathy for others and a belief that one is superior, unique and 'chosen'" (p. 225). White-collar criminals who show narcissistic traits of entitlement may think they will never get caught and will therefore not be deterred from committing offenses (Perri 2011). Rijsenbilt and Commandeur (2013) explored the aspects of the relationship between possible indicators of CEO narcissism and fraud. Highly narcissistic CEOs undertake challenging or bold actions to obtain frequent praise and admiration. Their narcissistic tendencies may result in a stronger likelihood of CEOs undertaking bold actions with potential detrimental consequences for their organizations. Rijsenbilt and Commandeur's sample consisted of all CEOs from the 500 largest corporations in the United States between 1992 and 2008 who had more than three years of tenure. The measurement of CEO narcissism was based on 15 objective indicators and fit the main conceptualization of narcissism. Enforcement releases of the Securities and Exchange Commission were the indicators of managerial fraud. The findings confirmed the expected influence of plausible proxies for CEO narcissism on fraud by showing a positive relationship. This confirms the psychological perspective of CEO narcissism as a potential cause of fraud.

5. Psychopathy

Every human being has personality traits, but people score differently on the scales that have been developed to measure these traits. Although these scores can be related to criminal behavior, this does not prove a causal relation. Causality does exist when scores on certain personality traits are so extreme that they lead to dysfunctional behavior. A personality disorder that is traditionally related to violent crimes but that recently has also been related to white-collar crime is psychopathy. People who have psychopathic traits are "callous, lack conscience, have an inability to empathize with others, and show no remorse for their actions when they violate the rights of others" (Perri 2011, p. 226).

Although psychopathy is not yet an official disorder in the *Diagnostic and Statistical Manual of Mental Disorders* (American Psychiatric Association 2013), several self-report measures of psychopathy (e.g., Psychopathic Personality Inventory [Lilienfeld and Andrews 1996] and Levenson's Self-Report of Psychopathy Scale [Levenson, Kiehl, and Fitzpatrick 1995]) exist, making it possible and promising to assess for this personality dimension in white-collar professionals. Babiak and Hare (2006) found relatively high levels of psychopathy among CEOs of large corporations. Some of the characteristics of a psychopath (i.e., charming and grandiose) emulate those features that make a successful business person (Babiak 2007). Although such "functional" psychopathy might not always lead to white-collar crime, the question remains how psychopathy is related to white-collar crime. According to Perri (2011), specific psychopathic traits that cause white-collar criminals to offend are egocentrism, manipulation, exploitation, deception, and an attitude that causes them to believe that the ends justify the means. Notably, psychopathic white-collar criminals appear to be more calculating and reflective of their actions compared to ordinary street-level offenders (Perri 2011).

Ragatz and Fremouw (2010) explored psychopathic characteristics and psychopathology of white-collar offenders compared with non-white-collar offenders. The study sample included 39 white-collar crime offenders (offenders who had committed only white-collar crime), 88 white-collar versatile offenders (offenders who previously had committed non-white-collar crime), and 86 non-white-collar offenders incarcerated in a federal prison. Groups were matched on age and ethnicity. Offenders completed self-report measures of criminal thinking, psychopathic traits, and psychopathology. Lifestyle criminality was gathered via file review. Results demonstrated that white-collar offenders had lower scores on lifestyle criminality but scored higher on some measures of psychopathology and psychopathic traits compared to non-white-collar offenders.

C. Summary

The various views of the actor of white-collar and corporate crime can be positioned along two axes: rationalistic versus deterministic and individual versus organizational. For each of these four positions, organizational characteristics are relevant but for different reasons. From an organizational deterministic view, corporate behavior is shaped by its organizational traits, even without explicit choices being made. From an individual deterministic view, individual behavior of employees is programmed by organizational factors, binding the rationality of this decision making. In the organizational rationalistic view, organizational properties are influencing the process and outcome of corporate decision making. Finally, in the individual rationalistic view, organizational factors are influencing individual choices of action of corporate officials. Furthermore, this organizational paradigm is challenged because evidence is accumulating that personality traits can be related to white-collar crime. More research is needed to investigate to what extent the personalities of white-collar criminals differ from those of their non-offending peers and whether and how these traits are causally related to criminal decision making.

III. Characteristics of the Situation

Opportunity theories of crime stress the importance of the situations in which decisions to commit crime are made by potential offenders. These situations can be starting points for preventative interventions. These general notions have been specified in theoretical frameworks such as crime pattern theory, routine activity theory, and situational crime prevention. Applications of these opportunity theories to the field of white-collar and corporate crime are scarce. Opportunity theory has been applied to medical billing fraud, identity theft, and environmental pollution (Benson and Madensen 2007; Levi 2008; Huisman and Van Erp 2013). However, Benson et al. (2009) stress the potential of opportunity theories for understanding white-collar crimes. A routine activity approach seems particularly appropriate for the study of white-collar crime because it is committed at the workplace and thus directly arises out of the routines of everyday life. Furthermore, as Felson and Boba (2010) have put forward to promote their routine activities theory for studying white-collar crime, because of their job and position, many white-collar offenders have specialized access to their targets, such as corporate assets. In fact, Benson et al. argue that an opportunity perspective to white-collar crime is more fruitful than an approach based on offender characteristics or motive: "Focusing on how is likely to be more productive than focusing on why" (p. 176). Benson and Madensen suggest that crime prevention via the alteration of opportunity structures represents "a more fundamental way of thinking about the problem of white-collar crime control" than those of competing schools of thought in the sense that it "implicitly underlies" other approaches (p. 623).

Central elements in these situational theories of crime are targets (a person or some kind of property, which has to be available and attractive), guardianship over these targets (which has to be absent or ineffective), and the time and the place at which these elements converge with motivated offenders. This is mostly true for street crime. For white-collar offenses, Benson and Simpson (2009) added three properties of these core concepts: (1) The offender has *legitimate access* to the location in which the crime is committed, (2) the offender is *spatially separated* from the victim, and (3) the offender's actions have a *superficial appearance of legitimacy*.

A. Targetless, Victimless Crime?

It is more difficult to define the "targets" of white-collar and corporate crimes compared to most street crimes, for which a target can be a wallet to steal, a house to burgle, or a person to attack. Because white-collar and corporate crime are generally considered to be economically motivated, the "target" of white-collar and corporate crime must represent some form of economic value. This value can take many forms and shapes, and the targets to which this value is attached are generally less tangible than objects or persons. Targets of white-collar crimes can be financial transactions that can be manipulated, contracts that might be obtained through bribery, or stocks that are bought or sold on the basis of insider information. When corporate or white-collar crimes are labeled as fraud, generally some form of deceit is used to access the target. Furthermore, although the notion of a "target" assumes a kind of action by which it is attacked, corporate crimes can also take the form of non-action. Many business regulations require corporations to take certain actions—for instance, to guarantee the integrity of financial accounting procedures, to guarantee safe working conditions, or to prevent environmental harm. Complying with such regulations costs extra time and money and complicates business processes, whereas noncompliance saves money and effort. In other words, violations can be the result of not taking action rather than the outcome of purposeful criminal activity. Such violations are crimes of *omission*—crimes that constitute *not taking* actions prescribed by regulation or, in other words, crimes that consist of *doing nothing* (Huisman and van Erp 2013). In this sense, criminal decision making is not taking a decision to act in a way that is illegal but is taking the decision not to perform the legally prescribed action. In a crime of omission, the target is to save money or avoid losing money.

Perhaps due to this abstraction of the target, white-collar and corporate crimes are often presented as "victimless crimes." This is far from true. On the contrary, the harm to society caused by white-collar and corporate crimes is generally assessed as being much higher than the harm due to street crime (Slapper and Tombs 1999; Friedrichs 2009, p. 50). White-collar and corporate crime also do not just produce harm and victimization in a financial sense. Although being motivated by financial benefits, physical harm might still be the outcome of white-collar and corporate crimes. Unsafe working conditions can lead to injuries, sickness, or even death of employees. Unsafe products can damage the health of consumers. Corporate crime producing physical harm is sometimes referred to as "corporate violence" (somewhat dramatically framed by Punch [2000] as corporations that murder and managers who kill). The criminal law system of the United Kingdom even has a special provision for "corporate manslaughter."

Although white-collar and corporate crime are far from victimless, for many reasons the victimization of white-collar and corporate crime can be less visible compared to the victimization of other types of crime. First, a relatively large number of people can be victimized by relatively insignificant harm. A great number of companies can be victimized by paying too much for raw materials when prices are fixed by a cartel of suppliers

(Simpson and Piquero 2001). Large numbers of consumers are only minimally harmed by offenses involving a small deficiency in a large number of goods (Croall 2009).

Second, harm can be difficult to individualize for other reasons, such as in the case of environmental crime, tax fraud, and bribery. Although green criminologists stress that the victimization of environmental crimes need not be defined in terms of human harm but, rather, as harm to flora, fauna, and the ecosystem as a whole, these "victims" do not file complaints (South and Beirne 2006). Either the government or the "taxpayer" can be seen as the victim of tax fraud. In either case, the victim is a rather anonymous collective entity. Furthermore, in some cases, the direct victims of corruptive transactions may be clear, such as competing companies that do not get a contract that was obtained through bribery by the winning company. However, because bribery is a consensual crime from which conspiring parties benefit, it is often not immediately clear who suffers harm (Huisman and Vande Walle 2010). This does not mean that corruption is a victimless crime. On the contrary, although the European Commission estimates the cost of corruption within the European Union to be as much as 120 billion Euros, the cost of corruption for developing nations is even higher (Méon and Sekkat 2005; European Commission 2014).

Third, individual victims might not be aware of their victimization—for instance, when consumers are unaware of the negative health impact that certain prohibited additives in food products have or when they are unaware of the risk of certain financial products that have not been properly explained to them. Even when harmful effects on physical or financial health are revealed, victims might not be aware of the fact that the actions by which they are harmed can be labeled as criminal and therefore not view themselves as victims of crime. Vande Walle (2012) highlights the "time–space gap" that blurs the causality between decisions made in the boardroom of a Western multinational corporation and the harmful consequences of that decision for people on the other side of the world for many years later.

Fourth, not all people run the same risk of being victimized by white-collar or corporate crime. For instance, according to a study by Vande Walle (2012), women, children, and inhabitants of developing nations have the highest risk of being victimized by corporate crime in the pharmaceutical industry. In addition to a higher level of victim proneness, such victims are also less able to respond to their victimization and, for instance, start class actions against companies. An interesting exception is the case of the lawsuit that farmers and fisherman from the Niger delta region in Nigeria initiated against Shell because of the detrimental effects of environmental pollution that oil production had on their livelihood (Huisman 2010).

Fifth, victimization can be further obscured when victims play an active role in their victimization. In many cases of white-collar crime, an element of "blaming the victim" can be observed. Victims of white-collar or corporate crime may be blamed for their self-interest and greed, for instance, when they invest money in highly speculative ventures that turn out to be fraudulent (Friedrichs 2009, p. 55). A clear example is the Ponzi scheme by Bernard Madoff. Investors "allowed greed to overrule advice and continued to flow in good faith, trusting only what they saw, i.e. the returns" (Gregoriou and

Lhabitant 2009, p. 15). Some investors suspected that Madoff earned his profits through trickery and deceit, but they made no further inquiries because they viewed themselves as the beneficiaries of his actions (van de Bunt 2010, p. 445). When ignoring the common wisdom "If it is too good to be true, it is generally not true," victims of fraudulent schemes are likely to also blame themselves for their victimization. Robert Chew, who invested $1.2 million with Madoff and lost all of his money in the collapse of the Ponzi scheme, expressed this nagging feeling: "We all hoped, but we knew deep down it was too good to be true" (as quoted in Van de Bunt 2010, p. 445). Research by Holtfreter, Reisig, and Pratt (2008) showed that routine consumer activities (e.g., remote purchases) and low self-control increase the likelihood of fraud targeting and victimization.

Sixth, much legal and moral ambiguity surrounds many white-collar and corporate crimes (Passas 1990; Nelken 1994). Due to the invisibility of (direct) harm and the "technical" nature of the offenses and the business regulations that are being violated, it is not always clear that laws have been broken. In many cases, the line between "criminal," "illegal," and "legal" is narrow and contested: "What is, for example, the distinction between a legal 'puff,' a 'misleading' description, a 'con' and a fraud?"(Croall 2009, p. 128). Moreover, forms of (very) harmful corporate behavior might be viewed as being "criminal" by many, even though no laws have been broken (Passas and Goodwin 2005).

This diffuse victimization as a character of white-collar crime and corporate crime is seen as a facilitator to criminal decision making. It helps to neutralize the harmfulness and the reprehensibility of criminal decisions (Coleman 1987; Stadler and Benson 2012). Diffuse victimization helps to detach the decision maker from the harmful effects of his or her decision. A neutralization technique is, in essence, a reasoning that allows people to violate laws or other normative standards without having to consider themselves to be deviant or criminal. Such neutralization techniques are deemed especially important in corporate crime (Slapper and Tombs 1999; Klenowski 2012). Most likely, officials holding white-collar positions view themselves as respectable, law-abiding citizens. They went to university, have made careers for themselves, and are likely to come from the middle or upper classes of society. Doing criminal harm will be far from their self-image of being respectable entrepreneurs or managers. To sustain this self-image, they will have to neutralize the harmfulness of their behavior, for which the nature of many white-collar and corporate crimes gives ample opportunity.

B. Formal and Informal Guardians

According to situational theories of crime, guardians are actors who have the potential to detect crime and to intervene (Reynald 2009; Felson and Boba 2010). Informal guardians can distinguished from formal guardians by the fact that exercising guardianship is the formal and professional duty of the latter. The role of formal control and enforcement in regulating businesses has been extensively studied, such as the practices of law enforcement agencies (Vaughan 1983; Hutter 1997; Kluin 2014) and other professionals whose explicit duty it is to exercise control, including compliance officers, internal auditors, and external accountants (Verhage 2011).

Almost all aspects of business and corporate operations are regulated by administrative laws, aimed to protect—among other things—the integrity of financial account, the safety of workers, the health of consumers, and the environment. Compliance with these regulations is monitored by various regulatory authorities and inspection agencies. Most industrialized countries will have a financial markets authority, a tax authority, an occupational health and safety agency, an environmental protection agency, a food safety agency, and so on. Depending on the particular legal system, the violation of these regulations might qualify as administrative offenses or criminal offenses. Regardless, various forms of white-collar crime, such as bribery and most actions that would be labeled as "fraud," are directly criminalized by criminal law. Thus, in addition to regulatory agencies, criminal justice agencies can act as guardians for white-collar and corporate crime as well. This also means that these formal guardians can use a wide array of sanctions against both individual white-collar offenders and corporations, such as administrative or criminal fines, jail sentences, community service, punitive damages, punitive settlements, and revoking licenses.

Notwithstanding this elaborate scheme of formal guardians, many empirical studies of white-collar crime control and regulatory enforcement show that enforcement is weak: Inspection rates are low, detection chances are low, sanction certainty is low, and sanction severity is low (Simpson 2002). Furthermore, a firm generally is more likely to face civil or regulatory procedures than criminal prosecution as a result of an illegal act (Clinard and Yeager 1980; Geis and Salinger 1998; Simpson 2006). The application of civil or administrative law for regulatory enforcement can have punitive or even incapacitating effects—for instance, by issuing administrative fines or revoking licenses (Huisman 2012). Nevertheless, the deterrence style is mainly associated with using criminal law. In practice, however, criminal prosecution of corporate offenders is rather scarce. Most cases of corporate crime are not prosecuted, or at best they lead to a settlement. The reasons for lack of priority compared to street crime are multilayered: Specialized expertise is needed because of the organizational and technical complexity of cases of white-collar crime; there are coordination problems due to the many agencies involved in the enforcement of economic laws; white-collar offenders and large corporations might be able to hire the better lawyers and "influence" prosecution policies; and there are legal difficulties, such as establishing who is liable in corporate entities (proving *mens rea*) as well as the legal ambiguity of many regulations aimed at businesses. Nevertheless, public blaming has increasingly led to prosecution and sanctions in spectacular cases, evidenced by accounting fraud at Enron, the Ponzi scheme of Madoff, and the large-scale bribery at Siemens. Because of political considerations of prosecutors, resource constraints, and evidentiary limitations, there is a greater likelihood that criminal sanctions for white-collar crimes will be brought against individual managers rather than criminal sanctions for corporate wrongdoing (Laufer 1999; Wells 2001; Simpson 2006).

In addition to formal guardians, clients, suppliers, financiers, shareholders, and competitors ("stakeholders") can act as informal guardians because they might observe rule-breaking behavior and might act upon these observations. These "third parties" are an important element of modern theories on the regulation of business (Gunningham, Gabrovsky, and Sinclair 1998). First, third parties can increase the likelihood of the detection of white-collar crimes because they are familiar with the operations of offending companies or professionals. However, because third parties often have a vested interest in their relation with a corporation, this may present difficulties in sounding an alarm or even showing that they are aware of illegal activities at all (i.e., exercising guardianship). Indeed, in the situation of health care fraud, the US government increased the likelihood of detection by encouraging natural surveillance. It provided an incentive to individuals not employed by the government (e.g., patients and physicians' office assistants) to provide information to fraud investigators (Benson and Madensen 2007). The diffuse relation between third-party complicity and guardianship is also apparent in illegal price fixing schemes and antitrust regulation. Widespread price fixing in the Dutch construction industry was reported by a whistleblower who previously participated in the cartel (van de Bunt 2010).

Second, stakeholders such as consumers can become active "co-producers" of market regulation (Gunningham et al. 1998). The aggregate market pressure from consumers' individual actions can result in third-party enforcement when consumers "punish" offending companies and "reward" firms with a good compliance status (Bardach and Kagan 1982). Shareholders, financiers, and other stakeholders take offense at the negative publicity about the corporation and consequently alter their behavior by, for example, no longer buying the corporation's products or discontinuing their investments in the corporation. Corporations are only sensitive to reputational damage if the market imposes such sanctions. Third-party enforcement does not derive its strength from its financial implications but, rather, from loss of prestige and public humiliation as a result of negative publicity (Fisse and Braithwaite 1983; Braithwaite 1989). Karpoff, Lee, and Martin (2008) showed that these market sanctions are not imposed in all cases of corporate misconduct. In cases of accounting fraud and other misconduct that harm stakeholders directly, costs to the corporation that result from reputational damage decrease the value of the corporation far more than costs resulting from legal sanctions. Other forms of corporate misconduct, such as environmental damage and bribery of foreign officials, do not usually lead to reputational damage. As long as the misconduct does not have a direct effect on their financial interests, clients, shareholders, and financers do not seem to be bothered.

C. Opportunity-Driven Crimes Versus Necessity-Driven Crimes

Situational crime prevention theory, routine activity theory, and crime pattern theory address how environments shape crime opportunities and subsequently how modifications in environments can diminish criminal opportunities. The "family" of opportunity-based theories are rooted in a rational actor approach in the sense that they regard offenders as purposive and crime as the outcome of a decision-making process, in which the offender weighs the costs and benefits of criminal behavior in a specific situation. As mentioned previously, this view fits well with the general perception of white-collar and corporate offenders.

The routine activity theory assumes the presence of motivated offenders and explains variation in crime as due to the availability of targets and guardians (Felson and Boba 2010). However, in white-collar crime theory, two types of situational conditions have been found to influence the motivation of offenders to commit white-collar crimes. Most theories of white-collar crime assume that the pursuit of individual material success or some kind of business advancement is the core motivation behind white-collar crime. Depending on both the person and the situation, this financial motivation can take two very different forms: profit maximization or loss minimization—in other words, the drive for more material gain versus the fear of losing what was already gained (Coleman 1987; Benson and Simpson 2009). The motivation for committing white-collar crime, greed or need, strongly depends on the situation—for example, situations in which criminal opportunities that are too strong to resist and situations in which law-breaking is perceived as unavoidable for economic survival.

1. *Opportunity-Driven Crimes*

A situation in which criminal opportunities that are too strong to resist is referred to as "lure" by Shover and Hochstetler (2006): "Lure is not criminal opportunity, but in the absence of credible oversight it is" (p. 28). Situations of lure seem to account for many instances of white-collar crime in the past. In these situations, white-collar crime is so widespread that not only the criminally disposed but also reputable businessmen and corporation are drawn to the lure. The widespread looting of the savings and loan thrifts in the 1980s in the United States, with losses of billions of dollars, is a well-published example (Calavita and Pontell 1990).

Although such inviting conditions might contribute to the explanation of criminal decision making on the micro-level of individual cases of white-collar crime, at least three types of situations on the macro-level have been identified in criminological study: inflated markets, war, and globalization.

An inflated, "bull" market refers to a situation of such strong economic growth that it seems every player on the market can prosper—a situation that leads to the general perception that even taking the highest risks will guarantee reward. Such market conditions tempt established, bona fide actors to take excessive risks while they also attract *mala fide* actors drawn to the lure, resulting in fraud schemes that contribute to implosion of these inflated markets. Studies by Robb (1992) and Wilson (2006) on fraud in the financial markets in Victorian England show a pattern that would reappear in modern European and American history. Due to industrialization and especially railway expansion, Victorian England witnessed a boom of the fairly new stock market. According to an observer at that time, the very same motivations of the modern speculator ("to make money easily and in a hurry") would also ensure the "inauguration, development and rapid progress of 'high art' crime" through the activities of those keen to exploit such exciting times (Evans 1859, as quoted in Wilson, 2006, p. 1075). The excitement of the intense stock market activity due to the railway boom, and the desperation of investors to make money, promoted empty and assetless "bubble" companies alongside legitimate rail schemes (Wilson 2006, p. 1076). In September 1845, *The Bankers' Magazine* warned that as many as three-fourths of investment opportunities were not intended to "devise good lines of railway" and, instead, sought to "rob and delude the public . . . and swindle their subscribers . . . by squandering and embezzling their deposit money" (Wilson 2006, p. 1076). The Victorian cases constituted the discovery of "financial crime" and led to the redefinition of certain business activity as being criminal activity in England (Wilson 2006).

The observation about the criminogenics of inflated markets is still as topical today as it was in Victorian England. Various studies attribute the widespread fraud with subprime mortgages that sparked the 2007 credit crisis to a combination of a boom in the market for subprime mortgages (and a booming economy in general), a cultural celebration of home ownership (even for the poor), and a governmental policy of deregulation of the financial markets (Friedrichs 2009, pp. 245–46).

A second situation that generates widespread opportunity for business-related crimes combined with a loss of control is war. It is not widely known that in his landmark book on white-collar crime, Sutherland (1949)—and later Clinard (1952)—devoted considerable attention to corporate crimes in the context of World Wars I and II. War effort creates an acute and huge demand for raw materials, products, and services while there is no time for public tendering procedures and negotiation. Companies can easily exploit these "no-bid" contracts. Many of America's largest manufacturers, corporations selling raw materials, and food and beverage processors and distributors engaged in war profiteering during World Wars I and II, for instance, by providing inferior products and overcharging for products (Galliher and Guess 2009). These practices have also occurred during recent wars. Recently, the multibillion-dollar company Halliburton has come under scrutiny for allegedly massively overbilling the US military for its services in Operation Restoring Freedom in Iraq and for systematically charging for services that were never provided (Rothe 2006).

Sutherland (1949) also noted how war contributed to the opportunity to commit antitrust offenses by the misuse of monopolies to inflate prices because of increased demand due to the war production. Some US companies even engaged in price fixing with the enemy. For example, after General Electric (GE) and Krupp (in Nazi Germany) signed an agreement, the price of the raw material tungsten carbide jumped from $48 per pound to $453 per pound (Galliher and Guess 2009). Controlling production in this manner was profitable for business on both sides of the military divide. GE paid royalties to the Nazis on every pound produced, thereby helping the German economy, and it informed the Nazis exactly how much tungsten carbide the US government was using in its buildup for war. In a court case, GE was fined only $20,000.

Finally, criminologists have attributed strong criminogenic effects to globalization (Friedrichs and Rothe 2014). In this view, globalization creates opportunities and motives for multinational corporations to commit crimes, and it reduces the possibility of combating these crimes. The world is small enough for corporations to conduct business on a global level, but it is too large for authorities to expand their control over business. According to Passas (1999), globalization multiplies, intensifies, and activates "criminogenic asymmetries" that lie at the root of corporate crime. Passas defines these asymmetries as "structural disjunctions, mismatches and inequalities in the spheres of politics, culture, the economy and the law" (p. 400). These are criminogenic in that they offer illegal opportunities, create motives to use these opportunities, and make it possible for offenders to avoid prosecution. For instance, globalization created the possibility to transport toxic waste to Third World countries, where it could be disposed of at a fraction of the cost and without the threat of law enforcement. Illicit opportunities are produced by the fragmentation of enterprises and transactions over more than one country. Price asymmetries create the incentive to move hazardous business activities to countries lower costs for disposal. In addition, regulatory asymmetries create the opportunity to reduce costs on environmental management and labor conditions while law enforcement asymmetries weaken social controls. In addition, globalization has fostered "competitive deregulation." Competition on global markets has driven corporations to "race to the bottom" to find low-cost services provided through poor environmental standards, low wages, and poor working conditions. Passas emphasizes that the illicit opportunities created by globalization are not counterbalanced by international forms of control of multinational enterprises or transnational business ventures.

2. *Necessity-Driven Crimes*

Lawbreaking is perceived as unavoidable for economic survival in situations in which individuals or corporations perceive that they are not able to achieve economic goals by using legitimate means. The inability to achieve economic goals is one of the most frequent explanations given for white-collar crime (for an overview, see Huisman 2016). In many texts, this causal factor is analyzed from the perspective of Merton's (1938) strain theory, which links crime to the strain generated from the blockage of success goals. Thus, assuming that the goals of corporations are profit maximization and market share expansion, the theory would predict that the motivation to engage in illegal behavior increases when these goals are more difficult to achieve by using legal means. Then, corporations opt for illegitimate means to achieve the goals set by a capitalist economy.

Most studies find a positive relation between economic strain and the occurrence of corporate crime. However, the available studies use a number of different ways to conceptualize and measure economic strain. Some studies find that assuming the goal of profit produces more strain than other types of organizational goals (Jenkins and Braithwaite 1993; Benson and Simpson 2009, p. 60). Results also vary by how profits are measured (e.g., stockholders' equity, return on sales, and return on assets) (Simpson and Rorie 2011). Several studies show a positive relation between level of competition in an industry and corporate lawbreaking. Companies in highly competitive markets experience more strain, resulting in more criminal decisions (Baucus and Near 1991; Martin et al. 2007; Wang and Holtfreter 2012; Ramdani and Witteloostuijn 2013).

According to Agnew, Piquero, and Cullen (2009, p. 39), financial stress is a rough surrogate for goal blockage. They state that studies have found that corporate crime is more common among companies with relatively low profits, companies with declining profits, companies in depressed industries, and companies experiencing other types of financial problems. Furthermore, they argue that crime may result not only from the inability to satisfy economic goals but also from the experience or threat of economic problems (Agnew et al. 2009, p. 43). Also, a number of variables may produce different levels of strain—for example, the magnitude of the gap between expected goals and actual achievement, the level of pressure put on organizational agents to achieve goals, and the availability of legitimate and illegitimate alternatives.

Strain can be experienced on the various hierarchical levels within the organization: by top management when it sets overambitious goals and by the shop floor when standard operating procedures are insufficient. Several studies show that strain is often experienced at the middle-management level, when middle managers are responsible for executing the ambitious targets set by top management while not being provided with the appropriate means of doing so (Clinard 1983; Dean, Beggs, and Keane 2010).

Whereas blocked goal attainment is often viewed as a situation that leads to criminal decision making by corporations, the risk of losing what has already been gained or achieved is more associated with individual white-collar crime (Coleman 1987; Wheeler 1992). In the rational choice perspective, benefits are typically conceptualized as gains. There is considerable psychological research, however, demonstrating that avoiding loss is a more powerful motivator than reaping a gain (Kahneman and Tversky 2000). Coleman suggested that the fear of failure is the inevitable correlate of the demand for success, and that it is a strong motivator in committing crime to prevent anticipatory loss. Wheeler argued that "it should be among those in fear of falling rather than those holding steady or on the rise, where a higher proportion of the white-collar offenders may be found" (p. 117). Weisburd and Waring (2001) labeled a group of low-frequency offenders of white-collar offenses as "crisis responders," engaging in criminality in response to some type of perceived crisis in their professional or personal lives. However, in a first attempt to empirically measure the fear of falling, Piquero (2012) found that the effect of fear of falling is significant, but it exerts a negative—and not the expected positive—effect on intentions to engage in white-collar crime.

D. Summary and Further Research

Because white-collar crimes and especially corporate crimes are generally viewed as more rational and more purposive than ordinary crimes, a focus on opportunities for white-collar and corporate crime seems logical. A better understanding of the situations in which these crimes are committed, and the opportunities that these situations generate, is fruitful for the understanding of both the *how* and the *why* of white-collar crime. Opportunities are related to particular settings, and with regard to white-collar crime, this means that much more research can be done to better understand the specific types of white-collar and corporate crime that are related, for instance, to specific branches of industry, specific markets, and specific products and services, such as the adulteration of food products (Spink, Elliott, and Swoffer 2013).

The application of criminological opportunity theories, such as routine activity theory and situational crime prevention theory, requires adjusting these general theories to the specifics of white-collar and corporate crime. Targets and victims have different meanings, and the conversion of time and place in the commission of a crime is less relevant for many white-collar crimes. Guardianship is very relevant, however, and because contemporary theories on the regulation of business stress the importance of corporate self-regulation and monitoring by third-party actors, much more empirical research on the working of corporate compliance officers and third-party monitors is desperately needed because these might have great potential in preventing white-collar and corporate crime.

A pitfall would be to view all business actors as amoral calculators who will seize every attractive illegitimate business opportunity to make money. Normally law-abiding corporate managers and business owners might only or especially be receptive to criminogenic opportunities when economic conditions compel them to do so. How these legitimate and illegitimate opportunities are perceived in the process of the evaluation of choice alternatives is explored in the next section.

IV. Perception and Evaluation of Choice Alternatives

Given the nature of the decision-making actor and the characteristics of the situation, the third element that determines the outcome of the choice is the perception and evaluation of choice alternatives by the actor. Even if the situation is given, this does not mean an actor is aware of its characteristics, such as utility of the outcome, probability of being caught, sanction probability and sanction severity, or reputation enhancement or damage. Also, not every actor weighs these factors in the same manner. Here, research on the assessments of costs and benefits of white-collar crime and corporate crime as well as its legitimate alternative—regulatory compliance—is discussed.

A. Perceived Costs and Benefits of White-Collar and Corporate Crime

As mentioned in section II, white-collar crime and corporate crime are generally viewed as calculated and instrumental actions that require some degree of planning and foresight. Paternoster and Simpson (1993) developed a rational choice theory of corporate crime that incorporates most factors that have been discussed in this chapter. They present a subjective expected utility model that privileges individuals over organizations as actors and decision makers but recognizes that the cost–benefit assessments will incorporate both individual and organizational factors. These factors include (1) perceived certainty and severity of formal legal sanctions as well as informal sanctions, (2) feelings of shame and guilt about the act, (3) perceived costs of rule compliance, (4) perceived benefits of noncompliance, (5) moral inhibitions, (6) perceived legitimacy and fairness regulatory requirements, (7) situational characteristics of the criminal event, and (8) prior offending history of the actor.

Both Paternoster and Simpson were involved in a number of vignette studies, further exploring the influence of these factors on offending decision making. Smith, Simpson, and Huang (2007) studied the interaction of morality, anticipated informal consequences, and legal sanctions with respect to decisions of corporate managers to engage in illegal and unethical conduct. Using the business ethics and deterrence literature as a guide, they hypothesized that formal sanctions could have a direct or indirect effect on corporate offending. They found that formal sanctions operated primarily through the perceived consequences of engaging in the violation (outcome expectancies) and moral evaluations. Those who perceived formal sanctions to be likely and consequential were also more apt to think that there would be substantial informal consequences for them if the acts were discovered within the firm. Similarly, respondents who thought formal sanctions were likely and severe were more apt to judge the illegal behaviors as morally wrong.

Smith et al. (2007) also discovered that morality and informal sanctions were directly associated with a lower likelihood of illegal conduct. However, moral evaluations also lowered offending risk through outcome expectancies (i.e., informal consequences). Respondents who objected to the acts on moral grounds were more apt to view the behaviors as having substantial informal costs that then affected offending considerations. In another vignette study, Paternoster and Simpson (1996) also found that moral considerations had a strong influence on managers' offending intentions. Only when moral obligations were weakened was compliance based on the perceived incentives and costs of crime. They concluded that some behaviors are "nonmarket areas" where moral inhibitions are so predominate that instrumental considerations are simply not salient. Other behaviors are then "market areas" where the decision to commit them is influenced by considerations of cost and benefit. Paternoster and Simpson further found that offending intentions were increased when managers thought the law was *illegitimate*. To the extent that regulatory laws are unreasonable and perceived by managers as harmful, even the morally inhibited may be swayed into committing corporate crime if there is "some appeal to a higher, more compelling, or more immediate moral principle" (Paternoster and Simpson 1996, p. 577).

The question is thus what factors can explain when and for whom certain actions are "nonmarket" areas. These might also be related to individual, organizational, and situational conditions. Furthermore, processes of socialization and normalization of deviance can draw nonmarket issues into the realm of "market areas" (Coleman 1987). Such processes may even make corporate complicity to gross human rights violations into a "market area," as it has been illustrated by various historical (van Baar and Huisman 2012) and contemporary cases of corporate involvement in war crimes, crimes against humanity, and genocide (Huisman 2010).

Smith et al. (2007) found that many of their respondents (most with significant managerial experience) indicated a willingness to offend even though the depicted behavior directly contradicted their moral code. In criminological theory on white-collar crime, this is explained by the use of neutralization techniques, as discussed in section II. Denial of responsibility and an appeal to higher loyalties are common rationalizations for white-collar offenders that view themselves as respectable managers (Stadler and Benson 2012). Smith et al. also speculated that following the dictates of one's superior within an organization would give individuals an excuse to morally disengage (Bandura 2002) while invoking a "role-based motive" (Kelman and Hamilton 1989, p. 209). In other words, within an organization, following the direct order of one's supervisor trumps individual moral responsibility. This process allows the actor to claim a duty to obey while denying personal responsibility for the action. Totally understudied is the question of whether gender has an effect on such assessment and moral valuation of choice alternatives, although the scarce research suggests that female managers are more ethical and are less inclined to commit white-collar crime (Piquero 2012).

The previous discussion suggests that chances of getting caught and formal sanctions have an indirect deterrent effect via the feelings of shame and guilt these might invoke. Moral considerations thus influence the assessment of costs and benefits and the attractiveness of choice alternatives. There is hardly any scientific evidence of more direct deterrent effects of law enforcement and formal sanction. Explicit within rational choice theories of corporate crime is the idea that a prospective offender weighs the benefits and costs of illegal behavior, including assessments of the threat (certainty and severity) of perceived formal sanctions. Nonetheless, research suggests that formal sanctions may not be perceived as very likely or consequential.

Further evidence is far from conclusive regarding whether corporate violators should be criminally prosecuted or whether other justice systems (civil or administrative) produce higher levels of corporate compliance or if sanctions should be directed toward the company, responsible managers, or both (Coffee 1980; Laufer 1994; Paternoster and Simpson 1996). Simpson (2006) stated, "Generally, these questions have generated more smoke than light because there is so little empirical research from which to draw firm conclusions" (pp. 69–70). In a first systemic review on corporate deterrence for the Campbell Collaboration Crime and Justice Group, in which 2003 studies of any intervention type (legal and otherwise) that focused on corporate crime prevention and control were included, Simpson et al. (2014) found hardly any significant effects. They concluded that it is premature to draw any conclusions from these findings and call instead for more methodologically rigorous and focused studies.

Indirect effects of general deterrence on corporate lawbreaking were found by Thornton, Gunningham, and Kagan (2005) in a survey study of 233 firms in several industries in the United States. Thornton et al. sought to answer whether, when severe legal penalties are imposed on a violator of environmental laws, other companies in the same industry actually learn about such "signal cases" and whether this changes firms' compliance-related behavior. It was found that only 42 percent of respondents could identify the "signal case," but 89 percent could identify some enforcement actions against other firms, and 63 percent of firms reported having taken some compliance-related action in response to learning about such cases. Overall, Thornton et al. concluded that because most firms are in compliance already (for a variety of other reasons), this form of "explicit general deterrence" knowledge usually does not serve to enhance the perceived threat of legal punishment, but it does serve as *reassurance* that compliance is not foolish and as a *reminder* to check on the reliability of existing compliance routines.

In a follow-up study of waste processing firms in the Netherlands, van Wingerde (2012) reached the same conclusion: Deterrent threats hardly have a direct effect on business compliance because the imposed sanctions and the probability of getting caught are too low. As far as sanctions influencing the compliance behavior of waste companies, this effect runs through the social environment. Negative publicity, reputational damages, and pressure from the local community are far more threatening than formal legal sanctions. Moreover, this research shows that sanctions can have an impact on those businesses that are already committed to complying with the law. Sanctions then serve as a reminder to check whether they are still in compliance and as a reassurance that compliance is the right thing to do and that bad actors are caught. This study also shows that this indirect effect depends on the degree of social responsiveness of the regulated actor. The more responsive the business firm, the sooner it views signals from outside the firm as meaningful to corporate compliance (van Wingerde, 2012).

B. Motivations for Compliance

From the previous discussion, it can be concluded that the traditional costs of crime that seem relevant from a rational choice perspective have only an indirect effect in the case of corporate crime. The effects sanction probability and severity depend on and are mediated by more general attitudes toward regulatory compliance. As mentioned previously, much corporate and white-collar crime constitutes the violation of business regulation. Criminologists examine the "dark side" of this compliance spectrum. A substantial number of studies have been performed on the "bright side"—the motivations to comply. This research is also relevant for the negative pole of the compliance spectrum and for understanding regulatory non-compliance and rule violation. Variations in regulatory compliance have been found to be related to variations in motivations for compliance. In this research, three types of motives for compliance and noncompliance are distinguished: economic, social, and normative motives (Parker and Nielsen 2011). Economic motives refer to the extent to which the firm is committed to maximizing its own economic or material utility, such as increasing turnover and profit. Social motives refer to the extent to which a firm is committed to earning the approval and respect of significant people with whom an actor interacts, including other businesses, trading partners, employees, customers, local communities, and the wider public. Normative motives refer to the extent to which the firm is committed to obeying the regulation for its own sake because of a sense of moral agreement with the specific regulation or a generalized sense of moral duty to comply. Empirical research has made it clear that a wide range of relevant motives interact with each other in reciprocal ways: Personal motives of managers are extrapolated to the motivations of the organization as a whole, and these shape the motivations of individual managers.

These types of motivations lead to different compliance outcomes between different actors and in different situations. Even economic motives can lead corporations to do more than is legally required—so-called "overcompliance" or "beyond compliance" (Pearce and Tombs 1997, p. 82). For example, Borck and Coglianese (2011) found that firms that join voluntary environmental self-regulation programs may increase sales to customers who value environmental protection, attract more productive employees, enhance the productivity of current employees who value working for an environmentally friendly firm, or win favorable treatment from the regulator in the enforcement of other mandatory environmental regulations. The proposition of regulatory scholars that affirmative motivations for compliance such as good intentions and a sense of obligation to comply can explain overcompliance (May 2004; Parker and Nielsen 2011) seems to fit well with rational choice perspectives on corporate crime that incorporate individual moral views into cost–benefit calculations and decision making regarding corporate crime (Paternoster and Simpson 1996; Gibbs 2012).

C. Summary and Further Research

Rational choice theory holds that the perception and evaluation of choice alternatives by an actor determine the outcome of the choice. Although the study of opportunities for white-collar crime in the previous section proved relevant for designing prevention techniques, research on the assessments of costs and benefits of white-collar crime is very relevant to white-collar crime deterrence. However, the recent and state-of-the-art systematic review on corporate deterrence by Simpson et al. (2014) may lead to the pessimistic conclusion that there is no empirical proof for the deterrence of corporate crime. Contemporary work on deterrence, however, does not consider whether sanctions affect compliance but instead considers the conditions under which sanctions affect compliance. This research focuses on individual and situational differences and emphasizes decision making under conditions of uncertainty (Loughran et al. 2011; A. Piquero et al. 2012). Although there has been little work in the corporate crime area using this approach, the management literature has been focused on risk and ambiguity and how these affect corporate decision making. Also, the approach can explain some of the contradictory findings in the corporate crime literature. For example, Simpson and Rorie found that corporate fraud occurs under conditions of both economic constraint and growth (Simpson and Rorie 2016).

Furthermore, a bias of criminology could be that criminologists consider only the dark side of human behavior because they usually take crime as the outcome of choice evaluations. For scholars of white-collar crime, the bright side of regulatory compliance studies is a very relevant field of research. Bringing together these research disciplines might produce new inspiration for research on white-collar offender decision making.

V. Conclusion

Although many criminological texts on white-collar crime and corporate crime begin with the observation that these topics have been rather neglected in mainstream criminology, it can be alternatively concluded that during the approximately 75 years since the introduction of the concept of white-collar crime by Edwin Sutherland, much knowledge has been produced. The controversy regarding the question of human or organizational agency has led to theoretical and empirical insights on organizational conditions that are related to white-collar and corporate crime. Economical strains, diffused organizational structures, and unethical corporate cultures contribute to offending decision making. Furthermore, the controversy between offender- and offense-based definitions of white-collar crime has led to much knowledge regarding the traits and profiles of white-collar criminals, who are predominantly male, white, middle-aged, and middle-class or higher class, and who use their occupational status and expertise to commit their crimes. Furthermore, the application of theories and methodologies from mainstream criminology has been proven fruitful to provide new insights into white-collar crime, such as the life course criminology on white-collar criminal careers and developmental trajectories and opportunity theories on situational conditions for white-collar crime. Finally, compared to ordinary street crime, the regulatory context of white-collar crime offers many more preventative and punitive interventions that may influence the outcome of criminal decision making.

This is not to say that no important work needs to be done. Most theorizing as well as empirical research has focused on large, corporate, for-profit organizations. More research needs to been done on causal factors of white-collar crime in the context of small and medium-sized business enterprises, as well as in the context of nonprofit organizations. Also, although much theorizing and case study research has been done on the influence of organizational characteristics and conditions on individual and corporate decision making that has criminal outcomes, more rigorous empirical research designs are needed to test the assumptions that have been deduced from this research. In addition, although preliminary findings suggest that white-collar criminals can be typified by certain personality traits—and perhaps even personality disorders—it remains unclear to what extent and in what ways these traits are causally related to white-collar criminal decision making.

The situational conditions for white-collar crime and corporate crime seem to fundamentally differ from those of street crimes and, therefore, challenge the usability of accepted opportunity theories of crime. Central notions from situational theories of crime need to be further translated and empirically studied in the field of white-collar and corporate crime. Motivated white-collar offenders often do not meet in time and place with suitable targets in the absence of guardians. Also, these targets are usually not tangible objects or persons but, rather, less tangible phenomena such as administrative processes and business transactions. Although serious and widespread cases of corporate crime are importantly due to deregulation and lack of compliance monitoring, these cases also lead to new or more potent regulatory agencies acting as formal guardians. Outside the United States, the capacity and powers of such agencies are not so much dependent on a shift in political power (Friedrichs 2009; Huisman et al. 2015). Furthermore, potential informal guardians in the context of business (employees, customers, and stakeholders) are omnipresent, and several studies have been done on their operations, but little empirical knowledge is available on how guardianship influences white-collar and corporate criminal decision making. However, it is clear that situational conditions can influence or even create the motivations to commit white-collar crime because certain business or organizational settings may create opportunities that are too attractive to resist or there is a perceived need for committing white-collar or corporate crime for economic survival.

Research on the perception and evaluation of choice alternatives by white-collar actors and their assessments of the costs and benefits of white-collar crime and corporate crime shows that formal sanctions are more likely to be effective if associated with the prospect of loss of respect of business associates, friends, and family. Because formal sanctions are indicative of society's views of the morality of certain conduct, they probably influence the individual's moral evaluations of the act. Simpson (2006) concludes that interventions that better familiarize managers with the law and that convey the moral opprobrium attached to illegal conduct may effectively inhibit white-collar and corporate crime. The impact of informal sanctions by stakeholders in response to corporate wrongdoing is potentially greater than the impact of formal sanctions, but this potential and its interaction with formal sanctions of white-collar and corporate crime need to be further explored. Doing right and doing what is expected not only serve as an inhibition to commit white-collar crime but also can be strong motives for corporations and their managers to comply with regulations and even to go "beyond compliance." Future studies should therefore examine not only offending decision making but also the full spectrum of compliance decisions in corporate and white-collar contexts.

NOTE

1. Helpful for the overview presented here were the master's thesis of Ronja Tuerlings and the PHD thesis of Joost van Onna, both supervised by the author.

References

Agnew, Robert, Nicole Leeper Piquero, and Francis T. Cullen. 2009. "General Strain Theory and White-Collar Crime." In *The Criminology of White-Collar Crime*, edited by David Weisburd and Sally Simpson, pp. 35–60. New York: Springer.

Alalehto, T. 2003. "Economic Crime: Does Personality Matter? *International Journal of Offender Therapy and Comparative Criminology* 47(3): 335–55.

American Psychiatric Association. 2013. *Diagnostic and Statistical Manual of Mental Disorders*, 5th ed. Arlington, VA: American Psychiatric Publishing.

Babiak, P. 2007. "From Darkness into the Light: Psychopathy in Industrial and Organizational Psychology." In *The Psychopath: Theory, Research, and Practice*, edited by H. Herve and J. C. Yuille, pp. 411–28. Mahwah, NJ: Erlbaum.

Babiak, P., and R. D. Hare. 2006. *Snakes in Suits: When Psychopaths Go to Work.* New York: HarperCollins.

Bandura, A. 2002. "Selective Moral Disengagement in the Exercise of Moral Agency." *Journal of Moral Education* 3:101–19.

Bardach, E., and R. A. Kagan. 1982. *Going by the Book: The Problem of Regulatory Unreasonableness.* Philadelphia: Temple University Press.

Baucus, Melissa S., and Janet P. Near. 1991. "Can Illegal Corporate Behavior Be Predicted? An Event History Analysis." *Academy of Management Journal* 34:9–36.

Benson, Michael L., and Elizabeth Moore. 1992. "Are White-Collar and Common Offenders the Same? An Empirical Examination and Theoretical Critique of a Recently Proposed General Theory of Crime." *Journal of Research in Crime and Delinquency* 29(3): 251–72.

Benson, Michael L., and Kent R. Kerley. 2001. "Life-Course Theory and White-Collar Crime." In *Contemporary Issues in Crime and Criminal Justice: Essays in Honor of Gil Geis*, edited by N. Pontell and D. Shichor, pp. 121–36. Upper Saddle River, NJ: Prentice Hall.

Benson, Michael L., and Sally S. Simpson. 2009. *White-Collar Crime: An Opportunity Perspective.* New York: Routledge.

Benson, Michael L, and Tamara D. Madensen. 2007. "Situational Crime Prevention and White-Collar Crime." In *International Handbook of Corporate and White Collar Crime*, edited by H. Pontell and G. Geis, pp. 609–26. New York: Springer.

Benson, Michael L., Tamara D. Madensen, and John E. Eck. 2009. "White-Collar Crime from an Opportunity Perspective." In *The Criminology of White-Collar Crime*, edited by Sally S. Simpson and David Weisburd, pp. 175–93. New York: Springer.

Blickle, Gerhard, Alexander Schlegel, Pantaleon Fassbender, and Uwe Klein. 2006. "Some Personality Correlates of Business White-Collar Crime." *Applied Psychology: An International Review* 55:220–33.

Blum, Richard C. 1972. *Deceivers and Deceived.* Springfield, IL: Charles C Thomas.

Borck, Jonathan C., and Cary Coglianese. 2011. "Beyond Compliance: Explaining Business Participation in Voluntary Environmental Programs." In *Explaining Compliance: Business Response to Regulation*, edited by Christine Parker and Vibeke Lehmann Nielsen, pp. 139–169. Cheltenham, UK: Elgar.

Braithwaite, John. 1984. *Corporate Crime in the Pharmaceutical Industry.* London: Routledge and Kegan Paul.

Braithwaite, John. 1989. "Criminological Theory and Organizational Crime." *Justice Quarterly* 6:333–58.

Braithwaite, John, and Brent Fisse. 1990. "On the Plausibility of Corporate Crime Theory." *Advances in Criminological Theory* 2:15–38.

Brockhaus, Robert. H. Sr., and P. S. Horwitz. 1986. "The Psychology of the Entrepreneur." In *The Art and Science of Entrepreneurship*, edited by D. L. Sexton, and R. W. Smilor, pp. 25–48. Cambridge, MA: Ballinger.

Bromberg, Walter. 1965. *Crime and the Mind: A Psychiatric Analysis of Crime and Punishment.* New York: Macmillan.

Bucy, Pamela H., Elizabeth P. Formby, Marc S. Raspanti, and Kathryn E. Rooney. 2008. "Why Do They Do It? The Motives, Mores, and Character of White-Collar Criminals." *St. John's Law Review* 82:401–571.

Calavita, K. C., and H. N. Pontell. 1990. "'Heads I Win, Tails You Lose': Deregulation, Crime and Crisis in the Savings and Loan Industry." *Crime Delinquency* 36:309–41.

Chandler, Alfred D. 1962. *Strategy and Structure: Chapters in the History of the American Industrial Enterprise.* Cambridge, MA: MIT Press.

Clinard, Marshall B. 1952. *The Black Market: A Study of White Collar Crime.* New York: Rinehart and Company.

Clinard, Marshall B. 1983. *Corporate Ethics and Crime: The Role of Middle Management.* Beverly Hills, CA: Sage.

Clinard, Marshall B., and Peter C. Yeager. 1980. *Corporate Crime.* New York: Free Press.

Clinard, Marshall B., and Richard Quinney. 1973. *Criminal Behavior Systems: A Typology*, 2nd ed. New York: Holt, Rinehart and Winston.

Coates, John M., and Joe Herbert. 2010. "Endogenous Steroids and Financial Risk Taking on a London Trading Floor." *Proceedings of the National Academy of Sciences* 105:6167–72.

Coffee, J. 1980. "No Soul to Damn, No Body to Kick: An Unscandalized Inquiry into the Problem of Corporate Punishment." *Michigan Law Review* 79:386–457.

Cohen, Deborah V. 1995. "Ethics and Crime in Business Firms: Organizational Culture and the Impact of Anomie." In *The Legacy of Anomie Theory*, edited by Freda Adler and William S. Laufer, pp. 183–206. Vol. 6 of *Advances in Criminological Theory*. New Brunswick, NJ: Transaction.

Coleman, James W. 1987. "Toward an Integrated Theory of White-Collar Crime." *American Journal of Sociology* 93:406–39.

Coleman, James W. 2002. "Organizational Actors and the Irrelevance of Persons. In *Corporate and Governmental Deviance: Problems of Organizational Behaviour in Contemporary Society*, edited by M. David Ermann and Richard J. Lundmann, pp. 95–110. New York: Oxford University Press.

Collins, Judith M., and Frank L. Schmidt. 1993. "Personality, Integrity and White Collar Crime: A Construct Validity Study." *Personnel Psychology* 46:295–311.

Cressey, D. R. 1973. *Other People's Money.* Montclair, NJ: Patterson Smith.

Cressey, D. R. 1989. "The Poverty of Theory in Corporate Crime Research." In *Advances in Criminological Theory*, vol. 1, edited by W. S. Laufer and F. Adler, pp. 31–55. New Brunswick, NJ: Transaction.

Croall, H. 2009. "White Collar Crime, Consumers and Victimisation." *Crime, Law and Social Change* 51(1):127–46.

Dean, Kathy Lund, Jeri Mullins Beggs, and Timothy P. Keane. 2010. "Mid-level Managers, Organizational Context, and (Un)ethical Encounters." *Journal of Business Ethics* 97: 51–69.

Dodge, M. 2009. *Women and White Collar Crime.* Upper Saddle River NJ: Prentice Hall.

Dugan, Laura, and Carole Gibbs. 2009. "The Role of Organizational Structure in the Control of Corporate Crime and Terrorism." In *The Criminology of White-Collar Crime*, edited by Sally S. Simpson and David Weisburd, pp. 111–28. New York: Springer.

Edelhertz, H. 1970. *The Nature, Impact and Prosecution of White-Collar Crime*. Washington, DC: US Department of Justice.

European Commission. 2014. *EU Anti-corruption Report*, Brussels, COM(2014) 38 final.

Felson, Marcus, and Rachel Boba. 2010. *Crime and Everyday Life*. Thousand Oaks, CA: Sage.

Fisse, B., and J. Braithwaite. 1983. *The Impact of Publicity on Corporate Offenders*. Albany: State University of New York Press.

Friedrichs, David O. 2009. *Trusted Criminals: White-Collar Crime in Contemporary Society*, 4th ed. Belmont, CA: Wadsworth.

Friedrichs, David O., and D. L. Rothe. 2014. *Crimes of Globalization: New Directions in Critical Criminology*. New York: Routledge Taylor and Francis.

Galliher, J. F., and J. F. Guess. 2009. "Two Generations of Sutherland's White-Collar War Crime Data and Beyond." *Crime, Law and Social Change* 51(1): 163–74.

Geis, G. 1991. "White-Collar Crime: What Is It?" *Current Issues in Criminal Justice* 3:9–24.

Geis, G. 2007. *White-Collar and Corporate Crime*. Upper Saddle River, NJ: Prentice Hall.

Geis, Gilbert, and Lawrence S. Salinger. 1998 "Antitrust and Organizational Deviance." In *Research in the Sociology of Organizations: Deviance in and of Organizations*, vol. 15, edited by Peter A. Bamberger and William J. Sonnenstuhl, pp. 71–110. Stamford, CT: JAI Press.

Gibbs, Carole. 2012. "Corporate Citizenship and Corporate Environmental Performance." *Crime, Law, and Social Change* 57:345–72.

Gregoriou, G. N., and F. Lhabitant. 2009. *Madoff. A Riot of Red Flags*. Nice, France: EDHEC.

Gunningham, Neil, Peter Gabrovsky, and Darren Sinclair. 1998. *Smart Regulation. Designing Environmental Policy*. Oxford: Clarendon.

Holtfreter, Kristy, Michael D. Reisig, and Travis C. Pratt. 2008. "Low Self-Control, Routine Activities, and Fraud Victimization." *Criminology* 46:189–220.

Huisman, W. 2010. *Business as Usual? Corporate Involvement in International Crimes*. The Hague, the Netherlands: Eleven International.

Huisman, W. 2012. "The Application of Administrative Law Against Organized Crime: Refusing and Withdrawing Licenses as Incapacitation." In *Incapacitation: Trends and New Perspectives*, edited by M. Malsch, M. Duker, and H. Nijboer, pp. 185–202. Farnham, UK: Ashgate.

Huisman, W. 2016. "Criminogenic Organizational Properties and Dynamics." In *The Oxford Handbook of White-Collar Crime*, edited by M. B. Benson, F. T. Cullen, and S. von Slyke, pp. 435–62. New York: Oxford University Press.

Huisman, W., and J. van Erp. 2013. "Opportunities for Environmental Crime: A Test of Situational Crime Prevention Theory." *British Journal of Criminology* 53(6): 1178–1200.

Huisman, W., J. van Erp, G. Vande Walle, and J. Beckers. 2015. "Criminology and White-Collar Crime in Europe." In *The Routledge Handbook of White-Collar and Corporate Crime in Europe*, edited by J. van Erp, W. Huisman, and G. Vande Walle, pp. 1–22. London: Routledge.

Huisman, W. and G. Vande Walle. 2010. "The Criminology of Corruption." In *The Good Cause: Theoretical Perspectives on Corruption*, edited by G. de Graaf, P. von Maravic, and P. Wagenaar, pp. 1342–69. Leverkusen, Germany: Budrich.

Hutter, B. M. 1997. *Compliance: Regulation and Environment*. Oxford: Clarendon.

Jenkins, A., and J. Braithwaite. 1993. "Profits, Pressure and Corporate Lawbreaking." *Crime, Law and Social Change* 20:221–32.

Kahneman, Daniel, and Amos Tversky. 2000. *Choices, Values, and Frames*. Cambridge: Cambridge University Press.

Kaptein, Muel. 2008. "Developing and Testing a Measure for the Ethical Culture of Organizations: The Corporate Ethical Virtues Model." *Journal of Organizational Behavior* 29:923–47.

Kaptein, Muel. 2010. "The Ethics of Organizations: A Longitudinal Study of the US Working Population." *Journal of Business Ethics* 92:601–18.

Karpoff, J., D. Scott Lee, and Gerald S. Martin. 2008. "The Cost to Firms of Cooking the Books." *Journal of Financial and Quantitative Analysis* 43:581–612.

Keane, Carl. 1995. "Loosely Coupled Systems and Unlawful Behavior: Organization Theory and Corporate Crime." In *Corporate Crime: Contemporary Debates*, edited by Frank Pearce and Laureen Snider, pp. 168–81. Toronto: University of Toronto Press.

Kelman, H. C., and V. L. Hamilton. 1989. *Crimes of Obedience: Towards a Social Psychology of Authority and Responsibility*. New Haven, CT: Yale University Press.

Klenowski, Paul M. 2012. "Learning the Good with the Bad: Are Occupational White-Collar Offenders Taught How to Neutralize Their Crimes? *Criminal Justice Review* 37(4): 461–77.

Klenowski, Paul M., H. Copes, and C. W. Mullins. 2011. "Gender, Identity, and Accounts: How White Collar Offenders Do Gender When Making Sense of Their Crimes. *Justice Quarterly* 28:46–69.

Kluin, M. 2014. *Optic Compliance: Enforcement and Compliance in the Dutch Chemical Industry*. Delft, the Netherlands: TU Delft.

Kolz, A. 1999. "Personality Predictors of Retail Employee Theft and Counterproductive Behavior." *Journal of Professional Services Marketing* 19:107–14.

Kramer, Ronald C. 1984. "Corporate Criminality: The Development of an Idea." In *Corporations as Criminals*, edited by in Eileen Hochstedler, pp. 75–95. Beverly Hills, CA: Sage.

Laufer, William S. 1994. "Corporate Bodies and Guilty Minds." *Emory Law Journal* 79: 649–732.

Laufer, William S. 1999. "Corporate Liability, Risk Shifting, and the Paradox of Compliance." *Vanderbilt Law Review* 54:1343–1420.

Lee, Matthew T., and M. David Ermann. 2002. "Pinto Madness: Flaws in the Generally Accepted Landmark Narrative." In *Corporate and Governmental Deviance: Problems of Organizational Behaviour in Contemporary Society*, edited by M. David Ermann and Richard J. Lundmann, pp. 277–306. New York: Oxford University Press.

Levenson, M. R., K. A. Kiehl, and C. M. Fitzpatrick. 1995. "Assessing Psychopathic Attributes in a Noninstitutionalised Population." *Journal of Personality and Social Psychology* 68: 151–58.

Levi, Michael. 2008. "Combating Identity and Other Forms of Payment Fraud in the UK: An Analytical History." In *Perspectives on Identity Theft*, edited by Megan M. McNally and Graeme R. Newman, pp. 111–131. Monsey, NY: Criminal Justice Press.

Loasby, Brian J. 2008. "Organizational Decision-Making: Economic and Managerial Considerations." In *Corporate and White-Collar Crime*, edited by J. Minkes and L. Minkes, pp. 122–40. London: Sage.

Loughran, Thomas A., Raymond Paternoster, Alex R. Piquero, and Greg Pogarsky. 2011. "On Ambiguity in Perceptions of Risk." *Criminology* 49(4): 1029–61.

March, J. G., and H. A. Simon. 1958. *Organizations*. New York: Wiley.

Martin, Kelly D., John B. Cullen, Jean L. Johnson, and K. Praveen Parboteeah. 2007. "Deciding to Bribe: A Cross-Level Analysis of Firm and Home Country Influences on Bribery Activity." *Academy of Management Journal* 50:1401–22.

May, Peter J. 2004. "Compliance Motivations: Affirmative and Negative Bases." *Law and Society Review* 38:41–68.

Méon, P., and K. Sekkat. 2005. "Does Corruption Grease or Sand the Wheels of Growth?" *Public Choice* 22:69–97.

Merton, Robert K. 1938. "Social Structure and Anomie." *American Sociological Review* 3:672–82.

Morgan, Gareth. 2006. *Images of Organization*. Thousand Oaks, CA: Sage.

Nelken, D. 1994. "White-Collar Crime." In *The Oxford Handbook of Criminology*, edited by M. Maguire, R. Morgan, and R. Reiner, pp. 355–92. Oxford: Clarendon.

Nguyen, T. H., and H. N. Pontell. 2010. "Mortgage Origination Fraud and the Global Economic Crisis." *Criminology and Public Policy* 9(3): 591–612.

Parker, Christine, and Vibeke Lehmann Nielsen, eds. 2011. *Explaining Compliance: Business Response to Regulation*. Cheltenham, UK: Elgar.

Passas, Nikos. 1990. "Anomie and Corporate Deviance." *Contemporary Crises* 14:157–78.

Passas, Nikos. 1999. "Globalization, Criminogenic Asymmetries and Economic Crime." *European Journal of Law Reform* 1:399–423.

Passas, Nikos, and Neva R. Goodwin. 2005. *It's Legal But It Ain't Right: Harmful Social Consequences of Legal Industries*. Ann Arbor: University of Michigan Press.

Paternoster, Raymond, and Sally Simpson. 1993. "A Rational Choice Theory of Corporate Crime." In *Advances in Criminological Theory: Routine Activity and Rational Choice*, vol. 5, edited by R. V. Clarke and M. Felson, pp. 549–83. New Brunswick, NJ: Transaction Books.

Paternoster, Raymond, and Sally S. Simpson. 1996. "Sanction Threats and Appeals to Morality: Testing a Rational Choice Model of Corporate Crime." *Law and Society Review* 30:549–83.

Pearce, Frank, and Steve Tombs. 1997. "Hazards, Law, and Class: Contextualizing the Regulation of Corporate Crime." *Social and Legal Studies* 6:79–107.

Perri, F. S. 2011. "White-Collar Criminals: The 'Kinder, Gentler' Offender?" *Journal of Investigative Psychology and Offender Profiling* 8(3): 217–41.

Piquero, Alex, Raymond Paternoster, Greg Pogarsky, and Thomas Loughran. 2012. "Elaborating the Individual Difference Component in Deterrence Theory." *Annual Review of Law and Social Science* 7:335–60.

Piquero, Nicole Leeper. 2012. "The Only Thing We Have to Fear Is Fear Itself: Investigating the Relationship Between Fear of Falling and White-Collar Crime." *Crime and Delinquency* 58:362–79.

Piquero, Nicole Leeper, Andrea Schoepfer, and Lynn Langton. 2010. "Completely out of Control or the Desire to Be in Complete Control? An Examination of How Low Self-Control and the Desire for Control Relate to Corporate Offending." *Crime and Delinquency* 56:627–47.

Piquero, Nicole Leeper, M. Lyn Exum, and Sally S. Simpson. 2005. "Integrating the Desire-for-Control and Rational Choice in a Corporate Crime Context." *Justice Quarterly* 22(2): 252–80.

Piquero, Nicole Leeper, Lynne M. Vieraitis, Alex R. Piquero, Stephen G. Tibbetts, and Michael Blankenship. 2013. "The Interplay of Gender and Ethics in Corporate Offending Decision-Making." *Journal of Contemporary Criminal Justice* 29(3): 385–98.

Punch, M. 2000. "Suite Violence. Why Managers Murder and Corporations Kill." *Crime, Law and Social Change* 33:243–80.

Ragatz, Laurie, and William Fremouw. 2010. "A Critical Examination of Research on the Psychological Profiles of White-Collar Criminals." *Journal of Forensic Psychology Practice* 10:373–402.

Raine, A., W. S. Laufer, Y. Yang, K. L. Narr, P. Thompson, and A. W. Toga. 2011. "Increased Executive Functioning, Attention, and Cortical Thickness in White-Collar Criminals." *Human Brain Mapping* 33(12): 2932–40.

Ramdani, Dendi, and Arjen van Witteloostuijn. 2013. "Bribery." In *Encyclopedia of Criminology and Criminal Justice*, edited by Jay S. Albanese and Jacqueline L. Schneider, pp. 1–5. Malden, MA: Wiley-Blackwell.

Reynald, D. 2009. "Guardianship in Action: Developing a New Tool for Measurement." *Crime Prevention and Community Safety* 11:1–20.

Robb, G. 1992, *White-Collar Crime in Modern England: Financial Fraud and Business Morality, 1845–1929*. Cambridge: Cambridge University Press.

Rothe, D. 2006. "War Profiteering and the Pernicious Beltway Bandits: Halliburton and the War on Terror." In *State–Corporate Crime: Wrongdoing at the Intersection of Business and Government*, edited by R. C. K. R. J. Michalowski, pp. 215–238. New Brunswick, NJ: Rutgers University Press.

Rijsenbilt, J. A., H. R. Commandeur, and A. G. Z. Kemna. 2013. "Narcissus Enters the Courtroom: CEO Narcissism and Fraud." *Journal of Business Ethics* 117(2): 413–29.

Shapiro, Susan P. 2005. "Agency Theory." *Annual Review of Sociology* 31:263–84.

Shover, Neal, and Andy Hochstetler. 2002. "Cultural Explanation and Organizational Crime." *Crime, Law, and Social Change* 37:1–18.

Shover, Neal, and Andy Hochstetler. 2006. *Choosing White-Collar Crime*. New York: Cambridge University Press.

Shover, Neal, and K. M. Bryant. 1993. "Theoretical Explanations of Corporate Crime." In *Understanding Corporate Criminality*, edited by M. B. Blankenship, pp. 141–76. New York: Garland.

Simpson, Sally S. 2002. *Corporate Crime, Law and Social Control*. Cambridge: Cambridge University Press.

Simpson, Sally S. 2006. "Corporate Crime and Regulation." In *Managing and Maintaining Compliance: Closing the Gap Between Science and Practice*, edited by H. Elffers, W. Huisman, and P. Verboon, pp. 63–90. The Hague, the Netherlands: Boom Legal Publishers.

Simpson, Sally S. 2011. "Making Sense of White Collar Crime: Theory and Research." *Ohio State Journal of Criminal Law* 8:481–502.

Simpson, Sally S., and Melissa Rorie. 2011. "Motivating Compliance: Economic and Material Motives for Compliance." In *Explaining Compliance: Business Response to Regulation*, edited by Christine Parker and Vibeke Lehmann Nielsen, pp. 59–77. Cheltenham, UK: Elgar.

Simpson, Sally S., and Melissa Rorie. 2016. "Economic Fluctuations and Crises." In *Oxford Handbook of White-Collar Crime*, edited by Shanna Van Slyke, Michael Benson, and Francis T. Cullen, pp. 326–44. Oxford: Oxford University Press.

Simpson, Sally S., Melissa Rorie, Mariel Elise Alper, Natalie Schell-Busey, William Laufer, N. Craig Smith. 2014. *Corporate Crime Deterrence: A Systematic Review*. Oslo, Norway: Campbell Collaboration.

Simpson, Sally S., and Nicole Leeper-Piquero. 2001. "The Archer Daniels Midland Antitrust Case of 1996: A Case Study." In *Contemporary Issues in Crime and Criminal Justice: Essays in Honor of Gilbert Geis*, edited by Henry Pontell and David Schichor, pp. 175–194. Old Tappan, NJ: Prentice Hall.

Simpson, Sally S., Nicole Leeper Piquero, and Raymond Paternoster. 2002. "Rationality and Corporate Offending Decisions." In *Rational Choice and Criminal Behavior*, edited by Alex R. Piquero and Steven G. Tibbetts. New York: Taylor and Francis.

Slapper, Gary, and Steve Tombs. 1999. *Corporate Crime*. Harlow, UK: Longman.

Smith, N. Craig, Sally S. Simpson, and Chun-Yao Huang. 2007. "Why Managers Fail to Do the Right Thing: An Empirical Study of Unethical and Illegal Conduct." *Business Ethics Quarterly* 17:633–67.

Spink, J., C. T. Elliott, and K. P. Swoffer. 2013. "Defining Food Fraud Prevention to Align Food Science and Technology Resources." *Food Science and Technology* 27(4): 39–42.

Soltani, B. 2014. "The Anatomy of Corporate Fraud: A Comparative Analysis of High Profile American and European Corporate Scandals." *Journal of Business Ethics* 120:251–74.

South, Nigel, and Peirce Beirne. 2006. *Green Criminology*. London: Ashgate.

Spelling, Lonell S. 1944. "Specific War Crimes." *Journal of Criminal Law and Criminology* 34:303–10.

Spencer, John C. 1965. "White Collar Crime." In *Criminology in Transition*, edited by E. Glover, H. Mannheim, and E. Miller, pp. 233–66. London: Tavistock.

Stadler, William A., and Michael L. Benson. 2012. "Revisiting the Guilty Mind: The Neutralization of White-Collar Crime." *Criminal Justice Review* 37(4): 494–511.

Sutherland, Edwin H. 1949. *White Collar Crime*. New York: Dryden.

Sutherland, Edwin H. 1983. *White-Collar Crime: The Uncut Version*. New Haven, CT: Yale University Press.

Szwajkowski, Eugene. 1985. "Organizational Illegality: Theoretical Integration and Illustrative Application." *Academy of Management Review* 10:558–67.

Thornton, D., N. Gunningham, and R. A. Kagan. 2005. "General Deterrence and Corporate Environmental Behavior." *Law and Policy* 27(2): 262–88.

Tombs, Steve. 1995. "Corporate Crime and New Organizational Forms." In *Corporate Crime: Contemporary Debates*, edited by Frank Pearce and Laureen Snider, pp. 132–47. Toronto: University of Toronto Press.

van Baar, A., and W. Huisman. 2012. "The Ovenbuilders of the Holocaust: A Case-Study of Corporate Complicity to International Crimes." *British Journal of Criminology* 52(6): 1033–50.

van de Bunt, Henk. 2010. "Walls of Secrecy and Silence: The Madoff Case and Cartels in the Construction Industry." *Criminology and Public Policy* 9(3): 435–53.

van de Bunt, Henk, and Wim Huisman. 2007. "Organizational Crime in the Netherlands." *Crime and Justice* 35:217–60.

van Erp, J., W. Huisman, and G. Vande Walle. 2015. *The Routledge Handbook of White-Collar and Corporate Crime in Europe*. London: Routledge.

van Onna, Joost, Victor van der Geest, Wim Huisman, and Adriaan Denkers. 2014. "Divergent Trajectories: Criminal Careers of White Collar Crime Offenders in the Netherlands. *Journal of Research in Crime and Delinquency* 51(6): 759–84.

van Wingerde, Karin. 2012. *De afschrikking voorbij. Een empirische studie naar afschrikking, generale preventie en regelnaleving in de Nederlandse afvalbranche*, Nijmegen, the Netherlands: Wolf Legal Publishers.

Vande Walle, G. 2012. "Conflict Resolution or Risk Management? Reflecting to a Study of Conflicts Between Victims and Businesses in the Pharmaceutical Sector. In *Social Analysis of Security*, edited by P. Ponsaers, pp. 32–55. The Hague, the Netherlands: Eleven International.

Vandivier, K. 2002. "Why Should My Conscience Bother Me? Hiding Aircraft Brake Hazards." In *Corporate and Governmental Deviance*, edited by M. D. Ermann and R. J. Lundman, pp. 102–22. New York: Oxford University Press.

Vaughan, Diane. 1983. *Controlling Unlawful Organizational Behaviour: Social Structure and Corporate Misconduct*. Chicago: University of Chicago Press.

Vaughan, Diane. 1999. "The Dark Side of Organizations: Mistake, Misconduct, and Disaster" *Annual Review of Sociology* 25:271–305.

Vaughan, Diane. 2002a. "The Challenger Space Shuttle Disaster: Conventional Wisdom and a Revisionist Account." In *Corporate and Governmental Deviance: Problems of Organizational Behaviour in Contemporary Society*, edited by M. David Ermann and Richard J. Lundmann, pp. 306–33. New York: Oxford University Press.

Vaughan, Diane. 2002b. "Criminology and the Sociology of Organizations: Analogy, Comparative Social Organization, and General Theory." *Crime, Law and Social Change* 37:117–36.

Verhage, A. 2011. *The Anti-money Laundering Complex and the Compliance Industry*. London: Routledge Taylor Francis.

Vieraitis, Lynne M., Nicole Leeper Piquero, Alex R. Piquero, Stephen G. Tibbetts, and Michael Blankenship. 2012. "Do Women and Men Differ in Their Neutralizations of Corporate Crime?" *Criminal Justice Review* 37:478–93.

Wang, Xia, and Kristy Holtfreter. 2012. "The Effects of Corporation- and Industry-Level Strain and Opportunity on Corporate Crime." *Journal of Research in Crime and Delinquency* 49:151–85.

Weisburd, David, Ellen F. Chayet, and Elin Waring. 1990. "White-Collar Crime and Criminal Careers: Some Preliminary Findings." *Crime and Delinquency* 36:342–55.

Weisburd, David, and Elin Waring. 2001. *White-Collar Crime and Criminal Careers*. Cambridge: Cambridge University Press.

Wells, Celia. 2001. *Corporations and Criminal Responsibility*. New York: Oxford University Press.

Wheeler, S. 1992. "The Problem of White-Collar Crime Motivation." In *White-Collar Crime Reconsidered*, edited by K. Schlegel and D. Weisburd, pp. 108–23. Boston: Northeastern University Press.

Wheeler, S., D. Weisburd, E. Waring, and N. Bode. 1988. "White-Collar Crimes and Criminals." *American Criminal Law Review* 25:331–57.

Wilson, S. 2006. "Law, Morality and Regulation: Victorian Experiences of Financial Crime." *British Journal of Criminology* 4:1073–90.

CHAPTER 33

....

ORGANIZED CRIME AND
PROTECTION RACKETS

....

PAOLO CAMPANA

TACKLING the issue of organized crime is not an easy task. One of the main challenges is posed by the ambiguity of the concept (Paoli 2002; Edwards and Levi 2008; Varese 2010). I briefly touch upon the problem of defining organized crime in the next section, but let me anticipate that this chapter adopts a rather narrow view of the phenomenon and focuses mostly on a specific set of criminal activities, namely protection rackets. This choice is in line with the works of Schelling (1971), Reuter (1983), Gambetta (1993), and Varese (2001, 2010). Protection rackets, and more generally the supply of illegal private ordering (i.e., illegal governance), possess a number of distinctive features that separate them from other criminal endeavors. This, in turn, points to a set of theoretical problems that are relevant to both scholars and practitioners—they will be explored in the remainder of the chapter. Moreover, teasing out the specificity of protection rackets provides a useful term of comparison for those studies seeking to explore other types of criminal activities that do not fall within this category but are nonetheless relevant and fairly common (e.g., instances of smuggling activities or, more broadly, the so-called "transit crime"; see Kleemans 2007 and Campana 2016). Finally, although this chapter relies mostly on studies conducted on the Italian and American Mafia, both the mechanisms and the theoretical problems discussed are by no means specific to these two mafia groups or territories. Scholars have pointed to the presence of protection rackets in countries as diverse as Japan, Russia, Georgia, Hong Kong, China, Mexico, Italy, and the United States, to name just a few examples (for reviews, see Paoli 2014; Varese 2014). Although on a much smaller scale, evidence of protection rackets has also been documented in countries that are not normally associated with this phenomenon, such as Sweden (Skinnari, Anders Stenström, and Korsell 2012).

This chapter proceeds as follows. The first section offers some clarification on the concept of organized crime, and section II discusses the factors that may lead to the emergence of illegal monopolies. Section III explores in some depth one of these monopolies, namely illegal protection. Section IV discusses the challenges that illegal protectors may face when running their operations. Section V critically assesses the interplay between globalization and organized crime. Finally, section VI reviews a new framework for interpreting transnational organized crime operations, and section VII offers some conclusions.

I. WHAT IS ORGANIZED CRIME?

Despite a century-long debate among scholars, practitioners, and policymakers, organized crime still remains a contentious concept (Levi 1998; Paoli 2002; von Lampe 2008; Varese 2010; Paoli and Vander Beker 2014). Scholars have so far failed to agree on a single accepted definition of what organized crime is, and they have instead produced a large number of often competing definitions. Varese (2010) lists 115 definitions, which have originated from a variety of sources between 1915 and 2009, and notes a sharp increase in their number from the 1960s onwards.[1]

In his groundbreaking work on the business of organized crime, Shelling (1971) defines the latter in terms of its attempt to gain monopolistic control over markets. According to Schelling (1971, pp. 72–73), monopoly—or exclusivity—is the defining characteristic that sets organized crime apart from other criminal organizations while placing it closer to legitimate governments in analytical terms. Organized crime is therefore not just "crime that is organized" but, rather, a set of organizations that seek governing authority in the underworld:

> From all accounts, organized crime does not merely extend itself broadly, but brooks no competition. It seeks not merely influence, but exclusive influence. In the overworld its counterpart would be not just organized business, but monopoly. And we can apply to it some of the adjectives that are often associated with monopoly—ruthless, unscrupulous, greedy, exploitative, unprincipled. (p. 73)

As with governments, organized crime groups alike need to have an element of monopoly as we "cannot all be obeying two conflicting sets of laws, two competing sets of trafficking lights, or two contradictory building codes, and paying taxes to maintain duplicate street systems or armies" (Schelling 1971, p. 74). Organized crime groups—and some legitimate governments for that matter—may not be entirely successful in their attempt to gain monopolistic authority; nonetheless, it is this attempt that separates them from other criminal groups operating in the underworld. However, isn't this attempt a common feature shared by all criminals? According to Schelling, the answer is no. He cites burglars as an example: They may associate in order to carry out their illegal activities, and they may even show some degree of internal coordination (i.e., organization). However, they tend not to exert monopolistic control over the market in which they operate. They are never seen to be fighting off other burglars to gain "exclusive control over their hunting grounds" (p. 74). It is only when we see a gang of burglars starting to police their territory against other burglars that we should "identify the burglary gang as *organized crime*" (p. 74, emphasis in original). Other examples of this kind cited by Schelling include bank robbers, motor vehicle thieves, shoplifters, muggers, embezzlers, and tax evaders.

Building on the work of Schelling, Varese (2010, p. 14) defines organized crime groups as entities that unlawfully regulate the distribution of a commodity or service in a given territory. The urban gang explored by Levitt and Venkatesh (2000) is an example of this kind. It controlled the distribution of drugs in a US inner-city neighborhood—initially a twelve-square block area that eventually doubled after a turf war with a rival gang. In its turf, the gang would either sell the drugs directly or give independent sellers the right to do so in exchange for a fee (i.e., market governance).

Within the broader domain of organized crime, there is a distinct subset of organizations whose speciality is to control the supply of a specific commodity, namely protection (Varese 2010). These organizations are commonly referred to as Mafia groups. Based on its manifestation in Sicily, Gambetta (1993, p. 1) defines the Mafia as an "industry which produces, promotes, and sells private protection." Mafia organizations have a wider scope than organized crime groups as they seek to "protect *any* transactions, not just those related to, say, drugs in a given domain" (Varese 2010, p. 17, emphasis in original).[2]

According to Paoli (2003, p. 156), in the "areas dominated by the 'Ndrangheta, nobody, not even the unaffiliated, is allowed to carry out any illicit activity without the authorization of the local mafia family." The Mafiosi's attempt to govern transactions may stretch beyond the illegal sphere and extend to legal markets. Examples of this kind have been documented in different areas of the world. Reuter (1987) examined the United States and found evidence of the role of the Italian American Mafia as a cartel organizer in a number of legitimate industries, including garbage collection and the carting industry in Long Island, New York. Similarly, Alexander (1997) explored the Mafia-enforced cartel agreements in the pasta industry in Chicago during the Depression (1931–34). Jacobs and Peters (2003) offered evidence of Mafia racketeering in the US labor market, particularly among manual workers employed on the waterfront. In Russia, Varese (2001) found evidence of illegal protection supplied by local Mafia groups to legitimate kiosk owners; this included protection against petty thieves, corrupt officials, and business competitors. In Hong Kong, Triads appear to be involved in suppressing competition (i.e., protecting existing economic actors) in the wholesale fish market as well as among minibus drivers and street hawkers (Chu 2000, chapter 5).

When can a collection of mafia groups be interpreted as a Mafia (collective entity)? Gambetta (1993, chapter 6) and Paoli (2003, chapter 2) both emphasize the importance of shared codes and rituals among Mafiosi. Paoli (2003, p. 66) notes that "it is in the interest of Mafia families to use symbols and rites extensively" as they allow these families "to exercise unconditional claims upon their associates and to create brotherhood ties among them." A key form of ritual often adopted by Mafia organizations is the initiation ceremony, during which novices are presented to the other members, the rules of the association are described, and the swearing of the oath is performed (Paoli 2003, p. 67). Varese (2010) maintains that it is precisely the sharing of common rituals and rules among distinct Mafia groups that creates a collective entity out of a set of otherwise separate groups. This is the case for the Sicilian Mafia, the Calabrian 'Ndrangheta, the Japanese Yakuza, and the Russian Mafia. There are also instances of Mafia-like organizations that have not managed to establish and sustain a set of shared rituals and rules and thus have failed to create a collective shared identity. An example of this kind is the Neapolitan Camorra (Campana 2011a; Catino 2014).

A Rational Choice Perspective on Organized Crime

A couple of years ago, I had the opportunity to interview a former Mafia member now turned state witness. Since the 1970s, his group has been running protection rackets in a town of approximately 30,000 people in southern Italy. However, lately, things have changed following a sweeping offensive by law enforcement. During the interview, I was struck by some remarks he made while describing the latest development in the local area:

> Shopkeepers are now charged less than €100 a month for protection. This is insane! Five, six or even seven years in jail for less than €100? Seriously? It makes no sense. In addition, one would hardly get away with this nowadays. They will get you at some point. In the past, shopkeepers always denied having made any payment, but now it is different. Now police collect evidence also against shopkeepers, so if they do not admit that they had paid, they too will face the consequences. So many more shopkeepers now admit paying the *pizzo* [protection fee].[3]

A rational choice perspective on criminal behavior immediately comes to mind (on rational choice more generally, see Elster 2007). According to this approach, offenders decide whether or not to commit a crime based on the benefits they expect to gain minus the expected costs of their actions. Becker (1968, p. 177) specifies a model for explaining the decision making behind committing a crime as a function of three distinct variables: the probability of conviction per offense, the level of punishment, and a third "portmanteau" variable capturing the income available to the potential offender from alternative activities as well as his or her individual propensity to break the law (for more details on Becker's model, see chapter 2, this volume). Let us consider again the reasoning of the Mafioso interviewed. He weighted the benefits from a *specific* illegal act, namely demanding protection money from a specific set of entrepreneurs, against the costs expected, based on both the criminal code in that specific jurisdiction and the likelihood of getting caught and sentenced. Finally, he concluded that asking for *that* amount of money from *that* specific category of entrepreneurs was not a good decision under *those* circumstances.

His case does not appear to be unique. A broad rational choice perspective has formed the basis of a number of works that have compellingly investigated the activities of Mafiosi, racketeers, and gang members in a number of different settings and geographic areas

(Schelling 1971; Graebner Anderson 1979; Reuter 1983, 1987; Jankowski 1991; Gambetta 1993, 2009; Gambetta and Reuter 1995; Decker and van Winkle 1996; Alexander 1997; Chu 2000; Varese 2001, 2011; Hill 2003; Morselli 2005; Campana 2011b; Campana and Varese 2013; Skarbek 2014). A rational choice model also underpins the vast literature on situational crime prevention (for its application to organized crime broadly conceived, see Bullock, Clarke, and Tilley 2010; see also von Lampe 2011).

More generally, the idea that criminal behavior may be the result of a rational calculation can be traced back to the pioneering works of Cesare Beccaria (*On Crimes and Punishments*, 1764) and Jeremy Bentham (*An Introduction to the Principles of Morals and Legislation*, 1789). A rational choice approach may or may not be the best candidate for explaining every type of crime; however, it appears to be a particularly appropriate way to make sense of organized crime operations. As Cornish and Clarke (2002, p. 41) stated, organized crime is "rational crime par excellence" due to a number of reasons, including its purposive nature and the often large amount of organization and planning involved.

Adopting a broad rational choice approach does not imply that criminals operate— and make their decisions—under perfect conditions. By the same token, it does not follow that criminals are necessarily good at making decisions. They face setbacks, failures, and often severe constraints in relation to their actions. Kleemans (2013, p. 626) reminds us that "organized crime is about criminal co-operation under difficult circumstances." Illegal markets are far from being efficient, information is often of poor quality, and trust among participants is rather low (Reuter 1985; Gambetta 2009; Campana and Varese 2013). Product illegality has significant consequences for how organizations operate, particularly due to the lack of enforceable contracts, the constant risk of asset seizure and forfeiture, and the risk of arrest and imprisonment for participants. From all of this, it follows that information—a key element in rational decision making as well as the well functioning of markets—cannot circulate freely and needs to be tightly controlled (Reuter 1983, chapter 5). Nonetheless, a broad rational choice perspective has the merit of making limits and constraints apparent, thus allowing us to shed light on the strategies adopted by criminals to overcome the problems posed by the difficult environment in which they operate.

II. Why Criminal Monopolies Emerge

The essence of organized crime is its attempt to monopolize markets. The attractiveness of monopolies for legal entrepreneurs was already clear to Adam Smith (*The Wealth of Nations*, 1776). Illegal entrepreneurs may find monopolies equally attractive. Schelling (1984) spells out a number of reasons why this may be the case. First, a single organization operating in a market can charge a monopoly price—which is higher than the price it would have otherwise charged under more competitive conditions—and this price will lead to an increase in the profit margin for the organization. The more inelastic the demand, the larger the increase in the profit margin. This is the case, for example, when consumers do not change their buying habits when prices increase.

Second, monopoly can lead to the formation of larger organizations. In turn, these organizations may be able to internalize formerly "external" costs and thus attempt to lower them. Violence is one of these costs: Racketeers have "a collective interest in restricting violence, as to avoid trouble with the public and the police—but the individual racketeer has little or no incentive to reduce the violence connected with his own crime" (Schelling 1984, p. 163). A large organization will internalize its control over the use of violence. However, when it is not feasible to set up a single organization, alternative mechanisms to enhance coordination may offer a viable solution. For instance, reducing violence was the main reason behind the establishment of the Commission among the Mafia families operating in New York (Critchley 2009). Similar considerations were at play when the same model was eventually exported to Sicily in the 1960s (Arlacchi 1993, chapter 13). Finally, large organizations are better placed in terms of building a "social capital" of corrupt relations with police and politicians; as this may require a long-term investment, it "can be undertaken only by a fairly large firm that has reasons to expect it can enjoy most of the market and get a satisfactory return on the investment" (Schelling 1984, p. 164).

There are sound reasons why one would expect monopolies to emerge in the underworld. However, not all criminal markets appear to be prone to monopolistic control. Moreover, they tend to be populated by small groups rather than large organizations (Reuter 1983; Paoli, Greenfield, and Reuter 2009; Catino 2014). What makes some illegal markets more prone to monopolization than others?

Key to exerting monopoly control over a market is the ability of a criminal organization to monitor all the transactions taking place in that market. At the same time, the organization should possess the ability to keep its competitors at bay. Monitoring transactions is often not an easy task for either criminal or legitimate entities (e.g., tax authorities). A crucial factor that impacts on the ability to monitor a transaction is the size of a market. For instance, the illegal sale of cigarettes to underage people is virtually impossible to monopolize as almost every individual older than the age of eighteen years can enter this market; as Schelling (1971, p. 76) notes, "the competition is everywhere." The size of the market makes the cost of keeping competitors at bay greater than the extra profit generated by monopolistic control. Bank robbers have no incentives to prevent all banks in a given territory from being assaulted by competitors: As banks can typically be robbed more than once, this would hardly be a cost-effective strategy. Other markets, however, show a different tendency. Protection rackets are the clearest example (Shelling 1971):

> Large-scale systematic extortion cannot really stand competition any more than a local taxing authority; I cannot take half the bookie's earnings if you took it before I got there. We can divide the bookies between us, territorially or otherwise, but if nine other mobs are demanding half his earnings, all ten are in trouble. (76)

Schelling (1971, p. 78) identifies a number of structural conditions that may increase the vulnerability of a given market to racketeering, including the inability of economic actors to adequately protect themselves, their inability to access the legal system, the cost of relocating their business, and the ability to hide their business from racketeers. Conversely, racketeers need to be able to identify the actors operating in a given market, to monitor the volume of their activity, and to quantify their earnings. Gambetta and Reuter (1995) examine Mafia-enforced cartel agreements in both Sicily and the United States, and they spell out the conditions that may favor the emergence of such cartels in legitimate industries, including low product differentiation, low barriers to entry, a low level of technology, the prevalence of an unskilled labor force, an inelastic demand, and a large number of relatively small firms.

III. Exploring Protection Rackets

As a product, protection possesses some rather distinct characteristics that make it akin to a natural monopoly. Indeed, the tendency of protection to create monopolies is evident well beyond the sphere of criminal markets.

Economic historian Frederic Lane (1958) argues that competing protection-producing enterprises would seek a monopoly over the use of force within a contiguous territory as a way to reduce costs and improve the product supplied. The evolution of societies in ancient and medieval times shows a tendency to move away from situations of competition over the use of force and toward the establishment of local monopolies. During feudalism, local monopolists would form "loosely organized cartels constantly bickering over the production and market quota of each" (Lane 1958, p. 411). Whereas modern democracies have finally reached a stage where violence is not only centralized but also under the control of their "customers," Mafia protection remains akin to feudal monopolies—localized, unaccountable, and with no consideration for justice. Paoli (2003) maintains that "up until the beginning of the modern period, neither governments nor business enterprises were formed in any of the ways that are now familiar to us" (p. 173). Building on Schumpeter (1942), she notes that the concepts of "state" and "private" enterprise cannot be meaningfully applied to the institutions of feudalism because "the state was in a certain sense the private property of a prince, just as the fief was the private property of a vassal" (p. 173). She then argues that in the case of Mafia organizations, the process of separation and differentiation between force-using enterprises and profit-seeking enterprises "has taken place only to a minimal extent" (p. 173). In addition,

> as in feudal institutions, the overlap between force-using and profit-seeking enter-prises is paralleled by a lack of clear boundaries between the private and public spheres. The mafia family is managed by its chief as a flexible tool to simultaneously

foster his own and the group's interest, and it is up to each leader to find a balance between different, sometimes diverging, interests. (p. 176)

According to Paoli (2003), "Italian mafia families . . . not only 'tax' the main productive activities carried out in their communities, but also claim a fully-fledged political power over their territory, which usually corresponds to a village or town, or to a neighborhood in larger cities" (p. 8). Adopting a focus on "governance," as suggested by Varese (2010), captures both the economic and the political dimension of Mafia organizations while "retaining the crucial distinction between producers of goods and services, and suppliers of forms of regulation, protection and governance" (p. 14).

Skaperdas (2001) equates organized crime groups with premodern forms of predatory states, and the competition among them is seen to be akin to that among lords, kings, and emperors. Organized crime presents a market structure that is similar to monopolistic competition.

Political philosopher Robert Nozick (1974) compellingly argues that a virtual monopoly will eventually arise in the market for private protection in a given territory due to the very nature of protection:

> The worth of the product purchased, protection against others, is *relative*: It depends upon how strong the others are. Yet unlike other goods that are comparatively evaluated, maximal competing protective services cannot coexist; the nature of the service brings different agencies not only into competition for customers' patronage, but also into violent conflict with each other. Also, since the worth of the less than maximal product declines disproportionately with the number who purchase the maximal product, customers will not stably settle for the lesser good, and competing companies are caught in a declining spiral. (p. 17)

The implication is that even if the production and supply of protection possesses the properties of a competitive market in the beginning, it will quickly evolve into a monopoly and thus become more akin to a system of taxation.

The production and supply of illegal protection presents both positive and negative externalities. In a setting in which some individuals are protected by a Mafioso, those who are not will experience some adverse effects on their business as an indirect consequence of the Mafioso existence (negative externalities). For instance, unprotected bookmakers operating in a market populated by Mafia-protected operators may see their operating costs increase because they will be more likely to become victims of swindling (Reuter 1983, p. 169). As Gambetta (1993) states, the more actors there are who are paying for protection, the higher the risk for the unprotected actors because "if protection is effective, predators will concentrate their efforts on the unprotected" (p. 30). Due to these negative externalities, even without any active attempt by a Mafioso to "persuade" the unprotected bookmakers, the latter might find themselves better off paying for protection rather than not (if we leave aside any consideration of the moral costs of the act; some individuals do find it morally wrong to pay a racketeer even if the economic benefits outweigh the costs). At the same time, protection also presents positive externalities. As argued by Gambetta (1993), if a market has a reputation for being protected by a Mafioso and outsiders are unable to easily identify who the protected ones are, then all actors will benefit even if only a few have actually paid for protection. In such a situation, a Mafioso would have an incentive to "tax" all participants in the market "for providing them with protection entails no further cost than that already incurred in protecting . . . a fraction of the market" (Gambetta 1993, p. 31).

A. Varieties of Protection

Illegal protection may take a variety of different forms, including protection against competition, enforcement of cartel agreements, settlement of disputes, labor racketeering, intimidation of workers and trade unionists for the benefit of employers, intimidation of lawful right-holders, protection against theft and police harassment, protection in relation to informally obtained credit and debt recovery, and protection against extortionists (Varese 2006, p. 412; see also Reuter 1983, 1987; Sabetti 1984; Arlacchi 1993; Gambetta 1993; Chu 2000; Varese 2001, 2010; Hill 2003; Paoli 2003; Campana 2011b; Wang 2014). The relationship between (illegal) producers and consumers of protection may also take different forms. Varese (1996, p. 134) identifies three distinct types of illegal protection agencies based on the nature of the service rendered (i.e., genuine or bogus) and their approach toward the sustainability of the businesses they protect. These types are predatory groups, extortionary groups, and protective groups.

Predatory groups show no consideration for the long-term sustainability of the businesses they supposedly "protect" and impose a fee so disproportionally high that it will quickly bring businesses to bankruptcy. Predatory groups do not supply any real protection services, merely bogus ones ("protection against a danger that the group itself might cause"; Varese 1996, p. 143). Extortionary groups generally charge a smaller fee than that charged by predatory groups, thus allowing for the survival of the businesses protected, but they do not provide any genuine service. Finally, protective groups supply a real service in exchange for a fee. This service may be of poor quality, but it is nevertheless genuine.

Based on his extensive fieldwork in the Russian city of Perm, Varese (1996) concluded that entrepreneurs operating in an area controlled by an extortionist group had little choice but to pay. However, he also discovered that a limited scope for decisions did indeed exist as entrepreneurs would "usually gather information in advance on the effectiveness of the group that was likely to protect him and tried to avoid predatory and extortionary groups. Rational business-people tried to locate their activity in areas controlled by groups that offered genuine protection" (Varese 2001, p. 134). Varese's prediction was that over time, only protective groups will be able to survive because they will attract more businesses than will predatory groups. These businesses would also be more prosperous economically as they would not be charged predatory fees while benefitting from genuine protection, for instance, against competitors. Pure predatory groups are thus likely to weaken over time and eventually disappear. As Leopoldo Franchetti, an Italian aristocrat who traveled to Sicily in 1876 to conduct an inquiry into the state of Sicilian society, stated, "If villains made use of their destructive abilities to an extreme degree, they would soon lack the very matter from which to steal" (Franchetti 1877, as quoted in Gambetta 1993, p. 33).

Under certain conditions, protective groups can stop offering genuine protection and turn into pure extortionists. A key factor is the time horizon of the protector: As it shortens, the incentives to oppress increase. As Gambetta (1993) argues, "As with all dealers, if the future looks uncertain, protectors will maximize present over future income. They will be more likely either to sell bogus protection or to charge extortionate prices for it, or both" (p. 33). The time horizon can also impact the decisions of consumers. If they credibly believe that the "life expectancy" of a Mafioso is sufficiently short, they may be more inclined to refuse to pay for protection. As a consequence, Mafiosi may need to resort to more "energetic forms of promotion"—that is, an increased use of violence (Gambetta 1993, p. 33). Increased pressure from law enforcement may shorten the time horizon and therefore have the unintended consequence of increasing the demands on consumers of protection. As Gambetta notes, the overall degree of stability of a protection industry is therefore a key variable in predicting the decision making of both Mafiosi and consumers (for a thorough discussion of the relationship between protection and extortion, see Varese 2014).

Smith and Varese (2001) developed a game theoretic model to examine the dynamics underpinning the repeated interactions between Mafiosi and entrepreneurs operating fixed establishments. They show that settings in which Mafias operate are inherently turbulent. The willingness of entrepreneurs to pay illegal protection encourages opportunistic behavior from non-mafia criminals (fakers). This in turn triggers the use of force from bona fide Mafiosi to re-establish their reputation. Succession disputes within Mafia families also tend to generate violence. In addition, Smith and Varese provide a game theoretic argument that an increase in the level of policing against a Mafia organization leads to a short-time increase in violence. Finally, they conclude that contrary to the widespread perception, racketeers may find it difficult to enforce territorial monopolies.

B. The Price for Protection

In addition to, deciding whether to supply a genuine or bogus service, racketeers also face a related choice: How much to charge for protection. Skaperdas (2001) argues that as a local monopolist, a racketeer will use his or her power "to extract a price for its protection that is not just at its monopoly level but is extortionist—the gang can name its price and its quantity" (p. 187). However, reality may appear rather different. Gambetta and Reuter (1995) maintain that the charges levied by Mafia members are "surprisingly modest, indeed well below extortionate levels" (p. 132), at least in settings in which the relationship between protector and industry is stable. In the mid-1980s, the Long Island carting industry was notoriously under the influence of the local Mafia: Racketeers would take no more than $400,000 annually, whereas the estimated profits for the carters was more than $10 million. In New York, the Mafia would fix prices of a concrete cartel and charge 2 percent of the contract price for its services (Reuter 1987; Gambetta and Reuter 1995). According to a relatively recent investigation into Mafia activities in Palermo, Mafiosi would charge up to 4.5 percent of the value of a contract for its bid-rigging role; however, 4 percent was kept by the organization and 0.5 percent was paid to politicians (Tribunale di Palermo 2008, p. 259). Varese (2011) offers evidence of a top-level Mafia boss in Calabria expressing concern at the excessive demands that the head of a neighboring family was imposing on the latter's victims. He was overheard by the police saying, "Do you know why I came here [to meet you]? Totò, be careful—when the human race, the people go against you, you will lose what you have achieved in thirty years! You just lose it! When you destroy the shop of one guy, burn the car of another, the people will rebel!" (as quoted in Varese 2011, p. 208, footnote 13). In addition, simple and fairly uniform arrangements would create a sense of "fairness" and thus help racketeers to run their businesses: As Schelling (1971) states, a victim "has to know that he is treated like other victims" (p. 78).

IV. Protector's Challenges: The Identification Problem and Threats to Cooperation

Decision-making processes underpinning protection rackets are affected by the cost and quality of the information available. In the world of such rackets, information tends to be costly to circulate, difficult to verify, and often of poor quality. This in turn generates a number of problems for participants, including identification problems for bona fide Mafiosi who need to keep impostors at bay. This problem is particularly acute in markets with a relatively large turnover of firms. By relying on signalling theory, Gambetta (2009) explores the strategies adopted by Mafiosi to overcome the identification problem, particularly when dealing with newcomers. One powerful strategy adopted by bona fide Mafiosi relies on signals that are cheap to produce for them while being expensive for impostors, as in the following case involving a request for protection made over the phone to a building contractor (Gambetta 2009):

> "You're well-advised to get in touch with *the friends* of Palizzi" (Palizzi is a small hill town of about one thousand families in southern Calabria, Italy). The contractor's reply must have been something like "Who the heck are they and where am I supposed to find them?" The counterreply, of which we have a record, was simple: "Ask around and you'll find out." (p. 191)

The rationale behind this strategy is to increase the cost for impostors to pass off as genuine racketeers while keeping the need for violent acts low. A direct request would not have been equally credible, and it would have been much easier to fake as anybody could claim to be "the friends of Palizzi." The bona fide Mafioso might find that his request would not be taken seriously. As a consequence, he would be forced to rely on more violent signals, such as placing a warning bomb at the construction site (which incidentally would also be more costly for the Mafioso). By adopting an indirect strategy, the "real" Mafioso will have his identity checked and vouched for by a potentially large number of independent sources (Gambetta 2009):

> If by asking people at random the contractor finds that everybody provides the name of the *same* man or men, he receives the implicit guarantee that the call must be one of the right "friends," those whose permission he must obtain if he wants to work in Palizzi without trouble. No impostor could persuade such an assortment of his fellow citizens to speak in unison and provide the same answer. (p. 192)

Cheating and swindling are not only an external threat for Mafia organizations. Fellow associates may also be reluctant to follow orders, may embezzle protection money, or may pass on information to the police. Campana and Varese (2013) explore the strategies that Mafia members may adopt to overcome the challenges to cooperation in settings characterized by illegality and a low level of interpersonal trust. They argue that cutting off options and taking hostages are two ways of establishing credible commitments among Mafia members. For instance, covering one's body with tattoos and cutting off fingers as a form of punishment—as in the Japanese Yakuza—may make it difficult for Mafia members to leave the group and re-enter legitimate society. Similarly, kin-based recruitment and sharing information about acts of violence are forms of "hostage-taking": They generate *information* that can be held hostage and eventually used against the "deviant" member to punish his actions (see also Schelling 1960, pp. 43–44; Gambetta 2009, chapter 3). Campana and Varese tested the impact of kinship and violence on fostering cooperation in two organizations—a Russian Mafia group and a Neapolitan Camorra clan—and found evidence that both factors enhance cooperation. In addition, they also discovered that violence has a much greater impact than kinship even in groups made up of relatives. They thus concluded that there is nothing ontological in the role of kinship in organized crime, and when better and more reliable mechanisms to increase commitment are available, criminals will resort to them, just as organizations in advanced societies tend to rely on merit rather than kinship.

V. MAFIAS IN A GLOBALIZED WORLD

Globalization and greater ease of travel are often perceived as facilitating factors for organized crime activities, and it is frequently suggested that such factors operate in a quasi-mechanical manner. The reasoning is usually as follows: Globalization increases the opportunities for organized crime groups, and these groups are often able to take advantage of these opportunities to a very large extent and with little effort. This in turn creates an even greater danger for Western societies than was the case in the past (Shelley 1999, 2006; Castells 2000; Williams 2001). Sterling (1994) goes as far as to suggest the existence of a "planet-wide criminal consortium" composed of the world's largest criminal syndicates, which are "pooling services and personnel" (p. 2). Castells (2000) shares this view, maintaining that a new phenomenon has emerged in our contemporary networked societies, namely "global crime," described as "the networking of powerful criminal organizations, and their associates, in shared activities throughout the planet" (p. 16). Among these organizations, Castells includes the Sicilian and American Cosa Nostra, the Camorra, the Yakuza, the Triads, and the Russian Mafia. The assumption underpinning this view is that organized crime groups possess an almost complete ability to seize opportunities generated by globalization; at the same time, costs and constraints associated with transnational operations are grossly overlooked. Greater ease of travel may increase the volume of specific cross-border criminal activities (e.g., vehicle crimes or other types of smuggling activities[4]); however, the interplay between globalization and organized crime *strictly conceived* (and particularly protection rackets) is considerably more complex than this view would lead one to believe.

A good way to explore this issue is to first consider the resources required to successfully run protection rackets and the constraints these resources may impose on the operations of such groups.

First, the ability to use violence is a constitutive element of organized crime groups; however, the actual use of violence may be rather costly, depending on the reaction from law enforcement authorities and their effectiveness in punishing violent acts. A newcomer may experience strict limits to the use of violence in a new territory if he does not wish to attract too much attention from the authorities (Campana 2011b; Campana and Varese 2013).

A credible reputation for being violent may decrease the need for the actual use of violence. Reuter (1982) examined the Mafia-controlled solid waste collection industry in New York and concluded that reputation is a particularly valuable asset for racketeers. Reputation deters competitors from entering a market, thus effectively creating barriers to entry while at the same time decreasing the actual use of violence. As a result, reputation increases the stability of illegal agreements. It also generates a dilemma for prosecutors and regulators: The more they attack a racketeer-controlled industry, the more notorious it becomes. Every investigation that falls short of eliminating the racketeer's influence on a given industry "adds to the bad name of the industry and further deters honest businessmen from considering entry" (p. 49). However, as noted by Reuter (1985, p. 22), the value of reputation is a function of the proximity between racketeers and the relevant population: The probability that an individual has heard about a reputation-enhancing act is higher the closer the individual is to at least one witness of such act—for example, through a continuous chain of personal contacts. Individuals living far away are less likely to be part of this chain. As it may be difficult for reputations in the underworld to travel, racketeers who wish to set up an outpost in a far removed locale must incur the cost of acquiring a reputation in that locale.

In addition, racketeers need to monitor the behavior of their agents. This is often a major task for large legal organizations; for illegal entrepreneurs, it can be even more daunting (Reuter 1983, pp. 127–28). They have to ensure that agents in distant locales work efficiently and "honestly." Distant agents can take excessive risks, thus exposing the entire organization to the danger of apprehension by law enforcement agencies, or they can misappropriate capital, both tangible and organizational, from the illegal enterprise (Reuter 1985, pp. 21–22). The monitoring problem is a crucial factor in explaining the limits to growth—both geographically and in size—that illegal enterprises experience (Reuter 1985):

> Although these incentives [to take excessive risk and misappropriate capital] exist for all agents of illegal entrepreneurs, the entrepreneur is less able to control the risk-taking and punish the misappropriation when the agent is in a remote location. He cannot force the agent to act cautiously since he is unable to observe the agent's behavior. He will have difficulty punishing informants since he has less information and control of force in remote locations. (p. 22)

Finally, gathering information on consumers and competitors alike is a crucial task for racketeers. This is done mostly through informal contacts. As Gambetta (1993) notes, "Building and managing an information network may be difficult, time-consuming and treacherous" (p. 36). From these considerations, it follows that the territory in which one was born or in which one has lived the longest is the most suitable territory in which to start a protection racket because a person would know "every resident and every street corner" in that territory (p. 37). In addition to collecting information in the new locale, racketeers also have to convey information across locales. This will in turn expose them to an increased risk of detection by law enforcement agencies.

Reuter (1985, p. 21) has concluded that illegal enterprises, and particularly protection rackets, tend to be "local in scope." Gambetta (1993) maintains that, like mining companies, Mafias are "heavily dependent on the local environment" (p. 251); the initial costs for setting up a Mafia-run protection racket in a new locale "can be met solely under a special combination of conditions since basic resources are expensive to produce in a void: Information gathering and advertising, for instance, exploit independent networks of kinship, friendship, and ethnicity" (p. 251). In other words, Mafias tend to be highly "embedded" in their territory of origin (Granovetter 1985; Kleemans and van de Bunt 1999).

VI. Making Sense of the Movement of Mafias: "Transplantation" and "Functional Diversification"

Varese (2011) has compellingly shown that, under specific circumstances, Mafias can relocate to new territories. He defines the successful relocation of protection rackets to new locales as "transplantation," namely "the ability of a Mafia group to operate an out-post over a sustained period outside its region of origin and routine operations" (p. 6). Varese spells out two sets of factors that may lead to transplantation: Supply-side fac-tors include generalized migration from Mafia hot spots and/or migration of individual Mafiosi. Demand-side factors (i.e., local conditions) include the level of trust and civic engagement in the new territory; the presence of existing illegal protectors; the size of the new locale; the presence of emerging or booming markets, including instances of newly formed market economies; and the presence of large illegal markets.[5] By rely-ing on a series of matched comparisons of case studies in Europe, the United States, and Asia, Varese concludes that generalized migration on its own cannot explain long-term Mafia transplantation in a new territory. The presence of Mafiosi is a necessary condition but not a sufficient one for a Mafia to transplant. It is the interplay between supply-side and demand-side factors that may lead to a successful movement into a new territory. Varese has also found that generalized trust plays no role in explaining Mafia transplantation—and more generally the emergence of Mafias. It is rather the inability of the state to govern markets—often as a consequence of unexpected booms in existing markets or the sudden emergence of new ones—that generates significant opportunities for Mafia organizations. If these opportunities are not met by existing protectors, then a Mafia may be in a position to successfully run a protection racket in the new territory. The work of Varese also illustrates that Mafias not only emerge during periods of transition when property rights are not adequately protected by the state—as in the case of Sicily, Japan, and Russia—but also emerge in well-function-ing market economies, and for reasons other than to ensure the protection of property rights (Varese 2011):

> A sudden boom in a local market that is not governed by the state can lead to a demand for criminal protection, even in countries where property rights are clearly defined, trust is high, and courts work relatively well at settling legitimate disputes among market actors. The presence of a supply of people trained in violence and capable of offering such protection might lead to the emergence of a mafia or the transplantation of a foreign group. Endogenous mafia emergence or transplan-tation, however, are not a mechanical product of sudden changes in the economy. Authorities and market operators can take actions to govern the transformation, thereby preventing the rise of a demand for mafia protection. (p. 195)

Furthermore, Varese (2011) also found clear evidence that Mafiosi tend to be stationary and entrenched in the territory they already govern. The decision to move to a new ter-ritory is often the consequence of state prosecution and court orders, internal disputes, and mafia wars: "What might appear the product of globalization is in fact the conse-quence of state repression exporting the problem to other countries (even mafia infight-ing can to an extent be the product of pressure put on the group by the state)" (Varese 2011, p. 8). Displacement effects driven by the action of law enforcement agencies have been identified, among others, in the case of Camorra groups (Campana 2011a), the Georgian Mafia (Slade 2013), and Albanian organized crime (Arsovska 2014).

The absence of a grand plan or an explicit strategy of criminal colonization does not imply that Mafiosi have no agency and that they just react to events. The decision-making process underpinning the movement of Mafia organizations is composed of two consecutive stages. In the first stage, Mafiosi have to decide whether to relocate their protection racket to a new territory or not. The evidence discussed previously shows that they tend to have a preference for not moving out of their old locale. When they do move outside the territory of origin, it is often because they are pressured into doing so. In the second stage, Mafiosi are faced with the decision regarding which territory to move into. When making this decision, they tend to collect information about potential contacts and opportunities as well as the legislation in the new territory (for evidence, see Campana 2011a). However, information gathering is often far from optimal and is based mostly on personal contacts established in the territory of origin.

The work of Varese has the undoubted merit of showing that Mafias also experience failures and are far from being invariably successful in their plans—whatever these may be. Acknowledging the difficulties in moving protection rackets into new territories does not imply that Mafia activities are necessarily confined to the territory of origin. Relying on a systematic analysis of phone conversations wiretapped by the police, Campana (2011b) carried out an in-depth study of the activities of a Camorra clan based near Naples, southern Italy, with outposts in Aberdeen, Scotland, and Amsterdam, the Netherlands. He showed that protection rackets were the core business of the group. However, despite a lasting presence abroad, the clan never managed to export these protection-related activities but, rather, diversified its activities by *investing* in both legal and illegal markets. The Camorra clan brooked no competition in its territory of origin, whereas it acted just like every other actor in the new locales. In addition, the clan did not resort to violence or large-scale corruption in Scotland and the Netherlands. A clear territorial specialization also emerged as a consequence of local conditions: The Scottish outpost was mainly devoted to investments in legal businesses (i.e., laundering revenues from illegal activities mainly conducted elsewhere), whereas the Dutch hub focused on illegal businesses (mostly the wholesale drug trade given the presence of local brokers). Nonetheless, the clan remained highly dependent on its territory of origin. This case showed that Mafia groups can adopt an alternative strategy to transplantation when operating across territories. This strategy is defined as "functional diversification," namely an instance in which "Mafia-like organizations do not move or expand their core business (protection) outside their territory of origin but instead diversify their activities across territories through investments in the legal and/or illegal economy" (Campana 2013, p. 318). Generally, Mafia organizations can carry out two distinct sets of activities: governing activities and trading activities (the former constitute their defining feature). Different activities have a different impact on the internal structure of the group. By using network analysis techniques, Campana (2011b) shows that the Camorra clan appears to be rather more centralized and hierarchical when it deals with the protection racket compared to its other trading activities. Trading in a market, as opposed to governing that market, requires less hierarchical organizational arrangements.

Finally, Campana (2013) has extended the analysis to the whole of the European Union and identified a presence of Italian Mafias in 22 countries. However, Mafias appear to be involved in trading activities in nearly all of the 75 cities considered.[6] Taken together, transplantation and diversification offer a new framework to interpret Mafia activities across territories and help identify early signs of potentially serious transitions from trading to governing.

VII. Conclusion

This chapter interpreted organized crime in terms of its attempt to govern markets, and it focused mainly on protection rackets. It first assessed the factors conducive to monopolization in illegal markets and then explored the specificity of protection as a natural monopoly. It then discussed the varieties of protection that can be traced in the underworld.

Protectors often have to make decisions in a hostile environment characterized by low trust and a low quality of the information available. This chapter examined how protectors can solve the identification problem—that is, how they can be correctly identified by the individuals who are supposed to pay them. In addition, it explored the difficulties that protectors face in preventing instances of cheating, wrongdoing, and defection among their fellow associates. The establishment of credible commitments may go a long way to address these problems and foster cooperation among criminals. The chapter also critically discussed the interplay between globalization and racketeering, highlighting the often severe limits to movement that racketeers face. Finally, it reviewed a new framework for interpreting transnational organized crime that separates instances of "transplantation" (i.e., when protection rackets are successfully moved or expanded into a new territory) from those of "functional diversification." I conclude with an attempt to sketch what the future may look like for racketeers.

Although it is next to impossible to formulate a definitive answer, there are some indications of emerging challenges that racketeers may have to face. A crucial one is posed by the increasing prominence of Internet-based transactions. This may impact on the ability of racketeers to monitor entrepreneurs' earnings and levy a protection "tax" accordingly (legitimate tax authorities are faced with the same problem). In addition, new communication technologies may increase the ability of entrepreneurs to move their businesses away from the control of the local racketeer while still keeping the same customer base. In addition, the Internet may widen the geographic reach of legitimate entrepreneurs. Previously highly localized businesses may now transact with customers in new and distant territories. In this scenario, racketeers will find it more difficult to offer genuine protection services, such as cartel enforcing and protection against competitors. Their services may eventually become superfluous, and they will be forced to turn into pure extortionists—with all the problems associated with sustaining pure extortion over prolonged periods. As discussed by Varese (2011, chapter 3), economies that are largely export-oriented have proven to be difficult for Mafiosi to penetrate. Finally, the scope for a monopolistic illegal governance of cyberspaces appears to be limited (Lusthaus 2013). Triad societies have been shown to face major challenges when entering new transnational criminal activities due to "deficiencies inherent in their traditional organizational structure" (Zhang and Chin 2003, p. 478). Adapting to structural changes is rarely an easy task—and this is also true for racketeers.

NOTES

1. See Paoli (2002), Paoli and Fijnaut (2006), von Lampe (2008), and Varese (2010) for a reconstruction of the debate around the concept, including its evolution over time and across jurisdictions.
2. For a broader discussion of the theoretical perspectives on organized crime, including a critique of the protection theory, see Kleemans (2014; see also Paoli 2003, chapter 4).
3. Author's interview with a former member of the Neapolitan Camorra now in the witness protection program, Carabinieri Police Regional Headquarters, Turin, Italy, February 2013.
4. The latter are also defined as "transit crimes," as opposed to "organized crime" or "racketeering" (Kleemans 2007).
5. At least to some extent, supply-side factors can be interpreted as "push factors" and demand-side factors as "pull factors" (on this point, see also Morselli, Turcotte, and Tenti 2011).
6. Some potential instances of protection rackets emerged in four cities mainly in connection with Italian restaurateurs and workers (labor racketeering). However, the evidence is far from conclusive.

REFERENCES

Alexander, B. 1997. "The Rational Racketeer: Pasta Protection in Depression Era Chicago." *Journal of Law and Economics* 40(1): 175–202.

Arlacchi, P. 1993. *Men of Dishonor: Inside the Sicilian Mafia—An Account of Antonio Calderone.* New York: Morrow.

Arsovska, J. 2014. "The 'G-local' Dimension of Albanian Organized Crime: Mafias, Strategic Migration and State Repression." *European Journal on Criminal Policy and Research* 20(2): 205–23.

Becker, G. 1968. "Crime and Punishment: An Economic Approach." *Journal of Political Economy* 76:169–217.

Bullock, K., R. V. Clarke, and N. Tilley, eds. 2010. *Situational Prevention of Organised Crimes.* Cullompton, UK: Willan.

Campana, P. 2011a. "Assessing the Movement of Criminal Groups: Some Analytical Remarks." *Global Crime* 12(3): 207–17.

Campana, P. 2011b. "Eavesdropping on the Mob: The Functional Diversification of Mafia Activities Across Territories." *European Journal of Criminology* 8(3): 213–28.

Campana, P. 2013. "Understanding Then Responding to Italian Organized Crime Operations Across Territories." *Policing* 7(3): 316–25.

Campana, P. 2016. "The structure of human trafficking: Lifting the bonnet on a nigerian transnational network." *British Journal of Criminology* 56(1):68–86.

Campana, P., and F. Varese. 2013. "Cooperation in Criminal Organizations: Kinship and Violence as Credible Commitments." *Rationality and Society* 25(3): 263–89.

Castells, M. 2000. *End of Millennium.* Oxford: Blackwell.

Catino, M. 2014. "How Do Mafias Organize? Conflict and Violence in Three Mafia Organizations." *European Journal of Sociology* 55(2): 177–220.

Chu, Y.-K. 2000. *The Triads as Business.* London: Routledge.

Cornish, D. B., and R. V. Clarke. 2002. "Analyzing Organized Crimes." In *Rational Choice and Criminal Behavior: Recent Research and Future Challenges,* edited by A. R. Piquero and S. G. Tibbetts, pp. 41–64. New York: Garland.

Critchley, D. 2009. *The Origins of Organized Crime in America: The New York City Mafia, 1891–1931.* London: Routledge.

Decker, S. H., and B. van Winkle. 1996. *Life in the Gang.* Cambridge: Cambridge University Press.

Edwards, A., and M. Levi. 2008. "Researching the Organization of Serious Crimes." *Criminology and Criminal Justice* 8(4): 363–88.

Elster, J. 2007. *Explaining Social Behavior: More Nuts and Bolts for the Social Sciences.* Cambridge: Cambridge University Press.

Franchetti, L. 1877. *Condizioni Politiche e Amministrative della Sicilia.* Florence, Italy: Barbera.

Gambetta, D. 1993. *The Sicilian Mafia.* London: Harvard University Press.

Gambetta, D. 2009. *Codes of the Underworld.* Princeton, NJ: Princeton University Press.

Gambetta, D., and P. Reuter. 1995. "Conspiracy Among the Many: The Mafias in Legitimate Industries." In *The Economics of Organized Crime,* edited by G. Fiorentini and S. Peltzman, pp. 116–136. Cambridge: Cambridge University Press.

Graebner Anderson, A. (1979). *The Business of Organised Crime.* Stanford, CA: Hoover Institution Press.

Granovetter, M. 1985. "Economic Action and Social Structure: The Problem of Embeddedness." *American Journal of Sociology* 91:481–510.

Hill, P. 2003. *The Japanese Mafia: Yakuza, Law and the State.* Oxford: Oxford University Press.

Jacobs, J. B., and E. Peters. 2003. "Labor Racketeering: The Mafia and the Unions." *Crime and Justice* 30:229–82.

Jankowski, M. 1991. *Islands in the Street: Gangs and American Urban Society.* Los Angeles: University of California Press.

Kleemans, E. R. 2007. "Organised Crime, Transit Crime, and Racketeering." *Crime and Justice* 35(1): 163–215.

Kleemans, E. R. 2013. "Organized Crime and the Visible Hand: A Theoretical Critique on the Economic Analysis of Organised Crime." *Criminology and Criminal Justice* 13(5): 615–29.

Kleemans, E. R. 2014. "Theoretical Perspectives on Organized Crime." In *The Oxford Handbook of Organized Crime,* edited by L. Paoli, pp. 32–52. New York: Oxford University Press.

Kleemans, E. R., and H. G. van de Bunt. 1999. "The Social Embeddedness of Organized Crime." *Transnational Organized Crime* 5(1): 19–36.

Lane, F. C. 1958. "Economic Consequences of Organized Violence." *Journal of Economic History* 18(4): 401–17.

Levi, M. 1998. "Perspectives on 'Organised Crime': An Overview." *Howard Journal of Criminal Justice* 37(4): 335–45.

Levitt, S. D., and S. A. Venkatesh. 2000. "An Economic Analysis of a Drugselling Gang's Finances." *Quarterly Journal of Economics* 115(3): 755–89.

Lusthaus, J. 2013. "How Organised Is Organised Crime?" *Global Crime* 14(1): 52–60.

Morselli, C. 2005. *Contacts, Opportunities and Criminal Enterprise*. Toronto: University of Toronto Press.

Morselli, C., M. Turcotte, and V. Tenti. 2011. "The Mobility of Criminal Groups." *Global Crime* 12(3): 165–88.

Nozick, R. 1974. *Anarchy, State and Utopia*. New York: Basic Books.

Paoli, L. 2002. "The Paradoxes of Organized Crime." *Crime, Law and Social Change* 37(1): 51–97.

Paoli, L. 2003. *Mafia Brotherhoods*. New York: Oxford University Press.

Paoli, L., ed. 2014. *The Oxford Handbook of Organized Crime*. New York: Oxford University Press.

Paoli, L., and C. Fijnaut. 2006. "Organised Crime and Its Control Policies." *European Journal of Crime, Criminal Law & Criminal Justice* 14:307–27.

Paoli, L., V. Greenfield, and P. Reuter. 2009. *The World Heroin Market: Can Supply Be Cut?* New York: Oxford University Press.

Paoli, L., and T. Vander Beker. 2014. "Organized Crime: A Contested Concept." In *The Oxford Handbook of Organized Crime*, edited by L. Paoli, pp. 13–31. New York: Oxford University Press.

Reuter, P. 1982. *The Value of a Bad Reputation: Cartels, Criminals, and Barriers to Entry*. Santa Monica, CA: RAND.

Reuter, P. 1983. *Disorganised Crime: The Economics of the Visible Hand*. Cambridge, MA: MIT Press.

Reuter, P. 1985. *The Organization of Illegal Markets: An Economic Analysis*. New York: US National Institute of Justice.

Reuter, P. 1987. *Racketeering in Legitimate Industries: A Study in the Economics of Intimidation*. Santa Monica, CA: RAND.

Sabetti, F. 1984. *Political Authority in a Sicilian Village*. New Brunswick, NJ: Rutgers University Press.

Schelling, T. C. 1960. *The Strategy of Conflict*. Cambridge, MA: Harvard University Press.

Schelling, T. C. 1971. "What Is the Business of Organized Crime." *Journal of Public Law* 20:71–84.

Schelling, T. C. 1984. *Choice and Consequence*. Cambridge, MA: Harvard University Press.

Shelley, L. 1999. "Identifying, Counting and Categorizing Transnational Criminal Organizations." *Transnational Organized Crime* 5:1–18.

Shelley, L. 2006. "The Globalization of Crime and Terrorism." E-Journal, US Department of State, February 2006: 42–45.

Schumpeter J. A. 1942. *Capitalism, Socialism and Democracy*. New York: Harper and Row.

Skaperdas, S. 2001. "The Political Economy of Organised Crime: Providing Protection When the State Does Not." *Economics of Governance* 2(3): 173–202.

Skarbek, D. 2014. *The Social Order of the Underworld: How Prison Gangs Govern the American Penal System*. Oxford: Oxford University Press.

Skinnari, J., A. Anders Stenström, and L. Korsell. 2012. *Otillåten påverkan mot företag*. Stockholm: Bra.

Slade, G. 2013. *Reorganizing Crime: Mafia and Anti-Mafia in Post-Soviet Georgia*. Oxford: Oxford University Press.

Smith, A., and F. Varese. 2001. "Payment, Protection and Punishment: The Role of Information and Reputation in the Mafia." *Rationality and Society* 13(3): 349–93.

Sterling, C. 1994. *Crime Without Frontiers: The Worldwide Expansion of Organized Crime and the Pax Mafiosa*. London: Little Brown.

Tribunale di Palermo. 2008. Sentenza nei confronti di Adamo Andrea + 57.

Varese, F. 1996. "What Is the Russian Mafia?" *Low Intensity Conflict and Law Enforcement* 5(2): 129–38.

Varese, F. 2001. *The Russian Mafia*. Oxford: Oxford University Press.

Varese, F. 2006. "How Mafias Migrate: The Case of the 'Ndrangheta in Northern Italy." *Law and Society Review* 40(2): 411–44.

Varese, F. 2010. "What Is Organised Crime?" In *Organized Crime: Critical Concepts in Criminology*, edited by F. Varese, pp. 1–33. London: Routledge.

Varese, F. 2011. *Mafias on the Move: How Organized Crime Conquers New Territories*. Princeton, NJ: Princeton University Press.

Varese, F. 2014. "Protection and Extortion." In *The Oxford Handbook of Organized Crime*, edited by L. Paoli, pp. 342–58. New York: Oxford University Press.

von Lampe, K. 2008. "Organized Crime in Europe: Conceptions and Realities." *Policing* 2(1): 7–17.

von Lampe, K. 2011. "The Application of the Framework of Situational Crime Prevention to 'Organized Crime.'" *Criminology and Criminal Justice* 11(2): 145–63.

Wang, P. 2014. "Extra-Legal Protection in China: How Guanxi Distorts China's Legal System and Facilitates the Rise of Unlawful Protectors." *British Journal of Criminology* 54(5): 809–30.

Williams, P. 2001. "Transnational Criminal Networks." In *Networks and Netwars: The Future of Terror, Crime, and Militancy*, edited by J. Arquilla and D. Ronfeldt, pp. 61–97. Washington, DC: RAND.

Zhang, S., and K. L. Chin. 2003. "The Declining Significance of Triad Societies in Transnational Illegal Activities: A Structural Deficiency Perspective." *British Journal of Criminology* 43(3): 469–88.

Index